Sir John Seeley memorably quipped that [...] *of absence of mind, and Sir Keith Hancock* [...] *'the nature of the British Empire defined* [...] *we can thank Wm. Roger Louis and Ends of British Imperialism for adding another aphorism on the history of the British Empire: 'Decolonization was the mirror image of the Scramble for colonies.'*

W. David McIntyre

A major work from the writer anointed by A. J. P. Taylor as 'the foremost historian of the British Empire and Commonwealth in his generation.'

Ends of British Imperialism illuminates the history of the Empire from the 1880s to the 1970s—from the Scramble for colonies in Africa to decolonization and the withdrawal of all troops East of Suez. The theme is British resistance to interference in its colonial affairs, whether by the League of Nations, the United States, or the United Nations. The test came at Suez in 1956, when 'Eden's war' violated the UN Charter. In the aftermath, the Labour Government of the 1960s reaffirmed Britain's commitment to the United Nations, broke with the United States over the war in Vietnam, and accelerated the transition of the Empire into the Commonwealth.

On the 50th anniversary of Suez, Roger Louis argues that the crisis can be viewed as a problem that began with the occupation of Egypt in 1882 and came to a close only with the death of Nasser in 1970 and the withdrawal of all British troops East of Suez in 1971. The events of Suez provided a moral compass for views about intervention in the non-Western world.

Full of original ideas and thought-provoking insights, *Ends of British Imperialism* brings together thirty-four essays spanning four decades of Professor Louis's writing on the history of the British Empire and its place in world affairs.

An Honorary Fellow of St. Antony's College, Oxford, and Editor-in-Chief of *The Oxford History of the British Empire*, Wm. Roger Louis, CBE, is Kerr Professor of English History and Culture and Director of British Studies at the University of Texas at Austin. His books include *Imperialism at Bay* and *The British Empire in the Middle East*. He has edited some 30 others, including *Adventures with Britannia, More Adventures with Britannia, Still More Adventures with Britannia,* and *Yet More Adventures with Britannia*. He is a past President of the American Historical Association and the present Chairman of the AHA's National History Center as well as Chairman of the US Department of State's Historical Advisory Committee.

Cover illustration by Sigismund Goetze,
Britannia Pacificatrix, courtesy of Marina Rainey.

Ends of British Imperialism

Books by Wm. Roger Louis

Ruanda-Urundi, 1884–1919 (1963)

Germany's Lost Colonies, 1914–1919 (1967)

(ed., with Prosser Gifford) *Britain and Germany in Africa: Imperial Rivalry and Colonial Rule* (1967)

(with Jean Stengers) *E. D. Morel's History of the Congo Reform Movement* (1968)

British Strategy in the Far East, 1919–1939 (1971)

(ed., with Prosser Gifford) *France and Britain in Africa: Imperial Rivalry and Colonial Rule* (1971)

(ed.) *National Security and International Trusteeship in the Pacific* (1972)

(ed.) *The Origins of the Second World War: A. J. P. Taylor and His Critics* (1972)

(ed.) *Imperialism: The Robinson and Gallagher Controversy* (1976)

Imperialism at Bay, 1941–1945 (1977)

(ed., with William S. Livingston) *Australia, New Zealand, and the Pacific Islands since the First World War* (1979)

(ed., with Prosser Gifford) *The Transfer of Power in Africa: Decolonization, 1940–1960* (1982)

The British Empire in the Middle East, 1945–1951 (1984)

(ed., with Hedley Bull) *The 'Special Relationship': Anglo-American Relations since 1945* (1986)

(ed., with Robert W. Stookey) *The End of the Palestine Mandate* (1986)

(ed., with Prosser Gifford) *Decolonization and African Independence: The Transfers of Power, 1960–1980* (1988)

(ed., with James A. Bill) *Musaddiq, Iranian Nationalism, and Oil* (1988)

(ed., with Roger Owen) *Suez 1956: The Crisis and Its Consequences* (1989)

(ed., with Robert A. Fernea) *The Iraqi Revolution of 1958: The Old Social Classes Revisited* (1991)

Leo Amery and the British Empire (1992)

(ed., with Robert Blake) *Churchill* (1993)

(ed.) *Adventures with Britannia* (1995)

(ed., with Michael Howard) *The Oxford History of the Twentieth Century* (1998)

(ed.) *More Adventures with Britannia* (1998)

(Editor-in-Chief) *The Oxford History of the British Empire* (5 vols., 1998–99)

(ed., with Ronald Hyam) *British Documents on the End of Empire: The Conservative Government and the End of Empire, 1957–1964* (2 parts, 2000)

(ed., with Roger Owen) *A Revolutionary Year: The Middle East in 1958* (2002)

(ed.) *Still More Adventures with Britannia* (2003)

(ed., with S. R. Ashton) *British Documents on the End of Empire: East of Suez and the Commonwealth, 1964–1971* (3 parts, 2004)

(General Editor) *Reinterpreting History: How Historical Assessments Change over Time* (AHA National History Center and Oxford University Press series, 2004–)

(ed.) *Yet More Adventures with Britannia* (2005)

(ed.) *Burnt Orange Britannia* (2005)

Festschrift

Robert D. King and Robin Kilson, eds., *The Statecraft of British Imperialism: Essays in Honour of Wm. Roger Louis* (1999)

ENDS OF BRITISH IMPERIALISM

The Scramble for Empire, Suez and Decolonization

Collected Essays

SECOND EDITION

Wm. Roger Louis

I.B. TAURIS
LONDON · NEW YORK

Published in 2006, on the 50th anniversary of the Suez crisis, by I.B.Tauris & Co Ltd
6 Salem Road, London W2 4BU
In the United States of America and Canada, distributed by
Palgrave Macmillan, a division of St. Martin's Press
175 Fifth Avenue, New York NY 10010
www.ibtauris.com

ISBN 1-84511-309-8 hardcover
ISBN 1-84511-347-0 paperback

Library of Congress Control Number 2006923303

Some of the essays that appear in this work were originally published in the *American Historical Review, English Historical Review, International Affairs, International Organization, Journal of African History, Journal of Modern History, Journal of Imperial and Commonwealth History,* and *Times Literary Supplement.*
    The following essays were originally published in other volumes: 'The Colonial Empires in the Late Nineteenth and Twentieth Centuries' in *The Oxford History of the Twentieth Century* (1998), edited by Wm. Roger Louis and Michael Howard; 'The Berlin Congo Conference and the (Non-) Partition of Africa, 1884–1885' in *France and Britain in Africa* (Yale, 1971), edited by Prosser Gifford and Wm. Roger Louis; 'E. D. Morel and the Triumph of the Congo Reform Association' in *Boston University Papers on Africa,* volume 2: *African History* (1966), edited by Jeffrey Butler; 'Trusteeship and Self-Interest: The British and the French Colonial Empire' (2006) in *États et sociétés en quête d'avenir: Le Moyen-Orient arabe des indépendances à aujourd'hui;* (Nadine Méouchy, ed., forthcoming) 'The Road to the Fall of Singapore, 1942' in *The Fascist Challenge and the Policy of Appeasement* (George Allen & Unwin, 1983), edited by Wolfgang J. Mommsen and Lothar Kettenacker; 'The Partitions of India and Palestine' in *Warfare, Diplomacy, and Politics: Essays in Honour of A. J. P. Taylor* (Hamish Hamilton, 1986), edited by Chris Wrigley; 'The End of the Palestine Mandate' in *The End of the Palestine Mandate* (University of Texas Press, 1986), edited by Wm. Roger Louis and Robert W. Stookey; 'Libya: The Creation of a Client State' in *Decolonization and African Independence* (Yale, 1988), edited by Prosser Gifford and Wm. Roger Louis; 'Prelude to Suez: Churchill and Egypt' in *Churchill* (Oxford, 1993), edited by Robert Blake and Wm. Roger Louis; 'An American Volcano in the Middle East: John Foster Dulles and the Suez Crisis' in *John Foster Dulles and the Diplomacy of the Cold War* (Princeton, 1990), edited by Richard H. Immerman; 'The United Nations and the Suez Crisis: British Ambivalence towards the Pope on the East River' (2006) in *Gurobaru Gabanansu no Rekishi-teki Henyo: Kokuren to Kokusai-seiji-si* (Sadako Ogata and Asahiko Hanzawa, eds., forthcoming); 'Public Enemy Number One: Britain and the United Nations in the Aftermath of Suez' in *The British Empire in the 1950s: Retreat or Revival?* (Palgrave Macmillan, 2006), edited by Martin Lynn; 'Mussadiq, Oil, and the Dilemmas of British Imperialism' in *Mohammed Mosaddeq and the 1953 Coup in Iran* (Syracuse, 2004), edited by Mark J. Gasiorowski and Malcolm Byrne; 'The Middle East Crisis of 1958' in *A Revolutionary Year: The Middle East in 1958* (Tauris; Woodrow Wilson Center, 2002), edited by Wm. Roger Louis and Roger Owen; 'The Origins of the Iraqi Revolution' in *The Iraqi Revolution of 1958* (Tauris, 1991), edited by Robert A. Fernea and Wm. Roger Louis; 'Robinson and Gallagher and Their Critics' in *Imperialism: The Robinson and Gallagher Controversy* (New Viewpoints, 1976), edited by Wm. Roger Louis; 'The Historiography of the British Empire' as the Introduction to *Historiography* (1999), edited by Robin W. Winks, volume 5 of *The Oxford History of the British Empire.*
    'Suez and Decolonization: Scrambling out of Africa and Asia' is published here for the first time.

Typeset, printed, and bound by Communication Specialists, Inc., Austin, Texas

To the memory of Albert Hourani

CONTENTS

THE MIDDLE EAST

HISTORIOGRAPHY

PREFACE

The approach of the fiftieth anniversary of the Suez crisis caused me to reflect that it would be a good time to collect my essays not only on Suez but on related subjects as well. 'Intervention' is a thread common to many of the essays, as is the connection between decolonization and the Scramble for colonies in the late nineteenth century. The emergent argument, the first of three theses or themes, holds that the Suez crisis can be studied as an episode in decolonization and that decolonization itself—specifically in the case of Suez, but also more generally—can best be understood in the context of the long colonial era extending from the British occupation of Egypt in 1882 to the death of Nasser in 1970 and the withdrawal of all troops East of Suez in the following year.

The focus on the Suez crisis explains the structure of the introductory essay. In reversing the order of conventional preliminary comment, it pulls together my ideas on the origins and consequences of Suez and then moves on to discuss the second theme: the principle of self-determination and the consequences of the shattering of the British Empire into independent and sovereign states—a development of profound, even revolutionary, significance, hardly foreseen either at the creation of the mandates system of the League of Nations in 1919 or indeed as late as the establishment of the trusteeship system of the United Nations in 1945.

In selecting the essays, I began to see that one of the neglected areas in the scholarship of decolonization, in my view, is the colonial issue at the League of Nations and later at the United Nations, especially in the 1950s, when the United Nations began its transformation from an institution for promoting peace to one promoting multiculturalism and multiracialism as well. The essays deal with British trusteeship in its national as well as its international manifestations—subjects in which I have long had an interest—beginning with a study of the Berlin Act of 1885 as an antecedent to the mandates system of the League of Nations, and continuing with attempts to show how Roger Casement and E. D. Morel contributed to the belief that the European powers had to be held responsible for the welfare of their colonial inhabitants.

The third theme deals with the dissolution of the British Empire and the efforts to convert formal colonial administration into informal control, or at least influence. The idea of the Commonwealth—the association of former British colonies voluntarily cooperating as independent and sovereign states—did not succeed as well in the decades after the Second World War, especially in the Middle East, as the British had hoped it might. Here as elsewhere I am concerned, as the title of the book suggests, with the ends of British imperialism: 'end' in the sense of decline and collapse and in the sense of motive, a general theme that runs throughout virtually all of the essays.

On the whole I have chosen essays of substance, but I have included a few reviews from the *Times Literary Supplement,* especially to convey my ideas on India and Palestine. But even in a book as comprehensive as this one I faced difficult choices about what to include. My selection ultimately rests on what I hope readers will find interesting. The historiographical section at the end has less to do with my attempt to demonstrate connecting themes in the literature on the Empire than it does with the hope that fellow historians and general readers might find those essays useful.

As an historian now approaching his forty-sixth summer at the Public Record Office (The National Archives), I know that some of the essays have found a general audience—one undeterred, I am glad to say, by footnotes appearing at the bottom of the page. I have also become aware of two other types of more specialized readers: those who read only the footnotes and some, apparently, who read only the index. As will be clear, I hope, there is something here for each. The essays themselves have been shaped largely by conversations and exchanges of ideas over many years at St. Antony's College and All Souls College as well as in the British Studies seminar at the University of Texas.

The jacket design is a curiosity. I thank Sir Adam Roberts for more than once calling the painting to my attention. It is by the Edwardian artist Sigismund Goetze. I am most indebted to his niece, Marina Rainey, for allowing me to reproduce it (and I wish to thank Kate Crowe of the Foreign and Commonwealth Office for her assistance). The mural was virtually complete on the eve of the Great War in 1914. Britannia clasps the hand of America, wearing the robe of stars and stripes and the cap of freedom. Next to America is Italy (with the fasces, an ancient Roman symbol of authority). Behind America are the other British allies: Romania (with a jar of oil), Greece (carrying the symbol of victory), France (with the tricolour and the sword pointing to broken weapons), Portugal (with a basket of grapes), and Japan (holding a spray of cherry blossoms). Russia (in a bearskin) hides her face in dismay.

Germany had been shown shaking hands with France and Britain in a preliminary sketch of the work, but was omitted from the final version after the events of August 1914. Goetze added Belgium in the shape of a ravaged young woman, and Montenegro as a devastated

child (in the arms of Serbia) at Britannia's feet. The youth with the trident is Newfoundland, and the robust young men on the right-hand
side of the painting are the original Dominions: South Africa (in a lion
skin), Canada (in maple briefs and crowned with wheat), Australia (in
a digger's hat), and New Zealand (draped with a sheepskin). The final
group includes a Swahili child representing Britain's dependencies in
Africa and, in Goetze's words, reminding 'us of our obligations and
possibilities in the dark Continent'; Prince Faisal, signifying Arabia;
and India in a knight's suit of armour. In the original painting India
had knelt before Britannia, but on the outbreak of war assumed an
upright position.

During the First World War—and especially once the Cabinet formally had to accept it—the mural had a troubled history. Lord Curzon, a member of the War Cabinet since 1916 and Foreign Secretary
(1919–24), protested that it was not art but melodrama. But the Prime
Minister, David Lloyd George, and other members of the Cabinet
prevailed; Curzon cast the sole vote against it. In more recent times,
Douglas Hurd, while Foreign Secretary, came to its defence: besides
having it cleaned and restored, he remarked that some of its critics
seemed to lack a sense of humour. It continues to hang in the grand
stairwell of the Foreign and Commonwealth Office.

All of the essays in this volume have been slightly reworked, some
of the titles have been changed, and the punctuation in a small number of quotations has been adjusted. For help in preparing the book,
I am much indebted in different ways to Lauren Apter, Whitney
Brown, Greg Harper, Alaine Low, Rene Harbison, and Barbara Sack—
and above all to Kip Keller. I also wish to thank Lester Crook and the
indomitable Iradj Bagherzade, whose view of the Goetze painting is
identical with Lord Curzon's. I have benefited from criticism of the introductory chapter—and indeed the whole range of my ideas—from
Michael Cohen, John Darwin, John Flint, Stephen Galpern, Ronald
Hyam, Keith Kyle, David McIntyre, Kenneth O. Morgan, Peter Sluglett, and Michael Thornhill. My wife, Dagmar, has borne the production of the book with characteristic good humour: she is the love of my
life, and had I not already dedicated a book to her, this one would be
for her.

In rereading these essays, some after many years, I have been reminded of my intellectual debts to A. J. P. Taylor, Margery Perham,
Jack Gallagher, Ronald Robinson, Michael Howard, and, from the
1950s to the present, Ernest May. But there is one person as an intellectual companion and friend to whom I owe more than anyone else:
a great historian of the Middle East, a creative, subtle, and ironic intellect, a gentle yet firm critic, a gourmet, and, not least, a student of

human foible. For years he was the best of friends, an inspiration, and a source of unfailing encouragement and fun. In his own phrase, though he never used it about himself, he was a 'creative achiever', enabling others to accomplish things they could not otherwise have done. I dedicate the book to the memory of Albert Hourani.

ABBREVIATIONS

Public Record Office (The National Archives), London:

CAB	Cabinet Office
CO	Colonial Office
DEFE	Ministry of Defence
DO	Dominions Office
FCO	Foreign and Commonwealth Office
FO	Foreign Office
PREM	Prime Minister's Office
T	Treasury
WO	War Office

Other abbreviations are explained in the footnotes in which they first appear.

SUEZ AND DECOLONIZATION:
SCRAMBLING OUT OF AFRICA AND ASIA

From the distance of fifty years it is difficult to recall the intensity of emotion about the end of the British Empire and its vital connection with the Suez invasion of 1956. For example, in the aftermath of the crisis, over pink gins in a bar in Aden, the following nuggets of conversation could be overheard:

'Don't you worry, old boy . . . we'll be here for another 30 years.'

'Mustn't take too much notice of Nasser, old chap. Flash in the pan, that's all.'

'Pity we didn't finish the job at Suez—could've done, too, except for those bloody Yanks.'

'Of course, they don't understand the wogs like we do.'[1]

From today's vantage point these views sound like caricatures, but they were commonplace, indeed alive and well, in the 1950s and 1960s. Such antiquated attitudes are hard to reconstruct, yet without understanding their enduring potency one cannot capture the spirit of the times.[2] Down to the last flicker of the old British colonial and social caste—and its cast of mind—as late as the fall of Aden in 1967, the belief persisted that the British Empire could continue to exist if only the Colonial Office, and above all the Cabinet, would buck up, show more determination and less defeatism.

---

[1] David Holden, *Farewell to Arabia* (New York, 1966), p. 20. In the same vein, see Caractacus [Norman Daniel], *Revolution in Iraq* (London, 1959); and Harold R. Isaacs, *The Tragedy of the Chinese Revolution* (London, 1938, 1961 edn.), p. 148, on the consequences of revolution: 'To have one's home turned upside down, to have to hastily lump a few belongings into a trunk or two and a suitcase and leave the rest behind to be looted or whatnot, is an unadulterated bother.'

[2] Such is the explosion of detailed scholarship on Suez that earlier books tend to be neglected; yet some of the works published close to the event convey not only the passion of the time but also exacting detail later confirmed, on the whole, by archival research. Here are the seven pillars of Suez scholarship written in the fifteen or so years after Suez: Paul Johnson, *The Suez War* (London, 1957); Merry and Serge Bromberger, *Les Secrets de l'expédition d'égypte* (Paris, 1957); Hugh Thomas, *The Suez Affair* (London, 1967; see especially the 1986 edn.); Erskine Childers, *The Road to Suez* (London, 1962); Terence Robertson, *Crisis: The Inside Story of the Suez Conspiracy* (New York, 1965); Kennett Love, *Suez: The Twice-Fought War* (New York, 1969); and Mohamed H. Heikal, *Nasser: The Cairo Documents* (London, 1972).

As if in dramatic retort, an equally determined set of voices urged the British to move with the times, to recognize as equals the natives (as they were still referred to in the 1950s), and to fulfil solemn and binding obligations, even though the Empire might be in a state of dissolution.[3] The idea of trusteeship, championed by Sir Frederick (Lord) Lugard in *The Dual Mandate* in the inter-war years and upheld no less vigorously by Margery Perham in the post-1942 era, continued to be taken seriously and deliberately by District Officers and by critics of British imperialism such as Leonard Woolf.[4] In 1964, James Craig, a Political Agent (the official designation for District Officers in parts of the Middle East), waxed lyrical about the traditions of the old British Raj in India and the continuity of British trusteeship in the Gulf. Craig, it will be noted, was, or rather is, a Scot:

> The title of Her Majesty's Political Agent . . . is an exceedingly ro-
> mantic one . . . The name, too, is rich in associations. It belongs with
> those other old and evocative titles: Collector, Resident, District
> Commissioner. It suggests remoteness in time and place. One feels
> that a Political Agent is (or should be) at the end of the line, one of
> those originals on whom the sun used never to set, the final execu-
> tive blood vessel in the network of arteries that stretched out, long,
> efficient, and complex, from the distant heart of the empire . . .
>
> The Agent sits in court . . . and sees the old procession of clerks and
> petition writers . . . He inspects gaols and pursues smugglers, runs
> hospitals and builds roads . . . He decides fishing disputes, negotiates
> blood-money, examines boundaries, manumits slaves . . . He ex-
> empts, pardons, appeases; exacts, condemns, ordains. Over a large

[3] One expression of dismay can be found in a major work by J. B. Kelly, whose impeccable scholarship conveyed a point of honour: the withdrawal from the Gulf amounted not only to a breach of trust, but also to a brazen and cynical scuttle: *Arabia, the Gulf and the West* (New York, 1980). The Foreign Office held Kelly's historical work in high but not uncritical esteem; see FCO 8/17.

[4] F. D. Lugard, *The Dual Mandate in Tropical Africa* (Edinburgh, 1922), was written in part as a handbook for District Officers but with the aim of conveying to the British public the dual responsibility of developing Africa for the benefit of Africans as well as for the British. Margery Perham, the most effective colonial publicist and scholar of her generation, carried on the tradition. In 1942, in the aftermath of the fall of Singapore, she courageously called for the abolition of the colour bar and for an egalitarian reconstruction of the British colonies; see W. R. Louis, *Imperialism at Bay* (Oxford, 1977), pp. 135–39. For Lugard and the tradition of trusteeship, see especially Kenneth Robinson, *The Dilemmas of Trusteeship* (London, 1965). Leonard Woolf's famous work, *Empire & Commerce in Africa: A Study in Economic Imperialism* (London, 1920), argues the radical case for international supervision of the colonies. For his later, mellower views, see his autobiography, *The Journey Not the Arrival Matters* (London, 1970).

but undefined field he in effect rules. All this will pass one day and . . . when it does it will indeed be the end of a very auld sang.[5]

The end came seven years later with the withdrawal of all troops East of Suez. As if in a straight line of descent, the process of decolonization that began in India in 1947 now reached a terminal point.[6]

In that linear, or Gibbonesque, interpretation, Suez destroyed Britain's position in the Middle East, and the only rational course was to liquidate the Empire as quickly and as systematically as possible. Sir William Luce, the last Proconsul in the Middle East, delineated the descent:

> India in 1947, our surrender of the Palestine mandate, our withdrawal from Jordan and the Sudan, our evacuation of the Suez Canal base, and our defeat at Suez in 1956. Whatever the reasons for each of these acts we have set in motion a process of abandoning British power in the Middle East and any attempt to arrest it in its last stage will merely bring us the worst of all worlds.[7]

This was indeed a contemporary view, but an opposite interpretation, also an outlook of the time, must be taken into account as well: the British Empire would revive, would re-create itself, even if in different form, to protect the vital centre of wealth in the oil-producing states of the Gulf. The microcosm of the Middle East in the period 1957–71 thus represents contrasting interpretations of decline and fall, on the one hand, and, on the other, revival, adjustment, and continued commitment to the idea of trusteeship.[8]

Lugard and Perham used the word 'trusteeship' mainly in a national context of accountability to the Colonial Office, the Cabinet, and Parliament—and in a broader sense to the British public. But

[5] A. J. M. Craig, 'Impressions of a Dubai Post', 27 September 1964, in S. R. Ashton and W. R. Louis, eds., *East of Suez and the Commonwealth, 1964–1971,* British Documents on the End of Empire (3 parts, London, 2004), pt. 1, #116.

[6] Troops remained in Hong Kong and Brunei, however, and the withdrawal from South-East Asia and the Indian Ocean proved to be a prolonged and complicated ordeal. See especially W. David McIntyre, *British Decolonization, 1946–1997* (Basingstoke, UK, 1998), chap. 5.

[7] The idea of the connection between Indian independence in 1947 and the consequences for decolonization are especially apparent in the papers of the Planning Department of the Foreign Office and in the minutes of John Thompson (in the FCO 49 series). For Luce, see especially Glen Balfour-Paul, *The End of Empire in the Middle East: Britain's Relinquishment of Power in Her Last Three Arab Dependencies* (Cambridge, 1991).

[8] See John Gallagher, *The Decline, Revival, and Fall of the British Empire* (Cambridge, 1982); and John Darwin, 'Gallagher's Empire', in W. R. Louis, ed., *Yet More Adventures with Britannia* (London, 2005).

from the time of the partition of Africa to the last days of British sway
in the Gulf, trusteeship also implied an international set of commitments, embodied in the Berlin Act of 1885, in the mandates system
of the League of Nations, and in the trusteeship system of the United
Nations. The radical version of this tradition reached its apex in the
1960s, in the Special Committee on Colonialism of the United Nations, eventually known as the Committee of the 24. Ideologically
driven, the Committee of the 24 denounced European colonialism,
and especially British colonialism, as a vicious system of exploitation
that would never willingly decolonize. At the United Nations, the British became Public Enemy Number One in the aftermath of the Suez
crisis. The agents of British imperialism, officials and intelligence officers in Aden for example, were condemned as torturers and mur-
derers. The essays in this volume embrace both themes: trusteeship as
a national system of accountability, and international trusteeship,
which the Colonial Secretary during the Second World War, Oliver
Stanley, described as a notorious procedure by which Britain's colonial
record would be judged—he added emphasis to express his revulsion—by a '*motley international assembly*'.[9]

The Suez crisis occurred at a critical time in the evolution of the two
traditions of national and international trusteeship, and in the process of decolonization. It is equally true that the Suez crisis itself was a
vital episode in the history of decolonization.[10] The British calamity
became a point of reference for subsequent events in the Middle East,
in the Cold War, and in the post-colonial world order at the United
Nations. The events of Suez also became a moral compass to help determine one's ethical stand on events stretching back to the British
occupation of Egypt in 1882. The powerful themes of Robinson and
Gallagher's *Africa and the Victorians* are relevant to the ending as well

[9] Louis, *Imperialism at Bay*, p. 99. The dual theme of the book is the transformation of the
British colonial empire during the Second World War and the creation of the UN trusteeship
system.

[10] For a discussion of the historical literature, see John Darwin, 'Decolonization and the End
of Empire', in Robin W. Winks, ed., *Historiography* (vol. 5 in the *Oxford History of the British Empire*, Oxford, 1999). McIntyre, *British Decolonization*, is a succinct account that brings to bear the
larger perspective of the Commonwealth. For Australia and New Zealand in the context of Suez,
see W. J. Hudson, *Blind Loyalty: Australia and the Suez Crisis* (Melbourne, 1989); and Malcolm
Templeton, *Ties of Blood and Empire: New Zealand's Involvement in Middle East Defence and the Suez
Crisis, 1947–57* (Auckland, 1994). For South Africa, see Ronald Hyam and Peter Henshaw, *The
Lion and the Springbok* (Cambridge, 2003), chap. 12; for Canada, Phillip Buckner, ed., *Canada
and the End of Empire* (Vancouver, 2005), especially chap. 3 by José E. Igartua; on Canada and
the United Nations, Michael Fry, 'Canada, the North Atlantic, and the United Nations', in
W. R. Louis and Roger Owen, *Suez 1956: The Crisis and its Consequences* (Oxford, 1989).

as the beginning of the colonial era.[11] The year 1956 is to 1882 as the end is to the beginning: just as 1882 marks the start of the occupation, so 1956 severs the link and can be seen as the end of the colonial era in Egypt and the beginning of the new Scramble out of Africa and the Middle East. We need not be concerned with the conceptual or causal fallacy in *Africa and the Victorians,* which argues that the occupation of Egypt sparked the Scramble for Africa. No one would claim that the Suez crisis led directly to massive decoloniza-tion. But, as these essays demonstrate, there is a remarkable similarity between the concern for protecting economic assets in Africa and elsewhere in the last decades of the nineteenth century, and similar preoccupations with oil and re-gional stability after the Suez crisis. Decolonization is a mirror image of the Scramble, and vice versa.

Each decade produces its own preoccupations. Contemporary anx-ieties find their way into historical analysis. From the mid-1950s until his death in 1970, there was no doubt that one of the central British fixations was on Gamal Abdel Nasser.[12] While writing *Africa and the Victorians* in the aftermath of the Suez crisis, Robinson and Gallagher pro-jected the nationalism of a later age onto the historical figure of Arabi Pasha, the 'proto-nationalist' who attempted to break the European grip over Egypt in 1881–82.[13] Arabi Pasha thus became a romantic

[11] Ronald Robinson and John Gallagher with Alice Denny, *Africa and the Victorians: The Offi-cial Mind of British Imperialism* (London, 1961). The second edition (1981) has a valuable intro-ductory 'explanation' by Robinson. For a work that imaginatively expands on and corrects their theme of collaboration, see Colin Newbury, *Patrons, Clients, and Empire: Chieftaincy and Over-rule in Asia, Africa, and the Pacific* (Oxford, 2003).

[12] But less of a fixation in the 1960s: 'What Castro and Che Guevara were to the 1960s, Nasser was for the 1950s' (D. C. Watt, 'Death of the Arab Nation—End of a Myth?' *New Middle East,* 25 [October 1970], p. 38). Nevertheless, Nasser's symbolic stature endured, even though, especially after the defeat of 1967, his fortunes declined. Along with Donald Cameron Watt, Elie Kedourie stands as the principal scholar who from the time of the crisis devoted sustained attention to Suez. For Cameron Watt, see *Succeeding John Bull: America in Britain's Place* (London, 1984); and his 'Demythologizing the Eisenhower Era', in W. R. Louis and Hedley Bull, eds., *The 'Special Re-lationship': Anglo-American Relations since 1945* (Oxford, 1986). For Kedourie, see the long intro-duction to his anthology, *Nationalism in Asia and Africa* (New York, 1970); and *The Chatham House Version* (London, 1970). David Pryce-Jones wrote in 1998 of Kedourie's seminal work: 'The shock of *The Chatham House Version* is still with me . . . In the dim and stagnant pond which British in-tellectual life had then become, at last there was a living creature' (David Pryce-Jones, 'A Master All His Own', in Sylvia Kedourie, ed., *Elie Kedourie, CBE, FBA, 1926–1992* [London, 1998], p. 38).

[13] Robinson and Gallagher had been anticipated by Tom Little, a journalist of long experi-ence in Egypt, in his classic and still useful work, *Egypt* (London, 1958), pp. 210–11: 'Nasser was remaking the Arabi rebellion all over again in more appropriate circumstances.' For a critique of Robinson and Gallagher's Egyptian interpretation, see A. G. Hopkins, 'The Victorians and Africa: A Reconsideration of the Occupation of Egypt, 1882', *Journal of African History,* 27 (1986); and Juan R. I. Cole, *Colonialism and Revolution in the Middle East* (Princeton, 1993).

and rather menacing, though less efficient, Nasser. At least this interpretation was a salutary corrective: after Nasser nationalized the Suez
Canal Company on 26 July 1956, comparisons in Britain were usually
drawn to Mussolini or Hitler.

Or, in another line of interpretation, Nasser was so obsessed with
British imperialism that he would sup with the devil in Moscow. In fact,
Nasser was at heart an Arab, indeed an Egyptian, nationalist, who had
no intention of becoming a Soviet stooge. But his ideas were neither
original nor careful: he often got carried away with his own rhetoric
and failed to think through the consequences. The larynx became the
mind, in the contemporaneous and often-quoted phrase. His denunciation of British imperialism placed Egypt and the Arab world
generally on the side of the Soviet Union in the propaganda of the
Cold War.

We now live in a post–Cold War age, and the menace of communist
domination seems to have been overdrawn; but it would be a mistake
not to see the source of danger as it was regarded in the 1950s.[14] It
would also be an error to minimize the significance of historical reasoning by which Nasser was viewed as the equivalent of a European
dictator of the 1930s—or as a misguided nationalist who might carry
Egypt into communism and Soviet rule. People in public life reason by
historical analogy.[15] In view of the great debate over appeasement during the 1930s and later, and of the paranoid anti-communist atmosphere of the 1950s, it would have been odd if such comparisons had
not been made. The Suez crisis seemed at the time, as it does in retrospect, to have universal significance: what to do about a dictator or tyrant, for such was the British view of Nasser, and when is intervention
justified?

Contemporary assessments of Nasser, and of Egypt, were ambiguous. Offsetting conventional thought, certain officials in the Foreign
Office, notably Sir Harold Beeley, regarded Nasser essentially as a rational figure, a nationalist working in the best interests of his own
country and in the cause of Arab nationalism. Nasser tried to subvert
British interests in the Middle East, but the menace could be held in
check. Sophisticated views about Egypt itself were also nuanced, indeed mixed, in part because Egypt's place in the history of the British

[14] For revelations from the Russian archives, see Christopher Andrew and Vasili Mitrokhin,
The World Was Going Our Way: The KGB and the Battle for the Third World (New York, 2005); for the
British and American side, Richard J. Aldrich, *The Hidden Hand: Britain, America, and Cold War
Secret Intelligence* (London, 2001).

[15] See Ernest R. May and Richard E. Neustadt, *Thinking in Time* (New York, 1986), which argues that historical analogies must not only be as accurate as possible but also provide insight:
for example, Nasser as Arabi Pasha, not Hitler. I have benefited from reading the unpublished
Harvard University 'Suez Crisis Case Book' prepared under May's supervision.

Empire was enigmatic. Egypt had always been part of the domain of the Foreign Office and was never technically a part of the British Empire except for a brief period, 1914–22, when it was a Protectorate. Nevertheless, Egypt had many of the attributes of a British colony.[16] For nearly three-quarters of a century after 1882, Egypt was part of Britain's informal empire of indirect control. Even though formal jurisdiction had ended in 1922, Egypt was known as the 'veiled protectorate'. At the one meeting between Nasser and Sir Anthony Eden— in the British Embassy in Cairo in February 1955—Nasser commented that he was glad to see the place from which Britain had governed Egypt. Eden gently corrected him: 'Not governed, advised, perhaps.'[17]

Eden was being arch, but his comment raised the question of how the British of the 1950s viewed the history of their relationship with the Egyptians. In so far as there was a consensus, it recognized that British rule in Egypt had been just as much a reality as that of the Raj in India. In fact, the British administrative structure in Egypt resembled India's. Sir Evelyn Baring (Lord Cromer), the Proconsul who governed Egypt from 1883 to 1907, had a background of administrative experience in India, as did many of his colleagues—and their upper-class lifestyle in Egypt was just as grand as their counterparts' way of life in India.[18] Cromer held a firm hand on finance and public works. But he was contemptuous of Egyptian national aspirations (a

---

[16] Beeley wrote, for example, in 1957 that the British had 'two immense assets'—'the widespread use of the English language' and 'social and cultural assimilation': 'If an Egyptian who can afford such things wants to complete his son's education, buy clothes for his wife, obtain specialist medical advice or simply escape the summer heat, he goes not to Moscow but to London or Paris' (minute by Beeley, Secret, 28 October 1957, FO 371/125445).

[17] Keith Kyle, *Suez* (London 1991), p. 60 (expressed in slightly different language in Mohamed H. Heikal, *Cutting the Lion's Tail: Suez through Egyptian Eyes* [London, 1986], p. 62). Kyle's is the indispensable work on Suez; the 2003 edition, with the subtitle *Britain's End of Empire in the Middle East,* adds important points of detail. See also his autobiographical account, 'To Suez with Tears', in W. R. Louis, ed., *Still More Adventures with Britannia* (London, 2003). See also W. Scott Lucas, *Divided We Stand* (London, 1991). Three recent important works are Nigel John Ashton, *Eisenhower, Macmillan and the Problem of Nasser* (Basingstoke, UK, 1996); Robert McNamara, *Britain, Nasser, and the Balance of Power in the Middle East, 1952–1967* (London, 2003); and Orna Almog, *Britain, Israel, and the United States, 1955–1958* (London, 2003). The key work on Britain and the origins of Suez is Michael T. Thornhill, 'Britain, the United States and the Rise of an Egyptian Leader: The Politics and Diplomacy of Nasser's Consolidation of Power, 1952–4', *English Historical Review,* 119 (September 2004); and Thornhill, *Road to Suez: The Battle of the Canal Zone* (Stroud, UK, 2006). There is a good recent bibliography in Bertjan Verbeek, *Decision-Making in Great Britain during the Suez Crisis* (Aldershot, UK, 2003); but see also the bibliography by Howard Dooley in the 1991 edition of Louis and Owen, *Suez 1956.*

[18] See Lord Edward Cecil, *The Leisure of an Egyptian Official* (London, 1921); and especially Hugh and Mirabel Cecil, *Imperial Marriage: An Edwardian War and Peace* (London, 2002).

disdain repaid decades later by Egyptian students in England who made pilgrimages to spit on Cromer's grave).[19] In the decades after Cromer, there was no agreement among the British themselves on the question of Egyptian nationalism, but it was usually beyond dispute that Cromer himself had ruled Egypt 'with good administration and even-handed justice'.[20]

Those were the words of Sir John Richmond, who, along with Sir Harold Beeley, deserves attention because of his grasp of Egyptian history and his knowledge of Islam. Richmond was in Houston, Texas, during the Suez crisis (alas, his views on Texas and the Texan reaction to Suez have not survived).[21] Richmond and most others knowledgeable about the Middle East shared a common outlook on British influence as a modernizing force in Egypt. They held as an axiom that the building of roads, railways, dams, banks, and hospitals—above all, the creation of a modern police force and courts of law—were all achievements in the tradition of Britain's Imperial mission. The Cromer legacy could be summed up, in Richmond's words, by stating that 'he gave Egypt a reasonably competent administration and a fair measure of stability.'[22]

Even as late as the 1950s there endured a sense of an intimate relationship between Britain and Egypt.[23] It was shattered by

---

[19] Roger Owen, *Lord Cromer: Victorian Imperialist, Edwardian Proconsul* (Oxford, 2004), p. vii. In a notorious definition, Cromer proclaimed a 'nationalist' in Egypt to be 'a demoslemised Moslem and an invertebrate European': 'The Egyptians are not a nation, and never can be a nation' (quoted in Ronald Hyam, *Britain's Imperial Century* [London, 1976, third edn. 2002], p. 186). For a more realistic assessment in the aftermath of the First World War, see Elie Kedourie, *Chatham House Version*, p. 121, quoting Lord Milner: 'There is undoubtedly an element of Egyptian nationalism which is anti-British, [yet] the better and stronger elements of it are not anti-British but simply pro-Egyptian.'

[20] Sir John Richmond, 'Nasser and Nasserism', Confidential, dated December 1964 and printed as a thirty-one-page Confidential Print, copy of which may be found in FO 371/183886. Richmond drew the distinction between Nasser as an individual and Nasserism as a systematic effort to dominate the Arab states and expand Egyptian influence into Africa. Richmond—and the British in general—attributed to Nasser's methods a coherence that Nasser himself would have found flattering, but in general Richmond's analysis sustains a high degree of accuracy.

[21] 'When Anthony Eden's misguided adventure at Suez ended in disaster and humiliation, it was Richmond's misfortune to be expected, as Her Majesty's Consul-General in Houston, Texas, to explain the British Government's motives to sceptical American audiences' (Michael Adams in Richmond's obituary, *Independent*, 11 July 1990).

[22] J. C. B. Richmond, *Egypt, 1798–1952: Her Advance towards a Modern Identity* (New York, 1977), p. 156.

[23] On which it is important to bear in mind the French perspective: see Jacques Berque, *Egypt: Imperialism & Revolution* (New York, 1972; original French edn., 1967), a remarkable work for its range and perception of Egyptian and British motives as well as for an understanding of the political economy. See also Jean and Simonne Lacouture, *Egypt in Transition* (London, 1958; original French edn., 1956).

Suez.[24] Elizabeth Monroe perhaps better than anyone else provided the epitaph when she wrote of Eden's 'fatal misjudgement of Arab nationalism', which marked the end of an era. She paid tribute to the British, who 'did good jobs in the fields at which they excel—on development, finance, dams, agriculture, drainage and other practical pursuits.'[25] 'Nightfall', the title she chose for the last chapter in the revised edition of *Britain's Moment in the Middle East,* reflected British disillusion in the post-Suez era.

A form of Imperial commitment or control was always in the background, but Egypt more obviously bore the brunt of the worst elements of British imperialism—economic exploitation and military occupation—while failing to receive the benefits of a colonial administration responsible to Parliament. This was the view of Sir Colin Crowe, a figure who played a prominent part in the Middle East in the 1950s and 1960s, both in Egypt and at the United Nations. Reflecting on British rule since Cromer, Crowe held that a clearer demarcation of authority would have been to mutual advantage:

> Until Nasser's revolution the British representative here [in Cairo], whether he was Consul-General, High Commissioner or Ambassador, was, or was thought to be, the ultimate source of power in Egypt. Our relationship would have been far healthier had we made Egypt a *colony* and the lines of authority been laid down clearly.[26]

In this interpretation, which runs through Foreign Office minutes through the Suez crisis and beyond, the British had intervened decisively from time to time in their own self-interest, for example, by installing a puppet government in 1942.[27] The Egyptian reaction to the great events from the 1940s onwards could be expressed in one word: humiliation. The 1942 incident, the victory of Israel in 1948, the with-

---

[24] So also were the bonds of close communication between Britain and the Old Dominions of Australia, New Zealand, South Africa, and Canada, because of Eden's deliberate withholding of information. The Commonwealth was never again the same after Suez. This is a theme that runs through recent essays and books by David McIntyre, but see especially *British Decolonization,* pp. 43–44. The pioneer work is James Eayrs, *The Commonwealth and Suez: A Documentary Commentary* (London,1964).

[25] Elizabeth Monroe, *Britain's Moment in the Middle East* (London, 1981 edn.), p. 219. For a general analysis of the Middle East in the post-war period, Malcolm H. Kerr, *The Arab Cold War* (London, 1965, but see especially the 1971 edn.) remains a key work. For the African equivalent of Monroe's book, see Andrew Roberts, ed., *The Colonial Moment in Africa* (Cambridge, 1986).

[26] Crowe to FO, Confidential, 9 February 1961, FO 371/158807 (emphasis added).

[27] On the 1942 incident, see especially Charles D. Smith, '4 February 1942: Its Causes and Its Influence on Egyptian Politics and on the Future of Anglo-Egyptian Relations, 1937–1945', *International Journal of Middle East Studies,* 10 (1979), pp. 453–79.

drawing of financial assistance for the Aswan High Dam in 1956, and the defeat of 1967 could be described—past, present, and future—in Richmond's phrase, as 'injured Islamic pride'.

The consequences of Suez became especially apparent in 1967, co-incidentally the fiftieth anniversary of the Balfour Declaration. In a se-ries of lightning strikes, the Israelis captured not only the West Bank but also the Gaza Strip, the Sinai Peninsula, and the Golan Heights, and shortly thereafter annexed East Jerusalem. As if in a flash, the fate of former British Palestine was sealed for at least four decades. The British now paid the ultimate price for Suez in what became known as 'THE BIG LIE'.[28] The speed and devastating force of the Israeli at-tacks, according to the Egyptians—in an interpretation quickly ac-cepted in Jordan and throughout the Middle East—could not have been possible without British and American assistance. The assump-tion of British or American aid was false; the Israelis managed to do it on their own, and it was all but forgotten that the Americans had saved the Egyptians from defeat in 1956. But from an Arab vantage point, the logic of British collusion seemed as compelling as it had been at the time of Suez.

The gist of the argument so far is that it is useful to regard the Suez crisis as an episode in decolonization, and decolonization itself as the mirror image of the Scramble for colonies three-quarters of a century earlier. The Suez crisis did not come to an easy or compre-hensive end. Beeley, one of the astutest observers, believed its spectre might reappear because of the Palestine question. He wrote the fol-lowing lines in 1961; it is a key quotation because it fixes the signifi-cance of Suez as it waxed and waned in popular memory, though leav-ing a permanent imprint on the peoples of the Middle East, especially the Egyptians.

> The events of 1956 have left behind a remarkably small residue of directly anti-British feeling, but at the same time they have greatly intensified the suspicion that in the event of any crisis in the rela-tions of Israel with her Arab neighbours the United Kingdom will be found on the Israeli side.[29]

---

[28] See Frank Brenchley, *Britain, The Six-Day War, and Its Aftermath* (London, 2005). See also especially Michael B. Oren, *Six Days of War: June 1967 and the Making of the Modern Middle East* (Oxford, 2002).

[29] Beeley to FO, Confidential, 18 July 1961, FO 371/158786. In the historical literature, Bee-ley usually appears as Ernest Bevin's lieutenant on the Palestine issue, but he also opposed Suez and served twice as Ambassador to Egypt in the 1960s. Before entering government service dur-

In 1967, the Arabs not only held the British responsible for Suez but also, especially in broadcasts heard throughout the region on transistor radios, violently reminded their people of the Balfour Declaration. The Suez crisis itself continued to be a symbol of anti-Western, specifically anti-British, defiance as well as an enduring source of suspicion of British motives, since the British had aligned themselves with the Jews.

Personalities, Traditions, and the Problem of Palestine

Leonard Woolf wrote in the last lines of *Empire & Commerce in Africa*—at the exact time when the great guns of London signalled the end of the Great War—that mankind had the capacity to act as a rational animal controlling the destiny of the world: 'individual men . . . govern the actions of men and nations, of Powers, of States, and of Leagues'.[30] This part of my introductory comment elucidates some of the themes of personalities and policies, of individuals and changing traditions, that run through the volume. It connects the issue of Suez with the consequent, or at least subsequent, enduring problem of Palestine.

The two personalities at the heart of the Suez crisis were, of course, Nasser and Eden, though in British demonology, John Foster Dulles stands close to Nasser.[31] It is illuminating briefly to depict Nasser in relation to the two great incidents leading to the Suez crisis. One was the creation in 1955 of the Baghdad Pact. It polarized the Middle East, in Nasser's view, between Western client states and those Arab states attempting to throw off the shackles of British and French imperialism.

---

ing the Second World War, he had been an academic historian. A Zionist writer summed him up, not unfairly:

> From the outset I found the man, with his cold, incisive intellect, to be an interesting study. He was of the type of person who, in spite of an icy temperament, develops an intensity of passion which holds him in a tight grip. He was not an anti-Semite. His grim, unyielding antagonism to Zionism arose from his assessment and appreciation of British Imperial interests in the East, and perhaps also from a modicum of romantic, and irrational, sympathy for the Arabs.

David Horowitz, *State in the Making* (New York, 1953), p. 38.

[30] Though he wrote those lines in 1918, the book was not published until 1920, and thus some of Woolf's powerful arguments—for example, the effective international control of colonies—had been overtaken by the peace settlement.

[31] See Herman Finer, *Dulles over Suez* (Chicago, 1964), the authoritative study of Dulles, overstated but invaluable.

The foremost British ally was Nuri es Said's Iraq, which Nasser regarded as a satellite of Britain.[32] The other momentous event was the Czech arms deal in the same year. By accepting Russian weapons and, later, advisers, Nasser brought the Cold War to the centre of the Middle East. From a British vantage point, he had taken a huge step towards the Russian camp, though from Nasser's point of view, the historic and immediate enemy was Britain, not the Soviet Union.

Nasser's anti-British attitude was understandable in view of the formative stages of his life.[33] In 1942 he had witnessed national humiliation when the British imposed a pro-Allied government. In 1948 in the war against Israel, he experienced Egypt's devastating defeat, which he attributed to the corruption of the old regime and specifically to King Farouk. As one of the Free Officers in the revolution of 1952, Nasser perfected the art of conspiracy. Those who met him were often struck by his transparent sincerity, but candour formed only one side of a complex personality. He was rational but also calculating and suspicious, especially of the British.[34] One of his achievements was to restore Egyptian pride and sense of dignity after decades of subjugation to the British. To most Egyptians, his embrace of the Arab vision also furthered the cause of Egypt. Nasser was first and foremost an Egyptian patriot, though also an impassioned and genuinely committed Arab nationalist. It is important to bear in mind the distinction as well as the ultimate priority. The two parts of his personality were not incompatible: Arab unity and Egyptian nationalism, if only for a decade or so, seemed inseparable.

Nasser was a charismatic orator whose rhetoric on pan-Arabism inspired his followers and caused Western observers to draw conclusions

[32] For the historical literature on Iraq, see Peter Sluglett, 'Formal and Informal Empire in the Middle East', in Winks, *Historiography;* for the Iraqi revolution, Robert A. Fernea and W. R. Louis, *The Iraqi Revolution of 1958* (London, 1991); see also especially Phebe Marr, *The Modern History of Iraq* (Boulder, Colo., 1985); and Charles Tripp, *A History of Iraq* (Cambridge, 2000).

[33] The best-rounded biography remains Robert Stephens, *Nasser: A Political Biography* (London, 1971). For Nasser and Arab (and Egyptian) nationalism, see especially Adeed Dawisha, *Arab Nationalism in the Twentieth Century: From Triumph to Despair* (Princeton, 2003); and an article of enduring significance by Fouad Ajami, 'The End of Pan-Arabism', *Foreign Affairs*, 57, 2 (Winter 1978–79). See also Joel Gordon, *Nasser's Blessed Movement: Egypt's Free Officers and the July Revolution* (Oxford, 1992); Joel Beinin and Zachary Lockman, *Workers on the Nile* (Princeton, 1987); R. Stephen Humphreys, *Between Memory and Desire: The Middle East in a Troubled Age* (Berkeley, 1999); and Michael Doran, *Pan-Arabism before Nasser: Egyptian Power Politics and the Palestine Question* (New York, 1999). See also especially P. J. Vatikiotis, *The History of Modern Egypt* (London, 1968; 4th edn. 1991); by the same author, see also *The Egyptian Army in Politics* (Bloomington, Ind., 1961); and *Nasser and His Generation* (London, 1978).

[34] 'I sometimes feel he approaches us rather like a police officer giving a reformed criminal the benefit of the doubt while more than half expecting to detect symptoms of recidivism' (Beeley to FO, Secret, 22 February 1963, PREM 11/4173).

about his ambitions. I myself remember—as a student who happened to be in Egypt when the Canal Company was nationalized on the night of 26 July 1956—his rich and melodious voice, which seemed to echo in endless cadences from speaker boxes attached to lamp posts in the streets of Cairo.[35] He had a captivating personality, conveyed not only by his rhetoric but also by the photographs of him that appeared in taxicabs and coffee houses throughout the Middle East. He was the hero of the Arab world, not least because of his defiance of the British. His aims were not modest, but neither were they especially coherent. As later events were to make clear, he was as perplexed and uncertain in the aftermath of the Suez crisis as were the British and Americans.[36]

There is no point of repeating here my interpretation of Eden and the Suez crisis, given at length in the essays, but it may be of interest to note some of the lingering ironies. Eden was often described as a lightweight, but he could hold his own in debate and in intense discussion.[37] He possessed an aesthetic rather than an analytical temperament; he was not by any means an intellectual. When John Foster

[35] On Nasser's decision to nationalize the Suez Canal Company and the coherence of his subsequent response, the comment by Stephen Humphreys repays careful attention: Nasser's actions during the canal crisis and afterwards 'can only be considered a triumph of daring but utterly rational policy making—rational in the motives that propelled it, in the goals it was intended to achieve, and in its estimate of the obstacles to be overcome' (*Between Memory and Desire*, p. 98).

[36] Richmond noted, in words that represented rare praise for Nasser within British circles: 'His personal life is blameless, his intelligence intensely practical, his capacity for work and his tenacity of purpose outstanding, his self-control above the average for his race, his only relaxation chess' (Richmond, 'Nasser and Nasserism', p. 8.) Richmond's interpretation can be usefully compared with that of John Voll:

> Nasser himself was a devout, practicing Muslim and encouraged an analysis of the Islamic bases for socialism . . . The great prestige of Nasser as a revolutionary nationalist and as the leading spokesman for the Arab cause helped to popularize the idea of Islam as being associated with Arab socialism.

John Obert Voll, *Islam: Continuity and Change in the Modern World* (Boulder, Colo., 1982), pp. 170–71.

[37] For example, Churchill remarked to his wife in 1936: 'I think you will see what a lightweight Eden is' (David Reynolds, *In Command of History: Churchill Fighting and Writing the Second World War* [New York, 2005], p. 107). Of the biographies of Eden, David Carlton's iconoclastic *Anthony Eden: A Biography* (London, 1981) has stood the test of time as a coherent and persuasive account. See also his *Britain and the Suez Crisis* (Oxford, 1989). The most recent biography is D. R. Thorpe, *Eden: The Life and Times of Anthony Eden, First Earl of Avon, 1897–1977* (London 2003), which is sympathetic and thorough. See also especially Jonathan Pearson, *Sir Anthony Eden and the Suez Crisis: Reluctant Gamble* (Basingstoke, UK, 2003). Of the memoirs, two of the most significant are Anthony Nutting, *No End of a Lesson* (London 1967); and Selwyn Lloyd, *Suez 1956* (London, 1978).

Dulles came to London, he preferred the fifth Marquess of Salisbury as a dinner partner over Eden because of the latter's lack of interest in abstract concepts and historical interpretation (not that Salisbury was a notable intellect, but his aristocratic charm helped create the impression that he was interested in ideas). Dulles mortally offended Eden on two occasions during the Suez crisis. At one point Dulles implied that the United States hoped to end the era of 'colonialism'. 'It was I who ended the "so-called colonialism" in Egypt,' Eden exclaimed.[38] He referred to the agreement with the Egyptians in 1954 to withdraw troops from the Canal Zone.[39] Slightly later in the Suez crisis, Dulles proclaimed that he had no intention of shooting his way through the canal, thus betraying the belief that the United States would support the British if force proved to be necessary. Eden never forgave him for what the British believed to be a deliberate deception. My own interpretation of Dulles, as will be seen, is that he did not deliberately mislead but hoped, rather like Nasser, that the crisis would peter out after never-ending debate. Dulles emerges from the subsequent crisis in 1958 slightly better than his ponderous, moralistic, and apocalyptic historical reputation might lead one to believe.[40]

There is a point of contrast between Eden and the grandfather of his colleague, Salisbury. The grandfather of the fifth Marquess was

[38] Iverach McDonald, *The History of 'The Times'* (6 vols., London, 1935–94), V, p. 368.

[39] On the strategic dimension of the withdrawal, see the introduction by John Kent, ed., *British Documents on the End of Empire: Egypt and the Defence of the Middle East* (3 parts, London, 1998), which should be compared with Michael J. Cohen, *Strategy and Politics in the Middle East, 1954–1960* (Abingdon, UK, 2005).

[40] Eisenhower's reputation, as it has emerged from the archives, has continued to rise, though there is a twist. In the post-Suez years Eisenhower became increasingly impressed with the need to accommodate black African nationalism as well as the nationalism he was more familiar with in the Philippines or even in its Egyptian manifestation. He was appalled at the thought of black African countries emerging from the colonial system as independent nations. This is a point that can be inferred from Peter G. Boyle, *The Churchill-Eisenhower Correspondence, 1953–1955* (Chapel Hill, N.C., 1990); and, by the same author, *The Eden-Eisenhower Correspondence, 1955–1957* (Chapel Hill, N.C., 2005); for a specific example, see Michael Graham Fry, 'Britain, France, and the Cold War', in Karen Dawisha and Bruce Parrott, eds., *The End of Empire?* (Armonk, N.Y., 1997), p. 153.

For the relationship between Eisenhower and Dulles, the key interpretation remains Robert R. Bowie, 'Eisenhower, Dulles, and the Suez Crisis', in Louis and Owen, *Suez 1956*. See also Cole C. Kingseed, *Eisenhower and the Suez Crisis of 1956* (Baton Rouge, La., 1995). For the Eisenhower administration and the emergence of the United States as a regional power in the Middle East, see Salim Yaqub, *Containing Arab Nationalism: The Eisenhower Doctrine and the Middle East* (Chapel Hill, N.C., 2004). See also especially Douglas Little, *American Orientalism: The United States and the Middle East since 1945* (Chapel Hill, N.C., 2002). I have had the benefit of reading a manuscript by Roby Barrett, 'The Cold War in the Middle East: United States Policies of Modernization and Reform, 1958–1963' (Tauris, forthcoming).

the great Lord Salisbury of the Victorian era. Eden's year of triumph was 1954, when, as Foreign Secretary, he had managed to bring to a successful conclusion the Persian oil crisis, to reach a settlement in Vietnam, and to find common ground with the Egyptians for dismantling the base at Suez. If he had retired from public life at that stage, Eden would be remembered as an accomplished practitioner of British statecraft. The withdrawal from Suez represented perhaps his greatest achievement, but in all those victories he relied on economic and military advisers. In the late nineteenth century, Lord Salisbury's supreme accomplishment was the partition of Africa without the outbreak of European war. His success can be traced in part to the head of the African Department of the Foreign Office, Sir Percy Anderson. Salisbury was in command of detail as well as fundamentals, but Anderson effectively executed Salisbury's policies.

In 1954 Eden in a similar vein relied on his lieutenants. After he became Prime Minister in late 1955, however, he increasingly failed to delegate responsibility as effectively as he had in the past. There were many reasons for the disaster of the Suez operation: one of them was the lack of coordination of military and political aims. The secrecy surrounding Israeli involvement further complicated an already intricate plan.[41] Eden needed experts and friends not only able to provide firm direction but also willing to challenge his assumptions, for example, about the Americans being willing to acquiesce in a successful military strike without being informed beforehand. He required colleagues whose nerve would not crack at the critical time of the invasion itself, as did Harold Macmillan's. Eden's own vanity together with his jealousy of Macmillan proved crippling, yet the Suez operation came close to succeeding, at least in the narrow sense of re-seizing the Canal Zone. Nothing fails like failure, but the outcome of the event has obscured what might have been a successful gamble: if the military strike had been completed, and if a quick negotiated settlement had been possible, with or without Nasser, the British public would have been much more forgiving—about both the intervention itself and the collusion with the French and the Israelis.

---

[41] At this stage of the crisis, Eden was also preoccupied with the prospect of an Israeli attack on Jordan, which might have brought Britain to war against Israel because of the Anglo-Jordan defence treaty; see Almog, *Britain, Israel and the United States*, pp. 84–90. For the Sèvres negotiations, see especially Avi Shlaim, 'The Protocol of Sèvres, 1956: Anatomy of a War Plot', *International Affairs*, 73, 3 (1997). For the Israeli side see, above all, Mordechai Bar-On, *The Gates of Gaza: Israel's Road to Suez and Back, 1955–1957* (Basingstoke, UK, 1994). Michael Brecher, *Decisions in Israel's Foreign Policy* (New Haven, 1975) remains valuable, as does his unique study, *India and World Politics: Krishna Menon's View of the World* (London, 1968).

After Nasser's nationalization of the Canal Company, the initiative lay with Eden to use force if necessary to restore international control—in effect, to demonstrate continuing British hegemony in the Middle East. But there was not a straight line towards military intervention. By September 1956 Eden had begun to play it both ways, wanting to be able to use force, but also to emerge, if necessary and if possible, as a man of peace supporting a solution at the United Nations. Eden spoke the truth in his famous television speech in November 1956, when he explained to the British nation that he had always been a League of Nations man, always a United Nations man. But his apologia needed a qualification. He was a League and UN man in so far as international organizations furthered British aims. The League could be regarded as a Britannic institution, but the United Nations far less so. That was part of Eden's problem.

Eventually the temptation to combine with the French and the Israelis in the late-October attack proved too seductive, though Eden was by no means the only one seduced.[42] There were different degrees of knowledge of the plans to invade Egypt, and Eden himself has often been blamed for a policy supported at the time by, among others, Macmillan, Salisbury, and, tacitly at least, R. A. Butler.[43] Nevertheless it remains astonishing at first sight that the Prime Minister and a handful of others could have virtually hijacked the government down the road towards Suez.[44]

Eden collapsed when his most reliable ally, Salisbury, began increasingly to reflect on Britain's commitment to the United Nations and Macmillan declared that there would be a breakdown of the economy. Eden called a halt to the operation while British forces were still occupying the Canal Zone. The stopping of the forward motion of the troops had great symbolic importance. His failure of the will puzzled the Americans at the time, just as it did his Tory critics. It raised far-reaching questions: Would the British persevere in crises of lesser

---

[42] Nye Bevan, who had a knack for going for the jugular, pursued that line of thought in the House of Commons in a famous comment about the French connection:

> Did Marianne take John Bull to a secret rendezvous? Did Marianne say to John Bull there was a forest fire going to start and did John Bull then say "we ought to put it out" but Marianne then said "No, let us warm our hands by it, it is a nice fire." Did Marianne deceive John Bull or seduce him?

Parliamentary Debates (Commons), 5 December 1956.

[43] On the degrees of knowledge, see especially John Barnes, 'From Eden to Macmillan, 1955–1959', in Peter Hennessy and Anthony Seldon, eds., *Ruling Performance* (Oxford, 1987).

[44] For this line of interpretation, see especially Saul Kelly and Anthony Gorst, eds., *Whitehall and the Suez Crisis* (London, 2000).

magnitude? Would 'Eden's war' have repercussions in the British colonies? Suez cast doubt on British military efficiency and probably exaggerated the strength of Arab nationalism. There was a deeper psychological dimension to the outcome of the Suez crisis. Sir Charles Johnston, the Governor of Aden, expressed it in regard to the Middle East in 1961:

> One of the worst things that has happened to us . . . particularly since Suez, is that in the Middle East we have lost confidence in our ability to deal with situations. This loss of confidence is a very odd thing —it is something which has happened inside ourselves and bears no particular relation to the facts as observed in the field. Our Suez fiasco seems, in effect, to have left a far deeper mark on ourselves than on the Arabs.[45]

It was an acute comment: the sense of humiliation of Suez reinforced anxiety about national decline.[46]

It is no whitewash of Eden to say that he became the scapegoat for a failed policy. His ideas were shared by many of his colleagues, and his policies were accepted by members of the Cabinet—despite some dissent and Eden's withholding of vital information. The overall configuration of political balance, in my view, requires a slightly different judgement than is commonly rendered. Eden does not by any means emerge as a statesman of the first rank. For reasons of temperament alone, he probably should never have become Prime Minister. But he was representative of his age. He believed that the British Empire would continue to survive as a Commonwealth and that Britain would remain a world power, as did many of his countrymen. He thought in historical analogies to the 1930s, as did many others. He had moral lapses, and perhaps the greatest part of his misfortune is that he betrayed himself and his country not by believing in the rightness of his cause, but by lying about his methods. Nevertheless, he deserves better than the treatment his colleagues gave him and merits more balanced consideration than the assessments of many historians. Eden must be held accountable as the captain of the ship, but Suez was very much a collective enterprise.

Eden's successor, Harold Macmillan, adroitly and even brilliantly

[45] Johnston to Sir Roger Stevens, Personal and Confidential, 16 March 1961, CO 1015/2185. This is a diagnosis in line with a post–Cold War assessment of the significance of Suez: Tony Judt, *Postwar: A History of Europe since 1945* (New York, 2005), p. 299: 'The lasting consequences of the Suez crisis were felt in British society.' On the military consequences, see Cohen, *Strategy and Politics in the Middle East,* chap. 10.

[46] For the issue of decline, see especially Peter Clarke and Clive Trebilcock, *Understanding Decline: Perceptions and Realities of British Economic Performance* (Cambridge, 1997).

managed the post-Suez crisis.[47] He effectively set in motion the disengagement from Africa and the Middle East while trying to protect the British lifeline to Aden and Singapore from 'the southward drive of Nasser and the Russians'.[48] His Edwardian theatrics may make him appear to be an improbable latter-day Lord Salisbury scrambling out of Africa, but in fact Macmillan played the Great Game just as deftly. Macmillan and Salisbury both were intellectuals in the sense of being men capable of entertaining large ideas.[49] Both were sensitive to the domestic consequences of expanding or contracting the Empire. But while Salisbury's historical reputation has continued to rise, in part because of the skill with which he presided over the Scramble for colonies, Macmillan's has suffered. Among other reasons, he created the impression of concealing British decline. His famous statement that the British people had 'never had it so good' came back to haunt him.[50] Yet Macmillan's slogans and showmanship should not be allowed to obscure the decisive part he played in the history of decolonization by appointing Iain Macleod Colonial Secretary in 1959.[51] Macmillan thereby dramatically accelerated the pace of independence, though not at all in the way he had intended; in his view, Macleod moved too fast, becoming in Africa the equivalent of Mountbatten in India. Macmillan's grand design was to reconvert the Empire into spheres of informal influence rather than direct control. But the

[47] For example, Simon Ball, *The Guardsmen* (London, 2004), p. 320: 'In a series of short-term manoeuvres, he [Macmillan] managed to lay the blame for the Suez crisis on Eden and Butler rather than himself. As a political adventurer it was his finest moment.' Alistair Horne, *Macmillan* (2 vols., London, 1988–89) remains the point of departure for understanding the complexity of Macmillan's personality.

[48] Minutes by Burke Trend, 1 March 1957, and 20 November 1958, PREM 11/2582. 'Inevitably', commented Trend, one of Macmillan's advisers, 'American money would have to finance the greater part of this policy.'

[49] 'Of all Queen Victoria's Prime Ministers, Lord Salisbury is, it seems to me, the only one who may be called an intellectual' (Elie Kedourie, 'Lord Salisbury and Politics', *Encounter*, 38, 6 [June 1972]). Nigel Nicolson, a Tory MP who lost his seat because of his protest against the Suez invasion, described Macmillan as 'the most intelligent Prime Minister of the century' (Nigel Nicolson, ed., *Harold Nicolson: The Later Years, 1945–1962* [New York, 1968], p. 331). Macmillan certainly was one of the best read of the twentieth-century Prime Ministers. In 1942 he had been a junior minister at the Colonial Office. For the extraordinary breadth of his reading on the Empire, see the Macmillan Papers in Bodleian Library c. 277, which reveals, among other curiosities, close attention to the writings of W. K. Hancock and Margery Perham.

[50] See Dominic Sandbrook, *Never Had It So Good: A History of Britain from Suez to the Beatles* (London, 2005).

[51] For Macleod and decolonization, see especially the introduction by Ronald Hyam in Ronald Hyam and W. R. Louis, eds., *British Documents on the End of Empire: The Conservative Government and the End of Empire, 1957–1964* (2 parts, London, 2000).

British wind of change blew through Africa with greater strength than it did in the Middle East and South-East Asia.[52]

Inwardly, Macmillan's moments of gloom were just as pessimistic as the black moods about the British Empire that had sometimes characterized Lord Salisbury's outlook. He had forebodings of a 'British Algeria' in central Africa and of being left in the last colonial ditch with Portugal. Yet Macmillan rose to the occasion, suggesting the very opposite of decline and fall. His dramatic Edwardian rhetoric, literary allusions, and grand talk of Britain's historic mission suggested optimism, adaptability, and progress. Time and again he gave the ebullient impression that Britain remained in control of her Imperial destiny, even in the Middle East.

Different people took different lessons from Suez, but Macmillan learned that he could not get back on good terms with the Americans unless he demonstrated that the British were contrite and no longer possessed a Suez mentality.[53] He drew the moral that Britain must always align herself with the United States, above all in the Middle East. But he did not change his ideas about Nasser. He believed that the fate of the Empire was balanced on a knife-edge, and that Nasser held the capacity to topple the remaining citadels of British power in the Middle East, including oil holdings in the Gulf—which would have been disastrous for the British economy. To Macmillan, Nasser symbolized the aspirations of the Arab people only in the analogical sense that Hitler was a typical German representing an aggressive and expansionist national spirit—and so he equated Nasserism with Nazism. This was a view poles apart from the later attitude of the Labour Government under Harold Wilson, and from that of George Brown, the

[52] For example, the irrepressible Arthur de la Mare, an Assistant Under-Secretary at the Foreign Office, wrote of the 'Wind of Change' in East and South-East Asia:

> It is quite untrue to say that the local people want us to go. They want us to stay . . . If we give the impression of losing interest in East Asia let us not imagine that that will be hailed locally with jubilation—it will cause regret, bewilderment, apprehension and eventually resentment.

Memorandum by de la Mare, 21 March 1967, FCO 49/10.

[53] On the 'Special Relationship', see, for example, Nigel J. Ashton, 'Harold Macmillan and the "Golden Days" of Anglo-American Relations Revisited', *Diplomatic History,* 29, 4 (September 2005), which has good and up-to-date bibliographical notes. See also especially W. Scott Lucas, 'The Cost of Myth: Macmillan and the Illusion of the "Special Relationship"', in Richard Aldous and Sabine Lee, eds., *Harold Macmillan: Aspects of a Political Life* (Basingstoke, UK, 1999). For Macmillan and France, see the important work by Peter Mangold, *The Almost Impossible Ally: Harold Macmillan and Charles de Gaulle* (London, 2005).

Foreign Secretary in the late 1960s who sympathized with Nasserism as a secular, pan-Arab political philosophy to which many Arabs legitimately aspired.[54] To Macmillan, Nasserism meant belligerent aims and an anti-colonial, anti-British movement that threatened to sweep the Middle East. But small gestures can sometimes be significant. Like Eden, Macmillan while Prime Minister met Nasser only once. It happened at the United Nations in September 1960. As a formality, and only as a formality, Macmillan extended his hand. It seemed to mark the beginning of a new era—rather like Lord Curzon clasping the hand of a Bolshevik in an earlier age.[55]

In the arena of British politics and the meaning of the aftermath of Suez in the eyes of the British public, it helps to focus briefly on the Tory side and on Julian Amery, who was at the Colonial Office as Under-Secretary for most of the time of Macleod's tenure, but who held a diametrically opposed outlook. Amery is of interest because he was *the* Imperialist of his generation in the same way that his father, Leopold Amery, had represented the ideals of the British Empire in a previous era.[56] For Amery, the Empire was not to be liquidated, but sustained, nurtured, re-created, and defended. Amery can also be taken as an arch-enemy not only of the United States but above all of the United Nations.

Amery held, for example, that the British should continue to occupy Aden as a city-port and military garrison despite an anarchic or hostile hinterland. The 'Gibraltar' of Aden would become the keystone in the new Imperial system, a fortress protecting Britain's position in the Gulf regardless of Aden or Arab nationalism. According to Amery: 'One of the greater heresies of contemporary thought is that a base is useless if situated amidst a hostile population.'[57] He believed

---

[54] See George Brown, *In My Way* (London, 1971), chaps. 7 and 9. Brown recognized, as few British observers did at the time, that Nasserism, though anti-imperialist, was anti-leftist and did not embrace Marxist assumptions such as the class struggle.

[55] 'It was Mr. Macmillan's handshake with President Nasser at the General Assembly in December [*sic:* September] 1960 which led to . . . a steady improvement of relations over the ensuing two years' (minute by R. S. Scrivener, 4 November 1964, FO 371/178597).

[56] See Noel Annan, *Our Age: Portrait of A Generation* (London, 1990), p. 32. On the Conservative right, see also Leon D. Epstein, *British Politics in the Suez Crisis* (Urbana, Ill., 1964); Ian Gilmour, *The Body Politic* (London, 1969); Philip Murphy, *Party Politics and Decolonization: The Conservative Party and British Colonial Policy in Tropical Africa, 1951–1964* (Oxford, 1995); and especially Sue Onslow, *Backbench Debate within the Conservative Party and Its Influence on British Foreign Policy, 1948–57* (Basingstoke, UK, 1997).

[57] Minute by Amery, 10 March 1959, CO 1015/1910. In the next year Amery conducted the negotiations with Makarios on the sovereign bases in Cyprus. On the Cyprus problem, the crucial and incisive work is Robert Holland, *Britain and the Revolt in Cyprus, 1954–1959* (Oxford, 1998).

that Aden could be effectively defended and to hell with the rest of the world. Were the world a different place—and if Amery's outlook had prevailed, as he and others still hoped it might as late as the 1960s—the British Empire would continue to exist today.

It is also useful to establish a dominant Labour perspective on Suez and its aftermath.[58] Labour opinion tended to be not only anti-Suez but also pro-United Nations—and pro-Israel. In the Labour Government of the 1960s, there was an underlying pro-Israel commitment, not least by the Prime Minister himself, Harold Wilson. This meant a shift in the overall balance of British policy towards the region. In the turbulent era of the 1960s, in the cultural and social explosion represented by the flower children, the campaigners for nuclear disarmament, and those who protested against the war in Vietnam, the Israeli victory over the Arab states in 1967 represented a watershed. The Israeli triumph also made clear the legacy of the Suez crisis for the ongoing problem of Palestine.

The aftermath of the 1967 war can be regarded as a missed opportunity. This was the view at the time of Cecil Hourani, Albert Hourani's brother, who spent part of his career as the adviser to Bourguiba of Tunisia. He thus had a view of the Palestine problem from the perspective of the former French empire and the Maghrib. The two Hourani brothers tried to make the Arab side of the Palestine controversy comprehensible to Western audiences.[59] In 1967 Cecil Hourani published an article in *Encounter* called 'The Moment of Truth'. Part of the article's significance is the debate it stirred up in the Foreign and Commonwealth Office, but it is important in its own right for historical insight. He argued that the end of the 1967 war represented a critical juncture in the history of the Arabs. 'At this moment when the destiny of the Arab nation is being decided', he wrote, 'it is the duty of every Arab thinker to witness the truth as he sees it.' With ruthless clarity he established the chronology and the principal Arab mistakes:

> The St. James's Conference in London in 1938 [*sic:* 1939] between the British Government and some of the Arab Governments led to the White Paper, which was in our favour but which we rejected. In

[58] For the Labour era of the 1960s and 1970s, see Kenneth O. Morgan, *Callaghan: A Life* (Oxford, 1997); and, by the same author, *Labour People* (Oxford, 1987). See also especially Stephen Howe, *Anticolonialism in British Politics: The Left and the End of Empire, 1918–1964* (Oxford, 1993).

[59] For Albert Hourani on the significance and consequences of the Suez crisis, see his essay in Louis and Owen, *Suez 1956*. His other relevant essays are 'The Anglo-Egyptian Agreement: Some Causes and Implications', in *Middle East Journal,* 9, 3 (1955); 'The Middle East and the Crisis of 1956', *St. Antony's Papers,* 4 (1958); 'Independence and the Imperial Legacy', *Middle East Forum,* 42, 3 (1966).

1948 we secured the evacuation of British civil and military authorities from Palestine but we did not take the necessary steps to take
their place. In 1948 again, after our first unsuccessful war, we could
have turned our military defeat into a limited political victory and
confined Israel to an insignificant territory.

When reality catches up with us, it is always too late. At every *débâcle* we regret that we did not accept a situation which no longer exists. In 1948
we regretted that we had not accepted the 1947 UN plan for partition. In May 1967 we were trying to go back to pre-Suez.[60]

The Arabs had suffered a grave defeat, but they could yet shape their
own future if they were honest with themselves and demonstrated a
collective will to resolve the Palestine question in the Arab tradition of
magnanimity. The greatest challenge that confronted the Arabs in
1967, he believed, would be to reject fanatical visions and demonstrate
that 'there is room in Arab society for the Jews'. 'Our greatest victory',
he concluded, 'will be the day when the Jews in Palestine will prefer to
live in an Arab society rather than in an Israeli one. It is up to us to
make that possible.'

Cecil Hourani's essay was read with great interest within the Foreign
and Commonwealth Office and by the Foreign Secretary himself,
George Brown. Sir Roger Beaumont, who shortly was to become Ambassador in Egypt, wrote as if releasing pent-up feelings of frustration
in dealing with the Arabs over a long period of time:

It has always seemed facile to compare the character and particularly
the shortcomings of the Arab governments to those of an adolescent
but this is precisely the conclusion to which Cecil Hourani's article
comes without saying so in as many words: wishful thinking (idealism, if you like), refusal to face facts, moral cowardice, love of slogans
and clinging to bogus principles, refusal to compromise, evasion of
responsibility, shifting of blame, emotional reactions which clash
with true interests and result in schizophrenic policies harming one-
self more than one's opponents.[61]

---

[60] Cecil Hourani, 'The Moment of Truth', *Encounter,* 29, 5 (November 1967), pp. 3–14. He
expanded on the critical importance of the year 1948 as a turning point:
   After 1948 Zionism was confined to a tiny territory which was strategically weak and
   scarcely viable economically. Had we consolidated the independence we had gained,
   we could have contained Israel, and with it World Zionism, for fifty years, after which
   Israel itself would have ceased to be a threat to us, and become just another Levantine
   state, part Jewish, part Arab, but overwhelmingly Oriental.
[61] Minute by Beaumont, 19 October 1967, FCO 17/95.

Beaumont and others in the Foreign and Commonwealth Office agreed with Hourani's main argument that the Arab governments should cooperate with the United Nations; but they rejected—as had their predecessors in the Colonial Office and Foreign Office since 1947—his implicit conclusion that, under UN tutelage, the West Bank should eventually become an independent Palestinian state. The proposal for a Palestinian state was still, in 1967, ahead of its time, and was viewed as little more than a potential home for anti-Western fanaticism. But Hourani was surely right in his remark about missed opportunity. He wrote some four months after the 1967 war: 'The point may soon be reached where the Arabs say "to hell with compromise, which leads nowhere" and then return to a more belligerent position.'[62]

One of the reasons the Suez crisis divided the British public was the issue of the United Nations. Paul Johnson, then a young editor at the *New Statesman,* caught the spirit of those who believed in the United Nations when he wrote a few months after Suez that Britain and France had been 'lurching towards a moral disaster'.[63] The historic comment at the time of the invasion was David Astor's apology in an *Observer* leader:

> We wish to make an apology. Five weeks ago we remarked that, although we knew our Government would not make a military attack in defiance of its solemn international obligations, people abroad might think otherwise. The events of last week have proved us completely wrong; if we misled anyone, at home or abroad, we apologize unreservedly. We had not realised that our government was capable of such folly and crookedness.[64]

The sentiment endured. The Labour Government of the 1960s reaffirmed its international commitments in such a way as to repudiate the deviant path of Sir Anthony Eden, the invasion of Egypt, and the flouting of the United Nations.

This re-embracing of the principles of the United Nations became apparent in one of the most difficult problems generated by the per-

---

[62] Cecil Hourani to Frank Brenchley, 20 October 1967, FCO 17/95.

[63] Johnson, *Suez War,* p. 95. On the other hand, those in favour of the war—more than half the British population—were not necessarily anti–United Nations, though there was a hard-core group of Members of Parliament, including Julian Amery and the 'Suez group', who could certainly be described as hostile, not least because of the belief, accurate enough, that the United Nations would increasingly interfere in the affairs of the British Empire.

[64] Quoted in Richard Cockett, *David Astor and 'The Observer'* (London, 1991), pp. 219–20. For the press and radio, see Tony Shaw, *Eden, Suez, and the Mass Media: Propaganda and Persuasion during the Suez Crisis* (London, 1996).

sistent, aggravating, and ideological criticism of the UN Special Committee on Colonialism, which, as already mentioned, became known as the Committee of the 24. One of the consequences of the Suez crisis was that, in the aftermath, virtually none of the Third World countries took the British at their word. Suez had shattered Britain's ethical position. One of the advantages that Sir Hugh Foot (Lord Caradon, as he will be referred to here) brought to the job as British representative on the trusteeship council, and subsequently as Ambassador to the United Nations itself, was that he had been a Colonial Governor who sympathized with nationalist aims. When he spoke to Asians and Africans in New York, he did not condescend but regarded them as equals. Caradon was wholeheartedly, enthusiastically, and spiritually committed to the United Nations, to such an extent that pro-UN attitudes became known as 'Caradonian'. The word 'Caradonian' came to mean total commitment to peace and decolonization, a repudiation of Suez, and a reaffirmation of UN principles.

Caradon would reply point by point to allegations of ulterior British motives and to the denigration of true ones, believing that every opportunity should be taken to establish the accuracy of the colonial record, of which the British had every right to be proud. He fended off proposals from within the British government to withdraw from the Committee of 24. He held that withdrawal would stand symbolically as Britain reverting to true form, especially in the eyes of enemies of British imperialism—as returning to the Britain of Anthony Eden and the invasion of Egypt. So powerful was the recent memory of Suez that no Labour Government wanted to give the impression of reversing course and re-establishing Britain as a reactionary power. The legacy of Suez thus steered Britain into reaffirming the United Nations as a principal feature of Britain's place in the modern world: Suez itself had been a gigantic aberration that proved the general rule.

Three Ideas

In this collection of essays there are three original ideas, or so I believed. The first idea is about decolonization as a mirror image of the Scramble and vice versa—about which I shall add only a point about 'the ends of British imperialism' and another about British decline. As the title of the book suggests, in a sense I am concerned with motive. This is a theme that runs through virtually all of the essays.

In another sense I am interested in periods of time and the way in which the dominant historical motif changes from one decade to the next. The Scramble came to a close at the turn of the twentieth century, only to be revived by the First World War. The inter-war years were those of formal colonial rule, though in regions such as the Middle East there were significant distinctions between formal colonies (such as Cyprus and Aden), mandated territories (Palestine, Jordan, and Iraq), and the 'Protected States', as they were eventually designated, in the Gulf. The period of dissolution lasted from Indian independence in 1947 to the withdrawal of all troops East of Suez in 1971 (certain important issues, of course, lingered on: above all, Rhodesia, the Falklands, Hong Kong).[65] The argument put forward in these essays is that it is useful to see the Suez era as extending to the death of Nasser in 1970 and the British withdrawal from the Gulf in the following year. An official of long-standing colonial experience, Sir Leslie Monson, could write as late as 1970: 'Public opinion in this country . . . [is] anti-Nasser [and] . . . still smarting over our rebuff at Suez.'[66] The magic of Nasser's rhetoric wore thin after his defeat in 1967; the civil war in the Yemen became, in the phrase of the day, Nasser's Vietnam, thus deflecting his attention from British imperialism.[67] Nevertheless, the aftermath of the Suez crisis came to a close only in the years 1970–71, thus marking the end of an epoch.

One further and final point to be made about the Suez crisis concerns not only decolonization but also the issue of economic and political decline. Eden was often much more candid with one of the editors of *The Times,* Iverach McDonald, than he was with colleagues. McDonald recalled that Eden was preoccupied above all with Britain's deterioration as a Great Power. The recollection is significant both because it connects the Suez crisis with the controversy of decline and because it very clearly sums up the contemporaneous view of the significance of Suez:

> In history the decline of a state's power in the world has often shown itself gradually over a long time. For Britain, still preserving much of the prestige won by its efforts and successes in the Second World War, the decline showed itself most dramatically during the few short hours in which the government decided to call off the Suez venture under international pressure.
>
> It thereby acknowledged that a British government, or the British and French together, no longer had the strength to carry out an in-

---

[65] For the 1967 decision to withdraw, in the sweep of British defence policy since 1945, see Saki Dockrill, *Britain's Retreat from East of Suez: The Choice between Europe and the World?* (Basingstoke, UK, 2002).

[66] Minute by Monson, 27 July 1970, FCO 49/295.

[67] See Clive Jones, *Britain and the Yemen Civil War, 1962–1965: Ministers, Mercenaries, and Mandarins: Foreign Policy and the Limits of Covert Action* (Brighton, UK, 2004).

dependent military venture, even one strictly limited in scope, if the
United States and other allies swung against the action.[68]

In the eyes of contemporaries, Suez punctured the mystique of British
power.

The second idea is the evolution of the concept of trusteeship in relation to the consequences of self-determination. My interest originated with a study of the Berlin Act of 1885 as a landmark in the tradition of trusteeship, which Roger Casement and E. D. Morel upheld
by attacking the abuses in King Leopold's regime in the Congo. The
Berlin Act and the Congo controversy leading to Belgium's annexation of the Congo in 1908 were precedents for the mandates system of
the League of Nations.[69] The mandates embodied the principle of
self-determination. The British endorsed the principle with calculation, as Lord Curzon made clear when he said that the natives would
determine in British favour because of their dislike of the French. Very
few in 1919, or for that matter 1945, foresaw that the consequences
of self-determination would lead to a world of microstates.[70] The

---

[68] McDonald, *History of 'The Times'*, V, p. 275.

[69] For useful recent works, see Michael D. Callahan, *Mandates and Empire: The League of Nations and Africa, 1914–1931* (Brighton, UK, 1999); and Susan Pedersen, 'Settler Colonialism at
the Bar of the League of Nations,' in Caroline Elkins and Susan Pedersen, eds., *Settler Colonialism in the Twentieth Century* (New York, 2005).

[70] According to the political philosopher Martin Wight, reflecting in 1960 on the Suez crisis,
the fault line on self-determination divided those (such as Eden) who believed in gradual independence and those (such as the late John Foster Dulles) who held that independence should
be granted as soon as possible:

> Some of Eden's critics seem to argue that the right policy is to grant independence to
> the rest of Asia and Africa as quickly as possible, and let the newly enfranchised mem-
> bers of the international society settle down to industrialize themselves and practise
> democracy with only such benevolent help from the older Powers as the newer them-
> selves will ask.

Wight went on to explain the relevance of the principle of self-determination to the Suez crisis:

> This may be a dream-transformation of the historical experience called Balkaniza-
> tion, which means a *Kleinstaaterei* of weak States, fiercely divided among themselves by
> nationalistic feuds, governed by unstable popular autocracies, unaccustomed to in-
> ternational law and diplomatic practice as they are to parliamentary government, and
> a battle-ground for the surrounding Great Powers. If it were clearer that this is not the
> future of the uncommitted world [as Dulles seemed to hope it would not], it would be
> clearer that Eden's analysis was wrong, however much he may be blamed for not find-
> ing policies whereby a declining Great Power can mitigate the evil.

Martin Wight, 'Brutus in Foreign Policy', *International Affairs*, 36, 3 (July 1960), pp. 308–09.

Colonial Office, however, eventually began to acknowledge that the genie of self-determination, released from the bottle, would have worldwide and revolutionary repercussions. Where would it all end, asked Christopher Eastwood, one of the more reflective of the Colonial Office mandarins—with independence for Pitcairn, with its minuscule population? 'Pitcairn Island, with 70 or 80 inhabitants, cannot really become independent.'[71] In 1956, on the eve of the Suez crisis, the membership of the United Nations had expanded from 51 to 67 and had not yet acquired its later reputation as an aggressive anti-colonial champion of self-determination. By 1967, at the time of the decision to recall all British troops East of Suez, the membership had grown to 133 (in 2006 it stands at 191). Clearly, the future lay with the wave of independent states.

The international system of today is the antithesis of the regional configurations that the Colonial Office had created in the 1950s and 1960s by constructing federations in the Caribbean, Nigeria, central Africa, Aden, the Gulf, and Malaysia—with mixed results. Aden is again a good example because it was the last major British bastion.[72] The building of the Federation of the Colony and Protectorate in 1963 symbolized one of the last acts of Britain's Imperial will. It took place at a time when comparable federations in the West Indies and central Africa either had collapsed or were on the brink of dissolution. The aim in Aden was admirable. It made geographic, economic, and administrative sense for the resources of the hinterland to be exploited by the vibrant economy of the city-port, and for the city-port itself to develop the hinterland rather than become an independent city-state on the model of Singapore.[73] The pooling of resources would allow for

[71] Minute by Eastwood, 20 October 1964, CO 936/925. Despite Eastwood's fears, Pitcairn Island, with a declining population—46 in 2006—has not yet become a member of the United Nations.

[72] See Spencer Mawby, *British Policy in Aden and the Protectorates, 1955–67: Last Outpost of a Middle East Empire* (London, 2005). I have had the benefit of reading the unpublished Ph.D. dissertation by John Allgood, 'Britain's Final Decade in South Arabia: Aden, the Federation and the Struggle against Arab Nationalism' (University of Texas, 1999). See also especially Simon C. Smith, *Britain's Revival and Fall in the Gulf* (London, 2004). The best historical survey is Rosemarie Said Zahlan's invaluable *The Making of the Modern Gulf States: Kuwait, Bahrain, Qatar, the United Arab Emirates, and Oman* (Reading, UK, 1998 edn.)

[73] In an exception to the general pattern—as will be seen in the essay on Hong Kong—Sir Alexander Grantham, the Governor of Hong Kong, made a critical decision in the early post-war years *not* to set Hong Kong on the path towards becoming a independent Commonwealth city-state. Grantham believed that Hong Kong was a Chinese port that must ultimately revert to China. He thus prepared the way for Hong Kong's later wealth and prosperity by assuring the Chinese Communists that the British had no plans for independence. See Steve Yui-Sang Tsang, *Democracy Shelved: Great Britain, China, and Attempts at Constitutional Reform in Hong Kong, 1945–*

the financing of large-scale development. But there was a hostile re-action from Yemen, Egypt, and the Arab world generally. Nasser pro-claimed an all-out war of liberation. When the High Commissioner, Sir Kennedy Trevaskis, visited New York in late 1963 in an attempt to prevent an adverse judgement at the bar of world opinion, he was treated to the full blast of anti-colonial sentiment from the UN Spe-cial Committee on Colonialism and told that Aden's jails were worse than Hitler's death camps. The public mood had changed: the British now felt beleaguered. Aden was regarded as a pariah colony at the United Nations, and Aden itself was in the throes of a terrorist insur-rection. The initiative passed to the leaders of the revolution. In Brit-ain, the collapse of the British position in Aden in 1967 marked the zenith of the anti-Empire spirit of the 1960s.

As I studied the archives from the 1960s, it seemed to me that the neglected dimension of decolonization lay in the transformation of international society at the United Nations.[74] In 1968, Conor Cruise O'Brien analysed the changing personality of the United Nations by showing how it had come to foster multiculturalism, multiracialism, and decolonization as well as peace.[75] The moral authority of the United Nations endowed it with a charisma and a quasi-religious qual-ity—with Dag Hammarskjöld as the secular Pope on the East River—and the new priorities in Turtle Bay took on an air that was at once sa-cred and chic. To those within the British government following these ideological developments, the consequences for the British colonies were dangerous because they were irrational yet compelling. Never-theless, the British public, on the whole, still believed that the United Nations symbolized the hope of humankind.

The third idea is the imperialism of decolonization, which means the reversion to indirect control or influence rather than direct colo-nial rule. Just as decolonization was the mirror image of the Scramble, especially in its economic motive, so too did the end of the colonial

---

1952 (Oxford, 1988). For Malaysia and Singapore, see Matthew Jones, *Conflict and Confrontation in South East Asia, 1961–1965* (Cambridge, 2002).

[74] But see A. W. Brian Simpson, *Human Rights and the End of Empire: Britain and the Genesis of the European Convention* (Oxford, 2001), a magnificent contribution to the study of Britain and the United Nations in the context of the history of human rights.

[75] Conor Cruise O'Brien, *The United Nations: Sacred Drama* (New York, 1968). On the signifi-cance of O'Brien's book, see Adam Roberts and Benedict Kingsbury, *United Nations, Divided World* (Oxford, 1993), p. 21. Two useful works dealing with important case studies are Alan James, *Brit-ain and the Congo Crisis, 1960–1963* (Basingstoke, UK, 1996); and Neil Briscoe, *Britain and UN Peacekeeping, 1948–67* (Basingstoke, UK, 2003). See also especially Brian Urquhart, *A Life in Peace and War* (New York, 1987).

era, specifically the part played by the United States, re-enact the economic origins of the Empire. The British Empire in theory was self-financing. It could hardly have been otherwise: the costs of colonial rule had to be accepted by the Treasury and ultimately the British taxpayer. The aim was not that Britain should sustain the Empire but that the Empire should sustain Britain. After the Second World War, when the British economy degenerated into virtual bankruptcy, Britain—and the British Empire—revived thanks to American wealth and power. The magnitude of the economic transfusion and the resulting effect of propping up the colonial system was one of the discoveries that Ronald Robinson and I made together over a period of six summers as we examined the archival evidence and worked out our argument. We became friends forevermore, but we also argued, continually and usually exuberantly. Such was the nature of our collaboration that it made me wonder how *Africa and the Victorians* ever saw the light of day. Eventually we agreed that neither metropolitan infirmity nor nationalist insurgency could explain the dissolution of the Empire without also taking into account the part played by the United States —and I would now give more emphasis to the United Nations. The British aim was to harness American capitalism to British purposes and to alter the structure of the Empire from formal rule to more indirect control, or at least influence. Such is the imperialism of decolonization.

Ronald Robinson had provided part of the argument in his essay 'The Imperialism of Free Trade', written with John Gallagher.[76] I had anticipated part of it in *The British Empire in the Middle East* when I tried to come to terms with the paradox of informal empire and intervention, covert as well as military. Subsequently I studied in considerable detail the overthrow of the Iranian government of Muhammad Musaddiq in 1953. We now know more about that combined operation of MI6 (the overseas arm of Britain's intelligence services) and the CIA than about any comparable post-1945 intelligence operation. MI6 archives remain even more tightly sealed than CIA records. But the accidental disclosure of a CIA official history—the account written by Donald Wilber, described in the Musaddiq essay—revealed an unprecedented amount of information about both intelligence agencies.

In studying the Musaddiq operation I began to reflect on my argument about intervention presented in *The British Empire in the Middle*

---

[76] John Gallagher and Ronald Robinson, 'Imperialism of Free Trade', *Economic History Review*, 2nd series, 6, 1 (1953).

East, and, more specifically, about Ernest Bevin. I wrote in 1984 about
'a theme that runs through Bevin's minutes':

> Quite apart from his perception of the economic crisis and the scar-
> city of resources, he judged that the British public would not tolerate
> colonial war or even prolonged suppression of resistance. To para-
> phrase both Burke and Tocqueville, he was fully aware that democ-
> racies and empires went ill together, and that the British system, if
> it were to succeed at all, would have to be dismantled and then re-
> constructed.
>
> The history of the British Empire in the Middle East during this pe-
> riod may be read as the unsuccessful attempt at conversion from for-
> mal rule and alliances to an informal basis of equal partnership and
> influence. Here there is a final paradox. The purpose of this trans-
> formation was the perpetuation of Britain as a great 'world power'.
> Non-intervention thus becomes intervention by other means.[77]

I now take the opportunity slightly to modify my views. I came to regard Ernest Bevin as the champion of non-intervention, as a man of
principle as well as common sense. He often said that the Middle East
could not be held by bayonets. But there was also a certain ruthless
quality to Bevin, as shown by his Palestine policy. He believed that the
peoples of Egypt, Iran, and elsewhere should rule themselves. He intended to convert the Empire into sovereign independent nations allied to Britain in common cause. Yet even though I have only circumstantial evidence, I now think that his faith in the new British Empire
was so great that he eventually would have gone to any length, even
intervention, to achieve his aims—including the overthrow of Musaddiq, and not only for reasons concerning the British Empire: Musaddiq seemed to be leading Iran into communist revolution and possible Soviet domination.

The point about intervention is of general significance because it
throws into relief the outstanding ethical as well as political quality
of the Labour Government of 1945–51. In 1951 Musaddiq nationalized the Anglo-Iranian Oil Company, thereby precipitating a debate
among Attlee and his colleagues whether to intervene. In 1953 the
Churchill government, together with the Eisenhower administration,
authorized a secret operation to remove Musaddiq from power—with
consequences to the present day. The overthrow of Musaddiq thus had
incalculably greater consequences than Eden's abortive reoccupation

[77] W. R. Louis, *The British Empire in the Middle East, 1945–1951* (Oxford, 1984), p. 15.

of the Canal Zone during the Suez war. As will be seen in the essays, decisions opposed to intervention can be just as difficult as those in favour. In the crisis over Iran in 1951, the Prime Minister faced chauvinistic and aggressive colleagues who wanted to invade. To his eternal credit, Attlee held firm against intervention.

THE LEGACY OF EUROPEAN COLONIALISM

1

THE COLONIAL EMPIRES
IN THE LATE NINETEENTH
AND EARLY TWENTIETH CENTURIES

In the late nineteenth and early twentieth centuries, colonial empires were associated with ideas of national greatness, competitiveness, and survival of the fittest. The colours painted on maps over vast areas of Asia and Africa symbolized national power, prestige, and destiny. Colonies seemed to enrich national character and to encapsulate national glory. The 'natives' were to be civilized, and the raw materials and other resources of the colonies would benefit the economy of the metropolitan country. But the popular view was not entirely optimistic or beneficent. Technological advance made it easy to believe in human progress throughout the world, yet humankind seemed trapped in an evolutionary struggle. Only the fittest nations and the fittest empires would survive. Great powers should possess great empires at the expense, if necessary, of lesser empires. Before 1914 the British Foreign Secretary, Sir Edward Grey, spoke of the Portuguese colonies as 'sinks of iniquity' and thought it would be merely a matter of time until they were partitioned between Germany and Britain. The possessions of the weaker colonial powers would be absorbed by the stronger, just as the territories of 'dying' nations of Turkey and China would be annexed by the more virile European nations. The drive for empire contributed to a spirit of ruthless militarism.

As William L. Langer wrote in *The Diplomacy of Imperialism* (1936): centuries hence, when general interest in the details of the European empires will perhaps have faded, historians will continue to record the phantasmagoric significance attached to colonies in the years before 1914. They will also note the frenzied energy of the explorers, adventurers, soldiers, missionaries, traders, and administrators who, for better or worse, tangibly extended European influence and affected the lives of non-Europeans throughout the world. Docks, roads, railways, plantations, and mines spread everywhere while Western goods and money were penetrating non-European societies. In that sense, the beginning of the century represented a Rubicon. Indigenous societies would never be allowed to continue their own natural evolution; they would be modernized and, in some cases, assimilated. Imperialism would be the engine of social and economic change.

Each nation with colonial possessions large and small both believed in the necessity of empire and possessed a sense of superiority as a governing race and a divine mission to civilize the non-European world. This was perhaps a rationalization, but it also became a galvanizing force. The ethic of empire created its own dynamic. As a contemporary writer inspired by Kipling described the British mission:

> To us—to us, and not to others,—a certain definite duty has been assigned. To carry light and civilisation into the dark places of the world, to touch the mind of Asia and of Africa with the ethical ideas of Europe; to give to thronging millions, who would otherwise never know peace or security, these first conditions of human advance.

In similar vein the most eloquent of British Proconsuls, Lord Curzon, wrote of the British Empire as the greatest instrument for good that the world had seen.

The creation of the modern colonial empires was the work of a single generation whose lifetime extended from the last decades of the nineteenth century through the period of the First World War. The antecedents of course were historical. Fundamentally, the empires were the product of the industrial revolution and Europe's consequent lead over the rest of the world in technology and weapons. Europe became a powerhouse, generating trade and commerce. In the last decades of the nineteenth century and until 1914, Europe expanded more rapidly than at any other time. Between 1800 and 1880, the colonial empires added some 6,500,000 square miles to their domains. In the next three decades, the empires grew by another 8,655,000 square miles, extending European sway to over 85 per cent of the world's land surface (up from 65 per cent). The British Empire alone extended over one-fourth of the globe and over one-fourth of its population. The revolution in medicine as well as technology enabled explorers to penetrate into the African interior and allowed Christian missionaries to establish stations throughout the tropics. The Western advance appeared irreversible. In Africa, railways reached Bamako in 1905, Katanga in 1910, Kano in 1911, and Tabora in 1912. Aeroplanes were used in the military campaigns in Libya in 1911 and Morocco in 1912.

With such a dramatic increase in territorial dominion, who made the profit? This was the principal question asked by John A. Hobson, the most outstanding writer on the subject of imperialism. Analysing the question of motive and profit during the period of the Boer War, he speculated in his book *Imperialism* (1902) that Europe's expansion in tropical Africa must be accompanied by profit, but his interpretation erred. He and others confused political expansion with economic investment, which continued to flow elsewhere, not least to the Americas, to China, and to Russia. Africa remained the bottom of the imperialist's economic barrel. Hobson's criticism was nevertheless influential. All theories of imperialism, including those of Rosa Luxemburg and Lenin, can be traced to his work. Hobson expressed the moral outrage of hundreds of other writers. The colonial empires did not lack critics, either liberal or revolutionary.

The origins of the twentieth-century empires were more haphazard than most theorists would concede, but one aim was to prevent rivals from acquiring sources of national wealth. In the Scramble for colonies there were a few lucky draws. Entrepreneurs and investors benefited from the diamonds and gold of South Africa, the copper of Katanga, the rubber of Malaya, the oil of the East Indies and the Middle East. Generally, however, the colonial possessions proved to be white elephants, not least in trade and commerce. In 1910 the German colonies accounted for less than 1 per cent of German trade, and in 1912 the Belgian Congo contributed only 1 per cent of Belgian trade.

The smallest of the colonial empires in the twentieth century was the Spanish. The loss in 1898 of Cuba, Puerto Rico, and the Philippines to the United States, and the Pacific islands to Germany, reduced the Spanish empire mainly to the Canary Islands, Spanish Sahara, a protectorate in part of Morocco, and Spanish Guinea in Equatorial Africa (the only colony of any economic value, mainly in cocoa). The tradition of the old Spanish colonial system nevertheless proved to be significant. It was authoritarian, legalistic, and paternalistic—the forerunner of the twentieth-century colonial regimes. Of the lasting Spanish legacies, perhaps the most remarkable was the assimilation of the Filipinos to Catholicism and the Spanish way of life. The effective colonizers were not the Spanish sea captains and conquistadors but the friars and monks who built churches and created parishes and schools. The class structure of the Spanish era remained intact, and the system of patronage continued into the era of independence.

The empires of the United States and Russia are beyond the scope of this essay, but it is useful to bear in mind that while the European colonial powers were expanding into Africa and the Pacific, the United States established a comparable empire on the remnant of the Spanish possessions, and that Russia continued to expand a vast land empire in Central Asia, completing a vast railway network linking Siberia with Vladivostok, the major Russian port on the Pacific, by the turn of the century. The colonial domain of the United States included Guam as well as the Philippines and Puerto Rico as well as the Virgin islands, which were purchased from Denmark in 1917. Because of its revolutionary and anti-imperial heritage, the United States never described these colonial possessions as colonies but as 'territories'. The acquisition of colonies in all but name caused ideological embarrassment. The United States and the Soviet Union were in this respect similar: both consistently demonstrated an anti-colonial attitude, though both had colonial empires of their own.

To contemporaries observing the fate of the Spanish empire, it seemed inevitable that the weak had given way to the strong. No one anticipated that the lifespan of the great colonial empires would be relatively short. The preponderant view at the turn of the century held that the new empires would last for at least a thousand years. Yet in 1991, within a hundred years of what the Spanish called the 'catastrophe' in 1898, even the Soviet empire began to collapse.

The German empire was the shortest-lived. Born in 1884, it was extinguished in 1919. Most of it was concentrated in Africa: German East Africa extended over 384,000 square miles (nearly double that of Imperial Germany), South-West Africa 322,000, the Cameroons 305,000, and Togoland 34,000. In the Pacific, German New Guinea consisted of 93,000 square miles. Germany also possessed lesser territories in Asia and the Pacific, including Kiau-Chau in China, the Bismarck Archipelago, part of the Samoan group, and the Caroline, Mariana, and Marshall islands north of the Equator. Only a few regions in South-West Africa and East Africa attracted settlers. Despite the brutal suppression of the Herero revolt in South-West Africa in 1904–07 and the Maji-Maji uprising in German East Africa in 1905–06, the Germans were no more, but no less, barbaric than the French in Algeria, the British in Kenya, or the Belgians in the Congo before 1908. A common fallacy held that colonies were vital to Germany's economic prosperity. Far from being assets, however, all of the German colonies before 1914 except Togoland (productive in cocoa and rubber) and Samoa (copra) required subsidies. German financiers as well as emigrants demonstrated a distinct preference for eastern Europe and the Americas rather for the colonies. In 1919, Germany lost her place in the sun and with it an unprofitable empire. In the 1930s it seemed possible that some of the colonies might be restored (or other territory in Africa ceded to Germany at the expense of Belgium and Portugal). It remains debatable how the social engineering of the Third Reich might have affected black Africa and whether the Holocaust might have taken a slightly different direction if places such as East Africa had been available as a dumping ground for Jews and Gypsies. The only thing that can be said with certainty is that after 1945 the Germans were spared the trauma of decolonization.

During the First World War, Britain and France emerged as major Middle Eastern powers and increased their colonial domains in Africa. The public mood changed. The European powers now paid lip service, at least, to the ideal that colonies would be held in trust until the native peoples could stand on their own. Germany not only lost her colonies but, through British propaganda, unjustly acquired a reputation as a barbarous power unfit to govern native peoples. The German colonies were overrun by the British (with the help of Indian troops), and by the French, Belgians, South Africans, Australians, New Zealanders, and Japanese. The Ottoman Empire was dismantled by the British and French, and to a lesser degree by the Italians. The smaller colonial empires of the Dutch, Belgians, and Portuguese remained intact. So also did the larger empires of France and Britain, but only because Britain was an ally of Japan. Japan's policing of the eastern seas enabled the British fleet to concentrate in European waters, thereby contributing to the Allied victory and the maintenance of the Allied empires.

After defeating China in 1894–95 and Russia in 1904–05, Japan annexed Korea in 1910, thus gate-crashing the white man's club of imperial domination. During the First World War, Japanese influence increased both in China and in the Pacific. In 1919 the German islands north of the Equator became Japanese-mandated territories. In the 1930s in Japan as in Germany, there emerged the doctrine that markets and raw materials were necessary for survival. After 1931 Japan occupied Manchuria. During the Second World War, the 'Greater Co-Prosperity Sphere' to the south aimed to secure Japanese economic and political hegemony in South-East Asia. In the early part of the war, the Japanese conquest of the Philippines, Malaya, and the East Indies, as well as its control of Indo-China, demonstrated the vulnerability of the Western regimes in Asia. Had the Japanese emerged undefeated from the Second World War, South-East Asia might have become part of an autarchic bloc not dissimilar from what the British had in mind with the sterling area. The islands north of the Equator would probably have been swamped with Japanese immigrants and might have been assimilated as an outlying territory of Japan. As it transpired, the Japanese left no legacy in Micronesia, no tradition of language or education, no statues or parks. The most enduring feature of Japan's colonial experience was the Koreans' profound bitterness at the violation of their 'national soul'. After 1945 the loss of colonial possessions demonstrated that Japan, like Germany, did not need a place in the sun to recover economically.

The Italian colonial empire was another casualty of the Second World War. At the turn of the century, Ethiopia had not only remained free from European control but also inflicted a humiliating defeat on the Italians at the battle of Adowa in 1896. Mussolini's invasion of Ethiopia in 1935–36 aimed at revenge as well as the establishment of a 'neo-Roman' East African empire. Italy's domain in East Africa included Eritrea (15,754 square miles and 4,188 Italians, according

to the 1931 census) and Italian Somaliland (194,000 square miles—
over one and three-quarters the size of Italy—and 1,631 Italians). The
numbers of Italians are significant because of the obsession with 'ex-
cess population' that characterized Italian public attitudes in the
1930s. The principal outlet for emigration was Libya, which Italy had
won by conquest from Turkey in 1911. In the inter-war years, Libya became Italy's 'Fourth Shore', and in 1938 had an Italian population of
89,098—a figure that bears comparison with 18,269 whites in Kenya,
386,084 Jews in Palestine, and 987,252 Europeans in Algeria. Libya
under Italian rule became one of the most urbanized countries of
North Africa, with concentrations of population in Tripoli and Benghazi. Some 30,000 Italian peasants also settled on the Gefara Plain of
Tripolitania. The Italian Fascist government built extensive harbours
and roads but resettled the local Muslim nomads nearer the desert,
thereby reducing their numbers drastically, perhaps by half. These
projects were pursued for the greater glory of the Fascist state, but in
the end they were a drain on the Italian budget and devastating to the
indigenous population.

The Second World War destroyed another colonial system of much
greater substance and longevity. The Dutch had held colonies since
the seventeenth century. In the West Indies their colonial possessions
included Surinam and Curaçao. In the East Indies, in the vast Indonesian archipelago (thirteen thousand islands extending 3,600 miles
from east to west), the Dutch had developed a colonial economy producing tobacco, tea, coffee, sugar, copra, tin, coal, rubber, and oil. In
neither the late nineteenth century nor the First World War did the
Dutch empire expand territorially; its scope in 1939 was the same as it
had been in 1815. But from the late nineteenth century onwards, the
expansion of the economy brought to the East Indies a new Dutch
population of businessmen and civil servants. By 1939, there were
240,417 Dutch, many of whom regarded the East Indies as their home,
raising their children, working, and retiring in the islands—and many
of them later became embittered during the post-war struggle leading to Dutch eviction. During the nineteenth century the size of the
indigenous population rose from 6 million to 30 million, and then to
70 million by 1940. Dutch rule in part reflected the problem of how to
govern such a vast and changing population; from early on they preserved native dynasties and ruled through them, though the expansion of European activities in the late nineteenth and twentieth centuries led increasingly to annexation. By the 1930s the Dutch held full
sovereignty over 93 per cent of Java and more than half of the outer
islands, but gave the administrative districts considerable autonomy.
Like the British system, and in contrast with the French, the Dutch

method was characterized by decentralization and indirect rule. Dutch influence was higher in densely populated areas such as Java, less pronounced in the outlying areas, where an indigenous bureaucracy buffered the peasant communities. The Japanese occupation after 1942 broke the continuity of Dutch rule: the Dutch were interned, and the Indonesian elite assumed administrative positions previously denied to them. By enlisting the support of both nationalist and Islamic leaders, the Japanese fostered the nationalist movement. After the war, the Dutch expected to reassert control, but a long and acrimonious struggle ended when the United States sided with the nationalists. The new nation of Indonesia achieved independence in 1949. In the West it was regarded as one of the two great Asian events of the year, the other being the emergence of the Communist regime in China.

We now come to the empires that endured into the latter part of the twentieth century, the Belgian, the French, the British, and the Portuguese. There were basic similarities. Each colony had a 'steel frame' of military, police, and administrative officers, who maintained order and defended the frontiers. A European outpost might consist merely of a district officer, a few interpreters, and a small military detachment. At the beginning of the century, the Portuguese, more than the others, lacked both military and administrative resources to go much beyond minimal occupation. Virtually all colonies developed revenue systems based on the taxation of crops, which sometimes involved forced labour or its equivalent. Each colonial power exported a simplified form of its own system of government and law, and each colony possessed a system of justice, though this often amounted to no more than the exercise of unrestricted and arbitrary authority. As administrative units of the European powers, the colonies were also nascent states, each in the process of acquiring modernizing characteristics. Each colonial system invested in ports, roads, and railways; in education; and in health measures—for example, against sleeping sickness. By midcentury, each had developed a network of government offices, complete with files, typewriters, and telephones. Earlier, it probably had not much mattered whether an African colony, for example, happened to be under one regime or another. By midcentury it mattered a great deal. Each colonial system came to possess distinctive characteristics that have endured from the post-colonial period to the present.

By 1950 the Belgian Congo had acquired a reputation as a model colony; it had not always been so. Under the autocratic regime of King Leopold, fifty years earlier, the Congo had been notorious. Leopold ruled in the Congo in his own right, not as King of the Belgians. His regime was exploitative and rapacious: Africans were compelled to collect a quota of wild rubber under a penalty of punishment that sometimes led to atrocities. Part of the reason lay in the nature of the early *Force Publique*, which resembled a mercenary army rather than a colonial police force. In 1905 it consisted of 360 European officers of various nationalities and 16,000 Africans. Leopold demanded profits, but his administrative apparatus proved too weak to prevent abuses. In 1908 Belgium annexed the Congo to remedy the evils of her King. The immense colony of the Congo extended over 902,082 square miles—around seventy-five times the size of Belgium. The African population was relatively small, some 9 million at the beginning of Belgian rule and 13,540,182 in 1958. The Belgians in the Congo numbered only 17,536 in 1940 and 88,913 in 1958. The resources included copper, diamonds, and uranium as well as tropical agricultural products such as rubber, palm oil, and cotton. Mining was the most valuable part of the economy. The profits on Belgian investment, however, were not high, yielding an annual return of only 4 or 5 per cent; before 1937 Belgium subsidized the colonial budget. By the standards of the time, Belgian rule was benevolent and efficient. No other colony had better labour conditions, health facilities, or primary education. No other, perhaps, was as paternalistic. Catholic missions provided a primary-school education to some 56 per cent of the African population, the highest percentage on the continent, but few students went on to secondary schools and fewer still to universities. By the time of independence, the Belgian Congo had produced only sixteen Congolese with university training. In December 1959, riots at Leopoldville shook the Belgian administration into a belated recognition of the strength of Congolese nationalism. The Belgians now made a fundamental miscalculation. Fearing that the troubles might escalate into the equivalent of the Algerian revolution, and nevertheless assuming that the Congolese could not manage without them, the Belgians decided in favour of granting immediate independence on 30 June 1960. The Congo quickly slid into anarchy. That summer will always be remembered as the time of one of the great disasters in European decolonization; the phrases 'Congo' and 'post-colonial chaos' became synonymous.

Before the Second World War, the French empire stood as the only worldwide empire comparable to the British. In 1939 it extended over 4,617,579 square miles and had a population of 64,946,975. Algeria, administered directly as part of France, was the major colony of settlement: its nearly 1 million Europeans and over 6 million Muslims had one of the highest rates of population growth in the world. Other parts of the North African and Middle Eastern empire included the protectorates over Tunisia and Morocco and the mandated territories of Syria and Lebanon. In South-East Asia the French held sway over Indo-China. In the Pacific, France possessed Tahiti (Oceania) as well as New Caledonia; along with Britain it administered the condominium of the New Hebrides. In the Caribbean, France retained the sugar colonies of Guadeloupe, Martinique, and French Guiana (but not Haiti, which had successfully revolted in 1804). Off Newfoundland, she held the fishing bases of St.-Pierre-et-Miquelon. In tropical Africa, the French domain was larger than that of any other power, extending from southern Algeria to the Congo and east to the Anglo-Egyptian Sudan. There were two main administrative units. The Federation of French West Africa included the colonies of Mauritania, Senegal, the Ivory Coast, Dahomey, French Sudan, French Guinea, Upper Volta, and Niger; French Equatorial Africa consisted of Chad, Gabon, the Middle Congo, and Ubangui Chari. France administered also the mandated territories of Cameroon and Togo. Nor is this long list exhaustive. French possessions further included French Somaliland, Madagascar, and island groups in the Indian Ocean. In all these territories the aim since the time of the French Revolution had remained the same: France's republican heritage and civilization would be offered to its subjects, allowing them to become assimilated as French citizens. The empire would be an integral part of France.

In the early part of the century it had already become clear that it would be difficult, probably impossible, to assimilate entire societies in such places as Algeria, Indo-China, and black Africa. In 1922 there were only 94 black French citizens in West Africa, though the figure rose to 2,000 by 1937. By 1936 only 7,817 Algerians had qualified for citizenship by renouncing Islam and traditional society. The project of transforming Arabs and black Africans into Frenchmen obviously had its limits. The idea of assimilation nevertheless did not disappear. The prominent French Colonial Minister after the First World War, Albert Sarraut, called for investment to develop the colonies and to make the colonial economies interdependent with the metropolitan economy. This was significant: the French proved themselves consistently more willing to provide money and to commit military forces than any of the other colonial powers. The universalist assumptions of French republican philosophy and the *mission civiliatrice* might have been impractical, but economic and military commitment helped the French produce a small assimilated elite devoted to French civilization. Assimilation was as much cultural as political, but the Arab *evolués* were not strong enough to prevent Syrian nationalists from defending their independence in 1945. The demise of France as a Middle Eastern power was a result of the Second World War, which also sapped French strength in Indo-China. The year 1954 marked a humiliating and decisive French defeat at Dien Bien Phu that effectively ended France's empire in Asia. In the same year, the French government reinforced Algeria with 20,000 troops, a number that would grow to a half-million by the end of the revolution in 1962. One of de Gaulle's supreme achievements, after his return to power in 1958, was the resolution of both the future of Algeria and the fate of the colonial empire. In 1958 he presented the Africans with a clear choice: they could decide in favour of independence and a privileged place within the French community, including the continuation of economic and military assistance, or in favour of unfettered independence and the abrupt severing of all links. Only Sekou Tourée of Guinea chose to break with France. The rest remained within the *Union Française*. In April 1961 de Gaulle survived a military revolt of the French army in Algeria and moved decisively towards 'Algérie Algérienne'. It was Algeria that captured the world's imagination, in part because of the movie *The Battle of Algiers*, which dramatically conveyed the message that nearly a half-million troops, sophisticated weapons, and torture could not destroy a revolution aimed at national freedom. On 3 July 1962 de Gaulle proclaimed Algeria independent.

The British Empire differed from the French colonial system above all by the possession of India and by the autonomous Dominions. At the turn of the century India constituted an empire in its own right, with a territorial scope of 1,802,629 square miles and population of 294,361,056. (In 1900, India alone had a population nearly five times that of the entire French colonial empire.) It is a measure not merely of firepower but of British confidence and prestige that India was administered by fewer than 1,000 members of the Indian Civil Service, which was almost exclusively British. By 1915 the percentage of Indians in the ICS rose to 5 per cent and by 1935 to 32 per cent. The Indian Army, with a core of 250,000 troops, made Britain the greatest military power in the East in the early part of the century. During that time the Dominions of Australia, New Zealand, Canada, and South Africa had become self-governing and virtually independent. By formally marking the birth of the Commonwealth, the Statute of Westminster of 1931 merely recognized the actuality of nations of kith and kin freely associating in self-interest. Until 1947 the Commonwealth remained an exclusive white man's club, representing only a small part of a still vast Empire, which had reached its greatest territorial extent in the inter-war years. In 1939, British colonies in the Caribbean included Jamaica, Trinidad, British Guiana, Honduras, the Leewards, the Windwards, the Bahamas, and Bermuda. In the Pacific, Britain administered Fiji, Tonga, and smaller island groups. In East and South-East Asia, British possessions included Hong Kong, Malaya, Burma,

Singapore, and parts of Borneo. In the Middle East, the Mediterranean, and the Indian Ocean, Britain ruled over Gibraltar, Malta, Cyprus, Palestine, Jordan, Aden, the Persian Gulf protectorates, Ceylon, Mauritius, and the Seychelles. The African territories included the Gambia, Sierra Leone, the Gold Coast, Nigeria, the Cameroons, the Anglo-Egyptian Sudan, British Somaliland, Kenya, Uganda, Tanganyika, Northern Rhodesia, Nyasaland, and Southern Rhodesia. Even this extensive list is not complete. The complex, worldwide system of the British Empire and Commonwealth stretched over 12.2 million square miles, roughly a quarter the earth's surface, and included territories acquired during every stage of colonization since the sixteenth century.

In retrospect the inter-war years represented the golden age of British colonialism, at least in the imagination. The District Officer inspired trust in his subjects as well as in the British public: colonial rule was believed to be just and enlightened, as portrayed in the movie *Sanders of the River*. The reality was more complicated, but the fictional accounts usually conveyed the essential point that British rule depended on indigenous authority. The India Office as well the Colonial Office monitored a decentralized and self-financing empire. The India Act of 1919 granted ministerial responsibility to the provinces and, through a system know as 'dyarchy', transferred to Indian hands authority in education, public health, public works, and agriculture while reserving to the British the crucial departments of justice, police, finance, and foreign affairs. Part of the purpose was to win the loyalty and collaboration of the Indian leaders. The India Act of 1935 granted further autonomy to the provinces and created a federal structure, including a Supreme Court, but, again, these measures were designed to prolong the Raj, not to end it, by consolidating British control at the centre of Indian government.

In Africa there emerged a similar design. In 1922 Sir Frederick Lugard's *Dual Mandate* developed the doctrine that local administration should be left to 'native authorities', preferably hereditary chiefs. As in India, the goal was to secure collaboration without weakening British control. The native authorities were self-supporting and therefore met the stringent fiscal requirements. Through indirect rule, the British would act as trustees and the Africans would retain their own identity, thus solving both an ethnic and an ethical problem of Empire. The difficulty was that the chiefs could not provide the leadership necessary for a modern colonial state. After the Second World War, the Colonial Office began to dismantle indirect rule and to democratize the Empire by systems of local government, thereby providing an outlet for nationalist ambitions. The aim was the same as in India: to win

over the nationalists before they became irreconcilables. For a while it
appeared that the strategy might succeed. In 1945 no one would have
believed that the end would come so quickly, though it was already
clear that India could not be held to the Empire. The Labour Government was committed to India's freedom, and in any event economic
and military weakness dictated retrenchment.

The dismantling of the Empire began first in Asia, with the granting of independence to India and Pakistan in 1947 and to Ceylon and
Burma in 1948. All except Burma remained in the Commonwealth,
providing a psychological cushion during the era of decolonization.
In 1948 the British were driven out of Palestine, in part because the
United States intervened in favour of the Zionists and the creation of
the state of Israel. It might be tempting to regard these events as the
beginning of a preordained decline and fall, but it did not seem so at
the time to those who hoped to rejuvenate the empire in the Middle
East and Africa. With India lost and Palestine shrugged aside, Britain
would develop Africa as a replacement for India, and the oil of the
Middle East would sustain Britain as a great world power. Imperial collapse would be prevented by genuinely coming to terms with African
and Middle Eastern nationalists as equals and not treating them as in-
feriors. The Sudanese were among the first beneficiaries of this new
approach, though they benefited as much from the Egyptian support
of their cause, and maybe even more. The Sudan became independent in early 1956; it is interesting to speculate how the end of the
British Empire might have come about had it not been for the Suez
crisis later in the same year. Suez revealed the extent of British military and financial weakness as well as the Empire's dependence on the
United States. In the wake of Suez, Harold Macmillan became Prime
Minister and proceeded to liquidate the Empire as a questionable
economic asset and a liability in Anglo-American relations. Above all,
Macmillan responded to the winds of African nationalism. He wanted
to avert colonial wars and 'a British Algeria' in central Africa. Independence for the Gold Coast and Malaya had already been planned
for 1957 and for Nigeria in 1960. But it was Macmillan's Colonial
Secretary, Iain Macleod, who dramatically stepped up the pace in
1959–61. Largely as a result of Macleod's accelerated timetables, Tanganyika, Cyprus, Sierra Leone, and Kuwait became independent in
1961; Uganda, Sierra Leone, Jamaica, and Trinidad in 1962; Kenya
and Zanzibar in 1963; and Nyasaland (Malawi), Northern Rhodesia
(Zambia), and Malta in 1964. There remained Aden and the protectorates in the Gulf; and the resolution of the Rhodesian problem was
left to another generation, twenty years later. But essentially the Empire—represented by those great expanses of red on the map—came

to an end within a four-year period after 1960. The calculation was ruthless and entirely in British self-interest. A prolonged British presence would have ended in colonial conflict. It was better to end colonial rule sooner, and hope for African good will and collaboration, rather than later, and guarantee ill will and bloodshed.

The Portuguese empire was the last to be liquidated, and it was in every sense an anachronism. Paradoxically, by the time that the other European colonial empires were in their death throes, the Portuguese had lost nothing until India seized Goa in 1961. The principal colonies were the immense territories of Angola (481,226 square miles) in western Africa, and Mozambique (297,654 square miles) in eastern Africa. These regions, first reached by Vasco da Gama and others in the fifteenth century, held a vital place in the national psyche. Portugal's other colonies included Portuguese Guinea in western Africa, the Cape Verde islands, the islands of São Tomé and Principe in the Gulf of Guinea, Macao off Canton, and Timor in the Malay archipelago. In the first decade of the twentieth century, the Portuguese were able to uphold their largely fictional claims to the vast hinterlands of Angola and Mozambique only because the other colonial powers did not want to see the territories fall into the hands of their rivals. By 1910 no more than a tenth of either colony was under actual Portuguese control. The effective colonizing instrument evolved in the shape of chartered companies or concessions, which were dominated by British capital. To develop plantations, the companies relied on forced labour, which roused international humanitarian protest until the reform of labour laws in 1926. Portugal acquired a reputation as a harsh and despotic colonial power, almost rivalling that of King Leopold's regime in the Congo, but the reason lay in Portugal's own poverty and the carrying over of nineteenth-century labour practices into the twentieth. Portugal was an underdeveloped country; the Portuguese had not experienced an industrial revolution and did not have a humanitarian movement. The critical period of modernization began with Salazar's Estado Novo in 1928. In the renaissance of the Portuguese state, the mystique of empire held a prominent place. Salazar presided over a period of colonial development that included the introduction of telegraphs and telephones, ports and railways, hospitals and schools. By midcentury the Portuguese colonies had been brought into line with other European colonies, though observers commented on the twenty-year time lag. There was less of a colour bar than in any of the other European colonies. The Portuguese viewed Angola and Mozambique as multiracial societies on the model of Brazil. They regarded the colonies as an integral part of the Portuguese state. But despite public subsidies to Catholic missions for education, by 1950 there were only 30,089 *assimilados* in Angola and only 4,353 in Mozambique. In 1961 a nationalist rising began in Angola. Further insurrections occurred in Mozambique and Guinea in 1964. For another decade Portugal fought rebel forces in all three of the African colonies. It is a measure of the vitality of the Portuguese colonial mission that the military commitment reached nearly 200,000 troops, a huge number of soldiers for a country with a population of only 8 million. The Portuguese devoted half the national budget to the colonial war effort. In the end, the Portuguese colonial empire in Africa died in 1974 as a result of revolution in Portugal, not defeat in the colonies.

In the aftermath of decolonization, the world has witnessed the rise and fall of such tyrants as Idi Amin of Uganda and Jean-Bedel Bokassa of the Central African Republic. It will long be debated how the European colonial powers might better have prepared the colonies for independence and the extent to which the new states are responsible for their own troubles. Many of the former colonies are hostages to the international economy, but the legacies of colonialism are cartographic, cultural, and aesthetic as well as economic and political. For better or worse, the boundaries that the colonial powers drew in Asia, the Middle East, and Africa a hundred years ago have proved remarkably durable. So also have the French, English, Spanish, and Portuguese linguistic blocs of the non-European world. French cultural influence probably exceeds British, though in the world of cricket and soccer the British have left a lasting legacy. The French have proved far more willing than the British and others to commit troops and economic assistance to the former colonies, not least to those torn by ethnic and religious strife. The political legacies, however, may in the long run prove less apparent than the aesthetic and even the culinary traditions. In the old French territories, red wine is still mandatory at lunch and dinner. In former British tropical colonies, one encounters mulligatawny soup, roast lamb, and steamed ginger pudding. Throughout the erstwhile world of French colonies, from Senegal to Tahiti, one of the most striking impressions is of French provincial houses and tree-lined streets. In Canada and South Africa as well as India, one is struck by the similarity of the public buildings and especially by the magnificence of the former Viceroy's Palace in New Delhi, designed by Lutyens. It could well be that architecture as well as language will serve as one of the conspicuous reminders of the colonial era.

THE SCRAMBLE FOR AFRICA AND THE CONGO

2

THE SCRAMBLE FOR AFRICA:
SIR PERCY ANDERSON'S GRAND STRATEGY

> The truth I believe is he has begun to think himself an African dictator but a dictator concealed who uses his power in secret, free of all responsibility.
>
> Sir John Kirk, 1894

During the last part of the nineteenth century the fate of the strategic regions of the Congo and Nile valleys was determined in large part by the British Foreign Office, whose policy was guided by Sir Percy Anderson.[1] Anderson was '*the* great and only African power'[2] of the Foreign Office. He was the African thinking-machine of the British government—'a complete focus of knowledge in regard to Africa'.[3] In his racy, pungent style, Anderson gave coherence to British policy during the crucial period of the Scramble for Africa: he was a civil servant immune to the vicissitudes of political fortune, a permanent fixture at the Foreign Office, valued by Conserva-

---

[1] Henry Percy Anderson, born 20 February 1831; educated Marlborough College, 1843–48; Christ Church, Oxford, B.A. 1852 (Hons.), M.A. 1865; appointed Junior Clerk, Foreign Office Slave Trade Department 1852 (see FO 366/512); British Legation in Washington, 1861–63; Senior Clerk, 1873; African Department head, 1883; British delegate, Berlin Congo Conference, 1884–85; K.C.M.G., 1885; conducted Anglo-German negotiations Berlin, 1890: K.C.B., 1890; Assistant Under-Secretary, 1894; died 19 July 1896. See *Foreign Office List(s)* and *The Times* obituary of 20 July 1896. The fullest description of Anderson's career is D. H. Simpson's 'A Forgotten Imperialist: Sir Percy Anderson, K.C.B., K.C.M.G., 1831–96', *Royal Commonwealth Society Library Notes*, new series, 44 (August 1960). See also Sir Harry H. Johnston, *The Story of My Life* (London, 1923), pp. 119–21, and the same author's novel, *The Gay-Dombeys* (London, 1919), in which Anderson appears as 'Sir Mulberry Hawk', pp. 143–44 (the authority for identifying Anderson as Hawk is Roland Oliver, *Sir Harry Johnston and the Scramble for Africa* [London, 1957], p. 83); Sir James Rennell Rodd, *Social and Diplomatic Memories, 1884–1893* (London, 1922), pp. 74–75; and Malet to Salisbury, 9 August 1890, Salisbury Papers, A/63 Christ Church, Oxford: 'His health during the middle period of his life was the stumbling block which prevented his advancement to the higher places in the Office.' For indications of Anderson's influence on the partition of east and west Africa, see A. J. Hanna, *The Beginnings of Nyasaland and North-Eastern Rhodesia* (Oxford, 1956); J. E. Flint, *Sir George Goldie and the Making of Nigeria* (London, 1960); J. D. Hargreaves, *Prelude to the Partition of West Africa* (London, 1963); Oliver, *Sir Harry Johnston;* and Ronald Robinson and John Gallagher, *Africa and the Victorians* (London, 1961). The other main aspect of Anderson's career beyond the scope of this essay is his role as administrator of the Foreign Office protectorates, for which see A. J. P. Taylor, 'Prelude to Fashoda: The Question of the Upper Nile, 1894–5', *English Historical Review*, 65 (1950), reprinted in his *Rumours of War* (London, 1952), p. 82. For another brief treatment of this problem, see Sir John Tilley and Stephen Gaselee, *The Foreign Office* (London, 1933), pp. 217–26.

[2] Lord Lugard's comment, quoted in Margery Perham, *Lugard* (2 vols., London, 1956–60), I, p. 556.

[3] Malet to Salisbury, 9 August 1890, Salisbury Papers, A/63.

tive and Liberal Governments alike. As one historian has commented, Lord Salisbury's supreme achievement, the peaceful partition of Africa, 'owed much to the extreme efficiency of Sir Percy Anderson'.[4]

When Anderson in 1883 became head of the African Department, which replaced the Slave Trade Department, the change signified the end of an epoch. No one was more representative of the new official Imperialism than Anderson; and there was no sharper contrast than that between him and his immediate superior, T. V. Lister,[5] an anachronism of the mid-Victorian period, when the slave trade was the main British concern in tropical Africa. Lister, in the anti-slave-trade tradition, saw foreign policy as a struggle between honesty and dishonesty, loyalty and disloyalty, and right and wrong; as a man of principle, he believed Britain should not hesitate to denounce the turpitude and treachery of other nations or be afraid 'of speaking the truth & shaming the French'.[6] Anderson was no less scrupulous, but his was a more complex world, a world in which Britain was no longer free to bully other nations with impunity, even on the straightforward issue of the suppression of the slave trade. He saw the Scramble for colonies mainly as a problem of maintaining British power and prestige. For each move made by Germany or France in Africa, Anderson countermoved; he had a first-class chessboard mentality. And for well over a decade he had the distinction of being the only Foreign Office official persistently to match wits with the shrewdest of all imperial chess players, Leopold II, King of the Belgians and sovereign of the Congo Free State. Throughout his career as the sage of the African Department, in 1894 as in 1884, Anderson played the dangerous game of trying to use King Leopold as a pawn to secure British interests against France. In 1894 Anderson audaciously attempted to push King Leopold's Congo State into the Nile Valley as a buffer between Britain and France; in 1884, after the collapse of the Anglo-Portuguese treaty, he helped create the Congo State itself, which eventually became a gigantic buffer state covering the heart of Africa and frustrating France's ambitions there. Fear of France was the unbroken thread that ran through Anderson's policy. 'If there is one thing dearer than another', he wrote in June 1883, 'it seems to be that the French have a settled policy in Africa, both on the East and the West Coast, and that policy is antagonistic to us. The progress of this policy is sometimes sluggish, sometimes feverish, but it never ceases.'[7]

[4] Algernon Cecil, in *The Cambridge History of British Foreign Policy* (3 vols., Cambridge, 1923), III, p. 613.
[5] Assistant Under-Secretary, 1873–94.
[6] Lister's minute of 13 March 1884, FO 84/1683.
[7] Anderson's minute of 11 June 1883, FO 84/1806.

Anderson's first job as head of the African department was to clean up the 'dreadful mess'[8] of proposals concerning the Anglo-Portuguese Congo treaty.[9] These negotiations had originated in the 1870s when the Portuguese, with curious prescience, had begun to feel that the winds of change might sweep them, along with their ancient and preposterous claims, off the African continent. The scheme itself was the product of the fertile brain of the British minister at Lisbon, Robert Morier. Morier's plan was simple. In return for British recognition of Portuguese claims northwards from Angola to 8° south latitude (in other words, including the mouth of the Congo River), Portugal would open up the whole of her West African possessions to free commerce and navigation. Linked with the negotiations of treaties concerning Goa and Portuguese East Africa, these provisions, Morier believed, would 'confer incalculable advantages on the Portuguese colonies and will in the course of a few years endow with life and health and wealth what are now mere malarious lagoons'.[10] Had these negotiations remained under the supervision of the able Lord Salisbury and not fallen under that of the dilatory Lord Granville, they might have been concluded before African questions had caught the eye of Bismarck and before King Leopold or the French had been able to make any pretence of sovereignty in the Congo; they might have extinguished many of the burning African territorial questions of 1882–85, and might have changed the entire history of tropical Africa.

As it happened, the Anglo-Portuguese negotiations stimulated rather than delayed the Scramble for Africa. The discussions were suspended in April 1881 owing to the Liberal government's irritation at anti-English sentiment in Portugal.[11] When they were revived in November 1882, British strategy had shifted from the offensive to the defensive: the French explorer Brazza had raised the tricolour of France at Stanley Pool.[12] The negotiations previously designed to rejuvenate Portugal's African empire were now aimed at keeping France out of the Congo.

The principal architect of the Anglo-Portuguese treaty was Percy

---

[8] Tenterden's minute of 26 May 1880, FO 84/1801.

[9] On the Anglo-Portuguese negotiations, see especially Roger Anstey, *Britain and the Congo in the Nineteenth Century* (Oxford, 1962), chaps. 3, 5–7; also S. E. Crowe, *The Berlin West African Conference* (London, 1942), chaps. 1–2; and Robert Stanley Thomson, *Fondation de l'État Indépendant du Congo* (Brussels, 1933), chap. 4.

[10] Morier to Granville, private, 17 May 1880, PRO 30/29/183.

[11] See Anstey, *Britain and the Congo*, p. 98. The question was bound up with the one of Lourenço Marques treaty, which the Portuguese parliament had refused to ratify.

[12] A point of great strategic importance because it is one of the first navigable parts of the Congo River. Thus Brazza's treaty with Makoko, the chief of the northern shore of Stanley Pool, was—so it was believed—a bid for control of the whole Congo basin.

Anderson. It was he who sorted out the proposals left by Robert Morier (who had been transferred to Madrid in 1881), and it was he who
clarified the purpose of the negotiations. The obvious goal, according
to Anderson, was to secure freedom for British trade by placing Portugal in nominal possession of the lower Congo and

> by inaugurating a liberal system on the lower waters, to make it diffi-
> cult for France to carry out an obstructive system in the upper waters.
> To secure this object it is essential that the guarantees should be
> binding and durable for if, through leaving a loophole or by any
> oversight we make it possible for the lower river to be barred or ob-
> structed, we shall play the game of the French.[13]

'I take it we shall have to be firm in pressing for better terms,'[14] he
wrote while transforming Morier's loosely worded suggestions into
such tightly binding clauses concerning freedom of trade and navigation that the Portuguese, in consternation, began to make secret overtures to the French.[15] Rebuffed by the French, the Portuguese were
forced to accept Anderson's highly distasteful terms. Since the Portuguese public regarded any concession in the realm of colonial affairs
as tantamount to treason—in part because 'large African Colonies
flatter their national vanity'[16]—the extent to which the Portuguese
government was willing to accept the British proposals indicates how
desperately they felt the insecurity of their African claims. 'The Portuguese are anxious for a treaty of some kind on any terms,' wrote one
Foreign Office official.[17] They gulped down dose after dose of humiliation: freedom of commerce on the Zambesi as well as on the lower
Congo; limitation of Portuguese claims in East Africa; and absolute religious liberty for missionaries.[18] 'The Portuguese Gov[ernment] have
given way upon one point after another,' Anderson wrote in October
1883. But there was one point on which the Portuguese were adamant:
they refused to establish an 'international commission' to ensure
freedom of navigation on the Congo. 'The idea of the commission',

[13] Anderson's memorandum of 19 February 1883, FO 84/1803.

[14] Ibid.

[15] De Serpa to de Laboulaye, 13 August 1883, included in no. 57, de Laboulaye to Challemel-
Lacour, 16 August 1883, *Documents Diplomatiques Français,* 1st series, 5, no. 79; Anstey, *Britain and
the Congo,* p. 144; Crowe, *Berlin West African Conference,* p. 19; Thomson, *Fondation de l'État Indépendant du Congo,* pp. 132–33.

[16] Lister's minute, no date, on King Leopold to Mackinnon, 4 June 1884, FO 84/1806.

[17] H. Austin Lee to Mackinnon, Private, 8 August 1883, Mackinnon Papers, London School
of Oriental and African Studies.

[18] The treaty is printed in *Accounts and Papers,* 56 (1884).

observed the British minister in Lisbon, 'is distasteful to the Portuguese as they think it savours of foreign tutelage, the very mention of which makes them frantic.'[19] The Foreign Office acquiesced in the proposal of a dual Anglo-Portuguese rather than an 'international' river commission. This was the hook on which the opponents of the treaty, both in England and abroad, began to hang their complaints.

Although the Portuguese eventually were willing even to agree to an 'international' commission, this would not have saved the treaty, which was signed (but never ratified) on 26 February 1884. It was unpopular both in England and Portugal.[20] 'Bah!' exclaimed the explorer (and King Leopold's agent) Henry M. Stanley, summarizing the British reaction, 'the very thought sickens me.'[21] In the words of a missionary, '[T]he extension of Portuguese sovereignty over both banks of the lower Congo is an unmitigated evil . . . In any case the King of the Belgians and not the King of Portugal is the man who ought to be entrusted with the guardianship of the gates of one of the greatest waterways in the world.'[22]

In the minds of his British followers, King Leopold stood for everything that Portugal did not: for freedom of trade in central Africa; for the suppression of slavery; for enlightened administration; for progress and civilization. However perverse this may seem in retrospect, it is a fact that King Leopold at this time seemed to represent all that was best in Europe's efforts to open Africa to trade and deliver it from barbarism. It was to him, not to the Portuguese, that British traders turned, and it was his ability to harness British energy, as well as Germany's sudden irruption into the colonial world, that resulted in the collapse of the Anglo-Portuguese treaty and the founding of the Congo Free State.

Percy Anderson had no illusions about what he called the 'Nature of the King of the Belgians Co[mpany]'.[23] However noisily King Leopold might proclaim himself the apostle of free trade, the treaties concluded by his agents in the Congo (copies of which had reached the Foreign Office) showed that his 'International Association of the Congo' was a 'private undertaking of a very abnormal kind',[24] which

[19] Baring to Sanderson, Private, 23 June 1883, PRO 30/29/183.

[20] See Lord Edmond Fitzmaurice, *The Life of Lord Granville* (2 vols., London, 1905), II, p. 345; Anstey, *Britain and the Congo*, chap. 6.

[21] Stanley to Johnston, 23 July 1883, quoted in Anstey, *Britain and the Congo,* pp. 251–52.

[22] H. Bentley of the Baptist Missionary Society, in the *Pall Mall Budget,* 23 May 1884.

[23] The title of his memorandum of 2 March 1884, FO 84/1809.

[24] Lister's minute of 28 February 1883, on King Leopold to Queen Victoria (copy), 22 February 1883, FO 84/1803.

aimed not only at sovereign rights, but also at an 'absolute monopoly of trade'.[25] Anderson was not concerned with King Leopold's morality as a trader, though there is no reason to assume that he did not believe, along with many other late Victorians, that sound commercial ventures were essential to the opening of tropical Africa. King Leopold entered into his calculations only to the extent that he was a force to be reckoned with in the problem of how to push the Anglo-Portuguese negotiations to a successful conclusion. 'Again and again', in Anderson's own words, he had dismissed King Leopold's African schemes as an alternative to the Portuguese solution of the Congo problem because 'the King, though repeatedly urged, has hitherto declined to form a Company—consequently no one clearly knows what is tangible . . . who is the head—or who is responsible . . . If the King stopped the supplies tomorrow the whole affair would crumble away —then who would be the claimants under the deeds of cession?'[26]

Nothing could have been more electrifying than the answer the Foreign Office received to this question in the spring of 1884. It came in the form of the Congolese-French pre-emptive agreement of 23 April, an arrangement by which *France* would be offered the option of the Congo if King Leopold decided to sell his possessions. Through this ingenious arrangement, King Leopold at one stroke had neutralized France and struck fear into the hearts of the Portuguese, who no doubt would have preferred even the puny King Leopold to the powerful French. 'Behind the Association [is] France,' Anderson wrote in May 1884.[27] This simple fact brought to a head the issue of territorial sovereignty in the Congo.

Only a day before the conclusion of the Congolese-French agreement, King Leopold had succeeded, through the agency of the former American minister in Brussels, General H. S. Sanford, in gaining American recognition of the flag of the Association as the 'flag of a friendly Government'.[28] Although this 'great act of folly'[29] was an implicit censure of the Anglo-Portuguese treaty, there was no mention of territorial sovereignty.[30] Indeed the main interest lay in the 'glaring contrast'[31] between it and the Congolese-French agreement. The United States Senate had supported King Leopold's Association in the

[25] Anderson's memorandum of 2 March 1884, FO 84/1809.
[26] Ibid.
[27] Anderson's memorandum of 18 May 1884, PRO 30/29/198.
[28] See Thomson, *Fondation de l'État Indépendant du Congo*, chap. 5; and the same author's 'Léopold II et Henry S. Sanford', *Congo*, 11 (1930), pp. 295–331.
[29] Lister's minute of 20 May 1884, PRO 30/29/198.
[30] Cf. Arthur Berriedale Keith, *The Belgian Congo and the Berlin Act* (Oxford, 1919), p. 54.
[31] *The Times*, 20 May 1884.

belief that this would help secure free trade on the Congo and that the goals of the Association were philanthropic and scientific. In President Arthur's words, 'it does not aim at permanent political control.'[32]

The American recognition of 'a friendly *Government*'[33] was not the recognition of a friendly (or unfriendly or indifferent) *state*. Although perhaps a move in this direction,[34] it was really a smokescreen for the pre-emption agreement with France. Peering through the philanthropic haze with his very large 'tortoiseshell-rimmed' spectacles,[35] Percy Anderson saw that, in contrast to the amorphous 'government' recognized by the United States, 'we shall have quite a different sort of body to deal with'—a 'nouvel Etat indépendant' backed by France.[36]

'It is . . . useless to argue against the agreement with France, for the agreement is signed,' Anderson wrote in May 1884.

> Last year the King was intriguing with France, France was negotiating with Portugal. Now we have the agreement with France completed by the King, and the Portuguese waiting to see whether we ratify the Treaty and ready, if we do not, to complete their negotiations with France . . . it is not improbable that if the Treaty is thrown out in the House of Commons, we may see two Powers and the Association sharing the spoils between them.

'It is my conviction that the whole of these secret intrigues are directed . . . against England . . .The net is closing round us.'[37]

To break out of the net, Anderson proposed laying the Congolese-French agreement before Parliament, which would then see the stark contrast between Congolese-French monopoly and Anglo-Portuguese free trade. Drafting a letter for Granville, Anderson challenged King Leopold to present the facts about the Association 'in their true light'. Would King Leopold object to Britain's laying the Congolese-French agreement before Parliament?[38]

Anderson had struck at the defensive armour of the Leopoldian

---

[32] *Foreign Relations of the United States, 1883,* p. ix.

[33] 'A great point gained!' (Sanford to Mackinnon, 1 April 1884, Mackinnon Papers). But was it? See J. Stengers, 'Léopold II et la fixation des frontières du Congo," *Le Flambeau,* 46 (1963), pp. 167–68.

[34] Sanford hoped it was; see his letter to Mackinnon of 18 April 1884, Mackinnon Papers.

[35] As Sir Harry Johnston described those worn by Sir Mulberry Hawk (Anderson) in *The Gay-Dombeys,* p. 144.

[36] Anderson's memorandum of 18 May 1884, PRO 30/29/198.

[37] Ibid.

[38] This idea was originally proposed in Anderson's memorandum of 18 May; cf. the draft of 20 May, PRO 30/29/198. For Anderson's shift in strategy as the time of the Berlin Conference approached, see Crowe, *Berlin West African Conference,* p. 88.

system of diplomacy: its secrecy. Parrying Anderson's thrust, King Leopold wrote to Granville that his agreement with France would become effective only in the event of the other Powers not recognizing
the Association. He begged Granville not to dwell in Parliament on
the imaginary dangers of the Congolese-French agreement but on the
vast advantages that a great independent Congo State based on principles of free trade would confer on Britain.[39] Granville did not immediately espouse the cause of the Association, but King Leopold had
won the round: the 'misrepresentations and lies'[40] of the Association
were not exposed by the British government. As Anderson had foreseen, 'the game . . . is . . . going dead against us.'[41]

By refusing to take a 'controversial'[42] line against the philanthropic
king of the Belgians, Granville was riding rapidly towards the disaster of France, Portugal, and the Association dividing the Congo basin among them—without the guarantees of free trade of the Anglo-
Portuguese treaty. This might well have happened had Germany not
intervened.

In the summer of 1884, Bismarck made his colonial debut. Exploiting the mine of colonial sentiment in Germany, grudging the niggardly
and dilatory British behaviour in South-West Africa, and coquetting
with France, Bismarck attempted to manipulate colonial issues for a
variety of reasons. Not the least of these was his desire to isolate and
embarrass Great Britain. He saw the Anglo-Portuguese treaty as a
veiled British attempt to control 'the Danube of Africa', and he had
no higher regard for 'Portuguese guardianship' than had the British traders and humanitarians. But despite his friendly overtures to
France, he had no intention of letting the Congo fall into the lap of
French protectionism. He looked upon King Leopold in much the
same way as the British looked upon the Portuguese. By binding King
Leopold's inchoate state to principles of free trade (as he did through
the Congolese-German agreement of 8 November 1884), he secured
German commercial interests; by helping establish the Congo State
as an independent buffer power, he blocked both Britain and France

[39] These views were not only developed in private letters from King Leopold to Granville (15
and 22 May 1884, PRO 30/29/198) but also through interviews at the Foreign Office by Mackinnon and King Leopold's agent, Colonel Strauch. See Strauch to King Leopold, 27 May 1884,
in J. Stengers, 'Rapport sur le dossier "Correspondance Léopold II-Strauch",' *Institut Royal Colonial Belge*, 24 (1953), pp. 1203–07; Pierre van Zuylen, *L'Échiquier Congolais* (Brussels, 1959),
pp. 86–87; Anstey, *Britain and the Congo*, p.171.

[40] Lister's minute of 20 May 1884, PRO 30/29/198.

[41] Anderson's memorandum of 18 May 1884, PRO 30/29/198.

[42] Sanderson's minute, no date, on Granville to King Leopold (draft), Private,
PRO 30/29/198.

from acquiring the supposed strategic advantage of controlling the heart of Africa.

From the British point of view, there was no basic reason why King Leopold's International Association should not be substituted for Portugal as the guardian of the Congo. King Leopold, despite his secret intrigues with France, his agitation against the Anglo-Portuguese treaty, his monopolistic treaties with the Congo chiefs—even despite his pre-emption agreement—was still widely regarded as a benevolent and disinterested philanthropist. 'Nobody doubts the aim of the King of the Belgians has had in view,' the Under-Secretary, Sir Julian Pauncefote, wrote in November 1884; 'Besides [and of greater importance] the Association will only be recognized on the conditions of free navigation and trade.'[43] With Germany's support, Britain could make King Leopold as accountable for free trade as Portugal would have been; but Bismarck would have to pay the price of British support on the Congo by recognizing British claims on the Niger.[44] 'I don't think we could steer a safer course,' Pauncefote commented on the eve of the Berlin Congo Conference of 1884–85.[45]

Pauncefote, not Anderson, was responsible for salvaging British Congo policy.[46] As in the Anglo-Portuguese negotiations, Anderson emerged as an executor, not an originator, of Britain's 'buffer state' policy, which in 1884 consisted merely of placing a scarecrow at the mouth of the Congo River to keep away France. Anderson's power rested on knowledge, not political inventiveness. Though he eventually helped change the nationality of the scarecrow from Portuguese to Belgian, he did not invent the device itself. So far as it is possible to trace the origins of Britain's 'buffer state' policy in tropical Africa, the artificer appears to have been Lord Salisbury in 1879–80.[47] Throughout his career, Anderson merely attempted to carry out Salisbury's policy.

In 1884–85 Anderson regarded the problem of the Congo as secondary to that of the Niger. As one of the British delegates at the

---

[43] Pauncefote's minute on Granville to Malet (draft), 15 November 1885, FO 84/1814.

[44] See Anderson's memorandum of 14 October 1884, FO 84/1813; Crowe, *Berlin West African Conference*, p. 127.

[45] Pauncefote to Granville, 14 November 1884, FO 84/1814.

[46] Pauncefote took the initiative in the policy leading to the recognition of the Association. See Granville to Malet (drafted by Pauncefote), 15 November 1884, FO 84/1814, with minutes by Lister and Pauncefote. The final decision to recognize was made by Granville on 1 December. See the Cabinet minutes on 'Recognition of International Association', 1 December 1884, PRO 30/29/144.

[47] By using 'the scarecrow of Egyptian sovereignty' against Italy (Agatha Ramm, 'Great Britain and the Planting of Italian Power in the Red Sea', *English Historical Review*, 49 [1944], p. 219).

Berlin Conference, he was willing to follow Bismarck's lead 'in placing the general control of the Congo trade on an international footing'— provided that 'we . . . take our seat as *the Niger Power.*'[48] The Niger and not the Congo was the main British concern at Berlin: '[V]ictory in regard to it [the Niger] has been the touchstone of our success in the Conference.'[49] That victory the British ambassador in Berlin, Sir Edward Malet, attributed entirely to Percy Anderson.[50]

Anderson himself recognized that the British delegation at Berlin owed its success to Bismarck: 'The Prince's [Bismarck's] influence is surprising: before he spoke we had not one friend; after his dictum we had not one opponent.'[51] But if the decisions at Berlin were made by Bismarck, it is no exaggeration to say, as Malet did, that Anderson was the 'moving spirit of the whole work' of the conference. Perhaps more than any other, it was the mind of Percy Anderson that reasoned what was practicable and impracticable in prevalent clichés of 'internationalization' and 'neutralization' of tropical Africa, yet also saw the humanitarian as well as the political precedent of the Berlin Act. The Berlin Act of 1885 has been variously described as a landmark in the history of 'trusteeship' and free trade on the one hand, and as a collection of humanitarian banalities and meaningless platitudes about freedom of commerce and navigation on the other. Even in 1884 the work of the conference was proclaimed as promoting 'lenient treatment and freedom of the natives, and . . . free navigation, free trade, and freedom for Europeans'.[52] Yet it was also denounced as 'philanthropic gabble about raising populations and promoting civilization': 'It scarcely seems necessary to have summoned some scores of distinguished personages together merely to reassert the old-fashioned doctrine that the strong ought to have their way.'[53] Since Percy Anderson was partly responsible for the Berlin Act, it is illuminating to know that he regarded it, above all, as a '*precious . . . triumph of common sense*'.[54]

Common sense to Anderson meant preventing France from acquiring the Congo basin; the recognition of British claims on the Niger; extending the principle of free trade as widely as possible; and, not least, taking steps to promote the welfare of the indigenous popula-

[48] Anderson's memorandum of 14 October 1884, FO 84/1813.

[49] Malet to Granville, 3 January 1885, FO 343/6.

[50] 'I fancy that if we have the Niger now, de facto, in our possession it is mainly due to the pains which he has bestowed upon the question' (ibid.).

[51] Anderson to Pauncefote, 31 January 1885, FO 84/1820.

[52] *Spectator,* 6 December 1884.

[53] *Saturday Review,* 29 and 22 November 1884.

[54] Anderson to Pauncefote, 31 January 1885, FO 84/1820; emphasis added.

tions. All of these were the formal and informal results of the conference. The Congo Free State was substituted for Portugal as a 'shadowy State'[55] at the mouth of the Congo; British claims on the Niger were consolidated; an enormous area, defined as the 'conventional basin of the Congo' and extending far beyond the political boundaries of the Congo State, was proclaimed open to free trade; and great emphasis was placed on the welfare of the natives.

The visionary goals of complete internationalization and neutralization of tropical Africa were not realized. As expounded by the American delegate,[56] these terms meant 'the international regulation of colonial occupations in Africa'[57] and the exclusion of tropical Africa from military operations in the event of war.[58] The European powers were unwilling to bind themselves to respect either of these interpretations, which, even if not actually inimical to their interests, were principles of untested value. In the final Act, international regulation of the partition of Africa appeared in the eviscerated form of provision for notification of annexations along the coast (and not the interior)—a common-sense clause mainly designed to prevent secret annexations.[59] Neutrality was left to the option of each of the powers—an innocuous clause conferring a privilege each nation already had. Its main significance is that it gave King Leopold a chance to proclaim the Congo State 'perpetually neutral' in the tradition of Belgian neutrality.

A half-year after the close of the Berlin Conference, King Leopold circulated his Declaration of Neutrality of 1 August 1885, which defined the frontiers of the Congo State. Technically there was no reason why Britain should not have protested against the description of these frontiers: the authority for proclaiming the Declaration of

[55] *Saturday Review,* 29 November 1884: 'Moreover, this power is of a highly peculiar and unprecedented description. It is a mere trading association such as the Dutch or English East India Companies would have been if there had been no State behind them. It will have neither a soul to be damned nor a body to be kicked.'

[56] For the participation of the American delegate, John A. Kasson, in the Conference, see Senate Executive Document 195, 49th Congress; also Edward Younger, *John A. Kasson: Politics and Diplomacy from Lincoln to McKinley* (Iowa City, Iowa, 1955), chap. 27; and David M. Pletcher, *The Awkward Years: American Foreign Relations under Garfield and Arthur* (Columbia, Mo., 1961), chap. 17.

[57] Younger, *Kasson,* p. 335.

[58] See Kasson's address to the Conference, included in no. 34, Kasson to Frelinghuysen, 20 November 1884, Senate Executive Document 196.

[59] 'The 3rd basis [effective occupation] is clearly intended to prevent the secret acquisition of new territories without occupation, but not to disturb existing titles' (Pauncefote's minute of 1 January 1885 on Stuart to Granville, 19 December 1884, FO 84/1818); cf. Crowe, *Berlin West African Conference,* chap. 6, which discusses this complicated point at length.

Neutrality was Article X of the Berlin Act, which itself did not mention territorial delimitation. Perhaps the Declaration of Neutrality slipped through the Foreign Office merely because Anderson happened to be on holiday in August 1885.[60] In any case, Anderson himself described the Foreign Office's failure to protest as a 'stupid blunder'. But he recognized this blunder six years too late—not when King Leopold circulated his Declaration of Neutrality but when Cecil Rhodes's agents began scrambling for Katanga. It was the same blind spot that plagued Anderson during the Mackinnon negotiations in 1890. He eventually recognized, but only in 1892, when King Leopold's troops appeared in the Nile Valley, that the Mackinnon agreement was also a blunder. In 1885 as in 1890, King Leopold was one move ahead of Sir Percy Anderson.

The Mackinnon agreement of 24 May 1890 was concluded between the Imperial British East Africa Company and the Congo State. Its purpose was to give King Leopold access to the Nile Valley and the British Company the right to a strip of territory from Uganda to Lake Tanganyika that would connect the British spheres in the north and south of Africa. This 'Cape to Cairo' scheme of Sir William Mackinnon, the director of the Company, stirred the imagination of the German and British press, and thus became a dominant issue in the Anglo-German East African negotiations of 1890.

> According to Sir William Mackinnon, the British 'sphere of influence' in East Africa is worth little except as a means of access to the Lake Country which lies beyond. If Germany gets into that country first, she will checkmate our movements alike from the south and from the east. It is no wonder, therefore, that Sir Percy Anderson's mysterious mission to Berlin is regarded with some alarm so far as British interests in East Africa are concerned.[61]

During his negotiations at Berlin in 1890, Anderson, following Salisbury's lead, was intent on securing Uganda and the sources of the Nile for Britain. He punctured Mackinnon's dream of a corridor to the south by declaring it 'impracticable',[62] seeing not only that the Germans would never accept exclusion from the Congo but also, in Salisbury's words, that 'trade does not willingly go across a continent.'[63] Not endowed with the imaginative powers of Mackinnon, Anderson believed the project so fantastic that he dismissed it irrevocably, and

---

[60] Professor J. Stengers presents that audacious interpretation in 'Léopold II et la fixation'.

[61] *Pall Mall Budget*, 22 May 1890.

[62] Anderson to Malet, 28 June 1890, included in Malet to Salisbury, 28 June 1890, *Accounts and Papers* 51. Cf. Lois Raphael, *The Cape-to-Cairo Dream* (New York, 1936), p. 317.

[63] *Parliamentary Debates*, 3rd series, 346, col. 1268.

four years later—at the time of the great blunder of his career—could not even remember, as will be seen, that the Cape-to-Cairo corridor had played any role at all in the Anglo-German negotiations.

To Mackinnon, the corridor was one of the vital stakes of the competition. Betrayed by Salisbury and Anderson, he turned to King Leopold. The Mackinnon agreement secured for Britain what the British government had abandoned: the 'bottle's neck' emptying into Lake Tanganyika. King Leopold received the left bank of the Nile up to Lado.[64]

Neither Salisbury nor Anderson saw the implications of this agreement, Salisbury perhaps because he might not have examined the actual terms of the territorial exchange,[65] Anderson perhaps because he was preoccupied with the Anglo-German negotiations.[66] Or perhaps they simply did not consider King Leopold a dangerous competitor for the Nile Valley. Salisbury wrote to King Leopold that he could see no difficulties in concluding the arrangement,[67] and, though he later modified his views, created the impression that the British government acquiesced in the agreement.[68] Anderson, though he noted that the approval of the agreement by the British government was a condition of its validity,[69] raised no protest. In September 1890, King Leopold, with characteristic secrecy, dispatched an expedition to the Nile Valley.

At the same time, King Leopold received a jolt that momentarily distracted his gaze from the Nile. The British South Africa Company was trying to poach on his Katanga preserve. Harry Johnston wrote to Salisbury in August 1890 that Katanga was 'an important piece of territory which we need to complete the new province of British Central Africa'.

> It is ruled by an important chief called Msiri, who is decidedly friendly to the British . . . [It] is the richest country in minerals (gold

[64] On the Mackinnon agreement, see 'Aus den Archiven des Belgischen Kolonialministeriums: Das Lado und Bahr-el-Ghazal Pachtgebiet des Kongostaates', *Deutsches Kolonialblatt*, 27 (1916); Frank Hird, *H. M. Stanley* (London, 1935), p. 275; Dorothy Stanley, ed., *The Autobiography of Sir Henry Morton Stanley* (London, 1909), pp. 412, 417–18; William L. Langer, *The Diplomacy of Imperialism* (New York, 1956 edn.), p. 119; W. R. Louis, *Ruanda-Urundi, 1884–1919* (Oxford, 1963), pp. 27–28.

[65] 'I don't think the cession of land near to Lado was in the draft I saw': Salisbury's comment on Anderson's minute of 8 March 1892, FO 84/2200.

[66] 'I was at Berlin when the King and the Co[mpany] put it in [i.e. sent the agreement to the Foreign Office]' (Anderson's minute of 10 March, added to his minute of 8 March 1892, FO 84/2200).

[67] Salisbury to Leopold, 21 May 1890 (copy), FO 84/2082.

[68] Salisbury to Leopold, Confidential (draft), 9 June 1890, FO 84/2083.

[69] Anderson's minute of 4 June 1890, FO 84/2082.

and copper) in all Central Africa. It is fairly healthy and has a fertile soil. Its peoples are peaceful and industrious. The King of the Belgians has no right to it.[70]

On the contrary, Katanga fell within the boundaries of the Congo State as described by the Declaration of Neutrality of 1885. 'I have always held', Anderson wrote in January 1891, 'that the Powers who . . . have never, during the five years, objected . . . have accepted the boundary.'[71]

Both Percy Anderson and King Leopold put great faith in paper rights: the latter when it served his own interests, the former even when it meant an abnegation of British interests. In May 1891, representatives of the South Africa Company asked Anderson whether they 'would be at liberty to hoist the British flag at Katanga and conclude a Treaty with Msiri conferring sovereignty'.

> I referred them to the King's Circular of August 1885, to which no Power had taken objection, and which had been accepted by France and Germany, and said that though the boundaries claimed in it were ill-defined and must be delimited, and though it was uncertain whether they included the whole of Msiri's territories, they unquestionably included the Katanga mining districts.[72]

So far as the Foreign Office was concerned, Anderson had closed the Katanga affair.[73]

The question of paper rights was raised again, in a much more acute form, when the Foreign Office in 1892 learned that 'the King of the Belgians is making for Lado'.[74] He justified this action by the Mackinnon agreement of 1890. Whatever Anderson thought of this engagement at the time it was concluded, he now regarded it 'most emphatically' as a 'wholly inadmissible' pretext for the Congo State's 'filibustering'. Explaining his views to the British Minister in Brussels (who, like King Leopold, failed to see the Foreign Office's logic), Anderson wrote that only a few days after Lord Salisbury had given his

[70] Johnston to Salisbury, 25 August 1890, quoted in Oliver, *Sir Harry Johnston,* p. 194, note 2.

[71] Anderson's minute of 5 January 1891 on Vivian to Salisbury, Very Confidential, 3 January 1891, FO 84/2118. This minute shows that Anderson confused the boundary set by the Declaration of Neutrality with those established by the bilateral agreements.

[72] Anderson's memorandum of 27 May 1891, FO 403/157; cf. Anderson's minute of 23 May 1891 on Johnston to Salisbury, 3 May 1891, FO 84/2114: 'This disposes of the Katanga disputes. No treaty has been made with Msiri.'

[73] See Stengers, 'Léopold II et la fixation', pp. 193–94.

[74] Anderson's minute of 3 March 1892, FO 84/2200.

'assent' to the Mackinnon agreement, 'the Anglo-German Agreement was published, in which Great Britain publicly claimed the Western Nile Basin'.

> This, if His Majesty correctly interpreted Lord Salisbury's expression, was a direct breach of faith. Why was Lord Salisbury not at once challenged? It is said that the Agreement was not formally communicated to Belgium nor to the Free State. But it was notorious; it attracted universal attention; the basin was marked as British on every map; no international Agreement contravening it was known to any publicist. Yet not a word of protest was uttered. The King cannot complain of the absence of communication, for His Majesty has never communicated to the Powers, to France, nor even to Belgium, the document by which he consented to alter the boundaries of the State which he notified in 1885; and yet His Majesty holds that document to be binding, at any rate so far as it is in his favour . . . . I need hardly go over the ground of the secrecy of the despatch of the Kerckhoven expedition [i.e. the Congolese expedition to the Nile], the mystery which has surrounded it, and the repeated refusals to give us any explanations respecting it. With all this you are quite familiar. I hope I have proved to you that our case is strong.[75]

King Leopold was outraged by the attitude of the Foreign Office: 'I will not admit that I am an aggressor, for I have committed no act of aggression . . . But of course . . . you are suspicious, not so much perhaps of me, as of my possible heirs and successors, the French.'[76]

Fear of France: King Leopold had placed his finger on the mainspring of British policy in Africa. In 1884 Anderson had penned the Anglo-Portuguese treaty in an effort to block French expansion in the Congo basin. A decade later he acquiesced in King Leopold's scheme for an agreement between Britain and the Congo State to keep France out of the basin of the Nile.

The Anglo-Congolese agreement of 1894 was the culmination of the Foreign Office's efforts to seal off the Nile Valley by diplomacy— a process begun by Salisbury's engagements with the Germans in 1890 (which closed the southern door of Egypt) and with the Italians in 1891 (barring penetration from the east coast of Africa), and continued by another convention with the Germans in 1893, concluded by Rosebery (which was supposed to have slammed the door to the Nile in the west). The last agreement was abortive. In March 1894 the French cut through these paper blockades by an agreement with

[75] The text of this quotation follows the Confidential Print, FO 403/188; cf. FO 10/594.
[76] Quoted in Monson to Rosebery, Secret, 28 January 1893, FO 10/598.

the Germans, which left the French free to advance to the Nile from the west. 'It is certainly probable', Anderson wrote during the course of these Franco-German negotiations, 'that . . . [the French] will now push towards the Nile.'[77] Nor was his anxiety merely concerned with the west of Africa: until 1894, the future of Uganda was uncertain. Writing 'in the highest jingo tune',[78] Anderson urged the retention of Uganda because of its strategic importance as the pivot of Foreign Office Nile policy.[79] His critics interpreted his motives as mere land hunger, but in fact Uganda and the sources of the Nile were vital for the defence of the Nile, Egypt, and the route to India.[80] Anderson was merely developing the strategy of his master, Lord Salisbury. Under the impetuous Lord Rosebery (who became Foreign Secretary in 1892), whose Francophobia surpassed even Anderson's, he drove this idea to its conclusion. Pressing for the retention of Uganda in the south, he also adopted King Leopold's plan for checkmating the advancing French in the west.

By his 'dangerously aggressive'[81] move towards the Nile, King Leopold had provoked Anderson's devastating attacks on the tenuous claims that the Mackinnon agreement gave him to the Nile Valley. Attempting to strengthen his position, King Leopold defended himself on grounds of a private conversation with Lord Salisbury.

> Many years ago [reported the British minister in Brussels] . . . when he [King Leopold] had first turned his mind to foreign enterprise of some sort, he had entered into a sort of preliminary negotiation with Rajah Brooke of Borneo for the acquisition of that Island.
>
> . . . The Foreign Secretary of the day, (Lord Granville, His Majesty believed) had answered 'Do not go there!'; and he relinquished the idea.

[77] Anderson's minute of 13 February 1894 on Plunkett to Rosebery, 11 February 1894, FO 10/614; quoted in Taylor, 'Prelude to Fashoda', p. 83, note 2.

[78] A. G. Gardiner, *The Life of Sir William Harcourt* (2 vols., London, 1923), II, p. 192; on the background of Anderson's memorandum, see Robert Rhodes James, *Rosebery* (London, 1963), p. 261.

[79] 'If we retain Uganda we ought to be able to settle the question of the Nile basin by prior occupation: if we withdraw we shall hardly be able to keep France out of it' (Anderson's minute of 6 September 1892, FO 84/2002).

[80] Thus, to my mind, Anderson represents the prototype of the Foreign Office official—and the official mind of British imperialism—of *Africa and the Victorians*. Yet Messrs. Robinson and Gallagher place the hardheaded Anderson in the same category as the muddle-minded Mackinnon, with the two together having 'large plans to seize the Upper Nile and the territory between Lakes Victoria and Tanganyika in pursuit of their fantasies of Cape to Cairo or Niger to Nile' (p. 202).

[81] Anderson's minute of 6 September 1892, FO 84/2202.

... Lord Salisbury, in the course of a very long conversation [in May 1890] during which the King explained in detail all his plans, [concerning the Nile Valley] stated distinctly that he saw no objection to them, and subsequently confirmed this statement in writing.

... Had his Lordship answered, as Lord Granville had done in the case of Borneo, 'do not go there', His Majesty would not have proceeded further.[82]

Recognizing the ludicrous depths into which these discussions were degenerating, Anderson wrote: '[T]he real point to be gathered ... is that the King still hopes to confront us with a *fait accompli,* the occupation of the Nile basin.'[83]

In 1894 Anderson changed his tactics. He did this partly because he had been unable to browbeat the sovereign of the Congo State into abandoning his Nile claims, partly because of the actual arrival of Congolese troops in the Nile Valley.[84] He also changed because in 1894 the Foreign Office saw the imminent danger of the French marching 'on Lado or Fashoda with an exceptionally well-organized expedition'.[85] There was no question that in the long run the French were a greater menace than King Leopold, or that the issue at stake even surpassed in importance that of the Congo in 1884; in the minds of Salisbury, Rosebery, and Anderson, the question of the Upper Nile was bound up with the one of Egypt and the route to India and therefore with the security of the British Empire itself. In the short run, the immediate problem facing the Foreign Office was the entrenchment of Congolese troops. To solve this problem, the Foreign Office—after two years of vigorous and persistent denial of the validity of Congolese claims—suddenly espoused King Leopold's idea that the Congo State would make a good 'buffer state' separating Britain and France in the Nile Valley. Regarding the Nile region as their own preserve, too important to be permanently entrusted even to a buffer power, the British decided to lease rather than give the territory to King Leopold— partly because of the problem of France's reversionary claims, but also because 'it was the ultimate intention of British policy to turn the Belgians out of the valley of the Nile.'[86]

[82] Monson to Rosebery, Secret, 28 January 1893, FO 10/595.

[83] Anderson's minute of 31 January 1893, FO 10/595.

[84] The arrival of Congolese troops at Lado was announced in *Le Mouvement Géographique,* 9 (27 November 1892), p. 130.

[85] Quoted in J. Stengers, 'Aux Origines de Fachoda: L'Expédition Monteil', *Revue belge de Philologie et d'Histoire,* 36 (1958) and 38 (1960), p. 1044.

[86] Taylor, 'Prelude to Fashoda', p. 85.

In March 1894 the Foreign Office befriended King Leopold, offering to lease to him the territories that he claimed along the western bank of the Nile by the Mackinnon agreement. King Leopold, who regarded occupation as nine-tenths of possession, jumped at the chance: '[T]he King is very anxious to come to terms with us', reported Rennell Rodd, who conducted the preliminary negotiations in Brussels, '[but] thinks it affords an opportunity for claiming a number of bargains wholly advantageous to himself, which at the same time perhaps he hardly expects to realize.'[87] Through the Anglo-Congolese agreement of 12 May 1894, the Foreign Office extended the Congo State into the Nile Valley to 10° north latitude, thus, in theory, blocking the French advance to the Nile.

Superficially, the Mackinnon agreement of 1890 and the Anglo-Congolese agreement of 1894 were practically identical. Both gave the left bank of the Nile to King Leopold, both gave a thin strip of territory running from Lake Albert Edward to Lake Tanganyika to Britain. In 1890 Mackinnon had been intent on securing the Cape-to-Cairo corridor for Britain, and from the British point of view this was the main purpose of the transaction. In 1894 Anderson was bent on securing the Nile Valley for Britain, and not the corridor. In 1890 Anderson had had nothing to do with the Mackinnon agreement; in 1894 he was responsible for the Anglo-Congolese negotiations.

He was responsible because by 1894 he had reached a position of considerable importance in the Foreign Office. In January 1894 Anderson had been appointed Assistant Under-Secretary. His influence in African questions was tantamount to that of the Foreign Secretary himself. This was not only because of his undisputed competence: it was also because of the transition occurring in the Foreign Office at the time. Rosebery had left to become Prime Minister; Sir Philip Currie, the Permanent Under-Secretary, had gone to Constantinople; Lister had retired.[88] Lord Kimberley became Foreign Secretary.

By becoming Foreign Secretary, the good Lord Kimberley—'a cautious statesman [who] . . . used black blotting paper to avoid the risk of having his letters read by spies'[89]—had fulfilled his lifetime ambition.[90] Philanthropic, loquacious, and endowed with a deep grain

---

[87] Rodd to Anderson, Private, 17 March 1894, FO 10/625.

[88] Lister retired in January 1894, and it was into his post that Anderson moved as Assistant Under-Secretary.

[89] Tilley and Gaselee, *The Foreign Office*, p. 138.

[90] Fitzmaurice, *Granville*, I, p. 180; *Cambridge History of British Foreign Policy*, III, p. 614. On Kimberley, see Ethel Drus, ed., 'A Journal of Events during the Gladstone Ministry, 1868–1874', *Camden Miscellany*, 3rd ser., 21 (1958).

of sarcasm, he was, in Granville's words, 'the least humbugging of men.'[91] Although attacked as being 'a mere clerk to the Premier',[92] he was a conscientious and forceful Imperial statesman in his own right, having served both as Secretary of State for India and as Colonial Secretary. The reason he cut 'an exceedingly poor figure'[93] as Foreign Secretary was primarily because of the Anglo-Congolese agreement. The responsibility for it was placed squarely and unjustly on his shoulders, and as a result he was charged with having 'set up in business without knowing the ABC of his trade': 'That Lord Kimberley probably trusted to some subordinate can hardly be urged as an excuse, as all the permanent officials in the African Department of the Foreign Office must be aware of the existence of . . . documentary evidence.'[94]

The subordinate of course was Sir Percy Anderson, and Kimberley, like everyone else, had implicit faith in his ability. So far as the Anglo-Congolese agreement is concerned, Kimberley had little to do with its inception. Anderson prepared it directly under the supervision of Rosebery. It was Anderson who drafted the treaty; it was he who conducted the final negotiations; it was he who neglected 'documentary evidence' of the 1890 Anglo-German negotiations that he himself had consummated. And it is therefore he and not Kimberley or even Rosebery who must be held accountable for the 'extraordinary and almost incredible blunder'[95] perpetrated during the negotiations. It was the great blunder of Anderson's career.

The blunder was not the move on the African chessboard to block the French advance to the Nile, though this created 'the vague feeling that Great Britain, with her stolid cunning, has stolen a diplomatic march upon the Powers that have portioned Africa.'[96] Nor was it even the lease to King Leopold, though he was perceptively recognized at the time as a 'tenant [who] resembles not so much a farmer as the devil, to whom it is dangerous to give even the tip of your little finger'.[97] The blunder was the Cape-to-Cairo corridor (Article III). The 'documentary evidence' to which the press referred was that which showed how the German government had defeated this scheme in the 1890 negotiations.[98] By exacting from King Leopold the concession of

---

[91] Granville to Morier, private, 17 July 1880, PRO 30/29/198.

[92] *Truth*, 25 October 1894.

[93] *National Observer*, 21 July 1894.

[94] Ibid., 21 July and 1 September 1894.

[95] *The Times*, 23 June 1894.

[96] *National Observer*, 16 June 1894.

[97] Translation from *Novoye Vremya* of 13 June 1894, FO 10/625.

[98] See Raphael, *The Cape-to-Cairo Dream*, p. 449, note 68.

a road from Lake Edward to Lake Tanganyika, Anderson had linked the British spheres in the north and south of Africa; he had 'encircled' German East Africa by British possessions and had cut it off from the Congo. Consequently, the assault on the Anglo-Congolese agreement came not only from France but also from Germany.

Was the Anglo-Congolese agreement a machiavellian scheme on Anderson's part to achieve a British Empire stretching from the Cape to Cairo as well as British supremacy in the Nile Valley? The answer is unequivocally no. Anderson had no more use for the sentimental vision of the Cape-to-Cairo route than had Lord Salisbury; in 1890 Anderson himself had curtly dismissed the idea as 'impracticable'. Why then was it included in the agreement? The answer is that Anderson thought King Leopold was getting too good a bargain. Handing over to the Congo State the territory along the west bank of the Nile (to which the Foreign Office had so acrimoniously denied King Leopold's claims) grated upon Anderson's chessboard mentality. He probably felt that the British were giving a *quid* without receiving a *quo*, even though King Leopold was willing to recognize sovereign British rights in the Nile Valley. He looked for concessions that might be extorted from the King, and consequently demanded frontier rectifications favourable to Britain in the Katanga region and telegraphic communication through the Congo State. King Leopold, though receiving more in the Nile Valley than he had ever dreamed he might, responded by demanding a port on Lake Albert. Anderson followed suit by exacting from King Leopold a port on Lake Tanganyika along with a road to connect it with Uganda. It was so much of an afterthought that the Lake Tanganyika scheme was not even discussed in the preliminary negotiations.[99]

Yet it was the Cape-to-Cairo corridor that greatly weakened the agreement by bringing Germany into a loose alliance with France in protest against it. From the German point of view, the corridor clause was no less than a deliberate, even provocative, British bid for hegemony on the African continent.

> They [the Germans] could not believe that the inclusion of Article III . . . was due to sheer inadvertence. But that was the fact. Percy Anderson . . . concentrated so narrowly upon the possibility of French opposition that the existence of objections on the part of Germany had simply been forgotten.[100]

---

[99] See W. R. Louis, 'The Anglo-Congolese Agreement of 1894', St. Antony's Papers 15 (1963).
[100] *The History of The Times, 1884–1912* (London, 1947), p. 149.

Throughout his career Anderson had been as tolerant of the Germans in Africa as he had been bigoted towards the French. In 1884–85 he was regarded by his Foreign Office colleagues as supporting a policy of 'complete surrender'[101] to German territorial claims, and on his return from the Berlin Conference, one official even described him as thoroughly 'Bismarckized'[102] at the expense of British interests. In part, Anderson's views towards German imperialism in Africa were probably conditioned by his notion of German free trade on the one hand and French monopoly on the other; but above all, his attitude after 1889 was determined by Salisbury's Nile strategy. The great victory of 1890 by which Salisbury and Anderson exchanged Heligoland for the sources of the Nile proved that Germany's overriding concern was Europe and not Africa; it proved that the main rivals of the British in Africa were not the Germans but the French. So little had he counted on German opposition to the Anglo-Congolese agreement that he was at a loss to explain it on any grounds other than 'unnecessary bullying'[103] by the Anglophobe director of the colonial division of the German Foreign Office, Dr. Kayser.[104] Through Article III of the Anglo-Congolese agreement, Anderson had unintentionally conjured up the bogey of the Cape-to-Cairo route; he failed to see why the Germans did not recognize it as a meaningless cliché. It was a failure of imagination.

Kimberley with great mortification had to admit that it simply 'did not . . . occur' to the British government that German interests might be prejudiced.[105] He cancelled the corridor clause on 22 June 1894.

At the same time, King Leopold faced perhaps the gravest crisis of his career. By creating a situation that could easily have led to an armed clash between French and Congolese forces as they raced to the Nile, King Leopold had brought the Congo State to the brink of war with France. The officers who would wage this war were officers of the *Belgian* army in the service of the Congo State, who, by engaging in hostilities with French troops, would jeopardize the neutrality

[101] Hill's minute of 7 December 1884, on Malet to Granville, 5 December 1884, FO 84/1815.

[102] H. Austin Lee to Mackinnon, Private, 13 May 1885, Mackinnon Papers.

[103] Anderson's minute of 29 May 1894 on Plunkett to Kimberley, no. 86 Africa, 28 May 1894, FO 10/618.

[104] On Kayser's role in the 1894 crisis, see Erich Eyck, *Das Persönliche Regiment Wilhelms II* (Zurich, 1948), pp. 112–13. I am again indebted to Professor Stengers for pointing out that Kayser himself was largely and personally responsible for the violent German attack on the Anglo-Congolese treaty and that therefore Anderson could have had no means of foreseeing events that might normally have never occurred. Perhaps this absolves Anderson to some extent, but Article III in any case was a grave miscalculation.

[105] Kimberley to Malet, 2 July 1894, FO 64/1332.

of Belgium herself.[106] Public opinion as well as the Belgian government turned against King Leopold; he 'could no longer hold out single handed against France, *and against pressure also in Belgium.*'[107] Confronted with ultimata from both the Belgian and French governments, King Leopold capitulated. On 14 August 1894 he and the French signed an agreement that left them free to advance to the Nile. The scheme for a Congolese buffer in the Nile Valley had collapsed.[108]

In 1894–96 the Congo State itself threatened to collapse. The crisis through which King Leopold was passing at this time was not limited merely to embroilment with France on the Upper Nile; it was a period of severe financial crisis as well. Having reached the limit of his personal resources, King Leopold was forced to consider handing over his African empire to Belgium.[109] The proposed annexation treaty of January 1895 produced a sharp division of colonial sentiment in Belgium; it also created a host of constitutional problems. Would the acquisition of a colony affect the neutrality of Belgium?[110] This was a weighty consideration, but there were others equally important. In Anderson's opinion: 'That [Congo] State cannot, by annexation, be placed in the position of an ordinary Colony. International obligations are imposed upon it by the Berlin Act.'[111]

Even more difficult was the question of France's right of preemption. As redefined in 1895: 'France may appropriate as much Congo State territory as she pleases [but] the other conterminous Powers, England, Germany & Portugal, cannot make even a slight rectification of frontiers without her assent. It is an abnormal situation, not easy to accept.'[112] Yet even the annexation question and the new pre-emption agreement dwindled in importance when compared to the other element in the Congo crisis of this period, which preoccupied Anderson during the last year of his life. In 1896 the foundations of the Congo State almost crumbled when the Stokes affair heralded

[106] See Stengers, 'Aux Origines de Fachoda', pp. 1056–61.

[107] Plunkett to Kimberley, Very Confidential, 11 August 1894, FO 10/617; quoted in Stengers, 'Aux Origines de Fachoda', p. 1063, note 4; Stengers's emphasis.

[108] But King Leopold's Nile claims were not settled until 1906. On this problem, see Robert O. Collins, *The Southern Sudan, 1883–1898* (New Haven, 1962), chaps. 3 and 4; and his article 'Anglo-Congolese Negotiations, 1900–1906', *Zaïre,* 62 (1958).

[109] See J. Stengers, 'La première tentative de reprise du Congo par la Belgique, 1894–1895', *Bulletin de la Société Royale Belge de Géographie,* 63 (1949).

[110] For Anderson's views on this problem, see his memorandum entitled 'Memorandum on the Effect of the Acquisition of the Congo State upon the Guarantee of the Neutrality of Belgium', 2 March 1895, FO 10/649.

[111] Ibid.

[112] Anderson's minute of 7 February 1895, FO 27/3234.

the later outcry over atrocities. This incident in a sense resulted from the financial and annexation crises: the Congo State had begun to enter its period of prosperity; with this change in his financial fortune, King Leopold, highly irritated moreover at the criticism of his 'Oeuvre Africaine', no longer favoured annexation. The scheme was dropped. King Leopold remained free of constitutional limitations; he remained, in fact, an absolute despot on the order of Louis XIV. The purpose of this kingdom was, among other things, to make money. Left free to pursue this pastime (which in fairness to him was for the benefit of Belgium rather than for personal gain), King Leopold continued to exploit and monopolize the ivory and rubber of the Congo. This was the basic cause of the Stokes incident, which demonstrated to Anderson, the Foreign Office, and the English public the true nature of the monstrosity they had helped create as a buffer state.

In January 1895 an officer of the Congo State, Captain Lothaire, hanged a British subject, an ivory merchant settled in German East Africa named Charles Stokes, on grounds of selling guns to the Arabs of the eastern Congo. Stokes was undoubtedly guilty of aiding the Arab enemies of the Congo State, but Lothaire's action was completely illegal. The complicated events surrounding Lothaire's trial and acquittal are beyond the scope of the present discussion,[113] but it is important to note that the judicial proceedings of the Congo State seemed to the Foreign Office 'little better than a farce'.[114] Nevertheless, the British attempted, in Henry M. Stanley's words, 'to deal mildly'[115] with the Congo State in regard to the Stokes affair—for the same reason that the Foreign Office had tolerated King Leopold's African empire almost from the time of its beginnings, and why in 1894 Britain had espoused the Congo State in an alliance: fear of France. 'It would, to my mind, be a grave mistake', wrote the British minister in Belgium, 'to make a bitter enemy of the Congo State . . . [this would] lead probably to dangerous discussions with France, under her claim to pre-emption.'[116]

Despite the shadow of France, the Stokes affair to British eyes was such a miscarriage of justice that it could not easily be dismissed. Nor was this the only indication of maladministration in the Congo: in

---

[113] See W. R. Louis, 'Great Britain and the Stokes Case', *Uganda Journal*, 28 (1964); and 'The Stokes Affair and the Origins of the Anti-Congo Campaign, 1895–1896', *Revue belge de Philologie et d'Histoire*, 43 (1965).

[114] Anderson's minute of 4 July 1896, FO 10/713.

[115] Stanley to Liebrechts, 2 September 1895, 'Der Fall Stokes 1895–1896', *Deutsches Kolonialblatt*, 27 (1916), p. 118.

[116] Plunkett to Anderson, Private and Confidential, 15 September 1895, FO 10/652.

May 1895 the British Congo Consul reported he was 'convinced that [other] . . . cases of brutal ill treatment actually occurred.'[117] In 1895–96, Sir Percy Anderson and the British Foreign Office began to taste the administrative fruit of the buffer tree that they had helped plant.

Sir Percy Anderson died suddenly towards the end of the Stokes affair, on 19 July 1896. No doubt he was haunted by the spectre of France on the Upper Nile and the Congo; no doubt his spirit did not truly rest until after the Fashoda showdown of 1898 and the Belgian annexation of the Congo ten years later. In a sense, these events were the successful outcome of his grand design against France, and it would have been as appropriate to say in 1908 as it had been in 1890 (as one Foreign Office official wrote at the close of the Anglo-German negotiations) that 'the great Sir Percy deserves well of his country!'[118] Yet he had a curious failing: he was shortsighted—as the disaster of the Anglo-Congolese agreement of 1894 abundantly proved. Concentrating narrowly on checkmating France, he lacked breadth of vision, unlike Lord Salisbury; and perhaps partly for this reason Lord Salisbury is remembered in history as a statesman and H. Percy Anderson only as a vaguely famous civil servant.

Like his fictional alter ego, 'though he might be short-sighted, [he] was exceedingly able. He was in some ways the wisest of men we have had in the Foreign Office.'[119] Yet despite his sagacity, it is doubtful whether Anderson ever recognized that King Leopold and not France was the true enemy of humanity and free commerce in tropical Africa. Had Sir Percy Anderson lived another decade and experienced the revelations of the anti-Congo campaign, he might have agreed with a comment made when he created a furore in 1894 with the Anglo-Congolese agreement: 'It never was a very heroic or a very wise game to play—this buffer-State game, in which the Congo was to be the buffer.'[120]

---

[117] Pickersgill to Kimberley, 27 May 1895, FO 10/731.
[118] H. A. Lee to Mackinnon, 20 July 1890, Mackinnon Papers.
[119] Johnston, *The Gay-Dombeys,* p. 144.
[120] *Saturday Review,* 18 August 1894.

3

THE BERLIN CONGO CONFERENCE AND THE (NON-) PARTITION OF AFRICA, 1884–85

In re-evaluating the history of the Berlin Conference of 1884–85, two dominant and neglected themes become apparent: the agitation of the British and French press over the questions of the Congo and Niger in relation to the major issues of international security and commerce in the late nineteenth century; and the legalistic approach of the Gladstone Government to colonial questions. Spurred by public opinion, the Foreign Office sought to establish British claims on the Niger and to protect British trade on the Congo; harnessed with the legal precepts of the Lord Chancellor, the British government espoused mid-Victorian juristic concepts that were imposed on the Conference and became embodied in the General Act. A new evaluation of the Berlin Conference from the perspective of Britain vis-à-vis France therefore must attempt to determine the nature of 'public opinion' and its influence on the policy-making process, and the legalistic preconceptions of the policy makers. This smacks of jargon, but deliberately so, for this essay, basically historical in approach, attempts to re-examine the work of Britain at the Berlin Conference by drawing occasionally on the disciplines of political science and international law. It also aims to give the deathblow to the persisting myth, recently restated by none other than Kwame Nkrumah, that 'the original carve-up of Africa [was] arranged at the Berlin Conference of 1884.'[1]

[1] Kwame Nkrumah, *Challenge of the Congo* (New York, 1967), p. x. The mythology of the Berlin Act is traced in part by J. Stengers, 'A propos de l'Act de Berlin, ou comment naît une légende', *Zaïre*, 8 (1953), pp. 839–44.

In writing this essay I have been indebted to Jean Stengers for placing at my disposal a large number of notes on the French press for 1884–85, which I have supplemented with my own research, even though my main focus is on British archives and newspapers. The British press usually referred to the 'Berlin Congo Conference': the major discussions concerned that region. In attempting to come to grips with that elusive concept, 'public opinion', I decided that it is best employed in accordance with its usage in 1884–85; in the words of the head of the African Department of the Foreign Office, it meant news and opinion 'published in the principal newspapers'. These are the French newspapers that occasionally had significant passages: *Echo de Paris, Economiste Français, Evénement, Figaro, Français, France, Gaulois, Intransigeant, Journal de Débats, Liberté, Messager de Paris, National, Revue des Deux Mondes, Temps, Télégraphe, République Française, Soleil,* and *Voltaire*. The British press debated the issues of the Conference much more extensively. I consulted the following newspapers: *Daily Chronicle, Daily News, Daily Telegraph, The Economist, Glasgow Herald, Globe, Leeds Mercury, Liverpool Courier, Liverpool Daily Post, Manchester Examiner and Times, Manchester Guardian, Morning Advertiser, Morning Post, Observer, Pall Mall Gazette, St. James Gazette, Saturday Review, Spectator, Standard, Sunday Times, The Times,* and *Truth*. The major problem facing the historian of the press is governmental influence on the news and editorial opinion, but that topic is irrelevant to the use I have attempted to make out of the press in this essay:

Conspiratorial theories were rife in 1884–85, and contemporary misconceptions about the nature of the Conference help explain the mythology of the European powers plotting Africa's fate only two years after Britain had occupied Egypt. Egypt remained foremost in the public's mind. A mere glance at the newspapers of 1884 strikes the reader with the importance of the continuing Egyptian emergency. But was there a causal connection between the British occupation of Egypt and the subsequent 'partition of Africa' with which the Berlin Conference is usually associated? Robinson and Gallagher in *Africa and the Victorians* argue forcefully that the British intervention sparked the 'Scramble' for Africa.[2] Their book is a landmark in the history of the expansion of Europe, above all because it demonstrates the crucial role of the Egyptian crisis in the grand strategy British statesmen formulated for the rest of Africa and, indeed, in the entire Eastern Hemisphere. Yet their single, basic explanation—Egypt—is as

---

to investigate European preconceptions of Africa in 1884–85. Anyone who works in the area of public opinion and foreign policy is indebted to Oron James Hale, whose *Publicity and Diplomacy* (New York, 1940) is a pioneering work, and to several works by E. Malcolm Carroll, of which the most relevant to this topic is *French Public Opinion and Foreign Affairs, 1870–1914* (New York, 1931).

[2] Ronald Robinson and John Gallagher, with Alice Denny, *Africa and the Victorians: The Official Mind of Imperialism* (London, 1961); important reviews related to western Africa and the Congo by C. W. Newbury and Jean Stengers, *Journal of African History*, 3 (1962), pp. 469–501. Robinson and Gallagher glide over the problems of the Conference and dismiss its importance by pointing out, 'At no time before, during or after the Berlin Conference was there a parliamentary debate about its aims or its results' (p. 177). For the details of the Conference and the significance of the Berlin Act, one must rely on the two most important works on the subject, both of which were written over a quarter of a century ago: S. E. Crowe, *The Berlin West African Conference* (London, 1942), and Geoffroy de Courcel, *L'Influence de la Conférence de Berlin de 1885 sur le droit colonial international* (Paris, 1935). See also especially Robert Stanley Thomson, *La Foundation de l'État Indépendant du Congo* (Brussels, 1933); K. O. Diké, *Trade and Politics in the Niger Delta, 1830–1885* (Oxford, 1956); J. E. Flint, *Sir George Goldie and the Making of Nigeria* (London, 1960); Henri Brunschwig, *Mythes et Réalités de l'Impérialisme colonial français, 1871–1914* (Paris, 1960); Roger Anstey, *Britain and the Congo in the Nineteenth Century* (Oxford, 1962); and John D. Hargreaves, *Prelude to the Partition of West Africa* (London, 1963). A standard French work that deserves special mention is by Maurice Baumont, *L'Essor Industriel et l'Impérialisme Colonial* (Paris, 1937). Chapter nine of William L. Langer's *European Alliances and Alignments* (New York, 1956 edn.) has a valuable bibliography; see also Jacques Willequet, 'Die Geschichte des Belgisch-Kongo, 1876–1960: Eine bibliographische Orientierung', *Jahresbibliographie Bibliothek für Zeitgeschichte*, 32 (1960), pp. 357–82. Otherwise dated monographs that still have occasional points of interest include A. B. Keith, *The Belgian Congo and the Berlin Act* (Oxford, 1919); Georg Königk, *Die Berliner Kongo-Konferenz 1884–1885* (Essen, 1938); J. S. Reeves, *The International Beginnings of the Congo Free State* (Baltimore, 1894); José Gonçalo Santa Ritta, *Conferência de Berlin de 1885* (Lisbon, 1916); Robert H. Wienefeld, *Franco-German Relations, 1878–1885* (Baltimore, 1929); and Howard E. Yarnall, *The Great Powers and the Congo Conference in the Years 1884 and 1885* (Göttingen, 1934).

unsatisfactory as the answer given by British journalists and officials of the 1880s, who thought more generally that France had conspired against England not only in Egypt but throughout the world.

Englishmen on the whole did not view the occupation of Egypt as the event that determined the course of the partition; and Robinson and Gallagher do not investigate why the English public held France responsible for the colonial rivalries that became the central theme of international relations in the 1880s and 1890s. The same observation (not criticism) applies to S. E. Crowe's book on the Berlin Conference, which will continue to remain the definitive study of official British policy. She also did not attempt to study the history of the era in relation to public opinion. This essay, in a sense, begins where both Robinson and Gallagher and Crowe stop—by asking these questions: Does a study of the British and French press as well as official documents throw light on what 'caused' the Scramble, or, in a broader and more ambitious sense, the First World War? Does an examination of the publicity as well as the diplomacy of the Conference reveal further the development of European attitudes towards Africa—Europe's image of Africa in the mid-1880s? Does this sort of investigation have any relevance for African as well as European history? The answers may be negative, but the questions are worth asking, if only to take a step towards the main task yet to be accomplished by the historian of the expansion of Europe: to recapture, as Felix Frankfurter once said in quite a different context, 'that impalpable thing, what was in the air' when Europe scrambled for colonies.

Who started it? 'The kettle began it, but who lighted the fire which started the kettle?' asked the *Glasgow Herald* surveying the Scramble (9 January 1885). 'We fear the solution will be as difficult as in the old game of Blackcap and Bluecap. Germany says England, England says France, France says Germany, and Spain says everybody.' The quotation accurately depicts British attitudes. For reasons that Englishmen failed to attribute to economic gain, the French 'colonial appetite' seemed to grow, in British eyes, with every new morsel of territory swallowed up in Africa and Asia. Glory and mischief, not profit, motivated the French in Tunis, Senegal, Madagascar, and Tonkin. According to *The Times* (25 May 1883):

> It has been said that France is always peeping through the keyhole to see what Prince Bismarck is doing; and that if at any time when she finds him looking the other way she sets off to amuse herself in her own old fashion in some unoccupied corner of the world. First it was Tunis, then the Congo, then Tonquin, and now the Madagascar adventure is in full activity.

Over a year later (4 June 1884), the *Daily Chronicle* reiterated the theme that summarizes the general English interpretation of French expansion from 1881: 'France, largely out of consideration for her reverses fourteen years ago and her decline as a European power, has been allowed a free hand—a too free hand, indeed—in divers quarters of the globe, and she has shown her gratitude to the Powers that have left her free to pursue a "spirited foreign policy" by ruthlessly trampling upon their interests when it has suited her to do so.'

When the *Daily Chronicle* voiced that typical indictment of French policy, Britain and France had been joined in the struggle for colonial supremacy by another major power, Germany. The colonial balance of power was shifting, but in which direction? Would English interests be damaged by the advent of Germany as a colonial power? Was England's 'natural ally' Germany or France? The following excerpt from the *Manchester Guardian* (2 January 1885) reflects the consensus of English opinion at the time of the Berlin Conference, when Anglo-German colonial rivalry was bitterest:

> Are we to continue to regard the friendship of France as the keystone of our foreign policy, even though, as in Egypt and in most other parts of the world at present, our interests are opposed to hers; or are we to maintain our traditional friendship with Germany, whose interests in Europe are identical with our own? So long as the Continental Powers were entirely absorbed in their own revolutions or unifications it was possible for England to go her own way, gradually building up a colonial empire, and paying little or no regard to the disputes by which the unsettled commonwealth of Europe was agitated.
>
> Those days are over. The other Powers seek to gratify a natural ambition for colonial extension. It is impossible for us to resist them all, and we should be wise to make up our minds without delay which is the Power whose interests lie nearest to our own, and which is the Power whom we should prefer in case of need to find upon the same side with ourselves.

France had provoked a colonial scramble; Germany had entered the race; and England's stance was indecisive. So ran the prominent ideas through the English press.

'Stands England where she did?' The question resounded throughout the years 1884–85. With the 'capitalists of Europe' ready to advance into the non-European world, would England be able to maintain her commercial supremacy? Possibly drifting towards war with France over Egypt, and facing recurrent crises with Russia over

Afghanistan, Englishmen questioned whether the 'immortal lyric' of having ships, men, and money continued to hold true. 'Britain still rules the waves', commented the *Globe* (21 March 1884), a newspaper that closely followed naval and colonial issues, but could England withstand an assault by a European alliance?

The industrial revolution led by England now seemed to be working against her: the European nations emerged as her competitors overseas and threatened her with alignments challenging her colonial supremacy. According to the Liberal newspaper most sensitive to colonial issues, the *Pall Mall Gazette* (30 July 1884): 'Day by Day the world perceptibly shrinks before our eyes. Steam and electricity have brought all the world next door. We have yet to re-adjust our political arrangements to the revolution that has been wrought in time and space.' The issue of England's ability to adjust to a changing world in turn gave rise to another fundamental question. Was the British Empire in a state of 'decline and decay'? In jingo tone, the *Morning Post* answer unequivocally (12 August 1884):

> England is still a great Power. Nay, more, in a very comprehensive sense, she is the greatest of Powers and the mother of great Powers both present and future. England has an empire in every quarter of the globe. Her fleet still commands the seas. Her fleet is saluted by all the world. She would fain go on calmly in the majesty of her strength, ready to welcome all in the paths of peace and progress. But if she be struck at she will strike back. Not once, nor twice, but until right be done. At least she can strike with a heart which has never quailed, and with an arm which does not know the meaning of defeat.

Such bluster might not seem surprising from such a conservative organ as the *Morning Post*, but similar effusions throughout the English press indicate the pangs of insecurity felt by the nation as a whole.

Frenchmen of course viewed the issues of overseas rivalry quite differently. Their attention in this regard mainly focused on Egypt, to a lesser degree on British 'obstruction' in the Far East and West Africa. Insults hurled at the British during the abortive Anglo-French Egyptian Conference of June 1884 typified French sentiments: the *Journal des Débats* referred to the 'chimerical time' when British troops would withdraw from the Nile, and labelled English promises as 'soap bubbles'; the *Télégraphe* entitled a leading article 'Egypt for the English'; the *National* accused Prime Minister Jules Ferry of 'excessive condescension' towards Gladstone; the *Gaulois* called the French Ambassador in London 'blind and incapable' in his dealings with the English; the *Messager de Paris* denounced the French policy of 'capitulation'; and the *France* caught the general polemical tone of the press by attacking the English as 'clever traders' who did not hesitate to take advantage of French interests throughout the world. A few journals, such as the *Liberté* and the *Voltaire,* expressed more moderate opinions, but all in all the French attitude towards England in mid-1884 was hostile, and by no means only because of Egypt. The *Journal de Débats* (12 October 1884) saw this as the heart of the matter: 'Not content with seizing the Nile, the English want to get their hands on the Congo and the Niger, those grand commercial routes.' To prevent British domination of those rivers, the French public generally supported the idea of Franco-German cooperation in colonial questions.

The French publicists who wrote on colonial questions in 1884–85 recognized that the Franco-German *entente* was a colonial understanding and not a permanent alignment designed to change or stabilize the European balance of power. Despite alarmist reports that Jules Ferry had been tricked by Bismarck into compromising France's security by again becoming embroiled in overseas ventures, the press on the whole emphasized that the two governments had merely reached an accord on the affairs of western Africa, and that this agreement was relatively insignificant. The chronological evolution of the issue in the public eye reflects this view. From April 1884, when Bismarck broached the subject of naval and colonial cooperation with France against England,[3] to August of the same year, when he concluded the *entente* with Ferry,[4] the French press continued to be engrossed in the Egyptian question. Not until shortly before the convocation of the Berlin Conference did other African issues become the main topic of discussion.

An editorial in the *République Française* of 10 October is a good example of a typical analysis of the Franco-German rapprochement and its implications for Europe and the colonial world:

> For our part we have never attached importance to the report of a Franco-German alliance against England. That there exists between

[3] See Courcel to Ferry, 25 April 1884, *Documents diplomatiques français* (*DDF* hereafter), 1st series, 5, pp. 267–71, no. 249. Bismarck's approach to France coincided with his commitment to protect German merchants in South-west Africa.

[4] See *DDF,* 1st series, 5, pp. 365 ff. The unpublished documents at the Ministère des Affaires Etrangères (MAE hereafter), and in the Section d'Outre-Mer, Archives Nationale (ANSOM hereafter) add but little to the published documents on Franco-German collaboration. For different interpretations, see Pearl B. Mitchell, *The Bismarckian Policy of Conciliation with France, 1875–1885* (Philadelphia, 1935), A. J. P. Taylor, *Germany's First Bid for Colonies, 1884–1885* (London, 1938), and a thorough, critical re-examination of the problem by Henry Ashby Turner, Jr., 'Bismarck's Imperialist Venture: Anti-British in Origin?' in Prosser Gifford and W. R. Louis, eds., *Britain and Germany in Africa: Imperial Rivalry and Colonial Rule* (New Haven, 1967). The fullest account of French policy at the Berlin Conference era is by Thomas F. Power, Jr., *Jules Ferry and the Renaissance of French Imperialism* (New York, 1966 edn.).

France and Germany a community of interests sufficiently important to give rise to an accord implying common diplomatic action is quite natural. But an alliance is quite another affair . . . France and Germany do not gravitate in the same political orbit.

'The bulk of public opinion', concluded the newspaper, was 'dead against this alliance, arrangement, or understanding' if it meant a permanent agreement about Europe. But the *République Française* admitted that there could be united action in tropical Africa. Most Frenchmen conscious of foreign affairs probably agreed. According to the *Journal des Débats* on 6 October: 'When certain newspapers talk of a *German alliance* it is impossible to ignore the fact that this is merely a play on words.' A permanent political alignment would be impossible; but there were certain places where Germany and France had common interests to defend, and it would be no sign of weakness or humiliation if France joined Germany in righting English wrongs in Egypt or in restraining English 'annexationist tendencies' in other parts of Africa. As the *Journal* affirmed: 'We can even make concessions to German colonial policy in the rest of Africa and support German colonial and commercial schemes where they do not run counter to ours.' Generally, Franco-German colonial cooperation would act as a check against Britain's maritime supremacy and would maintain equal access to territories not yet occupied; specifically, the French looked for German good will in Egypt, and in return would support Bismarck's colonial ventures in western Africa.

The Frenchman who publicly voiced his opinion on western Africa with greatest authority was the publicist-parliamentarian, Gabriel Charmes.[5] An expert on the affairs of Egypt, he had resented Britain's occupation in 1882, and since then, in signed editorials in the *Journal de Débats,* had repeatedly sounded alarms over British overseas activity elsewhere. He gave sustained attention to colonial issues, and the pattern of his thought makes him a representative of doctrinaire French imperial thought in the 1880s. He believed that the French government's preoccupation with Europe prevented the public from seeing that France could recover from the reverse of 1870 only by colonial expansion. Lagging in industrial development, France needed raw material and markets abroad. Colonial expansion would provide an outlet for surplus capital; moreover, it would give France the

[5] See his book, *Politique Extérieure et Coloniale* (Paris, 1885); also *L'Egypte* (Paris, 1891). For Charmes's background, see *Le Livre du Centennaire du Journal des Débats, 1789–1889* (Paris, 1889), the article by Etienne Lamy, pp. 376–83; also Agnes Murphy, *The Ideology of French Imperialism* (Washington, 1948), chap. 5. The other prominent publicist was Paul Leroy-Beaulieu, whose views are discussed later in this essay.

opportunity to mobilize the manpower of Africa and Asia, thereby perhaps eventually compensating for France's inferior size and population growth. In a word, the power and glory of France, in his opinion,
depended on overseas development.

Charmes's more specific views illustrate the temper of French opinion shortly before the Berlin Conference. One of the main purposes
of colonial enterprise, he thought, was to improve France's economy
and strategic potential against her Continental rival, but overseas she
found herself frustrated by Britain. Charmes wrote in the *Journal des
Débats* (7 October 1884):

> If we were always to remain separated from Prince von Bismarck, we
> ought to be united to England as her ally. For some years we were so
> united, and so long as this lasted, it was easy for us to hold aloof from
> Germany, because we had no interest to connect us with her. But
> everyone knows how the English alliance came to an end . . . We have
> explained why we no longer have an alliance with England, and why,
> in China as in Egypt, we shall perhaps be compelled to accept the
> support of Germany, which will cost us much more and will be less
> useful to us.

Charmes thus adjusted his ideas to changing circumstances. French
patriotism would not be compromised, he stated, if France and Germany worked together in western Africa. But French statesmen should
be cautious in their dealings with Bismarck, whose overseas aims differed from France's. According to Charmes, Bismarck's colonial policy until 1884 consisted of being clever enough to profit from the colonies of others while Germany had none herself. Since Germany had
'neither the cash nor inclination' to establish colonies in savage areas,
the solution was to let others create colonies and make sure that German merchants had trading rights. That explained Bismarck's motive
in wanting to collaborate on the Congo and Niger, and France clearly
had less reason to be enthusiastic.

'Regarding the Congo', Charmes wrote, 'France, thanks to the
courage and skill of M. de Brazza, possesses above the cataracts a vast
tract of territory extending along both banks, we believe one as well
as the other, but in any case a territory extensive enough so that we
have nothing to fear from our neighbors.' French rights to the Upper
Congo as well as to other areas in Africa rested on the basis of effective occupation. 'One can well understand how it is in Germany's interest to try to suppress these rights as well as those possessed by other
nations that have long fought on the seas. In this way a *tabula rasa*

would be created that would efface history.'[6] Germany might be permitted to advance in regions where no French interests existed, but why should Free Trade be established in territory claimed by France? Charmes therefore urged limited Franco-German cooperation, but saw that the aims of the two countries differed fundamentally. He demanded to know whether the Ministry of Foreign Affairs saw the dangers of Bismarck's proposals.

Bismarck's scheme essentially consisted of applying the principle of Free Trade to as much of western Africa as the French would agree to.[7] 'The German proposal', wrote Ferry, 'aims to provide for German goods and products free access, free traffic and free trade in regions not yet explored in central Africa.' The main territory in question was the Upper Congo region, commonly believed to have the greatest potential for trade. France had access to that area via the Ogooué River and Brazzaville, and if a differential tariff were established, protected French commerce would profit. But the Ogooué, unfortunately, was not the best entrance to the interior. The Congo provided a shorter and easier route to Brazzaville; if a railway could be built around the cataracts to the beginning of the Upper Congo (at Stanley Pool), the trade of the interior could be much more easily tapped. France therefore had an interest in seeing that railway privileges should be nondiscriminatory and in securing as free an access to the Congo as other nations enjoyed; in short, there were good reasons for applying the principle of Free Trade to the Congo and in cooperating with Bismarck in this regard—even though Germany would benefit from the pioneering of other countries. Bismarck's ideas about refusing to recognize new annexations lacking concomitant guarantees of Free Trade were obviously more problematical: there were advantages to be gained from the principle when foreign trading interests were predominant, disadvantages when French trade was supreme. Thus the French government had ambivalent feelings about espousing Bismarck's Free Trade proposals, but in any case his support could be used to wrench concessions from the British. To the Niger, concluded Ferry, should be extended the same principles applied to the Congo.[8]

The idea that the Niger was anything other than an 'English River' aroused indignation in England, where the issues of rivalry in western Africa were discussed with much greater intensity and frequency than

---

[6] *Journal des Débats,* 13 October 1884.

[7] See Ferry's memorandum of 22 August 1884, *DDF,* 1st series, 5, no. 376; supplementary material of interest in MAE Afrique, pp. 86, 108–09, and MAE Allemagne, pp. 59–62; and ANSOM Afrique VI/43–44.

[8] Ferry, *DDF,* 1st series, 5, no. 376.

in France. According to the *Globe* (17 October 1884): 'The Niger has
been a British possession in all but the form of having been declared
such, and in all the essentials of dominion it is as much part of our
Colonial Empire as Natal or the Cape.' In the same vein, the *Leeds Mercury* commented (16 October 1884):

> [T]he Niger is now to all intents and purposes an English river. Its
> mouths have been formally annexed by England; the river itself has
> been opened up by English explorers and English traders; peace is
> kept among the peoples on its banks by the patrolling of English
> gunboats, and it is the English Consul who is the recognized arbiter
> of all disputes.

In other words, the Niger was as English as the Senegal was French,
and if the Niger became the subject of an international conference,
why should not the Senegal also be discussed?

With 'French logic', Ferry and Bismarck seemed bent on 'interna-
tionalizing' the wrong river:

> It is difficult to see how France can justify her claim to undivided
> rights on the Senegal by arguments which England may not with
> equal force apply to her own position on the greater river. We do not
> mean that England should imitate her neighbour's use of her op-
> portunities. In the Senegal and the wide territories which it waters
> French trade enjoys exclusive privileges. In the Niger trade is as free
> to French and Germans as it is to Englishmen, as free as it is on the
> Hooghly or the Mersey ... The Niger cannot be rendered more free
> than it is at present.[9]

'The demand for free navigation', complained the *Standard* (15 November 1884), 'could be put forward much more cogently with respect to the Senegal; but . . . this magnificent stream is to remain
under the exclusive dominion of France, as well as the entire Upper
Niger from its source as far as Timbuctoo, over which France assumes
a shadowy protectorate.' The same point was also often made in comparing the Niger with the Congo: 'The claims of France in respect of
the Congo are doubtful, shadowy, and a subject for future ambition.
Those of this country in respect of the Lower Niger are real and actual.'[10] No doubt existed in the public's mind about British dominance on the Niger.

The doctrine of Free Trade—trade 'without restrictions, without

[9] *Daily News*, 20 October 1884.
[10] *Globe*, 1 December 1884.

preferential duties or private advantages of any sort' [11]—governed British attitudes and policy on both the Niger and Congo. As stated by the *Leeds Mercury* (16 October 1884), 'The policy of England in this matter is summed up in the good old phrase "A fair field and no favour".' In the words of the *Standard* (11 October 1884):

> 'The object [of the Berlin Conference]', we are told, 'is to extend the blessings of Free Trade and quality of rights to all nations interested in the trade of West Africa.' It would be impossible to frame a policy more distinctly in accordance with British views and interests. Our complaint is that all the world over the Governments that are called civilised are building up walls of hostile tariffs, to keep out the legitimate commercial enterprise of this country. Our ambition is to find markets, not to assert dominion; we do not want to extend our Empire, but to find outlets for our industries and avenues for our trade.

In that regard, the main point was that the Niger stood on an entirely different footing from the Congo. The Niger had been opened up by English explorers and traders. It was under the protection of the English government. By contrast, the Congo had only recently been explored and had become a cockpit of international rivalry. The English guaranteed Free Trade on the Niger, whereas the French threatened to seal off the Upper Congo by protective tariffs. Now, in collusion with Bismarck, the French also were attempting to introduce some sort of international regime on the Niger that would interfere with English trade and protection. According to the *Standard* (15 November 1884), 'Prince Bismarck and M. Ferry wish to oust British jurisdiction from a region where it has hitherto been indisputably exercised.' The *Daily Chronicle* (6 December 1884) thundered that for France and Germany to demand that Britain 'give up an administration it has cost her much time and wealth to build up, and in which fair treatment is meted out is, to the trader and native alike, not only an absurdity, but almost an impertinence.'

The *Globe* most cogently stated the difference between the two cases, in a leading article entitled 'The Congo and the Niger' (1 December 1884):

> Surveillance over the exercise of free commerce, navigation, and so forth, should not be made the business of an International body, that being the duty and privilege of England, as the chief, if not sole proprietary Power on the Lower Niger . . . There is . . . [a] failure

---

[11] *Manchester Examiner and Times,* 18 October 1884. This appears to have been the popular conception of Free Trade at the time.

to recognise the different international positions of the two rivers
—that is to say, the main principle involved in the whole contention,
so far as England is concerned. The equal neutrality of the two rivers,
and their equal control by the same Association, would be tantamount to a refusal to recognise English rights; and should no strongly
marked difference be made, then all the advantage we have obtained
on the Niger will simply have been thrown away . . .

Before we accommodate our position on the Niger to the commercial requirements of the world, we must at least have assurance that
we shall not be sufferers by the transaction. Any other course would
be the folly of Lear, who gave away all he had, and, having thence-
forth to depend on charity, was refused even the modicum of rights
that he nominally retained.

There was, the *Globe* concluded, an 'essential separation between the
Congo and the Niger—between the territory which does, and the territory which does not, call for international administration.' If the editorials of English newspapers reflected public opinion, Englishmen
were willing to establish an international regime to safeguard Free
Trade on the Congo, but were prepared to resist firmly, perhaps belli-
cosely, any attempt to place the Niger under international supervision.

English aversion to 'internationalization' explains why news of an
impending conference in Berlin was greeted with such hostility by
certain organs of the press. Taking the most extreme position, the
Morning Post (15 October 1884) denounced any form of international
control on either the Niger or Congo and stated with alarm that English participation in an African conference convened by France and
Germany would signify the decline and imminent fall of the British
Empire:

> The summoning of a European Conference to take counsel upon
> the future destination of Africa is, under the circumstances, one of
> the gravest warnings which have ever been uttered in the ear of a
> torpid and self-forgetful people . . . [The] African Conference is the
> most cruel, the most contemptuous, and the most dangerous blow to
> the reputation and influence of the British government in a sphere
> which used up to yesterday to be pre-eminently British.

The *Pall Mall Gazette* responded on the same day to that nearly hysterical view by pointing out that application to the Niger of the principles
of the Congress of Vienna would not impair British sovereignty at the
mouth of the river: 'Roumania is the undisputed Sovereign of the territory through which the mouths of the Danube find their way to the

sea, but there is an International Commission of the Danube, and our ownership of the delta is no bar to the establishment of an International Commission of the Niger.'

The *Standard* (18 October 1884) similarly ridiculed the idea 'that the Congo Conference is, in some occult fashion, the handwriting on the wall announcing the downfall of the English Colonial Empire, and the erection on its ruins of a Franco-German cosmopolitan understanding by which the world is to gain benefits not yet computed.' Other newspapers, such as the *Manchester Examiner and Times* (18 October 1884), interpreted the scheme of establishing an international commission on the Congo and Niger as a check to France:

> French merchants are to be treated no better than the merchants of other nations . . . It is proposed to apply to the navigation of the Congo and the Niger the principles adopted at the Congress of Vienna in order to ensure the freedom of navigation of several navigable rivers and afterwards applied to the Danube. France has assented to these proposals, but we do not gather that they were made by her, and there are some signs that she acceded to them with no exuberant willingness. The plain fact is that they effectually checkmate any policy which she might have contemplated carrying out for her own special advantage.

Despite such informed opinion, confusion existed about the precise form of 'internationalization' to be applied to the two rivers. Much of this confusion can be traced to the mystery surrounding the 'International Association'[12] founded by Leopold II, King of the Belgians, to bring 'civilization and the blessings of free trade' to the natives of tropical Africa.

The ambivalence towards King Leopold and his Association manifested itself by the repeated usage of the words 'philanthropic and beneficent' and 'shadowy and artificial'. There was widespread admiration for the king's attempt to introduce trade and civilization into tropical Africa; but how could an 'Association' become a state? The United States on 22 April 1884 had recognized the flag of the Association as the flag of a friendly government, and on the following day King Leopold signed the 'pre-emption' agreement with France,

---

[12] In the English press, only the most informed newspapers, such as *The Times* and the *Morning Post*, drew a distinction between the International African Association (founded in 1876) and the International Association of the Congo, one of Kind Leopold's subsequent creations. Usually the press merely referred to the 'International Association', which I use for convenience here. For a discussion of the evolution of King Leopold's various bodies that emerged finally as the État Indépendant du Congo, see especially Thomson, *Fondation de L'État Indépendant*.

whereby that country would acquire the territories of the Association in the event of the Association's demise.[13] The two transactions caused consternation in England. Later in the year, when Bismarck threw his support behind the Association by granting recognition from the German government on 8 November, the British public continued to regard the Association with a mixture of suspicion and enthusiasm. Was it wise to encourage the formation of a state that might fall to France? Or would the guarantee of Free Trade and the chances of King Leopold's success protect British commerce in that part of the world? As the *Morning Post* (19 November 1884) summarized Britain's apparent dilemma: 'Either the proposed Congo State is to be a mere despotism of irresponsible foreign traders—and in that case it could not be tolerated—or it must be the dependency of some foreign Power or Powers, and in that case England could not tolerate it without most serious guarantees.'

The *Morning Post* repeatedly denounced the agents of the Association as a gang of unscrupulous adventurers. But the mainstream of British opinion tended to hold the Association in higher esteem, above all because of King Leopold's reputation as a philanthropic Free Trader. The following extract from the *Daily Telegraph* (22 October 1884) typifies the praise the King received at the time:

> Leopold II . . . has knit adventurers, traders, and missionaries of many races into one band of men, under the most illustrious of modern travellers [Henry M. Stanley], to carry into the interior of Africa new ideas of law, order, humanity, and protection of the natives. There can be no doubt that from his initiative will arise a free State of the Congo, and that we shall see the new nationality neutralised like Belgium itself. Deprived, as the King by position is, of an opportunity of playing a great part in European politics, he takes his revenge nobly, applying his mind and money to a lofty end, and becoming the *Scipio Africanus* of our time.

Curiously enough, the *Morning Post* (13 December 1884) proved to be the best prophet when it stated that the Congo was being 'opened not to peace and progress but to the most horrible reprisals and massacres'.

Again, the leading Tory newspaper was accurate when it described the Association as essentially a commercial enterprise. Although there is no doubt exaggeration in the following quotation from the *Morning Post* (7 November 1884), it is of interest because it represents

---

[13] For clear chronology of these events, see Crowe, *Berlin West African Conference*, chap 8.

virtually the only vitriolic criticism of the Association in the English press in 1884 and is identical with the attacks made by the same newspaper twenty years later when it took the lead in the Congo reform campaign.

> There is really not the slightest essential difference between such a pretension [to territorial sovereignty by the Association] and the practice of Captain Kidd and other 'sea kings' who set up their picturesque ensign on one or another of the islets of the Caribbean and the Gulf of Mexico. The private ensign of sovereignty of the bold sea-rovers was, indeed, the Black Flag with the customary emblems and their large-minded operations were directed against all kinds of property which happened to suit them. The private ensign of the so-called 'International Association' sports nothing more terrifying than a star, and we understand that the operations of the adventurers are strictly confined for the moment to the acquisition of the property of the African tribes by no means more violent . . . than the threat of 'burning their villages over their heads'.

Yet that sort of caustic remark was never made at the time about King Leopold or the leader of the Association in the Congo, Henry M. Stanley. By their enthusiasm and propaganda they managed to persuade British traders and philanthropists of the altruistic aims of the Association, despite disquieting reports in the press of what was actually happening in the Congo.[14] In the interests of Free Trade and science, and under the philanthropic sponsorship of the King of the Belgians, Stanley would strike 'a white line across the dark continent'.[15] From the Atlantic to the Indian Ocean, in the recurrent phrase, 'peace, civilization, and the blessings of Free Trade will be brought to the dusky millions of the Congo.' Countless times King Leopold's publicists drove home that point, and it probably did much to conceal the real situation in the Congo, where agents were concluding monopolistic treaties with native chiefs, thereby alienating not only sovereignty but also the land and its produce to the Association. Stanley appeared in the public eye as the champion of Free Trade, struggling against French and Portuguese adversaries; in reality, he helped give birth to a state whose system of monopolies became the most vicious in Africa's history.

Except in general commentaries on French designs in central Africa, the issues of rivalry between Stanley and the French officer

---

[14] See for example the *Manchester Examiner and Times,* 28 November 1884.

[15] The title of King Leopold's propagandistic pamphlet, published anonymously in 1884. For sharp criticism, see the *Pall Mall Gazette,* 24 April 1884.

Savorgnan de Brazza for control of the Upper Congo aroused little comment in the English press of 1884. But publicists and statesmen alike recognized that the claims of the two explorers would shape in large part the political configuration of the region and would indirectly play an important role in the Berlin Conference. The reasons may be explained briefly. Brazza's treaties in 1880 with Chief Makoko claimed for France a sphere on the Upper Congo, in particular the right bank of Stanley Pool (where the Congo becomes navigable). The French Parliament approved the treaties in 1882, setting off a chain of reactions in England and in the Congo. The Foreign Office, perceiving a French threat to the Congo, renewed negotiations with the Portuguese to protect British commerce. English businessmen connected with the International Association felt indignantly that Brazza had 'stolen a march' on Stanley while Stanley himself was performing the service of building a road around the cataracts. Stanley retaliated by claiming for the Association the Kwilu district; this rich area on the north bank of the Lower Congo would, if left to the Association, block the growth of French influence from the Gaboon to the Upper Congo.

In French eyes, Stanley was wholly responsible for this check to legitimate French territorial aims, and because of his connections with English traders, he symbolized a danger to the growing French colonial empire. His efforts to 'Anglicize' the Association raised fears that were not dispelled even by the Franco-Congolese pre-emptive agreement of April 1884. Common phrases in the French press of that year referred to the 'peaceful' efforts of Brazza and the 'brutal' activities of Stanley. Various French newspapers, such as the *Journal des Débats,* began to maintain that Brazza's treaty extended to both sides of Stanley Pool, since Makoko's subjects resided there also and therefore were French subjects. In October 1884 the economist Paul Leroy-Beaulieu, author of the celebrated *Colonisation chez les peuples modernes,* wrote in the *Economiste Français* that the French government should not relinquish 'one atom of sovereignty over the territory on the Congo placed under French protection by King Makoko, or over any station where the French flag waves'. Although admitting that Danubian principles might be applied to the lower waters of the Congo and Niger, Leroy-Beaulieu felt that not only the Upper Congo but also the Upper Niger were 'peculiarly and wholly French'. That idea was most disturbing to Englishmen. To them, Brazza's treaties generally represented, in the words of the *Daily Telegraph* (22 October 1884), 'the old trick of tri-coloured pocket-handkerchiefs.' To the Foreign Office, the Tricolour planted on the Congo signified so great a danger that it might be worth letting the Portuguese in to keep the French out—a sentiment definitely not shared by Stanley and the International Association.

Stanley played a crucial role in arousing English opinion against Portuguese claims on the Congo. The negotiations leading to the abortive Anglo-Portuguese Treaty of February 1884 can be summarized to illuminate both his connection with its aftermath and the more well-known parts played by the International Association, France, and Germany. The scheme of recognizing Portugal's ancient claims to the mouth of the Congo in return for guarantees of Free Trade and other concessions originated in the 1870s, but the Foreign Office did not regard the matter as urgent until after the conclusion of Brazza's treaties with Makoko. As the *Manchester Examiner and Times* (22 November 1884) succinctly described the ensuing events in retrospect:

> It was obvious that our negotiations with Portugal were entered upon with a desire to forestall the action of other Powers. Our chief object was to put forward Portugal as a breakwater against the supposed designs of France, but Germany . . . had a West African policy, and our stealthy proceedings offended both Powers. The result was that Germany and France came to an understanding with each other on the West African question, and thenceforth took the lead. There is no doubt that we sustained a rebuff. The tables were turned.

Bismarck's refusal to recognize the Anglo-Portuguese treaty in June 1884 precipitated the events leading to the Berlin Conference. Germany and France refused to recognize Portuguese sovereignty over the Lower Congo, despite the guarantees of free trade; yet Portugal persisted in her claims, and it remained an open question whether the International Association could be made into a sovereign state.

In the three months preceding the Conference, the English climate of opinion turned enthusiastically in favour of the Association. Stanley, back from the Congo, gave interviews, wrote articles, and, most significantly, spoke before Chambers of Commerce. He denounced Portuguese maladministration and oppressive commercial policies, and emphasized that Portugal remained the only Western European nation trafficking in slaves. He presented facts about commerce on the Lower Congo: of the 165 European traders there, 25 were English, 24 Dutch, 1 Italian, 6 German, 12 Swedish, 22 Belgian, 8 French, and 67 Portuguese. Despite the comparatively large number of Portuguese nationals, three-fourths of the imports came from England, and only Portuguese table wine was imported from Portugal, for the consumption of Portuguese officials. In short, the Portuguese had done absolutely nothing since their discovery of the Congo four hundred years before except to ruin or injure trade. On the other hand, Stanley argued, the noble and disinterested King of the Belgians, with unbound

liberality and earnest devotion, was attempting to introduce civilization and plant commerce among the millions in the unknown interior
who thirsted for English trade. But his philanthropy would be frustrated if the Portuguese held the lower river. Those ideas Stanley reiterated before numerous audiences, and his speeches received widespread attention.[16] The *Daily Telegraph* (19 September 1884) caught
the mood of the English public when it proclaimed:

> It may be that the founders of the International Association are
> dreamers: but should it prove so, the blame will not rest on men who
> sought to light up the Dark Continent by the vivifying fires of peace
> instead of the destructive flames of war. It will fall upon the commu-
> nities, and their rulers, who will have shown that they could not rise
> from the low grounds of rivalries to support and stimulate an enter-
> prise which had for its sole aim the benefit of all.

To the English public, one of the main points of the Conference in
Berlin would be to determine whether King Leopold's idealistic experiment would succeed or fail.

There remains only one important point to make before passing on
to British official policy towards the Niger and Congo and discussing
the Conference itself. It is the vision of the Congo valley as projected
by Stanley and perceived by the English public. The reason for the importance of this image is that it provides the key to understanding the
setting and main issues at Berlin. There as in England, Stanley was li-
onized. He spoke authoritatively as one of the great explorers of the
nineteenth century. One newspaper referred to him as 'himself a Sovereign Power to be reckoned with', and the International Association
was often identified as 'Stanley's Association'. His herculean efforts on
the Congo and unsurpassed knowledge of central Africa demanded
respect; when he spoke, people listened. His message can be summed
up in one word: trade.

Echoing Stanley's remarks made before the London Chamber
of Commerce in September, the *Standard* (19 September 1884)
commented:

> Here, according to Mr. Stanley, is a River which is the greatest inlet
> to Africa, draining one million three hundred square miles of coun-
> try, permeated by vast waterways, peopled by forty million tribesmen,
> some fierce cannibals, but the majority ready for civilisation and
> eager for trade, abounding in ivory, cane-wood, India-rubber, and
> other wild products of the tropics, and capable of growing almost any
> crop suitable to such a climate.

[16] Most notably, his addresses before the London and Manchester Chambers of Commerce
were later published as pamphlets and reviewed extensively in the press.

Introducing Stanley to the Manchester Chamber of Commerce, the president of the Chamber, J. F. Hutton (one of the Association's prominent supporters), said that the explorer 'is here to tell us that these millions on the Congo are eager for our trade; he is here also to show us how the complete freedom of commerce may be established, and how all customs houses and all vexations and impediments to trade may be utterly abolished and swept away from the banks of the Congo (Cheers).' Speaking at a time when England feared a depression in the cotton industry, Stanley pitched his remarks at the growing manufacturing capacity and slackness of trade:

> Well, then, I come to you with at least one market where there are at present, perhaps, 6,250,000 yards of cheap cottons sold every year on the Congo Banks and in the Congo markets. I was interested the other day in making a curious calculation, which was, supposing that all the inhabitants of the Congo basin were simply to have one Sunday dress each, how many yards of Manchester cloth would be required; and the amazing number of was 300,000,000 yards, just for one Sunday dress! (Cheers). Proceeding still further with these figures I found that with Sunday dress and four-every-day-dresses would in one year amount to 3,840,000,000 yards, which at 2d. per yard would be of the value of £16,000,000.[17]

Although a few scoffed at Stanley's statistics,[18] to most Englishmen he described an overseas market that could have an adverse affect on

[17] *Manchester Examiner and Times,* 22 October 1884.

[18] The *Glasgow Herald* of 21 October 1884, carried a most incisive critique of Stanley's optimistic views on the Congo market:

> While one may enjoy the wonder of such visions as Mr. Stanley indulged in [at Manchester] one may doubt their practical value. There are unquestionably several millions of people in Central Africa who are naked. It does not follow that they desire clothes, or even that they need clothes, or that they would wear clothes if they had them, or that they could pay for them if they wanted them. And as for the moral influence of Manchester cotton, we must gauge it by the amount of sizing contained in the fabric, and the relation between the number of yards on the invoice and those in the bale. In sober earnest, there is a great deal of very businesslike talk about trade in Central Africa. Some people seem to think that the only thing to do is to 'annex' or 'open up' a country, and that orders will at once flow out in ceaseless streams to Manchester and Glasgow and Birmingham and Sheffield. Trade is elastic, but it has not such balloon-like capacity of rapid expansion. It must grow, and, as a rule, the more slowly it grows the sounder it is. It is possible, although we are not sanguine, that all the cotton which the vivid imagination of Mr. Stanley depicted may some day be saleable in the Congo Basin. But the day must be in the dim future, and before it can arrive there are a good many preliminaries to arrange. The old saying that 'trade follows the flag' has been heretofore known as true only in connection with a national flag. We doubt its applicability to an international one.

England's industrial development if England were excluded. Since this issue would be decided at the Conference in Berlin, the English press could state without hyperbole that 'To-day the Congo occupies a place in men's thoughts second only to the Nile,'[19] and that the Conference represented a 'turning point in the history of our Empire'.[20]

Much more is known about the Foreign Office's policy in the months preceding the Conference than about the attitudes of the press, so the diplomatic prelude to 'the extraordinary spectacle . . . at Berlin'[21] can be more succinctly surveyed. The main point is that French as well as British statesmen felt the pressure of 'public opinion', and that the prejudices colouring official views coincided with those expressed in the newspapers. In May 1884 the British Ambassador in Paris, Lord Lyons, wrote, 'So far as I can judge by the English Papers, the irritation in England against France is not less than that against England in this Country. The Newspapers on both sides of the channel seem to do all they can to fan the flame.'[22] Later in the year he wrote again on the same subject:

> Ferry complained bitterly of the English Press. He said in particular that the irritating lecturing tone of the 'Times' goaded the French to Madness; it used the same tone towards the Government of its own Country. I said that the Press on both sides of the Channel seemed to work as if for the express purpose of producing ill-will between the two Countries, but that certainly the English Government had no power to restrain it.[23]

Thus emerges one of the dominant themes in British documents relating to the origins of the First World War: the baleful influence of the press. Yet the Francophobe sentiments publicly expressed at this time hardly differed in substance or tone from the minutes written in the Foreign Office. Assistant Under-Secretary T. V. Lister once commented about French expansion:

> The feeling in France at this moment appears to be much in favour of Colonial expansion and enterprise. The French are jealous and bad colonists, they oppress the natives, repel foreign capitalists and have to fall back upon Slavery, slightly disguised, for the labour re-

[19] *Leeds Mercury,* 24 October 1884.
[20] *Globe,* 17 October 1884.
[21] *Morning Post,* 19 November 1884.
[22] Lyons to Granville, Private, 30 May 1884, PRO 30/29/174.
[23] Lyons to Granville, Private, 17 October 1884, PRO 30/29/174.

quired on their plantations. They are monopolists and protectionists and judge all other nations by their own standard.[24]

Though less politely expressed, Lister's ideas were the same as those of most other British officials. The thoughts in his minutes well illustrate the Foreign Office's low esteem of the French as colonizers and the tendency to hold them responsible for the Scramble.

So far as the British Cabinet considered the general affairs of tropical Africa at this time, it saw mainly the necessity of protecting the hinterlands of British territories on the west coast and safeguarding British trade on the Niger and Congo. It recognized the danger of French expansion, but did not detect a grand strategy whereby France would attempt to dominate the African continent. Like the editors of *The Times* (21 June 1883), Gladstone and his colleagues perceived a French 'feverish restlessness . . . on the Congo, in Tunis, in Tonquin, and in Madagascar . . . [that] have no relation to one another . . . [and] do not form part of any general scheme.'[25] But in the Foreign Office and the Colonial Office, where experts gave prolonged attention to the details of the partition, the pieces of the puzzle seemed to be falling into a comprehensible pattern. Apart from Brazza's treaty with Makoko, one event in particular appeared to signal the dangers of French imperialism in western Africa—the proclamation of the protectorate over Porto-Novo in Dahomey in January 1883.

That event provoked the head of the African Department, Percy Anderson, to write a comprehensive memorandum on Anglo-French rivalry. Anderson warned that unless immediate action were taken, British trade would be imperilled on the Oil Rivers and the Lower Niger.

> If we remain passive, we shall see our trade stifled, we shall find our traders furious, and we shall hardly escape grave complications with the French as successive Protectorates produce fresh irritation till, when the field is finally closed against us, we shall have to deal with chronic grievances and complaints.

To protect British commerce, Anderson argued that a general settlement with France should be reached in which Gabon would become British, France would acknowledge British rights on the Lower Niger

[24] Minute by Lister, 13 March 1884, FO 84/1683.

[25] The best succinct discussion of Gladstone's foreign policy is Agatha Ramm's introduction to *The Political Correspondence of Mr. Gladstone and Lord Granville, 1876–1886* (2 vols., Oxford, 1962).

and withdraw from the Gold Coast, and Britain in return would cede the Gambia. Such a policy would check the French scheme of ousting Britain from some of the most commercially valuable parts of western Africa. Of the scheme itself Anderson had no doubt. 'If there is one thing clearer than another', he wrote, 'it seems to be that the French have a settled policy in Africa, both on the East and West Coast, and that policy is antagonistic to us. The progress of this policy is sometimes sluggish, sometimes feverish, but it never ceases.'[26] In that conclusion lay the idea governing British policy during the partition: France was the main enemy. Where British and French aims directly collided, such as on the Niger, British claims would have to be consolidated. Where France threatened to take over territories where Britain had no traditional claims, such as on the Congo, minor powers such as Portugal would have to be put forward as a buffer.

Between July and October 1884, Consul E. H. Hewett concluded a series of treaties on the Oil Rivers and the Lower Niger that successfully placed those territories under British protection.[27] On the Congo, however, British plans misfired. The basic idea had been to allow Portugal to assert her authority over the mouth of the river in return for guarantees of free trade. The plan was intensely unpopular. In England, the philanthropists and trading community attacked it because of Portugal's tolerance of slavery and oppressive, corrupt colonial administration. Abroad, Portugal was denounced as a cat's paw of Britain. To make the treaty more palatable, the Foreign Office demanded that Portugal limit her claims to the southern bank of the Congo and agree to the establishment of an Anglo-Portuguese commission to ensure Free Trade. According to a British official at Lisbon, 'The idea of the Commission is distasteful to the Portuguese as they think it savours of foreign tutelage, the very mention of which makes them frantic.'[28] Nevertheless the Portuguese acquiesced. Their concessions made the treaty, in Anderson's words, 'an exceptionally liberal one, but . . . not . . . good enough for us.'[29]

So strong was anti-Portuguese sentiment that not even stringent guarantees of Free Trade could save the agreement. 'Manchester is up in arms,' reported the *Examiner*. So also was the House of Commons,

[26] Memorandum by Anderson, 'On the French Occupation of Porto Novo,' copy in FO 84/1806.

[27] See especially Hargreaves, *Prelude to Partition*, chap. 7.

[28] Baring to Sanderson, Private, 23 June 1883, PRO 30/29/183. For the Anglo-Portuguese negotiations, see Anstey, *Britain and the Congo*.

[29] Minute by Anderson, 13 July 1883, FO 84/1806.

where the Foreign Office detected King Leopold's effective lobbying against the treaty.[30] Granville protested to a peer active in West African trading circles: 'The agitation is being fomented by the King of the Belgians, which is not fair after the pains we are taking to safeguard his association.'[31] Granville wrote to King Leopold himself that Britain had acted 'in the general interest of the civilized world', and if the King did not cease his efforts to upset the treaty, threatened to reveal publicly what the Foreign Office knew about the monopolistic nature of the Association. It was an empty threat. King Leopold had the upper hand, as the Foreign Office gradually recognized in the spring of 1884. When Bismarck refused to assent to the treaty in June, Leopold merely played another card in the Congo game that had already, in Anderson's words, been going 'dead against us'.[32] Bismarck intervened decisively by refusing to accept the Anglo-Portuguese treaty and by working with France to convene the Berlin Conference. But in the whole affair it is King Leopold, not Bismarck, who deserves the epithet of wheeler-dealer.

King Leopold's tactics irritated the Foreign Office. The description of his Congo organization as a philanthropic free-trading association fooled no one in official circles. 'The King of the Belgians' Co.', Anderson wrote, '[is] a gigantic commercial monopoly.'[33] When the King began to put forward his plans of transforming the Association into an independent and sovereign state, Lister retorted that the proposal was absurd,

> [that] the 'Internat. African Assn.' has not, as far as we know, any recognized position, and that is does not appear to be controlled by, protected by or responsible to any govt. That it can have no right to make treaties which can claim to be respected by legitimate govts. That the offl. recogn. of the priv. flag wd. create a very dangerous precedent. That the treaties made by the 'Assoc' are drawn up in a spirit of the strictest monopoly. That the K of the B has bound himself to give the refusal of all the possessions of the 'Assoc' to one of the most exclusive and protectionist Govts in the world. And that it is therefore incumbent upon all Govts that value freedom of trade to abstain from recognizing the Assoc its treaties and its flag.[34]

[30] 'The King is agitating to upset the Treaty in the House' (minute by Anderson, 20 February 1884, PRO 30/29/198).

[31] Granville to Aberdare, Confidential (copy), 20 February 1884, PRO 30/29/148.

[32] Minute by Anderson, 18 May 1884, FO 84/1807.

[33] Memorandum by Anderson, 2 March 1884, FO 84/1807.

[34] Minute by Lister, 16 May 1884, PRO 30/29/198.

Lister held to his opinion that King Leopold's proceedings were 'absurdly irregular', but his colleagues came around to the view that Britain had no alternative but to support the Association.

Under pressure from the disaster of the Anglo-Portuguese treaty and the threat of joint French and German interference, the Foreign Office had to yield the initiative on the Congo in order to defend the Niger. Besides, King Leopold might be forced by international agreement to live up to his promises of Free Trade, and the Association might be buoyed up successfully as a buffer against France. Consequently, pre-emptive agreement worked to King Leopold's advantage: given the collapse of the Anglo-Portuguese treaty, the Foreign Office had an interest in seeing the Association succeed, and thus stay out of French hands. As usual, Anderson plotted the main strategy in this regard. Writing shortly after Bismarck issued invitations on 8 October to come to Berlin to talk about the Congo and Niger, Anderson wrote: 'it seems incontrovertible that . . . as regards the Congo, we can appear at the Conf. as one of many Powers interested, as regards the Niger we shld. take our seat as *the Niger Power.*'[35] Thus affairs were turning to King Leopold's favour, but not necessarily to Britain's. There was no guarantee that the other powers would permit England to pre-empt the Niger seat: as the Permanent Under-Secretary, Sir Julian Pauncefote, wrote, 'The Conference *may* end in smoke.'[36]

The Conference opened on Saturday, 15 November 1884. Fourteen nations were represented. Of them, only Britain, France, Germany, Portugal, the Association, and to a lesser extent the Netherlands, were directly concerned with West African questions. The rest were Austria-Hungary, Belgium, Denmark, Italy, Russia, Spain, Sweden and Norway, Turkey, and the United States—powers with such insignificant colonial interests that the *Morning Post* (19 November 1884) blasted the idea that Britain would condescend as 'the greatest colonial Power in the world . . . [to sit] at the board of the West African Conference like the simplest and least concerned of the States, while half a score of Powers with colonial possessions often insignificant enjoy each an equal representation.' But even the *Morning Post* agreed with the rest of the press that it was a 'brilliant assemblage'. The delegates met at Bismarck's official residence in the Wilhelmstrasse, where the last great international Congress had assembled six years earlier. Sitting at a large, horseshoe-shaped table whose open end overlooked the garden, the representatives could remind themselves of their immedi-

[35] Memorandum by Anderson, 14 October 1884, FO 84/1813.
[36] Minute by Pauncefote, 30 October 1884, FO 84/1814.

ate duties by gazing at a large map of Africa drawn by Kiepert. From this setting derived the myth that the Berlin Conference partitioned Africa.

At two o'clock Bismarck opened the first session and accepted the chairmanship. He stated that the purpose of the Conference was to promote the civilization of the African natives by opening the interior of the continent to commerce. He then attempted to define three specific goals: freedom of commerce on the Congo; freedom of navigation on the Congo and the Niger; and agreement about the formalities of valid annexation of territory in the future. Negatively, he said, the Conference would not concern itself with questions of sovereignty. Emphasizing that the Conference would serve the cause of peace and humanity, Bismarck ended his brief oration.[37] His remarks conveyed the impression of uncertainty and ambiguity. On the one hand, he appeared to put the Niger and the Congo on the same footing. On the other, a close study of his phraseology left it unclear exactly what he had intended. As the Foreign Office analysed what Bismarck had said, Lister wrote that his 'speech is extremely vague and it leaves it doubtful whether the Conference is to do more than register a few platitudes about freedom of commerce and navigation.'[38]

Bismarck's speech drew a rejoinder from the British Ambassador, Sir Edward Malet. His remarks set the tone and substance of British policy during the rest of the Conference. He said first of all that commerce was not the exclusive subject of the Conference: 'While it is desirable to secure a market in the Congo country, the welfare of the natives is not to be neglected.'[39] Coming to this main point, he emphasized that the situation on the Congo was 'entirely different' from

---

[37] First Protocol of the Conference. The proceedings are most conveniently available in *Accounts and Papers*, 55, United States Senate Executive Document 196 (49th Congress, 1st session), and the French Yellow Book, *Affaires du Congo et de l'Afrique Occidentale, 1884–85* (Paris, 1885).

[38] Minute by Lister, 19 November 1884, FO 84/1815. For a contemporary French interpretation of Bismarck's motives during the Conference, see especially the analysis by the French ambassador in Berlin:

Le prince de Bismarck a porté dans la politique coloniale où il se jette la même énergie d'impulsion, la même hauteur d'aspirations dont il a donné les marques dans sa politique continentale. On ne peut guère douter qu'il ne croie le moment venu de déposséder l'Angleterre de son hégémonie maritime, comme il a dépossé dé il y a quinze ans la France de l'hégémonie politique et militaire en Europe. Bien des indices tendent à prouver qu'il prépare contre la puissance anglaise une attaque à fond, calculée pour l'atteindre dans ses parties vitales, et pour la ruiner au profit de la grandeur industrielle et commerciale de l'Allemagne.

Courcel to Ferry, 19 January 1885, *DDF*, 1st series, 5, no. 528.

[39] First Protocol of the Conference.

that on the Niger. Her Majesty's Government would consent to the appointment of an International Commission to regulate the Congo, but a Commission on the Niger would be 'impracticable'. The lower and upper reaches of the river, he argued, were distinct geographical entities, and the Lower Niger was exclusively a British concern, over which Britain accepted responsibilities of administration. He stated flatly that the British Government would regulate the affairs of the Niger but would adhere to the principle of free navigation. Thus, to the public at least, the battle lines appeared to be drawn at the first session of the Conference. Britain refused to discuss the Niger on the same basis as the Congo. 'If in the course of a few days', commented the *Liverpool Daily Post* (18 November 1884), 'we do not hear that Sir E. Malet has withdrawn from the Conference, we may conclude that the English protest has done its work.'

In fact, the British hold over the Niger was so strong that it was hardly contested by the other powers. In the months immediately preceding the Conference, British commercial and political influence on the river had become supreme. On 1 November, George Goldie-Taubman of the National African Company wrote to the Foreign Office that the two French trading houses had sold out and that Britain 'stood alone on the Niger'—such welcome information that Granville greeted it with 'Hurrah'.[40] With British commercial paramountcy and the political claims established by Hewett's treaties, Ferry's proposal to establish an International Commission became little more than empty words. Why had the French government permitted the sellout of the two trading firms?[41] The commercial expert at the Foreign Office, Joseph Archer Crowe (who attended the Conference as one of the British delegates), quoted from published French documents to prove that the French did not hope to exploit the Lower Niger, but rather to gain control of the upper reaches of the river. Geographically, the Lower Niger was blocked from the interior by rapids; moreover, the Niger delta was unhealthy and infested with British commercial

---

[40] Minute by Granville *c*.3 November 1884.

[41] 'There is a mystery here' (Robinson and Gallagher, *Africa and the Victorians*, p. 176, note 5). Or was there?

> There is no 'mystery' . . . about the French government's indifference to the fate of the companies bought out by Goldie before the opening of the Berlin Conference. Throughout 1884 and 1885, Félix Faure, as Under-Secretary for Colonies, and Jules Ferry were concerned solely with the question of untariffed access through the Delta to the Upper Niger . . . All that mattered was freedom of communication with the coast.

C. W. Newbury, 'Victorians, Republicans and the Partition of West Africa', *Journal of African History*, 3 (1962), p. 496.

houses; therefore, the French would have to abandon their usual tactic of utilizing the mouth of the river and attempt to tap the trade of the Upper Niger via the Senegal. 'It seems clear', Crowe speculated, 'that if France comes into the Conference with these views . . . we need hardly expect much discussion from her as to our claims of preponderance in the Lower Niger.'[42] He guessed well. Compared with the French designs on the Upper Niger, their aim on the lower river in 1884 appears to have been merely a jab in the British belly.

In any case the move to internationalize the Lower Niger began to collapse when Bismarck gave his support to Britain on the day before the Conference. At that time Malet read his instructions from Granville, which included the passage about an international commission on the Niger being 'impracticable'.[43] Bismarck made no objection. The French Ambassador began to surmise that France would receive little support for the scheme to internationalize the Niger. Thus the Franco-German entente began to crumble even before the Conference began. Bismarck increasingly saw that Germany's goal of Free Trade coincided with Britain's and diverged from France's. In short, to achieve the most liberal extension of Free Trade on the Congo, he supported Britain on the Niger. This changing partnership resulted in British victory. Within two weeks after the Conference convened, Britain emerged pre-eminent on the Niger, and the threat of international interference evaporated. 'VICTORY ON THE NIGER'—as the English press emphasized in captions to leading articles—at once transformed a conference designed by Germany and France against Britain's interests into a congress in which Britain emerged as triumphant as in 1878.[44]

---

[42] Memorandum by Crowe, 7 November 1884, FO Confidential Print 5033. It is noteworthy, however, that Antoine Mattei, who sold most of the comptoirs, and General Faidherbe vehemently held that the sale of the commercial houses in no way transferred exclusive political rights in the Lower Niger to Britain. They argued that this was merely a normal business transaction and did not mean that France had lost political rights in the region. See Faidherbe, 'La Question du Niger,' *Revue Scientifique*, 3 (17 January 1885), p. 67; and Antoine Mattei, *Bas Niger, Benoue, Dahomey* (Grenoble, 1890), pp. 49–63. See also C. W. Newbury, 'The Development of French Policy on the Lower and Upper Niger, 1880–1893,' *Journal of Modern History*, 31 (1959). Also K. Vignes, "Étude sur la rivalité d'influence entre les puissances européenes en Afrique équitoriale et occidentale depuis l'acte general de Berlin jusqu'au seuil du XXe siècle,' *Revue française d'histoire d'outre-mer*, 48 (1961).

[43] The instructions are in Granville to Malet, No. 59 Africa, 7 November 1884, FO 84/1814.

[44] 'The British delegation came back from Berlin . . . nearly as happy as Disraeli had been seven years before. The difference was that they had not the same gift as Disraeli for the immortal historical phrase' (Jean Stengers, 'British and German Imperial Rivalry: A Conclusion', in Gifford and Louis, *Britain and Germany in Africa*, p. 338). Stengers is not entirely correct. In his own prosaic way, Granville stumbled on exactly the right word: Britain got on 'swimmingly'.

British diplomacy was almost as successful in the major problem facing the Conference—the future of the Congo. Here again Stanley played a crucial role. He attended the Conference as an American delegate, though in fact he was King Leopold's agent. He believed the aims of the Association should not conflict with the Free Trade policy of Britain. Speaking before the Conference 'in his own racy, humorous and vivacious English', he dwelt on the natural wealth of the Congo region, 'where Europeans could thrive as well as in their own temperate zone if they adopted their habits to the African climate'.[45] Emphasizing that Free Trade would benefit Africans and Europeans alike, he urged the desirability of establishing a Free Trade zone that was as large as possible. On 21 November he proposed to delimit the 'Geographical and Commercial' basin of the Congo by drawing the northern boundary as a line running from Fernando Vaz on the coast up the Ogooué, and the southern running from Coanza inland—thus including slices of territory claimed by France and Portugal. Seeing no reason why this geopolitical exercise should not be continued, the American delegate, John A. Kasson, on the next day proposed extending the line to the eastern coast of Africa from 5° north to the Zambesi, a proposal supported by the Germans as well as the British on the grounds that 'the greater the territory to which the principle is applied the greater will be the future to [German] trade.'[46]

This wild geographical interpretation of the Congo basin—an enormous chunk of territory running smack through the middle of the continent—astonished the British Foreign Office. One official said that it was geographically so confused that it would be comparable to drawing a map that put the Rhine in the basin of the Rhône.[47] Lister complained of 'these fancy definitions of the "basin of the Congo"' (which he regarded as 'absurd') and had a telegram sent to Malet, saying that Her Majesty's Government saw 'grave objections to definitions of the Congo which do not accord with geographical facts'.[48] The response from the British Ambassador in Berlin must have been enlightening: it was *Anderson* who had drawn the line and put the American delegation up to presenting it to the Conference.[49]

[45] *The Times,* 19 November 1884.

[46] See Malet to Granville, No. 21 Africa, telegram, 25 November 1884, FO 84/1815. See also Yarnall, *Great Powers and the Congo Conference.*

[47] Minute by Kennedy, *c.*22 November 1884, FO 84/1815.

[48] Granville to Malet, telegram, 25 November 1884 (draft by Lister), FO 84/1815.

[49] Malet to Granville, No. 92 Africa, 22 November 1884, FO 84/1815:

   I and the gentleman whom your Lordship has associated with me at the Conference thought that it would come with much greater weight before the members of the Commission if it were proposed by Mr. Stanley than if it were submitted by one of the

The scheme amounted to reserving as much of the interior as possible for Free Trade. Since most of the interior was unclaimed, none
of the powers had legitimate grounds for protest. The British refused
to mention the source of the Nile (an interesting reservation at such
an early date in the partition) and insisted that the Free Trade guarantees would not affect the sovereignty of the sultan of Zanzibar in
his mainland possessions. The French and Portuguese, on the other
hand, were forced into a defensive position and had to fight to get the
line pushed away from their spheres on the west coast. The French
and Portuguese ultimately acquiesced in a Free Trade area beginning at Sette Camma in the north and at the Loge River in the south,
thence looping in artistic ecstasy into the interior. The Foreign Office
continued to protest against the 'fantastic' definition of the Congo basin, but finally yielded feebly to the argument that it was a 'commercial' as well as geographical area. Engineered by Anderson, it was a
clever move that immediately caused the French to wonder why they
had agreed to attend the Conference in the first place.

The commentaries in the press well illustrate French disillusionment with the results of the Conference as early as the beginning of
December. Paul Leroy-Beaulieu complained that France 'has everything to lose and nothing whatever to gain from the proceedings of
the Conference.' He went on:

> Having already large dominions and larger claims in Africa, France
> will find, if the Conference has its way, that the claims will be denied,
> and that the dominions will be thrown open to the commerce of all
> the world. France will only have acquired colonies and dependencies
> in order to be forbidden to make any more use of them than any
> foreign nation which may choose to utilize them for commerce and
> trade.[50]

That typical comment from Paris indicates the sudden and unexpected adroitness of British policy, inspired not from London but
from the delegation in Berlin. Even the *Morning Post,* antagonistic
from the beginning, stated that the results of the Conference by early
December were 'amazing'—in a favourable sense.

At this stage of the Conference—late November to mid-December
—issues of territorial expansion and sovereignty that had been ex-
pressly excluded from the agenda nevertheless formed the back-

---

British Delegation . . . we have thought it right to waive any credit which might ultimately attach to Great Britain as the originator of the line.
[50] *Economiste Français,* 7 December 1884.

ground of the deliberations. Ultimately, these questions of sovereignty proved of much greater importance than the proclamation of Free Trade on the Congo and the Niger: the sovereign power, despite international agreement, could throw aside trade restrictions almost with impunity. Both the Niger and the Congo basins later became notorious as centres of monopoly—and in the latter, the monopolistic system of exploiting wild rubber gave rise to some of the worst atrocities in colonial history.

For the Niger, Britain assumed jurisdiction without international interference, and the Foreign Office attempted to hold British and other nationals responsible for their actions. For the Congo, the Conference provided for the creation of an International Commission to regulate the affairs of the region, but it was never established. Europeans in the Congo were responsible to no one other than an independent and irresponsible despotism, known in history as the Congo Free State. The Berlin Conference did not formally give birth to this bizarre child, but its delegates certainly sanctioned its existence. In Berlin, in the corridors outside the conference room, the delegates negotiated a series of bilateral treaties with the agents of the Association, transforming it into an independent and sovereign state. By taking the lead in their respective pre-Conference agreements of 22 April and 8 November, the American and German governments were instrumental in its creation. But British support was also necessary. Recognition at precisely the right time led to the British victory on the Niger. The British side of this story has never fully been told, and its telling makes a good study in the decision-making process of the Foreign Office in 1884 as well as in the history of the creation of the international monstrosity with which the formal Conference usually is erroneously identified.

On 19 November, Bismarck asked the British Ambassador to help the Association 'in its endeavour to become a State'. This was the critical moment of the Conference. British refusal would leave the Congo open to a territorial rivalry in which France and Portugal would probably be the winners, at the expense of Free Trade; and Bismarck probably would not support Britain on the Niger. On the other hand, British recognition might secure commercial liberty on the Congo and gain Germany's help on the Niger. But recognition entailed a significant departure from traditional international law, which grated against the conservative outlook of the Foreign Office and the Lord Chancellor. Moreover, the Foreign Office had no reason to be favourably disposed towards the Association, despite its trumpeting of Free Trade. The discovery of the treaties of monopoly, the pre-emptive agreement with France, and King Leopold's agitation against the

Anglo-Portuguese treaty all deepened the Foreign Office's suspicion, in Anderson's words, of 'the *bona fides* of the Association'. Nevertheless, on 16 December Britain granted recognition. Why? Who made the decision? To answer those questions, it is necessary to know precisely who was involved in the decision-making process during the Conference—who made the decisions in the delegation at Berlin and who in the Foreign Office, what was the interchange between these two groups and what was the role of the lobbying groups and public opinion.

To begin, both the delegation and the Foreign Office were bombarded with memorials from British traders and missionaries who were hostile to France and Portugal and who were intensely devoted to the ideals advertised by King Leopold. A trading delegation including the firms of Hatton and Cookson, John Holt and Company, and the Elder Dempster Company actually went to Berlin. They claimed to represent British 'public opinion'. They pressed their views on the official delegation. It was no secret that some of them were making a profit by investing in King Leopold's enterprise.[51] And it was also not hard to guess that if the delegation flouted their wishes, the press would erupt in London, Manchester, and Liverpool, and Britain's Congo policy would be condemned at the same time that the Foreign Office was being virulently denounced for caving in to the Germans in Africa and the Pacific. Thus, in this instance, 'public opinion' was a tangible part of the policy-making process.

How were decisions made within the delegation? It consisted of Sir Edward Malet, the Ambassador; H. Percy Anderson, the head of the African Department of the Foreign Office; Robert Meade, Assistant Under-Secretary of the Colonial Office; A. W. L. Hemming, principal clerk of the Colonial Office; Joseph A. Crowe, commercial attaché for Europe; and an unofficial delegate, a jurist, Sir Travers Twiss. Meade acted as Granville's private correspondent and liaison with Bismarck.[52] But the strongest members of the team were Twiss and Anderson. Twiss was fully won over to King Leopold and actually drafted the Congo State's constitution. An elderly gentleman who often lost the train of his thought when speaking, Twiss carried great weight with the Permanent Under-Secretary, Sir Julian Pauncefote, and with the Lord Chancellor. The three of them determined the legal aspects of British policy at the Conference.

---

[51] See especially Lister's minutes on British traders 'making large profits by supplying the Assocn. with goods' in FO 84/1815.

[52] The private correspondence about the Conference is in PRO 30/29/147, but it contains little of interest.

Anderson was important in a different sense. He, not the Ambassador, was the real British spokesman at the Conference. As Malet himself admitted the following February, 'I have been an automaton of which he has made the works.'[53] Anderson reasoned with the British traders, missionaries, and journalists in Berlin; he drafted the dispatches to the Foreign Office that later appeared in the Blue Books under Malet's signature; he represented the British delegation in the sessions where the real work was done, in the commissions; and he plotted the political strategy of Britain at the Conference. His motivation basically was Francophobic. He feared that France's expansion in Africa would cut off potential markets and increase her political and military power. To him, any neighbour in Africa, even the Germans, would be better than the French. To win German support against France, he was prepared to acquiesce in the Anglo-German disputes in South-West Africa, the Cameroons, and New Guinea—a policy labelled as 'complete surrender' and 'Bismarckized' by some of his colleagues. He willingly followed Bismarck's lead in making the Association into a state, hoping that with sufficient guarantees it would keep the Congo open to Free Trade and frustrate French ambitions. Above all, Anderson wanted to prevent France from meddling on the Niger, and this required Bismarck's support. To win it, he pushed hard in favour of the Association, despite his awareness of its sham philanthropic goals.

The actual decision to recognize the Association was made in London, not without strong protest from Lister. As Assistant Under-Secretary (Anderson's immediate superior), he closely followed the actions of the Association and was outraged at King Leopold's 'mischievous and shabby' behaviour. His subordinates at the time of the Conference were a senior clerk, Clement Hill, and a junior clerk, H. Austin Lee. Hill occupied himself with larger strategic and commercial aspects of the Scramble,[54] and had little to say about the Congo. Lee was too junior an official to influence policy, but nevertheless played an important role because he passed on Foreign Office

[53] Malet to Granville, 3 January 1885, FO 343/6, Malet Papers, and No. 129 Africa, 21 February 1885, FO 84/1822:

'He has been the moving spirit and my guide throughout the proceedings,' wrote the Ambassador. 'He has conciliated the traders and missionaries who have been here . . . I fancy that if we have the Niger now, de facto, in our possession it is mainly due to the pains which he has bestowed upon the question long previous to the meaning of the Conference, and . . . victory in regard to it has been the touchstone of our success.'

[54] See his memorandum of 9 December 1884, FO Confidential Print 5051.

secrets to Sir William Mackinnon, the director of the British and India Steam Navigation Company, who, as one of King Leopold's staunchest English supporters, in turn informed the Association's agents.[55]

In matters of routine, Granville followed Lister's advice and usually acted as a rubber stamp, casually approving the draft dispatches and telegrams. Lister, with his influence as a permanent official, perhaps would have been able to thwart Britain's recognition of the Association had it not been for Sir Julian Pauncefote, and to a lesser extent, the Parliamentary Under-Secretary, Lord Edmond Fitzmaurice. Pauncefote, in his capacity as Permanent Under-Secretary, attempted to give Granville's policy direction and precision. He overrode Lister's protests in almost every instance, and his voice was decisive. Two times in particular he spoke out in a way that paved the path towards recognition. First, on the opening date of the Conference, 15 November, a dispatch drafted by Pauncefote was sent to Malet:

> [T]he Association under existing circumstances does not present the conditions which constitute a State. But it no doubt possesses elements out of which a state may be created . . . The Association is still in its infancy; but having regard to the noble aims of its founder and to the liberal and enlightened principles which it is understood to advocate, Her Majesty's Government will watch with great interest and sympathy its effort to develop itself into a new State.[56]

This exchange had preceded the final draft of the dispatch:

> Lister: I think your [Pauncefote's] compliments to the Assocn. at the end of the Drt. go rather too far. The only evidence I have ever seen of its endeavours to promote freedom of Commerce & Navigation are the treaties it has made with the chief by wh. it secures itself an absolute monopoly.[57]

> Pauncefote: I cannot say that I concur . . . The passage can do us no harm as it stands & nobody doubts the aim which the King of the Belgs. has had in view. Besides the Assocn. will only be recognized on the condons. of free navigation & trade etc.[58]

Pauncefote wrote to Granville, 'I don't think we could steer a safer course.'

[55] The papers of Sir William Mackinnon at the School of Oriental and African Studies, University of London, reveal much about King Leopold's English connections.

[56] Granville to Malet, No. 78 Africa, 15 November 1884, FO 84/1814.

[57] Lister to Pauncefote, 14 November 1884, FO 84/1814.

[58] Minute by Pauncefote, FO 84/1814.

The second instance of Pauncefote's decisive influence came on 20 November, the day after the Foreign Office had received Malet's telegram stating Bismarck's request to help the Association become a state. Lister made this notation on the telegram:

> It is one thing to 'assist the Assocn. in its endeavour to become a State' and another to recognise it as being one. It is, I imagine, usual in recognising a new state to have a clear idea of its boundaries and even perhaps some proof of the validity of its claims to its territories. I shd. have thought that the proper mode of proceeding wd. have been for the Assn. to prove its title, to explain its constitution, to give assurances of its intentions as regards personal, religious and comml. freedom &c. &c. and then to petition the Confce. to recognise its sovereignty.[59]

Pauncefote retorted:

> Prince Bismarck has declared that the 'status' of the Association is not to be brought before the Conference & I doubt the expediency of urging that it should be discussed there . . . Outside of the Conference . . . the Association might be recognised not as an actual State, but as a State *in course of formation* & on certain defined conditions as to consular jurisdiction, religious liberty, freedom of trade &c. &c. . . . On those conditions it might be provisionally recognised for all practical and necessary purposes as an *inchoate State*. It would be a new feature in the practice of Nations, but I do not see any great objection to it under all the circes.[60]

Granville as usual merely noted 'I agree' on Pauncefote's minute.

Although Pauncefote succeeded in leapfrogging the legal obstacles, the British Government nevertheless continued to dawdle until directly threatened by Germany. On 1 December, Bismarck told Malet that unless Britain recognized the Association there would be 'a generally unfriendly attitude of Germany on matters of the greatest importance to us'—implying not only the Niger but also the Nile. Granville brought the matter before the members of the Cabinet. All favoured recognition. Their comments were brief, with the exception of the Lord Chancellor's. Stating that he did not want to stand out for 'mere form' and would acquiesce 'for practical reasons,' Granville wrote that he was not:

[59] Minute by Lister of 19 November on Malet to Grenville, No. 4 Africa, telegram, 19 November 1884, FO 84/1815.

[60] Minute by Pauncefote, 20 November 1884, FO 84/1815.

among those who expect that, in this or in any other matter in which we may have to yield to pressure from Prince Bismarck and deviate from the exact line of our own policy for the sake of conciliating him, we shall succeed in obtaining from him, as to Egypt or any other subject in which we have special interests, any equivalent.

Granville further noted: 'On several occasions I have urged concessions to a spoiled child, who happens, through Egypt, to have us a great deal in his power. In this case I think it is our policy as well as that of Germany, to strengthen the Association against France.'[61] On 2 December at 5:45 p.m. the Foreign Office telegraphed Malet that Britain would recognize the Association.[62] The delegation in Berlin was greatly relieved. Malet immediately informed Bismarck and wrote to Granville: 'The announcement of the intended recognition of the International Association has come at a very useful moment for us in the Conference, as it assures us the cooperation of the German, Belgian and United States Representatives in securing what we desire with regard to the Niger.'[63]

During the rest of the Conference, the Association fought for its political survival against the two powers with territorial claims on the Lower Congo, France and Portugal. Like the line of the conventional basin, the boundary of the Association was easy to draw in the interior, difficult to define along the coast and at the mouth of the river. France claimed the northern bank, Portugal the southern. If they realized their territorial ambitions, the new state would be cut off from the sea—'strangled at birth', as the representatives of the Association complained. After acrimonious negotiations, the French finally offered to limit their claim to 5°12', which included the Kwilu district on the northern bank but gave the Association a thin strip of territory running to the sea. King Leopold thought the French were dealing harshly with him. The British nevertheless urged him to capitulate. Malet wrote to the King:

I would give the French the line they ask, that is the parallel of 5°12'. They will not diminish their claim because they are sure that no pressure will be brought to bear on them to induce them to do so. The Germans will do nothing, and we shall do nothing beyond giving

[61] Minute by Granville, 1 December 1884, PRO 30/29/144; see also Pauncefote's memorandum of 2 December 1884, FO 84/1816.
[62] The agreement between Great Britain and the Association was finally signed on 16 December. See Crowe, *Berlin West African Conference,* p. 147.
[63] Malet to Granville, 5 December 1884, FO 343/6.

those platonic expressions of good will, which are often more irritating than expressions of hostility.[64]

Thus King Leopold was left to fend for himself. To Englishmen who had questioned the value of the Conference from the beginning, the situation now appeared ironical. According to the *Morning Post* (19 December 1884):

> [I]f France 'recognises' Mr. Stanley's Association, it will be in exchange for many a thousand square kilometres of African soil. But apparently England has 'recognised' the International Association from pure goodness of heart, and just to prove once more that the interests of the Empire are the very last consideration of a truly humanitarian statesmanship.

The delegation at Berlin responded to similar criticism by pointing out that the establishment of the Association as a legitimate power at least had the merit of temporarily preventing a French takeover of the Congo.

From the point of view of the French press, the unofficial results of the Conference also appeared paradoxical. Francis Charmes in the *Journal des Débats* (13 January 1885) attacked the Foreign Ministry for 'giving away' to the Association territories that rightly belonged to France:

> Because the Association has established a certain number of stations in the north at 5°12' it looks upon itself as the owner or, perhaps, the sovereign of the soil. Nothing could be more erroneous. The Association . . . is a mere tenant, and cannot claim any right of ownership. We contest that these territories belong to France, as far as the southern boundary of 5°12'. Moreover the treaty signed by M. de Brazza with King Makoko transferred to us a region near Stanley Pool extending along both banks of the great river. The International Association proposes an exchange of territories. We should give up what belongs to us on the left bank of the Congo, and the Association would give in barter what? Why the land it owns in the north at 5°12'. But it owns nothing at all![65]

Of course the argument in favour of French recognition was the preemption agreement. When the Association eventually collapsed —as was commonly assumed—the property would fall to France.

[64] Malet to King Leopold, Private and Confidential, 20 December 1884, FO 343/4.
[65] See also his article of 6 February 1885.

Nevertheless, the French drove a hard bargain. Finally, on 5 February 1885, France signed a convention with the Association that drew the boundary at Manyanga, a little more than midway up the Lower Congo. It was unsatisfactory from King Leopold's viewpoint because he failed to get compensation for the Association's stations in the Kwilu district; but he did gain limited access to the sea.

The Association did better with the French than with the Portuguese, who, as usual, were obstinate. They demanded even more than they would have received in the Anglo-Portuguese treaty. King Leopold, who had 'his heart set on getting both banks',[66] had to stand alone against the 'preposterous' Portuguese claims that extended not only to the Cabinda enclave but also to the port of Banana at the mouth of the river plus the territory along the southern bank up to Vivi instead of Noki. The King threatened to throw over the whole affair, burning his Congo boats and permitting France and Portugal to scorch the Lower Congo between them. According to his henchman, Henry S. Sanford of the American delegation:

> I consider the Association as practically abandoned by its friends, or those who should be . . . Great Britain has shown good will, but no power. She has apparently no influence in Portugal. Germany [is] now satisfied with what she has secured . . . If Portugal takes forcible possession today of Banana, Boma, Vivi—none will resist her—Your [British] Govt. will look on![67]

Britain indeed had little reason to intervene on behalf of the Association. When the question arose before the Cabinet in early February whether Britain should exert pressure on Portugal to come to terms with the Association, Charles W. Dilke, President of the Local Government Board, wrote in a minute that reflected the Cabinet's annoyance with the king: 'The K. of the Belgians has behaved badly throughout . . . & deserves in my opinion no consideration from us. I shd. stand aloof & not put prejudice on Portugal, but wash our hands of the bad business.'[68] Granville and the delegation at Berlin, however, continued to be sympathetic to the Association. Britain joined

[66] H. S. Sanford to Mackinnon, 12 January 1885, Mackinnon Papers. Sanford, King Leopold's American agent, secured recognition of the Association by the United States government. His Congo correspondence has been meticulously edited by François Bontinck, *Aux Origines de l'État Indépendant du Congo* (Louvain, 1966).

[67] Sanford to Mackinnon, 2 February 1885, Mackinnon Papers.

[68] Minute by Dilke of 4 February on Malet to Granville, No. 22 Africa, telegram, 3 February 1885, FO 84/1821.

Germany and France in presenting an ultimatum to Portugal.[69] On 15 February the Portuguese finally consented to have the boundary drawn at Noki. 'Harmless Portuguese authority', as the English press referred to it, thus became formally instated on the southern bank of the Congo, bringing to a close the territorial negotiations at the Conference. In that way the delegates created a nascent state whose boundaries resembled a gigantic funnel—its narrow spout emptying into the sea, its cone encompassing an enormous tract in the interior. The *Morning Post* (31 January 1885) commented that between France and Portugal the new state was 'almost hermetically sealed off from external intercourse'. But King Leopold *did* have access to the Atlantic; and in the interior, the boundaries of the Congo State stretched to Lake Tanganyika. In the words of the British Ambassador, the King now had 'an empire . . . sufficient for the grandest human ambition.'[70]

Dedicated to the ideals of Free Trade and the introduction of civilization in central Africa, the new state, it was hoped, would bring peace to the Congo. The notion was enthusiastically supported by the American delegate, John A. Kasson, who simplistically thought that peace could be achieved by avoiding war. He proposed to the Conference that the entire Free Trade area be neutralized.[71] From the Association's point of view, this suggestion was eminently sensible, for practical as well as idealistic reasons. In the event of war, the precarious new state would fall before the onslaught of even the puniest power—even Portugal. According to Stanley: '[W]e though a State are not strong, we cannot fight—because if we did the greatest harm would befall the natives'—and, needless to say, the new state. Stanley went on: 'We must be protected—how?—by a mutual agreement among the Powers that the territories of the Association shall be inviolate and considered neutral. Then and not till then shall I consider we are safe.'[72] The goal, then, would be to make the Congo State neutral in the tradition of its sovereign, the King of the Belgians.

Cui bono? Obviously the Congo State. But proximity gave France and Portugal every reason *not* to remain neutral. Bismarck favoured neutrality because, in wartime, German ships in African waters would be vulnerable to British sea power. For Britain, neutrality was a double-edged sword—useful if it checked France, annoying if it restricted

[69] See Crowe, *Berlin West African Conference*, pt. II, chap. 5, for the best account of these negotiations.
[70] Malet to King Leopold, Private and Confidential, 20 December 1884, FO 403/4.
[71] Fourth Protocol of the Conference.
[72] Stanley to Mackinnon, 16 December 1884, Mackinnon Papers.

British action in a general war. The Foreign Office was perplexed. Lister wrote: 'Why shd. one bit of W. Africa be exempt from warlike operons.? If the principle is good and practical why not extend it to all Colonies? Wd. it be advantageous to Engd. that such a principle shd. be partially or generally established?'[73] The Admiralty answered that in the case of the Congo neutrality would probably be desirable if belligerent ships could be prevented from coaling there.[74] The delegation at Berlin accordingly took that line, for reasons well analysed in broad perspective by Anderson:

> It seems clear that it would be dangerous for England if any enemy should have the power of using the Congo as a base of operations in the flank of what would be, in case of the closing of the Suez Canal, our sole communication with the East, and that it is consequently advantageous to us to place those waters under the neutral régime; but that this advantage would be more than counter-balanced if we surrendered the right of following an enemy into the waters without ample security against his making indirect use of them to our detriment.[75]

With reservations, the British delegation therefore supported the proposal to neutralize all the conventional basin. But France and Portugal would not agree, on grounds that it would be 'an infringement on their sovereign rights'.[76]

Finally, late in the Conference the delegates agreed to a compromise whereby a power possessing territory in the Congo basin had the option of proclaiming itself neutral. Thus, in a much watered-down form, neutrality found its way into the General Act and created confusion in the public mind about what the Conference had accomplished in this regard. To take one of many examples, the *Manchester Examiner and Times* (28 February 1885) commented that the 'neutralisation of the Congo Basin is . . . a decided gain to the world.' In fact, the Berlin Act did not neutralize the Congo basin, but merely created, in the words of the French delegate, 'a moral obligation' on the part of the signatories to respect the neutrality of any state that proclaimed it. The Foreign Office noted that the clause was 'innocuous' because it merely stated the truism that any state in time of war could claim

[73] Minute by Lister on Malet to Granville, No. 5 Africa, telegram, 19 November 1884, FO 84/1815.

[74] Minute by Northbrook, 26 November 1884, PRO 30/29/140.

[75] Memorandum by Anderson on Neutrality enclosed in Malet to Granville, No. 218 Africa, Confidential, 13 December 1884, FO 84/1817.

[76] See Malet to Granville, No. 104 Africa, 14 February 1885.

neutrality.[77] In the aftermath of the Conference only the Congo State invoked the neutrality clause. During the First World War, Belgians and Germans alike disregarded it.[78] But at the time of the founding of the Congo State, King Leopold's 'Declaration of Neutrality' contributed significantly to the myth reiterated at the close of the Conference—that he was sovereign of 'a neutral State given over to the world's free trade'.

The problem of neutrality played an important part in the third and final transaction of the Conference. Having established Free Trade on the Congo and the Niger as the first two bases of the general Act, the delegates in January attempted to formulate a third basis regulating the procedure of acquiring new territory in Africa. The main point hinged on the concepts of 'annexation' and—an idea gaining popularity at the time of the Conference—'protection'. The legal adviser of the British delegation, Twiss, wrote:

> [I]f the newfangled Protectorates are to come into fashion in the place of annexations, what is to be the status of a Protected State in time of War? Is it to follow the fortunes of the Protecting Power or is it to enjoy a Neutral character and to be exempt from hostile assault and if so, is the Protecting Power debarred from making it a base of belligerent operations and if so may the subjects of the enemy continue to trade with it as with any other State . . . these Protectorates are looming in the future as Neutral Coaling Stations![79]

If the term 'protectorate' merely meant a neutral annexation, then British sea power might be jeopardized in time of war. '"Protection" is a honeyed word', Twiss concluded, 'but a honeyed edge of the Cup does not guarantee the contents of the Cup to be innocent.'

The Foreign Office drew no clear distinction between annexations and protectorates. Nor did British officials have any precise ideas about the manner in which territories could or should be acquired. The answers to four questions that Lister posed to the Librarian of the Foreign Office, Sir Edward Hertslet, indicate the pragmatic and undoctrinaire way in which the British government regarded these issues:

1. T.V.L. Is there any generally recognised form for taking possession of an uninhabited island or district?
   Hertslet: There is no generally recognised form.

[77] See Pauncefote to Granville, 2 February 1885, FO 84/1822.

[78] See Jonathan E. Helmreich, 'The End of Congo Neutrality, 1914,' *Historian*, 28 (August 1966).

[79] Twiss to Pauncefote, 14 January 1885, FO 84/1817.

2. T.V.L. In cases of an annexation on the mainland, proclaimed only on the coast, how far inland does the annexation extend?
   Hertslet: There is no general rule on this point.
3. T.V.L. In cases of annexation of a coast, must the formalities take place on shore? And, if so, at how many points along a long line of coast?
   Hertslet: This formality has certainly not been gone through as a rule.
4. T.V.L. When the countries to be annexed are inhabited, is the consent of the natives in any way necessary to the validity of the annexation?
   Hertslet: Such consent would not appear to be necessary on all occasions. But there is a great difficulty in these days in making a clear distinction between annexation and protection.[80]

On one point at least, the Lord Chancellor, the Earl of Selborne, had a definite answer. His view determined the outcome of the last major business of the Conference. '*Annexation*', he wrote, 'is the direct assumption of territorial Sovereignty. *Protectorate* is the recognition of the right of the aboriginal or other actual inhabitants to their own country, with no further assumption of territorial rights than is necessary to maintain the paramount authority & to discharge the duties of the Protecting Power.'[81]

France and Germany, who resented British protectorates as 'dogs in the mangers', urged that protectorates as well as annexations should carry with them *jurisdiction*—in other words, not only authority but also responsibility. Although perhaps anti-British in sentiment, this proposal otherwise was made in good faith by delegates who wanted to curtail the rampant annexationist craze by ensuring that new territorial acquisitions were real, not sham. The British delegation supported the idea (with a few reservations on the part of Sir Travers Twiss). They reported that the scope of the legislation would be limited to avoid controversy. Malet pointed out on 7 January that the proposal was already so emasculated that nothing would be required but notification of new acquisitions on the coasts of Africa, which already were mostly under European control ('there will hardly be any territory to which the Declar. of the Confn. will attach,' Pauncefote noted).[82] The Foreign Office also favoured the idea. According to Pauncefote, 'The 3d basis is clearly intended to prevent the secret acquisition of new territories without occupation.'[83] Clearly, Britain had as great an interest as the other powers in preventing 'paper protec-

[80] 'Memorandum on the Formalities necessary for the effective Annexation of Territory,' 18 December 1884, FO 84/1818.

[81] Memorandum by Selborne (italics by Pauncefote), 3 January 1885, FO 84/1819.

[82] Minute by Pauncefote on Lister's draft telegram to Malet, No. 7 Africa, 17 January 1885, FO 84/1820.

[83] Minute by Pauncefote, 1 January 1885, FO 84/1818.

torates'. By refusing to accept the responsibilities flowing from protectorates, the British, again in Pauncefote's strong words, would 'incur great odium and suspicion'.[84] Malet put forward the same point:
'[R]efusal on our part [to accept the article on protection] would look
as if we were resolved to maintain the Dog in the manger policy of
simply giving Protection for the purpose of keeping other Powers out
of certain territories which we cannot use ourselves, but do not like
anyone else to use.'[85]

Nevertheless Britain, solely because of Selborne's objections, refused to adhere to the principle that protectorates involved administrative and judicial responsibility. In a manner unthinkable in a Salisbury government, England's participation in the partition of Africa
under Gladstone in this instance was determined by the Lord Chancellor. The Foreign Office circulated almost every important dispatch,
instruction, and telegram to him for approval; Granville deferred to
him absolutely, probably for the astute reason that feeble diplomacy
could be more easily defended if it had juridical sanction. For perhaps
the only time in the history of the Scramble, the Lord Chancellor of
England guided its course.

Selborne probably had as good a grasp of colonial and Imperial
constitutional issues as any other Lord Chancellor in the history of the
British Empire.[86] He certainly devoted more attention to them than
most of the others. He regarded the law of the Empire as unique, radically different in nature from that of the French or the embryonic
German colonial system. In his view, it probably made little difference
to the French or Germans whether they designated their overseas territories 'annexations' or 'protectorates'; but to the British Empire, the
failure to make that distinction would have momentous and undesirable consequences:

> [T]here is no substantial obstacle, in their case, to their treating the
> distinction between Protectorate and annexation as purely nomi-
> nal, so that by Protectorate they mean . . . annexation under another
> name. But it is otherwise with us; and that for reasons, some which
> are of peculiar force in Africa. If we annexed any territory, slavery
> must at once cease to exist. I am not aware that any other Power is
> embarrassed with this difficulty.[87]

[84] Pauncefote to Hill, 10 January 1885, FO Confidential Print 5080.
[85] Malet to Granville, 17 January 1885, FO 343/6.
[86] For Selborne's political views, see Roundell, Earl of Selborne, *Memorials Personal and Political, 1865–1895* (London, 1898).
[87] Selborne to Pauncefote, 23 January 1885, FO 84/1820.

The abolition of slavery was only one of many difficulties. In a protected state, Britain constitutionally *could not* exercise authority or jurisdiction because such a territory technically was not part of the Queen's dominions. As a 'Little Englander' and a most conscientious authority on constitutional law, Selborne saw every reason why Britain should fight against any declaration made by an international conference that would impose the duties of annexation in territories that Britain wished only to control and not to govern.

By refusing to apply jurisdiction to protectorates, British policy gave the impression of rejecting the principle of 'effective occupation'. In European eyes, Britain wanted to remain free to proclaim protectorates merely to prevent the legitimate advance of other powers. The British delegation quickly found itself isolated on this point, and feared that the negotiations over the third basis for the Act might rupture merely because of its 'captious objections.'[88] Britain would receive the blame. Moreover, the delegation thought there were other good reasons for accepting the protectorate clause: European suspicions of British territorial ambitions would be proved wrong, and 'effective occupation' would check French and German designs. In London, Pauncefote championed the proposal, and was distressed at the Lord Chancellor's intransigence. 'I cannot see the danger of adopting this Rule *in Africa*', he wrote, '—and indeed I think it a salutary one for it would prevent *Paper* Protectorates in those Regions.'[89]

Selborne did not regard his objection as 'captious' but as fundamental. 'It appears to me to be neither necessary, nor reasonable, nor expedient, that, in every case of a Protectorate, the Protecting Power should take upon itself an obligation "to establish and to maintain," in and throughout the protected territory, "a jurisdiction".'[90] He denounced 'our diplomatists at Berlin [who] place the smooth working of the Conference . . . upon a higher level than all other considerations connected with the question at issue.'[91] He attacked Pauncefote for not seeing the worldwide ramification of the issue:

> I always feel great respect for Sir Julian Pauncefote's opinions: but, in this case, I cannot but think, that it would be most fallacious and dangerous to assent to the rules & principles of the 'Projet' as to Africa, without being prepared to admit their application, practically, in other parts of the world also. If, in Africa, occupations &

[88] Malet to Granville, Africa No. 4 telegram, 7 January 1885, FO 84/1819.
[89] Pauncefote to Hill, 9 January 1885, ibid.
[90] Memorandum by Selborne, 8 January 1885, ibid.
[91] Selborne to Pauncefote, 23 January 1885, FO 84/1820.

Protectorates mean the same thing, and are to carry with them the same obligations, why not in the rest of the world also? Can we assent to such a principle there, where *possibly* it might work in our favour, and deny it, where it might work against us? [92]

In the Lord Chancellor's view the words 'recognise the obligation'—the crucial phrase of the proposal—would establish a principle applicable to all parts of the world and could not be restricted to Africa. The administrative and judicial burdens would be intolerable, especially to a Gladstonian government.

Curiously enough, that staunchest of all 'Little Englanders', Sir William Harcourt, the Home Secretary, challenged Selborne's opinion:

> I cannot concur . . . If a Protectorate is meant to carry with it the right to exclude other Powers from the territory, it in my judgment involves as a matter of course the obligations to do for other Powers what they could otherwise do for themselves, viz., protect their own rights and subjects within the territory. To appear to dispute this proposition, or to seek to cut it down, would in my opinion be at variance with the principles of international law, and would be highly inexpedient in regard to the question now so occupying the attention of Europe . . . Any other view would lead to indefinite '*Paper Protectorates*' . . .
>
> We should, I think, justly have all European opinion against us. The Powers would say England wants to engross the globe, to take just such advantages as she thinks fit, and to repudiate the corresponding duties. This I conceive at the present moment would be most unwise. [93]

Harcourt accurately perceived the prevailing sentiment in Berlin. On the same day he wrote those lines, 24 January, Bismarck warned the British Ambassador that he might adjourn the Conference without agreement on the third basis of the Act. Britain would be stigmatized with obstruction. British 'territorial greed', 'colonial hegemony', 'dog in the manger policy', and other such phrases would again echo in the European press. Granville consequently summoned a special meeting of the Cabinet. It overrode the Lord Chancellor's views. The Foreign Office on 26 January telegraphed Malet, instructing him to acquiesce. Nevertheless, Selborne triumphed: in the interim, Bismarck

---

[92] Note by Selborne, 11 January 1885, FO 84/1819.
[93] Memorandum by Harcourt, 24 January 1885, FO 84/1820.

had changed his mind. In an abrupt about-face, he dictated that the protectorate phrase should be modified. In final form, the clause appeared nearly meaningless to many, merely requiring notification of occupations along the African coasts. The British Ambassador thus could truly say in summary that the Conference had not been so bold as to attempt any daring innovations in international law. No 'new rules' were adopted; Selborne's 'Little Englander' philosophy emerged victorious over Sir William Harcourt's. In accordance with the law of the Empire, Britain could have the advantages of controlling protectorates yet remain untrammelled by the administrative and judicial responsibilities of the Crown's jurisdiction.

Why did Bismarck yield? Perhaps the answer is simple: with the Scramble at its height, there would be virtually no territories along the coast to which the declaration would apply. The British delegates, however, attributed his change of policy to their persistent efforts to prove that his suspicions of British territorial aims were unfounded and that Britain did not envy German colonial ambitions; they attempted to convince him of the difficulties of discharging precise administrative and judicial responsibilities in places such as South-West Africa. Would Germany be prepared to admit a direct and absolute responsibility under all circumstances for offences of the natives or crimes committed by Europeans? What was the purpose and function of German administration in a 'protected state'? Those questions gave force to the Lord Chancellor's argument that the world had gone along well enough in the past without the complication of turning protectorates into annexations, and probably gave Bismarck cause for thought.[94] In any case the British delegation took full credit for bringing Bismarck around. Anderson wrote to Pauncefote:

> Dropping water will pierce the hardest stone, and so our unceasing efforts, public and private, in season and out of season, pierced Bismarck's understanding, though he shewed no sign of yielding till the last moment.

> We have scored a triumph, the more precious as it is a triumph of common sense.[95]

It was an appropriate note on which to leave Berlin. 'Common sense' from the British point of view had won out in every major issue: free

---

[94] Bismarck's views are most fully expounded by Turner in 'Bismarck's Imperialist Venture'.
[95] Anderson to Pauncefote, 31 January 1885, FO 84/1820.

trade on the Congo; British control over the Niger; and the maintenance—at least in British eyes—of a sharp distinction between 'protectorates' and 'annexations'.

During the Conference, Stanley wrote that war might break out between the European powers if they could not settle the Congo issue.
Preoccupied with Africa, he misinterpreted the temper of the time.
Revanche, not the Congo or any other colonial question, remained the
central French concern. Europe, not Africa or the Pacific, continued
to govern Bismarck's policy. Even for England, the Congo and the Niger were secondary regions compared to places of highest imperial
importance: Egypt, the Cape, India, and Australia—the key points of
the 'Southern British World', as the press had already begun to refer
to it in 1884–85. With remarkable insight *The Economist* (15 November 1884) placed the rivalry in western Africa in perspective and detected the main historical significance of the Conference on its opening day:

> The English public is not interested in the Congo. The majority of
> the electors know little about the area and are completely unaware
> of any bearing it may have on British trade. Among the more in-
> formed, there is a certain disgust with the colonies and particularly
> with the African enterprises from the Egyptian expedition to the op-
> erations in Bechuanaland. They watch the Congo affair with more
> curiosity as to the machinations of Germany that anything else.
>
> Nonetheless, to those with an historical eye, the Conference is an
> important incident. It represents the first time that Europe as an in-
> formal group has assumed any jurisdiction over a large, uncivilized
> area . . . This distribution of land is perhaps the last to be made, the
> remainder of the globe being already parcelled out. Any further
> changes . . . will probably be the result of war.

For the next three decades the European powers continued to settle
African disputes by diplomacy. When war broke out in 1914, the 'concert of Europe' that had effectively regulated European activities overseas failed to function in Europe itself.

Yet it is also true that African issues exacerbated European relations
and created intense suspicion. According to a typical French view, that
of Francis Charmes in the *Journal des Débats* (11 March 1885):

> Prince von Bismarck does not desire wars and boulversements: but
> he would nevertheless like to see . . . everybody well occupied in
> the Sudan, Afghanistan, the Red Sea, the Balkans, and Tonkin, while

Germany remains severely and impassively presiding over the destinies of Europe with an eager eye to all profits or 'brokerage' likely to accrue.

Bismarck, as is well known, suspected that Britain tried to 'close in', 'encircle', wherever Germany attempted to colonize. But to the British, territories such as South-West Africa, the Cameroons, and New Guinea were traditional spheres of British influence being devoured by 'a boy who eats too much'. During the last two months of the Conference, Anglo-German colonial relations were extraordinarily bitter. The English press lampooned the Conference in articles with such titles as 'Dinner at Berlin'. According to the *Glasgow Herald* (19 January 1885) the feast included 'pickled Kangaroo from North New Guinea, lean (exceptionally lean) mutton from the Cameroons, and a barrel of very astonishing natives . . . from Wallfisch Bay'. Englishmen ridiculed Germany's advent as a colonial power, but welcomed her in preference to France. They blamed the English 'jellyfish politicians' as much as Bismarck for England's 'eating humble pie' in Africa and the Pacific. Although there was some debate whether Granville was 'a philistine or a sly diplomatic fox', most agreed that he should be held responsible for the 'open boot kissing' of the Foreign Office and the 'imbecility of English policy'. A few responsible organs of the press restrained their criticism of the Foreign Office and emphasized that Germany's overseas empire would not threaten Britain's security because, in the words of the *Liverpool Daily Post* (13 January 1885), 'Germany is no match for England at sea . . . every distant colony . . . is a vulnerable point at which any enemy that commands the sea can strike.' Along the same lines, the British Ambassador in Paris wrote a perceptive commentary that establishes the relevance of the colonial rivalries of the Berlin Conference era to the origins of the First World War:

> Bismarck used to say that Germany and England were like a wolf and a shark, both dangerous animals, but unable to get at each other. His new Colonial Policy is very much as if the wolf should put his paws into the water so as to bring them within reach of the shark.[96]

With empires go supporting navies; Bismarck's colonial policy launched Germany on a course of *Weltpolitik*.[97]

To the French, the Scramble was as much a race for markets as

[96] Lyons to Granville, No. 101 Africa, Very Confidential, 2 December 1884, FO 84/1816.
[97] See Turner, 'Bismarck's Imperialist Venture', p. 82.

a struggle for strategic position. At the beginning of the Conference, France appeared to have the upper hand. With Bismarck's concurrence, Ferry refused absolutely to discuss the application of the Free Trade principle to the Gabon, Guinea, or Senegal, and insisted that the Niger be considered along with the Congo. The Conference accomplished two-thirds of its major work by establishing freedom of navigation on the two rivers, along with freedom of trade on the Congo. But France emerged from the Conference having gained very little. Britain, on the other hand, succeeded in establishing a vast Free Trade zone in central Africa and in beating back the French attempt to impinge on British control of the Niger. In retrospect, the work of the Conference appears hollow in view of the commercial monopolies established despite the Berlin Act; but at the time, the accomplishments of the Conference appeared substantial, especially in British eyes because of the reverses suffered by France. All in all, the major achievement appeared to be that in the Congo 'a vast European, and especially British, trade will be opened'.[98] Compared with such jubilant comments, the tone of the French press was subdued. In one of the few lengthy commentaries on the results of the Conference, the *République Française* (14 April 1885) expressed the general feeling in French colonial circles when it unenthusiastically congratulated the government for securing the Ogooué and the right bank of the Upper Congo as 'our exclusive property'.

The third basis of effective occupation proved as ineffective in regulating the partition of the continent as the first two bases were in preventing monopolies on the Congo and the Niger. Yet the popular image of the Conference then as now is that it 'partitioned Africa'. Many captions in the press ran along the lines of 'Setting the Rules of the Grab'. Writers since then have assumed that because the Conference met during one of the Scramble's hottest phases, the delegates gave momentum to partition and 'plotted Africa's fate'. Since the Conference did not deal formally with questions of sovereignty, the interpretation is erroneous. But since the Conference did informally give birth to that bastard child, the Congo Free State, it can be loosely said that the Conference gave the Scramble 'international sanction', a vague phrase perhaps implying that Africa should be partitioned peacefully and in accordance with the principles of Free Trade.

Historians have often been sceptical whether the Berlin Act was effective as a political instrument or a legal precedent. Writing in 1942, Sybil Crowe stated that the events of the Scramble occurring at the time of the Conference 'must not be confused with any far-reaching

[98] *Standard*, 3 March 1885.

effect which the conference may have had, even indirectly, on international rivalry in Africa during the next fifty years or so. This appears to have been negligible.'[99] By contrast, a French scholar and diplomat, Geoffroy de Courcel, concluded seven years earlier in an important book overlooked by many writers on the subject (including Crowe):

> Au point de vue économique et juridique, on a parfois voulu considérer l'Acte de Berlin comme une Charte coloniale universelle. Cette conception s'était même manifestée au cours des débats et explique certaines des dispositions adoptées.
>
> Sans avoir cette portée, l'Acte de Berlin a tenté une expérience libérale intéressante et il a consacré, au double point de vue économique et juridique, l'abandon du système de Pact colonial: l'exploitation de la colonie ne devait plus se faire au profit exclusif de la métropole, mais avant tout au profit de la colonie elle-même, en y étendant la puissance, l'influence et la civilisation de la métropole . . .
>
> L'œuvre de la Conférence de Berlin a eu en définitive pour buts la paix, la prospérité et la civilisation.[100]

Which of the two writers held the more accurate view?

In a sense, neither was wrong. They viewed the Berlin Act differently from their respective disciplines of history and international law. As a historian, Crowe held that the provisions of the Act were flouted and proved totally ineffective. She argued cogently that the historical significance of the Conference lay in the preceding events rather than its influence on the Scramble. With equal force, Courcel proved that the Berlin Act reflected a consensus of the family of nations on a 'multiplicity' of issues that included, in addition to the three bases, protection of the natives, the slave trade, religious liberty, arbitrations, and even the Universal Postal Union. The Foreign Office lamented the inadequacy of these minor clauses, and some sections of the press attacked the Conference for its 'hollow humanitarianism' and 'philanthropic gabble'. Nevertheless, the Berlin Act, as Courcel emphasized, broached major questions and established precedents later elaborated in the Brussels Antislavery Act, the Convention respecting Liquors in Africa, and the conventions of St.-Germain-en-Laye. It should be

[99] Crowe, *Berlin West African Conference*, p. 5.
[100] Courcel, *L'Influence de le Conférence de Berlin*, p. 161. Cf. Boniface I. Obichere, *West African States and European Expansion: The Dahomey-Niger Hinterland, 1885–1898* (New Haven, 1971).

added, on the basis of evidence not accessible when Crowe and Courcel wrote, that the Berlin Act was relevant to the course of partition
and has a newly proven significance as precedent. From 1906 to 1908,
at the height of the Congo reform controversy, there was considerable
talk of reconvening the Berlin Conference to consider the maladministration of the Congo State. The Foreign Office prepared a 265-page
brief against King Leopold for having violated the 'spirit of the Berlin Act'.[101] Had Belgium not annexed the Congo in 1908, the Congo
probably would have become the subject of another international
conference, one to judge whether the Congo State should be partitioned between Germany, France, and Britain. The other revelation is
concrete, not speculative: documents recently released by the Foreign
Office establish beyond doubt that the precedent in the minds of British statesmen as they established the League of Nations mandates system was the Berlin Act.[102] The Trusteeship System of the United Nations thus descends from the Conference of 1884–85.

In the phrase 'the spirit of the Berlin Act', the historian perhaps
finds the clue to the meaning of the Conference for African as well as
European history. When African historians at some remote date re-
examine Europe's relations with Africa, they will probably look upon
the Berlin Conference as a curiosity. At no other time were European
attitudes towards Africa more marked with confidence, enthusiasm,
and idealism. Twenty years later, the reformer E. D. Morel described
the spirit of the Conference:

> Now, although international jealousies contributed very largely to
> the Berlin Conference of 1885, it is unquestionable that the spirit
> displayed at that Conference and the policy it laid down were alike
> inspired by humanitarian motives—*practical* humanitarian motives
> . . . there was throughout the deliberations which took place in the
> course of the framing of the clauses of the Act, a desire to protect
> the natives of Africa from injustice and expropriation; to guarantee
> them in the peaceful possession of their land and property; to check,
> as far as possible, inter-tribal warfare and the slave-raiding opera-
> tions of Arab half-castes and to maintain and develop trade. Par-
> ticular stress was laid upon the latter point, it being universally rec-
> ognised that commercial intercourse is, above all things, the surest
> medium for the advancement of arts and crafts, and generally speak-
> ing to a higher conception of life.[103]

[101] FO 371/117.

[102] W. R. Louis, *Great Britain and Germany's Lost Colonies* (Oxford, 1967), chaps. 3 and 4.

[103] Edmund D. Morel, *King Leopold's Rule in Africa* (London, 1904), pp. 3–4.

At the Berlin Conference, so the myth developed, King Leopold was appointed Europe's 'trustee' to introduce trade and civilization into the heart of the continent. With unbounded optimism, the English press reported on the success of his mission and on the conditions of the Congo.

There were of course a few sceptics, who jeered at the thought of Manchester's cotton being peddled to Congo cannibals, but this description by the *Standard* (2 March 1885) might be fairly taken as representative of Europe's image of the Congo in 1885:

> The Congo affords 4000 miles of navigable waterway, and on either side stretches a country of the most exuberant fertility. Palm oil, rubber, gums, coffee, copper—already smelted by the natives—ivory, camwood and orchella weed (both valuable for dyeing purposes), palm fibre, and hides are amongst a few of the chief articles of native trade, and there are besides vast areas covered with the most valuable timber such as ebony, mahogany, lignum vitre, teak, and redwood . . . there are 30,000,000 cubic feet of timber which will command the highest prices in the European market when the railway is made, and means of transport thus afforded. All kinds of European vegetables will grow luxuriantly, and both sugar and cotton are indigenous to many parts of the country.

Not only the products of the soil but also the animal life filled Europeans with enthusiasm:

> The greater part of the Free State is new country, and should be the paradise of sportsmen, containing as it does enormous numbers of elephants, lions, buffalos, hippopotami, crocodiles, antelopes, water bucks, lynxes and many other species of animals.

Above all the Africans hungered for European commerce:

> The wants of the natives are still more varied than their own products, and there is scarcely any branch of European industry which may not expect to benefit by the opening of this vast market. Cotton goods, blankets, crockery, muskets, gunpowder, hardware of all kinds, and cheap finery of every description are but a few amongst the goods in constant demand amongst them.

The press referred to the inspirer of those lines, Stanley, as 'the Clive of Africa', and quoted King Leopold in such rapturous phrases as 'I speak of Africa and golden joys'. 'In the name of Almighty God', the 'Congo Conference' had proclaimed the advent of civilization in the Dark Continent. Toasts were made to King Leopold, 'that noble-minded Sovereign who had the wisdom and the courage to begin the enterprise of the Congo which will be the bright centre to the new Federation of Freedom and Peace.' Having inspired such lofty sentiments, the Berlin Congo Conference should rightly be remembered in European colonial history as 'the most remarkable Conference that has ever been assembled'.[104]

France and Britain in Africa: Imperial Rivalry and Colonial Rule   1971

---

[104] *Leeds Mercury*, 28 February 1885.

4

ROGER CASEMENT AND THE CONGO

Roger Casement's role as Irish patriot has obscured his role as Congo reformer. Travelling in the interior of the Congo in 1903 as British Consul, he gathered evidence that enabled the British government to expose the maladministration of the Congo State. By providing detailed examples of 'wholesale oppression and shocking mismanagement'[1] in the Congo, he enabled the Foreign Office to take a decisive stand against the Congo State. He did not, however, regard action by the British government as sufficient to redress the wrongs of King Leopold's rubber trade. Convinced that only a humanitarian crusade could abolish the evils of the Leopoldian regime, Casement inspired E. D. Morel to found the Congo Reform Association. In his dual capacity as civil servant and humanitarian, he attempted, in his own words, to choke off King Leopold 'as a "helldog" is choked off'. His apocalyptic vision of evil in the Congo was no doubt exaggerated, but his influence was important in bringing about Belgium's annexation of the Congo in 1908.

The abuses that Casement exposed in 1903 had a long history. During the 1890s the British government protested sporadically to the Congo administration against the treatment of British West African labourers in the Congo; 'the loss of life has been very great', Consul Pickersgill reported in 1897.[2] Yet publicly the British government remained silent; when Sir Charles Dilke raised a question in the House of Commons about abuses in the Congo, he received only the bland answer that the British labourers were 'thoroughly contented, happy and well-treated'.[3] When a Congo agent illegally hanged a British subject named Charles Stokes in 1895, the faulty judicial and administrative system in the Congo was widely discussed throughout Europe; but at the end of the next year, public interest in the Stokes case had subsided. 'I think it is forgotten,' Lord Salisbury wrote.[4]

That the 'Congo atrocities' were not forgotten by the British public during the 1890s was due almost entirely to the efforts of one man: H. R. Fox Bourne, the secretary of the Aborigines Protection Society, a man 'well stricken in years and tortured with asthma, though very active and zealous'.[5] Fox Bourne campaigned so vigorously against the

---

[1] Casement to Lansdowne, telegram, 15 September 1903, FO 10/805.

[2] Pickersgill to Salisbury, 25 January 1897, FO 63/1336.

[3] *Parliamentary Debates,* 4th series, 45, 1897, col. 781.

[4] Salisbury's minute of [?] 2 November 1896, FO 10/716.

[5] E. D. Morel's unpublished history of the Congo Reform Association, Morel Papers, London School of Economics.

'Civilisation in Congoland'[6] that King Leopold himself was said to have called at the offices of *The Times* to beg the editors not to publish Fox Bourne's 'Congo letters'.[7] It was Fox Bourne who marshalled the evidence of missionaries to prove 'the ill-treatment of the aborigines' as well as the existence of trade monopolies in the Congo. Even the officials of the Foreign Office, with their inveterate suspicion of humanitarians, had to admit that Fox Bourne's indictments of the Congo State were 'temperately stated',[8] even if not justified. In Fox Bourne's view, the Congo State had violated the two main premises of the Berlin Act of 1885: permitting free trade and providing for the welfare of the indigenous population in the Congo basin. To remedy the evils in the Congo, he urged the Foreign Office to reconvene the Berlin Conference to discuss Congo affairs. 'We should be careful not to encourage any such scheme,' one distinguished British diplomat commented.[9] Lord Lansdowne, the Foreign Secretary, added with emphasis that 'we did *not* desire the reconvocation of the Berlin Conference.'[10]

Reconvocation of the Berlin Conference was a Pandora's box that the Foreign Office had no intention of opening; but the British diplomats were not unaware of the maladministration in the Congo. When Consul Pickersgill drew up a report in 1897 'respecting Congo atrocities',[11] Lord Salisbury commented, 'It is very horrible,'[12] and requested that a catalogue be prepared 'of all the brutalities imputed to the Congo Government'. 'It ought to be put in hand', Salisbury wrote in April 1900, 'for at any time we might need it.'[13]

Salisbury saw as early as the turn of the century that Britain eventually would intervene in the Congo, and the Foreign Office consequently began to debate Britain's legal rights there. 'What would be our *right*', Gosselin, the Assistant Under-Secretary, queried Davidson, the legal expert, 'as a signatory of the Berlin Act [of] 1885 as to interfering with the Congo Free State in the alleged ill-treatment of natives by Belgian officials?'[14] 'I do not think', Davidson replied, 'that we could do more than make a formal remonstrance with the Belgian Government on the ground that they were not fulfilling their treaty

[6] The title of his book published in 1903.
[7] Fox Bourne to Morel, 21 November 1903, Morel Papers.
[8] Farnall's minute on Fox Bourne to Salisbury, 27 March 1902, FO 10/773.
[9] Sir Martin Gosselin's minute of 21 May 1902, FO 10/773.
[10] Lansdowne's minute on Gosselin's memorandum of 5 June 1902, FO 10/773.
[11] 1 June 1897, FO 10/731.
[12] Salisbury's minute on Pickersgill's report of 1 June 1897, FO 10/731.
[13] Salisbury's minute of 30 April 1900, FO 10/754.
[14] Gosselin to Davidson, 10 May 1900, FO 10/754.

obligations as defined by the Berlin Act [of] 1885.'[15] Whatever intention the framers of the Berlin Act may have had, there was absolutely no provision in the treaty for international intervention. Lord Cranborne expressed the frustration felt by most Congo reformers when he said, 'Law Officers are prone to interpret a treaty rather too literally instead of reading its provisions in the light of the declarations made at the time of the conference.'[16] 'Beyond strong remonstrance', Davidson said bluntly, 'we have no further remedy short of the employment of actual force.'[17]

For this reason—legal impotence—the Foreign Office eschewed even the suggestion of reconvocation of the Berlin Conference. A conference also would reopen the whole question of the partition of Africa, which, Lansdowne observed, 'would not be desirable in our own interests'.[18] The Office's Congo expert, Harry Farnall, added, 'Neither this country nor any other is likely to take active steps in the matter unless more or less forced to do so by public opinion.'[19]

The Foreign Office was 'more or less forced to do so' when the House of Commons, moved by the humanitarian pleas of E. D. Morel (the editor of the *West African Mail*),[20] debated Congo affairs in May 1903. Herbert Samuel asked: if the administration of the Congo State was civilization, then what was barbarism?[21] Sir Charles Dilke said that the 'whole anti-slave world had been swindled by the administration of the Congo State':

> [T]he military system in the Congo State consisted of bringing in cannibal tribes, marching them without any commissariat through the country to be attacked, and rationing them on the bodies of the killed, carrying dried bodies with them for the purpose.[22]

The House of Commons, less concerned with legal niceties than the Foreign Office, resolved that the British government should confer with the other powers signatory to the Berlin Act in order 'to abate the evils' prevalent in the Congo.[23]

---

[15] Davidson to Gosselin, 16 May 1900, FO 10/754.

[16] Cranborne's minute of 19 May 1903, FO 10/805.

[17] Davidson to Gosselin, 16 May 1900, FO 10/754.

[18] Lansdowne to Dilke, 13 March 1902, Dilke Papers, British Museum Add. MS. 43917.

[19] Farnall's minute of 3 April on Fox Bourne to Salisbury, 27 March 1902, FO 10/773.

[20] 'The debate in the House of Commons last May was the first fruits of his devoted labours' (*Morning Post*, 24 March 1904).

[21] *Parliamentary Debates*, 4th series, 122, 20 May 1903, col. 1298.

[22] Ibid., col. 1304.

[23] Ibid., col. 1332.

This resolution has been interpreted as the turning point in the anti-Congo campaign.[24] In some respects it was, because it obliged the Foreign Office to explain its lack of action—and in consequence, its circular sent to the other European powers was written as much to 'the House of Commons . . . as it is to the powers'.[25] The reason why the Foreign Office had failed to intervene in the Congo was not, as Sir Charles Dilke put it, fear of being 'snubbed' by the other powers;[26] it was fear of being unable to prove its case. Here lies Roger Casement's contribution to the anti-Congo campaign.

The evidence possessed by the Foreign Office concerning atrocities in the Congo consisted mainly of clippings from the Belgian press. 'The newspapers are practically our only source of information,' lamented Farnall.[27] As a result, British protests had been 'neither many nor strong' because of 'the indirect nature of the evidence'.[28]

The reason for the lack of evidence was that until 1900 no British Consul had resided permanently in the Congo. Even after he took up residence in 1900, Casement was unable to spend any considerable period of time until the following year at Boma, the administrative capital of the Congo State, near the coast.[29] Even at Boma, Casement could provide little more than second-hand reports about the 'atrocities', since atrocities were committed in the interior and not at Boma. In 1902 he was forced to cancel a trip to the interior because of illness. Not until 1903 was he able to visit the rubber region of the upper Congo to confirm the 'hideous stories' of the rubber trade.[30]

Following the House of Commons debate of May 1903, Casement was instructed by the Foreign Office to travel to the interior to gather 'authentic information' about the alleged maladministration. Casement later claimed that he went up the Congo entirely on his own initiative. This is true in the sense that when he left for the interior, his trip had been planned for over a year; and it is revealing that the Foreign Office did not fully grasp the significance of the evidence he was about to gather: 'Casement's journey is of less importance than the completion of the representation to the Congo Government respecting the alleged ill-treatment of certain British subjects at and near

[24] Ruth M. Slade, *English-Speaking Missions in the Congo Independent State, 1878–1908* (Brussels, 1959), p. 273.

[25] Farnall's minute of 5 June 1903, FO 10/805.

[26] Dilke to Morel, 20 June 1903, Morel Papers; Slade, *English-Speaking Missions,* p. 274.

[27] Farnall's minute on Plunkett to Salisbury, No. 164 Africa, 18 June 1900, FO 10/754.

[28] Farnall's minute on Addison's memorandum of 11 May 1903, FO 10/803.

[29] See the memorandum of 10 February 1904, FO 10/807.

[30] Lansdowne's minute on Fox Bourne to FO, 5 May 1903, FO 10/803.

Boma.'[31] Contrary to common assumptions, Casement's famous trip followed the House of Commons debate more by accident than design. He could later say with some justification that he went up the Congo 'off my own bat'.[32]

When Roger Casement left on his historic journey in June 1903, he was almost thirty-nine years old, with nearly twenty years' African experience behind him. He had first gone to Africa in 1884, as he recalled to his own chagrin in 1904, as a volunteer

> in what was then represented as a philanthropic international enterprise . . . not the Congo State but a private association terming itself the 'Association Internationale du Congo' [which became the Congo State] . . . I left its service, of my own volition, as soon after it became a recognized government as I conveniently could—not without some little pecuniary sacrifice.[33]

In 1891 he received an appointment in the Niger Coast Protectorate, and in 1895 was promoted to British Consul at Lourenço Marques. In his own immodest words, referring to his Lourenço Marques experiences, 'I have served . . . with distinction and in posts of the highest confidence.'[34] When received by King Leopold in Brussels in October

---

[31] These cases had become so numerous by 1903 that the Foreign Office decided to address a strong representation to the Congo administration; 'I hope we are collecting materials for an indictment,' Lansdowne wrote shortly before the House of Commons debate in 1903 (Lansdowne's minute on Fox Bourne to FO, 5 May 1903, FO 10/803). The most important provable instance of maltreatment was that of a British subject called Mrs. Meyer, who had been robbed by the Congo police and then had her shop looted while under arrest. Her business was entirely ruined, and, after waiting in vain for her case to be settled in Boma, she returned to her home in Sierra Leone. Similar incidents were to form the basis of the Foreign Office's attack against the Congo State, but they were discarded in favour of Casement's report.

[32] Casement exaggerated in 1909 when he recalled the origins of his journey: 'I went up river, remember . . . not as a result of any order of theirs. I had started and was almost at Stanley Pool with all my measures prepared when they telegraphed out suggesting that in view of the debate of May 1903 I might start.' (Casement to Morel, Private and Confidential, 29 January 1909, Morel Papers.) The actual sequence of events was: Casement telegraphed on 8 May 1903: 'Leaving for interior end May'; the Foreign Office replied that he should remain in Boma; after the House of Commons debate on 20 May, the Foreign Office telegraphed that he should begin his trip to the interior as soon as possible; Casement received this order on 4 June and departed the next day (FO 10/804).

[33] Casement to Lansdowne, 9 October 1905, FO 10/815; see also Casement to Morel, 27 June 1904, Morel Papers; Peter Singleton-Gates and Maurice Girodias, eds., *The Black Diaries of Roger Casement* (New York, 1959), pp. 73–74; and Brooks Thompson, 'A Letter of Roger Casement in the Sanford Collection', *English Historical Review*, 77 (January 1962), pp. 98–102.

[34] Casement to Morel, 15 March 1905, Morel Papers.

1900 before taking up his duties as British Congo Consul, Casement made such a favourable impression on the Sovereign of the Congo State that 'His Majesty, in bidding me farewell, asked me to write him privately at any time, and to write frankly, should there be anything of interest I could, unofficially, advise him of for the advancement of the general situation on the Congo.'[35]

Casement's friend Herbert Ward, with whom he had pioneered on the Congo in the 1880s, wrote on the eve of Casement's emergence into the public eye: 'No man walks this earth at this moment who is more absolutely good and honest and noble minded than Roger Casement.'[36] E. D. Morel described him in the unpublished history of the Congo Reform Association:

> Very lithe and sinewy, chest thrown out, head held high—suggestive of one who had lived in the vast open spaces. Black hair and beard covering cheeks hollowed by the tropical sun. Strongly marked features. A dark blue penetrating eye sunken in the socket. A long lean, swarthy Vandyke type of face, graven with power and withal of great gentleness. An extraordinarily handsome and arresting face.

'Here was a man, indeed. One who would convince those in high places of the foulness of the crime committed upon a helpless people.'[37]

Did Casement go up the Congo as an unbiased British Consul, or did he begin his trip as a humanitarian, with the intention of 'having some influence on the side of right'? On 20 July 1903 he wrote to Lord Lansdowne that his goal was 'to place before your Lordship . . . a faithful and accurate representation of the state of affairs prevailing in this country'. But if he left Boma as an impartial observer, Casement returned, in his own words, as a self-appointed 'Criminal Investigation Department'.[38]

---

[35] Casement wrote these lines to the Foreign Office in justification of his bluntly stated personal letter to the Governor-General of the Congo State in 1904. Cf. Phipps to Lansdowne, No. 71 Africa, 20 September 1902, FO 10/773:

> Mr Casement's persistent animadversion on everything connected with the Congolese administrative methods is the more striking to me inasmuch as I found him, on the occasion of his interview with His Majesty some eighteen months ago, deeply impressed by the enlightened views entertained by King Leopold, who had urged him not to conceal whatever conclusions he might arrive at upon his arrival on the spot.

[36] Ward to Morel, 25 August 1903, Morel Papers.

[37] Unpublished history of the Congo Reform Association, Morel Papers.

[38] Casement to Lansdowne, No. 34 Africa, 15–16 September 1903, FO 10/805.

Casement was a man of tumultuous passion, which was exacerbated by the almost unendurable hardships of tropical Africa. 'I wish very sincerely . . . I were out of this horrid country—it is a nightmare,' he wrote to his friend Farnall in the Foreign Office.[39] There is more than one annotation by Foreign Office officials on Casement's dispatches to the effect that 'he will not stand the Congo climate much longer'.[40] In addition to his anxiety about his health, Casement was aware that 'the Congo Government here look on me with no friendly eye'. His official duties of criticizing the Congo authorities for maltreating British subjects made it difficult for him to keep on friendly personal terms with them. He felt he was regarded as a 'dangerous man'; once he even overheard a Congo official remark that '"cette canaille d'un Consul" was on their track'.[41]

Casement left the coast on 5 June for Stanley Pool, the jumping-off place for the interior. He left Stanley Pool on 2 July and returned two and a half months later, having travelled a surprising distance up the Congo, Lolongo, and Lopori rivers. The area he traversed was not large in comparison to the vast region of the Congo State, but it was one of the central—and also one of the most productive—rubber regions.

Casement's first problem was one of transportation. By limiting his travels to the regions served by the monopolized transportation system of the Congo government, he would be denied freedom of movement: 'the objects of my present journey could scarcely be served at all were I restricted to the use of those vessels.'[42] At his own personal financial risk, he chartered the *Henry Reed,* the steamer of the American Baptist Missionary Union, at £45 a month:[43] '[My] . . . journeys can now be undertaken independent of anyone else.'[44]

There is no point in relating the day-by-day events of Casement's trip, which are described in his report published by the Foreign

[39] Casement to Farnall, Private, 28 May 1903, FO 10/804.

[40] Gosselin's minute on Casement to Gosselin, Private, 16 May 1902, FO 10/773.

[41] Casement to Farnall, Private, 28 May 1903, FO 10/804. The theme of surveillance by the Congo authorities runs through Casement's dispatches. Reporting the results of his journey to the interior, Casement wrote: 'I was being "shadowed" wherever I went, and had I continued to seek to find out the truth by personal contact with the natives themselves the authorities would have intervened, under one pretext or another, to prevent my continuing in that course' (Casement to Lansdowne, No. 38 Africa, Very Confidential, 30 September 1903, FO 10/806).

[42] Casement to Lansdowne, No. 28 Africa, 20 July 1903, FO 10/805.

[43] Ibid.

[44] 'Mr Casement should be liberally treated in this matter . . . It is essential that [he] . . . should be able to move about freely and the less he is bound to use government boats the better his chance of seeing what is the true state of the country' (Farnall's minute on Casement's No. 28 Africa).

Office and are discussed at great length by his numerous biographers.[45] Casement's description of the expedition is misleading. It gives the impression of a man who studied the admirable Belgian steamers and stations as well as the administration's tax system; of a man who saw the flourishing plantations as well as evidence of murder and mutilation. It is easy to be misled: although for part of his journey Casement was indeed a dispassionate judge, carefully weighing both the merits and faults of the administration, this was not the important part of his trip. The important part, both for Casement personally and for the evidence he was to submit, occurred during early September 1903, when his moderate reports turned into 'febrile, almost hysterical despatches'.[46]

On 5 August 1903, writing from Lake Mantumba, far in the interior, Casement reported that it would take him several months to get 'to the bottom of things': 'There is much for me to see, and it were useless to rush round getting only superficial impressions; much better now that I am here to see one district thoroughly.'

> In the lake district things are pretty bad . . . Whole villages and districts I knew well and visited as flourishing communities in 1887 are today without a human being; others are reduced to a handful of sick or harassed creatures who say of the government: 'Are the white men never going home; is this to last for ever?' [47]

These lines are damning, but also moderately stated in comparison to those that followed a month later, when he had returned to Stanley Pool:

> Of all the shameful and infamous expedients whereby man has preyed upon man . . . this vile thing [the rubber trade] dares to call itself commerce . . . were I to touch on the subject of the treatment of the natives under the rubber regime, my indignation would carry me beyond the limits of official courtesy. One of the native labourers at the English mission at Bongandanga rejoiced, I was told, in the name of Esi Ambindo, 'The Father of Dirt'.

[45] Casement's report is in No. 1 Africa (1904). For biographies of Casement, see Denis Gwynn, *Traitor or Patriot?* (New York, 1931); Geoffrey de C. Parmiter, *Roger Casement* (London, 1936); more recent material in the Public Record Office and the Morel Papers has been used by Rene MacColl, *Roger Casement* (London, 1956); Giovanni Costigan's 'The Treason of Sir Roger Casement', *American Historical Review*, 60 (January 1955), and Galen Broeker's 'Roger Casement: Background to Treason', *Journal of Modern History*, 29 (September 1957) are scholarly efforts to trace and explain Casement's efforts during the First World War to gain German help for the cause of Irish nationalism—for which he was hanged for high treason in 1916.

[46] Phipps to Villiers, Private, 16 April 1905, FO 10/813.

[47] Casement to Farnall, Private, 5 August 1903, FO 10/805.

'That name more fitly applies to the Sovereign mind which gave birth to the ABIR [Anglo-Belgian India-Rubber] concession than to any naked unwashed, savage of the woods'[48]—a remark so extravagantly expressed that it caused someone in the Foreign Office to place an exclamation mark in the margin beside this passage of Casement's dispatch.

What turned the dispassionate judge into an indignant humanitarian? It is difficult to say precisely;[49] Casement emerged from the interior having seen a number of things that would twist the heart of any man. If one incident can be singled out, it was the case of Epondo—though Casement was later to deny that it had any especial significance. The Epondo case was 'the only one I had . . . the time or opportunity to personally investigate'.[50] On 6 September, Casement had been staying at the Congo Balolo mission of the Baptist Missionary Society, where he had arrived the previous evening from the Lopori River. A group of Africans came to see Casement, bringing with them a boy of about sixteen whose right hand was cut off at the wrist. The Africans said that a 'sentry' called Kalengo of one of the rubber companies had committed this crime simply to compel them to collect rubber. They said that Kalengo had similarly mutilated another boy.

Casement decided to visit the town where the atrocities had occurred. Accompanied by two missionaries, he found the second boy, named Epondo, who at once accused Kalengo of having lopped off his hand.

> [T]he entire community in my presence formally charged him with this and other grave offences. The sentry could make no reply to the accusation levied against him, and I informed him and the assembled natives that I should appeal for his instant punishment . . . to the highest quarter open to me in this country.[51]

In consequence of this appalling experience, Casement cancelled his plans for an extensive tour of the interior, though he knew that he had only 'touched on the outmost fringe of the horrible reality'.[52] 'I have seen enough,' he wrote.[53]

Physically exhausted, emotionally distraught, and plagued with

[48] Casement to Lansdowne, No. 33 Africa, Confidential, 6 September 1903, FO 10/805.

[49] One of the main difficulties is a gap in the evidence: Casement's No. 31 Africa was written on 5 August; No. 32 Africa, Confidential, on 5 September.

[50] Casement to Farnall, 20 February 1904, FO 10/808.

[51] Casement to Governor-General of the Congo State, 12 September 1903, FO 10/806.

[52] Casement to Lansdowne, No. 38 Africa, Very Confidential, 30 September 1903, FO 10/806.

[53] Casement to Lansdowne, No. 34 Africa, 15–16 September 1903, FO 10/805.

fears of being 'shadowed', he returned to Stanley Pool, where he took on himself the responsibility of writing his 'famous letter'[54] to the Governor-General of the Congo State, which contained the following lines:

> I am amazed and confounded at what I have both seen and heard; and if I in the enjoyment of all the resources and privileges of civilized existence know not where to turn to, or to whom to make appeal on behalf of these unhappy people whose sufferings I have witnessed and whose wrongs have burnt into my heart, how can they, poor panic-stricken fugitives . . . turn for justice to their oppressors.[55]

Casement was fully aware that this letter would be offensive to the authorities of the Congo State, who might well demand his recall.[56] But Casement regarded himself as being in a difficult moral situation: 'I thought the best course was to state exactly what I believed at all personal costs.'[57]

Thus ended the episode of Roger Casement's celebrated trip to the interior of the Congo State. The British Consul had 'broken into the thieves' kitchen'.[58]

'**M**y action has produced absolute consternation,' Casement wrote of the effect of his behaviour on the Congo authorities.[59] And the same might be said of the Foreign Office. Instead of returning for any length of time to Boma—'where Congo State authorities will try to diminish the significance of my disclosures'[60]—Casement paused there only long enough to dispatch his personal letter to the Governor-General, and then proceeded straight to the coast: 'I fear my return to the Congo, as Consul, is almost out of the question.'[61]

'It does not seem quite clear what Mr Casement wants to do,' E. A. W. Clarke, one of the African experts in the Foreign Office, noted on Casement's telegram announcing his return from the Upper Congo. Would Casement run a personal risk if he remained in the

[54] Phipps to Farnall, Private, 26 November 1903, FO 10/806.

[55] Casement to Governor-General, 12 September 1903.

[56] Cf. Farnall's minute of 2 November 1903, FO 10/806: 'I do not think that the Congo Government will demand Mr Casement's recall on account of this letter and if they do they will make their position worse than it now is.'

[57] Casement to Lansdowne, telegram, 5 October 1903, FO 10/806.

[58] Casement to Lansdowne, No. 34 Africa, 15–16 September 1903, FO 10/805.

[59] Ibid.

[60] Casement to Lansdowne, telegram, 15 September 1903, FO 10/805: 'I ought to place facts before you before submitting these to any partial and pretended local investigation.'

[61] Casement to Lansdowne, No. 33 Africa, Very Confidential, 30 September 1903, FO 10/806.

Congo? 'It is inconceivable that he would; the Congo people would never be so mad as to make away with a British Consul at the present moment.'[62]

Another unsentimental Foreign Office official, Assistant Under-Secretary F. A. Campbell, after reading some of Casement's dramatic lines, such as 'I do not accuse an individual, I accuse a system', noted that 'He has the system on the brain.'

> [H]e had better come home now, and prepare a circumstantial report here, where he can receive advice and assistance, in the direction of the elimination of violent diatribes against the Congo State which he has no evidence to support . . . He has—perhaps not unnaturally after all he has heard and seen—come to regard the whole matter as a personal one between himself and the Congo State; we ought to have as British representative someone not harder hearted, but harder headed.[63]

Lord Lansdowne sympathized with Casement's 'state of excitement': 'Making allowance for strength of feeling, these papers [Casement's dispatches] are a terrible indictment.' Despite the 'exuberant diction for which Consul Casement has a weakness', wrote E. A. W. Clarke, his reports provided an extremely effective weapon for attacking the Congo State. On 4 November 1903, Casement received a telegram from the Foreign Office instructing him to return to England to prepare a 'comprehensive report'.[64]

Casement's arrival in London on 1 December 1903 was anticipated as eagerly by the British press as it was anxiously by the Congo authorities in Brussels. E. D. Morel had learned from one of Casement's friends that Casement was touring the interior;[65] word was soon out that there was going to be an important development in the Congo controversy. The whole question turned on the matter of evidence. Until Casement's trip, most of the evidence about the state of affairs in the Congo had been produced either by missionaries and disaffected former employees of the Congo State or by the Congo administration itself. Since Casement fitted into none of these categories, the *Morning Post* observed (13 November 1903), but was a representative of the British government, sent to the Congo 'to ascertain the truth', then his report would carry great weight—so great that it would be possible

---

[62] Clarke's minute of 23 September 1903, FO 10/805.
[63] Campbell's minute of 18 October 1903, FO 10/805.
[64] Singleton-Gates and Girodias, *Black Diaries*, p. 179.
[65] See Morel to Dilke, 17 September 1903, Dilke Papers.

to say once and for all whether King Leopold's Congo enterprise was an 'ideal colony' or a 'disgrace to civilization'.

King Leopold feared Casement's report. So apprehensive was the Sovereign of the Congo State that he sent Sir Alfred Jones—'a noted Congophile',[66] the Consul for the Congo State in Liverpool, and director of the Compagnie Belge Maritime du Congo—to the Foreign Office on 9 and 20 December to warn the British that if they persisted in their attacks against the Congo State, he might be forced 'to hand over everything . . . to Germany'; Jones's visits were in fact trial balloons sent up by King Leopold to see whether the Foreign Office would suppress Casement's report under certain conditions—or even if it would hand over his report and evidence to an impartial 'International Commission of Inquiry'.[67] The possibility of a commission was discussed more seriously in the Foreign Office than is commonly known; but the British Parliament and public would never have permitted the Foreign Office to muzzle Casement—nor would Casement ever have let anyone muzzle him—regardless of the effect on Anglo-Congolese or Anglo-Belgian relations. 'We could not suppress Mr Casement's report,' Lord Lansdowne said simply.[68]

Lansdowne was favourably impressed when he met Casement on 3 December. After hearing some of Casement's Congo experiences, he commented, 'Proof of the most painfully convincing kind, Mr Casement,'[69] and said that he would like to have the report written with all possible speed. Within two weeks, Casement, with a furious burst of energy, produced a sixty-one-page printed record of his journey up the Congo, complete with documentary evidence. It was a report which, according to E. D. Morel, was 'to brand a reigning sovereign, allied by family connections to half the courts of Europe, with indelible infamy: . . . [a] report which, finally and for all time, was to tear aside the veil from the most gigantic fraud and wickedness which our generation has known.'[70]

Yet the tone of Casement's report was much less inflammatory than expected. Much to the astonishment of those in the Foreign Office,

[66] Clarke's minute of 19 September 1904, FO 10/811. Jones was a director of the Elder Dempster shipping lines, whose steamers plied between Antwerp and the Congo under contract with the Congo Government.

[67] See Villiers's memoranda of 10 December 1903, FO 10/806, and 21 December 1903, FO 10/807; cf. Casement to Fox Bourne, Private and Confidential, 15 October 1904, Papers of the Aborigines Protection Society, Rhodes House, Oxford; and Slade, *English-Speaking Missions,* pp. 287–88.

[68] Lansdowne's minute on Villiers's memorandum of 10 December.

[69] Singleton-Gates and Girodias, *Black Diaries,* p. 183.

[70] From the unpublished history of the Congo Reform Association, Morel Papers.

the report submitted by Casement was 'terse, full of matter and written in a quite dispassionate style'[71]—'free from all trace of exaggeration', admitted F. H. Villiers, the Assistant Under-Secretary.[72] It described in a straightforward way how Africans in the Congo State were worked very hard and how they were constantly exposed to harsh, often cruel treatment. It was not a verbally scathing denunciation of the Congo administration; it was, above all, understated. And for this reason it carried conviction—so much conviction that E. D. Morel was inspired to write the following passage:

> Its moderation of language threw the facts recorded into the boldest relief. The effect of the report was cumulative. One rose from its perusal in a sweat of rage. There was a subtle quality about it which stirred profoundly all who read it, however fortified by tradition and training against emotion. Men have confessed to me that certain passages moved them to tears less by their eloquence than from the painful manner in which they vividly illumined and brought home the human effects of specific conditions.[73]

When Casement submitted his report to the Foreign Office in mid-December it was by no means a foregone conclusion that it would be published. The 4th Marquess of Salisbury pointed out that '[t]he publication will make a great noise in England. The only thing that makes me uncomfortable is the possibility that those wretched blacks will be still worse used in consequence of publication.'[74]

Following Salisbury's line of thought (and also King Leopold's), Lord Percy, the Parliamentary Under-Secretary, urged not that the report should be suppressed, but that it should be given confidentially to an 'International Commission' appointed for the purpose of investigating the Congo State's administration. The commissioners would have to be given 'the fullest facilities to carry out the investigation on the spot into the charges of atrocity'. If King Leopold would agree to this scheme, then the British government could delay publication of Casement's report until after the conclusions of the commissioners had reached the various governments. Percy believed that this would satisfy Parliament and that '[w]e should be adopting a tangible and logical course of action.'[75]

The arguments against Percy's proposal were overwhelming. If

[71] Farnall's minute of 22 December 1903, FO 10/807.
[72] Villiers's minutes of 28 December 1903, FO 10/807.
[73] From the unpublished history of the Congo Reform Association, Morel Papers.
[74] Salisbury to Lansdowne, 26 January 1904, FO 10/807.
[75] Villiers's memorandum of 21 December 1903, FO 10/807.

Casement's report were suppressed, there would be a general agitation both in the House of Commons and throughout the country for
immediate publication; it would be commonly believed that the British government condoned atrocities. Casement's visit to the Upper
Congo was unexpected; the visit of a commission would be anticipated
and every precaution would be taken not only to prevent its members
from seeing fresh evidence of maladministration and cruelty, but also
to prove—even out of the mouths of Casement's own witnesses—that
the British Consul had been deceived. It was exceedingly doubtful
that King Leopold would sanction a commission meeting the British
requirements; in fact, the past experiences of the Foreign Office with
King Leopold gave no assurance even that he was to be trusted. Last
—and most importantly for Casement personally—by agreeing to a
commission, the British government would indicate that Casement's
evidence was untrustworthy: 'Mr Casement would be on trial rather
than the Congo Government.'[76] Even Lord Percy finally concurred
that there was no course other than publication. At the end of January
1904, Lord Lansdowne noted, 'We are I think all agreed that Mr Casement's report must be laid.'[77]

There remained the question of editing, a far more important point
than might appear at first sight. There developed out of this question
the 'names controversy', which embittered Casement and left him
feeling that he had been betrayed by the Foreign Office. Casement
thought that his report should be published with the names of the witnesses who had given him evidence.[78] Farnall, who pleaded Casement's case more than once in Foreign Office disputes, pointed out
that since the journey covered a relatively small area, and since it was
well known where Casement went, withdrawing the names of the witnesses would not effectively screen them—they could be identified
anyway. Without names, Casement's report would be equivalent to an
anonymous communication, which the Congo authorities could dismiss as not deserving attention.[79] Without names, 'the report loses
thereby much of [the] conviction it might otherwise convey.'[80] Casement's insistence on publishing the report with names was opposed

[76] Percy's memorandum of 21 January 1904, FO 10/807; Broeker, 'Roger Casement'.

[77] Lansdowne's minute of [?] 28 January 1904, FO 10/807.

[78] Except the names of the European Congo officials: 'It has been a pain to me all the way
through to have to refer to these poor men by name' (Casement to Farnall, 4 January 1904,
FO 10/807).

[79] Farnall's memorandum of 13 January 1904, FO 10/807.

[80] Casement to FO, telegram, 7 February 1904, FO 10/807.

vigorously by the same person who had felt that the report should not be published at all, Lord Percy: 'To publish the names of native witnesses is manifestly to expose them to the risk of reprisals.'[81]

Casement, who had 'fled to Ireland'[82] in late December, was ignorant of the elaborate discussions concerning the pros and cons of publishing the names. Since it was his report, he thought that *he* should have the right to determine the form in which it would appear; he thought, in fact, that the matter had been settled in accordance with his views. When Villiers telegraphed him in early February[83] that the names had been suppressed, Casement bombarded the Foreign Office with telegrams and letters explaining why he thought the names were an essential part of the report. 'The report will cease to be a faithful record . . . you make the report absolute fiction and worthless . . . the timidity of not speaking out plainly will, instead of doing good, only do harm . . . I cannot urge more than I have done,' he wrote in despair. 'Could I make [my protests] . . . any stronger without impropriety from me in my position?'[84]

Regardless of how violently Casement might have insisted, there is no reason to assume that he could have altered the Foreign Office's decision to suppress the names. Clearing the air with a gust of common sense, Lord Salisbury wrote:

> [A]ll names should be suppressed both of tyrants and victims— of tyrants because the papers will involve charges which of course have not been legally proved, of victims because of the danger of vengeance.[85]

Lansdowne agreed with Salisbury.[86] The report was published on 12 February with letters and symbols substituted for names and places.[87]

---

[81] Percy's minute on Villiers to Percy, 12 January 1904, FO 10/807.

[82] Casement to Fox Bourne, 25 January 1904, Papers of the Aborigines Protection Society.

[83] Villiers to Casement, telegram, 5 February 1904, FO 10/807.

[84] Casement to Farnall, 11 Feb. 1904, FO 10/808.

[85] Salisbury's memorandum of 26 January 1904, FO 10/807.

[86] Lansdowne's minute of [?] 28 January 1904, FO 10/807: 'This course has its disadvantages, but the publication of the names of the natives would certainly be criticized adversely.'

[87] 'How weak this continuous twisting of letters is!' (Casement to Farnall, 20 February 1904, FO 10/808).

The following telegram from the British Minister in Brussels with Lansdowne's minute explains the final timing of the publication date: 'Please manage to prevent issue of report by Casement until after 10th instant, date on which I must unavoidably encounter King of the Belgians. The publication will inevitably put me in an awkward position at court' (Phipps to Barrington, private telegram, 5 February 1904, FO 10/807); Lansdowne: 'I think we should postpone laying

Casement sent an eighteen-page letter of protest to the Foreign Office:

> You have issued a cooked and garbled report. I am . . . a good deal
> disgusted at the whole thing—its obvious irresolution and futility
> and playing with a subject that calls for a clear thought-out plan.

> Ringing changes of the alphabet cannot produce the same effect as
> putting the alphabet to its right use; and in the present case in no
> one of the changes made has the locality been hidden while in many
> cases the identity of the individual is still quite clear to anyone with
> local knowledge . . . By suppressing evidences of sincerity and alter-
> ing dates (or suppressing them rather) and omitting names, the For-
> eign Office has certainly rendered the task of the Brussels people to
> confute me easier than it would otherwise have been . . . I cannot well
> continue to serve a department which has so little confidence in me
> and so little regard for my opinion as . . . to make such vital changes
> in face of my strong protest.

> It would seem to me that my resignation is called for.[88]

Casement did not resign, but his attitude towards the 'permanent
gang'[89] at the Foreign Office remained bitter. 'They are not worth
serving', he once wrote to Morel, 'and what sickens me is that I must
go back to them, hat in hand, despising them as I do, simply to be able
to live.'[90] Casement's private letters contain abusive descriptions of his
Foreign Office colleagues—remarks so scurrilous that at first sight his
choice of language scarcely seems reconcilable with his education and
experience. Among his milder exclamations is his opinion of A. J. Balfour as a 'cur . . . incapable of any honest or straightforward act of human sympathy'.[91] He referred to Villiers as an 'abject piffler', which,
however true, was hardly an expression of gratitude towards one who
protected him from the attacks of his arch-enemy, Sir Constantine
Phipps—for whom Casement reserved the choicest of his vituperative
epithets.

---

the Blue Book until the 11th so as to make quite sure that the King receives his copy before the
contents get out here' (Lansdowne's minute on Phipps's telegram).

[88] Casement to Farnall, 20 February 1904, FO 10/808. Consistency was not one of Casement's virtues. Within one month he completely reversed his views on the point on which he
threatened to resign, urging that the names of his witnesses should not be given to the Commission of Inquiry because of the danger of vengeance. See Villiers to Lansdowne, 13 April 1904,
FO 10/808.

[89] Casement to Morel, 15 March 1905, Morel Papers.

[90] Casement to Morel, 2 February 1905, Morel Papers; Costigan, 'The Treason of Sir Roger
Casement', p. 287.

[91] Casement to Morel, 12 April 1905, Morel Papers.

Roger Casement and Constantine Phipps were as different in background and experience as they were in outlook on life. Casement had entered the British consular service through the back door of Africa, as an Irish adventurer who wandered in more by chance than ambition. Phipps was a career diplomat. Casement was emotional, undisciplined, and radical; Phipps was sophisticated, affected, and conservative to the core. Casement saw the 'Congo evil . . . [as] a special and extraordinary evil'.[92] Phipps sympathized with the Belgians in their efforts to civilize tropical Africa. 'I certainly myself', Phipps wrote shortly after Casement's report had been published, 'was loath to believe that Belgians, members of a cultivated people amongst whom I had lived, could, under even a tropical sky, have perpetrated acts of refined cruelty and of systematic oppression.'[93] As British Minister in Brussels, Phipps was responsible for reporting the views of the Congo administration to his government. 'You must not . . . think me irreverent or disloyal', he wrote to Farnall, 'in relating to you these possibly pardonable criticisms [of Casement's report] on the part of the gibbeted administration! It would be useless for me to retort with platitudes which would render my position even harder than it is.'[94] Casement took an entirely different view, regarding Phipps as 'the complacent mouthpiece' of the Congo administration. This opinion, privately expressed, was not difficult to detect from Casement's official dispatches; and Phipps not unnaturally resented it.

> I was obliged . . . today to take up Casement's frequently renewed assumption . . . that I 'support' the Congo cause. Writing from this country it is very difficult for me to join, or appear to join, in the general cursing! I should have thought that obvious.[95]

The point on which Phipps and Casement finally broke into an open quarrel was the case of Epondo. Epondo's truncated limb was of major importance in Casement's report because it was the only genuine atrocity of which Casement had first-hand evidence; the Congo authorities, however, immediately declared the Epondo story a pure fabrication and obtained evidence certified by an American missionary that the boy's hand had been bitten off by a wild boar and that he had lied to Casement.[96] 'The Epondo question', Phipps reported, 'appears to cause them a bitter satisfaction.' Phipps genuinely believed

[92] Casement to Morel, Private and Confidential, 13 February 1904, Morel Papers.
[93] Phipps to Lansdowne, No. 25 Africa, Confidential, 27 February 1904, FO 10/773.
[94] Phipps to Farnall, Private, 14 February 1904, FO 10/807.
[95] Phipps to Villiers, Private, 12 June 1904, FO 10/810.
[96] See Phipps to Lansdowne, No. 9 Africa, 12 February 1904, FO 10/808.

that Casement had been duped by a 'trumped-up story' and that the
Epondo case was legitimately refuted. Casement, extremely sensitive
to criticism, retaliated by mentioning in a letter (which reached
Phipps's eyes) to Sir Eric Barrington, Lansdowne's Private Secretary,
that the British Minister in Brussels was 'making hay' with his report
in league with the Congo authorities. Phipps had suffered much
provocation from Casement, and this was the last straw. In an angry
dispatch to the Foreign Office, he attacked Casement's 'discourteous
and sarcastic' remarks.[97] Villiers asked Phipps to withdraw the letter,
and received the following reply:

> There is nothing offensive to Casement in it but I have an opportu-
> nity of repudiating the charge, distinctly brought against me, of join-
> ing with the Congo Secretary in an attack on an official report laid
> before Parliament which was a weak one and that very Epondo case
> has been thrown in my teeth here as invalidating his report. The
> want of tact exhibited in his letter to the Governor also furnished the
> Congo government with a weapon, and both rendered my position
> very difficult . . . I fully agree in your estimate of Casement's ability
> but I absolutely deny his tact or his judgment.[98]

Phipps's judgement on Casement's tact may be taken as a generalization valid for the Foreign Office as a whole.

Casement's feelings about Phipps were even stronger:

> Please goodness I shall go for Phipps some day—I am biding my
> time in his respect—but when I get an opening I shall not spare the
> cur. He is beneath contempt—but I'd like to lay that same contempt
> on with a good thick Irish blackthorn.[99]

Roger Casement was as repelled by Constantine Phipps and the officials of the Foreign Office as he was attracted to E. D. Morel and the
Congo reformers.

Sir Arthur Conan Doyle called the meeting of Roger Casement and
E. D. Morel the most 'dramatic scene in modern history'.[100] Morel
himself later described their meeting in December 1903 as 'one of
those rare incidents in life which leave behind them an imperishable
impression'.

[97] Phipps to Lansdowne, No. 31 Africa (changed to Phipps to Villiers, Private), 16 April, 1905,
FO 10/813.

[98] Phipps to Villiers, Private, 24 April 1905, FO 10/813.

[99] Casement to Morel, [?] April 1905, Morel Papers.

[100] *St James Budget*, 28 October 1910.

> I [Morel] often see him [in retrospect] . . . as I saw him at that memorable interview . . . As the monologue [of Casement's Congo experiences] proceeded . . . the scenes so vividly described seemed to fashion themselves out of the shadows before my eyes. The daily agony of an entire people unrolled itself in all the repulsive terrifying details. I verily believe I *saw* those hunted women clutching their children and flying panic-stricken to the bush; the blood flowing from those quivering black bodies as the hippopotamus hide whip struck and struck again; the savage soldiery rushing hither and thither amid burning villages; the ghastly tally of severed hands.[101]

Morel had left his job as clerk in Sir Alfred Jones's shipping firm to carry on, as editor of the *West African Mail*, his crusade against the abuses of colonialism in Africa.[102] He was eloquent but not elegant in expression, well-informed but (as Sir Harry Johnston used to taunt him) without first-hand experience of Africa. Energetic as well as zealous, his tenacity won him the endearing nickname of 'Bulldog' from Casement.[103] The two men's temperaments, in short, were remarkably similar.

Though Morel was in England and Casement in Africa, they arrived at the same conclusion about King Leopold's rule in Africa: it had resulted in an 'extraordinary invasion . . . of fundamental human rights' of the Congo peoples.[104] They also agreed on how this evil should be fought:

> To unite in one Body the various influences at work against Leopoldianism . . . ; to appeal to a wide public on a single issue; to incorporate all men whose hearts were touched, whatever their standing, profession, political opinion and religious beliefs, in a common aim — that was the task.[105]

Casement was by no means a wealthy man, but he was so impressed by Morel — 'he wins me and charms me by his constancy and courage'[106] — and above all by Morel's eagerness to agitate for Congo reform, that without hesitation he wrote Morel a cheque for £100 — one-third of his annual income — to cover expenses for the founding of a 'Congo Reform Association'.

[101] Unpublished history of the Congo Reform Association, Morel Papers.

[102] See F. Seymour Cocks, *E. D. Morel: The Man and His Work* (London, 1920).

[103] Morel called Casement 'Tiger', and their letters to each other often began with the salutation 'Dear Bulldog' or 'Dear Tiger'.

[104] Casement to Dilke, Private, 1 February 1904, Papers of the Aborigines Protection Society.

[105] Unpublished history of the Congo Reform Association, Morel Papers.

[106] Casement to Fox Bourne, 25 January 1904, Papers of the Aborigines Protection Society.

Casement conceived of the Congo Reform Association as a special instrument designed to unite all Britain against the Congo State: 'It was the unique character of the Congo wickedness . . . which called for the formation of a special body formulating a very special appeal to the humanity of England.'[107] The British government would not move until moved by public feeling throughout the country; if Britain were roused, then the world would follow. Britain was to lead the crusade, and at the head of the crusade was to be the Congo Reform Association.

'I am afraid we do not agree at all,' Sir Charles Dilke replied to Casement's proposals about the strategy of Congo reform. In Dilke's view, Britain was already united: 'We are here dealing with a unanimous Parliament and a unanimous press, and the only difficulty in our way is that the more unanimous we are, the more tendency there is in France, and possibly on the continent generally, to oppose this as a purely English movement.'[108] 'Congo Reform Associations' should be formed in France or the United States, where public feeling had not been touched by the Congo atrocities.[109] In Britain, the main result would be merely to 'bleed and kill' the Aborigines Protection Society by competing with it for funds.[110]

No doubt this was one of the uppermost considerations in Fox Bourne's mind when he refused to answer Morel's telegrams of February 1904, urging him to cooperate in the founding of the Congo Reform Association; but he also had other solid reasons for spurning Casement's and Morel's proposals. In the eyes of the public, the Congo Reform Association, however unjustifiably, would be regarded as a rival to the Aborigines Protection Society; there would be an inevitable waste of resources. Since the Congo Reform Association was being formed at Morel's home in Liverpool, the movement would be open to charges of being a tool of British commerce; Morel had, in fact, already caused the British agitation for Congo reform to be denounced as hypocritical by mischievously suggesting that the best solution to the Congo problem would be simply to partition central Africa among the Great Powers.[111] The 'reckless haste' with which the Congo Reform Association was being formed only strengthened Fox Bourne's doubts about Morel's judgement. He himself had worked with the Congo problem long before Morel had taken it up, Fox

---

[107] Unpublished history of the Congo Reform Association, Morel Papers.

[108] Dilke to Morel, Private, 28 January 1904 (copy), Papers of the Aborigines Protection Society.

[109] Dilke to Casement, 12 February 1904 (copy), Papers of the Aborigines Protection Society.

[110] Ibid.

[111] In *The British Case in the French Congo* (London, 1903).

Bourne wrote with marked bitterness, and now Morel expected him 'on the spur of the moment to bow to your decision and submit to your friendship'.[112]

As the 'pre-eminent'[113] Congo reformer, H. R. Fox Bourne was genuinely respected by E. D. Morel. 'It would be sad indeed if you stood aside entirely,' Morel wrote to him in one of his lengthy letters. 'I entirely repudiate the idea that the movement would supersede in any degree the A.P.S.'s work.'[114] With 'deep personal sorrow',[115] Morel learned that Fox Bourne would refuse to cooperate in the establishment of the reform association, and composed an effusive letter that could just as well have been written by a son determined to persevere in a course in which his father firmly disapproved:

> Do please put it out of your head that the C.R.A. is going to be rival to the A.P.S. The very idea is absurd, and if you are annoyed at the C.R.A., shoot at me, don't shoot at Casement. He is one of the finest fellows in the world, and is consumed with a passion for those wretched people, which is a noble trait, and one but rarely met with. Shoot at me. They all do. I am used to bullets. I shall always play the straight game with you, and I shall always tell you what I think, and shoot you ever so hard . . . far from interfering with you, it will help out the cause, which it is part of your society's work to take up, and which you have fought for, for so long.[116]

Casement had less respect for Fox Bourne and was not as nervous about his attitude towards the C.R.A. After learning that Morel was determined to persist despite Fox Bourne, Casement telegraphed Morel: 'You have done splendidly . . . Bourne's movement is absurd';[117] 'it is clear to me', he later wrote, 'that the true objective on Fox Bourne's part (and Dilke's too) is . . . jealousy on behalf of the A.P.S.'[118]

The main burden of Congo reform in Britain thus fell on the shoulders of E. D. Morel—'Poor unceasing, ever-toiling . . . E.D.M.!'[119] It was an enormous task. '[It] . . . presses solely on you,' Casement warned him. 'It is clear to me that you will get *no* real support from Fox

---

[112] Fox Bourne to Morel, 1 February 1904, Papers of the Aborigines Protection Society.

[113] Casement to Fox Bourne, Private and Confidential, 12 February 1904, Papers of the Aborigines Protection Society.

[114] Morel to Fox Bourne, 30 January 1904, Papers of the Aborigines Protection Society.

[115] Morel to Dilke, telegram, 1 February 1904, Papers of the Aborigines Protection Society.

[116] Morel to Fox Bourne, 7 March 1904, Papers of the Aborigines Protection Society.

[117] Casement to Morel, telegram, 1 February 1904, Morel Papers.

[118] Casement to Morel, Private and Confidential, 13 February 1904, Morel Papers.

[119] Ibid.

Bourne or Dilke. They will lend it a moral sanction, but no more.'[120] Nor could Casement himself be of any more assistance; as a public official, he could not openly be associated with the C.R.A. 'I think it is my duty to hold myself aloof as much as I can,' he wrote to Morel.[121] Casement was not present at the public birth of the C.R.A. on 23 March 1904. E. D. Morel stood alone, holding the sword that Casement had forged for him. Casement left the battle by admonishing him that 'the Gods of ill die hard'.[122]

After the publication of his report and the founding of the Congo Reform Association, Casement's role in the Congo controversy changed. As the Congo expert, he continued to submit lengthy memoranda to the Foreign Office on Congo questions; as the 'sleeping partner'[123] in the Congo Reform Association, he continued to counsel Morel, to raise funds, and to recruit members. But he was no longer a driving force in either institution. He followed the issues passionately, but he was little more than an adviser.

Casement's report and his establishment of the C.R.A. contributed greatly to the eventual downfall of the Leopoldian system and the annexation of the Congo by Belgium. Yet he was disappointed by the immediate results of his campaign. His report was widely commented on throughout the British press, yet *The Times* failed to produce a leading article on the Congo scandals. His greatest disappointment was with the Foreign Office, which refused to travel down the paths he had blazed. As he wrote to Dilke:

> I regret to say that I believe no further action is likely to be taken by the Foreign Office in the matter, and the reason intimated to me was that neither Parliament, nor the press of this country has displayed the slightest interest—and that the Foreign Office could not be expected to stir either up . . . The whole thing has fallen flat.[124]

Casement exaggerated the attitude of the Foreign Office towards Congo reform, just as he exaggerated the attitude of the Foreign Office officials towards himself. 'It is Villiers, Phipps and Co. who have got control of the Congo question', he wrote in September 1904, 'and they are now vindictive . . . They are sincerely sorry I was born.'[125] He

[120] Casement to Morel, 13 February 1904, Morel Papers.
[121] Casement to Morel, 9 March 1904, Morel Papers.
[122] Casement to Morel, 24 March 1904, Morel Papers.
[123] Fox Bourne to Morel, 10 March 1904, Morel Papers.
[124] Casement to Dilke, Private, 4 May 1904, Papers of the Aborigines Protection Society.
[125] Casement to Morel, 8 September 1904, Morel Papers.

felt that he was being persecuted by the Foreign Office as well as by the Congo State.

Casement was an extraordinarily vain man. After his denunciation of the Congo administration, he could but expect that the Congo authorities would reciprocate by denouncing him. Yet he was stung not only by the pompous, silly articles of a Congophile named Lauzun-Brown—who wrote of Casement 'as a very superior person might write about a black beetle' [126]—but also by even faint suggestions in the press that he had perhaps been a 'too enthusiastic observer' [127] during his Congo journey. 'These wretched attacks on poor old you and poor old me', he wrote to Morel in one of his windy letters filled with self-pity, this one in reference to the articles appearing in the *Liverpool Journal of Commerce,* one of the very few British organs to plead the Congo State's case.

> They [the Foreign Office] shove me into the forefront, bitterly against my will—promising, too, that they would . . . stick up for me —and then they slink off and leave me exposed to vulgar abuses and openly expressed contempt . . . This they could easily have prevented . . . no finger has been lifted to back me up—no breath of half a voice to affirm their knowledge of my good faith and worth—not a syllable—only an ostentatious washing of their hands of as much responsibility for my report as they could wash off.

The Foreign Office had 'practically handed me over, defenceless, their own Consul, their own agent, their own mouthpiece, to be the world-wide butt of the very man [King Leopold] they publicly accused'.[128]

Through most of 1904 and 1905, the Foreign Office suspended action, though not judgement, on the Congo State, pending the outcome of King Leopold's Commission of Inquiry. There was never any suspension of judgement on Casement's work or ability; even Phipps admitted that Casement was an able man. Casement was unpopular at work, but there was no conspiracy against him. The Foreign Office did not defend him for the simple reason that the Congo government had not officially challenged his personal qualifications;[129] by not

[126] *Morning Post,* 19 July 1904.
[127] Casement to Morel, 8 September 1904, Morel Papers.
[128] Casement to Morel, 15 March 1905, Morel Papers.
[129] 'It is obvious that we cannot enter the arena with these people of whose misrepresentations Mr Casement complains [in reference to the articles appearing in the *Catholic Herald*] . . . I do not think we can do more than tell Mr Casement we are much obliged for his communications which will certainly provide us with ample material for reply should an *official* representation ever be addressed to us' (Clarke's minute on Casement to Lansdowne, 9 October 1905, FO 10/815, initialled by Campbell, Percy, and Lansdowne).

expressing publicly an opinion on his competence, the Office silently demonstrated the confidence in him that Casement longed to have proclaimed from the rooftops. Lord Edmond Fitzmaurice's defence of Casement in Parliament in 1906 was a highly unusual occurrence and a great compliment,[130] but one interpreted by Casement as a long overdue tribute: 'I am glad that after so long one Foreign Office official has had the decency to say publicly what they all had to believe in private.'[131]

During this lull in the Congo controversy of 1904–06, Casement was a Consul without a post, a desperate man, emotionally perturbed and financially in debt.[132] 'My own people have no inkling that I am hard up,' he wrote to Morel after he had been forced through illness to resign his new post in Lisbon. So filled with despair was Casement that he responded favourably to Morel's astonishing proposal that he return to the Congo to conduct an 'independent investigation' for the C.R.A.:

> Of course I realize fully the difficulties—not to say the dangers of the course in view—but frankly, it is *far* better than idling and eating my heart out—at least if I die out there I am doing something.[133]

> Once in Angola I could get away from the Coast quickly enough and could land up on Kasai where no one would know me.[134]

> [They might] hang me as they did Stokes—and one couldn't do better than be hanged in order to end that den of devils.[135]

The Congo journey remained a fantasy, for in August 1906 Casement received a consular assignment in South America. He never returned to Africa, and his role in the Congo controversy was reduced to occasional letters to Morel. With the annexation of the Congo by Belgium in 1908 and the death of King Leopold in 1909, Casement clearly recognized that 'the break-up of the pirate's stronghold [is] nearly

---

[130] '[A] deserved tribute of respect to an eminent British civil servant . . . Mr Casement had an exceedingly difficult task . . . That gentleman has been the object of many unjust attacks' (*The Times*, 4 July 1906).

[131] Casement to Morel, 24 January 1906, Morel Papers.

[132] See Broeker, 'Roger Casement'.

[133] Casement to Morel, Private, 16 July 1906, Morel Papers.

[134] Casement to Morel, 17 July 1906, Morel Papers.

[135] Casement to Morel, 4 July 1906, Morel Papers.

accomplished'.[136] 'The Congo reform movement is dead,' he wrote to Morel in June 1912.

> Its work is done—so far as the public interest and political effort to attain the public will are concerned. The Congo reconstruction movement has come—and that is necessarily a Belgian work—one in which you can scarcely take any part—no active part. You may influence Belgian minds still for good—but there is no *fight* to be fought there for you . . . The C.R.A. should quit the field with dignity and with no denunciation on its lips.[137]

The Congo Reform Association was disbanded on 16 June 1913, ten years from the time when Roger Casement had chartered a small mission steamer to carry him to the upper Congo.

E. D. Morel once commented with considerable understatement that Roger Casement was no ordinary Foreign Office official.[138] What distinguished Casement from the career diplomats like Phipps—and even the career humanitarians like Fox Bourne—was his apocalyptic vision of evil in the Congo. Like an enfrenzied prophet, Casement returned from the Congo in 1903 to preach the gospel of Congo reform, and it is perhaps the greatest indication of his ability that he could bridle his stormy emotions to produce a disciplined and restrained report that won over the Foreign Office as well as most of the British public. With his impressionable and talented disciple Morel, he founded the Congo Reform Association to turn the diplomatic skirmishes begun by the Foreign Office into an all-out humanitarian war. Neither the 'ineffective squibs' of the Foreign Office[139] nor the 'milk and water methods' of the Aborigines Protection Society could vanquish the enemy in the proper way: to seize King Leopold 'by the throat and choke him off as a "helldog" is choked off'.[140] Casement conceived of the founding of the Congo Reform Association as the beginning of a crusade that would end with the walls of the Leopoldian system crumbling before the trumpets of Congo reform; even during the dark days of 1905, when he felt 'practically ruined . . . [by] the Evil One',[141] Casement never lost his revelation that the forces of

---

[136] Casement to Morel, 13 June 1912, Morel Papers.

[137] Ibid.

[138] Unpublished history of the Congo Reform Association, Morel Papers.

[139] See Clarke's minute on Casement's telegram of 15 September 1903, FO 10/805.

[140] Casement to Morel, 4 January 1907, Morel Papers.

[141] Casement to Morel, 14 December 1904, Morel Papers.

righteousness and justice would prevail—'all will work out straight and white and clear'.[142] Casement and Morel were Manichaeans: they saw the world as a struggle between oppressors and oppressed, between the powers of darkness and light, between the forces of evil and good. As Casement expressed it in his simple formula to Morel, 'Leopold = Hades = Hell'.[143] Whether he was right or wrong, Roger Casement did more than any other person to convince the world that King Leopold had created a hell on earth in the Congo.

Journal of African History   1964

[142] Casement to Morel, 15 December 1904, Morel Papers.
[143] Casement to Morel, 21 August 1906, Morel Papers.

5

E. D. MOREL AND THE TRIUMPH
OF THE CONGO REFORM ASSOCIATION

A sort of gale is at present blowing upon the Congo State. This gale
has come from England.

M. Woeste in the Belgian Parliament, 1906[1]

I am convinced that when the whole story of the Congo has passed
into history the Belgian people will feel that the work of the Congo
Reform Association was a work of friendship and enlightenment in
their behalf.

Sir Roger Casement, 1913[2]

The paramount issues in the 'Congo controversy' of the early
twentieth century were constitutional government versus what
might be described euphemistically as benevolent despotism,
and colonial development for the benefit of the Congo versus exploitation of the Congo for the benefit of Belgium. The crucial years
of this controversy were 1905–08, between the time of the publication
of the report of King Leopold's Commission of Inquiry in November
1905 and the annexation of the Congo in November 1908. During this
period, the British movement for Congo reform reached full strength
and contributed greatly, even decisively, towards Belgium's momentous annexation of the Congo. The acceptance of colonial responsibility was perhaps the most important decision made by a Belgian government since the separation from Holland in 1830. For the Congo,
annexation was no less momentous: it marked the passing of the Leopoldian regime.

The outstanding feature of Leopold's rule in the Congo was an
anachronistic despotism. In an age of constitutional monarchs, his
critics frequently pointed out, the Sovereign of the Congo State could
say with more justification than Louis XIV, '*L'état, c'est moi.*'[3]

As criticism of his '*oeuvre Africaine*' grew, along with his dividends, as
he acquired the epithet '*le Roi Bâtisseur*' because of public works built
in Belgium with Congo funds, Leopold became less and less patient
with those who doubted his good faith, and more and more authori-

---

[1] *Annales Parlementaires, Chambre,* 27 February 1906.

[2] Casement to E. D. Morel, 11 June 1913, Morel Papers, London School of Economics; quotations from the Morel Papers by permission of the Librarian.

[3] Arthur Hardinge, *A Diplomatist in Europe* (London, 1927), p. 198; see also F. Cattier, *Étude
sur la situation de l'état indépendant du Congo* (Brussels, 1906), pp. 324–27; E. Vandervelde, *Souve-
nirs d'un Militant Socialist* (Paris, 1939), pp. 70–71; and Jean Stengers, *Belgique et Congo: L'Élabo-
ration de la Charte Coloniale* (Brussels, 1963), pp. 27–29.

tarian, perhaps not in his capacity as constitutional monarch of Belgium, but certainly in his role as Sovereign of the Congo State. As the personification of Belgian patriotism, he intended to transform the Congo into a Belgian colony; but as the revenues of the Congo State increased, he became less inclined to hand over his African empire. Why did he finally yield? In the period 1905–08 the Congo State was nearly wrecked on the shoals of public opinion. Leopold, the navigator, saw that the greatest danger was Great Britain. As E. D. Morel, the secretary of the Congo Reform Association, prophesied: '[I]f the British Government stands firm—the "Congo Free State" slaveship will break in pieces, and disappear beneath the waves of public execration.'[4]

The Congo reform movement (though it had its foreign counterparts) was essentially a British enterprise. The anti-Congo campaign was begun in the mid-1890s by the secretary of the Aborigines Protection Society, H. R. Fox Bourne, at a time when Europe and America were oblivious of what he called the 'Civilization in Congo-land';[5] it was ended two decades later, in 1913, by Morel, five years after the European powers and the United States began to regard the Congo controversy as a dead issue. On the basis of missionary reports and articles in the Belgian press, Fox Bourne and Morel (then editor of the *West African Mail*)[6] protested the system of commercial monopolies and the alleged cruelty to Africans in the Congo State—which in their eyes violated the two main premises of the Berlin Act of 1885: free trade and the protection of the indigenous population. The indignation at the 'Congo atrocities' stirred up by Fox Bourne and Morel had concrete results in March 1903, when the House of Commons passed a resolution 'to abate the evils' in the Congo.[7]

In accordance with the resolution, the British government on 8 August 1903 dispatched a circular on the alleged abuses in the Congo to the powers signatory to the Berlin Act.[8] From June to September of the same year, the British Consul in the Congo, Roger Casement, travelled in the interior of the Congo State.[9] The publication of his report in February 1904,[10] followed in March by the founding of

[4] *Official Organ of the Congo Reform Association*, August 1907.

[5] This was the title of his book published in London in 1903.

[6] For Morel's background as journalist, see F. Seymour Cocks, *E. D. Morel: The Man and His Work* (London, 1920), chap. 2.

[7] *Parliamentary Debates*, 132, 20 May 1903, col. 1304; on this debate, see Arthur Berriedale Keith, *The Belgian Congo and the Berlin Act* (Oxford, 1919), p. 131.

[8] No. 14 Africa (1903), *Accounts and Papers*, 62.

[9] See W. R. Louis, 'Roger Casement and the Congo', *Journal of African History*, 5 (1964), pp. 99–120.

[10] No. 1 Africa (1904), *Accounts and Papers*, 62.

Morel's Congo Reform Association (which in a few months included as members ten peers and over forty members of Parliament), marked an important point in the Congo reform campaign. 'No one reading this report', commented the conservative *Morning Post* (15 February 1904), 'can come to any other conclusion than that the system in force in King Leopold's kingdom rests on the enslavement of the native population.'[11]

Casement's report temporarily united the British public,[12] but by the end of 1904 the British agitation for Congo reform had subsided. According to one of the stalwart defenders of the Congo State, James J. Harrison (whom Casement once described as an 'addle-pated dwarf impresario'),[13] 'public opinion has veered round and begun to doubt the truth of all these countless atrocities.'[14] One reason for the temporary eclipse of the Congo reform movement was the reply by the Congo government to Casement's report.[15] The strength of Casement's inquiry—the reason it carried conviction—was his minute description of specific examples of maladministration, such as the one of the Congolese boy named Epondo, whose right hand, Casement reported, had been hacked off because of failure to fulfil a rubber quota. The Epondo case was of singular importance in Casement's report because it was the only atrocity that Casement had the opportunity to investigate personally.[16] When the Congo authorities in their reply produced evidence certified by an American missionary that Epondo had lied to Casement and that Epondo's hand had been bitten off by a wild boar, many Englishmen began to doubt the validity of other parts of his account.

There were other reasons for the waning of the reform agitation in late 1904. In December, Morel was temporarily discredited by an officer in the Congo State service, an unscrupulous Italian named Benedetti, whose disclosures that the Congo Reform Association had tried to bribe him gave the erroneous impression, according to the *Morning Post* (12 May 1905), that Morel was 'a suborner of witnesses and an

[11] Quotations from newspapers are from lead articles unless otherwise indicated.

[12] 'Nothing, indeed, is more remarkable in the movement for the reform of the Congo administration than the absolute unanimity with which the demand is advanced and supported by every section of public opinion in the country . . . Government and people are at one in demanding that an end shall be put to a state of things which recalls the worst days of the Spanish conquests in the new world' (*Morning Post*, 10 June 1904).

[13] Casement to Morel, n.d. (? May 1905), Morel Papers.

[14] Harrison to *The Times*, 1 October 1904.

[15] No. 7 Africa (1904), *Accounts and Papers*, 62.

[16] See Casement to Farnall, 20 February 1904, FO 10/808, in which Casement elaborates on circumstances concerning his report and protests against the Foreign Office's 'editing'.

atrocity monger caught red-handed in . . . his trade'.[17] At the same time, the Federation for the Protection of Belgian Interests Abroad, supported by such prominent Englishmen as Sir Alfred Jones and Sir Hugh Gilzean Reid, increased its attacks against the anti-Congo movement, alleging that the motives of King Leopold's British critics were 'if not the secret political ambitions of the British Government, at least the thinly veiled covetousness of the merchants of Liverpool, who look on the Congo as an easy prey'.[18] Between the accusations and counter-accusations of the association and the federation, even the most astute, impartial student of the Congo controversy could not ascertain the truth; as *The Times* complained on 25 January 1905, '[N]o one can have perused the voluminous correspondence on the Subject . . . without a certain feeling of hopelessness as to the utterly contradictory nature of the evidence given.'

The founders of the Congo Reform Association, Casement and Morel, were absolutely convinced of the justice of their cause. Moved by an apocalyptic vision of evil in the Congo, they set out in 1904 to organize a crusade 'with one clear, sole, determined end—namely to free the Congo people': 'They, poor beings, are being treated in a way in which no other human race on this earth is being treated—their case is a special one—their need an appalling one.'[19] Casement, as a civil servant, could not participate publicly in the Congo reform movement. As the 'sleeping partner' in the Congo Reform Association,[20] he was restricted, after 1904, to advising Morel.

Morel was a man of marked intelligence and prodigious energy who once, while organizing the association, wrote four hundred letters in ten days. He was an exceptionally gifted propagandist, able to persuade rationally as well as to excite emotionally. His contribution to the anti-Congo campaign was much more than rabble-rousing and tub-thumping. While Fox Bourne attacked the atrocities in the Congo, Morel attacked the system of administration that he believed inevitably led to atrocities. Morel saw the root of the Leopoldian system in the denial of the Africans' right to the land and its produce. In the words of one of the prominent figures of the reform movement, Sir Charles Dilke: 'You showed us that all depended upon the right of the original black inhabitants of the soil to own their property and carry

[17] For a different interpretation of the Benedetti affair, see F. Masoin, *Histoire de l'État Indépendant du Congo* (2 vols., Namur, Belgium, 1912), I, p. 143.

[18] *Morning Post,* 12 May 1905.

[19] Casement to Fox Bourne, 25 January 1904, Papers of the Aborigines Protection Society, Rhodes House, Oxford.

[20] Fox Bourne to Morel, 10 March 1904, Morel Papers.

on trade.'[21] As Morel wrote in *Red Rubber,* his most famous and widely read work, the Congo State's administration was based on the principle that 'the rubber which grows in the forest does not belong to the native. It belongs to King Leopold!'[22] The Africans were compelled to pay taxes. Since they had no means to pay, they were forced to work for the state (or the concessionaire companies) and to collect for its benefit the rubber and other forest produce as 'taxes in kind': 'So he [Leopold] claimed the labor of the people to bring him their wealth which he has pirated.'[23] The Congo government, as far as Morel was concerned, was a mere commercial enterprise, whose slogan might be expressed as, 'No rubber, no profit; no compulsion, no rubber'.[24] The result, Morel wrote in 1906, was that 'the "Congo Free State" has long ceased to exist . . . It has given place to a political monster and international outlaw . . . The reek of its abominations mounts to Heaven in fumes of shame. It pollutes the earth. Its speedy disappearance is imperative for Africa, and for the world.'[25]

In Belgium, Casement's report and the denunciations of the Congo State were received with almost universal scepticism. Leopold was at the zenith of his power. By everyone except the radicals and socialists, whose attacks he dismissed as contemptuously as he did those by British humanitarians, the commercial prosperity of the Congo State was admired throughout Belgium. The clerical government, devoting all its energies to preventing the advance of socialism, therefore allowed Leopold a free hand in the Congo. Belgium was ruled by a triumvirate: Leopold; Woeste, the leader of the ultraclerical, ultraconservative majority of the Belgian Parliament; and de Smet de Naeyer, the Prime Minister, through whose eminent financial ability were administered the sovereign's grandiose public-works projects.

Outwardly, Leopold's position was impregnable; nevertheless, the British anti-Congo campaign had a profound effect on his rule. His response to the indictment of the Casement report was to appoint, in July 1904, a Commission of Inquiry, the purpose of which, at least in the opinion of the Congo reformers, was to placate the Foreign Office. Leopold feared that the British might succeed in persuading the other powers to intervene in the Congo; the appointment of the Commission of Inquiry was a move to check this possibility; in Casement's view it was 'not intended and *never was intended* to find out anything

[21] Dilke to Morel, 6 February 1908, Dilke Papers, British Museum Add. Mss. 43917.
[22] E. D. Morel, *Red Rubber* (New York, 1906), p. 204.
[23] Ibid.
[24] *Morning Post,* 23 March 1904.
[25] Morel, *Red Rubber,* pp. 212–13.

detrimental to the Congo Government's interests'.[26] In Belgium, however, the appointment of the commission was interpreted as a genuine attempt by Leopold to sift the facts and arrive at the truth—to stifle his British critics by proving that their charges were false. Even those in the Congo government itself took the commission seriously: 'They express such confidence in the honesty of their commission', Sir Constantine Phipps, the British Minister in Brussels, reported, 'that I cannot believe any tricks will be played with the evidence.'[27] The commissioners, de Schumacher (Swiss), Janssens (Belgian), and Nisco (Italian) were suspected in Britain of having Congophile tendencies, but they were accepted nevertheless as men of integrity who would try to reach an impartial judgement. Only the Congo Reform Association regarded the commission as an utter farce.[28] Morel charged that its purpose was merely to soothe public opinion, and it did have this effect. The Foreign Office, as well as most of the British press, suspended judgement on Leopold's Congo, pending the commission's report.[29]

Leopold fully recognized the dangers of a censorious report from his own commissioners.[30] He attempted to diminish its impact in the same way that he had tried futilely to suppress the Casement report,[31] by striking a bargain with the Foreign Office. Leopold's agent in these negotiations was his Consul for the Congo State at Liverpool, Sir Alfred Jones.

Jones was the leading English opponent of the Congo reformers—in Casement's view, a 'poisonous serpent', 'a bold and original liar'.[32] In the eyes of his critics, he was the British equivalent of Leopold on a lesser scale, a curious mixture of patriot, philanthropist, and pirate. Even the Congophobe *Morning Post* admitted that Jones was 'a man respected in many walks of public life' (17 December 1904). He was president of the Liverpool Chamber of Commerce as well as Consul

---

[26] Casement to Fox Bourne, Private and Confidential, 15 October 1904, Papers of the Aborigines Protection Society (Casement's emphasis).

[27] Phipps to Campbell, Private, 30 September 1904, FO 10/811.

[28] See, for example, Morel's letter to the *Morning Post*, 21 March 1905.

[29] See, for example, *The Times*, 6 November 1905, and *Official Organ*, November 1905.

[30] See especially J. Stengers, 'Le Rôle de la Commission d'Enquête de 1904–5 au Congo', *Annuaire de l'Institut de Philologie et d'Histoire Orientales et Slaves: Mélanges Henri Gregoire*, 10 (1950), pp. 701–26.

[31] See F. H. Villiers's memos of 10 December 1903, FO 10/806, and 21 December 1903, FO 10/807; Casement to Fox Bourne, Private and Confidential, 15 October 1904, Papers of the Aborigines Protection Society; and Ruth Slade, *English-Speaking Missions in the Congo Independent State, 1878–1908* (Brussels, 1959), pp. 287–88.

[32] Jones as serpent: Casement to Morel, 14 December 1904, Morel Papers; lying 'is his chief asset in the game of life': Casement to Morel, 2 November 1905, Morel Papers.

for the Congo State; the latter position enabled him, in his own words, 'to promote the interests of civilization, good government, sanitation, and development of British commercial interests [in the Congo]'.[33] Under a contract with the Congo government, Jones's African Steamship Company (a subsidiary of the Elder Dempster Company) enjoyed a monopoly on the traffic between Belgium and the Congo. The head of a prominent Liverpool trading concern, John Holt (from whom the Congo Reform Association received much of its financial backing)[34] charged that Jones's 'steamers are employed in carrying the blood-stained rubber of the Congo to Antwerp'. Jones, in brief, was accused widely, in the words of an anonymous critic, of being the unprincipled agent of 'an enterprise piratical rather than commercial'.[35]

When goaded into public apology for his association with the Congo State, he emphasized the difficulties of introducing both trade and civilization into tropical Africa. The *London Star* commented, with an acumen valid for other Congophiles:

> Sir Alfred feels his position acutely. It is not a nice position. It is, as he says, a position of considerable odium . . . he ventures to hope that nobody who knows him would believe him to be callous or cruel, or capable of indifference to human suffering. That is true. His fault is less valiant. It is his moral patience which displeases his friends. It is his Christian tolerance which vexes them. It is his power of extenuating the crimes of others which saddens them. It is his ability to forgive wrongs done to others which saddens them.[36]

Jones, like the British Minister in Brussels, Phipps, believed that the best way to achieve reform in the Congo was to cooperate with Congo government:

> I have preferred to work in the way which seemed best to me for the maintenance of good relations between Belgium and England, and for the reform of the Congo administration, and I shall not rest satisfied until my efforts meet with complete success. As to the consulship, I will not retain this one day beyond the time when I

[33] Jones's statement to the Liverpool Chamber of Commerce, 29 October 1907, quoted in *Official Organ,* November 1907.

[34] See, for example, Casement to Morel, 12 May 1905, Morel Papers. Full evidence of Holt's support of the Congo Reform Association may be found in numerous letters from Holt to Morel in the Morel Papers. Holt himself had no financial interests in the Congo State but had suffered heavy losses in the French Congo. See E. D. Morel, *The British Case in French Congo* (London, 1903).

[35] Viator to *Morning Post,* 28 June 1906.

[36] Quoted in *Official Organ,* November 1907.

discover that I cannot use it for the good interests of humanity in that region.[37]

There is no reason to believe that Jones was insincere in his wish for Congo reform, but his financial connections with the Congo government made it difficult for him to persuade others of the purity of his motives (a position similar to Leopold's) and left him vulnerable to charges of being representative of the 'money-grubbing commercial spirit of the day'.[38]

Jones approached the Foreign Office in September 1905 with the following proposal: a British syndicate under his direction should take over the Anglo-Belgian India Rubber Company (ABIR),[39] the concessionaire company in the Congo most notorious for abuses. The company's territories extended over 30,000 square miles (around 60 per cent the size of England) in the Equator district of the Congo State; the concession amounted to a monopoly on the entire trade in the area and included the right to collect a tax from the Africans, payable in rubber through forced labour. Jones's proposal was that the administration would be entirely in the hands of Englishmen; the only role of the Congo government would be to provide an armed force for protection. In return, a yearly sum would be paid to the Congo government and a share of the profits would be given to the company until it was compensated for the loss of its concession. Jones was willing to accept Leopold's offer if he had the 'approval of the Foreign Office'.[40]

'This is a very puzzling question,' wrote Lord Lansdowne, the Foreign Secretary. On the one hand, if the concession were rejected, Britain would be criticized for failing to grasp an opportunity for remedying abuses to which the British themselves had constantly called attention. On the other hand, if a British syndicate were to take over the concession with the approval of the Foreign Office, the British government would incur definite responsibilities, 'some of which may be of a very inconvenient kind'.

It will not be possible for a syndicate formed in London to transform the administration by a stroke of the pen. Many of the present

[37] Jones's statement to Liverpool Chamber of Commerce 29 October 1907, quoted in *Official Organ,* November 1907.

[38] Casement to Morel, 25 April 1905, Morel Papers.

[39] The name is misleading. Although founded in part by British capital, control had passed into Belgian hands; the Congo State itself owned half the shares.

[40] F. H. Villiers's memorandum of 8 September 1905, FO 10/814. Jones's proposals on behalf of Leopold were made orally and are recorded in this memo. On 7 October the scheme was submitted to the Foreign Office in writing; See FO 10/815; cf. Slade, *English-Speaking Missions,* pp. 294–95.

local agents, natives and Europeans, will have to be retained, and unless they 'change their spots' very rapidly, we shall have complaints of cruelty, exaction, etc., for which we, and not the Belgian Government, will be held accountable.[41]

Other officials in the Foreign Office agreed:

The Belgians would watch our proceedings with an exceedingly critical eye, and exaggerate with joy any failures.[42]

Where a syndicate of Liverpool merchants have once tasted the sweets of 50 per cent, what prospect is there that they will voluntarily forgo these for the sake of the Congo native?[43]

'I cannot help doubting', Lansdowne said, 'whether the offer is not merely a clever move on the part of the Congo government intended to discount the report of the Commission [of Inquiry], and to place us in an embarrassing position.'[44] The Foreign Office refused to become entangled in Leopold's concession scheme.[45]

Jones handled these negotiations with an agility, not to say duplicity, worthy of his royal patron. When he approached the Foreign Office in September 1905, he was eager to accept Leopold's proposal: it was an attractive offer financially; apparently he was genuinely anxious 'to benefit the natives';[46] and he could hardly afford to offend Leopold, who might cancel his profitable steamer contract. A month later, however, Jones had altered his views: '[He] is now equally eager to obtain our assistance in backing out of it.'[47] The British syndicate scheme had been received hostilely in the British press;[48] and Jones had completely failed to gain the cooperation of the British missionaries in

[41] Lansdowne's minute of 10 September 1905, FO 10/814.

[42] Villiers's minute of 8 September 1905, FO 10/814.

[43] F. A. Campbell's minute of 11 October 1905, FO 10/815.

[44] Lansdowne's minute 10 September 1905, FO 10/814.

[45] For this decision, see E. A. W. Clarke's memorandum of 11 October 1905, minuted by F. A. Campbell and Lansdowne, FO 10/815.

[46] Villiers's minute of 8 September 1905, FO 10/814.

[47] Clarke's memorandum of 11 October 1905, FO 10/815.

[48] 'Doubtless King Leopold would have been prepared to admit a British syndicate into the ABIR territories if he could thereby have secured the continuance of his system in the rest of the Congo State. We are not at all sure, however, that the Sovereign of the Congo State will be pleased with Sir Alfred Jones's candid avowal that the syndicate would enjoy the exclusive right to all trade. Hitherto this has been disguised as the right of the state to the products of the soil on vacant lands. Now monopoly in trade emerges naked and unashamed' (*Morning Post*, 28 November 1905).

the ABIR region.[49] Steering between the Scylla of Leopold and the Charybdis of the British public, Jones decided that Leopold's concessionaire company was not worth the price of British condemnation. The Foreign Office's refusal to approve the scheme enabled him to save face with Leopold. The British syndicate project foundered along with Leopold's attempt to divert attention from the Commission of Inquiry report, which was released in November 1905.[50]

The *Manchester Guardian* (7 November 1905) interpreted the report as 'a complete vindication of those who have carried on a ceaseless agitation for investigation and reform'. The *Morning Post* (13 December 1905) called it 'one of the most damning indictments levelled at any government in modern times'. Yet on the surface the report was euphemistic, lavish in praise of Leopold's civilizing work in Africa and quick in defence of European officers of the Congo State accused of mutilating Africans. Casement himself, no doubt surprised that the report was less of a whitewash than he had expected, described it as 'a *very* queer production . . . I call it a series of half-truths each followed by its qualifying whole untruth!'[51] Casement's own report had been descriptive; it had not attempted to judge explicitly the good and bad features of the administration. It had shown through specific examples merely that Africans in the Congo State were forced to work hard, were often inadequately remunerated, and were frequently treated cruelly. By contrast, the Commission of Inquiry report was a lengthy, analytical (though in some places naive)[52] exegesis on good and bad colonial administration. The specific examples mentioned by the commissioners were given merely to substantiate their theories, not to create an impression of maladministration. The commissioners argued that forced labour was necessary and justified, but they objected to the brutal ways in which the Africans were compelled to collect rubber—the taking of hostages, the detention of chiefs, and the employment of sentries (armed Africans employed as overseers). They admitted as a 'most legitimate' principle the state's claim to all 'unoccupied and vacant lands'; but they concluded that 'over-restrictive interpretations and over-severe applications' of this principle had resulted in the administration's arrogating to itself nearly all

[49] See Jones's correspondence with Grattan Guinness of the Regions Beyond Missionary Union in *Morning Post,* 28 November 1905; Slade, *English-Speaking Missions,* pp. 294–96.

[50] 'The King was only waiting for Sir Alfred Jones's answer to authorize the issue of the report of the Commission of Inquiry' (Clarke's minute of 11 October 1905, FO 10/815). The report was published in *Bulletin Officiel de l'État Indépendant du Congo,* 1905, pp. 135–285.

[51] Casement to Morel, 18 November 1905, Morel Papers.

[52] See Stengers, 'Le Rôle de la Commission d'Enquête;' Cattier, *Étude sur la situation,* pp. 15–17; and A. Stenmans, *La Reprise du Congo par le Belgique* (Brussels, 1949), pp. 297–306.

the land and monopolizing the 'fruits of the soil'. This was the point that Morel was so fond of making: '[T]he root of the evil [will remain] untouched . . . till the native of the Congo becomes once more owner of his land and of the produce which it yields.' [53]

The Commission of Inquiry report proved conclusively to Belgians and Englishmen alike that abuses existed in the Congo. It vindicated the Congo reform movement, which gained strength not only in Britain but also on the Continent: 'the volume of disinterested opinion . . . all over western Europe is now rising in arms against the atrocities of a monstrous regime.' [54] In France, the Congo State was denounced by Anatole France and Pierre Mille.[55] In Italy, the Congo administration was discredited by disclosures that sums of money were given to certain newspapers to publish 'letters, articles and news in favour of the Congo Free State' and by adverse reports from Italian officers in the Congo service.[56] Most importantly, in Belgium itself Professor Cattier published a book called *Étude sur la situation de l'état indépendant du Congo,* in which he cogently argued as an acknowledged colonial expert that it was a 'fundamental error' to admit that the finances of a colony should be devoted to anything other than its exclusive development. 'Cattier's book is a great assistance to our cause,' Sir Charles Dilke wrote.[57]

The Belgian Parliament debated Congo affairs in February and March 1906. Emile Vandervelde, the leader of the socialist party, called on the members of all parties as patriots and humanitarians to reform the Congo administration:

> I ask you to forget the links which bind you . . . and to cling, above all, to that which your conscience dictates to you. In presence of facts denounced by all ministers of Christianity, Protestant and Catholic, you have no right to remain impassive, and to wash your hands of the blood which has been shed.[58]

Vandervelde denounced the 'reform commission' appointed by Leopold to consider the recommendations of the Commission of Inquiry. The reform commission was composed of fourteen members, seven of whom were officials of the Congo State, and one an administrator of the ABIR: 'It is precisely as though one called in a slave trader

---

[53] Morel's interview in *Morning Post,* 4 June 1907. For his immediate reaction to the Commission of Inquiry report, see *Official Organ,* November 1905.

[54] *Manchester Guardian,* 22 February 1906.

[55] See Pierre Mille, *Le Congo Léopoldien* (Paris, 1905).

[56] See *Morning Post,* 13 June 1905.

[57] Dilke to Lord Fitzmaurice (fragment), 16 February 1906, Dilke Papers.

[58] *Annales Parlementaires, Chambre,* 20 February 1906.

to a conference to abolish the slave trade!'[59] The attacks against the Congo State were vigorous, the defence feeble. The debate was a decided victory in the cause of Congo reform.[60]

In June 1906, Leopold responded to the mounting pressure for reform by decreeing 'some more admirable laws'.[61] Regardless of whether the reforms were intended to be 'illusory',[62] they were overshadowed by the King's haughty letter that accompanied them: 'My rights over the Congo are indivisible; they are the fruit of my labors and my expenditure . . . It is my duty to proclaim these rights to the world, since Belgium possesses none in the Congo beyond those which will come to her from me.'[63] Leopold said, in effect, that the Congo was entirely his own affair, which he would conduct as he saw fit. As to Belgian annexation, 'at present I have nothing to say.'[64] Spurning international as well as Belgian opinion, 'King Leopold tries to treat the rest of the world as cavalierly as Belgium.'[65]

Leopold's Congo administration was debated in the House of Lords a month later. Expressing the general mood of the debate, Lord Lansdowne, then out of office, with uncharacteristic vehemence emphasized that there was in the Congo 'the existence of bondage under the most barbarous and inhuman conditions, and maintained for mercenary motives of the most selfish character'.[66] As Foreign Secretary, Lansdowne, though genuinely appalled at reports of atrocities, had been hesitant and indecisive in prosecuting the anti-Congo campaign. 'Ghastly', he once wrote about the Congo maladministration, 'but I am afraid the Belgians will get hold of the stories as to the way the natives have apparently been treated by men of our race in Australia.'[67] Relieved of his official responsibilities at the time of the advent of the Liberal Government in December 1905, he became bolder: 'Lansdowne in opposition can talk bravely—Lansdowne in office was a belated wayfarer seeking a harbour of refuge to escape the pitiless gibes of Leopold and company!'[68] By contrast, Sir Edward Grey,

[59] *Annales Parlementaires, Chamber,* 20 February 1906.

[60] On this debate, see Stengers, *Belgique et Congo,* pp. 69–72.

[61] Fitzmaurice in the House of Lords, *Parliamentary Debates,* 159, 3 July 1906, col. 1584. See also *Bulletin Officiel,* 1905, pp. 226–86.

[62] *The Times,* 18 June 1906.

[63] *Bulletin Officiel,* 1906, p. 289.

[64] Ibid., pp. 287–98.

[65] *Manchester Guardian,* 20 June 1906.

[66] *Parliamentary Debates,* 159, 3 July 1906, col. 1584.

[67] Lansdowne's minute on Mackie to Lansdowne, 11 March 1905, FO 10/815.

[68] Casement to Morel, Private and Confidential, 4 July 1905, Morel Papers.

Lansdowne's successor, and Lord Fitzmaurice, the new Parliamentary Under-Secretary, were 'as emphatic as the most zealous of the reformers on the iniquity of the present system and the necessity for its abolition'.[69]

Grey was 'absolutely convinced of the shame of the thing'.[70] 'The Sovereign of the Congo State', he said in the House of Commons in July 1906, 'speaks less as a governor and more as if he were the owner of private property . . . It has become like a private possession.'[71]

> My own personal feeling is that we are justified in any measures which will result in taking the Congo out of the hands of the King. He has forfeited every claim to it he ever had; and to take the Congo away from him without compensation would be less than justice, for it would leave him still with all the gains he has made by his monstrous system.[72]

The object of Grey's Congo policy was the 'Belgian solution'—in other words, Belgian annexation. Where did this idea originate, and how did it become the grand design of the British anti-Congo campaign? It did not start, it seems, in the Foreign Office, which probably would not have moved towards any solution had it not been pressed by the strength of public sentiment.[73] It originated in the interchange of ideas between Morel and Sir Harry Johnston.

Morel had a one-track mind. He saw the 'Congo evil' as 'special and extraordinary'.[74] Johnston, as an Africanist of many years' experience in varied capacities (and one of the early Congo explorers), remembered that the early years of the Congo State's administration were 'positively beneficent'[75] and that Britain's own colonial record was 'very far from stainless'.[76] Morel clung to his views tenaciously and ferociously—as Casement remarked, like a 'bulldog . . . very dangerous and gripping and seeing red'.[77] Johnston had trouble making up his

---

[69] *Morning Post*, 5 August 1907.

[70] Emmot to Morel, 26 June 1904, Morel Papers. See also Grey's *Twenty-Five Years*, (2 vols., New York, 1925), p. 190: 'My own feeling was one of detestation of the system and its crimes and of the character of the man who was responsible for them.'

[71] *Parliamentary Debates*, 155, 5 July 1906, cols. 319–22.

[72] Grey to Hardinge, 28 February 1908, in George M. Trevelyan, *Grey of Fallodon* (London, 1937), p. 200. See also *Parliamentary Debates*, 184, 26 February 1908, cols. 1870–81.

[73] See, for example, Harry Farnall's minute of 3 April, on Fox Bourne to Salisbury, 27 March 1902, FO 10/773: 'Neither this country nor any other is likely to take active steps in the matter unless more or less forced to do so by public opinion.'

[74] E. D. Morel's unpublished history of the Congo Reform Association, Morel Papers.

[75] Johnston to Morel, Private and Confidential, 4 July 1907, Morel Papers.

[76] Johnston's introduction to Morel, *Red Rubber*, chap. 7.

[77] Casement to Morel, n.d. (May? 1905), Morel Papers.

mind whether to take a prominent part in the anti-Congo campaign.[78] Morel had a romantic vision of the pre-Leopoldian Congo, a prosperous Congo thriving in trade. Johnston disagreed: 'Oh *do* let us purge our minds of cant in these things,' he wrote to Morel.

> The pre-Bula Matari [pre-Congo State] trade you mention so often as having been so flourishing in western Congoland. Well! I have *seen* that trade being carried on by much slavery, much gin and rum drinking, and endless wearisome caprices and tyranny, and I have come out of Congoland—like Grenfell [the missionary]—in 1883 as much desirous of a European control (in the best interests of the natives) as he did.[79]

Johnston regarded Morel's ideas as sentimental and utopian. Morel, on the other hand, was utterly baffled about why Johnston had 'the slightest difficulty in accepting the [Congo] gospel I preach as the "ultimate" right thing to do'.[80] His efforts to proselytize Johnston were in vain: '[D]o leave me alone a little bit,' Johnston wrote. 'I don't think I shall ever become a crusader!'[81]

Yet it was Johnston who shaped the strategy of the Congo reform movement. 'Johnston's suggestion that Belgium should become nationally responsible for the administration of Congo affairs', Casement wrote to Morel in May 1905, 'would offer a practical line of advance for all—it would unite the most convinced opponents of Congo misrule with the lukewarm ones—for it is a suggestion capable of being taken up even in Belgium.'[82] This policy was accepted hesitantly by the rank-and-file Congo reformers, who were generally sceptical of Belgium's ability to administer the Congo. 'It was . . . with misgivings as deep as your own', Dilke wrote to Morel, 'that the Aborigines Protection Society . . . and myself . . . accepted the Belgian solution.'[83] It

[78] Compare the following two passages concerning a public meeting of the Congo Reform Association in June 1905: 'I took the chair, very unwillingly' (Johnston's introduction to *Red Rubber*, chap. 7); 'I saw Johnston, who jumped at it and will take the chair *con amore*' (Casement to Morel, 4 May 1905, Morel Papers).

[79] Johnston to Morel, Private, 8 September 1908, Morel Papers.

[80] Morel to Johnston, 10 September 1908, Morel Papers.

[81] Johnston to Morel, 8 September 1908; see also Johnston to Clarke, 3 April 1907, FO 367/68: 'I am never at any time very keen on "crusaders"; they so often cover either unreasonable sentimentalism or secondary and interested motives. At the same time, I have felt for some time past that the situation in the Congo was no ordinary case of African misgovernment.'

[82] Casement to Morel, 26 May 1905, Morel Papers.

[83] Dilke to Morel, 6 February 1908, Dilke Papers. See also Roland Oliver, *Sir Harry Johnston and the Scramble for Africa* (London, 1959), p. 348.

was a solution to which some Congo reformers never agreed.[84] It was a conditional solution, to be accepted only if Belgium would promise to abolish the Leopoldian system and to administer the Congo in the 'spirit as well as the letter' of the Berlin Act.[85] It was, above all, an expedient, an excellent way to prove that the Congo reform movement was not motivated by territorial or commercial greed.

If the Congo reformers accepted the 'Belgian solution' reluctantly, the Foreign Office pursued it eagerly and dogmatically. The attitude of the Foreign Office was of course determined by European as well as African considerations.[86] As an anonymous correspondent wrote to *The Times* (10 January 1905):

> Of late the historic position of Great Britain in Belgium has almost disappeared. The Belgian people believe, rightly or wrongly, that England has designs on the Congo State, and that the agitation fostered here by certain interests has the tacit support of the government. And so Belgium is looking to her continental neighbours for support . . . Her trade . . . with Germany has grown rapidly.

The Congo was an irritant in Anglo-Belgian relations. It was also an issue that could reopen the Scramble for Africa. 'Some are inclined to think', Morel wrote to Grey, 'that His Majesty's Government are bent

---

[84] A. Conan Doyle, *The Crime of the Congo* (New York, 1909), p. 123:

Can a solution be found through Belgium? No, it is impossible, and that should be recognized from the outset. The Belgians have been given their chance. They have had nearly twenty-five years of undisturbed possession, and they have made it a hell upon earth. They cannot disassociate themselves from this work or pretend that it was done by a separate State. It was done by a Belgian King, Belgian soldiers, Belgian financiers, Belgian lawyers, Belgian capital, and was endorsed and defended by Belgian governments. It is out of the question that Belgium should remain in the Congo.

Cf. Casement to Morel, 8 November 1909, Morel Papers:

I hold with Doyle that the Belgians are really unfit to govern a subject and defenceless race. But you cannot say that—and failing getting rid of the Belgians altogether, which I fear is out of the question for many years yet, the next best thing is to try and bind them fast and sure and not leave 'reforms' to be of their goodwill and fancy.

[85] Technically it could not be proved that the Congo State had violated the Berlin Act; legally (according to the interpretations by the Law Officers of the Crown of the Anglo-Congolese treaties), Britain had no basis for intervention and could only remonstrate that the Congo government had not fulfilled the spirit of the Berlin Act.

[86] 'For Belgium might have been driven into the arms of Germany' (Trevelyan, *Grey of Fallodon*, p. 196). For international complications, see also Casement to Morel, 2 November 1905, Morel Papers.

upon . . . securing a right of way through Congo State territory for the Cape to Cairo railway.'[87] This argument was used effectively by the Congo government in convincing the Belgian public of the sinister motives of Britain. According to Leopold himself:

> Good relations with England are of great importance to Belgium; but England, in pursuance of her Cape to Cairo policy, is bent upon the dismemberment of the Congo Free State, as she was bent on the destruction of the Boer republics. She sets up humanitarian pretexts in the one case, as she did the wrongs of the outlanders and natives in the other; and, if the Free State became a Belgian colony tomorrow, she would still complain of its misgovernment until she had secured her slice.[88]

Only by the 'Belgian solution' could the Foreign Office disclaim territorial ambitions in central Africa.

The 'Belgian solution' meant more than simple annexation of the Congo by Belgium. It signified the introduction of a humane native policy and the end of commercial monopolies; in the words of Morel, it meant 'reform, drastic reform—that is . . . the system under which the Congo natives are robbed and murdered, rooted up, and . . . the basin of the Congo thrown open to commerce'. During the summer and fall of 1906 it was by no means clear that this sort of radical reform would occur, or even that Belgium would annex the Congo. Leopold's June letter was interpreted in Belgium as well as in Britain as a declaration of absolutism; so was his didactic letter to Grey, which Leopold wrote after having been provoked by the British Parliamentary debates in July 1906;[89] so also was his famous interview published in the

---

[87] Morel to Grey, Private and Confidential, 28 December 1906, FO 367/68.

[88] As recounted in Hardinge to Grey, Africa No. 99, Very Confidential, 20 October 1906, FO 367/33.

[89] King Leopold to Grey, 17 July 1906, FO 367/32:

> If my views and dealings are not well known in England, the real state of things in the Congo is still less well known. Certain persons seem only to be occupied in finding or inventing faults and crimes. The natives' well-known propensity for lying greatly facilitates their task . . . The government of a state must be unique; it is alone qualified in its independence to insure the administration of the public interests of the state. Any other situation would give rise to a state of anarchy, of which the natives would take advantage to perpetuate their laziness and barbarous customs. As far as I am concerned I have always clearly and publicly defined my aspirations. When I entered the international field I have always said, and I repeat it, that I devoted my efforts to civilization, and to the free expansion of trade. I still hold to the same flag. You may, perhaps, find my letter too long and too outspoken. I belong to an independent country, the institutions of which are the most liberal in existence. I have served this country in public office for fifty-five years without interruption. I have devoted my attention

New York American on 10 December of the same year, which, *The Times* wrote, in its 'affectation of artless and engaging candor, is one of the most characteristic specimens of Congo tactics the world has seen' (17 December 1906).[90] When asked during this interview whether it was true that atrocious conditions existed in the Congo, Leopold replied: 'Of course not, as a system of government.' This remark was pregnant with meaning. It indicated to Leopold's critics that he believed that atrocities in the Congo were only sporadic and occasional, and that they resulted merely from individual officials who abused their powers, not from the system of exploitation on which the administration was based. Leopold believed that reform was possible within the system he had created. He believed, above all, that the Congo was entirely his own business—that, as Stengers has stated, he 'owned the Congo just as Rockefeller owned Standard Oil'.[91] Stung by criticisms, he publicly professed, sometimes arrogantly, sometimes disingenuously, his faith in the regime as well as in his absolute rights.

Leopold's extravagant utterances consolidated his opponents, though this was less true in Belgium than abroad. The June letter was generally considered a 'royal blunder', but Leopold's defenders in Belgium pointed out that the letter had to be read in the context of the violent attacks that had provoked it; that it was not a declaration of absolutism but a 'solemn recommendation'; and that Leopold should be admired for taking such a bold stand. Owing to the hostile reception in Britain of his June proclamation, Leopold was able to point forcefully to reasons for his continued rule in the Congo. 'The best way to keep Belgium out of international complications resulting from England's African ambitions', he said, 'is to put off the annexation of the Congo, with all its attendant financial problems, as long as possible, and let the King-Sovereign alone bear the brunt of the Brit-

---

to central Africa for twenty-six years, also uninterruptedly, animated with that Belgian sentiment which is neither blood-thirsty, despotic, nor unenlightened.

[90] Leopold said in his interview:

Financially speaking . . . I am a poorer man, not a richer, because of the Congo . . . They see me as a boa-constrictor squeezing the life out of the blacks to put gold into my purse. Why should I do such a thing? . . . I have sufficient money for my wants. I do not wish any more. I am not a business man.

Cf. Hardinge to Grey, No. 153 Africa, Confidential, 14 December 1906, FO 367/33: 'The astounding assertion that his philanthropic efforts in Africa had seriously impoverished His Majesty had been . . . really and deliberately made to this newspaper correspondent by the King.'

[91] J. Stengers, 'La Place de Leopold II dans l'Histoire de la Colonisation', *La Nouvelle Clio* (1949–50), p. 527.

ish attack.'[92] Contemptuous of parliamentary politics, Leopold did not want the Congo to be administered under parliamentary control. Staggered by the vast financial operations in the Congo, and hesitant to accept so complicated and onerous an inheritance, the Belgian Parliament procrastinated. Although shocked by the disclosures of the Commission of Inquiry's report, the leaders of the clerical and liberal parties were unwilling to antagonize their King, not so much on grounds of principle as because of Leopold's personal authority and their own timidity. Nevertheless, in late 1906, on the eve of the great parliamentary debate on the Congo, public pressure in Belgium for annexation was rapidly mounting; but this was not the immediate reason for Leopold's decision in favour of annexation.[93]

In November 1906, Edward Grey stated to a delegation of Congo reformers that 'it will be impossible for us to continue to recognize indefinitely the present state of things.'[94] As *The Times* commented (21 November 1906), 'That is the plainest warning yet addressed to King Leopold and it is one which he will do well to heed.' A few days later, news reached Europe that the American government had joined the anti-Congo campaign. Deluged by public petitions, and guided by a report from the American Consul in the Congo that the government there was 'nothing but a vast enterprise for exploitation',[95] Elihu Root, the Secretary of State, instructed the American representative in London to cooperate with Grey to bring about 'amelioration of conditions in the Congo'.[96] On 10 December, Senator Lodge introduced a resolution to the effect that the President would have the Senate's 'warm support' in whatever action might be necessary to achieve reform in the Congo State.[97] These rapid developments, especially those in the United States, came as a tremendous shock to King Leopold, who feared that the anti-Congo campaign was gaining such momentum that it would spread to still other countries. He yielded, mainly

---

[92] Quoted in Hardinge to Grey, No. 99 Africa, Very Confidential, 20 October 1906, FO 367/33.

[93] On this question, see J. Stengers, 'Quand Leopold II s'est-il Rallié à l'Annexion du Congo par la Belgique?' *Bulletin de l'Institut Royal Colonial Belge,* 23 (1952), pp. 783–824.

[94] *The Times,* 21 November 1906.

[95] Slocum to Secretary of State, 1 December 1906, *Foreign Relations of the United States, 1907.*

[96] Root to Carter, 10 December 1906, ibid.

[97] Originally the resolution was worded 'that the native inhabitants of the Congo Free State have been subjected to inhuman treatment'; but it was amended to read 'the native inhabitants of the Congo basin'. The results of this ingenious revision was to change a censure of Leopold into 'an insult to ourselves Britain and France and Germany' (Clarke's minute of 4 March 1907, FO 367/68). 'It appears that Senator Spooner, of Wisconsin, intended to draw the attention of the Senate to this change, but was dissuaded from doing so by the Belgian Minister, and that the majority of the Senators voted for the resolution without appreciating the real meaning of the change' (Howard to Grey, No. 32 Africa, Confidential, 19 February 1907, FO 367/68).

because of the stand taken by the British and American governments. In December 1906, King Leopold decided that Belgium should annex the Congo.[98]

The historic debate in the Belgian Parliament during the winter of 1906 was followed with avid interest throughout Europe and America. Seen from abroad, the main issues were the welfare of Africans and commercial freedom in the Congo. In Belgium, however, the point of paramount interest was not maladministration (as had been the case in previous debates), but the legal and constitutional implications of the June letter, which had imposed arbitrary conditions on the transfer of the Congo State.[99] Attacking these conditions, Paul Hymans, the liberal leader, asked de Smet de Naeyer whether annexation would occur by a unilateral act of the Belgian Parliament or by a bilateral convention between Belgium and the Congo State. In other words, would the Belgian Parliament be free to deal as it pleased with the future administration of the Congo, or would its freedom be fettered by obligations contracted with the King? De Smet de Naeyer conceded finally that the law establishing the future government of the Congo should be the work of the Belgian Parliament alone, thus throwing Leopold's autocratic June letter to the winds.[100]

Leopold, though having decided that it was in his best interests for Belgium to annex his African empire, by no means had intended to give up his sovereign rights as ruler of the independent state of the Congo. He was annoyed at de Smet de Naeyer for having surrendered so much. Throughout 1907 and part of 1908, Leopold struggled to have his own terms accepted. Even after annexation he was determined to influence, even still control, Congo affairs, and he intended that revenues from the Congo should continue to be allocated for public works in Belgium.

During this period, the British Congo reformers assumed the responsibility of enlightening the Belgians about the nature of the heavy

---

[98] See Stengers, 'Quand Leopold II'.

[99] *Bulletin Officiel,* 1906, pp. 297–98:

> In assuming the sovereignty of the Congo, with all property, rights, and advantages attaching to it, my legatee will, as is just and necessary, undertake to respect all engagements of the ceded state with respect to third parties, as well as the acts by means of which I have . . . provided for the endorsement of . . . the foundation of the Domaine de la Couronne, the establishment of the Domaine National. My legatee will also respect the obligation not to diminish in any way the integrity of the revenues of those institutions without granting them equivalent to the loss of revenue involved.

On the question of the 'domains', see J. Stengers, *Combien le Congo a-t-il Coûté à la Belgique?* (Brussels, 1957), chap. 3.

[100] Cf. Masoin, *Histoire de l'État,* I, pp. 206–07; Stenmans, *Reprise du Congo,* pp. 346–69.

burden they were about to acquire. 'Bearing no enmity to the Belgian people', Morel wrote in May 1907, 'we should deplore that the Belgian[s] . . . find themselves committed to annexation of the Congo without being in a position to judge the issues.'[101] The issues that the Congo Reform Association tried to place before the Belgian public were both political and economic. Politically, the Congo reformers, who by 1907 included most of the British press[102]—an important point, since the press was the main medium of communication with the Belgian public—feared that annexation on Leopold's terms would mean merely a perpetuation of the Leopoldian regime. The fall of de Smet de Naeyer's ministry in April 1907 (ostensibly on a matter of domestic politics, but really because of de Smet de Naeyer's inability to agree with Leopold on the Congo issue) was interpreted in Britain as a victory for Leopold in his efforts to maintain his authority in Congo affairs.

De Trooz, the new Prime Minister, *The Times* observed (4 May 1907), was an 'unqualified "King's friend"; with M. Renkin, the new minister of justice [who in 1908 became the first Belgian colonial minister] and M. Delbeke, who has been appointed minister of public works, he stands without concealment for the old regime, for absolutist government in the Congo, and opposition to all reform.' Further, 'They are understood to be there because they will do what is pleasing to the King, and everyone knows that what the King desires as regards the Congo is the perpetuation of the old system, the stifling of inquiry, and the annexation of the Free State only on such terms as will leave His Majesty in full possession of the absolutism he now enjoys.'[103] It is obvious, said the *Morning Post,* that the annexation of the Congo by Belgium 'can only be satisfactory if it is complete and unrestricted, if it gives the Belgian nation a free hand to carry out necessary reforms' (10 April 1908), and 'It is certain that public opinion in this country will not recognize any scheme of transfer that does not seem to provide for real and radical reforms' (4 June 1908). In the words of Edward Grey, annexation must be 'a reality and not a sham'.[104] As seen by *The Times* (4 May 1907), the crucial question involved in making the Congo transfer a reality was 'whether, if Belgium annexes the Congo, annexation can take place on terms that will make it a re-formed

---

[101] *Official Organ,* May 1907.

[102] With the principal exceptions of the *Catholic Herald,* the *Catholic Times,* and the *Daily Graphic.*

[103] Cf. Carton de Wiart, *Léopold II* (Brussels, 1944), pp. 159–64; Stenmans, *Reprise du Congo,* pp. 369–76.

[104] Quoted in *The Times,* 28 February 1908.

colony, or whether it may not have the sinister result of extending King Leopold's absolutism over a hitherto constitutional country.' [105]

'Absolutism' was one of the powerful shibboleths of the British anti-Congo campaign. Yet it was an extraordinarily imprecise battle cry. Even admitting that Leopold was 'the absolute ruler of the Congo', how he might remain so after annexation was at best a matter of speculation. However justified the fear of absolutism might have been, the concrete issues in the Congo controversy after the Belgian Parliamentary debate of December 1906 were more economic than political.

The real plague spots in the Congo were the regions handed over to the chartered companies. The Congo State, by investing in the companies that administered and exploited its territories, was the apotheosis of the chartered-company system of empire building:

> The body which was set up to govern was a body existing for private profit, and bent primarily on making the work of government pay dividends. It has no responsibility to the governed, nor to anyone else except the financial promoters, whose main interest it is that the governed shall be fleeced. [106]

'It cannot be too frequently asserted', commented the *Morning Post* (28 August 1906), 'that the anomaly that differentiates the Congo Free State from all other African communities is the fact that its vast territories are administered not in the interest of the inhabitants, but of a group of persons in Europe who for courtesy's sake are styled the Congo Government.' The rankest 'excrescence' [107] of this system of exploitation was unquestionably the Domaine de la Couronne, the private preserve of King Leopold. Lying west of Lake Leopold II, the Domaine de la Couronne was a territory twice the size of England. No other region in the Congo was more notorious for cruelty to Africans, and no other was richer in rubber; it was the best slice of the Congo cake. [108] According to Cattier in 1906, the Domaine de la Couronne had already yielded profits in rubber of nearly 3 million pounds sterling, a large proportion of which (as de Smet de Naeyer admitted) had been invested in real estate in the vicinity of Brussels and Ostende. The Domaine de la Couronne became the burning issue in the transfer of the Congo State to Belgium.

[105] See also *Official Organ*, October 1907: 'The bill proposed by the Belgian Government for the administration of the Congo is the very negation of national responsibility, the very incarnation of unfettered absolutism.'

[106] *Manchester Guardian*, 22 February 1906.

[107] *The Times*, 18 June 1906.

[108] See especially Cattier, *Étude sur la situation*, pp. 211–45.

Leopold's June 1906 letter had declared that the revenue from the Domaine de la Couronne after annexation must continue to be devoted to the construction and upkeep in Belgium of projects such as the ones described by *The Times* as 'gorgeous palaces of art and pompous public buildings' (21 December 1907).[109] This was a condition he would not yield. According to the draft treaty of cession published in December 1907, the Belgian government acquiesced in his demand. The revenues of the Domaine de la Couronne, however, could be maintained only under the Leopoldian system of forced labour, with all its attendant abuses. Without severely exacted forced labour, the colonial budget would show a deficit. If there were a deficit, could expenditures from Congo revenues be justified for architectural and other sumptuary purpose in Belgium? As far as both the Congo Reform Association and the Foreign Office were concerned, the Belgian government's concession to Leopold on the issue of the Domaine de la Couronne was tantamount to admitting that Belgium had no intention of making a real break with the past.

The tendency of the Foreign Office in regard to the Congo, as Roger Casement once observed, was to 'hope—hope for this, hope for that—never to resolutely think out what could be accomplished and then set to work to bring it about'.[110] Until 1907 there was a good deal of truth in this statement, though perhaps there was more in the comment by a Foreign Office official that the British policy was 'to avoid pin pricks while saving ourselves for a grand assault'.[111] In any case, in 1907 there was a hardening of thought about Belgium and the Congo.

The two people who contributed most to the Foreign Office discussion were Sir Arthur Hardinge and E. A. W. Clarke. Hardinge was the British Minister in Brussels (who had replaced Phipps in early 1906),

[109] In the mind of one British diplomat, Sir Arthur Hardinge, the issue of exploitation for the benefit of the metropole was the fundamental difference between the British and Congolese systems of administration:

> Our system was that the revenues of a dependency were to be devoted to its development, to its defence, and to the welfare of its population, and that any surplus was to be expended in it either on remunerative works of public utility, on paying debts, or on directly relieving the burden of taxation. The system of the Congo Government, on the other hand, seemed to be to extract as much revenue as possible from its African territories for the purpose of public works, improvements, etc., in Belgium, which however admirable in themselves, were of no benefit to the subject populations.

Hardinge to Grey, No. 129 Africa, 25 September 1907, FO 367/69.

[110] Casement to Morel, 16 August 1909, Morel Papers.

[111] Clarke's minute of 3 December 1906, FO 367/5.

a scholar as well as a diplomat who, while a fellow of All Souls, Oxford, had chosen diplomacy as a career. Clarke was the head of the African Department of the Foreign Office, an exuberant twentieth-century version of his predecessor, Sir Percy Anderson. An incorrigible conservative, Hardinge thought that the Foreign Office under the Liberal government was too susceptible to the 'sentimentalism' of the reformers.[112] By contrast, Clarke was closer in temperament to the Congo reformers. He was deeply disturbed by the reports of atrocities. 'We have supped full of Congo horrors', he once wrote, 'but I really don't think we have ever had anything in its way more horrible than that instance of ill-treatment of the child Katuma.' According to the British Consul in the Congo, Katuma was a Congolese boy of seven years who had been carried off by his parents to attend one of the Congo State's schools:

> No attempt whatever is made to teach him his letters but he is instead made to carry stones and because the wretched creature is unable to execute his tasks to the satisfaction of his masters he is not only put in chains but he is kept in them night and day for three months.[113]

Clarke, with Edward Grey's approval, instructed Hardinge to ask the Congo authorities about Katuma.

The results of this one incident reveal a good deal about Foreign Office attitudes towards Congo reform. Hardinge asked the Foreign Office to reconsider his instructions, not because there was no way of ascertaining the facts in the case, but also because there would be no practical results from a complaint to the Congo officials. Would the British government, he asked, protest a similar case if it had happened 'in Algeria or in a German African colony'?[114] Clarke retorted angrily: 'If no reform was ever begun until the reformer was absolutely *sure* his fiery speeches would have effect the world's history would be very different.'[115] Further, 'Of course we should not say anything about a similar case in Algeria or German East Africa: in the first place because *au fond* the French and Germans are boys too big to interfere with. It may be quite possible and one's duty to prevent a big boy bullying a small but it is quite another matter to stop a strong man beating a little.'

In some respects the behaviour of Britain towards Belgium over the Congo did (to straighten out Clarke's analogy) resemble a big boy

---

[112] Hardinge, *Diplomatist in Europe,* p. 194.
[113] Clarke's minute of 3 December 1906.
[114] Hardinge to Barrington, Private, 16 December 1906, FO 367/5.
[115] Clarke's minute of 21 December 1906, FO 367/5.

bullying a small one. According to the Law Officers of the Crown, the Congo State was an independent and sovereign state, which Belgium could annex without the consent of the other powers. Legally, Britain had no more right to interfere in the internal affairs of the Congo State than in those of France or Germany.[116] Yet Grey planned to 'regard the Congo as a territory without a government and equally open to every one', unless Belgium annexed it. 'I know there may be some technical difficulties in the way of the course I propose,' he wrote. 'But public opinion here will make light of technical difficulties and I consider that the state of slavery [there] . . . is such as to transcend technical difficulties and the letter of treaties.'[117]

As far as legality was concerned, France had pre-emptive rights over Congo territory through the Franco-Congolese agreements of 1884 and 1895. Grey foresaw that the state of affairs in the Congo could become so intolerable that France might have to exercise this right; to prevent international rivalry, he went as far as to suggest to the French Ambassador in London that France might easily come to an agreement with Germany to partition the Congo State between them.[118] This was, in any case, a proposal filled with uncertainties. In the minds of his colleagues, Grey, by disclaiming British territorial ambitions while encouraging those of France and Germany, had jeopardized Britain's strategic position in Africa. The British Ambassador in Paris wrote:

> I believe that the ambition and ultimate aim of Germany is to extend her African possessions from sea to sea, viz. from the Indian Ocean to the south Atlantic . . . If we begin by disclaiming all territorial desires we leave the cake to be cut up between France and Germany, and if later on we make objection to a prospective allotment between those two powers France would have reason to say you told me that so long as the natives were secured in their rights and the Berlin Act trade arrangements were observed you had no desires. What have you to complain of?[119]

[116] See, for example, W. E. Davidson's minute of 16 May 1900, FO 10/754: 'Beyond strong remonstrance we have no further remedy short of the employment of actual force.'

[117] Grey to Hardinge, 28 February 1908, in Trevelyan, *Grey of Fallodon*, pp. 198–200. Cf. Grey's statement in *Twenty-Five Years*, I, p. 192: 'We hoped we were making him [Leopold] uncomfortable; it was all we could do.'

[118] Grey to Bertie, No. 17 Africa, Confidential, 19 April 1907, FO 367/68. Cf. Clarke's memorandum of 13 December 1906, FO 367/68: 'We should not object, failing all else, to cutting the Congo up.'

[119] Bertie's memorandum of 25 November 1907, Private, with minutes by Clarke, Charles Hardinge, and Grey, FO 367/74.

The result of such a policy might be to give Germany the opportunity of making with France a bargain which would bring Germany in still further contiguity than now with British interest in Africa.[120]

Clarke recognized this as a 'suicidal course'.[121] Grey, modifying his stand, wrote:

I am not anxious personally to see us assume the responsibility for more territory in tropical Africa, but if France proceeds to make an [?arrangement] with Germany about the Congo we should have to consider how our frontiers would be affected and put in our word according to what our interests seemed to require.[122]

Britain would resist, in Clarke's words, 'anything which would enable Germany to bar the way definitely between our possessions in the South and Egypt and the Sudan'.[123]

These considerations about French and German territorial designs in Africa were largely academic. British policy was based on the assumption that Belgium *would* annex the Congo, but that Belgium herself could not be trusted to 'lay the foundations of the economic and moral regeneration of the native'.[124] The British public demanded guarantees. To secure them, Clarke proposed a reconvocation of the Berlin conference:

Personally I rather share Mr. Morel's views that no great good is likely to result from the annexation of the Congo by Belgium, even if that annexation takes place . . . A conference is certainly our best, if not our only, chance of seeing our wishes in regard to affairs in the Congo given effect to.[125]

Hardinge pointed out that the logical prelude to a conference—which should be a last resort—would be a policy of non-recognition:

[120] Bertie to Tyrrell, Private, 31 October 1907, FO 367/70. Also Johnston to Clarke, 3 April 1907, FO 367/68: 'I believe myself that behind Leopold and all the Congo trouble stands Germany . . . Germany is not at present in a position to stretch out her hand over the Congo Free State, so that it serves her purpose better that Leopold shall remain in possession of it.' See also Hardinge to Grey, No. 162 Africa, Confidential, 21 December 1906, FO 367/33.

[121] Clarke's minute of 2 December 1907, on Bertie's memorandum of 25 November 1907, FO 367/74.

[122] Grey's minute on Bertie's memorandum of 25 November 1907, FO 367/74.

[123] Clarke's minute of 2 December 1907.

[124] *Official Organ*, November 1907.

[125] Clarke's minute of 21 January 1907, FO 403/374.

> Before recognizing as a signatory of the Berlin Act the validity of the transfer we must ask for explicit and positive guarantees . . . our formal refusal to recognize the cession without the guarantees insisted on by the Congo Reform Association would satisfy the latter that we were acting energetically on the lines constantly urged by them, and were applying that impressive moral leverage in which they profess such touching faith . . . there might be no immediate cessation of all the grave abuses on the Congo; but this latter result can in no case be looked for unless Belgium at once voluntarily undertakes the work of reform.[126]

Arthur Hardinge, the scholarly diplomat who despised humanitarians, was responsible more than any other Foreign Office official for the perpetuation of the anti-Congo campaign until 1913. It was Hardinge who shaped the British policy of non-recognition.[127]

In January 1908, Hardinge, along with the American minister, Henry Lane Wilson, called at the Belgian Ministry for Foreign Affairs. Hardinge said that Britain would reserve the right of recognition of the transfer if the Congo were not administered 'in the spirit of the Berlin Act'. The Foreign Office demanded three specific reforms:

1. Relief of the natives from excessive taxation.
2. The grant to the natives of sufficient land to ensure their ability to obtain not only the food they require, but also sufficient produce of the soil to enable them to buy and sell as in other European colonies.
3. The possibility for traders whatever their nationality may be to acquire plots of land of reasonable dimensions in any part of the Congo for the erection of factories so as to enable them to establish direct trade relations with the natives.[128]

Once committed to making British recognition contingent on specific reforms, Foreign Office policy became inflexible. And by choosing to measure the 'spirit of the Berlin Act' by the yardstick of land and tax legislation, the Foreign Office denied itself the chance to appraise the Congo situation according to events of incalculable importance — such as King Leopold's cession of the Domaine de la Couronne (under the new name of the Foundation de la Couronne) in March 1908.[129]

The cession of the Foundation de la Couronne signified that Belgium had at last, to use Hardinge's phrase, succeeded in 'buying out'

---

[126] Arthur Hardinge to Charles Hardinge, Private, 20 December 1907, FO 367/70.

[127] See Wellesley's dissenting memorandum, n.d. (Dec. ? 1907), with minutes by Clarke, Langley, Charles Hardinge, and Grey, FO 367/70.

[128] No. 3 Africa (1908), *Accounts and Papers,* 62.

[129] On this point, see Stengers, *Belgique et Congo,* chap. 4.

King Leopold. The Belgian government agreed to subsidize King Leopold's public-works projects; but the funds were to come from the Belgian treasury. It was thus officially recognized that parks, museums, palaces, hippodromes, triumphal arches, and 'bathing cities unique in Europe' should not be built by funds raised in the Congo. It was a substantial triumph of the principle that the Congo should not be exploited for the benefit of Belgium.

The other major issue in the Congo controversy, absolutism, for all practical purposes had been killed by the Belgian Parliamentary debate of December 1906, which repudiated Leopold's autocratic June letter. Yet the issue lingered on, even through the annexation debates of the spring of 1908 and the actual enactment of annexation by the Chamber and Senate during August and September of the same year. Suspicion of the King's sinister influence died only with Leopold himself. His death in December 1909 profoundly affected Congo affairs, of course. From the Belgian point of view, the colonial administrators were left free to promote reforms and to govern the colony as they themselves were inclined; for the British, there was considerably less ground for suspicion that reforms were intended to be superficial and sporadic. But the Belgian administrators were unable to revolutionize the Leopoldian system immediately, and the Foreign Office could not ignore reports from their consuls in the Congo that there was little administrative improvement to be seen there. As Hardinge explained to King Albert, Leopold's successor, in July 1910: 'The confidence felt in England in His Majesty's good intentions and high ideals had largely allayed the old feelings of distrust, but . . . the extreme Congo reformers, who were slower to convince, demanded positive evidence of improvement . . . our consular reports had, unfortunately, so far not justified the hopes of those among us who believed in and wished well to the Belgian solution.' [130]

The Foreign Office wished to heal the wound in Anglo-Belgian relations, but agitation against Congo abuses, coming both in Parliament and from the humanitarians, meant that it could not acknowledge the transfer as legitimate until there was evidence that the abuses had been abolished. The Belgian government, for its part, while wishing genuinely to introduce adequate reforms, was unable to rectify quickly the evils of a system over two decades old. This placed the Belgian government in an extremely embarrassing position:

> The Belgians are a proud little people, very sensitive to the opinion of other countries, and the implied suggestion that they are not

[130] Hardinge to Grey, No. 133 Africa, Confidential, 22 July 1910, FO 367/213.

living up to civilized standards in the Congo is one which they feel
somewhat acutely. Their papers may now and then say 'we don't
care' . . . but the present situation is certainly galling to their national
self-esteem.[131]

As Casement wrote to Morel in 1910, 'the Belgian State cannot dis-
pense with the goodwill of mankind as the one-man machine of King
Leopold could do.'[132]

The continued agitation from Congo reformers was based on their
conviction that Belgium had 'no intention of reversing the . . . Leopoldian system'.[133] It could not be denied, Morel wrote in 1912, that
Africans were still not permitted to own land. In theory, most of the
land in the Congo still belonged to the state. Renkin, the Belgian Colonial Minister, tried to handle this bitter issue by avoiding theoretical
discussions of sovereign rights and concentrating on practical measures of reform. As far as he was concerned, colonial rule should not
be judged by controversial standards of property ownership, but by
the way in which Africans were treated. By 1913 the British government was obliged to accept this view; recognition could not be withheld from a benevolently ruled Congo in which freedom of trade had
been restored. According to Morel's biographer:

> By May 1913 very little was left to be done. The entire Leopoldian
> policy had been completely abandoned. The atrocities had ceased.
> The concessionaire companies had either vanished or had been re-
> duced to impotence, and with their disappearance the swarms of ir-
> regular levies which had terrorized the countryside had also gone. A
> responsible government had replaced an irresponsible despotism.[134]

Morel said in 1913 that 'the Association has failed in securing one only
of its objects . . . a specific act of the Belgian Parliament recognizing
the native tenure in land'.[135]

The happy ending to the drama of Congo reform was the general
recognition of E. D. Morel as the hero of the day. 'That damned old
scoundrel in Brussels must hate you with a pretty vigorous hatred,'
Casement wrote him in 1907.

> The King of Beasts to be beaten by a poor, lowly, unknown man!
> The pen in your case, in the hand of a very honest, very brave, and

[131] Hardinge to Grey, No. 101 Africa, Confidential, 10 June 1910, FO 367/213.
[132] Casement to Morel, 12 July 1910, Morel Papers.
[133] *Morning Post*, 23 December 1907.
[134] Cocks, *Morel*, p. 161.
[135] Quoted in *The Times*, 17 June 1913.

very unceasing human being has beaten the Principalities of Powers of Darkness out of their domains—Leopold has nothing, absolutely nothing, but his gold left.[136]

It was Morel who caused the name of King Leopold to reek 'in the nostrils of the civilized world',[137] who convinced the world that the real atrocity of the Congo was that 'the native owns nothing',[138] and who could claim, only half in jest, that the Congo exposures 'had permeated wherever civilization extended, and even beyond the pale of civilization—into the palace of the Sovereign of the Congo State'.[139] Within a year of his vindication by the Commission of Inquiry report, Morel had risen from the obscurity of a freelance journalist to the national prominence of a latter-day Wilberforce.

He was not universally admired, even in Britain or even in the councils of the Congo Reform Association itself. Harry Johnston regarded him as 'a visionary and next door to a lunatic'.[140] He was a quixotic figure, a knight errant in search of controversy as well as justice. He did overplay his emotional appeals to pity and imagination, as when he once described the plight of the Congo people at a public meeting:

> In the vast crown domain, two and one half times the size of England, the natives wandering distractedly through the gloomy forest, exposed to the attacks of wild beasts, to the inclemencies of the weather, to the hardships of all kinds, far from home and wife and child, shelterless, hopeless, searching for rubber, rubber, rubber, to minister to the disordered ambitions of Leopold II, his courtiers and his mistresses.[141]

But if he exaggerated, he did so in the conviction that he was justified by his Christian mission to turn 'the biggest pagan in Christendom out of his misused kingdom'.[142] He was sincere, and despite the 'dirty mud-slinging'[143] of the Leopoldian press, he emerged with his character untarnished. His honesty made him, in the eyes of his disciples, 'the conscience of humanity, especially British humanity'.[144]

[136] Casement to Morel, 16 October 1907, Morel Papers.

[137] *Official Organ,* August 1907.

[138] *Manchester Guardian,* 20 April 1907.

[139] *Morning Post,* 22 February 1908.

[140] Morel surmised this from Johnston's letter to him of 8 September 1908; the quotation is from Morel to Johnston, 10 September 1908, Morel Papers.

[141] *Official Organ,* November 1907.

[142] Casement to Morel, n.d., (1909), Morel Papers.

[143] Casement to Morel, n.d., Morel Papers.

[144] *The Times,* 17 June 1913.

Morel had been able to precipitate the 'tidal wave'[145] of British opinion against the Congo State. The sources of his strength were not the diplomatic machinations of the Foreign Office or the commercial ambitions of the Liverpool merchants. Nor was the Congo reform movement essentially either political or religious. At bottom, the secret to Morel's success was the shared belief of the British public that the Congo reform movement was the last great crusade against slavery. In the words of the Bishop of Exeter: 'The natives were living in the Congo in what was virtually a state of slavery, and such as was utterly unparalleled in the history of slavery in any civilized or almost any uncivilized, state, ancient or modern.'[146] At the dissolution of the Congo Reform Association in June 1913, the Bishop of Winchester said that Britain owed to Morel its success in 'freeing the natives of the Congo'.[147]

Whatever the truth of this assertion, and whatever credit should be given Morel in general, there can be little doubt that the Congo reform movement was a powerful force to be reckoned with by the British government. Morel did not exaggerate when he wrote that it was 'a movement which Mr. Asquith, Sir Edward Grey, Lord Lansdowne, Sir Harry Johnston and other eminent personages have, in varied language, described as the most remarkable British popular movement in the last half century'.[148]

Boston University Papers on Africa   1966

[145] *Official Organ,* May 1907.
[146] Ibid.
[147] *The Times,* 17 June 1913.
[148] Unpublished history of the Congo Reform Association, Morel Papers.

THE FIRST WORLD WAR
AND THE ORIGINS OF THE MANDATES SYSTEM

6

AUSTRALIA AND THE GERMAN COLONIES IN THE PACIFIC DURING THE FIRST WORLD WAR

> A first class Pacific Power watches every move of the game in commercial and territorial expansion and is ready to pounce down upon a quarrelsome neighbour, a helpless prey and an empty continent.
>
> Governor-General of Australia[1]

> Behind Mr. Wilson's vaguely philanthropic sentiments there stands the definite political purpose of safeguarding American interests in the Pacific against possible aggression on the part of Japan.
>
> *Auckland Star*, 29 January 1919

In the early days of the First World War, Japan intervened by presenting an ultimatum to Germany to get out of China. That action immediately brought to the surface Australian anxieties about Japanese ambitions in the Pacific. The *Hobart Mercury*, one of the very few Australian newspapers to escape severe censorship, commented that declaration of war by Japan against Germany should be regarded 'with somewhat mixed feelings' (13 August 1914) but that it need not '*necessarily* imply a fresh "Yellow Peril"' (19 August 1914). The censor compelled other Australian newspapers to be more restrained and to express their opinions by implication. If the more freely stated views of the New Zealand press may be used as a yardstick by which to measure the true sentiment of the editorial writers in Australia, the *Brisbane Telegraph* clearly intended the following comment to be interpreted in the opposite of its literal sense: 'That, in the issue, Japan will demand any *quid pro quo* [for her Kiaochow campaign], much less obtain it, that would be a menace to Australia or to the integrity of the white races anywhere is too ridiculous for serious consideration.' Along with many other Australians, the journalists of the *Telegraph* hoped that if Japan *did* expand she would do so 'in her own latitudes . . . there she can expand in accordance with her own national and racial traditions and ideals' (24 August 1914). What of expansion southward? That question summed up one of the crucial points in the history of the Pacific during the First World War and involved, above all, the fate of Germany's colonies.

Australasian and Japanese forces captured the German colonies in the Pacific within four months after the outbreak of war. On 23 August, Japan declared war on Germany and began the siege of Kiao-

---

[1] Munro Ferguson to Walter Long, Personal (copy), 25 October 1917, National Library of Australia, Canberra, Novar Papers, 4.

chow, an operation not completed, however, until early November. On 30 August, New Zealand troops occupied Samoa.[2] The Australians hoisted the British flag on German New Guinea on 13 September. During October the Japanese occupied the German islands north of the Equator. The subsequent destruction of the German cruisers *Emden, Scharnhorst, Gneisenau, Leipzig,* and *Dresden* ended German naval power in the Pacific.[3] 'With the British fleet in command of the seas', commented the *Perth Daily News,* 'Germany's hopes of colonial expansion must remain barren' (23 October 1914).

Only with Japanese support, however, did the British manage to retain control of the seas. The military operations in the Pacific demonstrated the extent to which the security of both the British Empire and Australia depended on Japanese sea power. In their war against Germany, the British now reaped the benefits of the alliance concluded over a decade earlier with Japan. Even Australians hostile to the Japanese began to see the value of the Anglo-Japanese alliance. According to the *West Australian* (10 October 1914):

It is no secret that that alliance has not in the past been viewed with whole-souled enthusiasm by every section of the Australian people; to-day it is highly important, for the sake of our national future, that we should venture upon some clear and cool thinking on this matter, and that we should look at the facts, not through a veil of sentiment and prejudice, but face to face . . . Britain has paralyzed German oversea commerce, and has kept her own trade routes clear, because she was able, in good time, to call her ships home to guard her own gateways; and it was the Japanese Alliance which enabled her to do this.

In the words of the *Adelaide Register:* 'Japan's interpretation of her duty under the treaty of alliance with England has for the time being

[2] The Australian press learned of the capture of Samoa by means of an American newspaper, illustrating the severity of Australian censorship. Even the censor, however, could not conceal, in the words of the Governor-General, that in Australia 'the occupation of Samoa by New Zealand rankles a little. It is felt that she got there thanks to the protection of the Australian Fleet, and can only remain there under the same protection. Australia regards the Pacific as her "duck pond" and scarcely admits New Zealand's right to a look-in' (Munro Ferguson to Lewis Harcourt, Personal [copy], 13 May 1915, Novar Papers, 4).

[3] These events may be followed by reading the official Australian history of the war in the Pacific, by S. S. Mackenzie, *The Australians at Rabaul: The Capture and Administration of the German Possessions in the Southern Pacific* (Sydney, 1938). Russell H. Fifield illuminates the problem of Japanese expansion in the Pacific as well as in China from the point of view of American foreign policy in *Woodrow Wilson and the Far East: The Diplomacy of the Shantung Question* (New York, 1952); see also another valuable work along the same lines, Roy Watson Curry, *Woodrow Wilson and Far Eastern Policy, 1913–1921* (New York, 1957).

extinguished all hopes of German aggression in the Pacific, and materially added to the safety of British colonies and trade in Eastern waters' (23 September 1914). But the Australasian press generally remained highly suspicious. In franker words than Australian censorship permitted, the *Lyttelton Times* of Christchurch, New Zealand, suspected very early in the war that Japan 'has her eye on the Carolines' (18 August 1914). The *Invergargill Southland Times* even more bluntly asserted that with the 'White Australasia' policy of New Zealand and Australia, 'we would feel safer with the Pacific islands under the flag of a white Power than under the emblem of the Rising Sun' (18 August 1914).

The Canberra archives reveal that the Australian government shared those sentiments. The Governor-General, Sir Ronald Munro Ferguson, cabled the Colonial Office in London on 25 November, inquiring whether the Australian expeditionary force in the Pacific should occupy the Caroline, Ladrones (Marianas), Marshall, and Pelew (Palau) Islands (all north of 'the Line'). The Colonial Secretary, Lewis Harcourt, replied on 3 December that the British government would be 'glad' if the Australians would confine their operations to the islands south of the Equator.[4]

Why did the British government run the risk of thus antagonizing the Australians in the same way as in the 1880s, when—as the Australasian press frequently pointed out during the war—the 'supine' behaviour of the Colonial Office had given Bismarck the chance to plant German colonies in the Pacific? Harcourt justified his government's action in the following letter to Munro Ferguson:

December 6, 1914

Private & Personal. Very Secret.

My Dear Ronald,

I telegraphed to you on the 3rd[5] that in view of the fact that the Japanese are in actual occupation of the German Pacific Islands *north* of the Equator, and in view of the great assistance they are rendering to us (at our request) with their fleet through the *whole* of the Pacific, it

---

[4] 'Pelew, Marianne, Caroline Islands and Marshall Islands are at present in military occupation by Japanese who are at our request engaged in policing waters Northern Pacific. We consider it most convenient for strategic reasons to allow them to remain in occupation for the present leaving whole question of future to be settled at the end of war. We should be glad therefore if the Australian expedition would confine itself to occupation of German Islands South of the Equator' (Harcourt to Munro Ferguson, Secret, cablegram, 3 December 1914, Commonwealth Archives Office, Canberra [hereafter cited as CAO], Governor-General's Office, 89/68).

[5] Ibid.

seemed to us here undesirable that the Australian Expedition should proceed anywhere north of the Equator at the present time.

I feel that I ought to give you *personally* some explanation . . . but I must impress upon you that this letter is for your eye only, and under no circumstances is to be seen by anyone else.

Our fleets were so fully engaged in the North Sea, Atlantic, Mediterranean, and in convoy of troops across the Indian Ocean that we could not spare enough to deal with the Pacific. We had therefore to call in Japanese aid.

It has even been in contemplation (and still is) that the Japanese fleet may in the future be employed in the European theatre of war.

All this has changed the character of the Japanese participation and no doubt of their eventual claims to compensation.

There is a considerable agitation in Japan against the present Govt. on the ground that they are giving much and getting nothing.

From information which reaches me I have very little doubt that it is the intention of the Japanese at the end of the war to claim for themselves all the German Islands North of the Equator. Of course we should absolutely refuse at this present time to make any admission of such a claim.

Our attitude throughout has been that all these territorial questions must be settled in the terms of peace and not before.

But it would be impossible at this moment to risk a quarrel with our Ally which would be the certain & immediate result of any attempt diplomatically to oust them now from those Islands which they are occupying more or less at the invitation of the Admiralty.

All this is a long story . . . but the moral of it is that you ought in the most gradual & diplomatic way to begin to prepare the mind of your Ministers for the possibility that at the end of the war Japan may be left in possession of the Northern Islands and we with everything south of the Equator.

I know that they won't like this, but after all the thing of most importance are those territories most contiguous to Australia, and it will be a great gain to add German New Guinea to Papua and to have the whole of the Solomon Isl. group under the British flag.

I fear I have set you a hard task but I am sure you will execute it with your usual skill & discretion.

I am writing this from my bed where I am nursing an overstrained heart, but I am getting better, and I have never missed a Cabinet since the War began!

Yours always,
L. Harcourt[6]

Munro Ferguson—whom Walter Long (Colonial Secretary, December 1916–January 1919) judged to be one of the great Governor-Generals in the history of the British Empire—had anticipated Harcourt's request. In January 1915 he wrote:

I am glad to be able to say that I had already done something in the direction of meeting your wishes re the post bellum Pacific situation, and in talking over the question with trustworthy leading men had suggested the Equator as a likely line between British and Japanese Spheres in the Pacific. When our Ally's Fleet went to the Carolines and Mariannes [Marianas] it seemed unlikely that it would again evacuate those Islands . . . I therefore sounded those with whom I am on confidential terms in naval, military and political circles . . . as to their views on the matter. None of these showed much antipathy to the suggestion—though we agreed our fractious U.S.A. Coz. wouldn't like it. They all rather accepted it as an inevitable sequence to the inestimable service rendered by Japan to Australia throughout the War.[7]

Four months later, however, Munro Ferguson wrote that the Prime Minister, Andrew Fisher, had become 'jumpy' about the 'Yellow Peril Scare'.[8] Though accepting Japanese occupation of the islands north of the Equator as an accomplished fact, the Australian government at that stage of the war had not assessed the strategic value of the former German possessions. Japan's 'twenty-one demands' on China during January–May 1915 again conjured up the spectre of Japanese expansion and with it the fear that the Carolines eventually might be used as a 'jumping off place' against Australia.

[6] Harcourt to Munro Ferguson, Private and Personal, 6 December 1914, Novar Papers, 6.

[7] Munro Ferguson to Harcourt, Personal (copy), 20 January 1915, Novar Papers, 4.

[8] Munro Ferguson to Harcourt, Personal (copy), 13 May 1915, Novar Papers, 4. Nevertheless, a few days later Munro Ferguson cabled Harcourt that Fisher 'anticipates no effective objection to continued occupation by Japanese of islands North of Line when question raised at end of war' (Munro Ferguson to Harcourt, Secret and Personal [copy], cablegram, 19 May 1915, Novar Papers, 19).

Australasian attitudes towards the German colonies during 1915–16 remain more obscure than those during the earlier or later stages of the war. When Harcourt's political head as Colonial Secretary rolled in May 1915, Bonar Law succeeded him. Unfortunately for the historian of the Pacific, Bonar Law did not regard colonial affairs as one of his life's callings. Until Walter Long became Colonial Secretary in December 1916, the Governor-General restrained his correspondence with his chief, and the Colonial Secretary wrote little of interest to his lieutenant in Australia. Nevertheless, the lines of controversy that developed in Australia during that time appear clearly enough. Opinion about the captured German territories divided itself roughly into two camps: those who regarded themselves as 'Little Australians' and those who thought that Australia had a 'Pacific destiny'. The former believed that the islands seized by Japan could only remotely endanger Australian security and that the ones taken by Australia, if annexed, would add an intolerable financial burden to a country that had not yet developed its own territory. The latter envisaged innovations in naval technology that could well make the Carolines a menace to Australia, and advocated an Anglo-American alliance to check Japanese expansion. 'An alliance between Great Britain and the United States would secure an Anglo-Saxon hegemony in the Pacific,' one official wrote later in the war.[9] With his usual prescience, Munro Ferguson had divined those tendencies in Australian thought at an early date. He argued that both schools missed the most important point. The real danger, he said, involved the 'White Australia' policy and its corollary of encouraging people mainly of English stock to colonize Australia. 'It leaves us an empty continent, while it invites occupation by other peoples. This fool's paradise needs a rude awakening, and if a Japanese naval base near the Line should act as a solvent then it would be a blessing in disguise!'[10]

Did Japanese occupation of the Carolines in fact jeopardize Australian security? According to the Minister of Defense, George F. Pearce:

> My view is that these Pacific Islands to the North of the Equator are not of very great value to Australia. Their commercial value is small; they have essentially a tropical climate and their distance from Australia renders them of little value to us from a strategical point of view. In fact they might be a source of weakness whereas, in the hands of another Power, they cannot be of much danger to us because of their distance from us and the intervention of other Islands.

[9] Memorandum by J. G. Latham, 12 July 1918, National Library of Australia, Latham Papers, 18.

[10] Munro Ferguson to Harcourt, Personal (copy), 6 April 1915, Novar Papers, 4.

On the other hand, he described the German islands south of the Line as being 'of incalculable value to Australia'.

> Their commercial value is already considerable and will be largely increased . . . Their strategic value is exceedingly great to Australia as forming a shield to the Northern portion of our continent. They may possess many good harbours. In addition New Guinea might be capable of carrying a considerable white population; the New Guinea native is capable of training for industrial pursuits and as a soldier and, because of this, the holding of these islands with Naval assistance is rendered fairly easy, and the holding of these Islands and outlying posts will ward off any invasion of Australia by a hostile Power.[11]

William M. Hughes, who became Prime Minister in October 1915, devoted much more serious thought to the problem of the former German colonies than had his predecessor.[12] During his visit to England in 1916, Hughes reported to Pearce the following gist of his conversations about that topic with Bonar Law and the Foreign Secretary, Sir Edward Grey:

> As to the Japanese problem. . . . all our fears—or conjectures—that Japan was and is most keenly interested in Australia are amply borne out by facts.

> The position is aggravated—I will not say it is critical—by the fact that Britain has approached Japan with a view to obtaining naval

[11] Pearce to Hughes, Secret, 14 January 1916, Australian War Memorial, Canberra, Pearce Papers. Peter Heydon quotes from this document in *Quiet Decision: A Study of George Foster Pearce* (Melbourne, 1965), p. 231. Often in discussions about strategy the military experts disagreed with their political superiors. In the case of the German colonial question in the Pacific, that did not prove to be so. For a powerful analysis of the situation in the Pacific from a military and naval point of view, see a minute by Brigadier-General Hubert Foster (Chief of the General Staff), 'German Possessions in the Pacific', 23 May 1917, CAO, Prime Minister's Department, SC 12.

[12] Munro Ferguson made the following comparison between the two Prime Ministers:
His [Fisher's] political armoury consists mainly of a vast collection of set opinions on all subjects. He has no elasticity of mind and is impervious to other people's ideas. His mind never 'sits down' to deal thoroughly with a subject . . . The new Prime Minister [Hughes] is quite a different person. In some respects not unlike his countryman Lloyd George. His judgment is better; his insight clear; his capacity for affairs great. He is highly strung and at times violent. I have always found him most agreeable. Few men are more entertaining and so far he has been perfectly frank with me. He stands out above his whole Party in intellect, courage and skill . . . He is the right man to be Prime Minister.
Munro Ferguson to Bonar Law, Personal (copy), 8 November 1915, Novar Papers, 4.

(and, or, military assistance)—say in the Mediterranean—and that the Japanese Government, while ready to grant this, asks for some evidence of Britain's friendliness to her in order possibly to justify her action or placate the opposition. And as Grey says,—if we say: Well we are friendly towards you and we want your aid to win this war—*but*—(1) you must not get any concessions in China: (2) your people cannot come into Australia: (3) you are not to be allowed most favoured nations treatment with Australia (or other parts of the Empire), Japan can hardly be expected to treat our protestations of friendship very seriously.

I told Grey that Australia would fight to the last ditch rather than allow Japanese to enter Australia. Upon that point we were adamant. *I told him that as to control of the Pacific after the war, we were prepared to consider favourably the Equator as a line of demarcation, giving us control of all Islands to the South.*[13]

During the rest of 1916 the Japanese continued to consolidate their position in the islands north of the Line. Munro Ferguson reported in August that Japan obviously intended 'to follow in the footsteps of Germany' in the Pacific and 'evidently means to become the dominant power'.[14] What could be done to offset increasing Japanese influence? Munro Ferguson reckoned that the first step must be to place the loose conglomeration of British Pacific territories under a tightly controlled central administration.[15] Beyond that, he toyed with the idea of bringing another first-class power into the mainstream of Pacific affairs. One way would be to yield the British share in the unhappy

[13] Hughes to Pearce, Strictly Confidential, 21 April 1916, Australian War Memorial, Pearce Papers (emphasis on last sentence added). That letter should be compared with one written by Hughes in 1915, quoted in Fifield, *Woodrow Wilson and the Far East*, pp. 60–61, and also with a much more important copy of a letter in the William M. Hughes collection (Australian National University, Canberra; hereafter cited as Hughes Papers), written to Lloyd George on 7 January 1919, marked 'file secret most carefully'. In the latter letter Hughes attempted to prove in regard to the Pacific settlement that he had merely 'acquiesced in something which had already been done'.

[14] Munro Ferguson to Bonar Law, Personal (copy), 3 August 1916, Novar Papers, 19.

[15] 'A consolidated control of British interests in the Pacific has become continuously more urgent in view of Japanese activities' (Munro Ferguson to Long, Personal [copy], 13 December 1916, Novar Papers, 4). 'There are at present half a dozen distinct British administrations, civil and military. Japanese affairs, on the other hand, are centrally controlled—and consequently ... it [is] urgently necessary to secure a unification of British Administration' (Munro Ferguson to Sir William MacGregor, Private and Personal [copy], 13 June 1917, Novar Papers, 19). When Milner became Colonial Secretary in 1919, his intellect quite characteristically seized upon the problem of the anachronistic administrative structure as the prominent British weakness in the Pacific (see Milner to Munro Ferguson, 26 March 1919, Novar Papers, 216).

administration of the New Hebrides to the French. He wrote to the Governor of Fiji (who also advocated this idea): 'It looks as if the Condominium had better be ended in their favour—in order to firmly establish a third Power in the Pacific and so end our *tête a tête* with Japan.'[16] Another way would be to strengthen the position of the United States in the Pacific, perhaps by letting the Americans take over the part of Samoa under the occupation of New Zealand.[17] As with similar ideas about a general shuffle of territories in Africa after the war, all those Pacific schemes failed, not least for local reasons. The British settlers in the New Hebrides no more wanted their administration transferred to the French than the New Zealanders desired to see Samoa ceded to the Americas—just as the Japanese had no intention of handing over the former German possessions north of the Equator to the Australians.

The frank recognition that Japan could not be ousted from those islands lay at the heart of the Anglo-Japanese understanding of February 1917. 'It would be practically impossible to induce her to surrender them,' Walter Long cabled Munro Ferguson on 1 February. 'We should not therefore in fact be giving up anything if we recognized [the] claim of Japan to the Islands.' Despite the 'great difficulty and complexity' of the China problem, the British government also proposed to support Japanese claims in Shantung. In return, of course, the Japanese government would acknowledge the British Empire's right to acquire the former German possessions south of the Equator. Infinitely more important from the point of view of the Imperial government and the general conduct of the war, Britain would secure additional Japanese naval support in the form of 'destroyers to cope with submarines in the Mediterranean and some additional light cruisers in [the] South Atlantic to deal with enemy raiders'.[18]

[16] Munro Ferguson to Sir Bicham Escott, Personal and Private, 13 January 1917, Novar Papers, 19.

[17] This idea can be associated especially with the governor of Fiji during a later stage of the war:

> For the same reason that it may be as well to strengthen the French in the New Hebrides, I would strengthen also the U.S.A. by handing over to them entirely Samoa. We do not require Samoa for any special purpose, and we cannot expect to have everything when the war is over. Fiji would be a far better outlet than Samoa for the energies of New Zealand if they find the limits of their own Dominion too confined.

Bicham Escott to Hughes, 4 May 1918, Hughes Papers.

[18] Long to Munro Ferguson, Secret, cablegram, 1 February 1917, CAO, Governor-General's Office, 89/216.

Recognizing the 'importance and delicacy' of the issues at stake, the Australian government acquiesced on 7 February; the New Zealand government had expressed its approval the day before.[19] On 2 March, Long transmitted to Munro Ferguson the text of the agreement relating to the Pacific: 'The Japanese Government have been informed that His Majesty's Government accede with pleasure to the request of the Japanese Government for an assurance that, on the occasion of any peace conference, they will support Japan's claim in regard to the disposal of Germany's rights in Shantung and her possessions in the Islands North of the Equator, it being understood that, in the eventual peace settlement, the Japanese Government will treat Great Britain's claims to the German Islands South of the Equator in the same spirit.'[20]

The Anglo-Japanese understanding represents one of the last 'secret agreements' of the First World War. Later in the same year the Russian Revolution popularized the slogan 'no annexations'. The publication of the Allies' secret treaties by the Russians, along with President Wilson's 'peace prattlings' (as the Australasian press called them), forced the British Prime Minister publicly to indicate that 'imperialism' did not motivate British policy. 'With regard to the German Colonies', Lloyd George proclaimed with some exaggeration in his famous 'war-aims' speech of January 1918, 'I have repeatedly declared that they are held at the disposal of a Conference whose decisions

[19] Bernard K. Gordon's *New Zealand Becomes a Pacific Power* (Chicago, 1960) makes two errors in that regard, which need to be corrected. On pp. 48–49 he states: (1) that 'New Zealand, in contrast to Australia, was not even consulted on the affair' and (2) that Britain concluded the arrangement with Japan and notified the Australian government 'on the same day'. On those false premises he reaches the incorrect conclusion that 'any Australian comment could have had no effect on British policy in any case'. What actually happened was this. On 1 and 2 February, Long cabled the Australian and New Zealand governments, respectively; moreover, he even showed a copy of the latter message to the Prime Minister of New Zealand, Massey (in London at the time), who 'expressed a favourable opinion'. The New Zealand government concurred on 6 February, the Australian government on the 7th. On 14 February the British Foreign Secretary informed the Japanese Ambassador that the British government had instructed the British Ambassador in Tokyo to make the statement subsequently transmitted to Munro Ferguson on 2 March (quoted above). In October 1918, Lord Robert Cecil (then Under-Secretary of State for Foreign Affairs) initialed a War Cabinet paper that summarized all of this correspondence in detail. He concluded: 'In 1917, when the Japanese Government were being pressed to accede to the Admiralty's appeal for additional naval assistance, the Governments of the Commonwealth and New Zealand were consulted, and their assent obtained, before the assurance respecting the Pacific Islands north of the Equator was given to the Japanese Government' (memorandum prepared by R. Cecil, Confidential, 15 October 1918, FO 371/3236).

[20] Long to Munro Ferguson, Secret (copy), 2 March 1917, CAO, Prime Minister's Department, SC 12.

must have primary regard to the wishes and interests of the native inhabitants of such Colonies.'

> None of those territories are inhabited by Europeans. The governing consideration, therefore, in all these cases must be that the inhabitants should be placed under the control of an administration, acceptable to themselves, one of whose main purposes will be to prevent their exploitation for the benefit of European capitalists or governments. The natives live in their various tribal organisations under Chiefs and Councils who are competent to consult and speak for their tribes and members and thus to represent their wishes and interests in regard to their disposal. The general principle of national self-determination is, therefore, as applicable in their cases as in those of occupied European territories.[21]

The application of the 'self-determination' principle to the former German colonies caused consternation in Australia, and the Cabinet quickly instructed Munro Ferguson to tell the Colonial Office that some of the natives of New Guinea 'can barely understand that the British are now their masters'.

> While such a policy would be applicable to colonies settled by a white or civilised population such conditions do not obtain in German New Guinea . . . The native inhabitants number from five hundred thousand to eight hundred thousand, and they consist of different races speaking different languages with numerous tribes constantly at war with each other on the larger islands, so that it can readily be seen how little cohesion may be expected from them.
>
> It would be quite impossible to get anything like a reliable expression of their wishes as regards future Government. Even after three years

---

[21] The day before Lloyd George's speech, Long dispatched a cablegram to Munro Ferguson that indicates more frankly the colonial aims of the British government:

> His Majesty's Government are firmly convinced that it is necessary for security of Empire after the war [that we] retain possession of German Colonies but owing to divergence of opinion amongst Allies it has not been possible to secure general acceptance of this view. During recent negotiations with Germans great stress laid by Russians on right of population of country to determine its future and proposal was made to apply this to German Colonies . . . I should be glad therefore if your Ministers could furnish me with statement suitable for publication if necessary containing evidence of the anxiety of natives of German New Guinea to live under British rule.

Long to Munro Ferguson, Secret, cablegram, 4 January 1918, CAO, Prime Minister's Department, SC 12.

military occupation by a small British force the natives have a very hazy idea of the state of affairs . . . To the native mind conquest by another nation means slavery of the conquered or a human feast.

Under all these circumstances it is not difficult to foresee what the result will be if the British Prime Minister's policy is carried out with regard to German New Guinea.[22]

Taking stock of the situation, J. G. Latham of the Royal Australian Navy (later the Chief Justice of Australia) wrote that regardless of the situation in New Guinea, the peace settlement would probably be influenced by humanitarian ideals and 'by considerations which might be described as sentimental, as well as by direct and obvious European interests'. He therefore suggested that Germany's 'injustice, cruelty, or carelessness of native rights or disregard of native feelings should be ascertained with all possible corroborative detail'. On the positive side, Latham recommended that 'public expressions of native opinion in favour of the British should be recorded and preserved. Where a favourable result can be relied upon, opportunities for such expressions might be made by tactful officers who understand the native mind and who are acquainted with the leaders of native opinion—in cases where there is any such thing as native opinion. If any action be taken upon the lines suggested it is essential that the utmost secrecy should be observed in relation to the various activities mentioned.'[23]

Wilsonian idealism thus spurred British politicians, military experts, and colonial administrators to establish as a matter of historical record that Britain ruled in the interests of the indigenous inhabitants of her colonies. If the British clearly promoted 'native welfare' more than any other colonial power, what justification could there be of returning the lost colonies of 'the Hun'? Lord Robert Cecil, speaking in the House of Commons in May 1917, stated: 'We did not, of course, attack these Colonies in order to rescue the natives from misgovernment, but, having rescued them, are we going to hand them back?' The British public and government also feared the military threat posed by an 'unregenerate' Germany possessing colonies. 'Germany wants colonies as military and naval bases to suit her aggressive designs against her neighbours,' the *Yorkshire Herald* proclaimed (23 April 1917). A great German colonial empire, according to the *Daily Graphic*,

---

[22] Official Secretary to Governor-General, Secret, 7 January 1918, CAO, Prime Minister's Department, SC 12.

[23] Minute by J. G. Latham, 'Former German Colonies in the Pacific', Secret, 16 January 1918, Hughes Papers. Latham's superiors enthusiastically endorsed his minute and forwarded it on to the Prime Minister.

'could produce one of the most powerful armies the world has seen. [Native] armies may be trained so large that, properly led by whites and properly equipped, they may be a danger to civilisation itself' (23 May 1917). Ideas such as those led to the conviction in certain British as well as American circles that the peace settlement should prevent the 'militarization' of colonial territories. The British Labour Party believed that the best way to do that and to achieve other noble goals, such as rooting out 'imperialism' as a cause of war, would be to place European colonies under international administration.

On the other side of the political fence, the *Morning Post* and its conservative followers demanded outright annexation of the former German colonies. The sympathies of the Colonial Secretary lay with the latter. Long thought that only a strong British Empire could guarantee world peace—and that strengthening the Empire meant the tightening of the Imperial lines of communication by tying the conquered German colonies to England and the Southern Dominions. The following passages from Long's letters reveal the development of his thought on that question as well as the general lines of the German colonial controversy during the latter part of the war:

> The question about which I am most anxious is the retention of the Colonies and possessions which we have taken from Germany. There is a ridiculous idea in many quarters that this means territorial acquisition and therefore ought in the spirit of self-denial to be abjured by us. In my judgment it has nothing to do with territorial acquisition, but solely with the question of how we are to establish a permanent peace and to make certain of the security of the British Empire in the future.[24]

> We must stick it out and secure a real and conclusive victory. The more help we can get from the Dominions upon these questions, the better for ourselves in every way. I regard it as essential to the Empire that the Colonies should be retained under our own control. Their return to Germany is unthinkable, and I at least do not believe that any system of international control is possible, or will bear the smallest real examination.[25]

> I think the position of the German Colonies question has immensely improved. I was almost alone at the beginning, now I have immense support, and I think that, subject to any difficulty we may have with President Wilson, there is no doubt that in the interests of the peace

[24] Long to Munro Ferguson, Personal and Confidential, 11 October 1917, Novar Papers, 6.
[25] Long to Munro Ferguson, Personal and Confidential, 8 February 1918, Novar Papers, 6.

of the world the conviction is generally shared that they must not be returned to Germany.[26]

How to cope with President Wilson? The answer to that question came from one of the most incisive minds in the War Cabinet.

On the eve of the Peace Conference, General Smuts of South Africa took the matter in hand and instructed one of his subordinates, Sir Erle Richards, to prepare a 'brief' on the German colonies.[27] After the composition of that lengthy memorandum, Smuts wrote to Long in November the following letter, which outlined British tactics to be used in Paris.

> I entirely share your difficulties against any joint international control of the African Colonies.
>
> I have gone through Richards' brief and omitted or toned down certain passages, so that the effect now is that the unconditional annexation of the German Colonies should be pressed for to the utmost. In case that contention should fail, we should continue to hold them subject to the control of the League of Nations in regard to certain specified subjects (liquor, arms, military training, fortifications, etc.). Such control should be laid down in an Act of a general character, so that the French and others are bound in the same way as ourselves. You will see there is here nothing left about joint control, and a small concession is made about the League of Nations which might have the effect of securing the support of the United States to our holding on to these Colonies if our other lines of argument fail. *Our Delegates will, of course, not make this concession until it becomes necessary to carry President Wilson with them.*[28]

The British Empire delegation at Paris did find it indeed necessary to make that concession to President Wilson: 'He [Wilson] is entirely opposed to our annexing a little German colony here or there, which pains me deeply and will move Billy Hughes to great explosions of righteous wrath.'[29]

In his own way, Hughes held firm convictions so replete with moralism that they can be compared with those of Wilson himself. Far from

[26] Long to Munro Ferguson, Private and Personal, 11 October 1918, Novar Papers, 6.

[27] A copy of that important document may be found in the papers of Sir George Foster, National Archives of Canada, Ottawa.

[28] Smuts to Long (copy), 28 November 1918, University of Cape Town, Smuts Papers, vol. 101, no. 49.

[29] Smuts to M. C. Gillet, 20 January 1919, quoted in W. K. Hancock and Jean van der Poel, eds., *Selections from the Smuts Papers* (Cambridge, 1966), p. 889. I am indebted to Dr. van der Poel for allowing me to see the page proofs of this work.

being merely a 'noisome demagogue'[30] (though he certainly mastered the art of demagoguery), Hughes regarded himself an Old Testament prophet as much as Wilson saw himself a New Testament disciple. On 17 January 1919, Hughes wrote in his 'biblical Welsh' style (as Munro Ferguson described it):

> Wilson is the god in the machine to the people outside: but his stock declines daily in spite of much fulsome and persistent puffing. Between ourselves he is rather a stick when it comes down to the facts of life. He is great on great principles. As to their application he is so much like Alice in Wonderland that I suspect him of being [*sic*] sat in a former incarnation for that dear little lady to Lewis Carroll.

> I'm working up the case for the ex-German Colonies and the Pacific. Wilson's against us on this point . . . But I hope we shall convince him. I think we shall for he is a man firm on nothing that really matters. He regards the League of Nations as the great Charter of the World that is to be and sees himself through the roseate cloud of dreams officiating as the High Priest in the Temple in which the Sarcophagus or Ark containing the body or ashes of this amazing gift to Mankind is to rest in majestic seclusion for all time. Give *him* a League of Nations and he will give *us* all the rest. Good. He shall have his toy![31]

On 23 January the Prime Ministers of the Southern Dominions presented their annexationist cases before the Supreme Council of the Peace Conference, and Hughes quickly discovered that the President intended to take seriously the question of the Pacific islands. Parrying Wilson, Hughes thrust forward two lines of argument that he had pursued since he had become Prime Minister: (1) that the war had been fought for security, and from the point of view of Australians, their safety rested on the control of the islands which 'lie like ramparts to the north and east'; and (2) that Australia deserved the privilege of administering the New Guinean and other natives because Australian colonial rule compared favourably with that of any other power. He demanded 'unfettered control' of the islands conquered by Australian troops. Wilson, on the other hand, insisted that those territories should be placed under the control of the League of Nations. The dispute between the Australian David and the American Goliath came to a head on 30 January.[32] When Wilson asked whether the Aus-

---

[30] As he is described by Seth P. Tillman, *Anglo-American Relations at the Paris Peace Conference* (Princeton, 1961), p. 407.

[31] Hughes to Munro Ferguson, Personal, 17 January 1919, Novar Papers, 9.

[32] Hughes's biographer, L. F. Fitzhardinge, uses the well-chosen description of the 'puny, raucous-voiced David aiming his sling at the President of the United States' in an unpublished

tralasians insisted on presenting an ultimatum to 'the whole civilised world', Hughes impudently replied, 'That's about the size of it, President Wilson.'[33]

Nevertheless, Hughes backed down. He finally agreed that the Pacific islands should be placed under 'mandatory control'. Why did he do so? Had he maintained a bold stance merely because, in the words of the *Christchurch Sun* (25 January 1919), 'this strident little man is suffering from a swelled head'? No doubt Hughes's vanity and desire for the limelight partly explain why he challenged Wilson. But that by no means provides a full explanation either of Hughes's behaviour or of Australian policy towards the German colonial question at the Peace Conference. To understand that, one must study the extent to which Australian opinion supported Hughes, the instructions he received from his Parliament and Cabinet, and, perhaps most important of all, his views about problem of Australian security.

Assuming that the journalists who wrote the leading articles in the antipodean newspapers reflected the views of the Australasian public (sometimes a dubious assumption), Hughes clearly did not have an unqualified mandate to demand the annexation of the Pacific islands. The *Melbourne Age* expressed the 'Little Australian' sentiment: 'If, like Alexander the Great, our statesmen sigh for new worlds to rule, their attention may very properly be directed to the old worlds of our own that they have failed to rule with success' (3 February 1919).

On the other hand, the *Brisbane Courier* emphasized Australia's 'Pacific destiny' (30 January 1919):

> Months ago, when the finger of destiny pointed to the approaching collapse of Germany, Mr. Hughes raised his voice in favour of an Australian 'Monroe Doctrine' in the Pacific, and this captivating phrase has been on his lips ever since.

> It must be our business to teach the native, who is too lazy to work unless he has to, that his physical and moral salvation lies in having an occupation which imposes on him a physical tax. The islander has too long been mollycoddled and made a subject merely of sentimental

---

typescript, 'W. M. Hughes and the Treaty of Versailles, 1919' (Institute of Advanced Studies, Australian National University, Canberra, March 1964).

[33] Several versions of this episode exist. I follow the one given by Fitzhardinge in his paper cited in the preceding footnote. Volume 3 of *Foreign Relations of the United States, 1919: The Paris Peace Conference* contains the crucial discussions of the major colonial problems at the peace conference. Among the many books that have dealt with the founding of the mandates system, Paul Birdsall, *Versailles: Twenty Years After* (New York, 1941), and H. Duncan Hall, *Mandates, Dependencies, and Trusteeship* (Washington, 1948), remain among the best.

concern. The island population is diminishing chiefly because of the enervating effects of idleness.

Which of those two views predominated? According to Munro Ferguson in mid-January 1919: 'Mr. Hughes did his best to lash Australia into a desire to possess and administer the Pacific Islands, but the subject is not much mentioned at public meetings or in Labour Halls.'[34] Nevertheless, the theme of security emerged as the foremost consideration not only in the Australasian press but also in the Australian Parliament and government and in the mind of Hughes. '*Our representatives have been bitten with the bug of strategy,*' commented the *New Zealand Observer* in a remark applicable to the statesmen of both antipodean Dominions (8 February 1919; emphasis added). That consideration had motivated the Australian Parliament in mid-November 1918 to resolve that the German colonies in the Pacific should not 'in any circumstances' be restored to Germany.[35]

The Australian Cabinet, no less concerned about 'security', in late November cabled Hughes instructions that contained three major points: '(1) We are against international control. (2) The islands should pass to the British Empire. (3) Control should be vested in the Commonwealth of Australia.'[36] In view of that cablegram, Hughes's actions at the Peace Conference demonstrated that he faithfully if vociferously followed the instructions of his government to the letter.[37] Following his presentation of Australian claims before the Supreme Council on 23 January, Hughes continued his opposition to mandatory control in the meetings of the British Empire delegation. In one of those frank sessions, Hughes later claimed that he lashed out at Lloyd George 'with some burning words about men, who, forgetful of the dignity of their high office, the great traditions of the British people

[34] Munro Ferguson to Milner, Personal (copy), 17 January 1919, Novar Papers, 9.

[35] *Commonwealth of Australia, Parliamentary Debates*, 86 (1918), 7784–7801, 7833–44, 7858–89, 7929–47.

[36] Watt to Hughes, Secret, cablegram (copy), 30 November 1918, CAO, Prime Minister's Department, SC 12.

[37] The Australian cabinet recognized that. The acting Prime Minister, Watt, cabled Hughes: 'Your colleagues hope that your strong representations will meet with the success which they deserve' (Watt to Hughes, Secret, cablegram [copy], CAO, Prime Minister's Department, SC 12). Despite that expression of confidence, an important difference of opinion existed in the highest levels of the Australian government, perhaps because Hughes kept the acting Prime Minister 'in the dark' about the peace conference. In a sense, Hughes and Watt represented the 'Pacific Destiny' and 'Little Australian' schools of thought. Munro Ferguson wrote during the peace conference: 'I hear that Mr. Watt is not favourable to the financial burden of administering the Pacific Islands being cast on the Commonwealth' (Munro Ferguson to Milner, Personal [copy], 4 February 1919, Novar Papers, 5).

and their heroic valour and immense sacrifices in the war, prostrated themselves in meek subservience before the representative of America—for whose people he was no longer entitled to speak.'

> And then having exhausted my stock of vituperative language in English, I fell back upon Welsh—the ideal language for giving full expression to the emotions and passions. And believe me, as our friends in America would put it, I said 'a mouthful'. My words poured out in a foaming cataract: they were highly personal, the kind of words even the most conventional of men would on occasions dearly love to use, but for what the prim and proper people all round them would think. To the members of the Cabinet staring at me open mouthed, they were words full of sound and fury without any definite meaning, but they hit Lloyd George between wind and water. He knew what they meant all right; but he had not heard any thing like them since he was a boy! [38]

In his calmer moments, Hughes asked whether Wilson had any definite ideas about the precise application of 'mandatory control'. To that query he received a negative answer. At a meeting of the British Empire delegation on 27 January, 'General Smuts said that he was satisfied that President Wilson had no tangible idea on the subject.' On the 28th, Lord Robert Cecil assured Hughes that Australia would have 'absolute security' under the mandates system, but that the Australian government would have to 'report annually' to the League of Nations. Hughes brushed aside that requirement as 'an appeal from the men who knew to those who did not know'. That obligation did not seem to bother him.

What did concern Hughes? He showed his hand on the next day, the 29th—after Lloyd George announced to the British Empire delegation that he 'feared a deadlock' and that unless a compromise could be reached, Wilson might depart for the United States. Hughes asked whether 'the laws of Australia' would apply to the territories entrusted to Australia under the mandates system—so that the 'White Australian policy' could be enforced.[39] The answer to that question was affirmative. Through an ingenious plan apparently devised by Smuts, Hankey (secretary of the British Empire delegation), and Latham (now one of Hankey's assistants), the mandates would be divided into ·

---

[38] W. M. Hughes, *Policies and Potentates* (Sydney, 1950). Hughes evidently based that passage on a post-Second World War memorandum entitled 'Mandate and Racial Equality Clause' (Hughes Papers).

[39] This chronology and interpretation of events follows the minutes of the British Empire delegation, which can be studied in the Latham Papers, National Library of Australia, Canberra, and other collections of private papers.

three classes: the 'A' mandates of the Middle East; the 'B' mandates of tropical Africa; and the 'C' mandates of South-West Africa and the Pacific. The latter would be administered as 'integral portions' of the Southern Dominions and Japan. From the Australasian point of view, that meant the closing of the 'open door' (which in the other classes of mandates remained 'open' in the sense of providing equal commercial opportunity for traders of all nations), and—much more importantly—it ensured the control of immigration. Hughes had triumphed. The Japanese would not be allowed to 'infiltrate' into the islands under Australian control, a point in which the Japanese themselves later acquiesced.[40]

Wilson reluctantly agreed to the compromise, and the Supreme Council created the three-pronged mandates system on 30 January.[41] Why had the President so vehemently resisted Australasian attempts to annex the Pacific territories? Did he suspect Australia and New Zealand of harbouring territorial ambitions that somehow might endanger American security in that vast ocean? Or did he merely believe that 'imperialism' had to be ended in the Pacific as in other places in order to secure world peace? Perhaps both those thoughts ran through Wilson's complex mind, but according to the Australasian press, a more important idea motivated him. According to the *Melbourne Age* (1 February and 30 January 1919):

> The Dominion delegates believe President Wilson's firm stand was due to a fear that the Japanese occupation of the Pacific Islands would cause a great outcry in America. [His] predilection for the internationalisation of the German colonies is based rather upon Japan's progress across the Pacific than from a desire to thwart the British acquisition of the islands.

And the *Grey River Argus* concluded that 'President Wilson prefers internationalisation to Japanese expansion in the Pacific' (29 January 1919).

---

[40] For a discussion of that and other important points in Australian-Japanese relations, see especially E. L. Piesse, 'Japan and Australia', *Foreign Affairs*, 4 (April 1926), pp. 475–88. The Piesse Papers, now at the National Library of Australia, Canberra, form the basis of a Melbourne University M.A. thesis entitled 'Attitudes to Japan and Defence, 1890–1923' (1956) by D. C. S. Sissons. I am indebted to the historian of the Department of External Affairs, Mr. J. S. Cumpston, for allowing me to study the Piesse Papers, and to Dr. Sissons for permitting me to read his thesis.

[41] The peace conference did not allocate the mandates, however, until May. At that stage of the conference, Wilson finally yielded to the sharp demands to sit down and 'carve Turkey' and other parts of the world.

By placing the former German colonies in the Pacific under international control, Wilson—according to the Australasian press—believed he could prevent the Japanese from fortifying those islands and from building naval bases there (those requirements were part of the obligations of the 'C' mandatory contract). He could also avert domestic criticism that he had handed over strategically important territories to Japan. And through the device of the annual reports to the League of Nations, the United States would have a means of intelligence about Japanese activities that otherwise would not be available. In short, through mandatory control exerted by the League of Nations, Wilson hoped to check Japanese militarism.

Hughes no less than Wilson was worried about Japan, and he and his advisers in the Australian government spent considerable time and effort evaluating Wilson's ideas of how best to deal with the islands now under Japanese occupation. Both Wilson and Hughes aimed at the same thing: security in the Pacific. From the Australian point of view, the Wilsonian solution in many ways made more sense than the annexationist one. Outright annexation of the former German territories could force Australia to counter Japanese activities, and this would mean building Equatorial military and naval bases, which would be vulnerable in defensive operations and of questionable value in offensive manoeuvres. On the other hand, if a demilitarized buffer zone under international control—and backed by American power—could be created north of Australia, the Japanese threat obviously would be minimized. Why then did Hughes not accept Wilson's logic? The answer in part lies in the cautious and curious nature of Hughes's mentality. Viewing the mandates system as a 'leap in the dark', he safeguarded himself from possible criticism in the future by making it quite clear that he became a party to the scheme only under great duress. But another and much more important sort of logic also motivated Hughes. As Wilson himself once pointed out at the Peace Conference, Hughes had '*a fundamental lack of faith in the League*'. Had the United States joined the League and had the League actually proved effective in preventing the Japanese from fortifying the Pacific islands, history would have taken a different course. What of history as it actually happened? In the words of L. F. Fitzhardinge, 'History surely supports Hughes.'[42]

[42] Fitzhardinge, 'W. M. Hughes and the Treaty of Versailles, 1919'.

7

THE REPARTITION OF AFRICA
DURING THE FIRST WORLD WAR

A. J. Balfour: The French and the Italians. They are not in the least out for self-determination. They are out for getting whatever they can.

Lord Robert Cecil: They are Imperialists.

A. J. Balfour: Exactly.   December 1918[1]

I am inclined to value the argument of self-determination because I believe that most of the people would determine in our favour . . . if we cannot get out of our difficulties in any other way we ought to play self-determination for all it is worth wherever we are involved in difficulties with the French, the Arabs, or anybody else, and leave the case to be settled by that final argument knowing in the bottom of our hearts that we are more likely to benefit from it than anybody else.
                                        Lord Curzon, December 1918[2]

O n the eve of the Paris Peace Conference, the British government decided in principle to accept the proposal for a 'mandates system'. The reason for this decision was complex. In former wars, Britain, like other powers when victorious, had pursued the straightforward procedure of acquiring territories believed to have strategic or commercial importance. These considerations weighed no less heavily in the deliberations of the British statesmen at the end of the First World War than at the close of the Napoleonic Wars. But in 1919 the urge for simple territorial aggrandizement was checked by the popular belief that 'imperialism' was a cause of war and that the rivalry of the Great Powers in Africa, the Middle East, and Asia jeopardized the peace of the world.

---

[1] Eastern Committee Minutes, Secret, 18 December 1918, Milner Papers, New College, Oxford. On the Eastern Committee, see Richard H. Ullman, *Intervention and the War* (Princeton, 1961), p. 307, note 16. The Milner Papers most recently have been used by A. M. Gollin in an incisive study of Lord Milner: *Proconsul in Politics: A Study of Lord Milner in Opposition and in Power* (London, 1964). The main source upon which this article is based is a collection of unbound documents in a dispatch box marked 'Mandates Peace Conference' in the Milner Papers, not used by Gollin (or to my knowledge by any other historian); they reveal for the first time the full details of the British role in the African peace settlement of 1919. Subsequent references to the Milner Papers are to this set of unbound documents unless otherwise indicated. I am grateful to the Cabinet Office for allowing me to publish excerpts from them. All quotations from unpublished official British documents are derived from the Milner Papers and other collections of private documents.

[2] Eastern Committee Minutes, Secret, 5 December 1918, Milner Papers.

President Wilson championed this point of view. He believed that a just peace was one without annexations. He doubted, nevertheless, whether Germany's colonies should be restored. Perhaps he believed that the Germans had forfeited their moral right as colonial rulers; perhaps he thought that the elimination of Germany from colonial affairs would contribute towards a stable world; or perhaps he merely recognized that the Allied Powers would never permit the return of the German colonies. In any case Wilson urged that the former Turkish territories and German colonies be administered as a 'sacred trust of civilization' under the League of Nations.[3] By accepting mandates, the British seemed to bring their aims into alignment with the non-annexationist policy of the United States.

Wilson himself did not define mandatory obligations precisely. As interpreted by the members of the British Imperial War Cabinet, mandates did not mean international administration but merely a sort of international control. According to the Minutes of the Imperial War Cabinet:

> As to the precise distinction between the occupation of territory in a 'possessory' and in a 'mandatory' capacity . . . it was generally agreed that 'mandatory occupation' did not involve anything in the nature of condominium or international administration, but administration by a single Power on certain lines laid down by the League of Nations. These lines would naturally include equality of treatment to all nations in respect of tariffs, concessions, and economic policy generally.[4]

By attaching this meaning to mandates, the British Prime Minister, David Lloyd George, believed that the British could get their share of

[3] On Wilson's views of colonialism, see George Curry, 'Woodrow Wilson, Jan Smuts, and the Versailles Settlement', *American Historical Review*, 66 (July 1961), pp. 968–86. On Wilson's advisory staff, see Lawrence E. Gelfand, *The Inquiry: American Preparations for Peace, 1917–1919* (New Haven, 1963); and W. R. Louis, 'The United States and the African Peace Settlement of 1919: The Pilgrimage of George Louis Beer', *Journal of African History*, 4, 3, (1963), pp. 413–33; on the development of 'the idea of colonial trusteeship' during the First World War, see Henry R. Winkler, *The League of Nations Movement in Great Britain, 1914–1919* (New Brunswick, N.J., 1952).

[4] Imperial War Cabinet Minutes, Secret, 20 December 1918. Copies of these minutes may be found in several collections of private papers, but they are most easily accessible in those of Sir Robert Borden and Sir George Foster, National Archives of Canada. In final form, commercial equality was secured only in the 'A' and 'B' mandates of the Middle East and tropical Africa and not in the 'C' mandates of South-West Africa and the Pacific islands. The other prominent anomaly was the French 'nigger army' clause (Lloyd George's phrase), by which France reserved the right in the Cameroons and Togoland to raise troops 'in the event of a general war'. On these points, see Paul Birdsall, *Versailles: Twenty Years After* (New York, 1941), chap. 3; and H. Duncan Hall, *Mandates, Dependencies and Trusteeship* (Washington, D.C., 1948), pp. 66–69 and passim.

the spoils, but not commit themselves to obligations any more stringent than those Britain had already incurred in tropical Africa under
the Berlin and Brussels Acts of 1885 and 1890.[5] By accepting mandates
along the lines of these acts, he hoped to pay little for an object of
great value: American friendship in colonial affairs. He calculated that
it would be wise to invite the Americans themselves to accept mandatory responsibilities: 'If America were to go away from the [Peace]
Conference with her share of guardianship, it would have a great effect on the world . . . by making the offer to America we would remove
any prejudice against us on the ground of "land-grabbing".'[6]

The other powerful advocates of an Anglo-American colonial understanding were Sir Robert Borden of Canada, General Jan Smuts
of South Africa, and Lord Milner (War Secretary during the last part
of the war, Colonial Secretary during the Peace Conference). Borden,
like Wilson, did not believe that the war had been fought 'in order to
add territory to the British Empire'. He was prepared to support the
annexationist claims of the Southern Dominions (South Africa, Australia, and New Zealand), but he thought that if the result of the war
was merely a scramble for territory by the Allies, 'it would be merely
a prelude to further wars.' Borden, like Lloyd George, urged that the
conquered enemy's colonial territories (apart from South-West Africa
and the former German colonies in the Pacific) be entrusted to mandatory powers under the League of Nations. He hoped that the United
States would accept 'world wide responsibilities in respect of undevel-
oped territories and backward races'.[7]

By contrast, Smuts conceived of American participation in a mandates system in which responsibilities would be limited to the fallen
empires of Eastern Europe:

> The thing would work out like this. The League of Nations, for the
> larger purpose, would step into the shoes of the old Turkish and Rus-
> sian Empires. These peoples, so far as they are of any vitality, would

---

[5] In this connection, see W. R. Louis, 'African Origins of the Mandates Idea', *International Organization*, 19 (Winter 1965), pp. 20–36, which attempts to trace the origins of the mandates in
relation to the Berlin and Algeçiras Acts.

[6] Imperial War Cabinet Minutes, Secret, 20 December 1918; David Lloyd George, *The Truth
about the Peace Treaties* (2 vols., London, 1938), I, p. 118. That Lloyd George published this and
other similar quotations in his memoirs bears evidence that he tried to fulfil his boast of publishing his account of the Peace Conference without 'suppression or distortion of any relevant
fact or document'. So far as colonial problems are concerned, he seems to have suppressed little.
But owing to the limited number of sources he appears to have had at his disposal when he wrote
his memoirs, his account is now of interest less because of the evidence presented than because
of the insight it gives into his personality.

[7] Imperial War Cabinet Minutes, Secret, 26 November and 20 December 1918.

> become little autonomous States . . . some particular Power be-
> longing to the League of Nations should be indicated as the tutelary
> Power, the guardian Power, in respect of one or the other of these
> States.

> The result would be, supposing America were to undertake this job,
> [that] America would keep a large general control over Georgia . . .
> in such a way that the general supervision which America exercises
> over Georgia would be in the general interest not only of Georgia,
> but of the world as a whole . . . My point is to try and get America on
> to our side.[8]

By late 1918 Smuts was also willing to include parts of German Africa in this scheme. Along with Borden and Milner, he was especially
anxious for America to have a share (to use one of Milner's favourite phrases) in the 'white man's burden'. All three attached supreme
importance to an Anglo-American 'colonial alliance'. According to
Milner: '[T]he future peace of the world depended on a good understanding between us [Britain and the United States], and [he] regarded this policy of a mandate by the League of Nations, not as a
mere cloak for annexation, but as a bond of union . . . between the
United States and ourselves.'[9]

Smuts and Milner, however, were reluctant to establish the United
States as the mandatory power in German East Africa. In Smuts's
opinion:

> The British Empire was the great African Power right along the
> eastern half of the continent, and securing East Africa would give us
> through communication along the whole length of the continent—
> a matter of the greatest importance from the point of view of both
> land and of air communications . . . It was not only on the grounds
> of our conquests and sacrifices, but on the obvious geographical sit-
> uation, that we were entitled to make a strong claim to being the
> mandatory in that region. Personally he [Smuts] would give up very
> much in order to attain that . . . He would prefer to see the United
> States in Palestine rather than East Africa.[10]

[8] Eastern Committee Minutes, Secret, 2 December 1918, Milner Papers; see also Lt. Gen. the
Rt. Hon. J. C. Smuts, *The League of Nations: A Practical Suggestion* (New York, 1919), and Sir Keith
Hancock, *Smuts: The Sanguine Years, 1870–1919* (Cambridge, 1962), chap. 20.

[9] Imperial War Cabinet Minutes, Secret, 20 December 1918; Lloyd George, *Truth about the
Peace Treaties*, I, p. 122.

[10] 'Mr. Balfour suggested that the line of argument pursued by General Smuts was perhaps
playing a little fast-and-loose with the notion of mandatory occupation' (Imperial War Cabinet
Minutes, Secret, 20 December 1918; quoted in Lloyd George, *Truth about the Peace Treaties*, I,
pp. 119–20).

Lloyd George objected to this proposal. Though he originally had supported the idea of shoving the United States into Palestine, by December 1918 he had changed his mind:

> It would involve placing an absolutely new and crude Power in the middle of all our complicated interests in Egypt, Arabia, and Mesopotamia. Everyone with any complaint to make against British administration would rush off to the United States, who would not be able to resist the temptation to meddle. Every Bedouin would be going to the Americans, and we should be put into the humiliating position of continually giving in to the Americans on every complaint raised by them, up to a point when we could stand it no longer, and then might find ourselves involved in a serious quarrel.[11]

Lord Milner thought that Armenia might be a possible American mandate: 'The mere fact that we did not want it ourselves was no reason for not assigning the responsibility of it to the United States.'[12] Winston Churchill considered, however, that it would be dangerous to entrust even Armenia to the Americans: 'If America were introduced in the heart of European politics, in Armenia, or anywhere else in the Mediterranean region, this would be an incentive to her to make herself the greatest Naval Power.'[13] If the British had to give up any territory to the Americans, Churchill was 'strongly in favour of giving up German East Africa.'[14]

The Imperial War Cabinet thus did not agree on where the United States should become a 'mandatory power'. In any case the point remained theoretical because the United States never offered to accept mandates.[15] There was complete accord in the Imperial War Cabinet,

---

[11] Imperial War Cabinet Minutes, Secret, 20 December 1918.

[12] Ibid.

[13] 'Admiral Wemyss supported this argument, and said the Admiralty would regard a large American fleet in the Mediterranean with greater apprehension than anywhere else. An American occupation of Palestine, or Armenia, would inevitably lead to her building up a fleet in the Mediterranean, with bases and lines of communication' (ibid.).

[14] Ibid.; Lloyd George, *Truth about the Peace Treaties*, I, p. 121.

[15] Wilson's colonial adviser, George Louis Beer, urged that the United States should assume mandatory responsibility in the Cameroons. This scheme failed, not only because of Wilson's reluctance to see the United States become involved in colonial affairs, but also because the French had no intention of giving up the Cameroons. See the typescript copy of Beer's diary at the Library of Congress. This manuscript is invaluable in tracing the attempts made to cement the 'Anglo-American colonial alliance' and in understanding the American role in the African peace settlement. The Edward M. House Papers and the Sir William Wiseman Papers, Yale University, are also useful in this regard. Unfortunately the Woodrow Wilson Papers, Manuscript Division, Library of Congress, are difficult to use for so specialized a topic as this because of the cumbersome classification system.

however, on two other important points: that President Wilson's principle of self-determination had little or no relevance for territories outside Europe and the Middle East; and that South-West Africa and the former German colonies in the Pacific should not be placed under the mandates system, but annexed by the British Dominions that had conquered them. A. J. Balfour, the Foreign Secretary, stated in December 1918 in regard to the first point:

> We must not allow ourselves to be driven by that broad principle [of self-determination] into applying it pedantically where it is really inapplicable, namely, to wholly barbarous, undeveloped, and unorganised black tribes, whether they be in the Pacific or Africa. Self-determination there, I do not say it has not even a real meaning, but evidently you cannot transfer formulas more or less applicable to the populations of Europe to different races.[16]

Later in the same month, Prime Minister William Hughes of Australia stated emphatically that any attempt to apply 'self-determination' to South-West Africa or the Pacific islands would be 'futile'. He thought that any sort of mandatory interference in the former German colonies in these regions would jeopardize the security of the British Empire.

> As regards the German colonies in the Pacific, he [Hughes] thought that the President was talking of a problem which he did not really understand. New Guinea was only 80 miles from Australia.[17]

[16] Eastern Committee Minutes, Secret, 5 December 1918, Milner Papers. The most prominent British humanitarian who denounced German 'colonial atrocities' during the war, John H. Harris, Organizing Secretary of the Anti-Slavery and Aborigines Protection Society, was more confident. 'Upon the outbreak of War', Harris wrote in March 1917, 'the German administration, which is always militarist, hanged without trial very large numbers of native chiefs, not upon any definite charge, but merely upon the suspicion that they were friendly to the Allies.'

> If this were so upon suspicion, one trembles to think what would happen on the restoration of the Colonies to Germany. No International safeguards the mind of man could conceive would save other Chiefs. From the information in our possession, and it increases every month, the native chiefs in the occupied territories have assisted the 'conquerors' in a wholehearted manner, supplying money, carriers, foodstuffs and even soldiers, and have thus quite unwittingly laid themselves open to trial for treason, and you can be quite sure that such trial and sentence would be vigorously carried out.

In those circumstances Harris knew that the native chiefs would opt for British rule—a triumph of the logic of self-determination (Harris to J. G. Alexander, 2 March 1917, Anti-Slavery and Aborigines Protection Society Papers, D 3/16, Rhodes House, Oxford. These papers are especially valuable in tracing the development of the mandates idea during the course of the war.).

[17] Imperial War Cabinet Minutes, Secret, 30 December 1918.

. . . To the northward lie the teeming millions of Asia . . . Australia is deeply convinced of the strategic importance to her of the islands which lie like ramparts to the north and east . . . Australia must have unfettered control.[18]

As is well known, Hughes's unyielding attitude on this point brought him into head-on collision with Wilson, and in January 1919 nearly disrupted the Peace Conference.[19] With great reluctance Hughes and his colleagues from New Zealand and South Africa finally yielded to Wilson's fervent insistence that all conquered colonial territories be placed under the mandates system. As Hughes had feared, he found himself, in his opinion, being 'dragged quite unnecessarily behind the wheels of President Wilson's chariot'.[20] On 30 January the Peace Conference decided to place the German colonies as well as the former Turkish territories under the mandates system.

Yet Wilson's triumph was not all he might have wished. He forced the conference to accept a universal application of the mandates system, but he did not succeed in establishing 'self-determination' as the basis of this system.[21] And in return for the acceptance of the mandates system by the representatives of the Southern Dominions, he acquiesced in Smuts's proposal that there should be various types of

[18] Hughes memo, Secret, 6 February 1919, Milner Papers.

[19] Among the more important works that have dealt with the mandates negotiations at the Peace Conference are Ray Stannard Baker, *Woodrow Wilson and World Settlement* (3 vols., New York, 1922); Robert Lansing, *The Peace Negotiations: A Personal Narrative* (Boston, 1921); David Hunter Miller, 'The Origin of the Mandates System', *Foreign Affairs*, 6 (January 1928), pp. 277–80; *The Intimate Papers of Colonel House*, ed. Charles Seymour (4 vols., New York, 1926–28); Quincy Wright, *Mandates under the League of Nations* (Chicago, 1930); Seth P. Tillman, *Anglo-American Relations at the Paris Peace Conference of 1919* (Princeton, 1961); and the works cited in footnotes above. The best general work on the subject is Hall, *Mandates, Dependencies and Trusteeship*. For a discussion of these and other works concerning the mandates system, see my chapter in *British Empire–Commonwealth Historiography: Reassessments and Prospects*, ed. Robin W. Winks (Durham, N.C., 1966).

[20] Imperial War Cabinet Minutes, Secret, 30 December 1918.

[21] If indeed this was Wilson's intention. The slippery term 'self-determination' was interpreted in a great variety of ways. On the one hand, it could mean the eventual independence of the peoples concerned; on the other hand, it could merely take into consideration the interests and welfare of the indigenous inhabitants. In the mandates charter (Article 22 of the League Covenant), 'self-determination' was implicit in the clauses relating to the peoples of the Middle East but not in those concerning Africa and the Pacific islands. Wilson apparently resigned himself to the absorption of those latter regions by the mandatory powers—provided this was the wish of the indigenous inhabitants. As he illustrated this point before the Council of Ten: 'It was up to the Union of South Africa to make it [natural union between the two territories] so attractive that South-West Africa would come into the Union of their own free will . . . if successful administration by a mandatory should lead to union with the mandatory, he would be the last to object.' On this point, see Hall, *Mandates, Dependencies and Trusteeship*, pp. 123–24.

mandates. The 'simple and straightforward' 'C' mandates of South-West Africa and the Pacific islands, according to Milner, would differ in little other than name from normal colonial possessions. The 'B' mandates of tropical Africa and the 'A' mandates of the Middle East bound the mandatory powers to more stringent obligations,[22] but

[22] There has been so much written on the mandates negotiations at the Peace Conference that it seems unnecessary to give a detailed exposition of them here. The basic published source is *Papers relating to the Foreign Relations of the United States: The Paris Peace Conference, 1919* (13 vols., Washington, D.C., 1942–47); for a lucid account, see Tillman, *Anglo-American Relations*. The Milner Papers nevertheless provide such interesting supplementary information that perhaps it is justified to give a brief summary of Milner's views about mandates. In a powerfully written memorandum of 8 March 1919, he stated: 'in the C mandate the obligations incurred by the mandatory Power, the limitations to its sovereignty, are very few and simple.' Apart from obligations to combat the slave trade and the arms traffic, and to refrain from erecting fortifications, 'this class of mandate contains no restrictions upon the legislative and administrative authority of the mandatory Power.'

> The country handed over to it becomes an integral part of the territory of that Power. It follows, that the commercial and fiscal system prevailing in the existing territory of the mandatory Power may be applied to the mandated territory without reservation or restriction.

The 'B' mandates of tropical Africa (designed for German East Africa, Togoland, and the Cameroons) were more complicated than the 'C' mandates. In Milner's opinion there were two important differences between the two classes:

> (1) Under mandates of the 'C' Class the laws of the mandatory Power are *ipso facto* applicable to the mandated territory, whereas in mandates of the 'B' Class the mandatory Power is only made 'responsible for the administration' of the mandated territory. This no doubt implies that the mandatory Power may make laws for the territory . . . But this will have to be special legislation, and must in practice differ materially from the laws in force in the country exercising the mandates.
> (2) In Class 'B' mandates the mandatory Power is under very much more extensive obligations than in mandates of Class 'C', especially with regard to fiscal and commercial matters . . . It thus appears that under mandates of the 'B' Class, the position of a mandated territory very much resembles, if it is not absolutely identical with, that of certain existing British Protectorates such as Nigeria and East Africa, in which equality of trade conditions has already been established under existing treaties.

If the 'B' mandates were more complex than those of the 'C' group, there was also, in Milner's words, a 'broad distinction in character' between these two classes on the one hand and the 'A' class on the other. The 'B' and 'C' mandates of tropical Africa and the Pacific for all practical purposes could be regarded as colonial possessions. They were trammelled only by certain international obligations, such as those to combat the slave trade, to submit reports to the League of Nations, and, in the case of the 'B' mandates, to ensure equality of commercial opportunity. Once the principles of the mandates system had been accepted by the Peace Conference in regard to the 'B' and 'C' territories, the delegates had little difficulty in drafting the terms of the mandatory obligations. This was entirely untrue of the 'A' mandates of the Middle East, which were, in Milner's words, 'by far the most difficult and complicated'.

these were accepted by the French as well as the British with the conviction that there was 'no real difference between a colony and . . . [a] mandated area'. 'You will see', said one of the French delegates to Wilson's colonial adviser, 'what these mandates will develop into in ten years.'[23]

The purpose of the above remarks has been not only to illuminate British attitudes towards the founding of the mandates system, but also to explain why Britain simply did not annex the German colonies and to provide the background of the territorial settlement. During the war as during the Peace Conference, in the Pacific as in Africa, British territorial ambitions remained fairly constant. The basic aim was to absorb German territories in the vicinity of the Southern Dominions. In 1915 the Colonial Secretary, Lewis Harcourt, in a memorandum aptly entitled 'The Spoils', had written: 'It is out of the question to part with any of the territories now in the occupation of Australia and New Zealand . . . German South-West Africa . . . must obviously be retained as part of the British Empire.'[24] These words were echoed in the report of the Imperial War Cabinet's Committee on Territorial Desiderata of April 1917:

> The restoration to Germany of South-West Africa is incompatible with the security and peaceful development of the Union of South Africa, and should in no circumstances be contemplated . . .

It is really impossible to frame a single form of mandate which would be applicable, or even approximately applicable, to all the Territories in question. They differ so radically from one another in essential particulars that no one system of Government can be devised which will suit them all . . . When we have settled the number of states into which the Turkish Empire is to be divided, the question of the boundaries between these states will arise, and here there is . . . room for the greatest difference of opinion . . . Ethnic affinity will no doubt be regarded as a basic principle, but this alone affords very insufficient guidance, for in almost every case, notably in that of Armenia, different, and indeed hostile races are intermixed. On the other hand we have in fixing the boundaries of Syria and Mesopotamia, to deal with the exactly opposite problem, viz., how to escape or at least to minimise the administrative difficulties of dividing authority over one and the same race between two different mandatory Powers.

Milner memo, 'Mandates', Secret, 8 March 1919, Milner Papers. The solution to the problem of the drafting of the 'A' mandates eluded the ingenuity even of Milner, and the Middle Eastern settlement was not concluded until long after the Peace Conference had adjourned.

[23] Beer diary, 7–13 July 1919.

[24] Harcourt memo, Secret, 25 March 1915, Herbert H. Asquith Papers, Bodleian Library, Oxford. The Asquith Papers are essential for understanding colonial problems at the beginning of the war.

> The retention of the German islands and colonies in the Pacific south of the Equator, in order to eliminate all possible future German naval bases in this region, is required for the security of the British Australasian Dominions.[25]

The British government at the beginning of the war had agreed to permit Japanese occupation of the German islands north of the Equator. With a bitterness recalling that of the 1880s (when in an analogous way the Colonial Office had restrained the Queensland government from annexing eastern New Guinea), the Australians and New Zealanders watched the Japanese take over Pacific islands that they regarded as a threat to their security if occupied by a hostile power.[26] At the Peace Conference, the remaining islands south of the Equator were apportioned in the way that had been obvious since practically the beginning of the war: Samoa to New Zealand, the rest to Australia. Nor was there any doubt about South-West Africa: in 1919 not even Wilson challenged South Africa's claim.[27]

In the other African settlements, Britain was the only power with interests at stake in both the east and the west of the continent. The French claimed part of Togoland and most of the Cameroons, the Belgians part of German East Africa. The Portuguese and the Italians, though they had conquered no territory in Africa, nevertheless demanded a share of the spoils. The Italians justified their claims on the basis of the Treaty of London of 1915 (which promised the Italians 'equitable compensation' in colonial areas). The Portuguese had no treaty engagement, but could see no reason why their empire should not grow at Germany's expense along with those of the other powers. The French and the Belgians held a far stronger position: their troops actually occupied African territory. By contrast, however, with the Bel-

[25] Committee on Territorial Desiderata, Report, Secret, 28 April 1917, Austen Chamberlain Papers, Birmingham University. This is one of the very few collections of private papers—perhaps the only one—containing the minutes of this committee.

[26] There is no satisfactory account of Anglo-Japanese relations during the First World War, but on the problem of the Pacific, see especially Russell H. Fifield, *Woodrow Wilson and the Far East* (Hamden, Conn., 1965 ed.), and Roy Watson Curry, *Woodrow Wilson and Far Eastern Policy, 1913–1921* (New York, 1957).

[27] Nor did Wilson interfere in the issues concerning Egypt and Morocco. The settlement of these questions followed the basic pattern of the *Entente* agreement of 1904: Britain received recognition of the protectorate declared over Egypt in 1914; France strengthened its hold over Morocco and in addition regained in full sovereignty the two slices of the Cameroons ceded to Germany by the 1911 Moroccan agreement. (These points are discussed in Louis, 'United States and the African Peace Settlement'.) The Peace Conference not only founded the mandates system, but also consolidated and extended the European empires in Africa.

gians (who had tried in vain to make a bargain with the British before the beginning of the Peace Conference), the French even possessed agreements by which Britain recognized French rights to administer 'provisionally' parts of Togoland and the Cameroons.[28]

The origins of the Anglo-French West African agreements are still obscure. Perhaps these arrangements resulted merely from the necessity to establish provisional spheres of administration, but probably (at least in regard to the one concerning the Cameroons) they were connected with the problem of the Middle East. In West Africa, the French tentatively received, in Milner's phrase, 'the lion's share'—half of Togoland, nine-tenths of the Cameroons—even though a large part of the Cameroons, including the port of Douala, had been overrun by British troops. Following the traditional pattern, the British gave way in the west of the African continent to secure their lines of communication in the east. In 1917 Smuts thought that

> [i]f there were a choice between keeping German East Africa or the German West African colonies, he [Smuts] considered it much more important to make sure of the safety of the eastern route from South Africa, more particularly as the retention of German East Africa included the provision of a land communication with Egypt, and also secured the Red Sea route to India.[29]

About the importance of West Africa itself, opinion was divided between the officials in England and those in the British West African territories. According to the Colonial Secretary in 1918, Walter Long, Douala was 'the best port on the West Coast of Africa, and possessed great importance as a potential base for coal and supplies, and a wireless station'. In the opinion, however, of the Governor-General of Nigeria, Sir Frederick Lugard: 'The portions of the Cameroons we had from time to time been anxious to get were of little value, and he [Lugard] would be inclined to give the whole of the Cameroons and Togoland to France.'[30] In 1919 this conflict of views was resolved along the lines of the recommendation of the Imperial War Cabinet's Committee on Territorial Desiderata:

[28] See the copies of the Anglo-French agreements of 13 September 1914 and 28 February 1916 for Togoland and the Cameroons, respectively, in the Records of the American Commission to Negotiate Peace, National Archives, 185.115/24. On the Cameroons agreement, see Margery Perham, *Lugard* (2 vols., London, 1956–60), II, pp. 544–45.

[29] Minutes of the Second Meeting of the Imperial War Cabinet Committee on Territorial Desiderata, Secret, 18 April 1917, Chamberlain Papers.

[30] Imperial War Cabinet Minutes, Secret, 20 December 1918; for Lugard's earlier views, see Perham, *Lugard*, II, pp. 544–45.

The Committee concluded that the Cameroons should not be restored to Germany under any circumstances except those of imperative necessity, and that in our dealings with France the utmost importance should be laid on the greatness of the concession made to France, and its provisional character insisted on to secure, at the least, the [boundary] modifications specified by the Colonial Office.[31]

The issues at stake were not great. As a representative of the Admiralty had pointed out in 1917, 'in French hands Duala might be a very great inconvenience to us, though he could hardly call it a very serious menace.'[32] By December 1918 the British had resigned themselves to handing over most of the German West African territories to the French. Smuts pointed out that 'it was really only a question of boundaries.'[33]

The settlement of these West African 'boundary' questions took place in Paris during the spring of 1919.[34] Like the other African territorial problems, they were mainly dealt with, in Milner's phrase, 'out of court'—not as part of the formal conference. On 7 March, Milner met with Henri Simon, the French Colonial Minister, to discuss the Cameroons and Togoland: 'M. Simon stated that his Government would be found very accommodating in the Cameroons, but could not adopt the same policy in Togoland.'[35] In the Cameroons, the French willingness to accommodate the British amounted to making boundary adjustments, which were necessary, according to Milner, because (writing in reference to Togoland and German East Africa as well as the Cameroons),

> the boundaries between the different spheres of occupation are haphazard and, as a permanent arrangement, would be quite intolerable.

---

[31] Minutes of the Second Meeting of the Imperial War Cabinet Committee on Territorial Desiderata, Secret, 18 April 1917, Chamberlain Papers.

[32] Ibid.

[33] Imperial War Cabinet Minutes, Secret, 20 December 1918.

[34] Though the decision to establish the mandates system was taken in late January, the mandates were not allocated until May. Wilson attempted to postpone this question as long as possible, partly because he wanted to avoid the impression of dividing the spoils at the Peace Conference, partly in order to retain bargaining power. Unable to withstand the increasingly sharp demands of the French and British delegates, he finally yielded. On 7 May he agreed that the German colonies should be 'entrusted' to Britain and France—an arrangement that ignored the claims of Italy, Belgium, and Portugal and that brought the colonial question again to the fore. The British and French delegates had already begun the technical process of partition; see especially Milner memo, 'Cameroons and Togoland', 7 March 1919, Milner Papers.

[35] Ibid.

They cut across tribal and administrative divisions, take no account of economic conditions, and are in every way objectionable.[36]

Apart from several minor adjustments designed to make this partition less artificial, the final settlement between Britain and France in the Cameroons was substantially the same as the provisional one of 1916.[37] The Togoland negotiations were more acrimonious:

> As to Togoland, M. Simon said that, to be quite frank, France wanted the whole of it.[38]

The French justified this claim on grounds that Dahomey had only a small seaboard 'and urgently required more'. Simon believed that Togoland was 'an entirely artificial creation', a situation best rectified in his opinion by French annexation. Milner did not respond favourably to this suggestion:

> Lord Milner observed that he had the impression that in return for extreme accommodation on our part in the Cameroons, the French were shewing great exigence in Togoland.[39]

Milner and Simon finally agreed that the best solution would be simply to partition Togoland between Britain and France, but to improve, as in the Cameroons, the 'very hastily fixed' provisional boundary of 1914. France received the larger part (60 per cent of the territory, containing approximately four times the population of the British sector), which included the only good port in the colony, Lomé, and the railways running to it. Summarizing these negotiations, Milner wrote:

> While ... the settlement is generous to France, and while we can well afford to take credit for it in any other negotiations with the French about territorial adjustments—in Syria for instance—the position from the British colonial point of view is not a bad one. We shall not, indeed, have added much to our possessions in West Africa, either in the Cameroons or in Togo. But the additional territory we have gained, though not large in extent, has a certain value in giving us better boundaries and bringing completely within our borders native

[36] Milner memo, 'Mandates', Secret, 8 March 1919, Milner Papers.

[37] See Milner memo, 'Cameroons and Togoland', 29 May 1919, Milner Papers, which was written shortly after he had reached agreement with Simon on these questions. The final details, however, were not settled until late June.

[38] Milner memo, 'Cameroons and Togoland', 7 March 1919, Milner Papers.

[39] Ibid.

Tribes which have hitherto been partly within British territory and partly outside it.[40]

Neither the Cameroons nor Togoland lay contiguous to a British Dominion, a geographical fact that largely explains the relatively indifferent British attitude. Yet German East Africa, which also fell into this geographical category, was crucial to British security. In Smuts's opinion, German East Africa was less important than German South-West Africa, but nevertheless 'very materially concern[ed] the safety of the British Empire as a whole'.

> He [Smuts] drew attention to the evidence which had been produced with regard to German designs of creating a great Central African Empire, which, in conjunction with German control over Turkey, might eventually be used to threaten the British position in Egypt. He also attached great importance to the securing of continuity of territory by land between British South Africa and British North Africa.[41]

German East Africa was the 'missing link' in the chain of British possessions from the Cape to Cairo; this consideration preoccupied British statesmen throughout the war, as is indicated by the sustained interest shown by Harcourt:

14, Berkeley Square, W.1.
February 13th, 1919

My dear Milner,

I think I ought to warn you, as I did your two predecessors [Bonar Law and Walter Long], that in the Peace settlement of German East Africa the province of Ruanda at the North-western corner of G.E.A. should on no account go to the Belgians or in any way pass out of British control. It is the only possible route for the Cape to Cairo railway, if that project is ever realised . . .

Yours very sincerely,
(sgd) Harcourt[42]

In conjunction with the British offensive against German East Africa of 1916, Belgian troops had moved into the north-western part of

---

[40] Milner memo, 'Cameroons and Togoland', 29 May 1919, Milner Papers.

[41] Minutes of the First Meeting of the Imperial War Cabinet Committee on Territorial Desiderata, Secret, 17 April 1917, Chamberlain Papers.

[42] Milner Papers.

German East Africa, occupying territory that extended to Lake Victoria in the east and Tabora in the south, and that included the western part of the central railway to Lake Tanganyika. Following occupation, the Belgian government demanded British recognition of the Belgian right to dispose of this territory for advantages elsewhere. The British refused on these grounds:

1. because the successful invasion of the north-west part of German East Africa by the Belgians was only made possible by British assistance and as the result of British efforts;

2. because the Belgian view was contrary to the agreement by which all conquered territory was to be held for disposal in the peace negotiations;

3. because there are reasons specially affecting the future of British rule in East Africa which made it imperative to avoid any recognition such as the Belgians sought of their position in the territory occupied by them. (Among these reasons are:—(i) the difficulty of administering German East Africa without the north-west provinces, which form an integral part of the German Protectorate, (ii) the necessity of maintaining our land communications between the south and the north (Uganda and the Sudan) on the one hand, and between the east and the west (the Indian Ocean to Lake Tanganyika) on the other, (iii) the importance of our sharing equally with the Belgian Congo the control over Lake Tanganyika and the communications on the Lake).[43]

Whatever the validity of these reasons, Belgian occupation rankled the British mainly because the Belgians had secured 'the richest and most populous districts of German East Africa' and had blocked the Cape-to-Cairo route.[44] In Milner's opinion, this was 'intolerable'.[45]

He so informed the colonial adviser to the Belgian Foreign Ministry, Pierre Orts, on 12 May 1919.[46] He argued that the extension of Belgian dominion into German East Africa was objectionable because it would violate the 'natural frontier' between East and Central Africa, and he stated 'most emphatically' that the British would not tolerate the Belgians 'sitting' on their 'lines of communication from East to West and from North to South'. Orts, after considerable skirmishing, 'admitted the force' of Milner's argument. He said that his government was prepared to hand over the territory necessary for British

[43] Colonial Office memo, No. 1066 Africa, Confidential, 'Belgian Occupied Territory in German East Africa', 27 October 1918, Milner Papers.

[44] Ibid.

[45] Milner memo, 'Negotiations with Belgium about German East Africa', n.d. [May 1919], Milner Papers.

[46] These negotiations are discussed in detail in W. R. Louis, *Ruanda-Urundi, 1884–1919* (Oxford, 1963), chap. 21.

'communications', but that Belgium must retain most of the districts of Ruanda and Urundi. This concession satisfied Milner so far as strategic considerations were concerned, but he was far from happy about Belgian retention of Ruanda and Urundi:

> The districts of Ruanda and Urundi, though small in extent, are in some respects the best part of all German East Africa. They are healthy highlands, very fertile, and well cultivated as East African cultivation goes. They have a very large population, something like 3 millions, which is about 40% of the total native population of German East Africa. They are also particularly rich in cattle.[47]

Still, Milner was willing to concede these districts to Belgium:

> I should be prepared, especially in the case of a small power like Belgium, to err if I must err on the side of generosity; and I feel that with the enormous extent of mandated territory which the Peace settlement is likely in any case to leave in our hands, we can well afford to do without Ruanda and Urundi.[48]

Milner knew, however, that the Belgians were merely using Ruanda and Urundi as a pawn. What they really wanted was not part of East Africa but a strip of territory at the mouth of the Congo on the west coast.

> They are extremely embarrassed by the very narrow sea front of their enormous Congo territory, and by the fact that they only possess one, —the Northern—bank of the Congo.

> If they could get a strip of land on the south of that river, extending as far as Ambrizette, I believe that they would be willing to give up almost the whole of Ruanda and Urundi, and this would be from every point of view the best solution.[49]

This proposed solution to the 'East African tangle' (as Milner referred to it in his diary) involved persuading the Portuguese to part with the southern bank of the Congo.[50] They would do this only in return for a substantial quid pro quo elsewhere. Milner therefore proposed to give the Portuguese some territory in the south of German East Africa:

[47] Milner memo, 'Negotiations with Belgium about German East Africa', n.d. [May 1919], Milner Papers.

[48] Ibid.

[49] Ibid.

[50] Entry for 14 May 1919, Milner Papers.

thus Belgium would receive the southern bank of the Congo River; Portugal would expand into southern German East Africa; and Britain would acquire Ruanda and Urundi. This bargain failed to materialize, however, because the Portuguese refused to be bought off, in their opinion, with worthless territory. After 'troublesome and time wasting' negotiations, in Milner's words, Belgium was left with Ruanda-Urundi,[51] as was agreed upon by Orts and Milner on 30 May 1919. Despite the protest of the American representative, George Louis Beer, and of the Anti-Slavery and Aborigines Protection Society, the Milner-Orts agreement proved final.[52]

Thus, far from being willing to give up the southern Congo bank for part of German East Africa, the Portuguese demanded the southern portion of the latter territory as a mandate. Milner thought this was preposterous:

> The Portuguese have in my opinion no claim whatever to receive a mandate for any portion of German East Africa on the score of what they have done in the conquest of it . . . they even failed to defend their own boundaries against Von Lettow [-Vorbeck, the German commander in East Africa], when our operations rendered his position in East Africa untenable, and by that failure prolonged the war in East Africa about a year.[53]

At a meeting of the Mandates Commission on 12 July 1919, the Portuguese were told that they could have no part of German East Africa as a mandate, but to silence them, they were given full sovereignty over a scrap of territory called the 'Kionga Triangle' in northern Mozambique, which rounded off the Portuguese territory at the natural frontier of the Ruvuma River.[54] This was done, in Milner's words, 'as a matter of grace and convenience'.

[51] Except for a strip of territory in eastern Ruanda that was handed over to Belgium in 1923.

[52] At the meeting of the Mandates Commission on 16 July, Beer pointed out 'its [the Milner-Orts agreement's] absurdity from the geographical, ethnographical and political standpoints'. He later wrote: 'This agreement cannot be defended except on grounds of merest expediency. It is contrary to the fundamental principles upon which these colonies were to be disposed of in that no attention at all was paid to native interests' (Beer diary, 13 July–4 August 1919). The Anti-Slavery and Aborigines Protection Society protested that 'past experience of Belgian proceedings in the Congo does not encourage an extension of the rule of that nation over large portions of Africa,' and Harris complained that talk of the 'sacred trust' in this regard was 'manifest hypocrisy'. On Beer's and Harris's attempts to influence the territorial settlement, see Louis, 'United States and the African Peace Settlement'.

[53] Milner memo, 29 May 1919, Milner Papers.

[54] See H. B. Thomas, 'The Kionga Triangle', *Tanganyika Notes and Records*, 31 (July 1951), pp. 47–50.

The Portuguese were extremely suspicious of the machinations of the other imperial powers. It is now clear from the British records that these suspicions were justified. At the Peace Conference, the Portuguese learned that the Italians were pressing the British to support their efforts to establish a 'trading company' in Angola. According to a British memorandum written in March 1919:

> The Italian Delegate was unable to explain satisfactorily why the good offices of H.M.G. should be required in order to enable them to carry on trade with a Portuguese Colony. On being pressed however it appeared that . . . the real aim was political. The Italian Delegate has now explained that Italy wishes H.M.G. to conclude with Italy an agreement similar to the secret agreement with Germany of 1898, whereby in the event of a disruption of the Portuguese colonial possessions part would fall to H.M.G. and part (including Angola) to Germany.[55]

The British refused on the grounds that 'Imperialism' was dead. 'Such an arrangement in the present altered state of the world', wrote a Colonial Office official, 'would be quite unthinkable.'[56]

Though the British rebuffed Italian overtures regarding the Portuguese colonies, they were bound by the Treaty of London to consider the more general problem of 'equitable compensation' for Italy in Africa. On 7 May 1919, the Supreme Council appointed an Inter-Allied Committee, composed of Milner, Simon, and an Italian delegate, Silvio Crespi, to discuss Italian territorial claims, which extended over a large part of north-eastern Africa. Most of the regions claimed by Italy were, as Milner described them, 'mainly desert', but even so the British and the French were reluctant to hand them over to the Italians. The remarkable feature that struck Milner about Italian ambitions was the extent to which they involved British territory:

> [F]rom the first it was Great Britain that was asked to make the principal sacrifices. In Libya the area claimed from Great Britain was three or four times as large as that claimed from France . . . In asking for the whole of British and French Somaliland, Italy was asking us to give up a country ten times as large as France was asked to give

---

[55] Italy similarly demanded a 'free hand' to trade in Abyssinia: 'In this matter as in others the Italian Government are using trade as a cloak for political aims' (R. Sperling memo, 11 March 1919, Lothian [Philip Kerr] Papers, Scottish Record Office, Edinburgh. These papers contain valuable information about the creation of the mandates system as well as the settlements in Africa and the Middle East.).

[56] Ibid. On Italian colonial aims in the First World War, see Robert L. Hess, 'Italy and Africa: Colonial Ambitions in the First World War', *Journal of African History*, 4, 1 (1963), pp. 105–26.

up. Finally in Jubaland the territory asked for by Italy was exclusively British.[57]

Milner was willing only to make a rectification of the Libyan frontier in Italy's favour and to cede the region in the north of British East Africa called the Juba Valley, which he described as 'a fertile district capable of growing large quantities of cotton'. In Somaliland, Milner 'declined to budge', on grounds that Britain had already given away more than France. He did not see 'why we should continue to make all the sacrifices'. In fact, he wanted to yield as little as possible:

> I may say I was rather glad that the French took up an uncompromising attitude about Jibuti (French Somaliland), as if they had been more yielding about it, I might have found it difficult to refuse Berbera [in British Somaliland] and the part of British Somaliland adjoining it.

'Ultimately I presume', Milner wrote, 'Italy will have to be satisfied with what France and Great Britain are prepared to give up.'[58] The main points of the final settlement included only the cession of the Juba Valley by Britain and a few oases in the Sahara by France.[59]

This niggardly attitude of Britain and France was largely determined by the putative strategic importance of north-eastern Africa and the unsettled state of affairs in Abyssinia. According to Milner: 'As long as the fate of Abyssinia, which is one of the most serious international problems of the near future, remains undecided, neither France, Italy nor England can be expected to give up any positions now held by them, from which they can exercise an influence on the future of that country.'[60]

At the bottom of the Abyssinian problem was the question of the Nile:

> We . . . have one absolutely vital interest; it is to safeguard the head waters of the Blue Nile . . . When the time comes to liquidate the Abyssinian situation, we must be in a position to stipulate for the security of this water supply.[61]

> It is vitally important to Egypt to retain undisputed control of the Nile.[62]

---

[57] Milner memo, '"Equitable Compensation" for Italy in Africa', 30 May 1919, Milner Papers.
[58] Ibid.; see also Milner's memo in Lloyd George, *Truth about the Peace Treaties*, II, pp. 898–901.
[59] See Hess, 'Italy and Africa'.
[60] Milner memo, '"Equitable Compensation" for Italy in Africa', 30 May 1919, Milner Papers.
[61] Ibid.
[62] Sperling memo, 11 March 1919, Lothian Papers.

As in the days of Lord Salisbury, British statesmen at the Peace Conference believed that the power in possession of the Nile Valley controlled Egypt and the route to India. By the end of the First World War, the ramifications of Salisbury's Nile policy had led Britain into becoming the 'mandatory power' in a large part of the Middle East and German East Africa. Even in the disposal of the former German West African colonies, protection of the 'other' route to India was a primary consideration. As Balfour said in December 1918: 'Every time I come to a discussion—at intervals of, say, five years—I find there is a new sphere which we have got to guard, which is supposed to protect the gateways of India. Those gateways are getting farther and farther from India.'[63]

Apart from the representatives of the Southern Dominions, British statesmen in 1919 did not regard the establishment of the mandates system as a threat to the security of India or of the Empire as a whole. Nor did the apportionment of the mandates affect the repartition of Africa. The continent was divided mainly along the lines of conquest. To the regret of the British delegates at the Peace Conference, there was little room for manoeuvre. According to Cecil: 'I know that if Mr. Balfour or myself makes any proposition with regard to Africa, we shall be told that it is the oldest colony, or it will bitterly offend some New Zealand politician if we don't, or something of that kind. It is always the same.'[64]

Thus the First World War ended in the same way as other wars, in Balfour's words, with 'a map of the world with more red on it'. In his opinion, the reason was geographical. But the expansion of the British Empire, he said, 'might not be ascribed in other countries to its geographical cause'.[65]

Whatever its cause, imperialism was not easy to disguise at the Peace Conference, even by the founding of the mandates system. The fate of the Turkish territories and German colonies was determined, in Milner's frank words, by 'a huge scramble'. From their superior geographical position, the British merely led the race.

---

[63] Eastern Committee Minutes, Secret, 9 December 1918, Milner Papers. 'Why should England do this?' asked Lord Curzon. 'Why should Great Britain push herself out in these directions? Of course, the answer is obvious—India' (ibid.).

[64] Ibid.

[65] Eastern Committee Minutes, Secret, 24 April 1918, Milner Papers.

8

THE UNITED STATES
AND THE COLONIAL SETTLEMENT OF 1919

*It has constantly been asserted that the determining principle . . .
should be the welfare of the natives.[1]*

George Louis Beer

Of all the sideshows at the circus of the Paris Peace Conference of 1919, the African peace settlement perhaps attracted the least attention. In the words of one of the ringmasters, President Wilson, 'the disposition of the German colonies was not vital to the life of the world in any respect. It was the determination of the pressing European questions which was all-important.'[2]

Africa was no longer of central concern in European diplomacy; but it would be a mistake to underestimate its significance. The First World War had revived the Scramble for Africa; in the minds of many Europeans, 1919 had renewed, not ended, an imperial era. And the new era differed from the old not only because of larger empires, but also because of the mandates system, which was implemented in Africa at the insistence of the United States.

Mandates were not a new experiment in Africa, though the new status of the former German colonies obviously differed in some important respects from the anomalous position of the Congo Free State. As George Louis Beer, the American authority on colonial issues at the Peace Conference, pointed out, the twofold purpose of the mandates—welfare of the indigenous population and free trade—was essentially the same as that of the Berlin Act of 1885. Unlike the scheme set up by Berlin Act, the mandates system (theoretically anyway) safeguarded international intervention, if necessary,[3] and started from the premise of eventual self-government,[4] a premise unheard of in 1885, and so far as Africa was concerned, not taken seriously in 1919. Curiously, of the multitude who have written about the establishment of the mandates, Lord Lugard is one of the very few who have emphasized the important connection with the Berlin

[1] Beer to E. M. House, 21 July 1919, House papers, Yale University.

[2] *Foreign Relations of the United States, 1919: The Paris Peace Conference,* III, p. 771.

[3] 'What sharply distinguishes the mandatory system from all such international arrangements of the past is the unqualified right of intervention possessed by the League of Nations' (G. L. Beer, in H. W. V. Temperley, ed., *A History of the Peace Conference of Paris* [6 vols., London, 1920], II, p. 236).

[4] See especially Parker Thomas Moon, *Imperialism and World Politics* (New York, 1926), chap. 18.

Act.[5] The connection is clear enough: less than a quarter of a century earlier, the spirit of international trusteeship had been caricatured in one of the great disasters of modern history, King Leopold's Congo. But by the end of the First World War, the controversies of the past were blurred, even forgotten. As the Great Powers blithely (King Leopold, after all, had been dead for almost a decade!) re-subscribed to the principle of trusteeship at the Paris Peace Conference, the Belgians tried to purge the Congo of the last vestiges of international control. As the Berlin Act did in King Leopold's time, the mandates controversy in 1919 showed that 'trusteeship' meant all things to all men.

George Louis Beer's good friend and colleague at the Peace Conference, Professor James T. Shotwell, claims that Beer himself was the first to use the term 'mandate' in the sense in which it appeared in the treaty.[6] But it would be pointless to attempt to give Beer credit for the invention of the mandates system; indeed, the controversy about who 'invented' mandates is as barren as the one about their antecedents. The notion of mandates was in the air in 1919, and was the result of the course of the war as much as the brainstorm of any one person.

[5] F. D. Lugard, *The Dual Mandate in British Tropical Africa* (Edinburgh and London, 1929), pp. 48–51; for Beer's views on international control in Africa, see part III of his *African Questions at the Paris Peace Conference,* ed. Louis Herbert Gray (New York, 1923), which is a collection of memoranda by Beer written for the Commission of Inquiry. Cf. David Hunter Miller, 'The Origin of the Mandates System', *Foreign Affairs,* 6, (January 1928), pp. 277–89.

Cf. also the remarks of Professor Stengers in a letter to me of 1 March 1963:

Dans la controverse entre Léopold II et l'Angleterre, il y a un point, à mon avis—et c'est d'ailleurs peut-être le seul—où Leopold II avait raison: c'est lorsqu'il soutenait que l'origine de l'Etat du Congo, juridiquement, n'avait rien à voir avec l'Acte de Berlin, et que l'Etat du Congo n'etait en rien un Etat 'international'. Sur ce terrain juridique, je le répète, Leopold II avait à mon sens raison à 100% et ce qu'ecrit Lugard ne tient pas. D'un point de vue purement historique, d'autre part, je puis vous dire qu'après avoir lu tout l'essentiel des documents diplomatiques, publiés et inédits, relatif à la Conférence de Berlin, je ne trouve nulle part l'idée d'un 'mandat', d'un 'international trusteeship' en 1884–1885. Ce n'est pas, à man sens, une idée de l'époque. C'est une idée née au début du XXe siècle chez ceux qui ont quinze ans après, interprété l'Acte de Berlin.

However erroneous the interpretation of the Berlin Act by the Congo reformers may have been, it is clear that 'King Leopold [as] the greatest "fraudulent trustee" whom the world had seen' (*Official Organ of the Congo Reform Association* [November 1907]) was in the minds of those who conceived of the mandates system during the First World War. Discussing the 'neutralization and internationalization' of tropical Africa, E. D. Morel (who had led the anti-Congo campaign in Britain) wrote in 1917 that his proposals were '*substantially an amplification and precision of the purposes of the Berlin Act*' (*Africa and the Peace of Europe* [London, 1917]; Morel's emphasis).

[6] In *George Louis Beer: A Tribute to His Life and Work in the Making of History and Moulding of Public Opinion* (New York, 1924), p. 86; this book is a memorial volume published after Beer's death.

The best summary of the causes that led to the founding of the mandates system is given by an American historian:

> The modern opposition to territorial conquests and annexations and to the use abroad of colored colonial troops, together with the modern practice of condominium, the ideal of self-determination, and the policy of the open door in colonial territory, as embodied in the Roosevelt-Root mandate plan for Morocco under the Act of Algeçiras of 1906, converged, through the writings of the Round Table group in England in 1915–1917 (especially Hobson), in the mind of General Smuts in 1917–1918, were then and there reenforced by the Wilson principles for the peace settlement, cast into the terminology of the mandate and formulated in the Smuts 'Suggestions' on 16 December 1918. From here they were taken up by President Wilson, and, by decisions of the Supreme Council, the Commission on the League of Nations, and the Peace Conference itself, were written into Article XXII of the Covenant of the League and the Treaty of Versailles.[7]

Whether Wilson seized on Smuts's idea of a mandates system for the defeated empires in Europe[8] and 'universalized it' by applying the principle to the German colonies,[9] or whether the idea was already ripe in his mind, it is clear that the hard core of thought which formed the basis of the system originated with neither Wilson nor Smuts. It originated with the British Labour Party,[10] and, more immediately, with the forum of British Imperial idealism, the *Round Table*. George Louis Beer was a member of the Round Table group. In December

---

[7] Pitman B. Potter, 'Origin of the System of Mandates under the League of Nations', *American Political Science Review*, 16 (November 1922), p. 583; cf. Potter's 'Further Notes', *American Political Science Review*, 20 (November 1926), pp. 842–46; Luther H. Evans, 'Some Legal and Historical Antecedents of the Mandatory System', *Proceedings of the Southwestern Political Science Association* (March 1924); David Hunter Miller, 'Origin of the Mandates System'; Quincy Wright, *Mandates under the League of Nations* (Chicago, 1930), chaps. 1 and 2; Elizabeth van Maanen-Helmer, *The Mandates System* (London, 1929), chap. 2; Ernest B. Haas, 'The Reconciliation of Conflicting Colonial Policy Aims: Acceptance of the League of Nations Mandate System', *International Organization*, 4 (November 1952), pp. 521–36; and Seth P. Tillman, *Anglo-American Relations at the Paris Peace Conference of 1919* (Princeton, 1961), chap. 3.

[8] Jan C. Smuts, *The League of Nations: A Practical Suggestion* (London, 1918). Smuts did not intend the mandates scheme to be applied to Africa; cf. Sir Keith Hancock, *Smuts: The Sanguine Years, 1870–1919* (Cambridge, 1962), pp. 501–02, 507, 543–44.

[9] Ray Stannard Baker, *Woodrow Wilson and World Settlement* (3 vols., New York, 1922), I, pp. 265–66.

[10] Henry R. Winkler, *The League of Nations Movement in Great Britain, 1914–1919* (New Brunswick, N.J., 1952); chap. 8 of this work is a full discussion of the idea of colonial trusteeship in Britain during the war, correcting the erroneous impression that the Round Table group carried the burden of campaigning for international trusteeship. See especially p. 205.

1918 an article called the 'Windows of Freedom'—'one of the most eloquent statements of responsible idealism to be found in any of the literature at the close of the war'—for which Beer was partly responsible, appeared in the *Round Table*.[11] The gist of the article, so far as the African settlement is concerned, was that the success of the Peace Conference would depend on the role of the United States:

> The allies in Europe ought not to be made answerable to a League of Nations for the whole of the regions outside Europe now severed from the German and Turkish Empires. The future of the system depends upon whether America will now assume her fair share of the burden, especially in the Near East and even in German East Africa.[12]

Whatever the role of the United States, it was clear to the writer of 'Windows of Freedom' that the mandates system would never be a success if African questions considered at the Peace Conference were dealt with in the same way as at the Berlin African Conference of 1884–85. After the Berlin Conference had 'dispersed in a cloud of rhetoric', Leopold II had '"banged, bolted, and barred" the door against all but his own traders, and under his rule some of the worst features of slavery were developed'.[13] How could this have been prevented? The answer was simple: by making the guardian strictly responsible by treaty to a League of Nations. This was idealism tempered by the experience of the Scramble for Africa; it was the idealism of President Wilson.

Wilson supported trusteeship fervently, but his ideas were fuzzy. In the words of George Louis Beer, 'Wilson is strong on principles a sophomore might enunciate, but is absurdly weak on their application.'[14] At the beginning of the Peace Conference, Wilson's notion of trusteeship had not developed much beyond his Olympian proclamation that there must be a 'free, open minded, and absolutely impartial adjustment of all colonial claims'.[15] Wilson believed this principle right, and he would fight for it. But how was it to be applied? Wilson's staff of specialists, the Commission of Inquiry (established by Colonel

[11] The article, which was written by the editor, Lionel Curtis, appeared as 'Windows of Freedom', *Round Table*, 9 (December 1918), pp. 1–47; for the quotation, see James T. Shotwell, *At the Paris Peace Conference* (New York, 1937), p. 90, note 2.

[12] 'Windows of Freedom', pp. 35–36. The German East Africa proposal was Curtis's, not Beer's, idea.

[13] Ibid., p. 26.

[14] Entry for 5 April 1919, from a typescript copy of G. L. Beer's manuscript diary, deposited in the Library of Congress.

[15] Wilson's fifth point; cf. the Cobb-Lippmann memorandum in Harry R. Rudin, *Armistice, 1918* (New Haven, 1944), pp. 414–15.

Edward M. House in 1917 to provide details on issues that would require settlement at Paris),[16] was responsible for the answer to this question; they were to shape Wilson's ideas on specific issues. Wilson, of course, had many more important questions to settle than the details of the peace in Africa—questions 'so complex and far-ranging that no mortal mind could master them'.[17] On matters of minor importance he expected the Inquiry simply to provide him with the necessary information; then he could make a sound judgement. Wilson's brain trust for Africa was the American colonial expert, George Louis Beer.

George Louis Beer was a representative 'of the New World at grips with the legacy of the Old World's problems'.[18] He was a man of leisure, an Anglophile, a scholar from Columbia University who had made substantial contributions to British colonial history. He was able and engaging, but devoid of humour and imagination. One of his Belgian colleagues commented that he was 'a typical American'.

Beer left New York on 4 December 1918 aboard the *George Washington,* together with President Wilson and a 'highly undemocratic and unsociable' peace delegation ranging from ambassadors and plenipotentiaries to members of the Inquiry.[19] On the seventh day of the voyage he attended a presidential conference, where Wilson expounded the main goal of the colonial settlement: the German colonies were to serve as cement for the League of Nations, the common property which would hold it together; they would be administered by small nations—a highly disturbing thought to Beer—since otherwise the German colonies might cease to be League property by becoming absorbed into the old empires. The United States was interested only in fair settlements, not in boundary issues: 'Firm on broad general principles, but flexible as to their precise application.' Beer was impressed with the President's candour, charm, and wit; he was alarmed at the vagueness of the President's ideas: '[The] talk demonstrated he had not gone into details—he frankly said so—and that he had not thought out everything.'[20]

[16] See especially Shotwell, *At the Paris Peace Conference,* chap. 1; also Sidney Edward Mezes, 'Preparations for Peace', in E. M. House and Charles Seymour, eds., *What Really Happened at Paris* (New York, 1921), pp. 1–14.

The scholarly 'Inquiry' group, many of whom were academics, was unkindly regarded by the State Department as a dangerous rival, and at the beginning of the Peace Conference its position was entirely uncertain. Beer recorded with relief in his diary on 22 December 1918: 'Our position on [the] Inquiry has been greatly strengthened and virtually the entire burden of giving information has been thrust upon us; [the] President seems to regard us as his personal staff.'

[17] Thomas A. Bailey, *Woodrow Wilson and the Lost Peace* (New York, 1944), p. 83.

[18] A. E. Zimmern, in *George Louis Beer,* p. 54.

[19] Beer's diary, 9 December 1918.

[20] Ibid., 10 December 1918.

Beer frankly regarded Wilson's notion of mandates for small nations as muddled. He felt that a small nation such as Norway, with no experience in colonial administration, could hardly be expected to assume responsibility for vast regions in tropical Africa. On the other hand, it would be even more undesirable to add to Belgium's or Portugal's already heavy burdens, even if Belgian and Portuguese colonial history commended this course of action—which most certainly was not the case. Only the Great Powers had the colonial experience and resources to administer the German colonies. And Wilson's 'very dangerous and academic type of thinking'[21] must have been shattering to Beer for yet another reason: Wilson's scheme would have ended Beer's dream of a United States mandate for the Cameroons.

The idea of the United States accepting mandates in Africa had originated in Beer's correspondence during the summer of 1918 with three members of the Round Table group, Lionel Curtis, Lord Eustace Percy, and Professor Reginald Coupland of Oxford.[22] So far advanced—in Beer's mind at least—was the plan at the beginning of the Peace Conference that he recorded in his diary: 'A decision on this point means a turning-point in the world's history and momentous things hang upon it.'[23] On 21 December, Beer took Curtis to see two of the American plenipotentiaries, General Bliss and Colonel House:[24]

---

[21] Shotwell, *At the Paris Peace Conference*, p. 75; cf. Paul Birdsall, *Versailles Twenty Years After* (New York, 1941), p. 42: 'the proposal to entrust colonial administration to small states was a desperate device to avoid even the semblance of a division of spoils at the Peace Conference.'

[22] Shotwell, *At the Paris Peace Conference*, p. 90, note 2. Cf. Professor Gaddis Smith's remarks in a letter to me of 13 September 1963:

> This idea was also strenuously championed by Prime Minister Sir Robert Borden and other Canadians. Borden was distressed at the idea that the British Empire would come out of the war with vast reaches of new territory. At the Imperial War Cabinet in 1917 and 1918, but especially in 1918, Borden was a vocal anti-annexationist. He wanted the United States to have African mandates (1) to relieve the British Empire of the onus of territorial gain; (2) to give the United States a specific job to do and thus help bind the United States to the British Empire, and the postwar international organization.

[23] Beer's diary, 22 December 1918.

[24] Beer's diary, 24 December 1918:

> [The] President has done no work since [his] arrival . . . there has been no meeting of [the] commissioners at which [the] President expressed himself on fundamental questions of policy—in fact, no such meeting at all. This explains General Bliss's ignorance of [the] President's attitude towards international administration and his ideas of a mandatory under [the] League of Nations in his conversation with me and Curtis.

'Both were much impressed with [the] views advocated and expressed no dissent. Apparently, the matter is up to Wilson alone and depends entirely on his decision about small states as mandatories.' Curtis was to discuss Beer's project with Philip Kerr (Lloyd George's Private Secretary), Lord Milner (the British Colonial Secretary), and Lloyd George (the British Prime Minister).

Beer was convinced that he had British support for a United States mandate in the Cameroons: 'I have hopes that Lloyd George may induce Clemenceau to persuade Wilson.'[25] The question, he thought, turned completely on Wilson: 'Wilson was the crucial point and . . . [the] British could not bring pressure upon him without France's cordial and entire support.'[26] The attitude of France would determine Wilson's decision, and it was France's attitude that Beer therefore attempted to influence.

On 11 January 1919, Beer explained to Louis Aubert, one of the technical experts in the French delegation,[27] 'the necessity of getting [the] U.S.A. to take their share in caring for derelict territories and peoples', and according to Beer, 'Aubert was very responsive and caught the point.'[28] A few days later, while lunching with Beer and Curtis, Aubert avoided the question of the Cameroons, but brought up the future of German East Africa. Beer explained that the great distance from America would make it difficult for the United States to assume a mandate there; 'We unquestionably made an impression on Aubert.'[29] Two days later Beer talked to Mille, the colonial editor of *Le*

Beer's diary, 15 January 1919: '[Bliss] . . . is evidently of the opinion that [the] U.S.A. should not mix up in the details of the European and colonial settlements beyond seeing that American principles are *not* violated and the U.S.A. should under [the] League of Nations be responsible for order in the western hemisphere.'

Beer's closest association with House was through the Mandates Commission, to which House was the American delegate and Beer the alternate delegate. The following revealing passage is recorded in Beer's diary on 7–13 July 1919:

Although House was very modest and said very little, allowing me to do all the talking, his presence was a handicap and I am sure that I could have accomplished more had he not been present. He is inclined to give in rapidly and to defer to Milner and Cecil. I never felt sure that he would not leave me in the lurch and could not devote my undivided attention to the work and the argument.

[25] Beer's diary, 29 January 1919.
[26] Ibid., 11 January 1919.
[27] Aubert was Director of the Service of Research and Information in the Commission on Franco-American Affairs of War.
[28] Beer's diary, 11 January 1919.
[29] Ibid., 14 January 1919.

Temps, expounding the same ideas;[30] *Le Temps* subsequently reversed its policy and supported Beer's scheme of a United States African mandate.[31] On 28 January, Beer surmised that Aubert had 'evidently persuaded Tardieu'; the only problem would be French compensation for withdrawal from the Cameroons.[32] The 'psychological moment' had arrived.[33] Beer asked Shotwell 'to have Curtis immediately get [the] British to work with [the] French' to convince Wilson.[34]

Wilson proclaimed on 30 January 1919 that he was prepared to have the United States accept mandates.[35] To Beer, this was, of course, a remarkable triumph, and the following passage from his diary reveals the extent to which he considered himself responsible.

> Sequence interesting. My letters to Percy, Coupland and Curtis in 1918. Curtis's article in December *Round Table.* Our talks with House and Bliss about it. My campaigns with Aubert and Millet [*sic,* Mille]. Complete *volte-face* of *[Le] Temps.* Aubert's conversion and that of Tardieu and influence of Clemenceau.[36]

Aubert assured Beer that complete agreement was not far distant: '[He] does not hesitate about [the] Cameroons and agrees that compensation could be arranged in five minutes between Lloyd George and Clemenceau.'[37]

Beer's disillusionment came rapidly. He recorded uneasily on 30 January that 'Wilson's announcement that he was prepared to have [the] U.S.A. assume mandates aroused no excitement and its significance was not noticed.' Two days later he discovered why; on 1 February, Beer met Henri Simon,[38] the French Colonial Minister. Simon, in contrast to Curtis and Aubert, wielded power in colonial affairs.

In this 'very interesting talk', Beer broached the question of the Cameroons: 'Simon says it is absolutely essential to French Equatorial Africa, as Duala is [the] natural point of ingress.'[39] On 5 February at the French Colonial Ministry, Beer continued his discussion about the United States and the Cameroons. 'Probably little hope of [the]

[30] Beer's diary, 16 January 1919.

[31] Ibid., 30 January 1919.

[32] Ibid., 28 January 1919.

[33] Ibid., 29 January 1919.

[34] Ibid., 28 January 1919.

[35] Or at least this was Beer's inference; cf. *Foreign Relations, 1919,* III, pp. 788 and 807.

[36] Beer's diary, 30 January 1919.

[37] Ibid.

[38] '[Simon] is a southerner, rather testy, of sharp temper, but business-like and does not make speeches. His manner is quite vehement' (Beer's diary, 13 July–4 August 1919).

[39] Ibid., 1 February 1919.

French Colonial Office [*sic*] agreeing to this,' he concluded.[40] There are no more references in Beer's diary to his 'Cameroon project'.[41] Beer had learned what Wilson had begun to grasp during his dramatic encounters in the Supreme Council in late January—that Africa had already been repartitioned, without the help of the United States.

Until the European archives divulge their secrets, the whole story of the repartition of Africa will not be known. The documents shown to the Americans at the Peace Conference revealed merely the arrangements made between France and Britain for the provisional administration of German West African colonies;[42] the discussions between the European governments as to the future of Africa remain obscure. In any event, the ultimate fate of the German colonies was determined by one of the quickest decisions of the conference. With almost no previous discussion of the evils of German colonialism, President Wilson commented to the Council of Ten on 24 January that he thought all were agreed that the German colonies should not be returned to Germany.[43] There followed the famous clash of wills between President Wilson and the representatives of Britain's Southern Dominions and of France. The basic question was whether the German colonies should become mandates under the League of Nations or whether they should be annexed. As Beer recorded in his diary, '[The] whole question [is] a test case and vital to [the] League of Nations. It is absolutely fundamental.'[44]

The details of the mandates controversy are so well known that it is unnecessary to dwell at length on them here.[45] In brief, the first day of discussion, 24 January, was mainly noteworthy for the blasts from the trumpets of Imperialism blown by Hughes (Australia), Massey (New Zealand) and Smuts (South Africa). 'Smuts spoke convincingly against the mandatory system in German South-West Africa'; the country was a desert and could be developed only if it were incorporated into the

[40] Ibid., 5 February 1919.

[41] '[O]ur taking the Cameroons—soon revealed its utter impossibility, but it should be mentioned now in passing to show how far away from subsequent tendencies were even some of the clearest-sighted men of that day. The flush of promise had not yet faded from all our war-time ideals' (Shotwell, in *George Louis Beer*, pp. 102–03).

[42] See the paraphrases of the Anglo-French agreements of 13 September 1914 and 28 February 1916 for Togo and the Cameroons respectively, in the Records of the American Commission to Negotiate Peace, National Archives of the United States, 185.115/24. Margery Perham throws some light on this dark subject in *Lugard* (2 vols., London, 1956–60), II, pp. 544–45; see also Lloyd George's *Memoirs of the Peace Conference* (2 vols., New Haven, 1939), I, p. 71.

[43] *Foreign Relations, 1919*, III, p. 718.

[44] Beer's diary, 28 January 1919.

[45] Many of the works listed in note 7 deal with this subject in detail, but also see especially Birdsall, *Versailles Twenty Years After*, chaps. 2 and 3.

Union of South Africa.[46] As the debate raged through 27 January—
'All the speeches were rhetorical, inaccurate and not to the point'[47]—
it became clear that the Prime Ministers of the British Dominions
were no more willing to give up their war spoils than Wilson was his
mandates system. On the morning of 28 January, Lloyd George, the
key to the compromise that resulted in the establishment of the mandates system, said that he was willing to accept Wilson's mandates proposal, provided the Dominions' case was considered 'special'. But in
the afternoon, Simon claimed Togo and the Cameroons in full sovereignty for France, promising only the *porte ouverte*. Wilson then said it
looked 'as if the roads diverged' and that the discussion so far had been
no more than a negation in detail of the whole mandates system.[48]

Balfour, the British Foreign Secretary, came to the rescue by suggesting that the terms of the mandates should differ (so that the Dominions could have their new colonies in all but name); Clemenceau
followed by repudiating Simon and accepting the mandate principle.[49]
By 30 January, Lloyd George, who was unwilling to quarrel with Wilson over the Pacific islands, had bullied the Dominions into accepting a watered-down version[50] of Wilson's mandates scheme, which
Wilson reluctantly accepted.[51] The precise terms of the mandates were
to be drafted by the colonial experts of the conference.[52] Wilson had

[46] Beer's diary, 24 January 1919; *Foreign Relations, 1919*, III, pp. 722–23.

[47] Beer's diary, 27 January 1919.

[48] *Foreign Relations, 1919*, III, p. 763; Beer's diary, 27 and 28 January 1919.

[49] *Foreign Relations, 1919*, III, pp. 763–69; Beer's diary, 28 January 1919.

[50] *Foreign Relations, 1919*, III, p. 796:

> [T]here are territories, such as South-West Africa and certain of the islands in the
> South Pacific, which, owing to the sparseness of their population, or their small size,
> or their remoteness from the centers of civilization, or their geographical contiguity
> to the mandatory state, and other circumstances, can be best administered under the
> laws of the mandatory state as integral portions thereof, subject to the safeguards
> above mentioned in the interests of the indigenous population.

[51] Ibid., pp. 795–96. House wrote that 'If I had been in his place I should have congratulated
them over their willingness to meet us more than half way' (Charles Seymour, *The Intimate Papers
of Colonel House* [4 vols., Boston, 1928], IV, p. 299).

[52] The business of drafting the mandates extended far into the conference. Apart from 'the
absurdity of putting Pacific islands and South-West Africa in the same class' (Beer's diary, 28 June
1919), there was no problem concerning the 'C' mandate of South-West Africa, which for all
practical purposes became part of South Africa. During the discussion on 30 January, Clemenceau insisted 'on the right to raise troops [in Togo and the Cameroons] in case of general war'.

> Mr Lloyd George said that so long as M. Clemenceau did not train big nigger armies
> for the purpose of aggression, which was all the clause was intended to guard against,
> he was free to raise troops . . .

won what appeared to be a remarkable triumph in the face of almost unanimous opposition.[53] Beer later learned why the French had
acquiesced: in the frank words of Henri Simon, '[there is] no real
difference between a colony and . . . [a] mandated area.' 'You will
see what these mandates will develop into in ten years,' Beer's exuberant French colleague, Peretti, commented to him.[54] Wilson had
his mandates; his opponents had their new colonies, or pretty close
to them.

After the historic decision on 30 January to accept the mandates system, there followed a lull in colonial affairs at the conference. During
this time Beer was primarily concerned with Liberia, which, though
out of the mainstream of negotiations, posed in a different way the
problem of international trusteeship.

Liberia was the skeleton in the United States colonial closet. 'Can
we afford to bolster up this corrupt oligarchy?' Beer wrote in his diary
on 2 February:

> There we already had obligations, and if we were to insist that France,
> England, Belgium and Italy should be responsible to the League of
> Nations for their trusteeship in the case of the lands they held in Af-
> rica, there was much force in the contention that the power which
> stood behind the oligarchical negro government of Liberia should
> be in some degree answerable as well to the same international su-
> pervision. This argument was enforced by the common charge that
> the existing government of Liberia was notoriously corrupt; a charge
> which, true or not, placed the U.S. in an invidious light so long as it
> seemed to shield the native government from the very kind of over-
> sight which it was imposing upon others.[55]

President Wilson said that Mr Lloyd George's interpretation was consistent with the
phraseology.
Foreign Relations, 1919, IX, p. 543. Beer, who was present at the meeting, thought that 'Clemenceau understood the agreement in a diametrically opposite sense from that of Wilson and Lloyd
George'; in any case, Beer regarded the privilege of raising troops in mandates for use in France
as 'a queer idea and queer times for a mandates area', and tried to block the French 'black army'
scheme during the discussions of the Mandates Commission. The agreement of 30 January was
explicit, however, and led to the peculiar result that the mandates given to the French for the
Cameroons and Togo contained a clause (not included in any of the other mandates) giving
them the right 'to raise troops in case of general war'; see Miller, 'The Origin of the Mandates
System'.

[53] Cf. Robert Lansing, *The Peace Negotiations* (New York, 1921), chap. 13.

[54] Chief of the African section in the French Foreign Ministry.

[55] Shotwell, in *George Louis Beer,* p. 103.

To prevent European annexation of Liberia by 'peaceful penetration through economic measures',[56] the United States had devised the international receivership agreement of 1912, which was administered jointly by the German, French, British, and American governments with an American receiver general. As in other instances of international control, the general results (as well as the financial returns) were discouraging; by 1919 the Germans had been ousted, and the French and British were ready to sell out to the United States. The main interest of France and Britain in Liberia in any case was not financial, but in maintaining order on the borders of their colonies: 'The anarchical conditions in the hinterland are a constant source of annoyance to them.'[57] To rehabilitate Liberia, the British and the French frankly urged the Americans to accept a mandate or to establish some form of protectorate.[58]

On 1 February, Lansing, the American Secretary of State, instructed Beer to conclude an arrangement with the Liberian delegates to the conference: 'The idea is to keep [the] Liberian situation as a whole out of the peace conference.'[59] Beer was to negotiate a treaty between the United States and Liberia, as well as one between the United States, Britain, and France.[60] The next day Beer began his tedious work

[56] Secretary of State to Assistant Secretary of the Treasury, 28 November 1919, *Foreign Relations, 1919*, II, p. 494.

[57] Commission to Negotiate Peace to Acting Secretary, no. 1873, 30 April 1919, ibid., p. 476.

[58] Memorandum of 27 March, enclosed in Grew to Acting Secretary, 17 April 1919, ibid., p. 473.

[59] Beer's diary, 1 February 1919.

[60] Ibid., 27 March 1919:

I am to draw up a draft agreement between Great Britain, France and the U.S. This agreement is to contain a renunciation on the part of Great Britain and France of their rights to appoint receivers in Liberia and also of any claim to participate in the financial programme . . . we are to guarantee on the one hand the open door, and, further, the protection of native rights. This agreement concluded, we have to conclude an agreement between Liberia and [the] U.S.A., and then, if possible, to secure the sanction of the League of Nations to this arrangement. The question of the mandate is quite difficult and may possibly be met by our agreeing, provided Great Britain and France so desire at any future time, to submit this entire arrangement, that between France, Great Britain and [the] U.S. to [the] League of Nations for its formal sanction and embodiment in a mandate. [The] other difficulty is that France in return for her renunciation wants us to assume definite responsibility and wants to have recourse to us in case of any difficulties on the border . . . The whole situation is absurdly complex for so trifling a matter as many difficulties must be overcome. How, for instance, can Liberia sign [the] peace treaty and at the same time be mandated ? Yet we are proposing what is virtually a protectorate while at the same time asserting the sovereignty of Liberia.

with C. D. B. King (the principal Liberian delegate), 'a diplomatic old beggar'[61] who bitterly resented the interference of France and Britain —'Evidently he wants our money and advice, while preserving intact Liberian independence.'[62]

Beer drafted an American-Liberian treaty, but it was flatly rejected by the State Department:

> In view of the fact that your proposed treaty would establish American control by American officers in practically every important department of the Liberian government—a control which is more extensive and intimate than the control of the U.S. in the Caribbean countries—it is believed by us doubtful if the Senate would approve such a treaty for a country in Africa.[63]

The State Department viewed Liberia mainly as a financial problem to be solved in consultation with the United States Treasury; Beer regarded it as a problem of trusteeship to be solved with France and Britain: 'before withdrawing from the international receivership and disinteresting themselves in the future of Liberia, England and France desire the United States to assume in some form or other responsibility for effective administration.'[64]

The Liberian negotiations were not concluded at the Peace Conference. They were lifted from Beer's hands; he was glad to be relieved of the whole 'boresome matter'.[65] He thought that the United States was not assuming proper responsibilities: 'A mandate would be the best solution.'[66] He was also convinced that the State Department had 'botched' his work and had failed to understand French diplomacy: 'now the French had all they wanted from us in Africa, that is Togo and the Cameroons', Beer wrote on 28 May, 'they would probably be less agreeable about the Liberian business';[67] 'One cannot but be disgusted with French foreign policy.'[68]

---

[61] Ibid., 4 February 1919.

[62] Ibid., 2 February 1919.

[63] Acting Secretary to Commission to Negotiate Peace, 24 April 1919, no. 1722, *Foreign Relations, 1919,* II, p. 474.

[64] Commission to Negotiate Peace to Acting Secretary, 30 April 1919, no. 1873, ibid. p. 476.

[65] Beer was left dangling by the State Department without instruction, unable to respond to the proposals of his British and French colleagues, throughout the rest of the conference. A loan credit of $5,000,000 was eventually negotiated between the United States and Liberia, but was blocked by the U.S. Senate in 1922. See Raymond Leslie Buell, *The Native Problem in Africa* (2 vols., New York, 1928), II, chaps. 100–103.

[66] Beer's diary, 31 May 1919.

[67] Ibid., 28 May 1919.

[68] Ibid.

During his talk with Simon on 1 February, Beer had gathered that Morocco was the main French concern: '[They] would like [the] Algeçiras Act abolished except for the open door.'[69] From an American point of view, the revision of the Algeçiras Act of 1906 was one of the more important African questions to arise at the Peace Conference. It was the Algeçiras Act—described by Walter Lippmann in 1915 as 'the most hopeful effort at world organization made up to the present'[70] —that regulated economic activity in Morocco; it was the Algeçiras Act, not the Berlin Act, that many Americans regarded as embodying the mandate principle in Africa—because of the American participation in the Algeçiras conference.[71] For this reason Beer did not think that it should be abrogated, 'but that the international administration should be abolished and their functions entrusted to France'—'to leave [the] façade intact and cut out the interior.'[72]

On 25 February, Peretti presented 'a highly disingenuous plan'[73] before the Council of Ten for the abrogation of the Algeçiras Act ('which imposed upon Morocco an internationalization directed against France'),[74] promising only the open door. Henry White, one of the American plenipotentiaries who had been a signatory to the Algeçiras Act, astonished even the French by tentatively agreeing to the French proposal: 'he made some damaging admissions as he does not see [the] significance of this act re mandatory principle and also the place it holds in liberal thought in America.'[75] Beer advised White a couple of days later to refer the matter to a commission without mentioning the French scheme;[76] on 28 March the Moroccan Commission was appointed, including Beer and Peretti as members.

The work of the Moroccan Commission proceeded smoothly until Lansing's intervention. On 14 April, Lansing instructed Beer to draft a blanket clause for divesting Germany of all rights outside Europe.[77] Lansing had been provoked by a memorandum from the British del-

---

[69] Beer's diary, 1 February 1919.
[70] Lippmann, *The Stakes of Diplomacy* (New York, 1915), p. 149.
[71] Beer's diary, 25 February 1919.
[72] Ibid., 28 February 1919.
[73] Ibid., 25 February 1919.
[74] See *Foreign Relations, 1919*, IV, pp. 131–37.
[75] Ibid., pp. 127–31; Beer's diary, 25 February 1919.
[76] 'This afternoon [I] had a talk with Henry White about [the] Algeçiras Act and explained my views to him. He concurred in them. I found him very amiable and [a] good listener' (Beer's diary, 1 March; see also 2 March).
[77] Ibid., 14 April 1919.

egation, requiring, in effect, Germany to recognize the British protectorate over Egypt and renounce extra-territorial rights there.[78] The purpose of Lansing's blanket clause was not only to nullify all German rights outside Europe, but also to prevent an endless number of colonial questions from being raised at the Peace Conference. By making this suggestion, he interrupted the proceedings of the Moroccan Commission.

> De Peretti was intensely annoyed at [the] postponement of [the] Moroccan clauses and said that if a blanket clause were substituted he would write an article showing its injustice to Germany . . . Of course Lansing's proposal is absurd and cannot be carried out.[79]

Lansing, with almost all of the Council of Ten arrayed against him, obstinately insisted on his blanket clause.

> Lansing then took up the matter and spoke in his characteristically querulous, irritating manner, annoying everybody by his petulance . . . he even drove me into opposition in feeling towards him. He must always be treated like a spoiled child.[80]

Finally Lansing admitted that Morocco and Egypt warranted special treatment in the form of special clauses; his opponents agreed to the blanket clause. The Moroccan Commission was instructed to include as much as possible in a general clause,[81] but in addition to draft

---

[78] A commission on Egypt was not formed; the British were as anxious to keep Egyptian affairs out of the conference as the Americans were those of Liberia. The main reason for finally dragging Egypt into the treaty at all was to give recognition to the protectorate declared by Britain in 1914. Once it had been decided to include Egypt in the treaty, the clauses had to be elaborate; otherwise they would be adversely compared in the British Parliament 'with the elaborate Moroccan articles'; see Beer's diary, 16 April 1919. Beer was responsible for the Egyptian draft clauses, for which he mainly followed those drafted for Morocco (as noted in his diary on 17 April):

> Hurst [the British legal expert] . . . adopted all my suggestions, but had re-drafted them radically. He was, however, quite cool to me and was evidently annoyed at me for calling attention to the gross inadequacy of their original clauses and suggesting the necessary additions. He has, it seems to me, overlooked the necessity of calling for a renunciation by Germany of rights in Egypt derived from treaties between Germany and Turkey.

[79] Ibid., 15 April 1919.
[80] Ibid., 17 April 1919.
[81] See *Foreign Relations, 1919,* IV, p. 569.

specific clauses, including ones for Egypt and Liberia, as well as for Morocco.[82]

The acceptance of the report of the Moroccan Commission by the Council of Ten on 17 April ended a distinct phase of the African settlement of the conference.[83] Whatever might be said of Liberia, Egypt, and Morocco, they were questions of secondary importance, secondary to the question of what was to become of the German colonies. In April and May 1919 the attention of the colonial delegates turned again to the problem of the repartition of Africa.

To some extent the outcome of the repartition was a foregone conclusion, even to Wilson (who had stopped talking about mandates for small nations) and Beer (who had stopped talking about United States trusteeship in the Cameroons): it was clear that the peace settlement would follow the lines of conquest. The British and the French would administer Togo and the Cameroons; South Africa would control South-West Africa; and Britain would receive most of German East Africa. But Belgium held the north-west of German East Africa, and presumably the future of that colony could not be determined without consulting her. It was also clear that the Treaty of London of 1915 gave Italy the right to participate in the African settlement.[84] For these reasons—the rights of Belgium and Italy—the decision of the Council of Three on 7 May, as far as Africa is concerned, was the most cynical of the conference—a naked example of territorial greed.

On 7 May the British Empire and France arrogated to themselves the German colonies. The other colonial powers—Italy, Belgium, and Portugal—were left in the cold.

The delay in the allocation of the German colonies had been due to President Wilson, who 'was very anxious to avoid the appearance of a division of the spoils being simultaneous with the Peace'.[85] Exactly why Wilson finally yielded at this particular time is not clear; perhaps he simply could no longer withstand the sharp demands of Lloyd George and Clemenceau.[86] Nor is it clear exactly why he acquiesced

[82] For the clauses in their final form, see Beer, *African Questions at the Peace Conference*, annex C.

[83] 'Sonnino [the Italian Foreign Minister] condemned the economic clauses severely, saying that it was going back 200 years to seize private property of [the] enemy and that he objected to Italy saying that France *should* do certain things in Morocco which Italy would not do herself. He spoke like a gentleman, quietly, but forcibly and effectively' (Beer's diary, 17 April 1919).

[84] Article 13 of that treaty stipulated that if Britain and France increased their territories in Africa at the expense of Germany, Italy was entitled to compensation.

[85] *Foreign Relations, 1919*, V, p. 473.

[86] Beer was in London at the time. On 9 May he learned that he should return 'immediately as I was urgently needed . . . Hughes had written to House about [the] necessity of Australia

entirely in the British and French territorial demands; perhaps he did not even know of the claims of the other three powers.

In any case, the Italians, unlike the Portuguese and the Belgians, were in a position to complain immediately, since Italy was a member of the Council of Four. The decision to give the German colonies to Britain and France had, in fact, been made behind Italy's back: 'It is apparent . . . that the Three wished to dispose of this question before Orlando and Sonnino had returned.'[87] Orlando protested at once; Lloyd George generously said that he was prepared to consider Italy's claims.[88] In view of the unyielding attitude towards almost all questions on the part of the French Colonial Minister, Simon, the burden of reaching a settlement fell on the shoulders of the British Colonial Secretary, Lord Milner, the only person, Lloyd George observed, capable of piloting these matters to a conclusion.[89]

Milner, one of the British plenipotentiaries to the conference, had returned from Paris to London in late March after learning that Wilson wanted to delay the assignment of the mandates. When Lloyd George heard in May that Milner had not pre-arranged the African settlement, he was 'quite annoyed',[90] and curtly re-summoned him to Paris: 'I earnestly hope that you will not find it necessary a second time to leave Paris without achieving a decision on the important questions entrusted to your charge.'[91]

Discussing the Italians with Milner on 14 May, Beer, as had been his habit throughout the conference, 'helped them on a bit'[92] by remarking about the modesty of the Italian claims.[93] In fact, the Italian aims in Africa by May 1919 had been drastically curtailed. During the war, the Italians had developed colonial ambitions on such a grandiose scale that one cannot but be reminded of the territorial fantasies of the Portuguese during the 1880s and 1890s. The Italian Colonial Ministry had its eyes not only on a major part of the Sahara (the 'Libyan hinterland'), but also on control of the Red Sea and a free hand

---

receiving an immediate mandate for the islands south of the equator, and House had promised him a speedy answer. Hence the call for me. In the meanwhile, the Council of Three had already on Tuesday disposed of this question by allocating the German colonies. Evidently House knew nothing of this' (Beer's diary, 9 May 1919).

[87] Ibid.

[88] *Foreign Relations, 1919,* V, p. 507.

[89] Lloyd George to Milner, 14 May 1919, in Beaverbrook, *Men and Power* (New York, 1956), pp. 330–31.

[90] Beer's diary, 12 May, 1919.

[91] See the letter cited in note 89.

[92] Beer's diary, 4 April 1919.

[93] Ibid., 14 May 1919.

in Ethiopia.[94] But since the Italians (like the Americans) were not in actual occupation of these lands, they received little more than rebuffs from the British and French whenever they broached the question of territorial aggrandizement. By May 1919, Beer reported, the Italians 'expected only to get a hinterland for Libya': 'They had no longer any hopes for Djibouti [the strategic port on the Red Sea possessed by the French], did not want British Somaliland, and had only faint hope of securing Kismayu [the British port].'[95]

Even Milner, not to mention Simon, was reluctant to appease the Italians;[96] 'he could not give to Italy any part of Egypt, as Egypt did not belong to England.'[97] There were also difficulties in ceding Kismayu and Jubaland to the Italians because of the British settlers there: 'These Englishmen had left their places on outbreak of war and they would raise a howl, if now when they returned to their homes, they suddenly found that they had been turned over to the Italians.'[98] Simon refused absolutely to cede Djibouti.[99]

The most Italy could expect to receive was a slight rectification of the Libyan frontier in the hinterland—giving her access to trade routes—and 'a slice of eastern British Somaliland'. In other words, practically nothing.[100]

The Italians threatened to bring the issue before the Council of Four; in desperation, the colonial experts looked for a solution. The most imaginative answer was to let Italy rejuvenate the sick man of Africa: '[to] give an Italian company the right to develop Angola. But I do not see how in decency the Italians can be foisted upon the Portuguese. It is too d[amnab]ly barefaced.'[101] The Portuguese, who were no fools when it came to hard colonial bargaining, had ambitions of their own, and did not intend to see the Italians take over Angola. For

[94] Robert L. Hess deals fully with the Italian aims in 'Italy and Africa: Colonial Ambitions in World War I', *Journal of African History,* IV, 1 (1963) pp. 108–26.

[95] Beer's diary, 12 May 1919.

[96] See especially Milner's letter to Lloyd George, 16 May 1919, in Lloyd George's *Memoirs,* II, pp. 583–85.

[97] Beer's diary, 27 May 1919.

[98] Ibid., 14 May 1919.

[99] '[T]he Djibouti railway to Addis-Ababa is all the more important that it is the only railway existing on the east coast of Africa and Ethiopia. France, to whom credit is due for having built this line, would lose, by giving it up, the economic interests and influences she has acquired for herself in Ethiopia' (Simon's statement in the 'Report of the Inter-Allied Commission delegated to study the conditions of the application of Article 13 of the Treaty signed at London on April 26, 1915', in the Records of the American Commission to Negotiate Peace, 181.22502/1, National Archives).

[100] Beer's diary, 14 May 1919.

[101] Ibid., 21 May 1919.

this reason the Italian plan for Angola collapsed, and Italy was forced to accept the modest concessions of France: Ghadames, Ghat, and Tummo in the Sahara; and of Britain: rectification of the Libyan-Egyptian frontier and cession of Kismayu and part of Jubaland. The bitter pill was made palatable only by the British cession of the Juba valley, which, the Italians were told, was 'a rich valley susceptible of great development, particularly in cotton'.[102]

The Portuguese territorial claims, in contrast to the Italian, which were based on treaty rights, were founded on nothing more than the traditional Portuguese policy of expansion whenever possible. Unlike the Belgians, the Portuguese had not invaded German East Africa, but like the Belgians, they had ingeniously devised a justification for their demands. The Portuguese case for territorial aggrandizement in the south of German East Africa rested on Germany's forcible usurpation in 1894 of the Kionga triangle in northern Mozambique, a slice of territory south of the mouth of the Rovuma River, inhabited by about 4,000 people.

> [This] has caused a very painful and lasting impression . . . The Portuguese people have never resigned themselves to a loss which although unimportant by value of the territories taken, represented . . . an act of violence.[103]

The Portuguese claims were presented to the Commission on Mandates on 12 July 1919. There was 'substantial unanimity' that the Kionga district should be handed over to the Portuguese: 'It appears from the published treaties and diplomatic documents that Germany virtually forced Portugal to cede this area in 1894.'[104] Since the region was insignificant in size and population, there was no question of a mandate; it was given to Portugal in full sovereignty.[105]

The Portuguese, however, aimed at more than what was, essentially, justice on the historical issue of Kionga; they also demanded a mandate over part of German East Africa on the grounds that if Belgium were allowed to have a mandate, Portugal should have one too. As Beer observed, the Portuguese claim 'hinges upon questions of national

---

[102] Minutes of the Commission on Colonies, 15 May 1919, in the Records of the American Commission to Negotiate Peace, 181.22501/1.

[103] Portuguese memorandum in the American Commission records, 185.115/48.

[104] Beer to Grew, 25 July 1919, Polk Papers, Yale University; Beer to House, 18 and 21 July 1919, House Papers.

[105] Cf. the editorial note to H. B. Thomas's 'The Kionga Triangle', *Tanganyika Notes and Records,* 31 (1951), pp. 47–50, which emphasizes the commercial and strategic value of the district.

dignity, pride and prestige . . . [it] is wholly untenable.'[106] A Portuguese mandate over German East Africa was not even seriously considered by the conference.[107]

Both Italy and Belgium tried to expand their colonial empires at the expense of Portugal. Both had Angolan designs, the Italians with hopes of a chartered company, the Belgians with hopes of annexing the southern bank of the Congo. Both schemes failed for the same reason: the Portuguese simply refused to cooperate.

The Belgians regarded control of the southern bank of the Congo as vital to the security of their colony; without it the Congo was bottled up, with only limited access to the ocean. To acquire the Congo bank, the Belgians were prepared to pay almost any price—even the evacuation of the north-west of German East Africa. They proposed a three-sided deal: they would hand over their occupied territory in German East Africa to the British; the Portuguese would cede the southern Congo bank to them; the British would compensate the Portuguese by giving them more territory in the south of German East Africa.[108]

If the Portuguese refused to consider the scheme (as they eventually did), the Belgians, so the Belgian Foreign Ministry thought, would at least be left with the north-west of German East Africa, in particular with the densely populated and mountainous countries of Ruanda and Urundi. To their great dismay, they learned in early May that all of German East Africa had been given to Britain.

The Belgians were disgracefully handled by the Great Powers at the conference. Their pleas before the Council of Ten in January had been disregarded;[109] the letter from Clemenceau that they had received in May stating that Belgian colonial claims would be respected had proved meaningless.[110] The Belgians were being robbed of the prize they thought they had justly won; and to be told by an observer such as George Louis Beer that they should not receive Ruanda-Urundi because their colonial history was worse than that of the Portuguese must have been especially insulting.[111]

[106] Beer to House, 21 July 1919, House Papers.

[107] See Milner to Duasta, 14 August 1919, *Foreign Relations, 1919,* VIII, p. 363; and Lansing to American Commission to Negotiate Peace, telegram, 9 August 1919, American Commission records, 185.1111/7.

[108] I have discussed these plans and the Anglo-Belgian Ruanda-Urundi negotiations in detail in *Ruanda-Urundi, 1884–1919* (Oxford, 1963).

[109] *Foreign Relations, 1919,* III, pp. 809–12.

[110] Ibid., V, p. 420.

[111] Beer's views, through no fault of his own, were known even to the Belgians: 'those who showed the *procès verbal* [of the Mandates Commission] to the Belgians were guilty of a gross breach of faith' (Beer's diary, 13 July– 4 August 1919).

Beer was not convinced that the Belgians had reformed their colonial rule: 'They have more of Africa than they can administer properly.'[112]

> The matter is, in my opinion, a very serious one. From the geographical standpoint the areas [of Ruanda and Urundi] . . . jut across the physical backbone of Africa and from this standpoint the [proposed] arrangement is indefensible. Furthermore, the population of this area is ethnographically closely connected with that of the British Protectorate of Uganda on its northern border. In my opinion, the native states of Ruanda and Urundi should be governed by means of the native institutions. This system of government is entirely unknown in the Belgian Congo. It is true that the administration of the Belgian Congo has improved greatly since the days of King Leopold, but the colony is still regarded mainly as a plantation of the mother country and the native is looked upon chiefly as a source of labor supply. I very much fear that the Belgian administration will use the large population of these new areas for the purpose of recruiting labor for their plantations and mining enterprises.[113]

Whatever his conclusions, there can be little doubt that this was the attempt of an honest man trying to look at the problem objectively, but to some extent he must have been biased as well: 'These small nations with intense national feelings bore me,' he wrote in his diary on 19 February.[114] Whatever the basis of his views, he set out to block the Belgian acquisition of Ruanda-Urundi with all the fervour of Woodrow Wilson crusading for the mandates system.

On 9 May, Beer recorded in his diary that the Belgians were 'highly indignant' that the German colonies had been disposed of without consulting them. A few days later he explained to his friend Curtis 'what the Belgian claim in east Africa meant'.[115] Then he took the matter to Lord Milner himself:

> [I] found Lord Milner quite perplexed about [the] Belgian claim. He agrees entirely with me that it is impossible to turn over these four million natives to the Belgians. But he does not know how to handle the situation. He suggested having a Commission appointed to handle the question, as he had proposed some months ago. But I said that this would only reopen the entire question which had

[112] Ibid., 3 May 1919.

[113] Beer to House, 21 July 1919, House Papers.

[114] This remark was made in reference to eastern Europe, but it expresses Beer's attitude towards Belgium as well.

[115] Beer's diary, 12 May 1919.

already been decided by the Council of Four and would only lead
to a deadlock. France, having secured what she wanted in the Cameroons and Togo, would probably side with Belgium. Milner said he
wanted us there as neutrals to give dispassionate opinion.[116]

'[Milner] did not attempt to disguise his lack of relish of the job that
Lloyd George had given him.'[117]

Milner, of course, was as concerned with the peace in Europe as
in Africa. Even Beer recognized the political danger of alienating
Belgium by frustrating her central African ambitions. Belgium had
suffered much during the war; 'England . . . did not want to appear
greedy as regards a small nation like Belgium.'[118] For these reasons,
Milner signed the Milner-Orts agreement of 31 May 1919, which
handed over Ruanda-Urundi to Belgium: 'It is quite obvious that if
the welfare of the natives had been the sole, or even the chief, consideration, no candid or impartial student would turn these natives
over to Belgium.'[119]

Beer protested. On his advice, Wilson recommended that the Mandates Commission consider the Belgian claims. The commission met
on 16 July.

> The Belgians presented the agreement of 30 May between Orts and
> Milner giving Belgium under mandate Ruanda and Urundi with over
> 3 million natives, probably 3 and 1/2 million. In view of this agree-
> ment the meeting was quite perfunctory, all accepting an Anglo-
> Belgian agreement as definitely disposing of the matter. They took

[116] Beer's diary, 14 May 1919. Beer also tried to convince Milner that part of German East Africa should be given to India: 'Milner said that he agreed to this in principle provided it were
practicable. He did not want the chief [cheap?] Indian dealers and traders, but only genuine
settlers . . . he was opposed to giving India [a] mandate and any hand in the administration . . .
Milner as usual was very modest and frank.'
 Cf. R. Meinertzhagen, *Army Diary* (Edinburgh and London, 1960), pp. 248–49:
> It would be difficult to conceive a more disastrous policy [of giving German East Af-
> rica to India] . . . The experience of the Indian in Africa has been an unhappy one. It
> has been the history of vice, crime, unrest and general political intrigue; he has been
> unpopular with the local governments concerned, with the white settlers and with the
> Africans, and God help the natives of German East if the Indian government becomes
> its mandatory power.
Despite the differences of opinion, there are many similarities between Beer's and Meinertzhagen's outspoken diaries.
[117] Beer's diary, 14 May 1919.
[118] Ibid., 13 July–4 August 1919.
[119] Ibid.

no interest in it at all. It was not their concern, but solely an Anglo-Belgian affair. I was the only one who spoke about it, pointing out its absurdity from the geographical, ethnographical and political standpoints.[120]

In a final attempt, Beer wrote to Colonel House on 21 July, saying that only President Wilson could reverse the decision of the Mandates Commission:

> [W]ere President Wilson to take such a stand considerable resentment against the U.S. would be aroused in Belgium. On the other hand, the welfare of nearly three and one half million voiceless natives should not be lightly disregarded.[121]

But House did nothing. In his opinion, 'siding against Belgium giving those lands to Great Britain would strengthen the anti-British opposition to the Treaty'. As Beer noted ruefully, 'By such things is the fate of three and a half million human beings determined!'[122]

The Ruanda-Urundi agreement shocked Beer to the core. As a man of principle, he was genuinely dismayed to see flouted the principles on which he thought the African settlement should be based. Yet he was realistic enough to know that his solution had no chance of being accepted. Beer was a deeply religious person,[123] but he was a sceptic as well, and his observation about Woodrow Wilson could just as well apply to him: he was an idealist, but a cynical one.

At no time during the Peace Conference did these two aspects of Beer's personality emerge more clearly than in his last venture, the revision of the Berlin and Brussels Acts, when his greatest triumph followed his greatest defeat. The main point involved here was that the Belgians were trying to free themselves from the 'servitudes' of these international agreements by establishing their complete sovereignty in the Congo. Beer waged a fierce battle, and succeeded in defeating the Belgians on many important points, such as 'the theory that these acts had lapsed, that commercial equality and all other provisions should cease absolutely in ten years, that the colonizing state had full control over all vacant native lands, that the state could establish for

---

[120] Ibid.

[121] Beer to House, 21 July 1919, House Papers.

[122] Beer's diary, 13 July–4 August 1919.

[123] 'Friday, March 21, 1919 . . . Beer explained that the basis of his personal confidence in the ultimate solution [of peace in Europe] is his religion' (Shotwell, *At the Paris Peace Conference*, p. 223).

itself monopolies'.[124] But Beer was the only opponent of the Belgians, and all the rest of the commission sided with them. When the Belgians introduced an amendment concerning navigation on the Congo—which would have compromised much of his work—Beer was forced into a difficult situation: the other delegates volunteered to get instructions from their governments and he was scheduled to depart within a few days. He consequently decided 'to frighten' Louwers, the Belgian delegate.[125]

He invited Louwers to lunch and casually asked him, '[W]hat was the state of [the] Ruanda and Urundi claim of Belgium?'

> He said that he understood it was disposed of definitely in their favor. I replied that such was not my understanding and that the settlement would have to be approved of by the heads of the governments and that this question of the navigation of the Congo might have some effect upon the decision. By this time Louwers was thoroughly frightened and said 'Vous m'inquietez beaucoup'. I could hardly keep a straight face . . . Louwers then said: 'But I don't see any connection between the two questions.'

> I said, 'It's very simple. Here we are erecting the mandatory system and you claim a mandate in East Africa, but at the same time you are insisting upon undermining an analogous system established in the Congo basin.'

> Louwers finally saw the light and said he had a proposal to make. I asked him to write it down and gave him pencil and paper. I told him that it was not satisfactory, but that it might be modified and that we could go after lunch to my study and see what could be done. By that time he was ready for anything. I sat at my table and wrote out in French a clause giving them the right in the interest of public safety to control the navigation of those parts of the river not necessary for [the] two states provided there was no discrimination against

[124] Beer's diary, 13 July–4 August 1919.

[125] After one of his 'passages at arms' with Louwers, Beer wrote in his diary (13 July–4 August 1919):

> I could make no impression on Louwers. In the first place broad questions of principle and statesmanship, of policy in a big way, make no appeal to such delegates. They receive positive instructions from their Colonial Ministry [*sic*] to get a certain measure adopted. If they succeed, they may move up one rung in the official ladder; if they fail, they have a black mark against them. Besides this personal factor, they are swayed by national considerations predominantly. Hence I was not surprised that I could not budge him.

ships and people on the grounds of nationality. He spoke of the
necessity of securing the consent of the Colonial Ministry . . . When
the matter came up [in the commission] he made a long speech, offered his new proposal which all accepted and had a great diplomatic
triumph. After the meeting de Gaiffier [another Belgian delegate]
thanked me for accepting the proposal. There was really nothing
in it that was not in the original text before the Belgians tried to
change [it].[126]

Despite his success in the Berlin and Brussels Acts Commission,
Beer obviously failed in his quest to secure colonial justice at the Peace
Conference. As he remarked about the Ruanda-Urundi arrangement,
which to him epitomized the worst features of the African settlement:
'This agreement cannot be defended except on grounds of merest expediency. It is contrary to the fundamental principles upon which
these colonies were to be disposed of in that no attention at all was
paid to native interests.'[127] Beer was as powerless to alter this bargain
as he was in his efforts to acquire an African mandate for the United
States. The United States, he learned, was much more of an observer
than a participant in the African settlement; the American influence
was negligible. Yet Beer's own impact on colonial affairs was considerable, and perhaps no greater tribute to him as a statesman could have
been paid than his selection as the first Secretary of the Permanent
Mandates Commission of the League of Nations. 'There is no doubt',
Lord Milner wrote after Beer's premature death in 1920, 'that Beer
had a strong sense of the duty which the more advanced nations owe
to the more backward . . . [He] appreciated the spirit in which we were
trying to carry "the white man's burden".'[128]

Journal of African History   1963

[126] Ibid. The work of the Berlin and Brussels Acts Commission was embodied in the Treaty
of St.-Germain-en-Laye; see Beer, *African Questions at the Peace Conference*, annex G.
[127] Beer's diary, 13 July–4 August 1919.
[128] *George Louis Beer*, pp. 128–29.

9

THE BEGINNING OF THE MANDATES SYSTEM
OF THE LEAGUE OF NATIONS

The decision of the Supreme Council of the Paris Peace Conference in January 1919 to place the German colonies and Turkish territories under the supervision of the League of Nations raised serious political and legal questions to which no one had satisfactory answers. But very few scholarly essays have analysed the aftermath of the Peace Conference's deliberations on international colonial affairs, although numerous recent studies mention in passing the origins of the mandates system. The opening of the archives of the government of Britain after 1919 provides a good opportunity to review the subject and to examine what the unpublished records reveal about international supervision in colonial areas.

This mandatory topic has a vast literature.[1] In the words of William E. Rappard of the Permanent Mandates Commission, 'no subject in the realm of the social sciences . . . in the brief space of ten years, has given rise to a greater number of publications.' He did not exaggerate when he added that the number of works on the subject was already overwhelming.[2] Since the Second World War, writing on the mandates system has declined as studies on its successor body, the Trusteeship Council of the United Nations, have

---

[1] In reviewing the extremely voluminous literature on the subject in relation to recently released archival material, the author has cited only the most relevant and useful works. Far and away the best books on the topic remain H. Duncan Hall's *Mandates, Dependencies and Trusteeship* (Washington, 1948); and Quincy Wright's *Mandates under the League of Nations* (Chicago, 1930). *Empire by Mandate: A History of the Relations of Great Britain with the Permanent Mandates Commission of the League of Nations* (New York, 1954), by Campbell L. Upthegrove, is an uncritical, territory-by-territory account of Britain's relations with the Permanent Mandates Commission, but it is nevertheless useful. Other works that remain especially valuable are by Freda White, *Mandates* (London, 1926); J. Stoyanovsky, *La Théorie Générale des Mandats Internationaux* (Paris, 1925); D. F. W. van Rees, *Les Mandats Internationaux* (2 vols., Paris, 1927); Elizabeth van Maanen-Helmer, *The Mandates System in Relation to Africa and the Pacific Islands* (London, 1929); and Aaron M. Margalith, *The International Mandates,* (Baltimore, 1930). For the administration of the mandates in tropical Africa (with the exception of Ruanda-Urundi), see Raymond Leslie Buell, *The Native Problem in Africa* (2 vols., New York, 1928). For a succinct official summary of the history of the first decade of the system, see League of Nations Secretariat, *Ten Years of World Co-operation* (London, 1930), chap. 10. For a short bibliographical essay discussing the founding of the mandates system and the trends of historical interpretation of the work of the Permanent Mandates Commission, see Robin W. Winks, ed., *The Historiography of the British Empire–Commonwealth: Trends, Interpretations, and Resources* (Durham, N.C., 1966), pp. 296–311.

[2] William E. Rappard's introduction to Benjamin Gerig, *The Open Door and the Mandates System: A Study of Economic Equality before and since the Establishment of the Mandates System* (London, 1930), p. 11.

grown.[3] Nevertheless, the mandates continue to interest political scientists, international lawyers, and scholars of other disciplines, as well as historians, and the subject, as Rappard put it, is in a constant state of rejuvenation. This article therefore reviews the literature of the mandates system in addition to discussing the political and legal problems that arose immediately as a consequence of the creation of the mandates.

Where did sovereignty reside in regard to mandated territories? What was the nationality of mandated subjects? British statesmen in 1919 thought those questions were almost unanswerable; but the creation of the League demanded precise answers to them and to a host of other complicated issues. What steps, for example, were required to give 'international validity' to the position of the mandatory powers? What procedure was necessary to enable the British Dominions to administer their mandated territories legally? Who conferred the mandate? Did authority derive from the Crown, the Dominion parliaments, or the League?

The very nature of the mandates system needed clarification before those questions could be answered, and the process of analysing the application of international supervision in non-European territories in turn gave rise to other questions of fundamental importance. What was the purpose and function of the Permanent Mandates Commission? What action could be taken by the League in the event of a violation of a mandate? The thin line between legal and political problems led British officials to consider further how the establishment of the mandates system would affect the balance of power in the Pacific, Africa, and the Middle East, and how the United States, with a traditional suspicion of European 'imperialism', would view the implementation of the mandates system—a question that became acute after the US Senate's rejection of the Treaty of Versailles. To those perplexing problems, the British government had no clear-cut answers, and the lengthy memoranda prepared by the Foreign Office and the Colonial Office make evident the great difficulty in arriving at even makeshift solutions.

The fundamental questions of sovereignty and nationality, although of much academic interest to international lawyers, were largely ignored by the colonial experts responsible for the establishment of the mandates system.[4] But they could not entirely avoid the problem.

---

[3] The best work on this subject is James N. Murray, Jr., *The United Nations Trusteeship System* (Urbana, Ill., 1957).

[4] 'I leave it to lawyers to say where the "sovereignty" will in any case reside.' See the memorandum by Lord Milner (Colonial Secretary), 'Mandates', Secret, WCP-211, 8 March 1919, CAB 29/9/1. For questions of sovereignty and nationality, see especially two articles by Quincy

Decisions had to be made, above all, about the symbol of sovereignty and nationality, the flag of the mandated territories. Should the flag of the mandatory power or a League flag be flown? Lord Robert Cecil, the British statesman who championed the League's cause, felt strongly that the symbolism of a 'trustee flag' would foster the idealism that had contributed to the founding of the mandates system. The Colonial Office, however, objected vigorously to that proposal. One official wrote that a League flag 'wd. have a confusing effect on the primitive natives of Tropical Africa & [would] probably prejudice our position.'[5] Another official wrote:

> Unless the insignia of the League are made subsidiary to the Flag of what is really the Protective State, the result on the natives of the Tropical African Mandated territories will be to form the opinion that (in the expressive lingo of the West Coast) 'British flag, no dam good Sar!'[6]

Mainly for that reason the British government dropped the idea of a 'trustee flag' and decided to fly the Union Jack—a decision that reflected the British official tendency to associate sovereignty with the mandatory power rather than with the League. In an abstract sense, the British government was willing to admit that the inhabitants of the mandated territories had, in the words of the Colonial Secretary, Lord Milner, 'a divided "sovereignty".' But in 1919 the point did not seem important.[7] The overriding concern during the period following the Peace Conference was not how to establish the nationality of the inhabitants of the mandated territories but how to terminate German and Turkish sovereignty.

To rescind Germany's and Turkey's legal titles to their former possessions, sovereignty had to be transferred. The problem arose first of all in regard to the 'C' mandates of South-West Africa and the Pacific. British officials assumed that German and Turkish sovereignty could

---

Wright, 'Sovereignty of the Mandates', *American Journal of International Law*, 17, 4 (October 1923), pp. 691–703, and 'Status of the Inhabitants of Mandated Territory', *American Journal of International Law*, 18, 2 (April 1924), pp. 306–15. Also see James C. Hales, 'Some Legal Aspects of the Mandate System: Sovereignty—Nationality—Termination and Transfer', *Transactions of the Grotius Society*, 38, pp. 85–126.

[5] Minute by H. J. Read, 5 March 1919, FO 608/242.

[6] Minute by Charles Strachey, 5 March 1919, FO 608/242. See also various minutes by the legal adviser to the Foreign Office, Sir Cecil J. B. Hurst, who wrote: 'The idea of a flag for the League of Nations would tend to strengthen the idea that the League was a supra State, an idea which would endanger its existence' (6 March 1919, FO 608/242).

[7] Two years later, however, the nationality question became controversial. It will be discussed below in relation to South-West Africa.

be annulled simply by a proclamation of the Allied and Associated Powers and the conferral of the mandates (in the British case) by the Imperial government or the Dominion parliaments.[8] The British government thus attempted to reject out of hand the idea that authority to govern—one of the touchstones of sovereignty—should derive from the League. Confronted with the opinion of international jurists, however, the British Cabinet in August 1920 acquiesced in a general report submitted to the League Council by Paul Hymans of Belgium. Hymans successfully argued that the mandatory powers exercised their functions on behalf of the League and that 'the legal title held by the Mandatory Power must be a double one: one conferred by the Principal Powers and the other conferred by the League of Nations.'[9] British officials were never entirely happy with this definition of sovereignty, for reasons well stated by the first British representative on the Permanent Mandates Commission and later Under-Secretary of State for the Colonies, David Ormsby-Gore:

> [T]he main obstacle . . . was the lack of sense of security in the title of the Mandate. Practically all the troubles and difficulties had arisen from that fact . . . [People] were suspicious of it. They had it in the back of their minds that such territories might possibly go back to Germany.[10]

The 'C' Mandates: Jurisdiction and National Security

Despite agreement in British circles that the role of the League in the question of sovereignty should be kept as subordinate as possible, an important controversy did develop within the British Empire that has relevance to today's dispute over South-West Africa. On 23 August 1919, the Governor-General of New Zealand sent an 'Urgent' telegram to the Colonial Secretary in London, asking whether legislative authority to govern the former German Samoan Islands should be conferred by the New Zealand Parliament or whether the Imperial government would issue an Order in Council under the Foreign Jurisdiction Act.[11] Here was an issue of fundamental importance: If the

[8] See the full correspondence on this point in CAB 24/94 and CAB 24/97.

[9] League of Nations, *Official Journal*, 1, 6 (September 1920), pp. 336–37.

[10] Quoted in *Journal of the Royal Society of Arts*, 72, 3736 (27 June 1924), p. 550. For the mandates question in relation to Germany, see especially Wolfe W. Schmokel, *Dream of Empire: German Colonialism, 1919–1945* (New Haven, 1964).

[11] Lord Liverpool to Milner, Urgent, 23 August 1919, CAB 24/94. The reason for the urgency was the unrest in Samoa. For an outstanding discussion of the Foreign Jurisdiction Act and other points of British Empire law in historical perspective, see Claire Palley, *The Constitutional*

New Zealand Parliament conferred legislative authority, ultimate responsibility for Samoa would rest with the New Zealand government; but if the mandate were conferred by Order in Council, ultimate responsibility would rest in London.

The New Zealand government, guided by Sir John Salmond, a legal adviser inclined towards a conservative interpretation of Imperial law, urged that an Order in Council be issued. But the Prime Minister of South Africa, General Jan C. Smuts, objected strenuously to this proposal:

> I . . . question whether proposed Order in Council is correct procedure. Mandate over Samoa is given not to United Kingdom, but to New Zealand; that is to say, to His Majesty not in his British Government, but in his Dominion Government. King in his British Government or Privy Council is not concerned, therefore, and British Order in Council is beside the point. It would only apply where effect is to be given to mandate like German East Africa, which was conferred on His Majesty in his British Government, and it is not clear that Foreign Jurisdiction Act applies even there. Any Act purporting to confer jurisdiction over mandated territories like South West Africa or Samoa must emanate from His Majesty in his Dominion Government, on whom alone mandate was conferred, and who has, I assume, some prerogative to extend jurisdiction as King in his British Government.[12]

Smuts argued, in short, that the South African Parliament was the proper and competent authority to abrogate German sovereignty by enacting legislation for South-West Africa—an argument, he said privately, that ultimately derived from right by conquest.

The law officers of the Crown, whose views reflected the trends of thought that led to the Statute of Westminster of 1931, concurred in Smuts's opinion:

> No formal Act or Instrument such as the proposed Order in Council on part of His Majesty is necessary to enable the Union of South Africa or other Dominion concerned to make provision for execution of Mandate but Parliament of Dominion concerned is competent to make such provision.[13]

History and Law of Southern Rhodesia, 1888–1965, with Special Reference to Imperial Control (Oxford, 1966).

[12] Lord Buxton to Milner, quoting J. C. Smuts, Private and Personal, telegram (paraphrase), 15 November 1919, CAB 24/94.

[13] Milner to Liverpool, 'Telegram Citing Law Officers' Opinion' (paraphrase), 3 February 1920, CAB 24/97.

The British government thus agreed that ultimate authority for South-West Africa resided in South Africa.[14]

The Southern Dominions of South Africa, Australia, and New Zealand were given much more far-reaching privileges in their mandated territories than were Britain, France, and Belgium in theirs. The 'C' mandates were administered as 'integral portions' of the mandatory states and were subject to the legal and fiscal regulations of the mandatory powers. The 'C' mandatory contracts lacked the 'free trade' clauses imposed on the 'B' and 'A' mandates of tropical Africa and the Middle East. By thus closing the 'open door', British officials hoped to protect Britain's interests in the Pacific, where, in the opinion of Prime Minister William M. Hughes of Australia, 'Japan is and has been long working to oust [the British] Empire and Australia . . . and to secure trade for herself.'[15]

The Australians also feared Japanese 'infiltration' into the islands south of the Equator, and the representatives of Australia and New Zealand agreed to accept mandates only on the condition that the 'White Australia' policy would apply to the islands under their control. According to Sir Eyre Crowe of the Foreign Office, the 'C' mandates were 'specially designed to enable them [the Southern Dominions] to apply their protective tariffs and their legislation for excluding coloured immigrants'.[16] The adamant determination of the Australians and New Zealanders not to admit Japanese influence south of the Equator formed the dominant theme of the Pacific island negotiations.

During the discussions that led to the creation of the mandates system in January 1919, the Japanese delegate had not protested against the restrictive clauses of the 'C' mandates. But in the meetings of the

[14] For the procedure of conferring the 'C' mandates, see especially Mary Boyd, 'New Zealand's Attitude to Dominion Status—1919–1921: The Procedure for Enacting a Constitution in Her Samoan Mandate', *Journal of Commonwealth Political Studies*, 3, 1 (March 1965), pp. 64–70.

[15] William Hughes to David Lloyd George, Secret and Confidential, telegram, 26 September 1919, CAB 24/94. The Australian attitude towards the mandates is well discussed by L. F. Fitzhardinge, 'W. M. Hughes and the Treaty of Versailles, 1919' (typescript seminar paper, Institute of Advanced Studies, Australian National University, March 1964). See also Peter Heydon, *Quiet Decision: A Study of George Foster Pearce* (Carlton, Australia, 1965); and E. L. Piesse, 'Japan and Australia', *Foreign Affairs*, 4, 3 (April 1926), pp. 475–88.

[16] Minute by Sir Eyre Crowe, 8 September 1921, FO 371/7051. The unpublished Foreign Office documents provide interesting reading for those concerned with the charge, made repeatedly in the 1920s and 1930s, that the 'C' mandates were 'veiled annexations'. One of the best discussions of this point is by Luther Harris Evans, 'Are "C" Mandates Veiled Annexations?' *Southwestern Political and Social Science Quarterly*, 7 (March 1927), pp. 381–400. For the opposite view, see, for example, Herbert Adams Gibbons, 'The Defects of the System of Mandates', *Annals of the American Academy of Political and Social Science*, 96, 185 (July 1921), pp. 84–90.

Mandates Commission [17] during the following July, the Japanese began to raise objections to the discriminatory clauses on the grounds that they were 'contrary to the spirit of the League of Nations'. None of the other mandatory powers agreed, but the Japanese persisted, and their protest caused a long delay in the conferral of the 'C' mandates. In November 1920, the Governor-General of Australia expressed 'great surprise' at renewed Japanese proposals to introduce more liberal regulations, and sent the following telegram to the Colonial Secretary:

> The Japanese Government is endeavouring to amend conditions of mandate to introduce thin end of wedge of racial equality and the conditions obtaining for class 'B' mandates in regard to trade. Both these proposals will be resolutely resisted by Commonwealth Government.
>
> Commonwealth Government cannot agree to grant any rights to Japanese subjects inconsistent with the general policy of the Commonwealth in regard to islands. They cannot entertain the suggestions that there should be a recognition of so-called vested rights and interests, either such as were in existence prior to August 1st 1914, or subsequently. We are starting with clean slate. [18]

By starting with a 'clean slate', however, the Japanese found themselves faced with the possibility of being treated less favourably than if the Germans had retained the islands. That obvious fact lay behind Japan's protest.

The British government, although willing to express sympathy for the Japanese plight, was bound to support Australia and New Zealand. The Foreign Secretary, Lord Curzon, frankly told the Japanese Ambassador that the granting of 'most favoured nation treatment' to the Japanese south of the Equator would be regarded by the Dominions 'as a breach of faith on our part, and would be doomed to immediate and angry refusal'. [19] The Japanese continued to insist that Japanese subjects in such places as New Guinea should enjoy the treatment they had received under German rule; but they eventually agreed to limit their proposals in order merely to secure certain privileges, such as

---

[17] The purpose of the Mandates Commission was to draft the mandates and to study the problems involved in establishing the Permanent Mandates Commission. The best discussion of the Commission's work is in the dissenting opinion of Judge Philip C. Jessup in *South West Africa Cases, Second Phase, Judgment, I.C.J. Reports 1966*, pp. 356 ff.

[18] Governor-General of Australia to Colonial Secretary (paraphrase copy), 15 November 1920, FO 371/4787.

[19] Lord Curzon to Sir Charles Eliot (Tokyo), No. 266, 7 July 1920, FO 371/4766.

the right of Japanese vessels to load and unload copra at Rabaul. They were also willing to prevent Japanese immigration to New Guinea. As the time approached for a reconsideration of the Anglo-Japanese alliance, the minor issues concerning the 'C' mandates appeared more and more trivial.

So conciliatory did the Japanese become that the Foreign Office in December 1920 reported that the 'real desire of the Japanese was not so much to raise fundamental objections to the terms of the Mandate, but rather to discover some formula that would preserve their dignity.'[20] Following Australian assurances that Japanese interests in New Guinea would be treated as well as they had been under the Germans, the Japanese in mid-December 1920 agreed to the issuance of the 'C' mandates with the restrictive clauses.[21] Japan thus paved the way for a general Anglo-American-Japanese understanding about the balance of power in the Pacific.[22]

To prevent the 'C' mandate negotiations from disrupting the Washington Naval Conference of 1921–1922, Japan also had to yield to American demands for cable privileges on Yap—an island described by President Woodrow Wilson at the Peace Conference as an important international communications centre. Situated between the Philippines and the American islands of Guam and Wake, Yap appeared to be an essential link in the developing US system of communications in the Pacific. The Japanese at first refused to grant American concessions on Yap because the Peace Conference, they argued, had explicitly given Japan the island as a mandate. The American press, ignorant of the Conference's proceedings and misunderstandings, viewed the issue jingoistically. The *Nation* commented:

> Give us Yap! Give us Yap!
> The Yanks have put it,
> The Yanks have put it,
> The Yanks have put it,
> On the Map!

'We will not attempt to write the [further] verses', the periodical continued, 'but . . . we must have Yap.'[23] Under the 'gentle pres-

[20] Gerald Spicer (reporting for the British Empire delegation at Geneva) to the Foreign Office, 16 December 1920, FO 371/4768.

[21] The 'C' mandates were then confirmed by the Council of the League, and the mandates were entered into force on 17 December 1920. The publicists who concerned themselves with the issue at the time were well aware of the causes of the delay. See especially T. Baty, 'Protectorates and Mandates', in *British Year Book of International Law, 1921–22* (London, 1922), pp. 109–21.

[22] See James B. Crowley, *Japan's Quest for Autonomy: National Security and Foreign Policy, 1930–1938* (Princeton, 1966), p. 27 et seq.

[23] *Nation*, 109, 2827 (6 September 1919), p. 328.

sure'[24] of Britain and the United States, on 11 February 1921 Japan and the United States signed a treaty that conferred cable rights on Yap on the Americans.[25] Once again the Japanese displayed a conciliatory attitude. But these concessions by no means dispelled growing distrust of Japanese ambitions in China and the Pacific.

The problem facing Britain at this time consisted of checking Japanese 'imperialism' while dealing with American suspicions of the Japanese alliance: while the British handled the delicate 'C' mandate negotiations, they also fundamentally reviewed the problem of power in the Pacific. As far as the mandated islands were concerned, the Japanese might use them as bases for expansion despite the demilitarization clause of the 'C' mandates. 'Japan desires and intends to expand both in China and in the Pacific,' a Foreign Office memorandum concluded in 1920.[26] If so, that course of action would probably bring Japan into collision with the United States. Britain would then be placed in an extremely awkward position. Regardless of Japan's ultimate aims, the Americans' interpretation of Japanese policy forced Britain into the role of mediator. In the words of one official:

> Owing to Japan and the United States being apparently irreconcilable, it is very difficult for us to work a policy in the Far East conjointly with both of them, while it is essential to us, owing to our Naval weakness in the Pacific to have a friendly Japan.[27]

According to another analysis of the situation:

> The interests of Japan and the United States clash at every point, and the future of the Far East and the Pacific is likely to become more and more the theatre of rivalry between these two countries. At present,

[24] See especially the Foreign Office memorandum circulated by Curzon to the Cabinet, 'The United States and Mandates', dated July 1921, FO 371/7050.

[25] The best discussion on the Yap negotiations remains that by Harold and Margaret Sprout, *Toward a New Order of Sea Power: American Naval Policy and the World Scene, 1918–1922* (Princeton, 1940), pp. 91–93; see also A. Whitney Griswold, *The Far Eastern Policy of the United States* (New York, 1938), pp. 264ff; and George H. Blakeslee, 'The Mandates of the Pacific', *Foreign Affairs*, 1, 1 (September 1922), pp. 98–115. The published documentary source is Department of State, *Papers relating to the Foreign Relations of the United States, 1921* (2 vols., Washington, D.C., 1936), II, pp. 263–87; *Foreign Relations of the United States, 1922* (2 vols., Washington, D.C., 1938), II, pp. 599–604.

[26] 'Foreign Office Memorandum on Effects of Anglo-Japanese Alliance upon Foreign Relations', 28 February 1920, FO 371/3816, in E. L. Woodward and Rohan Butler, eds., *Documents on British Foreign Policy, 1919–1939* (first series, 12 vols., London, 1956; hereafter cited as *Documents on British Foreign Policy*), VI, p. 1017.

[27] John Tilley to Beilby Alston (Tokyo), Private and Confidential (copy), 11 December 1919, FO 371/3816. Cf. *Documents on British Foreign Policy*, VI, p. 880.

however, Japan is far too weak to embark single-handed upon a war with the United States, and she is well aware of this.

Our future course lies between our ally with whom our interests conflict, and our friend who is united to us by race, tradition, community of interests and ideals. It will be difficult for us to steer a straight course; both parties will no doubt reproach us, as they have done in the past, for not giving them more wholehearted support against the other, but this course must be steered—our interests demand it . . . we must content ourselves with . . . alliance with Japan; intimate friendship and co-operation with the United States of America and France.[28]

The situation in the Pacific reflected these uneasy relations.

The 'C' island mandates were, essentially, the result of British co-operation with the United States against Britain's ally, Japan. If neutralized and placed under international control, the islands could not, theoretically, be utilized by the Japanese as military bases; and by means of the annual reports submitted to the League, the United States and Britain would have an important source of information about Japanese activities in the islands. But would Japan adhere to the regulations of the mandates system? As early as October 1919, a British official in Tokyo warned:

I question if the League of Nations is really understood in this country or if much confidence is reposed in it; on the contrary it would appear to be regarded in many quarters with suspicion.[29]

Japanese mistrust of the mandates system, and British and American fears about Japanese intentions in the mandated islands, remained a persistent theme in the history of the Pacific during this era.[30]

In the 'C' mandate of South-West Africa, the Union of South Africa's government held similar suspicions about the intentions of the German settlers. South-West Africa contained the only substantial

[28] *Documents on British Foreign Policy*, VI, p. 1017.

[29] Alston to Tilley, Private and Secret, 7 October 1919, FO 371/3816. Cf. *Documents on British Foreign Policy*, VI, pp. 761–65.

[30] For the point of view of the League and the Western powers on this matter, see especially Hall, *Mandates, Dependencies and Trusteeship*. The principal accusation of Japan's violation of the mandate is by a former official in the Mandates Section of the League Secretariat, Huntington Gilchrist, 'The Japanese Islands: Annexation or Trusteeship?' *Foreign Affairs*, 22, 4 (July 1944), pp. 635–42. He writes: 'The character of Japan's attack on Pearl Harbor is clinching evidence that she had set up bases in the islands. Her gross violation of the terms of the mandate amply justifies its termination' (p. 640).

number of Germans who remained in former German territory—
about 6,000. By three years after the Armistice, South African immigrants totaled over double that figure, but the Germans continued to
be a problem. They protested obstreperously against the Union's attempts to submerge them in ever-increasing numbers of South Africans. In September 1920, the German community in Windhoek urged
Prime Minister Smuts to preserve German institutions, encourage the
return of German settlers and capital, and, in effect, establish a semi-
autonomous German colony, one only loosely connected with South
Africa.[31] There thus were many similarities in the attitudes of the Germans in South-West Africa after the war to the outlook of the Boers
two decades earlier in South Africa. Smuts furthermore adopted the
policy pursued by the British, that of reconciliation. He urged the
Germans to become part of the South African community. At the same
time, he bluntly stated that South-West Africa would be incorporated
into the Union in accordance with the legal and fiscal provisions of the
'C' mandate and that the territory would for all practical purposes be
another of the Union's provinces. 'In effect', he said frankly, 'the relations between the South-West Protectorate and the Union amount to
annexation in all but name.'[32] As to the problem of the German settlers, the best solution, according to Smuts, was 'wholesale naturalization', a proposal he later modified to give those concerned a chance
to decline Union citizenship. This policy brought to a head the controversy of the nationality of mandated subjects.

The Union as well as the other mandatory states all agreed that the
nationality of the native inhabitants in the 'B' and 'C' mandates was
not affected by the terms of the mandate.[33] The 'natives' became 'protected persons' without the conferral of nationality. But what of the
resident Europeans? According to the legal adviser to the Foreign
Office,

---

[31] For a perceptive discussion of these points, see Maynard W. Swanson, 'South West Africa
in Trust, 1915–39', in *Britain and Germany in Africa: Imperial Rivalry and Colonial Rule,* ed. Prosser
Gifford and W. R. Louis (New Haven, 1967), chap. 21. Swanson also deals at length with the Bon-
delzwarts uprising of 1922, which is not discussed here because the British government was not
directly involved. For the trusteeship theme and South-West Africa in the inter-war years, see
also Robert L. Bradford, 'The Origin of the League of Nations' Class "C" Mandate for South West
Africa and Fulfilment of the Sacred Trust, 1919–1939' (Ph.D. diss., Yale University, 1965).

[32] League of Nations, Permanent Mandates Commission, Minutes (2nd session), 1–11 August 1922, annex 6, p. 92 (League of Nations Document A. 35. 1922. VI).

[33] The 'A' mandates recognized the nationality or local citizenship of the inhabitants. See
'National Status of the Inhabitants of the Territories under B and C Mandates' (League of
Nations Document C. 546. 1922. VI); and League of Nations, *Official Journal*, 4, 6 (June 1923),
p. 604. For a summary and references, see Hall, *Mandates, Dependencies and Trusteeship*, p. 78.

the wholesale naturalisation envisaged by the South African Commission [appointed in October 1920 to consider the future government of South-West Africa] was contrary to the spirit of the Treaty of Versailles, as it amounted to practical annexation.[34]

Apart from South Africa, the mandatory powers held that the

special conditions relating to administration as an integral part of the Mandatory's territory where they occur should not affect the nationality of *European* inhabitants of the mandated territory.[35]

But the Union maintained successfully that the large number of Germans in South-West Africa created a unique danger not present in other mandated territories. How could subversive Germans be tried for treason if their nationality was of an indeterminate nature?[36] Similar questions touching on 'security'—the dominant theme of the postwar era—made even staunch defenders of international organization more sympathetic to the Union's point of view. In April 1923 the Council of the League of Nations stated explicitly that it had 'no objection' to the Union's proposal to naturalize the Germans of South-West Africa who did not decline by declaration within six months.[37] The League thus demonstrated its tendency to bow to the mandatory powers on questions of national security.

The 'B' Mandates: Anglo-French Friction in Tropical Africa

The B mandates of tropical Africa also raised an important point of security. During the Peace Conference, the French premier had insisted

---

[34] Minutes of an interdepartmental meeting held at the Colonial Office, 28 October 1921, CO 732/5.

[35] See minutes of interdepartmental meeting held at the Colonial Office, 23 November 1921, attended by members of a subcommittee of the Permanent Mandates Commission, CO 649/23.

[36] The question was important because under the Roman-Dutch law of South Africa, treason could be committed only against a sovereign power. In 1924 the Supreme Court of South Africa ruled that the mandatory government possessed sufficient sovereignty 'to justify the obligation of allegiance by the inhabitants of the [mandated] territory' (Norman Bentwich, *The Mandates System* [London, 1930], p. 127). See also E. L. Mathews, 'International Status of Mandatory of League of Nations: High Treason against Mandatory Authority', *Journal of Comparative Legislation and International Law*, 3rd series, 6, 4 (November 1924), pp. 245–50.

[37] League of Nations, *Official Journal*, 4, 6 (June 1923), pp. 603–04; discussed at length by Wright, *Mandates under the League of Nations*, pp. 522–29. Only about 250 persons filed declarations declining naturalization; 2,900 automatically became South African citizens. See *Report of the Administrator of South-West Africa for the Year 1924* (League of Nations Document C. 452. M. 168. 1925. VI).

on the right 'to use black troops from the mandated area in the same way that he had used black troops from the French colonies during the last war'. As one official summarized these proceedings, the reason why the British and American delegates acquiesced in the French demand did not seem apparent in retrospect, 'but it is pretty clear that both President Wilson and the Prime Minister [David Lloyd George] agreed that there was nothing to prevent this.'[38] A special clause was therefore included in the 'B' mandates assigned to France, conferring this privilege. One Colonial Office official viewed these 'nigger army' provisions with alarm:

> So far as defence of British & French Possessions & Protectorates in West & Equatorial Africa is concerned, it might be said:—
>
> (a) The only enemy the French have to fear is Great Britain & that this is a provision directed against us
>
> (b) That in view of the enormous extent of the French territories in West & Equatorial Africa, we need the right to recruit troops to defend Br W Africa from French aggression far more than the French need the reciprocal right to defend French W Afr against us.[39]

L. S. Amery, Under-Secretary at the Colonial Office at this time, more accurately held that the French 'want nigger conscripts not against us but to hold down Arabs & Germans'.[40] Britain therefore had no reason to object to the French plans, especially since events in East Africa might require the Tanganyika administration to recruit African troops. 'We shall, possibly', wrote Amery, 'want a reasonable liberty to use K[ing's] A[frican] R[ifle]s raised in Tanganyika territory in B[ritish] E[ast] A[frica] or Nyasaland for police purposes.'[41] Unlike the French, the British did not insist on the formal right to raise troops in mandated areas, because if military or police operations did become necessary, they calculated that 'no-one is likely to challenge our action.'[42]

---

[38] Memorandum by Hurst, '"B" and "C" Mandates', 20 July 1920, FO 371/4767. Chapter 3 of Paul Birdsall, *Versailles Twenty Years After* (New York, 1941), remains a useful commentary on this point.

[39] Minute by A. J. Harding, 26 January 1920, CO 649/21.

[40] Minute by L. S. Amery, 2 February 2 1920, CO 640/21.

[41] Ibid.

[42] Minute by E. S. Machtig, 16 January 1920, CO 649/21.

The War Office dissented, arguing that the war had changed the British military position in India and that the British government therefore would have to look to Africa for troops:

> The French are aware of the potential value of these African troops, of the comparative immunity and peace of the territories in which they will be raised, and of the great assistance they can render in more disturbed areas elsewhere . . . For instance, troops raised in the Cameroons will add greatly to French strength in West Africa, already so much superior to our own. On the other hand, inability on our part to raise troops in German East Africa except for internal purposes, would cripple at the outset any serious endeavour to utilise the native man-power resources of Eastern Africa either for the defence of any mandatory areas elsewhere, or for relieving the general military burden of the United Kingdom or India.[43]

The view of the Colonial Office prevailed, and Britain did not request the right to raise troops in East Africa. The extensive discussions on this point nevertheless indicate how carefully British officials weighed each humanitarian clause of the mandates in relation to military strength and security.

The French had accepted the mandates system at the Peace Conference only for reasons of political expediency. When it became apparent that the United States might not join the League, the French proposed to Britain that the West African mandates be dropped and that Togo and the Cameroons be annexed according to the divisions agreed upon by Lord Milner and the French Colonial Minister, Henri Simon, on 10 July 1919.[44] The British at first were willing to go along with the French proposal. According to Lord Milner in November 1919:

> The French want to get out of having any 'mandate' at all for their part of Togo and Cameroons, but are willing to pledge themselves by a formal declaration (which they wish us to join in making) to carry out such of the conditions of the draft 'B' Mandate as they do not object to . . .
>
> Personally I have always thought that the application of the mandatory system to the strips of Togo and the Cameroons, which we are to

---

[43] Memorandum by the General Staff, 'External Employment of Troops Raised in Mandatory Territory', 22 December 1920, CAB 24/117. There has been almost nothing of substance written about colonial manpower in relation to European security, but see D. K. Fieldhouse, *The Colonial Empires: A Comparative Survey from the Eighteenth Century* (London, 1966), p. 272 et seq.

[44] Text of agreement and lengthy minutes in CO 649/21.

take over, was a useless complication. There was not much harm in it, and I was quite willing to accept it rather than raise a controversy, which might cause difficulties in getting the question of the disposal of the ex-German Colonies settled. But, as the French are evidently determined not to have a mandate for their share of Togo and Cameroons, if they can possibly avoid it, and as there is no British interest, that I can see, involved in forcing them to submit to a mandate . . . I think there is more chance of arriving at an early settlement by falling in with their proposal than by falling out with them over it.[45]

The important point was to ensure that France stood on the same footing as Britain. If the French 'escaped' from having mandates, the British in equity should also be relieved of their obligations. Otherwise the French would exploit the British disadvantage.

Unless the French are themselves put in a glass (mandated) house somewhere, they will almost certainly amuse themselves by throwing stones at our mandated houses whenever they are annoyed with us or want something from us. But if they are liable to attack as a Mandatory Power they will probably leave us alone lest we retaliate on them . . . The ideal solution would of course be to have no mandates (or a form of Mandate C) for Togoland and the British portion of the Cameroons but for the French to accept Mandate B for the French Cameroons, just as we accept Mandate B for German East Africa.[46]

As Lord Milner later candidly observed in public, the implementation of the mandates system was accompanied by 'a return of the old rivalries and ambitions'.[47]

The French plan to avoid mandatory responsibility quickly encountered strong opposition from the United States. The Department of State regarded Article 22 of the League Covenant (the charter of the mandates system) as a binding international contract, regardless of the American position vis-à-vis the League. The State Department moreover insisted firmly that the United States, as one of the Allied and Associated Powers, had to be a formal party in any arrangements made about the disposition of the former German colonies.[48] For the

[45] Minute by Lord Milner, 26 November 1919, CO 649/21.

[46] Minute by A. J. Harding, 18 November 1919, CO 649/18.

[47] Quoted in 'The Mandate System and the British Mandates', *Journal of the Royal Society of Arts*, 72, 3736 (27 June 1924), p. 548. For this theme in relation to the Middle East, see especially Henry H. Cumming, *Franco-British Rivalry in the Post-War Near East: The Decline of French Influence* (London, 1938).

[48] The American insistence on this point led to a long series of agreements negotiated between the United States and each of the mandatory powers and covering almost all the mandated territories. See Walter Russel Barsell, 'The United States and the System of Mandates',

same reason that the French had accepted the mandates system in the first place—to conciliate the United States—they now dropped their scheme of jettisoning the 'B' mandates, but proposed instead to accept them as 'C' mandates. France would thus escape from the free-trade requirements of the 'B' mandates. The British once again were inclined to fall in with the French, this time on grounds that it would be administratively more convenient.

> The French proposal is more suitable for the circumstance of the British spheres of the Cameroons & Togoland than Mandate B. Those spheres must in practice be administered as 'integral portions' of Nigeria & the Gold Coast—and the French sphere of Togoland will undoubtedly be administered as part of Dahomey—and it will be more honest to recognise the facts.[49]

By supporting the French, however, Britain would run into trouble with the Belgians, who would demand that a 'C' mandate be conferred on Ruanda-Urundi. After a lengthy conversation with an official of the Belgian government, Sir Cecil Hurst reported 'that Belgian opinion would be very much moved if Belgium received a less favourable type of mandate than that awarded to France' and that the Belgians would not submit their draft mandate for the League's approval until after the West African 'B' mandates were formally accepted.[50]

Caught between 'the "Devil" of the Americans, and the "deep blue sea" of the French'[51] and also threatened with untold complications with the Belgians, Britain decided it would be best to tolerate the 'fiction' of 'B' mandates in West Africa. The issue was resolved mainly because of the unyielding attitude of the Americans, who insisted that the original stipulations of the 'B' mandates be adhered to. In mandatory affairs as well as in issues concerning more general problems of international organization, the European powers at this time tended to yield to the United States. Sir Cecil Hurst wrote in June

---

International Conciliation, 213 (October 1925), pp. 269–315; Quincy Wright, 'The United States and the Mandates', *Michigan Law Review*, 23, 7 (May 1925), pp. 717–47; Wright, *Mandates under the League of Nations;* for a basic chronology, see Hall, *Mandates, Dependencies and Trusteeship,* pp. 136–43. The United States continued to be critical of European administration of the mandates, especially those under British control. For one of the most biting British responses to the American attitude, see Margery Perham, 'African Facts and American Criticisms', *Foreign Affairs,* 22, 3 (April 1944), pp. 444–57.

[49] Minute by A. J. Harding, 26 November 1920, CO 640/21.
[50] Hurst to Foreign Office, 16 December 1920, CAB 24/117.
[51] E. J. Harding to Colonial Office, 23 September 1921, CO 640/23.

1921: 'The whole policy of the League at present is to cringe to the United States.'[52]

The 'A' Mandates: Oil, Strategy, and the Palestine Problem

As far as mandates were concerned, the British felt American pressure most strongly in the Middle East. There the Americans suspected that Britain intended to secure its grip over strategic territories that it would also be able to exploit economically by a monopoly given to the British-controlled Turkish Petroleum Company. The State Department protested specifically against the San Remo Oil Agreement of 1920, by which Britain agreed that France should have a 25 per cent share in the petroleum development in Mesopotamia in return for permission to build a British pipeline across French mandated territory to the Mediterranean. The United States, pursuing the traditional American policy of the 'open door', accused Britain of violating the free-trade arrangements of the 'A' mandates even before the mandates became formally operative.

The State Department's dispatches were couched in idealistic language emphasizing 'the spirit of the Covenant'; but the Foreign Office thought that the United States aimed at more than the achievement of international idealism. According to one British document, 'the United States Government, impelled by the important Standard Oil interests, [desires] to acquire a share in the Mesopotamia oil-fields.'[53] The British, basing their case on the sanctity of international agreements, argued that the Turkish Petroleum Company had vested, pre-war interests that remained valid. The Americans, emphasizing the equality of commercial opportunity as secured by Article 22 of the League Covenant, denied the legitimacy of the Turkish Petroleum Company's claims. After a series of lengthy and heated exchanges—in one of which Lord Curzon, the Foreign Secretary, denounced the US oil policy in the West Indies and Latin America as being out of line with the American 'open door' policy in the Middle East—it became increasingly clear that the mandates negotiations had become bound up with the acrimonious issue of Anglo-American oil rivalry in the Middle East. The Foreign Office had scant regard for the State Department's pretext for intervention: 'the standpoint taken up by the United States Government on the general question is devoid of legal

---

[52] Minute by Hurst, 4 June 1921, FO 371/7050.

[53] Foreign Office memorandum, 'The United States and the Mandates', dated July 1921, FO 371/7050.

foundation and of logic.'[54] By yielding to the United States on minor points concerning the Middle East mandates and by acquiescing in a certain amount of American investment in the Turkish Petroleum Company—deemed desirable for the economic development of Iraq—the British generally managed to conciliate the Americans. At the same time, the British-controlled oil company remained dominant. The diplomacy of the United States merely succeeded in securing American participation in a monopoly, not in achieving the open door.[55]

To British eyes, American 'interference' in the Middle East blocked the peace settlements and in large part caused the long delay in the issuance of the mandates. The basic difficulty arose from President Wilson's insistence that the principle of self-determination should be applied to the peoples of the Middle East. How to reconcile the self-determination principle with the Sykes-Picot agreement of 1916, which partitioned the Middle East into British and French spheres of influence? How to cope with the conflicting ambitions of the British, French, and Italians—and the Arabs and Jews—and at the same time satisfy the Americans that 'imperialism' had ended? Shortly after the signing of the Peace Treaty, Arthur J. Balfour made this analysis:

> The language of the Covenant assumes or asserts that in the regions we are discussing, as in other portions of the Turkish Empire, there are in the advanced chrysalis state 'independent nations' sufficiently 'developed' to demand 'provisional recognition', each of which is to be supplied by the Powers with a mandatory till it is able to stand alone. Where and what are these 'independent nations'? Are they by chance identical with Syria, Mesopotamia, and Palestine? If so, the coincidence with the Sykes-Picot arrangement is truly amazing, for no such idea was present to the minds of those who framed it. They started from the view that France had ancient interests and aspirations in Western Syria; that Britain had obvious claims in Bagdad and Southern Mesopotamia; that Palestine had a unique historic position; and that if these three areas were to be separately controlled, it was obviously expedient that none of the vast and vague territory

---

[54] 'The United States and the Mandates', July 1921, FO 371/7050.

[55] These negotiations are traced in lucid detail by John A. DeNovo, *American Interests and Policies in the Middle East, 1900–1939* (Minneapolis, 1963), chap. 6. See also Elizabeth Monroe, *Britain's Moment in the Middle East, 1914–1956* (Baltimore, 1963), chap. 4; and Edward Mead Earle, 'The Turkish Petroleum Company—A Study in Oleaginous Diplomacy', *Political Science Quarterly*, 39, 2 (June 1924), pp. 265–79. The American documentary source on this issue is *Foreign Relations of the United States, 1920* (3 vols., Washington, D.C., 1936), II, pp. 649–74; *Foreign Relations of the United States, 1921*, II, pp. 71–123; *Foreign Relations of the United States, 1922*, II, pp. 333–52; and *Foreign Relations of the United States, 1923*, II, pp. 240–64.

lying between them, which had no national organisation, should be under any foreign influence . . . It never occurred to them that they had to deal at all with nations in the modern and Western sense of the term.[56]

Balfour then went on to consider the main problem apart from the one of Mesopotamia—that of Syria and Palestine:

> Let us assume that two of the 'independent nations' for which man-datories have to be provided are Syria and Palestine. Take Syria first. Do we mean, in the case of Syria, to consult principally the wishes of the inhabitants? We mean nothing of the kind. According to the uni-versally accepted view there are only three possible mandatories —England, America, and France. Are we going 'chiefly to consider the wishes of the inhabitants' in deciding which of these is to be se-lected? We are going to do nothing of the kind. England has refused. America will refuse. So that, whatever the inhabitants may wish, it is France they will certainly have. They may freely choose; but it is Hob-son's choice after all.[57]

In Balfour's opinion, there was an even greater contradiction between the principle of the Covenant and the policy of the Allies in Palestine than in Syria: 'For in Palestine we do not propose even to go through the form of consulting the wishes of the present inhabitants of the country.'[58] Yet the Peace Conference had authorized the appointment of an 'international commission' to visit the Middle East and report on the wishes of the inhabitants. As Balfour complained, the Commission 'began by being international, and ended up by being American'.

The British, and to a much greater extent the French, upon closer examination of the danger of the Arabs publicly voicing their senti-ments, began quietly to place obstacles in the way of the appoint-ment and functioning of the Commission. Wilson finally dispatched two prominent Americans to lead an investigation, in which the Brit-ish and French did not participate, but ultimately the President did not act on the Commission's recommendations.[59] Had he done so, the United States might have become a mandatory power for one or more territories in the Middle East, and the presence of American influence

[56] Memorandum by Balfour, 'Respecting Syria, Palestine, and Mesopotamia', 11 August 1919, FO 406/41.

[57] Ibid.

[58] Ibid.

[59] See *Papers relating to the Foreign Relations of the United States: The Paris Peace Conference, 1919* (13 vols., Washington, D.C., 1942–47), XII. The work of the Commission is treated fully in Harry N. Howard, *The King-Crane Commission: An American Inquiry in the Middle East* (Beirut, 1963).

would have proved to Britain, at least, that behind American idealism lurked imperial ambition.

Britain had no doubt about French and Italian designs in the Middle East. The French were determined to establish permanent civil control over Syria and to end their military occupation. According to one British document:

> [T]he French were very anxious to get the Syrian mandate approved by the [League] Council in order to replace their military administration by a civilian government and to reduce their expenditure in that part of the world.[60]

But the Italians, jealous of the growth of their historic rival's influence in the Middle East, obstructed the proceedings of the Council by refusing to accept a French mandate in Syria. The French in turn would not agree to a settlement in Palestine until the Syrian mandate became final.

Together with the American protests against the issuance of the mandates, these triangular quarrels between the Italians, French, and British explain why the 'A' mandates did not come into force until over four years after the signing of the Peace Treaty. From the point of view of the League, the situation was intolerable. After several minor modifications in the draft mandates were made to suit the Americans, the United States by mid-1922 was finally willing to agree to the issuance of the Palestine mandate. But Italy persisted in its attempts to thwart France in Syria. In July 1922, Lord Balfour addressed the League Council and gave the following résumé:

> The Italian Representative was bound by the instructions of his Government to oppose the discussion of the mandate for Syria. The French representative was similarly bound to oppose the discussion of the mandate for Palestine, if the mandate for Syria were not taken at the same time. It followed that unless the Italian Government could be induced to modify its attitude, the Council would be unable to make any progress, and a most deplorable delay would ensue. The Council would thus be obliged to confess its impotence, and would cut a very poor figure before . . . the Assembly.[61]

---

[60] Balfour's comment at an interdepartmental conference held at the House of Commons, Secret, CP 2604, 17 February 1921, CAB 24/120.

[61] 'Provisional Minutes of a Private Meeting of the Council of the League of Nations held at St. James's Palace', Confidential, CP 4114, 19 July 1922, CAB 24/138. Cf. the minutes of the nineteenth session of the Council, in League of Nations, *Official Journal*, 3, 8, pt. 2 (August 1922), p. 801.

By opposing the French, the Italians were indirectly causing a delay in the settlement of the Palestine mandate. Under British pressure, the Italians yielded. On 24 July 1922 the Italian representative on the Council paid tribute 'in a moral sense' to Balfour.[62] The British documents clearly reveal that Balfour's patient and skilful diplomacy contributed greatly to the final issuance of the 'A' mandates for Syria and Palestine on 29 September 1923.

Balfour emerged within official British circles as the champion of the mandates system. Time and again he reminded his colleagues that Britain had assumed serious international responsibilities, which had to be fulfilled. These obligations could not be avoided, he reminded the Colonial Secretary, Winston Churchill, merely by carrying on with the de facto administration of territories such as Palestine and Mesopotamia in the hope that the mandates system would eventually collapse.[63] But as Churchill pointed out, the British did have to cope with apparently insoluble problems in the Middle East, where international supervision often seemed to be merely another complication. Summarizing the difficulties confronting Britain in that part of the world, Churchill wrote:

> whereas in Mesopotamia we have been able to study the wishes of the people and humour their national sentiment, we are committed in Palestine to the Zionist policy against which nine-tenths of the population and an equal proportion of the British officers are marshalled.[64]

In Palestine, the British had to assume the role of mediators between the increasingly hostile Jewish and Arab communities; in Mesopotamia, Britain had to prove that the word 'mandate' did not imply veiled annexation; to the League, Britain had to demonstrate that mandatory obligations were being fulfilled; and among themselves, British statesmen had to make sure that mandates would not jeopardize British security. Again, Balfour, more than any other member of the Cabinet, as Curzon once put it, 'interested himself keenly' in these questions. Uppermost in Balfour's mind as he grappled with the problem was how to reconcile international supervision in the Middle East with the prospect of 'connecting Mesopotamia with the Mediterranean by rail and pipe-line through all-British protectorates'.[65]

---

[62] League of Nations, *Official Journal*, 3, 8, pt. 2 (August 1922), p. 825.

[63] See the correspondence in FO 371/7053; also minutes in FO 371/7051.

[64] Churchill to Balfour, 12 October 1921, FO 371/7053. Richard Meinertzhagen, *Middle East Diary, 1917–1956* (London, 1959) has several illuminating comments in this regard.

[65] Memorandum by Balfour, FO 406/41.

The Mesopotamian issue brought to a head the debates about British strategic priorities much as the East African question had done in the 1880s and 1890s. Apart from oil (which could be exploited by Britain without a formal mandate), the major reason for the occupation of this Middle Eastern territory remained the traditional need to protect the route to India. To statesmen such as Curzon, who valued India as the permanent *raison d'être* of the British Empire, almost any territory in the Eastern Hemisphere could be envisaged as an outpost necessary for India's defence. But other officials, such as the Secretary of State for India, E. S. Montagu, thought that movements for independence in places such as Egypt and Ireland would inevitably contribute to unrest in India and would weaken, even end, Britain's hold over its most important colonial possession—thereby destroying one pretext for control over such places as Mesopotamia.[66] To borrow a comparison made by Professor John Gallagher of Oxford, Britain's occupation of Mesopotamia resembled the homeowner who took out fire insurance while his house was burning down.

The key to official British thought in the series of recurrent crises in the immediate post-war years was to keep territories such as Ireland, Egypt, and Mesopotamia *'within the British Imperial system'*. If that goal entailed unorthodox steps, the British were prepared to take them. Curzon—commenting on Egypt, but expressing a thought that held true for all British territories, whether Crown Colonies, Protectorates, or mandates—once wrote:

> The Egyptians are giving us a great opportunity by the superstitious and almost insane significance which they attach to the phrase protectorate. In their eyes it connotes servitude of a degrading character, inconsistent with the glorious Wilsonian discovery of self-determination as the future guiding principle of mankind. Why should we not humour them? Why worry about the rind if we can obtain the fruit? I take it that what we all have in view is that Egypt would remain inside rather than outside the British Imperial system. If the best way to do this is to drop the word protectorate and conclude a treaty of alliance with her, as we did with the Indian Princes a century ago . . . why not do it?[67]

Faced with intense dislike of the conception of a 'mandate' in Mesopotamia—which carried with it the implication of a nation not yet able to stand on its own feet—Britain transformed the draft mandate into

---

[66] See E. S. Montagu's memorandum 'Ireland', Secret, 10 November 1920, CP 2084. For Montagu's views on Egypt in this connection, see especially his memorandum 'Egypt', Secret, 19 October 1920, CP 2000, CAB 24/112.

[67] Memorandum by Curzon, 'The Egyptian Situation', Confidential, CP 2589, 14 February 1921, CAB 24/119.

a bilateral treaty that amounted to the same thing.[68] Iraq remained within the 'British Imperial system' and in 1932 became a member of the League of Nations. The British thus attempted to hold their Empire together and at the same time to reconcile Imperial demands with the idealism that had inspired the League.

British ambivalence towards the idealism of Article 22 manifested itself most clearly in the negotiations that led to the creation of the Mandates Section of the League Secretariat and the Permanent Mandates Commission. Sir Cecil Hurst and his colleagues in the British government thought that the Secretariat, in Hurst's words, consisted 'of gentlemen whom I know by experience to be extremely pernickety and apt to be tiresome if not obstructive'.[69] Britain nevertheless gave warmer support to the head of the Mandates Section, a Swiss named William E. Rappard, than did any other nation.[70]

The British also took the lead in defining the purpose and function of the Permanent Mandates Commission. The recently released documents show that British statesmen thought that anything in the nature of a 'roving commission' would be 'very objectionable' and that, in Lord Milner's words, 'the sole duty' of the Permanent Mandates Commission should be merely 'to examine the reports presented by the Mandatories, and to ascertain if the Mandatories were carrying out their Mandates'.[71]

[68] The text is printed in Wright, *Mandates under the League of Nations,* pp. 595–600. In this connection, see two articles by Luther Harris Evans, 'The Emancipation of Iraq from the Mandates System', *American Political Science Review,* 26, 6 (December 1932), pp. 1024–49; and 'The General Principles Governing the Termination of a Mandate', *American Journal of International Law,* 26, 4 (October 1932), pp. 735–58.

[69] Minute by Hurst, 13 January 1922, FO 371/7775.

[70] There are numerous minutes about this in the Foreign Office files, of which the following is a good example. After a visit to London by a subcommittee of the Permanent Mandates Commission chaired by Rappard, Hurst wrote:

[T]he sub-committee were very pleased with the reception which they have had in London and with the efforts of [the] British Government to meet them and help them in every way. In Paris, on the other hand, the sub-committee was not well received, and the officials whom they met adopted an air of resentment at the intrusion of the Mandates Commission.

Minute by Hurst, 23 November 1921, FO 371/1053. There are numerous letters by Rappard in the Papers of the Anti-Slavery and Aborigines Protection Society (Rhodes House, Oxford) that discuss the difficulties of the establishment of the mandates system from the League's point of view, and the recurrent theme in them is gratitude for British cooperation. For Rappard's views on the beginning of the mandates system, see William E. Rappard, *International Relations as Viewed from Geneva* (New Haven, 1925), chap. 2.

[71] 'Conference of Representatives of H.M. Government, the British Dominions and India', minutes, Secret, 9 November 1920, CAB 29/28/2.

The Meaning of the Mandates System

What could be done if a mandate were violated? Lord Robert Cecil summed up the consensus of British official opinion:

> We did not think the League of Nations should attempt to interfere with Mandatories . . . The Commission should enquire into any grave complaint made in a mandated territory, but should not undertake administration. If, for instance a complaint was received to the effect that a country was carrying on slavery, the Commission should inform the country in question of the complaint, and ask for a reply. *In the last resort it could not do more than call the attention of the public . . . to the matter.*[72]

From first to last the British viewed 'mandates' merely as 'a self-imposed limitation of sovereignty' and saw that the ultimate success of the mandates system would depend on the amount of publicity given to it. In Balfour's words, the most important achievement of the mandates system consisted of making 'it quite impossible that any transaction of general interest should take place except in the full glare of the noonday sun of public opinion'.[73]

The Legacy of the Mandates

Did international supervision in the inter-war years make any difference? And does the mandate experience have any relevance to international affairs today? The answers to those questions are difficult and paradoxical. In the half-century since the establishment of the mandates system, experts in international affairs have witnessed revolu-

---

[72] Ibid; emphasis added. The British government thus held that the League's power of intervention was much more severely limited than did the American colonial expert, George Louis Beer, who wrote that 'what sharply distinguishes the Mandatory System from all such international arrangements of the past is the unqualified right of intervention possessed by the League of Nations' (H. W. V. Temperley, ed., *A History of the Peace Conference of Paris* [6 vols., London, 1920], II, p. 236). An eminent authority on British constitutional law at the time, Professor Berriedale Keith, much more accurately held:

> The true mode of securing the just carrying out of the system lies in bringing to bear on any abuses the public opinion of the League, and especially of the country whose methods are pronounced faulty.

'Mandates', *Journal of Comparative Legislation and International Law*, 3rd series, 4, 1 [February 1922], p. 80.

[73] Balfour to Secretary to the Cabinet, Confidential, 17 May 1922, FO 371/7776.

tionary developments undreamed of by the statesmen of 1919; yet the trusteeship areas in which national security remains an international issue are the same territories where the Peace Conference consented to the most elaborate security precautions—the Pacific islands and South-West Africa. In those areas, the historic themes of security and self-determination are by no means yet played out.

In the 'A' mandates of the Middle East, the self-determination principle had its most rapid and successful fulfilment within the boundaries established at the Peace Conference, a triumph of Wilsonian idealism. The statesmen of Paris miscalculated, reckoning that idealistic slogans were either harmless or could be used to their advantage. In Lord Curzon's celebrated statement, well worth requoting:

> I am inclined to value the argument of self-determination because I believe that most of the people would determine in our favour . . . If we cannot get out of our difficulties in any other way we ought to play self-determination for all it is worth wherever we are involved in difficulties with the French, the Arabs, or anybody else, and leave the case to be settled by that final argument knowing in the bottom of our hearts that we are more likely to benefit from it than anybody else.[74]

History records President Wilson, not the British or French imperialists, as more accurately foreseeing the future of the Middle East. If nothing else, Article 22 embodied Wilson's prophetic plea that the peoples of the Middle East should and eventually would be independent.

The inter-war publicists who wrote so voluminously on the subject of mandates attached great importance to the League's humanitarian and economic accomplishments in tropical Africa. For example, one prominent authority, C. K. Webster, wrote that the free-trade clauses limited 'to some extent the range of action of competing economic imperialisms which have been, and are, such a menace to world peace'.[75] Historical research bears him out. Benjamin Gerig, in the most important work on the subject, declined to state definitely whether the economic development of the mandates would have been different had they never been subjected to international supervision, but he did conclude that the mandates system 'is undoubtedly the most effective instrument yet devised to make the Open Door effective'.[76] Much

[74] Eastern Committee Minutes, Secret, 5 December 1918, CAB 27/24; W. R. Louis, *Germany's Lost Colonies, 1914–1919* (Oxford, 1967), p. 6.

[75] C. K. Webster, *The League of Nations in Theory and Practice* (London,1933), p. 290.

[76] Gerig, *The Open Door and the Mandates System,* p. 199.

more detailed, comparative research is needed before definitive conclusions can be reached about the impact of the mandates system on economic development and administrative policies; but recent work by Professor Ralph Austen of the University of Chicago suggests that the League's public scrutiny induced the colonial regimes to make their mandated territories 'model colonies' and that the attention given to the mandates by colonial writers played a crucial role in the development of the ideology upon which the Trusteeship Council of the United Nations was founded.[77]

In the Pacific islands and South-West Africa, the issues of power politics created by the First World War appear to be as vital as ever. Today the islands south of the Equator have lost their strategic value; New Zealand has granted Samoan independence and the United Nations is pressing Australia to accelerate New Guinean self-determination. But the United States holds Micronesia as a 'strategic trust'—described by one authority as a 'somewhat bastard and contradictory' conception, giving the United States even more complete control than Japan had under the 'C' mandate.[78] The future?—51st state or independent Micronesia? In the meantime, the phrase 'annexation in all but name' —the charge so often leveled against the European powers—is as applicable to the Pacific dependency of the United States as to the former territories under mandatory control. The United States will probably continue to receive from the United Nations, in Balfour's phrase, 'the full glare of the noonday sun of public opinion' before the future of Micronesia is determined: ample proof of the efficacy of the mandates system as conceived by one of its principal founders.

In South-West Africa, the issues arising from the mandates system demonstrate themselves most vividly. When the United Nations dramatically—and, it would appear, futilely—terminated the mandate in October 1966, South Africa stood indicted before the world as a violator of one of civilization's sacred trusts. The charge is hotly denied in South Africa, and South African scholars point to the minutes of the Paris Peace Conference for historical justification for dealing with the territory as an 'integral portion' of their country. The relevant passage contains this remark by President Wilson to Generals Botha and Smuts of South Africa:

[77] Ralph A. Austen, 'African Territories under French and British Mandate', in Prosser Gifford and W. R. Louis, eds., *France and Britain in Africa: Imperial Rivalry and Colonial Rule* (New Haven, 1971).

[78] Rupert Emerson, 'American Policy toward Pacific Dependencies', in Rupert Emerson et al., *America's Pacific Dependencies: A Survey of American Colonial Policies and of Administration and Progress toward Self-Rule in Alaska, Hawaii, Guam, Samoa and the Trust Territory* (New York, 1949), p. 9. See also A. Hugh McDonald, ed., *Trusteeship in the Pacific* (Sydney, 1949).

It was up to the Union of South Africa to make it so attractive that South-West Africa would come into the Union of their own free will. Should that not be the case, the fault would lie with the mandatory.[79]

In other words, say the South Africans, was the President not giving South Africa a free hand for eventual annexation? And who, they say, can dispute the sincerity and tenacity of purpose that guides South Africa's effort to create a stable and structured society attractive to blacks and whites alike? Their interpretation is erroneous. President Wilson could not have anticipated that apartheid and South African determination to retain control of the territory would frustrate the process of self-determination. There lies the nub of the problem. The civilization South Africa is attempting to create differs radically from the societies that now characterize most of the Western world. Viewed conservatively, from within the narrow and static legalism characteristic of the Permanent Mandates Commission's proceedings, South Africa's case rests on the claim of a scrupulously legal fulfilment of the mandatory contract. On the other hand, measured by the school of international idealism that demands an evolution of legal and social institutions for the betterment and equality of all mankind, South Africa stands guilty of turning backward to racism and Boer nationalism and against the main currents of Western liberal thought. South Africa, by implication at least, holds that apartheid best fulfils its sacred trust; but the overwhelming consensus of international opinion interprets true trusteeship in a spirit reminiscent of the Wilsonian idealism on which the mandates system was founded.

International Organization   1969

---

[79] *Papers relating to the Foreign Relations of the United States: The Paris Peace Conference, 1919*, III, pp. 740–42.

10

THE BRITISH AND THE FRENCH COLONIAL EMPIRE: TRUSTEESHIP AND SELF-INTEREST

The British attitude towards French colonialism can be summed up in a single sentence by A. J. Balfour, the last of the Victorian Prime Ministers and later Foreign Secretary during the First World War. Subjecting the French to the indignity of placing them in the same category as the Italians, he remarked: 'All the troubles of the Foreign Office, since I have been a member of it, have been brought about by matters raised by officials looking after the twopenny-halfpenny and very often very corrupt interests of France or Italy.'[1] This is a persistent theme in British thought. Whenever troubles arose in Asia or Africa, they could usually be traced to the French.

Yet the British did not have an entirely clean conscience. Part of the underlying purpose of the Balfour Declaration in 1917, to give but one example, was to keep the French out of Palestine by promising the Jews a national home. Nor could the British help but reflect, at least occasionally, that they persistently undermined French aims. For example, during the Second World War, would not the British, by sponsoring the independence of Syria and Lebanon, help consolidate Arab anti-French sentiment? Yet the British attempted to collaborate as much as possible with the French (and the Belgians and the Portuguese) in tropical Africa—as long as collaboration did not damage Anglo-American relations. The crisis at Suez in 1956 marked a turning point in this historic relationship. Though they were contemptuous of French colonialism and they believed, with conviction, that British colonies were better ruled and better guided towards self-government, the British eventually had to acknowledge that the French were making a success of decolonization and of modernizing their national economy. While Britain lost an empire and appeared to be lost at sea (as Dean Acheson famously put it), France took the lead in creating the European community. Britain, by contrast, seemed to enter a period of national decline. The ultimate irony is that the British noted, at the high point of decolonization in the early 1960s, that French sway in their former colonies far surpassed their own influence in the Commonwealth. Contempt thus became transformed into grudging admiration.

The British of course were well aware of an enduring French conviction, which could be epitomized in the phrase 'Perfidious Albion'—

---

[1] Eastern Committee Minutes, Secret, 9 December 1918, CAB 27/24, quoted in W. R. Louis, *Germany's Lost Colonies* (Oxford, 1967), pp. 127–28.

attributed to Napoleon, but in use at least since the seventeenth century. In the colonial or imperial history of the two countries, nothing could divert attention from the glaring fact of the British occupation of Egypt in 1882 or the consolidation of the British position in Africa as a result of the Fashoda crisis in 1898. Giving way in the western part of Africa to secure the eastern backbone of the continent, recognizing French supremacy in the Maghrib and parts of western Africa in order to protect the lifeline to India, seemed to be a pattern reasonable enough to the Foreign Office. But British predominance rested on the assumption that France would put European priorities ahead of colonial aims, and thus that the French would back down in Africa or Asia because their principal enemy was in Europe. Nevertheless, France was Britain's most dangerous colonial rival. This competitive relationship seemed to be more than a fact: it was an attitude, a tradition, espoused, for example, by that most knowledgeable and eloquent of British imperialists, Lord Curzon, Viceroy of India at the turn of the twentieth century and member of the War Cabinet during the First World War. But there was an opposite and equally compelling line of reasoning in the tradition of Sir Edward Grey and the Entente Cordiale. In the decade before the First World War, it seemed to Grey and others that the British and French ought to close ranks against Germany and that both powers should subordinate petty colonial quarrels to the higher cause of good and close mutual relations. The long-standing belief in the necessity of Anglo-French amity can be juxtaposed with that of antagonism and Francophobia—and both points of view must be taken into account in considering British attitudes towards the United States. Might not Anglo-French friendship prove in the end to be more durable than an Anglo-American 'special relationship', as it became known? Was there not a risk in placing faith in the unreliable, indeed fickle, Americans? This was a question raised in both world wars.

During the early part of the First World War, Grey tried to diminish French suspicion that the British were collecting colonial spoils around the world, notably the German colonies, while the French bore the brunt of the fighting on the western front. For example, he proposed to yield—surrender, in the view of his critics—most of the Cameroons to the French. He drew the wrath of the Colonial Secretary, Lewis Harcourt, who pointed out that British and French aims collided throughout the world, in the Pacific as well as Africa, and that the territories in West Africa should at least be used to extract from the French certain concessions. Harcourt wrote in March 1915, in a minute that well illustrates a habitual way of thinking at that time:

We want from France two things—

    (a) their share of the Condominium in the New Hebrides;

    (b) their small settlement of Jibuti opposite Aden, which controls the mischievous arms traffic to Abyssinia and Central Africa.

To obtain these we can offer France—

    (c) three-fourths of the Cameroons (instead of one-half), *plus* our half share of Togoland;

    (d) or, if we wish to retain all of Togoland and acquire Dahomey, we can offer France all the Cameroons except Mount Cameroon and Duala, and in such a wide settlement we could throw in the Gambia, which is an object of great desire by the French; but the cession of the Gambia would be very unpopular in this country, and arouse much public and Parliamentary criticism and agitation.

Alternatively, we might surrender to France *our* share of the New Hebrides Condominium as compensation, with nearly the whole of the Cameroons, for our possession of Togoland and Dahomey.[2]

Such were the points of territorial tension, which had political, economic, and even psychological ramifications. One landmark in this regard deserves special comment because it stood forevermore as a symbol of British and French imperialism in the Middle East: the Sykes-Picot agreement of 1916 partitioned the region into shades of British and French influence or control, though the British uneasily acknowledged that the agreement was not easy to reconcile with assurances to the Arabs for an independent state.[3]

Lord Curzon commented in December 1918 on the historical differences in national character that inevitably brought the two countries into conflict:

A good deal of my public life has been spent in connection with the political ambitions of France, which I have come across in Tunis, in

---

[2] Memorandum by Harcourt, 'The Spoils', Secret, 25 March 1915, Harcourt Papers.

[3] For a recent, detailed study that tends, in the author's own phrase, to 'vindicate the British Government of the day', see Isaiah Friedman, *Palestine: A Twice-Promised Land? The British, the Arabs, and Zionism, 1915–1920* (London, 2000).

Siam, and in almost every distant region where the French have sway. We have been brought, for reasons of national safety, into an alliance with the French, which I hope will last, but their national character is different from ours, and their political interests collide with our own in many cases. I am seriously afraid that the great Power from whom we may have most to fear in the future is France, and I almost shudder at the possibility of putting France in such a position. She is powerful in almost all parts of the world, even around India.[4]

Moreover, there were military considerations. A. J. Balfour, also writing at the end of the First World War, believed that the currents of international power would sweep the United States into a new position and that American aims would offset the imperialist ambitions of the French. The solution to the danger of French military and colonial expansion might lie in President Wilson's championing of the principle of self-determination:

> With Germany practically wiped off for a generation we must deal with France. France is a great military Power. We know the character of French policy in the past, and what it may be in the coming generation again. France may be our great problem, and there it seems to me that we must try to make friends with America. That is the line of policy for us to pursue . . . America is not out for anything except for the larger issue of world settlement, depending upon the League of Nations . . . [and] the principles of autonomy and self-determination.[5]

The price for American friendship in colonial affairs would be the acceptance of the mandates system and with it the principle that subject peoples should be allowed eventually to stand on their own. By agreeing to the mandates system, the British endorsed the principle of what became known as the Pax Anglo-Americana.

As Lord Milner put it, the Anglo-American 'colonial alliance' would not be 'a mere cloak for annexation, but . . . a bond of union . . . between the United States and ourselves'.[6] Milner was the Colonial Secretary at the time of the colonial settlement at the Paris Peace Conference of 1919. Though he tried to improve the colonial relations of France and Britain, he believed that Britain's natural partner in developing the non-Western world would be the United States. As for the principle of self-determination, sufficient evidence could be found

---

[4] Eastern Committee Minutes, Secret, 2 December 1918, CAB 27/24.
[5] Ibid.
[6] Ibid., 20 December 1918.

that the indigenous inhabitants of Africa and Asia would determine in favour of the British—so ran the British line of thought—if only because the natives disliked the French even more.

In the aftermath of the 1914–18 war, as in the wake of the Second World War, the British studied the problem of the colonial empires with an eye towards the security of the British Isles as well as the Empire at large. At both times, the British needed a strong French government and a stable French empire as a safeguard against resurgent German militarism and revolutionary Russian communism. In the 1920s, however, France herself appeared to be a military danger. Pondering the advance in military technology, Lord Curzon drew a pessimistic conclusion. He remarked, after glancing at a map of the world:

> France has potential submarine bases in Tonquin, West Africa, the Red Sea and on both sides of the Mediterranean, in addition to the bases on the English Channel and the Western coast of France which are all close to British sea routes. Great Britain would consequently in a war with France require a very large force of destroyers and small craft to cope with large French submarine flotillas.[7]

And not only submarines. According to British military intelligence, the French air force could easily bombard London, while the army could acquire military superiority on the European continent because of the additional black African manpower gained as a result of the war. The doctrine that France was a permanent or potential enemy thus continued to jostle with the principle that France could or should be Britain's natural ally.

The same contradictory ideas tormented the British during the Second World War. They needed a resuscitated, vigorous French government, and they relied on the French colonial empire as a stabilizing force in world affairs. If Indo-China were placed under international trusteeship—the solution favoured by Franklin Delano Roosevelt—then what might be the fate of such colonies as Malaya or Hong Kong? As in the time of the 1914–1918 war, the British after 1940 were torn between conflicting impulses: either fall in with American plans for trusteeship or protect and resuscitate the French colonial empire. In self-interest, the British tried to defend the integrity of the French colonies, but knew that they would have increasingly to rely on American economic and military assistance. For the same reason that they had accepted the mandates system, the British now acquiesced in the

---

[7] Curzon to Balfour, 23 November 1921, quoted in W. R. Louis, *British Strategy in the Far East, 1919–1939* (Oxford, 1971), p. 101.

trusteeship system of the United Nations. It seemed a small price to pay in order to win American support, even if it was sceptical and conditional, for the continuation of the British Empire.

The true enemy of French colonialism during the Second World War was not Britain but the United States—indeed, the President himself. It is important to note Roosevelt's attitude in order better to understand the British view towards the French colonies during the wartime era. Roosevelt despised French colonialism. It is a repeated theme in his wartime conversations. He thought the French had attempted little at all, for example, for the peoples of Indo-China: 'The French had been there for nearly one hundred years and had done absolutely nothing with the place to improve the lot of the people.'[8] He thought the French themselves to be decadent and corrupt. In summing up his attitude, he remarked in 1943 that the French in Indo-China were 'hopeless'—at which point Sir Alexander Cadogan, the Permanent Under-Secretary, observed, not incorrectly, that the President might regard the British as almost as hopeless in Malaya.[9] British self-interest in the cause of the European colonial mission thus worked to French advantage. Oliver Harvey, a Foreign Office official who later became Ambassador to France, summed it up: 'If we weaken the French in Syria, we weaken our own position.'[10] British military support of the French, specifically in the reoccupation of Indo-China, helps explain the restoration of the French colonial system in 1945.[11]

Roosevelt's disposition was not only generally anti-French but also specifically anti–de Gaulle. To him, de Gaulle represented the narrow nationalism of the previous era and the resurgence of French imperialism. At the time of Roosevelt's death in April 1945, the British knew that the United Sates would continue to pursue anti-colonial goals. Nevertheless, the dogged persistence of thwarting French aims was now no longer embodied in the President. Harry Truman also carried forward the military and economic plans of the Pentagon and State

[8] Pacific War Council minutes, 21 July 1943, Roosevelt Papers, Map Room, Box 168. The latest work to place colonial goals in the general context of the war is Victor Rothwell, *War Aims in the Second World War* (London, 2005).

[9] Minute by Cadogan, 2 February 1944, FO 371/41723. Cadogan continued: 'In what way were they [the French] hopeless? When stricken at home, they could not, of course, defend it [Indo-China]. But was their peace-time record so bad? . . . if the French are to be turned out, what is to be put in their place? . . . Who would be better off?'

[10] Oliver Harvey Diaries, 29 October 1944, British Library Add. MSS 56400.

[11] The most recent account of 'brazenly pro-French policy' of the local British commander, General Douglas Gracey, is Mark Atwood Lawrence, *Assuming the Burden: Europe and the American Commitment to War in Vietnam* (Berkeley, 2005), chap. 3.

Department, but to the relief of the British, he did not, with the exception of Palestine, demonstrate much interest in colonial issues. Indo-China and other French colonial territories were eventually restored to France in full sovereignty and were not, as Roosevelt had hoped, placed under international trusteeship.

The conception of colonial trusteeship, for the French no less than for the British, had a substantial and intrinsic meaning quite apart from trusteeship as an issue in power politics.[12] Writers of international history tend to regard Second World War trusteeship schemes as a sort of international receivership or as a makeshift device to block the takeover of a colonial territory by a rival. There is a good deal of truth in this partial view, if only because de Gaulle and Churchill saw it as the essence of American colonial designs.

For de Gaulle's part, it is paradoxical that he regarded the Brazzaville Conference of January–February 1944 as a step towards tying the colonies more firmly to the metropole, when in fact the conference stands in colonial history as one of the seminal events in the resurgence of French colonial trusteeship (and in French decolonization). To de Gaulle, the unity of the empire and the metropole was one of the keys to the restoration of French grandeur and represented tangible evidence of France's rank as a world power. But the actual agenda of the Brazzaville conference, which the British followed closely, was much more mundane. The conference dealt with technical questions of tropical medicine, colonial agriculture, and economic self-sufficiency. On larger issues, as the British were aware, there was a critical ambiguity. The conference addressed itself to the issue of political change. But would it be change towards increasing local autonomy or towards the reassertion of metropolitan control? One of the shrewdest American observers of the French colonial empire, Ralph Bunche, noted that at the conclusion of the conference, the phrase 'self-government' had been rendered in English, as if it had no equivalent in the French language or in the French conception of the proper relationship between the colonies and the metropole.[13] In any event, for the French as well as the British, the Second World War marked a rejuvenation of the French colonial mission, a mission that would be controlled by France and not by the United States or the United Nations. At the San Francisco conference that created the United Nations, George Bidault spoke indignantly of 'a campaign of

[12] See W. R. Louis, *Imperialism at Bay* (Oxford, 1977), pp. 38–47.
[13] Ralph J. Bunche, 'The French African Conference at Brazzaville', 6 April 1944, US Department of State, Notter Files, Box 36, National Archives.

ignorance and calumny' against the French colonial empire. He said emphatically that 'France would be her own trustee'.[14]

It is ironic that while the British were coming to the assistance of the French in the reoccupation of Indo-China, they were moving in the opposite direction in Syria and Lebanon. In the face of riots and a full-scale uprising in Damascus, the British military commander in May 1945 presented an ultimatum to French troops to return to their barracks. The humiliating outcome was well expressed by the French commander: 'the whole affair reminded him of Fashoda'.[15]

It is useful to trace briefly the origins of the Syrian crisis in the last months of the war because the British archival records illuminate the motives as well as the goals of the British in the French dependencies. One source in particular is remarkably candid and revealing. The head of the Eastern Department of the Foreign Office, Robin Hankey, committed to paper his inner thoughts on the predicament with the French. At the beginning of the crisis in the Levant in the spring of 1945, Hankey had thought the French might ultimately prevail:

> English and American people in the Levant States tend to talk rather loosely, but with pleasurable anticipation, of the French being thrown into the sea, but my own impression, after consulting the Army Commander and other people, is that the French would maintain themselves, though with difficulty, until reinforced; and that we should probably have to support the French in order to prevent Europeans and Christians being murdered, when it came to the point.[16]

Hankey was also frank about local sentiment towards the French:

> The French only see their own stooges, which is bad for them. Everyone . . . without exception, hates the French like poison and denounces them, lock stock and barrel, often quite unreasonably—but the French have a very bad record. The locals certainly behave as provocatively to the French as they dare and an outburst of Gallic impatience is always possible.[17]

On the other hand, Oliver Harvey held unorthodox and acute views that were probably much closer to the reality in the Middle East: 'The Syrians hate us as much as they hate the French, but they think

---

[14] Louis, *Imperialism at Bay,* p. 46.
[15] Quoted in W. R. Louis, *The British Empire in the Middle East* (Oxford, 1986), p. 165.
[16] Minute by Hankey, 3 March 1945, FO 371/45575.
[17] Minute by Hankey, 28 February 1945, FO 371/45561.

they can use us. Our long term interests and those of the French are identical.'[18]

One of the merits of the British minutes is the utter frankness of expression. Hankey for example did not want the French to be entirely kicked out of the Levant, because the British themselves might require bases in Syria. If the British moved in as the French moved out, how could the British sincerely maintain that they had no imperialistic aims? Hankey's solution would be to allow the French to remain in the Levant with a hand on their collar, and at the same time to fetch the Americans to the general cause of defence. In a moment of inspiration, Hankey thought that the United Nations might provide the solution:

> The only hope that I can see of getting the acquiescence of the Levant States in the continued presence of French forces is . . . [to] say to them that in the post-war world the principal United Nations will have bases everywhere. America will have bases in the West Indies and in Indo-China. We already have bases all over the world. The French will participate in the maintenance of security in the Eastern Mediterranean and will have to have a base in Syria.[19]

But the actual areas occupied by the French would be strictly circumscribed, and thus would not be a cause of alarm to the 'locals'. The French for their part would have the chance to perfect the art of desert warfare:

> The French base should not be near any centre of population . . . The troops would be confined to the base and would not be able to go elsewhere except for training in the surrounding desert. The number of troops would be limited to a low figure . . . We should aim at keeping French troops away from the places where they can be used to intimidate Governments and Parliaments.[20]

Hankey also took into account the arguments in favour of siding with the French:

> It could be argued that we should only help the French to remain in Syria if we could be sure that they would use their influence there in a useful way—e.g. to help us keep the Arabs quiet in the event

[18] Harvey Diaries, 4 December 1943, British Library Add. MSS 56400.
[19] Minute by Hankey, 3 March 1945, FO 371/45575.
[20] Ibid.

of trouble in Palestine or not to oppose our policy as regards Arab unity.[21]

He did not however believe that the argument of supporting the French outweighed the dangers of Arab hostility.

The Foreign Secretary himself, Anthony Eden, was well aware that the world at large would accept 'the French story' that in the eastern Mediterranean 'this is a struggle between France & ourselves for the control of the Levant States in which we have made use of France's weakness to entrench ourselves.'[22] The British were careful to point out that they championed the cause of Syrian and Lebanese independence. Yet it is easy to detect less admirable characteristics. There is a tone of *schadenfreude* in the British minutes about French troubles in the Levant at the close of the war. The French, their old colonial rivals, in the words of one official, had 'now finally cooked their own goose'.[23] The British were quite aware that by sponsoring Arab independence they would appear 'to the logical and suspicious French mind as deliberate and perfidious'.[24] There was no 'Sykes-Picot' in the Second World War.[25]

It is important to recall the general intellectual attitude in both Britain and America towards the French colonies after 1945: it was generally dismissive. In Britain, belief in the superiority of the British colonial system was seldom challenged, and even in the United States the cult of the District Officer—the admiration for colonial-service officers helping less fortunate peoples in remote outposts—tended to offset anti–British Empire sentiment. By contrast, Anglo-American feelings towards French colonies, rather in the tradition of Franklin Delano Roosevelt, were usually contemptuous. The French were regarded as imposing a centralized and exploitative bureaucracy over unwilling subjects, though some intellectuals admired the French policy of assimilation and willingness to grant citizenship and equality to the elites of the colonies.

In the two departments of the British government most concerned with the French colonies—the Colonial Office and Foreign Office—there existed of course a much higher level of knowledge than among the general public, and some officials genuinely respected the French

[21] Minute by Hankey, 16 March 1945, FO 371/45561.

[22] Minute by Eden, 21 May 1945, FO 371/45570.

[23] Sir Terence Shone to Foreign Office, Top Secret and Personal, 27 August 1945, FO 371/45582.

[24] Minute by Harvey, 3 October 1945, FO 371/45583.

[25] See Louis, *British Empire in the Middle East,* p. 167.

civilizing mission. Within the Colonial Office the person most knowledgeable about the French colonies was Kenneth Robinson of the International Relations Department. Robinson took the lead in promoting cooperation between the two countries on technical issues of agriculture and public health.[26] Shortly after the end of the war, he left government service to become a Fellow of Nuffield College, Oxford, and later became Director of the Institute for Commonwealth Studies in London. His single book, *The Dilemmas of Trusteeship*, a seminal work, deals with British colonial administration; but in his time he was the foremost British authority on the French colonial system, and in intellectual circles at least, his sophisticated vision served to correct the outlook of those who took a simplistic view of French colonialism.[27]

Within the Foreign Office, the principal authority on the French colonies in the 1950s was Adam Watson, who, like Robinson, had an academic temperament and later distinguished himself as an historian of international relations.[28] In 1956, Watson was the head of the Foreign Office's African Department, which then included Egypt. He was thus at the centre of the Suez crisis, though below those making critical decisions. It is worthwhile briefly to focus on Watson because of his views on the French during the crisis of 1956 and because shortly thereafter he became Ambassador to several of the newly independent French African states.

To Watson, the plan of the British and French ministers to invade Egypt, and eventually to include Israel as part of the anti-Egyptian combination—or collusion, to use the phrase of the time—bore the characteristics of an alliance 'made in Paris'.[29] He observed that the French demonstrated greater resolve and that they worried that the British lacked the determination necessary to make the invasion a success. The French, quite erroneously in Watson's judgement, viewed Nasser as the source of the trouble in Algeria. Egypt seemed to resemble an octopus whose tentacles stretched throughout North Africa —a monster that could be killed only by decapitating the head. In effect, the British and French, with Israeli assistance, would be restoring

[26] See John Kent, *The Internationalization of Colonialism: Britain, France, and Black Africa, 1939–1956* (Oxford, 1992), pp. 173–74.

[27] See, for example, K. E. Robinson, 'Experts, Colonialists, and Africanists', in J. C. Stone, ed., *Experts in Africa* (Aberdeen, 1980).

[28] See, for example, Hedley Bull and Adam Watson, eds., *The Expansion of International Society* (Oxford, 1984).

[29] See Adam Watson, 'The Aftermath of Suez: Consequences for French Decolonization', in W. R. Louis and Roger Owen, eds., *Suez 1956* (Oxford, 1989).

European dominance in the Middle East. From his vantage point in the Foreign Office, Watson, like virtually all of his colleagues, thought the alliance with the French—and the Israelis—to be ill judged and bound to backfire. Later he was equally certain that the French felt betrayed when the British caved into American economic pressure and stopped the invasion. 'Les Anglo-Saxons', he later wrote, had demonstrated that they were more interested in each other than in France or Europe.

The Suez crisis was a turning point in the history of modern Europe. The emotional disappointment of Suez helped turn France away from Britain to create the Paris-Bonn axis and the European community. If nothing else, Suez demonstrated how closely the British were tied to the Americans. The British had proved their unreliability at Suez. For the British, however, there was another interpretation, which fell in line with their traditional tendency to blame whatever was wrong in the world on the French: Suez was a disaster because the French began it. Marianne had seduced John Bull. Though a caricature, of course, the essence of a caricature is that it contains an element of truth: John Bull's outlook in 1956 was reflected in the postmortems on Suez.

Within the British government, those who observed French decolonization detected early on what they believed to be the significance of transferring political power to French-educated elites while retaining considerable economic, political, and cultural influence in the newly independent countries. In giving the new states a clear choice to retain or break the connection with France, de Gaulle offered substantial financial and administrative aid. The wave of independence that swept the former French colonies in 1960 demonstrated very clearly to the British that French decolonization differed dramatically from British transfers of power. The French colonies remained much more dependent because, in the British view, they were too weak to stand alone. But in 1960 no one could have anticipated how far the French would exceed the British in continuing to provide economic and military assistance to most of their former dependencies. Over time, the British came to see that French influence in the former colonies far surpassed that of the British in the Commonwealth.

États et sociétés en quête d'avenir—
Le Moyen-Orient arabe des indépendances à aujourd'hui   forthcoming

SINGAPORE AND HONG KONG

11

THE ROAD TO THE FALL OF SINGAPORE, 1942:
BRITISH IMPERIALISM IN EAST ASIA
IN THE 1930S

Reflecting on the consequences of the Manchurian crisis, the British Ambassador in Japan, Sir Francis Lindley, in late 1932 drew an analogy based on Britain's experience in the Boer War. At the turn of the century Britain had stood in isolation, vilified by the European powers and generally denounced throughout the world for a war fought to aggrandize the British Empire. The absorption of the two Afrikaner republics into the Empire marked a turning point in British imperialism just as the creation of Manchukuo represented a landmark in the history of Japanese expansion. Britain had not altered her policy in South Africa because of international pressure, nor could Japan be expected to change course in similar circumstances.[1] Lindley had a sense of the historic drift in Anglo-Japanese relations. He implied that things probably would be worse and definitely not better unless Britain adopted a sympathetic attitude towards an expansive Japan, whose problems were, after all, not dissimilar to those of the British Empire only a few decades earlier.

This historical perspective is not especially profound, but it was common in the circles of a 'good solid Englishman' (as one contemporary described Sir Francis Lindley) who lamented the decline of Anglo-Japanese friendship. And it is useful in illuminating the salient aspects of the relations between the two island empires. In the same year that Britain concluded peace in South Africa, the long era of 'splendid isolation' closed with the conclusion of the Anglo-Japanese Alliance of 1902. During the First World War, the British fleet was able to concentrate in the Atlantic because of Japanese support in the

---

[1] Lindley to Simon, 1 January 1933, enclosing his annual report for 1932 (FO 371/17158). For a work sympathetic to Lindley's point of view, see Malcolm D. Kennedy, *The Estrangement of Great Britain and Japan, 1917–35* (Manchester, UK, 1969). Recent scholarly accounts of Britain in the Far East in the 1930s include Christopher Thorne, *The Limits of Foreign Policy: The West, the League and the Far Eastern Crisis of 1931–1933* (London, 1972); Ann Trotter, *Britain and East Asia, 1933–1937* (Cambridge, 1975); Stephen Lyon Endicott, *Diplomacy and Enterprise: British China Policy, 1933–1937* (New York, 1975); Bradford A. Lee, *Britain and the Sino-Japanese War, 1937–1939: A Study in the Dilemmas of British Decline* (Stanford, Calif., 1973); Aron Shai, *Origins of the War in the East: Britain, China, and Japan, 1937–39* (London, 1976); and Peter Lowe, *Great Britain and the Origins of the Pacific War: A Study of British Policy in East Asia 1937–1941* (Oxford, 1977). My own work, *British Strategy in the Far East* (Oxford, 1971), surveys the inter-war period on the basis of recently released archival material. The present essay draws from it, but further explores the archives and develops the theme of assumptions about Japan and China as well as the background to the collapse of British power.

Pacific. The Alliance ceased at the time of the Washington Conference of 1921–22 for reasons that remained controversial in the 1930s. For those Englishmen who tended to be pro-Japanese, appeasement of the United States and misguided views about the League of Nations had brought about the alienation of Japan. At the end of the Manchurian crisis, relations between Japan and Britain nevertheless remained better perhaps than between Japan and any other major power.[2] During the 1930s a powerful group of British statesmen, including Neville Chamberlain (Chancellor of the Exchequer, 1931–37, Prime Minister, 1937–40) attempted to improve Anglo-Japanese relations and to resuscitate the spirit of the Alliance. This effort ended in failure. Far from managing to conciliate Japan, the British in only a matter of years found themselves faced with the disastrous possibility of a war in Asia fought against a former ally now acting in concert with their arch-enemy in Europe. The history of Anglo-Japanese relations in the 1930s is thus the history of one important part in the origins of the Pacific war; moreover, it is a cardinal theme in the story of the decline and fall of the British Empire. The British failed to check the erosion of British military and economic power and, not least, that incalculable basis upon which the British Empire in Asia ultimately rested, prestige. With the fall of Singapore on 15 February 1942, the Japanese dealt the British Empire a blow from which it never recovered.

The perspective is no less illuminating from the angle of the British Minister in China, Sir Miles Lampson (later Lord Killearn). Lampson, also reflecting in the aftermath of the Manchurian crisis, emphasized, as had his predecessors, that the entire problem of the Far East could be summed up as Japan's position in China. He held strong views about the recent history of China and the interaction of Japanese and British aims on the Asian mainland. He believed that individuals as well as nations possessed the capacity to make decisions at certain 'turning-points' in their national history. These decisions had far-reaching consequences. This tenet held true for Lampson's own career in China. He was the key figure in the British revision of the 'unequal treaties' and indeed in the general Western accommodation of Chinese nationalism. He represented the nineteenth-century proconsular tradition of assuming unquestioned British authority. He possessed a sense of self-confidence associated with such Victorian heroes as General 'Chinese' Gordon. Lampson later became a paramount

---

[2] 'It is not much comfort to the Americans that in spite of everything [i.e. Manchuria] we still stand better with the Japanese than any other nation' (minute by Richard Allen of the Far Eastern Department of the Foreign Office, 25 March 1933, FO 371/17158).

figure in Egypt and the Sudan before and during the Second World War and afterwards in South-East Asia—in other words, two of the most sensitive and important assignments in all of the British Empire. His views are of particular importance here because he left what might be called the 'Lampson legacy' in China. He believed that Britain should not yield an inch to nationalist or anti-British forces. British policy would adjust and accommodate in kind, but the strength and prestige of the British Empire would be maintained against all comers, whether Chinese nationalists or Japanese imperialists.

Lampson defined the object of British policy in China as 'our determination not to permit ourselves to be deprived by forceful action of our treaty rights, and, on the other hand, our readiness at any moment to negotiate the revision of the old treaties in a peaceful spirit.'[3] He believed in firmness combined with a sense of British justice, and he brought to bear an absolute determination not to capitulate to anti-British influences in commerce or diplomacy. He drove a hard bargain. By mid-1931 he could look back with considerable satisfaction on the negotiations with the Chinese by which Britain yielded nineteenth-century privileges in return for twentieth-century safeguards for British trade and commerce. Japan's intervention in Manchuria in September 1931 and the attack on Shanghai in February 1932 brought his work of treaty revision to a standstill. In one of his moments of contemplation on what the British Empire represented in Asia and other parts of the world, he philosophically asked himself whether there might be historical explanations for Japan's actions. He identified four momentous 'decisions' on the part of the Japanese leaders. He presented a distinctly British interpretation that is all the more interesting for the purposes of this essay. His analysis serves obliquely as a commentary on adverse developments for British imperialism and the origins of the Pacific war.

Lampson thought that the first turning point was the Sino-Japanese War of 1894, from which Japan emerged as an Asian power. Japan had the opportunity of 'playing the role of the champion of the yellow race in the fight for freedom against the Imperialist powers of the west'. Instead Japan chose the opposite course and joined the imperialist powers, herself imposing treaty rights on the 'decadent' government in Peking. This choice was a deliberate decision on the part of Japanese leaders, and one to which British statesmen at the time did not object. 'In those days, before and after 1900', Lampson continued, 'Russian penetration was the principal menace to British interests in the Far

[3] Lampson to Simpson, 24 August 1933, FO 371/17064.

East, and we looked to the cooperation of Japan in preserving the integrity of China.'[4]

The second turning point occurred during the First World War, when Japan, with the twenty-one demands of 1915, obtained special concessions in China that exceeded those of the Western powers. Again, this was essentially a decision to pursue an imperialist course, but now the British had cause for alarm. 'It was at this time', Lampson wrote, 'that we were first led to suspect that Japan's ambitions might be nothing less than to dominate China and become the leader of Asia against the White races.' This period was brought to a close by the end of the First World War. Here Lampson made a surprising omission in his historical survey. At the Paris Peace Conference, the Americans together with the British deprived Japan of formal assurance of 'racial equality'. He certainly was not oblivious of the explosive nature of the racial issue. Indeed he suspected that the Japanese might exploit it to anti-British advantage. 'There is reason to believe', he wrote, 'that they, the Japanese, have in fact already [by 1933] made approaches to certain quarters in China, and that these approaches have been along the lines of pan-Asian doctrines and the alliance of the Yellow races under the leadership of Japan.'[5]

The third juncture was the era of the Washington Conference of 1921–22, when Japan reluctantly agreed to preserve the integrity of China and the doctrine of the 'Open Door'. In Lampson's view, Japan's conciliatory attitude was deceptive. The Japanese remained adamant about maintaining special rights in Manchuria; and despite a seemingly complaisant attitude towards treaty revision, their attitude towards China continued to harden. Japan, according to Lampson, remained 'unaffected by this post-war mentality' of anti-imperialism. Japan, in contrast to Britain and the United States, 'saw no reasons to give up her treaty rights and privileges except in so far as they could be used as bargaining factors to obtain her political objectives. In these circumstances a head-on collision between Japanese policy and Chinese nationalism was hardly to be avoided.' The result was the fourth turning point, the Manchurian crisis of 1931–32, which Lampson could only describe as an incalculable setback for Britain. He wrote in June 1933:

> Japan's great military adventure has, it seems, met with a full measure of success. She has seized, and to all intents and purposes secured, a

[4] Lampson to Simpson, 24 August 1933, FO 371/17064.
[5] Ibid.

protectorate over Manchuria, rounded off her conquest by the occupation of Jehol, defied the behests of the League of Nations, and
. . . forced the Chinese to admit military defeat and to accept, at least
tacitly and for the time being, the loss of Manchuria and the *de facto*
position created by the Japanese army.[6]

Lampson speculated that it might be best for the British to reconcile
themselves to the Japanese takeover in Manchuria because it was preferable for Japan to expand there rather than in the Pacific towards the
white Dominions. But this line of thought did not appeal to him. The
greater the Japanese successes on the mainland, the greater would be
the Japanese appetite for more aggrandizement. Lampson's attitude
is important for understanding British policy during the rest of the
1930s. Though British officials continued to emphasize their generosity in treaty revision and assistance to China, in fact British policy became less flexible because of suspicion of Japan. On this point the explanation of the origins of the Pacific war as one of a clash of empire
certainly holds true for Anglo-Japanese relations in China. The British
were determined to hold their own, and Sir Miles Lampson personified this determination.

It would do Lampson an injustice to suggest that he always painted
the situation in China in such black and white (or rather, perhaps, yellow and white) colours, but there was a consistency to his views, and
they were representative of certain British attitudes. Many of Britain's
difficulties in Asia could be traced to Japanese economic, political, and
military aggression. Rather than 'turning points', it might be more accurate to describe Lampson's junctures as representing stages in the
growth of virulent Japanese imperialism. Though it might assume different guises, and sometimes appear more conciliatory than at other
times, Japanese imperialism was a constant ingredient in the power
politics of the Far East. In short, Japanese imperialism might lead to
the subjugation of all of China. Should this prove to be the case, then,
in Lampson's judgement, there would be no future 'for British political influence in Asia, east of Singapore'. To prevent this catastrophe, Britain would have to throw her weight behind China. 'A united
China, master in her own house, could hardly be dominated by Japan
or any other power,' Lampson concluded. China would respond to
moral support against Japan and to specific acts of British friendship,
such as technical and financial aid, by developing into a nation—if
not exactly a nation along Western lines, at least a pro-British nation.

[6] Ibid.

Despite setbacks, Lampson and Foreign Office officials persistently held out hope throughout the 1930s for a united, prosperous, and friendly China.

The Foreign Office was of course only one governmental department. The Colonial Office had its own empire in the Far East, and it would be no less interesting to trace the turning point of the 1930s as seen, for example, through the eyes of officials in Hong Kong—officials who were in daily contact with the traders and missionaries who formed just as real a part of the British Empire as did the officials themselves. Of the military branches of the government, the Admiralty had the most pronounced views about the strategic situation in the Far East. The policy of the Treasury at times rivalled the Foreign Office's, in part because of the severe problems resulting from the Depression. The India Office and the Board of Trade were also concerned with Asian commercial issues. The Dominions Office attempted to coordinate and represent the views of Australia and New Zealand. Various Cabinet committees (notably the Committee of Imperial Defence) and the Cabinet itself intervened in the affairs of the Far East from time to time. In short, it is possible to regard the British Empire in Asia as composed of several constituent parts rivalling among themselves for ascendancy.

Of those various bodies, the Foreign Office possessed the longest official memory and greatest continuity of policy in Asia. Like the British government itself, the Foreign Office was a complex institution. Of the various internal branches, the Far Eastern Department probably ranked behind its American and European rivals in prestige and influence. Nevertheless, the Far Eastern Department had acquired a tradition and an intellectual distinction associated with the half-dozen of its members who had had careers in Asia or had long experience in the department itself. For example, Sir John Pratt (who retired in 1938) and Sir John Brenan (1937–43) had served with distinction in the consular service in China. Their expertise commanded the respect of their principals. Though the interests of the Permanent Under-Secretary, Sir Robert Vansittart, lay primarily in Europe, the Far Eastern experience of the supervising Deputy Under-Secretary, Sir Victor Wellesley, stretched back to the days of the First World War, and he continued to follow Asian affairs with an incisive eye until his retirement in 1936. The head of the Far Eastern Department was Charles W. Orde, who, like Lindley and Lampson, holds a particular place in the history of Britain and the origins of the Pacific war. He was an official of balanced and moderate inclination who saw the complexity of Britain's situation in the Far East probably as acutely as any of his contemporaries. His minutes reflect an agony of careful choices, and his reluctance to take a firm stand either pro-Chinese or anti-Japanese (or vice versa) characterizes another important strand of Foreign Office policy of the 1930s.

Orde was a person of supreme rationality, a virtue that, along with a certain aridity of character and style, perhaps explains why his reasoned views were sometimes misinterpreted as lacking in decisiveness. He was not popular among his peers, and climbed the ladder of the Foreign Office only to arrive at the less-than-lofty pinnacles of Riga and Santiago. He was willing to grant the Japanese a rationality denied by many of his colleagues. 'Proud and excitable as the Japanese may be', he wrote in December 1933, 'they have shown caution and self-control in the major crises of their history.' He thought it understandable that the Japanese, with a population growth of one million a year, felt a need for places to send emigrants—but he ranked the necessity for emigration below the need for trade and the control of raw materials. On the point of emigration, he wrote: 'It is the stigma of racial differentiation, with its implication of inferiority, that they resent rather than the need of [emigration] facilities in practice.' This was a shrewd psychological insight that eluded many of his contemporaries. At the same time, Orde argued that it was equally important to recognize Japan's real necessity for raw materials and trade outlets. But rather than possibly cause a war, these economic needs might help keep the peace, at least with the United States and Britain. In the early 1930s, for example, the United States took 80 per cent of Japan's raw silk export, her most valuable export commodity. In return, Japan depended largely on the United States for raw cotton. Her trade with India was less important, but nevertheless acted as a similar deterrent to war with Britain. In other words, Japan had powerful economic reasons for remaining peaceful. How realistic, then, were common British fears that Japan intended to dominate China and extinguish British trade? Was there no hope that British and Japanese economic aims in China could be reconciled?

Britain's economic stake in China can be stated briefly. Though the old myth of the China market lingered on, by 1933 only 2 per cent of the world's trade went there, and Chinese purchases from Britain were less than half of India's. In the same year, 1933, China absorbed 2.5 per cent of Britain's total exports, ranked sixteenth on the list of British customers, and accounted for only 5.9 per cent of Britain's total foreign holdings. Almost 77 per cent of British investment in China was in Shanghai. By contrast, Japan was China's best customer. Beyond any doubt, Japan's interest in China was infinitely greater than Britain's.

Britain's needs in China, according to Orde, could be summed up in a single word, 'prosperity'. A prosperous China need not necessarily be a strong China. Britain would continue to pursue the policy of conciliation initiated by that landmark in British diplomacy in the Far East, the December memorandum of 1926, or, in other words, the basis of peaceful treaty reform. Chinese friendship would be the best protection against 'the aggressive instincts of Japan'. Only over a period of many years, however, would there be the possibility of a strong and independent China. In the meantime China might 'muddle along much as she has been doing in the last few years without much "reconstruction" and without relapsing into chaos'.[7] This was not a cause for alarm. Japan would have her hands full in Manchuria for the foreseeable future. This also should not cause any particular worry for Britain, provided Japan was not unduly provoked. 'There is no need to go out of our way', Orde wrote, 'to obstruct her plans in Manchukuo, and it will be a mistake to oppose her trade expansion, except where it comes into serious conflict with our own trade.'[8]

Orde's reasoned opinion may be taken as representative of British foreign policy in the early 1930s, at least in the sense that it reflected the consensus of the experts in the Far Eastern Department. It could be described as mildly anti-Japanese, yet it was not without sympathy. It looked out for British interests. 'We should recognize the real needs of [the] Japanese economy', Orde wrote, 'avoid any appearance of deliberate antagonism and confirm our action within essential defensive limits.' On the other hand, this balanced view was not stalwartly pro-Chinese, and it held that the Chinese themselves were quite as capable as any of the other powers of adversely changing the situation in the Far East . There was the danger that too much aid and comfort to China would arouse Japan: 'Our policy should be to work for China's *prosperity,* but *not,* except with great caution, for China's political and military strength, the prospect of which must always be abhorrent to Japan.' Orde's outlook may be summed up in his own balanced words, which appeared to some to be indecisive but in fact were resolute: 'We should continue our policy of avoiding antagonising either country.'[9]

The Foreign Office generally tried to pursue the course of moderation, but that policy won neither unanimous respect nor consensus in the decade before the Second World War. Laurence Collier, the head of the Northern Department, for example, upheld the extreme view that power politics consisted of the perpetual clash of rival imperialisms. He espoused a view of British realpolitik in the tradition of Lord

[7] Minute by Orde, 13 July 1933, FO 371/17158.
[8] Minute by Orde, 16 September 1933, FO 371/17081.
[9] Ibid.

Palmerston: Britain had no eternal friends or enemies but only eternal interests. He believed that Japan, like Germany, was by nature an aggressive power: 'I use the word ["aggressive"] not in the moral sense, but in the sense of wanting to expand at the expense of others.' Collier wrote those words shortly after the proclamation of the 'Amau doctrine' of April 1934, which the British interpreted as a Japanese Monroe Doctrine for Asia, or, in Collier's words, Tokyo's declaration 'warning other powers off China'. He believed that Britain should respond by vigilantly maintaining the status quo throughout the world. Accommodation with either Japan or Germany would be an impossibility: 'A Power vitally interested in the maintenance of the *status quo*, as we are, can keep on tolerable day-to-day terms with Japan, as with Germany, but cannot hope to do more than that, in the long run, and ought not to want to do so.'[10] He thought that any suggestion of bargaining for security in China should be condemned. If Britain acquiesced in Japanese control of China, or a Japanese attack on Russia, any hope of Britain thereby improving her own position should be regarded as a dangerous fallacy, comparable to the illusion that German attention would be diverted from Britain by encouraging the Germans to swallow Austria: 'In either case the "aggressive" Power, having increased its strength, would in the long run become an even greater danger than it is now.'[11]

Collier represented an important element in the Foreign Office's intellectual make-up. Japanese expansion should be resisted, just as the imperialist ambitions of Germany should be checked. Unstinting efforts should be made in Asia as in Europe to protect the British Empire:

> Japan is the determined enemy of all European interests in China, including our own, and . . . an understanding with her to safeguard those interests is therefore impossible . . . unless we are prepared to sacrifice our whole position in the Far East, with effects which would not be confined to those regions—unless, indeed, we are prepared to contemplate losing most of our trade with Asia as a whole, and holding all our Asiatic possessions on sufferance from Japan, we must take every possible step to keep Japan in check—build up the Singapore base, cultivate good relations with the Americans, the Dutch, the French and all others whose interests are threatened with a view to concerted measures against further Japanese aggression, and . . . see to it, as far as we can, that Russia is kept where she now is, in the Franco-British orbit, and not allowed to drift into the German-Japanese orbit.[12]

[10] Minute by Collier, 20 April 1934, FO 371/18184.
[11] Ibid.
[12] Minute by Collier, 30 October 1934, FO 371/18169.

The chronology of this clear warning about a possible Japanese-German link is significant. During 1934 British attitudes hardened. Analogies began to appear in the minutes of Foreign Office officials about the possibility of a 'Hitlerite revolution' in Japan. Again in Collier's words, Japanese policy 'is directed by nationalist-military elements preaching a philosophy of expansion by force even more openly than Herr Hitler preaches it in Germany'.[13] He penned those thoughts linking the philosophy of Hitler with the ideology of the militarists of Japan at a key time in the history of British rearmament, February 1934.

February 1934 is a convenient landmark because at that time Sir Robert Vansittart, the Permanent Under-Secretary at the Foreign Office, signed his name to a report on defence deficiencies by the Defence Requirements Committee (a subcommittee of the Committee of Imperial Defence).[14] He did so along with Sir Warren Fisher, the Permanent Secretary at the Treasury. Vansittart and Fisher together constituted two of the most powerful voices in the civil service. The report identified Germany as the long-term potential enemy of the British Empire. The corollary of that proposition was the necessity of remaining on good terms with Japan, though it is important to note that the report also urged the completion of the Singapore base. Both Vansittart and Fisher were obsessed with Germany; they differed in their attitude towards Japan. Vansittart, wishing to devote all energies towards Germany, was less assertive in his views about the Far East. In general he followed the line of the Far Eastern Department and the Deputy Under-Secretary, Sir Victor Wellesley. For example, Vansittart concurred in the following minute by Wellesley:

> The Anglo-Japanese Alliance was abrogated for several very good reasons. In the first place it had outlived its usefulness and had degenerated into a sort of umbrella under which the Japanese considered themselves safe to perpetrate every kind of iniquity in China which was bringing us into bad odour with the Chinese. Secondly the renewal of the Alliance would have gravely endangered our relations not only with America, which were at the time considered, and I think still are, of paramount importance, but with Canada also. But for the disappearance of the Alliance there would have been no Washington Naval Agreement in 1922.[15]

[13] Minute by Collier, 16 February 1934, FO 371/18176.

[14] The other members of the Committee were the three Chiefs of Staff and Sir Maurice Hankey, Secretary to the Cabinet and the Committee of Imperial Defence. For the Defence Requirements Committee and the problem of rearmament at this time, see especially Norman H. Gibbs, *Grand Strategy: Rearmament Policy* (London, 1976), chap. 4.

[15] Minute by Wellesley, 9 February 1934, FO 371/18184.

Vansittart agreed with Wellesley and Orde that although nothing should be done to antagonize either Japan or China, nothing also should be done to try to realign Britain's policy to Japan's advantage. Vansittart was more flexible in his attitude towards Japan than towards Germany, but he disfavoured concessions that might appear to the Japanese to be a sign of weakness. He believed that the Japanese had their hands full in Manchuria and could be restrained from further aggression by a stiff attitude on the part of the other Great Powers concerned with China. 'Vansittartism' in the Far East was thus a moderate but firm force, and it was rather vague in its application. Often as not it carried a philosophical or moral message. For example: 'If we show that we are really about to rehabilitate ourselves as a nation —until others cease to impose the crude test—we shall be able to look after ourselves and our interests without serious challenge.' 'If we don't', he concluded, in the Far East as elsewhere, the British would have to admit that they were 'impotent'. More concretely, Vansittart wished simply to avoid a collision with Japan. In a remark that sums up his general ideas in the mid-1930s, he wrote that 'we are in no condition to have trouble with Japan. The state of Europe is far too delicate and dangers are perhaps far too near.'[16]

By contrast, Sir Warren Fisher believed that Britain should take active and specific steps to reverse the drift into Anglo-Japanese antagonism.[17] To Fisher's restive and creative mind, there was one obvious and imperative truth about the defence of the British Empire. It surpassed all others; it recurred in his writings: '*We cannot simultaneously fight Japan and the strongest European naval Power.*'[18] Though he agreed with Vansittart and the Foreign Office that the British should not negotiate with the Japanese from a position of weakness, he saw no reason whatsoever to prepare for a war in the Far East. The danger lay nearer to home: it could be summed up in the phrase 'the German menace'. That danger would be considerably lessened if the British fleet were free to strike in European waters. With that object in view, Fisher was prepared to go to almost any length to win Japanese friendship: '[W]e not merely cannot afford further to alienate Japan, but it is an imperative and pressing need for us to effect a genuine and lasting reconciliation with her.'[19] Thus, to Fisher the stakes could not have been higher or the issues clearer. Britain's survival against Germany

[16] Minute by Vansittart, 28 July 1935, FO 371/19287.

[17] For an essay central to this theme see D. C. Watt, 'Britain, the United States and Japan in 1934', in *Personalities and Policies* (London, 1965).

[18] See, for example, his memorandum of 19 April 1934 (*Documents on British Foreign Policy* [hereafter *DBFP*], 2nd series, VIII, appendix I).

[19] Ibid.

depended on a benevolent or at least neutral Japan. With an insight that proved to be historically accurate, he saw that the British Empire could not survive an onslaught in Asia while fighting for survival in Europe and the Middle East.

Fisher knew of course that an Anglo-Japanese rapprochement would create an adverse reaction in the United States. He was entirely willing to run this risk. Indeed a distinctly anti-American sentiment runs through his minutes. Not since the days of Lord Curzon had any British official articulated such exasperation at the unpredictability and fickleness of Americans. Expressing his ideas about the United States in relation to Japan and Germany, he wrote:

> It is common ground that we cannot successfully fight both Japan and Germany at the same time. The first essential, therefore, to our own safety is that we must be free to concentrate our strength where it is most needed . . . What, then is the prime condition for attaining this essential object of definitely relieving ourselves of any danger of being involved in a war with Japan? I suggest that the first and, indeed, cardinal requirement for this end is the disentanglement of ourselves from the United States of America.[20]

To the dismay of both Fisher and the Admiralty, the battle cry 'Rule, Britannia!' had been replaced by the degrading slogan 'Rule, Columbia!' at the Washington Conference. The Americans had actively promoted Anglo-Japanese discord. They wanted to possess 'an unlimited luxury armada' for reasons that ultimately could be described only as arrogance and vanity. Such rhetorical excesses did not blind Fisher to an important point: it seemed quite improbable that the United States would attack the British Empire. The Americans could not be depended on to come to Britain's aid, and in any case probably would do nothing; but they would not become a belligerent in the event of war. Thus it seemed clear to Fisher that Britain should take whatever risks might be necessary regarding Anglo-American relations in order to bring about 'a thorough and lasting accommodation with the Japanese'.

Neville Chamberlain's ideas were in line with Fisher's and were only slightly more cautious. Since 1931 Chamberlain had been Chancellor of the Exchequer. He conceived of his office as one responsible for the resources of the British Empire at large rather than as being limited to purely financial questions. He did not hesitate in attempting to find solutions for difficult general problems such as rearmament. Like

---

[20] Memorandum by Fisher, 19 April 1954, *DBFP*, VIII, appendix I.

Fisher, he recognized that rearmament could proceed only at a slow pace and that Britain could never be adequately prepared to wage war simultaneously in Asia and Europe. He also shared with Fisher a scepticism about the United States. '[D]on't let us be browbeaten by her,' he wrote in September 1934. 'She will never repay us for sacrificing our interests in order to conciliate her and if we maintain at once a bold and a frank attitude towards her I am not afraid of the result.'[21]

Chamberlain hoped that the Naval Conference of 1935 could be used as an opportunity to bring about a closer understanding with the Japanese. Specifically he thought it possible and desirable to build into the Naval Conference not only an agreement about rearmament and technical naval issues, but also 'a gentleman's understanding' between Britain and Japan (and the United States) 'not to fight one another for the next ten years'. In short, Chamberlain argued for a non-aggression pact with Japan. 'The main point to be kept in mind', he wrote to the Foreign Secretary, 'is that the *fons et origo* of all our European troubles is Germany.' Whether it was a matter of two, five, or ten years, Chamberlain believed that trouble with Germany would come, and that Japanese friendship might determine the future of not only Great Britain but the whole of the British Empire.

Chamberlain together with Sir John Simon explored the possibilities of drawing closer to Japan. 'I can't help reflecting', the Chancellor wrote to the Foreign Secretary, 'that if you could bring off an agreement with Japan . . . it would stamp your tenure of office with the special distinction that is attached to memorable historical events, and, incidentally would add greatly to the prestige of the National Government in the most difficult of all fields.'[22] Simon was receptive to these ideas. The experience of the Manchurian crisis had driven home to him the difficulties of cooperating with the United States and supporting the League. For his efforts to steer a balanced course, he had been reproached for working behind the back of the Americans and undermining the principles of the League. Though he had no high personal regard for the 'yellow men' of the 'anthill' (his phrase), he grasped the complexity of the Manchurian problem and refused to heap all the blame on Japan. He wanted to be pro-League without being anti-Japan. He wished to protect British trading interests without antagonizing China. He hoped to patch up minor quarrels with Japan without offending the United States. He recognized the Japanese sense of national pride as a legitimate force in international affairs. He thought it undesirable to try to impose on the Japanese a naval quota

[21] Chamberlain to Simon, 1 September 1934, *DBFP*, VIII, no. 14.
[22] Ibid.

that they would regard as unfair. As with racial equality, so with naval parity, which he believed the Japanese regarded as a matter of national prestige. 'I do not believe that Japan will accept an inferior ratio imposed by Treaty,' Simon wrote to Vansittart. 'Japan feels the impulses of "equality of status" as much as Germany.' Along with Chamberlain, Simon hoped that a revival of the 'atmosphere' of the Anglo-Japanese Alliance might alleviate some of Japan's anti-Western sentiment and help stabilize the situation in the Far East. 'As regards [a] non-aggression pact', he wrote, '*why not?*'[23]

Simon and Chamberlain emerged as the two leaders of the pro-Japanese movement within the Cabinet. From their respective vantage points of the Foreign Office and the Exchequer, the two of them could argue a vigorous case on grounds of economy as well as on the need to lessen tensions in the Far East. The attitude of the Cabinet as a whole was characterized by a concern for the cost of armaments, as reflected in the decision to accept only one-third of the Defence Requirements Committee's projected expenditures.[24] The British public and Parliament would not tolerate an extensive programme of rearmament. The Cabinet's priority lay with the development of the air force for protection against Germany, which meant that only inadequate defence measures could be taken against Japan. In Chamberlain's writings as in Fisher's there ran the dominant proposition 'that we cannot provide simultaneously for hostilities with Japan and Germany and that the latter is the problem to which we must now address ourselves'.[25] To Chamberlain as to Fisher, this conclusion led to the clear-cut necessity for rapprochement with Japan. Simon accepted the logic of the pro-Japanese stand, but he was less resolute. Characteristically, he weighed both sides of the question: a non-aggression pact with Japan would be misunderstood by the Americans, and he saw that British security in the Pacific in the long run would rest with the United States. In this sense, history proved Simon to be just as right as Chamberlain. Chamberlain perceived that a hostile Japan would destroy the British Empire in Asia, but Simon saw that the Empire's ultimate protector and means of resurrection would be the United States.

Simon and Chamberlain hoped to achieve a quasi-recognition of Manchukuo, phrased so that it would not blatantly appear to contradict the non-recognition policy of the United States and the League. Japan would guarantee the integrity of China proper, signifying the end of Japanese ambitions for expansion. On the naval side of the

[23] Simon to Vansittart, 20 August 1934, *DBFP*, VIII, no. 8.
[24] For the DRC report, see Gibbs, *Rearmament Policy*, chap. 4.
[25] Keith Feiling, *The Life of Neville Chamberlain* (London, 1946), p. 258.

equation, the British hoped that a non-aggression pact might discourage both the Japanese and the Americans from a programme of unlimited building.[26] The project eventually foundered because of Japanese scepticism and the stalemate in the naval discussions of late 1934; but long before then it had suffered heavy attacks within British circles.

These assaults influenced Simon more than Chamberlain. Simon perceived the pro-American sentiment of the Prime Minister, Ramsay MacDonald. He listened sympathetically to Sir Maurice Hankey (Secretary to the Cabinet and the Committee of Imperial Defence), who argued that dependence on Japan would mean the end of the sea power of the British Empire. And he faced strong criticism within the Foreign Office itself. Though he tried to keep his permanent officials at arm's length, he recognized the strength of their arguments, especially those of Charles Orde. These varied influences help explain why Simon responded to the idea of Anglo-Japanese rapprochement at one moment as 'a flash in the pan', at another with mild enthusiasm, and most often with that indecisiveness that critics have identified as a fault in his character.

Though by no means an 'Imperial' statesman by interest or temperament, Simon clearly saw the issues at stake in the Far East for the Empire-Commonwealth as a whole. His broader vision is apparent in a document written in November 1934, when General J. C. Smuts of South Africa was in London. Smuts attended a meeting at the Dominions Office on an occasion when Simon candidly expounded the dilemmas facing the British. Smuts brought to bear on the discussion his wide knowledge of the First World War and its legacies as well as his views on the Commonwealth and the League of Nations. There was a vigorous exchange of ideas.

After explaining the complex and detailed issues of the naval conversations, Simon stated that the Japanese believed that they had nothing to lose by having no naval agreement at all. They demanded equality with the other Great Powers, and if they failed to reach it through international agreement, would attempt to achieve it on their own. There would be increasing antagonism between the Japanese and the Americans. Simon predicted a bleak picture of the Pacific basin —in short, anarchy that would exacerbate the European situation because France and Italy also belonged to the Washington treaty system. Smuts responded to Simon's reasoned exposition with questions that indicated his reluctance to believe in the severity of the crisis. He asked whether Japan might be bluffing. He inquired whether there might be a way of enabling her to 'save her face'. He stated that in any event the

[26] Memorandum by Chamberlain and Simon, 16 October 1934, *DBFP*, VIII, no. 29.

British Empire should keep company with the United States. At this stage of the discussion, Simon did not necessarily agree. 'The British Empire did not want to stand in with the United States of America', he said, 'if by doing so she made a certain enemy of Japan.'[27]

Smuts then made it pointedly clear that if there was ultimately going to be a war in the Pacific, then the British Empire should unite with the United States. Far from being a danger to the British fleet, the size of the American navy should be a comfort. If Japan were truly an aggressor, then the British Empire would have to stand up and fight; there could be no appeasement.[28] Smuts drew a parallel with the Roman Empire: the frontiers of the Roman Empire had been land frontiers, while those of the British were sea frontiers.

> Naval defence went to the roots of her Imperial defence system. If Japan was now out to establish a mastery in the East, and to this end intended to build nearer to the British [naval] strength, it became a very serious matter for the Empire. There was then a threat to the whole Imperial system. If the British Empire made concessions to Japan which went too far, then she would become a second rate Power and go the way that the Roman Empire had gone.[29]

Smuts argued forcefully that the British must keep their position in the race and maintain good relations with the United States. Simon now yielded to Smuts's line of argument, saying that friendship with the Americans was a sine qua non. He lamented American unpredictability, but there was no question that he and most other Englishmen of the mid-1930s, when pressed to their ultimate position, hoped that over the long haul the British Empire would stand side by side with the United States.

An Anglo-Japanese reconciliation might rupture the tenuous Anglo-American friendship, and it would also affect the entire network of international relations in Europe as well as the Far East. Within the Foreign Office, the weightiest analysis of a rapprochement came from the pen of Charles Orde. Orde pointed out that at the other end of the ideological spectrum, Russia was the key. Despite the ideological antipathy shared by most British (as well as American) officials towards the Soviet regime, they regarded Russia as a valuable counterweight against both Japan and Germany. Anything that Britain might do to weaken Russia in the Far East would increase the danger from

---

[27] Notes of a meeting of 13 November 1934, *DBFP*, VIII, no. 55.

[28] Smuts did not use the word 'appeasement' during this particular discussion, but for his ideas in this regard see W. K. Hancock, *Smuts: The Fields of Force* (Cambridge, 1968), p. 272.

[29] Meeting of 13 November 1934.

Germany. 'An Anglo-Japanese pact', Orde wrote, 'can hardly have any other effect.' It might also encourage Japanese designs for an attack on Russia, which, if successful, might lead to further Japanese aggression in South-East Asia: 'A pact will surely bring nearer the day when she will attack Russia and then, after a pause for recovery from the effort, proceed against the East Indies.'[30]

Not least, in Orde's view, an Anglo-Japanese combination would lead to a revival of anti-British sentiment in China. 'A pact pure and simple could hardly fail to arouse consternation and violent resentment in China', he wrote, 'which could only be removed by explanations which would show the Chinese that we were afraid of Japan.' Such an indication of British anxiety would increase Japanese influence and, at the same time, encourage the Chinese to attack British interests. There were still further considerations. A non-aggression pact would represent to the world at large no less than a repudiation of the principles of the League of Nations. These were powerful thoughts. They were summed up in Orde's conclusion that an Anglo-Japanese pact would 'increase the chances of a Russo-Japanese war and of a weakening of Russia'. Moreover it would entail 'violent Chinese resentment against us, a diminution in the authority of the League, and most likely a worsening of our relations with the United States'.[31] Thus the long-term results of an Anglo-Japanese pact would be almost entirely undesirable.

The pessimistic assessment of the Far Eastern Department was shared by Sir George Sansom, Commercial Counsellor to the Embassy in Tokyo. Sansom is of particular interest in the debates of the 1930s because he was, in Simon's words, 'generally acknowledged to be the greatest living authority' on Japan, with over thirty years' experience with that country.[32] Sansom believed that the only conditions on which the British could gain relief from trade competition in Asia would be to give political support to Japan. Thus the question arose whether Japan had any economic advantages 'sufficient to justify our mortgaging —for good or for evil— our political future in the Far East'. Sansom doubted it. 'Even assuming a genuine intention on the part of the Japanese Government to moderate Japanese competition in foreign markets', he wrote, 'it would [not] be possible for them in practice to enforce upon their industry any trade restrictions which would satisfy us.' In Sansom's opinion the recent history of Anglo-Japanese relations provided no ground for optimism: 'Since 1931 Japan has been a

[30] Memorandum by Orde, 4 September 1934, *DBFP*, VIII, no. 15.
[31] Ibid.
[32] Memorandum by Simon, 11 January 1935, CP 8 (35), CAB 27/596.

very difficult country to deal with, in matters both of diplomacy and commerce. The attitude, now aggressive, now intractable, of the officials with whom we have to do business has made negotiations on large and small matters extremely trying.'[33]

Putting the issues in their most exaggerated form, Sansom on another occasion wrote that in 1935 a mission of visiting Englishmen representing the Federation of British Industries had given rise to wild speculations. These rumours included the hope on the part of the Japanese that Britain might be prepared to recognize Manchukuo in return for trade concessions, that she might be eager to renew the Anglo-Japanese Alliance, and, moreover, that Britain might be ready to 'tell the USA to go to the devil, split up China, desert the League of Nations, and (I suppose) ensure the peace of the Far East by encouraging Japan to have a whack at Russia and thus precipitate another world war.'[34] These ideas went beyond those entertained even by Chamberlain and Fisher, though they were not entirely incompatible. Sansom thought they were alarming. Intelligent Japanese officials might not place any credence in them, but such rumours nevertheless encouraged lesser and still dangerous hopes. Sansom summarized the Japanese mood in late 1934: 'In their present frame of mind the Japanese conception of friendship is give-and-take; we give and they take.' On Anglo-Japanese rapprochement, he wrote: 'I am all for friendship. I am all against wantonly offending Japan or scoring points for the sake of scoring them. But . . . it would be folly on our part in the name of this abstraction [friendship] to surrender to Japan all that she wants in order to make her position such that our friendship is not necessary to her.'[35]

Sir Warren Fisher resented such remarks as a caricature of his position. But there can be no question that his views were diametrically opposed to Sansom's and the Far Eastern Department's. In January 1935, Fisher erupted with anger when Simon circulated a memorandum to the Cabinet enclosing critiques of the situation by Sansom and Orde. Orde not only challenged the Treasury's assumption that trade relations with Japan could be improved, but also questioned the moral validity of drawing closer to the power responsible for the twenty-one demands and 'the rape of Manchuria'. 'We cannot morally afford in the present-day world to put ourselves in the same camp with an exponent of such policies,' Orde concluded.[36] To Fisher, these

[33] Memorandum by Sansom, 29 October 1934, enclosed in memorandum by Simon, 11 January 1935.
[34] Sansom to Crowe, 12 October 1934, copy in T 172/1831.
[35] Ibid.
[36] Memorandum by Orde, 7 January 1935, enclosed in Simon's memorandum cited in note 32.

words were misguided as well as offensive. They conveyed a lack of
realism about power politics and represented a weak effort to justify
a policy of drift. He referred to Orde's recent writings as 'a revised
version of the Book of Lamentations'. Fisher's reaction indicates the
pitch of emotion on the subject of Japan. He wrote to Chamberlain:
'Orde can, I think, best be described as a pedantic ass, admirably
suited to join the eclectic brotherhood of Oxford or Cambridge.' He
denounced the head of the Far Eastern Department's condemnation
of Japan with biting words: Orde's pedantry was 'only equalled by his
quite obvious ignorance of human nature, and at the same time he is
obsessed with the fixed idea that original sin is monopolized by Japan,
and our only proper attitude is, therefore, never to soil ourselves by
contact with such impiety.'[37] To Sir Warren Fisher, the original sin of
his generation was the failure to recognize the transcendent danger
of Germany.

Fisher and Chamberlain persevered in the quest for security with
Japan. Coupling a rich political inventiveness with a faith that economic expertise could solve the problems of the Great Depression
in Asia as well as in Europe, they embarked on a project to put China
on a sound financial footing through Anglo-Japanese cooperation.
They acted in response to the Chinese currency crisis of late 1934 and,
in Fisher's words, to 'the wholly selfish silver policy of the US government'.[38] The Chinese requested a loan of £20 million. So complex and
serious was the economic situation in China that the Treasury urged
the appointment of an economic adviser to be sent to the Far East to
give expert advice. The Foreign Office agreed that the appointment
of an expert was desirable. Then, to the astonishment of the Foreign
Office, the Treasury designated none other than the Chief Economic
Adviser to the British government, Sir Frederick Leith-Ross. His status
rivalled that of a Minister of State. The effect of his appointment created the impression that Britain would in effect have two Ambassadors
in China. This was the beginning of the 'dual diplomacy' conducted
by the Treasury on the one hand, and the Foreign Office on the other.
The Foreign Office continued to try to balance friendship with both
China and Japan, to protect economic interests while taking account
of Britain's strategic vulnerability. The Treasury pursued a 'forward'
policy of active friendship with Japan while stabilizing China with a
currency loan.

With a confidence not shared by the Foreign Office, the Treasury
believed that British economic genius, as personified by Leith-Ross,

[37] Memorandum by Fisher, 21 January 1935, T 172/1831.
[38] Memorandum by Fisher, 28 March 1935, FO 371/19240.

could resuscitate China and provide a basis for cooperation between Britain and Japan. In financial straits, China might accept economic aid upon which Britain and Japan could mutually agree. China might be persuaded to recognize Manchukuo. Britain and Japan might reach an agreement about naval disarmament, and Japan might even return to the League of Nations. With such hopes in mind, Leith-Ross sailed for the Far East in August 1935. He discovered that the Japanese were even more profoundly suspicious of his mission than the Far Eastern Department had warned, and that the Chinese would not willingly submit to foreign financial control. Nor would the Chinese listen to the concrete suggestion that might have helped reconcile Japan and Britain, the recognition of Manchukuo. Leith-Ross therefore began to work on the technical part of his mission first. He devised a complicated scheme for currency reform that won the admiration of his fellow economists. But it had the opposite of the intended political effect. The greater his involvement in China, the more sceptical he became about the good faith of the Japanese. The longer he stayed in China, the more he became intrigued by the potential of the China trade for Britain. Political friction with Japan, rather than accommodation, was the result. Sir John Pratt wrote in November 1935: 'We set out to win the good will and the cooperation of Japan but in Japanese eyes the Leith-Ross mission must appear as an attempt to assert and strengthen Great Britain's influence in China, and as a challenge to the position claimed by Japan.'[39]

The 'forward' policy of Leith-Ross and the Treasury consisted of economically bolstering the Chinese government to prevent its collapse. The leading British firms in China hailed this 'stronger' stand as an indication that the British government did not intend to abandon them. On the other hand, the Ambassador in Tokyo warned that the Japanese would regard a British loan as an attempt to subjugate China to British economic control. They would respond by tightening their grip on northern China, possibly resulting in political as well as economic separation. Rather than strengthening China, Leith-Ross was pursuing a course that might bring about disintegration and Japanese hostility. In late 1935 this danger materialized with dramatic swiftness. The Japanese responded to anti-Japanese sentiment in China, which was not unconnected with the prospects of the loan. They began to mass troops in Manchuria; the Chinese attitude stiffened. The British found themselves likely to be caught between Japanese impe-

---

[39] Memorandum by Pratt, 25 November 1935, FO 371/19247. For the Leith-Ross mission, see Endicott, *Diplomacy and Enterprise,* chaps. 5 and 6; and Trotter, *Britain and East Asia,* chaps 8 and 9.

rialism and Chinese national resistance. Leith-Ross continued to press forward with the loan. The Foreign Office judged that the Treasury had landed British policy in 'a rare mess'. Vansittart wrote that he could not understand 'the working of Sir Warren Fisher's mind'.[40] The Treasury had constantly urged reconciliation with Japan, but no move could be more calculated to stir up Japanese hostility than British intervention in China. The Japanese would never be convinced that the purpose of an economic loan was not to make the Chinese government the puppet of Britain. Sir Victor Wellesley wrote in a remark that summarizes the attitude of the Far Eastern Department:

> All this is the result of allowing our Far Eastern policy to drift into the hands of the Treasury. It is very dangerous. I have always sympathized with Sir F. Leith Ross for being sent out on a wild goose chase. It is high time he came home for as long as this bull remains in the China shop there is no knowing how much political crockery may be broken.[41]

The British retreated. Neville Chamberlain instructed the Treasury that no action should be taken that might antagonize the Japanese. The failure of the Leith-Ross mission helps explain why a policy of appeasement did not work in the Far East. Though the pro-Japanese faction in the British government was willing to recognize Manchukuo (and indeed believed that recognition would create more prosperous opportunities for British trade), recognition would undermine Britain's position in China. At best the British would substitute some measure of Japanese friendship with unmitigating Chinese hostility. In China proper the British believed that they had little to give. The situation was not analogous to the Ethiopian case or that of the former German colonies. In Africa the British were prepared to yield, though at the expense of others—the Ethiopians, the Belgians, or the Portuguese. In China they stood by their treaty rights. They paid lip-service to the ideology of the open door and the dismantling of the unequal treaties, but neither the Treasury nor the Foreign Office intended to give the Japanese an economic advantage. And there was more than commercial interest at stake. What might be the effect, Wellesley asked, 'of abandoning our interests to the Japanese?' What would be the effect on 'the whole Oriental world?'[42] For that matter, how would a collapse in China affect Britain's status as a Great Power?

[40] Minute by Vansittart, 29 October 1935, FO 371/19245.
[41] Minute by Wellesley, 22 January 1936, FO 371/20215.
[42] Minute by Wellesley, 25 September 1935, FO 371/19287.

Though more remote geographically from England than Central Europe or Ethiopia, China impinged more directly on the British Empire. Part of the question of Britain's position involved prestige, as Wellesley's minute suggests. Part of it can be traced to anxiety about British economic competitiveness, or lack of it. In profits, British companies in China continued on the whole to prosper, but in expansion and innovation, the Japanese were gaining the upper hand. The British were determined to hold their own, but their economic drive appeared to be failing. Perhaps this says something about the decline of the British Empire. In any case, the Japanese noted that the British seemed more enthusiastic about making trade concessions to the Germans or Italians than to them. Though the Japanese protested new restrictive tariffs in the wake of the Ottawa Conference of 1932, the British did not undertake any serious study of tariff revision in, for example, Nigeria and the Gold Coast. In short, political appeasement sounded appealing in principle, especially because it seemed like a reasonable price to pay for strategic security, but it became more and more elusive when examined in the light of concrete steps to achieve it. The British did not yield easily when the issues boiled down to specific economic concessions. The great act of appeasement did not occur in the Far East, but eventually in Central Europe, where the British Empire had no direct involvement.

By the time of the publication of the German-Japanese anti-Comintern pact in November 1936, the Leith-Ross mission had died a natural death. Leith-Ross claimed credit for alleviating the Chinese currency crisis,[43] but the 'forward' policy of the Treasury certainly had not succeeded in bringing about a reconciliation with Japan. Instead, Japan had moved towards the German orbit, though the significance of the anti-Comintern pact for the British Empire was not clear-cut. Laurence Collier believed that it should be regarded definitely as 'inimical to British interests'.[44] But Anthony Eden, now Foreign Secretary, did not take the matter 'too tragically' and refused to take an alarmist view. Nor did Charles Orde, who gave the matter sustained thought. Like Eden, he attached little importance to ideology. Orde believed that the pact amounted to little more than anti-communist propaganda, though he did grant that it might have 'psychological' effects that could eventually lead to a military alliance.

Orde's views are again of interest at this particular time—less than a year before the resumption of Japanese-Chinese hostilities in 1937 —because they represented the triumph of the Foreign Office's tradi-

---

[43] For example, see his memorandum of 4 September 1936, PEJ 251 (36), CAB 27/296.
[44] Minute by Collier, 26 November 1936, FO 371/20285.

tional policy. That policy can be described as essentially passive and opportunistic, as a policy of carefully attempting to maintain friendship with China rather than to rupture Chinese relations in a gamble with Japan. He believed that Japan would remain preoccupied with Russia, essentially for strategic reasons, and that the anti-Comintern agreement had not altered the balance of power in the Far East. On the other hand, a military pact between Germany and Japan, as opposed to an ideological one, would truly be a cause for Russian and British alarm. No one could predict what Japan might do if both those countries were simultaneously engaged in a war against Germany. But Orde had no doubt at all about Japan's action if either Russia *or* Britain were to go to war against Germany: 'If one [i.e. Russia or Britain] were engaged there could be little doubt that Japan would attack that one.' Since circumstances might change quickly and unpredictably, Britain's only safeguard, Orde concluded, 'will come from the completion of the Singapore Base and the possession of a really strong fleet based upon it'.[45]

The phrase 'Singapore Base' conveys the great illusion of British security in Asia during the 1930s. Since 1923, British defence in the Far East had been based on the proposition that the fortress—Churchill once used the word 'citadel'—at the tip of the Malayan peninsula would form the linchpin of protection for Australia and New Zealand as well as the Far Eastern empire. The slogan 'Main Fleet to Singapore' became an almost unquestioned writ, despite anxiety about Germany in the Atlantic and Italy in the Mediterranean. According to the Singapore strategy, a British fleet could arrive at Singapore within forty-eight to seventy-two days to handle a defensive emergency against Japan, and still retain control of European waters. Misguided though this scheme might seem in retrospect, in the 1930s it was defensible as a rational strategy. The French could be expected to help neutralize Italy and to deny Japan air and sea bases in Indo-China. After the fall of France in 1940, the British were left alone to deal with Japan, Italy, and Germany. Long before then, however, the grand design for the defence of the Far Eastern empire had been called into question not only by sceptics in London but also by those most vitally concerned, the Australians and New Zealanders.

At the Imperial Conference of 1937 the First Lord of the Admiralty, Sir Samuel Hoare, discussed the Singapore issue with a candour that at once assured and alarmed the antipodean delegates. He took full measure of the responsibilities of the Imperial government for the defence of the Empire, yet he also surveyed the dangers of an aggressive

---

[45] Memorandum by Orde, 19 November 1936, FO 371/20287.

Japan in a way that surpassed British alarm even at the time of the Manchurian crisis. Hoare's blunt assessment of the issues of Imperial security and the response of the participants of the Imperial Conference in May–June 1937 well indicate the temper of the British Empire on the eve of the war between China and Japan.

Hoare took an extreme position. He represented the view (also shared by Sir Maurice Hankey and Sir Ernle Chatfield, the First Sea Lord) that the defence of the eastern Empire as a priority ranked second only to the defence of the British Isles. He believed that the loss of a British colony such as Hong Kong would be disastrous to British prestige. Failure to stand up to the Japanese might lead to the break-up of the Empire. Hoare emphasized the dangers of Japanese imperialism as well as the necessity for the Dominions to stand together with the Imperial government. He requested the conference to ponder the worst possible circumstances. What might happen, he asked, if Japan were left free to exercise her sea power in the Far East, unopposed by the British fleet? 'Let me assume', he continued, 'that, in these circumstances, Japan decides to invade Australia and launches an expedition covered by the full strength of her naval forces and her naval air forces.' The very existence of the Pacific Dominions would be imperilled.

> I am convinced that, if this act of aggression took place, no measures of local defence, no Army and no Air Force which the Commonwealth of Australia could conceivably maintain could save her from invasion and defeat at the hands of the Japanese. The Dominion of New Zealand would be exposed to exactly the same danger, and every word I have said about Australia is equally applicable to New Zealand.[46]

Nor was the Japanese menace restricted to Australia and New Zealand. Hoare also tried to place the fear of Japan in the hearts of the South African, Indian, and Canadian delegates:

> With Australia and New Zealand dominated by the Japanese and the Indian Ocean under the control of Japanese sea power, where would be the security of the Union of South Africa and of the India Empire? Or let me suppose that Japan casts her eyes eastward across the Pacific, what is to deter her from action against the Dominion of Canada?[47]

---

[46] Imperial Conference minutes, 5th meeting, 24 May 1937, CAB 132/28. For the Conference, see Rainer Tamchina, 'In Search of Common Causes: The Imperial Conference of 1937', *Journal of Imperial and Commonwealth History*, 1, 1 (October 1972).

[47] Imperial Conference minutes, 5th meeting, 24 May 1937, CAB 132/28.

He now came to the main point. In the event of a Far Eastern emergency, Britain unequivocally would dispatch the fleet to the Far East. *"[W]e believe that the very existence of the British Commonwealth of Nations as now constituted rests on our ability to send our fleet to the Far East, should the need arise."*[48]

If Hoare had been more candid, he might have added that the Empire was so overextended that only an optimistic assessment would hold that it *could* be defended—even with the wholehearted support of all the Dominions. One set of risks had to be balanced against another. The defence of Singapore and the antipodean Dominions rested on the mobility of the fleet. For obvious economic reasons, an effective fighting force could not be maintained simultaneously in both the Western and Eastern hemispheres (though at the Imperial Conference, the New Zealand Prime Minister had irreverently asked why, if the fleet could be sent to Singapore in time of emergency, could it not from time to time be stationed there in time of peace?). Singapore consequently suffered in priority, despite the view of ranking strategists such as Hankey and Chatfield that it was second only to home defence. At the time of the Imperial Conference of 1937, the Dominion representatives had prevalent doubts whether the Imperial government could or would support the Singapore strategy. Hoare's powerful speech was calculated to reassure, but everyone present knew that British involvement in a Far Eastern war would be influenced, even determined, by European circumstances.

In fact, the key to Imperial defence in the Far East lay in the Mediterranean.[49] Insecurity in the Middle East could paralyze British policy in China and Japan. By 1939, as a result of the Abyssinian crisis, Britain's Far Eastern strategy had to be carefully calculated around considerations of Italy. The principal British naval base in the Mediterranean, Malta, appeared to be increasingly vulnerable to Italian air power. Hence Hankey's view that the British 'should grasp the hand held out by Signor Mussolini, however repugnant it may be'. The courting of Italy, 'Europe's most expensive whore', thus lay at the bottom of Britain's defence in Asia.[50]

The 'Eastern' outlook that characterized the 1937 Conference

---

[48] Ibid. (emphasis added). For Hoare's autobiographical account, see Viscount Templewood, *Nine Troubled Years* (London, 1954), which refers occasionally to matters of Far Eastern interest.

[49] This is the theme of Lawrence R. Pratt, *East of Malta, West of Suez: Britain's Mediterranean Crisis, 1936–1939* (Cambridge, 1975).

[50] For Hankey and problems of imperial defence at this time, see Stephen Roskill, *Hankey: Man of Secrets, 1931–1963* (London, 1974), vol. 3.

stands in contrast to Churchill's view of the paramount importance of the Mediterranean and the balance of power in Europe. When Churchill later altered British priorities from Singapore and the Far East to Egypt and the Mediterranean, he endorsed a political as well as a strategic principle. The Empire meant different things to different men. What counted most? The unity of the Dominions? The Empire as opposed to the Dominions? The Far Eastern as opposed to the Middle Eastern and African empires? Evolution of the colonies into self-governing Dominions such as Australia and New Zealand? Or, as Churchill would have it, the continuing power and prestige of the Empire itself? Could the Empire live compatibly with the Chinese and Japanese (as Chamberlain hoped)? Or should the Empire respond to the Chinese with contempt and the Japanese with suspicion (as was in fact Churchill's private attitude)? These sorts of general questions were seldom given direct answers. But they have a direct bearing on the question of 'appeasement'. If the Japanese were unscrupulous and imperialistic, should they nevertheless be accommodated because of the pre-eminent danger of Germany? Or should the Empire-Commonwealth be prepared to wage war in both hemispheres?

According to the Chiefs of Staff in June 1937, the British should hold their own in the Far East, even at great risk in Europe and elsewhere. The commitment to Australia and New Zealand was absolute. Even the defence of Hong Kong, a controversial point, was held to be in the vital interest of Imperial security. In the event of war with Germany, the British had two choices in Hong Kong: evacuate, cut losses, and avoid commitments in China; or defend a strategically indefensible outpost, knowing full well that the Japanese would eventually conquer the colony. The argument for defence prevailed:

> [T]he evacuation of an important fortress on the outbreak of war would itself entail a very serious loss of prestige, not only in the Far East, but throughout the world; and might influence other potentially hostile Powers to form an exaggerated idea of the weakness of our position, and to throw in their lot against us.[51]

Hong Kong would be held as long as humanly possible. Not only would Britain's pledge to Australia and New Zealand be upheld, but the circumference of the Far Eastern empire would also be defended. These sorts of arguments worked in favour of those who wanted to preserve the Empire and avoid commitment in Europe. As Michael

[51] 'Appreciation of the situation in the Far East, 1937, by the Chiefs of Staff Sub-Committee', FO 371/20952.

Howard has pointed out, the burden of the Empire's worldwide defence was so great that it lessened Britain's ability to intervene in Europe.[52]

Yet commitment to home defence and the eastern Mediterranean made it increasingly improbable that the Singapore strategy would actually work—especially with an Arab revolt in Palestine occurring at the same time as the Abyssinian crisis. Should the Dominions be candidly told about Britain's dilemmas? Chamberlain feared that frank discussion would cause political rupture within the Commonwealth. South Africa and Canada, for different reasons, were isolationist. Australia was alarmed at Japan, and pressed for greater defence measures. New Zealand remained loyal to the ideals of the League and collective security. How could the Dominions be convinced of the need for a common front on the issue of Imperial security, especially when there was no agreement within the Imperial government? Though the plight of the statesmen and strategists in London might seem understandable in retrospect, the Dominion leaders later believed that the discussions about Imperial security had been less than honest.[53]

From the vantage point of the Foreign Office, the most important conclusion of the Chiefs of Staff's assessment was the decision to defend Hong Kong. 'Decisive weight', Charles Orde wrote on 2 July 1937, 'is given to considerations of prestige and our ultimate position in China.'[54] When the Defence Plans Committee (a subcommittee of the Committee of Imperial Defence) discussed the issue of Far Eastern security, Eden stated that he was 'very glad, for political reasons, that the Chiefs of Staff had decided that Hong Kong should not be evacuated'.[55] Chamberlain, now Prime Minister, agreed. But between Eden and Chamberlain there existed an important difference about the political future of the Far East. Eden believed that one of the large issues would be the importance of gaining American cooperation. Only by asserting a sort of combined Anglo-American 'white race authority' (his phrase) could the British preserve their influence. Chamberlain continued to distrust the United States and to hope for an accommodation with Japan, even at the risk of disorder or 'chaos' in China. The resumption of hostilities between the Japanese and Chinese in July 1937 eventually made Chamberlain's position untenable.

---

[52] Michael Howard, *The Continental Commitment* (London, 1972), p. 138.

[53] Roskill, *Hankey*, III, p. 395; on this general theme, see Ritchie Ovendale, *'Appeasement' and the English Speaking World: Britain, the United States, the Dominions, and the Policy of 'Appeasement', 1937–1939* (Cardiff, 1975).

[54] Minute by Orde, 2 July 1937, FO 371/20952.

[55] Minutes of the DPC, 13 July 1937, FO 371/20952.

The 'moderate' forces in Japan did not inspire confidence. But the clash of outlook within the government in London persisted. Estimates of American reliability continued to be a divisive issue.

In September 1937, Eden requested Sir Alexander Cadogan to assess the possibility of Anglo-American cooperation in the Far East. Cadogan had served as Ambassador in China (1933–36). On Victor Wellesley's retirement, he became Deputy Under-Secretary and in January 1938 he succeeded Vansittart as Permanent Under-Secretary. Though Vansittart now held the position of 'Chief Diplomatic Adviser', a revolution had occurred at the Foreign Office. In contrast with Vansittart, who obsessively dwelt on the need for stalwart resistance to Hitler, Cadogan believed that all the 'gangster belligerents' should be treated with an attitude that would neither provoke nor give an impression of impotence. 'If you are too bellicose', Cadogan once wrote about Mussolini, 'you provoke Dictators into doing something irrevocable. If you are too passive, you encourage them to think they can do anything.'[56] In this vein, he reflected in September 1937 about the danger of provoking Japan with sanctions: 'If we *and the US* cut off all trade with Japan, the latter would be faced with the most serious consequences. So serious, that she might "see red" and, in that event, *we,* and not the US would bear the first brunt, at any rate, of her attack.'[57] With such realistic points in mind, Cadogan continued to analyse the dangers as well as the benefits of concerted action with the United States.

Cadogan believed that the Americans would 'recoil in horror' at the idea of joint action with Britain. 'US public opinion', he wrote, 'is a very unpredictable element.' The sentiment for non-intervention appeared to be waxing rather than waning. And without American support, the British in the Far East were powerless:

> I think it really all comes back to this, that if the US won't play, there is nothing really effective to be done. If they really come in with both feet, the situation might be very different, but we must be frightfully careful not to scare them: they must be allowed (if they will) to come round to it themselves—and probably take all the credit if they do!

Cadogan went on to note the incongruity of American indecisiveness:

> Here indeed is a case where, I should have thought, with no risk to themselves, and with comparatively little material loss, the Americans

---

[56] David Dilks, ed., *The Diaries of Sir Alexander Cadogan* (New York, 1972), p. 171.
[57] Minute by Cadogan, 23 September 1937, FO 371/20956.

would have a golden opportunity of putting into practice all their preaching about collaboration for the prevention of the horrors of war![58]

But he concluded that there was little hope for American action. Though open-minded, Cadogan had experience in the Far East: at this stage his judgement tended to confirm Chamberlain's pessimism about the United States rather than Eden's guarded optimism that the two powers might work together to restrain Japan.

Roosevelt's 'quarantine' speech of October 1937 encouraged even Chamberlain to hope that the United States might at last be moving away from isolation. Chamberlain doubted whether the Americans would invoke effective sanctions against Japan (as he interpreted the implicit threat of Roosevelt's speech), but he said to the Cabinet that he did not underrate the importance of the President's statement, 'especially as a warning to the Dictator Powers that there was a point beyond which the United States of America would not permit them to go'.[59] Nevertheless Chamberlain's scepticism predominated in his overall judgement of the situation in late 1937. Privately he wrote: 'It is always best and safest to count on nothing from the Americans but words.'[60] Eden, again in contrast, emphasized the necessity of working together with the Americans and avoiding the accusation that Britain would remain passive in the Far East to preserve the British Empire. The ghost of the Manchurian crisis visited both Chamberlain and Eden in different incarnations. Chamberlain remained wary of the Americans and was determined not to give the Japanese the impression that they would again be put 'in the dock' by the League of Nations; Eden feared another American reproach that 'England has let us down'.

At the time of the Manchurian crisis, the British had thrown their support behind the League and had earned the enmity of Japan. They had attempted to cooperate with the United States but had won American moral disapproval for failure to adopt a policy of non-recognition of Japanese claims. They had placed themselves in a position of seeming not to sympathize with China. Eden now resolved not to repeat those mistakes. At the Brussels Conference of November 1937 (attended by most of the major and minor powers concerned with China, but boycotted by Japan), he took the line that the British would

---

[58] Minute by Cadogan, FO 371/20956.
[59] See Cabinet minutes of 6 and 13 October 1937, CAB 23/89.
[60] Feiling, *Chamberlain*, p. 325.

follow American initiatives. The Americans produced none. Roosevelt's speech about quarantining Japan had misfired. The American representatives could not commit themselves to anything that might lead to foreign difficulties, or even to a domestic debate about isolationism. The Conference produced little other than a few platitudes deploring the use of force. Eden nevertheless created a spirit of co-operation between the American and British delegations. He had an intuition about the President's purpose. He sensed that Roosevelt was 'deeply perturbed at the prospects in the Far East' and perhaps even more alarmed at the possibility of the United States having to bear the brunt of an Asian war.

The attack by Japanese aircraft on the British gunboat *Ladybird* and the sinking of the American *Panay* in December 1937 acutely raised the question whether the British fleet should be mobilized in protest and, again, whether joint action with the Americans was possible. With mild astonishment the British learned of Roosevelt's response. He did not wish to precipitate a crisis leading to a war for which the American public was not prepared. Softening the public protest (against the advice of some of his advisers), he wished to step up the naval armament programme and secretly to move closer to the British. He talked vaguely of an economic and naval blockade against Japan and, more specifically, about secret staff talks between the two navies. The British Ambassador in Washington reported to London:

> You may think that these are the utterances of a hare-brained statesman or of an amateur strategist but I assure you that the chief impression left on my own mind was that I had been talking to a man who had done his best in the Great War to bring America in speedily on the side of the Allies and who now was equally anxious to bring America in on the same side before it might be too late.[61]

Plans for the staff talks were made immediately. On New Year's Day 1938, Eden greeted Captain Royal E. Ingersoll of the United States Navy in London. The Ingersoll mission represented a landmark in Anglo-American relations in the Far East. The British discussed the state of readiness and possible movements of the fleet as well as general strategic policies with Roosevelt's own emissary. Though the talks were technical rather than policy-oriented, they marked, as Eden

---

[61] Lawrence Pratt, 'The Anglo-American Naval Conversations of the Far East of January 1938', *International Affairs*, 47, 4 (October 1971), p. 752; for Roosevelt's ideas, see also especially J. M. Haight, 'Franklin D. Roosevelt and a Naval Quarantine of Japan', *Pacific Historical Review*, 40, 2 (May 1972).

noted in his memoirs, the beginning of the alignment of power of the United States and Britain against that of the dictator states.[62]

In the midst of the controversy between Chamberlain and Eden, Cadogan noted in his diary that they exaggerated in opposite directions.[63] Both had accurate perceptions of the dangers to the British Empire. 'We are a very rich and a very vulnerable Empire', Chamberlain wrote in January 1938, 'and there are plenty of poor adventurers not very far away who look on us with hungry eyes.'[64] Chamberlain, of course, had in mind the Italians as well as the Germans. By recognizing Italy's claims in Ethiopia, perhaps as part of a comprehensive settlement, he hoped not only to detach Italy from Germany but also to make the position in the Far East more secure by neutralizing the Italian threat in the Mediterranean and the Red Sea. After the Italian intervention in the Spanish Civil War, Chamberlain and the Admiralty became increasingly preoccupied with the western as well as the eastern Mediterranean. Italy was a delicate problem. For this reason, in part, Chamberlain did not respond enthusiastically to Roosevelt's intrusion in January 1938, when the President put forward his good offices to cooperate with the British in establishing a general basis for peace in Europe.

Eden believed that it would be no less than a calamity for the British Empire not to work together with the United States, with whom, he thought, Britain should properly share the hegemony of the western Pacific. He was away from the Foreign Office briefly in January 1938, and not consulted by Chamberlain. He regarded the Prime Minister's attitude towards Roosevelt's initiative as a setback for satisfactory progress in Anglo-American relations as well as an affront to his conduct of foreign affairs. The Americans were bound to be suspicious of any settlement with Mussolini. If Britain recognized Italian claims in Ethiopia, the United States might regard this step as a prelude to British accommodation with Japan. Chamberlain and Eden thus were indeed pulling in different directions, though both of them had a firm grasp of the essential issues. Eden's resignation in February 1938 represented a protest, in part, over the persistent inclination on the part of the Prime Minister to accommodate Japan—despite Chamberlain's own recognition that 'the Japs are growing more and more insolent and brutal'[65]—and in part over the question of appeasement in Europe and the issue of the control of foreign policy.

[62] Anthony Eden, *Facing the Dictators* (Boston, 1962), p. 620.

[63] *Diaries of Sir Alexander Cadogan*, p. 37.

[64] Feiling, *Chamberlain*, p. 323.

[65] Ibid., p. 336.

If Japan could not be appeased, at least she ought not to be provoked. This was Chamberlain's premise, and it provided continuity in
British policy when Lord Halifax succeeded Eden as Foreign Secretary. To the Admiralty, this outlook appeared to be more realistic and
less dangerous than Eden's estimation of the Far Eastern situation.
Eden had believed that, after the *Ladybird* and *Panay* incidents, part of
the fleet should be sent to Singapore. Like Churchill, he believed that
the Japanese would be daunted by a show of force. Since only a few
months earlier at the Imperial Conference the First Lord of the Admiralty had given a firm assurance that the 'Singapore strategy' was
designed to meet any emergency created by Japan, Eden's response
was not unreasonable. The Admiralty however now had grave reservations. Chatfield informed Cadogan in November 1937 that the dispatch of capital ships to the Far East would 'denude' the Mediterranean.[66] Moreover, unless the Americans could be depended upon to
mobilize their fleet also, then British ships at Singapore could undertake only a defensive strategy. Indeed, such a movement of the fleet
might provoke rather than deter further Japanese action. Again the
British faced the recurring dilemma: the greater their difficulties in
Europe, the less their ability to defend the Empire. The failures to
reach an accord with the United States exacerbated the dilemma: the
greater the danger in the Far East, the less latitude they had for manoeuvre in Europe. In other words, there were powerful Asian reasons
for an appeasement policy in Europe.

In a sense, Halifax unimaginatively pursued the objectives of both
his Prime Ministers, Chamberlain and Churchill (the latter from May
to December 1940), but there was also an internal consistency to his
own views. It can perhaps be best described in the phrase associated
with British Imperial history in India, where Halifax had served as
Viceroy from 1926 to 1931—'masterly inactivity'. Events would determine themselves with discreet and sometimes decisive British influence in the background. To the problems of the late 1930s, Halifax
brought to bear certain suppositions that had served him well in India:
with proper guidance, non-Western nations, Japan as well as India,
eventually might develop along the same lines as the Western democracies; the Japanese, like the Indians, must be kept 'in play' until they
could be convinced of Britain's goodwill and desire for peace. Keeping the Japanese 'in play' became one of Halifax's paramount goals.
In the eyes of some of his critics, he had 'sipped tea with treason'
with Gandhi. He demonstrated similar patience, even obliquity (again

[66] Memorandum by Cadogan, 29 November 1937, FO 371/20960.

according to his critics), with the Japanese. Halifax was a great believer in conciliation, a virtue that afforded him distinction in his career as wartime Ambassador to the United States. The value he placed on conciliation also explains his relative failure with the dictators of the 1930s.

The permanent staff at the Foreign Office needed no persuasion about the desirability of a policy of 'masterly inactivity'. 'I trust we shall not get involved in negotiations between the two parties,' Charles Orde had written shortly after the outbreak of war between China and Japan. If Britain were to intervene and help bring about peace, any settlement that had any chance of stability would be regarded as a 'betrayal of China' by the world at large as well as by the Chinese. There were also dangers in trying to tilt the balance in favour of China: again in Orde's words, 'the Chinese are such inveterate wrigglers and self-deceivers that they are really best helped by leaving them to face hard facts by themselves.'[67] Despite such reservations about the ethical defects of the Chinese people, the sentiment of the Foreign Office was pro-Chinese. Apart from expressing moral sympathy, Orde and others, including Halifax, believed that the staying power of the Chinese should not be underestimated: 'The kind of spontaneous, passive, elastic resistance of which the Chinese are perhaps the world's greatest masters will continue.'[68] In the end, Chinese resistance would perhaps defeat Japanese imperialism; the Japanese would become bogged down in China. In the long run, China, as a diversion to Japan, would be of incalculable importance. 'It is not to our disadvantage', Orde wrote, should Japan find herself 'unable to cope' with the situation in China. He expressed the consensus of the Foreign Office when he wrote the following words in late 1937: 'The best effect on Japan would I believe be produced by a failure in China without assistance to China from other countries.'[69]

The Far Eastern Department of the Foreign Office did not, on the whole, sympathize with the policy of 'appeasement', indelibly associated with Halifax's name. The general attitude of the Department remained the same as it had during the mid-1930s—'generosity towards China, firmness towards Japan'—despite a change in personnel. In the spring of 1938, Orde was relegated to the Baltic (perhaps through the influence of Sir Warren Fisher?) and Sir John Pratt retired.

[67] Minute by Orde, 29 July 1937, FO 371/50951.

[68] Minute by Orde, 22 November 1938, FO 371/20559.

[69] Minute by Orde, 20 October 1937, FO 371/20951. Orde went on to note that in dealing with China there was, as usual, a paradox: if China were to defeat Japan without foreign assistance, Chinese xenophobia could be expected to increase.

Sir John Brenan emerged as the leading authority on China. Brenan was a former Consul-General of long experience at Shanghai. Like Pratt, he was respected for his independent and vigorous ideas as well as his knowledge of Asia. His views generally found support in Orde's successor, Robert Howe (head of the department, 1938–1940), who had served at the Embassy at Peking. During part of this period, Sir George Sansom was in London and acted as adviser in the Far Eastern Department. Sansom's knowledge of Japan's economic affairs was unsurpassed, and he also held strong ideas abut political trends. Each of these three officials believed that Japan could not be appeased by Britain's giving way in China. They held that it was a false hope to think that moderate opinion in Japan might predominate over that of the extremists. There was no way for Britain—or any other foreign power—to bolster the moderates. The extremists would have to be defeated by outside forces. Later, after war had broken out in Europe, Brenan expressed a thought that represented the sentiment of the Far Eastern Department in the 1938–42 period: 'China is fighting our battle and is doing us great service by exhausting a dangerous potential enemy. It is obviously in our interest to give her all the help we can spare from our own war effort.'[70]

The project of economic assistance to China (the initial proposal was a loan of £20 million) first met with failure, despite its support by Halifax. 'China is fighting the battle of all the law-abiding States,' he wrote to the Chancellor of the Exchequer in May 1938.[71] This line of argument did not appeal to the Treasury; nor was the Cabinet persuaded. Chamberlain feared the dangers of a clash with Japan at the especially inauspicious time of the impending crisis in Czechoslovakia. Cadogan noted that it was 'all very well' for Brenan and others in the Far Eastern Department to press for aid to China, but that they did not have a sufficient grasp of the 'awful situation in Europe'.[72] The Far Eastern Department, though disappointed, was not surprised. 'We did our best for the Chinese over the question of a loan', Ronald Howe wrote to the British Ambassador in China, 'but . . . the Powers-that-Be felt that in the existing critical situation in Europe they would not be justified in taking any risk, however slight, of provoking the Japanese to take further, and possible more direct, action against us in the Far East.'[73] Halifax had followed the lead of the Far Eastern Department,

[70] Minute by Brenan, 21 May 1940, FO 371/24661.
[71] Lowe, *Origins of the Pacific War,* p. 41; for the question of later assistance, see appendix D. As Lowe notes, the aid was more in the realm of moral support than supplies and money.
[72] *Diaries of Sir Alexander Cadogan,* p. 86.
[73] Howe to Clark Kerr, 19 July 1938, Halifax Papers, FO 800/299.

but had then wavered in the face of such arguments as the hostility of Japan and the futility of intervention on the Chinese side. One critic pointed out that the only predictable aspect of the situation was the certainty that the Chinese would ask for more. Halifax clearly sympathized with the Chinese, but in weighing the various considerations, he chose to act with caution. He also chose not to make clear-cut decisions and, perhaps unconsciously, adopted an attitude of what one historian has aptly described as an air of 'puzzled rectitude'.[74]

At roughly the same time as the Chinese loan question, the Cabinet decided to acquiesce in Japan's insistence that the customs revenues at Shanghai and Tientsin be placed in a Japanese bank. The amount of money involved was only enough to pay the interest on Chinese foreign loans, and thus was relatively trivial. But there was more at stake than might be apparent. The British and Americans feared further takeovers. What began with the usurpation of customs revenues might end with the appropriation of the internal concessions. British and other Western traders might be ousted from the China coast. The British and American governments protested accordingly, but they did not match their protests with threats of retaliation. The British in particular were more inclined to accept Japan's assurances that the customs revenues would be dealt with equitably by the Japanese bank. To the Chinese, it seemed clear that the British were more interested in protecting their finances than in defending the Chinese administration; to the Foreign Office, it was a disagreeable but not intolerable concession. It could in fact be defended as a test to see whether the Japanese would keep their word and as an attempt to curb more extreme Japanese action. In May 1938 the Foreign Office thus announced that the customs revenues would be administered by the Hokohama Specie Bank.[75] The agreement hardly compared with the bargains being contemplated with the European dictators. But it is instructive in judging the impact in the Far East of Britain's appeasement policy in Europe. It helps reveal Halifax's general handling of Far Eastern problems. A minor point had been conceded to Japan without much loss of British honour or prestige. The Japanese were being kept 'in play'.

On Far Eastern questions, Halifax was temperamentally inclined to follow the guidance of the experts in the Far Eastern Department, some of whom held just as strong feelings about Germany as about Japan. On the other hand, Halifax loyally attempted to pursue Cham-

---

[74] A. J. P. Taylor, *English History, 1914–1945* (Oxford, 1965), p. 372.
[75] On this issue see especially Lee, *Britain and the Sino-Japanese War,* pp. 116–19.

berlain's line of appeasement. The goal of maintaining a balance of power in Europe was not always compatible with that of preserving the British Empire in Asia and other parts of the world. Just as Halifax was sometimes torn between the Prime Minister and the Foreign Office, so also on broader scale did he feel the conflicting pressures in the Commonwealth. Both Chamberlain and Halifax knew that war with Germany in 1938 would split the Dominions. Australia and New Zealand would enter reluctantly, but South Africa and Canada probably would refuse to enter at all. Halifax was also sensitive, in a way that Chamberlain was not, to the sentiment of the dependent Empire. There was an important moral element involved. The British, not least Halifax and his advisers, believed that the British Empire in Asia and Africa rested on a moral foundation. If Britain were to conclude a dishonourable agreement in the name of appeasement, the repercussions would be felt throughout the empire. 'I'd rather be beat than dishonoured,' Cadogan wrote on 24 September 1938. Contemplating the terms of Hitler's demands on Czechoslovakia, he continued: 'How can we look any foreigner in the face after this? How can we hold Egypt, India, and the rest?' [76]

It is clear from Cadogan's diary, among other sources, that such ethical questions weighed heavily on Halifax's mind during the great Czechoslovakian crisis of September 1938, and that Cadogan himself persuaded the Foreign Secretary to take a firmer stand against Hitler than Chamberlain liked or anticipated. Cadogan acted as a check on Halifax's conciliatory impulses in Asia as well. As the Foreign Secretary's principal adviser, he could sometimes exert decisive influence. Since he had served as Ambassador in China, his minutes reflected a greater knowledge of China than Japan, but they did not reflect any particular bias in favour of the British trading community in China. Indeed he wrote in the aftermath of the Munich crisis—when he attempted a general review of the major issues facing Britain at the time —that the China trade was probably important as much for the 'prestige' of the Empire as for its economic significance—and thus trading interests intrinsically were probably not worth the risk of war with Japan. His ideas coincided with Halifax's in the hope that China would continue to divert Japan and prevent her from turning southwards towards the vital part of Britain's eastern Empire, Malaya, and beyond Singapore, to Australia and New Zealand. Most importantly of all, the Permanent Under-Secretary and the Foreign Secretary were at one in the view of the United States as the ultimate protector of Britain's position. '[T]he shadow of possible trouble with America', Cadogan

[76] *Diaries of Sir Alexander Cadogan*, p. 104.

wrote in October 1938, 'has undoubtedly restrained Japan in recent times from doing as much damage as she would like to do to our interests in the Far East.'[77] Perhaps more than anything else, anxiety about future American action acted as a brake on appeasement in the Far East. Cadogan wrote on another occasion that 'making up to Japan' not only would be morally offensive to the British themselves but would also alienate the Americans: 'We have America to consider, and we should lose the last shreds of respect and sympathy that we may enjoy in that country if we did so.'[78]

The fall of Hankow and Canton in October 1938 and Prince Konoye's subsequent proclamation of a 'New Order in Asia' caused Sir John Brenan to remark that events in the Far East had now taken a truly ominous course. According to the Japanese, the Chinese nationalist government now no longer existed except as a mere local regime. The 'New Order' would be founded on a tripartite bloc of Japan-Manchuria-China, a bloc from which Britain would be more and more excluded unless she proved to be more cooperative. Brenan, for one, did not believe that the Japanese were offering any real choice. His analysis of the situation is of particular interest for the immediate pre-war period because he disliked the policy of appeasement in Europe and believed that it would be even less effective with Japan. The Japanese would regard British willingness to negotiate as a sign of weakness, not strength; their demands would only increase. In Brenan's view, the best response would be to maintain British rights and give way only under protest—to keep Japan in play, short of provoking war. This firm line towards the Japanese stands in contrast to British appeasement in Europe, but it carried Halifax's endorsement.[79] As with all oriental peoples, the Japanese would have to be dealt with firmly.

The word 'prestige' occurred frequently in the deliberations about Japan. When the Tientsin crisis erupted in 1939, one of the paramount concerns was the stripping and searching of British subjects as they entered and left the British concession. Stripping was a dramatic affront to Imperial prestige. There is nothing so undignified as a naked Englishman, or so at least the Japanese appeared to think. And they had other motivations. They were incensed at Chinese guerrillas using the settlement as a haven, and angered at long-standing British economic policies supporting Chinese currency. Tientsin was a symbol of resist-

---

[77] Ibid., p. 119.
[78] Minute by Cadogan, 23 December 1938, FO 371/22110.
[79] See Halifax's memorandum of 29 November 1938, FO 371/22110.

ance to the 'New Order'. The Japanese blockaded the concession in mid-June. Emotions rose quickly. British subjects were slapped and kicked as well as forced to submit to the indignity of stripping. Halifax informed the Japanese Ambassador that such measures were 'unworthy' of a civilized people. Even Chamberlain spoke of the Japanese insults as being 'almost' intolerable. Nevertheless he was prepared to be humble in order to avoid war, in Asia as well as Europe. Halifax and his advisers were only slightly less willing to accept a loss of prestige. In Brenan's words, '[I]t is desirable to secure a local *détente* if it can be done without too great a sacrifice of principles.'[80] If they would not suffer too great a loss of face, the British were prepared to negotiate on the concessions, which the Far Eastern Department regarded more in the nature of liabilities than assets. In time of war, they could not be defended; in time of peace, they provided provocation to both Japan and China. They were remnants of nineteenth-century British imperialism. The British would act firmly, but they would also act prudently, again in Brenan's words, on these questions concerning the 'excrescences' of a bygone era.

The Englishman responsible for trying to bring the Japanese to reason was Sir Robert Craigie, Ambassador in Tokyo since August 1937. Craigie recognized the logic of appeasement towards Japan and came close to endorsing it. He stood apart, in virtual isolation, from the consensus of Foreign Office opinion. He thought that the moderates in Japan were sympathetic to Britain and that their position against the extremists would be strengthened if the British adopted a more conciliatory attitude towards Japanese aims in China. Craigie was a friend of Sir Warren Fisher, and he agreed with Fisher's views of the necessity of Anglo-Japanese friendship. Though he had no previous experience in Asia, part of his career had been devoted to naval disarmament, and thus he had definite ideas about the strategic situation in the western Pacific. He shared Neville Chamberlain's distrust of the United States. Chamberlain in turn regarded Craigie's efforts as a valuable corrective to the anti-Japanese bias of the Foreign Office. During the Tientsin crisis, the Prime Minister wrote in praise of the Ambassador's calm attitude and his disposition 'never to get rattled'. Craigie's critics, on the other hand, detected a lamentable inclination to accept Japanese assurances at their face value and a refusal to recognize that the Japanese intended to dominate Asia at the expense of the British Empire. With a certain pomposity of character, Craigie worked to revive the spirit to the Anglo-Japanese Alliance.

[80] Lowe, *Origins of the Pacific War*, p. 73.

Sir Archibald Clark Kerr, Craigie's counterpart in China, expressed almost the opposite sentiments about the general situation in the Far East. Clark Kerr was sympathetic to the ideas of the political left. He was optimistic about Chiang Kai-shek's ability to prolong the struggle against the Japanese, and he had faith in the vitality and greatness of the Chinese people. He attached great importance to Britain's moral responsibility. In the Far East as elsewhere, British honour and decency counted as a force for good in world affairs. 'I am in a difficulty and I need your fearless guidance,' he wrote to Halifax in May 1939 about four Chinese nationalists at the British concession in Tientsin. The Japanese demanded that they be handed over for punishment as terrorists. Clark Kerr wrote that if the British acquiesced in this demand, they would for ever reflect upon it with shame. Here was a clear-cut case of appeasement versus resistance to Japanese imperialism.

Or so it seemed to Clark Kerr. From Craigie's vantage point, it appeared, on the basis of Japanese evidence, that the four Chinese were guerrillas guilty of blowing up railroads and other acts of sabotage. To Clark Kerr, this crime appeared to be that of fighting for their country. To Craigie, they were terrorists, and refusal to hand them over to the Japanese would further strain Anglo-Japanese relations. In a sombre tone he warned that the incident might even lead to war. The blockade demonstrated that the Japanese were prepared to take extreme measures. To those in London, some of the measures were little short of intolerable. The stripping of British subjects provoked indignation in the press as well as in the government. When word reached London that even an English*woman* had been subjected to this indignity, Chamberlain and Halifax recognized the extent of the crisis. There was a point beyond which even the appeasers would not go. Seeking to avoid 'a very humiliating position', in Halifax's phrase, the Cabinet devised a formula: the Japanese had a right to maintain order in the areas under their occupation, but the British government refused to acknowledge any general change in the policy of taking a firm line towards Japanese aggression. The British thus were able to avoid the semblance of a Far Eastern Munich.[81]

The outbreak of the European war in September 1939 did not seem at the time necessarily to mean a turn for the worse in Far Eastern affairs. The Nazi-Soviet non-aggression pact of 23 August, though a setback for Britain, had far worse implications for Japan. Russian aims would now preoccupy the Japanese and might divert them from such conflicts as the Tientsin controversy. The Japanese were also certainly

---

[81] For a discussion of this general subject, see Shai, *Origins of the War in the East.*

not unaware of growing American support for the British war effort in Europe, and the consequences of such support for Asia. In the words of the British Ambassador in Washington:

> If the United States is to rely upon Great Britain to prevent totalitarian Europe from entering the Atlantic through the Straits of Gibraltar and the exits from the North Sea, the United States must themselves underwrite the security of the British Empire in the Pacific because they cannot afford the weakening of Great Britain itself which would follow the collapse of her dominions in the Pacific.[82]

Another element of hope in the Far Eastern crisis was the resilience of the Chinese. According to Sir Robert Craigie, 'Japan has her hands far too full in China and is too apprehensive of the United States in its present mood to think seriously of any move involving danger to Australia and New Zealand, or to territories in which those Dominions are interested.'[83] These were the sorts of optimistic comments used to buck up the Dominions. But they are indicative of genuine hopes held by the British in the 1939–40 period. The Japanese might decide, in the words of a Foreign Office assessment of the situation, that the best course would be 'to sit on the fence'; or rather, they might be forced to do so, not only because of the United States and Russia but also because of China. In these various possibilities, one certainty appeared to be the tenacity of the Chinese. The greater Japan's involvement in China, the less likely would be the chances of a general Far Eastern war. Hence Britain's interest in a prolonged Chinese-Japanese conflict. Sir John Brenan wrote in December 1939: '[I]t seems to me obvious that the longer Japan is embroiled in China the less likely is she to take the opportunity of fishing in troubled waters of the world war, and that our policy, far from bringing about a patched-up peace, should still be to encourage Chinese resistance until we can again enter the Far Eastern theatre with something of our former influence.'[84]

The British stance can also be regarded as a calculated gamble that Japan would remain neutral. To win the gamble, some officials, such as Sir Robert Craigie and R. A. Butler, at this time Parliamentary Under-Secretary, believed that little as possible should be done to antagonize Japan and that economic concessions should be made to improve relations. In the spirit of reconciliation of Chamberlain and Fisher, Butler

---

[82] Lothian to Halifax, No. 747, 10 November 1939, FO 371/23562.

[83] Foreign Office, 'Appreciation of Probable Japanese Policy in the Far East', 15 November 1939, FO 371/23562.

[84] Minute by Brenan, 13 December 1939, FO 371/23551.

wrote in September 1939: 'I have never been happy since the Japanese Treaty was allowed to lapse . . . I believe there is in the Japanese a desire to improve their relations with us. I believe that they are a nation who keep their words when given.'[85] Butler hoped that Japan's economic situation might be eased by agreements about raw materials, possibly in exchange for war supplies. Rather than standing by and letting Japan 'explode' into South-East Asia, he wanted to administer certain 'therapeutic' measures that would enable the Japanese to resolve their economic and political problems by peaceful means—notably, by Britain facilitating a negotiated peace between Japan and China. Peace in China would help put Japan on a more moderate course, and Butler believed this might be accomplished without sacrifice of principle on Britain's part.

Thus there were two strategies to survival. The one, urged by Butler and to some extent by Sir Robert Craigie, held out hope for a neutral Japan, where the moderates might prevent the extreme militarists from waging war against Britain. The other, expressed most articulately by Sir George Sansom and Sir John Brenan, was based on the premises that the extremists in Japan held the upper hand and that they would be turned back only because of military failure in China. Sansom wrote in December 1939: 'The so-called moderate elements in Japan are unimportant. The only thing that can conceivably give them importance or increase their numbers is a manifest failure of extremist policies. No concessions to Japan, by us or by anybody else, can help the moderates, whatever they may tell us.'[86] Sansom had observed earlier, in lines of persistent analysis:

> All Japanese want a 'new order' in Asia, and a 'new order' involves the ultimate displacement of Great Britain in the Far East. The difference between the extremists and the moderates is not one of destination, but of the road by which that destination is to be reached and the speed at which it is to be traveled.[87]

That is the interpretation that eventually predominated in London, even among latter-day appeasers such as Butler. As for the idea of a negotiated peace in China, Brenan expressed a growing sentiment in the Foreign Office when he wrote at the time of the fall of France: 'Japan is a potential enemy and it is not in our interest to get her out

[85] Lowe, *Origins of the Pacific War,* pp. 106–07.
[86] Minute by Sansom, 12 December 1939, FO 371/23551.
[87] Minute by Sansom, 3 August 1939, FO 371/23529.

of the Chinese morass in order that she may be better able to take advantage of our difficulties in the European war.'[88]

When Churchill became Prime Minister in May 1940, he faced an upheaval in Europe that simultaneously had undermined Britain's position in the Far East. The Singapore strategy rested on the axiom that France would help hold the Mediterranean if the British fleet were engaged in Eastern waters. After the occupation of the Low Countries and the collapse of France, there now existed the danger of a Japanese takeover of the Dutch East Indies and Indo-China. Control of the latter territory would give the Japanese a land approach to Singapore. Churchill nevertheless minimized the possibility of an attack on Malaya, either by land or by sea. He had long-held preconceptions about the Japanese, and he greatly underrated their ability to wage war on the British Empire. In 1925 he had written: 'Japan is at the other end of the world. She cannot menace our vital security in any way . . . The only war it would be worth our while to fight with Japan would be to prevent an invasion of Australia.'[89] He continued to entertain such ideas. In short, he held that if worse came to worse, the British could cut their losses in the Far East and settle with the Japanese after the war. He respected Japan as a minor military power that would not be so unwise as to go to war against Britain.

His respect was mixed with a contempt for oriental peoples. His racial bias helps explain his blind spot in the Far East. Churchill miscalculated the forces of Asian nationalism while maintaining an almost nineteenth-century notion of the prestige, even if not the power, of the British Empire. He once wrote when contemplating the broader dangers of war in Asia: 'As for India, if the Japs were to invade it would make the Indians loyal to the King Emperor for a hundred years.'[90] As for China, 'Japan has done for the Chinese people what they could, perhaps, never have done for themselves. It has unified them once more.'[91] As for the Far East in general, he recounted in his memoirs that 'nothing we could have spared at the time . . . would have changed the march of fate' in Malaya, the Dutch East Indies, and other territories overrun by the Japanese.[92] Though many of his critics have challenged that view as entirely misguided, it stands as an accurate reflection of his attitude in the 1940–41 period.

Churchill's sense of inevitability hinged on the distinct possibility

[88] Minute by Brenan, 17 May 1940, FO 371/24661.
[89] Martin Gilbert, *Winston S. Churchill* (London, 1976), V, p. 26.
[90] Stephen Roskill, *Churchill and the Admirals* (London, 1977), p. 126.
[91] Gilbert, *Churchill*, V, p. 938.
[92] Churchill, *The Second World War*, vol. III: *The Grand Alliance* (Boston, 1950) p. 588.

of US inaction. His Far Eastern policy aimed at aligning Britain and America and avoiding war with Japan as long as possible. He also wished to strengthen China, but just as he put the Far East generally low on his list of priorities, so also he regarded assistance to China as a relatively unimportant or futile matter. On the other hand, he saw great value in prolonging the war between China and Japan as an inexpensive means of keeping the Japanese occupied. The Chinese were succoured, both materially and morally, by supplies reaching them from Burma. In June 1940, shortly after the collapse of France, Churchill learned that the Japanese threatened war with Britain unless the supplies ceased. The Chiefs of Staff reported that it was 'doubly important' to avoid war with Japan now that Britain had lost her principal ally. The Foreign Office was under no illusion: Japanese demands would increase in proportion to the intensity of the crisis in Europe. 'The severity of the actual pressure applied to us', Brenan noted, 'would fluctuate with British fortunes in Europe.'[93] The Foreign Office invented an ingenious solution, which the Japanese accepted. Britain closed the Burma road for a period of three months, with the face-saving provision that there would be a genuine search for peace. Once again the Japanese were being kept in play, with only a little sacrifice of British principle. Chamberlain wrote in July 1940: 'I was relieved and gratified to find that Winston, with the responsibilities of a P.M. on his shoulders, was firmly against the bold line.'[94] If war were to come, Churchill wanted the United States to bear the brunt of it. In the meantime, he hoped for a continuation of hostilities between China and Japan. 'I have never liked the idea of our trying to make peace between Japan and China,' he wrote in July 1940. He noted that he had yielded to the formula of a search for peace in exchange for the temporary closing of the Burma road, 'but it is certainly not in our interests that China and Japan should end their quarrel'.[95]

Hoping for the best in the conflict between the Japanese and Chinese, Churchill adopted a passive role for Britain. He reversed the Singapore strategy of the mid-1930s. After the defence of the British Isles came the Middle East and the Mediterranean, not the Far East, which in Churchill's estimate ranked at the bottom of strategic priorities. He was consistent in outlook. In September 1939, as First Lord of the Admiralty, he had written, for the guidance of the Australians, an appreciation of the situation at Singapore. He believed that there was no need to fear an attack from Japan because the Japanese were

---

[93] Minute by Brenan, 8 July 1940, FO 371/24725.
[94] Lowe, *Origins of the Pacific War,* p. 129.
[95] Minute by Churchill, 17 July 1940, FO 371/24661.

'a prudent people' who would not embark on such a 'mad enterprise'. He assured the Australians that a battle fleet would be sent to Eastern waters to act as a deterrent to Japan if the need arose, and in the meantime he thanked the Australian government for the 'loyal and clairvoyant strategy' whereby Australian forces were deployed where needed most—in other words, in the Middle East. As a consequence, Singapore had been left, in his own phrase, 'denuded', but Australian troops were serving in 'decisive' battlefields.[96] Churchill continued to believe that the Japanese could be deterred by a show of force. When he insisted on sending the two great ships to Singapore in order to restrain Japan, he overrode the advice of the Admiralty and those less contemptuous than he about the fighting prowess of the Japanese. The loss of the *Prince of Wales* and *Repulse* in December 1941 represented more than a failure to assess Japanese air power, just as the fall of Singapore reflected more than a deficiency in defence preparations. Churchill persistently underestimated the fighting capability of the Japanese.

In the 1940–41 period, the Far East remained at the end of the list of strategic imperatives. The Prime Minister adopted a cavalier attitude towards the Singapore strategy, yet he gave repeated assurances to the Australians that the Middle East would be sacrificed 'for sake of kith and kin' if Australia were threatened by Japanese invasion. If Churchill was able to keep a clear conscience about the commitment to Australia and New Zealand, the Far Eastern Department of the Foreign Office was not. M. E. Dening (who during the war served as political adviser at the South-East Asia Command and later as Ambassador to Japan) wrote in July 1940:

> I think we have been a little dishonest . . . because before September 1939 the potential menace of Germany and Italy made it necessary to retain all our main forces in the Atlantic and Mediterranean. On the outbreak of war and the subsequent entry of Italy, it must have been apparent even in Australia that we had no fleet to spare. Australia may well feel that she has been induced to send troops to the Near East and to England on false pretenses.[97]

Churchill was not disposed to ponder the niceties of past commitments. In his persistent view, Japan would be restrained if necessary

[96] Memorandum by Churchill, 17 November 1939, DMV (39), 3, CAB 99/1.

[97] Minute by Dening, 10 July 1940, FO 371/24725; for discussion about Australia, see especially John M. McCarthy, *Australia and Imperial Defence, 1918–39: A Study in Air and Sea Power* (Brisbane, 1976); Glen St John Barclay, 'Australia Looks to America: The Wartime Relationship, 1939–1942', *Pacific Historical Review*, 46 (May 1977); and Ovendale, *'Appeasement' and the English Speaking World*.

by the dispatch of capital ships—a disastrous miscalculation. On the other hand, his political and strategic instinct served him well by placing all bets on the Americans. He foresaw that only the United States could make a decisive stand in the struggle against Japan and at the same time tilt the balance in Europe. His transcendent purpose was to bring America into the war on the side of Britain. He wrote shortly after Japan joined the Axis powers in September 1940: 'The entry of the United States into the war either with Germany and Italy or with Japan is fully conformable with British interests . . . if Japan attacked the United States without declaring war on us we should at once range ourselves at the side of the United States and declare war on Japan.'[98] To the time of the Japanese attack on Pearl Harbor, British policy aimed at tightening economic restrictions on Japan without provoking her into a war that would involve only Britain. Though the Japanese onslaught proved to be calamitous for the British Empire in the Far East, it was a godsend for the British cause. In Churchill's famous phrase: 'So we had won after all.'

The collapse of British power in the Far East ended an era in which the political influence of the British had outlived their military strength. 'We lived on bluff from 1920–1939', Sir Alexander Cadogan wrote in July 1940, 'but it was eventually called.'[99] Though a few perceptive observers had been uneasily aware of the discrepancy between British power and British pretension, most people in Britain, not least Churchill, believed that the prestige of the British Empire still counted as an intangible and powerful force in Asia. The word 'prestige', as Sir John Brenan once pointed out, is an abused word. In its contemporary usage it meant, in his phrase, 'respect inspired by military strength'. The sinking of the *Prince of Wales* and *Repulse,* along with the fall of Singapore, brought an end to the illusion of both the power and prestige of the British Empire in the Far East.

The Fascist Challenge and the Policy of Appeasement   1983

---

[98] Minute by Churchill, 4 October 1940, FO 371/24729.
[99] Minute by Cadogan, 27 July 1940, FO 371/24708.

12

HONG KONG: THE CRITICAL PHASE, 1945–49

The Hong Kong handover at midnight, 30 June 1997, closed the last major chapter in the history of British imperialism. Although there are remnants of empire such as Gibraltar and the Falklands, there are no more significant British dependencies. Hong Kong itself holds a unique place in the history of the British Empire, not merely because of its astonishing economic success. As a possession acquired in 1842 by the Treaty of Nanking (with the tip of the Kowloon peninsula and Stonecutters Island annexed in 1860, and with leased territories added in 1898), it enjoyed a formal status as a Crown Colony, but it lacked, until recently, certain distinguishing characteristics of the era of British colonial rule, identifiable in almost all other principal colonial territories: the development of a nationalist movement and an advance towards self-government. 'Hong Kong Man', as he came to be known, was a phenomenon of the 1980s—especially of the end of the decade, when the men and women of Hong Kong were galvanized into acute political consciousness by the Beijing Massacre of 4 June 1989.[1] The people of Hong Kong thus acquired a sense of identity and, in the early 1990s, a certain amount of democratization. The new era that began in 1997, however, poses a question that had confronted them at a similar time of uncertainty, in 1949: how long can it last?

Everything, now as then, depends on China. Therein lies the particular way in which the history of Hong Kong as a part of the British

I am grateful to Christopher Patten, Governor of Hong Kong, 1992–97, for allowing me access to Hong Kong Secretariat records not in the public domain. I also wish to express my appreciation to the archivist, Simon F. K. Chu, and the staff of the Government Records Service. The Secretariat records appear in the notes without an archival prefix number but with the original Secretariat file number, for example HK Secretariat 5/1162/465 [1162 = Chinese affairs]. Documents at the Hong Kong Government Records Service bear an archival prefix, for example HKRS 41. I have also studied the relevant files in the Australian Archives, Canberra (hereafter, AA), and the National Archives of New Zealand, Wellington (hereafter, NZ). The Post Files of the US Consul in Hong Kong (Record Group 84, China, Hong Kong Consulate General, 1946–49, National Archives II, College Park, Maryland) are abbreviated USSD HK. I wish to thank John Cell, Ronald Hyam, and Warren Kimball for critiques of my argument. On the Chinese dimension of the article, I am especially indebted to Jonathan Spence and Nancy Bernkopf Tucker as well as my colleagues at the University of Texas, William Braisted and Edward Rhoads, who gave me valuable advice and provided me with translations from some of the historical literature in Chinese. I am grateful above all to my colleague at St. Antony's College, Oxford, Dr. Steve Yui-Sang Tsang, for discussion of all aspects of the subject.

[1] 'Hong Kong Man' is the phrase coined and given currency by the anthropologist Hugh D. R. Baker in 'Life in the Cities: The Emergence of Hong Kong Man', *China Quarterly*, 95 (September 1983), pp. 469–79.

Empire can be best understood. Hong Kong today possesses, as much as ever, the characteristics of the China port system of the nineteenth and twentieth centuries, up to the fall of Shanghai in 1941 (or, in an extended sense, 1949). Under the formula of 'one country, two systems', devised in 1984 as the basis for the transfer, Hong Kong is subject to its own law. Despite the reversion to China, it is not any easier for Chinese nationals to visit or settle there. No revenues are sent to Beijing. The territory retains its own currency and judicial system. No one knows how long the present system will last, but that was also true of one of the turning points in Hong Kong's modern history, 15 October 1949, when Chinese Communist troops arrived in Canton. Two days later they halted at the northern border of the British colony. They did not, as was feared, take Hong Kong at bayonet point, in part perhaps because the British had resolutely decided to defend the colony. What were the British calculations in reaching the decision to hold fast? That became one of two critical questions in the course of my research.

If Hong Kong continued to function as a port of entry into China, it nevertheless possessed a colonial administration that would have been recognized instantly as 'British', just as the colonial regimes in Malaya, Ceylon, Nigeria, or Jamaica would have been at any time up to independence.[2] Hong Kong was also a colonial autocracy. In its power to tax and to administer justice, in its police force, and in the defence of its frontiers, Hong Kong had all the attributes of the 'colonial state'.[3] It was, however, a nascent city-state rather than a nation-state. Therein lay my second question. After the reoccupation at the end of the Second World War, the British briefly contemplated launching Hong Kong on a course that might have given the colony a national identity much earlier than the 1980s and might have secured its independence within the Commonwealth. Hong Kong might have become an independent city-state analogous to Singapore. What inspired that vision in the years after 1945 and why did it fade?[4]

[2] This interpretation should be compared with the one put forward by John Darwin, who argues that the formal status of Hong Kong as a Crown Colony has obscured the informal nature of the treaty port, with 'informal empire' thus masquerading as 'formal empire' (John Darwin, 'Hong Kong in British Decolonisation', in Judith M. Brown and Rosemary Foot, eds., *Hong Kong's Transitions, 1842–1997* [London, 1997], p. 30).

[3] For the idea of the 'colonial state', see especially Crawford Young, *The African Colonial State in Comparative Perspective* (New Haven, 1994), reviewed by the present author in *American History Review,* 101 (October 1996), pp. 1257–58.

[4] The point of departure for the post-war years is Steve Yui-Sang Tsang, *Democracy Shelved: Great Britain, China, and Attempts at Constitutional Reform in Hong Kong, 1945–1952* (Oxford, 1988). See also Lanxin Xiang, *Recasting the Imperial Far East: Britain and America in China, 1945–*

Chinese and British perspectives on Hong Kong differ dramatically, it would seem, but there is one British insight into the Chinese attitude that helps establish the historical background. In late 1945, the head of the China Department at the Foreign Office, George Kitson, proposed that Hong Kong be returned to China as a gesture of friendship in the new post-war era. As will be seen, the suggestion was met with a ringing rejection, but Kitson had a shrewd sense of the way the Chinese regarded the British position in Hong Kong. He was an old China hand who knew the Chinese languages and admired Chinese art and literature. He had begun his career in Beijing in 1922 and had risen through the ranks of the China service to become Consul in Shanghai in 1939. He believed that the British needed to establish 'moral leadership' and to demonstrate to 'left-wing opponents of British imperialism' that the old system of exploitation was dead. The restoration of Hong Kong would not merely prove that the British had had a change of heart but might also avert confrontation over the territory. In arguing the case, Kitson developed what became known in British official circles as the 'Isle of Wight analogy', which carried a powerful historical parallel:

> The Chinese feelings towards Hong Kong can perhaps be most easily described by using the Isle of Wight analogy. Supposing the Chinese had taken the island against our will 100 years ago and covered it with pagodas, etc., and developed it by means which they had invented and we had not learned to use, doing all this for their own purposes, although talking a great deal about the material advantages to the United Kingdom, and all the time emphasising the value of this haven of good government, a protection against insecurity, in the Isle of Wight.

> Even if they had created a heaven on earth in that small island we should have only one feeling about it. We should want it back.[5]

1950 (Armonk, N.Y., 1995); James T. H. Tang, 'From Empire Defence to Imperial Retreat: Britain's Postwar China Policy and the Decolonization of Hong Kong', *Modern Asian Studies*, 28 (1994), pp. 317–37; Qiang Zhai, *The Dragon, the Lion, and the Eagle: Chinese-British-American Relations, 1949–1958* (Kent, Ohio, 1994); and Zhong-ping Feng, *The British Government's China Policy 1945–1950* (Keele, UK, 1994). For background, other important works include Norman Miners, *Hong Kong under Imperial Rule, 1912–1941* (Oxford, 1987); Aron Shai, *Britain and China, 1941–47* (London, 1984); and Edmund K. S. Fung, *The Diplomacy of Imperial Retreat: Britain's South China Policy, 1924–31* (Hong Kong, 1991). The standard and reliable reference work is G. B. Endacott, *A History of Hong Kong* (Hong Kong, 1958, rev. edn., 1973).

[5] George Kitson, memorandum, 'The Future of Hong Kong', 28 February 1946, FO 371/53632.

The Chinese undeniably felt the same way about Hong Kong.[6] *The Economist* expressed this proposition in a slightly different way: 'Chinese memories are almost as long as Irish.'[7]

The questions how and when the Chinese would attempt to get the island back remained contentious. For example, Sir Alexander Grantham, Governor of Hong Kong from 1947 to 1957, believed that the British might hold their own against the Nationalist Party (Kuomintang), but that if China were brought under Communist control, 'then it will be only a matter of time before some kind of rendition campaign is started.'[8] It is therefore important to clarify, as further prelude to the British side of the story, the views of Chiang Kai-shek as the leader of the Kuomintang and of Mao Tse-tung as the leader of the revolutionary Chinese Communist movement.

It is beyond the scope of the present discussion to consider Chiang Kai-shek's crumbling position at the end of the Second World War, but it should be pointed out that when the Japanese surrendered in August 1945, the Chinese Nationalists had crack troops from two separate corps only 300 miles from Hong Kong.[9] They could muster a combined strength of 60,000 men, many of whom had been trained and equipped by the Americans. General Albert Wedemeyer, Chiang's

[6] Steve Tsang, *Hong Kong: An Appointment with China* (London, 1997), pp. 57–60. In general excellence, Tsang's work is in a class by itself among the books on Hong Kong published in the run-up to the handover. It is based on Chinese as well as English sources and, among other virtues, has a comprehensive bibliographical list of articles and books in Chinese. Jung-Fang Tsai, *Hong Kong in Chinese History* (New York, 1993), is useful for background from the Chinese perspective. For a discussion of recent books on Hong Kong, see the anonymous review 'All Change in Hong Kong', *The Economist*, 19 April 1997, review section, pp. 3–4; Jonathan Mirsky, 'Looking Forward, Looking Back', *The Times*, 26 June 1997; and Brian Hook, 'Was There Another Way Out?' *Times Literary Supplement*, 18 July 1997, pp. 28–29.

[7] 6 March 1948.

[8] Alexander Grantham to Arthur Creech Jones (Secretary of State for Colonies), Top Secret, LM [Loose Minute] D31149, 3 May 1949, FO 371/15780. In the same month, Communist documents seized in Hong Kong revealed that the Chinese Communists 'are aiming at a quick military solution of the civil war . . . Foreign trade is to be conducted, without foreigners as much as possible, since to rely on foreigners is a relic of imperialism' (C. B. B. Heathcote-Smith, minute, Secret, 10 May 1949, HK Secretariat 6/3571/48). Most British officials nevertheless doubted whether Communist forces could constitute a threat against Hong Kong in the immediate future. The Consul-General in Canton, G. F. Tyrrell, wrote, for example, in 1948, 'I daresay we shall see no actual fighting in this part of the world at all' (Tyrrell to D. M. MacDougall [Colonial Secretary in the Hong Kong administration], Confidential, 3 December 1948, HK Secretariat 5/1400/47). The US Consul-General in Hong Kong also reported that Communist forces were 'not sufficiently well organized' to carry out a concerted action against Hong Kong (Raymond P. Ludden to Lewis Clark, Secret, 19 October 1948, USSD HK, Box 6, File 800). I am grateful to David Fado for his assistance in the National Archives.

[9] For the general military situation, see especially E. R. Hooton, *The Greatest Tumult: The Chinese Civil War, 1936–49* (London, 1991), chap. 7.

American chief of staff, supported Nationalist aims and opposed British plans for reoccupation. He planned to use those troops to attack the Japanese in the Canton–Hong Kong region in November 1945. But the sudden end of the war forced Chiang to decide on priorities. As will be discussed later, the British managed to secure American support for the reoccupation of Hong Kong. Chiang could have seen a humiliating setback in the Anglo-American collusion on Hong Kong, but he aimed to secure international recognition of China as a leading power in the post–Second World War era. British as well as American support had been essential for China's receiving a high place in the new United Nations. There was, furthermore, an even more compelling reason why Chiang decided not to act. The Communists had an effective guerrilla force, known as the East River Column, in the vicinity of Hong Kong. A Nationalist advance against the British might have precipitated a showdown with the Communists over Hong Kong. Chiang had more important priorities: if he were to re-establish control over northern China, he needed to redeploy troops as quickly as possible along the railway lines and in the large urban and industrial areas to the north. Hong Kong would have to wait. Chiang thus took the line that the issue of Hong Kong would be resolved according to international treaties and in the context of amiable relations with the British.

Mao did not recognize the legitimacy of British claims to Hong Kong. He refused to be bound in any way by the 'unequal treaties' concluded in the nineteenth century. Like Chiang, he had much more pressing priorities than Hong Kong. According to a British journalist in 1946, Mao's thoughts seemed far removed from the issue of Hong Kong's future:

> I am not interested in Hong Kong; the Communist Party is not interested in Hong Kong, it has never been the subject of any discussion amongst us. Perhaps ten, twenty or thirty years hence we may ask for a discussion regarding its return, but my attitude is that so long as your [British] officials do not maltreat Chinese subjects in Hong Kong, and so long as Chinese are not treated as inferior to others in the matter of taxation and a voice in the Government, I am not interested in Hong Kong, and will certainly not allow it to be a bone of contention between your country and mine.[10]

As long as the British remained neutral in the Chinese civil war, Mao would not pursue the issue of Hong Kong. By not recognizing the legitimacy of British claims, he would continue to hold the initiative.

[10] Tsang, *Appointment with China,* p. 69, which should be compared with Xiang, *Recasting the Imperial Far East,* p. 101.

Mao, in short, espoused a 'Middle Kingdom' view of world politics, in which China proper was much more important than the peripheral or border areas. Foreign countries such as Britain, the United States, and even the Soviet Union seemed comparatively remote. Mao and his successors were content to let Hong Kong provide the People's Republic of China with technology, capital investment, and, eventually, one-third of its foreign-exchange earnings, as well as with critical financial services. Mao held a representative Chinese outlook, which had ramifications extending to the handover in July 1997.[11]

There were two Governors in the period under consideration, Sir Mark Young (1946–47) and Sir Alexander Grantham (1947–57). Both exerted a lasting influence, but since the former was in office for only a year and the latter for a decade, the comparison might seem odd if not for the legacy of political reform that Young left to Grantham. Young succeeded in committing the Colonial Office to the principle of municipal self-government. He believed that Hong Kong could eventually develop a British identity as a city-state within the British Empire and Commonwealth. Grantham, by contrast, thought that Chinese cultural affinity and the proximity of the colony to China would prevent the development of a British allegiance, but he was bound to some extent by the commitment his predecessor made. Although there were other important differences between the two Governors, Grantham summed up the overriding principle of British policy: Britain must maintain 'friendly relations with whatever government is in power in China' but should never make concessions merely for the sake of concessions—in other words, never appease for the sake of appeasement, resist when possible, and give way only when necessary.[12] Hong Kong,

[11] Problems of the present often influence the interpretation of the past. When the archives become accessible, they may reveal that the British, not the Chinese, triggered the set of events leading to the transfer of the territory in 1997. According to this controversial interpretation, related here in its barest bones, the British had their own reasons for wanting to terminate their administration in Hong Kong, not least being the responsibility for 6.2 million people. British anxiety greatly increased after the Tiananmen Square repression in June 1989. This is a plausible argument and must be taken seriously until evidence to the contrary appears. And another nearly mythic British view must also be questioned. The British took as an article of faith that the Chinese had always objected to the democratization of Hong Kong because of fear that it might fortify the pro-democracy movement in China. The Chinese certainly did object to the moves towards representative government in Hong Kong introduced by Governor Patten, but the projection of the Chinese attitude of the 1990s backward onto previous decades is anachronistic. This has a direct bearing on the argument of this article. There is little or no evidence that the Communists ever protested against the proposed democratization of Hong Kong in the 1940s; Tsang independently makes the same point (*Appointment with China,* p. 117).

[12] Grantham to CO, No. 372, Secret, 11 April 1950, CO 537/6045. Grantham's general views emerge clearly in his memoir, *Via Ports: From Hong Kong to Hong Kong* (Hong Kong, 1965).

in Grantham's robust view, could be effectively defended, despite military opinion to the contrary.[13]

There was a certain continuity of high policy in the period 1945–49, although earlier, during the wartime years, the status of Hong Kong had been fiercely debated between the Colonial and Foreign Offices in London. The axiom of holding Hong Kong within the Empire yet remaining on terms as friendly as possible with China subsequently became refined when the British, over time, in the words of a later Governor, came 'to know our enemy rather better'.[14] As the British got to know the enemy more intimately, however, their views were transformed. Until late 1947, it was the Nationalist Party of Chiang Kai-shek that seemed to menace the British presence in Hong Kong.[15] Since 1927 the British had pursued a course of conciliation with Chinese nationalism as represented by the Kuomintang; after 1949 the British attempted to apply the same principle to the new Communist regime. But there have remained puzzling questions. How did the

---

[13] Naval and military commanders in Hong Kong at the end of the Second World War reported that the colony was 'considered undefendable against a serious attack by a major power in occupation of the Mainland of China' (Hong Kong Defence Plan, Top Secret, No. 58/2, 24 December 1945, FO 371/53629). (This is an example of a vital document that appears neither in the Hong Kong registry nor, it would appear, in the CO files.) The air defence of Hong Kong seemed to pose singular problems:

> [D]emobilized and disgruntled young air crews of any nationality may easily be tempted by love of adventure coupled with a promise of high emoluments. Soldiers of fortune of this category are capable of introducing an element of leadership, skill and courage into an air force of poor quality . . . it is [therefore] considered that defensive air forces in Hong Kong should be designed to be slightly stronger than is necessary for defence against local air forces.

Hong Kong Defence Plan. For the inter-war background of Hong Kong in the evolution of British strategic plans, see Christopher M. Bell, '"Our Most Exposed Outpost": Hong Kong and British Far Eastern Strategy, 1921–1941', *Journal of Military History*, 60 (January 1996), pp. 61–88. For post-war defence issues, see Malcolm H. Murfett, *In Jeopardy: The Royal Navy and British Far Eastern Defence Policy, 1945–1951* (Oxford, 1995).

[14] R. B. Black to Secretary of State, No. 130, Secret, 21 January 1959, CO 1030/590. For the decade of the 1950s, see especially Steve Tsang, 'Strategy for Survival: The Cold War and Hong Kong's Policy towards Kuomintang and Chinese Communist Activities in the 1950s', *Journal of Imperial and Commonwealth History*, 25 (May 1997), pp. 294–317.

[15] My judgement on late 1947 as the turning point is based on the records of the Hong Kong Secretariat. After the resumption of civil war in 1946, there were many comments speculating on the outcome; but the basic shift in view about the ultimate enemy began to take place in late 1947, when, for example, the political adviser (adviser on foreign affairs) wrote of 'the not impossible event of the Chinese Communists gaining control of China'. He concluded, not unreasonably, 'I do not think a Communist Government in China would be at all well-disposed towards Hong Kong' (Heathcote-Smith, 13 December 1947, HK Secretariat 1/1166/47C).

British official mind perceive the connections or interactions among local problems in Hong Kong, regional issues concerning Britain and China, and the place of Hong Kong in the late-1940s Cold War? Why did the British overrate the power and influence of the Kuomintang? How would the British respond, in the words of the head of the Hong Kong Department in the Colonial Office, to 'the hordes of Chinese refugees' after the collapse of the Nationalist government?[16] What were the changing assumptions about the Communists' power and the implications for Hong Kong? How is it that the British in some ways found the Chinese Communists more accommodating than the Kuomintang on the issue of Hong Kong? What were the relative weights in the triangular process of shaping British policy in the Hong Kong Secretariat, the Colonial Office, and the Foreign Office? What were the sources of information or the intelligence networks on which the British relied? To what extent did the personality or influence of the Governor in Hong Kong make a difference? In short, what do the archival sources reveal about Hong Kong's survival as a British colony in the critical phase of 1945–49?

In answering those questions, it is useful to bear in mind the problems following the Japanese seizure of the colony in 1941 as well as those of the 1950s, when officials occasionally reflected on the crisis of the late 1940s. In the 1940s, as at any time, certain demographic, geographic, and economic facts had to be borne in mind. The population of Hong Kong at the time of the British reoccupation in 1945 was 800,000, of which 97 per cent was and remained Chinese.[17] In 1946, the population increased to over 1 million. The colony consisted of the island of Hong Kong (35.5 square miles), the peninsula of Kowloon on the mainland opposite the island (3.25 square miles), the New Territories (355 square miles), running north from Kowloon for about twenty miles, and a number of islands. The frontier with China extended about twenty miles across a neck of land dividing the

---

[16] J. B. Sidebotham to Grantham, Secret, 14 May 1948, HK Secretariat 54436/48. Grantham used the conventional figure of 600,000 Chinese refugees who fled to Hong Kong in 1949–50. When the crisis approached, the Hong Kong administration estimated that the colony could accommodate 4,800 British subjects evacuating Shanghai and that 'one camp to accommodate 240 persons could be erected every 48 hours by working continuously day and night' (MacDougall to Sidebotham, Top Secret, 30 December 1948; and J. L. Hayward, minute, 11 February 1949, HK Secretariat 5/1400/47 TS).

[17] On the situation in the aftermath of the Japanese occupation, there is a vivid description in the Hong Kong archives in an account called 'Food and Fuel Position', October 1945, HKRS 41/1/547/7410/45: 'The Japanese left no appreciable stocks of . . . food. Peanut oil, fish, beef, vegetables, sugar and salt all are in seriously short supply . . . As to firewood, Hong Kong is living off floors and doors.'

colony from the mainland. There was no marked geographical feature to form a natural frontier. Until 1950, the Chinese and others in Hong Kong moved more or less freely to the adjoining Chinese province of Guangdong and vice versa. Transient labourers provided a vital part of the Hong Kong workforce. The Governor in the immediate post-war period, Young, commented on one of the adverse effects of the fluctuating population: 'The geographical position of . . . Hong Kong inevitably makes for a transient population subject to great influxes of the least desirable classes in times of economic and political trouble in China.'[18]

Britain held the island of Hong Kong and the tip of the Kowloon peninsula in absolute sovereignty. The New Territories had been leased, rather than annexed, from the Chinese in 1898 for a period of ninety-nine years; the expiration date was thus 1997. The terminal date applied only to the leased territories, which constituted, however, 90 per cent of Hong Kong's total area. It was therefore inconceivable that the terminal date would not apply to the territory as a whole. The colony had become administratively indivisible. Even assuming that the British might continue to hold Hong Kong island and the lower part of Kowloon, they would be dependent on China for water and food. To the Hong Kong government and the Colonial Office in 1945, there thus existed a unique situation. Here was a colony with an established timetable for the end of British rule. Relinquishing it to China seemed to most British observers to be inevitable. But there were important exceptions, notably Young.

Grantham later reflected in his memoirs that Shanghai had been 'a great cosmopolitan centre' and that Hong Kong in comparison was 'a small village'.[19] Before 1941, the total trade and investment in Shanghai was ten times that in Hong Kong. After 1949, however, Hong Kong became the heir to Shanghai.[20] Refugees from the civil war infused the colony with energy and wealth. Grantham summed up the critical

[18] Mark Young to Secretary of State, No. 255, Secret, 7 February 1947, FO 371/63387.

[19] Grantham also remarked that the expatriates in Hong Kong in the pre-war period possessed the same racial arrogance and claims to privilege as in Shanghai. Such attitudes died hard, but by 1947 Grantham could say that there was a 'marked decline' in the arrogance that had been typical of expatriates in Shanghai; by 1965, he could claim that 'the age of the "blimps" is over' (Grantham, *Via Ports*, p. 104).

[20] For the Shanghai connection, see Nicholas R. Clifford, *Spoilt Children of Empire: Westerners in Shanghai and the Chinese Revolution of the 1920s* (Hanover, N.H., 1991), which begins: 'Seventy years ago, Shanghai occupied a position very much like that of Hongkong today' (p. xi). See also especially Frederic Wakeman, Jr., *Policing Shanghai, 1927–1937* (Berkeley, 1995). For the later period, another useful recent book is Maochun Yu, *The D.S.S. in China: Prelude to Cold War* (New Haven, 1990).

development in the aftermath of Communist victory: '[T]he refugees from the North . . . brought with them some refugee capital, many new techniques and a commercial shrewdness and determination superior even to that of the native Cantonese.'[21] Most of the refugees had no place else to go. The *Far Eastern Economic Review* commented on their plight: 'Passport and visa difficulties make their further travel practically impossible. Thus Hongkong, for better or worse, has become their home and new place of commercial and industrial venture.'[22] Hong Kong's economic resilience had roots in these refugees' necessity to start a new life.

In 1949, Hong Kong was on the verge of rapid economic growth and industrialization, but business opinion at the time was uncertain. In view of the civil war, no one knew what the future would hold. A visitor from Shanghai, writing in February 1949 in the *China Weekly Review,* however, was generally optimistic:

> [T]here is undoubted prosperity . . . Real wages have increased an estimated 25 percent as compared with pre-war, the building trades are booming, and the high prices for food have benefited the farmer . . . There is no dearth of fine motor cars, fine food, and good things in the shops; and if business is actually at middling levels, the men of business are most certainly enjoying their indifferent prosperity.

> With all the present tensions, Hongkong presents a welcome freedom from the hovering clouds of suspicion, distrust and star chamber proceedings met with elsewhere [notably in Shanghai].[23]

Business opinion may have been jittery, though optimistic, but the period up to 1949 and beyond reveals substantial commercial and industrial expansion. Hong Kong was a member of the sterling bloc, that is, its currency was based on the pound sterling, but it was also a free port, with an open market for US dollars. The total value of trade reached the level (in Hong Kong dollars) of HKD 2.767 billion in 1947, which increased in the next year by nearly 16 per cent to HKD 3.2 billion—an almost 100 per cent increase over the 1946 level of HKD 1.7 billion and 133 per cent higher than the 1940 figure of HKD 1.375 billion. The figure for 1949 was HKD 5.069 billion, and for 1950, HKD 7.503 billion—almost 135 per cent above the 1948 level.[24]

[21] Grantham to Secretary of State, LM 210/54, Confidential, 22 December 1954, CO 1030/292. For the Hong Kong Secretariat's assessment of immigration problems since 1947, see, for example, HK Secretariat 1/1166/47C.

[22] 19 January 1949.

[23] 19 February 1949.

[24] Tsang, *Democracy Shelved*, pp. 78, 141.

It is important to note the contemporary British assessments of Hong Kong's value. *The Economist* commented in September 1949 that most British merchants in China 'are probably going to be ruined' and that 'this reduction of our stake in China is occurring at a time when the problems presented by our export trade and the balance of payments are graver than ever before in our history.'[25] The estimates of Britain's loss of assets in China from 1949 vary from a high of £1 billion in Shanghai alone to a low of £125 million for all of China. The loss of £200-300 million worth of assets is the conventional figure.[26] Nevertheless, the low figure of £125 million is useful as a point of comparison because British investments in Hong Kong in 1949 were assessed at £156 million. As a point of reference, the figure of £125 million is useful for another reason: the value of Britain's share of oil in the Middle East fell into the same category as did that of trade and commerce in China. Hong Kong was frequently described as one of the empire's largest cities and the largest entrepôt in Asia. After the Second World War, the refinery at Abadan in Iran was the largest of its kind in the world. In the British government, the Ministry of Fuel and Power estimated the replacement cost of the British plant at Abadan at £120 million—'not much less than the estimated cost of retooling and modernising the coal industry in this country'.[27] Hong Kong thus stood up to comparison with one of Britain's most valuable assets.

At the height of the wartime struggle in 1942, the British government had considered whether cession of the colony to China might not be more effective sooner rather than later. With the same motive that inspired the British to offer post-war Dominion Status to India in return for Indian support of the war effort, the Foreign Office held that a return of Hong Kong to the Chinese would help forge an alliance between the British and the Kuomintang. According to this line of argument, which was developed in the aftermath of the fall of Singapore, Hong Kong could already be regarded as a lost cause. The gesture of cession would demonstrate to the Americans that the British were not fighting the war for the reactionary purposes of preserving the British Empire.[28] The proposal had a long pedigree: as early as the First

---

[25] 24 September 1949.

[26] See Aron Shai, 'Imperialism Imprisoned: The Closure of British Firms in the People's Republic of China', *English Historical Review*, 114 (1989), p. 88. Wenguang Shao, *China, Britain, and Businessmen: Political and Commercial Relations, 1949–57* (London, 1991), is also an exceptionally useful work.

[27] Quoted in W. R. Louis, *The British Empire in the Middle East* (Oxford, 1984), p. 55.

[28] For the broader background in Anglo-American discussions, see Christopher Thorne, *Allies of a Kind: The United States, Britain, and the War against Japan, 1941–1945* (London, 1978).

World War, the British Minister to China, Sir John Jordan, had argued that Hong Kong should be returned as part of the peace settlement, thereby helping the British come to terms with ascendant Chinese nationalism.[29] During the inter-war period, Sir John Pratt, the principal authority on China at the Foreign Office, had continued to press the case on grounds that Britain could retain by treaty the advantages of trade and commerce without the provocation of a territorial enclave.[30] After the outbreak of fighting between China and Japan in 1937, the prospect of holding the colony for another half-century probably seemed increasingly remote. After the surrender of Hong Kong and the fall of Singapore a few years later, it certainly did.

In the aftermath of the Japanese conquest of Hong Kong in December 1941, the Foreign Office pursued the logic of relinquishing the colony for the sake of friendly Anglo-Chinese relations.[31] The British, already powerless against the Japanese, would be equally impotent against resurgent the Chinese nationalism represented by the Kuomintang, especially if Chiang Kai-shek were supported by the United States.[32] In mid-1942, the Colonial Office reluctantly agreed that Hong Kong might be ceded as part of a post-war settlement. But by mid-1945, the assessment of the Hong Kong issue had shifted. By then it was clear that the reassertion of Nationalist authority in China would be possible only with American military and political support. Hong Kong became an issue of contention between Franklin Delano Roosevelt and Winston Churchill. The President made it clear that the British, in his view, upheld an antiquated colonial system and that the restoration of Hong Kong would help bolster Chiang Kai-shek's China

[29] This is one of the themes of W. R. Louis, *British Strategy in the Far East, 1919–1939* (Oxford, 1971).

[30] See Sir John Pratt, *War and Politics in China* (London, 1943).

[31] The wartime debate about the future of Hong Kong can be traced in CO 825/38/20; CO 825/42/B15; FO 371/31671; FO 371/35824; FO 371/41657; FO 371/46251; FO 371/46257; FO 371/46259; and FO 371/53629. See Lau Kit-ching Chan, 'The Hong Kong Question during the Pacific War (1941–1945)', *Journal of Imperial and Commonwealth History*, 2 (1973–74), pp. 56–78; and, by the same author, 'The United States and the Question of Hong Kong, 1941–1945', *Journal of the Hong Kong Branch of the Royal Asiatic Society*, 19 (1979), pp. 1–20.

[32] For example:

> Americans who have no special knowledge of the Far East naturally know and care very little about Hong Kong . . . [I]f at any time the question of the future of Hong Kong were raised in the United States it is pretty certain that the American public, taking a sentimental view of China, and being generally critical of colonial rule, would side against Great Britain and with China.

'American Opinion regarding Hong Kong', FO Memorandum, 7 August 1943, FO 371/35824.

as one of the 'four policemen' (along with Britain, the Soviet Union, and the United States) of the post-war order. Churchill made it equally clear that he would not yield Hong Kong and that he regarded Nationalist China as a puppet of the United States.[33] In this instance, Churchill held the upper hand. By early 1945, a sea change had taken place in the American security plans, which became policy after Roosevelt's death in April.[34] Instead of insisting on the liquidation of the British Empire, the United States increasingly saw advantages in sustaining an ally that held bases and colonies with strategic resources throughout the world.[35] The US government, without abnegating its historic role as intermediary between the forces of European imperialism and emerging Asian nationalism, now tended, not always (as in the case of Palestine) but generally, to support the British. At the end of the Pacific war, President Harry Truman agreed to the Japanese surrender of Hong Kong to British forces.[36] On 30 August, Admiral Sir Cecil Harcourt re-established British control over Hong Kong with the cruiser *Swiftsure,* the battleship *Anson,* two aircraft carriers, eight destroyers, and eight submarines.[37]

The British reoccupation of Hong Kong and other Asian dependencies, including Malaya, took place under the umbrella of American military supremacy. So also did Chiang Kai-shek's attempt to reassert control over China. Hong Kong was, in comparison, a minor issue. By late 1945, 100,000 Nationalist troops had passed through Hong Kong for deployment in the north. According to the commander of British troops in the China theatre, Major-General L. C. Hayes, '[O]ne was left with an impression that the Chinese have not only accepted without rancour our return to Hong Kong but are even relieved to find us there ready to lend a helping hand in any way we can.'[38] Chiang took the expedient view that Hong Kong was Chinese territory merely under temporary British administration. In the meantime, Nationalist troops, using transportation facilities of the US Army, Air Force, and Navy, managed temporarily to secure key cities

[33] The most recent comprehensive analysis of these questions is by Warren F. Kimball, *The Juggler: Franklin Roosevelt as Wartime Statesman* (Princeton, 1991), chap. 7.

[34] For the shift in American policy from the dominance of the 'trusteeship' idea to that of security, see W. R. Louis, *Imperialism at Bay* (Oxford, 1977).

[35] See W. R. Louis and Ronald Robinson, 'The Imperialism of Decolonization', *Journal of Imperial and Commonwealth History,* 22 (September 1994), pp. 462–511.

[36] See *Foreign Relations of the United States, 1945: The Far East, China,* VII, p. 509.

[37] For the events of the surrender and its aftermath in Hong Kong, see especially Louis Allen, *The End of the War in Asia* (London, 1976), pp. 251–54.

[38] L. C. Hayes to G. A. Wallinger (Chunking), 26 November 1945, FO 371/46259.

and most railway lines in eastern and northern China. But Communist troops occupied much of the hinterland in the north and in Manchuria. Such was the shadow of the Chinese civil war over Hong Kong.

The military administration lasted some eight months from the end of the Pacific war, after which Sir Mark Young resumed a broken Governorship. In his earlier tour of duty, he had arrived in Hong Kong from service as Tanganyika's Governor only a few months before the Japanese invasion in December 1941.[39] On Christmas Day, he became the first Governor ever to surrender a Crown Colony, but he had personified the Churchillian spirit of resistance in its East Asian manifestation with his message before the fall of Hong Kong: 'Fight on! Hold fast for King and Empire! God bless you all in this your finest hour!'[40] Young had been educated at Eton and King's College, Cambridge. By no means an intellectual, he was a stern and rather autocratic personality who nevertheless exuded good will. He was respected by the British community in Hong Kong as a natural leader. A contemporary recalled that he was 'very authoritarian' and 'intimidating'.[41] He could also be charming and persuasive.[42] Despite Foreign Office qualms that his reincarnation as Governor would signify a continuation of the old Imperial system, he again took control of the civil administration in May 1946. His tenure lasted only until July of the next year, but it is significant for the present analysis because of the way he dealt with the Kuomintang in Hong Kong and because of his attempt to democratize the Hong Kong government. Had he remained Governor more than a mere year, he might have set Hong Kong on a course towards responsible or representative government, which might in turn have changed not merely the colony's subsequent political evolution but its relationship with China.

Young vigorously proposed constitutional reform as a means of preventing the absorption of the colony by China. It is important to grasp the motive behind his scheme as well as the reaction to it in London, especially in the Foreign Office but also in the Colonial Office. Officials in the Colonial Office, with one important exception, tended

[39] After a brief internment at the Peninsula Hotel in Hong Kong, Young spent the rest of the war as a prisoner of war in Manchuria. The continuity in the civil administration had been maintained by Franklin Gimson (Colonial Secretary), who with great courage and discipline provided leadership of the British prisoners of war at Stanley Camp, Hong Kong. The Foreign Office even in 1942 had recognized in Gimson a man of exceptional character. See L. H. Foulds, minute, 7 October 1942, FO 371/31671. Gimson later became Governor of Singapore.

[40] Quoted in Jan Morris, *Hong Kong: Epilogue to an Empire* (1988; Harmondsworth, 1993), p. 246. Morris's book is a popular but informed and perceptive account.

[41] Tsang, *Democracy Shelved*, p. 196.

[42] For example, see his minutes and letters in the Legislative Council files, HK Secretariat 5/1136/49.

to defer to the Governor. The exception was N. L. Mayle, the head of the Hong Kong Department, who, by virtue of his position, was able to brake the speed with which Young hoped to move. Mayle appears to have had grave doubts about the Chinese capacity for representative government. With more sophistication, various officials in the Foreign Office implied that Young's proposal would have the opposite of the intended effect. Would not the introduction of democracy into a China port merely provoke the Chinese government? The Chinese, whether Nationalist or Communist, might well tolerate an enclave administered by Britain, but how would they respond to a grand design to hold Hong Kong in the British Empire and Commonwealth by popular consent? Especially in the Foreign Office, Hong Kong was viewed against the wider background of Anglo-Chinese relations: British measures of self-government would be interpreted as an attempt to install a collaborative and permanently hostile regime.[43] The evidence on this point is often more implicit than explicit, but there was an underlying pattern in the British response, especially in the Foreign Office, where Hong Kong was regarded as a China port involving intricate complications with China. Naturally enough, the Colonial Office, wary of China in a different way, viewed Hong Kong much more as a British colonial dependency and was more sympathetic towards measures of self-government.

Young's instinctive response to the question of Hong Kong's future was in line with the traditional Colonial Office policy of introducing representative government in gradual stages. Colonial subjects were allowed step-by-step to manage their own affairs. Young's formative years in the Colonial Service had been in Ceylon. He had also served in Sierra Leone, Palestine, Barbados, and Trinidad, in addition to Tanganyika. The weight of his administrative experience led him to apply the same lessons of constitutional progress that he had experienced elsewhere, especially in Ceylon, and even perhaps to think of the Chinese of Hong Kong as an 'advanced people', in Young's phrase, like the Sinhalese of Ceylon, who would develop a British allegiance. Young in fact did not know much about the Chinese. Shortly after his arrival in Hong Kong in 1941, he was interned by the Japanese. Grantham, by contrast, had begun his career in Hong Kong and had served there from 1922 to 1935.[44] Grantham held much more of a Foreign Office

---

[43] This is the interpretation cogently argued by N. J. Miners, 'Plans for Constitutional Reform in Hong Kong, 1946–52', *China Quarterly*, 107 (September 1986), pp. 463–82: 'Communist China could live with a colony ruled by British administrators but would not long have tolerated one which offered opportunities for its political opponents to attain power' (p. 482).

[44] The contrast between the two governors is developed fully in Tsang, *Democracy Shelved*, chap. 7.

than a Colonial Office viewpoint and believed that Hong Kong was essentially a Chinese port.[45] He certainly did not think that the Hong Kong Chinese would ever develop a British allegiance. They would merely be content to prosper under British rule. At the time, Grantham's assessment seemed realistic enough. Indeed, it was not until late in the day, in the 1980s, that the Chinese of the colony truly began to develop a 'Hong Kong identity'. On the other hand, Young's plan for democratization, had it been successful, might have promoted a similar sense of identity at an earlier stage.

To understand the question of British aims, and Young's specific motives, a word on the constitutional background is necessary. Hong Kong was a Crown Colony. The principle of Crown Colony rule was that the colony was responsible to the Imperial authority in London, not to representatives either appointed or elected. Hong Kong was ruled by a Legislative Council, which was presided over by the Governor. It consisted of official members (officers of the colonial government) and unofficial members (appointed by the Governor). There was also an Executive Council, which was a policy-making body more or less the equivalent of the British Cabinet, again with official and unofficial members. Young wanted to leave this system intact but to establish at a lower level a representative Municipal Council. The Legislative Council would continue to consist of 'loyal British subjects', but the municipal council would be elected on a popular franchise.[46] In British constitutional parlance, this was a form of dyarchy, or parallel government, which had been developed in India. The British administration would continue to control such vital functions of government as finance and security, but the creation of a municipal council would allow the inhabitants of Hong Kong a fuller share in the management of their own affairs, as they already had, for example, in the rather restricted area of municipal sanitation.[47]

Young believed in the gradual 'transfer of responsibility' as he had experienced it in Ceylon. In his own words, Hong Kong needed 'to develop an active sense of citizenship and to become capable of openly expressing and giving practical effect to the general desire of its

---

[45] Grantham held such emphatic views on the subject of Hong Kong and China that one can only wonder whether CO officials assessing his credentials at the time of his appointment as Governor took his outlook into account. The decision itself appears to have been determined mainly by Grantham's administrative record as one of the outstanding colonial civil servants of his generation.

[46] Young to Creech Jones, No. 255, Secret, 7 February 1947, FO 371/63387.

[47] 'Whatever its constitutional backwardness in other respects', John Darwin has written, 'Hong Kong recognised the principle of no sanitation without representation' (Darwin, 'Hong Kong in British Decolonisation', p. 20).

inhabitants [if it were so] to remain under British rule and to resist absorption by China'.[48] Part of Young's plan reflected British colonial policy dating back to the lessons learned from the American Revolution: by giving colonial subjects a voice in their own affairs, they would be co-opted as collaborators in the Imperial system. Nationalists would be conciliated before they could turn into anti-British extremists. In Hong Kong, however, there was good reason to doubt whether Young's use of conventional wisdom would apply to a population that was almost entirely Chinese. Young himself admitted that there were dilemmas virtually beyond solution. He rejected out of hand the idea that the members of the new Municipal Council should be restricted to the British. But what would be the proportion of the Chinese representation? What would prevent the Kuomintang from penetrating the Municipal Council and subverting it into an instrument for incorporation with China?[49] Young's answer to the question of possible subversion was as follows: 'There can be no shadow of a doubt that Chinese political parties would seek to use the Municipal Council for their own ends. It is consequently most necessary . . . that the constitution should be framed as to preclude the possibility of the Council concerning itself with political matters, particularly in relation to the future status of the Colony.'[50] In other words, in matters of political importance, the colonial administration would remain an autocracy.

Young's plan for constitutional reform met with resistance, for different reasons, in the Colonial Office and Foreign Office, though in Hong Kong itself the general response was apathetic. A small number of politically articulate Chinese supported the plan, but there was an element that feared the influence of the Kuomintang and corrupt politics at the municipal level. At the Colonial Office, the proposal encountered a host of objections, not least from the Secretary of State himself, Arthur Creech Jones, who disliked the plan for a Municipal Council and thought that the Legislative Council itself ought to be democratized.[51] In essence, he proposed as an alternative the gradual creation of a ministerial government, a miniature of the Westminster system. Creech Jones had the reputation of having his heart in the right place but also, at least on occasion, of connecting his mind to his

---

[48] Young to Secretary of State, Confidential, 22 October 1946, CO 537/1651. See the illuminating and useful editorial comment by Frederick Madden and John Darwin, eds., *The Dependent Empire, 1900–1948: Colonies, Protectorates, and Mandates—Select Documents on the Constitutional History of the British Empire and Commonwealth* (Westport, Conn., 1994), VII, pp. 389–93.

[49] These issues are raised in Young to Secretary of State, 7 February 1947, FO 371/63387.

[50] Young to Secretary of State, Confidential, 22 October 1946, CO 537/1651.

[51] See, for example, his minutes in CO 537/1651 and also the revealing file in the Creech Jones Papers, Box 57.

political instincts in a fuzzy sort of way. He was capable of sustained and creative thought, but on Hong Kong his proposals did not cohere. Perhaps he was too preoccupied with the problem of Palestine, which in 1947 was all-consuming. In any event, Young brought the full weight of the Hong Kong Secretariat into play and secured the acquiescence of the Colonial Office in the plan for a Municipal Council. This was a watershed. Once committed to the plan, neither the Colonial Office nor Young's successor could disavow it. Young's scheme to liberalize the constitution by broadening the franchise for the election of the Municipal Council was made public in July 1947.

The plan's critics, whose voices became more articulate with the passing of time, perceived a danger in the cultivation of Hong Kong nationalism, or what Young referred to as a sense of identity.[52] Nothing would provoke Chinese reaction more quickly than an attempt by the British to create either a sense of separatism or something equivalent to a city-state that would reject the eventual re-absorption of Hong Kong into China. Britain could continue to rule in Hong Kong only with the acquiescence of the power controlling China, whether Nationalist or Communist. Young proposed to travel a different road, which might eventually have led to confrontation. The inaction of the British government, brought about mainly by Young's successor, Grantham, shaped the course for the next four decades. Grantham held the counter-assumption: Hong Kong would revert to China in 1997 and would not become a self-governing British city-state within the Commonwealth. His view in the long run proved to be accurate. Despite minor constitutional adjustments made by Grantham himself, and by successive Governors, Hong Kong remained decidedly unrepresentative until the last years of British administration.

The basic criticism of the Young plan, to which Young himself had no effective riposte, was that a democratically elected Municipal Council might fall under the control of the Kuomintang. In the immediate post-war years, as has been noted, the Hong Kong Secretariat continued to regard the Kuomintang as the principal enemy. It represented not merely the ruling party in China; Chiang Kai-shek also offered an alternative to the British administration in Hong Kong. It is now clear that the Hong Kong administration greatly exaggerated Chiang's effectiveness, agility, and general guile, and that a considerable amount of the inflated significance can be traced to the writings of the offi-

---

[52] For the complicated evolution of British views on democratization into the 1970s and later, see Tsang, *Appointment with China*, especially p. 117, and note 11 above. For an FO summary of the proposals for constitutional reform, see N. C. C. Trench, minute, 18 December 1950, FO 371/92213; for the Hong Kong administration's views, see Secretariat to CO, 7 November 1950, HK Secretariat 5/1136/49.

cial designated as the expert on China, the acting Secretary for Chinese affairs, Thomas Megarry. The key adviser on Chinese politics and culture, Megarry held the position equivalent to 'Oriental secretary' in other parts of the world. He possessed a reductionist and lively intellect, perceiving a gigantic conspiracy on the part of the Kuomintang. He believed that Chiang's influence in Hong Kong had significantly increased during the period of Japanese occupation. Operating in unoccupied China, the Kuomintang had secured 'a foothold in the Colony' by enlisting men of the Triad societies, or criminal gangs— 'underground desperadoes', as the British called them—to carry on subversive activities against the Japanese. The British administration attempted to counter the lingering underground influence of the Kuomintang 'by buying off the Triad bands', but there remained a larger philosophical and cultural problem: 'The Kuomintang has always put the education of Chinese youth in its political tenets, which of course are those of its founder Dr. Sun Yat Sen, in the forefront of its programme of propaganda. It is estimated that in Hong Kong the party has some thirty-five private schools under its influence.'[53] The Kuomintang, according to Megarry's analysis, attempted to intimidate and control by 'systematic blackmail' the Hong Kong newspapers and to dominate the seamen's unions: 'The method is to support individual unions in disputes as to wages and labour conditions.'[54]

Chiang Kai-shek would have been extremely pleased if the Kuomintang's influence had been anywhere near as great as that described in British secret reports, specifically in Megarry's. The exaggerated quality of the political reporting of the Hong Kong Secretariat at this time would not have been so significant had it not been for the Governor's relative lack of knowledge of Hong Kong and China. Partly because of his lack of expertise on China, Young relied on Megarry, whose reports in turn caused alarm in the Colonial Office. With only a few exceptions, officials in the Colonial Office generally knew less about Hong Kong than any other dependency.[55] The Colonial Office

[53] Megarry, memorandum, 27 November 1946, CO 537/1658.

[54] Ibid. For labour conditions, see the extensive report by C. K. Hawkins, the Labour officer in the Hong Kong administration, 10 June 1947, CO 537/2188. The views of Hawkins are useful among other reasons as a corrective to those of Megarry. So also are the minutes throughout the HK Secretariat files of D. M. MacDougall, the Colonial Secretary (equivalent more or less to the Permanent Under-Secretary in the Colonial Office). MacDougall was the mandarin of the colonial administration, a man of wide knowledge of China, sympathy with Chinese sensitivities, and clear judgement. Nevertheless, on the subject of Chinese political aims, Megarry's views carried weight.

[55] One notable exception was (Sir) Sydney Caine, who had served in Hong Kong as Financial Secretary before the Second World War and who became the foremost economic adviser in the Colonial Office after the war. (He eventually became director of the London School of Eco-

was thus deficient in the vital function of intelligence. There was a certain corrective by the Foreign Office, but in general, Colonial Office views on Chinese politics up to the end of the Young administration in May 1947 were paranoid and distorted.

Publicly, the Hong Kong administration consistently aimed at doing nothing that would dignify or inflate the significance of the Kuomintang in the eyes of Hong Kong Chinese. Young wrote in March 1947, at the end of his tenure, that it was important to keep all public recognition of Kuomintang officials at a distance, as if they were 'not a matter of great importance to this Government'.[56] Young's successor, Grantham, pursued the same tactic. 'The policy I have consistently followed since my arrival [in July 1947] in the Colony', Grantham wrote, 'has been to refrain studiously from anything which will give the Kuomintang "face" in the eyes of the Chinese population.'[57] Grantham, like his predecessor, was determined to prevent the Kuomintang from creating, in Megarry's words, 'an "imperium in imperio" . . . undermin[ing] the foundations of our administration.'[58] Grantham, however, often used public rhetoric that disguised his actual views. He held a much more realistic assessment of the influence of the Kuomintang than did his predecessor and, most assuredly, than did Megarry. Grantham did not believe that the leaders of the Kuomintang (as distinct from local functionaries) wished to destabilize Hong Kong or that Chiang had plans for a campaign of immediate retrocession. Grantham correctly judged that Chiang was occupied with more pressing issues.

Grantham once remarked that he faced two problems as Governor. The first was the tradition of the British community in Hong Kong to defer to him as an almost godlike figure. The other was the opposite tendency of the Colonial Office, to regard him as a sub-department. There is little if any evidence that the deference to his position caused Grantham any distress, but he emphatically resented his treatment by the Colonial Office. He held that Hong Kong would have been much better off if it had been under Foreign Office rather than Colonial Office jurisdiction. In Grantham's view, Hong Kong from beginning

---

nomics.) In general, the career pattern of officers in the Colonial Service did not produce, as in the Foreign Office, 'old China hands'. For the Foreign Office, China was a major concern; for the Colonial Office, Hong Kong was an exotic though lucrative appendage.

[56] Young to Secretary of State, No. 13, Top Secret, 17 April 1947, FO 371/63388.

[57] Grantham to Secretary of State, No. 19, Top Secret, 28 May 1948, HK Secretariat 5/1162/46.

[58] Megarry, memorandum, 27 November 1946, CO 537/1658. Megarry waxed almost lyrical on the danger of the Kuomintang: the British must be vigilant 'to secure that this Party shall not . . . manoeuvre a unilateral resumption of the territory and meanwhile batten on its wealth and bend the populace to its will by methods of subtle intimidation'.

to end should always have been viewed as part of China, and thus relations with China were always paramount, not issues of the Legislative or Municipal Councils. With a deft use of the technique of the blind eye, whereby he ignored or manipulated the Colonial Office bureaucracy, Grantham often got his way. He had a buccaneer streak in his personality but was also outgoing and friendly. Having spent his formative years in the colony, he moved easily in Hong Kong business circles. He was consistently sensitive to charges that the Europeans in Hong Kong were reactionaries and that the Hong Kong administration was an autocracy. For example, he wrote in 1954: 'It is quite untrue to think of Hong Kong, as she is not infrequently represented, either as a happy hunting ground for dubious commercial adventurers who are only too ready to play China's game so long as their own interests benefit thereby, or as a reactionary quasi-Police State where exotic liberalism soon withers in the mid-day sun.'[59]

By virtue of his ten-year tenure (1947–57), Grantham acquired one of the longest service records in modern British colonial history as Governor of a single colony. During this time he witnessed the fall of the Nationalist government at the capital of Nanjing, the expulsion of the British community from Shanghai, the British recognition of the People's Republic, and the Korean War. Towards the end of his term, he was able to draw a comparison between the events of the Hungarian revolution in 1956 and the revolution he had witnessed in China.[60] For the history of Hong Kong, he is significant for the part he played in the stabilization of relations between the colony and the People's Republic, but that outcome was by no means obvious when he took charge in July 1947, during the Chinese civil war.[61]

Grantham was at ease not merely with the merchants of Hong Kong, Chinese as well as British, but also with some of the generals and leading political figures of Nationalist China. His principal point of contact was with T. V. Soong (the brother of Madame Chiang Kai-shek), who had served as one of Chiang's principal ministers and was appointed Governor of neighbouring Guangdong province in October 1947. With a political touch that enabled him to form alliances with unlikely figures, Grantham became an ally of sorts with Soong.

[59] Grantham to Secretary of State, LM 210/54, Confidential, 22 December 1954, CO 1030/292.

[60] 'The world conscience which has recently been roused by the plight of about 100,000 refugees from Hungary might well be awakened to the situation of five to six times that number who fled into Hong Kong in 1949–50' (Grantham to Secretary of State, 23 December 1956, CO 1030/384).

[61] On Britain and the Chinese civil war, see especially James Tuck-Hong Tang, *Britain's Encounter with Revolutionary China, 1949–54* (London, 1992); and Brian Porter, *Britain and the Rise of Communist China* (London, 1967).

It was Soong who took the initiative, pointing out to Grantham that having the Communists as a common enemy eclipsed the historic enmity between the Kuomintang and the British. Soong urged cooperation in such matters as police intelligence in Canton and Hong Kong. The British, he remarked to Grantham on one occasion, 'would not wish one of her Colonies to be used as a base for subversive activities against a friendly power'.[62] At another time Soong commented: 'I would like you to discuss with my men how Hongkong can assist us in return. You must realise that in helping us you are helping yourselves, because if the Communists come here God help Hongkong.'[63] Such conversations laid the basis for limited but significant cooperation between the Chief Inspector of Police and officers in the Special Branch, or security service, in Hong Kong and their counterparts in Canton. Grantham himself during his first year made three visits to China, one of them to confer with Chiang Kai-shek.[64] Visits by members of Grantham's staff included that of the political adviser (equivalent to a Minister of Foreign Affairs) to Nanjing and Shanghai, and of the Financial Secretary to confer with officials of the Central Bank of China. The Governor thus quickly created the equivalent of an intelligence network at every level of administration and invigorated the Colonial Service, not least by impressing on cadet officers 'the importance of a knowledge of Chinese'.[65]

Although Grantham by nature was dynamic, gregarious, and slightly pugnacious, his decision to improve relations with the Nationalist Chinese expressed not so much his activist temperament as his calculated assessment of a shift in priorities in the Kuomintang. He had no intention of creating a special relationship; he merely judged that the Chinese Nationalists were now attempting to bring the British, and the Americans, into an alliance against the Communists. He wrote in May 1948 on how the local presence of the Kuomintang represented larger political trends: 'In political matters the Kuomintang in Hong Kong has concentrated on an anti-Communist line. Its chief aim has been to present the menace of Communism in such a way as to rally British and American feeling in support of the Nanking regime.' Grantham was certain that the conflict in China was connected in one way or another with the crisis in Europe and with the hardening of attitudes of

[62] Grantham to N. L. Mayle, Confidential, 22 November 1947, HKRS 41/9/5701/47.

[63] Grantham to Secretary of State, Secret, 7 July 1948, HK Secretariat 1276/45.

[64] 'I came away with the impression that the Generalissimo was surrounded by a court that cut him off from knowledge of the real state of affairs in China' (Grantham, *Via Ports,* p. 129).

[65] Grantham to Secretary of State, No. 190, Confidential, 3 August 1948, HKRS 41/9/5701/47.

both the British and the Americans towards the Soviet Union. Within the local compass of Hong Kong, the energies of those who sympathized with the Kuomintang had been redirected: 'So long as the present civil strife continues in China, the energies of the local [Kuomintang] Party are more likely to be concentrated towards counteracting Communist propaganda and boosting Nanking than towards embarrassing this [Hong Kong] Government.'[66]

In widening their contacts with the Nationalist Chinese, the British expected neither the Kuomintang to change their political philosophy nor the Chinese to base their actions on anything other than political calculation. 'It is common knowledge', Grantham wrote in early 1948, 'that this Colony has gone to great lengths to cooperate with China since the reoccupation, without receiving any recognition or thanks.'[67] The Chinese might well have made the same observation about the British, whose attitude towards the Kuomintang may have been less severe or suspicious than earlier, but it too was certainly based on self-interest. However, the British now began to believe that collaboration with the Nationalists would in any event have a short life. In January 1948, Grantham concluded on the basis of conversations with Nationalist military leaders that the civil war would spread to South China within three months.[68] Some months later, he commented to T. V. Soong that 'it was really a race against time, whether he [Soong] could solidify South China before there was a break-up in the North.'[69] By mid-1948, the answer had become obvious: Grantham reported Soong as saying in July 'that the National Government is slowly disintegrating'.[70] Soong believed that Chiang Kai-shek was still 'the only

[66] Grantham to Secretary of State, No. 19, Top Secret, 28 May 1948, HK Secretariat 5/1162/46. There was nevertheless one major incident that continued to strain Kuomintang–Hong Kong relations. In late 1947, the Hong Kong police evicted the residents of the Kowloon Walled City, a small compound of six acres in the Kowloon peninsula over which the Chinese continued to claim sovereignty. In the view of the Hong Kong administration, the 'Walled City' (the 'walls' had long been razed) was a health menace and a haven for criminals, but after the police fired on squatters, Chinese protesters in Canton burned down the British Consulate in January 1948. The circumstances of an international incident deriving from 'squatters and criminals' occupying a congested plot of land, the legal title to which was obscure, led to unending exasperation in the Hong Kong Secretariat and inspired a piece of doggerel: 'I saw a City stone-wall bound, / A little one that can't be found. / It wasn't there again today, / I wish that it would go away' (HK Secretariat 1/1166/47).

[67] Grantham to Secretary of State, 17 January 1948, FO 371/69577.

[68] Grantham to British Ambassador in Nanking, No. 4, Secret, 16 January 1948, HK Secretariat 3/1167/47.

[69] Grantham to Mayle, Secret, 5 April 1948, HKRS 41/9/5701/47.

[70] Grantham to Sidebotham, Secret, 2 August 1948, enclosing a note on a talk with Soong of 31 July 1948, CO 537/3326.

man in China' who could save the situation, but the British took Soong's remark merely as another example of the accumulating and overwhelming evidence that the Nationalist position was now hopeless.

The thrust of my interpretation so far has been that the complex and sometimes subtle interaction between the Governor of Hong Kong, the Colonial Office, and the Foreign Office determined the overall policy of the British government. On many matters, the Governor often had his way. The government in London, not surprisingly, deferred to local expertise on financial, defence, and political issues unique to Hong Kong. The question of constitutional reform and representative government is a case in point. Young's command of the situation in Hong Kong and his tenacity in pursuing the issue in London allowed him to achieve a victory in favour of his scheme for broadening the franchise and electing a municipal government. Grantham succeeded in reversing course through a combination of evasive action and a commitment to a different sort of constitutional reform. He had a different set of priorities. He upheld the principle of the Legislative Council and believed that the Hong Kong version of it might be made more representative in minor ways. But he also believed that Hong Kong, a port and a part of China, could never support the Westminster model in the same way that colonial policy had evolved earlier in his career in Jamaica, Nigeria, and even Fiji. (None of those territories, it should be added, were foremost in the movement towards self-government during Grantham's years of service.) On the other hand, Grantham was concerned, in the words of his constitutional adviser, not to make Hong Kong's Legislative Council a 'laughing stock'.[71] Grantham introduced minor reforms to prove that he was not retrograde, and it is significant that, building on the design of his predecessor, he acquired the reputation of a forward-looking Governor. On the whole, however, he was 'very much inclined', as he wrote in 1951, 'to agree with the F.O.' and to put constitutional reform 'in cold storage'.[72] Perhaps it was a blessing in disguise for the British, at the time and later, that Grantham sabotaged Young's project of democratization and the fostering of a British allegiance in a city-state that was to be an integral part of the Empire and Commonwealth. Assuming

[71] W. J. Carrie, minute, 24 August 1950, HK Secretariat 5/1136/49.

[72] Grantham, minute, 14 January 1951, and Grantham to J. J. Paskin, Secret, 12 February 1952, HK Secretariat 5/1136/49. In 1950, Grantham had visited London and conducted extensive discussions with officials in the Colonial Office and the Foreign Office. See, for example, the important notes dated 4 July 1950, in Ronald Hyam, ed., *British Documents on the End of Empire: The Labour Government and the End of Empire, 1945–1951* (4 vols., London, 1992), II, no. 172.

it was even possible, would the achievement of Young's purpose have been countenanced by the People's Republic? Grantham, for one, thought not.[73]

On the issue of the critical year 1949 and the fate of Hong Kong, one might be tempted to believe that here, too, the Governor realized his goal of prodding the British government into defending the colony. It was Grantham who challenged London to prove that the British had the willpower not to scuttle. On this as on other issues, however, there was a discrepancy between Grantham's public pronouncements, his advice to the Colonial Office, and his own assessment. He was less alarmed than many of his contemporaries at the prospect of a Communist takeover, and his public statements as well as his admonitions to the British government appear to have been made with the motive of reassuring the British community in Hong Kong. The key decisions, however, were made in London, where the Governor's influence, and indeed that of the Colonial Office, played only a minor part.

To understand the decisions made on Hong Kong in 1949, one must look to the upper reaches of the Labour Government, particularly to Clement Attlee, the Prime Minister, and Ernest Bevin, the Foreign Secretary. Bevin dominated all discussions on foreign affairs and, to a large extent, colonial matters when they impinged on foreign policy. He attempted on all issues to work in concert with Attlee, who, Bevin noted, was 'deeply involved' in the issue of Hong Kong because of the ongoing economic review of defence commitments.[74] Usually, but not always, Attlee followed Bevin's lead. Tough-minded, efficient, and succinct to the point of abruptness, Attlee held independent views

[73] The Chinese side remains a matter of speculation. As has been mentioned previously (note 11 above), Mao Tse-tung did not venture a view one way or another about the proposed democratization of Hong Kong. Indeed, he and Chou En-lai (Foreign Minister) were not only vague on the subject but seemed to have, not surprisingly, only a rudimentary knowledge of the British colonial system, in which colonies progressed through stages of self-government to achieve Dominion Status or independence within the Commonwealth. There can be no doubt, however, that Young and Grantham recognized the alternative goals of keeping Hong Kong within the Empire or anticipating its eventual return to China. As the issue developed in later decades, it was a reasonable assumption that the Chinese would have objected in the strongest terms to Hong Kong becoming an independent city-state within the Commonwealth. See Tsang, *Appointment with China*, pp. 117–19, which draws on Chinese sources and offers a slightly different interpretation.

[74] Bevin, minute, *c.*19 March 1946, FO 371/53632. Attlee, who himself was Minister of Defence (as well as Prime Minister) until December 1946, used the Defence Committee of the Cabinet as the executive arm of the Cabinet to discuss such issues. See, for example, CAB 131/1. On Bevin, see Alan Bullock, *Ernest Bevin: Foreign Secretary, 1945–1951* (London, 1983), especially p. 720.

and sometimes did not trust Bevin's judgement—as, for example, on the question of India. He had to be persuaded that Bevin had devoted his mind to a problem and had integrated it into what they both regarded as the basic philosophy of the Labour Government. On the question of Hong Kong, the Prime Minister and Foreign Secretary saw eye to eye. When the two of them linked up with another minister, in this case A. V. Alexander (First Lord of the Admiralty until December 1946, then Minister of Defence), it was usually an unbreakable combination.

Since 1946, Bevin had followed the Hong Kong issue only sporadically. When it did command his attention, he usually concurred in the views of the Permanent Under-Secretary at the Foreign Office, Sir Orme Sargent, an official who in a sense personified the post-war consensus on the lessons of the 1930s. In 1946, Sargent and Bevin were provoked by George Kitson's 'Isle of Wight analogy' and the proposal to hand over Hong Kong to China as a gesture of friendship. Sargent wrote that it would be 'a complete delusion' to believe that concessions in Hong Kong would 'buy Chinese good will'.[75] In words that summed up one side of the controversy over Hong Kong's future, he continued:

> The fact is that if we do abandon any part of our present position in Hong Kong, including the New Territories, it will be either because we have no longer the physical means (military and financial) to maintain our position or because we anticipate that sooner or later the Chinese Government will be able to hold us to ransom by paralysing our trade and administration in Hong Kong.[76]

Bevin noted, 'I agree with Sargent,' thus closing, not quite for ever but almost, the protracted wartime debate whether Hong Kong ought to

[75] Sargent, minute, 19 March 1946, FO 371/53632. Two years earlier, G. F. Hudson, one of the leading British historians advising the Foreign Office on East Asia during the war, had written:
> [W]e should get no gratitude from China for a unilateral 'gesture' of rendition. But it is important that the rendition, if it is to be made, should be made on principle as recognition of China's services to the cause of the United Nations [i.e. the wartime alliance], and not on grounds of geographical and ethnic claims by China; otherwise it would serve as a precedent for Gibraltar.

Hudson, minute, 10 July 1944, FO 371/41657. Hudson was a Fellow of All Souls College, Oxford. His books included *The Far East in World Politics* (London, 1937).

[76] Sargent, minute, 19 March 1946, FO 371/53632.

be returned to the Chinese.[77] Bevin did not, however, suggest at this stage anything other than a negative, defensive stance whereby the British would do nothing and say nothing about the status of Hong Kong. For the next two years the Colonial Office, in response to requests from Governor Grantham for a more assertive public statement, importuned the Foreign Office, but with the same result.[78] As a Foreign Office official summed it up, 'The Colonial Office have pressed at intervals since 1946 for an authoritative statement on the Colony's future and we have advised the Secretary of State to resist.'[79] In the judgement of the Foreign Office, it was best to let the issue lie dormant.

With public interest roused because of deteriorating conditions in China, the Foreign Office in the summer of 1948 faced parliamentary inquiries about the future of Hong Kong. The Assistant Under-Secretary supervising Far Eastern affairs, Michael Wright, wrote: 'Our object is to retain Hong Kong for as long as we can, but we have to face the fact that it is in the power of the Chinese whether by boycott or otherwise to render our position in Hong Kong untenable.' He therefore advised that the issue should be kept as quiet as possible by persuading members of Parliament to withdraw questions about the future of the colony: 'This seems to be a classic case of the wisdom of letting sleeping dogs lie.'[80] Sargent held a much more aggressive view, in part because of the moral to be drawn from the story of appeasement in the late 1930s. He, too, wanted to avoid public debate, but if it proved necessary, then the Foreign Office should concur with the Colonial Office and make it clear to the world that Hong Kong was and would remain British: 'If we once begin to hedge and qualify we shall not only demoralise our friends in Hong Kong—not to mention the British officials there—but we shall also encourage the Chinese hot-heads to start an agitation in the hope of pushing us still further down the slope of appeasement.'[81] On this occasion Bevin did not

[77] For later reassessments of Britain's position in Hong Kong and the resumption of the debate, see Tsang, *Appointment with China*, chaps. 4–5.

[78] For the debate in the Colonial Office and Grantham's assertion that the Chinese in Hong Kong believed that 'in a showdown', the British would 'desert the Colony', see CO 537/3702, particularly the minute by Sidebotham, 11 June 1948. See also minutes in HK Secretariat 1/1166/47C.

[79] Peter Scarlett (head of the Far Eastern Department of the Foreign Office), minute, 8 June 1948, FO 371/69582A. For the corresponding debate in the Colonial Office, see CO 537/3702.

[80] Michael Wright, minute, 8 June 1948, FO 371/69582A. For similar American estimates of deteriorating conditions in China, based on intelligence reports of 'incompetence, corruption and lack of popular support' of the Nationalist government, see Nanking to Washington, No. 701, Secret, 27 April 1948, USSD HK, File 800, Box 7.

[81] Sargent, minute, 8 June 1948, FO 371/69582A.

follow the advice of the Permanent Under-Secretary. Bevin was watching the course of the Chinese civil war, in which he wished to stay as neutral as possible. He did not want to stir up either side on the issue of Hong Kong. His temperament did not allow him to leave things to chance, but he moved with caution. He would go no further than agreeing to an announcement in Parliament on 7 July 1948: the British government anticipated no change in the status of Hong Kong.

In mid-1948 the Colonial Office was swept into the mainstream of debate, though with the Colonial Secretary as a junior partner to the Foreign Secretary. Creech Jones stood in the shadow of Bevin. 'Creech', as he was known in Labour circles, had long regarded himself as a lieutenant to Bevin in the Labour movement, and the relationship continued in the affairs of the Labour Government. The Colonial Secretary thus resisted pressure from the Governor and from within the Colonial Office to make a strong statement that the British would hold their own in Hong Kong.[82] He wanted to avoid confrontation in Cabinet discussions, in which Bevin would predominate. 'I do not relish a decision against us,' Creech Jones wrote to his staff.[83] He concurred in Bevin's view that the colony might be held if the British could keep on as good terms as possible with the Communists yet convince them that Hong Kong could not be taken without stiff resistance.

The mood in the Colonial Office was sombre—indeed, alarmist—as revealed especially in the reaction of officials to a newspaper report entitled 'War Threat to Helpless Hong Kong'. The author was Patrick O'Donovan, a columnist respected in the Colonial Office for balanced views. O'Donovan wrote in December 1948 that the British in Hong Kong seemed to be 'tiptoeing between two extremes'. In a passage that was underscored in ink in the Colonial Office, the article stated:

> Certainly the administration's task is delicate. There are more than 1,500,000 Chinese in the colony, and a few thousand Britishers, Portuguese, Eurasians and Indians. *Only a few hundred Chinese feel any profound loyalty to the Crown.*

[82] There was one prominent exception to the consensus in the Colonial Office that Hong Kong should be held. Sir Charles Jeffries, the constitutional authority, believed Hong Kong to be so exceptional that it should be administered by Britain as a 'free city' under 'a special trusteeship'. See Jeffries, memorandum, 25 May 1949, Creech Jones Papers, Box 57, file 1. This was the last flicker of the old wartime controversy whether Hong Kong ought to be returned to China, perhaps with UN trusteeship as an intermediary stage. Some members of the Cabinet found this solution attractive, at least as a fall-back position. Bevin resisted it, though did not entirely rule it out. See Hyam, *British Documents on the End of Empire*, II, no. 170.

[83] Creech Jones, minute, 22 June 1948, CO 537/3702.

The last war demonstrated the extreme vulnerability of the island. The present garrison is scarcely sufficient to maintain law and order. The island could be crippled instantly by a Communist-called general strike.[84]

On the sentence about loyalty, one Colonial Office official commented: 'One of the few press articles I have seen which really faces the hard facts.'[85]

The 'hard facts' were much more ambiguous. Grantham did not believe that the Chinese who now took down portraits of Chiang Kai-shek would be any more inclined to espouse the cause of communism or that underlying Chinese sympathies in Hong Kong would change in any way. He thought that the Chinese population of Hong Kong favoured British rule, though he kept a close eye out for subversive elements within the administration, especially in the police.[86] Grantham knew that the Communists in the past had not attempted to destabilize Hong Kong, and he believed that they probably would not do so in the immediate future. He was far less concerned with ideological issues than were officials in the Colonial Office and the Foreign Office. To Grantham, what mattered was the efficiency and discipline of the Communists. They had to be persuaded that it would be in their own interest not to interfere in Hong Kong. He made aggressive public statements, but his purpose was to steady the Europeans as well as the Chinese in Hong Kong and to demonstrate that the British would not desert them. At the same time, he feared that the Labour Government might indeed abandon the colony—thus, his demands for a statement that the British would hold Hong Kong come what may. In the spring of 1949, he increasingly argued that such a public reassurance was imperative, especially in view of the disastrous *Amethyst* incident.[87]

In April 1949, Chinese Communist troops had opened fire and grounded a British gunboat, HMS *Amethyst,* on its way up the Yangtze from Shanghai to Nanjing. The captain, Lieutenant Commander B. M. Skinner, died of his injuries. Rescue attempts by the Royal Navy proved futile. The Communists held the *Amethyst* captive until late July, when it managed to escape by night downriver under the command of an

[84] Patrick O'Donovan, 2 December 1948, in CO 537/3702 (emphasis in the original). O'Donovan was the special correspondent of the *Daily Post* in Hong Kong.

[85] Minute, 6 December 1948, CO 537/3702.

[86] See the intelligence assessment in Chiefs of Staff (49) 12, 7 January 1949, DEFE 5/13, which reported Grantham's view that 'Chinese members of the Police Force cannot be regarded as wholly reliable.'

[87] See Malcolm H. Murfett, *Hostage on the Yangtze: Britain, China, and the 'Amethyst' Crisis of 1949* (Annapolis, Md., 1991).

assistant naval attaché at the British Embassy in Nanjing, Lieutenant Commandeer J. S. Kerans. The *Amethyst* broke free from the coast and sailed to Hong Kong, where the crew received a tumultuous, jubilant reception. In England, the press and public regarded the escape as a daring act of bravery, but in fact the *Amethyst* episode had humiliated the navy. Far from the anti-Communist victory depicted in the newspapers, a British ship had been held hostage for over a hundred days and had managed to escape only under cover of darkness. It was during the time of the *Amethyst* captivity that the Cabinet made the critical decisions on Hong Kong. There was a prevailing sense of anger and frustration. (One is reminded of the statement by Winston Churchill in the 1920s: 'Punishing China is like flogging a jelly fish.') Grantham described the mounting anxiety in Hong Kong in May 1949: '[T]he public reaction here to the crossing of the Yangtze, the fall of Nanking, and the forthcoming fall of Shanghai . . . have had a profound effect on public opinion.' The attack on the *Amethyst* had 'gravely aggravated' an already troubled public mood.[88]

In the forefront of official deliberation was the impression conveyed by the Governor that Hong Kong must now batten down and prepare against a possible Communist onslaught. Grantham, as has been seen, was in fact less alarmist than the Colonial Office, but his measured rhetoric was effective. Would the British government now at last issue a determined and vigorous statement that the colony would be held at any cost? Would such a declaration rouse the United States to support the British position in Hong Kong? According to a report drawn up on the basis of intelligence sources in Hong Kong in early 1949, the Communists in the colony itself were quiescent, but in view of the crumbling Nationalist position, the British would have to anticipate an attack:

> It still remains the policy of the Communists in Hong Kong to lie low and to avoid a head-on collision with the administration which would hamper their more overt activities . . . How long this policy will be maintained depends entirely on circumstances, but, as the Communist advance South of the Yangtze develops, a change to a more active attitude of hostility may be anticipated, and at any moment a decision by the Communist higher command to turn to the direct offensive [might also be anticipated].

[88] Grantham to Creech Jones, Top Secret, 3 May 1949, FO 371/75780. The dispatch provoked a comment in the Foreign Office on Grantham's 'bellicose' attitude (P. D. Coates, minute, 14 May 1949, FO 371/75780).

This would mean strikes internally and possibly guerrilla or direct military attack externally.[89]

The attack might not come in the immediate future, but the British would have to prepare for it. Grantham wrote in May 1949: 'Since the beginning, last summer, of the Chinese Communist armies' sweeping successes, there has been a growing though for the most part latent uneasiness, both in European and in Chinese circles here, about the future of this Colony.' He made it clear publicly that he detected an infirmity of will on the part of the British government. Unless a committed and determined attitude were struck, public morale would be undermined and the colony lost before it could be saved: 'The events of 1941, when the Hong Kong . . . defence [was] undertaken with an inadequate regular garrison, are freely recalled.' The matter was of utmost gravity: 'It is being said that neither British prestige nor British military strength is any longer adequate to safeguard British interests in the Far East.' Did Britain have the 'will' to defend Hong Kong?[90]

With the sweep of the Communist armies southward, the issue now rose to the highest levels of the British government.[91] In the context of Bevin's China policy, Attlee took the initiative in the Cabinet. The Prime Minister worked closely with the Defence Minister, A. V. Alexander, the Labour Government's stalwart on issues of defence. Steady, slow, and sound, the former First Lord of the Admiralty moved through the waters of the Far Eastern crisis with thoroughness and balanced judgement. He shared assumptions about the nature of Chinese Communism that were representative of members' of the Labour Government in the late 1940s.[92] Attlee, Bevin, and Alexander all believed that

[89] 'Report on Communist Activities in Hong Kong', in Grantham to Secretary of State, Secret, 23 February 1949, FO 371/75779. For a comparable American intelligence report on the 'overwhelmingly more capable and powerful' Communist position and corresponding danger to Hong Kong, see Nanking to Washington, No. 11, Secret, 1 April 1949, USSD HK, Box 10, File 350.2.

[90] Grantham to Secretary of State, Top Secret, 3 May 1949, FO 371/75780.

[91] For an acute comment, written before the release of archival material but informed by private papers, see D. C. Watt, 'Britain and the Cold War in the Far East, 1945–58', in Yonosuke Nagai and Akira Iriye, eds., *The Origins of the Cold War in Asia* (Tokyo, 1977), pp. 99–100; see also Feng, *British Government's China Policy*, pp. 117–22. There is a brief but comprehensive analysis of the problem by Hyam in the introduction to *British Documents on the End of Empire*, I, pp. liii–liv.

[92] The extensive minutes of Guy Burgess on the theory of Communism and the issue of Hong Kong are of interest in this regard. Burgess appears to have been at pains to depict 'the rigid and essential orthodoxy of Chinese Communist policy' (minute, 5 August 1949, FO 371/75749), a view that coincided with that of Bevin and others. No one reading Burgess's minutes would have anticipated, in my judgement, his later defection to the Soviet Union.

the Chinese Communists adhered to the philosophy of 'Marxist Le-
ninism', that they were aligned with the Soviet Union, and that the collapse of Hong Kong would lead to the fall of Malaya and the general
British position in South-East Asia.[93]

Attlee made the key statement defining British policy to the Cabinet on 26 May 1949. In the meeting itself there was powerful dissent.
Sir Stafford Cripps, the Chancellor of the Exchequer, thought that
Hong Kong ought to be abandoned, principally on grounds of economy but also because, like others, he believed holding it to be untenable: internal subversion combined with external pressure had created
a situation similar to that in Berlin but without any guarantee of American or, for that matter, Commonwealth support. Most members of
the Cabinet regarded Cripps's argument as defeatist. Attlee skilfully
marshalled a consensus by urging on his colleagues the proposition
that 'failure to meet this threat to the security of Hong Kong would
damage very seriously British prestige throughout the Far East and
South-East Asia'. He rested his case on the necessity to resist aggression. In the course of the discussion, there emerged three significant
points that he found most persuasive: 'Practical evidence of our determination to defend Hong Kong would have important consequences.
First, it might well deter the Communist forces from making a direct
attack on the Colony. Secondly, it would rally to our side the wavering
elements among the local population and would substantially reduce
the threat to internal security. Thirdly, it would strengthen the anti-
Communist front throughout South-East Asia.' The Cabinet discussion struck a note that echoed the lessons of appeasement and formed
part of the emerging domino theory: 'The maintenance of our trading position in Hong Kong was doubtless important; but even more
important at the present time was the political question whether we
must not somewhere make a stand against Communist encroachment
in East Asia. If we failed to make this stand in Hong Kong, should we
not find it much harder to make it elsewhere in South-East Asia?'[94]

[93] As almost in a litany, Attlee explained in a telegram to the Australian Prime Minister:
'Leaders of Chinese Communist Party are orthodox Marxist Leninists and there is no doubt that
their present strongly pro-Soviet policy constitutes serious threat to our political and economic interests not only in China but also in South East Asia' (Attlee to J. B. Chifley, Top Secret,
20 August 1949, AA 3318/1, L49/3/1/22/1). On the views of the Hong Kong Secretariat on the
theory of Communism, in HK Secretariat 21/3571/49, see, for example, G. A. Aldington, minute, 23 January 1952.

[94] Cabinet Minutes (49) 38, 26 May 1949, CAB 128/15; this and other important documents
are reproduced by Hyam, *British Documents on the End of Empire*, II, nos. 164–72. For the background of Attlee's decision, see PREM 8/945, especially Norman Brook, minutes, 12 and 19 May
1949. For the Foreign Office view at this time, see the minutes by Bevin's principal adviser on East
Asia, (Sir) Esler Dening, FO 371/75754, especially his comment of 13 May 1949. Dening and

The argument for the British holding fast can be summed up in Attlee's statement that 'the whole common front against Communism in Siam, Burma and Malay[a] was likely to crumble unless the peoples of those countries were convinced of our determination and ability to resist this threat to Hong Kong.'[95]

The extent of the commitment to defend Hong Kong remained debatable. Alexander had stated in the House of Commons on 5 May 1949 that Britain would strengthen the garrison in the colony, but the statement, though robust, was studiously vague. What would be the extent of the British reinforcement? How could the United States be drawn in to support the British cause? On the other hand, would not American support alienate the Chinese Communists still further? Could Australia and New Zealand be persuaded to contribute troops, ships, and aircraft? What of morale within Hong Kong? Could the colony be expected to defend itself? Alexander and Creech Jones debated the appointment of a Military Governor to replace Grantham.[96] Should there in any event be a unified command structure?

To answer those questions, Alexander left on 2 June for a marathon trip to the Far East, arriving in Hong Kong four days later. He conferred with the Governor and the military authorities, examining from all angles the central question: how far could Hong Kong be defended by its own forces and how much reinforcement would be necessary? The Minister of Defence aimed to convince the Governor that there needed to be a unified command structure in which the Commander-in-Chief could take immediate and effective action. Alexander explained the rationale:

> [T]he rapid advance of the Chinese Communist Forces made it imperative to ensure that any military or security measures could be taken without delays, which would go far to render them ineffective, and might lead to disaster in circumstances which would gravely affect the whole of the position in South-East Asia.[97]

---

others hoped that China might become 'another Yugoslavia' and thus more amenable to the British position in Hong Kong. See especially his further minute of 16 August 1949, FO 371/75766.

[95] Cabinet Minutes (49) 38, 26 May 1949, CAB 128/15. For the parallel between China in 1945–49 and Vietnam in 1961–65, see the sustained argument by Ernest R. May, *The Truman Administration and China, 1945–1949* (Philadelphia, 1975).

[96] See 'Disadvantages of Replacing the Civil Governor by a Service Governor', memorandum, Creech Jones Papers, Box 57, file 1, n.d. [probably May 1949], in which the Colonial Office successfully argued that replacing Grantham 'might well be interpreted as indicating that we regard an external attack on the Colony as inevitable. This would be bad for the morale of the population of Hong Kong and moreover might make an external attack more likely.'

[97] Alexander, memorandum, Top Secret, 17 June 1949, CAB 129/35; CO 537/4838.

After a sleepless night during which Grantham pondered the consequences of relinquishing part of his virtual dictatorship, he agreed to
the creation of a new post of Commander-in-Chief. (Grantham nevertheless reserved the right of appeal.) There was one further major
point of friction. In other colonies, notably Malaya, immigration controls and such security measures as the registration of all inhabitants
had proved to be the first steps towards effective internal security.
Grantham believed that similar measures in Hong Kong would stifle
trade and 'kill off the corpse'—in other words, the colony itself, which
would suffer a slow, perhaps even a quick, death and make the defence
more difficult because of the opposition that registration would arouse
among the Chinese. Alexander in effect wanted to close the border.
'We should lose all our trade with China,' Grantham remarked.[98] On
this point, the Governor held his ground, even though frontier controls were subsequently introduced in May 1950 to reduce the number of immigrants.

Alexander formed a high opinion of the Governor, but he found
the British business community in Hong Kong to be far less admirable,
especially on the issue of defence:

> The business people want the best of both worlds. They want ade-
> quate defence provided for their interests and persons, but nothing
> said about it, and to go on making money, indifferent to the ques-
> tions of principle which arise . . . Yet no successful defence of Hong
> Kong can be conducted which does not have regard to the dominat-
> ing position of the trading interests in the Colony.[99]

Alexander deferred to Grantham's judgement that the British community 'would be willing to play their part', yet Grantham himself was
sceptical regarding how long Hong Kong business firms would sustain financial losses before urging a compromise peace with the Communists.[100] In general, Alexander concluded that Hong Kong had
the capacity to demonstrate 'our will to resist aggression and . . . the
onward rush of communism in South-East Asia.'[101] Grantham believed that, with reinforcements, Hong Kong's position could be held
'indefinitely'.[102]

[98] Grantham to Secretary of State, No. 579, Top Secret, 14 June 1949, CO 537/4838.

[99] Alexander, memorandum, 17 June 1949.

[100] Grantham to Secretary of State,14 June 1949.

[101] Alexander, memorandum, 17 June 1949.

[102] Grantham to Secretary of State, 14 June 1949. Grantham and others, including the military planners, made this assessment by assuming that the Soviet Union would not intervene. In
the event of 'appreciable Russian help', Hong Kong would be 'indefensible'. See the extensive
estimate by Commanders-in-Chief, Far East, Top Secret Guard ['Guard' = not for American
eyes], 7 October 1949, COS (49) 330, DEFE 5/16.

Attlee and Alexander thought that the Australians and New Zealanders might see it in their own interest to contribute to the defence of the colony, perhaps with a battalion of troops, an aircraft carrier, and naval forces directly from Australia, perhaps by shifting a squadron of Mustang fighter planes from Japan, perhaps by naval support from New Zealand. The New Zealand Prime Minister, Peter Fraser, immediately volunteered the modest support of three frigates.[103] The Australian Labour Government of J. B. Chifley, however, declined the invitation, in the belief that Hong Kong would prove impossible to defend and that British action might lead to 'full-scale war' in China.[104] The British had held rather extravagant hopes for Australian support, which now had to be extracted from slender British resources. Depending on how one juggled the statistics, the reinforcement of Hong Kong might reduce the home defence of the British Isles to a single infantry brigade. In any case, it would involve the transfer of engineer and signal forces from Germany as well as a Royal Marines Commando brigade and an armoured regiment from the Middle East.[105] In the event, troop strength in Hong Kong increased from a few thousand to well over a division, including a Gurkha regiment, and by the autumn of 1949 there were some 30,000 troops supported by tanks, land-

[103] The developments on the New Zealand side can be traced in the file on Hong Kong NZ AAEG 950/389A (300/3/1); see especially Fraser's full exposition of the problem in Peter Fraser to J. B. Chifley, Top Secret and Personal, No. 77, 15 June 1949. See Ian McGibbon, *New Zealand and the Korean War* (2 vols., Auckland, 1992), I, pp. 37–38, for New Zealand's 'first peacetime defence commitment in South-East Asia'. I am grateful to Dr. McGibbon for his assistance in the New Zealand National Archives. For the reaction of other Commonwealth countries, especially India but also Canada, see Hyam, *British Documents on the End of Empire*, I, nos. 166–69.

[104] Chifley to Attlee, No. 85, Top Secret Personal, 15 June 1949, AA 3318/1, L49/3/1/22/1. H. V. Evatt, the Attorney General and Minister for External Affairs, played the key part in the Australian refusal. Evatt criticized both Britain and the United States as well as the Soviet Union for sustaining tensions in the Cold War. From the British perspective (and the American), he aimed to establish Australia as the successor to the British in the Pacific region. Evatt had been in London in the spring of 1949 and had led the British to believe that Australian support for Hong Kong would be forthcoming. On his return to Australia, however, he reversed himself. In any event, his refusal to support the British was in line with Chifley's disinclination. There is a valuable contemporary analysis of the sequence of these events by the New Zealand Permanent Secretary for External Affairs, A. D. McIntosh (memorandum, 16 June 1949, NZ AAEG 950/389A [300/3/1]). See David Lee, *Search for Security: The Political Economy of Australia's Postwar Foreign and Defence Policy* (Canberra, 1995), pp. 103–04; and Christopher Waters, *The Empire Fractures: Anglo-Australian Conflict in the 1940s* (Melbourne, 1995), pp. 183–88; see also E. M. Andrews, *Australia and China: The Ambiguous Relationship* (Melbourne, 1985), pp. 135–38. For Hong Kong in British-Australian-New Zealand strategic planning, see W. David McIntyre, *Background to the Anzus Pact: Policy-Making, Strategy and Diplomacy, 1945–55* (Basingstoke, UK, 1995), especially pp. 118, 141–42, 176. I am indebted to Dr. David Lee for his help in the Australian Archives.

[105] See, for example, Chiefs of Staff Committee, Joint Planning Staff, JP (49) 50 (Final), 17 May 1949, DEFE 6/9.

based fighter aircraft, and a substantial naval unit, including an aircraft carrier.[106] The scale of mobilization thus compared in significant
measure with that in Palestine, where a year previously the British had
been armed to the teeth: 100,000 troops, one soldier for every city
block in Jerusalem.

Through reinforcement, Hong Kong came to symbolize resistance
to communist expansion, acquiring a Cold War status comparable to
that of Berlin. Although the blockade against Berlin had been lifted,
the danger persisted. Attlee informed the Commonwealth Prime Ministers in September 1949 in a clipped and urgent telegram:

> In some respects situation is similar to that which faced us—and
> to some extent still faces us—in Berlin. Just as we cannot foresee
> with certainty how future of Berlin will develop but are convinced of
> necessity of remaining there, so we are impelled to remain in Hong
> Kong without any clear indication of extent or duration of military
> commitments involved. In both cases the threat of Russian and Com-
> munist expansionism necessitates holding what we have and not
> withdrawing.

Hong Kong was therefore one of the principal pillars of Western defence that might fall in Asia.

> For political and strategical reasons we cannot permit South East
> Asia to be dominated by Communism, and from an economic point
> of view it would be a disaster if the area were cut off from rest of the
> world. Any weakening before Communists in Hong Kong would be
> regarded by peoples of South East Asia as beginning of a general re-
> treat and they would immediately turn their thoughts towards mak-
> ing terms with the new power of Communism.[107]

The significance of Hong Kong was thus defined in the highest terms
of the Cold War.

The Americans proved receptive to the argument that the colony
should be held, but they did not commit themselves. In September
1949, the Foreign Secretary met with the American Secretary of State,
Dean Acheson. Previously lukewarm, Acheson now became more sym-

---

[106] Against which the Chinese Communists might marshal some 65 warships (including 7 destroyers and 15 gunboats) and 250 aircraft 'of all types'. The naval vessels and aircraft had been
seized mainly from the Nationalists. The Chinese Communist army was estimated at 2.25 million. These estimates were passed on to the Pacific Dominions (for example, A. N. Snelling to
Fraser, Top Secret, 28 June 1949, NZ AAEG 950/389A [300/3/1]).

[107] Attlee to UK High Commissioners, telegram, No. 326, Top Secret, 7 September 1949,
CO 537/4805.

pathetic to the plight of Hong Kong. The British record of the meeting includes the following exchange:

> *Mr. Bevin* said . . . if there was aggression against Hong Kong, this would be resisted with all available forces . . . The authorities [in Hong Kong] were now confident of their ability to face armed aggression, economic blockade or subversive activities from within.

> *Mr. Acheson* said he thought the policy described by Mr. Bevin was a sound and reasonable one, which should receive the support of the United States Government.[108]

In a discussion ranging over South-East Asia and India as well as Japan and China, Bevin and Acheson in fact did not give sustained attention to the problem of Hong Kong. It appears that Bevin aimed to secure general American endorsement for the British stand but to leave it at that. The military consequences, on which the US Navy would have had substantial comment, were not discussed. Even though Acheson accepted Bevin's line of argument, the British did not receive an American military guarantee. After the outbreak of the Korean War, however, President Truman in June 1950 ordered the Seventh Fleet to the Taiwan Straits.[109] The proximity of the Seventh Fleet, the British believed, acted as a deterrent against possible Chinese moves on Hong Kong.[110]

Partly because of inflated British rhetoric, Hong Kong from 1949 became known as 'the Berlin of the East'. But to those who gave close thought to the proposition, it was ironic. To the Governor of Hong Kong, at least, the purpose was precisely the opposite. Hong Kong needed to be defended but not become a centre of ongoing crisis.[111] Economic prosperity would depend on keeping the colony on peaceful terms with China and at the same time redirecting Hong Kong's trade and industry towards the West. A prosperous Hong Kong might

[108] Record of meeting, Top Secret, 13 September 1949, CO 537/4805. For the US account, see Dean Acheson, memorandum, 13 September 1949, *Foreign Relations, 1949*, IX, pp. 81–85, which confirms that Acheson used the phrase 'sound and reasonable'.

[109] See Nancy Bernkopf Tucker, *Patterns in the Dust: Chinese-American Relations and the Recognition Controversy, 1949–1950* (New York, 1983), pp. 23–24, and the detailed discussion of source material in the notes, pp. 216–18. See also Edwin W. Martin, *Divided Counsel: The Anglo-American Response to Communist Victory in China* (Lexington, Ky., 1986), chap. 25.

[110] See, for example, Sir Robert Black to Sir Hilton Poynton (Permanent Under-Secretary at the Colonial Office), Top Secret and Personal, 30 October 1962, CO 1030/1300.

[111] This interpretation is successfully argued in Tsang, 'Strategy for Survival', but it should be compared with Feng, *British Government's China Policy*, which upholds the view that the British sustained Hong Kong as an outpost in the Cold War.

benefit both China and Britain; in the long run, this proved to be the Communist view as well. At the time, Bevin calculated on the basis of intelligence reports from Hong Kong and elsewhere that Communist forces in 1949 were too disorganized to attempt a concerted effort against the colony. Whatever the short-term motive, Communist troops stopped at the northern border on 17 October 1949 and did not attempt to move further.

One might reflect that Hong Kong as 'the Berlin of the East' did not suit the purpose of Attlee or Bevin any more than it did the Governor of Hong Kong. Bevin's China policy finally crystallized in the summer and autumn of 1949. It had two purposes. The first was to demonstrate to the Chinese Communists that the seizure of Hong Kong not only would be a costly venture but would destroy a commercial and industrial entrepôt that otherwise might benefit China's own economy. In Grantham's words, 'all they would get would be an empty shell.'[112] The other aim was to keep on good terms with the People's Republic by according recognition as soon as possible and thus reducing the danger, so it was hoped, of British commercial firms being taken over or expelled from the mainland. British recognition took place in January 1950 despite the chasm in outlook that existed between the United States and Britain.[113] Although the British succeeded in holding Hong Kong, recognition of the People's Republic did not prevent the gradual squeezing out of British firms from China by 1954.[114]

It has now been close to half a century since the British made the critical decision to defend Hong Kong, and one can contemplate the wider significance by looking at archival evidence that extends to the 1960s. What do the British records reveal about Chinese motivation and intent? Reflecting on events of 1949, Sir Robert (Robin) Black, Grantham's successor, wrote a decade later that 'there has been no [Chinese] suggestion of an intention to "liberate" Hong Kong at an early date.' Black was Governor from 1958 to 1962. His contemporaries respected his gift for political analysis, and his judgement is thus a matter of some interest. He believed that Grantham had set the course

---

[112] Grantham, *Via Ports,* p. 172.

[113] See especially Ritchie Ovendale, 'Britain, the United States and the Recognition of Communist China', *Historical Journal,* 26, 1 (1983), pp. 139–58; Tucker, *Patterns in the Dust,* chap. 2; and Martin, *Divided Counsel,* part 2.

[114] See Aron Shai, 'Imperialism Imprisoned: The Closure of British Firms in the People's Republic of China', *English Historical Review,* 104 (1989); I have also benefited from reading the draft chapter on China by Jürgen Osterhammel in the *Oxford History of the British Empire* (vol. 4, in progress), which concludes: 'At least symbolically, with the removal in 1954 of Jardine Matheson & Co., the old agency house of opium trade times, an epoch had ended.'

necessary for the colony's survival by being bold yet giving way when necessary, by being firm yet taking care not to provoke.[115] Black acknowledged that however firm might be the British stand, it was the American Seventh Fleet that acted as the immediate deterrent. The People's Republic did not seize the colony in part because 'an attack upon Hong Kong might precipitate a war with the United States'.[116] But he also believed that the Chinese, by using a variety of tactics, could eventually have overcome the danger posed by the American forces had they calculated it to be in their national interest. As a Chinese priority, Hong Kong fell well below Tibet and Taiwan.[117] But there were further reasons. The economic value of Hong Kong to the People's Republic was of obvious importance: 'The Chinese Government derives advantage both from the foreign exchange which it earns here and from the financial facilities available here.'[118] Beyond that were two powerful and overriding calculations that caused Beijing, on the whole, to remain silent.

The first was the Chinese assessment, so the British believed, that the issue of Hong Kong should be kept between China and Britain and not become a confrontation involving the United Nations: 'China, no less than Britain, would deplore United Nations' sponsorship and initiative for a change of the status of Hong Kong.'[119] From the Chinese vantage point, there was nothing to be gained from the internationalization of the issue and much to be said in favour of keeping Hong Kong a purely bilateral matter beyond the competence of the UN. The second calculation concerned, in Black's phrase, China's 'undaunted sense of time'. The British presence in Hong Kong had a terminal date of July 1997. 'There are no explanations', Black wrote, for China's 'failure to press her claims on Hong Kong hitherto, other than a conviction that time will not derogate from those claims and an assessment that her immediate interests counsel restraint. It is on this slim thread that the stability and, indeed, the security of Hong Kong depend.' Black made one final observation that endorsed his prede-

[115] Black to Secretary of State, Secret, 21 January 1959, CO 1030/590.

[116] Ibid.

[117] For example, see L. H. Lamb (Peking) to C. H. Johnston, Confidential, 17 June 1952, HK Secretariat 26/4841/52, for the view that the Chinese 'recovery' of Hong Kong would come after the 'liberation' of Tibet and Taiwan. It was the Taiwan problem that preoccupied the Hong Kong Secretariat: some Kuomintang 'personages' in Hong Kong were 'merely trying to keep a backdoor open to help them save their skins when the Communists invade Formosa' (J. F. Nicoll [Colonial Secretary, Hong Kong] to Secretary of State, Top Secret, No. 23, 17 July 1950, HK Secretariat 5/1162/46).

[118] Black to Secretary of State, Secret, 21 January 1959, CO 1030/590.

[119] Black to Poynton, Top Secret and Personal, 30 October 1962, CO 1030/1300.

cessor's lack of enthusiasm for broadening the franchise and democratizing Hong Kong: '[T]here has been no substantial or sustained movement towards self-determination and self-government in Hong Kong . . . There is emphatically no emotional popular support for such a course.' He rejected out of hand Governor Young's plan for the creation of a city-state with a British allegiance.[120] In Black's judgement, as in Grantham's, as long as the British did not attempt to create in Hong Kong a separate political identity and an independent city-state, the People's Republic would tolerate the temporary existence of a British administration.

---

[120] 'People who have, from time to time, advocated such a course have been generally dismissed as unrealistic, irrational or disingenuous' (Black to Poynton, 30 October 1962).

INDIA, PALESTINE, AND EGYPT

13

THE GOVERNING INTELLECT:
L. S. AMERY, THE BRITISH EMPIRE,
AND INDIAN INDEPENDENCE

Giving his own twist to a popular remark, A. J. P. Taylor once commented that Leo Amery would have been Prime Minister had he not been two inches too short and his speeches two pages too long. As the long-awaited publication of these valuable diaries (*The Empire at Bay: The Leo Amery Diaries, 1929–1945*) makes clear, height was less of a problem than abstract intellect. Amery had an academic turn of mind. 'Rather high brow stuff,' he wrote of one of his own speeches. At his best, eloquent and devastating, he rose to the historic occasion. In May 1940 he denounced Neville Chamberlain in the House of Commons by invoking Cromwell's dismissal of the Long Parliament. Thanks to Amery, Cromwell's words are for ever associated with the fall of the Chamberlain government: 'You have sat too long here for any good you have been doing. Depart, I say, and let us have done with you. In the name of God, go!' Such judgements carried weight: Amery was a man of undisputed integrity. Churchill once said that he was 'the straightest man in public life'. Lord Wavell, Viceroy of India, wrote in 1945: 'What a gallant, loyal, straight little man he is, but a little detached from realities and more occupied with ideas and theories than persons and facts.'

Born in 1873, Amery was a year older than Churchill. Their careers ran parallel. When the two first encountered each other at Harrow, Churchill pushed Amery, fully clothed, into the swimming pool, the 'Ducker'. After Amery retaliated, Churchill apologized but observed that Amery was 'small'. ('My father, too', explained Churchill as he retrieved the situation, 'is small though he also is a great man.') On that occasion as on others, Amery held his own. During one of the Parliamentary debates on India in 1934, he convulsed the House by exposing Churchill's reactionary position. He wrote in his diary that he had 'given Winston the best ducking he has had since he first pushed me into Ducker in 1889. But he remains unsinkable and will no doubt bob up again after a bit.' Amery too had buoyancy and pugnacious spirit. During the Second World War, Hugh Dalton (then President of the Board of Trade), noted that in Cabinet meetings Amery refused to be bullied by Churchill and yelled back at him. Amery recorded that his colleagues were 'partly shocked and partly delighted that Winston should be spoken to in straight terms'. Beneath the schoolboy boisterousness of the two, there was a point of real divergence: 'His [Churchill's] attitude towards me has always been affected by a complete difference of outlook on almost every subject affecting the Empire.'

The present instalment of Amery's diaries covers the years 1929–45, but allusions to his formative years explain the clash with Churchill. The latter's romantic ideas about the British Empire never advanced from the time he served in India with the Malakand Field Force in 1897. Amery by contrast was committed to the cause of Imperial unity and an integrated economic system of the British Empire even before he went to Oxford. His election to All Souls in 1897, on a second try, gave him unrivalled opportunity to develop sophisticated ideas and to advance his career. He described All Souls as the place 'where the world of intellect and that of active life outside come together in the happiest intimacy'. He also once half jokingly referred to it as 'a world-wide secret society pledged to see to it that its members are ensconced in all the key positions of public life'. The All Souls influence can be seen in all stages of Amery's career, but it would be a mistake to believe that he owed his success to it. Amery created his own opportunities.

From 1899 to 1909 he served on the editorial staff of *The Times* and was mainly responsible for *The Times History of the South African War,* which the historian H. A. L. Fisher described as 'a history with a mission': 'Its aim is to defend Imperialism in the past, to make Imperialists in the present, and, by displaying not only the virtues but also the faults of British organization, to strengthen the Empire against the perils of the future.' Amery himself probably could not have provided a better description of his goal while Member of Parliament for the South (later Sparkbrook) division of Birmingham from 1911 to 1945. During these thirty-four years he held the vital 'Imperial' Cabinet posts: he served as First Lord of the Admiralty (1922–24), Secretary for the Colonies (1924–29), Secretary for the Dominions (1925–29), and, finally, Secretary for India and Burma (1940–45). 'Sidetracked' was Amery's word to sum up his predicament when Churchill offered him India. Winston wished to keep Leo out of the mainstream of the conduct of the war. Yet it was a curious appointment: India was one of the principal issues on which they violently quarrelled.

Other persistent sources of disagreement were the economy and the political goals of the Empire and Commonwealth. Amery believed Churchill held doctrinaire 'Free Trade' views and had no understanding whatever of the principle of colonial self-government. He wrote of him in 1941: 'He has always hated Dominion self-government . . . and hates it still more as applied to India. Similarly he accepted Free Trade in early youth and has never been able to understand the conception of national protection or of Empire Preference.' By self-government, Amery meant that all units or peoples within the Empire gradually should come to manage their own affairs. By 'Empire Preference', he meant the development of the Empire and Commonwealth through common economic policies. Amery drew his inspiration from Joseph Chamberlain's 'dream of a United Empire' and Lord Milner's version of an 'Imperial' economic and political system in the 'Southern British World', stretching in an arc from South Africa through Egypt and the Middle East to India and on to the antipodean Dominions. In the First World War, Amery served a Prime Minister who at least understood those goals. Lloyd George's 'radical imperialism' was close to Amery's own. In the Second World War, Amery despaired of Churchill. In fascinating passages of the diary, he compares the two wartime leaders:

> Ll.G.'s great qualities were that he was interested in every part of the field of national endeavour and was increasingly human and accessible to everybody as the war went on . . .

> Winston understands war better and strikes the high note more truly, but holds forth the whole time and does not like to listen to others or be argued with. That is a real weakness . . .

> Ll.G. was purely external and receptive, the result of intercourse with his fellow men, and non-existent in their absence, while Winston is literary and expressive of himself with hardly any contact with other minds. Again Winston is a retrospective Whig of the period 1750–1850, with very little capacity for looking forward, while Ll.G. was a constructive Radical, with essentially the same kind of outlook, allowing for differences of upbringing, as Joe [Chamberlain] or Milner, or for that matter myself.

Pursuing the principles of Chamberlain and Milner, Amery had attempted to modernize the British economic system. He had helped shape the agreements on protective tariffs in Ottawa in 1932; Churchill referred to the result as 'Rottawa'.

Amery believed that trends in world trade would lead to competitive economic blocs. 'In the world of today', he once wrote, 'there is no room for the small unit politically or economically.' He recognized Hitler's 'New Order' as a rational response to the economic problems of the Great Depression. If the British could develop a comparable system tied to sterling and based on British territories throughout the world, there would be nothing to fear from a European bloc. The real danger would come from the United States. 'Free Trade' and other 'lunatic' phrases of Cordell Hull (the Secretary of State for whom Amery reserved vituperative language) amounted to no more than 'American Lebensraum' at British expense. During the war, Hull denounced the Ottawa accords as 'economic aggression'. Amery was outraged at this assessment. Britain and the Dominions at Ottawa had attempted to bring about agreements based on timber, metals, tobacco, wheat, beef, mutton, lamb, bacon, sugar, cocoa, coffee, fish, apples. Amery's obsession with such commodities may have demonstrated, to the Americans at least, a large British appetite, but in his own view the modest bilateral agreements of the Ottawa system were by no means as effective or far-reaching as he wished. Amery believed that members of the Empire and Commonwealth should develop a common agricultural and industrial policy as well as a common currency. Otherwise Britain would eventually be reduced to the status of an economic satellite of the United States.

'Economic Preference', as Amery espoused it, was as much a political as an economic programme. It rested on the assumption that the British Empire could remain a great world power only if British statesmen possessed the will and courage to adapt to changing circumstances. Amery always attempted to take a realist's view of how shifts in world politics might affect British security. Above all he stressed the need to retain British mastery of the eastern Mediterranean. As early as 1936 he warned of the danger of a Japanese-Italian-German combination that might jeopardize the British Empire. He thought it folly to alienate Japan over Manchuria. He publicly pledged not to send 'a single Birmingham lad to his death for the sack of Abyssinia'. He did not believe that the ascendancy of Germany in Europe would necessarily lead Germany into conflict with Britain. Here he pursued a dual policy of sympathy and sternness: 'non-encirclement' of Germany yet no return of her former colonies (though at one stage he was prepared to cede the Solomon Islands or the New Hebrides as a symbolic gesture to placate the Germans). He wrote in 1938 that he favoured 'Anglo-Italian rapprochement' to secure the British position in the Mediterranean, and that he was prepared to give Germany 'a freer hand in the East, at any rate as against Russia and in the Baltic States'. He deplored 'the blundering and humiliation' over Czechoslovakia and had 'deep misgivings at the extent to which we have let down the unhappy Czechs', but he did not see the outcome as unfavourable to British security.

Yet rational appeasement could work only if pursued with rational men, or at least those who kept their promises. 'When I think of the outrageous conduct of Germany', he wrote, 'I cannot help seeing red, and reason tells me that there can be little permanence in a settlement won by sheer threat of violence.' Amery did not oppose the Munich settlement over Czechoslovakia, but he was sceptical. The following passage sums up his premonitions and his faith: '[W]e may find ourselves besieged in Hong Kong, and Singapore, driven out of Egypt and Palestine, with most of London and our chief munition works in ruins. But perhaps the same national character that has got us into this mess will see us through to the end. Anyhow thank God we are not Germany and capable of being led by a man like Hitler.' Amery had absolutely no doubt about British honour and justice pitted against 'all the powers of darkness, gangsterism, brutality, persecution, mendacity'.

The urgent need for rearmament brought Amery and Churchill into common cause. They saw eye to eye, as Amery put it, on the disastrous policy of 'fatuous disarmament'. He recalled that the overriding issue of war and peace had linked them as comrades-in-arms since the Boer War: 'So now Winston and I are once more working together in the third war,' he wrote as early as 1938. The camaraderie had its light-hearted moments. Amery prided himself on athletic fitness. In 1929 he had scaled 19,940-foot Mount Amery, the peak in the Canadian Rockies named in his honour. In his later years he had to guard his health. Churchill twitted him: 'If only you had drunk and smoked like me you would be both better and happier!' Amery nevertheless enjoyed life to the full, relishing evenings at home reading Kipling or discovering new historians—for example, 'a young man called [A. J. P.] Taylor', whose *Germany's First Bid for Colonies* in 1938 fortified Amery's belief that the German colonial empire should not be restored. All Souls provided Amery with conviviality and the opportunity to exchange ideas with his peers—men such as Sir John Simon (his direct contemporary), Lord Halifax (Foreign Secretary in Chamberlain's War Cabinet) and Geoffrey Dawson (Editor of *The Times*)—as well as the younger Fellows: A. L. Rowse was 'a shrewd likeable fellow and much the ablest and most constructive among them'. Amery also had an eye for intelligent and beautiful women, among them Margery Perham, 'a clever and rather good-looking girl', whose work on Africa he encouraged through the Rhodes Trust. Moreover he liked to sing. At All Souls he intoned the 'Swapping Mallard Song' from the roof of the College. He was good-hearted and bore no grudges (except, perhaps, towards John Maynard Keynes and other economists who differed with him over 'Empire Preference'). Though in overall competence he regarded himself as better qualified than Churchill to conduct the war, he noted in March 1940: 'Winston with all his failings is the one man with real war drive and love of battle.'

Some of those details will be familiar because Amery used his diaries as the basis of his three volumes of memoirs, *My Political Life*, which cover the years 1896–1940. The reader of this instalment of the diaries will thus find the wartime section the most absorbing, but the freshness of the wartime material does not diminish the value of the entries over the whole period. In the introduction to the previous set published in 1980, Julian Amery quite rightly emphasizes that his father's diaries constitute the fullest day-by-day record of the period compiled by any British public figure of the front rank. The editors, John Barnes and David Nicholson, deserve high praise for their perseverance over the past eight years in producing this huge book, in which, as a bonus, they provide extensive historical introductions to each chronological period. Some readers may find these learned and lengthy comments a distraction rather than a bonus, but they can be read separately as a helpful analysis. One point reinforced in the 1940–45 section is Amery's administrative competence. He could not resist clearing up muddles, even if they were not his direct concern. The didactic letters and memoranda he wrote to his colleagues during the war were not always welcome. Another compelling impression of the wartime period is Amery's indefatigable tenacity, especially on the issue of 'Empire Preference', which continued to form one of the main themes of his life. By continually hoeing the same row, at various levels with different people, Amery was effective, even with Churchill: 'There is no doubt that if one stands up to Winston and argues with him . . . the argument [often] sinks into the subsoil and comes out as a Winstonian flower later on.' Amery's Victory Garden of ideas extended over the whole range of grand strategy and party politics. But in this inner history of the war, the most luxuriant fruits are to be found in his own plot, India. Amery was the only one who could stand up to Churchill's truculence on India. 'Winston will have to give way', he wrote in characteristic vein about persistent tactics, 'but he is really not quite normal on the subject of India.' A few days later, again in characteristic vein, Churchill said, '"I give in," adding sotto voce: "When you lose India don't blame me".'

Here emerges a point of profound importance in the history of the partition of India. As early as 1940, Amery began to write of the eventual transfer of power. Yet more than anyone, perhaps, he wished to preserve the British connection. It was imperative to him that India remain in the Commonwealth. Eventually he was prepared to sacrifice the unity of India to achieve that end, even though he regarded the 'break up of India, on Ulster and Eire lines . . . [as] a disastrous solution'. The more he studied the possibility of partition, the less catastrophic it appeared. He consciously decided, almost immediately on assuming office, that for military and political reasons the British must remain on good terms with the Muslims. He wrote explicitly of a pro-Muslim British policy. There was an element of realpolitik in Amery's thought. It was not difficult for him to adjust to the idea that Indian

freedom might lead to more than one new member of the Commonwealth. Amery in fact appears as the key figure within the British Government in the tilt towards a separate Muslim State. If one pursues this
proposition to *reductio ad absurdum,* the real father of Pakistan was not
Mohammad Ali Jinnah but Leopold Stennett Amery.

The critical period in Amery's tenure as Secretary of State for India
occurred in 1942 in the aftermath of the fall of Singapore. In March,
the War Cabinet decided to send a Labour emissary, Sir Stafford
Cripps, to India to prove British good intentions by offering independence at the end of the war. To keep India on Britain's side, there
needed to be a dramatic indication of change of heart, or at least a
firm assurance that Indian independence was a near and not a remote
reality. At first volunteering to go himself, Amery became persuaded
in conversation with Churchill that it would be best to let 'this dangerous young rival' take on the impossible job 'of squaring the circle
of India'. (Some of these conversations were flavoured by Churchill's
helping himself 'to two or three small brandies to illustrate how much
better off and happier he was'.) The gamble was fraught with political risk. Cripps might succeed in reaching an accommodation with
the leaders of the Congress by offering them an acceptable share in
the management of the war they were helping wage. The downfall
of Cripps on this occasion is too complicated to relate here, but the
Cripps mission collapsed when Amery, Churchill, and Lord Linlithgow (the Viceroy) created the impression that Cripps had played into
the hands of the Congress leaders, who would be satisfied with nothing less, in Amery's words, than 'the whole government of India . . .
handed over to them here and now'. The failure of the Cripps mission
was an entirely satisfactory outcome for Amery, who then and for ever
after argued that the British had put forward a reasonable proposal—
independence after the war—which the Indians had rejected. 'We can
now go ahead with a clear conscience,' Amery wrote in March 1942.

In the diary entries after the fall of Singapore and during the Cripps
mission, it becomes clear that Amery was prepared if necessary to put
his ideas about Indian freedom into cold storage for the rest of the war
and to rule with an iron hand. Would it not be better, he asked himself in February 1942, 'for the moment at any rate to go back more
to the spirit of Mutiny days and revive British Rule in its more direct
and, if necessary, ruthless form'? Here there was no disagreement with
the Prime Minister or the Viceroy. When the challenge to British rule
came in August 1942 in the form of the 'Quit India' movement, Amery
steadied Cabinet sentiment behind Linlithgow's merciless and effective quelling of the revolt. He regarded this as the critical moment to
hold firm at all costs. In the midst of the August rebellion he reflected

on the loss of confidence in Britain's Imperial mission and the danger
of the flabby wartime idealism of the Atlantic Charter:

> This appalling defeatism about our mission in the world horrifies
> me. The place seems full of people who really think that the solution
> of everything after the war is to hand it over to the Americans, or the
> Chinese, or the Russians, or some mixed committee of all of them.
>
> I only wish sometimes I were in a free position to say what I think
> about the Atlantic Charter and all the other tripe which is being
> talked now, exactly like the tripe talked to please President Wilson.

Yet such passages must not be allowed to obscure Amery's genuine
efforts to plan, in his own words, for 'Indian independence' within the
British Commonwealth. To move forward the constitutional issue, he
persuaded Linlithgow to appoint a young Fellow of All Souls, H. V.
Hodson, to the post of Reforms Commissioner (constitutional adviser
to the Viceroy). At the same time, he persuaded another Fellow of the
college, the Beit Professor of the History of the British Empire, (later
Sir) Reginald Coupland, to make a study of the Indian constitution:
'It does rather look as if I were perpetrating the mutual jobbery which
is sometimes charged against All Souls!' To achieve a breakthrough in
the political issue, however, Amery had to await the appointment of a
Viceroy who would accelerate the pace of constitutional change faster
than Linlithgow.

The diaries reveal that Amery had nothing to do with the appointment of Lord Wavell as Viceroy in July 1943. Wavell was Churchill's
idea of a stopgap. As a soldier, he could be relied upon merely to hold
the lid down. Amery immediately saw that Churchill had miscalculated: 'From what I know of soldiers', Amery wrote, 'it by no means follows that Wavell may not prove more radical before long than most
politicians.' Amery and Wavell in fact had similar ideas on the need
to move India as rapidly as possible towards full self-government and
independence. They now formed a united front against Churchill,
who resisted them every inch of the way. Any proposal put forward
by Wavell and backed by Amery would produce an explosion in the
Cabinet. Here is a representative exchange that took place at a Cabinet meeting in August 1944, when 'Winston in a state of great exulta-
tion' described what he would do about India after the war. He would
carry out:

> a great regeneration of India based on extinguishing landlords and
> oppressive industrialists and uplift[ing] the peasant and untouch-
> able, probably by collectivization on Russian lines. It might be nec-
> essary to get rid of wretched sentimentalists like Wavell . . .

Naturally I [Amery] lost patience and couldn't help telling him that I didn't see much difference between his outlook and Hitler's which annoyed him no little. I am by no means sure whether on this subject of India he is really quite sane.

Amery carried on with his own plans, together with Wavell, 'to make it clear that we intend to concede to India . . . full and unqualified independence within the Commonwealth'. When Amery left office in July 1945 he was disconsolate about India, quite convinced that 'the real wrecker' of British plans was Churchill.

How does one assess Amery on India? These diaries provide invaluable evidence about his motives, ideas, and plans, but it is useful to bear in mind how he was judged by his contemporaries. According to Hugh Dalton, who also kept a diary, Amery unfairly acquired the reputation of a reactionary merely because he was associated with Churchill. Dalton wrote in August 1944: 'Amery—as many outside would be surprised to find—is always in Cabinet the warmest advocate of a "sympathetic" and "constructive" policy in India . . . Amery always stands up for India and the Indians and, as the P.M. said this afternoon, "You [Amery] . . . have become, like Wavell and Linlithgow . . . more Indian than the Indians, [and yet you] are attacked in the House of Commons as being a narrow-minded old-fashioned reactionary! It serves you right!"'

There is one aspect of Amery's life that it not fully brought out in the diaries. The editors have excluded almost all references to Amery's eldest son, John, who was executed for high treason in Wandsworth prison in December 1945. There is a note by Amery, produced as an appendix, that explains how this son believed 'the Communist peril' to be the greatest danger of the future and how, finding himself in occupied Europe and Germany during the war, he attempted to raise a brigade among British prisoners of war to fight against the Soviet Union—emphatically not against Britain, but rather 'to save the British Empire'. For this tragedy, Rebecca West's *Meaning of Treason* is still a useful account, but there is an entry in the diaries that gives an indication of the agony suffered by Amery and his wife, Brydde, when they heard their son speak from Berlin in November 1942: 'After dinner B. and I faced the miserable ordeal of listening in to John's broadcast . . . It is all pretty beastly but there is at any rate the consolation that our friends are very good to us.'

14

THE PARTITIONS OF INDIA AND PALESTINE

The year Lord Linlithgow became Viceroy of India, 1936, was also the year of the Arab revolt in Palestine. 'With my Indian experience', he reflected on one of his visits to the Middle East, '[I] gained the feeling that I was witnessing an example of the dangers of alienating a peasant people from their lands.' A year later, in 1937, writing in response to the conclusion drawn by the Peel Commission that Palestine should be partitioned (yet retain economic links between the parts and provide the British with strategic facilities), Linlithgow observed that 'Willie Peel' and his colleagues appeared to have made the best of a bad situation.[1] A separate state might prove to be a good solution after all—a thought that found an echo in most British official circles in 1947, perhaps more in regard to Pakistan than Palestine.

Both problems had their immediate origins a decade earlier, and events in Palestine were much on the minds of those in India: 'I fear that in certain parts of the country, e.g. NW India', Mohammed Iqbal wrote to Mohammed Ali Jinnah in May 1937, 'Palestine may be repeated.'[2] In this critical year, moderate Zionists took heart at the recommendations of the Peel Commission ('Today we laid the basis for the Jewish state' were the words of Chaim Weizmann, the President of the World Zionist Organization, after a conversation with the principal architect of the scheme, Professor Reginald Coupland of Oxford).[3] In Palestine itself, the partition proposal signified to the Arabs an attempt at colonization comparable to that of the French in Algeria

[1] Linlithgow to Zetland, Private and Personal, 24 September 1936 and 2 August 1937, Linlithgow Papers (India Office Library). There is a helpful biography of Linlithgow by his son John Glendevon, *The Viceroy at Bay: Lord Linlithgow in India, 1936–1943* (London, 1971). The best scholarly study of Linlithgow as Viceroy is Gowher Rizvi, *Linlithgow and India: A Study of British Policy and the Political Impasse in India, 1936–1943* (London, 1978). For a discussion of trends in interpretation with which the present essay is concerned, see C. H. Philips and M. D. Wainwright, eds., *The Partition of India: Policies and Perspectives, 1935–1947* (London, 1970); and A. K. Majumdar, 'Writings on the Transfer of Power, 1945–47', in B. R. Nanda, ed., *Essays in Modern Indian History* (New Delhi, 1980). For historiographical comment on the Palestine literature, see the essay by Robert W. Stookey in W. R. Louis and R. W. Stookey, eds., *The End of the Palestine Mandate* (Austin, Tex., 1985).

[2] In a letter of 28 May 1937, in Syed Sharifuddin Pirzadi, ed., *Quaid-e-Azam Jinnah's Correspondence* (Karachi, 1977), p. 139. For this crucial period in Jinnah's life, see especially Stanley Wolpert, *Jinnah of Pakistan* (New York, 1984), chap. 11; and Ayesha Jalal, *The Sole Spokesman: Jinnah, the Muslim League, and the Demand for Pakistan* (Cambridge, 1985), chap. 1.

[3] N. A. Rose, *The Gentile Zionists* (London, 1937), p. 128; Aaron Klieman, ed., *Letters and Papers of Chaim Weizmann* (Jerusalem, 1979), XVIII, p. x.

or the Italians in Libya—'Hebrewstan', as it was called by some Indian newspapers. In India, as Penderel Moon and many others have argued, the crucial point was the Muslim League's response to the implementation of provincial autonomy under the India Act of 1935 and the electoral successes of the Indian National Congress in February 1937.[4] The ten-year ring to the Indian and Palestinian developments—with 1937 and 1947 as the critical years—also had a resonance over three decades. If one were to pursue a Whiggish comparison, taking the Montagu Declaration of 1917 as the Indian point of departure and the Balfour Declaration of 1917 as the Zionist, then the story would end with only a one-year difference between Indian and Israeli freedom.[5]

Reginald Coupland (for the present discussion, a central figure because of his involvement in both Palestinian and Indian affairs) stated in 1946 that 'the Indian problem . . . with all its obvious differences, is similar at root to that of Palestine. Muslim minority like the Jewish is fired with consciousness of "nationhood" which will not submit to a majority rule by another "nation".'[6] Coupland was increasingly apprehensive about the consequences of full-scale civil war in Palestine. Full political sovereignty imposed by the Jews on their own terms would lead to economic catastrophe, at least for the Arabs. If Palestine was to be partitioned, it would best be done quickly and decisively in 1937, with political as well as economic provisions (Haifa as a 'free port', for example) to ensure stability. Here perhaps was the lesson for India. 'Partition', Coupland had written in his exhaustive study, *The Indian Problem,* during the war, 'means that the Moslem State or States would be relatively weak and poor,' the same point he had emphasized about

---

[4] Penderel Moon, *Divide and Quit* (Berkeley and Los Angeles, 1962), pp. 13–14. See, however, the sophisticated challenges to various of Moon's arguments by Ayesha Jalal and Anil Seal, 'Alternative to Partition: Muslim Politics between the Wars', *Modern Asian Studies*, 15, 3 (1981). For the India Act of 1935, see especially R. J. Moore, *The Crisis of Indian Unity, 1917–1940* (Oxford, 1974).

[5] For the Montagu Declaration, see especially Richard Danzig, 'The Announcement of August 20th, 1917', *Journal of Asian Studies*, 18, 1 (November 1968); for the Balfour Declaration, see Mayir Vereté, 'The Balfour Declaration and Its Makers', *Middle Eastern Studies*, 6, 1 (January 1970); and for a rigorous analysis applicable to both, see Conor Cruise O'Brien, 'Israel in Embryo', *New York Review of Books*, 15 March 1984.

[6] As reported in the *Hindustan Times*, 6 May 1946. Coupland was writing shortly after the publication of the report of the Anglo-American Committee of Inquiry on Palestine. He feared, as did the Viceroy, Lord Wavell, that the Muslims and Hindus might find common cause against the British as they had after the First World War, when the terms of peace with Turkey had abolished the Khilafat (see Gail Minault, *The Khilafat Movement* [New York, 1981]). Coupland had served on the Palestine Royal Commission of 1936–37 and had assisted the Cripps mission to India in 1942. His Indian diary at Rhodes House, Oxford (MSS. Brit. Emp. S.15), is an invaluable background source for the themes of the present essay.

Arab Palestine. 'Will not Moslem Patriots say what those Arabs said: "What does it matter how weak and poor our homelands are if only we are masters in them?"'[7] Could not rationality yet prevail over the fanaticism of partition? As late as the spring of 1946, Coupland and, as will be seen, many officials within the British government refused to give up hope that outright partition in both Palestine and India might be averted.

The two cases are so dissimilar that analogies can be little more than tangential; but it is nevertheless possible to explain, from the British vantage point, why the Palestine episode ended so disastrously and why the accession to the Commonwealth by both India and Pakistan appeared at the time to be one of the great achievements of the Labour Government. An examination of the two cases helps explain the changing character of British imperialism in its response to nationalism, the Labour initiative, and the circumstances of possible American intervention. The two situations developed so differently in part because of the attitude of the US government. The possibility of American support for Indian nationalists appeared as a shaft of light in 1942 but flickered only intermittently thereafter. By contrast, the spotlight turned on the Palestine issue by the American Zionists, at least from the time of the Biltmore resolution calling for an independent 'Jewish Commonwealth' in May 1942, illuminates a main theme down to the time of Israeli independence in May 1948. The Indian and Jewish struggles against the British sustain the analogy, yet the intensity of the Palestine issue in Anglo-American relations was without parallel. One of Churchill's frequent complaints in the post-war period was that Palestine, a territory the size of Wales, held down four to five British divisions—nearly 100,000 men, or roughly the equivalent of one-tenth of the Indian Army in 1947 (coincidentally, the figure 100,000 was the estimated size of the non-military European population in India). Viewed from the 'Imperial' perspective of India as the centre of the British Empire, Palestine was disruptive out of all proportion to its size or significance.

In 1946 the *Hindustan Times* (a newspaper of interest for present purposes because its editor, Gandhi's son, Devadas, appeared to have a keen appreciation of Palestinian affairs) denied that there could be any comparison between Palestine and India simply because of the difference in demographic scale: 'Except in the one respect that both are creations of British imperialism, there is no parallel between them

---

[7] Reginald Coupland, *The Indian Problem: Report on the Constitutional Problem in India* (Oxford, 1944), III, p. 99.

. . . The total population of Arabs and Jews in Palestine is less than the number of Indians officially acknowledged to have died in the Bengal famine of 1943.'[8] (The conventional British figure for the number of victims was three million.) It is a point worth bearing in mind. In 1945 the respective Jewish and Arab populations of Palestine were 560,000 and 1,200,000. In the Punjab alone, a province over seventeen times the size of the Palestine mandate (minus Transjordan), there were some 16,000,000 Muslims and 7,500,000 Hindus plus an almost solid block of 4,500,000 Sikhs. Nor was the demographic difference the only striking contrast. Using Churchill's comparison of the size of Palestine and Wales, if one superimposes an Indian map over one of the British Isles and Europe, with Wales in the western part of Baluchistan (a province itself some sixteen times larger than Palestine), then Peshawar will be in northern Norway, Calcutta will be east of Moscow, and the southern tip of India will fall somewhere between Greece and eastern Libya. Such comparisons would not have impressed the Zionists. The Jewish nationalists were driven by the messianic aspiration to return to 'Eretz-Yisrael', and they were above all obsessed with the six million Jews murdered by the Nazis, a unique event in human history, surpassing all other considerations.

If the Holocaust provided the main post-war drive for Jewish nationalism, it was the immigration question that distinguished the Palestine problem from that of India. Immigration in the inter-war years increased the Jewish community from 83,000 to 444,000—to some 30 per cent of the total inhabitants. Part of the British purpose behind the 1939 White Paper was to stabilize the population at about one-third Jewish and two-thirds Arab.[9] Jewish immigration would be limited to 75,000 during the next five years, and thereafter would depend on Arab consent. The White Paper also prohibited land sales in some areas and placed further restrictions in others. To the Jews, of course, the White Paper represented appeasement of the Arabs as well as betrayal of the Zionist cause, an abandonment of the Balfour Declaration of 1917, which promised the Jews a national home in Palestine. Like the Jews, the Indian Princes in 1947 also detected a British willingness to sacrifice historic commitment. British pledges were reinterpreted according to prevailing circumstances. In 1939 the White Paper aimed not only to secure the Arab good will necessary to hold the eastern Mediterranean, but also to avert partition. To the Foreign

[8] 7 May1946. See M. S. Venkataramani, *Bengal Famine of 1943* (Delhi, 1973).
[9] For the 1939 White Paper, see especially Michael J. Cohen, *Palestine: Retreat from the Mandate* (New York, 1978); and Walid Khalidi, *From Haven to Conquest* (Beirut, 1971).

Office, at least, the positive purpose was the creation of a binational state that guaranteed political and economic rights for the Jewish minority. The White Paper drew inspiration from the historical experiences of Canada and South Africa, and it anticipated the formulas that the Cabinet Mission in 1946 attempted to devise in order to keep the Muslims within a unified India. The wartime response of David Ben Gurion reveals a profound difference between the Jewish struggle and the Indian, whether Hindu or Muslim: 'We shall fight the War as if there were no White Paper, and the White Paper as if there were no War.' [10] To the Jews, a Nazi victory would be the ultimate catastrophe. It was not at all the same for the Indians, or for the Arabs.

Besides Palestine, there is another Middle Eastern parallel that is significant for the issue of British power and the question of loss of 'Imperial' nerve. In 1942 the British held firm in Egypt as well as India. In the spring of that year, German forces opened a campaign against Egypt. If successful, it might have snapped the 'spinal cord' connecting Britain and the short route to India, and it might have led to preponderant German influence in the Middle East. The protagonist of this episode was Sir Miles Lampson, the Ambassador in Cairo. Lampson was soon to be raised to the peerage as Lord Killearn in part because of his decisive stand. He is a figure of considerable interest in the Britain–Middle East–India connection because in 1943 Churchill attempted, unsuccessfully, to make him Linlithgow's successor as Viceroy. In February 1942 Lampson surrounded the Egyptian Royal Palace with British tanks. He presented an ultimatum to King Farouk: abdicate, or purge the court of Axis influences and install a pro-British Wafd regime.[11] The successful intervention, like Linlithgow's clampdown on the 'Quit India' movement a few months later, had far-reaching consequences. At the time, at least to diehard Tories, it seemed to prove that Egypt could be ruled indefinitely—if necessary, by bayonets. The British Empire could endure through political willpower combined with adequate military force. Lampson, in short, personified Britain's dominant position in the Middle East. The younger generation of Egyptian nationalists, who rankled at the humiliation of 1942, proved to be exceedingly sceptical whether the post-war Labour Government would end the unequal relationship. The mystique as well as the reality of British determination and ruthlessness left a permanent imprint on Egyptian nationalism at a critical time.

It is helpful in getting a bearing on Linlithgow's response to the

[10] Barnet Litvinoff, *Ben-Gurion of Israel* (London, 1954), p. 132.
[11] See Gabriel Warburg, 'Lampson's Ultimatum to Faruq, 4 February 1942', *Middle Eastern Studies*, 11, 1 (January 1975).

emergency in India to know that he regarded Killearn and Churchill as reactionaries.[12] Linlithgow is a much-misjudged Viceroy, in part because he is seldom assessed according to his own goals and Tory code of conduct. '[H]eavy of body and slow of mind, solid as a rock and with almost a rock's lack of awareness,' was Nehru's judgement.[13] H. V. Hodson made a shrewd comment when he observed that Linlithgow's heaviness of style belied a decisiveness and vigour of mind.[14] Like Killearn, Linlithgow sought to preserve British supremacy, but he believed that the British in India could remain dominant only by adjusting to changing circumstances and keeping the game constantly in play. He was more vigorous than Killearn in attempting to align 'collaborators' of all political colours, Hindu, Muslim, Sikh, or 'untouchable', and just as determined to prevent any anti-British extremist from gaining the upper hand. In holding the balance in Indian politics, his main adversaries were the Congress leaders, of whom, before the war, he regarded Gandhi as distinctly more reasonable and pragmatic than the doctrinaire and 'radical' Jawaharlal Nehru. Linlithgow's political lodestar was the India Act of 1935, to which he had contributed substantially as chairman of the Joint Select Committee that guided it through Parliament despite the opposition of Churchill and other diehards. Linlithgow had an unrivalled knowledge of the Act's details and implications. Its purpose was to set up a federal structure integrating the Princely States into a united India. In John Gallagher's words, it signified an adjustment in the method of keeping the Indian connection 'while retaining intact most of its fundamental advantages'.[15] Linlithgow believed in self-government, provided the British retained control over such areas as defence and foreign affairs, and perhaps he genuinely subscribed to the idea of Dominion Status—but in the remote future, probably the twenty-first century. In the 1936–39 period, he concentrated much of his efforts on persuading the Princes to accept the 1935 Act. He was not unduly dismayed when it had to be shelved because of the war.

Percival Spear has written that in 1939 'Pakistan was in the air'.[16] The Linlithgow Papers substantially confirm the details of the drift in

---

[12] 'I regard him as a very unsuitable choice,' Linlithgow wrote, though he opposed Lampson at least as much on grounds of inability to change with the times as on political outlook (Linlithgow to Amery, 3 December 1942, in Nicholas Mansergh et al., eds., *The Transfer of Power, 1942–1947* [12 vols., London, 1970–83], III, p. 329).

[13] Sarvepalli Gopal, *Jawaharlal Nehru, 1889–1947* (Oxford, 1975), p. 225.

[14] H. V. Hodson, *The Great Divide* (New York, 1971), p. 110.

[15] Quoted in J. F. C. Watts, 'The Viceroyalty of Lord Irwin, 1926–31', (Oxford, D.Phil. thesis, 1973), p. iii.

[16] Percival Spear, *India: A Modern History* (Ann Arbor, 1961), p. 394.

Indian politics more than the atmosphere, in part because of the Viceroy's wariness in dealing directly with Indian politicians. 'I feel no doubt', Linlithgow wrote in March 1939, 'that the Muslims are beginning to feel increasingly uneasy at what Jinnah described as "Hindu arrogance", and increasingly apprehensive of the fate of a minority— even a minority of 90 million people—under the scheme of the [India 1935] Act.'[17] Linlithgow did not believe that the Muslim League or the Princes had the power to block the Act. His basic strategy was to play the Muslim League and the Princes off against the Congress. He made a serious misjudgement in underestimating Muslim sentiment before the outbreak of the war. He did not take the idea of 'Pakistan' seriously. After the adoption of the March 1940 Lahore resolution, calling for the creation of a separate state or states of Pakistan, he wrote: 'My first reaction is, I confess, that silly as the Muslim scheme for partition is, it would be a pity to throw too much cold water on it at the moment.'[18] Linlithgow surmised that what Jinnah feared was a federal India dominated by Hindus. Part of the purpose of the famous British 'August offer' of 1940 was to assure the Muslims that they would be protected against a 'Hindu Raj' as well as to hold over the discussion of the 1935 Act and a 'new constitution' until after the war. The game of politics continued, in Linlithgow's judgement, with Jinnah and Gandhi as the principals and 'no other leaders in sight'.[19] Nehru he had written off as a hopeless Anglophobe extremist bent on Marxist revolution. Of the principal danger, the Viceroy had no doubt: 'Congress will I fear have to be beaten in the present trial of strength before we can get forward.'[20] Such was Linlithgow's outlook in 1940, the year Churchill became Prime Minister.

Both Churchill and his Secretary of State for India, Leopold Amery, were Zionists.[21] By contrast with their attitude towards Palestine, they both rejected outright the idea of a separate Muslim state in India. Even Linlithgow responded less rigidly. Though contemptuous of the plan, he could nevertheless use it as a card to keep Jinnah in play. To

---

[17] Linlithgow to Zetland, Private and Personal, 28 March 1939, Linlithgow Papers F125/7.

[18] Quoted in Uma Kaura, *Muslims and Indian Nationalism: The Emergence of the Demand for India's Partition, 1928–40* (New Delhi, 1977), p. 170.

[19] Minute by Linlithgow on Amery to Linlithgow, Private, 27 August 1941, Linlithgow Papers F125/10.

[20] Minute by Linlithgow on Amery to Linlithgow, 13 December 1940, Linlithgow Papers F125/9.

[21] By 1943, however, Amery had retreated to the position that there should be an autonomous Jewish state only within a larger Arab confederation. Churchill was much less pro-Zionist than has been commonly believed. See the historical revision by Michael J. Cohen, *Churchill and the Jews* (London, 1985).

Amery, partition would be 'disastrous', 'fatal', the prelude to civil war and anarchy (though he rationalized it in 1942 as being compatible with Dominion Status). Linlithgow's and Amery's ideas in general must be distinguished from Churchill's. Both the Viceroy and the Secretary of State in contrast with the Prime Minister were enlightened Tories. Linlithgow had more of a commitment to the general development of India than any Viceroy since Curzon. Amery was truly dedicated to the long-range Dominion Status of a unified India and was willing eventually to accept *two* Dominions. Churchill's celebrated denunciation of the India Act of 1935 reveals his general attitude: 'a gigantic quilt of jumbled crochet work, a monstrous monument of shame built by pigmies'.[22] As for Indian leadership, Churchill believed that it consisted of no more than a clique of the 'Hindoo priesthood', who were opposed by the peasant masses, the untouchables, the Princes, the Muslims, and other minorities. The Indian peoples therefore depended on British guardianship. 'When you learn to think of a race as inferior beings it is difficult to get rid of that way of thinking,' he later reflected.[23] He applauded the 'Hindu-Muslim feud' as 'the bulwark of British rule'.[24] Despite the chasm in outlook that separated him from Amery and Linlithgow, Churchill could rely on both of them to defend the Raj against all comers, American as well as Japanese.

As Robin Moore has written, one way of viewing the Cripps mission of March 1942 is as the attempt by British Labour, at one stage with American assistance, to break the Churchill-Amery-Linlithgow throttlehold on India.[25] Clement Attlee, at this time Lord Privy Seal in the coalition government, once called Linlithgow a 'defeatist'. It was a perceptive remark. He saw that Linlithgow merely intended to uphold the status quo rather than to make political progress. 'We need a man to do in India what Durham did in Canada,' Attlee wrote to his colleagues in the War Cabinet.[26] Sir Stafford Cripps, a patriot as well as a Labour statesman committed to Indian independence, hoped to hold Indian loyalty by offering de facto Dominion Status (or, in other words, self-determination and the possibility of Pakistan) and the Indianization of the Executive Council of the Indian government in all areas except the critical one of defence. He arrived in India after the fall of Singapore and the loss of Britain's Far Eastern empire, after

[22] See Martin Gilbert, *Winston S. Churchill* (London, 1976), V, chap. 31.

[23] Lord Moran, *Winston Churchill: The Struggle for Survival* (London, 1966), p. 394.

[24] On this point, see especially M. S. Venkataramani and B. K. Shrivastava, *Quit India: The American Response to the 1942 Struggle* (New Delhi, 1979), pp. 20–23.

[25] See R. J. Moore, *Churchill, Cripps, and India, 1939–1945* (Oxford, 1979).

[26] WP (42) 59, 2 February 1942, in *Transfer of Power*, I, p. 112; quoted in R. J. Moore, *Escape from Empire: The Attlee Government and the Indian Problem* (Oxford, 1983), p. 10.

the conquest of most of Burma by the Japanese, and at the time of a possible invasion of the Orissa coast and southern India—and at the same time, roughly, to keep the Middle Eastern parallel in mind, that Rommel was advancing towards Egypt and Killearn had clamped down on Farouk. For present purposes, Cripps made two critical errors: underestimating Linlithgow's ability to block a settlement with the Congress leaders, and entertaining a misguided hope for decisive support from President Roosevelt's representative in India, Colonel Louis Johnson.

Churchill, Amery, and Linlithgow of course saw a propaganda purpose in the Cripps mission. In Amery's words to Churchill, the aim was to provide something that would satisfy 'Moslems and *just possibly* some of the Congress, as well as Americans and Left Wing here'.[27] By the phrase 'just possibly', Amery expressed the doubt that Congress would accept a formula in which the military command of the war would remain firmly in British hands. This was the principal point on which the Cripps mission broke down, despite Cripps's gamble that he could pull the Americans with him (through Colonel Johnson) in a proposal to admit Indian participation in the running of the war. Churchill supported the Viceroy and the Commander-in-Chief, General Wavell, in refusing to admit Indian influence in the command of the war. The Churchill-Amery-Linlithgow-'plus Wavell' axis thus blocked the Cripps-Johnson initiative to create an Indian national government that might have had the support of Jinnah as well as the Congress leaders. The significance was profound. One of the premises of the 1942 offer was that India might be held together by the union of the Congress and the Muslim League fighting against the Japanese.[28] The collapse of the Cripps mission meant that Jinnah could pursue the alternative option of not joining a unified India after the war. It is arguable that if Roosevelt had leaned on Churchill, and Churchill in turn had been obliged to tone down Linlithgow and Wavell's objections, then Congress might have been able to participate in a 'national' government and Pakistan might not have become a mass issue.

Two Indian historians, M. S. Venkataramani and B. K. Shrivastava, have dealt at length with the American dimension of the problem.[29] As they point out, Roosevelt was getting advice from not only Louis Johnson in Delhi but also Harry Hopkins in London. As usual, FDR was hedging his bets. From my own rereading of the Roosevelt Papers at Hyde Park, he genuinely anticipated not only a Japanese

[27] Amery to Churchill, 5 March 1942, in *Transfer of Power*, I, p. 324.
[28] See Gopal, *Nehru*, chap. 17; and Moore, *Churchill, Cripps, and India*.
[29] See *Quit India*.

invasion of India but also possible revolution.[30] This was the gist of some of the warnings he received from Louis Johnson. But Harry Hopkins had his ear, and the voice was an echo of Churchill's. Churchill was well aware that FDR suspected that the British were unwilling to grant the equivalent of self-government and that a compromise might be found on the issue of control of defence affairs. FDR was no doubt moved by Churchill's passionate eloquence. But he also made decisions that corresponded with his highest priorities in winning the war. By insisting on Indian self-government (about which Roosevelt himself had doubts) at this stage of the war—four months after Pearl Harbor—not only would he have caused dismay among his own military advisers such as Henry L. Stimson, but he would also have driven a wedge into the Anglo-American alliance. It was better to keep on good terms with Churchill than with Gandhi. No one can say for certain whether FDR's support of Johnson and Cripps might have won the allegiance of the Indian National Congress and thus might have helped defeat the Japanese. What can be said is that Roosevelt's intervention in the Indian issue would have had drastic repercussions in Anglo-American relations.

After the collapse of the Cripps mission, the next juncture was the 'Quit India' movement of August 1942. Linlithgow, from a Tory vantage point, rose to the occasion. The day after the fall of Singapore (15 February 1942), he had written that 'the key to success in this war is now very largely in my hands'.[31] After the fall of Rangoon on 8 March, he apprehended that Gandhi was organizing an all-out effort to undermine the authority of the government. He feared the danger of the Mahatma's 'Pétainism'. He had taken all precautions against the 'open rebellion' of the Congress. The day after the All India Congress Committee's demand for immediate departure of the British, Gandhi and other prominent Congress leaders were arrested. The rebellion was quelled within six weeks. By the end of the year there had been 1,000 killed, 3,000 injured, and more than 60,000 interned (the conventional British figures). '[If] we had [not] struck as swiftly and as decisively as we did', Linlithgow wrote to Amery, 'we might have found ourselves faced with an extremely awkward situation, wholly revolutionary in character, well organised by people working underground

[30] For example, the prominent journalist Louis Fischer noted after a confidential conversation with Sumner Welles (Under Secretary of State) that if 'things get much worse', in other words, if India appeared to be moving towards revolution, 'we might have reason to deal with the matter' (memorandum by Fischer, 25 September 1942, Fischer Papers, Franklin D. Roosevelt Library, Hyde Park, New York).

[31] Linlithgow to Amery, 16 February 1942, in *Transfer of Power*, I, p. 186.

and deterred by no considerations of non-violence or the like.'[32] Linlithgow felt that he was entirely entitled to claim that he was suppressing the most serious rebellion since 1857, indeed since the American Revolution.[33]

At no time, of course, could the High Commissioner for Palestine have made such a claim. The comparison would be the crackdown on the Jewish nationalists in mid-1946, (2,700 interned) and, in July of the same year, the explosion at the King David Hotel in Jerusalem, which took 90 lives—British, Arab, and Jewish. Yet as long as the Palestine issue festered, Britain's security was threatened throughout the Middle East. There lies the reason why the Palestine emergency is comparable on a large scale to that of India. In India, the key to British resolution of the problem partly lay in Churchill, Amery, and Linlithgow's success in preventing the internationalization of the issue. The quelling of the 1942 disturbances proved to most Americans, including Roosevelt, that in India the British could manage their own affairs and would resist to the bitter end any American interference. By contrast, after 1945 the British had to rely on American assistance in dealing with Palestine. This assessment is not to minimize the place held by India in American calculations during the war itself. Auchinleck's biographer, John Connell, has written:

> Their stand-point was one of cold, vigilant, businesslike and rather naive detachment; but above all they were concerned with the subcontinent's strategic and logistical utility. By contrast the British . . . knew India . . . and the Americans did not; and for the time being they ruled India.[34]

One may rightly infer that most Americans believed that the British Empire was in an impending state of dissolution in India and at least parts of the Middle East.

Roosevelt did not change his mind on not intervening in India, and he was kept well informed. Louis Johnson's successor was William Phillips, a former Under Secretary of State who is a figure of considerable interest in the India-Palestine analogy because he later served on the Anglo-American Committee of Inquiry in Palestine in 1946. Phillips regarded Linlithgow as a chip off the old block of George III.

---

[32] Linlithgow to Amery, 17 August 1942, in *Transfer of Power,* II, p. 740.

[33] For the analogy of 1857 and 1942, see Francis G. Hutchings, *India's Revolution: Gandhi and the Quit India Movement* (Cambridge, Mass., 1973).

[34] John Connell, *Auchinleck* (London, 1959), p. 727.

Phillips was appalled at the pomp, extravagance, and arrogance of the Raj. He believed it a serious mistake on the part of Linlithgow not to keep open channels of communication with the Congress leaders and not to seek a course of conciliation. Yet Phillips remained a 'perfect gentleman' (Amery's phrase) and acquiesced in Linlithgow's dictum to 'keep off the grass'. Phillips did so not out of sympathy with British rule in India but because this was Roosevelt's policy. As long as the war lasted, Roosevelt was content to let the British uphold the status quo. Changes would come later. In his last dispatch from Delhi in May 1943, Phillips ruefully reported that the British were 'sitting "pretty" . . . [and] have been completely successful in their policy of "keeping the lid on" . . . There is to be no change'—at least not so long as Linlithgow remained Viceroy.[35]

When Lord Wavell became Viceroy in October 1943, his outlook in some ways resembled Linlithgow's. Wavell was not anti-Hindu, but he was profoundly mistrustful of Gandhi and the Congress leaders. In his view, Gandhi was a purely negative force, incapable of imposing or inventing a positive solution. Wavell was sensitive to Muslim sentiment. It is his Middle Eastern background that I wish to stress in order to sustain the Palestine theme, and here it is useful to contrast Wavell's general outlook with Cripps's.

Despite Cripps's intellectual arrogance, he and the Congress leaders established a rapport that never existed to the same degree with any other British statesman, certainly not Attlee and definitely not Wavell. Cripps believed that it was of transcendent importance for Britain to remain on good terms with the 400 million Indians—one-fifth of humanity—and therefore with its majority, the Hindus, and the 'Hindu leadership', led by Nehru and Patel (with of course Gandhi as the spiritual, even if not the guiding political, figure). In other words, Cripps pursued a line of conciliation, which in the eyes of his critics was one of appeasement.

Before his Viceroyalty, Wavell had become Commander-in-Chief in India after a lifetime of military service, mainly in the Middle East. He certainly did not minimize the importance of keeping on good terms with the Hindus, but he attached just as much significance to maintaining good relations with the ninety-million-Muslim minority in India, a group larger than the combined population of the Arab states of the Middle East. Wavell regarded the 'Muslim world' as stretching in a loose sense all the way from Morocco to Indonesia. From this angle, the Muslim minority in India could be regarded as part of the

---

[35] Quoted in M. S. Venkataramani and B. K. Shrivastava, *Roosevelt, Gandhi, Churchill: America and the Last Phase of India's Freedom Struggle* (New Delhi, 1983), p. 149.

overall majority, and the Hindu majority in India as a minority in the predominant majority. All of this had grave implications for the British Empire and Commonwealth unless the majorities and minorities (regardless of how one looked at the problem) could somehow be reconciled. It was by no means clear that an even-handed policy would work. Cripps believed that the British should tilt towards the Hindus, while Wavell's inclinations propelled him towards the Muslims.

'[T]he really fatal thing for us', Wavell wrote in regard to the analogy between the Middle East and India, 'would be to hang on to responsibility when we had lost the power to exercise it, and possibly to involve ourselves in a large-scale Palestine.'[36] By late 1946, perhaps even earlier, Britain stood on the verge of being drawn into civil war not only in Palestine but also in Greece. In Palestine, Britain and the United States would find themselves on opposite sides. In India the British could count on American support, even in the event of partition, provided they worked to prevent further 'balkanization' and attempted to ensure stability by a peaceful transfer of power. It was imperative for the British to maintain American good will in the eastern Mediterranean and throughout the world. Attlee's phrase 'world-wide commitments' helps explain both Palestinian and Indian dilemmas.

Are there further commonalities? This is not the place to analyse the details of the Simla conference of 1945 and the Cabinet Mission of 1946, on the one hand, or, on the other, of the Anglo-American Committee of Inquiry of 1945–46 and the conferences held by the British and the Jews and Arabs in 1946–47. One may, however, put forward two generalizations about the policy of the Labour Government:

1. The goal was to avoid partition in both India and Palestine;
2. If the goal proved unobtainable after every possible effort had been made at reconciliation, then the aim would be to cut losses strictly in terms of British self-interest.

It was on the latter point, as will be seen, that Wavell found himself out of step with the Labour Government's method of doing business. His pessimistic outlook on Indian politics contributed to his sacking as Viceroy.

The Palestinian and Indian issues were handled entirely separately, the former by Ernest Bevin as Secretary of State for Foreign Affairs, and the latter by a Cabinet Committee on India and Burma with Attlee and Cripps as the driving forces within it. Significantly enough, Bevin was not on the India and Burma committee. It was commonly

---

[36] Wavell to H.M. King George VI, 24 February 1947, in *Transfer of Power*, IX, p. 807.

alleged that he knew little of the Jewish mentality, and it may be added that he probably knew even less of the Hindu. Richard Crossman once stated that it was a godsend that Bevin had no hand in India because he would have mucked it up as well.[37] Bevin wished to keep India within the British Empire, though with a shift towards an 'equal relationship' (in his view synonymous with Dominion Status) similar to the one he was attempting to bring about in Egypt. He entirely dominated the Palestine question. His solution was essentially the one of the 1939 White Paper, in which there would be Jewish autonomy within a larger Arab federation. Like Wavell and Mountbatten in India, he was willing to negotiate the terms of the federation (or its variations of 'provincial autonomy' along the lines of Swiss cantons), but his goal was to create a binational society with Palestine remaining essentially an Arab country. He encountered the stone wall not only of Jewish nationalism but also of the President of the United States and his advisers. The Zionists, notably Weizmann, had managed to win President Truman over to their side, and the President, not the State Department officials sympathetic to the Arabs, determined American policy. Truman once candidly stated that his pro-Zionist attitude could be explained by his having no Arab constituents.[38] He also had few Indian constituents, which perhaps explains his relative indifference to the question of India. When Bevin visited America in late 1946, he was astonished at the extent to which Palestine had become an issue in American politics. The Zionists were able to wage a successful crusade not only because they captured the President but also because they won a substantial amount of public sentiment. The struggle against the British struck a responsive chord in the memory of America's own revolutionary history, as well as with other ethnic groups, notably the Irish.[39]

Despite the powerful Zionist and American opposition to his policy, Bevin nevertheless hoped to form a common front with the Arabs, who, after all, were the dominant majority in the neighbouring Middle Eastern states as well as Palestine. It was the failure to carry the Arabs with them—a breakdown of the 'collaborative mechanism', in Ronald Robinson's phrase—that led Bevin and Attlee in late 1946 and early 1947 to refer the issue to the United Nations, where they still hoped that the aim of creating a binational state—in other words, an unpartitioned Palestine—would carry the majority.[40] It lost by only a few

[37] See the New York tabloid *P.M.*, 26 October 1947.

[38] See Evan M. Wilson, *Decision on Palestine: How the U.S. Came to Recognize Israel* (Stanford, 1979), p. 58.

[39] See, for example, Isaiah Berlin, *Personal Impressions* (New York, 1981).

[40] See, for example, David Horowitz, *State in the Making* (New York, 1953), p. 143.

votes on 29 November 1947. The British had already decided to cut their losses, but only after all options had been tried and all possibilities exhausted. In the end, Palestine was judged to be a drain on the British economy and a military liability. In the Cabinet deliberations on how best to minimize American and Arab antagonism, the case for an even-handed withdrawal was overwhelming.

When the British evacuated Palestine in the spring of 1948, the withdrawal was remarkably similar to the 'breakdown plan' drawn up by Wavell two years earlier in India. By 'breakdown', Wavell did not necessarily mean to imply defeat, but rather the possibilities and probabilities of British withdrawal as a result of unwavering Indian opposition. He foresaw a prolonged stalemate between the Congress and the Muslim League, which might paralyze the administration and eventually lead to mass disturbances. One of the lessons of the 1942 'Quit India' movement was the possibility that it might happen again. This time the British might not be able to contain it successfully. As an administrative and military precaution, Wavell's plan for possible withdrawal was a rational and necessary measure. As a matter of policy for the Labour Government, it was unacceptable. It seemed to Attlee, not to mention Bevin and others who denounced Wavell as a defeatist, to be prejudging or moving towards the most undesirable outcome without finally exhausting the possibilities of a political settlement. Until the constitutional negotiations had proved to be futile, Attlee refused to despair.[41] There was an element of the Major Attlee of the First World War, who was contemptuous of military officers' capacity for political judgement. Attlee and Cripps became increasingly intent on a political settlement with the leaders of the Congress and the Muslim League, even if it meant the upheaval of partition. The scepticism whether Wavell could salvage the situation led to Lord Mountbatten's succession in March 1947. By late 1946, India, as Wavell himself admitted, seemed to be going the way of Palestine, but without the determined effort to turn the tide.

In 1946 there were certain turning points in both India and Palestine, perhaps points of no return. In February, sailors of the Royal Indian Navy mutinied in Bombay. The mutiny had critical implications for British security throughout India. In March, the Cabinet Mission failed to produce agreement on a sophisticated 'three tier' system of government that attempted to strike a communal balance in part by groupings of Hindu- and Muslim-majority provinces (a scheme not dissimilar to some of the variants of the 'provincial autonomy' plan in

[41] See 'Notes by Mr Attlee', [November 1946], in *Transfer of Power*, IX, pp. 68–69.

Palestine). After the Muslim League's 'Direct Action' and the Calcutta massacre of 6,000 in August, all hope was lost (in the consensus of British historical opinion) for a united India. The comparable turning points on the Palestine side may also be briefly stated. The report of the Anglo-American Committee of Inquiry in April recommended that Palestine be neither a Jewish nor an Arab state (in other words, the implicit premise was that of a binational state) and called for the immediate admission of 100,000 Jewish refugees. There followed a concerted military effort by the Zionists aiming to force Britain into a political settlement; but there was also the explosion at the King David Hotel in July, caused by the extremists. Ernest Bevin continued to hold out hope for a binational solution, but the extreme Zionists were on their way to proving that a campaign of terrorism might be successful.

Even though terrorism might be successfully combated (as some British military officers believed it could), prolonged conflict would turn Palestine into an immense 'Bevingrad', in other words, a territory under harsh military occupation with troops bivouacked behind barbed wire. British forces would be compelled to wage guerrilla warfare in an urban setting against the survivors of Nazi Germany (as in fact proved to be the case). Quite apart from the demand on the manpower of the British Army, the strain on morale would be severe, even in a territory the size of Wales. According to one calculation, there was one British soldier for every city block.[42] If the Jews could do it, why not the Hindus or the Muslims, whose chances for success were far greater? Lord Wavell thus had good reason to be apprehensive of a 'large-scale Palestine' in India. Even if the willpower of a Killearn or a Linlithgow could be reasserted, where could the manpower be found?

'Up to now', Field Marshal Sir Claude Auchinleck (Commander-in-Chief, India) stated in June 1946, 'it had been possible to rely on the loyalty of the Indian army.' The Hindu-Muslim rift now cast doubt on the reliability of Indian units even outside of India itself. 'This even applies to Gurkha units,' according to the Chiefs of Staff.[43] Should the Indian armed forces be disaffected, it would require no less than four to five additional British divisions to restore the situation. Where were the additional troops to come from? No British troops would remain in Greece. British forces in Germany would be halved. The reserve division in Italy would be removed. And the entire question of Indian forces in Indonesia would have to be reviewed. Not least there would

---

[42] The classic indictment of the British administration in Palestine as a 'police state' is Jorge García-Granados, *The Birth of Israel* (New York, 1948).

[43] Chiefs of Staff report, 12 June 1946, in *Transfer of Power*, VII, p. 892; Cabinet Minutes, 5 June 1946, ibid., p. 815.

be insufficient troops to keep the peace in Palestine.[44] Nor was there complete agreement on priority. According to Field Marshal Lord Montgomery, who became Chief of the Imperial General Staff in July 1946, 'the provision of the divisions would be impossible in view of the present situation in Palestine and Venezia Giulia.'[45] If there was one particular year when the sun never appeared to set on the troubles of the British Empire, it was probably 1946.[46]

If that year in some respects seemed to represent an 'Imperial' nadir, then 1947, Palestine aside, was Britain's year for a miracle (hyperbole was not restricted to the creation of the state of Israel). India and Pakistan agreed to Commonwealth membership. In Palestine, all talk of a Jewish 'Dominion' had stopped in 1939, even before. India and Pakistan resembled a phoenix arising from the ashes of the British Empire of a past age. 'This does not look like quitting,' wrote J. C. Smuts, the Prime Minister of South Africa.[47] Indeed, at one stage it appeared as if the British might more or less preserve the unity of India, with two Dominions under one Governor-General, who would coordinate defence issues and thus preserve Britain's status as a great 'world power'. Pakistan and India would continue to link the Empire and Dominions in the East in defence affairs as well as on the map, which would continue to be painted British red. As Partha Gupta has argued, the defence issue was at the heart of the matter for the British.[48] When Mountbatten learned that Patel and Nehru would be prepared to accept, as an interim measure at least, Dominion Status (and to muffle the Congress battle cry of an 'independent sovereign Republic') in return for an early transfer of power, Churchill and the Tories as well as the Labour Government leapt at 'the greatest opportunity', in Mountbatten's ringing words, 'ever offered to the Empire'.[49] The terminal date of British rule, which Wavell had insisted upon and the British Cabinet had fixed at no later than June 1948, would be moved forward, eventually to 15 August—a date Mountbatten chose, in his precipitous effort to move as quickly as possible, not merely because it signified the anniversary of the end of the Second World War, but also because he foresaw the collapse of British authority.

These concluding comments will approach the actual transfer of

---

[44] See *Transfer of Power*, VII, pp. 894–95.

[45] Ibid., p. 965, note 11.

[46] See John Gallagher, *The Decline, Revival, and Fall of the British Empire* (Cambridge, 1982), pp. 145–50.

[47] *Transfer of Power*, X, p. 988.

[48] Partha Sarathi Gupta, 'British Strategic and Economic Priorities during the Negotiations for the Transfer of Power in South Asia, 1945–47', *Bangladesh Historical Studies*, VII (1983).

[49] *Transfer of Power*, X, p. 699.

power by viewing it in a Middle Eastern and American context, and finally by drawing a comparison between the territorial partitions of Palestine and India. One of the key decisions was taken by Attlee and Bevin after Christmas 1946, when they decided to withdraw troops from Greece and, almost simultaneously, as has been mentioned, to refer the Palestine question to the United Nations. A study of this juncture is rewarding because it indicates the common motive in both Palestine and India: the refusal to be drawn into civil war. In early 1947 the United States acquired a commitment to defend the eastern Mediterranean, thereby relieving the British of immense economic and military burdens and enabling them to concentrate on the 'British' Middle East. The sudden expansion of American power worked to British advantage in India. The Congress leaders were suspicious, in the words of Krishna Menon, of 'American absorption'—the Americans 'wished to capture all the markets, to step in and take the place of the British'.[50] Mountbatten played on those anxieties, just as he emphasized to Jinnah that Commonwealth membership could not be taken for granted.

The accession to membership by India and Pakistan has to be seen, in other words, both against the background of the developing Cold War, and as a result of Mountbatten's ingenuity and the calculations of self-interest on the part of the Indians. The grandiose ambitions of the British to remain a 'world power' with the support of India and Pakistan were soon dispelled by Jinnah's insistence on becoming Governor-General of Pakistan (thus dashing Mountbatten's hope of coordinating defence affairs from a central position) and by the crisis in Kashmir; but could anyone else have 'bounced' (a word used in Whitehall) India and Pakistan into the Commonwealth? His achievement is not easy to compare with the other colonial emergencies of the era. One Colonial Office official—to take a random example—lamented in 1950 that there was no one to 'bounce' the Cypriots into position in Mountbatten style.[51]

The British decision to withdraw from Palestine was made on 20 September 1947 (little over a month after the transfer of power in India) in the wake of the sterling convertibility crisis and, more directly, the majority report of the United Nations Special Committee on Palestine, recommending partition. According to the minutes of the British Cabinet:

> The Prime Minister said that in his view there was a close parallel between the position in Palestine and the recent situation in India. He

[50] Mountbatten's conversation with Menon, 22 April 1947, in *Transfer of Power*, X, p. 372.
[51] See minute by Mary Fisher, 31 January 1951, CO 531/7453.

did not think it reasonable to ask the British administration to continue in present conditions, and he hoped that salutary results would
be produced by a clear announcement that His Majesty's Government intended to relinquish the Mandate and, failing a peaceful settlement, to withdraw the British administration and British forces.[52]

As in India, the pace was quickened and the final date for the termination of the mandate finally set at 15 May 1948. Once the evacuation (and its concomitant of partition) had been decided upon, then
it would be, the British hoped, quick and decisive, with most of Arab
Palestine absorbed by Transjordan. The principal calculation was that
the Jews might be held to the coastal plain and contained in the areas
allocated to them by the United Nations Special Committee on Palestine (which included the desert area of the Negev). The UN map, in
the phrase used at the time, resembled a 'portrait by Picasso'. During
the war of 1948 the Israelis were able to paint it mainly in their own
colour by force of arms. The Jewish state was won on the field of battle;
the frontiers were so determined. The Israeli triumph was curtailed
only by an American ultimatum in January 1949. In contrast to the
partition of India, there was no division of assets, no problem of dividing an army, and no dissolution of the civil service. Much of the Israeli
success may be attributed to careful administrative as well as military
planning. From the British vantage point in 1949, nothing was left 'but
the dismal wreck of Arab Palestine'.[53]

The boundary award in India at least had the continuity of one
pen and one man's effort to delimit Muslim and Hindu majority areas.
Sir Cyril (later Lord) Radcliffe, by having to adjudicate among the
boundary commissioners as Chairman, ruthlessly applied the geographical principles of Mountbatten's political maxim of equal self-
determination—in Radcliffe's phrase, 'the fundamental principle of
contiguous areas'.[54] Radcliffe himself remains somewhat of an enigma,
but Mountbatten's aim in the partition is quite clear. He wished to
avoid the impression of having anything to do with the boundary
award, thereby ensuring his reputation for impartiality, and he hoped
to postpone the announcement of the award until after the independence ceremonies. This he managed to do, and he later defended to
the hilt his decisions about the pace, though he seems to have had
pangs of conscience about the consequences. 'To be thoroughly candid and callous and brutal', Mountbatten states in his final set of oral

[52] Cabinet Minutes (47) 76, 20 September 1947, CAB 128/10.

[53] Michael Wright (Foreign Office) to Sir Ronald Campbell, 30 March 1949, FO 371/75064.

[54] For a detailed assessment of the 'specialist surgeon', see S. A. Akanda, 'The Bengal Boundary Commission and the Radcliffe Award, 1947', *Bangladesh Historical Studies*, VII (1983).

memoirs (published in 1984), only 0.01 per cent of the total population of 400 million were killed: 'That's the first thing to realize.' To reiterate his central explanation: 'I was afraid of not, 200,000 people, but two or three million dead which could easily have happened with civil war, easily.'[55]

If there is one point more than any other that emerges emphatically in Mountbatten's oral testimony, it is his determination in the summer and autumn of 1947 not to engage units of the British army. He was determined at any cost not to be drawn into civil war; otherwise he would not only risk his reputation for impartiality but would inevitably lose the good will of one side or the other and probably both. There lies the contrast with Palestine, where the British left with the ill will of the Jews and with only the cold comfort of knowing that the Arabs at least held the Americans to be largely responsible for the creation of the State of Israel. There is at least one remarkable feature of these massive British disengagements from India, Palestine, and, it should be added, Greece. This is perhaps best established in relation to the bald statistics of the end of British tutelage in Palestine and India: there were over one million Arab refugees in Palestine; in India some six to seven million Hindus and Muslims changed sides, and at least 200,000 were killed.[56] With the exception of the disastrous RAF incident in January 1949 (in which four Spitfires on reconnaissance in the Negev were shot down by the Israelis), British forces emerged from these upheavals virtually unscathed. In India, Mountbatten proved himself to be a consummate practitioner of disengagement. He was quite right about the implications of Indian independence. If the British could avoid being drawn into civil war and manage to bring India and Pakistan into the Commonwealth, it would immensely enhance Britain's 'prestige' (at least among other Western powers). Walter Lippmann, for one (and he was perhaps the most influential of the post-war journalists), confirmed that judgement when he wrote a few weeks before the actual transfer of power that for the British, this was indeed their 'finest hour'.[57]

Warfare, Diplomacy, and Politics: Essays in Honour of A. J. P. Taylor   1986

[55] Larry Collins and Dominique Lapierre, *Mountbatten and Independent India, 16 August 1947–18 June 1948* (New Delhi, 1984), pp. 19–20, 24.

[56] 'Plus or minus 50,000', in Mountbatten's final judgement. Collins and Lapierre, *Mountbatten and Independent India*, p. 24.

[57] *Washington Post*, 7 June 1947; see Philip Ziegler, *Mountbatten* (London, 1985), p. 428.

15

TAKING THE PLUNGE
INTO INDIAN INDEPENDENCE

The flames of controversy still blaze forty years after India's partition, not merely in scholarly circles but among all those who hold strong views about the end of the British era in India, whether they see it as a catastrophe or as a glorious new beginning. Shahid Hamid's *Disastrous Twilight* (1986) is a sustained attack on Lord Mountbatten, who as Viceroy in 1947 presided over the division of the subcontinent. 'Mountbatten, and Mountbatten alone, will have the blood of all these innocent people on his hands,' Hamid wrote in June 1947, anticipating the mass slaughter in the Punjab two months later. R. J. Moore's *Making the New Commonwealth* (1987) is a scholarly assessment of the consequences of partition and of the creative effort to salvage the smouldering remnants of the British Raj. The British attempted to remain neutral in what Moore describes as 'the communal holocaust' of Sikhs and Muslims. Virtually by an act of will the Labour Government managed to reconstruct out of the rubble the new Commonwealth, which, in Moore's judgement, has become Britain's 'greatest contribution to civilization'.

Hamid was an Indian Army officer who in March 1946 became private secretary to Sir Claude Auchinleck, Commander-in-Chief of the Indian Army. Auchinleck is the hero of *Disastrous Twilight,* Mountbatten the villain. 'He is flirting with the Congress leaders,' Hamid wrote about Mountbatten when the latter passed through Delhi while still Supreme Allied Commander South-East Asia, some nine months before he became Viceroy. At the same time, May 1946, Auchinleck rose to the rank of Field Marshal. Hamid served with him until August 1947 and remained in close contact until December, the crucial months in the aftermath of partition. He kept a diary, which forms the substance of *Disastrous Twilight.* He patiently recorded the straightforward, honourable, and courageous impulses of Auchinleck, and, in his own words, the 'devious', 'ignoble', 'sinister' motives of Mountbatten. This, then, is a highly subjective account. It is nevertheless a useful and revealing one.

Disastrous Twilight helps restore perspective on Auchinleck. Hamid, accurately reflecting popular sentiment, describes him as the embodiment of the Indian Army before its dissolution by Mountbatten in August 1947. 'He is more Indian than British,' Hamid noted in 1946. 'His lasting achievement will always be the creation of a genuinely Indian Army.' There is much to be said for this point of view. 'The Auk' was not only one of Britain's greatest soldiers, but also one of the truly distinguished military commanders of the Second World War. He was a soldier's soldier, always most at ease with his troops—living with them, eating the same food, sleeping on the ground, setting an example of camaraderie, dignity, and courage by his own conduct. In the old Indian Army there was unquestionably greater affection for him than for any other commander. Unlike Mountbatten, Auchinleck believed that a 'recording angel' would establish his place in history and thus that he had no need to defend or explain his actions.

In an elegant and incisive introduction to *Disastrous Twilight,* Philip Ziegler points out that Hamid's account is valuable not only for its coherence but also because it represents a radically different interpretation from the one that has predominated in Britain (and, one might add, in the United States). In view of Ziegler's own recent biography, *Mountbatten,* which in essentials is contradicted by Hamid's strictures, this is a generous statement in the service of historical scholarship. The diary is internally consistent and transparently honest. There is much more at stake here than the reputation of Auchinleck as an honourable soldier attempting to maintain the unity of India and to prevent the division of the Indian Army, or the portrayal of Mountbatten as a tricky politician who becomes little more than a puppet manipulated by leaders of the Indian National Congress, Jawaharlal Nehru and Vallabhbhai Patel. These are simplistic views, and the immensely complicated problem of India's partition cannot be reduced to personalities. But Hamid's interpretation leads to an issue of genuine historical controversy. Auchinleck believe that the Indian Army and, if necessary, British troops could have been used to prevent or at least ameliorate the massacres in the Punjab. In Auchinleck's view, Mountbatten's decision to leave precipitately in August 1947—in effect, to scuttle—was a calamitous and unnecessary mistake. Mountbatten, then and for ever after, held that a quick departure was necessary to prevent an even greater explosion.

Seldom have the two conflicting interpretations been so sharply drawn. Hamid goes for the jugular in his indictment of Mountbatten. He wrote in March 1947, a few days after Mountbatten's advent as Viceroy:

> Soon after the arrival of Mountbatten there was a point of disagreement between him and the Auk. The latter maintained that in order to uphold British prestige, British troops must be used to save lives. The Provinces were continuously demanding them for internal security duties.
>
> Mountbatten, however, was of the opinion that they must be sent away before the date of handing over. Behind this he had a sinister

motive. He thought that their withdrawal would help in keeping
both India and Pakistan in the Commonwealth as the two countries
would not be too confident of their defence capabilities and probably would bank on His Majesty's Government's assistance. Besides he
was frightened of being blamed for any action the British troops may
take in putting down disturbances.

The quotation is a good example of the subjective quality of the diary.
Mountbatten was supremely self-confident. It is grotesque to describe
him as frightened or lacking in nerve. Nevertheless, Hamid was on to
something when he pondered the military consequences of the partition. As Moore substantiates in his new book, both India and Pakistan
feared that leaving the Commonwealth would give military advantage
to the other.

'Why this hurry?' Hamid asked after Mountbatten's announcement
that power would be transferred on 15 August 1947. 'Why this shock
treatment? What is at the back of it?' Those questions led to even more
fundamental ones: 'Why is he bulldozing everything and leaving no
time for an organized handover? Does he not realize that things done
in such a desperate hurry can lead to chaos, confusion and shambles?'
And lastly: 'Is he trying to show the world that he has succeeded in
finding a solution and has managed to keep the two States in the Commonwealth?' On the ethics of the Viceroy's determination to leave
quickly and decisively, *Disastrous Twilight* is unequivocal: 'I think he is
prepared to accept bloodshed and human miseries.' 'Sheer irrespon-
sibility' was the phrase Hamid used to sum up Mountbatten's head-
long plunge into Indian independence. There is nothing said in the
Viceroy's defence. But what does emerge clearly (and it can be veri-
fied independently in the Auchinleck Papers at the Rylands Library at
the University of Manchester) is that Auchinleck would have pursued
a slower and steadier pace, and that he would have deployed troops
from the British as well as the Indian Army to try to keep the peace. In
the event, his counsel was ignored.

The Viceroy had a poor opinion of the Field Marshal's political
judgement. 'Mountbatten is reported to have said', Hamid wrote, 'that
the Auk lacks political sense!!' It must be said that Mountbatten was
not entirely wrong. In one of the most astonishing documents reproduced in *Disastrous Twilight,* the Field Marshal writes to the Viceroy
in September 1947 that the Sikhs are up to even more trouble in the
Punjab, planning to step up the communal war and to create an independent Sikh state, 'Sikhistan'. This was no doubt being tried,
though not with the ruthless and systematic efficiency attributed by
Auchinleck to one of the Sikh leaders, Tara Singh, nor, as Auchinleck

believed, with the connivance of the Indian Government. In what must rank as one of the great conspiracy theories of modern Indian history, Auchinleck traced the troubles of independent India to the ambitions of the Congress leaders to establish a 'Hindu Raj' that would re-incorporate the lost Muslim provinces:

> [T]he Sikh plans are much what I have always thought they would be. Briefly, they intend to make Simla the capital of a Sikh State, in which there will be very few if any Muslims and possibly not many Hindus either . . .

> The Muslims of Lahore and the border districts are in a very jumpy state and firmly believe in the coming Sikh 'invasion'. The theory is that the Indian Government would not sponsor any such aggression but would make a show of trying to hold the Sikhs back without actually doing very much. If the attempt failed they would disown them and say 'we did our best to hold you back—now you have had it'. They (the Hindus) would then set about the Sikhs properly and destroy their cohesion.

> If the attempt succeeded, it is probable that the Indian Government would back them up and use the chance to destroy the Pakistan Government and so bring Pakistan to an end, substituting a Brahmin 'Raj' for the whole of India including Pakistan.

Auchinleck here demonstrates the stereotypes of the British military mind in its Indian setting. The Auk was a great soldier, and second to none in service to the Indian Army; in high politics he was out of his element.

In perhaps the most controversial part of *Disastrous Twilight,* Hamid sustains the frequent accusation that Mountbatten intervened in the boundary award to Pakistan and India, to the latter's advantage. Specifically, so runs the indictment, Mountbatten persuaded Sir Cyril Radcliffe, the boundary commissioner, to alter the boundary of the Gurdaspur district of the Punjab to provide India with a strategic corridor to Kashmir. Without such access by land, Kashmir might not have gone to India. In Hamid's view, the Kashmir dispute would have been avoided at the outset by Kashmir acceding to Pakistan, for legitimate demographic, ethnic, religious, and geographical reasons.

The evidence adduced by Hamid to prove the point of Viceregal interference is a provisional sketch-map sent, a few days before the award, by Radcliffe to Sir Evan Jenkins, the Governor of Punjab. It was later discovered in his safe by his successor, Sir Francis Mudie, who became Governor of West Punjab in the new state of Pakistan. The sketch-map indicated a line favourable to Pakistan, denying the Gurdaspur corridor to India. Before the actual award, the map was altered—according to Hamid, because of the Viceroy's wish to appease Nehru. The award itself ceded the critical corridor to India. Unfortunately for those who would like to convict the Viceroy of tilting towards India, his complicity cannot thus far be proved. Nevertheless a sceptical mind cannot but ask whether Mountbatten might have skilfully covered his tracks.

One of the opening chapters of *Making the New Commonwealth* examines the Gurdaspur dispute in detail. Moore is a cautious historian whose writings are dispassionate and judicious. He notes that Mountbatten once remarked that Kashmir might go either way, but that if it were to become part of India, then the eastern part of Gurdaspur, in effect the corridor, would have to be awarded to India. Moore thus sets the stage for historical detective work. Did Mountbatten in fact intervene? What of Radcliffe and his motives? What weight should be given to the sketch-map? What of its recipient, Sir Evan Jenkins? In view of the importance of the Kashmir issue both for India and Pakistan and as a historic problem before the United Nations and in world politics, Moore's answers are of considerable interest.

The evidence seems to lead away from convicting Mountbatten, though it does not especially enhance his reputation for integrity. One of the members of his staff, W. H. J. Christie, noted on 9 August 1947 (several days before the boundary award) that the Viceroy was 'having to be strenuously dissuaded from asking Radcliffe to alter his award'. Mountbatten apparently had to be reminded that it was in his own interest, whatever the outcome, to let Radcliffe bear 'the odium of arbitration'. The Viceroy, along with his Chief of Staff, Lord Ismay, did meet with Radcliffe. Mountbatten later had irresistible urges to meddle with the evidence. He later thanked Ismay for persuading him not to intervene. Ismay had to record that his recollections of the meeting with Radcliffe were 'far different' from Mountbatten's and that there was no need for byzantine historical reconstruction. 'Our consciences are perfectly clear,' Ismay wrote, because Radcliffe himself claimed that the award represented his own 'unfettered judgement'. Here is a clue, though it may be misleading. It confirms Radcliffe's reputation as a man of high ethical standards. In any event, the integrity of Sir Evan Jenkins is beyond question. He accepted the map for what it was, merely a provisional and rough indication of the boundary. He later stated that he would have solved the Gurdaspur problem in exactly the same way as Radcliffe. Thus the evidence seems to point to Mountbatten's acquittal; he appears not to have intervened. Moore himself seems to deliver the Scots verdict of not proven.

Until now my own view has been that Mountbatten's staff succeeded in restraining him, but that in any event Radcliffe would have not have listened. Having read Hamid's book, and having thought again about the circumstantial evidence, I now believe that Mountbatten might have persuaded Radcliffe to alter the boundary award.

Moore thinks that Radcliffe revised the boundary on his own initiative after taking into further consideration the local railways, rivers, and canals. He judged that taking the Sutlej River as a natural frontier should outweigh the principle guiding the overall division, that of 'contiguous Muslim nationalities'. The award could be justified within its own local circumstances, without reference to Kashmir. All of this is exceedingly complex, but Moore's conclusion, drawn after exhaustive study of contemporary maps and demographic figures, may be clearly stated in his own words:

> Radcliffe's award, which was finally published on 17 August [1947], is not to be understood in terms of the consistent application of simple principles such as the ascertainment of contiguous Muslim majorities . . . or predominant national interests in canal headworks.

> It may be safely said that the modifications to the contiguous-majority principle consistently deprived Pakistan of territories to which that principle entitled her, and that 'other factors' had the effect of enabling the Sikhs to consolidate themselves securely in East Punjab.

The conclusion is profoundly important, not merely for the 1947 settlement but for the evolution of the Sikh problem since then.

Mountbatten devoted most of his attention to solving the conflict between the Congress and Muslim League; he did not spend much time reconciling the Sikhs to the partition of their homeland. Radcliffe thus found himself in the position of having to provide a 'paramilitary' solution to the Sikh problem. According to Moore, Radcliffe felt duty-bound to do justice to the Sikhs: 'His award is consistent with that obligation above all others. It gave to India those "debatable" areas . . . in which Sikhs were a substantial contiguous majority, approaching 25 per cent of the population.' Once it is understood that Radcliffe was attempting to provide a settlement as acceptable as possible to the Sikhs, then his boundary award in the Punjab becomes comprehensible. Here Moore is substantiating the interpretation, derived from much scantier evidence, Professor Hugh Tinker put forward ten years ago. The Pakistanis, needless to say, were not sympathetic to the underlying logic of the award. They regarded the outcome as a 'parting kick of the British to Pakistan'. I myself do not think that

Radcliffe had any particular bias against the Muslims. But he had such a high-powered and balanced intellect that he may well have provided an Indian corridor to Kashmir while attempting to solve, as best he could, the problem of the Sikhs, to the slight disadvantage of the Pakistanis. He destroyed his papers, so we may never know for certain.

If Auchinleck was a soldier's soldier, R. J. Moore is a scholar's scholar. *Making the New Commonwealth* is an erudite monograph, diligently researched and laconically written. So economical is Moore's prose that even an attentive reader must devote full concentration to grasp the argument along with the detail. It is by no means an easy read, but it is a rewarding one. Moore is a reliable guide through the crises of Kashmir and Hyderabad, the problems of post-war defence and the Cold War, the question of transforming the old 'White Man's Club' into a multiracial Commonwealth. (Sir Gilbert Laithwaite, a prominent official throughout the period, remarked in 1948: 'There may be some advantage, given the great Negro population of the Colonial Empire, in avoiding any suggestion that the Commonwealth is a White Man's Club.') One sympathizes with the author's frustration in trying to breathe life into the arid documents of Commonwealth constitutional history. Slowly he succeeds. *Making the New Commonwealth* takes on a dramatic quality when the Prime Minister decides, in the buccaneering spirit of the Labour Government, that, come what may, India must continue to be a member of the Commonwealth. 'There is . . . nothing inherently impossible in a republic forming part of a monarchy,' Attlee wrote in early 1948.

The heart of Moore's work is an explanation of Nehru's motives for wishing to remain in the Commonwealth (even though India would become a republic); the constitutional gymnastics involved in reconciling an Indian republic with the British Crown; and the difficulties of persuading both old and new members of the Commonwealth to go along with the solution. Ernest Bevin, the Foreign Secretary, put the question squarely when he asked whether it was worth keeping India in. 'Her rulers are not animated by the same sentiments of kinship and loyalty as are those of the older Dominions,' he wrote. Outside the government, Lord Salisbury, in a letter not quoted in Moore's book, expressed the Tory objections most lucidly: 'So far as I can see, India's continued association with the Commonwealth does not help us in any way . . . She will not agree to any coordinated foreign policy. She is definitely hostile to our colonial policy. She reserves the right to stab us in the back at any moment at the United Nations.'

Gradually, Bevin and other members of the Cabinet became converted, not for sentimental reasons, but because they saw the advantages in having close links with India in the deteriorating circumstances of the Cold War. Similar motives could be found on the Indian side, in part because of Nehru's mistrust of the United States. He thought it 'astonishing how naïve the Americans are in their foreign policy' and suspected them, as did the British themselves, of economic imperialism. Against this danger, among others, India's pure self-interest would be better served in the Commonwealth than out. Slowly and with grave deliberation, Australia, New Zealand, South Africa, Canada, and, not least, the new members, Pakistan and Ceylon, decided, each for slightly different reasons, that granting India membership outweighed the disadvantages of kicking her out over what Attlee described as the 'theoretical' constitutional issue. Finally the solution was found: India as a sovereign and free republic would nevertheless recognize the King as head of the Commonwealth—the King, in other words, as a symbol of freely associated and independent states. For those who wish to pursue the constitutional details of the founding of the new Commonwealth in April 1949, Moore's book will be an indispensable companion. It is tantalizing in its clues for further research on the economic, strategic, and political transformation of the Empire into the Commonwealth.

Making the New Commonwealth ends on a wishful note, with Lord Rosebery exclaiming in 1884 that 'the Empire is a commonwealth of Nations', and with another quotation emphasizing that the Commonwealth expresses 'the England of Kipling or even of Dickens!' The Commonwealth continues today, according to Moore, to represent 'peace, liberty, and progress'. No doubt that is true. But the contemprary Commonwealth is a far cry from what Mountbatten had in mind —and here the suspicions of *Disastrous Twilight* are justified—when he secretly spoke of the Commonwealth as a means of keeping India within the Empire.

Times Literary Supplement   28 August 1987

16

THE END OF THE PALESTINE MANDATE

The key to the problem of Britain and the end of the Palestine mandate lies in an understanding of the thought and motivation of the Foreign Secretary, Ernest Bevin. He often referred to British Palestine policy as 'his' policy, and he was right in doing so, even though the contributions of the Prime Minister, the Chiefs of Staff, and the Colonial Secretary were substantial. Bevin was in overall control, and he followed developments with a grasp of detail and force and personality unrivalled by his British contemporaries. He has often been denounced as anti-Semitic. As Alan Bullock has pointed out, however, Bevin reached the age of sixty-four before anyone suspected him of harbouring an anti-Jewish prejudice.[1] It was rather the reverse. Bevin's 'anti-Semitic' reputation developed from policy, not personal sentiment.

Bevin consistently attempted to avert partition. He wished to create a binational state in which Arabs and Jews would live and work together as equals. He temperamentally tended to regard those who disagreed with him as enemies. Thus the Zionists from the beginning became his adversaries. When he was frustrated, he often became angry, and he sometimes rose in wrath against the Americans as well as the Zionists. For example, at a Labour Party conference in June 1946, he exclaimed that the Americans supported the proposal to admit 100,000 Jewish refugees into Palestine because they did not want any more Jews in New York. Bevin's outbursts must not be allowed to obscure the creative thrust and coherence of his purpose. Paradoxically, there is truth in the view that his 'pro-Arab' disposition helped bring about the creation of the state of Israel. Zionists throughout the world were able to unite in vilifying him.

Bevin had in mind Commonwealth precedents for the binational state in Palestine. It was a common British view, in the words of W. K. Hancock, who helped build part of the theory that the Labour Government attempted to put into practice, that 'the experience of Canada and South Africa is written into the mandate'.[2] Towards the end of his life, Bevin referred to Lord Durham's solution of responsible self-government for the French and British in Canada and to Sir Henry

---

[1] Bevin's attitude towards the Jews of Palestine is discussed at length in Alan Bullock, *The Life and Times of Ernest Bevin: Foreign Secretary, 1945–1951* (London, 1983), and in W. R. Louis, *The British Empire in the Middle East, 1945–1951: Arab Nationalism, the United States, and Postwar Imperialism* (Oxford, 1984). The present essay draws from the latter work, though not without a fresh examination of the archival records and reflection on the specific issues of concern here.

[2] W. K. Hancock, *Survey of British Commonwealth Affairs, 1918–1939* (2 vols., London, 1937, 1940), I, p. 473.

Campbell-Bannerman's peace of reconciliation with the Boers as two of the three 'milestones' in the history of the Commonwealth. To Bevin, 'partition' symbolized a bankruptcy of policy, the end of the road, and an admission of failure—though sometimes unavoidable, as in the case of India. The granting of freedom to India and Pakistan was the third of Bevin's milestones.[3] In Palestine he pursued the goal of the binational state with such tenacity that one wonders what might have happened if he had become Secretary of State for India in 1945 rather than Foreign Secretary. In the view of his principal critic on Palestine in the House of Commons, Richard Crossman, the result might have been disastrous. One will never know. The point of the comparison is that the original goal was the same, a unified India on the one hand, a binational state in Palestine on the other. A divided India would split the Indian Army and erode Britain's power in Asia. With a divided Palestine, Arab nationalism would continue to fester and would bring about the end of Britain's paramount position in the Middle East. In sum, Bevin's motivation must be found in areas of military power and economic resources, as well as in the idealism of the Commonwealth.

Bevin believed that the answer to the problem of Jewish refugees and displaced persons should be sought in Europe rather than in Palestine, which he regarded as a predominantly Arab country. He found himself caught between a Jewish nationalism supercharged by the emotions of the Holocaust, and the anti-Zionism of the Arabs, without whose good will the British Empire in the Middle East would be doomed. The British could not support a Jewish state without alienating the Arabs. Nor could the British impose a settlement acceptable to the Arab countries without antagonizing the United States. The Middle East, in Bevin's view, was second in importance only to Europe; but in order for Britain to remain the dominant regional power, both Arab cooperation and the support of the United States were vital. Without them, Britain's influence would decline, and not only in the Middle East. Britain would sink to the status of a second-class European power like the Netherlands. That anxiety helps explain the emotional energy that Bevin and other British leaders expended on the regeneration of the British Empire in the Middle East and Africa. In this larger context, Palestine represented the principal stumbling block.

[3] Bevin's concluding speech at the Colombo conference, 14 January 1950, as recorded in the minutes of the Commonwealth Meeting on Foreign Affairs at Colombo, 15 January 1950, FO 371/84818.

In view of the overriding priorities of Arab collaboration and American assistance, the accusations against Bevin—for example, that he was callous to Jewish suffering—become more comprehensible. In short, he was pursuing a grand 'Imperial' strategy in which Palestine played only a small but most irritating part.

Churchill once described Bevin as 'a working class John Bull'. Like all good caricatures, this one contains an element of truth. With his working-class background and his concern for the welfare of common people, Bevin saw no contradiction between the development of the oil and other resources of the Middle East and what he hoped would be the future prosperity of the British Commonwealth. He believed, as did many of his generation, that the British Empire was a beneficent force in world affairs, though the word 'Empire' would have to be replaced in the Middle East with something that suggested less exploitation and more equality. The British and the Arabs could work together to develop the region to common advantage. Economically, the Middle East, together with Africa, offered just as alluring a prospect as India had in the past. Militarily, the countries of the Middle East could be brought into a system of defence that would help offset the manpower and military potential of the Soviet Union. Such, in brief, was Bevin's vision. He combined political, economic, and military strands of thought into a coherent general policy that sought to preserve Britain as a Great Power. The Middle East was the principal pillar of Britain's position in the world.

Bevin could not systematically have pursued his Middle Eastern aims without the effective partnership of the Prime Minister, Clement Attlee. Bevin was careful to square his ideas with Attlee's before airing them in Cabinet meetings. Together the two of them often made an unbreakable combination, though Attlee was much more sceptical about Britain's economic and military capacity to remain a 'Great Power' in the Middle East. To a far greater extent than Bevin, Attlee was willing to acknowledge the diminution of British power, to contemplate general withdrawal from the area, and, specifically, to cut losses in Palestine.[4]

Apart from those in the military chain of command, the other figure who requires a brief comment is Arthur Creech Jones, who was Parliamentary Under-Secretary for the Colonies from July 1945 until October 1946, and then Colonial Secretary until his defeat in the general election of February 1950. Both Attlee and Bevin respected

---

[4] For an extensive discussion of Attlee and Palestine, see Kenneth Harris, *Attlee* (London, 1982), chap. 22.

Creech Jones and listened to his advice, though Attlee lamented his political ineffectiveness and came to regard his appointment as a mistake. 'Creech Jones despite much hard work and devotion', Attlee wrote in 1950, 'had not appeared to have a real grip of administration in the Colonial Office.'[5] 'Creech' (as he was known to his friends) was sympathetic to the aims of the moderate Zionists (though he himself never endorsed the idea of a state as large as the one that came into existence in 1948). He was overshadowed by both the Prime Minister and the Foreign Secretary, and his ability to work harmoniously with them explains why the Palestine issue within the Labour Government remained relatively non-controversial. The Colonial Office and the Foreign Office, the two offices of state mainly concerned with Palestine, often clashed over many issues, but when Creech Jones, Bevin, and Attlee agreed on ministerial policy, it was virtually invulnerable to challenge by other members of the Cabinet or by the Chiefs of Staff. The Bevin–Attlee–Creech Jones combination helps explain why the pro-Zionist voices in the Cabinet—including those of Hugh Dalton, Aneurin Bevan, and Emanuel Shinwell—remained ineffective, and why the policy of the Labour Government in practice appeared to be at variance with the Labour Party's publicly proclaimed sympathy with the Zionist cause.

In getting a bearing on the tacit as well as the explicit British postwar assumptions about Palestine, it is useful to dwell briefly on the relationship between Creech Jones and Bevin and the responsibilities of the Colonial Office and the Foreign Office. Throughout his career, Creech Jones was associated with Bevin, first in the Transport and General Workers' Union and later as Bevin's Parliamentary Under-Secretary at the Ministry of Labour during the war. The facts of that connection, however, fail to do justice to Creech Jones's passionate and long-standing interest in colonial affairs. In 1940 he founded the Fabian Colonial Bureau with Rita Hinden. With his knowledge of the colonies, especially the ones in Africa, he came to his position as Colonial Secretary thoroughly prepared. He was responsible for endorsing the Labour Government's new direction in colonial policy, which later culminated in the transfer of power in Africa. He is remembered as the epitome of British decency and good will towards 'colonial' peoples. It is therefore ironic that he had to devote so much of his time to Palestine, which was by no means a typical colonial dependency. At first he was not unoptimistic, but eventually he came to believe that it was impossible to come to terms realistically with the

---

[5] Attlee's notes, 1950, ATLE 1/17, Attlee Papers (Churchill College, Cambridge).

Zionists. He later took pains to emphasize that he and Bevin were ultimately at one on Palestine.[6]

Since 1922, Palestine had been a Colonial Office responsibility. In the late 1930s its relatively minor significance as a mandated territory of the League of Nations was transformed because of the crisis in Europe; it became a major political and strategic concern of the Foreign Office and Chiefs of Staff as well. In the 1945–48 period, the Foreign Office and the Colonial Office shared responsibility for Palestine: the former for the international dimension of the problem, the latter for the mandate's administration. Both departments responded to the strategic demands of the Chiefs of Staff: the Colonial Office in relation to Palestine as a strategic territory (and as a fallback from Egypt), the Foreign Office in regard to broader aspects of the defence of the Middle East and the global security of the Empire and Commonwealth. In these intricate relationships, Creech Jones played a critical part. During his tenure as Colonial Secretary, he favoured partition as a solution, but on this and other important issues he eventually yielded and followed Bevin's lead. On the whole, Bevin found in Creech Jones a supporter as faithful as he could have expected in the head of another major, and in some senses rival, government department.

In Parliament, Bevin confronted Churchill, who was not only his most powerful and persistent adversary in Imperial and foreign affairs, but also his principal critic on the tactics and timing of withdrawal from Palestine. Churchill was important in the background of the Labour Government's policy towards Palestine because after the First World War he himself as Colonial Secretary had penned the official elaboration of the Balfour Declaration. The declaration of 1922 established Transjordan as an Arab territory distinct from Palestine. Palestine itself, in words that followed the Balfour Declaration, was not to be a Jewish 'national home', but there was to be a national home in Palestine. Jewish immigration would be allowed, in Churchill's own phrase, up to the limit of 'economic absorptive capacity', which was to be judged by the mandatory power. The declaration of 1922 served as the basis of British policy for nearly two decades. When the White Paper of 1939 attempted to curtail and stabilize the Jewish population of Palestine at one-third of the total population (with further immigration after five years dependent on Arab acquiescence), Churchill denounced it as a breach of faith with the Jews. Throughout his career, with varying degrees of enthusiasm and scepticism, Churchill

---

[6] See Creech Jones to Elizabeth Monroe, 23 October 1961, Creech Jones Papers (Rhodes House, Oxford).

remained a moderate Zionist. As Prime Minister during the war, he became the moving spirit behind the solution of partition and its possible corollary of an independent Jewish state. But he always kept his Zionism subordinate to his Imperial priorities. He never became a convert to the idea that Palestine might be substituted strategically for Egypt. And he always believed that relatively minor conflicts, or 'wars of mice', between Arabs and Jews (in comparison with the struggle in India) should never disrupt the Anglo-American alliance. In August 1946 he summarized his indictment of the Labour Government's handling of the Palestine problem: '[I]t is our duty . . . to offer to lay down the Mandate. We should . . . as soon as the war stopped, have made it clear to the United States that, unless they came in and bore their share, we should lay the whole care and burden at the foot of the United Nations organisation.'[7]

Anglo-American cooperation over Palestine proved to be perhaps the single most frustrating and elusive goal of the Labour Government. A major disagreement developed in August 1945 when President Truman requested the admission of 100,000 Jewish refugees into Palestine. This issue is discussed in the next section of this essay. It is mentioned here because to the British it constituted the point of departure for the post-war controversy. Bevin later reflected that 'had it not been for a succession of unfortunate actions on the part of the United States' following the demand of the 100,000, the question might have been settled. His point was that if the United States and Britain had acted together immediately and decisively at the end of the war, the Palestine drama might have had an entirely different denouement.

One might question whether it was not rather late in the day for the British to make such bold assertions about decisive chronology. For the British, at least, was not the White Paper of 1939 the turning point? Could not its constitutional provisions, which for better or worse were never developed, have led to a binational state? Or for that matter, what of the recommendations of the Royal Commission of 1937? Might they not have prepared the way in the opposite direction for the creation of a Jewish state at a much earlier date? To pursue the chronology still further, Bevin might have lamented the lost opportunity of 1922, when the Arabs rejected measures that, as in other British dependencies, might have started Palestine down the path of self-government. The British were entirely willing to share the blame for failure in Palestine with the Arabs as well as the Jews, and with the

---

[7] *Parliamentary Debates* (Commons), 1 August 1946, col. 1253. For Churchill and Palestine, see especially Michael J. Cohen, *Churchill and the Jews* (London, 1984).

Americans as well as the Russians. On the question of chronology and points of departure in the story, Bevin was emphatic on one subject: the Balfour Declaration, in his view, was no more than 'a unilateral declaration' that 'did not take into account the Arabs & was really a Power Politics declaration'.[8] It was the source of all the trouble. In Bevin's opinion, it was the greatest mistake in Britain's Imperial history.[9]

The 100,000 and the Anglo-American Committee of Inquiry

When President Truman called for the admission of 100,000 Jewish refugees into Palestine in August 1945, the population of the country itself, according to British estimates, comprised 550,000 Jews and 1,200,000 Arabs. It could be that the British made a tactical blunder by not accepting the additional 100,000 as a final quota. In any case, the Foreign Office believed that a sudden influx of Jewish immigrants would destroy any last chance of reconciling the two communities. It is important to emphasize the thrust of Foreign Office thought, which upheld the principles of the White Paper of 1939 and the solution of the binational state, rather than the consensus of Colonial Office opinion, which tended to support the opposite solution—partition, recommended by the Royal Commission in 1937 and reaffirmed by Churchill during the war. The Foreign Office predominated, not least because of Bevin. One is struck by the continuity of official sentiment, which responded to the White Paper of 1939 not as 'appeasement' of the Arabs (and still less, at least by implication, of the Nazis) but rather as the basis of a constructive and just solution. The head of the Eastern Department of the Foreign Office, C. W. Baxter, wrote about 'the constitutional proposals envisaged in the 1939 White Paper':

> It was then considered essential that Jews and Arabs should learn to
> work together as part of a single Palestine State. It was realised that
> the Jews would never attempt to work with the Arabs in a joint Arab-

[8] Minute by Bevin, *c*.1 February 1946, FO 371/52509. For an interpretation, with which Bevin himself might have agreed, of the motives and meaning of the Balfour Declaration, see Mayir Vereté, 'The Balfour Declaration and Its Makers', *Middle Eastern Studies*, 6, 1 (January, 1970), pp. 48–76.

[9] Sir Harold Beeley, 'Ernest Bevin and Palestine' (unpublished Antonius Lecture, St. Antony's College, Oxford, 14 June 1983), p. 9. This was in fact a common British view. See Elizabeth Monroe, *Britain's Moment in the Middle East* (London, 1963), p. 43: 'Measured by British interest alone, it was one of the greatest mistakes in our imperial history'; and, in a slightly different vein, 'Arnold Toynbee on the Arab-Israeli Conflict', *Journal of Palestine Studies*, 2, 3 (Spring, 1973), p. 3: 'I will say straight out: Balfour was a wicked man.' For the opposite tradition, that of defending the commitment to the Jews, see N. A. Rose, *The Gentile Zionists: A Study in Anglo-Zionist Diplomacy* (London, 1973).

Jewish State, so long as they hoped that, by the continuance of Jewish immigration, the Jews would eventually become a majority in Palestine, and be able to press for a Jewish State. There must therefore be some finality as regards Jewish immigration and the size of the Jewish National Home . . .

Unhappily, owing to the war, the White Paper's constitutional proposals were never put into force. The 1939 policy has thus not been given a fair trial. If it is now decided to pursue the idea of a joint 'binational' State, it would seem necessary to decide now, once and for all, what the size of the Jewish National Home in Palestine is to be.[10]

The phrases 'finality as regards Jewish immigration' and 'the size of the Jewish National Home' (as opposed to 'Jewish State') are thus keys to official British thought.

Bevin has been accused of having succumbed to entrenched Foreign Office prejudices after July 1945. This was not the case (the accusation could be more accurately levelled against Creech Jones in 1946 in regard to general colonial policy). The archival records reveal that he took a strong and independent line from the beginning, that he was influenced by the Chiefs of Staff as well as the Prime Minister, and that his natural sympathies flowed towards the Arabs. He regarded them as an indigenous people who were being dislodged by the equivalent of white settlers in Algeria and Kenya. He was quick to remind his critics in the House of Commons that he was not lacking in sympathy for the Jews. But he wished to find a solution to the problem of the survivors of the Holocaust elsewhere—in other words, in Europe, the United States, and 'other countries' besides Palestine.[11] He was convinced that he could persuade the Americans of the reasonableness of that point of view. He also had great confidence in his ability to resolve difficult problems by negotiation, a skill he believed was apparent from his success in the trade-union movement in Britain. This sense of assurance, some would say arrogance, helps explain his incautious statement when announcing the appointment of the Anglo-American Committee of Inquiry in November 1945: 'I will stake my political future on solving the problem.'[12] Churchill was right in saying later that 'no more rash a bet has ever been recorded in the annals of the British turf.'[13]

[10] Minute by Baxter, 14 January 1946, FO 371/52504.

[11] The words 'other countries' were those of Bevin himself, scrawled onto a Foreign Office memorandum on the subject (see note by Robert Howe, 6 October 1945, FO 371/45380).

[12] *Parliamentary Debates* (Commons), 13 November 1945, col. 1934.

[13] Ibid., 29 January 1949, col. 948.

Bevin's preconceived ideas help explain his later policy. He laboured under certain misapprehensions, as did many of his contemporaries. He believed, for example, that there would be, to use his own words, 'a certain amount of re-emigration' of Jews from Palestine back to Europe.[14] A record of his thoughts in September 1945 also reveals his conviction that if the Palestine question were submitted to the General Assembly of the United Nations, 'the Arabs would have a chance to state their case.'[15] The United Nations would endorse British policy. These of course proved to be misguided judgements. But he was not far wrong in believing that an independent committee of inquiry might recommend the creation of a binational state. One of the major conclusions of the Anglo-American Committee of Inquiry, which was composed of six British and six American members, was that the Palestinian state should be neither Arab nor Jewish. On the other hand, the other principal recommendation of the committee, which reported in April 1946, came as a jolt to the British. It called for the immediate admission of the 100,000 Jewish refugees.[16] President Truman precipitately and publicly accepted this part of the report without referring to its 'binational' recommendations. He made this announcement unilaterally, without discussing it with the British. Bevin had assumed that the British and American governments would be able to work closely together on the Palestine question and that there would be a correlation between the policies endorsed by the White House and the State Department. Both those assumptions proved to be false. In the year following the end of the war, Bevin learned that the Americans would not follow his lead in resolving the Palestine issue and that President Truman would respond to the pressures and opportunities of American politics more than to the dilemmas of the British.

To preserve British paramountcy in the Middle East, Bevin needed the economic underwriting and, if necessary, the military support of the United States. The Jews, in his eyes, threatened to poison his relations with both the Arabs and the Americans. The report of the Anglo-American Committee of Inquiry and Truman's further demand for the 100,000 made things worse, not better. A minute by Sir Walter

[14] Foreign Office minutes, 6 September 1945, FO 371/45379.

[15] Ibid., 10 September 1945.

[16] For a detailed assessment of the committee's work, based on full use of archival sources, see Amikam Nachmani, 'British Policy in Palestine after World War II: The Anglo-American Committee of Inquiry' (Oxford D.Phil. thesis, 1980); see also William Travis Hanes III, 'Year of Crisis: British Policy in the Palestine Mandate, January 1946–February 1947' (University of Texas, M.A. thesis, 1983), which is based in part on the papers of the American chairman, Joseph C. Hutcheson, at the Humanities Research Center at the University of Texas.

Smart, the Oriental Secretary at the British Embassy in Cairo, reveals the Arab side of the dilemma:

> I am much struck by the superficiality and intellectual dishonesty of this Report . . . the Committee demands the admission within less than a year of 100,000 immigrants (i.e. a larger number than have ever been brought in within such a short period at any time in the past) without making any mention of the question of Palestine's economic capacity to absorb them. It must have been perfectly obvious to the members of the Committee, as it is to all of us, that their proposals must result in acute political and military conflict between the Arabs and the Jews in Palestine and the Arab countries round it.[17]

On the other hand, if the British refused to yield on the issue of the 100,000, then the Zionists would be able to exploit the volatile anti-imperialist sentiment of the American public. According to Sir Nevile Butler, who had served as head of the North American Department during the Second World War, 'The American "anti-imperialist" feeling . . . is traditional and profound and it is in these areas that the Russians are trying to drive their wedge.'[18] He wrote that minute in April 1946, a critical time in the development of the Cold War as well as in the Palestine conflict. It was also the time of the British Cabinet Mission to India. A false step in Palestine could lead to disaster in the larger areas not only of Anglo-Arab relations but also of American support of the British Empire, the transfer of power in India, and the confrontation with the Soviet Union.

It was a perilous time. Most British officials and statesmen, including Attlee and Bevin, would probably have agreed with the analysis, though not the sentiment, of an American critic of the British Empire who was a member of the Anglo-American Committee, Frank Buxton (editor of the *Boston Herald*): 'There was a time . . . when England was so strong that muddling-through and stupidity were not especially harmful to her; she had so much reserve strength that she could retrieve her blunders. But now . . . stupidity and shortsightedness are unforgivable sins and may inflict wounds from which she cannot recover.'[19] The quotation is significant because the unpublished British records yield the overall impression that, far from 'muddling-through', the policy of the Labour Government on the Palestine ques-

---

[17] Minute by Smart, 2 May 1946, FO 141/1090 (Cairo Embassy files).

[18] Minute by Butler, 5 April 1946, FO 371/51630.

[19] Buxton to Felix Frankfurter, 6 June 1946, Frankfurter Papers, Library of Congress. This quotation is taken from a file in the Frankfurter Papers that I was not able to study while writing *The British Empire in the Middle East*, and I am glad to be able to provide an excerpt from it.

tion was a painstaking attempt to keep in balance the vital Arab and American parts of the equation. It was the need for American as well as Arab support that explains the British retreat to a position of even-handed withdrawal.

The Critical Period: Summer 1946 through February 1947

Zionist terrorism offers a basic explanation of why the British were forced to retreat. On 22 July 1946 the Irgun Zvai Leumi (one of several mandate-era Jewish paramilitary organizations) blew up the British military headquarters at the King David Hotel in Jerusalem, with heavy loss of British, Arab, and Jewish life. It is a melancholy fact that the explosion polarized the Palestine conflict. Everyone in the British civil administration or army had a friend or acquaintance killed at the King David. It stirred up powerful and conflicting emotions among the British: terrorism should be repressed and, at the same time, the British should withdraw because of Jewish ingratitude. The chief of the Imperial General Staff, Field Marshal Bernard Montgomery, wrote two days after the incident, 'We shall show the world and the Jews that we are not going to submit tamely to violence.'[20] Churchill, on the other hand, represented a wide current of public thought when he questioned the wisdom of further loss of British life in Palestine. The blowing up of the King David explains much about the public mood on Palestine in the summer of 1946: emotions were running high.

The explosion at the King David occurred while officials in the British and American governments were attempting to salvage the recommendations of the Anglo-American Committee of Inquiry by implementing a scheme of provincial autonomy. It would have provided an ambiguous compromise between the two extreme solutions of partition and a binational state. There would have been a large measure of Arab and Jewish autonomy, with certain powers reserved to the central administering authority. Britain would continue indefinitely as the trusteeship power. It is not important to dwell on the details, because the scheme was unacceptable to both Arabs and Jews. It might have been remotely feasible if both the United States and Britain could have agreed upon it. In the event, according to the dominant British interpretation, President Truman became apprehensive about Palestine as a campaign issue in the 1946 congressional elections and feared that he would be accused of 'ghettoizing' the Jews in Palestine. So ended the plan for provincial autonomy, which, if it had been implemented decisively, might eventually have led to a binational state

[20] Montgomery to Dempsey, Personal and Top Secret, 24 July 1946, WO 216/194.

or, perhaps, to a more peaceful partition. Yet one can only agree with one of the first authorities who wrote dispassionately on the subject, J. C. Hurewitz: by 1946 it was too late.[21]

British leaders, then and later, recognized President Truman's statement on the eve of Yom Kippur as a turning point. On 4 October 1946 he expressed the hope for a compromise between the British and Zionist proposals. The Zionists, however, publicized the part of the statement in which the President appeared to support 'the creation of a viable Jewish state'. Attlee and Bevin at this time correctly believed that the Zionist movement was in disarray, at odds with itself over the extremist demand for a Jewish state in all of Palestine. They still hoped that the Zionist 'moderates' might negotiate if the Americans would support the solution of a binational state. Then came news of the 'Yom Kippur statement'. Attlee had attempted to prevent another unilateral move on the part of the President, but Truman refused to wait. He drew a rebuke from Attlee that must rank high in memorable exchanges between British Prime Ministers and American Presidents. The flawless handwritten draft of Attlee's letter, which is among his papers at the Public Record Office, still radiates white-hot anger:

> I have received with great regret your letter refusing even a few hours' grace to the Prime Minister of the country which has the actual responsibility for the government of Palestine in order that he might acquaint you with the actual situation and the probable results of your action.
>
> These may well include the frustration of the patient efforts to achieve a settlement and the loss of still more lives in Palestine.
>
> I am astonished that you did not wait to acquaint yourself with the reasons for the suspension of the Conference with the Arabs. You do not seem to have been informed that so far from negotiations having been broken off, conversations with leading Zionists with a view to their entering the Conference were proceeding with good prospects of success.[22]

It did not amuse Attlee and Bevin to learn that Truman had made the statement on the eve of Yom Kippur (with no mention of the congressional elections) for the reason that the Jewish people on their day of atonement 'are accustomed to give contemplation to the lot of the

---

[21] See J. C. Hurewitz, *The Struggle for Palestine* (New York, 1950), chaps. 18 and 19.

[22] See PREM 8/627/5, Attlee to Truman, 4 October 1946; *Foreign Relations of the United States, 1946* (Washington, 1969), VII, pp. 704–05.

Jewish people' and that he therefore hoped to relieve 'their feeling of depression and frustration'.[23]

The conference mentioned in Attlee's letter to Truman was the London conference on the Middle East, which met sporadically from September 1946 to February 1947. The Arabs stood by the letter and spirit of the assurances of 1939 and would agree to nothing less than Palestine as an Arab state. The Jews boycotted the proceedings because of the denial of the opposite premise of a Jewish state. They conducted unofficial simultaneous negotiations with the British. Bevin and Creech Jones provided the basis of discussion by presenting to both groups in essence the plan for provincial autonomy. It was as close as British ingenuity could come to reconciling Arab and Jew and preserving British influence. The Arabs rejected the British plan because they believed it to be a move towards partition. The ghost of the 1930s haunted the conference. Since the British had proclaimed finality in 1939, why should the Arabs believe them in 1946?

For the British, the hardening of the Jewish position was symbolized by Chaim Weizmann's fall from formal political power at the Zionist Congress in Basel in December. When David Ben Gurion met with British officials shortly thereafter, he stated that Weizmann was 'still first in moral standing' but that his political defeat had come about because of 'his blind trust in Britain'.[24] Those who now led the Zionist movement did not believe that the British would leave Palestine unless they were pushed out, though Ben Gurion made it clear that he hoped for as peaceful a nudge as possible. The Jews judged the plan for provincial autonomy in exactly the opposite way than did the Arabs: to the Zionists, it was a step in the direction of an Arab Palestinian state.

In November 1946, Bevin paid a visit to New York in order to attend the meeting of the Council of Foreign Ministers. Dock workers refused to handle his luggage. He was jeered at during a football game by a crowd that remembered his statement about Americans not wanting any more Jews in New York. He met with President Truman, who, though sharing a common sense of humour at the expense of the Jews, unfortunately was struck by Bevin's resemblance to John L. Lewis, the leader of the United Mine Workers of America. Bevin also had a conversation with Rabbi Abba Hillel Silver, the anti-British leader of the American Zionist movement. He told the rabbi that if the Jews

[23] Truman to Attlee, 10 October 1946, enclosed in a memorandum by Acheson to Truman, President's Secretary's Files Box 170, Truman Papers (Independence, Missouri); *Foreign Relations 1946*, VII, pp. 706–08.
[24] 'Note of Interview with Mr. Ben Gurion at the Colonial Office', 2 January 1947, copy in FO 371/61762.

pressed the issue of partition, the British 'would give up the mandate' and hand it over to the United Nations. 'At this', Bevin reported to Attlee, 'Doctor Silver showed signs of distress.'[25] This was more than a warning: it was an articulation of what might be called the British 'United Nations strategy'.

The game at the United Nations was one that the British believed they could win. In the autumn and winter of 1946, when Bevin's ideas crystallized during discussions at the Council of Foreign Ministers and the United Nations, it would have taken a bold prophet to anticipate Zionist success in mobilizing two-thirds of the members of the General Assembly to support the creation of a Jewish state. It required the unlikely combination of the American and Russian voting blocs and what seemed to British and American officials alike to be the flouting of a fundamental principle of the organization itself—the imposition of a form of government opposed by the majority of the inhabitants. With such thoughts in mind, Bevin and his advisers hoped that the United Nations might endorse the solution of a binational state. Bevin himself continued to be sceptical about partition because he believed that the Arab opposition would be so great that it would undermine Britain's entire position in the Middle East.[26] Nevertheless, he began to give serious thought to the possible military and strategic consequences of the division of Palestine as well as to a possible political solution through the United Nations. 'Partition' was generally in the wind in the British Cabinet. A meeting of 25 October 1946 concluded: 'several Ministers said that they were glad that the possibility of Partition was not excluded . . . and expressed the view that this would in the end be found to be the only practicable solution of the Palestine problem.'[27]

The Chiefs of Staff held that Britain could not successfully impose a solution by force if actively resisted by both communities. If compelled to choose between Arab and Jew, there could be no doubt whatsoever

[25] Memorandum of conversation, 14 November 1946, FO 371/52565.

[26] Although Bevin was consistent in his opposition to partition, the records in London, Washington, and Jerusalem make it clear that he did not have a closed mind. In an especially revealing conversation with Nahum Goldmann of the Jewish Agency in August 1946, he talked about partition as a 'possibility' but added that he was troubled about the prospect of a Jewish 'racial state' ('I got annoyed at that,' Goldmann noted, and he pointed out to Bevin that 300,000 Arabs would be included, 'with equal rights'). Bevin emphasized several times that he 'never ruled out partition'. Goldmann for his part believed that he detected a more fair-minded attitude than the one usually attributed to Bevin. But he told him, 'You have treated us abominably.' Bevin responded by saying that he had always wanted to be fair to the Jews, and that 'he knew the Jewish tragedy and their sufferings' (memorandum by Goldmann, 14 August 1946, Central Zionist Archives [Jerusalem] Z6/17/21).

[27] Cabinet Conclusions 91 (46), 25 October 1946, CAB 128/6; see minutes in FO 371/52563.

of the imperative need to preserve Arab good will. The Chiefs of Staff wrote in the aftermath of the publication of the 'disastrous' report by the Anglo-American Committee of Inquiry:

> All our defence requirements in the Middle East, including mainte-
> nance of our essential oil supplies and communications, demand that
> an essential feature of our policy should be to retain the co-operation
> of the Arab States, and to ensure that the Arab world does not gravi-
> tate towards the Russians . . . We cannot stress too strongly the im-
> portance of Middle East oil resources to us both in peace and war.[28]

When it became clear in mid-1946 that British military, air, and naval forces might be withdrawn from Egypt, the Chiefs of Staff attached emphatic importance to the retention of strategic rights in Palestine.

The Chiefs of Staff believed that Jewish terrorism could be quelled. Police and military authorities attempted to break the back of Jew- ish resistance by searching for arms caches and interning prominent leaders of the Jewish Agency. The British Army hoped at the minimum to neutralize the Jews' ability to attack. Those tactics had the opposite of the intended effect on Jewish morale, though the military effective- ness of the Haganah (forerunner of the Israeli Defense Forces) was no doubt weakened. After the King David Hotel explosion, the Brit- ish commanding officer, General Sir Evelyn Barker, ordered British troops to have no 'social intercourse with any Jew' and to punish the Jews 'in a way the race dislikes as much as any, by striking at their pock- ets and showing our contempt for them'.[29] He accused prominent Jews of 'hypocritical sympathy' with the terrorists. By August the Colonial Office feared that Palestine would be plunged into a bloodbath.

The Prime Minister himself steadied British nerves. Attlee believed that firmness against terrorism would strengthen the 'moderates', with whom it might be possible to work out a political solution. He stuck by his maxim of trying to accommodate the more 'sensible' of the leaders of the Jewish Agency in order to prevent the extremists from precipitating, in Jewish eyes, a war of liberation. Curfews and house- to-house searches were relaxed. Barker was reprimanded for his non- fraternization order and eventually replaced (before his departure, he pissed on the soil of Palestine as if in symbolic disgust). Attlee's 'ap- peasement' did not please the Chief of the Imperial General Staff, Montgomery, who continued to believe that military force would and

---

[28] CP (46) 267, 10 July 1946, CAB 129/11; see also minutes in FO 371/52563.
[29] For an extensive discussion of British army policies, see Michael J. Cohen, *Palestine and the Great Powers, 1945–1948* (Princeton, 1982), chap. 4.

should prove to be the only answer in Palestine. Montgomery stated in late 1946:

> The policy of appeasement which had been adopted during the last few months had failed. Searches had been discontinued and internees had been released with no consequent improvement in the position, which in fact had deteriorated. The police and military forces were placed in a most difficult position . . . He felt that what was required was a clear directive by His Majesty's Government to the High Commissioner to use all the forces at his disposal to maintain strict law and order.[30]

Montgomery had a high opinion of British capability of imposing a peace with bayonets. His memoirs veil only slightly his contempt for Attlee's and Bevin's capitulation to the Jews, and for Creech Jones's 'spineless' handling of Palestine he reserved a special rancour.[31]

In London, the Palestine crisis gained momentum in December and January of 1946–47 and reached a climax in February. The decisions took place against the background of the great emotional debate about India, the general deterioration of Britain in the Middle Eastern 'northern tier', the collapse of new defence arrangements with Egypt, a sense of impending economic disaster, and one of the worst winters in British history. Two great offices of state, the Foreign Office and the Colonial Office, clashed over the interpretation of 'trusteeship'. Trusteeship for whom? Arab or Jew? The Chiefs of Staff continued to answer that question with 'the British' and to press for the retention of Palestine as a permanent strategic possession. The salient feature of this period was the persistent British effort, especially by Ernest Bevin, to support the Arabs and thereby to sustain British power in the Middle East. As a case study in decolonization, Palestine demonstrates the convergence of ethical sympathy for the Arabs and political calculation of how best to maintain British influence.

The two men making the critical decisions about timing and cutting losses were Bevin and Attlee. There was tension between them. 'I do not think', Attlee wrote to Bevin in December 1946, 'that the countries bordering on Soviet Russia's zone viz Greece, Turkey, Iraq and Persia can be made strong enough to form an effective barrier. We do not command the resources to make them so.'[32] When the two of them agreed that British troops should be withdrawn from Greece,

[30] Chiefs of Staff (46) 169, 20 November 1946, copy in FO 371/52565.

[31] Montgomery's contentious discussion of his part in the Palestine controversy is in *The Memoirs of Field-Marshal the Viscount Montgomery of Alamein* (Cleveland, 1958), chap. 29.

[32] Attlee to Bevin, Private and Personal, 1 December 1946, FO 800/475. These are the Bevin Papers, that is, Private Office Papers.

Attlee viewed this problem above all as one of economic and military retrenchment. Bevin, by contrast, regarded the crisis in the eastern Mediterranean not only as an economic and military emergency, but also as an opportunity to win American commitment to a 'northern tier' that would provide a shield for British defence and development of the 'British' Middle East. By late 1946 Bevin and his advisers had begun to devise a strategy whereby referring Palestine to the United Nations might win international support for both the British and the Arabs.

The Greek and Palestine crises interlocked. The Bevin Papers, now accessible at the Public Record Office in London, make clear an important point of chronological detail that previously remained elusive. Two days after Christmas 1946, Attlee and Bevin agreed not only on the question of withdrawal from Greece but also on the issue of submitting the Palestine problem to the United Nations. Bevin had become disillusioned with the Egyptians as well as the Greeks and Jews. His grand design for a defence arrangement about the Canal Zone now lay in shambles because of nationalist sentiment in Egypt. The more precarious the British position in the eastern Mediterranean appeared to be, the more attractive was the potential of Libya as the future linchpin of the British Empire. The following consensus between the Prime Minister and the Foreign Secretary after the latter's return from New York is revealing: 'The Prime Minister agreed [with Bevin] that if we had Cyrenaica, there would be no need to stay in either Egypt or Palestine.'[33]

The Chiefs of Staff continued to advise that British troops could impose a solution by force upon one community in Palestine but not both. In their view, the extreme solution of partition would, in bluntest terms, destroy Britain's position in the Middle East. The Chiefs of Staff presented their case in a Cabinet meeting of 15 January 1947:

It was essential to our defence that we should be able to fight from the Middle East in war . . . In future we should not be able to use India as a base for . . . deployment of force: it was the more essential, therefore, that we should retain other bases in the Middle East for this purpose.

Palestine was of special importance in this general scheme of defence. In war, Egypt would be our key position in the Middle East; and it was necessary that we should hold Palestine as a screen for the defence of Egypt.[34]

[33] Note by J. N. Henderson, 28 December 1946, FO 800/475.
[34] Cabinet Minutes (47) 6, Minute 3, Confidential Annex, 15 January 1947, CAB 128/11.

Far from wishing to relinquish Palestine for mere reasons of political discontent, the Chiefs of Staff wished to retain a naval base at Haifa, at least two army garrisons, and a major air base. Dividing Palestine would create indefensible borders. To the traditional British military mind, treaty rights with a binational state would provide, under the circumstances, the best answer to the strategic problems of the British Empire in the eastern Mediterranean.

Creech Jones presented the Colonial Office's case for partition. The Chancellor of the Exchequer, Hugh Dalton, observed that the Palestine issue was now being discussed mainly in relation to the United Nations. Dalton is of interest because before the Labour landslide victory in 1945 he had been the moving spirit behind the Labour Party's endorsement of the Zionist cause. He wrote in his diary in mid-1947 about the Cabinet deliberations:

> On Palestine a number of us have been shouting for partition—Creech Jones is very good on this and much more decisive than his predecessor. E.B. and the P.M. try to tangle up the merits of various solutions with hypothetical conclusions of who would vote for this or that at U.N.O. I have been trying to keep these disentangled and have been urging that partition is the least objectionable of all policies.[35]

If Dalton had been Colonial Secretary in 1947, the solution of partition might have stood a better chance. Creech Jones could not stand up to Bevin, nor could the Colonial Secretary negotiate skilfully enough with the Jews to put a more persuasive case before the British Cabinet. In the end, he reconciled himself to Bevin's policy as 'inevitable'. Bevin for his part took care not to make it difficult for Creech Jones. The Foreign Secretary used the effective argument that partition was untenable because of overriding reasons of British security.

Bevin argued the case relentlessly in the discussions of the Cabinet. He emphasized the repercussions of partition on the Arab states. One of his deputies perhaps pressed the argument to its fullest global dimension:

> To how great an extent partition would result in an estrangement between Great Britain and the Arab peoples it is not possible to estimate. But the consequences of such an estrangement would be so grave that the risk of it should be a major consideration in the examination of partition as a possible policy. The loss of Arab good will would mean the elimination of British influence from the Middle

---

[35] Dalton Diary, 17 January 1947, Dalton Papers (London School of Economics).

East to the great advantage of Russia. And this in turn would greatly weaken the position of the British Commonwealth in the world.[36]

In the end, the argument about 'the British Commonwealth in the world' was one that Attlee as well as Bevin had to bear in mind.

The key to Attlee's (and Bevin's) thought lies in a statement he made to the Cabinet in late November 1946. Though partition might have a powerful attraction as an immediate and decisive solution, Attlee said, 'His Majesty's Government should not commit themselves to support of this solution before all the alternatives had been fully discussed in the . . . proceedings of the Palestine Conference.'[37] The Jews and Arabs would be given the chance to agree or disagree with all reasonable proposals, including the extremes of partition and a binational state. If no solution were found, then they and not the British would bear the main brunt of failure. Attlee and Bevin independently arrived at the same conclusion: they did not want to be held responsible in Arab eyes for a policy of partition. If there could be no agreement, then the British government would continue to play the same hand at the United Nations, where a showdown could not be avoided (if only because of the indeterminate status of the mandate in international law). The British would appear to assume an impartial position, but in fact they would allow the pro-Arab majority of the General Assembly to decide the issue for them. That calculation explains Dalton's comment in mid-January 1947 about Attlee's and Bevin's preoccupation with UN votes.

In the last stages of the London conference, which still dragged on formally and informally until mid-February, Bevin continued to guide the discussions towards a plan for provincial autonomy. With an ostensibly even hand, he exhausted possibilities of concessions that might be interpreted as a step towards either partition or a binational state. The more the details of partition were examined, the more the problem seemed to be insuperable. With a stalemate impending, Bevin and Creech Jones then put forward their last proposals, for a binational Arab-Jewish state. In what became known as the 'Bevin plan', the United Nations would supervise a five-year trusteeship regime that would prepare Palestine for independence as a binational state. Instead of provincial autonomy, there would be 'cantons' determined by the size of Jewish or Arab majorities. Bevin had in mind alliances of Jewish and Arab groups based on communities of economic interest.

[36] Memorandum by Robert Howe, 21 January 1947, FO 371/61858.
[37] Cabinet Conclusions 101 (46), 28 November 1946; see also CO 535/1787.

As Sir Harold Beeley has written, 'Bevin's plan was in essence a return to the White Paper of 1939,' though close to 100,000 Jewish immigrants would be admitted within a period of two years. Jewish and
Arab local and self-governing institutions would be 'rooted in the lives
of the people'. The Bevin plan represented the last effort to solve the
problem of Palestine in the tradition of British trusteeship: ameliorat-
ing ethnic differences within the framework of a single state.[38]

At the end of the London conference, the Arabs refused to consider Jewish self-government in any form or any further Jewish immigration. Thus the British confronted one impasse. The Jews regarded
the boundaries of the 'cantons' as totally unacceptable and would not
agree to any scheme not based on the premise of an eventual Jewish
state. Thus the British presided over final deadlock.

In mid-February 1947, Bevin and Creech Jones together submitted
to the Cabinet a report anticipating difficulties at the United Nations.
They emphasized that once the British made the decision to refer the
Palestine controversy to the United Nations, they would have to act
with all possible speed to bring about a resolution; otherwise the administration in Palestine itself would face renewed outbreaks of terrorism and possible civil war. At this stage, the British considered, but
rejected with a ring of self-confidence, the possibility of evacuation.
They did not wish to leave the Arabs, the Jews, the Americans, and
the United Nations stewing in their own juices. Such an abnegation
of responsibility, according to Bevin and Creech Jones, would be ignoble and would amount to a repudiation of the 'sacred trust' of the
mandate: 'We do not recommend the adoption of this humiliating
course.'[39] Creech Jones re-emphasized that point in the subsequent
Parliamentary debate: 'We are not going to the United Nations to surrender the mandate.'[40]

Evacuation and the End of the Mandate

The rapid deterioration of British moral suasion and military power
in Palestine took place against the background of political drama in
the United Nations. It was accompanied by the rising danger of anti-
Semitism in England and by increasingly virulent anti-British sentiment in New York. In Palestine, Jewish 'terrorism' and British 'oppression' reached symbolic heights. In July the Irgun brutally hanged two

[38] Beeley, 'Ernest Bevin and Palestine', treats the 'Bevin plan' with sympathetic insight.

[39] Memorandum by Bevin and Creech Jones, 13 February 1947, CP (47) 59; for minutes, see
CO 537/2327–2328.

[40] *Parliamentary Debates* (Commons), 25 February 1947, col. 2007.

British sergeants and placed booby traps on their bodies. They became martyrs. Bevin told the American Secretary of State, General Marshall, that the executions 'would never be forgotten' and that, as a result, 'anti-Jewish feeling in England now was greater than it had been in a hundred years.'[41] The Jews also had symbolic figures, and they appealed to a much greater public conscience. In the same month, British authorities turned away some 4,500 Jewish refugees aboard the *Exodus 1947*. In one of his 'black rages', Bevin decided 'to teach the Jews a lesson'. The passengers aboard the *Exodus* would be returned to their port of embarkation in France. As it transpired, the Jews refused to disembark, and the British, blundering from one position to another, wound up sending these survivors of the Nazi murder camps back to Germany.[42]

When the members of the United Nations Special Committee on Palestine (UNSCOP) visited Palestine in the summer of 1947, they found the British community in a state of siege. Wives and children had been evacuated. The number of British police and military forces together with contingents of the Arab Legion now rivalled the symbolic figure of the 100,000 Jewish refugees who were still interned in European displaced-person camps. The United Nations committee observed 'Bevingrads', the British redoubts in the centre of Jerusalem and other places, where British personnel were bivouacked behind barbed wire. One-tenth of the armed forces of the entire British Empire now occupied a territory the size of Wales. There was one soldier for every eighteen inhabitants in the country, or, as one observer calculated, one for every city block. The drain on the economy for military upkeep alone amounted to close to £40 million a year. 'There is the manpower of at least 100,000 men in Palestine', Churchill stated in Parliament, 'who might well be at home strengthening our depleted industry. What are they doing there? What good are we getting out of it?'[43] When Britain experienced a severe economic crisis in 1947, a broad consensus of public, Parliamentary, and Cabinet opinion developed around military withdrawal as an economic as well as a political and ethical imperative.

The general crystallization of British sentiment in favour of withdrawal did not necessarily contradict the Foreign Office's hope of preserving Britain's political and strategic position by relying on probable

---

[41] See *Foreign Relations, 1947*, V, pp. 1285–87.

[42] For the *Exodus* episode from the British vantage point, see especially Nicholas Bethell, *The Palestine Triangle: The Struggle between the British, the Jews, and the Arabs, 1935–48* (London, 1979), chap. 10.

[43] *Parliamentary Debates* (Commons), 31 January 1947, col. 1347.

UN action. It was a rational and indeed ingenious calculation, as the Zionists at the time recognized. It assumed that even biased or obtuse observers would not endorse partition, because the creation of a Jewish state would precipitate civil war. The Foreign Office also assumed that the Soviet Union and the United States would, as usual, gravitate into opposite camps and that such influences as Catholicism would militate against the Jews. The British, in short, hoped that the United Nations would support an independent binational state in which Jewish rights would be guaranteed and the promise of a national home more or less fulfilled. As it turned out, the British merely reconfirmed that UN special committees as well as the General Assembly did not operate on British rational assumptions.

The struggle for the Jewish state, as the British discovered, was fuelled not only by a sense of historical necessity deriving from the Holocaust, and by genuine humanitarian sentiment, but also by worldwide animosity against British imperialism. Anti-colonialism, as it has been traditionally understood, was a conspicuous force in the summer and autumn of 1947. The opportunity to disrupt the British Empire in the Middle East certainly helps explain Russian motivation. Though the American aim was the opposite, a tacit alliance emerged between the United States and the Soviet Union in favour of the Jews. The anti-colonial movement found vociferous representation on UNSCOP, which, the British could later sadly reflect, was the first of many UN bodies dedicated to the exposure of the evils of colonialism. The UNSCOP majority voted in favour of partition. This development triggered the British decision in September 1947 to evacuate.

Montgomery and a few others continued to believe that a Pax Britannica could be maintained by British bayonets. On the whole, however, the British by this time were ready to quit. They were responding to a combination of international, local, and domestic pressures. From the United Nations, and from the United States, they were subjected to demands for the creation of a Jewish state. In Palestine itself they faced a skilful campaign of Zionist terrorism. In England a certain current of public protest, guided by Richard Crossman (who was assistant editor of the *New Statesman* as well as a Member of Parliament), expressed revulsion against suppressing a people who had suffered unspeakable atrocities under the Nazis.[44] All of this was occurring while the British feared the impending collapse of their economy. Decisions on Palestine were being made during the convertibility crisis. Underlying economic anxiety thus provides a key to the mood of

---

[44] See especially Khalid Kishtainy, *The 'New Statesman' and the Middle East* (Beirut, 1972), chaps. 6 and 7.

September 1947. By then the British had concluded that the only way to resolve the international, local, and metropolitan tensions was to evacuate Palestine. The same interaction of similar forces triggered transfers of power in Asia and Africa. In the case of Palestine, the Labour Government decided that the crisis could be resolved only by evacuation pure and simple.

What inspired the actual decision to evacuate? There can be no doubt that the UNSCOP report precipitated it, but the international annoyance only catalysed more fundamental discontent. The minutes of the Cabinet meeting of 20 September 1947 starkly convey the sense of relief at arriving at a firm decision marking the end of years of frustration. 'This', Dalton wrote in his diary, 'if we stick to it, is a historic decision.'[45]

The Foreign Secretary again stated the case against endorsing partition. He was not willing, Bevin re-emphasized in a remark that became his public theme in the coming months, 'to enforce a settlement which was unacceptable' to either side.[46] The Colonial Secretary, who by now was thoroughly embittered at Jewish terrorism, had resigned himself to 'leaving Palestine in a state of chaos'. Creech Jones would instruct the staff of the Colonial Office to begin making plans for the withdrawal of some 5,200 British subjects in the civil administration.[47] The Minister of Defence, A. V. Alexander, was not hopeful about maintaining law and order over the whole of Palestine for an indefinite period of time. The army could, however, protect the oil installations and the airfields without additional military reinforcements.[48] The Minister of Health, Aneurin Bevan, hoped that British withdrawal would finally demonstrate to other powers, notably the United States, that the British 'did not wish to retain forces in Palestine for imperialist reasons'. The Labour Government would at last live up to its pledges. The Minister of Fuel and Power, Emanuel Shinwell, stressed the importance of an 'orderly' evacuation to avoid the impression of British 'weakness'. There was apprehension that leaving Palestine in 'chaos' might not be compatible with British 'dignity'. The Chancellor of the Exchequer emphasized that the continuing presence of British troops 'merely led to a heavy drain on our financial resources and to

---

[45] Dalton Diary, 20 September 1947.

[46] Cabinet Minutes (47) 76, 20 September 1947, CAB 128/10; PREM 8/859/1; see also CP (47) 259, 18 September 1947, CAB 129/21.

[47] The dilemmas facing the Colonial Office and other ministries are outlined in a memorandum by the Official Committee on Palestine, DO (47) 83, 5 November 1947, Creech Jones Papers, CAB 134/4.

[48] See memorandum by Alexander, 'Military and Strategic Implications', 18 September 1947, CP (47) 262, CAB 129/21.

the creation of a dangerous spirit of anti-Semitism'. Dalton, more-over, introduced the theme of a timetable: 'He . . . felt that a date for the withdrawal of British administration and British forces should be announced as soon as possible.'[49] This was the key to the problem as it had also crystallized in the mind of the Prime Minister.

Attlee was determined to liquidate Palestine as an economic and military liability. In the aftermath of the transfer of power in India, he began more and more to apply the same formula to Palestine. He wrote, for example, three days before the decision on evacuation by the Cabinet:

> We should . . . state that we will withdraw our administrative offi-cers and troops from Palestine by a definite date which should not be longer than six months, even if no other mandatory has been ap-pointed and no agreement has been come to between the Arabs and the Jews.[50]

Only by imposing a definite time limit would there be any hope of forcing the Arabs and the Jews to make arrangements for their own political future, as had been proved, Attlee believed, in the analogous case of India. The minutes of the meeting of 20 September record Att-lee's train of thought:

> *The Prime Minister* said that in his view there was a close parallel be-tween the position in Palestine and the recent situation in India. He did not think it reasonable to ask the British administration in Pales-tine to continue in present conditions, and he hoped that salutary results would be produced by a clear announcement that His Maj-esty's Government intended to relinquish the Mandate and, failing a peaceful settlement, to withdraw the British administration and Brit-ish forces.[51]

The Indian solution thus played a prominent part in the evolution of the thought of the Prime Minister. It was duly applied to Palestine, with sanguinary results, only on a smaller scale.

After September 1947, the influence of the British diminished. They stayed on, of course, for some eight months, until the expiration of the mandate on 14–15 May 1948. It would be possible to examine in

---

[49] CM (47) 76, 20 September 1947, CAB 128/10.
[50] Minute by Attlee, 17 September 1947, FO 371/61878.
[51] CM (47) 76, 20 September 1947, CAB 128/10.

detail the circumstances of the end of the mandate by drawing attention to such memorable episodes as the singing of 'Auld Lang Syne' as
well as 'God Save the King' when the Union Jack was hauled down for
the last time in Jerusalem. But such a recounting of events might detract from the larger continuity of post-war British imperialism. The
termination of the mandate was only part of the story; the paramount
aim was to remain on good terms with the Arabs as well as the Americans. The British could not do so as long as Palestine continued to poison the atmosphere. Arab nationalism, frustrated in Palestine, could
not be appeased. In British eyes, the American failure to curb militant Zionism was at the heart of the trouble. But British perceptions
and misperceptions about the motives of the other powers, the nature
of Zionism, and the responsibility of the United States all played a part
in the outcome.

Before the historic UN vote on 29 November 1947 in favour of partition, Ernest Bevin wrote one of his rare personal letters, in which he
discussed Soviet motives. Among other things, it reveals that he shared
the belief, not uncommon in British official circles, that the Jewish
state would eventually become communist:

> I was not surprised when the Russians supported partition . . . There
> are two things operating in the Russian mind. First of all, Palestine. I
> am sure they are convinced that by immigration they can pour in suf-
> ficient indoctrinated Jews to turn it into a Communist state in a very
> short time. The New York Jews have been doing their work for them.

> Secondly, I shall not be surprised if Russia, to consolidate her po-
> sition in Eastern Europe, does not break up all her satellite States
> into smaller provinces, reaching down to the Adriatic. Thus partition
> would suit them as a principle . . . You must study very carefully
> Stalin's work on nationalities to realise how his mind works, and then
> you will learn that he would have no compunction at all in exploit-
> ing these nationalities to achieve his object by means of a whole se-
> ries which Russia could control.[52]

On another occasion, Bevin used the phrase 'international Jewry', with
its connotation of conspiracy, as an explanation of what had gone
wrong.[53] If he did not implicitly subscribe to the equivalent of a conspiracy theory, at least he believed that the Jews might be fitting into

[52] Bevin wrote this letter to his Minister of State, Hector McNeil, and designated it 'Confidential and Personal'. 'Please burn it after you have read it,' Bevin instructed him (15 October 1947,
FO 800/509). Fortunately, the carbon copy was not destroyed. As will be seen, McNeil played an
important part in discussing unpleasant but unavoidable facts about Palestine with Bevin.

[53] See Minutes of Foreign Office Middle East conference, 21 July 1949, FO 371/75072.

Stalin's plan for eventually absorbing Jewish Palestine into the system of Soviet satellites. Bevin's ideas on this subject were not idiosyncratic. British apprehensions about the Jews and communism can be traced to the time of the Russian Revolution in 1917. The world of the early twentieth century abounded in conspiracy theories about Freemasons, Papists, international financiers, and, not least, Jews. Revolutionary Jews were believed to have been decisive in the overthrow of the tsar. There later appeared to be a similarity between the collective farms in the Soviet Union and the kibbutzim in Palestine. Such stereotyped ideas, absurd as they may seem in retrospect, help explain British attitudes towards the Zionists in 1947–48. During the 1948 war, Czechoslovakia supplied arms and ammunition to the Jews; British intelligence reports indicated that refugees from Eastern Europe included indoctrinated communists.[54] Thus Bevin's attitude and his suspicions, though misguided in retrospect, are at least comprehensible.

Bevin twice attempted to influence the territorial outcome of the struggle. In early 1948 he encouraged King Abdullah of Jordan to take over most of 'Arab Palestine'. In the last stage of the 1948 war, he attempted to secure part of the Negev as a connecting strip between Egypt and the other Arab states. At no time did he consider the possibility of an independent Arab Palestinian state, which the Foreign Office feared would be too small to be viable and moreover would probably fall under the control of extremists led by the anti-British leader of the Palestinian Arabs, the Mufti, Hajj Amin al-Husseini. During the 1948 war, the head of the Eastern Department of the Foreign Office, Bernard Burrows, wrote of 'the disadvantages of a separate Arab state under the Mufti':

> It would be a hotbed of ineffectual Arab fanaticism and after causing maximum disturbance to our relations with the Arabs would very likely fall in the end under Jewish influence and be finally absorbed in the Jewish state, thereby increasing the area of possible Russian influence and excluding the possibility of our obtaining strategic requirements in any part of Palestine.[55]

Bevin pinned his hopes on the takeover of most of 'Arab Palestine' by the Arab Legion of Transjordan, led by Sir John Bagot Glubb. Glubb acted as interpreter between Bevin and the foreign minister of Transjordan, Tawfiq Pasha Abul-Huda, in a critical meeting in March 1948. 'I can to this day almost see Mr. Bevin sitting at his table in that splendid room' at the Foreign Office, Glubb recalled later. Commenting on Transjordan's intention to occupy the West Bank, Bevin said, 'It seems

[54] This point is established by Bullock, *Bevin: Foreign Secretary*, chap. 16, sec. 6.
[55] Minute by Burrows, 17 August 1948, FO 371/68822.

the obvious thing to do,' then repeated, 'It seems the obvious thing to do . . . but do not go and invade the areas allotted to the Jews' under the UN partition plan.[56] The British records do not sustain the view that Bevin intended to reduce the Jewish part of Palestine into a 'rump state' that would be forced to throw itself on British mercy, though it is clear that he wished to salvage, in the retrospective words of one of his lieutenants, 'the dismal wreck of Arab Palestine'.[57]

The long-range goal was the preservation of as much as possible of 'Arab Palestine', mainly by its absorption into Transjordan; the short-range aim was to hold the ring for the Arabs from September 1947 until mid-May 1948 so that 'Arab Palestine' would not be overrun by the Zionists before the expiration of the mandate. The fall of Haifa on 22 April 1948 was a critical blow, militarily and psychologically, to both the British and the Arabs. Bevin complained angrily that he had been 'let down by the Army', which led to a row between him and Montgomery.[58] The political purpose was at variance with the military risk of British casualties. Bevin was not merely concerned with the loss of military position; he was also alarmed at the Arab mass exodus that had been precipitated earlier in the month, on 9 April, by the Irgun's massacre of the Arabs of a village called Deir Yasin. The High Commissioner, General Sir Alan Cunningham, had written three days afterward of 'that brutal Jewish attack on Deir Yassin where 250 Arab civilians were butchered, half being women and children'. He went on to explain to the Colonial Secretary the reasons why the British had not intervened, in Deir Yasin and in other places, against the Zionist offensives:

> This village is still in the hands of the Jews as I write. I wanted the soldiers to attack it, if necessary with all the power they can produce and turn out the Jews. But I am told that they [the British Army] are not in a position to do so, or indeed do anything which may provoke a general conflict with either side as their troops are already fully committed. This is only one example out of many where the Civil Government has to stand idle while its authority is flouted in all directions.[59]

From the point of view of the High Commissioner, the tragedy of the massacre was matched by the calamity of British impotence during the last weeks of the mandate. To some British officials, though by no means to all, the atrocity at Deir Yasin came as a revelation about the

---

[56] John Bagot Glubb, *A Soldier with the Arabs* (London, 1957), pp. 63–66.

[57] Michael Wright to Ronald Campbell, 30 March 1949, FO 371/75064.

[58] See *Memoirs of Field-Marshall Montgomery*, pp. 424–26.

[59] Cunningham to Creech Jones, Private and Personal, 12 April 1948, Cunningham Papers (Middle East Centre, St. Antony's College, Oxford).

nature of the new Jewish state. Sir John Troutbeck, the head of the British Middle East Office in Cairo, wrote that 'Deir Yassein is a warning of what a Jew will do to gain his purpose.'[60]

On the eve of the Arab-Israeli war the British were apprehensive about its outcome, but virtually no one anticipated the extent of the Arab collapse and the Israeli victory. The British associated themselves with the Arab cause as one that was ultimately compatible with their own sense of mission in the Middle East, and during the course of the war they became convinced that a grave injustice was being perpetrated because of American support of the Israelis. The resentment towards the United States still smoulders in the files at the Public Record Office. It existed as the main sentiment underlying official policy, and it was perhaps most indignantly expressed by Troutbeck, who held that the Americans were responsible for the creation of a gangster state headed by 'an utterly unscrupulous set of leaders'.[61] Even if one disregards such intemperate and indeed unbalanced comments, the anti-Israeli and anti-American tone of the telegrams, dispatches, and minutes cannot be ignored. This sense of moral outrage reached a climax in late 1948 with the collapse of the 'Bernadotte plan'. A brief concluding comment on this episode serves to place some of the more controversial issues concerning the birth of the state of Israel into British perspective.

The Bernadotte plan essentially would have given the Negev to the Arabs in return for a Jewish Galilee. The British believed this to be a geographically sound solution that would at least help placate the Arab world. They argued that a Jewish 'wedge' driven between Egypt and the Arab countries would give the Soviet Union the opportunity to exploit Arab discontent. They held that only by American pressure could militant Zionism be curbed and Arab irredentism be mitigated. The long and the short of the interlude is that there was an abrupt change of American policy from supporting the Bernadotte plan to championing the Israeli claim to the Negev. President Truman wrote to President Weizmann to this effect on 29 November 1948, the anniversary of the UN vote. The British believed, in the words of Hector McNeil (who was then acting as Bevin's lieutenant on Palestine affairs), that they had been 'double-crossed'. This was not the first time he had used that phrase to describe the reversal of State Department policy by the President. Furthermore, he used the expression passionately and angrily. The Jews would not hold on to the Negev *and* Galilee. Nevertheless, it was McNeil who wrote to Bevin in early

[60] Troutbeck to Wright, Personal and Secret, 18 May 1948, FO 371/68386.
[61] Troutbeck to Bevin, Secret, 2 June 1948, FO 371/68559.

1949 that that time had come to face realities. The British would have to recognize that the Israelis held frontiers that they had the military capacity to defend, and that the United States would refuse to rein in militant Zionism.

'This is not a happy situation for us,' McNeil wrote to Bevin. 'Indeed it is so unhappy, that whenever some new offence or indignity is given to us, or some further disadvantage is imposed upon the Arabs, we are tempted to act unilaterally.' By pretending still to be the masters of the Middle East, the British tended to neglect the overriding importance of retaining American good will. American collaboration in the Middle East and the rest of the world remained the paramount consideration: 'It is essential even when the Jews are most wicked and the Americans most exasperating not to lose sight of this point.' It was irritating to reflect that each time the British had attempted to work in concert with the Americans, the President had intervened—to repeat McNeil's phrase, had 'double-crossed' them: 'Each time the Americans have shifted. One way of explaining this is to point to the undoubted weakness of their President. Another way of explaining it is that each time the Jews have been permitted too much time so that they have been enabled to put the screw on Truman.'[62] Whatever the explanation, it always led McNeil to the same conclusion, which he now pressed on Bevin: 'As long as America is a major power, and as long as she is free of major war, anyone taking on the Jews will indirectly be taking on America.' Since the Americans would not cooperate, the only alternative would be for the British themselves to fight in the Negev. McNeil ruled out this possibility for a simple and compelling reason: 'Our public would not stand for it.'[63] British policy had thus led to a dead end. There was nothing left but to accommodate the Jews on their own terms.

Bevin's tempestuous response to the events of late 1948 and early 1949 sums up his exasperated thoughts as well as what might be called the final 'British perspective' on the Palestine problem. He wrote that the American attitude appeared to be not only 'let there be an Israel and to hell with the consequences' but also 'peace at any price, and Jewish expansion whatever the consequences'.[64]

---

[62] Minute by McNeil, 14 January 1949, FO 371/75337. The Permanent Under-Secretary, Sir Orme Sargent, added to this assessment that Truman was 'a weak, obstinate, and suspicious man' (minute by Sargent, 17 January 1949, FO 371/75336).

[63] Minute by McNeil, 14 January 1949.

[64] Bevin to Franks (draft), 3 February 1949, FO 371/75337.

DECOLONIZATION

17

THE IMPERIALISM OF DECOLONIZATION

(*with* RONALD ROBINSON)

I t ought to be a commonplace that the post-war British Empire was more than British and less than an imperium. As it survived, so it was transformed as part of the Anglo-American coalition. Neglecting the American role, historians of empire often single out British enfeeblement as the prime cause of imperial demise.[1] The presumption is that an imperial state caved in at the centre like Gibbon's Rome, with infirmity in the metropole and insurgency in the provinces. For the 'Gibbonians', the Empire therefore ends with political independence. Dependent though they remained in other ways, the new states are said to be decolonized.[2] Historians of the Cold War necessarily take more account of invisible empires, but the imperial effects of the trans-Atlantic alliance are not their concern, except for some writers who suspect that the expansion of American capitalist imperialism swallowed up the Empire.[3] Far from being decolonized, in this view, the British system was neo-colonized more intensively under new management. Each of these interpretations may be true in some instances, given a particular definition of empire. The overall picture is nonetheless confusing. To see the transformation of an imperial coalition as if it were the collapse of an imperial state is like mistaking the melting tip for the iceberg. Without defining the relativities of imperial power, it is hard to tell how much metropolitan infirmity,

---

[1] Paul Kennedy, *The Rise and Fall of the Great Powers* (New York, 1987), pp. 367 ff. For themes of 'decline' directly relevant to the present article, see John Darwin, 'Imperialism in Decline? Tendencies in British Imperial Policy between the Wars', *Historical Journal*, 23 (1980), pp. 657–79; B. R. Tomlinson, 'The Contraction of England: National Decline and Loss of Empire', *Journal of Imperial and Commonwealth History*, 11 (October 1982), pp. 58–72; R. F. Holland, 'The Imperial Factor in British Strategies from Attlee to Macmillan, 1945–63', *Journal of Imperial and Commonwealth History*, 12 (January 1984), pp. 165–86; and W. W. Rostow, 'Beware of Historians Bearing False Analogies', *Foreign Affairs*, 66 (Spring 1988), pp. 863–68. See also especially the major new work by P. J. Cain and A. G. Hopkins, *British Imperialism* (2 vols., London, 1993). We are generally in agreement with their interpretation of the issue of decline (for example, II, pp. 311 ff.) but, as will be seen, we do not agree with their explanation of the motives of British imperialism (II, p. 297; also, for example, I, pp. 393, 395).

[2] John Darwin provides a shrewd analysis of the historiographical problem in *The End of the British Empire* (Oxford, 1991) and in *Britain and Decolonisation* (London, 1988). See also R. F. Holland, *European Decolonization, 1918–1981* (London, 1985); and John D. Hargreaves, *Decolonization in Africa* (London, 1988).

[3] See especially Roger Owen and Bob Sutcliffe, eds., *Studies in the Theory of Imperialism* (London, 1972); and Wolfgang J. Mommsen and Jürgen Osterhammel, eds., *Imperialism and After* (London, 1986).

nationalist insurgency, and American or Soviet expansion contributed to whatever happened to the post-war Empire.

The difficulty of attributing the fall to British decline is that it leads us into paradox. Colonial emancipation is not necessarily a sign of metropolitan weakness. Virtual independence was conceded to Canadian, Australasian, and South African nationalists before 1914, when Britain was at her strongest. Conversely, when she was much weaker, during the inter-war years, the Empire reached its greatest extent, with the addition of much of the Middle East and more of Africa. By 1940, when there was scarcely strength to defend the home islands, the British were able to crack down on nationalists in India, Egypt, and Iran and mobilize the Empire for war. When peace came, a bankrupt metropole somehow reconstructed the imperial system in the familiar Victorian style of trade without rule where possible, rule for trade where necessary. The 'imperialism of free trade', or rather of the sterling area, continued. Weak or strong, the metropole was clearly not the only source of imperial strength. Gibbon will not help us with these difficulties. How is the survival of the Empire to be explained? Was it in fact decolonized by the 1960s, or informalized as part of the older story of free-trade imperialism with a new American twist? It is with the answers given by British and American officials at the time that this article is concerned.

A more refined notion of the ingredients of imperial power is required to explain the Empire's capacity for regenerating on alternative sources of strength and for exchanging informal and formal guises. In peacetime, the British government invested relatively few resources in imperial upkeep. The British state provided military forces in emergencies, a string of bases from Gibraltar to Singapore, and not least the necessary prestige. Whitehall monitored what was in effect a self-generating and self-financing system. It could not have been otherwise. Had ministers tried to project so vast an empire with metropolitan resources, they would have been driven from office before they ruined the country. At the centre of an imperial economy, the international financial and commodity markets of London held the system's bread and butter together, whether the branches were politically dependent or not. Most of Britain's chief trading partners belonged to the sterling area;[4] imperial preferences encouraged their exchanges.

[4] On the sterling area, a useful recent article with an extensive bibliography is Gerold Krozewski, 'Sterling, the "Minor" Territories, and the End of Formal Empire, 1939–1958', *Economic History Review*, 46 (1993), pp. 239–65. Works essential to our argument include Alec Cairncross and Barry Eichengreen, *Sterling in Decline* (London, 1983); Susan Strange, *Sterling and British Policy* (London, 1971); J. O. N. Perkins, *The Sterling Area, the Commonwealth, and World Economic Growth* (Cambridge, 1970); Diane Kunz, 'British Postwar Sterling Crises' (British Studies Distinguished

Tight state controls over capital and commodity movements persisted from wartime into the mid-1950s. No longer the hub of a global economy, London remained the central banker and market for the world's largest trading area.[5]

Our hypothesis suggests that more than a project of the British state, imperial sway by 1939 derived mainly from profit-sharing with business and power-sharing with indigenous elites overseas. At the country level, the system relied on unequal accommodations with client rulers or proto-nationalists, who multiplied British power locally with their own authority for their own advantage.[6] Contracts could not be too unequal or else collaborators would lose their constituents and the system would break down. As local subcontractors became better organized, the terms for cooperation turned progressively in their favour. The final settlement would be with national successors, who would secure British economic and strategic assets under informal tutelage. Local bargains could not be struck to imperial advantage if other Great Powers competed in the bidding. International alliances —at least 'hands-off' arrangements—were essential if the Empire were to be defended and the imperial balance sheets kept out of the red. The object was not that Britain should sustain the Empire, but that the Empire should sustain Britain. From Canning to Churchill, British geo-strategists looked to 'the continuous creation of new sources of power overseas to redress the balance of the Old World'.[7] They once sought those sources of power in Latin America. They found ample reward in India. In the 1900s they looked to the Japanese alliance and the Anglo-French and Anglo-Russian ententes. They were to turn to the United States. The various local coalitions depended on international alignments to tilt internal and global balances in their favour.

Finally, the system required the tolerance of the British voter. Terms for the metropolitan contract were those of 'empire on the cheap'— that taxpayers should not be asked to meet the cost at the expense of

Lecture: Austin, Texas, 1992); and, of lasting value in the context of Empire, J. D. B. Miller, *Survey of Commonwealth Affairs: Problems of Expansion and Attrition, 1953–1969* (London, 1974), especially chap. 12.

[5] In the post-war years, between 36 per cent and 49 per cent of global merchandise trade was conducted in sterling (Imanuel Wexler, *The Marshall Plan Revisited* [Westport, Conn, 1983], p. 166).

[6] On the collaborative system, see Ronald Robinson, 'Non-European Foundations of European Imperialism', in Owen and Sutcliffe, *Studies in the Theory of Imperialism*. On the origins of the idea, see Anil Seal's preface to John Gallagher, *Decline, Revival and Fall of the British Empire* (Cambridge, 1982), pp. viiiff.

[7] War Cabinet Memorandum by L. S. Amery, 'Notes on Possible Terms of Peace', GT-448, Secret, 11 April 1917, CAB 24/10. W. R. Louis, *In the Name of God Go! Leo Amery and the British Empire in the Age of Churchill* (New York, 1992), p. 68.

their home comforts; that a benign imperial image assuage the latent forces of anti-imperial opinion; that British industry remain strong enough to drive the imperial economy; and that the economic prizes to be won were worth more than the imperial cost of winning them. The state of imperial power at different places and times may therefore be measured in the contracts required to win collaboration and head off resistance at international, metropolitan, and local levels. Bargains were interdependent.[8] As we have argued in an earlier essay,[9] an alteration of terms at one level implied corresponding changes on the others. The Second World War overthrew the balance of pre-war terms; a different Britain re-formed the post-war Empire in another world.

Clement Attlee's government faced devastating problems of economic recovery in the period 1945–46. When American Lend-Lease ended, he protested that the very living conditions of people in the British Isles depended on the continued flow 'both of food and . . . raw materials' from the United States.[10] There were no dollars to pay for them.[11] The cumulative shortfall on current accounts stood at £10 billion. Even if the economy could be re-jigged to export 75 per cent above pre-war levels, the estimated balance-of-payments deficit would still be running at over a billion pounds in 1951. Fifteen billion dollars

[8] It seems to us that Cain and Hopkins (*British Imperialism*) overstate the case by arguing that 'Gentlemanly Capitalism' was the primary cause of British expansion and contraction. The stock exchange is obviously an entrepreneurial business, the success of which depends on partnerships on the periphery.

[9] W. R. Louis and R. E. Robinson, 'The United States and the Liquidation of the British Empire in Tropical Africa, 1941–1951', in Prosser Gifford and W. R. Louis, eds., *The Transfer of Power in Africa* (New Haven, 1982), pp. 31–55.

[10] Attlee to Truman, 1 September 1945, *Foreign Relations of the United States, 1945* (Washington), VI, p. 115.

[11] Cabinet Memorandum by Lord Keynes, 13 August 1945, CAB 129/1, CP (45) 112, in *British Documents on the End of Empire*, series A, vol. 2: *The Labour Government and the End of Empire, 1945–1951*, ed. Ronald Hyam, Part II (London, 1992), pp. 1–5 (hereafter *BDEEP—Labour Government*). For further British documentation, see A. N. Porter and A. J. Stockwell, eds., *British Imperial Policy and Decolonization* (2 vols., London, 1987 and 1989). For the economic context, see W. K. Hancock and M. M. Gowing, *British War Economy* (London, 1949), chap. 19; Richard N. Gardner, *Sterling-Dollar Diplomacy* (Oxford, 1956); Sir Richard Clarke (Sir Alec Cairncross, ed.), *Anglo-American Economic Collaboration in War and Peace, 1942–1949* (Oxford, 1982); and, especially for our argument, L. S. Pressnell, *External Economic Policy since the War*, vol. 1: *The Post-War Financial Settlement* (London, 1986). See also Robert A. Pollard, *Economic Security and the Origins of the Cold War, 1945–1950* (New York, 1985); Robert M. Hathaway, *Ambiguous Partnership: Britain and America, 1944–1947* (New York, 1981); and Alan P. Dobson, *The Politics of the Anglo-American Economic Special Relationship, 1940–1987* (New York, 1988).

was owing to Washington. Three billion pounds was due to sterling countries, especially to India and Egypt for defence costs. The British were no longer the creditors but the debtors of the Empire. John Maynard Keynes, the Treasury's most influential adviser, concluded: 'We cannot police half the world at our own expense when we have already gone into pawn to the other half.'[12]

There was no recourse but to go cap in hand for a dollar grant or loan. With or without the American loan, ministers had to choose between financing their domestic recovery and their imperial commitments. To reduce food rations further was not practical politics. In 1945–46, as in every budget thereafter, the promised welfare state competed with the Empire for scarce resources.[13] The Treasury warned: '[A] straight issue would be reached with the Middle East and India. Either they would have to lend us the money for our troops there, or we should have to move our troops out.'[14] Keynes emphasized that 'the American loan is primarily required to meet the political and military expenditure overseas.' Without it, 'a large-scale withdrawal . . . [from our] international responsibilities' was inevitable.[15]

On what terms would Washington, with its plans for global free trade, agree to underwrite Britain and the Empire?[16] During the eighteen months between the end of the hot war and the beginning of the cold, most Americans regarded empires as obsolete. British claims to world power seemed pathetic. To save their wartime ally from 'starvation corner', Congress wrote off the Lend-Lease debt, but saw no reason to rescue the Empire. In return for a dollar loan of £3.75 billion, which the Canadians topped up to £5 billion, the British were forced to make the pound convertible into the dollar within twelve months. The imperial economy, in effect, was to be dismantled.[17] Meanwhile, nationalist protests against stringent economic controls

---

[12] Quoted in M. W. Kirby, *The Decline of British Economic Power since 1870* (London, 1981), p. 93.

[13] See A. K. Cairncross, *The British Economy since 1945: Economic Policy and Performance* (Oxford, 1992), chap. 2.

[14] Minute by R. W. B. Clarke to Sir David Waley, 'What happens if we do not get the US Loan?' 15 February 1946, in Clarke, *Anglo-American Economic Collaboration*, p. 147.

[15] Minute by Lord Keynes to Sir David Waley, 'If Congress rejects the Loan', 22 February 1946, Clarke, *Anglo-American Economic Collaboration*, p. 152.

[16] On the ethnic opposition to the loan in the United States and the countering anti-communist argument, see John Rourke, *Congress and the Presidency in U.S. Foreign Policymaking: A Study of Interaction and Influence, 1945–1982* (Boulder, Colo., 1983), pp. 43–48.

[17] On American motives for the loan, see especially *Foreign Relation of the United States, 1945*, VI, pp. 54, 110 ff. For British reactions, see Alan Bullock, *Ernest Bevin: Foreign Secretary, 1945–1951* (London, 1983), pp. 201–05.

erupted throughout the dependent Empire. Imperial contracts were falling apart at all levels in the 1945–47 period, as Attlee recognized. 'It may be', he foresaw in March 1946, 'we shall have to consider the British Isles as an easterly extension of a strategic [arc] the centre of which is the American continent rather than as a Power looking east-wards through the Mediterranean to India and the East.' In Attlee's forthright estimate, '[W]e cannot afford . . . the great sums of money for the large forces involved.'[18] His acidic foreboding of Britain re-duced to a small Empire in Africa seems, in retrospect at least, more realistic than the case made by his Foreign Secretary, Ernest Bevin, for holding the Middle East.[19] Much depended on 'what the Americans are prepared to do'.[20]

The Cabinet debate echoed in the Colonial Office, where J. S. Ben-nett argued that 'the United States cannot be expected to underwrite the British Empire either *in toto* or unconditionally. In consequence, the system and objectives of [pre-war] colonial administration . . . no longer correspond to the realities of the situation.' Either the British could 'hang on' until international and related internal pressures be-came overwhelming, as in India, or they could wind up colonial com-mitments in the Middle East and South-East Asia in return for 'maxi-mum practical' support from the United States; 'The Colonial Empire . . . would thus be reduced to Africa, the Pacific and the Caribbean.'[21] But British recovery depended largely on the imperial cohesion of the sterling area. From the economic standpoint, Hilton Poynton com-mented: 'The point surely is that USA must help the British Empire to underwrite the world.'[22] The issue remained in doubt up to the end of 1947.[23] By that time the Americans were doing a great deal to prop up the Empire, especially in the eastern Mediterranean and the Middle East.[24] Meanwhile the Cabinet withdrew the troops fighting

[18] Memorandum by Attlee, 'Future of the Italian Colonies', 2 March 1946, DO (46) 27, CAB 131/2.

[19] Memorandum by Bevin, 13 March 1946, DO (46) 40, CAB 131/2.

[20] Attlee to Bevin, 1 December 1946, FO 800/475, *BDEEP—Labour Government*, III, p. 222.

[21] Memorandum by J. S. Bennett, 'International Aspects of Colonial Policy—1947', 30 April 1947, CO 537/2057, *BDEEP—Labour Government*, II, pp. 418–19. For the antecedents of these themes in the wartime period, see W. R. Louis, *Imperialism at Bay* (Oxford, 1977). For domestic politics, see Stephen Howe, *Anticolonialism in British Politics: The Left and the End of Empire, 1918–1964* (Oxford, 1993).

[22] Marginal note by Poynton on Bennett, 'International Aspects of Colonial Policy—1947', 12 May 1947, *BDEEP—Labour Government*, II, p. 418.

[23] For the ministerial discussion on the Mediterranean issue, see *BDEEP—Labour Government*, III, pp. 215–348.

[24] In October 1949, Bevin reported that 'American policy towards the Middle East has for some time past been crystallising on lines similar to our own . . . The United States Government has undertaken to help His Majesty's Government to maintain their position in the Middle East.'

the communists in Greece and gave up the Turkish commitment. They were determined to leave India, Burma, and Ceylon, and they were soon to abdicate in Palestine.

Attlee felt morally obliged to concede Indian independence. For all that, the British were being driven out. In the 1930s the National Congress had gained the momentum to become a popular movement, but the outbreak of war put an end to provincial power-sharing with Indian ministers.[25] After crushing the 'Quit India' rising of the Congress in 1942, the Raj relied on Muslim collaborators for the war effort and alienated its remaining indigenous support. By 1945 the Viceroy, Lord Wavell, could no longer rely on Indian loyalty in the army and public services. The pre-war contracts for local cooperation had run out of time. In John Gallagher's irreverent metaphor, nationalists and imperialists were propping each other up like punch-drunk boxers, lest they both fall into chaos. One question only remained—how to find a viable and amenable successor. At the Indian elections of 1946, the avowed British intention to leave in 1948 evoked not one possible successor but two. Fearing entrapment in a terrible communal war, Attlee and Lord Mountbatten, the last Viceroy, brought the departure date forward to 1947. The emergency enabled Mountbatten to settle with Congress for a strong central government over most of the subcontinent. In exchange, Congress yielded to Jinnah's claims to Pakistan.[26] Both new states unexpectedly joined the Commonwealth, which now began its uncomfortable mutation from an English-speaking club into a multiracial association.[27]

There had been no significant superpower intervention in India, as there was to be in Palestine. Since the Indian empire had always drawn its strength from local allies more than from the metropole, the idea that the British 'transferred power' is a half-truth. The other half is that the divided communities once articulated by the Raj had become nationalized. It was the emergence of two national fronts of

---

Cabinet Memorandum by Bevin, 'The Middle East', 19 October 1949, CAB 129/37/1, CP (49) 209, *BDEEP—Labour Government*, III, p. 383.

[25] See John Gallagher, Gordon Johnson, and Anil Seal, eds., *Locality, Province and Nation* (Cambridge, 1973); Sarvepalli Gopal, *Jawaharlal Nehru,* (Delhi, 1975), vol. 1; B. R. Tomlinson, *The Indian National Congress and the Raj* (London, 1976); R. J. Moore, *Escape from Empire: The Attlee Government and the Indian Problem* (Oxford, 1983); Ayesha Jalal, *The Sole Spokesman: Jinnah, the Muslim League and the Demand for Pakistan* (Cambridge, 1985); Anita Inder Singh, *The Origins of the Partition of India, 1937–47* (Delhi, 1987).

[26] For documentation see Nicholas Mansergh et al., eds., *Constitutional Relations between Britain and India: The Transfer of Power, 1942–1947* (12 vols., London, 1970–83).

[27] See Cabinet Minutes on India's future relations with the Commonwealth, 8 February–27 April 1949, *BDEEP—Labour Government*, IV, pp. 187–203; R. J. Moore, *Making the New Commonwealth* (Oxford, 1987).

non-cooperation that drove the bitter transition to a relatively stable and scarcely revolutionary succession. A partition that left the Indian Army[28] divided between two hostile states was the solution that the British had tried above all to avoid.[29] Informal affiliations nonetheless continued to serve imperial objectives in unforeseen ways.

In Palestine, there were no effective power-sharing contracts to expire.[30] Separate administrative arrangements with the Arab and Jewish communities had been incompatible, especially after the Arab revolt in 1936. As Bevin complained, President Truman's intervention on behalf of Jewish refugees and Zionist aspirations exacerbated the conflict. When the plan for partition gained momentum in 1947, Attlee and Bevin were ready to throw in their hand. Even Churchill insisted on withdrawal: '[T]here is the manpower of at least 100,000 men in Palestine who might be at home strengthening our depleted industry . . . What good are we getting out of it?'[31] After the attempt at convertible sterling in July 1947 turned into a disastrous run on the pound and exhausted almost all the American loan, the imperative to leave Palestine became overwhelming. On 15 May 1948 the British withdrew from an imbroglio in another communal war that was disrupting their Arab alliances throughout the Middle East.[32] Against the advice of the Secretary of State, George C. Marshall, Truman immediately recognized the state of Israel. An American-sponsored government had taken over much of the British Mandate. Zionist contracts with the White House had prevailed. Two can make viable imperial contracts; three is a crowd; four is an impossibility. Palestine showed how

---

[28] In 1941 the Indian Army had 418,000 personnel, of whom 155,000 (37 per cent) were Muslim and 263,000 were Hindus and other religions, including 51,000 Sikhs. (General R. M. Lockhart, memorandum, 25 February 1942, India Office Library, L/PO/6/106b). The Muslim element was greatly expanded during the war. See Gowher Rizvi, _Linlithgow and India: A Study of British Policy and the Political Impasse in India, 1936–43_ (London, 1978), p. 176.

[29] Though the British attempted to retain as much influence as possible over the defence policies of both Pakistan and India. See the important article by Partha Sarathi Gupta, 'British Strategic and Economic Priorities during the Negotiations for the Transfer of Power in South Asia, 1945–47', _Bangladesh Historical Studies_, 7 (1983), pp. 39–51.

[30] See the chapter by W. R. Louis in W. R. Louis and R. W. Stookey, eds., _The End of the Palestine Mandate_ (Austin, Tex., 1986); Michael J. Cohen, _Palestine: Retreat from the Mandate_ (London, 1978), and _Palestine and the Great Powers_ (Princeton, 1982); Martin Jones, _Failure in Palestine: British and United States Policy after the Second World War_ (London, 1986); and Ritchie Ovendale, _Britain, the United States, and the End of the Palestine Mandate, 1941–1948_ (Woodbridge, UK, 1989). On the absence of power-sharing contracts, see Bernard Wasserstein, _Herbert Samuel: A Political Life_ (Oxford, 1992), pp. 262, 266–67.

[31] _Parliamentary Debates_ (Commons), 31 January 1947, col. 1347.

[32] For documentation, see _BDEEP—Labour Government_, I, pp. 31–79.

an intrusive superpower allied with a nationalist revolt could upset the collaborative equations of Empire.

The ensuing Arab-Israeli war eventually forced the Americans to resume their partnership with the British. Washington felt morally obliged to defend Israel, and the British were treaty-bound to defend Transjordan.[33] Washington and London could easily have been drawn into the war by proxy on opposite sides. 'This must not be allowed to happen,' Truman vowed after his election in November 1948.[34] He compelled the Israelis to withdraw from Egyptian territory by ultimatum,[35] though they acquired the territory of the Negev. At Bevin's request, Truman appeased the Arabs by agreeing to incorporate Arab Palestine into British-allied Jordan.[36] The Anglo-American schism over Palestine had to be repaired to bring about an armistice and a de facto territorial settlement.

As the Cold War intensified from 1947 to 1951, competition between the two superpowers came to the rescue of the Empire. Faced with the Czech crisis and the Berlin blockade, the United States hastened to strengthen Britain and France in defence of Western Europe. As Senator Henry Cabot Lodge, Jr., testified at Senate hearings on the North Atlantic Treaty, '[W]e need . . . these countries to be strong, and they cannot be strong without their colonies.'[37] After the fiasco of

[33] Message from Attlee to Truman, 15 November 1948, *Foreign Relations of the United States, 1948,* V, pt. 2, pp. 1585–89. For earlier discussions of the danger, see ibid., pp. 865-1038. On the British side, see, for example, Bevin to Amman and other posts, Top Secret, 12 July 1948, FO 371/68572. For themes of the war relevant to our argument, see Mary C. Wilson, *King Abdullah, Britain and the Making of Jordan* (Cambridge, 1987); Benny Morris, *The Birth of the Palestinian Refugee Problem, 1947–1949* (Cambridge, 1987); Avi Shlaim, *Collusion across the Jordan* (Oxford, 1988); for the consequences, see Ilan Pappe, *Britain and the Arab-Israeli Conflict, 1948–51* (London, 1988).

[34] Account of conversation with the President, Lewis Douglas to Acting Secretary of State, 12 November 1948, *Foreign Relations of the United States, 1948,* V, pt 2, p. 1572.

[35] Acting Secretary of State to US Representative (McDonald) in Israel, 30 December 1948, ibid., 1704.

[36] Acting Secretary of State to Stabler in Amman, 3 January 1949, *Foreign Relations of the United States, 1949,* VI, p. 604. For the British side, see especially minute by Sir Orme Sargent (Permanent Under-Secretary), 17 January 1949, FO 371/76336.

[37] Hearings in Executive Session on Vandenberg Resolution and the North Atlantic Treaty, 2 June 1949, *Senate Committee on Foreign Relations,* 81st Cong., 1st sess., 1949, p. 256. According to an estimate by the Central Intelligence Agency in 1947: 'Existing British overseas commitments are so extensive and important that their precipitate liquidation would create conditions prejudicial to security interests of the United States' (CIA, Office of Reports and Estimates, 'Review of the World Situation', 26 September 1947, Secret), in Michael Warner, ed., *CIA Cold War Records: The CIA under Harry Truman* (Washington, 1994), pp. 144–45.

convertibility, the dollar underwrote the sterling area up to 1951 and at need thereafter.[38] Under the Truman Doctrine, American power reinforced the traditional imperial 'Great Game' of checking Russian advances into the eastern Mediterranean and the Middle East.[39] By the end of 1947, the American Chiefs of Staff had recommended 'all feasible political, economic, and if necessary military support . . . to the United Kingdom and the communications of the British Commonwealth'.[40] In the wake of the Maoist triumph in China and the stalemate of the Korean War, Washington relied on the British and French empires to block Sino-Soviet expansion into the lands on the rim of southern and western Asia. Much as some American officials disliked it, the State Department and the Pentagon found their 'most important collaborators' in the British and their Empire-Commonwealth.[41]

After 1947 the Americans subsidized the imperial system generously in one way or another as a measure of national defence. Robert Hall of the Cabinet Office summed up the tally in 1951: 'We have had . . . an average of over a billion dollars a year . . . since 1946 and of course under Lend/Lease we had a great deal more. In fact our whole economic life has been propped up in this way.'[42] Keynes had earlier underlined the imperial effect: 'America . . . was underwriting British policy in other parts of the world.'[43] Marshall Plan aid and the Mutual Security programme[44] met the otherwise prohibitive charge on the balance of payments required to sustain British power overseas. The British voter could have his imperial cake and eat at the same time. In

[38] On the origins of US support, see Clayton's memorandum, 27 May 1947, *Foreign Relations of the United States, 1947*, III, pp. 230–32. On the British side, see Alec Cairncross, ed., *The Robert Hall Dairies, 1947–53* (London, 1989), pp. 138–39, 269–71.

[39] A work that helps correct the bipolar vision of the Cold War as a purely American-Soviet conflict is Anne Deighton, ed., *Britain and the First Cold War* (London, 1990). See especially the chapter by John Kent, 'The British Empire and the Origins of the Cold War'. See also Ritchie Ovendale, *The English-Speaking Alliance: Britain, the United States, the Dominions, and the Cold War, 1945–51* (London, 1985). On the American side, we have found especially useful John Lewis Gaddis, *The Long Peace* (Oxford, 1987); and Melvyn P. Leffler, *A Preponderance of Power: National Security, The Truman Administration, and the Cold War* (Stanford, Calif., 1992).

[40] Agreed State Department–Joint Chiefs memorandum, endorsed by Truman; James F. Schnabel, *The History of the Joint Chiefs of Staff* (Wilmington, Del., 1979), I, p. 93 and chap. 3.

[41] See Top Secret Minutes of 7th Meeting of the Policy Planning Staff, 24 Jan. 1950, *Foreign Relations of the United States, 1950*, III, pp. 617–22. According to George Kennan: '[T]he dissolution of the [British] empire was not in our interest as there were many things the Commonwealth could do which we could not do and which we wished them to continue doing' (ibid., p. 620).

[42] *Hall Diaries, 1947–53*, 20 July 1951, p. 161.

[43] Quoted in Strange, *Sterling and British Policy*, p. 274.

[44] See Alan S. Milward, *The Reconstruction of Western Europe, 1945–51* (Berkeley, 1984); and Michael J. Hogan, *The Marshall Plan: America, Britain, and the Reconstruction of Western Europe, 1947–1952* (Cambridge, 1987).

return, Bevin undertook to assume the lead in saving Europe for social democracy and in taking 'primary responsibility' for defending the Middle East.[45] With Anglo-American joint policies in Europe and mutual support in Asia,[46] the Empire could rely on the US shield against Sino-Soviet intervention. British policy was aligned with Washington's Cold War strategy, and the keystone of the reconstituted imperial system became the Middle East, a region honeycombed with British air bases and military installations. The oilfields there were as vital to European defence as they were to British prosperity. So too were the tin and rubber of Malaya. Whitehall relied largely on the sterling countries between Suez and Singapore for the dollar earnings required to make up the British trade deficit.[47] The potential of Africa's minerals and vegetable oil was also linked more and more to British recovery. With India and Pakistan hived off and Palestine shrugged aside, the Empire reasserted itself in the Middle East and Africa.

Much of the pre-war Empire survived locally and was slotted into the post-war design. Even so, local continuities masked the basic discontinuity. At the metropolitan and international levels, British imperial power was substantially an Anglo-American revival. Neither side cared to publish the fact, the one to avoid the taint of imperialism, the other to keep the prestige of Empire untarnished. An imperial coalition was as unnatural for the Americans as it was demeaning for the British. Congress may have needed a communist devil to assure the American people of the innocence of their global expansion;[48] it could not afford to be implicated as well in London's Great Game of Empire. Endless talks were devoted to straddling the divergence in order to permit concerted action. A consensual, though perhaps not a common, official mind worked to achieve the 'overlap' of interdependence in the Cold War. It was not merely a question of 'he who pays the piper'.[49] As Bevin analysed the situation in October 1949:

[45] Summary of Pentagon Talks, 16 October–7 November 1947, in Bullock, *Bevin*, pp. 468–75; Kennan memorandum, 24 February 1948, *Foreign Relations of the United States, 1948*, V, pt. 2, pp. 655–57; key British files: FO 371/61557–59.

[46] See *Foreign Relations of the United States, 1949*, VI, 50ff. There were 'points of asymmetry' in individual countries, but they were 'superimposed on an area of broad agreement' (ibid., p. 62). See also minute by Michael Wright, 14 November 1947, FO 371/61559.

[47] Richard Clarke memorandum, 'The World Dollar Crisis', 16 June 1947, Clarke, *Anglo-American Economic Collaboration*, pp. 168–74.

[48] H. W. Brands, *The Devil We Knew: Americans and the Cold War* (Oxford, 1993): 'The ideological gulf between the United States and the Soviet Union gave the geopolitical rivalry unprecedented urgency' (p. 32).

[49] Though it was so argued at the time: 'After all', Sir Roger Makins of the Foreign Office wrote, 'they [the Americans] are paying the piper, and in the last analysis we are dependent on general American support for our security' (Makins memorandum, 'Some notes on British for-

Western Europe, including its dependent overseas territories, is now patently dependent on American aid . . . The United States rec- ognises that the United Kingdom and the Commonwealth . . . are essential to her defence and safety. Already it is, apart from the economic field, a case of partial inter-dependence rather than of complete dependence. As time goes by [in the next ten to twenty years] the elements of dependence ought to diminish and those of inter-dependence to increase. The United Kingdom in particular, by virtue of her leading position both in Western Europe and in the Commonwealth, ought to play a larger and larger part in a Western system.[50]

Bevin accepted that '[i]n all fields in which the United States makes the major contribution, whether financial, military or otherwise, it is in- evitable that proportionate (although not always determining) weight must be given to her views.'[51] Dependence could weaken imperial ties; interdependence could strengthen them. A study of some regional crises will show how much and how little the Anglo-American alliance disturbed the balance of imperial contracts locally.

So long as the Cold War left tropical Africa aside, the Americans had few interests and exerted little influence in colonial management there. In 1948, Attlee's ministers faced a crisis in British West Africa when riots in Ghana[52] and strikes in Nigeria threatened colonial con- trol. Dissatisfied with low prices from colonial marketing boards and inflated charges for British imports, the dollar-earning cocoa farmers and palm-oil collectors were turning for economic relief to national leaders. Drs. Nkrumah and Azikiwe campaigned for immediate inde- pendence. The British took account of American and international anti-colonial opinion.[53] But the balance-of-payments deficit, together

eign policy', 11 August 1951, FO 371/124968, *BDEEP—Labour Government*, II, p. 375, note 1). The Foreign Secretary at the time, Herbert Morrison, disliked the emphasis on US dependence. The sentence was deleted in the official version of the note.

[50] Cabinet memorandum by Bevin, 'European Policy', CAB 129/37/1, CP (49) 208,18 Octo- ber 1949, *BDEEP—Labour Government*, II, pp. 344, 347.

[51] Ibid., p. 346.

[52] For the background, see Dennis Austin, *Politics in Ghana* (London, 1964); Richard Rath- bone, 'Political Intelligence and Policing in Ghana in the late 1940s and 1950s', in David M. An- derson and David Killingray, eds., *Policing and Decolonisation: Politics, Nationalism and the Police, 1917–65* (Manchester, UK, 1992), pp. 84–104. A useful work for comparative perspective is John Kent, *The Internationalization of Colonialism: Britain, France, and Black Africa, 1939–1956* (Oxford, 1992).

[53] See Anglo-American official and ministerial talks, *Foreign Relations of the United States, 1950*, III, pp. 950–53, 1097–1103. Creech Jones to Creasy, 18 March 1948, CO 537/3558, *BDEEP —Labour Government*, III, pp. 38–39.

with the Labour Party's expectations of a better deal for African workers, convinced the Cabinet that the iron hand of economic control required the velvet glove of power sharing.[54] The quasi-democratic reforms of 1951–52 in Ghana and Nigeria were aimed at bringing conservative chiefs and their moderate nationalist spokesmen into the executive government, strengthening the popularity of these traditional allies of colonial administration against their radical critics.[55] By this route, the two dependencies were expected to achieve self-government 'within a generation'.[56] Their connection with the imperial economy eventually would be within the Commonwealth, albeit politically informal.

In British Central Africa, it was white rather than black nationalists who brought about a crisis from 1949 onwards. Roy Welensky, the European leader in the dependency of Northern Rhodesia, could halt the copper mining on which the British economy and large American stockpiling contracts depended. Sir Godfrey Huggins, the Premier of self-governing Southern Rhodesia, controlled the railways required for mineral export. To expand the dollar-earning capacity of the region, Britain had to appease the European miners and tobacco farmers. By 1953 a Tory government had shaped the velvet glove of power sharing around a white Rhodesian federation imposed on the black majority.[57]

Under the impact of the Far Eastern crisis in 1949–51, imperial Anglo-Americanism solidified, though with many a crack, from Europe and the Middle East to eastern and southern Asia. Once the People's Republic had driven the Kuomintang regime out of main-

[54] Cabinet memorandum by Creech Jones, 'Gold Coast Constitution', 8 October 1949, CP (49) 199, CAB 129/36/2, ibid., III, pp. 46–49. For the origins of the new African policy, see ibid., pp. 38–69. See also Ronald Robinson, 'Andrew Cohen and the Transfer of Power in Tropical Africa', in W. H. Morris-Jones and G. Fischer, eds., *Decolonisation and Africa* (London, 1980); R. D. Pearce, *The Turning Point in Africa* (London, 1982); and Ronald Hyam, 'Africa and the Labour Government, 1945–1951', in Andrew Porter and Robert Holland, eds., *Theory and Practice in the History of European Expansion Overseas* (London, 1988), pp. 148–72.

[55] Or, in the Foreign Office's more general statement of the proposition applicable to the entire non-Western world, the British would attempt 'to prevent nationalism getting out of control . . . by creating a class with a vested interest in cooperation' (FO memorandum on 'The Problem of Nationalism', 21 June 1952, CO 936/217, in *British Documents on the End of Empire*, series A, vol. 3, *The Conservative Government and the End of Empire, 1951–1957*, David Goldsworthy, ed., pt. I [London, 1994], p. 18 [hereafter *BDEEP—Conservative Government*]).

[56] Report of the Committee on the Conference of African Governors, CO 847/36/1, 22 May 1947, app. II, *BDEEP—Labour Government*, pt. I, p. 199.

[57] For documentation, see *BDEEP—Labour Government*, IV, pp. 246–374. On the motives for confederation, see Ronald Hyam, 'The Geopolitical Origins of the Central African Federation: Britain, Rhodesia and South Africa, 1948–53', *Historical Journal*, 30 (1987), pp. 145–72.

land China, Soviet-allied power seemingly dominated the Eurasian land mass. As the global balance shifted in July 1949, Dean Acheson, the Secretary of State, accepted Bevin's invitation to make 'a trip around the world . . . in a matey sort of way' to see whether Britain and the United States might pursue a common policy against the spread of communism in the Far East.[58] In a series of private talks, they reached a workable consensus in every area but one. To save the Hong Kong trade and to accommodate India's championing of the principle of pan-Asian self-determination, the British insisted on recognizing Communist China. The Americans, by contrast, still recognized and protected Chiang Kai-shek's Nationalist government on Taiwan. With the unexpected outbreak of the Korean War in June 1950, the two policies undercut each other. Taiwan now acquired strategic significance in the American defence of Japan and the Pacific. Acheson told Bevin that if the British wanted their global common front, they had better not keep asking the Americans to abandon Taiwan.[59]

The vicissitudes of the war widened the rift in late 1950, despite the common UN cause. A token British force belatedly joined the Americans in repelling the North Korean invasion. But 'it was almost universally felt in England that MacArthur had provoked the [subsequent] Chinese attack in N. Korea' by advancing to the Yalu River and bombing North Korea.[60] Consequently, the left wing of virtually all of Attlee's government feared that General MacArthur, perhaps even President Truman (who admitted considering the use of atomic weapons), was bent on reconquering China for Chiang Kai-shek. Much more importantly, the NATO allies bristled at the prospect of the

---

[58] Acheson to Douglas, 20 July 1949, *Foreign Relations of the United States, 1949*, IX, p. 50. Acheson had a good working relationship with Bevin and, on the whole, admired the Labour Government for its moderation and for its resistance to 'jingo pressures' (Dean Acheson, *Present at the Creation* [New York, 1969], p. 508).

[59] See Top Secret messages between Acheson and Bevin, 10–15 July 1950, *Foreign Relations of the United States, 1950*, VII, pp. 347–90. A work relevant for our argument is Callum MacDonald, *Britain and the Korean War* (Oxford, 1990), especially pp. 95–96. See also D. Clayton James, *Refighting the Last War: Command and Crisis in Korea, 1950–1953* (New York, 1993); Bruce Cummings, *The Origins of the Korean War* (Princeton, 1981); and L. F. Stone, *The Hidden History of the Korean War* (New York, 1952), especially pp. 192–98. Stone makes the point that the right wing in Britain was the first to question British involvement in the fall of 1950.

[60] *Hall Diaries, 1947–53*, 8 December 1950, p. 135. The Central Intelligence Agency foresaw that a UN military conquest of North Korea would split the Allies and convince Asians 'that the US is, after all, an aggressive nation pursuing a policy of self-interest in Asia. The invading forces might become involved in hostilities with the Chinese Communists' (CIA memorandum, 18 August 1950, *Foreign Relations of the United States, 1950*, VII, p. 601.) For British documentation, see Roger Bullen and M. E. Pelly, eds., *Documents on British Policy Overseas*, series II, vol. II (London, 1987).

United States becoming absorbed in a major Asian war that could leave Europe undefended.[61]

It was usually the Americans who warned the Europeans of the penalties for aggressive imperialism in the Cold War, but when Attlee flew to Washington in December 1950, the imperial boot was on the other foot. The Prime Minister in effect admonished the President against allowing MacArthur any more scope for what most European socialists and Asian nationalists regarded as American imperialist intervention in China.[62] If the American people could not rely on their allies' support in the East, Truman remarked, they would no longer subscribe to a common front in the West.[63] Nonetheless, the two leaders agreed to put real teeth into NATO. Attlee undertook the trebling of British defence expenditure over the next three years.[64] The Americans promised to 'pick up the tab' on the balance-of-payments costs.[65] Much of the Anglo-American wartime apparatus for allocating strategic supplies globally was reactivated in the Korean emergency. The reuniting of priorities was symbolized by the recall of MacArthur from Korea four months later and the advent of Eisenhower as Supreme Commander, Europe.[66] The Prime Minister and the President agreed to differ over China for the sake of their 'identity of interests generally throughout the world'. In view of 'Korean aggression', their subordinate officials laid the ground for dealing with the other Soviet-inspired 'Koreas' anticipated in Greece, Germany, Iran, and South-East Asia.[67]

[61] Bruce to Acheson, 5 December 1950, *Foreign Relations of the United States, 1950*, VII, pp. 1387–89. See Alan Bullock's analysis of the European context in *Bevin*, chaps. 21 and 22.

[62] US Delegation Minutes of Fifth Meeting of President Truman and Prime Minister Attlee, Top Secret, 7 December 1950, *Foreign Relations of the United States, 1950*, VII, pp. 1449–62. Alex Danchev, *Oliver Franks: Founding Father* (Oxford, 1993), chap. 6, is essential on the British side. Franks was Ambassador in Washington.

[63] From the British perspective, however, if the Anglo-American combination held, then it would give the British opportunity to consolidate their position in the Middle East. According to a Foreign Office minute by A. Rumbold, 27 September 1950, FO 371/81967: 'because we have a base in Egypt we ought to take the initiative and bear the initial burden if any operation has to be undertaken in the Eastern Mediterranean similar to the Korean undertaking.'

[64] On this point, see especially Kenneth O. Morgan, *Labour in Power, 1945–1951* (Oxford, 1984), pp. 430 ff.

[65] *Hall Diaries, 1947–53*, pp. 136, 139, 142, 150–53.

[66] The merging of priorities might have been taken one step further had a proposal been accepted to appoint Lord Mountbatten as British High Commissioner for the Far East. He was described by John Strachey (Secretary of State for War) in a letter to Attlee as 'a man who is, at one and the same time, strong and yet is genuinely and at heart in sympathy with the new Nationalism of Asia.' Attlee considered but did not act on Strachey's suggestion (Strachey to Attlee, 11 December 1950, PREM 8/1406/2, *BDEEP—Labour Government*, III, pp. 204–05).

[67] 'Present World Situation', Top Secret, 25 July 1950, *Foreign Relations of the United States, 1950*, III, p. 1658ff.

Washington's ambivalence about being considered a centre of Western imperial power[68] emerged sharply in 1949, when Secretary Acheson and Ernest Bevin discussed the domino effect of a Communist China on South-East Asia. In 'a turmoil of revolutionary nationalism' left by the Japanese retreat, the French in Indo-China as well as the Dutch in Indonesia were fighting to regain colonial control. Their intransigence, the State Department believed, was 'doomed to ultimate failure'. They were driving nationalists into the arms of the communists at the cost of draining men and money away from 'the revitalization of Western Europe'. On the other hand, it was feared, 'the only alternative to imperial rule is chaos in Indonesia and communism in Indochina'. European 'self-support' depended on the 'economic attachment' of these areas to their respective metropoles. America could not ride 'rough-shod' over European pride without straining vital NATO alliances;[69] that was to be the American dilemma wherever colonial empires became involved in the Cold War.[70]

Bevin agreed with Acheson on the only way to square the circles of local and international collaboration in this region. They fruitlessly pressed the French and Dutch to follow the American example in the Philippines and do what the British had done in India and were doing in Malaya.[71] The French and Dutch colonial presence would have to take on the mantle of an informal association: anything that looked

---

[68] It is useful on this point to compare Thomas McCormick, '"Every System Needs a Center Sometimes": An Essay on Hegemony and Modern American Foreign Policy', in Lloyd C. Gardner, ed., *Redefining the Past* (Corvallis, Ore., 1986), pp. 195–220. See also William Appleman Williams, *The Contours of American History* (New York, 1973 edn.) and, by the same author, *Empire as a Way of Life* (New York, 1980). For our purpose, significant works on similar themes are Emily S. Rosenberg, *Spreading the American Dream* (New York, 1982); and Michael J. Hogan, 'Corporatism', *Diplomatic History*, 10 (Fall 1986), pp. 363–72.

[69] Quotations from staff paper by George Kennan, PPS/51, 29 March 1949, *The State Department Policy Planning Staff Papers, 1949* (New York, 1983), III, especially pp. 42–44; revised version in *Foreign Relations of the United States, 1949*, VII, pt. 2, pp. 1128 ff.

[70] See the analysis by Miles Kahler, who encapsulates the ambivalence of American policy towards the subjects of colonial empires in three images—those of counterrevolutionary ally, imperial rival, and anti-colonial spokesman—in 'The United States and the Third World: Decolonization and After', in L. Carl Brown, ed., *Centerstage: American Diplomacy since World War II* (New York, 1990), pp. 104–20.

[71] See Cabinet memorandum by Bevin, 'Review of International Situation in Asia', 30 August 1950, CP (50) 200, CAB 129/41. For these themes, see especially Robert J. McMahon, *Colonialism and Cold War: The United States and the Struggle for Indonesian Independence, 1945–49* (Ithaca, N.Y., 1981); George McT. Kahin, *Intervention* (New York, 1986). On Malaya, see especially A. J. Stockwell, 'Policing during the Malayan Emergency, 1948–60: Communism, Communalism and Decolonisation', in Anderson and Killingray, *Policing and Decolonisation*, pp. 105–26. For South-East Asia generally, see Nicholas Tarling, *The Fall of Imperial Britain in South-East Asia* (Oxford, 1993).

like imperialism or Western dictation, Bevin warned, would alienate the newly independent countries of southern Asia. But the Western Allies, with their strategic priorities in Europe and the Far East, had few resources left for the area. South-East Asia had to be persuaded to defend itself, with Indian support.[72] Given political independence, the nationalists would stand on their own feet against the communists. A relatively small amount of economic and military aid from the West would win their alliance and secure Europe's economic assets. Then, as British and American officials agreed, the Western powers could 'keep out of the limelight' and 'pull the strings whenever necessary'.[73]

American anti-colonialism evidently did not extend to informal sway; nor, after the outbreak of the Korean War in June 1950, did it run to handing over colonies to communists or to chaos. American subsidies for the defence of Indo-China against the communist Viet-Minh by 1954 fell little short of the French investment. Washington blessed the British colonial campaign against Chinese communists in Malaya. Yet in January 1949 the Americans had threatened to end Marshall aid to the Netherlands in order to forestall a Dutch reconquest of an anti-communist nationalist regime in Indonesia.[74] Ideally, the United States preferred 'independence' and covert influence to colonialism. In practice, the Americans gave priority to anti-communism over anti-colonialism. It was admittedly for the Europeans to decide. Determined not to commit American ground troops to mainland Asia after the Korean truce, Washington necessarily pursued the Cold War through imperial proxies. At the local level, the Americans, under protest, acted as sleeping partners in the British and French empires wherever the latter had to cope with local communist subversion.

In South Asia, the Americans relied chiefly on Britain and the Commonwealth to take the major responsibility. 'We are becoming engaged in a competition with the USSR for the favor and resources of South

[72] The division of the Indian Army, however, had shattered the original British plan for the defence of South and South-East Asia: '[T]he standard [of the Indian Army] has deteriorated considerably, and inevitably so. The division of the Indian Armed Forces between India and Pakistan caused very serious problems . . . the Indians have yet to show that they can produce a standard of leadership comparable to that provided by the British officer' (Sir Archibald Nye [High Commissioner in India] to Lord Ismay, Secret, 16 November 1951, FO 371/92870).

[73] Anglo-American official talks, Washington, 12 September 1949, *Foreign Relations of the United States, 1949*, VII, pt. 2, p. 1199. There was good reason for American influence to remain as inconspicuous as possible. According to Sir Archibald Nye, the High Commissioner in Delhi: 'The power of America has drawn on to her much of the odium that formerly attached to Britain as the ruler of this part of the world, and there is deep suspicion of American capitalism' (Nye to Gordon Walker, Top Secret, 17 May 1951, DO 35/2976).

[74] Memorandum of conversation with the Ambassador of Netherlands, 11 January 1949, *Foreign Relations of the United States, 1949*, VII, pt. 1, p. 139.

Asia,' the State Department and the Joint Chiefs of Staff reported in 1949. 'Bearing in mind our commitments elsewhere, it would appear to be in our interest for the British to bear as great a share of this burden as they possibly can.'[75] The demise of the imperial Raj served the purpose in unforeseen ways. Despite Jawaharlal Nehru's policy of 'non-alignment', a powerful Indian buffer state stood in the way of Sino-Soviet expansion.[76] A successful Indian democracy would show the rest of Asia that Mao's path was not the only road to modernization. To support Nehru in this involuntary role—and of course to compete with Moscow—Washington first supplemented and soon surpassed the inadequate supply of British and Commonwealth aid.[77] From 1953 to 1961 the foreign-exchange costs of Delhi's five-year plans were subsidized by the United States to the extent of two and a half billion dollars.[78] Meanwhile, the British retained a strong market for their exports.[79] India remained an important member of the Commonwealth. From 1949 onward, the Pentagon joined the War Office in the traditional imperial Great Game of securing the subcontinent's frontiers from Kabul and Herat to Rangoon and Singapore. As F. P. Bartlett, Director of South Asian Affairs in the State Department, observed, Curzon's strategy in 1889 for containing Russian expansion in Central Asia 'applied very much today'.[80]

Unlike the Indians, the Pakistanis joined the Baghdad and SEATO (South-East Asia Treaty Organization) defence pacts, under direct and indirect Anglo-American auspices, and provided strategic air bases.[81]

[75] Report, 'U.S. National Interests in South Asia', Top Secret, 19 April 1949, *Foreign Relations of the United States, 1949,* VI, pp. 8–31 (the quotations are on pp. 14 and 28).

[76] See National Security Staff Study, 17 May 1951, *Foreign Relations of the United States, 1951,* VI, pt. 1, pp. 44–45. For ramifications of the idea of India as a buffer, see, for example, Nye to Gordon Walker, Top Secret, 17 May 1951, DO 35/2976; see also especially the book by Olaf Caroe, *Wells of Power* (London, 1951). Caroe's book helped popularize the view that Western (or American) defence of the Middle East should be based on Pakistan, just as British defence had previously been based on control of the subcontinent.

[77] See memorandum for Cabinet Economic Committee, 22 March 1950, CAB 134/225, *BDEEP—Labour Government,* II, pp. 142 ff. A key file at the Public Record Office for the evolution of this problem is PREM 11/2726.

[78] See *U.S. Overseas Loans and Grants and Assistance from International Organizations: Obligations and Loan Authorizations, July 1, 1945–September 30, 1989, CONG-R-0105* (Washington [Agency for International Development], 1989), p. 16.

[79] But see Michael Lipton and John Firn, *The Erosion of a Relationship* (London, 1975), for the gradual deterioration of the economic connection between Britain and India.

[80] Memorandum of 19 January 1959, *Foreign Relations of the United States, 1958–60,* XV, p. 154.

[81] See Robert J. McMahon, *Cold War on the Periphery: The United States, India, and Pakistan* (New York, 1994); Ayesha Jalal, 'Towards the Baghdad Pact: South Asia and the Middle East Defence in the Cold War, 1947–1953', *International History Review,* 11 (August 1989), pp. 409–33; and especially for the strategic dimension, Richard Aldrich and Michael Coleman, 'Britain and the

In return, they received two billion dollars of military and economic aid in the 1950s.[82] They were soon affiliated more closely with the United States than with the Commonwealth. Under the shadow of the Cold War, a region of the former British Empire modulated strategically into an Anglo-American field of influence, and thence into a predominantly American commitment. Similarly, in the ANZUS pact of 1951, the American 'off-shore island' chain around Communist China took in the Australasian Commonwealth.[83] Australia and New Zealand, nonetheless, continued to be bound up with Britain financially and commercially in the sterling area up to 1960.[84]

At the centre of the post-war Empire, paramountcy in the Middle East worked through a network of client dynasties that were in the political, military, and financial grip of British diplomatic missions, military bases, and oil companies.[85] Americans within the 'open door' tradition objected to these discriminatory satrapies; in 1945 the State Department regarded them as 'outmoded' and 'dangerous to peace'.[86] The Kings and Emirs asked for American help to escape the imperial thrall. By the end of 1947, Marshall had undertaken with Bevin to restrain the oil rivalry and to abstain from intervening competitively in British relations with Egypt, Iraq, Jordan, and the Gulf States.[87] Communist encroachment threatened the security of the Middle East,

---

Strategic Air Offensive Against the Soviet Union: The Question of South Asian Bases, 1945–49', *History*, 74 (October 1989), pp. 400–26. See also Richard J. Aldrich, ed., *British Intelligence, Strategy, and the Cold War, 1945–51* (London, 1992).

[82] *U.S. Overseas Loans*, Statistical Annex 1, p. 26.

[83] See *BDEEP—Labour Government*, III, pp. 414–19.

[84] See David Lee, 'Australia, the British Commonwealth, and the United States, 1950–1953', *Journal of Imperial and Commonwealth History*, 20 (September 1992), pp. 445–69.

[85] See W. R. Louis, *The British Empire in the Middle East, 1945–1951* (Oxford, 1984).

[86] Memorandum by Loy Henderson, 28 December 1945, *Foreign Relations of the United States, 1946*, VII, p. 2. In the Foreign Office, Sir Orme Sargent (Permanent Under-Secretary) had written a few months previously, in almost a mirror-image of mutual suspicion, of

> the uphill task of maintaining ourselves as a world power in the face of the United States, who now for the first time is prepared to assume this position with the help of the almighty dollar, export surpluses . . . civil aviation, and all the other instruments which they can if necessary use in order to 'penetrate' the world.

Minute by Sargent, 1 October 1945, FO 371/44557. For the immediate post-war crisis, see Fraser J. Harbutt, *The Iron Curtain: Churchill, America, and the Origins of the Cold War* (New York, 1986).

[87] Anglo-American Pentagon Talks of 1947, Top Secret, October–November 1947, *Foreign Relations of the United States, 1947*, V, pp. 575–625; Louis, *British Empire in the Middle East*, pp. 109–12. It was the emergency in Greece that caused the Americans to be more favourably disposed to the general position of the British in the Middle East: 'The principal result of the Washington [Pentagon] talks is that for the first time American policy has crystalised on the lines of supporting British policy' (minute by Michael Wright, 20 January 1948, FO 371/68041.

especially the oilfields of the two allies. By July 1950, British and American officials agreed that a Soviet attack on Iran would 'raise the question of a general war'. The northern Iranian frontier was the 'stop line', equivalent to the 38th parallel in Korea. No less importantly, the Middle East had become an area of Anglo-American interdependence in oil. Any conflict between Middle Eastern client governments and the oil companies could open the way to Soviet influence. Early in 1951, Washington urged on the British, as a precaution, the wisdom of conceding a fifty-fifty share in the Anglo-Iranian Oil Company's profits to the Shah's government. The American oil company in Saudi Arabia (Aramco) had already yielded as much.[88] The British company, however, did not follow the American example until it was too late.[89] In May 1951 the Iranian premier, Mohammed Musaddiq, put Anglo-American solidarity to the test by nationalizing the Anglo-Iranian concession.[90]

A legacy of the British Great Game in south-western Asia, the Pahlavi dynasty in Teheran had been in every sense a creation of the British. Under the Shah, Mohammad Reza, Iran produced more oil than all the Arab states combined and figured largely in the sterling balance of payments. If Musaddiq were 'allowed to get away with it', Emanuel Shinwell, the Defence Minister, warned Attlee's Cabinet that other clients would nationalize their way to financial freedom: 'The next thing might be an attempt to nationalise the Suez Canal.'[91] But to reoccupy the Abadan oil fields would be costly and militarily precarious.[92] Washington warned that use of force could provoke a communist rising with Soviet backing in northern Iran.[93] With Ameri-

---

[88] See especially Irvine H. Anderson, *Aramco, the United States and Saudi Arabia: A Study of the Dynamics of Foreign Oil Policy, 1933–1950* (Princeton, 1981), chap. 6.

[89] The Aramco precedent had repercussions throughout the world and in areas other than the petroleum industry. Though the nationalization at Abadan was not a Colonial Office concern, it alarmed the Colonial Secretary, Oliver Lyttelton, and caused him to consider abolishing royalties in mining and other enterprises (for example, hydroelectric development) in favour of local investment. See Colonial Secretary to Governors, 13 May 1952, *BDEEP—Conservative Government*, III, p. 163.

[90] See James A. Bill and W. R. Louis, eds., *Musaddiq, Iranian Nationalism, and Oil* (Austin, Tex., 1988).

[91] Confidential Annex to Chiefs of Staff [COS] (51) 86, 23 May 1951, DEFE 4/43.

[92] Confidential Annex, COS (51) 84, 21 May 1951, DEFE 4/43; Cabinet Conclusions, 12 July 1951, CAB 128/20. See also *BDEEP—Labour Government*, I, pp. 87–96; and James Cable, *Intervention at Abadan: Plan Buccaneer* (London, 1991).

[93] For American fears that Iran would become 'another Korea' if the British did not accommodate Iranian claims to a greater share of the profits of the Anglo-Iranian Oil Company, see State Department memoranda, 21 September–20 December 1950, *Foreign Relations of the United States, 1950*, V, pp. 593–635. British assessments tended to be more cautious, with assumptions

can cooperation, the British resorted to blockading Iran's oil exports. When Musaddiq refused to talk to the British any longer in October 1952, the Americans attempted to broker a settlement.

The Americans now feared that strangling Iran's main revenue would prove a double-edged weapon. If rising economic discontent destroyed Musaddiq's popularity, he could turn only to the pro-communist faction for support; Moscow in that case might bail out his regime. On several occasions American officials, such as Defense Secretary Robert Lovett, argued for going it alone and lifting the oil embargo to save Musaddiq, the only non-communist leader in sight; but as a British official put it to Acheson, 'the choice before you is whether Iran goes Commie, or Brit[ain] goes bankrupt'.[94] Acheson decided that 'only by correlating our efforts with the British' could the Middle East be stabilized.[95] The Anglo-American blockade continued. In March 1953, President Eisenhower's National Security Council, like Truman's before it, first considered settling with Musaddiq without the British. Charles Wilson, the Defense Secretary, asked 'whether [the United States] were not in fact in partnership with the British in Iran'. John Foster Dulles, now Secretary of State, acknowledged that 'this had been the case until fairly lately, but that the British had now been thrown out'. The President stated that he 'certainly [did not] . . . want a break with the British'.[96] Dulles eventually decided that selling out to Musaddiq might have grave effects on US oil concessions in other parts of the world. 'We cannot force the British hand,' he concluded.[97]

In August 1953 the critical problem of saving Iran from communism without damaging the British required a desperate gambit. A coup promoted by British and American intelligence services restored the Shah to power on the shoulders of the army of General Fazlollah

---

based on Soviet unwillingness to embark on global war during the time of the Korean conflict. See, for example, memorandum by Pierson Dixon, 18 May 1951, FO 371/ 91459.

[94] Acheson to State Department, 10 November 1951, *Foreign Relations of the United States, 1952–54*, X, p. 279.

[95] Acheson to Defense Secretary Lovett, 4 November 1952, ibid., p. 512.

[96] Memorandum of discussion, National Security Council, 4 March 1953, ibid., p. 695. In the view of Anthony Eden (Foreign Secretary in the Churchill government, 1951–55), Eisenhower was 'obsessed' with the danger of a communist Iran. See Eden's minutes in FO 371/104613 and 104614.

[97] Memorandum of National Security Council discussion, 11 March 1953, *Foreign Relations of the United States, 1952–54*, X, p. 713. The British welcomed Dulles's attitude, but there was considerable scepticism on how long it would last. Some British observers of the different branches of the American government found the CIA much more inclined to adopt a firm line, but in the State Department, according to C. M. Woodhouse of MI6, there was a lingering 'silliness' that Musaddiq could be appeased (C. M. Woodhouse, *Something Ventured* [London, 1982], pp. 118, 121).

Zahedi.[98] American military aid consolidated the regime and strengthened the Iranian buffer in the northern tier of Middle Eastern defence. Washington willy-nilly had taken over the senior part of partnership in Iran. The consequent oil settlement in 1954 registered the shift in local collaborative terms. The percentages of the consortium were Anglo-Iranian Oil Company, 40 per cent; Royal Dutch-Shell, 14 per cent; Standard Oil of New Jersey, 7 per cent; Socony Vacuum Oil Company, 7 per cent; Standard Oil of California, 7 per cent; Gulf Oil Corporation, 7 per cent; Texas Company, 7 per cent; Compagnie Française des Pétroles, 6 per cent; and a 5 per cent interest by a group of nine American independents. Much of the British oil stake had been saved, but the Americans now held 33 per cent of the Iranian market. Even though the percentage of the American independents was minor, the reason for their inclusion was significant. If they were left out, warned, Lewis Douglas, a former Ambassador to Britain who had oil contacts, the US Senate would blow the new consortium into 'little bits as effectively as a hydrogen bomb'.[99]

There was complaint in some British circles that the Americans had taken over a British monopoly. But the Americans had ousted the British in Iran; they had taken over when the British could no longer cope. Lord Salisbury, the influential Tory minister, warned against recrimination: 'If we give the impression in Washington that we are only concerned with our oil to the exclusion of . . . keeping Persia in the anti-communist camp, we may lose all control over American actions. That would be disastrous.'[100] The Americans were highly sceptical of the ability of the Anglo-Iranian Oil Company to adjust to twentieth-century conditions, but Eisenhower, like Truman before him, was certain that 'US-UK agreement is necessary for any settlement of Middle Eastern problems'.[101] Vulnerable to Soviet pressure in the Middle East,

---

[98] See Mark J. Gasiorowski, 'The 1953 Coup d'Etat in Iran', *International Journal of Middle East Studies*, 19 (August 1987), pp. 261–86; and Moyara de Moraes Ruehsen, 'Operation "Ajax" Revisited: Iran, 1953', *Middle Eastern Studies*, 29 (July 1993), pp. 467–86. The Americans were 'agog for action', the British Ambassador in Washington reported in the run up to the coup (Franks to Eden, Secret, 24 August 1952, FO 371/98694).

[99] Douglas to Sir William Fraser (AIOC), 24 October 1953, FO 371/104642. For the consortium, see Daniel Yergin, *The Prize* (New York, 1991), pp. 475–78; David S. Painter, *Oil and the American Century* (Baltimore, 1986), pp. 192–98; and especially for the Iranian side, Mostafa Elm, *Oil, Power, and Principle: Iran's Oil Nationalization and Its Aftermath* (Syracuse, N.Y., 1992).

[100] Minute by Salisbury, 22 August 1953, FO 371/104577.

[101] At talks in Washington in January 1952, Churchill had stressed that Anglo-American co-operation in the Middle East would 'divide the difficulties by ten'. Truman had declared that 'US-UK agreement was necessary for any settlement of Middle Eastern problems' (*Foreign Relations of the United States, 1952–54*, IX, pt. 1, p. 176).

the British had to keep in line with America's Cold War strategy, just as American strategy had to be aligned on the strong points of the British Empire. If Washington forced the British to change their unrealistic imperial policies in Iran, Egypt, and elsewhere, Dulles admitted in April 1954, it would 'have the effect of tearing the free world coalition to pieces'. Nevertheless, he continued, the Americans could not 'go on forever' avoiding these great issues: 'The peoples of the colonial states would never agree to fight Communism unless they were assured of their freedom.'[102] For the British, the Iranian crisis had demonstrated another, equally compelling, principle: if Musaddiq's view had prevailed, then nationalists throughout the world might abrogate British concessions. Intervention could be effective, but as a precedent for Suez, the British lesson from the Persian oil crisis was disastrous.

In the Tory governments of 1951–57, first Churchill and then Eden fell increasingly out of step with their wartime comrade Eisenhower. In the Far East the allies divided bitterly over Communist China, Taiwan, and Quemoy. To Washington's dismay, London and Paris took advantage of the advent of 'peaceful co-existence' to initiate dealings with Moscow. They went to Geneva in 1954 and partitioned Indo-China with Chairman Mao. Dulles lamented, 'We can no longer run the free world.'[103] For the Americans, the British appeared far too ready to ensure their eastern Empire at the expense of 'free world' territory. Tory ministers in Whitehall did indeed resolve to rebuild imperial strength, which they regarded as the main opportunity for national solvency. American financial aid dwindled from 1952 to 1956. Despite recovery, British exports could not balance overseas payments under the overload of debt, social welfare, and massive rearmament. Two solutions were discussed in 1952. One was to expand exports to hard-currency markets by £600 million a year at the expense of

[102] Memorandum of National Security Council discussion, Top Secret, 6 April 1954, *Foreign Relations of the United States, 1952–54*, XIII, pt. 1, p. 1259. The Foreign Office essentially agreed with this assessment and with the American view of the magnitude of the threat; Colonial Office officials were more sceptical. 'We are having a lot of difficulty', a Foreign Office official wrote somewhat later, 'in convincing the Colonial Office . . . that the Communist threat to Africa is as serious as we believe it to be' (I. T. M. Pink to Sir C. Stirling, FO 371/118677, *BDEEP— Conservative Government*, I, p. 240).

[103] National Security Council memorandum, 24 June 1954, *Foreign Relations of the United States, 1952–54*, II, pt. 1, pp. 694–95. In May 1953, Bedell Smith (Under Secretary of State) observed: 'our relations with the British Government [are] . . . worse than at any time since Pearl Harbor' (ibid., IX, pt. 2, p. 2076). On Dulles, see Richard H. Immerman, ed., *John Foster Dulles and the Diplomacy of the Cold War* (Princeton, 1990).

austerity at home and power abroad.[104] The other was to develop dollar earnings and savings in the sterling system through tighter imperial control.[105] Washington prodded London towards convertibility and the General Agreement on Tariffs and Trade. As Harold Macmillan put it, 'This is the choice—the slide into a shoddy and slushy Socialism [as a second-rate power], or the march to the third British Empire.'[106] In the continual fear of a run on the pound, the Churchillians marched to the imperial drum up to 1956. International confidence in sterling seemed to depend on Britain acting as a great imperial power: 'Our economic survival in the next year or two will largely depend upon world confidence in sterling.'[107] This might have been muddled economics, but it was good Tory politics.

At the same time, the British relied on Washington not to retaliate against their discriminatory imperial economy.[108] They hoped that American capital would share in developing sterling-area assets.[109] They needed Washington to back sterling countries with economic and military aid to stabilize them against Soviet influence.[110] In the last resort, the Cabinet relied on American strategic cover in Europe and the world at large.[111] Yet the British aspired to a sterner, less dependent imperialism. By their own reckoning, they were caught between their vision of the Britishness of the Third British Empire and their actual dependence on the Americans.

[104] Cabinet memorandum by R. A. Butler, 'The Balance of Payments Outlook', C (52) 172, 23 May 1952, CAB 129/52; *BDEEP—Conservative Government*, III, pp. 37–43.

[105] Memorandum by Macmillan, 'Economic Policy', 17 June 1952, ibid., pp. 47–50.

[106] Ibid., p. 50.

[107] Ibid., p. 44.

[108] Macmillan remarked: 'I doubt . . . whether the American attitude to such a Sterling Area policy will be determined . . . mainly by economic considerations. The real interest of the United States is that Britain should make the maximum contribution to the common defence and that the British Commonwealth should be strong' (ibid., p. 49).

[109] 'The largest source of investment capital is, of course, the U.S.A. . . . [w]e should spare no effort in trying to persuade the Americans . . . to back it [sterling area development]' (ibid., p. 48).

[110] American official aid increasingly played this role from 1955 onwards in India, Pakistan, and other Colombo Plan countries as well as in the Middle East and eventually in Africa. American aid to the development of British colonies, however, remained small through the 1950s. In 1951 the Colonial Office did not expect 'U.S. assistance to be more than marginal nor would it be desirable politically for them to play the principal part'. Nevertheless, '[h]elp to U.K. or sterling area enables U.K. to help Colonies.' American aid to the colonies was thus considerable but indirect. See 'Colonial Development', CO brief for Churchill, December 1951, CO 537/7597, ibid., p. 159.

[111] Or as Macmillan put it, 'If we decide to reject, as essential to our economic needs, G.A.T.T. (and all that G.A.T.T. implies), it is all the more important that we should be true to N.A.T.O.' (ibid., p. 45).

Friction was acutest in the Middle East. Anxious to keep up international confidence in sterling, especially after losing Abadan, London meant to confront 'nationalists sapping at our position as a world power'.[112] On the other side of the Atlantic, influential officials were bending policy in favour of substituting direct American alliances for British influence in the Arab states. For a time in 1953, Dulles pressed the British to evacuate the Suez base unconditionally as a way to win the good will of General Neguib and Colonel Nasser.[113] The Americans expected the British to concede the Buraimi oasis to please the new King of Saudi Arabia, Saud Ibn Abdul Aziz al-Feisal, thereby protecting Aramco and the US-Saudi connection. To Churchill and Eden, the Americans seemed far too eager to woo Arab nationalists away from Soviet blandishments at imperial expense. Washington certainly looked forward to some such outcome in the long run. But the Pentagon and the Treasury wanted the British to bear the burden in the Middle East. The State Department did not want to weaken NATO. Given the heavy demand on American resources, and in view of Eisenhower's conservative fiscal policies, it seemed wiser for the time being to rely on the existing imperial positions in Libya, Jordan, Iraq, and the Gulf states.[114]

Despite the deviations, the Americans generally returned to supporting British positions in the Arab states. Along with the French, the British and Americans doled out arms supplies to the region and so regulated the balance of power. Aided by the Americans, the British in 1954 at last achieved a Suez base treaty with a right of re-entry in case of war.[115] Together, the two allies had tried and failed to entice

[112] Foreign Office memorandum, 'The Problem of Nationalism', Secret Guard [Guard = not for American eyes], 21 November 1952, CO 936/217, with extensive CO minutes. See David Goldsworthy, 'Keeping Change within Bounds: Colonial Policy during the Churchill and Eden Governments, 1951–57', *Journal of Imperial and Commonwealth History*, 18 (January 1990), pp. 81–108.

[113] For the British side of the issue, and for defence policy generally, see especially David R. Devereux, *The Formulation of British Defense Policy towards the Middle East, 1948–56* (New York, 1990). For changing naval strategy, see E. J. Grove, *Vanguard to Trident* (London, 1988).

[114] For the reluctance of the Eisenhower administration 'to fight in the Arctic and in the Tropics; in Asia, the Near East, and in Europe; by sea, by land, and by air; with old weapons and with new weapons', see H. W. Brands, 'The Age of Vulnerability: Eisenhower and the National Insecurity State', *American Historical Review*, 94 (October 1989), pp. 963–89 (quotation from Dulles on p. 973).

[115] The military side can be followed in the files of the Chief of the Imperial General Staff series WO 216; for naval dilemmas in the wake of the thermonuclear tests in Bikini in March 1954, see 'Future Strategy', 6 May 1954, in the First Sea Lord's Records in ADM 205/102. On the base negotiations, see W. R. Louis, 'The Anglo-Egyptian Settlement of 1954', in W. R. Louis and Roger Owen, eds., *Suez 1956: The Crisis and Its Consequences* (Oxford, 1989), pp. 43–71; and Ritchie

Egypt into joining the Western alliance and making peace with Israel. Despite misgivings, Washington backed the military association of Iraq with Iran and Turkey under British auspices in the Baghdad Pact.[116] It was not the Americans but the British who finally tried to go it alone when the rivalry between the American Cold War and the Great Game of the Empire came to a head in 1956. The Suez Crisis thus becomes a touchstone of the inquiry into the nature of post-war imperial power.

Once the evacuation of some 80,000 troops at Suez had been scheduled, the British had few cards to play in Cairo except remote control of the White Nile in Uganda.[117] Throughout the Arab Middle East, anti-British feeling combined with resentment against American sponsorship of Israel. The Egyptians united behind Gamal Abdel Nasser. Like Musaddiq, Nasser skilfully played the American and Soviet ends against the British middle. Unlike the Iranian leader, he had no oil that could be embargoed, and the Russians agreed to buy his cotton. By November 1955 the Egyptian premier had clinched a Czech arms deal with Moscow and upset the regional power balance. The Soviets were dangling the possibility of economic aid for his Aswan dam project as well as arming his Syrian allies, and offering munitions to Saudi Arabia and Yemen. As the Americans admitted, the communists had executed 'a brilliant series of economic forward passes' and mounted a 'new and monumental threat' to the Middle East.[118] Eisenhower saw the beginning of a great struggle between the communist and free-world economies for control over the development of the Third World.[119] Dulles averred that no cleavage between British and

---

Ovendale, 'Egypt and the Suez Base Agreement', in John W. Young, ed., *The Foreign Policy of Churchill's Peacetime Administration, 1951–1955* (Leicester, 1988), pp. 135–58. On the American side, see especially Peter L. Hahn, *The United States, Great Britain, and Egypt, 1945–1956* (Chapel Hill, N.C., 1991); and Steven Z. Freiberger, *Dawn over Suez: The Rise of American Power in the Middle East, 1952–1957* (Chicago, 1992).

[116] See especially Brian Holden Reid, 'The "Northern Tier" and the Baghdad Pact', in Young, *Churchill's Peacetime Administration*, pp. 159–79.

[117] 'In any show-down with Egypt, the control Uganda gives us of the source of the White Nile must clearly be of paramount importance' (minute by Alan Lennox-Boyd [Colonial Secretary], 23 November 1955, CO 822/1195).

[118] C. D. Jackson to President's Special Assistant, Nelson Rockefeller, 10 November 1955, *Foreign Relations of the United States, 1955–57*, IX, p. 8.

[119] President to Secretary of State, 5 December 1955, *Foreign Relations of the United States, 1955–57*, IX, pp. 10–12. In this momentous confrontation, Eisenhower even more than Dulles had to mute his aversion to British imperialism, which is ironic because to the British it was Dulles who seemed to personify the spirit of anti-colonialism. In the words of a contemporary critic, Dulles had a 'hypocritical obsession with the evils of British colonialism' (Hugh Thomas, *The Suez Affair* [London, 1986 ed.], p. 174).

American policy could be allowed if the Middle East and Africa were not to become another Communist China.[120]

It had long been evident, according to Sir Humphrey Trevelyan (the British Ambassador in Cairo) that the British retained their position in the Middle East only because of the relatively low level of Russian intervention.[121] Anthony Eden commented: 'We are [now] compelled to outbid them, or lose the main source of [oil] on which our economy depends.' Only by enlisting the Americans and their money could the British stave off Russian influence in Cairo and over the canal. 'On our joint success in excluding the Russians from this [Aswan] contract', Eden wrote to Eisenhower in November 1955, 'may depend the future of Africa.'[122] A joint bid of 330 million American dollars and 80 million British pounds was entered.

London and Washington saw eye to eye on the danger that the Egyptian ruler represented. By June 1956 he was being viewed as an involuntary pawn of the Russians; he was inciting the Arab states to rise against Western domination. Eisenhower and Dulles feared not only for 'the jugular vein' of Western Europe's oil; they also believed that Nasser was rallying the Arabs for a final assault on Israel.[123] To Eden, the Egyptian 'Mussolini' with his pan-Arab ambitions threatened to become 'a Caesar from the Atlantic to the Gulf . . . It is either him or us.'[124] From March 1956 the British Cabinet set in train plans to reinvade Egypt.[125] Three months later the Anglo-American offer for the Aswan dam was cancelled; it was no longer possible to get Congressional aid for so menacing a regime. In riposte, after the last British troops had left the Suez base on 26 July, Nasser nationalized the Suez Canal Company. British and French control of the canal was the final emblem of his country's bondage. The result was explosive; the canal carried two-thirds of Europe's oil supply.

The Americans also wished for Nasser's downfall, but as Eden was repeatedly told from April 1956 onwards, they were unalterably opposed to military intervention. Dulles suspected a British attempt to manoeuvre Washington into reasserting British imperial supremacy

[120] Dulles, Report to National Security Council, 21 November 1955, *Foreign Relations of the United States, 1955–57*, XIV, p. 797.

[121] See, for example, Trevelyan to Macmillan, Secret, 24 October 1955, FO 371/113680.

[122] Eden to Eisenhower, 26 November 1955, FO 371/112739. This was a recurrent theme in Eden's thought: 'If the Russians get the contract we have lost Africa.' Quoted in Robert Rhodes James, *Anthony Eden* (London, 1986), p. 430. See also especially David Carlton, *Anthony Eden: A Biography* (London, 1981).

[123] National Security Council memorandum, 28 June 1956, *Foreign Relations of the United States, 1955–57*, XII, p. 308.

[124] Quoted in David Reynolds, *Britannia Overruled* (London, 1991), p. 203.

[125] See especially Keith Kyle, *Suez* (London, 1991), chap. 5.

in the Middle East.[126] If Egypt were invaded, the President predicted, every Arab state would swing towards Moscow. Revenge would be taken on American as well as British oil companies, and the British thus would lose the assets and the prestige they hoped to secure.[127] Washington preferred covert methods, of a kind familiar from US actions in Latin America. They had succeeded in Tehran, and the CIA was already plotting a coup against the pro-Nasser regime in Damascus. The Americans had every reason to dissociate themselves publicly from British military action.

The Great Game was now being played for the highest stakes in the Cold War. Eden's ministers agreed with the Bank of England that Egyptian 'piracy' on the canal 'imperils the survival of the U.K. and the Commonwealth, and represents a very great danger to sterling'.[128] An expedition was prepared 'to bring about the fall of Nasser and create a government in Egypt which will work satisfactorily with ourselves and other powers'.[129] Harold Macmillan, Chancellor of the Exchequer, pointed out that Nasser, like Arabi Pasha in 1882, would block the canal in self-defence. In that case, American finance would be needed to meet the dollar cost of alternative oil supplies from Venezuela and the Gulf of Mexico.[130] The British presumably took it for granted that their ally would gladly accept and pay for a fait accompli. There is only circumstantial evidence that they meant to stage a 'Boston Tea Party' in reverse on the Nile. At Eisenhower's request, the British waited to see if Dulles could persuade Nasser to 'disgorge the canal' to international management. The indefatigable Dulles failed on this occasion. Keeping Washington in the dark, the British decided to go it alone, or rather, with the French and the Israelis. On 5 November 1956 an Anglo-French expedition landed on the canal in the guise of peacekeepers come to stop a second Israeli-Egyptian war.

In the event, forebodings were realized. The canal was blocked,

---

[126] Dulles's statement at a meeting of the National Security Council, 21 November 1955, *Foreign Relations of the United States, 1955–57*, XIV, p. 797.

[127] Memorandum of conference with the President, 31 July 1956, *Foreign Relations of the United States, 1955–57*, XVI, pp. 62–68.

[128] Quoted in Diane B. Kunz, 'The Importance of Having Money', in Louis and Owen, *Suez 1956*, p. 215. See also the same author's *Economic Diplomacy of the Suez Crisis* (Chapel Hill, N.C., 1991). According to a Foreign Office minute: 'If Middle East [oil] supplies are cut off altogether . . . it is difficult to see how we could manage to avoid major economic disaster' (minute by Denis Wright, Top Secret, 27 August 1956, FO 371/120799).

[129] Memorandum by Macmillan, Top Secret, 7 August 1956, EC (56) 8, CAB 134/1217.

[130] For Macmillan and the crisis, see Alistair Horne, *Macmillan, 1894–1956* (London, 1988), chap. 15.

pipelines were sabotaged, and the oil ceased to flow. Far from saving sterling, the intervention set off a disastrous run on the pound. As the reserves ran out, Macmillan presented his colleagues with two alternatives: either to float the pound—a 'catastrophe affecting not merely the [British] cost of living but also . . . all our external economic relations'; or to ask for massive American aid.[131] Only after Eden had agreed to leave Egypt unconditionally did Eisenhower rescue the pound, with a billion dollars from the International Monetary Fund and the Export-Import Bank.[132] As the expedition took to its boats, Nikita Khrushchev rattled the nuclear sabre over London and Paris. Eisenhower shielded his errant allies with a similar threat against Moscow.[133]

It was the Americans, not the Russians, who had vetoed the Anglo-French effort at imperial reassertion in the Middle East and North Africa. At the peak of the crisis, Dulles told the National Security Council, in a now famous comment, that for many years the United States had been 'walking a tight rope' between backing Europe's empires and trying to win the friendship of countries escaping from colonialism. Unless the United States now asserted leadership, all those countries would turn to the Soviet Union.[134] Eisenhower asked: 'How can we possibly support Britain and France if in doing so we lose the whole Arab world?'[135] The Americans insisted that their major European

[131] See 'Sterling', 19 November 1956, T 236/4189. See also especially the minutes in T 236/4188 and T 236/4190.

[132] See Diane Kunz, *Economic Diplomacy*, chap. 7. George Humphrey, Secretary of the Treasury, remarked that 'if the United Kingdom did not look out, it would bust itself to a point of bankruptcy and of no return' (National Security Council discussion, 8 November 1956, *Foreign Relations of the United States, 1955–57*, XVI, p. 1077). On the British side of the financial crisis, see especially *Hall Diaries, 1954–61*, pp. 85–87; and, specifically on the Treasury, Lewis Johnman, 'Defending the Pound: The Economics of the Suez Crisis, 1956', in Anthony Gorst et al., eds., *Post-War Britain, 1945–64* (London, 1989).

[133] Eisenhower remarked: 'The British realized that it [the Russian threat] is partly a propaganda effort but nevertheless they are scared.' The risk was too great to 'discount the possibility that the Russians would actually move into the area with force' (memorandum of 7 November 1956, *Foreign Relations of the United States, 1955–57*, XVI, p. 1049) On the weakness of the Soviet position, see Galia Golan, *Soviet Policies in the Middle East* (Cambridge, 1990), pp. 47–53. For the British assessment, 'Soviet Motives and Objectives in the Middle East', Secret, 2 October 1957, FO 371/127737; PREM 11/2404. For the American appreciation, see Special National Intelligence Estimate, 'Soviet Actions in the Middle East', Secret, 29 November 1956, in Scott A. Koch, ed., *CIA Cold War Records: Selected Estimates on the Soviet Union, 1950–1959* (Washington, 1993), pp. 147–52.

[134] Memorandum on National Security Council discussion, 1 November 1956, *Foreign Relations of the United States, 1955–57*, XVI, p. 906.

[135] *Foreign Relations of the United States, 1955–57*, XVI, 910. Dulles stated: 'We had almost reached the point of deciding today whether we think the future lies with a policy of re-asserting

allies give priority to the Cold War over their empires. Yet the prize of Arab friendship eluded the righteous. The Arabs gave the credit for defeating imperialism mostly to the Egyptians and the Russians. Nasser and Nasserism were exalted; it was Eden who was toppled. American anti-imperialism in the Middle East provoked anti-Americanism in Europe and threw NATO into disarray. It was difficult not to fall off Dulles's tightrope.

A triumph for the non-aligned nations, the Suez fiasco was a disaster for the Empire. It ended British aspirations to imperial dominance in the Middle East. It showed that international confidence in the sterling empire still rested on the alignment of Anglo-American aims. Once and for all, it was established that Britain had to work in concert with the United States in the 'peripheral regions' no less than in Europe or suffer humiliating consequences. What Dulles called the 'violent family quarrel' over Suez had exposed the American essentials underlying British imperial power for all to see. The colonial periphery of the First Empire had become the centre of the Third.

In 1957 at Bermuda, and later in Washington, Macmillan, now Prime Minister, and Eisenhower hastily revised and renewed the Anglo-American contract. Once more, as in 1947, the British were cutting their European and imperial commitments to save their payments balance.[136] Once again, the Americans repaired British power as the 'core of the [revitalized] NATO alliance and . . . an important element in SEATO and the Baghdad Pact'.[137] Like Attlee and Truman before them, the two leaders pledged 'joint policies' over the whole range of world affairs.[138] Bevin had looked forward to equality, but this time the Prime Minister spoke of British 'junior partnership' and declared 'interdependence'. With the Soviet Sputnik signalling nuclear parity

by force colonial control over the less developed nations, or whether we will oppose such a course of action by every appropriate means' (p. 906).

[136] Eden had noted on the eve of the Suez crisis: '[W]e must now cut our coat according to our cloth. There is not much cloth' (PR [56] 11, 13 June 1956, CAB 134/1315). For Macmillan's explanation at Bermuda, see *Foreign Relations of the United States, 1955–57*, XXVII, pp. 749–52.

[137] Northern European Chiefs of Mission Conference, 19–21 September 1957, *Foreign Relations of the United States, 1955–57*, IV, p. 610. On the need for the United States to support sterling, see State Department memorandum, 26 November 1956, *Foreign Relations of the United States, 1955–57*, XXVII, pp. 668–72. For the British Treasury's view of the problem in the aftermath of Suez, see T 236/4189.

[138] Dulles on agenda for Washington Talks, 17 October 1957, *Foreign Relations of the United States, 1955–57*, XXVII, pp. 789–91.

with the United States, 'no country can do the job alone'.[139] The extreme danger of the allies acting at cross-purposes in Suez fashion had become undeniable.

The understandings reached at Washington in 1957 initiated a concerted Anglo-American strategy in Asia and Africa to match the closer relationship in Europe. Eisenhower equipped the British with ballistic missiles and agreed to covert joint leadership in NATO. In return, Macmillan undertook not to negotiate with Moscow over disarmament or Germany without the Americans. He also agreed to keep his troops on the Rhine. As an American official put it, 'They can't ask for a 50 per cent interest in the political profits and then draw down their share in the firm's assets from 30 to 10 per cent . . . if . . . sterling is really heading to disaster, we will have to bail them out in our own interests.'[140] There would be no more British talk of seating Communist China at the United Nations. It was understood that independence for cooperative nationalists was the best chance of saving Africa from communist subversion. Under the Eisenhower doctrine, which carried with it an allocation of up to 200 million dollars a year for the Middle East, the Americans were taking over the lead there as elsewhere.[141] Nevertheless, the British position in Iraq and the Gulf states was to be respected and supported. The oil there was vital to British prosperity, Washington noted, and the British would fight for it.[142] Along those lines, the President and the Prime Minister subscribed to 'coordinated effort

---

[139] Macmillan to Eisenhower, 10 October 1957, *Foreign Relations of the United States, 1955–57*, XXVII, p. 785. Implicit in the new British approach was a subtle lesson from Suez on the use of force. According to Sir Harold Caccia, the British Ambassador in Washington:

> In American eyes the use of force by others is justifiable in almost any circumstances when it can be shown to be directed against communism; but that, conversely, when the connection cannot be clearly shown, there are almost no circumstances in which they can be counted on to support it openly.

Caccia to Hoyer Millar, Secret and Guard, 10 September 1957, FO 371/126888.

[140] Memorandum by Merchant for Dulles, 19 October 1957, *Foreign Relations of the United States, 1955–57*, XXVII, p. 795.

[141] For the consequences of the Eisenhower doctrine in the Middle East, see especially Malcolm Kerr, 'The Lebanese Civil War', in Evan Luard, ed., *The International Regulation of Civil Wars* (New York, 1972), especially pp. 72–74. British officials viewed the Eisenhower doctrine as a loosely worded statement designed to win Congressional support for the American initiative in the post-Suez era. They were amused but not comforted when Dulles described it as 'an attitude, a point of view, a state of mind' (as recorded in Caccia to Lloyd, 23 April 1957, FO 371/127896).

[142] See National Intelligence Estimate, 'British Position in Persian Gulf and Arabian Peninsula', 19 February 1957, *Foreign Relations of the United States, 1955–57*, XIII, pp. 486–88. On the British side, see Bernard Burrows, 'The Future of the Persian Gulf States', Secret, 27 May 1957,

and combined planning in the field of production, defense and economic warfare' towards a global common front.[143] In 1958 they faced
the sequel of the Suez crisis together.

Eisenhower found the root of the trouble in 'Nasser's capture of
Arab loyalty and enthusiasm throughout the region'.[144] A Nasserite
coup had ejected Soviet influence from Damascus and merged Syria
with Egypt in the United Arab Republic. Pan-Arab disturbances, seemingly directed from Cairo and Damascus, were undermining every ally
of the West from Beirut to Kuwait and Aden. In the spring of 1958, the
Americans prepared for military action with British participation in
support of President Chamoun in Lebanon. To strengthen their clients, the British in turn had supported the proposal of their most loyal
collaborator in the Middle East, Nuri es Said of Iraq, to form a union
of Iraq and Jordan. On 14 July, however, another 'pro-Nasser, anti-
Western coup' swept away the pro-British regime and the Hashemite
dynasty in Baghdad.[145] Would Brigadier Abdul Qasim's revolutionary junta join forces with Nasser's United Arab Republic, or would he
oppose Nasserite aggrandizement with communist support?[146] The
question had wide ramifications. The British had lost their Iraqi air
bases, they might lose their Iraqi oil fields,[147] and worse still, Qasim

---

FO 371/126916. Burrows was Political Resident in the Gulf and played a key part in these events.
See his memoir, *Footnotes in the Sand: The Gulf in Transition, 1953–1958* (Wilton, UK, 1990).

[143] As anticipated by Dulles in agenda for Washington Talks, 17 October 1957, *Foreign Relations of the United States, 1955–57*, XXVII, p. 791.

[144] President to George Humphrey, 22 July 1958, *Foreign Relations of the United States, 1958–
60*, XI, p. 365.

[145] As described by William M. Rountree (Assistant Secretary of State), 14 July 1958, *Foreign
Relations of the United States, 1958–60*, XI, p. 228. The British Ambassador in Baghdad, however,
believed initially that 'it is essentially an Administration of liberal reformers' (Sir Michael Wright
to Lloyd, Secret, 23 July 1958, FO 371/134200).

[146] The British assessment of the revolution in relation to the United States is particularly
instructive:

> The question arises as to whether a Communist controlled Iraq would be more inim-
> ical to our interests than a Nasserite controlled Iraq, the point being that against a
> Communist controlled Iraq American help could be rallied, and perhaps the whole
> Arab Nationalist movement turned into a patriotic anti-Communist feeling.

Minutes of a meeting at 10 Downing Street, 21 December 1958, PREM 11/2735. For the Iraqi
revolution in this context, see Robert A. Fernea and W. R. Louis, eds., *The Iraqi Revolution of 1958*
(London, 1991).

[147] Sir Gerald Templer, Chief of the Imperial General Staff, believed that Arab nationalism
in general 'had become a tool of Soviet policy' (12 August 1948, COS [58] 71, ADM 205/116);
see also Templer's minutes in WO 216/917. Sir Michael Wright, however, offered this assessment:

> There is no one in sight, other than Abdul Karim Qasim . . . able to keep Iraq inde-
> pendent and united. This is so important not only for the benefit of the Iraqis but also

might invade Kuwait, which was now the chief supplier of oil to the sterling area.[148] The Americans feared that if the King of Jordan fell, the Israelis would move into the West Bank and start a general war in the Middle East.[149]

Now it was Eisenhower's turn to fulminate against 'the struggle of Nasser to get control of these [petroleum] supplies—to get the income and power to destroy the Western world'.[150] Like Eden in 1956, he felt that 'the most strategic move would be to attack Cairo'[151] and 'turn Israel loose on . . . the head of the snake'.[152] Unlike Eden, the President knew 'of course [that] this can not be done'. Critics in Congress and the world at large, Foster Dulles added, would say that 'we are simply doing what we stopped the British and French from doing'.[153] But pro-Western rulers from Turkey and Israel to Saudi Arabia and Pakistan had requested immediate American or Anglo-American military support. Either the United States and Britain would have to respond, according to Eisenhower, or they would have to 'get out of the Middle East entirely'.[154] On the day of the Baghdad coup, brushing aside the Prime Minister's idea of a joint expedition to clear up the whole situation in the Middle East, the President ordered the marines into Lebanon.[155] By agreement, the British sent a contingent to Jordan as insurance for the King and a warning to Qasim.

Most of Asia and much of Africa condemned the military intervention. 'If we stay on', Eisenhower was advised, 'the USSR will beat us to death in public opinion. We must adjust to the tide of Arab nation-

---

for the future of the oil industry, for British interests generally in the Arab world and for the staving off of the Russian advance into the Middle East that it seems desirable to give Qasim the benefit of the doubt.

Wright to Lloyd, Confidential, 4 December 1958, PREM 11/2735.

[148] Nuri, too, had threatened Kuwait. See Macmillan's comment, 9 June 1958, *Foreign Relations of the United States, 1958–60*, XII, p. 302. On the vital importance of Kuwait oil to sterling, see Frank Brenchley, *Britain and the Middle East: An Economic History* (London, 1989), chap. 12. For Qasim's attack on Kuwait in 1961 and the consequent British intervention, see Mustafa M. Alani, *Operation Vantage: British Military Intervention in Kuwait, 1961* (Surbiton, UK, 1990).

[149] For American reactions to the Iraqi coup, see Editorial Note, *Foreign Relations of the United States, 1958–60*, XII, pp. 307–08; 'Briefing Notes by Director of Central Intelligence', 14 July, 1958, ibid., pp. 308–11.

[150] Memorandum of Conversation between President and Vice-President, 15 July 1958, *Foreign Relations of the United States, 1958–60*, XI, p. 244.

[151] Conference with President, 14 July 1958, ibid., p. 214.

[152] Conference with President, 16 July 1958, ibid., p. 310.

[153] Conference with President, 14 July 1958, ibid., pp. 214–15.

[154] Conference with President, 14 July 1958, ibid., p. 213.

[155] Telephone conversations and messages between Eisenhower and Macmillan, 14–15 July 1958, ibid., pp. 231–42. The British records of these conversations are in PREM 11/2387.

alism . . . before the hot heads get control in every country. The oil companies should be able to roll with the punches.'[156] Such were the guidelines of American and Anglo-American policy thereafter. In October 1958, Eisenhower's marines left Lebanon. Macmillan in turn withdrew the troops from Jordan, and Washington provided most of the money needed to support the King with a credible army.

It was recognized after 1958 that friendly regimes, if only to survive, had to temper their pro-Western stance and share power with the more moderate pan-Arabs.[157] As Macmillan put it, the Cold War in the Middle East and elsewhere had become a question of winning the battle against 'so-called neutralism'.[158] The British accordingly dismantled their formal controls over Kuwait.[159] They trod warily in Iraq, where Anglo-American cooperation aimed at encouraging Qasim 'to resist pro-communist and pro-Nasserite forces equally'.[160] Qasim renounced his British defence treaty, left the Baghdad Pact, and accepted military aid from Moscow. But the Iraqis resisted Soviet pressure to nationalize the British and American oil concessions through the 1960s. Qasim's army had to be paid; forewarned by Musaddiq's fate, even revolutionary nationalists could not afford to lose three-quarters of their revenue.[161] In Iraq and Iran the politics might be nationalized, but the invisible empire of oil remained.

Throughout the 1950s, Anglo-American strategy rested on an oil cartel that allegedly fixed prices and divided 'producing and market-

[156] Memorandum of National Security Council discussion, 24 July 1958, *Foreign Relations of the United States, 1958–60,* XI, p. 384. According to the Foreign Office: 'Like Nuri, Qasim also wants an independent Iraq, in which Kurds and Arabs, Shias, Sunnis and other minorities will be united and which will be developed in accordance with a long-term economic plan, financed from the oil royalties paid by the Iraq Petroleum Company' (Annual Report for Iraq, 1958, FO 371/140896).

[157] See National Intelligence Estimates, 'The Outlook for Lebanon', 10 May, 1960, *Foreign Relations of the United States, 1958–1960,* XI, pp. 649–53; 'The Outlook for Jordan', 10 March 1960, ibid., pp. 681–87.

[158] Memorandum of conversation with President, 21 March 1957, *Foreign Relations of the United States, 1955–57,* XXVII, p. 710.

[159] See Jill Crystal, *Oil and Politics in the Gulf* (Cambridge, 1990), pp. 81–86. For the political side of the Kuwaiti crisis of 1960, see especially George Middleton (Bahrain) to Sir Roger Stevens, Secret, 10 September 1960, FO 371/152120: 'We cannot see the Americans taking over the lead from us [in the Gulf], for they even more than we are tarred with the capitalist brush and are objects of peculiar suspicion.'

[160] Record of conversation between Lloyd and Dulles, 4 February 1959, FO 371/141841; memorandum of conversation between Eisenhower and Macmillan, 22 March 1959, *Foreign Relations of the United States, 1958–60,* XI, p. 216.

[161] The Soviets offered no alternative market for Iraq's oil until 1969. See Michael E. Brown, 'The Nationalization of the Iraqi Petroleum Company', *International Journal of Middle Eastern Studies,* 10 (1970), pp. 107–24.

ing territories' for 85 per cent of the world's supply outside the United States.[162] The five American and two British multinationals involved represented the substance of Empire in the Middle East. Their interests were so enmeshed with Western economic and strategic security that American anti-trust proceedings against them hung fire throughout the decade.[163] The more highly capitalized American companies expanded their areas of production in the region more than the British. As the American consortium opened new oilfields, American influence eroded British sway in much of the Middle East and North Africa.[164] Most of the 'British' Middle East became an Anglo-American concern after 1958. Only in the Gulf States and the Red Sea could British power cope single-handed. It was not a matter of simple metropolitan enfeeblement: all the combined influence of the United States and Britain proved insufficient to shape the turmoil of pan-Arabism into stable informal sway.

The new Tory government of 1957 under Harold Macmillan set its sights on an empire in the post-colonial world. A system of influence was to be won by converting discontented subjects into loyal allies. The strategy was nothing if not Anglo-American. Imperial defence was realigned on joint plans for bypassing the canal and rerouting Europe's oil supplies around Africa. As the 'air barrier' over the eastern Mediterranean 'thickened', the only sure way to reinforce the security of the Gulf states and the Indian Ocean seemed to be a string of airfields connecting Kano (in northern Nigeria) to Nairobi and Aden.[165] Control in the Red Sea became the pivot of the scheme. The Middle East Command moved its headquarters to Aden—the only major base left in the Arabian peninsula. The Colony also housed the regional oil refinery of the Anglo-Iranian Oil Company (now British Petroleum).

---

[162] Memorandum by Legal Adviser (Hager) to State Department, 11 April 1960, *Foreign Relations of the United States, 1958–60,* IV, pp. 630–33. For an earlier assessment, see British and American joint review, 'Middle East Problems Bearing upon the Supply of Oil to the Free World', *Foreign Relations of the United States, 1955–57,* X, pp. 682–89.

[163] See memorandum of National Security Council discussion, 9 May 1960, *Foreign Relations of the United States, 1958–60,* VI, pp. 633–36.

[164] 'The *official* policy of the State Department is not unfriendly towards the maintenance of British interests. At the same time . . . the American oil companies are fiercely competitive . . . and, since we do not have the same . . . economic resources as the Americans, we tend to lose ground all along the line' (George Middleton to A. D. Ross, Personal and Confidential Guard, 20 December 1956, FO 371/121238).

[165] Cabinet memorandum by Burke Trend, 1 March 1957, PREM 11/2582. For the changing naval dimension of the problem, see Peter James Henshaw, 'The Transfer of Simonstown: Afrikaner Nationalism, South African Strategic Dependence, and British Global Power', *Journal of Imperial and Commonwealth History,* 20 (1992), pp. 419–44.

But the local nationalists listened to the 'Voice of the Arabs' broadcasts from Cairo and could no longer be kept at bay with colonial gradualism. In 1958 the Colonial Secretary, Alan Lennox-Boyd, set about yoking the trade-unionized port to the clutter of tribal sheikdoms inland in an unlikely scheme to form a federation that would be weighted in favour of collaboration with the British after independence.[166] In Aden the British were gambling against the odds for high strategic stakes.[167]

During the Scramble into Africa in the 1890s, the great Lord Salisbury had worked at keeping hostile powers away from the Upper Nile region and the Horn of Africa.[168] Six decades later the British were pursuing a similar plan in the colonial scramble out of Africa; only the method and the enemies had changed. In 1957 the members of Macmillan's government were bent on erecting buffer states against 'the southward drive of Nasser and the Russians' towards the projected trans-African lifeline to Aden and Singapore. It was thus essential for the British and Americans to persuade the peoples of Somalia and Ethiopia 'to live together as good neighbours'. Ethiopian cooperation depended largely on American subsidies to Emperor Haile Selassie: 'Inevitably, American money would have to finance the greater part of this policy.'[169]

At first the Nile Valley had been sealed off in the Sudan, where the British had advanced the anti-Egyptian party to independence by 1956 in the course of outbidding Cairo and the pro-Egyptian party for Sudanese loyalty. Two years later General Ibrahim Abboud's coup in Khartoum reopened the way for Nasserite influence. For 'a counterpoise' the British turned to the Somalis.[170] In the familiar style, Macmillan's government bought nationalist cooperation with imperial

---

[166] Memorandum by Lennox-Boyd, 'Aden Colony and Protectorate', Secret, 14 August 1959, C.P.C. (59) 12, CAB 134/1558. See especially Glen Balfour-Paul, *The End of Empire in the Middle East: Britain's Relinquishment of Power in Her Last Three Arab Dependencies* (Cambridge, 1991).

[167] A comment made by W. L. Gorrell Barnes of the Colonial Office reveals how the interplay of local and international circumstances had to be borne in mind while assessing the strategic aim in Aden: 'Our own general [colonial] policy and the fashion of anti-colonialism is of course a factor, but only insofar as local conditions create a situation which these considerations can exacerbate' (minute by Gorrell Barnes, 24 April 1959, CO 1015/1912).

[168] See Ronald Robinson and John Gallagher, *Africa and the Victorians: The Official Mind of Imperialism* (London, 1981, 2nd edn.).

[169] Minutes by Burke Trend, 1 March 1957 and 20 November 1958, PREM 11/2582.

[170] Record of conference between East African Governors and Secretary of State, Entebbe, 7–8 October 1957, Secret, CO 822/1807. In the event of the Sudan falling under Nasser's sway, 'the threat will reach to the borders of Uganda and Kenya' (minute by Trend to Prime Minister, 20 November 1958, PREM 11/2582).

strategy at the price of independence. After the United Nations decreed independence for Italian Somalia in 1960, the Cabinet, with American support, united the British Somali clans with their neighbours into a greater Somali state. Given their national aspirations, Lennox-Boyd judged, 'the moderate political parties and the mass of the people would cooperate fully' with the Western powers.[171]

British officials concentrated on independence for tropical Africa after 1957—independence in the north-east, independence in the west—above all independence to prolong imperial sway and secure British economic and strategic assets. It was increasingly urgent to exchange colonial control for informal Empire.[172] To turn this trick, the last aces in the African colonial hand would have to be played before they were forced. In West Africa the game had already been played out with some success, despite errors. The constitution that Attlee's government had introduced into the Gold Cost (Ghana) in 1951 had been designed to allow the British to share power with conservative chiefs and nationalists.[173] It was a British initiative. However, the psephology proved mistaken, and Kwame Nkrumah's young 'Independence Now' party won an unexpected majority in the Legislative Assembly; he had to be let out of jail and endowed with the executive power intended for his 'elders and betters'.[174] First as 'Leader of government business' and soon as Prime Minister, Nkrumah won prestige as the next ruler of Ghana. His Convention People's Party undermined the chiefs' hold over their local communities and won more elections. The British Governor had 'only one dog in [his] kennel'.

[171] Lennox-Boyd to Macmillan, Secret and Personal, 12 February 1959, PREM 11/2582; 'Policy in Aden and Somaliland', Secret, 17 November 1958, CPC (58) 19, CAB 134/1557. It is of interest that at the time of the First World War and the Peace Conference, Lennox-Boyd had no clearer idea than his predecessors about the status of Somalia or Tanganyika in international law. 'Incidentally', he once asked, 'where does "sovereignty" lie . . . ? The Queen is not Queen of Tanganyika under international law is she?' (minute of 11 July 1957, CO 926/1054).

[172] Even the more diehard Colonial Governors had begun to recognize, in the words of Sir Edward Twining in Tanganyika, that there would be a time 'when we pass out of the phase of control into the phase of influence'—though he thought that it would be 'a generation or so before control gives way to influence' (Twining to Gorrell Barnes, 12 November 1956, CO 822/912, *BDEEP—Conservative Government*, II, p. 272). The principle, however, had long been established in the Colonial Office. For example, one official wrote in 1953: '[A]s the Secretary of State progressively loses direct control of the Colonies, he must increasingly rely on influence and advice to them' (minute by A. E. Drake, 3 October 1953, ibid., III, p. 306).

[173] Cabinet memorandum by Arthur Creech Jones, 'Gold Coast Constitution', 8 October 1949, CAB 129/36/2 (*BDEEP—Labour Government*, III, pp. 46–49).

[174] Arden-Clarke to Cohen, Personal, 5 March 1951, CO 537/7181. For the full story, see Richard Rathbone, ed., *British Documents on the End of Empire*, series B, vol. 1: *Ghana* (London, 1992), Part I, 1941–1952, (henceforth *BDEEP—Ghana*).

As the only effective collaborator with the colonial administration in sight,[175] the Ghanaian leader was able to bargain his country's way to political, even if not economic, independence by 1957.[176] White-hall was consoled that Ghana had been stabilized under British influence.[177] But as Lord Home, the Commonwealth Secretary, observed, Nkrumah 'sees himself as a Messiah sent to deliver Africa from bondage'.[178] He was becoming the Nasser of black Africa.

According to the French, Nkrumah's progress spawned nationalists and discouraged the friends of colonial gradualism throughout West Africa and beyond.[179] Concessions yielded in Accra were immediately demanded in Lagos and Dakar. Colonial governors warned that if the claims to power of 'responsible' national leaders were denied, they would lose their followers to revolutionaries.[180] Step-by-step behind the Ghanaians, the Nigerians, followed by the Sierra Leonians, advanced to political independence in 1960 and 1961 respectively. A Nigerian federation was negotiated to yoke the radical Yoruba and Ibo leaders of the southern provinces to the conservative pro-British emirs in the Muslim north. By installing their 'very good friend'[181] Abubaker Balewa, the northern leader, as federal Prime Minister, the British had done their best to construct a reliable and congenial succession. Partly as a result of the domino effect, but chiefly because of the writing on the wall in Algeria, the French followed the British example in West Africa in 1960.[182] The accelerated schedule of independences made

[175] 'We have only one dog in our kennel, all we can do is to build it up and feed it vitamins and cod liver oil'; it could be replaced only with one 'of even more extremist nationalist tendencies' (Arden-Clarke to Cohen, 12 May 1951, quoted in Hyam's note on Cohen minute, 11 June 1951, *BDEEP—Labour Government*, II, pp. 73–74).

[176] To obtain Nkrumah's collaboration, the Governor, Sir Charles Arden-Clarke, promised to consider virtual internal self-government within five years, and to make him Prime Minister with control over all domestic departments. The Governor's object was to win time for the emergence of a moderate political party that would win the next election. Sir John Macpherson, Governor of Nigeria, commented: 'The thought that two or three years . . . would be sufficient to achieve this, seems the dreamiest [pipe dream] I have ever heard of' (Macpherson to Lloyd, 8 January 1952, CO 967/173). For the policy of constitutional advance in Ghana and Nigeria generally, see *BDEEP—Labour Government*, III, pp. 38–78; for Ghana, see *BDEEP—Ghana*, II.

[177] 'Africa: The Next Ten Years', Interdepartmental Report, June 1959, FO 371/137972.

[178] Home hoped that 'the emergence of Nigeria . . . will cut him down to size' (memorandum by Home, 1 June 1959, PREM 11/2588).

[179] C. de Brabant, 'Anglo-French Colonial Cooperation, Principally in West African Affairs' (unpublished M.Litt. thesis, Oxford University, 1989).

[180] See Ronald Hyam's preface to Cabinet memorandum by James Griffiths (Colonial Secretary), 'Nigerian Constitution', 3 May 1950, CAB 129/39, CP (50) 94, *BDEEP—Labour Government*, III, 52 ff.

[181] The phrase of Iain Macleod in a minute to Macmillan, 9 May 1960, PREM 11/3047.

[182] Sir Anthony Rumbold in Paris wrote at the time of Algerian independence: 'There are not wanting Frenchmen today to evoke memories of Fashoda . . . We must particularly avoid giv-

sport of imperial timetables. In the 1930s the Colonial Office had expected the tropical African empire to last into the twenty-first century, and in 1945, for another sixty years. By 1950 the end of colonial rule in Nigeria and Ghana was predicted for the 1970s. In fact, the span of imperial longevity in West Africa was cut off within a decade.

The pace of events in this region owed little to direct pressure from the superpowers. Until 1960, Soviet intervention remained prospective rather than actual. With little leverage in tropical Africa, Eisenhower and Dulles found that 'we must tailor our policies . . . to . . . our overall relations with the metropolitan powers' in NATO: 'Premature independence would be as harmful to our interests . . . as . . . a continuation of nineteenth century colonialism.'[183] Paris was thus enabled to ignore American advice and continue the Algerian war, with American financial support.[184] London proceeded single-handed with its own collaborative arrangements in tropical Africa. From 1956 onwards, nonetheless, Washington, fearing a build-up to another Suez, pressed the colonial powers to consult and coordinate their African policies with the Americans in the councils of NATO.[185] Anglo-American diplomacy barely calmed the Graeco-Turkish struggle over Cyprus, which imperilled a vital Western base and the integrity of NATO and CENTO (Central Treaty Organization).[186] Salvation took the form of rule by the once-exiled Archbishop Makarios over an

---

ing any ground for ever-present French suspicions of an Anglo-Saxon drive to replace their influence in Africa' (Rumbold to Lord Home, Confidential, 23 May 1962, FO 371/161371).

[183] 'Statement of U.S. Policy Toward Africa South of the Sahara', 23 August 1957, *Foreign Relations of the United States, 1955–57*, XVIII, pp. 79–80; see also assurances to Macmillan at Bermuda Conference, 23 March 1957, ibid., pp. 55–57. Despite the consensus, the British were worried that the client states would attempt 'to play us and the Americans off against each other . . . It is not always easy to get the Americans to discuss these things with us' (minute by A. D. M. Ross, 19 March 1957, FO 371/127755).

[184] See *Foreign Relations of the United States, 1955–57*, XVIII, pp. 219–302, for American frustration over the situation in Algeria. For the British side, see, for example, FO 371/161371.

[185] Until 1956 the Americans had usually refused in principle to adopt joint policies with Britain and France in colonial and quasi-colonial affairs to avoid the taint of imperialism. As a result, the Europeans were free to divert forces, and incidentally American aid, to regional imperial purposes and to involve the United States in confrontations with the Soviets without Washington's authorization. After Suez, Dulles pressed the NATO Council of Ministers, with little success, to coordinate European policies in the 'peripheral regions'. Otherwise, he feared, NATO would be torn apart (*Foreign Relations of the United States, 1955–57*, IV, pp. 78ff, 109, 200–01, 265ff). The alignment of British and US views on Africa began at a meeting between Dulles and Selwyn Lloyd at the Brize Norton airfield in October 1958; see minute by Adam Watson, 15 June 1959, FO 371/137952.

[186] For the turning point in 1955 and the beginning of the debate in the Colonial Office about a possible 'Anglo-Greek-Turkish condominium' or 'even a N.A.T.O. solution', see minutes in CO 926/257.

independent Cyprus in 1960.[187] Coordinating the African policies of the NATO powers proved even harder.

At Dulles's request in June 1959, Macmillan instructed his officials to survey the African endgame in a comprehensive interdepartmental report under the auspices of the Africa Committee of the Cabinet, which was chaired by Burke Trend of the Cabinet Office and composed of representatives of the Colonial Office, Foreign Office, Commonwealth Relations Office, Treasury, and Ministry of Defence.[188] Written as a possible basis for Anglo-American consensus, the document testified to the shared belief that Africa's future would be shaped by the relationship between Britain and America.[189] British officials approached the crisis of African independence with no solid belief in the potentiality of black nationalism among so many divided ethnic communities. They regarded the freedom movements as essentially anti-European, not to say racist. What impressed them was the speed with which handfuls of urban nationalists were stirring up popular black resentment against white rule.[190] 'Africanism', as some preferred to call it,[191] was spreading from the Niger to the Zambesi and the Nile. The agitation could be contained at local levels, but the use of force would defeat the object. As the Colonial Office noted:

> It would be difficult for us to create some new authoritarian force artificially, and if we tried to do so . . . to the exclusion of people like Nkrumah or [Obafemi] Awolowo [in Nigeria] or [Julius] Nyerere

[187] See *Foreign Relations of the United States, 1958–60*, X, pp. 564–835. For the key British files on Cyprus in relation to other dependent territories, see CAB 134/1558 and CAB 134/1559 (Colonial Policy Committee, 1959 and 1960). For recent interpretations of Cyprus in the 1950s, see Robert Holland, 'Never, Never Land: British Colonial Policy and the Roots of Violence in Cyprus, 1950–54', and David M. Anderson, 'Policing and Communal Conflict: The Cyprus Emergency, 1954–60', both in *Journal of Imperial and Commonwealth History*, 21 (September 1993), pp. 148–207.

[188] 'Africa: The Next Ten Years', June 1959, FO 371/137972. For the interdepartmental discussions, see CAB 134/1353. The quotations are from the copy in FO 371/137972, which is a complete document, but see CO 936/572 and PREM 11/2587.

[189] 'This is the first time', the head of the African Department of the Foreign Office noted, 'that an effort has been made to see the picture as a whole . . . Hitherto the different areas of Africa have been regarded as largely in water-tight compartments' (minute by Adam Watson, 15 June 1959, FO 371/137952). Christopher Eastwood of the Colonial Office recognized the urgency of 'high level talks with the Americans' in his minute of 3 July 1959, CO 936/572.

[190] 'Africa: The Next Ten Years', June 1959, FO 371/137972.

[191] Notably Lord Hailey in *An African Survey* (London, 1957 edn.); see John W. Cell, *Hailey: A Study in British Imperialism, 1872–1969* (Cambridge, 1992), pp. 301–02.

[in Tanganyika]—it would probably lead to the creation of a revolutionary force against the set-up that we had created.[192]

The good will of amenable national leaders had to be won before independence if they were to be allied after independence.

Anticipations of Soviet intervention and the fears of an alliance between Nkrumah's pan-Africanism and Nasser's pan-Arabism multiplied the significance of local nationalist agitation. In the Cabinet Office's analysis, Moscow was alert to every chance of promoting African freedom movements. The Russians would be competing with the West for the sponsorship of every ex-colonial state. They were already making overtures in Ghana and Guinea as well as Ethiopia. The well-worn phrases of Anglo-American discourse ran through the Cabinet Office report: 'If the Western Governments appear to be reluctant to concede independence . . . they may turn [African opinion] towards the Soviet Union; if . . . they move too fast, they run the risk of leaving large areas . . . ripe for Communist exploitation.'[193] Only independent countries headed by nationalist leaders could form a 'strong, indigenous barrier to the penetration of Africa by the Soviet Union and the United Arab Republic'.[194] The American analysis of African prospects followed similar lines.[195] Washington was as sure as London that tropical Africa was far from ready for independence. Every other consideration pointed to the necessity of keeping in step with African national aspirations.

By the late 1950s, British hopes for the economic future were veering away from the Empire and towards Europe. Sterling was on the verge of full convertibility. The preferences and financial controls of the imperial economy had given way to freer world trade. In 1957, Macmillan had requested a 'profit and loss account'[196] for the colonies, and it found, ambiguously, that British trade might be better served if independence came sooner rather than later. Two years later colonial controls were clearly no longer indispensable to metropolitan prosperity. The inevitable political informalization of the Empire

---

[192] Colonial Office officials went on to draw the lesson they had learned from the Iraqi revolution: '[W]e would gain nothing by trying to back authoritarians against public opinion' (minutes of a meeting at the Colonial Office, Secret, 20 May 1959, CO 936/ 572).

[193] 'Africa: The Next Ten Years', June 1959, FO 371/137972, p. 6.

[194] Ibid., p. 29.

[195] See National Security Council 5818: 'US Policy Toward Africa South of the Sahara', approved by President, 26 August 1958, *Foreign Relations of the United States, 1958–60*, XIV, pp. 23–37.

[196] See especially CO 1032/144, CO 1032/146, and CO 1032/147.

in its final stages went hand in hand with the desirable economic in-formalization of the sterling area.[197]

The economics of dependence after political independence was the key to the Cabinet Office's plan for an African informal empire. Since 1957, British and American officials had agreed that the African dependencies must evolve 'towards stable self-government or inde-pendence' as rapidly as possible, but 'in such a way that these [succes-sor] governments are willing and able to preserve their economic and political ties with the West.'[198] Economic and military aid adminis-tered by technical advisers would bind the new states to their former rulers. The Americans would underwrite this ambitious plan for Af-rica.[199] It was all to the good that they had few economic interests and large Cold War stakes in the continent. The British would share in the profits of American investment. They were relying a great deal on the Americans financially and strategically for the imperial future in Af-rica.[200] Although some of his officials were talking about an African Marshall plan, Eisenhower and the Treasury wanted the British and French to carry the burden of assistance, 'with the Americans picking up the slack'.[201] Whatever the source, the influence to be won from aid would go to the donor. If there were to be an African informal em-pire, the British Cabinet Office report implied, it would be increas-ingly Anglo-American rather than British.

Everything now depended on winning and keeping African good will. It would all be lost, the Colonial Office feared in 1959, unless the struggle for independence between black majorities and white

[197] Cf. Cain and Hopkins, *British Imperialism,* II, pp. 281 ff.

[198] Agreed US-UK paper, 'Means of Combatting Communist Influence in Tropical Africa, 13 March 1957', *Foreign Relations of the United States, 1955–57,* XXVII, p. 759.

[199] 'Africa: The Next Ten Years', June 1959, FO 371/137972, pp. 25–26.

[200] The interest of the Americans in Africa was rapidly increasing: 'Their main concern is po-litical and strategic . . . If we are prepared to co-operate with the Americans, we have an oppor-tunity to influence their thinking and benefit from their growing interest in Africa, which is bound to become a major factor in the future of the continent' ('Africa: The Next Ten Years', June 1959, FO 371/137972, pp. 19–20). This optimistic assessment was in marked contrast to the view held two years earlier: 'United States investment in tropical Africa . . . will naturally depend on economic as well as political factors—the investment must look profitable as well as secure against expropriation. It seems unlikely that there would be any great rush of American capital' (R. W. Bailey to Adam Watson, Confidential, 20 March 1957, FO 371/125304). In 1952 the Co-lonial Secretary, Oliver Lyttelton, had written that it was important to lure American capital into Africa but not to hold out false hope: 'Lead the horse to the water', he admonished the Colo-nial Governors in Africa, 'but do not lead him up the garden path' (circular despatch by Lyttel-ton, 22 August 1952, CO 537/7844, *BDEEP—Conservative Government,* III, p. 168).

[201] For the stalemate in American policy over aid to Africa, March–December 1960, see *For-eign Relations of the United States, 1958–60,* XIV, pp. 93–171.

minorities in Kenya and the Central African Federation could be resolved:[202] 'If we fail to . . . demonstrate that we are not seeking an unqualified white supremacy [there], we may lose West Africa as well.'[203] African good will rested on the outcome of the racial struggle in East and Central Africa. Since 1921 a few thousand European settlers in Kenya, with the racial sympathy of British voters, had vetoed African advancement by threatening revolt.[204] After British troops had put down the Mau Mau rising in the early 1950s, Whitehall had more control over the situation. Even so, Downing Street was reluctant to impose black majority rule on British kith and kin: it might lose the next British election, and it would certainly alienate white Southern Rhodesia and the Union of South Africa from the Commonwealth. Yet the Africa Committee report of 1959 argued that unless the British could build 'a viable non-racial state' in Kenya, the entire African position would be jeopardized.[205]

Until late 1959, nonetheless, Macmillan and Lennox-Boyd were determined that British authority in East Africa would prevail for at least another decade. It seemed vital to secure the air bases at Nairobi and Entebbe and the sea base at Mombasa. Peter Ramsbotham, the Foreign Office liaison with the Chiefs of Staff objected: 'Are we to adopt a political policy in East Africa which is almost certain to poison our future relations with Africa as a whole because of a possible strategic need outside Africa?'[206] By May 1960 it was not practical politics for the Nigerians to give the British base rights in Kano. According to Iain Macleod, who had become Colonial Secretary in October 1959: 'They would be very glad to see their airfields used to help us in a struggle in which we supported Blacks against Whites but might not like them used if we supported Whites against Blacks.'[207] When Belgian rule collapsed in the Congo and the Soviets intervened, the trans-African reinforcement route to the Red Sea and the Gulf proved to be an illusion.[208] Amphibious forces on a scale that Britain could not afford would be needed when the East African bases were lost. The projected

[202] There were two dangers: the bedrock American anti-colonial mentality, now manifested 'by the negro vote', and the Afro-Asian bloc vote at the United Nations ('Africa: The Next Ten Years', June 1959, FO 371/137972, pp. 19, 29–30).

[203] Ibid., p. 23.

[204] For the background, see Ronald Robinson, 'The Colonial Office and the Settler in East-Central Africa, 1919–63', in E. Serra and C. Seton Watson, eds., *Italia E Inghilterra Nell'Eta Dell Imperialismo* (Milan, 1990), pp. 195–212.

[205] 'Africa: The Next Ten Years', June 1959, FO 371/137972, p. 16.

[206] Minute by Ramsbotham, 27 February 1959, FO 371/137951.

[207] Macleod to Macmillan, 9 May 1960, PREM 11/3047.

[208] Minutes by War Office and Air Ministry, 11 May 1960, PREM 11/3047.

informal empire in the Red Sea and the Gulf would eventually then depend largely for defence on the US Navy.

British Central Africa presented the gravest prospects of racial conflict. Since 1953 the British dependencies of Northern Rhodesia (Zambia) and Nyasaland (Malawi) had been subjected to a federal government dominated by the virtually independent European minority in Southern Rhodesia (Zimbabwe). A quarter of a million whites were consolidating their rule over six million blacks. Reacting to the federal imposition, the Africans organized national parties and worked for black majority rule. In response to the British abdication in West Africa, the Europeans demanded white independence for the whole federation before they were submerged under an 'uncivilized' African government. By mid-1959 the Colonial Office feared that 'the Federation may simply break up under the mounting pressure of the internal conflict'.[209] At worst, the white Southern Rhodesians would declare independence unilaterally with the support of the South Africans. At best the British hoped that the Federation would become a 'primarily multi-racial community' that could act as a 'shock-absorber' between South African apartheid and the emerging black states in the north. But if white domination were maintained by force, 'the whole of the Western position in black Africa, even in those territories (such as Nigeria) which are . . . well-disposed towards us, will be gravely shaken.'[210] Given the possible domino effects of pan-Africanism, questions of local racial collaboration had broadened into great matters of continental balance, involving the interdependent interests of Europe and the United States.

In January 1960 the Prime Minister set out on a tour of African capitals in search of African partners and British influence. Macmillan assured the new rulers in Lagos and Accra that the British were on the side of black Africa. In Cape Town and Salisbury (Harare), he warned the Europeans against resisting the 'Wind of Change' from the North.[211] The intransigent Premier of the Federation, Sir Roy Welensky, suspected that, if need be, Macmillan would break up the Feder-

---

[209] 'Africa: The Next Ten Years', FO 371/137972, p. 17.

[210] Ibid., p. 18.

[211] Significantly, Eisenhower had used this metaphor for the national aspiration of underdeveloped countries in his second Inaugural Address in January 1957 (Dwight D. Eisenhower, *The White House Years: Waging Peace, 1956–1961* [New York, 1965], p. 103). In the Suez crisis, Eisenhower and Dulles had feared that the British and the French might 'commit suicide by getting deeply involved . . . in an attempt to impose their rule by force on the Middle East and Africa' (memorandum of conversation with Dulles, 24 October 1956, *Foreign Relations of the United States, 1955–57*, XVI, p. 774). By 1959 this concern had become part of Macmillan's creed.

ation to appease pan-Africanism.[212] African appeasement was certainly Macmillan's overriding aim. From this standpoint, it seemed to him that 'the Africans are not the problem in Africa, it is the Europeans who are the problem.'[213] As the new Colonial Secretary, Iain Macleod, remarked, 'The pace of events in Somalia, Tanganyika, Uganda, and above all the Congo' was overtaking the timetables of mid-1959.[214] In an effort at saving the Central African Federation, Macleod ended Federal police rule in Nyasaland and Northern Rhodesia. Hastings Banda and Kenneth Kaunda, the African nationalist leaders, were released from prison.[215] But African hatred of the white Federation was such that, within four years, Federal government was to end in African rule in independent Malawi and Zambia. Macmillan wanted to avoid a British Algeria in Central Africa. But in 1965, Premier Ian Smith was to declare independence unilaterally in order to perpetuate white supremacy in Southern Rhodesia, with disastrous consequences for British relations with the Afro-Asian members of the Commonwealth.

Early in 1960, Macmillan and Macleod promoted a compromise intended to clear the way for independence in Kenya. If the settlers would accept African majority rule, the Africans would guarantee the Europeans' land and commercial stake in the country. Michael Blundell, the leader of the multiracial New Kenya Party, was chosen to persuade the settlers. Macmillan told him that 'if the multi-racial approach failed the likelihood was that the whites would be driven out of Africa and this could only be of profound detriment to the black.'[216] In March 'a tacit conspiracy'[217] between Macleod and Julius Nyerere's unrivalled TANU party led to Tanganyikan independence in 1961. Uganda followed a year later, after a federal compromise was reached between the dominant Baganda and the rest of the country.[218] After one year more, the suspected Mau Mau leader Jomo Kenyatta was

[212] Through a leak in the intelligence supplement to *The Economist,* Welensky had learned something of the contents of 'Africa: The Next Ten Years' and of Anglo-American discussions about it (record of Meeting with Welensky, 20 January 1960, PREM 11/3065).

[213] Minute by Macmillan, 28 December 1959, PREM 11/3075.

[214] Macleod to Macmillan, Secret, 8 February 1960, PREM 11/3030.

[215] Macleod had written to Macmillan: 'If we go on with this emergency which as you know rests on the shakiest of grounds, political conditions are bound to worsen' (27 January 1960, PREM 11/3030); see also 3 April 1960, PREM 11/3076).

[216] Note of Meeting, 17 February 1960, PREM 11/3031.

[217] John Darwin's phrase: see his account in *Britain and Decolonisation,* chap. 6. See also Cranford Pratt, *The Critical Phase in Tanzania, 1945–1968* (Cambridge, 1976); and John Iliffe, *A Modern History of Tanganyika* (Cambridge, 1979).

[218] See D. Anthony Low and R. Cranford Pratt, *Buganda and British Overrule* (London, 1960).

to rule in Nairobi.[219] The British were scrambling out of colonialism before the combination of anarchy, pan-Africanism, and pan-Arabism opened the door for Soviet penetration.[220] The collapse of Belgian rule and its consequences in the Congo lent speed to British heels.[221]

By the summer of 1960 the darkest scenario of Anglo-American planning was realized in the Congo (Zaire). Western relations with a score of newly or prospectively independent African governments were at stake in the crisis. If the Congo disintegrated, radical anti-Western Congolese factions would bid for Soviet support, which would have repercussions in western, eastern, and southern Africa. The supreme test of Anglo-American solidarity in Africa would be to hold the Congo together and keep it aligned with the West. After prohibiting political activity for decades, in 1959 the Belgian administration, faced with riots and revolts, offered self-government within four years. Diverse political parties emerged. The anti-colonial coalition that insisted on independence in June 1960 soon fell to pieces. Premier Patrice Lumumba's radical centralists quarrelled with President Kasavubu's federalists, who represented various ethnic and provincial societies. When the Force Publique dismissed its Belgian officers and mutinied, civil order broke down entirely. Belgian troops returned to protect the lives of the 100,000 Europeans. Shortly thereafter, Moise Tshombe declared the secession of Katanga province, taking with him the bulk of the country's revenue and mineral wealth.

The rump of the Congolese government in Leopoldville required foreign aid to restore its authority. Yet the divided ministers favoured different helpers. Justin Bomboko (Foreign Minister) welcomed the return of the Belgians and looked to Brussels for assistance.[222] Lu-

---

[219] See Gary Wasserman, *Politics of Decolonization* (Cambridge, 1976); B. Berman and J. Lonsdale, *Unhappy Valley: Conflict in Kenya and Africa* (London, 1992).

[220] See the Colonial Secretary's account of progress in Africa, Cyprus, Malta, and West Indies: minute by Macleod to Macmillan, 31 May 1960, PREM 11/3240.

[221] For the connection between the Congo and the independence of the British East African territories, see CO 822/1451, especially the minutes of a meeting of 16 November 1959 at the Colonial Office:

> There had been a great upward surge of nationalism in the Belgian Congo which had not been foreseen . . . On the whole these developments had not greatly influenced the thinking of the leading political people in Tanganyika because their minds had been directed to their own internal political problems. But if H.M.G. failed to produce an acceptable answer to those problems, then it could not be expected that Tanganyika would remain immune from the trend of events elsewhere in Africa.

[222] Herter to US Congo Embassy, 12 July 1960, *Foreign Relations of the United States, 1958–60*, XIV, p. 299. Madeleine G. Kalb, *The Congo Cables: The Cold War in Africa—From Eisenhower to Kennedy* (New York, 1982) remains essential. For the memoirs of the British Ambassador, see Ian

mumba excoriated both the Belgian return and the Katanga secession as parts of a Western capitalist plot for a colonial reoccupation. At first Lumumba fruitlessly solicited aid in Washington. The Americans took the initiative in assembling a UN peacekeeping force, chiefly from African states, and called upon the Belgians to withdraw. Afro-Asian opinion sided with Lumumba. Anti-imperial resentment against the Belgian invasion was sapping the good will that the West had cultivated so sedulously in black Africa. The Belgian forces merely withdrew to their bases, and the Belgians remained in Katanga. When the United States and the United Nations failed to respond to Lumumba's plea to throw the Belgians out immediately, he called for Soviet aid and appealed to the non-aligned powers for support. Brussels protested that the 'US was seeking [to] cut Belgium off and out from [the] Congo entirely, and injuring NATO in [the] bargain'.[223] General de Gaulle supported the Belgians. The activities of the UN officials in the Congo represented an Afro-Asian menace to the influence of the French over their neighbouring ex-colonial territories. King Leopold's Congo Free State had been set up in 1885 to exclude international rivalry from the heart of Africa; the disintegration of the state brought about the alliance of indigenous factions with rival powers and involved the whole of tropical Africa in one way or another in the Cold War.

Eisenhower and Macmillan agreed that Lumumba must be removed or 'fall into a river full of crocodiles' before he handed over the richest country in the region to Russian managers and technicians.[224] Covert plans to ensure his disappearance were laid.[225] Meanwhile there was another possibility that tested Macmillan's resolve to placate black nationalism in Central Africa at the expense of alienating European feeling. Katanga formed part of a multinational mineral empire (much of it British and American and controlled by interlocking directorships) that ran by rail to the Zambian copper belt and the Johannesburg gold mines. The company directors were influential in

Scott, *Tumbled House: The Congo at Independence* (London, 1969). For the United Nations and the Congo, see the magisterial and revealing account by Brian Urquhart, *Ralph Bunche: An American Life* (New York, 1993), chaps. 22–24.

[223] US Mission at United Nations to State Department, 14 July 1960, *Foreign Relations of the United States, 1958–60,* XIV, p. 305.

[224] Memorandum of conversation between the President and Lord Home, 19 September 1960, *Foreign Relations of the United States, 1958–60,* XIV, p. 495; memorandum from Board of National Estimates to Director CIA, 22 August 1960, ibid., pp. 435–42. The evidence on the British side is fragmentary, but see minute by H. F. T. Smith in the Foreign Office on 'ensuring Lumumba's removal from the scene by killing him' (minute of 28 September 1960, FO 371/146650).

[225] Director CIA to Station Officer, 26 August 1960, *Foreign Relations of the United States, 1958–60,* XIV, p. 443; cf. memorandum on National Security Council discussion, 18 August 1960, ibid., p. 421, note 1.

the right wing of the Conservative Party. Welensky saw the chance of allying Tshombe's Katanga with his Federation. Why not back the secession and leave the shell of the Congo to Lumumba and the Soviets? Washington also kept the possibility open as a last resort.[226]

For a time, the Americans vetoed the entry of UN forces into Katanga in an attempt to restore unity in NATO. In the end, Eisenhower and Secretary of State Christian Herter stood for the integrity of the Congo. Not to be tempted, Macmillan stood with them. Like his Foreign Secretary, Lord Home, he feared that the Congo would become another 'Korea'. According to Home:

> The great danger of the Congo situation has always been the danger of outside intervention & the creation of a situation very similar to that which occurred in the Spanish Civil War & Korea . . . the only hope of averting that was intervention by U.N. & our line has been to give complete support to Mr Hammarskjold.[227]

The Under-Secretary at the Foreign Office, Lord Lansdowne, who served as envoy to the Congo, wrote: 'I cannot emphasise too strongly how unrealistic . . . is the theory that an independent Katanga can exist along side a truncated Congo.'[228] The Congolese could not afford to lose Katanga. The Americans would not tolerate such a disastrous move in the Cold War; independent black Africa as a whole would be alienated.[229] The British, after much debate on the dilemma of the wealth of the copper belt versus the larger issue of the Congo and the Cold War, did not want to risk their chances of informal Empire in black Africa.[230] The Congo crisis showed that the Western allies could lose all of their interdependent interests if they were to act independently. Post-colonial sway in Africa would have to be maintained in concert as part of the Western coalition under American leadership.

The Congo held together. Zaire became, for better or worse, a vast client state of the United States. The Congolese type of breakdown, however, was soon matched in the Nigerian civil war and later with Sino-Soviet intervention in Portuguese Africa and Rhodesia. Latter-day Lumumbas abounded. Castro, as Macmillan remarked, became

[226] Memorandum on National Security Council meeting, 18 August 1960, *Foreign Relations of the United States, 1958–60*, XIV, p. 424.

[227] Minute by Home, *c.*14 September 1960, FO 371/146644.

[228] Memorandum by Lansdowne, 26 September 1961, PREM 11/3/91.

[229] National Estimates memorandum, 22 August 1960, *Foreign Relations of the United States, 1958–60*, XI, pp. 435–42.

[230] See Cabinet Conclusions 74 (62), 11 December 1962, CAB 128/36/2.

Eisenhower's and Kennedy's Nasser,[231] and Panama their Suez. Cuban forces were to fight in Angola. The Cold War fed upon internal instability, whether through colonial or ex-colonial proxies.

In conclusion, we have given an account of what officials believed was happening to the Empire. Their evidence has its limitations. Groping among their illusions for the reality at times of crisis, they did not always find it where they expected. For all that, where the estimates proved unrealistic, they were soon corrected. It is the corrections that offer the surest evidence of how the Empire was being made, unmade, and remade.

If the assessments of Attlee and his Treasury advisers in 1945 are credible, the collaborative basis of the pre-war Empire went down in the Second World War. The calculus of Bevin and Marshall suggests that the post-war system was regenerated through American wealth and power. Compared with this reinforcement, the loss of India in the imperial Great Game seems almost derisory.[232] With economic recovery and a brief respite from overseas-payments deficits, the system under Churchill and Eden regained a tentative dynamism of its own, until in 1956 Eisenhower jolted Eden into realizing that imperial dynamics were still reciprocal. Until the late 1950s, British prosperity relied on an imperial economy whose discriminatory integrity required toleration, dollar underwriting, and strategic protection by the Americans. In all these ways, the post-war Empire represented not a continuation, but a more formidable and a more vulnerable innovation. If the system were to succeed in securing and developing the sterling area, it had to operate as a project of the Anglo-American coalition. Such was the common prayer in Whitehall and Downing Street from Attlee to Macmillan.

By comparison, the liturgy in Washington dissented in faith and conformed in works. Imperialism was Beelzebub. Ancient antagonism and historic bonds underlay the arguments of exclusive national interest that ostensibly justified the imperial coalition. From ingrained prejudices, the Americans were reshaping the Empire in the revolutionary image of the thirteen colonies in 1776. The British were welcoming the Americans back into the British family of nations and, informally at least, into the Commonwealth, to which the shared tra-

---

[231] Macmillan to Eisenhower, 22 July 1960, *Foreign Relations of the United States, 1958–60*, VI, p. 1005, note 6. For a major reassessment, see 'The Future of Anglo-American Relations', 5 January 1960, FO 371/152112.

[232] Cf. D. A. Low, 'The Asian Mirror to Tropical Africa's Independence', in Gifford and Louis, *Transfer of Power in Africa*, p. 3.

dition of civil liberties had contributed. Anti-colonialism constrained both sides. For a time, however, America's Cold War aims ran broadly parallel with British imperial purposes, despite the rifts over Communist China and Suez. Committed heavily in the Far East and Europe, and anxious to keep its major allies, Washington depended on imperial proxies in other regions. For all the 'holier than thou' attitudes of the Americans, the British and French empires were propped up in the democratic cause of saving the global free market from communist annexation. The Americans looked forward in the long run to turning Europe's colonies and client regimes into national states and allies. So, in their own good time, did the British. One by one the imperial barriers tottered. Only then did Washington invest its power directly and exert effective influence in local management. Even then the Americans backed the British and French in their efforts at exchanging formal control for informal tutelage. None of the Western powers intended to 'decolonize' their dependencies, because they feared 'neo-colonization' by the communists. The relationship between Britain and the United States largely offset British decline in the international system. But at the local level, as Bevin foresaw in 1949, the more American aid that was required to compete with the Sino-Soviet bloc for nationalist good will, the more British imperial areas came under American influence.[233]

It follows that the dismantling of the visible Empire is not to be explained in monolithic terms of metropolitan infirmity. With American support or acquiescence, the British had resources enough to deal with local insurgencies. Coercion was often threatened; force was used in Cyprus, Aden, and Malaya with Washington's blessing, and without it in Kenya, Suez, and the Buraimi oasis. The Americans restored much of the British oil fief in Iran, and they refrained from interfering with those in Iraq and the Gulf Emirates. In British calculations, the necessity for heading off resistance and winning local collaboration governed the colonial retreat at different speeds in different territories. Just as local imperial authority had multiplied through divided indigenous alliances, so it dwindled in the face of popular national organization. The process had long historical roots. Pre-war power-sharing contracts expired in South Asia without significant superpower intervention, but in Palestine there was American interference. The collaborative arrangements in Egypt had come to an end before the Soviet irruption into the Middle East. Post-war colonial contracts were reaching their term in Ghana and Nigeria before the Russian aid

---

[233] For the geographic spread of American military and economic aid, see *U.S. Overseas Loans and Grants*.

offensive in tropical Africa. Until 1956 the presence of superpowers was by no means the imperative for imperial retreat. Soviet and at times American competition thereafter helped frustrate the conversion of British pre-war clientships into informal tutelage in most of the Middle East. In tropical Africa after 1958 the danger of Soviet sponsorship multiplied the weight of black nationalism and hastened the dismantling of white supremacy in the eastern and central regions. After Suez, the British concurred with the Americans at last in setting their sights on the post-colonial era. To assert colonial power became counter-productive when it came to bidding against the Soviets for nationalist alliances after independence. According to Anglo-American calculations, the strategic significance of pan-Arabism, pan-Africanism, and the non-aligned nations in the Cold War motivated the final dismantling of formal empire.

It should be a commonplace, therefore, that the post-war Empire was more than British and less than an imperium. As it survived, so it was nationalized and internationalized as part of the Anglo-American coalition. It operated more like a multinational company that after having taken over other peoples' countries, was hiving them off again, one by one, as associated concerns. In this, at least, the Empire after 1945 hewed to its original mid-Victorian design. Like the Americans, the Cobdenites in their day had worked for a revolutionary, worldwide commercial republic, held together by economic attraction rather than political subordination.[234] Long before Truman and Eisenhower, Palmerston and even Gladstone had discovered that the international economy required imperial protection. Combining the two principles, Victorian imperialism withdrew from countries as reliable economic links and national organizations emerged—while it extended into others in need of development. Such was the genius of British free-trade imperialism.[235]

The formal Empire contracted in the post-war years as it had once expanded, as a variable function of integrating countries into the international capitalist economy. Under Anglo-American auspices, the remains of the system were progressively nationalized and—in tropical Africa, even if not in India and the Middle East—informalized. Only now the American economy would drive the economic development of the system. The ex-colonial powers would share the dividends and the burdens. Most of the new states would have to cooperate with

---

[234] See Bernard Semmel, *The Rise of Free Trade Imperialism* (Cambridge, 1970).

[235] See John Gallagher and Ronald Robinson, 'The Imperialism of Free Trade', *Economic History Review*, 2nd series, 6 (1953), pp. 1–15. For a critique, see W. R. Louis, ed., *Imperialism: The Robinson and Gallagher Controversy* (New York, 1976).

one side or the other in the Cold War if they were to fulfil their national aspirations. Though some might choose aid from the Soviet bloc, prospects of development generally depended on the superior economic capacity of the West. After 1956 the British fell in with the American design for Western alliances with freer trade and free institutions. Such was the imperialism of decolonization.

The prescription for British informal sway worked well enough as long as sterling remained central to the economies of many underdeveloped countries. It was ill suited to the 1950s and 1960s, when the rouble and the dollar were contending for the economic and military contracts as well as the doctrinal loyalty of the Third World. Competition devalued, when it did not entirely debase, the currencies of informal sway. President Kennedy's 'New Frontier' began where Europe's imperial frontiers had ended. In competition with communist political economics, the Anglo-American alliance during the 1960s was dedicated to Third World development under the aegis of the United Nations and the World Bank. As things turned out, the new world order took shape under a good deal of old-fashioned imperial and financial intervention along with economic lures. Visible empires may be abolished; the thraldom of the international economy remains. There was no conspiracy to take over the Empire: American influence expanded by imperial default and nationalist invitation.

Journal of Imperial and Commonwealth History   1994

18

LIBYA: THE CREATION OF A CLIENT STATE

'W e are now reaching the culminating point in a three-years' political operation of great delicacy and complexity,' Sir William Strang wrote on the eve of the birth of the Libyan state. Strang was the Permanent Under-Secretary at the Foreign Office and one of the architects of Libyan independence. This was a moment of uneasy jubilation: 'We cannot even now say that nothing will go wrong: but we have good hopes. We have kept faith with the Amir, and he with us.'[1] He made that comment when the Amir, Sayyid Muhammad Idris, was about to assume leadership as King of the first African state to emerge free from formal colonial rule in the post-war period. On 24 December 1951, Libya became one of the five independent states of Africa, thus achieving the same status as Egypt, Ethiopia, Liberia, and South Africa.

The Libyan state was a British creation within the context of Anglo-American collaboration and United Nations sponsorship. Its formation reveals the classic themes of British imperialism, recast in a post-war mould: the search for indigenous support, in this case with the Senusi of Cyrenaica; the quest for minimal yet necessary funds for the military occupation and administration during a period of prolonged British economic crisis; and the attempt to gain the cooperation of the United States and the United Nations to secure British strategic rights. This, then, is a study of British efforts to harness a nationalist movement and come to terms with the economic and strategic dilemmas facing the post-war Labour Government as well as to resolve the perplexities of post-war anti-colonialism.

The paramount goal was to secure Cyrenaica, the eastern province of Libya, as a strategic area that might serve as a substitute for the base at Suez. In the post-war period, as in the days of the Scramble for Africa three-quarters of a century earlier, Egypt was the driveshaft in a vast geopolitical machine. When the British began to recognize that it might be desirable, and perhaps necessary, to terminate the occupation of the Canal Zone, Cyrenaica emerged as the most suitable alternative.[2] In winning this strategic position, the British competed in

---

[1] Minute by Strang, 8 December 1951, FO 371/90350. The principal historical studies of Libya are Majid Khadduri, *Modern Libya: A Study in Political Development* (Baltimore, 1963); John Wright, *Libya* (New York, 1969); and Wright, *Libya: A Modern History* (Baltimore, 1982). See also esp. Lisa Anderson, *The State and Social Transformation in Tunisia and Libya* (Princeton, 1986), chap. 12.

[2] An opposing school of thought had held that British power was shifting from the Mediterranean to the Indian Ocean and that Kenya rather than Cyrenaica should become the principal strategic base in the Eastern Hemisphere. The champion of this point of view was Sir Philip

a cockpit of international rivalry for supremacy in the eastern Mediterranean. The solution had to be acceptable to Britain's European neighbours, France and Italy, as well as the United States. At a critical time in 1949, the British rallied to an American plan for 'independence' that would simultaneously satisfy the traditional aim of American anti-colonialism and check the danger of Soviet expansionism. Libyan independence proved to be satisfactory to the parsimonious and dyspeptic British Treasury as well as the sceptical British public because the subsidy to the Libyan government (eventually £2.75 million a year in budgetary aid and an annual grant of £1 million for development) would be modest in comparison with expenditures elsewhere, and in any case a small price to pay for strategic security in the eastern Mediterranean.

Not least, the solution was agreeable to Idris, the leader of the Senusi, but in making these arrangements, the British found themselves confronted with problems of bolstering a weak monarch and devising a formula for both provincial and national stability; they were drawn ever deeper into internal as well as international complications. The British initiative in implementing the American scheme of Libyan independence would not have been possible without the active collaboration of the agent of the United Nations, Adrian Pelt.[3] Yet it would appear in historical reappraisal that Libyan independence was less of a UN or US makeshift operation and more of a sustained British effort. 'It is still difficult to convince the French, Americans and Italians that we do not in some mysterious way still administer Libya,' the first British Ambassador, Sir Alec Kirkbride, wrote some months after the actual date of independence.[4]

In Libya as much as in any other territory under British sway, the viability of the regime after 1945 can be assessed in relation to the worldwide decline of the British Empire, the ascendancy of the Labour Party in domestic politics, and the advent of the nationalist movements in Asia and the rest of Africa.[5] Regarding Libya after the end of the Second World War, the British domestic part of the equation was never absent, because of the sentiment within the Labour Government

---

Mitchell, Governor of Kenya. He wrote bitterly in 1948 after the Cyrenaican strategy had been endorsed by the Defence Committee of the Cabinet: 'I suppose that the nation that built Singapore could hardly be expected to refrain from building another one in Cyrenaica' (Mitchell to Poynton, 29 June 1948, CO 537/3514).

[3] See his monumental account, *Libyan Independence and the United Nations: A Case of Planned Decolonization* (New Haven, 1970).

[4] Kirkbride to Bowker, 17 May 1952, FO 371/97269.

[5] W. R. Louis and Prosser Gifford, eds., *The Transfer of Power in Africa* (New Haven and London, 1982), p. 53.

that it might be best to cut losses, withdraw from the Mediterranean, and concentrate on developing tropical Africa, where there were fewer dangers of international interference and less-volatile problems of nationalism. This tendency to retrench, however, was kept in check by those who believed that Britain's position as a 'world power' could be upheld. This was notably true of Ernest Bevin, the Foreign Secretary during the period 1945–51. Apart from the question of the transfer of power in India, Bevin was the dominant figure in Imperial as well as foreign affairs. His policy in Libya was systematically to strengthen the relationship with the Senusi and to adjust British policy to changing international circumstances so that the British position in Cyrenaica would be secured, whether by backing Cyrenaica as a trusteeship territory or by promoting independence for Libya as a whole.

It is important to bear in mind the debate about the significance of Libya, which had taken place within the British government intermittently since the end of the war. 'What do we mainly want?' asked Ivor Thomas, the Parliamentary Under-Secretary for Colonies in 1947. 'Is it strategic rights in Cyrenaica? Or the exclusion of Russian influence from Africa? Or the friendship of the Arabs of Tripolitania and Cyrenaica? Or the restoration of good Anglo-Italian relations? Or the maintenance of the Entente Cordiale with France?'[6] Those questions could not be answered without taking into account a Cold War issue that impinged on the Libyan controversy. The head of the East African Department of the Colonial Office, Andrew Cohen, realistically summed it up when he acknowledged that African questions had to be kept subordinate to grand strategy because Italy had to be kept 'on the right side of the iron curtain.'[7] The Italian demand for colonial restitution led Bevin to endorse a proposal (known as the Bevin-Sforza Plan) that would have partitioned Libya into its three constituent parts of Tripolitania, the Fezzan (that is, the south-western province under French occupation), and Cyrenaica. The three provinces would have been administered as Italian, French, and British trusteeship territories respectively. This plan had the virtue of securing the strategic rights in Cyrenaica at little expense (assuming that the British would have managed to convert Cyrenaica into a 'strategic trust' territory comparable to the American islands in the Pacific), but it was narrowly defeated (by only one vote) in the General Assembly of the United Nations in May 1949 as smacking of old-fashioned Western imperialism. Bevin now reversed course, and he could do so having proved that he

---

[6] Minute by Thomas, 24 July 1947, CO 537/2087.

[7] Comment by Cohen in an interdepartmental meeting of 24 January 1947, minute in CO 537/2083.

had at least tried to win concessions for the European Allies. 'We are coming to the conclusion', he wrote in July 1949, 'that the solution for Libya must be independence.'[8] This was an adroit, though machiavellian, affirmation of the American solution. 'Independence' was the principal issue, indeed the only one, on which all parties directly concerned could agree.

This exercise in British state building was forged against the realities of Libyan geography and demography. Libya, the fourth-largest state in Africa, is two and a half times the size of Texas, but it is 95 per cent desert. In 1945 it possessed a population of 880,000, of which about 68 per cent was Muslim and about 5 per cent Italian. During the war, the Italians had been driven out of Cyrenaica, and the Italian community of some 40,000 was now concentrated in Tripolitania. There was a substantial Jewish population, about 30,000. J. S. Bennett of the Colonial Office once made a penetrating observation that established the wider significance of the white settler community and the legacy of Italian colonization. His comment connected the Libyan question with the Palestine controversy. He wrote in 1946:

> I believe it is now a choice between treating the Arab world as a whole (in which case we can look for good relations with it), or having a series of 'bridgeheads' along the Mediterranean coast into a hostile Arab interior. You can't play both policies at once. The French and the Zionists (and previously the Italians) frankly go for the 'bridgehead' policy. I don't believe that, with our wide Middle Eastern interests, we can afford to.[9]

Until 1949, Bevin's Libyan goals, as he himself acknowledged, were out of line with his general 'pro-Arab' policy. After the defeat of the Bevin-Sforza Plan (which had been denounced throughout the world as blatant support for the re-establishment of an Italian colonial regime), Bevin put British policy back 'on the rails' (his own phrase) towards the creation of an Arab state.[10]

Let there be no mistake that the dominant motive was the estab-

---

[8] Bevin to Franks, No. 7222, Secret, 20 July 1949, PREM 8/921.

[9] Bennett to J. S. Majoribanks, 15 June 1946, FO 371/57181.

[10] Bevin made that revealing remark after the defeat of the Communists in the Italian elections of April 1948 (minute by Bevin, c.7 April 1948, FO 371/69331). During this crucial period in European as well as post-war African history, he was clearly aware of the tension in his policy of appeasing the Italians and attempting not to alienate the Arabs. In other words, he was playing the game both ways; only after the dramatic defeat in the United Nations of the Bevin-Sforza Plan did he shift decisively towards the Arab solution. What is remarkable is the dogged persistence with which he moved towards his goal in Cyrenaica.

lishing of a strategic base in Cyrenaica. Bevin and the members of the
Labour Government foresaw eviction from Egypt. To secure Cyrenaica, they were prepared to pay a high price, perhaps by bartering the
other former Italian colonies of Eritrea and Somaliland, which were
also under British military occupation, perhaps by accommodating the
Italians and the French as well as the Americans, or perhaps by constructing a vast national edifice that would be based on Cyrenaica and
would extend over Tripolitania and the Fezzan. All of those possibilities were studied by the Labour empire builders with an exuberant
calculation worthy of their Victorian predecessors. It was the last that
proved to be the most attractive, for two reasons that went beyond the
need to comply with the resolutions of the United Nations. During the
war, the Americans, at considerable expense—the figure usually cited
is $100 million—had constructed an air base at Mallaha (Okba bin
Nafi, east of Tripoli), which they wished to revive and expand into a
major installation; it eventually became known as Wheelus Field. The
money paid to the Libyans for base rights and rent would go a long
way towards subsidizing a Libyan state. The other reason why a Libyan
polity proved to be feasible was because of an advantageous link between the British and the Senusi, which developed into an effective
political alliance. Here was a state that was to be subsidized largely by
the Americans, held together by the Senusi, and controlled indirectly
by the British.

Though Cyrenaican nationalism did not command loyalty in Tripolitania before the Second World War, after 1945 it generated an appeal that extended throughout all of Libya. Was this because of the dynamism of the Senusi reformist movement and the influence of Sayyid
Idris, or the fear of the possible return of the Italians? There was a remarkable scholarly contribution to the contemporary understanding
of these problems. In 1949 the anthropologist E. E. Evans-Pritchard
published *The Sanusi of Cyrenaica,* an important book that appeared at
exactly the time British officials were pondering the meaning of Sufi
mysticism and the *Ikhwan*. What was the significance of the Senusi order for the development of Middle Eastern or African nationalism?

Sir William Strang welcomed Evans-Pritchard's book as 'excellent'. It helped clarify the nature of Senusi society and the struggle of
the Senusis against the Italians. In the words of Michael Brett, who
has translated the anthropological essence into the idiom of African
history:

> The warfare of the Cyrenaicans against the Italians . . . appears [to
> be] the perfect example of the ability of a stateless society, that of

the beduin, to generate the rudiments of a state in the face of external attack, and by the same token, of a primary resistance to colonial
penetration which became a movement for independence.[11]

Nationalism in Libya thus had deep roots in the colonial era rather
than merely in the shallow subsoil of post-war power politics. The
question, however, was whether Cyrenaican nationalism could unite
all of Libya. According to Evans-Pritchard, there might be insuperable
geographical as well as other obstacles:

> The people of Cyrenaica are linked to the classical Arab world of
> the east, to Egypt and the Jazirat al-Arab (Arabia, Palestine, Iraq and
> Syria) rather than to the Maghrib . . . The desert comes down to the
> sea at the Gulf of Sirte and separates Cyrenaica from Tripolitania and
> these two countries have always gone each its own way.[12]

When Cyrenaica was linked to Greece and Egypt, Tripolitania had
belonged to Phoenician Carthage: 'Cyrenaica went with Byzantium,
Tripolitania with Rome.' When the Senusi order came to power in
Cyrenaica, the Tripolitanians had responded with animosity. The inference to be drawn from Evans-Pritchard's work was that the geographical, cultural, and religious differences between Cyrenaica and
Tripolitania would prove too great to bridge. Sir William Strang preferred to regard this interpretation as 'not decisive'.[13]

The chances of unifying Libya would depend in large part on the
ability, drive, and charisma of the Senusi leader. Here there was cause
for scepticism. Evans-Pritchard wrote of Idris:

> Nurtured, as were all the Sanusi family, in piety and learning in oasis
> retreats and accustomed to a refined and sedentary life, he has never
> been a man of action . . . That he is vacillating and evasive cannot be
> denied, and though these characteristics may sometimes have been
> a wise response of the weak negotiating with the strong . . . they seem
> to be weaknesses to which he is temperamentally prone and to have
> become an aversion to directness in either thought or action.[14]

Unfortunately for the British, Evans-Pritchard's description appeared
to be all too true. It strengthened the impression of the Foreign Office
that Idris was hardly a hearty enough nationalist to manage his own

---

[11] Michael Brett, 'The U.N. and Libya', *Journal of African History*, 13, 1 (1972), pp. 168–70.
[12] E. E. Evans-Pritchard, *The Sanusi of Cyrenaica* (Oxford, 1949), pp. 46–48.
[13] Minute by Strang, 22 July 1947, FO 371/73892.
[14] Evans-Pritchard, *Sanusi*, p. 269.

affairs, still less to extend his sway over all of Libya. According to a Foreign Office assessment:

> While he has the interest of his people very much at heart, he has . . . no very strong personal ambition to rule them . . . The fact that the small circle surrounding him is psychologically as much out of contact as he is himself physically with the local inhabitants means that more often than not the advice he receives is unsound. Having taken advice, however, he can be obstinate in refusing to go back on any decision reached.[15]

This appraisal also mentioned Idris's 'innate indolence', his temptation 'to throw his hand in and retire', and his 'taste for a quiet life'.

Ernest Bevin had no use for 'tame Arabs'. Here was one who did not appear to have the backbone or the fire in his belly necessary to make the British venture in Libya a success. Nationalist leaders were usually made of sterner stuff. In making their plans regarding Idris, the British had to rely on their own resourcefulness and resign themselves philosophically to a situation that in other circumstances might have been much worse. '[I]f Amirs and Princes were archangels', wrote George Clutton, the head of the African Department of the Foreign Office, 'there would be little place in this world for either foreign servants or pro-Consuls.' With British inspiration, Idris might prove to be a satisfactory leader after all: 'The Amir is far from being a perfect character, but I doubt very much whether he is much more imperfect than many Eastern rulers who, under British guidance, have ended their days as respected benefactors of their people.'[16]

It would perhaps satisfy the wish to see a sense of purpose in history to be able to regard Libyan independence as the triumph of a nationalist leader, as part of a march towards colonial freedom, or at least as the logical outcome of planned decolonization. The broader vision was there, but as will be seen, it was negative, focusing on the possible reaction of the Arab states and new members of the Commonwealth, who might regard the Libyan experiment as a continuation of the system of unequal treaties, or, as it was later known, the dependency relationship. There was no intention of setting a precedent for other African dependencies. Libya was merely a case where informal methods were preferable to formal. The aim throughout was to maintain Britain's position as a world power. Specifically, the transfer of power in Libya was intended to sustain British influence through King Idris

[15] Minute by I. W. Bell of the African Department of the FO, 20 December 1948, FO 371/73829.
[16] Minute by Clutton, 20 December 1948, FO 371/73829.

and to establish a state that would provide both Britain and the United States with the right to station land and air forces on Libyan soil. The case of Libya thus forms part of the grand strategy of disengagement from Egypt. And it also indicates constant improvisation in response to rapidly changing combinations of local, metropolitan, and international pressures.

1949: Resolution of the International Issue

In February 1949, Ernest Bevin asked for weekly reports 'on all matters affecting Cyrenaica'.[17] As if anticipating rapidly developing and disagreeable events, he did not wish to be caught off guard either by the French or the Italians, still less by the Americans, or by what he referred to as the 'Arab-Moslem-Asiatic bloc'.[18] Until the opening of the British archives, it was difficult to ascertain the extent of Bevin's influence and the counterweight of the permanent officials. It is now clear that his grasp of policy was of the calibre of the great Lord Salisbury's during the original partition of Africa. Bevin played the same game with relatively fewer resources. It was he, not the permanent officials or even the other members of the Cabinet, who called the shots in this new Scramble for influence, even if not for territory. In all significant questions concerning the future of the Italian colonies, Bevin made sure that he had the concurrence of the Defence Committee and, when necessary, the Cabinet. And he regarded the matter as so important that he delegated authority only to trusted lieutenants.

Hector McNeil, the Minister of State, was one of them. McNeil played a vital part in trying to put Bevin's ideas, in McNeil's own phrase, into the 'conceited skull' of the Italian Foreign Minister, Count Sforza, and by serving as Bevin's personal emissary at the UN discussions on the subject.[19] McNeil believed that the key to British success would lie in getting an American commitment in Tripolitania, either by persuading the Americans to take on trusteeship responsibility (a misguided hope) or by convincing them of the desirability of stationing troops there. 'Palestine is no parallel,' he wrote about the possibility of Anglo-American collaboration.[20] In telling words, he once summed up his impression of the Libyan question and the tactics to be used with the Americans: 'Our need is great: our case is not good. We must therefore be as naive as possible.'[21]

[17] See Minute by Clutton, 7 February 1949, FO 371/73829.
[18] Bevin to Franks, 20 July 1949, PREM 8/921.
[19] See Minute by McNeil, 6 August 1949, FO 371/73885.
[20] Minute by McNeil, 22 February 1949, FO 371/73856.
[21] Minute by McNeil, 28 July 1949, FO 371/73838.

On Bevin's instructions, the Permanent Under-Secretary himself kept abreast of the Libyan question and attempted to weave the complex strands into a coherent pattern. During a visit to the Middle East in the spring of 1949, Strang paid a call on Idris in Benghazi. He made it clear that the British people were grateful for the support of the Senusi during the war. There were utterances about the 'happy and mutually beneficial relationship'. Nevertheless, Strang's task was not an easy one. He had to explain to Idris why the British had allied themselves with the Italians and the French in what amounted to a repartition under the guise of trusteeship—the Bevin-Sforza agreement. 'It had however failed; thank God!' Idris told Strang.[22] And a disastrous confrontation with the British military administration had been only narrowly averted (just a week before Strang's visit). In mid-May 1949 a crowd of three hundred had assembled in front of the British Military Administration headquarters in Tripoli, carrying banners and shouting anti-Italian slogans. Shots were fired, and were returned by the police. Each day the crowds grew, up to a strength of eight thousand by the end of the week, and had to be dispersed with tear gas and baton charges.[23] These local demonstrations were critical in the defeat (as will be recalled, by only one vote) of the Bevin-Sforza Plan at the United Nations. Here was a clear case of misjudging the extent of local anti-Italian sentiment and miscalculating the politics at the United Nations. The lesson was not lost on Strang, McNeil, or Bevin. After the riots of May 1949, Bevin frequently re-emphasized a premise of his Libyan policy, which seemed to be all the more important after the disturbances: no solution would be imposed by force. In Bevin's own celebrated phrase, the Libyan problem would not be resolved by 'British Bayonets'.

Until the riots in Tripoli and the setback at the United Nations, Bevin had planned on keeping on good terms not only with the Italians in Tripolitania but also with the French, by backing their claim in the Fezzan. He now held that the Italians would have to be content with Somalia. The French were another matter. Though he regarded French cooperation as 'very much less important' than American, he believed that any settlement that adversely affected the French position in North Africa might eventually have repercussions in British Africa.[24] It was a British axiom not to weaken the French Empire. According to the Chiefs of Staff in an appreciation written in 1947, '[I]t

[22] Memorandum by Strang, 24 May 1949, FO 371/73835.

[23] For the British military administration's account of the riots, see the report of 18 May 1949, FO 371/73860.

[24] See minute by Strang, 1 April 1949, PREM 8/921.

is essential that we hold securely the North coast of Africa.' Therefore it was mandatory, in Bevin's own words, that 'Tunisia, Algeria and
French Morocco should remain under French control'. Whatever the
'shortcomings and mistakes of French colonial policy' might be with
regard to the nationalist aspirations, the British would not intervene.
The temptation to lecture the French, still less to meddle, would be
resisted. 'I cannot see why we should interfere with the French', Bevin
had noted in 1947, by 'fishing in troubled waters.'[25] These 'troubled
waters' by 1949, however, included the oases of the Fezzan. The strategic points of Ghat and Ghadames were essential for French intercep-
tion of the arms flowing into Algeria.

Events in the spring of 1949 compelled the British to reassess the
French position in North Africa. The appraisal of nationalism in Tunisia, Algeria, and Morocco caused some British officials to reflect that
they had much more in common with the French than with the Americans. 'What is at stake', observed Ivo Mallet of the African Department
of the Foreign Office, 'is not merely the suddenly inflamed ambitions
of a few thousand Arabs, but the security of North Africa and our relations with France and Italy.'[26] The agitated tone of Mallet's minute
arose from the American response to the disturbances in Libya and
the debacle at the United Nations. The Americans now believed, as
a matter of urgency, that independence for all of Libya would be the
best solution and that if the French could be coerced into making
plans for decolonization as well, then so much the better. Thus the
Libyan problem had wide implications. Mallet wrote about an 'independent' Libya:

> [T]he creation of half-baked Arab states which have no traditions
> and no opportunities of remaining viable is hardly calculated to fur-
> ther our policy of increasing tranquillity and stability in North Africa.
> The catchword 'independence', regardless of the conditions in the
> country in question . . . is not one by which the State Department
> should allow itself to be led astray . . .
>
> [W]hen it comes to bringing pressure on the French to institute mea-
> sures towards independence in their North African territories, the
> proposal becomes sheer madness . . . I can say of Morocco with com-
> plete conviction that if it was given independence in the near future
> the result would be immediate chaos. Moroccan nationalism is not a
> real force.[27]

[25] These memoranda and minutes are summarized and quoted in a memorandum by I. Mallet, 18 July 1949, FO 371/73892.

[26] Minute by Mallet, 31 May 1949, FO 371/73880.

[27] Minute by Mallet, 14 July 1949, FO 371/73892.

'Dangerous' was the word Mallet used to sum up American ideas about North African 'independence'.

The reassertion of the American anti-colonial attitude at this time was a direct response to the riots in Tripoli and the remorse of guilt by association with the British at the United Nations. By giving reluctant support to the British plan for Italian, French, and British trusteeship administrations, the Americans had lost, in the judgement of the State Department official responsible for Libyan affairs, 'a large amount of the reserve of good will which we enjoy among the Asiatics as the result of our treatment of the Philippines'.[28] It appeared to the British that the same naive panacea for the ills of the colonial world of the wartime years had now resurfaced with a vengeance. For now the Americans made no secret that independence, beginning in Libya, would eventually sweep through all of north-western Africa. In the American view, these developments would be 'inevitable'. 'The Americans will welcome and press for early independence in Libya', wrote George Clutton, 'not merely as the only practicable solution, but also because they realise its effects on the French position in Tunisia, Algeria and Morocco. The State Department have made no effort to conceal this from us.'[29]

Some of Bevin's most influential advisers attempted to persuade him to hold out against the Americans. For example, Gladwyn Jebb at this time was Deputy Under-Secretary and especially concerned with Western European and UN affairs. He wrote:

> As for 'independence' for Libya being 'inevitable' within the next year or two, I should have thought that was really carrying defeatist determinism too far! After all the string of rather backward Arab and Berber communities along the fringe of the Mediterranean are strongly penetrated by Latin Colonists who do, on the whole, represent the civilising influence; and to *encourage* them along the road towards 'independence' in the name of some obscure national morality or alternatively, out of a romantic love for Arab Sheikhs seems to me to be the height of folly.[30]

The State Department, to Jebb's exasperation, continued to press the idea of Libyan independence and the hope that pressure on the

[28] See memorandum by Joseph Palmer, Secret, 27 May 1949, records of the U.S. State Department (National Archives), 865.014/5–2749, Box 770, printed in *Foreign Relations of the United States, 1949*, IV, pp. 542–43. The developments in American policy are much better known than those in the British, and can easily be traced in the *Foreign Relations* series.

[29] Minute by Clutton, 31 May 1949, FO 371/73880.

[30] Minute by Jebb, 2 June 1949, FO 371/73880.

French might force them to move in the same direction in Tunisia, Morocco, and even Algeria. Jebb returned to the charge in protest against an independent Libya that might be no better than another Burma:

> I am myself rather alarmed by the prospect of a real row with the French . . . I simply don't believe that an 'independent Libya' will be likely to be anything much better than a new Burma on a smaller scale or that undue fostering of 'independence' in the rest of North Africa would produce anything but chaos.[31]

Jebb's minute was discussed by Strang, McNeil, and Bevin. Though it helped to precipitate Bevin's decision, it was not in the direction Jebb desired.

Bevin held to his former view that there could be no question of bringing pressure to bear on French colonial policy, though he had no doubt that 'we are in for trouble with the French'. He was 'not disposed to resist' a UN resolution that would provide for Libyan independence 'by about 1953'.[32] This was a turning point. It is clear in retrospect that Bevin's acquiescence in July 1949 was one of the decisive moments in actually bringing about the birth of the Libyan state. As Sir William Strang noted later, it was obvious, at least to the Foreign Office, that Libya would need 'to be the client of some Power'.[33] The task now was to make sure that Libya would become a British client state.

The other chronological landmark for Libya in 1949 was the UN resolution on 21 November. It must not be assumed that Bevin's path towards it was clear and straight. He was sceptical, in this case, about the Americans' reliability as well as their motives, and neither he nor anyone else had devised a satisfactory method of dealing with the anticolonialism of the United Nations. The Americans seemed 'to be anxious to land us with responsibilities for the defence of the whole of Libya', Bevin is recorded as saying in words that deserve to be emphasized, '*and in fact to use us as their mercenaries to ensure their own strategic requirements.*' Bevin thus had no illusions about what he believed to be the reality of American independence proposals. As for the UN side of the question, 'Egypt and India seem to be concerned to get us out of Libya, and with this object in view the Egyptians are apparently quite ready to gang up with the Italians.'[34] Until a few days before the

[31] Minute by Jebb, 13 July 1949, FO 371/73892.
[32] As recorded in minute by Strang, 14 July 1949, FO 371/73892.
[33] Minute by Strang, 24 November 1949, FO 371/73840.
[34] Minute by Barclay, 24 October 1949, FO 371/73890.

United Nations voted on the resolution, Bevin kept an open mind whether it might not be better to try to sabotage it in the hope of being able to work out a treaty unilaterally with Sayyid Idris. Increasingly, it became a choice of the lesser of evils: going along with the United Nations and having to accept conditions for Libyan independence dictated by the anti-colonial bloc, or going it alone in defiance of both the United Nations and the United States. Ultimately the UN scheme stood the test of British self-interest, though not before it had survived the assault by the Chiefs of Staff.

Less than two weeks before the Libyan issue came to a vote in the General Assembly, the Chiefs of Staff felt it their duty to emphasize the 'strategic implications of an independent and united Libya'. This was a major assessment, in which they viewed Libya as an essential part of the Middle Eastern 'pillar of British strategy'. The fate of Libya would shortly be decided at the United Nations (the reason for the timing was the deadline imposed by the failure by the Council of Foreign Ministers to resolve the issue of the Italian colonies). The Chiefs of Staff believed that the resolution of this momentous issue had nothing to do with the well-being of the inhabitants or the peace of the world, except negatively. The enemies of the British Commonwealth and Empire at the United Nations aimed, indirectly at least, at the altering of the political and strategic balance of power in North Africa and the Mediterranean. The Chiefs of Staff therefore wished to make it unequivocally clear how Britain's position as a 'world power' might be affected:

> Today, we are still a world power, shouldering many and heavy responsibilities. We believe the privileged position that we, in contrast to the other European nations, enjoy with the United States and the attention which she now pays to our strategic and other opinions, and to our requirements, is directly due to our hold on the Middle East and all that this involves.

> If we surrendered that hold and the responsibilities which it entails, we would automatically surrender our position as a world power, with the inevitable strategic and economic consequences. We should join the ranks of the other European powers and be treated as such by the United States.[35]

It would be up to the British to hold the Middle East in the event of war with the Soviet Union. The United States would continue to respect

---

[35] Chiefs of Staff, 'Strategic Implications of an Independent and United Libya', COS (49) 381, 10 November 1949, DEFE 5/18.

Britain as a 'world power' only as long as the British could defend the
Middle East alone, at least initially: '[W]e must find a way of holding
the Middle East at the beginning of a war with our own resources and
of developing offensive action against Russia from that area. We believe this can be done. It must be done.'

It could be done only, the Chiefs of Staff held, by maintaining forces
in the Canal Zone at Suez at the level of 9,500 fighting troops (with additional auxiliaries) and a balance of 11,000 troops in Cyrenaica. This
was a time when the British military authorities believed that the Canal
Zone negotiations with the Egyptians could still be resolved by reducing numbers rather than by evacuating. In any case there would have
to be a redistribution of troops in Cyprus, Malta, the Sudan, and above
all in Cyrenaica.

> Lying adjacent to Egypt, forces stationed in Cyrenaica can most easily
> co-ordinate their higher training with our garrison in the Canal Area
> or, in an emergency, be moved quickly into the Delta either overland
> or by a short sea route. The climate is good and the country provides
> better training areas for the type of warfare we anticipate than else-
> where in the theatre.[36]

Cyrenaica was thus an area of critical military significance. 'We are
counting on a treaty with Amir Idris to retain these facilities for us when
Cyrenaica attains her independence,' the Chiefs of Staff reiterated.

Ernest Bevin essentially accepted the logic of the Chiefs of Staff,
though not all of their conclusions. His own ideas had been developing in the same direction since the end of the war. 'The first priority
must be the accommodation of our forces in Egypt,' i.e. in the Canal
Zone, he stated in November 1949. 'The second priority should be
Cyrenaica. Tobruk should be the base and our military and Air Force
establishments should be economically built.'[37] Bevin's thoughts thus
continued to reveal not only his optimism about the Canal Zone but
also the way in which the Libyan question could be reduced, as far
as the British were concerned, to a strategic and military issue. If the
worst came to the worst, the Suez base could be evacuated and Cyrenaica would become Britain's principal base in the Middle East. Bevin's principal difference with the Chiefs of Staff was that he believed
the goal could best be achieved in cooperation with the United Nations, even though his own advisers as well as the military authorities

---

[36] 'Strategic Implications of an Independent and United Libya', 10 November 1949,
DEFE 5/18.

[37] As recorded in a minute by Strang, 26 November 1949, FO 371/73895.

found the UN conditions highly disagreeable.[38] He characteristically attempted to turn adverse circumstances to British advantage. In late 1949, Bevin decisively implemented British policy in Libya under the umbrella of the United Nations.

On 21 November, the British voted in favour of the United Nations resolution, which included:

1. That Libya, comprising Cyrenaica, Tripolitania and the Fezzan, shall be constituted an independent and sovereign State;
2. That this independence shall become effective as soon as possible and in any case not later than 1 January 1952.

The resolution passed with a vote of forty-nine to none, with nine abstentions. The abstentions included the Soviet Union, which denounced the British and French 'puppet governments'. France also abstained, maintaining that the solution departed from 'common sense'. 'It was the French who were likely to be our friends in this matter,' Bevin noted afterwards.[39] It could be argued that the Russians, the French, and the British each in their own way held realistic attitudes. With the perspective of some thirty-five years and the benefit of archival sources, it is the Egyptian outlook, among others, that appears to have struck a note of false optimism: '[M]illions of people in Africa . . . looked to the United Nations for justice and liberty.'[40]

1950–51: Idris, the United Nations, and the United States

'I think he will make a good King of Libya,' a member of the British Residency at Benghazi, Malcolm Walker, wrote of Sayyid Idris in an assessment that took full measure of the Amir's diffident character. The British on the whole were willing to give Idris the benefit of the doubt (though as will be seen, severe criticism was not lacking) and believed that he might develop into an effective political leader. In Walker's judgement, based on extensive Middle Eastern experience:

[38] For these discussions, see minutes in FO 371/73893. Sir Roger Makins (Deputy Under-Secretary) commented: 'I am now convinced that if the Resolution goes through . . . we shall not get a treaty with Cyrenaica alone, and that the choice will lie between a treaty with the whole of Libya or no treaty at all' (minute of 20 October 1949). Bevin noted, 'I agree.'

[39] See minute by Strang, 26 November 1949, FO 371/73895. For the important memorandum drawn up for the Defence Committee of the Cabinet in the aftermath of the UN resolution, see 'Future Developments in Libya', DO (49) 85, 19 December 1949, CAB 131/7.

[40] Quoted in Pelt, *Libyan Independence,* p. 106.

> He will always be a bit remote and, by comparison with Ibn Saud or
> King Abdullah, perhaps rather inaccessible . . . But I am not sure that
> this matters. His influence comes after all primarily from his reli-
> gious position as Head of the Senussi Sect and it is not unreasonable
> that a religious leader should be rarely seen by his followers.

Despite his aloofness, his influence extended throughout Libya, into
Tripolitania as well as in the Fezzan, and most Libyans agreed that he
was the only figure who might lead a united Libya into independence,
even though they passionately disagreed on what form of government
the new state should have. Part of the reason for the acceptance of his
leadership in the Fezzan arose from fear of Tripolitanian domination.
In Cyrenaica, Idris was identified with the older generation of nationalists, who wished to see Cyrenaica itself become an independent state,
and to his intimates he did not conceal his contempt for the Tripolitanians. Yet he remained on good terms, generally, with the younger
nationalists of the Omar Mukhtar Clubs (named after the guerrilla
leader hanged by the Italians in 1931), who aspired to a united Libyan
nation. His leadership was respected among the Bedouin as well as in
Benghazi. '[I]n many ways he seems to have his finger very firmly on
the Cyrenaican pulse,' Walker concluded.[41]

Nevertheless, the contemporary tendency was to underestimate
Idris as a political figure. This was true of the British and Americans
as well as his Tripolitanian and Egyptian adversaries. Only in the post-
independence period did the British fully acknowledge that the King
possessed the drive and determination as well as the acumen to hold
the Libyan state together. The Kingdom of Libya lasted for eighteen
years, until the revolution of 1969. A member of the African Department of the Foreign Office thus made an accurate prediction in 1952
when he reflected that Idris 'will be the most permanent force in Libya
and the only man who, in the last resort, could hold the Federation together'.[42] This was also the view of Sir Alec Kirkbride, the first British
Ambassador, who arrived in Libya from Jordan after having requested
a transfer following King Abdullah's assassination. Kirkbride had a
lifetime's knowledge of Arab politics and took issue with those who believed that Idris suffered from a deficiency of character:

> As I get to know him better, I realise that some of the descriptions of
> his [weak] character in common circulation are incorrect. It is said
> for instance that he never makes decisions. It is true that he takes a

[41] Walker to Michael Stewart, 13 December 1950, FO 371/81034.
[42] Minute by A. G. L. Baxter, 23 April 1952, FO 371/97267.

long time to reach a decision but, when he does they often seem to be right; he is also capable of taking quite a strong line, and sticking to it in a crisis.[43]

Since part of the fascination of the study of the transfer of power in Libya (as elsewhere in Africa) lies in the long-range as well as the immediate consequences, another contemporary British comment is striking in its accurate prognosis of the flaw in Idris's regime that ultimately contributed to the Libyan revolution:

> One of the most unfortunate things about this country is the Senussi family. They are almost as numerous as the House of Saud and quite as grasping. Individually they are nice enough, but I fear they closely resemble a plague of locusts and much of the substance of the country is bound to be devoured by them.[44]

'I can see no immediate solution,' Malcolm Walker added, in words that were even more perplexing and urgent in the 1960s than the 1950s.

In the period before the transfer of power, Idris's political stamina was certainly misjudged by his foremost political rival, Beshir Saadawi. Beshir was the Tripolitanian nationalist who attempted to forge a unitary state that would draw its inspiration from Egypt and the Arab League rather than Britain and the United States. To Idris and the British he represented a formidable challenge. Two-thirds of the Libyan population lived in Tripolitania. If Beshir could provide cohesive leadership, then, according to Kenneth Younger (Minister of State at the Foreign Office), 'we shall probably find ourselves faced in a year or so with a Government in Tripolitania which is closely linked with Egypt and the Arab League and strongly opposed to Western influence. We shall not get a Federal Libya under the rule of the Amir of Cyrenaica who is friendly to us. This will endanger our strategic plans in the Middle East at a time when our arrangements in Egypt are precarious.'[45]

Beshir had a chequered political and personal history. The catalyst in his early life had been the Italian invasion in 1911. While in exile during the inter-war period, he became head of the Libyan Defence Committee, and his name became indelibly associated with pan-Arab extremists, including the Mufti of Jerusalem. Though no one doubted

---

[43] Kirkbride to Bowker, 31 March 1952, FO 371/97267.
[44] Walker to Stewart, 13 December 1950, FO 371/81034.
[45] Minute by Younger, 27 April 1951, FO 371/90385.

his patriotism, everyone regarded him as a political opportunist of the first rank. So often did he switch his allegiances that he was distrusted among Tripolitanians as well as pan-Arabs, even though he could maintain that he was entirely consistent in his anti-British attitude. Thus he could explain that before the war he had briefly allied himself with the Italians in the belief that Arab liberation could be best achieved by cooperation with the Axis powers. His enemies believed that he had been bribed to abandon his pro-Italian position. In any case, the British in the post-war period possessed evidence that he was in the pay of the Egyptians. According to an appraisal written by the British Resident in Tripolitania, 'he is regarded as a paid tool of Egypt—a mercenary who will sell himself at any time.' [46] This did not lessen his potential for damaging the British position. Beshir had considerable demagogic powers. For the British, the question was how to minimize his influence, perhaps by banishing him. In mid-1950 he threw things into confusion by proclaiming that he would support Idris as head of a federal state. Beshir believed he could ultimately control Idris by coming into alliance with him, and this proved to be a miscalculation, though in view of Idris's reputation as a weak political leader, it seemed a credible gamble. To the British, this veiled bid to take over the future Libyan state became one of the gravest dangers of the transfer of power.

Besides Idris and Beshir, the third principal protagonist in the drama of Libyan independence was the ubiquitous Adrian Pelt, a UN representative of almost mythic dimensions. As in most cases, the legend is larger than the historical figure, though Pelt has a good claim to be described as one of the fathers of the Libyan state. The initial British reaction to his appointment as UN commissioner in December 1949 was one of scepticism. 'We are clearly going to have some difficulty with him,' wrote the head of the African Department.[47] Another member of the same department wrote later that Pelt was the 'villain' of the piece because of his 'anxiety to present Libya as a perfect theoretical example of international cooperation [which] has led him to canvass support for ideas which, though superficially attractive, are fundamentally unsound and as dangerous to Libya's own interests as to those of H.M.G.' [48] There was inevitable tension between Pelt and the British because of the anti-colonialism of the United Nations. But there emerges from the British archives a theme that is quite subdued in Pelt's book on Libyan independence. He knew from the beginning

[46] Memorandum by T. R. Blackley, 7 May 1951, FO 371/90386.
[47] Minute by Clutton, 30 January 1950, FO 371/81014.
[48] Minute by Stewart, 19 April 1951, FO 371/90361.

that for his mission to succeed, he would have to work closely with
the British on all points of detail as well as principle, strategic as well
as financial. 'Collaboration' is an apt word to describe the working
relationship.

In February and again in March 1950 Pelt had extensive discussions
in London with Sir William Strang and Roger Allen (Clutton's successor as head of the African Department). These talks were highly satisfactory to the British. They received assurances from Pelt on the following points, among others:

   (a) [He] agrees with our objectives in Cyrenaica, and is prepared to
       help us obtain a long term agreement with the future State of Libya
       in respect of Cyrenaica on the lines we desire . . .
   (b) He is prepared to support such an agreement in due course before
       the General Assembly of the United Nations . . .
   (c) He favours a loose federal constitution for Libya, and he considers
       that the Amir of Cyrenaica is the only possible Head of the future
       Libyan State . . .[49]

This was not a one-way street. Pelt insisted in turn that the British wait
to conclude a treaty with Idris until *after* independence, which meant
a delay in strategic arrangements. Nevertheless, the accord was so mutually beneficial that it developed into an effective partnership. From
the outset there was a remarkable acknowledgement that Pelt and
the British would work to serve each other's interests, but it should be
noted that an occasional note of brutal determination crept into British minutes. Bevin himself remarked that nothing should be kept back
from Pelt, but that 'our policy should go through'.[50] And at a later
stage Allen noted that 'Mr. Pelt should be left in no doubt that we are
prepared to run him down if he does not join the band-wagon.'[51]

The critical constitutional issue on which the British and Pelt were
agreed was that Libya should have a federal rather than a unitary government. 'The immediate problem', Strang wrote, would be to establish 'a simple form of government, not of a centralised type, but of a
federal type.' Pelt believed that if the government of the new state
were to be 'too centralised, it would lack stability'.[52] This was identical
with the British view. A stable Libyan state would depend on strength
at the provincial levels. And the greater the degree of autonomy in Cyrenaica and the Fezzan, the greater the degree of British and French

[49] Memorandum by Allen, 6 April 1950, FO 371/81018.
[50] Minute by Bevin, *c.*8 March 1950, FO 371/81018.
[51] Minute by Allen, 14 June 1951, FO 371/90363.
[52] See memorandum by Strang, 20 February 1950, FO 371/81015.

influence; the more centralized the power in Tripolitania, the greater
the influence of Beshir Saadawi and the Egyptians. As Pelt later pointed
out, the problem of federation versus unitarism ran like a leitmotiv
through all of the 1950–51 period.[53] This is not the place to relate in
detail the history of the Libyan constitution, but it should be pointed
out that in the Advisory Council appointed by the United Nations, the
British, French, and Americans together with Pelt and Idris indirectly
had sufficient influence to keep in check the unitarists (principally,
Beshir along with the Egyptian and Pakistani representatives on the
Advisory Council). It was above all the British-UN (i.e. Pelt) combination that proved effective in defeating the aim of Beshir and the Arab
states to create a highly centralized state that would, perhaps, be less
vulnerable to foreign influence.

American involvement in the building of the Libyan state was deliberately kept as low-key as possible. 'I think we must be extremely
careful', wrote Andrew Lynch, the Consul-General in Tripoli, not to
give the impression 'of coming into Libya in [a] high-powered manner.'[54] Supporting the British indirectly bolstered the American position. Like the British, the Americans were wary of the possibility of
a unitary state that might fall under extremist or Egyptian influence.
The air base at Wheelus Field gave the United States a vested interest
in Tripolitania. The plan for a federated state, however, might work
out less well for the Americans than for the British. If the federation
collapsed, then the Americans in Tripolitania would be left to face
Beshir and the radical nationalists. According to a British minute that
related the American anxiety:

> [T]he Americans are uneasy because . . . it is they who would suf-
> fer most if there were a breakdown of the Federation since they had
> put all of their eggs into the Tripolitanian basket. They evidently feel
> that, if there is a breakdown, we would retire gracefully to Cyrenaica
> and leave Tripolitania in confusion.[55]

That comment, written shortly after the actual transfer of power, accurately indicated American suspicions before and after Libyan independence.

The two allies were making separate calculations in secret. What
the Americans did not know was that the British military planners now

---

[53] Pelt, *Libyan Independence*, p. 316. The most incisive contemporary British treatment of
the constitutional issues is in a memorandum by Roger Allen, 'Libya', 19 February 1951,
FO 371/90382.

[54] Lynch to Acheson, 20 July 1951, *Foreign Relations of the United States, 1951,* V, p. 1332.

[55] Minute by A. G. L. Baxter, 23 April 1952, FO 371/97269.

regarded the barracks built by the Italians in Tripolitania as more and more attractive because of the expense involved in building new ones in Cyrenaica.[56] What the British did not know was the projected scope of the American military commitment. Wheelus Field might eventually include seven additional airfields, a US Navy communications facility, supply and service centres, and five hundred square miles for an amphibious training area for the Army and Marine Corps.[57] Wheelus Field had the potential of becoming an American military area or 'base' in Libya comparable to the British 'base' at Suez. It would be smaller but almost as complex. This was a delicate issue. With their tradition of anti-colonialism, the Americans were apprehensive that these plans might be misunderstood. Even the existing installation at Wheelus evoked nationalist protest. 'We are being accused of being new imperialists who plan to take over all of Libya,' Andrew Lynch ruefully reported.[58]

Adrian Pelt did not know of the magnitude of possible American expenditure until June 1951 (in other words, six months before independence), but from the outset he had assumed that the British and Americans would subsidize the Libyan state in return for strategic facilities. This was the key to the collaborationist relationship. '[I]t appears that Mr. Pelt considers that the only way in which Libya can become self-supporting is by leasing bases to ourselves, the Americans and the French,' were the words of the original British revelation in February 1950. 'If these are really Mr. Pelt's views, then we can be much franker with him.'[59] That was indeed Pelt's outlook. He often reiterated, for example, that 'he would do his best to safeguard our strategic interests in Cyrenaica in the form of a long term lease of bases.'[60] Pelt also assumed, correctly, that the Americans would be equally interested in bases, and, to their annoyance, fostered the idea among the Libyans that the United States might be prepared to purchase base rights in Tripolitania for huge sums of money. When Andrew Lynch attempted to explain to the Libyans the purpose of the modest amount of aid available, there was an 'obvious lack of interest';[61] they were much more interested in annual cash payments for base rights. During a visit to Washington in June 1951, Pelt learned that $1,500,000 would be available annually for economic assistance and that the pending legislation for the mutual security programme would

---

[56] See ibid. and other minutes in FO 371/97269.

[57] See, for example, *Foreign Relations of the United States, 1951,* V, p. 1363.

[58] Lynch to Acheson, 30 October 1951, ibid., p. 1358.

[59] See minute by Clutton, 18 February 1950, FO 371/81016.

[60] Minute by R. S. Schrivener, 25 March 1950, FO 371/81017.

[61] Lynch to Acheson, 2 June 1951, *Foreign Relations of the United States, 1951,* V, p. 1326.

greatly ease the problem of the Libyan budget. This was the origin of the United States–Libyan agreement of 1954, which provided $42 million over the period 1954–71. The British figure in comparison, as has been stated above, was £2,750,000 per annum, which was about the same as the annual subsidy to Jordan.[62]

The near falling-out of the collaborationists occurred over the question of Libya and the sterling area. This was one of the principal concerns of the head of the African Department of the Foreign Office when he visited Libya in the spring of 1951, when all of the vital issues about the impending transfer of power appeared to be coming to a head. Allen listened to Andrew Lynch pronounce a representative American view, referring to 'the dead hand of the sterling area'.[63] Allen replied in kind, telling Lynch that he was an 'imperialist' of a well-known American type who wished to take over the British Empire by economic means.[64] Pelt despondently observed that the British had persuaded Idris of the virtues of sterling; this was their ace; they were in dead earnest. Britain's status as a world power depended on holding the Middle East, but this position could be sustained only by economic recovery, and this in turn meant the protection of the sterling area. The British therefore put the screws to Idris, who made it clear to the Americans, the United Nations, and not least the French, that Libya would join the sterling area. This was the context in which Allen made the comment, quoted above, that if Pelt attempted to block Libya's entry into the sterling area, then the British would 'run him down'.

'Nobody besides ourselves wishes to support the Libyan budget', Allen wrote, 'except the Egyptians.'[65] That somewhat disingenuous justification was received with varying degrees of scepticism. Pelt, for example, was also wary of the Egyptians, but he warned the British that their attempt to control the Libyan budget—to provide 'the money and the advice on how it is to be spent'—was exceedingly unwise. It would be denounced in the United Nations and elsewhere 'as the thinly disguised form of economic imperialism'.[66] It was precisely the British method that fired Beshir Saadawi's imagination and rhetoric about 'economic imperialism'. By the spring of 1951, the British

[62] The Libyan agreements with Britain and the United States are reproduced in Khadduri, *Modern Libya,* apps. IV and V.

[63] Memorandum by Allen, 9 May 1951, FO 371/90386.

[64] These were accusations that by no means ended at the time of Libyan independence. Allen wrote later that Lynch continued to be 'bitterly opposed to our financial control over [the] Libyan economy'. Allen told him in reply that he could only be described as 'an unashamed imperialist' (memorandum by Allen, 17 April 1952, FO 371/97267).

[65] Memorandum by Allen, 2 July 1951, FO 371/90364.

[66] Ibid.

judged Beshir's anti-imperialism to be a danger not only in Tripolitania, the most populous and relatively prosperous of the three provinces, but also to the future Libyan state itself. Here was a classic case of the British forced to confront extremist opposition during an impending transfer of power.

In July 1950, as will be recalled, Beshir had declared his support for a federal state under Idris as ruler. This was a reversal of his previous position. Might it be a plot for a future coup from within? Or was it mere opportunism? In any case, in December, after a visit to Egypt, Beshir again reversed himself. Now he proclaimed himself once more in favour of a unitary form of government, according to a secret British report, as 'demanded by his Egyptian paymasters'. He organized anti-British and anti-American demonstrations, two of which interfered with the inauguration of the provisional government in March 1951. He subsidized two Arabic newspapers that were violently anti-federal and anti-British. The British accepted the following figures as the sources of Beshir's 'nefarious activities' in the period 1949–50:

Egyptian Foreign Office	£13,000
Arab League Secretariat	£10,000
Syrian Government	£ 4,000
Lebanon Government	£ 3,000
Saudi Arabian Government	£30,000

In January 1951 he was understood to have received an additional £120,000 from the Egyptian government for 'propaganda purposes'.[67] Beshir lived well. He had three automobiles in Tripoli, an extravagance that did not go unnoticed by his fellow nationalists. Though he was himself a Tripolitanian nationalist, he carried a Saudi Arabian passport. Technically, he was vulnerable. The question for the British was whether to take action against him.

The African Department balked at the idea of an outright cash bribe to buy off Beshir. There was the alternative of finding him a lucrative position in the administration, but whether he could be permanently silenced by a sinecure was open to question. Michael Stewart believed he was too volatile a personality, who, moreover, possessed 'genuine ability as a political agitator and rabble-rouser'. In Stewart's view, he could probably be 'neutralised' only by expulsion. For that, the British would need the excuse of 'a more or less serious breach of the peace', which could be 'artificially contrived or at least fostered by

---

[67] Memorandum by T. R. Blackley (Resident in Tripoli) entitled 'The Personal History of Beshir Bey Saadawi', 7 May 1951, FO 371/90386.

the administration'.[68] The debate about such tactics reached the highest levels of the Foreign Office. Kenneth Younger wrote: 'One is very tempted to suggest that the best way to get rid of Beshir would be that he should die from natural causes! This is, however probably either impracticable or too dangerous a peace-time precedent to be attempted!'[69] Younger favoured expulsion. Herbert Morrison was now Foreign Secretary. He noted, 'I agree,' and cautioned that 'we should do it thoroughly while we are about it.'[70]

The British did not in fact find a favourable enough opportunity to expel Beshir, and thus the Labour Government in its last months adhered to a policy of non-intervention, almost despite itself. Adrian Pelt is on record as having told the British that he would oppose the expulsion of Beshir.[71] Throughout 1950–51 he was a restraining influence and, in retrospect, probably a wise one. From the beginning, he urged the British to have more confidence in the political ingenuity of the Libyans themselves, to allow them to find their own solutions, and to interfere as little as possible. In the case of Beshir, he undoubtedly gave sound advice. In 1952, King Idris himself expelled Beshir.

As the date of Libyan independence approached, the British went through what might fairly be described as a case of the political jitters. It was brought about in part by the assassination of King Abdullah in July 1951. General Sir Brian Robertson, the commander of British forces in the Middle East, visited Libya shortly after the murder. He felt compelled to report his 'serious anxiety' to London. His judgement of Idris was hardly reassuring:

> The weakness of the Amir and his [provisional] Government is our greatest source of trouble. Quite frankly the Amir is a coward. He knows that the Arab League and the Egyptians would like to see him eliminated ... Now that King Abdullah has been assassinated, he feels that he will be the next and he is terrified.[72]

The head of the African Department did not entirely agree with that alarmist assessment. Allen admitted that Idris was 'a great weakness' in the plan for 'independence', but that there was nothing to do but hope for the best. His comment provides the most illuminating British assessment of Idris in the last months before independence:

[68] Memorandum by Stewart, 26 April 1951, FO 371/90385.
[69] Minute by Younger, 27 April 1951, FO 371/90385.
[70] Minute by Morrison and Barclay (recording Morrison's instruction), 1 May 1951, FO 371/90385.
[71] Memorandum by Stewart, 26 April 1951, FO 371/90385.
[72] Extract from a letter by Robertson, 27 July 1951, FO 371/90346.

It is perhaps not quite fair to describe him simply as a coward. He
is a holy man, and of a quietist sect at that, turned politician. He has
a certain natural shrewdness and caution. He is friendly to us and
committed in every way that he can be committed on our side. But
he is not courageous physically or I should say morally, he is not a
commanding personality, he does not really want to be a King, he
is an elderly man in poor health, and he has no obvious heir. But
the plain fact is that there is no other person who can be head of the
future State, and therefore we must deal with the Amir and make the
best of him too.[73]

Allen had to confess that he shared Robertson's anxiety. '[T]he future
of Libya', Allen wrote, 'is in my view balanced on a knife edge.'[74]

Idris proclaimed Libyan independence on 24 December 1951. The
British remained unobtrusively in the background. There was a real
transfer of power in the sense of the creation of a sovereign state, but
in the sense of 'independence', at least to the British, things would remain much the same. According to a Foreign Office minute, 'we know
that the Libyan Prime Minister expects to receive in the future precisely the same services from us that Tripolitania and Cyrenaica have
received in the past.'[75] The goal of British policy, Roger Allen had
written in early December, would now be to make sure that 'the future
Libyan Government is well advised, principally by British advisers in
the key posts, and supported by British funds.'[76] Rather than describing the new state as the child of the United Nations, which is its traditional epithet, it would probably be more appropriate to regard it as
a puppet of the British Labour Government. At least that was the aim
inherited by the Conservatives when they returned to power in the autumn of 1951. It was Anthony Eden, now again Foreign Secretary, who
had helped with the genesis of the new state by his wartime pledge
to the Senusis some ten years earlier. He now presided over the creation of an artifice not entirely to his liking. He would have preferred
a Cyrenaican rather than a Libyan state. But as he surveyed the work
of the officials of the African Department, he marvelled at the way they
had 'played their hand skilfully and patiently'. 'Personally', he wrote,
he would have felt 'safer' if the arrangements had been limited to Cyrenaica: 'However we are now embarked on wider deserts. Let us hope
that all will yet be well.'[77]

[73] Minute by Allen, 11 August 1951, FO 371/90346.
[74] Ibid.
[75] Minute by General R. G. Lewis, 10 October 1951, FO 371/90394.
[76] Minute by Allen, 7 December 1951, FO 371/90350.
[77] Minute by Eden, 9 December 1951, FO 371/90359.

Among the immediate architects of the new state, it was the head of the African Department who perhaps best expressed the significance for British self-interest. Here was a country, Allen wrote, that was being given its independence 'long before it is ready for it'. There was the complication of the United Nations, 'with its impractical doctrinaire idealism'. Over those elements in the situation the British had no control. They could only make the best of them. It could be, Allen continued, 'that nationalism, xenophobia and the intrigues of our enemies will get their way, and that the country will in effect lapse into chaos'. On the other hand—the other side of the knife-edge—the British had always recognized the danger of chaos and had attempted to guard against it by making sure that Libya, despite the United Nations, would 'be kept to some extent under our tutelage and that we should be able to make of her, if not an entirely satisfactory independent country, at least a reasonably stable and orderly one.'[78]

Measuring the meaning of 'independence' against those aims, the actual date held little significance. For the British, the test would be the continuity in Libyan collaboration and the stability of the new state. Looking back nearly a year after the date of independence, Allen could thus reflect that at least the situation had not deteriorated. The new state had not collapsed, nor had it fallen under the influence of Britain's enemies, nor were things entirely satisfactory: 'There is no drastic or complete solution for the Libyan problem, and we must therefore resign ourselves to a long period of patch-work. We shall just have to go on doing our best to keep Libya afloat and well disposed to us.'[79]

Had the descendants of the fabulous artificers of the last continent reached their last desert, only to be reduced to a policy of improvisation and patchwork? Or did the patchwork reflect ingenious improvisation in response to the exigencies of ever-changing combinations of international, metropolitan, and Middle Eastern or African circumstances? If Libya may be regarded as a case study in the transfer of power in Africa as well as the Middle East, it would appear that the latter-day British imperialists were merely reverting to more informal methods in order to achieve traditional aims.

Decolonization and African Independence:
The Transfers of Power, 1960–1980   1988

---

[78] Minute by Allen, 11 August 1951, FO 371/90346.
[79] Minute by Allen, 21 November 1953, FO 371/103038.

19

THE COMING OF INDEPENDENCE IN THE SUDAN

'After Uganda and Kenya it is a drop into an abysm of backwardness': Margery Perham thus recorded her dominant impression of the southern Sudan during her first visit, in February 1937.[1] Like an Edwardian travelogue, her diary records her thoughts with unguarded candour and reveals a romantic and inquiring mind. To those accustomed to think of her as the wise and committed defender of African causes in the 1960s, some of her early reactions to black Africans in the Sudan might appear out of character. She wrote about the mountains of Jebel Mara in Darfur:

> We are in a great wide basin, ringed by peaks of pointed or domed rock. It all seems so un-African that I was quite surprised, and perhaps almost disgusted, to meet negroes in this Paradise. For whatever I may feel about negroes, they are not romantic. Their appearance and their generally servile character must always from this point of view, put them in a category apart from Red Indians, Polynesians or Arabs.[2]

Certainly her diary entries do demonstrate how far she travelled from the age of Lugard and Hailey to the time of Oliver and Fage, when she was elected the first President of the African Studies Association a quarter of a century later in 1963. Yet it is also true that she never wholly lost the intense preoccupation with 'racial' differences, an interpretation that is a striking feature of her first encounters with Africa. There is also an irrepressible element of fun in her diaries of the 1930s, a sense of the absurd that must have confounded some of her more proper British hosts in the Sudan and elsewhere. There is, she once pronounced, 'something difficult as well as unaesthetic about swimming in a helmet'.[3]

From the outset, she distinguished the Sudan from all other African dependencies. On her first visit, she landed at night on a flight from Uganda at Torit in Equatorial Province. She recorded as one of her first impressions 'the two flags flying in the light of the flares, one on each side of the bonnet, the Union Jack for England, and a green flag with a crescent for Egypt'.[4] Though the administration of the Sudan was British, its status was half Egyptian. The Agreement of 1899 between Britain and Egypt established the Sudan as a Condominium but

[1] Uganda-Sudan Diary, 24 February 1937, Perham Papers, Rhodes House, Oxford, Box 49/7.
[2] Ibid., 21 February 1938.
[3] Ibid.
[4] Ibid., 19 February 1937.

conferred on Britain administrative control. 'The two flags, which can be seen today flying on all public buildings in the Sudan', she wrote later, suggested 'equal status', but the Governor-General's 'almost un-fettered power' was the principal element of British administration.[5] Britain ruled the Sudan, in one of her phrases, as a benevolent autoc-racy. It was an autocracy, however, that did not come under the Co-lonial Office but the Foreign Office. This bureaucratic arrangement contributed to the distinctive nature of the Sudan Political Service, the corps of officers who presided over the country's administration. The Foreign Office was acutely sensitive to Egyptian influence, which cata-pulted the Sudan into independence at a far earlier date than Margery Perham believed to be desirable. The Sudanese were able to play the British off against the Egyptians.

On her second visit to the Sudan, at the end of 1937, she travelled through Egypt. She was conscious that, as a woman, she placed Egyp-tian politicians and officials in an uncomfortable position. After a talk with the head of the Egyptian Agricultural Society in Cairo, she noted that 'he was making a great effort to do something almost as diffi-cult and ludicrous as standing on his head in having a serious political talk with a woman.'[6] She spent Christmas Day 1937 in Luxor. Her de-scriptions of Egyptians, again, were not flattering. At the Office of An-tiquities she encountered 'a fat official in a tarbush', which led her to generalize that 'all Egyptian "effendies" are fat with a triangular extension of the paunch and the face.' After trudging through 'filthy crowded streets', she summed up her overall reaction by stating that 'everything run by Egyptians was dirty and disorderly'.[7] These dispar-aging remarks would not be noteworthy were it not for the lasting con-trast with the Sudan. She travelled with American companions as she crossed the frontier:

> I was thankful to leave this [Egypt]; with its sordidness, dirt, unspeak-able lavatories, and dishevelled and indifferent officials, and to en-ter the atmosphere of efficiency, intelligent paternalism and cleanli-ness which marks the Sudan.[8]

> I bade the Americans note the order and comeliness that reigned under British rule, and the sudden end of that long chorus of

[5] Margery Perham, 'The Sudan Emerges into Nationhood', *Foreign Affairs* (July 1949); re-printed in *Colonial Sequence, 1949–1969* (London, 1970), p. 3.
[6] Sudan Diary, 22 December 1937, Perham Papers 50/3.
[7] Ibid., Christmas Day 1937.
[8] Ibid., 26 December 1937.

'bakshish' ['tips'], and the clean and soignés uniforms of all officials, white and coloured.[9]

The injunction to the Americans is significant. She was never hyper-sensitive to American criticism; but especially in the case of the Sudan, she took what she believed to be a justifiable pride in sound colonial administration.

First impressions are sometimes lasting impressions. Throughout her writings the seat of government in the Sudan, the Palace at Khartoum, acquires an almost symbolic significance as a stabilizing and civilizing influence, in marked contrast to the average Government House elsewhere in British Africa. She similarly regarded the Sudan Political Service as distinctly a cut above the Colonial Service. She recorded her first reactions to the colour and vivacity of the Palace on her arrival in Khartoum:

> It stands right over the Nile on the four mile river-front along which most of Khartoum's large solid buildings are placed . . . I must confess . . . that I was never in a Government House where things were done so efficiently and impressively.

> The women here exhibit a high standard of looks and dress . . . The whole social tone is upon a higher level than the Colonial Service. The Black Watch officers, with their striking dress uniforms, contribute another mass of colour to the parties.[10]

Before the Second World War, she believed that the Palace would last as a centre of benevolent British authority for the indefinite future. Ten years later, however, she reflected on the same landscape along the Nile:

> I felt suddenly an intense regret for what was passing or at least beginning to pass. This solid building, these statues of the man the Sudanese murdered [Gordon] and the man who conquered them [Kitchener]—the men *we* honour—all these great buildings, the banks, the smart police, this structure of efficient, honest government—these are the outward signs of British rule set up in the years of our high confidence in our own power, the priority of our interest, our certainty of the justice and welfare we had to bring. In 5, 10, 15 years what will remain?[11]

[9] Ibid., 28 December 1937.
[10] Ibid., 29 December 1937–9 January 1938.
[11] Sudan Diary, 22 Feb. 1948, Perham Papers 53/2.

It was a perceptive foreboding. British authority began to collapse only five years later, in 1953.

Her attachment to the Sudan, of course, went much deeper than her aesthetic appreciation of the buildings along the Nile. She developed loyalties and lasting friendships, above all with Sir Douglas Newbold. When she first met him in 1938 he was Governor of Kordofan. He later became Civil Secretary, the highest post in the Sudan Political Service. He grew into a legendary figure, in part through her own efforts after his early death in 1945.[12] Her analysis of his method of colonial government demonstrates her own command of local detail and administrative procedure, above all at the district level, but extending through general financial, legal, defence, and educational policies. It is clear from her papers that Newbold gave her unrivalled and complete access to the records of the Sudanese government. At one time she hoped to write a major work on the Sudan, but she got only as far as outlines and a few draft chapters; one can only lament that the book was never finished. Wartime circumstances caused the Foreign Office and Colonial Office to believe that Britain might become involved in the long-term administration of Ethiopia. Margery Perham was thus requested to write a book examining the problems in historical perspective. In 1948 she published *The Government of Ethiopia,* which analyses the history and institutions of the country from a Western vantage point. There can be no doubt that the book on the Sudan would have been a far more significant work.

She once wrote that two men had a marked influence on her life, Sir Frederick (Lord) Lugard and Newbold. Her friendship with the latter gave her description of his work a warmth and insight that raises her comment to a level of historical significance. In a broad political context, the Sudan becomes a microcosm of the British colonial experience, with its past errors, present problems, and future hopes. Newbold is the protagonist, the archetypal colonial administrator as District Commissioner, Provincial Governor, and Civil Secretary. He faces problems resembling those from an earlier age in India and, more recently, in Nigeria:

> We can see him [Newbold] dealing, in the very special and rather isolated situation of the Sudan, with the same main problems which had confronted Britain in India and were still demanding solution in nearly all the colonies.
>
> Following the establishment of law and order . . . had come the construction of a system of local government for both tribal and urban

[12] See her introduction to K. D. D. Henderson, *The Making of the Modern Sudan* (London, 1953). Her introduction is reprinted in *Colonial Sequence, 1949–1969,* pp. 47–67.

groups; and the juxtaposition, if not the harmonization, of two systems of law and of law-courts; the delicate tasks of fitting Western education upon societies formed in a wholly different physical and mental environment; and the introduction of Western economic principles into communities of peasant farmers or semi-nomadic pastoralists.[13]

The universal problems of colonial administration thus manifest themselves in Sudanese circumstances.

One problem had become especially pressing. Newbold had to deal with the dual culture, Arab and black African, the long-term relationship of an Arab and Muslim north with a black African pagan and partly Christianized south. Under the direction of Sir Harold Mac-Michael, the Civil Secretary from 1926 to 1933, there had developed a 'southern policy' that attempted to exclude northern Sudanese and Arab influence from the south. In the Perham Papers, Newbold can be seen hesitantly trying to develop a more harmonious and constructive policy. The fate of the south became a cause of anguish to Margery Perham as the political pace quickened and as the Sudan administration attempted to adjust, in her words, 'the future relationship of an Arab and Moslem north with a Negro and pagan south'.[14]

In the 1930s she came to grips with the issue of 'Indirect Rule', which MacMichael had implemented in the Sudan (with the Nigerian model in mind). Newbold began to adjust the principle to circumstances of local government. It was Newbold's work in the district and the province that stirred her imagination. She believed him to be 'the ideal District Commissioner', who, despite an exasperating fault of procrastination, did an admirable job in difficult circumstances. He brought humour, balance, and common sense to his work. Despite her use of the word 'ideal', she did not idealize him, but she did regard him as a person of such integrity and humanity that his attitudes became a touchstone of her own judgement.

Newbold himself adopted a mildly sceptical and teasing attitude towards the phenomenon of an Oxford female don with boundless energy coming his way by chance at El Obeid (the provincial capital of Kordofan), but he obviously enjoyed her company and found her intellectually engaging. He wrote the following 'Ode' to her in 1938 after witnessing her prodigious research in his files on the problem of 'Native Administration', or administrative units of indirect rule. He used her family nickname, 'Pro'. Newbold described the circumstances of his authorship: 'Written in sweat & agony while buried

---

[13] Ibid., pp. 53–54.
[14] Letter to the *Manchester Guardian*, 22 December 1955; *Colonial Sequence, 1949–1969*, p. 129.

in files on town lands, witchcraft, aerodromes, bloodmoney, & soap factories.'

ODE to the 'PRO'

Margery P. lives on weak tea,
Refuses to eat pies or red meat.
But *she'd* travel miles, to devour old files.
Like Oliver Twist, to her mill all is grist,
And shouts Hip! Hooray! when she tastes some N.A.[15]

For her, Newbold was a lasting source of inspiration. She wrote of her joy in his companionship in 1938: 'We played tennis in the afternoon and talked until late at night. Newbold is marvellous. He . . . was acute and humorous and as idealistic as ever. It renews my faith and my hopes for Africa to stay with him. We could not stop talking.'[16]

The Post-War Sudan

Both Lugard and Newbold died in 1945, making the year a landmark not only as the end of the war but also in her personal life. During the war years she had not been able to follow the affairs of the Sudan as closely as she might have liked, and now she had the task of Lugard's biography thrust upon her.[17] It became obvious that her book on the Sudan would have to be a long-term rather than an immediate project. In any case, the time for the kind of book she had originally planned was already past. Though the country continued to be one of her principal interests, she knew that the post-war Sudan would be radically different from the benevolent autocracy of her pre-war visits. Perhaps the most lucid example of the combination of her old and new ideas can be found in a letter written in 1946 to one of the officers in the Sudan Political Service. She restated the theme that the Sudan represented a microcosm of the British Empire and that the Condominium would be in the vanguard of colonial change. But now the time had come to cease ruling and begin yielding power:

> I think the Sudan Service has got a hard task in front of it for the next few years, but if you will forgive me for being platitudinous, this

[15] Dated 22 March 1938, Perham Papers 536/6.

[16] Sudan Diary, 7 March 1938, Perham Papers 50/7.

[17] She wrote in 1945 about her decision not to carry on with the Sudan book: 'Lord Lugard died, and very strong pressure was brought upon me from the highest quarters to start work on his Life.' Presumably she referred to Lugard's brother, Major Edward Lugard (Perham to Robertson, 1 June 1946, Perham Papers 536/7).

phase is a great test of all that has gone before, not only in the Sudan, but elsewhere in the Empire.

It is clear we have got to switch over from ruling to helping and advising, and if the British can manage the transition, it will be a most wonderful achievement.[18]

The idea that the Sudanese would be managing their own affairs in 'the next few years' was a fundamental departure from her pre-war views.

The change in outlook can be traced to her stock-taking after the fall of Singapore in February 1942, when she saw more clearly than most other contemporary observers that the old British Empire was a thing of the past and that the British would have to adjust rapidly to a new order.[19] After the war she was still optimistic about the Sudan and generally about the future of the other British dependencies in Africa. The handling of the question of Sudanese independence, however, caused her to have grave misgivings. I shall argue that the management of the transfer of power in the Sudan failed, from her point of view, to take into account some of the lessons she had drawn as early as the fall of Singapore.

The storm clouds were already on the Egyptian horizon in 1946. In October of that year, the Foreign Secretary, Ernest Bevin, attempted to negotiate with the Egyptian Prime Minister, Sidky Pasha, an agreement that would revise the Anglo-Egyptian Treaty of 1936 and end the dispute over the British military presence in Canal Zone. To find common ground with the Egyptians, Bevin yielded to Sidky's insistence that Egypt and the Sudan shared, and would share, the same sovereignty. In essence. this meant that Egypt and the Sudan would be as two states under a 'common crown'—that is to say, under an 'Egyptian' crown. Bevin believed that this theoretical or juridical concession to the Egyptians would not interfere with the Sudan's right of self-determination, but there were riots in Khartoum. The discontent was not restricted to the Sudanese. The British officers in the Sudan Political Service believed that they had been betrayed by the Foreign Office. All of this is common historical knowledge. What is new, on the basis of the Margery Perham Papers, is the way that Newbold's successor as Civil Secretary, James Robertson, turned to her for help in mobilizing public sentiment in Britain against the proposed agreement with the Egyptians.

'It is extremely improper', Robertson wrote to her in November

---

[18] Perham to K. D. D. Henderson, 29 July 1946, Perham Papers 536/1.

[19] Letters to *The Times* of 13 and 14 March 1942; *Colonial Sequence, 1930–1949* (London, 1967), pp. 225–31. See W. R. Louis, *Imperialism at Bay* (Oxford, 1977), pp. 135–39.

1946, 'for me as one of the senior officials of the Sudan Government to write to you in this way but the gravity of the situation . . . make[s] it imperative that people at home should know what the danger is.' They had previously met only over 'a very hurried and uncomfortable lunch'. But he now divulged his inner thoughts on the crisis in the Sudan. He described the way in which the protest against the proposed agreement with Egypt had nearly led, in Khartoum, to a 'serious breakdown of public security'. Should the future of the Sudan be decided without consulting the Sudanese? This appeared to him to be a violation of the principle on which British rule rested. Robertson was obviously nervous about writing to her in this manner. But he did so in the hope 'that you [and] . . . your many influential friends' would not wish to see the 'betrayal' of British pledges that the Sudanese would determine their own future.[20]

He need not have worried about his plea falling on unsympathetic ears. '[Y]our letter', she responded, 'gave me sufficient confidence and information.' She was inspired to write a letter to *The Times,* which was published on 10 December 1946.[21] In it she cogently pointed out the contradiction between the premise that people should determine their own fate and the assumption of the projected Anglo-Egyptian accord, whereby Britain 'has signed away her share of sovereignty and given it solely to Egypt'. There were some things that she thought were best left unsaid in public. She had always believed that the officials in the Sudan underestimated the danger of the British and Egyptian governments' undermining the colonial order in the Condominium. Now the reality had to be faced. The Foreign Office might sacrifice the Sudan for security in the Canal Zone. 'At the moment', she wrote to Robertson, 'I fear that you must all have an overwhelming sense of bitterness and disillusionment.'[22] In the event, the plan for shared sovereignty was scrapped because of the protest by the Sudanese.

She became a comrade in arms with Robertson. Such was the extent of his trust that each month he sent her secret intelligence reports. In his judgement, she could be relied upon to put forward sympathetically the point of view of the Sudan Political Service. 'I shudder to think what might have happened if it had not been for the influence of people like you,' he wrote to her in 1952.[23] Sometimes he flattered her. One can also detect strains of tension in the correspondence. An official point of view does not necessarily coincide with the outlook of

[20] Robertson to Perham, 25 November 1946, Perham Papers 538/2.
[21] 'The Anglo-Egyptian Treaty'; *Colonial Sequence, 1930–1949,* pp. 292–93.
[22] Perham to Robertson, 10 December 1946, Perham Papers 538/2.
[23] Robertson to Perham, 7 May 1952, Perham Papers 536/7.

a scholar, even though in this case she believed the Sudan administration to be almost beyond reproach. 'It is probably the most considerate and honest foreign government that history has ever seen,' she declared in early 1947.[24] That judgement on the past must strike one as romantic, even naive. From it derived idealism about the future: 'What is needed is the building up of a new vision, a new positive task of friendly cultural cooperation in which we give freely what they want in a way which allows them to accept it.'[25] Her thought can also be translated into the language of realpolitik: nationalists should be given power, not given the opportunity to seize it.

Robertson from time to time tried to restrain her enthusiasm. She was a worthy ally, but he and others in the Sudan Political Service thought that her zeal sometimes exceeded her knowledge. She was herself aware of the limitations on her expertise imposed by other commitments. The Sudan was only a part, though a vital one, of her African concerns. The pace of Oxford life, the research on the Lugard biography, and the press of committee work gave her a sense of frustration in coming to grips with the problems of the Sudan. 'I do wish we could meet,' she wrote to a Sudan official.

> It is this eternal pressure of overwork plus all the little worries and extras of life to-day that leave no margin for friendship or other things that matter. I am generally . . . so exhausted at the week-end that I want to crawl into a corner and hide. Unfortunately everyone descends on Oxford at week-ends, eager for official business, so that the week's work simply goes on into the week-end.[26]

Yet she always found time to meet Robertson's requests to provide information, for example, on colonial constitutions.

After the breakdown of the 1946 negotiations with Egypt, the devising of the future constitution became her principal Sudanese preoccupation. From the vantage point of the 1990s, it is not easy to recall or understand why people forty years ago devoted such time and energy to drafting African constitutions. For Margery Perham, it was a time for the planning of Africa's future. It was an age in which she, for one, hoped that the British could ensure a stable and durable order in the post-colonial era by giving the Sudan and other British African territories the benefit of Britain's own political tradition. In retrospect

[24] Perham to John Monro, 1 January 1947, Perham Papers 538/2.
[25] Sudan Diary, 22 February 1948, Perham Papers 53/2.
[26] Perham to R. Davies, 14 December 1946, Perham Papers 538/2.

it appears clear that it was rather Anglocentric to believe that the 'Westminster model' would provide a pattern along which ex-colonial states would or should develop. But it would be a mistake to underestimate the importance that she and others attached to constitutional development as the key element in colonial planning. Here was her basic idea:

> People cannot be fundamentally changed in 50 years. But if we can keep a vital relationship with these people we may continue to be able to help them in many ways, especially if they maintain a constitution based on our model.[27]

With the benefit of hindsight, again, it is clear that she attached too much significance to the Sudanese adopting British parliamentary ceremony, and that she was too optimistic about their 'natural dignity and courtesy' prevailing indefinitely once they learned 'House of Commons procedure'.[28] Nevertheless, her constitutional instincts were sound. 'It seems to me', she wrote to Robertson in March 1947,

> that when a backward country makes a sudden [constitutional] advance like this, it is very important that the executive should be as strong and independent as possible . . . The danger surely in a country like the Sudan is a weak administration following the firm administration of the former regime, and the fear of an utter collapse of good government.[29]

The problem was that the pace of events seemed to be moving too rapidly to allow time for the constitution to be accepted as the supreme law of the land. Political ambition seemed to be outstripping prudent planning. She had written a year earlier that she was reduced 'almost to tears by the utter unreasonableness of young coloured nationalism'.[30]

During the war she had briefly had as a student in Oxford a young Sudanese official who gave her considerable intellectual pleasure but who also caused her anguish about Sudanese nationalism. This was Mekki Effendi Abbas, one of the most outstanding of her African students. He had an incisive mind, buoyant vitality, and an infectious laugh. After his return to the Sudan in 1940, both she and Newbold kept in touch with him. He became in turn a member of the Local

[27] Perham to W. H. T. Luce, 24 May 1954, Perham Papers 536/1.
[28] 'Parliamentary Government in the Sudan'; *Colonial Sequence, 1930–1949*, pp. 329–32.
[29] Perham to Robertson, 19 March 1947, Perham Papers 536/7.
[30] Perham to Henderson, 29 July 1946, Perham Papers 536/1.

Government Advisory Board, the Advisory Council for the Northern Sudan, and various conferences set up to advise on Sudanization. But in 1947 he resigned from his official post to espouse 'radical' political views and began editing what she described as a 'pro-Egyptian' weekly newspaper (*El Raid*). This was undoubtedly one of her most painful experiences with a student, but he helped her develop a perceptive understanding of Sudanese politics when she visited the country from February to April 1948. It was her longest visit to the Sudan, and although two months may not seem like a long time, she was able to compress interviews and research into the time available with a remarkable intensity. This journey certainly left the most lasting impression on her, and in some ways was traumatic because of her meetings with Mekki Abbas.

Mekki gave her insight into the religious and historical traditions behind the two leaders in Sudanese politics, the Sayed Ali Mirghani and the Sayed Abdel Rahman el Mahdi, the latter the son of the Mahdi who, in British Imperial history, is indelibly associated with the death of Gordon. The Sayed Ali Mirghani, or 'S.A.M.', was associated with the Ashigga, or pro-Egyptian party. The Sayed Abdel Rahman el Mahdi, or 'S.A.R.', was the force behind the Umma, or independence party, which, in her view, might lead the Sudan into a new Mahdist dictatorship. She described the two Sayeds as religious figures who divided the allegiance of Muslims and infused politics with the religious zeal of the sects in northern Sudan. She later distilled her thoughts into a formal political analysis, of which the following extract is useful because of its insight into the two figures dominating Sudanese politics at the time.

> Sayed Sir Ali Mirghani [was] pious, aging, delicate and retiring in disposition . . . [and] he had neither desire nor capacity to lead a political party, but as a rival to the other outstanding religious leader, he became, inevitably, the symbol round which opposition was grouped.

> On the other side stood Sir Abdel Rahman el Mahdi, the Mahdi's son, who had by this time become a great public figure, winning his way by his moderate and astute political leadership and the great wealth he had amassed from growing irrigated cotton.[31]

Those two descriptions help make comprehensible some of the salient issues in her conversations with Mekki. He challenged the good faith of the British government. He believed that the British did not wish to grant independence to the Sudan, at least in the immediate future:

[31] 'Sudan Emerges into Nationhood'; *Colonial Sequence, 1949–1969*, p. 7.

We talked for over 2 hours and it was even more painful than I expected . . . The whole mind of the most intelligent, sensitive and liberal Sudanese [Mekki] who has yet been developed, torn between his admiration and respect for the British and his sense of having been deceived by them.

He sees with a dreadful clarity the danger of his country between the Egyptian menace on the one side and the threat of a new Mahdia from S.A.R. and his family, who would establish something like an Egyptian pashadom in the Sudan. The people remember the horrors of the Mahdia, whereas the Egyptian oppression is becoming a matter of history.[32]

She acknowledged that Mekki helped her understand the Ashigga, 'the so-called Egyptian party', better than she had before. 'I gather', she wrote, 'that Egypt means no harm to the Sudan and that . . . they [the Sudanese] can have a status like that of a British dominion.'[33] She had a frank discussion with him over the range of Sudanese politics. But there were some issues on which she could not be candid. Even though he had been her student at Oxford, certain subjects were still taboo or too sensitive to debate. She could not discuss with him, for example, the question of religion and the saving of 'Southern negroes . . . from Islam and female circumcision'. Mekki told her that political issues could never 'affect his friendship for me, and his trust, and once or twice his grand laugh rang out'. But she came away 'deeply depressed'.[34]

Yet she still refused to lose faith in Mekki or in the hope of winning him back to the cause of gradualism. On her return to England, she helped him obtain one of the first studentships at Nuffield College and a grant from the Rhodes Trust. 'I am playing Lord Elton here', she wrote of the Trust's chairman, 'but have not yet landed him . . . he is very Right wing and is worried about Mekki's political views.'[35] Under her supervision, Mekki eventually completed his B.Litt. thesis on 'the Sudan question', and later she went to great lengths to secure its publication, contributing a generous introduction of her own.[36]

The main object of Margery Perham's 1948 visit was to respond to the invitation of the Civil Secretary, Robertson, and the Principal of

[32] Sudan Diary, 27 February 1948, Perham Papers 53/2.

[33] Ibid., 28 March 1948, Perham Papers 53/3.

[34] Ibid.

[35] Perham to V. N. Griffiths, 13 May 1948, Perham Papers 537/3.

[36] See M. Abbas, *The Sudan Question* (London, 1952).

Gordon College (which became in 1951 the University of Khartoum) to advise on the future training of Sudanese administrative officers and the development of the School of Administration of the College. Her wartime correspondence with Newbold shows that they had both come to accept the principle that Sudanese officials should replace the British administrative officers.[37] She had abandoned her earlier support of the 'scaffolding theory', which argued that the administrative service established by the British should dissolve on their departure. The functions would be transferred to local government and judicial officials, on a British domestic model.[38] She was not only concerned about the initial courses for administrative officers. The British, she hoped, would leave in place a system of administrative training for officials of all departments, who would continue throughout their careers to take refresher courses. She had always been impressed by

> the spirit of cooperation and friendship between British and Sudanese in the partnership in administration [but] it is inevitable that this partnership should feel the strain of that most testing of all political operations, the transfer of power . . . But at least these conceptions of conscious and continuous training 'on the job' will, far more than any attempt to turn lectures on government into sermons on social obligations, make it possible for the British officials to communicate to their Sudanese colleagues the high qualities which a non-official may be permitted to recognise in their own service to the Sudan.[39]

She was also beginning to address herself intensely to the wider aspects of 'the problems of the *transfer of power*'.[40] In the year following the independence of India and Pakistan, the phrase came naturally enough. What is remarkable is the clarity of her vision: seeing that the end of British rule would come quickly and that the Sudanese would have to be granted independence, in her view, before they were actually ready for it. There is a paradox here. She pressed the Sudan officials to move forward rapidly, but she was haunted with fear about the consequences of 'premature' independence. Yet unless the British moved quickly, the initiative would pass to the 'extremists'. She explained her contradictory impulses in a way that went to the heart of the matter:

[37] See, for example, Newbold to Perham, 18 May 1940, and extracts from Newbold's reports, in Henderson, *Making of the Modern Sudan*, pp. 139 and 512.

[38] Margery Perham, *Native Administration in Nigeria* (London, 1937), p. 361.

[39] Notes for discussion on report, Khartoum, 9 March 1948, Perham Papers 583/3.

[40] Sudan Diary, 27 February 1948, Perham Papers 53/2; emphasis added.

> I have a dreadful feeling that we are missing the psychological mo-
> ment in this country's history by being, as we nearly always are, just
> too late and too grudging in our constitutional concessions.

> If we lose the last moment when we have some good will left among
> the moderate elements we shall be forced into much larger surren-
> ders of power in an embittered atmosphere when they will do little
> good.[41]

The resolution of the paradox thus becomes the yielding of power
quickly in order to preserve as much good will and influence as possible among the moderates—but not so quickly as to throw them into
disarray. She debated this proposition with everyone she encountered:
Robertson, the Sayed Abdel Rahman el Mahdi, Mekki Abbas. She was
impressed with the relentless logic with which Mekki pursued the same
point. 'As Mekki said to me bitterly', she recorded in her diary, 'it is
no good the British waiting until the Sudan is a Utopia before they
hand over.'[42]

There are two especially poignant passages in her 1948 diary, one
about a church service, the other describing a dinner. In the atmosphere of the church, she believed she witnessed the spirit of a van-
ishing age. She experienced the exuberance of the Sunday service attended by the British community in Khartoum. She noted that 80 per
cent of the congregation consisted of British troops: 'They seemed
very young and clean in their newly ironed biscuit coloured linen
shorts & tunics and their very red faces and legs.' They sang the old
hymns 'with enormous zest'. She thought it was probably nostalgia
for home that caused most of them to attend.[43] For her, on the other
hand, the church in Khartoum on more than one occasion became a
place to reflect on the meaning of the British presence in the Sudan.

> Whatever may come, the age of confidence and power has passed,
> and it has been very brief as the history of Empires goes—too brief
> to have affected the hearts and minds of these people [the Suda-
> nese] deeply . . .

> [W]hat a difficult and delicate act of judgment is asked of the men
> in this secretariat! The yielding of power and the timing of that yield-
> ing, and by men formed in a tradition of authority whose only rea-
> son for their presence here is confidence in what they are doing.[44]

[41] Sudan Diary, 5 March 1948, Perham Papers 53/3.
[42] Ibid., 29 March 1948.
[43] Ibid.
[44] Ibid., 22 February 1948.

'The glory', as she reiterated on another occasion, 'the glory of absolute confidence not only in our beneficent autocracy but in its indefinite duration, is departing.'[45]

The transience of the British era was also a theme when she wrote about less sombre things than churches and soldiers. On the eve of her departure she attended a dinner at the Palace. It was held out of doors because of the heat. It is probably fair to say that she only half lamented the passing of the British era. The part of her that resisted the new era relished the entertainment characteristic of an earlier age. She had an eye for pomp and Imperial circumstance. Her diary would probably have been read with interest by critics of British imperialism at home and abroad, the ones who believed that the end of the British Empire would come none too soon. In any case, her comments would have provided good ammunition for Evelyn Waugh.

> Lamps in silver candle-sticks lit the long table and lamps hung on the palm trees and flowering shrubs. Everything was of the highest English standard—the standard of 20 years ago—beautiful silver, glass and flowers, luxurious food in many courses, perfect service, wines, liqueurs, bon-bons.

> The women were, of course, in full evening dress, a little pale and tired with the heat, but responding to the growing coolness of the evening and the wine. I felt like a watcher at a well produced play—admiring the scenery, the dresses, the actors—and wondering how long the run would last.[46]

On her last day, she accepted an invitation to sail up the Nile and swim. 'I knew I ought not to do it,' she wrote. 'But on this whole tour I have hardly had one hour of recreation and this was the last day.'

The Crisis of Sudanese Independence

'I have followed constitutional events in the Sudan with almost breathless interest,' she wrote to Robertson about the developments in the year following her visit in 1948.[47] Within the next few years, the creation of the superstructure of what she described as 'Western democratic institutions' seemed to be complete. She wrote that the British had helped create in the Sudan 'an elective two-chamber legislature, a Cabinet system, Westminster parliamentary procedure, and an

[45] Ibid., 10 March 1948.
[46] Ibid., 21 April 1948.
[47] Perham to Robertson, 15 Feb. 1949, Perham Papers 536/7.

independent judiciary and Civil Service'.[48] Had the British in the Sudan Political Service and the Sudanese then been left to themselves to develop those institutions, the result, in her view, would have been far more satisfactory than what actually transpired. In the event, the question of the Sudan's future, as she had feared, became entangled once more with the problem of the Canal Zone.

I shall not attempt to describe the sequence of events leading to the Sudanese declaration of independence in late 1955. There are, however, two landmarks that are important to recognize in order to make the problem of the transfer of power comprehensible from her vantage point. The first is the unilateral renunciation of the 1899 Agreement by the Egyptian government in late 1951 and the proclamation of King Farouk as King of Egypt and the Sudan. The second is the Egyptian revolution of 1952. These were momentous external events. In 1951 the Egyptians aimed at breaking the British grip over the Sudan by repudiating the legal foundation of the Condominium. After the revolution in July 1952, the military officers who ousted Farouk abandoned the ancient slogan of 'unity of the Nile Valley' and proclaimed that the Sudanese would be free to determine their own future. She wrote about General Mohammed Neguib, the prominent leader of the revolution, and the problems of the Sudan in 1952:

> General Neguib, by the refreshing contrast between his personality and methods and those of his predecessors [of King Farouk's regime], seems to have so captured the good opinion of the British Press and public that neither seems in the mood to scrutinize his recent [proposals] . . . on the Sudan with the care that our responsibilities for that country require.[49]

The faint praise of Neguib was in fact a veiled warning. She feared a Foreign Office sell-out to Egypt.

Her suspicions of the Foreign Office were deep-seated. She had no doubt at all that the Sudan would be sacrificed to Egypt if the strategic needs of the British Empire demanded it. She wrote in 1951 about the plans to bring Egypt into a 'Middle East Defence Organisation' that would complement NATO: 'Let us hope that the fate of the Sudan is not going to be the pawn in North Atlantic strategic interests.'[50] Unlike the Colonial Office, the Foreign Office, in her view, had

---

[48] 'Delicate Transfer of Rule in the Sudan', *The Times*, 16 June 1954; *Colonial Sequence, 1949–1969*, p. 90.

[49] 'The Choice before the Sudan', *The Times*, 17 November 1952; *Colonial Sequence, 1949–1969*, p. 72.

[50] Perham to Creech Jones, 11 October 1951, Perham Papers 23/1.

no tradition of protecting indigenous inhabitants from external pred-
ators, Egyptian or otherwise. 'I don't trust the Foreign Office in these
matters,' she once wrote to Robertson. 'Their tradition is all against
what I should regard [as] a properly open and democratic way of handling these situations.'[51]

The mistrust was reciprocated. Willie Morris, the head of the Sudan
Department of the Foreign Office, diligently read her letters to *The
Times*. He was not one of her admirers. Morris was later Ambassador
in Cairo. He was one of the ablest Foreign Office officials of his generation. His annoyance at her gratuitous advice to the Foreign Office
boiled over in response to her letter to *The Times* about Neguib and the
implication that the Foreign Office did not take seriously the commitment in the Sudan. He commented sarcastically about her suggestion
that there might be a premature transfer of power:

> It is entirely appropriate that she should do it [make the suggestion],
> since no one has done more to foster the illusion that if only we never
> contradict the politically ambitious amongst African peoples when
> they claim to be ready for the highest responsibility, if only we show
> unlimited sympathy, and never remind them of harsh practical facts
> which might offend, then they will somehow rise to the occasion and
> show an equivalent sense of responsibility.[52]

If she had been able to read the Foreign Office minutes, her fears
would have been confirmed. 'I think this price is worth paying,' the
Permanent Under-Secretary, Sir William Strang, wrote about yielding to the Egyptians on the Sudan to resolve the problem of the Canal Zone.[53]

She did not know, of course, of the secret Foreign Office calculations. Nevertheless she had, in her own phrase, 'a great suspicion' that
the business about the Canal Zone might throw out of step the already
rapid yet measured stride towards a transfer of power in the Sudan.
One of the remarkable features in her correspondence with Robertson was the comparison with India:

> The experience of India seemed to show that the act of transfer
> is not one that can be easily performed, but takes a tremendous
> amount of energy, determination and good will, on the side of the
> transferring power . . . I cannot help thinking that the more quickly

[51] Perham to Robertson, n.d. but January 1952, Perham Papers 536/7.
[52] Minute by Morris, 18 November 1952, FO 371/96912.
[53] Minute by Strang, 4 December 1952, FO 371/96915.

we act, the greater the likelihood of our retaining the good will of the moderates.[54]

She hoped that the Sudan, like India and Pakistan, would become a member of the Commonwealth, or at least would be treated more or less the same as other members through a treaty of alliance. She wrote to Robertson: 'If there is still any chance of bringing the Sudan, if not into the Commonwealth, into a kind of alliance with us, it would allow us to go on helping them.'[55] There was in fact never any prospect that the Sudan might be encouraged to join the Commonwealth. The Foreign Office officials, among other things, were wary of complications with Egypt.[56] Robertson knew of the Foreign Office's reasons, but in his letters to Margery Perham he preferred to emphasize the Sudanese rather than the British motives not to press for Commonwealth membership: 'These [Sudanese] chaps are all so ignorant and hidebound, mention of membership of the Commonwealth means to many of them continued British domination—and the phrase "dominion status" seems to prove that.'[57]

The Indian example appealed to her in part because of the skill of Mountbatten and the pageantry of the transfer of power in 1947. Was not the Sudan worthy of similar attention and ceremony? Mountbatten had captured her imagination, though not entirely positively. She wrote again to Robertson:

> Do you not think it might be a good idea if some big political figure came over to Cairo and Khartoum to carry through the hand-over? Don't for a moment imagine that this means that I have not got 100% confidence in you personally but I feel that these terribly difficult transfers have to be carried through with a certain amount of drama.
>
> Would not a Mountbatten help, especially if he were a little less ruthless and tempestuous in his methods?[58]

Her choice of the person to 'do a Mountbatten' in the Sudan was her friend Arthur Creech Jones, the former Secretary of State for the Colonies in the Labour Government. She believed that Creech Jones had the stature, the sympathy with Africans, and the sense of timing that would allow him to rise to the occasion. As Colonial Secretary, he

---

[54] Perham to Robertson, 6 December 1951, Perham Papers 536/7.
[55] Ibid.
[56] See, for example, FO 371/96852.
[57] Robertson to Perham, 28 January 1952, Perham Papers 536/7.
[58] Perham to Robertson, 27 November 1952, Perham Papers 536/7.

had taken the measure of African nationalism and had become convinced that it was better to take the risk of moving forward too quickly rather than yielding, as she once put it, 'too little and too late'.[59] In her judgement, he had handled the nationalist movement in the Gold Coast in a manner that would inspire confidence for a similar performance in the Sudan. She pointed out to Robertson the importance of drawing lessons from the Gold Coast experience:

> In almost all our dealings with the development of self-government (coloured people) we tend to underrate the psychological factors. I am following Gold Coast affairs very closely and I really think that we owe it to the Labour Government that we took the plunge there at the right moment.

> The immense good will that we have gained and the sense of responsibility that has been shown by Nkrumah have made me realise that if we give away gracefully in time what we have to give away we gain something quite new and of immense importance.[60]

Again, Robertson felt it necessary to dampen her enthusiasm. The lessons of India and the Gold Coast did not inspire the Foreign Office, which made no effort to find someone to do for the Sudan what Mountbatten had achieved at the time of Indian independence. Nor was the Sudan administration at first responsive, though Robertson did eventually arrive at a similar conclusion.[61] It must be said that if her suggestions had been followed, the events of Sudanese independence might have been more satisfactory from both the British and the Sudanese vantage points.

Instead, the Anglo-Egyptian Agreement on the Sudan of February 1953 came as a terrible blow to her. To pave the way towards agreement on the Canal Zone, the Foreign Office made concessions in the Sudan. These included speeding up the Sudanization of the administration, appointing an international commission (including Egyptian representatives) to supervise the process of self-determination—to be completed no later than the end of 1955—and setting a target date for independence shortly thereafter. These were terms, of course, that the Sudan political parties accepted wholeheartedly. As Robertson wrote in his diary, 'There seems little point in struggling, if all the

[59] Sudan Diary, 4 March 1948, Perham Papers 53/3.

[60] Perham to Robertson, n.d. but January 1952, Perham Papers 536/7.

[61] Robertson eventually wrote: 'Someone like Lord Mountbatten, General Templer or Mr Eden himself is what I have in mind' (memorandum by Robertson, 1 July 1954, FO 371/108324). He failed to persuade the Foreign Office.

[Sudanese] political parties are with Egypt.' [62] The Sudanese would be allowed to choose independence or union with Egypt (the option to join the Commonwealth was added to placate the British public, but was not seriously pursued).

The agreement of February 1953 was a turning point. Then and for ever after it signified to her the negative lessons to be learned about the management of African independence. One is reminded of her sober assessment at the time of the fall of Singapore, when she stated that experience was a rough teacher. For her personally, the calamity in the Sudan caused a comparable amount of soul searching. At Singapore, the Japanese had been a recognizable enemy; the military collapse precipitated a moral crisis within the British Empire. In the Sudan, the real enemy, as she had suspected, turned out to be the Foreign Office. The diplomatic collapse, as she viewed it, demoralized the Sudan Political Service and called into question the capacity of the British government to deal with the general problem of the transfer of power in Africa. At one stroke the Foreign Office nullified, in her judgement, the good work of half a century.

The charge is serious and the issues are complex, but essentially what happened was the dismantling of the colonial administration *before* independence. Here was her own description of the agreement as she analysed it in a letter to *The Times:*

> Under the terms of the agreement of February 1953, which the Foreign Office made with Egypt in the vain hope of easing the Suez Canal dispute, the British in the administration, the Defence Force and the police are to leave *before* the date set for self-determination . . . The terms of the agreement are unfortunate: they leave men tied to posts which are becoming difficult to hold, and entrust the initiative to discharge and the arrangements for cancellation and compensation to a Sudanese Ministry which has hitherto shown more complaisance towards Egypt than towards Britain. [63]

The last sentence is slightly cryptic but critical. She referred to the officers of the Sudan Political Service whose contracts could be cancelled: they now faced an abrupt termination of their careers. In her view, leaving the civil servants of the Sudan Political Service to fend for themselves was no less than a feckless abdication of responsibility

---

[62] Sir James Robertson, *Transition in Africa* (London, 1974), p. 151. In Robertson's view, the real villains in the piece were the Americans, who had pressed the British to settle with the Egyptians, thereby 'selling the Sudan' (p. 150).

[63] 'Delicate Transfer of Rule in the Sudan', *The Times,* 16 June 1954; *Colonial Sequence, 1949–1969,* p. 91.

by the Imperial government. There was also one regional problem to which she was especially sensitive. A British exodus would 'spell misery to the primitive south, where the tribes need expert and sympathetic handling'. She referred generally to 'a bitter conclusion to our partnership with a fine people'.

She visited the Sudan for a week in the month following the conclusion of the February 1953 agreement. Her diary is filled with words of bitterness, remorse, and despair. She immediately went to see Robertson:

> We went to the bone of our subject, and saw it in all its horrible shape. The end of one of the finest chapters in humane and efficient administration by one people of another that the world has ever seen.

> Everything crumbling—everything threatened with more or less ruin. If the F.O. had gone ahead [with the plans for elections without Egyptian interference] . . . they would have had a Sudanese Parliament and could have laughed at Neguib.

> But now the way was open for Egyptian interference and she [Egypt] was going to see the administrative service, the keystone of the arch, knocked out in 3 years.

> Now how could they [the officers in the S.P.S.] hold on for so long? Why should they? The service was full of bitterness—soon it would not be a service at all.

> Their misery, personal and professional and, deeper still, their love of the country and people, chimed in with my realization of all that may happen of collapse and bitterness and I went wretchedly to bed.[64]

She found nothing to be optimistic about. But she admired the fortitude of the officers of the Sudan Political Service: 'These people are the salt of the earth—or at least of our imperial world.'[65]

If her thoughts appeared to be morose or melodramatic, they were no more so than those of the officers who felt that they had been betrayed. A Sudan official wrote to her in 1954:

> You have struck the nail right on the head when you lay the Agreement or the blame for the authorship of the Agreement solely on the Foreign Office . . . the work of fifty years in the Sudan was thrown

[64] Sudan, Kenya, Uganda Diary 1953, 6 March 1953, Perham Papers 54/2.
[65] Ibid., 8 March 1953.

away in the hope that Egypt might toe the line over the Suez Canal issue.[66]

There is of course another side to the story. Willie Morris and others in the Foreign Office would have warmly denied her interpretation of scuttle. The British withdrew from the Sudan, rather as they would from a Middle Eastern than from an African country, and remained on good terms with the Sudanese. But from her point of view it was a calamitous example to set for the rest of Africa. She watched with distaste the approach to independence and the way in which the men of the Sudan Political Service were forced to wrangle over the severance of their salaries: 'Certainly the way our administration is running out slowly and rather sordidly, with all these arguments about pay and so on, is very disheartening.'[67]

'The Sudan has declared its independence,' she wrote to *The Times* in December 1955. She earnestly wished the Sudanese well in the future. The birth of the new state had not been auspicious, because of the serious revolt in the south, where unrest has persisted in one form or another to the present day. At the time, she lamented 'an appalling personal and professional loss' of British officers in the Sudan Political Service, since they might have reduced the killing.[68] About the insurgency itself, she believed that it might have been prevented only by a radically different policy towards the south, and one begun much earlier. On the other hand, there were some things that she was certain could have been prevented, above all the Foreign Office's treating the Sudan as 'the pawn in our Egyptian policy'.[69] To her, the high politics of the British government seemed to have reverted to the days of the Scramble for Africa. Yet it is worth recalling the confidence she had expressed a few years earlier that the British effort would not have been in vain. She had written in 1946 to Robertson:

> I feel sure that none of the good work that the British have put into the Sudan will be wasted. You have trained some good men and true among the Sudanese, and you have established standards of administration, and though they will certainly decline under Sudanese or Egyptian rule, the situation will never be as though they had not been established. I am certain these things enter into the fabric of society and are not lost.[70]

[66] R. C. Mayall to Perham, 16 June 1954, Perham Papers 536/5.
[67] Perham to Mayall, 30 June 1954, Perham Papers 536/5.
[68] Letter to *The Times; Colonial Sequence, 1949–1969*, pp. 128–29.
[69] Perham to Mayall, 23 June 1953, Perham Papers 536/5.
[70] Perham to Robertson, 10 December 1946, Perham Papers 538/2.

This fundamental optimism was characteristic. By 1952, however, a new note of disillusion tempered her outlook. The Sudanese had shrewdly manipulated the Egyptian and British governments to achieve their own independence. They had received Egyptian support, but it was the Sudanese themselves who kicked out the Sudan Political Service; gratitude was not a characteristic of colonial nationalism. That she already knew, but the point was now driven home with a vengeance. It was a sadder and a wiser Margery who wrote: 'Strange, that nothing short of the final act of transfer ever satisfies the nationalist.'[71]

Margery Perham and British Rule in Africa 1991

---

[71] Sudan, Kenya, Uganda Diary 1953, 11 March 1953, Perham Papers 54/2.

20

TAXING TRANSFERS OF POWER IN AFRICA

Sir Lewis Namier once stated that good history combines 'the great outline and the significant detail'. J. D. Hargreaves was Namier's junior colleague at the University of Manchester from 1948 to 1952. Namier disapproved of his decision to devote his career to Africa; Hargreaves had taught in Sierra Leone before becoming professor of African History at Aberdeen. *Decolonization in Africa* vindicates the commitment not only to African history but also to the subject in which both of them shared an interest, the growth of modern nationalism. As with Namier, so with Hargreaves: a meticulous concern for accuracy and a distrust of political ideas. The book can be read as an investigation into the motives of those who liquidated the colonial regimes—'how they consorted together', in Namier's famous phrase.

In the 1920s the European powers viewed the colonial future with confidence: no significant opposition existed either externally or internally—or, at least, so they believed. The economic dislocation of the 1930s, to which Hargreaves devotes extensive comment, caused the British and the French to introduce reforms and to begin to alter the political relationship in Africa from one based on force to one seeking collaboration. The critical period was that of the Second World War, when anti-colonial forces gained momentum above all in Asia but also in Africa. Between 1940 and 1945 the Colonial Office developed programmes of social engineering designed to reconstruct African societies in accordance with the ideals of the welfare state in Britain and the aims of a rapidly changing Commonwealth. The French, much more ambiguously, began to think of decolonization within the framework of a new French Union, with full assimilation for some communities and autonomy for others. Hargreaves is quite sober in his assessment of African nationalism within the context of European calculations. He is aware that he is going against the grain of contemporary historiography, which emphasizes the primacy of African initiatives in the collapse of the European regimes. His point is that to explain the phenomenon of decolonization, the historian must carefully assess how international forces, the changing circumstances in the metropolitan countries, and developments in Africa itself all interact. Neglect of any of these three dimensions will lead to distortion. On the other hand, Africanists have long been aware of the complexity of decolonization, and Hargreaves's assessment of the various dimensions may fail to convince them that any of the other forces are nearly as important as insistent African nationalism itself.

He is firm in his judgement that at the end of the Second World War 'the initiative still rested with those who sought a slow and controlled decolonization.' How then does he explain the dramatic transformation within the next fifteen years? This is the most original part of the book. The focus is mainly on the French and British colonial empires, though he does not neglect the Belgian Congo. Both the French and the British pragmatically sought economic and defence agreements, which were concluded mainly as bilateral treaties. The French, however, were much more willing to commit economic and military assistance to independent Francophone Africa. Hence the economic and military links between France and her former colonies are much stronger today than those between Britain and the former British dependencies.

When Harold Macmillan became Prime Minister in 1957, he tipped the balance against those who wished to give Africa the same sort of economic priority that the French gave it. In 1956, as Chancellor of the Exchequer, he had attempted to cut expenditure on colonial development; in 1957 he ordered a cost-benefit analysis: 'something like a profit and loss account for each of our colonial possessions, so that we may be better able to gauge whether, from the financial and economic point of view, we are likely to gain or lose by its departure.' Macmillan's directive led to sober reassessments that ironically bucked up Tory diehards in their determination not to abandon Imperial possessions while also steeling the Labour Party not to prejudice existing policies by hasty withdrawal. But as Hargreaves points out, the British situation differed substantially from the French. After the Suez crisis of 1956, Britain's straitened circumstances caused a tightening of financial and military resources at the expense of Imperial commitments in Africa.

Ultimately, the main thrust of the shifts described in *Decolonization in Africa* is the attempt to shed the costs of colonial rule while perpetuating the advantages. Those who liquidated the colonial empires did not regard the motive of self-interest as dishonourable. In the tradition of their predecessors, they believed in a harmony of interests, so that former subjects as well as former rulers would benefit from the new relationship. From the vantage point of the 1980s, the idealism of the 1950s and 1960s appears grotesquely naive. What went wrong? How can the wide discrepancy between hopes and results be explained? On the British side, Hargreaves gives a measured answer. It was not the plan for a rapid transfer of power that was wrong, nor the way it was implemented. The fault lay with later British governments that indifferently squandered the moral and political heritage of the British era in Africa.

Trade union and co-operative advisers, teachers in schools and universities, many younger officers in the administrative and technical services, had without deliberate intent built a capital of goodwill which . . . was a priceless asset to statesmen seeking to terminate colonial rule and prepare for continuing cooperation. The practical help and moral support offered from within the UK by many politicians, university teachers, clergy and journalists worked in the same direction.

Having been a university teacher himself in Africa, Hargreaves writes with understandable bitterness about the declines of Britain's educational and cultural ties with Africa, engendered by the short-sighted mentality of cost accountants.

At another level, *Decolonization in Africa* finally attempts to answer a basic historical question. Why were the Europeans, particularly the British, compelled to grant Africans independence faster, and with less preparation, than had been intended? Hargreaves does not respond as boldly as the reader might wish, but part of the answer lies with the hero who emerges in the last part. He is the Yorkshire-born Scottish Highlander Iain Macleod, who became Macmillan's Colonial Secretary in October 1959. For me, this was the revelation of the book, though Hargreaves does not make the analogy that sprang into my own mind: Macleod was to Africa as Mountbatten had been to India.

Macleod possessed a razor-sharp intellect and a moral passion that convinced him that the problem of decolonization consisted in being able to move fast enough: 'Sensitive both to the moral challenge of African nationalism and to the political perils of resisting it, Macleod concluded . . . that the dangers of over-rapid decolonization were less than those of moving too slowly.' He provided the 'genuine moral conviction' necessary to disengage politically. In suppressing the ambitions of the white-settler communities, he was more successful in Kenya than in Rhodesia, but in both cases he demonstrated 'a capacity for coolly ruthless calculation' as well as a will of iron. He brought about African independence in a much shorter time than almost any of his contemporaries believed possible. John Hargreaves judges that he was justified in taking the political risk. One of the ironies of the aftermath was the betrayal of Macleod's legacy by later British governments.

Times Literary Supplement   10 February 1989

21

THE DISSOLUTION OF THE BRITISH EMPIRE
IN THE ERA OF VIETNAM

My purpose is threefold: to reflect on British imperialism in South-East Asia in the 1950s and 1960s; to establish a connection between the British colonial experience and the American presence in Vietnam; and to pursue the idea of memory, time, and place in the context of those themes.

The Vietnam War is of course within living memory, though it is perhaps worth bearing in mind that it is as remote to our students as the First World War was to me as a young assistant professor at Yale in the 1960s. The liquidation of the British Empire is also a matter of the immediate past, especially if one brings the end of it down to the reversion of Hong Kong to China in 1997. My points of concentration in the 1960s will be the legendary naval base and colony, Singapore, and the creation of the state known today as Malaysia, or 'Greater Malaya'. I also mention, as part of the background, Aden and Rhodesia as two other major colonial problems of the 1960s. Aden was the colony and protectorate at the tip of the Arabian peninsula. Some commentators at the time described Aden as Britain's Vietnam—though part of my conclusion will be that Malaysia's confrontation with Indonesia in the mid-1960s was, at least potentially, a much more serious conflict. Rhodesia (today's Zimbabwe) was the breakaway, self-governing African colony that in 1965 unilaterally declared independence, on the model of the United States of America. Rhodesia held a much more prominent place in British consciousness than did Singapore, Malaysia, or Aden, but all are examples of what has been called the death rattle of British imperialism. In a more general way, my analysis concerns memory, time, and place; the passions of the 1960s in our collective memory; and the continuity as well as the different shapes of British imperialism in South-East Asia, the Middle East, and Africa.

Discussing such controversial subjects will force me to take a position, and I shall develop the argument that the events in Vietnam, Singapore, and Malaysia were not merely interconnected but can be studied in such a way as to illuminate the spirit of the age—a deeply anti-imperial age, but then as now not without its champions of the British Imperial mission or the American cause in Vietnam. The ideological currents of the Vietnam War and decolonization are at last ebbing, though there are certain fixed ideas. In the popular view, the Empire came clattering down—Churchill's phrase—in the 1960s. Yet the withdrawal of all forces East of Suez was not completed until 1971, and the major issue of Rhodesia was not resolved until 1980. The

Empire continues today in such places as Gibraltar, the Falklands, scattered islands throughout the world, and, some would say, Northern Ireland. Though concerned with the 1960s, by concentrating on South-East Asia, or for that matter the Middle East, I run the risk of conveying the impression that the Empire came to an abrupt end. Like the beginning, the end was complex: a broader unfolding could begin at least as far back as Indian independence in 1947 and extend to the present.

In 1968 the US Secretary of State, Dean Rusk, commented that he was 'profoundly dismayed' by the British intention to evacuate all forces from South-East Asia and the Middle East:

> This represented a major withdrawal of the UK from world affairs, and it was a catastrophic loss to human society. These decisions involved the highest level of judgment and of instinct about where the human family was going. We were facing a difficult period in world affairs and Britain was saying it would not be there.[1]

His lament, of course, has to be understood in the context of Vietnam, where the United States found little support among Western countries other than Australia and New Zealand. A perceptive British observer of American politics commented: '[M]ost Americans feel rather lonely about Vietnam.'[2] The year 1967 saw the publication of Bertrand Russell's *War Crimes in Vietnam*, and one British politician commented in retrospect that 'the feeling against the war in Vietnam was so strong that [the] Labour [Party] . . . regarded [it] as the most immoral act since the Holocaust.'[3]

Lyndon Baines Johnson was once described by a distinguished American historian as 'a President who talks like a Baptist preacher and who inherited his disaster from a Secretary of State [Dean Rusk] who was also a ruling elder of the Presbyterian Church'.[4] That com-

[1] Memorandum of Conversation, 11 January 1968, *Foreign Relations of the United States, 1964–1968*, XII, p. 608.

[2] N. C. C. Trench to J. E. Cable, Confidential–Guard [Guard = not for American eyes], 13 August 1965, FO 371/180543. Part of Trench's job in the British Embassy in Washington was to gauge the reaction of the American public to the war. Another official commented: '[W]hat the President wants is for a few British soldiers to get killed in Viet Nam along-side the Americans so that their photographs can appear in the American press and demonstrate to American public opinion that the principal ally of the United States is contributing to a joint effort' (minute by A. M. Palliser, 28 July 1965, FO 371/180543).

[3] Roy Hattersley, *Fifty Years On: A Prejudiced History of Britain since the War* (London, 1997), p. 184.

[4] John K. Fairbank, 'Assignment for the '70s', *American Historical Review*, 74 (February 1969), p. 879.

ment was not unrepresentative of British views as well. The British Prime Minister, Harold Wilson, was always studiously polite to LBJ, and LBJ in turn referred to Wilson in public as 'Shakespeare'.[5] But at other times Wilson had to endure the President's sanctimonious and earthy invective. Once asked why he put up with it, and why Britain did not take a stronger line against the war in Vietnam, Wilson gave an entirely candid reply: 'Because we can't kick our creditors in the balls.'[6] In that single crude phrase he went to the heart of the matter.[7] In the 1960s the United States still propped up the faltering British economy, which in three successive decades had lurched from the convertibility crisis of 1947, to devaluation in 1949, to economic haemorrhage during the Suez emergency in 1956–57, and again to devaluation in 1967. British trade deficits plunged to their worst level in history in October 1967, the month of the 50,000-strong march on the Pentagon and anti-war demonstrations throughout the world. On 28 November 1967 the Prime Minister announced that the pound

---

[5] Or, to place Wilson much more accurately in British political tradition: '[H]e had an almost Gladstonian belief in his own righteousness . . . He was [also] somewhat like David Lloyd George' (Chris Wrigley, 'Now You See It, Now You Don't: Harold Wilson and Labour's Foreign Policy, 1964–70', in R. Coopey, S. Fielding, and N. Tiratsoo, eds., *The Wilson Governments, 1964–1970* (London, 1993), pp. 126–27.

[6] Philip Ziegler, *Wilson: The Authorised Life of Lord Wilson of Rievaulx* (London, 1993), pp. 228–29. The other major biography is Ben Pimlott, *Harold Wilson* (London, 1992). Both biographers assess Wilson favourably, though not uncritically. It is useful to bear in mind severer appraisals, for example:

> Wilson was . . . a mediocre but ruthless man . . . The Labour government which Wilson led . . . was immolated morally by its support of a war of atrocity and aggression in Vietnam and immolated politically by its fetishisation of an impossible and illusory position for sterling . . . The price exacted by Lyndon Johnson for support of sterling was that British Labour lent its vanishing prestige to his Indochina adventure. This was and remains a worse historical humiliation even than Suez.

Christopher Hitchens, 'Say What You Will about Harold', *London Review of Books* (2 December 1993). See also Clive Ponting, *Breach of Promise: Labour in Power, 1964–1970* (London, 1989). For Wilson's own memoir, see Harold Wilson, *The Labour Government, 1964–1970: A Personal Record* (London, 1971).

[7] As did Philip Toynbee in the *New Statesman*, 5 January 1968:

> We protest against the government's wretched support for the American crime in Vietnam . . . [But] we are economically dependent on the US. If we incensed the American government either by withdrawing from our East-of-Suez commitments or by condemning the Vietnam war, then the Americans would make it unbearably hot for us economically.

Reprinted in Kingsley Amis, ed., *Harold's Years: Impressions from the 'New Statesman' and the 'Spectator'* (London, 1977), pp. 56–60.

would be devalued by 14.3 per cent to \$2.40.[8] Devaluation, as the British rediscovered, is one of the most serious steps a government can take. It not only causes anxiety about inflation and savings but also impinges on national self-esteem. In Britain in 1967, the public mood reflected a general sense of national decline.[9]

The decision to devalue sterling in 1967 merely accelerated a process long underway of liquidating the major remnants of the Empire, but the economic crisis gave the impression, then and for ever after, of precipitating a scuttle. The Minister of Defence, Denis Healey, described the defence budget as a 'runaway train'. To reduce expenditures and minimize the danger of holding a military base in Asia, he had already decided in the previous year to close down the Singapore base—not immediately, but at some point in the mid-1970s, perhaps in ten years.[10] In mid-1967 these debates on military and colonial retreat took place against the background of momentous events in the Middle East and in the context of possible British entry into the European Common Market. In June the Six Day War disrupted the flow of oil and further strained the economy.[11] The members of the British

[8] For the background to the decision in both Washington and London, and generally on Anglo-American economic relations in the 1960s, see Diane B. Kunz, *Butter and Guns: America's Cold War Economic Diplomacy* (New York, 1997), chap. 6. Other useful works on Anglo-American relations that are relevant to my themes are C. J. Bartlett, *'The Special Relationship': A Political History of Anglo-American Relations since 1945* (London 1992); John Baylis, ed., *Anglo-American Relations since 1939: The Enduring Alliance* (Manchester, UK, 1997); and Alan P. Dobson, *The Politics of the Anglo-American Economic Special Relationship, 1940–1987* (Brighton, 1988).

[9] For the sense in the American government that 'British political culture was permeated by a kind of defeatist and disenchanted apathy', see John Dumbrell, *The Making of US Foreign Policy* (Manchester, UK, 1990), p. 224. On the general subject of decline, see Peter Clarke and Clive Trebilcock, eds., *Understanding Decline: Perceptions and Realities of British Economic Performance* (Cambridge, 1997).

[10] See above all Karl Hack, *Defence and Decolonisation in Southeast Asia: Britain, Malaya and Singapore, 1941–1968* (Richmond, UK, 2001); and two carefully written and useful articles by Simon J. Ball, 'Harold Macmillan and the Politics of Defence', *Twentieth Century British History*, 6, 1 (1995), and 'Macmillan and British Defence Policy', in Richard Aldous and Sabine Lee, eds., *Harold Macmillan and Britain's World Role* (London, 1996). See also C. J. Bartlett, *The Long Retreat: A Short History of British Defence Policy, 1945–70* (London, 1972); Phillip Darby, *British Defence Policy East of Suez, 1947–1968* (Oxford, 1973); Michael Dockrill, *British Defence since 1945* (Oxford, 1988); and Michael Carver, *Tightrope Walking: British Defence Policy since 1945* (London, 1992).

[11] The Middle Eastern war revived a long-standing analogy, used by the Chinese themselves, about the Chinese of Singapore as 'the Jews of Asia . . . Singapore was to become "Little Israel", a diminutive, bellicose, indigestible socialist state bracketed by the bigger, predominantly Muslim sister-nations of Malaysia and Indonesia' (Dennis Bloodworth, *An Eye for the Dragon: Southeast Asia Observed, 1954–1986* [Singapore, 1987], p. 306). In October 1967 the government of Singapore recruited Israeli military advisers (under the official designation of 'Mexican agricultural advisers') to train the armed forces. See T. J. S. George, *Lee Kuan Yew's Singapore* (London, 1973), p. 170: 'Singapore's decision to follow the Israeli pattern . . . suggested that the confrontation

Cabinet now proved to be bitterly divided not only on the liquidation of the Empire but also on Europe.[12] Those who took a robust view, not least the Prime Minister himself, hoped that it might still be possible to transform the defeatist mood of decline and instill a revived sense of national purpose.[13] Regardless of Britain's future relationship with Europe, might the Empire continue to exist in a new or informal guise, extending in an eastward arc from Britain to Aden to Singapore?

British sway in the Malayan peninsula can be traced to Stamford Raffles and the founding of a trading settlement at Singapore in 1819, but since my subject deals in part with living or collective memory, I take as my point of departure the Malaya of Somerset Maugham, who was to Malaya as Kipling was to India. In Maugham's Malaya of the inter-war years, Singapore society was orderly, stable, and calm on the surface, but rotten underneath. British civil servants as well as the owners of the rubber plantations often led dissolute lives of drink, gambling, horses, and womanizing.[14] Though a caricature, the notion of moral degeneracy became indelibly associated with the fall of Singapore to Japanese forces on 15 February 1942.[15] The sense of ethical decadence or culpability lived on from one generation to the next. Sir Arthur de la Mare, a British official who at one stage of the Vietnam War presided over the South-East Asia Department of the Foreign Office, reflected late in his career that Singapore exerted a strange fascination, at once attractive and repellent: attractive because of its 'vigour,

between the Chinese of Singapore and the non-Chinese of neighbouring countries was similar to that between the Jews and the Arabs.'

[12] See John Darwin, 'Britain's Withdrawal from East of Suez', in Carl Bridge, ed., *Munich to Vietnam: Australia's Relations with Britain and the United States since the 1930s* (Melbourne, 1991).

[13] Roy Jenkins, Chancellor of the Exchequer, 1967–70, recalls the pro-Empire members of the Cabinet as 'worthy of a conclave of Joseph Chamberlain, Kitchener of Khartoum and George Nathaniel Curzon'. In 1967 their counterparts would have been George Thompson (Commonwealth Secretary), Denis Healey (Minister for Defence), and George Brown (Foreign Secretary) —though Jenkins, alas, did not make direct individual comparisons (Roy Jenkins, *A Life at the Centre* [London, 1991], pp. 224–25).

[14] As a corrective to Maugham's Malaya, see especially T. N. Harper, 'The Passing of the Somerset Maugham Era', chap. 1 of *The End of Empire and the Making of Malaya* (Cambridge, 1999). For the African equivalent, see Bruce Berman and John Lonsdale, *Unhappy Valley: Conflict in Kenya and Africa* (London, 1992). The closest Asian parallel is that of Shanghai. See Robert Bickers, 'Shanghailanders: The Formation and Identity of the British Settler Community in Shanghai, 1843–1937', *Past and Present,* 159 (May 1998).

[15] There is an abundant and ever-growing literature on the fall of Singapore. For important recent essays, see Malcolm H. Murfett et al., eds., *Between Two Oceans: A Military History of Singapore from First Settlement to Final British Withdrawal* (Oxford, 1999); and Christopher M. Bell, 'The "Singapore Strategy" and the Deterrence of Japan: Winston Churchill, the Admiralty and the Dispatch of Force Z', *English Historical Review,* 116 (June 2001).

industry, bustle and thrust', repellent 'because I am reminded of the shame of 1942'. He emphasized the word 'shame' in a passage describing the sense of guilt at the worst military defeat in British history.

> [E]very day I am reminded of the shame of 1942. It was as a diplomatic prisoner in Japan that, on my birthday, I heard of Singapore's surrender. Mercifully for all of us held captive in the enemy's capital we were then too numbed and too uninformed to realise that what had taken place was not only an appalling military disaster but the most shameful disgrace in Britain's imperial history.

> It was only later that we heard of the irresolution, the incompetence and the bungling of those charged here [Singapore] with the duty of defending not merely Britain's military interests, but her very name. One may or may not regret the passing of Empire but no loyal British subject living in Singapore can forget that it was here that the hollowness of the imperial ethos was so cruelly and so shamefully exposed.[16]

I have quoted de la Mare's lamentation at length because it is an interesting merger of memory, time, and place. Some three decades after the fall of Singapore, the memory and the pain for the British remained as vivid as ever, just as for us the memory and the pain of Vietnam have not faded after three decades. And in a different way the events of 11 September 2001 will influence our interpretation of earlier historical episodes. In the cases of Singapore and Vietnam, collective memory became legend or myth—which in a positive sense can inspire imaginative understanding of the past. But myth also obscures historical reality.

Memory, time, and place: two of my subjects are Singapore since 1942 and Malaya's independence in 1957, leading to the later creation of Malaysia. According to the heroic rendition, the British after 1945 redeemed themselves for the fall of Singapore by resolution,

---

[16] De la Mare to Foreign and Commonwealth Office, 2 October 1970, FCO 24/885. Those were stern words, and de la Mare regretted equally the signs of hedonism in the post-colonial Singapore of the early 1970s. It is thus ironic not only that today's Singapore bears permanent features of Britain's architectural legacy—the Raffles Hotel, for example, has been restored to a degree of garishness and luxury that Somerset Maugham would have found virtually unrecognizable—but also that the government of Singapore enforces a severe disciplinary code for the abuse of drugs and in general a certain puritanical standard of behaviour. Lee Kuan Yew (Prime Minister of Singapore, 1959–90), once commented on three hippies whose hair had been cut off by Singapore police: 'Things like this happen in the best of places. If any embarrassment has been caused, we can send them three wigs. We make wigs here' (quoted in Thomas J. Bellows, 'Big Fish, Small Pond', *Wilson Quarterly*, 7 [Winter 1983], p. 80). See also, by the same author, *The People's Action Party of Singapore: Emergence of a Dominant Party System* (New Haven, 1970).

selfless dedication, and hard work in Malaya. During the insurrection of 1948–60, known as the 'Emergency', the British defeated communist guerrilla forces, developed the rubber and tin industries that made Malaya a significant part of the world economy as well as a vital component of Britain's post-war economic recovery, and built both the infrastructure and the polity of a modern nation.[17] In this version of history, the British thus fulfilled their dual mandate to develop Malaya for the benefit of the indigenous peoples as well as for the British themselves.[18] This is a myth that cries out for reassessment. The British had not come to Malaya, in the words of a recent historian, 'to collect butterflies'.[19]

In the 1950s the British were confronted with an insurgency, which provided the motivation to build a unified state and attempt the reconciliation of the indigenous Malays with the Malayan Chinese. Bear in mind these round figures. In 1957, Malaya was a country with a population of six million and an area of fifty thousand square miles, about one-fifth the size of Texas. The island of Singapore had a population of nearly 1,500,000, more than twice the population of Houston at that time! Singapore's population was predominantly—three-fourths —Chinese. In the 1960s the British feared that Singapore might become a Chinese Cuba. How then did the British manage to defeat the communist insurgents so efficiently that Malaya became a model for the Americans in Vietnam, to create a political union of the patchwork of Malay states strong enough to endure after independence in 1957, and to resolve, if only by acquiescence, the problem of Singapore?

In answering those questions, it helps to deploy the fertile concept of the 'colonial state', which, like Hobbes's Leviathan, set out to raise taxes, suppress revolt, defend the frontiers, and forge a unified economic and political structure.[20] All this amounted to one of the most ambitious state-building projects in the post-war era. In 1945–49 the British pumped £86 million in grants and loans into Malaya's economic development, a huge amount in view of the Labour Government's scarce resources. Malayan rubber and tin production reached

---

[17] For a careful examination of the extent to which the insurrection was inspired or led by communists, see A. J. Stockwell, '"Widespread and Long-Concocted Plot to Overthrow Government in Malaya"? The Origins of the Malayan Emergency', *Journal of Imperial and Commonwealth History*, 21, 3 (September 1993).

[18] On this theme, see Robert Heussler, *British Rule in Malaya, 1942–57* (Singapore, 1983).

[19] Harper, *End of Empire and the Making of Malaya*, p. 58.

[20] See especially Crawford Young, *The African Colonial State in Comparative Perspective* (New Haven, 1994); for the colonial Leviathan, see Ronald Hyam, 'The British Empire in the Edwardian Era', in Judith Brown and W. R. Louis, eds., *The Oxford History of the British Empire: The Twentieth Century* (Oxford, 1999), pp. 58–61.

record heights at the time of the Korean War; windfall revenues from the boom financed the war against the guerrilla insurgents.[21] Malaya was the top producer of the world's rubber—rubber plantations covered two-thirds of the colony's cultivated soil—though its position as a ranking supplier of rubber eroded later in the decade.[22] Malaya in the 1950s also provided 50 per cent of the world's tin. While Malaya's economy boomed, Singapore made major leaps forward as a thriving trade and manufacturing entrepôt. The number of people employed by the Malayan government increased from 48,000 in 1948 to 140,000 a decade later.[23] This was state building with a vengeance, but Singapore remained apart as a separate colony.

As a consequence of 1942–45 wartime planning, the Colonial Office after the war detached Singapore from Malaya, establishing it as an autonomous colony with its own Governor. There was an underlying logic to this decision. Merging Singapore, an extremely populous and predominantly Chinese city, with Malaya might intensify Malay suspicions of a Chinese takeover. On the other hand, Singapore as a separate colony might remain an impregnable military and naval fortress for ever under British paramountcy. Commercially, it might become a Hong Kong of the south. Yet there was a counter-logic. Singapore was a city 'as large in relation to the country as a whole as London is in relation to the United Kingdom'.[24] Keeping the city separate was no more reasonable than sealing off London from the rest of Britain. Economically, socially, and geographically, Singapore was an integral part of the Malayan peninsula. A causeway joined it to the mainland by road and rail.

The two contradictory patterns of logic eventually intersected. The

---

[21] See Richard Stubbs, 'The Malayan Emergency and the Development of the Malaysian State', in Paul B. Rich and Richard Stubbs, eds., *The Counter-Insurgent State: Guerrilla Warfare and State Building in the Twentieth Century* (London, 1997).

[22] See especially Nicholas J. White, *Business, Government, and the End of Empire: Malaya, 1942–1957* (Kuala Lumpur, 1996), which portrays the vulnerability or fragility of the Malayan economy and the ambivalent relations between business and government. For the modernization of the rubber industry in the 1950s, see Martin Rudner, 'Malayan Rubber Policy: Development and Anti-Development during the 1950s', *Journal of Southeast Asian Studies*, 7, 2 (September 1976).

[23] Richard Stubbs, *Hearts and Minds in Guerrilla Warfare: The Malayan Emergency, 1948–1960* (Singapore, 1989), p. 263. This number included some 500 former members of the Palestine Police, who helped transform the Malayan police into an effective paramilitary force. See A. J. Stockwell, 'Policing during the Malayan Emergency, 1948–60: Communism, Communalism, and Decolonisation', in David M. Anderson and David Killingray, eds., *Policing and Decolonisation: Politics, Nationalism, and the Police, 1917–65* (Manchester, UK, 1992).

[24] Minute by Sydney Caine, 1 December 1943, in A. J. Stockwell, ed., *Malaya* (*British Documents on the End of Empire* [*BDEEP*], series B, 3 vols., London, 1995), I, p. 63. This British documentary series is indispensable for all aspects of British colonial history since 1945.

colony would develop autonomously, but later on—assuming Singapore did not remain a permanent British colony—it might form part of a federation with Malaya. This idea could be traced to the 1940s or earlier, and then as later it seemed to be a compelling vision: 'a substantial block of territories with Singapore as its centre of trade and communication . . . [possessing] a potential strength which would offer promise of economic and political development.'[25] Virtually no one in the 1940s or 1950s anticipated Singapore's future as an independent city-state. The general sentiment in the city could be summed up in the words of a contemporary Singaporean verdict: 'Nobody in his senses believes that Singapore alone, in isolation, can be independent.'[26] In 1959 Singapore became self-governing, but the British retained rights to the base as well as control over foreign affairs and internal security.

In the 1950s, British forces in Malaya had fought a bitter and ultimately successful war against the insurgents by regrouping some 500,000 rural Chinese into 'new villages', where the British attempted to win 'hearts and minds'. This is a phrase that Americans associate with Vietnam, but it had its origins in Malaya with General Sir Gerald Templer.[27] To mobilize the totality of the colonial state against the insurgents, Templer was given unparalleled plenipotentiary military and civil powers, as if he were a 1950s Cromwell.[28] Templer's unrelenting drive and ruthless efficiency contributed to the defeat of the communist guerrilla forces and also to the construction of a powerful, unitary state. This transformation was accompanied by certain comic interludes. Once when addressing the Chinese inhabitants of one of the new villages, Templer said: 'You are all bastards.' The Chinese interpreter translated: '[H]is excellency says none of your parents were married.' Templer: 'And I can be a bastard too.' Chinese interpreter: '[H]is excellency says his parents were also unmarried.'[29]

During the 1950s, the infrastructure of Malaya was extended into

[25] Quotation from a 1942 Colonial Office document in A. J. Stockwell, 'Colonial Planning during World War II: The Case of Malaya', *Journal of Imperial and Commonwealth History*, II, 3 (May 1974), p. 338.

[26] Quoted in C. M. Turnbull, *A History of Singapore, 1819–1988* (Singapore, 2nd edn., 1989), p. 267.

[27] See Stubbs, *Hearts and Minds in Guerrilla Warfare*.

[28] 'With the powers of a Cromwell at his disposal, he often looked like the Lord Protector, albeit in his English rather than his Irish role' (Anthony Short, *The Communist Insurrection in Malaya, 1948–1960* [New York, 1975], p. 386). Short's book is the classic work on the insurgency. For the military campaign, see especially Richard L. Clutterbuck, *The Long Long War: Counterinsurgency in Malaya and Vietnam* (New York, 1966).

[29] Heussler, *British Rule in Malaya*, p. 186.

remote parts of the country, and grew to include airfields, roads, bridges, canals, radio networks, power lines, and electrification. In this complex process, war and economic development forged a new sense of national identity. The British had anticipated the rapid growth of Malayan nationalism, so in the mid-1950s, when they assessed the possibility that the movement for independence might veer out of control, they decided to yield to moderate nationalist demands before it was too late. By granting—or yielding to—the independence of Malaya in 1957, the British avoided the fate of the Dutch in Indonesia and the French in Indo-China.

The British were able to defeat the communist guerrillas primarily because the full force of the colonial state could be brought to bear on the insurgents—in contrast to Vietnam, where the United States was not the colonial master and could exert, in the phrase of the day, only leverage rather than control.[30] The winning of hearts and minds in the reconstructed villages of Malaya occurred because it was undertaken—in British self-interest—as a sustained, dedicated effort that held out the promise of a better life to the rural inhabitants. This vast experiment in social engineering secured improved living conditions, local representation, and, above all, legal entitlement to the land. Nevertheless, the lessons from Malaya's social revolution were difficult to apply to the very different circumstances in Vietnam, even though the Americans tried hard to do so, having studied closely the British methods of counter-insurgency as well the techniques and aims of reconstructing rural villages.

In the early 1960s the British worked in concert with the Malayan Prime Minister, the Tunku (Prince) Abdul Rahman, to achieve a federation of 'Greater Malaysia'.[31] The motivation was in part the need to cope with the increasing instability and radicalism of Singapore. On the left of Singapore's political spectrum there was articulate and stalwart sympathy for the People's Republic of China. The British saw the danger of subversion in the active and well-organized trade unions. Federation with Malaya seemed to be the answer: not only could

---

[30] For other critical differences, including those of geography and ethnic composition of the two countries, and for comparisons as far afield as Algeria and the Congo, Clutterbuck, *The Long Long War* is unconventional and useful despite its insistent Cold War tone.

[31] See Matthew Jones, *Conflict and Confrontation in South East Asia, 1961–1965: Britain, the United States and the Creation of Malaysia* (Cambridge, 2002), a major new work on which I have relied for my own interpretation. See also especially S. J. Ball, 'Selkirk in Singapore', *Twentieth Century British History*, 10, 2 (1999). For the Tunku in Malaysian politics, see Mohamed Noordin Sopiee, *From Malayan Union to Singapore Separation: Political Unification in the Malaysia Region, 1945–65* (Kuala Lumpur, 1974).

internal security be controlled from the capital at Kuala Lumpur, but federations were also the grand design of the 1950s and 1960s in the Middle East, Africa, and the Caribbean as well as South-East Asia. Larger territorial units, in this case Malaysia, would be more economically viable than fragmented pieces of empire such as Singapore, which represented the type of 'micro-state', as they became known, that everyone wanted to avoid.

The plan for a greater Malaysian federation included, besides Singapore, territories in neighbouring Borneo to balance the ratio of Malays and Chinese. The Malays were thus to be reassured that the Chinese would not outnumber them. Malay suspicion of the Chinese, however, could not be quenched. Just as the Africans in the Central African Federation had been apprehensive about the supremacy of the white settlers, so the Malays feared dominance by the Chinese, whatever their numerical proportion.[32] The Chinese, for their part, resented their treatment, at least on the mainland, as second-class citizens: their franchise was restricted and they bore the brunt of a different scale of taxation. Just as the Malays saw themselves as an ethnic group who, by kinship and sentiment, were related to the peoples of Indonesia and the greater Malay world of South-East Asia, so the Chinese of Singapore were conscious of their cultural heritage, though they were bitterly divided on the issue whether Singapore should defy the West and turn to Communist China. The British High Commissioner in Malaysia summed up this complex society in a manner hardly profound yet nevertheless revealing of the British perception: 'Right-wing Chinese hate Left-wing Chinese, Malays are frightened of Chinese, and the Left-wing Malays dislike the Tunku's régime.'[33]

Two dominant but conflicting visions of Malaysia become apparent in the ambitions of the Tunku Abdul Rahman—known universally to the British simply as 'the Tunku'—and the politician who emerged as the leader of Singapore, Lee Kuan Yew. The Tunku cultivated a reputation for having the 'Edwardian outlook' of an Anglicized Malay of an older generation. In a way, the Tunku was to Malaya as Harold Macmillan was to Britain. The British came to regard the Tunku as a comrade-in-arms, the 'brown brother' often sought as a collaborator but seldom found. But he was not a stooge. When dealing with the highly intelligent Lee Kuan Yew, he sometimes gave the impression of being out of his depth, but in fact the Tunku knew what he wanted and tenaciously stuck to his goals. Sometimes charming and ebullient, at

---

[32] See especially Albert Lau, *A Moment of Anguish: Singapore in Malaysia and the Politics of Disengagement* (Singapore, 1998).

[33] Lord Head to Commonwealth Relations Office, 11 December 1963, FO 371/175065.

other times pugnacious and emotional, he aimed to incorporate Singapore into a greater Malaysia to prevent the city from gravitating into the orbit of Communist China.[34] But there were great risks. In a united Singapore and Malaya, the Chinese would outnumber the Malays. Thus the Tunku planned to include the three British territories on the island of Borneo—Brunei, Sarawak, and North Borneo—to preserve a non-Chinese majority.[35] As a precondition for the new state, the Tunku insisted that leaders of the radical left-wing Barisan Sosialis (Socialist Front) and other political enemies in Singapore be jailed indefinitely. This demand for repressive action caused soul searching on the part of the British. The evidence for subversive activity was slender or non-existent, nor did the British believe that there was any immediate danger of a communist takeover. But they agreed eventually to the lock-up.[36]

Lee Kuan Yew had studied law at Cambridge. He was tough mannered and clear minded. The characteristic British view was that personally he demonstrated 'no warmth, humanity or humour'.[37] Publicly

[34] The following passage well reflects both the contemporary and retrospective British view of the Tunku, who served as Prime Minister of Malaya (1957–63) and Malaysia (1963–70):

> The Tunku was straightforward, steady and slow . . . No one could have survived in office for so long without political skills of the highest order . . . Perhaps it was the fact that many of them [the British] looked down on him intellectually—he always consulted the racing calendar before agreeing to an official engagement—that made them so fond of him.

Brian Lapping, *End of Empire* (London, 1985), pp. 188–90.

[35] The populations of the territories were as follows: Brunei: 118,000 (mainly Malay); Sarawak: 750,000 (including, among others, 130,000 Malay, 230,000 Chinese, plus 238,000 Sea Dyaks [Ibans] and 58,000 Land Dyaks); and North Borneo: 450,000 (104,000 Chinese and the rest indigenous peoples). The total Chinese population of the Borneo territories was calculated generally as being less than 350,000. In round figures, the Chinese in the new federation of Malaysia would be 3.7 million and would be outnumbered by 4 million Malays. In dealing with these nominal and, in the case of Borneo, highly hypothetical figures, Lee Kuan Yew preferred a calculation that would establish an equal number of 4 million Chinese and 4 million Malays. But in any estimate, the additional Indians, indigenous peoples, and others would constitute a non-Chinese majority.

For North Borneo (Sabah), see M. H. Baker, *Sabah: The First Ten Years as a Colony, 1946–1956* (Singapore, 1965); for Sarawak, Vernon L. Porritt, *British Colonial Rule in Sarawak, 1946–1963* (Kuala Lumpur, 1997); for Brunei, Donald E. Brown, *Brunei: The Structure and History of a Bornean Malay Sultanate* (Brunei, 1970); and David Leake, Jr., *Brunei: The Modern Southeast-Asian Islamic Sultanate* (Jefferson, N.C., 1989).

[36] See Matthew Jones, 'Creating Malaysia: Singapore Security, the Borneo Territories, and the Contours of British Policy, 1961–63', *Journal of Imperial and Commonwealth History,* 28, 2 (May 2000).

[37] Minute by T. J. Bligh reporting the views of the British Commissioner-General South-East Asia, Lord Selkirk, Secret, 16 May 1962, PREM 11/3735. C. Northcote Parkinson, the distin-

he was a 'firebrand'.[38] Though the British regarded him as habitually cold and ruthless—and as lacking the Tunku's sentimental attachment to Britain—Lee had a genuine dedication to building a new state of Malaysia based on absolute equality between Chinese and Malays. The Tunku, on the other hand, viewed the new state essentially as an extension of Malaya, which would include as well the built-in system or tradition of privilege and class distinctions.[39] Lee Kuan Yew and the Tunku mistrusted each other. The Tunku believed that Lee aimed eventually to become Prime Minister of Malaysia, and Lee thought that the Tunku wanted to replace him, perhaps subversively. Nevertheless, an uneasy but indispensable partnership emerged in the early 1960s to build the new state. Lee saw no less acutely than did the Tunku that it would be to their mutual advantage to imprison the ringleaders of the political opposition, including the key activists of the Barisan Sosialis.

The pretext for the lock-up—in Lee Kuan Yew's phrase, a 'heaven-sent opportunity'—was provided by an insurrection in one of the three Borneo territories.[40] In December 1962 a rebellion broke out in the oil-rich protectorate of Brunei; it was quickly suppressed. Its origins had little to do with political unrest in Singapore, but rather with the unpopularity of the local Sultan and an attempt to overthrow British rule in favour of union with Indonesia. Both the Tunku and Lee claimed that the uprising would lead to trouble in Sarawak and North Borneo, spreading in turn to Malaya and Singapore. The British gov-

---

guished historian of the British Empire and also the inventor of Parkinson's law—which, applied to this essay, would state that footnotes expand to fill the amount of space allocated to them, and then some—once wrote of Lee: 'Utterly without charm, his expression is one of barely concealed contempt for his opponents, for his followers, perhaps for himself . . . One cannot imagine that . . . he is even capable of friendship' (C. Northcote Parkinson, *A Law unto Themselves: Twelve Portraits* [London, 1966], p. 174). This is a harsh judgement, but it reveals a certain strain of British opinion. Harold Wilson, on the other hand, got on well with Lee and admired his intellectual sophistication; see, for example, Wilson, *The Labour Government*, p. 195. Lee Kuan Yew's own autobiography (*The Singapore Story: Memoirs of Lee Kuan Yew* [Singapore, 1998]) is remarkably charitable and, on the whole, honest. Though silent on certain points, it clearly reveals that his passion was the building of Singapore.

[38] So described by Sir Robert Scott (Commissioner-General in South-East Asia, 1955–59), quoted in John Drysdale, *Singapore: Struggle for Success* (London, 1984), p. 148.

[39] For his own rather fragmented autobiographical account, which throughout emphasizes horse racing, football, the virtues of the Malayan aristocracy, and the general theme that 'we in Malaysia are among the happiest people in the world', see Tunku Abdul Rahman Putra Al-haj, *Looking Back: Monday Musings and Memories* (Kuala Lumpur, 1977), p. 332. Beneath the platitudes lay a shrewd grasp of Malaysian politics. Lee's contempt for the Tunku as a man whose purpose in life was 'to preserve the orchid from wilting' was a radical misperception; see George, *Lee Kuan Yew's Singapore*, p. 167.

[40] See Jones, 'Creating Malaysia'.

ernment in London now authorized the arrests in Singapore urged by the Tunku and Lee Kuan Yew. In February 1963 some two dozen members of the Barisan Sosialis and over a hundred other suspects were imprisoned.[41] During the same period, the Prime Minister, Harold Macmillan, took the initiative in overriding Colonial Office objections to pressing the Borneo territories into the new federation. The Colonial Office believed that the peoples of Borneo were being compelled to join before they were ready to determine their own future. To use Macmillan's phrase, Malaysia was very much a 'shotgun wedding'.[42] Brunei remained apart, but Sarawak and North Borneo were fused into the union: in September 1963, the new state of Malaysia was born.

At this point it is worth bearing in mind the British purpose in helping create Malaysia. The federation would be more viable than the individual units, but there were other reasons, including preventing a communist takeover in Singapore and hastening colonial and military withdrawal. By incorporating Sarawak and North Borneo (Sabah) as well as Singapore into an independent state, the British would be bringing the era of their colonial rule in South-East Asia virtually to an end.[43] Though not entirely dismantled (a few units might stay on), the Singapore base would be closed down, thus relieving an immense strain on the British defence budget and averting the danger, at some point in the future, of a possible clash with a radical socialist or revolutionary regime in Singapore. Immediately after the launching of the new state, however, Malaysia came into conflict with Indonesia in what was known as 'Konfrontasi' in the jungles of Borneo. Fearing also Indonesian raids on the Malayan peninsula itself,[44] the British deployed forces on behalf of the nation of Malaysia, a country of 8 million, against Indonesia, a country of 100 million. Some 50,000 British, Malaysian, and Australian soldiers eventually fought in jungle theatres, backed up by one-third of the British fleet. Along with the campaign in Aden, the conflict with Indonesia in Borneo was one of two

---

[41] They included Lim Chin Siong, the spokesman of the Chinese working class of Singapore and a vital figure in the opposition. See T. N. Harper, 'Lim Chin Siong and the "Singapore Story",' in Tan Jing Quee and Jomo K. S., eds., *Comet in Our Sky: Lim Chin Siong in History* (Kuala Lumpur, 2001). This is a seminal essay.

[42] See Ronald Hyam and W. R. Louis, eds., *The Conservative Government and the End of Empire, 1957–1964* (*BDEEP*, series A, 2 vols., London, 2000): I, pp. lviii–lx, 718–49. See also especially Nicholas Tarling, *The Fall of Imperial Britain in South-East Asia* (Singapore, 1993), pp. 199–201.

[43] The British Protectorate in Brunei continued until 1984, when Brunei became an independent sultanate within the Commonwealth. North Borneo was renamed Sabah in 1963.

[44] See John Subritzky, *Confronting Sukarno: British, American, Australian and New Zealand Diplomacy in the Malaysian-Indonesian Confrontation, 1961–65* (London, 2000); Greg Poulgrain, *The Genesis of Konfrontasi: Malaysia, Brunei, Indonesia, 1945–1965* (London, 1998); and J. A. C. Mackie, *Konfrontasi: The Indonesia-Malaysia Dispute, 1963–1966* (Kuala Lumpur, 1974).

ferocious colonial campaigns that the British fought while the Americans were waging war in Vietnam. Far from resolving Britain's colonial and military problems in South-East Asia, the new federation intensified them.

From the American vantage point, the creation of Malaysia seemed to be a dangerous venture from the beginning. Sukarno, the charismatic leader of Indonesia and hero of the revolution against the Dutch, put forward irredentist claims to the British Borneo colonies as lost provinces of the homeland.[45] He denounced the new state as an artificial construction of British 'neo-colonialism'.[46] There was some sympathy for the Indonesian point of view in Washington, in part because turmoil in Indonesia might lead to the takeover of the American oil companies Caltex and Stanvac, which had some $500 million worth of holdings in the country. On the other hand, American good will towards Sukarno was tempered by his dependence on the powerful Indonesian Communist Party (the PKI) for support. He now moved to forge closer ties with Beijing. In the British view, the traditional American attitude towards Indonesia could be summed up in a few words: 'to keep the largest country in the area non-Communist

[45] The balanced and judicious study by J. D. Legge, *Sukarno: A Political Biography* (London, 1972) repays rereading in this context. For example, from the Indonesian perspective (p. 364):

In social terms Malaya, with no revolution to launch her into the modern world, appeared a conservative, aristocratic country as compared with Indonesia's radical nationalism. Symbolizing this difference of temperament was the personal contrast between the Tengku [the Tunku] and Sukarno—the English-trained, racehorse-owning, Malay prince and the Jacobin leader drawn from the lower aristocracy of Java and trained through the long struggle against Dutch rule.

[46] The considered definition of neo-colonialism by the Foreign Office is of interest: 'that the West will seek to recapture by economic means the predominance which it once held by arms' (Foreign Office memorandum, 5 May 1961, FO 371/161230). Note also the carefully constructed definition of 'anti-colonialism' by Sir Robert Scott, who had served in China before becoming Commissioner-General South-East Asia:

It is a frame of mind, resentment at patronage, resentment at fancied Western assumptions of superiority whether in social status or culture, reaction to the Western impact on Asia in the past centuries. This frame of mind, expressed in terms of opposition to Western control or interference, explains the paradox of 'anti-colonialism' in countries that have never been colonies, directed against countries that have never had them. Americans are sometimes baffled to find that Asian sentiment towards Britain, the greatest colonial power of all, is apt to be more cordial than towards the United States despite their remarkable record of generosity and altruism in dealings with Asia.

Scott to Macmillan, Secret, 13 November 1959, FO 371/143732.

even if quasi Fascist'.[47] By the summer and autumn of 1965, however, it was by no means clear that Sukarno, whether fascist or veering towards communism, could continue to master the tempestuous economic and political challenges to his rule. As a confrontation with the British, Sukarno's aim to 'smash Malaysia' had international origins, but it was above all a domestic crisis, which tested to the ultimate degree his political skill at balancing the PKI against the army. The army supported Sukarno in the initial stage of the confrontation crisis, but in September 1965 turned against him. Neither the British nor the Americans could anticipate the outcome, but both eventually had good reason to be pleased with the emergence of the army as the decisively dominant force and with the ruthless destruction of the communist party and its followers.

Preoccupied not only with Vietnam but also with arms control and European affairs, the Kennedy administration wanted as little trouble as possible in Indonesia. The creation of Malaysia threatened to destabilize the entire region: by bringing the Western powers, including Australia, into a major war over Borneo, the 'confrontation' might end in the disintegration not only of Malaysia but of Indonesia itself. When LBJ became president after Kennedy's assassination, he took a much tougher line towards Sukarno, whom the President believed to be an expansionist, aggressive, bombastic, unstable, and dangerous dictator. He agreed with the British that Sukarno was an Asian Hitler. But Johnson too was preoccupied with Vietnam. He resented the lack of British support in Vietnam, and at the same time he did not want to provoke Indonesia, the largest Muslim country in the world, into open opposition to the United States. In a moment of anger, he told Harold Wilson that the United States would take care of Vietnam and the British would have to look after Malaysia: 'I won't tell you how to run Malaysia and you don't tell us how to run Vietnam.'[48]

One detects a sense of British desperation in the archival records. The British earnestly warned that the Indonesian conflict could prove to be much more serious than the war in Vietnam; they needed American support. A comment made later in the context of Vietnam applied just as well to Indonesia: Michael Palliser—who eventually rose to the position of Permanent Under-Secretary in the Foreign Office —stated: '[W]e have . . . opened our hearts' to the Americans.[49] Sentiment counts for little in international politics, but in this case the

---

[47] Minute by J. O. Wright, 22 January 1964, PREM 11/4906. Wright was Private Secretary to the Prime Minister and later Ambassador in Washington (1982–86).

[48] Record of telephone conversation, 11 February 1965, PREM 13/692. Wilson, *The Labour Government*, p. 80.

[49] Minute by Palliser, 18 March 1966, FO 371/185917.

British used every argument available to drive home their commitment to Malaysia. They pleaded with some cogency that, in relation to national resources, the number of British troops in Borneo compared favourably to the number of US military advisers in Vietnam. By late 1964 there were already 8,000 British troops in Borneo and 20,000 on the Malaysian mainland. Borneo, or Malaysia itself, had the potential of becoming to Britain what Vietnam was to the United States.

At the beginning of the confrontation, Indonesian mobs had sacked the British Embassy in Jakarta.[50] On a note of defiant contempt, the Scots military attaché marched up and down during the assault, playing bagpipes—to the Indonesians, an intolerable act of British colonial arrogance. In Kuala Lumpur the Tunku urged the British to counter-attack Indonesia in the outer islands, thereby sparking anti-Sukarno sentiment throughout the country and breaking up Indonesia itself.[51] In this early part of the conflict, the British were of two minds. They could not commit themselves to full-scale or even formal war without running the risk of bankrupting their own economy, not to mention the problem of explaining to a sceptical British public the need for all-out war over Borneo. In 1964 things began to turn in favour of the British. LBJ swung increasingly against Sukarno. Sukarno himself denounced the United States as well as Britain with shrill and extravagant rhetoric. In August, Indonesian raids reached islands off the Malaysian peninsula. According to a British assessment in October 1964: 'Events and Sukarno's own actions have moved the Americans a long way in the last few months without much assistance from us.'[52]

In March 1965, a month after the United States began bombing North Vietnamese military and industrial targets in the operation called 'Rolling Thunder', LBJ committed himself—so the former British Foreign Secretary, Patrick Gordon Walker believed—to the British position against Indonesia. Gordon Walker wrote: '[A]t the end of the day, should it become necessary, he [Johnson] would be ready for major war against Indonesia if she raises the stakes too high. *This is most confidential.*'[53] Gordon Walker got the gist of Johnson's views indirectly

[50] The British Ambassador commented on the destruction of his automobile, a Leyland 'Princess': 'The charred corpse of my poor old Princess is causing an elegant traffic-jam.' The Prime Minister minuted: 'I hope the historian will not misunderstand this' (minute by Macmillan on Djakarta to Foreign Office, 17 September 1963, PREM 11/4310).

[51] The Tunku had expansionist aims of his own. Malay ties of kinship extended to Indonesia. He believed that the Sumatran and other Malay rulers in Indonesia would welcome intervention and that they would spontaneously join their 'Malayan cousins' to bring about 'an all-embracing Federation of all the Malaysian countries' (Jones, *Conflict and Confrontation*, p. 214).

[52] O. G. Forster to Foreign Office, 21 October 1964, FO 371/176454.

[53] Record of conversation, Secret, 6 March 1965, PREM 13/693; Robert Pearce, ed., *Patrick Gordon Walker: Political Diaries 1932–1971* (London, 1991), pp. 303–04. Gordon Walker was

through Dean Rusk, and probably the account became exaggerated in the telling.[54] Nevertheless this was an explosive conflict that has largely been lost sight of in the overall context of Vietnam. It bears emphasizing that the United States might have lent support to Britain in a catastrophic war against Indonesia if Sukarno had not followed a path of self-destruction.

Sukarno was a romantic revolutionary. He held a heroic place in the history of Indonesia's struggle against European imperialism. He had ruled the vast archipelago country since 1949. He was authoritarian, but to Indonesians he represented not only the liberation of their country but a national renaissance. By the early 1960s, however, his powers were waning for various reasons, including the deterioration of his health. He confronted Malaysia when Indonesia itself laboured under severe inflation, suffered from food shortages, and hovered on the verge of economic collapse. His crusade against British neo-colonialism and his rhetoric about the class struggle in Indonesia served to rally the PKI, which was the largest non-ruling communist party in the world and one of the main sources of his strength.[55] More and more, however, he alienated the Americans, who feared revolutionary communism in Indonesia, and those in Indonesia itself who believed that the country stood at a crossroads of domestic economic reform and foreign confrontation. Above all, Sukarno faced a showdown with the Indonesian army, which in the autumn of 1965 intervened decisively in the internal struggle for control.[56] The army's *coup d'état* released deep cultural as well as political enmities and led to the killing of hundreds of thousands of communists and communist

Foreign Secretary for two months, November–December 1964, before resigning after the loss of his Parliamentary seat in a by-election the following January.

[54] He admitted later that he was 'not very good at taking records', but the point must have stood out in Gordon Walker's mind: he wrote that Rusk had made it 'with great emphasis'. See Wright to Henderson, Secret, 11 March 1965, FO 371/180540. I have not had any luck on the American side in tracing the conversation.

[55] See Rex Mortimer, *Indonesian Communism under Sukarno: Ideology and Politics, 1959–1965* (Ithaca, N.Y., 1974).

[56] See Harold Crouch, *The Army and Politics in Indonesia* (Ithaca, N.Y., 1978). For the destruction of the myth that the CIA engineered the coup in a major way, see H. W. Brands, 'The Limits of Manipulation: How the United States Didn't Topple Sukarno', *Journal of American History*, 76, 3 (December 1989). The article by Brands was written before the publication of *Foreign Relations of the United States, 1964–1968*, XXVI, which deals with Indonesia. The documentary record largely confirms his account. The CIA's part in the coup was minimal, involving little money or advice, but afterwards the CIA helped provide equipment to the army as well as information about communist leaders. The question remains open about the extent of CIA involvement in Indonesian affairs after October 1965.

sympathizers—'one of the bloodiest massacres in modern history'.[57] After the virtual destruction of the PKI, Sukarno gradually yielded political control to General Suharto. Indonesia emerged with an anti-communist military government. The era of confrontation came to an end in 1966, to the immense relief of the Americans as well as the British.

For the British there was a crisis within the crisis. In the midst of its confrontation with Indonesia, Malaysia had expelled Singapore from the federation. Since the time of the creation of the new state in 1963, communal tension had risen both on the mainland and in Singapore. The great historian Arnold Toynbee commented at one point that the real danger in all of Asia lay in 'the Malay peninsula where the Malays and the Chinese could fall into a race war'.[58] Lee Kuan Yew's own rhetoric contributed to a tense and troubled atmosphere. He undoubtedly thought that Singapore's future lay with the federation, which offered economic opportunity in a common market for goods and services. He continued to hope that a Malaysian society could eventually be created on the basis of equality and mutual respect. Nevertheless, he adopted, perhaps in spite of himself, a belligerent and condescending attitude towards the Malays. He attempted to consolidate Chinese political support on the mainland. In April 1964 he backed candidates there from the People's Action Party—his own party in Singapore—in a federal election, despite his pledge not to do so for at least five years after the merger. Lee's decision to participate in the federal election—on the mainland—was a catalyst for the eventual separation, not least because of the accompanying rise of Chinese ethnic chauvinism. In July 1964 there were communal riots in Singapore; more than 20 people were killed and 450 injured. From this point on, Lee and the Tunku were on a collision course. Lee calculated in round figures, '40–40–20'—in other words, a roughly equal number of Malays and Chinese, and 20 per cent Indians, indigenous peoples, and others on the peninsula and in the Borneo territories. He believed that he could win enough support to become Prime Minister of Malaysia. The Tunku took the stand that communal politicking would lead to further bloodshed. He had no doubt that Lee aimed to replace him as Prime Minister. In August 1965 the Tunku made the decision to expel Singapore from the federation.

Lee Kuan Yew was dismayed. During his explanation to the public in Singapore, he broke into tears and said in a famous line that it was

---

[57] Legge, *Sukarno*, p. 399.
[58] As paraphrased by George, *Lee Kuan Yew's Singapore*, p. 157.

his 'moment of anguish'. The Tunku was much more down to earth. In identifying Lee's participation in mainland politics as one of the basic reasons to sever the tie, the Tunku later used a vivid though brutal physical metaphor. With political gangrene spreading to the main part of the body politic, he explained, Singapore had to be excised: 'If you have a bad leg, the best thing is to amputate it.'[59]

The British played no part in the separation of Singapore from Malaysia. The decision had been made in secrecy. Even Lee Kuan Yew's acquiescence was kept secret from the British, though the High Commissioner, Lord Head, learned of the impending rupture at the last minute. Both the Tunku and Lee had their reasons: the Tunku wanted to avoid British pressure to keep the union intact, and Lee feared, quite erroneously, that the British would seize the opportunity to reassert Imperial control over Singapore.[60] At this stage in his career, he still had the reputation of a fiery, coruscating left-wing politician who passionately denounced Western imperialism—above all, American imperialism.[61] No one could predict in August 1965 whether Lee might turn to Communist China. In fact, he rapidly adjusted his political orientation when he learned that the British would move immediately to secure Singapore's membership in the Commonwealth as an independent state.

As the decade progressed, Lee Kuan Yew proved to be an adept politician and a staunch enemy of both Communist China and Indonesia. He quickly espoused the principle that Singapore would prosper only under the protective umbrella of Britain, the Commonwealth, and the United States. According to a typical comment, Lee wanted a continuing British military presence. This remark is also of interest because it reveals Lee's developing outlook that the American presence in South-East Asia had prevented a takeover of the region by Communist China:

> Mr. Lee Kuan Yew . . . said that he hoped the British would remain in Singapore for a considerable time . . . He did not seem upset at his own forecast that the United States would be fighting a bloody and losing battle in Viet Nam for many years. His point was that only the presence of Western forces could provide a screen against Chinese

[59] Quoted in Lee Kuan Yew, *Singapore Story*, p. 662.

[60] See, for example, George, *Lee Kuan Yew's Singapore*, pp. 90–91.

[61] For Lee Kuan Yew's denunciation of the Americans for, among other reasons, 'their lack of civilisation', see James Minchin, *No Man is an Island: A Study of Singapore's Lee Kuan Yew* (London, 1986), p. 158.

expansion, whether by aggression or subversion, behind which the indigenous forces of Asia might be mobilised.[62]

At an early stage, Lee articulated the argument that the United States was losing the battle in Vietnam but winning the war in South-East Asia.[63]

He was appalled in 1967 to learn of the British decision to dismantle the vast naval and military complex in Singapore. Though the British did mostly withdraw in 1971, Lee succeeded in arranging a protracted disengagement that enabled a few British military detachments to stay on and thus to contribute to both Singapore's security and the local economy. The British maintained a military and naval presence but at negligible risk and expense; the final withdrawal did not occur until 1976.[64] In the meantime, British-Malaysian defence arrangements had been replaced by the five-power security treaty entered into by Britain, Australia, New Zealand, Malaysia, and Singapore.[65]

Singapore's independence in 1965 coincided with a sea change in British strategic and technological calculation. The Royal Navy and the other branches of the armed services now viewed bases on or near the Asian mainland as liabilities—at best as 'filling stations' to service aircraft carriers and other vessels that no longer needed traditional facilities.[66] The Singapore base had become an anachronism. It was also the largest defence expenditure East of Suez. Confronted with an economic emergency at home and mounting defence expenditures

[62] Minute by J. A. Thomson, 22 April 1966, FO 371/185920.

[63] The champion of the view that America lost the battle in Vietnam but won the war in the region is W. W. Rostow; see, for example, 'The Case for the War: How American Resistance in Vietnam Helped Southeast Asia to Prosper in Independence', *Times Literary Supplement*, 9 June 1995.

[64] For the extended British withdrawal, see Hack, *Defence and Decolonisation in Southeast Asia*, chap. 9.

[65] In 1971 the Five Power Defence Arrangement provided for a joint British–Australian–New Zealand fleet to be stationed in Singapore and for an integrated air-defence system for Malaysia. See Chin Kin Wah, *The Defence of Malaysia and Singapore: The Transformation of a Security System, 1957–1971* (Cambridge, 1983), chaps. 8 and 9. For a succinct discussion of these issues in relation to the British Indian Ocean Territory (Diego Garcia) and the British 'abracadabra' strategy, see W. David McIntyre, *British Decolonization, 1946–1997: When, Why and How did the British Empire Fall?* (London, 1998), chap. 5.

[66] 'The Chiefs of Staff [believed] . . . that by the exercise of strategic mobility—and with the nuclear deterrent discreetly in the wings—Britain could continue to play a starring part on the international stage' (Anthony Verrier, *Through the Looking Glass: British Foreign Policy in an Age of Illusions* [London, 1983], p. 173). See also Ian Clark, *Nuclear Diplomacy and the Special Relationship: Britain's Deterrent and America, 1957–1962* (Oxford, 1994).

abroad, the British decided to withdraw, despite American protests.[67] It was clear that LBJ felt that it would be 'little short of treachery for us [the British] to sound a retreat . . . by abandoning our existing position before we are forced to do so.'[68] The British detected a certain American bitterness:[69] they were abandoning Singapore, and they had sent no troops to Vietnam. According to the British Ambassador in South Vietnam, the Americans regarded their behaviour as 'negative, defeatist and hypocritical'.[70] Still, in retrospect the British could claim that the war in Vietnam paled in comparison with what might have happened in Indonesia: '[T]he East Asia watershed is not ahead of us in Vietnam but lies behind us in Indonesia.' The end of confrontation in 1966 was Britain's 'greatest success' of the decade.[71]

The expulsion of Singapore from Malaysia was an event of comparable significance. In the 1960s, peoples throughout the world demanded the right to determine their own future, and since then the pattern has been towards ever-greater fragmentation. Malaysia is a partial exception. Since 1965 the federation has survived, minus Singapore. In the case of Singapore itself, independence came unwillingly —to repeat the phrase, in a moment of anguish—but the people of Singapore were among the first to demonstrate that a microstate can survive and prosper.

It is doubtful whether this would have happened if there had been all-out war with Indonesia. One piece of archival evidence struck me immediately when I saw it, though I mention it hesitantly because I have done what an historian should never do: I have lost my citation. But I mention it because it is burned into my memory. It was short and

---

[67] For the connection of these issues, see John Dumbrell, 'The Johnson Administration and the British Labour Government: Vietnam, the Pound and East of Suez', *Journal of American Studies*, 30, 2 (1996); and Alan Dobson, 'The Years of Transition: Anglo-American Relations, 1961–1967', *Review of International Studies*, 16, (1990).

[68] Memorandum, 'Indo-Pacific Policy', 10 May 1966, CAB 148/28.

[69] For example, in a conversation between Dean Rusk and Louis Heren of *The Times* of London:

> We had all had enough to drink, and he [Rusk] came over and asked me why Britain had not sent troops to Vietnam. He knew well enough, but rather lamely I began to repeat the obvious. He cut me short and said, 'All we needed was one regiment. The Black Watch would have done. Just one regiment, but you wouldn't. Well, don't expect us to save you again. They can invade Sussex, and we wouldn't do a damned thing about it.

Louis Heren, *No Hail, No Farewell* (New York, 1970), p. 230.

[70] Gordon Etherington-Smith to Foreign Office, 15 July 1966, FO 371/186331.

[71] Foreign Commonwealth Office memorandum, no date (but March 1967), FCO 15/4.

to the point, almost inadvertent. It revealed a chilling prospect. It said simply that the British would follow closely the American bombing of North Vietnam because similar action might be necessary against Indonesia.[72]

As for my comment on Vietnam, it will be brief. I limit my thoughts to the essential points of both the British involvement and the contemporary British analysis of the significance of the struggle.[73] First, the war had the same divisive effect in Britain as in the United States, though of course to a much lesser degree. Both within the British government and in the public debate, there was no agreement on the fundamental premise of self-determination. Those who protested

[72] As events transpired, the British were able to keep the Borneo campaign a 'low intensity conflict' despite its fierceness. According to Denis Healey, the Defence Secretary: 'At a time when the United States was plastering Vietnam with bombs, napalm, and defoliant, no British aircraft ever dropped a bomb in Borneo' (Denis Healey, *The Time of My Life* [London, 1989], p. 289). Quite a different perspective is given in Verrier, *Through the Looking Glass*, p. 254:

> The war was fought by British, Gurkha, and Malay troops with obsolescent weapons and inadequate equipment, and it was no comfort to these men on the spot to know that V bombers from Singapore (armed with 'conventional' bombs) could easily reach Indonesian targets. This subaltern's and platoon sergeant's war was won by troops whose units were under strength, made up to the order of battle by cross posting on a scale which revealed the strain on Britain's most valuable strategic resource: trained men.

[73] On the United States and Vietnam, I have found it useful to reread or in some cases read for the first time the following works: David L. Anderson, *Trapped by Success: The Eisenhower Administration and Vietnam, 1953–1961* (New York, 1991); Larry Berman, *Lyndon Johnson's War: The Road to Stalemate in Vietnam* (New York, 1989); Lloyd Gardner, *Pay Any Price: Lyndon Johnson and the Wars for Vietnam* (Chicago, 1995); William C. Gibbons, *The U.S. Government and the Vietnam War* (4 vols., Princeton, 1985–95); George C. Herring, *America's Longest War: The United States and Vietnam, 1950–1975* (New York, 1979; 1996 edn.); Gabriel Kolko, *Anatomy of a War: Vietnam, the United States, and the Modern Historical Experience* (New York, 1985); Walter LaFeber, *America, Russia, and the Cold War, 1945–1975* (New York, 1967; 1997 edn.); George McT. Kahin, *Intervention: How America Became Involved in Vietnam* (New York, 1986); John Prados, *The Blood Road: The Ho Chi Minh Trail and the Vietnam War* (New York, 1999); Andrew J. Rotter, *The Path to Vietnam: Origins of the American Commitment to Southeast Asia* (Ithaca, N.Y., 1987); and Marilyn B. Young, *The Vietnam Wars, 1945–1990* (New York, 1991). I have benefited especially from Robert D. Schulzinger, *A Time for War: The United States and Vietnam, 1941–1975* (New York, 1997), both because it is a state-of-the-art study of the Vietnam conflict and because of its pursuit of certain literary themes—for example, Graham Greene's portrayal of a CIA operative in Vietnam in *The Quiet American* (London, 1955), and William Lederer and Eugene Burdick's prototype of committed American pacification officers (as they were later known in the 1960s) in *The Ugly American* (New York, 1957): 'As political propaganda setting the stage for a war, *The Ugly American* had an impact similar to that of Harriet Beecher Stowe's *Uncle Tom's Cabin* in the years before the American Civil War' (Schulzinger, *Time for War*, p. 98).

against the war usually believed that the catchword 'communism' distracted attention from aggressive American aims, and in any event that the Vietnamese themselves should be allowed to determine their own fate. Those within the government tended to think that the principle of self-determination would be subverted by the expansionist ambitions of Communist China. 'It is this we ourselves are really frightened of', commented a member of the Labour Government: 'Chinese domination of the Saigon Government.' [74]

Even within official circles no consensus existed on a fundamental point: would the fall of South Vietnam lead to the loss of South-East Asia—i.e. was it true, to put it on a grander scale, as did Sir Robert Thompson, Britain's protagonist in the Vietnam struggle, that 'Vietnam is one of the vital issues to the latter half of the twentieth century'? [75] In attempting to reconcile contradictory assessments into a coherent policy, the South-East Asia Department of the Foreign Office doubted whether the countries of South-East Asia resembled dominoes that might topple, and even whether Vietnam itself was particularly significant. The strongest exponent of this scepticism was James Cable, an official of long experience in the region. Cable had participated in the 1954 Geneva Conference, which established a temporary truce at the 17th parallel after the French defeat at Dien Bien Phu.[76] 'If we had our way in 1954', Cable wrote, 'it [South Vietnam] would have been written off as politically untenable by being exposed to elections under international supervision.' [77] Britain's status as Co-Chairman of the Geneva Conference (along with the Soviet Union) led to the hope in the mid-1960s that Harold Wilson might be able

[74] Minute by Lord Walston, 27 July 1966, FO 371/186331. Walston was Parliamentary Under-Secretary.

[75] Thompson to Peck, Secret and Guard, 22 April 1964, FO 371/175496. For Thompson, see especially his memoirs, which are written with subtlety, humour, and extraordinary comparisons. For example, he wrote of one of the great British soldiers of the twentieth century—and also one of the last Viceroys in India—Sir Archibald (Lord) Wavell, in comparing him with one of the leading American military figures in Vietnam, General Creighton Abrams:

> I found him [Abrams] . . . to be a quiet, thoughtful, kind but rather dour person, not
> unlike Lord Wavell . . . Classical music was his solace, as poetry had been Wavell's . . .
> I came to regard him as one of the greatest American Generals of this century.

Sir Robert Thompson, *Make for the Hills: Memories of Far Eastern Wars* (London, 1989), p. 159.

[76] See his own historical account, James Cable, *The Geneva Conference of 1954 on Indochina* (London, 1986); see also especially R. B. Smith, *An International History of the Vietnam War: Revolution versus Containment, 1955–61* (London, 1983), chap. 2. For a contemporary, sustained attack on successive British governments for supporting the United States, see William Warbey, *Vietnam: The Truth* (London, 1965).

[77] Minute by Cable, 25 April 1964, FO 371/175496.

to act as a broker. But British failure to influence either the United States or the Soviet Union only deepened British despair. The British Ambassador in South Vietnam wrote: 'It is only too clear that over all our efforts hangs the black cloud of our own military and economic weaknesses.'[78]

As part of a pattern of analysis that may be taken as representative of mainstream British official thought, James Cable took issue with the theory that the fall of Vietnam would send a fatal shock wave through to Malaysia. Here is a point that deserves clarification. How did the British see the connection between the fate of Vietnam and the future of Malaysia? Cable wrote: 'What is at stake is not South Viet Nam, but American prestige in South East Asia.' He believed that 'Saigon is emphatically not worth a world war.'[79] The principal reason that Britain endorsed American aims in Vietnam was the need for American support in Malaysia (though Cable did not say so explicitly, the British could also provide an excuse for not sending troops to Vietnam by playing up their commitment to Malaysia). As for the Vietnam War itself, Cable wrote in June 1965 that it 'cannot be won at all'.[80] He took a severe view of American prospects, but there were others who at least believed that the American presence in South-East Asia had permitted the region to develop economically and had provided an element of stability. Michael Palliser wrote that 'the Americans have succeeded for the past ten years in preventing Indo-China from going communist —as I take it would have happened if the Americans had not propped up South Vietnam. This represents ten years gained.'[81]

The unrivalled British authority on Vietnam was Sir Robert Thompson, who had served in Malaya during the insurgency in the 1950s as the civilian in charge of Malayan defence. From 1961 to 1965 he headed the British Advisory Mission to Vietnam, which was created in 1961 and consisted of four British officers, all with Malayan experience.[82] Thompson eventually had the ear of three American Presidents

---

[78] Etherington-Smith to Foreign Office, Confidential, 14 January 1964, FO 371/175065.

[79] Minute by Cable, 25 April 1964, FO 371/17596.

[80] Minute by Cable, 2 June 1965, FO 371/180595.

[81] Minute by Palliser, 29 June 1964, FO 371/175092. Palliser's thought flowed in the same direction as that of Walt Rostow, who believed, then as later, that the presence of the United States in South-East Asia provided the necessary security for the region to develop economically. See Rostow, 'The Case for the War': 'The pain, loss and controversy resulting from Vietnam were accepted for ten years by the American people. That acceptance held the line so that a free Asia could survive and grow.'

[82] See Ian F. W. Beckett, 'Robert Thompson and the British Advisory Mission to South Vietnam, 1961–1965', *Small Wars and Insurgencies*, 8, 3 (Winter 1997). See also especially Alastair Parker, 'International Aspects of the Vietnam War', in Peter Lowe, ed., *The Vietnam War* (London, 1998).

—Kennedy, Johnson, and Nixon—and won friends in the CIA, the Department of Defense, and the State Department. He came into contact with numerous American journalists and academics.[83] His acquaintances in Washington were interested in what had been learned about counter-insurgency in Malaya and in how the idea of the reconstructed rural villages, now known as 'strategic hamlets', might be adapted to Vietnam.[84] In Vietnam itself, Thompson met with mixed success, both with the American military advisers and with the South Vietnamese Army, though his influence was widely acknowledged and to some he represented a sort of evil genius guiding American efforts. Noam Chomsky, one of the most prominent critics of the war in Vietnam, referred to him with inimitable irony as 'one of Britain's gifts to the Vietnamese people'.[85]

Thompson's fundamental idea, based on his experience in Malaya, was that the police were just as important as the army and that the pre-eminent function of the police was to protect the public, rural and urban. In Malaya, one of the keys to British success in the insurgency had been the gradual assertion of state control over all parts of the country. Regardless of whether people stayed in one place or were relocated, officials continued to record births, marriages, and deaths.[86] The villagers came to believe that they were being protected in all vital respects. No less important were Thompson's doctrines and techniques of counter-insurgency, for which he became famous, but he always returned to the underlying premise that one supreme authority should exercise civilian control. In Malaya there had been 'one plan and one man'. In Vietnam, the Pentagon, CIA, and State Department formed, in his view, an unholy trinity. The rivalries among them often prevented effective action. There was an acute deficiency of institutional memory; there was no American equivalent of Gerald Templer. Nor could there be, since South Vietnam was an independent country and not, like Malaya, a colony.[87]

---

[83] For an example of his exchange with American intellectuals, see Richard M. Pfeffer, *No More Vietnams? The War and the Future of American Foreign Policy* (New York, 1968). Thompson regarded Bernard Fall as his most formidable intellectual adversary. See Bernard B. Fall, *The Two Viet-Nams: A Political and Military Analysis* (New York, 1963).

[84] See especially Roger Hilsman, *To Move a Nation: The Politics of Foreign Policy in the Administration of John F. Kennedy* (Garden City, N.Y., 1967), pp. 429–39, 461–63, and 522–25.

[85] Noam Chomsky, *The Backroom Boys* (London, 1973), p. 116.

[86] On this point, see Short, *Communist Insurrection in Malaya*, p. 500: '[P]ara-normality . . . created at least the impression of stability and this both encouraged and was reinforced by the fact that, for the most part, District Officers, police, planters, tappers, peasants and miners remained where they were in spite of often continuous danger.'

[87] Daniel S. Papp, ed., *As I Saw It by Dean Rusk as told to Richard Rusk* (New York, 1990), pp. 453–54:

Thompson's thought reflected gradual disillusionment and despondency. At first he genuinely believed that the war in Vietnam could be won, but he began to think that the Americans were too warm-hearted, impatient, and impulsive to be sufficiently single-minded and pitiless. 'Fighting communist terrorism is a tough, dirty, ruthless business,' he once wrote.[88] The heart of the problem, however, did not lie with the Americans but with the South Vietnamese. 'We are stuck with the legally constituted Government,' he lamented.[89] The aims of the South Vietnamese were incompatible with those of the United States because the South Vietnamese government intended, in his view, not to reform but solely to perpetuate itself. By 1965 the principal element of public safety—police protection—still did not exist. When the American bombing of North Vietnam began in the same year, Thompson despaired.[90] He did not think that the bombing raids would have any positive effect at all. As in the United States, there were many views in Britain on the prospect of American defeat, or victory, but Thompson's ideas probably expressed a consensus, as far as one existed, among those who gave serious thought to the subject. His opinions fluctuated, but from 1965 onwards Thompson essentially believed that the United States had lost the war.[91] The arrival of Ameri-

We discussed turning Vietnam into a theater of operations, as we had done for World War II, and concentrating all authority in the theater commander, with the ambassador as the political adviser. We decided against that because such an arrangement might have downgraded the Vietnamese role and Americanized the war even further. Also, the Koreans, Australians, South Vietnamese, and other allies might not have liked an 'American warlord' running the war.

[88] Thompson to Foreign Office, Secret, 30 October 1963, FO 371/170102.

[89] Thompson to Foreign Office, Secret, 9 October 1963, FO 371/170102.

[90] Thompson's 'gloomy', 'depressing', and 'deeply pessimistic' outlook (words used by others to describe his views) can be traced mainly in records of conversations with him after his departure from Vietnam. See, for example, minute by James Cable, 21 March 1966, FO 371/186351; Trench to Murray, Secret and Guard, 25 March 1966, FO 371/186350; and minute by D. F. Murray, 21 April 1966, FO 371/186351.

[91] For the fluctuation of Thompson's views, see Neil Sheehan, *A Bright Shining Lie: John Paul Vann and America in Vietnam* (New York, 1988), p. 734. Thompson later believed that 1968 was the critical year, and his views evolved in a certain manner parallel, at least until the late 1960s, to those of John Paul Vann, the subject of Sheehan's book. In conversations with American officials as well as in his essays and books, Thompson tempered his pessimism. See especially Robert Thompson, *Defeating Communist Insurgency: The Lessons from Malaya and Vietnam* (New York, 1966), and *No Exit from Vietnam* (New York, 1969). To the Americans, Thompson must have seemed eternally optimistic. He wrote to Henry Kissinger as late as 1975, on the eve of the fall of Saigon: 'South Vietnam has played its part in a manner unsurpassed in history . . . It is ready to continue fighting and, given the minimum of support . . . [can] hold out successfully.' See the report submitted by Thompson to Kissinger, 23 February 1975, White House Operations File, National Security Adviser, Gerald R. Ford Presidential Library. I am indebted to John Prados for this quotation.

can ground troops, and therewith the Americanization of the war, deflected the incentive to reform the South Vietnamese government.

As an historian of the British Empire, I see a connection between the ethical code of conduct of the British District Officers in Malaya and the idealism of the Americans in the civilian and military pacification programmes in Vietnam. The job of the District Officer was not only to collect taxes and administer justice but also to help with purification of water, to improve crop production, and to build schools and hospitals. These were also the duties of the American pacification officers, who assumed, whether implicitly or explicitly, that the American presence would be the equivalent of a benevolent colonial power. This was Thompson's point: after 1965, pacification programmes were eclipsed by the intensification of the war.[92] Even if the Americans emerged militarily victorious, which he privately doubted, they had forfeited the chance to win the hearts and minds of the Vietnamese peasantry through an American-sponsored social revolution. But there is a paradox. If there were ever any chance of Americans functioning as District Officers, it disappeared when the war escalated in the mid-1960s. Nevertheless, the largest US investment in quasi–District Officer programmes came after 1965, and Robert 'Blowtorch Bob' Komer drove them.[93] The commitment to pacification manifested itself in initiatives of the US Administration for International Development, the CIA, and not least the US Marine Corps; the attempt to win hearts and minds continued to the end of the war.[94] And the

[92] This was also the view of Robert Komer, the chief US pacification officer in Vietnam. See Robert W. Komer, *Bureaucracy at War: U.S. Performance in the Vietnam Conflict* (Boulder, Colo., 1986), pp. 140–41 ('Pacification Takes a Back Seat—1965 to 1966') and p. 152: '[I]t seems clear that a *predominantly counterinsurgency-oriented strategy would have had its best chance for success prior to 1964–1965*, before insurgency escalated into a quasiconventional war' (emphasis in the original). On the dark side of Komer and pacification, see Young, *Vietnam Wars*, pp. 212–13. Young's work has a searching originality in demonstrating the brutality of the war and thereby the senseless violence of all wars.

[93] The classic work is Douglas S. Blaufarb, *The Counterinsurgency Era: U.S. Doctrine and Performance* (New York, 1977). See also especially Richard A. Hunt, *Pacification: The American Struggle for Vietnam's Hearts and Minds* (Boulder, Colo., 1995); and Jefferson P. Marquis, 'The Other Warriors: American Social Science and Nation Building in Vietnam', *Diplomatic History*, 24, 1 (Winter 2000), which is a comprehensive review emphasizing social science and political change. In view of this theme, it seems worth mentioning that Sir Robert Thompson, in his own words, 'would not touch political reform in these territories [South-East Asia] with a barge pole—and I certainly would not touch it with an American political scientist' (Pfeffer, *No More Vietnams?* p. 244).

[94] From the British perspective, see Thompson, *Make for the Hills,* chap. 16. Thompson believed that in the Nixon era 'the emphasis in Vietnam had at last been placed on pacification, that is regaining Government control over the populated areas of the countryside, and Vietnamization, that is the handing of the war back to the Vietnamese' (p. 160). But by then it was too late.

idealistic commitment manifested itself in another way, which for ever left its mark on the consciousness of the American public. According to the British Embassy in Washington, young American journalists—'including David Halberstam of the New York Times'—had 'made it their sacred duty to reveal the truth' about the conduct of the war.[95]

I now come full circle to the issues raised in my introductory comments about the passions of the 1960s in our collective memory. LBJ's decision to escalate the war in 1965 summoned memories in Britain of the Suez crisis of 1956, when the British government had found itself denounced by the United States as well as by many countries throughout the world as an aggressive, imperialistic power flouting the United Nations. In the British collective memory, which exists to the present, Britain was condemned for attacking Egypt. The British public was acutely aware that their country was regarded as an international pariah. Harold Wilson in 1965 now warned that there was 'a real danger of the moral authority of the United States diminishing very sharply'. He himself believed that all-out war against North Vietnam would also place the British government in an intolerable situation. Though the British had committed no troops, they had lent moral support. Britain would now be denounced as an American satellite, indeed as 'the 51st State'. On the American side, the United States would become 'morally isolated', like the British at Suez.[96]

Memory, time, and place. We now remember the 1960s not only because of the war in Vietnam but also, of course, because of the civil rights movement and student protests. The student takeover of Columbia University had its British equivalent in the student occupation of the London School of Economics.[97] In Britain, the debate about the Vietnam War confirmed Harold Wilson's prophecy that many of the British, and not only those of the student generation, believed on the whole that the United States had betrayed its own principles. The debate spilled over into issues of decolonization. By the 1960s the reputation of the British Empire had reached its nadir. With the exception of Rhodesia, which continued to hold the public's attention because of the kith and kin of the white settlers, the dismantling of the Empire took place in Aden, Sarawak, and North Borneo with hardly

---

[95] Trench to Foreign Office, 13 August 1965, FO 371/180543. See David Halberstam, *The Making of a Quagmire* (New York, 1964); and, by the same author, *The Best and the Brightest* (New York, 1969).

[96] Record of conversation, 12 March 1965, FO 371/180540.

[97] But at the other extreme: 'Neither the Cultural Revolution nor undergraduates succeeded in penetrating All Souls' (David Caute, *The Year of the Barricades: A Journey through 1968* [New York, 1988], p. 354).

a flicker of attention from the British public, as if the general sentiment conveyed 'good riddance'. Nostalgia for the British Raj in India lay ahead; in the 1960s it was the issue of apartheid in South Africa that cast a long shadow. Those who protested against South Africa saw themselves as comrades-in-arms with those who fought for civil rights in the United States, though there was not much immediate contact. The interaction between the American civil rights movement and British decolonization is only now being assessed through archival research.[98] But the comparison is fundamental for an understanding of the era. Even though the currents were parallel and not directly connected, the rivers of decolonization and civil rights flowed in the same direction.[99]

Presidential Address to the American Historical Association

American Historical Review   2002

---

[98] For background on the American side, see Penny M. von Eschen, *Race against Empire: Black Americans and Anticolonialism, 1937–1957* (New York, 1997).

[99] I owe the metaphor to Brian Urquhart (former Under-Secretary at the United Nations), with whom I taught a course on the Middle East at the University of Texas LBJ School of Public Affairs in 1988—an extraordinary experience. Since then I have found it a useful concept to explore both in teaching and in writing. See Brian Urquhart, *Decolonization and World Peace* (Austin, Tex., 1989); and, by the same author, *Ralph Bunche: An American Life* (New York, 1993). Bunche's life was devoted in about equal measure to civil rights and decolonization. In an earlier work, John Hope Franklin wrote:

> Negroes were heartened . . . when Ralph Bunche . . . joined the United Nations to work with the Trusteeship Council [in 1946]. They hoped that this Negro specialist would, somehow, be able to advance substantially the welfare and interests of those people who would be unable to promote their own interests.

From Slavery to Freedom: A History of American Negroes (New York, 1947), p. 585.

On the British side, see Stephen Howe, *Anticolonialism in British Politics: The Left and the End of Empire, 1918–1964* (Oxford, 1993), p. 308, which stresses 'betrayed hopes'. This interpretation should be compared with that of Kenneth O. Morgan, 'Imperialists at Bay: British Labour and Decolonization', in Robert D. King and Robin W. Kilson, eds., *The Statecraft of British Imperialism: Essays in Honour of Wm. Roger Louis* (London, 1999), p. 253: 'To adapt Alan [A. J. P.] Taylor's controversial phrase (originally applied to Munich) it [decolonization] was a triumph for all that was best in British life.'

SUEZ

22

AMERICAN ANTI-COLONIALISM, SUEZ, AND THE SPECIAL RELATIONSHIP

The catastrophe of decolonization, according to those who lament the passing of the Pax Britannica, has led to deprivation, famine, civil and tribal war, even genocide. The United States, having helped bring about the collapse of the British Empire, has not replaced Britain as a guarantor of world order. The downfall of the British and other colonial regimes has created a political void that the United States has not filled. Despite the 'special relationship' with the British, and the opportunity to learn from them the lessons of managing world affairs, the United States continues to rely on antiquated doctrines of the American Revolution, amounting to little more than the unsatisfactory proposition that good government is no substitute for self-government. The Pax Britannica has disappeared; the Pax Americana had yet to emerge. The principal proponent of this point of view is Lord Beloff, who carries the authority of one who has written a substantial and useful history of the British Empire, *Imperial Sunset*.[1] Have the failures of the United States, he asks, been those of the intellect or the will?[2] Other pertinent questions might be asked. Was it ever the intention to create an American equivalent of a Pax Britannica? Motive aside, was there any realistic expectation on the part of the British that the Americans would or should follow in their footsteps?

This essay will pursue the question of American motive and strength of purpose and will link the Anglo-American 'special relationship' with the issue of anti-colonialism by examining certain chronological themes and the case of the Suez crisis.

It is useful to bear in mind the Commonwealth perspective. There are recurring British themes of bewilderment, frustration, and despair about American attitudes from the time of the First World War onwards. According to the Prime Minister of New Zealand, William F. Massey, at the Imperial Conference of 1921:

> As for America's future, I consider that the future of America itself is the biggest problem of the world to-day. No one can look at all those mixed races in the United States; 13 million Negroes and millions of people from Southern Europe, Northern Europe, all sorts of

[1] Max Beloff, *Imperial Sunset* (2 vols., London and Basingstoke, 1969–89).
[2] Lord Beloff, 'The End of the British Empire and the Assumption of Worldwide Commitments by the United States', in W. R. Louis and Hedley Bull, eds., *The Special Relationship: Anglo-American Relations since 1945* (Oxford, 1986), p. 250.

conditions of men and women, without wondering what the population will be like in another forty or fifty years from now or even a much shorter period, and I say it is quite impossible for anybody to predict the result.[3]

During one of those discussions the Prime Minister of Australia, the inimitable William M. Hughes, remarked that it was difficult to establish the authentic 'voice of America': 'Who is able to say what is the voice of the American people? It is said that the voice of the people is the voice of God'—at which point Massey interjected, 'Not always'. Hughes continued: 'Precisely, you cannot tell whether the God speaks or merely rumbles in uneasy slumbers, or peradventure, speaks with a forked tongue saying many and quite inconsistent things.'[4]

One thing certain at this juncture in world affairs in 1921, on the eve of the naval disarmament conference in Washington, D.C., was that the British faced an excruciating choice between Japan and America. According to the British Prime Minister, David Lloyd George, the Japanese were becoming wary of the British:

> They are getting suspicious of us in Japan, and they think we are doing something. They say, 'Well, they are white races, they are the cousins of the Americans. They quarrel amongst themselves, but when trouble comes they act together.' This is true, the last war showed it. When there is trouble they begin to feel that we are nearer to the Americans than we are to them. The people who govern in America are our people. They are our kith and kin. The other breeds are not on top. It is the men of our race who govern in America. I do not know whether they are in the minority or not, but in the main they are on the top.[5]

Those statements raise a number of interesting questions worth examining in the latter context of the Anglo-American 'special relationship'. What was, or is, the 'voice' of America, or for that matter the United States government? Was the 'elite' of the post–Second World War period as Anglophile as the one of the previous generation? Clearly the British believed that their relationship with the Japanese before the First World War had been 'special'. It was just as important then as the American-Japanese relationship later became after the Second World War.

---

[3] Quoted in W. R. Louis, *British Strategy in the Far East* (Oxford, 1971), p. 72.
[4] Ibid., p. 66.
[5] Ibid., p. 77.

My preliminary reading of some of the 1954 files at the Public Record Office suggests that after the Second World War, the critical years for shaping the American-Japanese combination as well as the new American-German relationship were the early 1950s. This was the same time that the American anti-colonial campaign seemed to be reviving. The British Ambassador in Washington, Sir Roger Makins, like Lord Beloff, raised the question of motive:

> There is on our side a very understandable suspicion that the Americans are out to take our place in the Middle East. Their influence has greatly expanded there since the end of the Second World War, and they are now firmly established as the paramount foreign influence in Turkey and in Saudi Arabia. They are gaining a similar ascendancy in Persia, and it now seems that Pakistan may to some extent be drawn into their orbit . . . Are the Americans consciously trying to substitute their influence for ours in the Middle East?[6]

Makins also asked whether the political influence of the United States in such places as the Middle East was an 'inevitable' consequence of America's growing military and economic power. One is struck by the similarity of questions asked three-quarters of a century earlier, when Bismarck launched Germany on a disastrous colonial course that led to Anglo-German naval rivalry and thereby contributed indirectly to the origins of the First World War.

At the end of that war, George Louis Beer wrote of Woodrow Wilson: 'While he [the President] is in a fighting mood and is prepared to fight for a just peace, absolute justice in any specific instance was not attainable . . . Firm on broad principles, but flexible as to their precise application.'[7] Beer was Woodrow Wilson's adviser on colonial affairs at the Paris Peace Conference. He was an Anglophile in the sense that he sympathized with the aspirations of the Round Table group—in other words, to see the Empire evolve into a Commonwealth that would be a progressive force in world affairs. Lord Milner, the Colonial Secretary at that time, hoped that Beer might become the head of the mandates secretariat at Geneva and help promote Anglo-American cooperation in colonial affairs (an abortive plan because of the failure of the United States to join the League of Nations and Beer's premature death). Partly because of Beer's admiration for Milner, the United States and Britain saw more nearly eye to eye on the colonial situa-

---

[6] Memorandum by Makins, 25 January 1954, CAB 129/66.

[7] See W. R. Louis, 'The United States and the African Peace Settlement of 1919', *Journal of African History*, IV (1963).

tion at the close of the First World War than at the end of the Second, though at both times the British distrusted the application of general principles to complex colonial problems.

One of the 'broad principles' to which Beer referred was self-determination. 'Flexibility' became manifest in the case of South-West Africa. Wilson was prepared to allow South Africa to incorporate it if the South Africans could prove that the South-West Africans wished it. Self-determination proved to be more than a 'broad' principle. It was, to use one of Ernest Bevin's celebrated phrases, a Pandora's box that contained Trojan horses. Roosevelt no less than Wilson would have been astonished to have seen the 'headhunters' of New Guinea determining their own future only three decades after the Second World War. Both Wilson and Roosevelt were gradualists: both held that colonial peoples would and should eventually determine their own future, but neither foresaw the abrupt end of the European colonial system. The speed of the liquidation is a key point, as will be seen, in the question of responsibility for the aftermath.

FDR was a rogue Wilsonian. He believed in the same goals as Wilson, or so it seemed because of his frequent reiteration of some of Wilson's principles. He used Wilsonian rhetoric, but his aim was different. He wished to reshape the League of Nations into an effective force for preserving the peace. Yet his scheme for the 'four policemen' (the United States, Britain, the Soviet Union, and China) resembled the old spheres of influence, which Wilson had hoped to abolish. On the issue of security, Roosevelt went in the opposite direction from Wilson. Never again would nations such as Germany and Japan be allowed to menace the peace of the world. Disarmament had proved to be a broken reed; regional security would be the foundation of the future. In the Pacific, the United States would administer the Marianas, Marshalls, and Carolines as a trust territory of the United Nations, but would remain free to fortify them or use them as testing sites. The ideology of trusteeship was easily forged into a weapon of American defence. Ideology serves self-interest: American anti-colonialism was always reconciled with the needs of security.

In the case of Palestine, the Zionist crusade fused with the anti-colonial campaign. Palestine was hardly a typical colonial dependency, but the troubles of the 1945–48 period revealed prevalent attitudes in both Britain and America. To the British, the Jews were ungrateful. To most Americans, the Jews were struggling for self-determination. As Donald Watt has written, Anglo-American relations can be understood only by comprehending the nature of the elites in both countries, by studying their misperceptions and fixations, and by examining their unspoken assumptions.[8] By the end of the Second World War, Lloyd George's view about the men of 'our race' ruling America was no longer true. Yet there were certain continuities. Americans did not admire British imperialism. One wartime manifesto certainly caught the collective sentiment of the American public: the 'Open Letter to the People of England', published by *Life* magazine in October 1942 at the time of the 'Quit India' movement:

> One thing we are sure we are *not* fighting for is to hold the British Empire together. We don't like to put the matter so bluntly, but we don't want you to have any illusions. If your strategists are planning a war to hold the British Empire together they will sooner or later find themselves strategizing all alone . . . In the light of what you are doing in India, how do you expect us to talk about 'principles' and look our soldiers in the eye?[9]

The ideology of the American anti-colonial campaign was more than a reflection of self-interest. It was a force in itself that helped shape the substance of defence, economic, and foreign policy. It was a set of principles that most Americans upheld. The essence of it was the belief that colonial subjects had the inherent right to become independent and to rule themselves.

It would be unjust to the protagonists of the Second World War era, both American and British, to assume that they were unaware of the potential as well as the limits of their ideological assumptions, or the danger of conceding political principles. 'Our war aims . . . [are] practical weapons,' Wendell Willkie once said privately.[10] When Churchill and Roosevelt (and their respective advisers, Sir Alexander Cadogan and Sumner Welles) penned Article III of the Atlantic Charter in August 1941, each party in the transaction knew precisely how far these weapons could be employed within the context of the Anglo-American alliance. The Americans were insistent on a statement that the war was being fought to uphold the right of self-determination. Churchill acquiesced, but the ambiguity of the phrasing allowed him to argue afterwards that the aims of restoring self-government applied only to those countries subjugated by the Nazis. The principle of self-determination was a double-edged sword. In Churchill's hands it proved to be a suitable weapon for defending, negatively, the British

---

[8] D. Cameron Watt, *Succeeding John Bull: America in Britain's Place* (Cambridge, 1984).

[9] Quoted in W. R. Louis, *Imperialism at Bay* (Oxford, 1977), p. 198.

[10] In an interview with Louis Fischer, 13 August 1942, Louis Fischer Papers, Franklin D. Roosevelt Library, Hyde Park, NY.

Empire and the status quo. If the doctrine were applied to the Middle East, Churchill stated, the Arabs might claim by majority that 'they could expel the Jews from Palestine'.[11]

Within the American government, the key official who dealt with colonial affairs was the Under Secretary of State, Sumner Welles. He harboured a deep-seated animosity towards what he believed to be the malignant forces of British imperialism. It is now clear from the historical records that his influence extended beyond official circles into behind-the-scenes manouevres designed to weaken the British presence throughout the world. Welles is thus a good example of Lord Beloff's point about a concerted American effort to undermine the British Empire. Welles was pro-Zionist as well as anti-British. After he resigned as Under Secretary in 1943, he carried his campaign against the British Empire into the public arenas of newspaper controversy and, later, into the politics of the United Nations. At first sight it might therefore seem surprising that at the time of the signing of the Atlantic Charter, Welles did not attempt to seize the initiative by insisting on, for example, liberating India as a means of breaking up the British Empire by universally applying the self-determination principle. Welles's attitude in fact was identical with Roosevelt's. It was a question of priorities. The war was being fought against Germany and Japan. He judged that the war effort as a whole might be disrupted by the discord injected into the Anglo-American alliance by an anti-colonial crusade.

Roosevelt himself did not miss any opportunities to press for economic advantage (though he too subordinated economic as well as colonial issues to the higher purpose of winning the war). Nor did Churchill miss any chance to strengthen the Anglo-American alliance while simultaneously attempting to check American ambitions on the British Empire. In the short run, Churchill had the better part of the game. The principal reason why American anti-colonialism during the Second World War proved to be ineffective was that Churchill, L. S. Amery (Secretary of State for India), and Oliver Stanley (Secretary of State for the Colonies) managed to contain it to the limited yet symbolic area of international trusteeship affairs. But it should not be forgotten that the game was being played for the highest stakes. One cannot read the files of the Presidential correspondence at the Roosevelt Library without recognizing that Roosevelt and his advisers in 1942 were apprehensive of revolution in India. From a Tory point of view, the sturdy response of Lord Linlithgow, the Viceroy of India, in jailing the Indian nationalist leaders in 1942 was necessary, decisive, and

---

[11] Winston S. Churchill, *The Hinge of Fate* (Boston, 1950), p. 890.

admirable. The Americans were given no opportunity to meddle in what the British regarded as an internal affair.

Did the Americans foresee replacing the British Raj with American political and economic influence? They certainly drove hard bargains at British expense. They knew that the expansion of American power during the war would enable them to play a greater part in world affairs. But the reduction of Britain, still less India, to satellite status was a British suspicion, not an American motive. The emergence of the United States as one of the two superpowers, and the eclipse of British power, was a result of the Second World War. If the post-war period can be described as a Pax Americana, it was not modeled after the Pax Britannica.

American anti-colonialism was a sentiment easily reconciled with defence requirements and economic opportunities. It was also always subordinate to the more urgent problem of anti-communism. Yet anti-colonialism could not be dismissed merely as a self-serving or shallow slogan. It was a genuine sentiment—so believed informed observers of both countries at the time—amounting to an article of faith on the part of the American people, who believed that 'independence' should be the end result of colonial rule. So long as the British seemed to be making progress towards 'colonial independence', then the colonial issue was relatively unimportant in Anglo-American relations. In 1954 the British evacuation of the Suez base signalled a major effort to accommodate Egyptian nationalism. By contrast, the 1956 crisis, in American eyes, represented a return to the old imperialism, which, it was thought, should have died with the Second World War. Here there was indeed a question of the 'act of will'—the question of whose will would prevail in Britain and whose will would prevail between Britain and America. The Suez crisis itself helps explain the final decline of the Pax Britannica, and it also indicates some of the reasons why a Pax Americana of the same order has not arisen to take its place.

Prelude to Suez

At the end of the Second World War, Americans in general did not by any means believe that British 'colonialism' should be supported in Egypt. Beneath expressions of distress about deteriorating relations between the British and Egyptians there was a sense of American alarm at the mutual distrust. There was the danger that the Americans would not be able to remain on friendly terms with the Egyptians because of the British. In 1947 the US Ambassador in Cairo, Loy Henderson, commented on the problem of British troops in Egypt:

Their [military] presence is poisoning the atmosphere of the whole Near and Middle East rapidly and to such an extent that unless some indication is given in the near future that British troops are to be withdrawn from Egypt unconditionally . . . the relations of the Arab world with the Western world may be seriously impaired for many years to come.[12]

Henderson had therefore welcomed the Labour Government's initiative in 1946 to withdraw all troops from Egypt into the Canal Zone and to reduce the number in the base itself to the 10,000 stipulated by the 1936 agreement. Furthermore, the Labour Government held out hope that eventually the base might be handed over to the Egyptians, if they would agree to a military alliance. For the United States, this would have been a satisfactory outcome. Indeed, the Labour Government's suggestion contained the beginnings of the proposal of the early 1950s for a 'Middle East command', whereby Britain, Egypt, and other Middle Eastern countries (and perhaps even the United States) would, under British leadership, form an alliance comparable to NATO.

During this first period of the immediate post-war era—one which might be called the 'Henderson period'—the Americans were disappointed but nevertheless heartened by Bevin's initiative to resolve the Sudan problem by upholding the principle of self-determination (by the somewhat devious means of recognizing theoretical 'Egyptian sovereignty' over a Sudan in which the inhabitants would determine their own future). The other British aim was to move troops out of the Canal Zone altogether (or, better still, staying on as an 'equal' ally). Bevin was an egalitarian and a champion of social democracy. He believed that Egyptians should be treated as equals. His attitude struck a responsive chord in Washington and in American circles in Cairo. When he failed in 1946, Americans tended to blame the Egyptians and to credit Bevin and the British in general for having made an attempt, at least, to adjust the old Imperial relationship to one in which the Egyptians would be genuinely regarded as equals.

The second period, the late 1940s and early 1950s, might, from an American perspective, be called the Jefferson Caffery era. Before his posting as Ambassador in Cairo, Caffery had served as the first postwar American Ambassador in Paris. He had a reputation as one of the most distinguished, and also most formidable, members of the US

---

[12] Memorandum by Henderson, 28 August 1947, *Foreign Relations of the United States, 1947*, V, pp. 800–02. See also especially the memorandum by Gordon Merriam (head of the Near Eastern Affairs Division in the State Department), 28 March 1947, NA 741.83/302847 (National Archives, Washington, D.C.).

Foreign Service. He was certainly well informed, and on the whole well disposed to the British—but more to the British in Cairo than in Khartoum. In his opinion, the situation had deteriorated so badly by 1950 that 'keeping the Egyptians talking' in order 'to ride out the storm' was the most important thing to be done. With American help, Caffery believed, the British might be able to conciliate Egyptian nationalism. He had in mind arms supplies, guarantees of Egyptian sovereignty, the 'façade' at least of military consultation, an assurance that the British and the Americans were aware of the dangers of 'militant Zionism', and British withdrawal from the Sudan.[13]

The offer of the Sudan was the most important element in the bargain, which has to be understood against the background of the Korean War. Caffery viewed the deteriorating situation in the Canal Zone as an urgent problem in the defence against communism. In his opinion, the only way the British (and eventually the Americans) might stay on in Suez would be to make the Egyptians a substantial offer. Why not hand over the Sudan to the Egyptians in return for a secure footing in the Canal Zone? His idea, in short, was to accommodate the Egyptians in the Sudan, thereby facilitating a settlement for an 'international' (British, Egyptian, American) base at Suez. The project never got off the ground, not least because of the Egyptian suspicion that the 'international' base would merely be a continuation of the British occupation. For putting forward such proposals, Caffery was later denounced by Sir James Robertson (the Civil Secretary of the Sudan administration) for 'selling the Sudan'—for not appreciating 'our [British] concern for . . . "ten million bloody niggers".'[14]

Robertson's comment was aimed as a rebuke to America. Was the complaint not similar to Williams M. Hughes's indictment of the American god who spoke with a forked tongue, saying contradictory things? Quite apart from Robertson's sarcasm about the American blind eye turned towards segregation in the United States (a recurrent theme in British comment on 'colonialism' in the early 1950s), how could 'appeasement in the Sudan' (the British phrase used to describe the American attitude) be reconciled with the tradition of anti-colonialism? Even Caffery, with his contempt for British colonialism, hardly believed that Egyptian administration in the Sudan would be better than British rule. He responded to criticism in the same way as Roosevelt's defenders during the war: it was a question of priorities. The crusade against communism and the defence requirements of

---

[13] Caffery to Acheson, 25 November and 11 December 1950, *Foreign Relations of the United States, 1950*, V, pp. 323–24, 329–30.

[14] Sir James Robertson, *Transition in Africa* (New York, 1974), p. 150.

the West came first. The question of 'colonialism' (and the problem of the Sudan) would be solved later. From the American perspective, one of the most unfortunate aspects of the Suez crisis was the conjunction of revolution in a communist state, Hungary, and 'extreme colonialism' (Eisenhower's phrase) in Egypt.

The collision of 1956 with the United States was precisely what the British had attempted since 1945 to avoid. Britain, of course, was aware that in Egypt, as elsewhere, success depended on American support. One of the shrewdest officials at the Foreign Office, Sir Pierson Dixon, wrote in 1952:

> Thinking over our difficulties in Egypt, it seems to me that the essential difficulty arises from the very obvious fact that we lack power. The Egyptians know this, and that accounts for their intransigence . . . Power, of course, is not to be measured in terms alone of money and troops: a third ingredient is prestige, or in other words what the rest of the world thinks of us.
>
> Here the dilemma arises. We are not physically strong enough to carry out policies needed if we are to retain our position in the world; if we show weakness our position in the world diminishes with repercussions on our world wide position.
>
> The broadest conclusion I am driven to is therefore that we ought to make every conceivable effort to avoid a policy of surrender or near surrender. Ideally we should persuade the Americans of the disaster which such a policy would entail for us and for them, and seek their backing, moral, financial, and, if possible, military, in carrying out a strong policy in Egypt.[15]

There was an unspoken psychological dimension to the problem of power. Rationally, the British might acknowledge that they needed American support, and they might genuinely attempt to create an 'equal partnership' with the Egyptians. Yet they still regarded themselves as masters of the Middle East. The underlying purpose was to sustain themselves as a great 'world power'. This was still true in 1956, and here lies the principal significance of the Suez crisis: Dixon wrote later that the main result of the Suez fiasco was that Britain at one stroke had been reduced 'from a 1st class to a 3rd class power'.[16]

Two general developments need to be emphasized as background to the crisis itself. The first is the Egyptian revolution of July 1952. It

[15] Minute by Dixon, 23 January 1952, FO 371/96920.

[16] Piers Dixon, *Double Diploma: The Life of Sir Pierson Dixon* (London, 1968), p. 278.

set in motion the solution to the Sudan problem—to British disadvantage—by recognizing the Sudanese right of self-determination. In Egypt, the British now faced a revolutionary regime committed to social reform and, at the same time, to the extinction of British imperialism. John Hamilton, the Oriental Secretary at the British Embassy in Cairo, wrote in his assessment of events six months later:

> In Egypt the omens are disquieting. I believe General Neguib means well and that he is the best man the country has produced for years. But he is committed to the total evacuation of our forces and internally he may well prove to be the Kerensky of Egypt . . .
>
> I believe that we are up against a determined anti-British movement. The young officers think we are on the decline as a great power, they have a real hatred politically for us in their hearts and they will accept assistance and guidance from any party or persons who will aid them in turning us completely out of Egypt. No amount of concession or evacuation on our part will evoke the slightest gratitude in return. Whoever Egypt may want in the future as an ally, it will not be us.[17]

This was an astute analysis. It illuminates the rationale of the agreement concluded in 1954 for British withdrawal from the Canal Zone. The British had to accept the best terms they could get. They could not expect any Egyptian nationalist to be pro-British. This logic leads to some of the principal questions about the 1956 Suez expedition. What was the ultimate aim: A friendlier Nasser? Egypt returned to status as a client regime, which had produced unsatisfactory results in the past? Perhaps the ultimate aim was unclear. Perhaps Eden's plans might have led to another British occupation of Egypt.

The other development was the revolution in nuclear warfare signified by the American and Russian explosion of hydrogen bombs in November 1952 and August 1953. No longer could nuclear weapons be regarded as an extension of conventional warfare. Now the Canal Zone could be destroyed at one blow. According to the Permanent Under-Secretary at the Foreign Office in 1954:

> I do not believe that in this atomic age we shall have either the wish or the ability to reactivate the base. We will be sufficiently occupied struggling for survival. And in . . . time the power and the numbers of these frightful weapons will be so great that the chance of our wanting to conduct a campaign in the Middle East will be less than it is to-day.[18]

[17] Memorandum by Hamilton, 15 February 1953, FO 371/102764.
[18] Minute by Kirkpatrick, 26 July 1954, FO 371/108424.

The author of that minute was Sir Ivone Kirkpatrick, accurately identified in American documents in 1956 as one of the key figures behind
the scenes in the Suez emergency. Like Eden, he believed Nasser to
be a Hitler of the Middle East who had to be stopped. Kirkpatrick had
been posted to Germany in 1953. 'Humiliation' was a word that frequently appeared in his minutes: 'If we seek to hang on', he once wrote
in regard to the Sudan, 'we may end by being expelled, and that would
be humiliating.'[19] On Egypt as well as on general issues of defence,
Kirkpatrick saw eye to eye with Eden.

The 1954 agreement between Britain and Egypt, which provided
for Britain's right of re-entry into the Canal Zone in the event of an attack on an Arab state or Turkey, was the culmination of British policy
since the Second World War. It represented the Middle Eastern equivalent of the transfer of power in India. In Albert Hourani's words, it
was 'the greatest change that had occurred in the Middle Eastern balance of power since 1923', when the former Ottoman Empire had
been reduced to a rump Turkish state.[20] As Sir Harold Beeley has written, it recognized the Egyptians as equals, thereby signifying the triumph of Bevin's Middle Eastern policy.[21] The Middle East would have
been a very different place if the 1954 agreement had remained the
foundation of Anglo-Egyptian relations and had not been destroyed
by the events leading up to the Suez adventure.

In the records on the Suez crisis, an element of Lord Beloff's argument about the 'act of will' can be found among the inner core of British ministers and officials who wanted to reverse what they saw as a
process of decline. Eden could not do it alone. He needed the support
not only of the Cabinet and Parliament but also of the Ministry of Defence and the Foreign Office. The Foreign Office was a delicate problem because the members of the African and other Departments were
sceptical about whether toppling Nasser would lead to anything other
than another British occupation of Egypt. It was Kirkpatrick who effectively sealed off usual channels of Foreign Office telegram traffic, at
all levels, to conduct an ultra-secret operation. Not only was he highly
intelligent and efficient, but he also had fixed ideas and a will of iron.
He would not crack.

In his memoirs, Selwyn Lloyd, the Foreign Secretary who served
as Eden's stalwart lieutenant during the crisis, comments that the

[19] Minute by Kirkpatrick, 14 June 1954, FO 371/208378.

[20] Albert Hourani, 'The Anglo-Egyptian Agreement: Some Causes and Implications', *Middle East Journal*, 9 (Summer 1955).

[21] Sir Harold Beeley, 'Ernest Bevin and Palestine' (Antonius Lecture, St. Antony's College, Oxford, 14 June 1983).

American response was a combination of 'anti-colonialism and hard-headed oil tycoonery'.[22] This was a shrewd though misguided assessment. The Americans contemplated curtailing the oil supplies to halt the British and French, not to make short-term profit. Nevertheless, the crisis revealed that anti-colonialism and long-range economic self-interest are easily reconciled, and also that the mixture of those elements with another powerful ingredient, anti-communism, can lead to deadly results. In this case, the combination proved almost fatal for the British. This argument can be tested against the American records. The Eisenhower and Dulles Papers at the Eisenhower Library will be drawn upon here briefly for evidence about the 'special relationship' and anti-colonialism.

The American Response to the Crisis

'For many years now', John Foster Dulles stated to the National Security Council on 1 November 1956, in one of the first full discussions about the Anglo-French-Israeli invasion,

> the United States has been walking on a tightrope between the effort to maintain our old and valued relations with our British and French allies on the one hand, and on the other trying to assure ourselves of the friendship and understanding of the newly independent countries who have escaped from colonialism.

The United States, according to the Secretary of State, now faced overwhelming pressure from former 'colonial' peoples throughout the world. The Eisenhower administration therefore confronted a challenge, which Dulles posed in emotional and moralistic language:

> Unless we now assert and maintain this leadership all of these newly independent countries will turn from us to the USSR. We will be looked upon as forever tied to British and French colonialist policies.

> In short, the United States would survive or go down on the basis of the fate of colonialism if the United States supports the French and the British on the colonial issues. Win or lose, we will share the fate of Britain and France.

Dulles was distressed that world opinion was diverted from the Hungarian uprising against Soviet domination by this reassertion of 'colonial' control 'by force' over the Middle East:

[22] Selwyn Lloyd, *Suez 1956* (London, 1978), p. 78.

> It is no less than tragic that at this very time, when we are on the point
> of winning an immense and long-hoped-for victory over Soviet colo-
> nialism in Eastern Europe, we should be forced to choose between
> following in the footsteps of Anglo-French colonialism in Asia and
> Africa, or splitting our course away from their course.[23]

At that point Eisenhower attempted, according to the minutes of
meeting, to break the 'tension', but Dulles later returned 'with great
warmth' to the subject of colonialism: '[W]hat the British and French
had done was nothing but the straight old-fashioned variety of colonialism of the most obvious sort.' Unless the United States championed the cause of the 'lesser-developed nations' at the United Nations,
then the initiative would be lost to the Soviet Union.

In many ways, those statements reveal vintage Dulles: the same
Dulles who, with a missionary twist, had withdrawn economic assistance for the Aswan dam a few months earlier after refusing to be
'blackmailed' by Nasser's threat to turn to the Russians. He clearly had
not anticipated Nasser's response of nationalizing the Suez Canal
Company on 26 July 1956, nor had he foreseen that the British and
the French might bomb the airfields around Cairo and invade the Canal Zone. The element of surprise was critical for both Dulles and
Eisenhower. And in this regard it is for the President, much more than
for his Secretary of State, that the Eisenhower Papers change the nuance of historical interpretation.

The fatal British miscalculation was in supposing that Dulles controlled American policy and that both Dulles and Eisenhower would
cooperate in the overthrow of Nasser.[24] Those assumptions are of utmost importance for understanding the 'special relationship' then
and thereafter. As had been the case in Palestine, presidential involvement in a 'colonial' issue can make a decisive difference. In the
case of Suez, the British were not merely wrong about Dulles, they
were also wrong about Eisenhower. Eisenhower, not Dulles, controlled foreign policy. Dulles gave it a certain legal and moralistic tone

---

[23] National Security Council, 302 Meeting, 1 November 1956, Eisenhower Papers, Whitman
File. For Anglo-American relations at the time of Suez, see especially Herman Finer, *Dulles over
Suez* (Chicago, 1964); and Townsend Hoopes, *The Devil and John Foster Dulles* (Boston, 1973).
Both books were written before the opening of the collections at the Eisenhower Library. The
best general accounts are Kennet Love, *Suez: The Twice-Fought War* (New York, 1969); and Donald Neff, *Warriors at Suez* (New York, 1981). The most important recent analysis, based in large
part on documents made accessible by the Freedom of Information Act, is William J. Burns, *Economic Aid and American Policy toward Egypt, 1955–1981* (Albany, N.Y., 1985).

[24] See Stephen E. Ambrose, *Eisenhower: The President* (New York, 1984), chap. 15; see also especially Robert A. Divine, *Eisenhower and the Cold War* (New York, 1981), chap. 3.

that made it all the more objectionable to the British, but ultimately it was Eisenhower who dominated. Unlike some other American presidents (and more so even than FDR), Eisenhower studied the problems of foreign affairs until he had mastered the essentials. He gave latitude to his subordinates, but he himself set the direction and laid out the substance of policy. In the case of Suez, he proved to be just as anti-colonialist as his Secretary of State.

Eisenhower's years before the war had been spent in the Philippines. He did not have profound insight into Filipino politics or history, but he was convinced that the United States had governed the Philippines both wisely and well by preparing them for independence and, almost as importantly, by setting a timetable for independence. By granting independence, Eisenhower once said, the United States had enabled the Filipinos to achieve a 'fierce pride'.[25] He believed that the British should be following the American example. During his first term in office, he had written about Churchill clinging to the office as Prime Minister: 'He talks [in January 1953] very animatedly about certain . . . international problems, especially Egypt and its future. But so far as I can see, he has developed an almost childlike faith that all of the answers are to be found merely in British-American partnership.'[26] Eisenhower had little use for the 'special relationship' in this connection. He believed that the United States was the natural leader of the newly independent countries of the post-war era. Thus he erupted in anger—'barrack room language', in the euphemism repeated in the documents—when he learned of the Anglo-French-Israeli attack at Suez. Indignation in turn became mixed with sorrow. His reproaches to Eden conveyed anger as well as a genuine lament for the lost partnership.

Eden and at least some of his colleagues calculated that by keeping the United Sates in the dark, they might succeed in gaining Dulles's acquiescence because of his antipathy towards Nasser. Eisenhower might not intervene either because of his sympathy for long-range British plans or possibly because of the impending presidential election. Those miscalculations have to be recorded among the ranks of memorable blunders of modern history. 'Anthony, have you gone out of your mind?' Eisenhower asked in a transatlantic telephone call: 'You've deceived me.'[27] That was the ultimate miscalculation, even

[25] Ambrose, *Eisenhower*, p. 378.

[26] Robert H. Ferrell, *The Eisenhower Diaries* (New York, 1981), p. 223.

[27] Elizabeth Monroe, *Britain's Moment in the Middle East* (London, 1981 edn.), p. 209. Apparently this was Eisenhower's first telephone call to Eden, which was mistakenly put through to William Clark, the press officer at 10 Downing Street (according to Monroe, based on Clark's testi-

insult. Eden had offended Eisenhower's personal code of honour by
not keeping him informed. The ruthless crushing of the British by
threatening to deny emergency oil supplies, and the refusal of financial support, has to be explained at least in part by Eisenhower's sense
of betrayal. According to a typescript of a meeting at the White House
on 29 October 1956:

> The President thought that the British are calculating that we must go
> along with them (he thought they were not banking too heavily on our
> being tied up in the election, but are thinking in longer range terms).
> He thought we should let them know at once of our position, telling
> them that we recognize that much is on their side in the dispute with
> the Egyptians, but that nothing justifies double-crossing us.[28]

The British had 'double-crossed' the Americans not merely by the secret attack. It is clear from the records that Eisenhower no less than
Dulles believed that the British and the French were now demonstrating a brutal type of 'colonialism' comparable to Russian methods in
Hungary. This was the low ebb of the special relationship.

The 'Special Relationship' and the End of the British Empire

'The British Empire is pre-eminently a great Naval, Indian and Colonial Power', according to a celebrated statement that illuminates
that nature of the Pax Britannica.[29] The United States can today perhaps be regarded as a 'colonial' power in the sense of exercising indirect political control and dominance throughout much of the world,
but there has never been the American equivalent of British India.
The United States is a great naval, air, and military power, but the bipolar rivalry with the Soviet Union and the existence of nuclear weapons make the world of the twentieth century quite different from the
one of the nineteenth century, when the Maxim gun proved to be an
effective weapon for keeping the peace as well as making conquests.
     From FDR to Eisenhower, the Americans attempted to impress on

---

mony). The President thus spoke those words before he realized that he had the wrong person
on the line. This may explain part of the conflicting stories about what Eisenhower actually said
or did not say initially to Eden. For a critical assessment of Eden and the crisis, see especially David
Carlton, *Anthony Eden* (London, 1981), chap. 11. Anthony Nutting, *No End of a Lesson* (New York,
1967), remains indispensable for understanding the crisis within the British government.

[28] Memorandum of Conference with the President, 29 October 1956, Dulles Papers, Eisenhower Library.

[29] First report of the Committee of Imperial Defence (1904), quoted in Lord Hankey, *The Supreme Command, 1914–1918* (London, 1961), I, p. 46.

the British the lessons, psychological as well as technological, to be drawn from the confrontation between European imperialism and indigenous nationalism. In 1882 the British had succeeded in occupying Egypt; by the end of the Second World War they faced a nationalist movement that even sophisticated weapons could not indefinitely suppress. By the early 1950s the Americans foresaw communist revolution throughout the Middle East. In Dean Acheson's blunt words to Churchill and Eden in 1952:

> The Middle East presented a picture that might have been drawn by Karl Marx himself—with the masses a disinherited and poverty-stricken proletariat, no middle class, a small and corrupt ruling class pushed about by foreigners who sought to exploit priceless resources, whether oil or canal. Was there ever such an opportunity to invoke inherent xenophobia to destroy the foreigner and his system and substitute the Communist solution? Anglo-American solidarity on a policy of sitting tight offered no solution, but was like a couple locked in warm embrace in a rowboat about to go over Niagara Falls. It was high time to break the embrace and take to the oars.[30]

Behind Acheson stood a whole generation of Americans who held similar views—the '[George] McGhee's', as Selwyn Lloyd indignantly remarked.[31]

McGhee had been Assistant Secretary for Near Eastern, South Asian, and African Affairs (1949–51) and then Ambassador to Turkey. He was one of the most outspoken yet friendly critics of British colonialism. The trouble was, as he frequently explained, the British continued to think in 'nineteenth-century' terms. Unless they changed their ways and accepted Asian and African nationalism as the prevailing force, then the consequences would be catastrophic for both the British and Americans. This attitude did not make McGhee popular among the British, but it expressed a quintessential American point. The Pax Britannica was dead. Nothing comparable would arise to take its place. The Americans would have to do the best they could in a volatile world. The difficult nature of the task, perhaps even more its unpopularity, may explain why no one gets up enthusiasm singing 'March on Americans, march on in the world', or, indeed, 'Arise, Pax Americana'.[32] The most basic reason of all was the doubt that there

[30] Dean Acheson, *Present at the Creation* (New York, 1969), p. 600.

[31] Lloyd, *Suez 1956*, p. 78. See George McGhee, *Envoy to the Middle World* (New York, 1983).

[32] The Permanent Under-Secretary at the Foreign Office wrote in 1952: 'The Americans . . . cannot bring themselves to believe that people do not like them.' Eden noted, 'True' (minutes by Strang and Eden, 5 February 1952, FO 371/96922).

should be a Pax Americana, which implies world dominance as well as order and stability.

Did the Americans, wittingly or by accident, help bring about the post-war world of balkanization and unrest by dismembering the British Empire? The American influence on its dissolution is difficult to measure, but it must have been small. Through the trusteeship system at the United Nations, the United States may have helped advance the dates of independence for some trusteeship territories—for example, by setting a ten-year goal in the horn of Africa so that Somalia became independence in 1960. But it would require an imaginative leap to conclude that international influences precipitated the wave of African independence of the 1950s. The British were responding to the full current of African nationalism and were making their own calculations about the financial and moral cost of holding colonial dependencies against both overseas and domestic sentiment. In 1985, David Fieldhouse completed a study in which he concludes that the dependencies in Africa in the late 1950s were no longer as important to the British economy as they had been in the period of economic recovery. The British had their own reasons for precipitous decolonization: hoping to retain economic and political influence in return for a quick transfer of power.[33] If this analysis is correct, then the British as much as the Americas are responsible for the aftermath, in Lord Beloff's indictment, of instability and deprivation, civil and tribal war, famine, and even genocide.

Has the failure to replace the Pax Britannica by a Pax Americana been caused by infirmity of the 'will'? In some of the American as well as British literature dealing with the post-war economic crisis and its consequences, there runs the theme that the decline of British power might have been prevented if the British had been more determined or the United Sates had supported Britain more resolutely. The failure of this 'act of will' is an alluring interpretation for those seeking the reasons for the decline and fall of the British Empire. Here is an example of the way in which an American writer, Theodore H. White, brings this idea to bear on the devaluation crisis of September 1949. He relates a conversation with Sir Edmund Hall-Patch, one of the principal economic authorities at the Foreign Office:

> [H]is task humiliated him. Begging for the American buck was not
> his style . . . [he] was talking from the heart. America must move to

[33] D. K. Fieldhouse, 'Arrested Development in Anglophone Black Africa?' in Prosser Gifford and W. R. Louis, eds., *Decolonization and African Independence: The Transfers of Power, 1960–1980* (New Haven, 1988).

save and take over the British economy . . . or Britain would fade from power . . . He doubted whether England had the stomach to go the rough road it must go if it went alone—to cut the Empire adrift, to repudiate its distant and inner obligations, to hold on only to military command of the oil resources of the Middle East . . .

If scarcely occurred to me then . . . that, ultimately we would drive the British from the Middle East . . . and leave all of America's economy and civilization in debt to, and uncertainly dependent on, the oil of the Middle East sheikhs and strong men, whom the British had previously policed for us.[34]

A sense of lost opportunity is thus fused with self-recrimination for failure to rescue the British Empire. This is a grotesque lament. In the post-war period there was precious little sentimentality, in official American circles at least, about the British failure to solve their own colonial problems, especially at the time of Suez.

And on the British side? Was there a failure of 'will' during the Suez crisis? Some held that Anthony Eden should have persisted. Others believed in Ernest Bevin's maxim that it requires just as great an act of will not to intervene in the affairs of small nations—or in this case, to exercise restraint—as it does to impose a peace by bayonets.

The comparable point in American history was the loss of confidence during the Vietnam War, when national sentiment was divided and national purpose questioned. Yet in a sense, the Suez crisis was a watershed for the Americans as well as for the British: many of the world's problems can be directly traced to the policies pursued by the Eisenhower administration. Americans might take pride in Eisenhower's robust anti-colonialist stance at the time of Suez, but as Michael Howard has written, there was a dark side to the Eisenhower era.[35] Eisenhower did not hesitate to employ the subversive capabilities of the Central Intelligence Agency in the holy war against communism, few holds barred. The greater the frustrating restraint of nuclear weapons, the more tempting the use of covert methods. Eisenhower's policy of external interference, pursued by his successors, almost certainly contributed to the Iranian revolution and led to the replacement of Britain by the United States as the 'great Satan'. The global reputation of the British Empire as a satanic force has ebbed; the United States as a diabolical and ubiquitous influence is a popular perception throughout much of the world today.

---

[34] Quoted, with comment in a Middle Eastern context, in W. R. Louis, *The British Empire in the Middle East* (Oxford, 1984), p. 14.

[35] Michael Howard, 'Keeping the Team Together', *Times Literary Supplement,* 8 February 1985.

Eisenhower was in fact as on guard against possible excesses of the CIA, just as he was against those of the American military; nevertheless, his administration endorsed the clandestine operations of the CIA and other American agencies in such places as Guatemala and Iran. The President himself was perhaps under the impression that a Pax Americana of sorts could be created and sustained by such methods. If so, there must have been a delicate balance between hoping that the United States could preserve freedom by subversive means (or 'ruling indirectly', American style) and believing that small nations have the right to conduct their own affairs. In any case, Eisenhower's attitude gives support to the view that in the competition in the American mind among the 'special relationship', 'anti-colonialism', and 'anti-communism', the last always prevails. As for the more precise connection between the 'special relationship' and 'anti-colonialism', Dean Acheson perhaps best expressed the consistent American attitude: 'As we saw our role . . . it was to help toward solving the colonial-nationalist conflict in a way that would satisfy nationalist aims and minimize the strain on our Western European allies.'[36]

[36] Acheson, *Present at the Creation*, p. 671.

23

PRELUDE TO SUEZ: CHURCHILL AND EGYPT

'Whose finger on the trigger?' The question referred to the choice between Winston Churchill and Clement Attlee during the election campaign of 1951, but it has an eerie relevance to the Suez crisis of 1956. Shortly before he became Prime Minister for the last time, Churchill said: 'Least of all do we want a fumbling finger.'[1] He had very little to do with the Suez crisis itself, but earlier he had not flinched from pursuing a bellicose course. He believed that the Egyptians, like other 'Oriental' peoples, should be handled with firmness at all times and with force if necessary. If anything, his attitude towards the Egyptians was even more contemptuous than his regard for Indians. 'Degraded savages', he commented characteristically in his Egyptian mood.[2] He wrote those words in anger in 1952, when British subjects had been murdered in Cairo, but the phrase represented views he had held since he first visited Egypt more than half a century earlier. He never wavered from his Victorian opinion that the Egyptians were an inferior and essentially cowardly people. He was persistently bullying and truculent in his attitude. Nevertheless, he did, towards the end of his career as Prime Minister, decide in favour of evacuating British troops from Egyptian soil and the peaceful resolution of the issue of the Canal Zone. As in the case of India, he ultimately took a magnanimous view that placed him on the side of disengagement and reconciliation.

That good will was no substitute for power was a theme running through his thought. On this point he differed fundamentally from the leaders in the Labour Party, above all Attlee and Ernest Bevin. Churchill believed—at least until 1953 or 1954—that the Canal Zone would continue to provide Britain with a commanding bastion in the East despite the irrevocable loss of India. Suez, in his view, remained the geographical keystone of the Middle East and indeed one of the supreme geopolitical positions in the world. He never forgave the Labour Government for proposing to withdraw British troops from Egypt in the spring of 1946. He also used the word 'scuttle' to describe the British evacuation from the Iranian oilfields and the refinery at Abadan in 1951. He occasionally made exceptions—notably on Palestine—but in general he denounced as tantamount to treason any suggestion of withdrawal from any British position in any part of the world.

---

[1] D. E. Butler, *The British General Election of 1951* (London, 1952), p. 55; Martin Gilbert, *Winston S. Churchill* (Boston, 1988), VIII, p. 643.

[2] Churchill to Eden, Private and Personal, 30 January 1952, PREM 11/91.

Why then did he change his mind in 1954 about Suez, which, to use his own phrase, he regarded as the 'lifeline of the Empire'?

Churchill had a picture in his mind's eye of Egypt as he had known it around 1900. He had been eight years old at the time of the British occupation of Egypt in 1882, eleven at the time of the death of Gordon, and he was present at the battle of Omdurman with Kitchener in 1898.[3] He made no secret of the influence of his past experience and indeed took unabashed pleasure in holding what he granted was an old-fashioned view. It was a view that seemed to others, then as now, more a caricature than a true picture. But as he listened to military and political advice, and as he placed his ideas in a larger setting of Anglo-American relations and of technological change, he slowly and almost imperceptibly altered his outlook. In 1954, when he stated in the House of Commons that he now favoured British evacuation from the Canal Zone, Attlee was astonished. Churchill, the foremost critic of the Labour Government's conciliatory policy, now seemed compelled, in Attlee's phrase, to reverse himself. What were the stages, to rephrase the question, at which Churchill adjusted his thought to the necessity of withdrawing troops from Egypt? Or to pitch the question still higher, when did he reconcile himself, in the words he had employed previously in regard to India, to the sad spectacle of the British Empire in the Middle East 'clattering down . . . with all its glories, and all the services it has rendered to mankind'?[4]

The answer must begin with his preconceptions and, closer to hand, his policy towards Egypt during the Second World War. In his mind from the beginning was a picture of the unquestionable benefits brought by British rule and influence, which had continued in one form or another since the British occupation in 1882. The modern landmark was the Treaty of 1936, whereby Britain acquired the right to station 10,000 troops in the Canal Zone. The Treaty would expire in 1956, a fact never far removed from Churchill's calculations: it was the legal basis of the British presence. As wartime Prime Minister, he had made it clear that the Canal Zone and indeed Egypt itself was vital to British security. In early 1942 he supported to the hilt the aggressive tactics of the Ambassador in Cairo, Sir Miles Lampson (Lord Killearn), who surrounded the Royal Palace with armoured cars to coerce King Farouk into forming a pro-British Egyptian government. Later in the same year Churchill made the famous statement that he had not become the King's First Minister to preside over the

---

[3] See Raymond A. Callahan, *Churchill: Retreat from Empire* (Wilmington, Del., 1984), for a survey of Churchill's early life and career with the Imperial theme as the focus.

[4] *Parliamentary Debates* (Commons), 6 March 1947, col. 678.

liquidation of the Empire, in which, clearly, Egypt was one of the pillars. What might appear to others as British 'imperialism' was to Churchill an entirely natural and worthy enterprise. From the time of Lord Cromer the British had stood for economic progress and had imposed a peace that restrained the ruling class of 'Pashas' and landlords from exploiting the peasants, or fellahin. The belief that British influence was good for the Egyptians remained a constant ingredient of Churchill's basic assumption, which no Egyptian nationalist ever succeeded in altering.

'Egypt owes us a great debt,' Churchill stated in the House of Commons in 1946. 'Since the days of Cromer we have done our best to shield her from the storms which beat about the world.' The Egyptians, or at least the great bulk of the people in Egypt, had cause for gratitude for internal reasons as well.

> We have done a great deal, though not nearly as much as we ought to have done, to force forward the lot of the fellaheen and the masses of the people. We have been hampered by our respect for the authority of the Egyptian potentates and assemblies and by not wanting to interfere too much in the affairs of the country. But it is a shocking thing how little progress there has been among the great masses of Egyptian fellaheen.[5]

Churchill consistently demonstrated a concern for the welfare of the common people of Egypt. His attitude was paternalistic but nonetheless genuine. 'Unhappily', he concluded at another time, Egyptian prosperity was 'shared almost exclusively by the rich and well-to-do classes, while the peasantry seemed to remain in very much the condition in which I saw them when I first went to Egypt as a young officer towards the end of the last century.'[6] Again, his outlook never changed. 'It is most important', he wrote in 1952 in a minute that summed up his attitude towards social change in Egypt, 'that we should not appear to be defending the landlords and Pashas against the long overdue reforms for the fellaheen.'[7]

The British presence was, in Churchill's view, essentially benevolent but by no means supine. Ingratitude would be repaid in kind. Earlier in his career he had remarked that punishing China was like flogging a jellyfish. The same sense of frustration characterized his attitude towards Egypt after 1945, when he wished to teach Egyptian nationalists a lesson. His bellicose impulse was checked by the fear of being pulled

[5] Ibid., 7 May 1946, col. 895.
[6] Ibid., 30 July 1951, col. 981.
[7] Minute by Churchill, 26 August 1952, PREM 11/392.

into another full-scale occupation. Churchill's picture of Egypt was tinged with realism, but his sentiments remained constant. One of the first entries in the diary of Evelyn Shuckburgh (Under-Secretary in charge of Middle Eastern affairs at the Foreign Office) relates a late-night meeting in December 1951 of Churchill, Anthony Eden (then Foreign Secretary), and various Foreign Office officials. They discussed Egyptian attacks on the British position in the Canal Zone. After heated exchanges—and a considerable amount to drink—Churchill concluded the meeting by giving strong advice on how to respond to the Egyptians. According to Shuckburgh, he provided comic relief: 'Rising from his chair, the old man advanced on Anthony with clenched fists, saying with the inimitable Churchill growl, "Tell them that if we have any more of their cheek we will set the Jews on them and drive them into the gutter, from which they should never have emerged".'[8]

Before, during, and after the Egyptian revolution of July 1952, Churchill urged Eden not to be intimidated by threats of violence from the Egyptians. 'If . . . you make what looks like a surrender to violence and evacuation of forces by threats and atrocities', Churchill wrote in a minute that reveals his concern with the Iranian oil crisis as well as Suez, 'it may cause deep resentment in that element of British public life whose regard sustains you, and also mockery from the Party that scuttled from Abadan.'[9] In the summer of 1952, Farouk was deposed and Mustafa Nahas, the leader of the nationalist party, the Wafd, was thrown into disgrace. The champion of the new regime was Colonel Mohammed Neguib. Churchill was sceptical. Be it Farouk, Nahas, or Neguib, the Egyptian national character would not change. He again linked the question of the Canal Zone with the previous 'scuttle' from Iran a year earlier:

> I am quite sure that we could not agree to be kicked out of Egypt by Nahas, Farouk or Neguib and leave our base, worth £500 millions, to be despoiled or put in their care . . . How different would the position have been if the late [Labour] Government had not flinched . . . at Abadan.[10]

There was a powerful logic in this position. Had the Labour Government held firm in Iran, there would be no crisis in Egypt. If Churchill

---

[8] Shuckburgh Diaries, 16 December 1951. References are to unpublished Shuckburgh Diaries (privately held) unless the excerpt appears in the published version, Evelyn Shuckburgh, *Descent to Suez: Diaries 1951–1956* (London, 1986).

[9] Churchill to Eden, 15 February 1952, PREM 11/91.

[10] Minute by Churchill. 19 August 1952, PREM 11/392.

did not draw the line in Egypt, the end would be in sight. Shuckburgh summed up Churchill's reasoning: 'If we go out of the Sudan and Egypt it will be another stage in the policy of scuttle which began in India and ended in Abadan. It will lead to the abandonment of our African colonies.' [11]

For well over a year after returning to office, from October 1951 until sometime in 1953, Churchill held views essentially unchanged from his in 1946, when he had protested against the attempt made by the Labour Government to reach a settlement with the Egyptians whereby British troops would be withdrawn from the Canal Zone. In 1946 he had stated in the House of Commons: 'Things are built up with great labour, and cast away with great shame and folly . . . we know that there is no satisfactory method of keeping the Canal open, and making sure that it is kept open, except by keeping troops there.' [12] He now wrote in 1952: 'I do not think that we should in any case give up the Treaty rights which we possess and which we have the power to enforce . . . We should stay where we are in the Canal Zone.' [13] If anything, he became even more obdurate than before because of the indignation he experienced on 'Black Saturday' in January 1952, when mobs in Cairo burned down Shepheard's Hotel, a symbol of British and other foreign privilege, and murdered nine British subjects at the Turf Club. He wrote in response to these 'murders and massacres' that the Egyptians 'cannot be classed as a civilized power until they have purged themselves'.[14]

After the Egyptian revolution in July 1952, Churchill momentarily entertained the possibility that the military officers who had overthrown the old regime might now be able to lead Egypt back to the ranks of 'civilized powers' and might prove to be more accommodating over the issue of British troops in the Canal Zone. It was a fleeting moment, but he nevertheless thought that military men might be impressed with British resolution to fire 'the decisive volley'. On the other hand, British willingness to deal with the revolutionary regime would depend on the capacity of the new Egyptian government to pursue economic reform. Here is Churchill's minute in which he took measure of the leader of the revolution:

> I am not opposed to a policy of giving Neguib a good chance provided he shows himself to be a friend.

[11] Shuckburgh, *Descent to Suez*, p. 76.
[12] *Parliamentary Debates* (Commons), 7 May 1946, cols. 781 and 894.
[13] Minute by Churchill, 24 March 1952, FO 371/96928.
[14] Churchill to Eden, Private and Personal, 30 January 1952, PREM 11/91.

I hope he will do something for the fellaheen, but we must not be afraid of him or be driven by the threats of cowards and curs from discharging our duty of maintaining the freedom of the Suez Canal for all nations until we can hand it over to some larger, more powerful combination.[15]

It took only a few months for him to revert to form and conclude that Neguib was 'a military dictator of about the feeblest nation alive'.[16] The 'Dictator Neguib' became the epithet that Churchill now used to imply that the situation in Egypt had taken another turn for the worse. He wrote in February 1953: 'This military Dictator is under the impression he has only to kick us to make us run. I would like him to kick us and show him that we did not run.'[17]

When Churchill referred to 'the freedom of the Suez Canal for all nations' and his desire to hand it over to a larger combination, he expressed the hope that a military defence pact comparable to NATO might be created in the Middle East. There would be a British rather than an American commander, but the United States would be a principal partner. The Canal Zone would be converted into a base occupied by American as well as British and Egyptian and other troops. The formula of Britain *plus* the United States *plus* Egypt would allow a settling of the Canal Zone dispute in a manner that would, in Churchill's view, benefit all parties. In fact, this solution never had a chance of success because, among other reasons, the Egyptians regarded the presence of British troops on Egyptian soil as a continuation of the occupation that had gone on for some seventy years. British forces in new camouflage would be unacceptable. Nevertheless, the new defence plan was the key to Churchill's thought. After taking office in 1951, he had proposed to state in the House of Commons that there should be a 'token' presence of American troops in the Canal Zone. Shuckburgh, who helped draft the speech, was sceptical. He suggested that the reference to token American forces be omitted because the Americans simply would not assent and would be irritated by being asked in public. 'No, you silly owl', Churchill shouted at him, 'That is the whole point'—to put pressure on the Americans to deploy troops at Suez.[18]

In the spring of 1953, during Eden's prolonged illness, Churchill took direct control over the problem of the Suez base. He read telegrams with a sharp eye, determined not to be jockeyed or rushed by

---

[15] Minute by Churchill, 19 August 1952, PREM 11/392.

[16] Minute by Churchill, 19 October 1952, PREM 11/398.

[17] Minute by Churchill, 20 February 1953, PREM 11/392,

[18] Diary entry, no date but probably December 1951, Shuckburgh Diaries.

Foreign Office officials pursuing a policy of reconciliation. He spoke of 'appeasement', according to Shuckburgh, 'saying that he never knew before that Munich was situated on the Nile'.[19] Churchill nevertheless accepted that in principle there must be a settlement. At best it would consist of the continued presence of British troops in the Canal Zone; at worst the British would evacuate but would be allowed to return in the event of war. 'It seems that the old man is now changing his ideas on Egypt,' Shuckburgh wrote in August 1953. 'He has come round to thinking that we must have an agreement to evacuate the Canal Zone and seems to have dropped his previous idea that we could not possibly go until a lot of people had been killed.'[20] This was a turning point. From the spring and summer of 1953, Churchill fought a rearguard action to assure that the withdrawal did not amount to 'dead-level scuttle'.

He sent his own chosen emissary, Robin Hankey of the Foreign Office, to Egypt to ensure a robust outlook at the British Embassy in Cairo. 'The Prime Minister asked me to dinner this evening', Hankey wrote shortly before his departure, 'and over a period of well over an hour explained his view about the policy we should pursue in Egypt. He was most categorical . . . At one point he said I should be a "patient sulky pig".'[21] Hankey further stated that Churchill's bellicosity had not diminished: 'The Prime Minister said he was not afraid of physical trouble. Although we should not of course say so, he would in some ways welcome it. It would do the Egyptians no end of good.'[22] Churchill trusted Hankey, in part because he too held right-wing views, in part because he was the son of Lord Hankey, the legendary Secretary of the Committee of Imperial Defence and now one of the directors of the Suez Canal Company. Lord Hankey had convictions about the British Empire that were as unyielding as Churchill's. The younger Hankey, however, began to see the Egyptian side of the case. He mistrusted the Egyptians as much as anyone else, but he believed that they had their own reasons for wishing to reach a settlement over the Canal Zone and, moreover, that the leaders of the revolution possessed a 'standard of integrity . . . very much higher than anything that has been known in Egypt for years'.[23] It would do Churchill a disservice to believe that he was impervious to such views. If nothing else,

[19] Shuckburgh, *Descent to Suez*, p. 75.
[20] Ibid., p. 95.
[21] Memorandum by Hankey, Secret, 22 May 1953, FO 371/102765.
[22] Ibid.
[23] Hankey to Roger Allen (head of the African Department of the Foreign Office), Confidential, 24 September 1953, FO 371/102706.

they brought home the point that his leading advisers, including those he appointed personally, believed that the time had come to resolve the dispute over the Canal Zone.

The person responsible more than anyone else for wooing Churchill away from a diehard position was perhaps General Sir Brian Robertson. Robertson was Commander-in-Chief, British Middle East Land Forces. He had served in that tour of duty since 1950. During the war he had been a key figure in the logistical success of the Abyssinian campaign and later had won distinction as Field Marshal Alexander's chief administrative officer in Italy. After the war he became Military Governor and Commander-in-Chief of the British Zone in Germany. The son of the Field Marshal of the 1914–18 war, he had a clear intellect, a commanding presence, and considerable powers of persuasion. In April 1953, Churchill announced to the Cabinet that Robertson would be the principal military representative to discuss issues of the Canal Zone with the Egyptians. Churchill respected Robertson's points of view and listened to his arguments. Robertson believed, among other things, that the Suez base was becoming strategically obsolete and that British forces should be deployed elsewhere in the Middle East, notably in Libya and Jordan. In the spring of 1953, Churchill seemed, very slowly, to acknowledge the advantages of redeployment. Then in June he had a stroke.

During Churchill's convalescence the political direction of the Suez problem was delegated to Lord Salisbury, who held the position of Lord President of the Council and commanded respect not merely as a leader of the Tory Party but also as a person of considerable experience in foreign affairs. Salisbury was impressed with 'the immense strain, both military & economic, which the keeping of 70,000 men on the Canal imposes on us'.[24] He now began to work with Robertson. By the time Churchill had recovered some months later, Salisbury and Robertson had established a basis for withdrawal; it included the British right to reactivate the base in the event of war. There would be a time limit for the evacuation of British troops, which in the event took place by mid-1956. Faced with the powerful combination of Salisbury and Robertson—and, above all, Eden, when he returned in October 1953—Churchill may have seemed to have no alternative but to acquiesce. In fact, his previous attitude sometimes reasserted itself. He continued to play a central part, which was marked by suspicion and obstruction. 'He starts confused and wrong on almost every issue,' Shuckburgh wrote in December 1953. Even though evacuation might be necessary, Churchill still wished to teach the Egyptians a lesson.

[24] Minute by Salisbury, 9 September 1953, FO 371/102816.

'Always he has wished a war with Egypt', Shuckburgh concluded, 'after which we would march out and leave them.'[25]

Sometimes Churchill's written comments, not to mention his utterances, failed to do justice to his actual assessment, which was more flexible and far-seeing than some contemporary observers believed. He had gradually shifted in his outlook. By the end of 1953 his views were not far removed from those of Salisbury and Robertson or, for that matter, Shuckburgh. 'He hates the policy of "scuttle" which the Foreign Office and Anthony have persuaded him to accept about the Suez Canal', his doctor, Lord Moran, wrote in October, 'but tries to console himself with the fact that the eighty thousand troops can be used elsewhere, and that it will mean a substantial economy.'[26] His natural inclination was to take an emphatic stand against evacuation, and his exclamations made it easy to caricature his true position. He also relinquished his original ideas only after prolonged resistance. The final blow came when he failed, utterly and unequivocally, to persuade President Eisenhower of the merits of holding on to the Canal Zone.

It is illuminating to review briefly the exchange of views between Eisenhower and Churchill because it reveals the latter's methods as well as his aims. From 1951, as has been shown, Churchill hoped to resolve the issue of the base's future by bringing in American help. The problem in part was one of expense, which was significant. The Chancellor of the Exchequer demanded prodigious cuts in defence expenditure, eventually of £180 million. The upkeep of the military installations in the Canal Zone alone cost £56 million a year. Only with American financial assistance could the British hope to continue over a long period. Churchill was well aware of this dimension of the problem. But there was another, no less important aspect: only if confronted by a unified Anglo-American stand might the Egyptians be willing to concede a continuing occupation by the forces of a regional defence organization. Making a persuasive case to Eisenhower thus became a transcendent priority.

'My dear Friend', he wrote to the President in February 1953, 'There is no question of our seeking or needing military, physical, or financial aid from you.' The British had sufficient military strength, he assured Eisenhower, 'to prevent a massacre of white people and to rescue them' in both Alexandria and Cairo. Emphasizing a repeated theme, Churchill drove home the point that there was 'no question of our needing your help or to reinforce the 80,000 men we have kept at

[25] Shuckburgh, *Descent to Suez*, pp. 112 and 121.
[26] *Churchill: Taken from the Diaries of Lord Moran: The Struggle for Survival, 1940–1965* (Boston, 1966), p. 513.

great expense on tiptoe during the last year.' What he did request, however, was joint action: '[W]e should present to the dictator Neguib an agreed plan.'[27]

Eisenhower was puzzled at the tone of urgency as well as by the course of action urged on him. He drew the letter to the attention of the National Security Council. He stated that he was concerned about the 'somewhat frightening phraseology' used by the Prime Minister.[28] He did nothing to encourage Churchill, who then pursued the matter in the following month. 'My dear Friend', Churchill began again, 'I am very sorry that you do not feel that you can do much to help us about the Canal Zone.' Churchill now spoke of the danger of 'the bear' (the Soviet Union) and of his own determination 'not to be bullied any further by Neguib'. 'I have reached my limit,' Churchill wrote.[29] This time Eisenhower responded immediately. 'Dear Winston', he wrote, 'I am a bit puzzled as to the real meaning of your note to me.' He now told Churchill explicitly that the United States would not become involved in the dispute between Britain and Egypt unless invited to do so by the Egyptians.[30]

Churchill was by no means deterred by Eisenhower's studied determination not to become embroiled. He now wrote of the 'unity of the English-speaking world' and the way in which 'Anglo-American unity' might have solved the Canal dispute 'to the general advantage of the free world'. He felt that an opportunity had been missed. 'You have decided', he wrote to the President, 'that unless invited by Neguib, who like all dictators is the servant of the forces behind him, we cannot present a joint proposal.' He warned Eisenhower that many in the Labour opposition held 'that we ought to abandon Egypt altogether'.[31] Churchill also communicated with General Bedell Smith, now serving as Under Secretary of State. 'My dear Bedell', he wrote, 'There is a point of detail on which I shall have to insist': if the British were to agree to withdraw from the Canal Zone, the British military personnel left 'to guard or look after the base' must be permitted to wear British uniforms and carry arms. Otherwise they would remain defence-less and 'at the mercy and good faith of any Egyptian dictator who

---

[27] Churchill to Eisenhower, Private and Confidential, 18 February 1952: *Foreign Relations of the United States, 1952–1954*, IX, part 2, p. 1990. The significant exchanges have been published in *Foreign Relations*, which I cite for convenience. I follow, however, the punctuation, spelling, and form of the originals in the PREM series.

[28] 24 February 1953: ibid., pp. 1997–98.

[29] 18 March 1953: ibid., p. 2026.

[30] 19 March 1953: ibid., pp. 2027–28.

[31] 5 April 1953: ibid., pp. 2042–43.

may jump or crawl into office overnight'.[32] Churchill, moreover, sent a telegram to the Secretary of State, John Foster Dulles, protesting against American military assistance to Egypt. Did Dulles not know, he asked, that Neguib had engaged 'German Nazis' to train guerrillas to sabotage the British position in the Zone? 'Do you wish to give them American arms as well at a moment when so much hangs in the balance?'[33]

Eisenhower himself responded to Churchill's telegram about military equipment. He had looked into the matter himself, he reported, and judged it to be only 'a meager quantity of arms'. The Egyptians had pressed hard for military assistance, and it had been long delayed. If the United States refused, it would be a breach of faith. Why should the British object to the transfer of such items as helmets and jeeps? 'I hope my comments do not offend,' he wrote to Winston.[34] Eisenhower was, in fact, alarmed at the deteriorating situation. In May 1953 it looked as if the British and the Egyptians were on a collision course. What might happen, he asked the members of the National Security Council, if the Egyptians managed to kick the British out? 'Do we expect the Russians to take over? Would the Russians supply the Egyptians with arms? Would we blockade Egyptian ports to prevent these arms from reaching Egypt?'[35] No one could answer those questions. But Eisenhower himself had views on how to resolve the Anglo-Egyptian imbroglio. The demands on the Egyptians, he wrote to Churchill in June 1953, should be kept to a minimum. Otherwise the British—and the Americans—would find themselves at odds 'with the very strong nationalist sentiments of the Egyptian Government and people'.[36]

Eisenhower's message constituted a clear warning that it was better to evacuate quickly, thereby retaining as much good will as possible. To Churchill, this seemed to embody a defeatist attitude. 'My dear Friend', he wrote to Eisenhower in June, shortly before the debilitating stroke, 'We have been disappointed not to receive more support.' In Churchill's view, the Egyptians were playing the Western partners off against each other. 'Dictator Neguib', Churchill continued, 'is emboldened to translate his threats into action, [with] bloodshed on a scale difficult to measure.'[37] Eisenhower was now genuinely alarmed

[32] 15 April 1953: ibid., p 2049.
[33] 8 May 1953: ibid., pp. 2060–61.
[34] 8 May 1953: ibid., pp. 2061–62.
[35] 20 May 1953: ibid., p. 2076.
[36] 10 June 1953: ibid., p. 2089.
[37] 15 June 1953: ibid., p. 2095.

that Churchill might go off the deep end. Churchill himself apparently thought that he had pitched his rhetoric too high, because he now promised to express himself 'less belligerently'.[38] Eisenhower was glad of that. He confined himself in his response to saying that there were 'certain passages' in Churchill's letter 'which I fail to understand', but that they could be resolved orally at a meeting planned for late June in Bermuda. The rendezvous did not take place because of Churchill's illness. Eisenhower welcomed Lord Salisbury's less flamboyant approach.

The Churchill–Eisenhower exchange of views on the Canal Zone now lapsed until much later in the year. Churchill still believed that 'unequivocal American support' would force the Egyptians to yield to the continued presence of at least 'a few thousand British troops'.[39] He thus returned to the charge in December, relating the Egyptian issue to other questions and protesting against American economic assistance to Egypt. 'My dear Friend,' Churchill began again, the 'Socialist Opposition' would exploit the issue of American aid to Egypt as an opportunity 'to press for the inclusion of Red China in U.N.O.' Would Eisenhower, with his 'immense responsibilities', get much help on these matters from a socialist government in Britain? It was something to think about, Churchill suggested.[40] Indeed it was. Eisenhower decided to respond patiently and firmly, issue by issue:

> You state that the Socialist Opposition would be bitterly resentful of American economic aid to Egypt because of American objection to trade with Communist China. It has been my understanding that Britain has continued to carry on trade in economic non-strategic items with Red China, and we do not now propose more with respect to Egypt than beginning to help develop its economy. Consequently, I am at a loss to understand the basis on which the Socialists could make a logical attack.

> You likewise mention that the Opposition would resent any economic aid to Egypt so bitterly that they would urge you to press for inclusion of Red China in the UN. By implication this would seem to mean that if we do not extend economic aid to Egypt, you are prepared to stand firm with us in opposing the inclusion of the bloody Chinese aggressor into the councils of peaceful nations, at least until Red China withdraws her invading armies, ceases supporting the

---

[38] 17 June 1953: *Foreign Relations of the United States, 1952–1954,* IX, part 2, p. 2096.

[39] Cabinet Conclusions (53) 72, 26 November 1953, CAB 128/26.

[40] 19 December 1953: *Foreign Relations of the United States, 1952–1954,* IX, part 2, p. 2177.

Indo-China war and begins to act like a civilized government. Could you confirm this to me?[41]

Eisenhower made a tart comment in this letter: 'I assume, of course, that you are genuinely anxious to arrange a truce with Egypt.'

Churchill now attempted to defend his comments about socialists, Egyptians, and Chinese Communists, but he only made things worse: 'It is always difficult to explain the internal politics of one to another and I have not succeeded this time.' He did not mean, really, what Eisenhower thought he had said about the socialists, or about China. In fact he backed down and, in effect, apologized, thereby acknowledging that he had been wasting the President's time with breezy ideas that had not been clearly thought out. He then made the mistake of resorting to sentiment. He invoked the spirit of the 'special relationship'. He mentioned that '50,000 British graves lie in Egypt and its approaches'. If only Britain and the United States had made common cause against the Egyptians, 'all might well have been settled six months ago.'[42] Eisenhower was irritated. He asked Dulles whether he had seen 'the latest one' from Winston. Eisenhower had to confess, he told Dulles, that he was 'very annoyed'. He responded briefly but courteously to Churchill, expressing hope that the dispute with the Egyptians would soon come to an end. 'Dear Winston', he wrote, 'I am anxious to find a way for us to conform as far as possible to your views on Egypt.' After a few other platitudes, Eisenhower wished Winston a 'Merry Christmas'.[43] He thereby ended the Churchill–Eisenhower correspondence over Suez at the close of 1953.

By early 1954, Churchill found his military and political advisers as well as the President of the United States urging him to acquiesce in a settlement with the Egyptians. His preference was still to retreat at British convenience, to maintain troops in the Canal Zone in any event, and, if provoked, to break off relations with the Egyptians. It is clear from the historical record that he would have welcomed a fight. He wished to give the Egyptians a military thump, then to redeploy British forces in Libya and Jordan. At one stage it appeared that events might be moving in the direction he preferred. In early 1954, Gamal Abdel Nasser challenged Neguib's control of the Egyptian government, though Nasser did not in fact consolidate his own power until later in the year. 'Neg-wib's gone,' Churchill said in his inimitable lisp

[41] 20 December 1953: ibid., pp. 2178–79.
[42] 22 December 1953: ibid., p. 2183.
[43] 22 December 1953: ibid., p. 2184.

to Shuckburgh. When it was pointed out that Nasser might not be an improvement, Churchill responded, 'No, no. Much worse. That's the point. Perhaps he will bring it to a head. I have been afraid they [the Egyptians] might agree.' When Shuckburgh reflected on what the Prime Minister meant by Nasser's forcing matters to a head, he concluded that Churchill 'can only mean attacking our troops, so that we have an excuse for fighting'.[44]

One of the issues at stake, which troubled Members of Parliament as well as the Prime Minister, was the possible decline of British nerve. Those who protested against caving in to the Egyptians became known as the 'Suez rebels'. They were led by Captain Charles Waterhouse, who bitterly opposed withdrawal because it would represent sagging will and failing confidence in British purpose. Churchill did not publicly support the extreme right-wing Tories who opposed the evacuation from Egypt, but privately he encouraged them. 'You keep it up', he said to the son of Leo Amery, Julian, who was now an MP and the intellectual force in the 'rebel' movement, 'You're on the right lines.'[45] According to the younger Amery, British forces could be reduced to 10,000 'teeth troops' and the Canal Zone held indefinitely. Churchill was attracted to this point of view. Unfortunately for him, the Chiefs of Staff were not; they regarded 'teeth troops' as mere 'hostages of fortune'.[46] Churchill concurred, formally even if not in spirit, in their judgement. To Julian Amery, he commented ironically that 'it is not worthwhile keeping the Suez Canal when you Amerys have given away India'—a return to the controversies of the Second World War, when Churchill had acrimoniously blocked Leo Amery's plan to grant Dominion Status to India.[47]

The Leo Amery Diaries provide a right-wing view of Churchill's changing moods as well as the essential questions surrounding Suez. Leo Amery complained that Churchill had never really possessed an 'imperial' or 'Commonwealth' intellect: 'That the Suez Canal might make all the difference to keeping not only India and Pakistan but also Australia and New Zealand in the Commonwealth does not fit in with his mentality.'[48] Thus in Amery's judgement Churchill failed to see some of the larger issues and was able to justify the withdrawal from the Canal Zone by arguing the need for 'redeployment'. Both Leo and Julian Amery regarded redeployment as a misguided venture that

---

[44] Shuckburgh, *Descent to Suez*, p. 136.
[45] Brian Lapping, *End of Empire* (London, 1985), p. 255.
[46] See, for example, minutes of Meeting of Ministers, 8 February 1954, PREM 11/701.
[47] Leo Amery Diaries (privately held), 16 November 1953.
[48] Ibid.

would drive British troops from African pillar to Middle Eastern post until nothing was left. It would be better to detach the Canal Zone from Egypt and hold on to it at any cost as an enclave. There were more than the military issues at stake. 'If only we stand firm now', Leo Amery wrote in 1953, 'it may be a turning point in the whole psychology of the Empire.'[49]

'Better for us to run our own show', Amery exclaimed, 'than to be mixed up with the Americans.' Here was a fundamental point of difference between Churchill and the Amerys. Churchill believed that the British, at the minimum, would have to gain at least the acquiescence of the United States in any Middle Eastern settlement; Leo Amery, by contrast, lamented 'sucking up to Ike'.[50] Amery thought, in other words, that it was still possible for Britain to act independently of the United States. Churchill did not, as has been shown in his correspondence with Eisenhower. Of the two points of view, Churchill's was certainly the more realistic, as was to be demonstrated in the Suez crisis. But Amery's instinctive reaction represented a mainstream of British thought, which resented American ascendancy and Egyptian recalcitrance. 'Will the British worm never turn?' Amery asked.[51] He believed that Britain's position in the Middle East could be reasserted and maintained indefinitely if there were bold leadership and strength of will. Churchill's own stewardship in the spring and summer of 1954 he regarded as 'lamentable'.[52]

The Anglo-Egyptian settlement may have been deplorable from a true-blue Tory point of view, but from Churchill's own perspective it proved to be one of his finest hours. The agreement provided for the withdrawal of British troops but with the provision of re-entry in the event of war. It might have been humiliating for Churchill to defend in Parliament such an accord, which went against his views on the British Empire and his attitude towards the Egyptians. He managed, however, to wring victory out of potential disaster during the great debate on the consequences of the hydrogen bomb tested by the Americans on 1 March 1954. No one who has studied Churchill's letters and speeches at this time can doubt the genuine concern he felt about the 'bloody invention' and the harm it could do 'to society and to the race'.[53] He believed that thermonuclear warfare would be a turning point in the history of mankind. But to those involved in the Suez

---

[49] Ibid., 12 May 1953.
[50] Ibid., 15 January 1954.
[51] Ibid., 10 March 1953.
[52] Ibid., 27 July 1954.
[53] Moran, *Struggle for Survival*, p. 566.

issue, the hydrogen bomb appeared as a deus ex machina that allowed Churchill to solve the problem of the Canal Zone in an entirely unexpected way. As Julian Amery put it, 'I cannot help feeling that this mention of the hydrogen bomb was introduced as a political camouflage.'[54] In any event, Churchill joined wholeheartedly in the Cabinet consensus that

> our strategic needs in the Middle East had been radically changed by the development of thermo-nuclear weapons . . . Our withdrawal from Egypt could be presented as a part of a redeployment of our forces in the Middle East based on a re-assessment of our essential strategic needs in that area.

For his own part, Churchill made it clear to his colleagues in the Cabinet, once again, that he regretted 'abandoning the position which we had held in Egypt since 1882'.[55] To those in his immediate circle, his comments had become somewhat sentimental about India as well as Egypt: 'We have thrown away our glorious Empire, our wonderful Indian Empire, we have cast it away'.[56]

The great Parliamentary debate took place in the last week of June 1954. There was considerable uneasiness among Churchill's associates. He was now approaching the age of eighty. In March, Eden had said: '[H]e is gaga; he cannot finish his sentences.'[57] This was not a single impression; 'gaga' was the word used by others as well.[58] How then might he respond in the House of Commons, where he would be under attack by rebels in his own party as well as from leaders of the Opposition? Attlee, for one, had no intention of giving him an easy time. He quoted Churchill's words from 1946: things had been built up with labour and thrown away with folly. Churchill had previously believed that the only way of keeping the canal open was to station British troops there. Why then had he changed his mind? Attlee thought it was inexcusable to brush away the earlier position with an easy reference to 'his hydrogen bomb'. For years Churchill had thrown about the word 'scuttle'. Now that he was Prime Minister, he had to face the realities. There was a great difference, Attlee concluded, between Churchill in and Churchill out of office. They now witnessed Churchill having 'to eat humble pie'. He was leading

---

[54] *Parliamentary Debates* (Commons), 29 July 1954, col. 780.
[55] Cabinet Conclusions, 22 June 1954, CAB 128/27.
[56] Shuckburgh, *Descent to Suez,* p. 173.
[57] Shuckburgh, *Descent to Suez,* p. 157; 'We are under the dictatorship of an old dotard' (Shuckburgh Diary, 6 July 1954).
[58] See Gilbert, *Churchill,* VIII, p. 961.

Britain into a new era in the Middle East, an eventuality that had been foreseen almost a decade earlier by the Labour Government. Attlee wished it to be clear to everyone that Churchill emerged with little credit.[59]

That view was also shared by the Tories belonging to the Suez group. 'I and my friends had feared that there would be a sell-out,' stated Captain Waterhouse. 'This is not a sell-out. It is a give-away. Instead of having physical control of a great base, instead of having troops on the major waterway of the world, we have got this piece of paper in our hands.' With stinging words he went on to say that if he had foreseen 'this piece of paper' at the time of the last election, he and his colleagues 'would not now be sitting on this side of the House'.[60] In what must be taken as the ultimate rebuke, Waterhouse indicted the Tory Government for 'losing our will to rule'. A further speaker made a point that was close to Churchill's own heart. The British should have intervened at the time of the rioting during 'Black Saturday' in January 1952: 'We could have gone into Egypt then and taught the pashas and the very small class of educated Egyptians a lesson which they would not have forgotten for a decade.'[61]

Churchill finally rose to respond. He did so briefly and eloquently, and demonstrated that his mind had been open to recent changes:

> I have not in the slightest degree concealed in public speech how much I regretted the course of events in Egypt. But I had not held my mind closed to the tremendous changes that have taken place in the whole strategic position in the world which make the thoughts which were well-founded and well knit together a year ago utterly obsolete, and which have changed the opinions of every competent soldier that I have been able to meet.

He then placed the issue of the Canal Zone in the perspective of larger problems:

> I should be prepared . . . to show how utterly out of all proportion to the Suez Canal and the position which we held in Egypt are the appalling developments and the appalling spectacle which imagination raises before us. Merely to try to imagine in outline the first few weeks of a war . . . would, I am sure, convince hon. Gentlemen of the obsolescence of the base and of the sense of proportion which is vitally needed at the present time, not only in military dispositions but

[59] *Parliamentary Debates* (Commons), 29 July 1954, cols. 731–37.
[60] Ibid., cols. 739–40.
[61] Ibid., col. 748.

in all our attempts to establish human relationships between nation and nation.[62]

Churchill spoke for only four minutes, but he captured the House of Commons. 'It was a triumph,' he said the next day. 'If I never speak again in the House I can say I have done nothing better.'[63]

It is ironic that Churchill, having all along objected to the evacuation, deserves large credit for the settlement achieved between Britain and Egypt in 1954. He was acclaimed by all parties for rising to the occasion, even though his critics, of course, continued to disagree with him. Leo Amery, like Julian, believed that the argument about the hydrogen bomb was camouflage to cover up a disagreeable decision. It was a deplorable outcome, Leo noted in his diary. He concluded that the British were 'abdicating our responsibilities in the Middle East'.[64] Nevertheless, Amery recognized that Churchill, for all his lapses, continued to demonstrate the qualities of a statesman. 'Balancing pros and cons', Amery wrote later in the year, 'I dare say lack of continuous grip in the Cabinet may be more than offset by his reputation and power of broad statesmanlike utterance when required. What a maturing from the aggressive young political swashbuckler of . . . 50 years ago.'[65]

On the eve of the invasion of Suez in early November 1956, Churchill issued a public statement explaining his reason for supporting the Eden government. Britain's aim, he emphasized, was 'to restore peace and order' in the Middle East. He expressed confidence 'that our American friends will come to realize that, not for the first time, we have acted independently for the common good'.[66] He said later that 'I would never have dared to do it without squaring the Americans, and once I had started I would never have dared stop.'[67] Had he reflected on his exchanges with Eisenhower, he would have known that American cooperation or acquiescence was the one thing he could never have secured. On the other hand, the whole history of Churchill's career certainly bears testimony that he would never have stopped.

Churchill: A Major New Assessment of His Life in Peace and War   1993

[62] *Parliamentary Debates* (Commons), 29 July 1954, col. 750.

[63] Moran, *Struggle for Survival*, p. 622; Gilbert, *Churchill*, VIII, p. 1037.

[64] Amery Diary, 27 July 1954.

[65] Ibid., 18 October 1954.

[66] Gilbert, *Churchill*, VIII, pp. 1220–21.

[67] Ibid. p. 1222, note 2. Another version of this remark is 'I am not sure I should have dared to start; but I am sure I should not have dared to stop' (Hugh Thomas, *The Suez Affair* [London, 1986 edn.], pp. 182–83).

24

A PRIMA DONNA WITH HONOUR:
EDEN AND SUEZ

The rehabilitation has begun: the onslaught continues: the historical reputation of Anthony Eden has reached a critical point. The publication in 1986 of *Anthony Eden* by Robert Rhodes James and *Descent to Suez* by Evelyn Shuckburgh coincides with the thirtieth anniversary of the Suez crisis: both are important works that will cause reassessment and further controversy. Robert Rhodes James has written an authorized biography based on the Eden Papers. Sir Evelyn Shuckburgh's diaries cover the years 1952–54, when he was Eden's Private Secretary, as well as 1955–56, when he was in charge of Middle Eastern affairs at the Foreign Office. At times it is difficult to believe one is reading about the same person. Both stress the element of Greek tragedy in Eden's downfall, but they reflect quite different interpretations.

Rhodes James is an experienced biographer, and *Anthony Eden* is his best book yet. Even those hostile to Eden will be astonished at the effectiveness of this rounded and perceptive narrative. Because the book gives full measure to Eden's life, Suez, as if an unfortunate incident, can be seen in the perspective of his achievement. Yet Suez occupies almost one-third of a book of over 600 pages. Rhodes James has met the challenge head-on, without flinching before damaging evidence. The chapters on Suez are based on both private and official records to which no other historian has had access.

Even though the immediate interest of this book will be the revelations about Suez, it would be unfair not to assess Rhodes James's account of Eden's boyhood at spacious and elegant Windlestone Hall; the artistic temperament and volcanic disposition of his father; the selfishness and profligacy of his mother. His tutor at Eton described Eden as 'distinctly intelligent without being brilliant'. In January 1919 his commanding officer wrote: 'A young but capable and energetic Brigade Major. Cool and resourceful in battle and possessed of a staying power his appearance doesn't suggest.' At Oxford, Eden studied Persian and Arabic. He described Persian literature in his presidential address to the university's Asiatic Society: 'It is the charm and melody of its verse, with its depths of mystic richness, its descriptive and varied vocabulary, the subtlety of its thought, couched in a language as beautiful as it is expressive, that gives it its unique power.' He may have been aware of the richness and subtlety of language, but Rhodes James makes a telling remark about his subject's own powers of expression: 'Eden's capacity for writing was limited, even on artistic subjects on which his knowledge and enthusiasm were manifest. His style was clear, but deficient in excitement, and sometimes came close to the banal.' The young Eden emerges as high-strung, complex, and shy, and constantly worried about his slender financial resources; his distinguished and brave military service during the First World War was a more formative experience than his years at Oxford. This then is the familiar Eden, but one whose personality is much more comprehensible because of the nuanced interpretation. The author writes of Eden's father and the creation of the garden at Windlestone: 'The garden was soft, for William Eden hated harsh colours, and was scented with lavender, rosemary and sweet briar.' Such also are the colour and scent of the book.

The colours may be soft, but they nevertheless portray finely a man of delicate but volatile temperament. 'He seems to be two men', were the words of one of his subordinates: 'one was charming, kind and deeply impressive—the other impossible.' 'Gusts of impatience and prone to constitutional irritability', was how another official summed up the character defect of hot temper. He was himself aware of his abusive petulance. 'Don't forget that I am just a bloody prima donna,' he once said with disarming candour.

Eden became Foreign Secretary at the age of thirty-eight. He had chosen the political 'Curzon' route rather than that of the career diplomat. Rhodes James writes with verve about Eden and the House of Commons, and as pure biography, this is the best part of the book, relating the development of his political philosophy (a 'property-owning democracy'), his mastering of foreign affairs by dint of hard work, and his identification with the League of Nations, disarmament, and the quest for peace. 'If he was generally perceived as the one who actually made the League work', writes Rhodes James, 'this was the truth.' The passages on Neville Chamberlain and Eden, culminating in the latter's resignation, establish themes that later connect with the Suez crisis. Eden detected in Mussolini 'a gangster mentality'. Chamberlain wished to negotiate. Eden noted in his diary in February 1938:

> N.C. became very vehement, more vehement than I have ever seen him, and strode up and down the room saying with great emphasis 'Anthony, you have missed chance after chance. You simply cannot go on like this.' I said, 'Your methods are right if you have faith in the man you are negotiating with.' N.C. replied, 'I have.'

Eden had no faith in Mussolini, just as later he distrusted Nasser. Indeed he drew comparisons between the two. But the disagreement about Mussolini was by no means the only reason why Eden resigned.

Chamberlain had slighted the United States, and he had disregarded the advice of the Foreign Office: 'One of the real mysteries of 1956 is why Eden made the same mistakes as Chamberlain did in 1937–39.'

How much substance was there behind the glamorous public image and bland speeches? Upon his resignation as Foreign Secretary, 'Eden by his manifest integrity and years of working, albeit vainly, for an ordered and reasonable world, had touched a particular chord . . . The British people sensed something . . . honourable and brave. In this they were right.' During the war, Churchill, who had previously commented that Eden was a 'lightweight', came to regard him as his 'outstanding Minister'. In 1940, at one of the critical moments of Britain's history, he became Secretary of State for War. He was one of the few in the Cabinet entrusted with the secrets gained by breaking the German Enigma cipher.

As Foreign Secretary from 1941 to 1945, he pursued his own goals, which were not by any means identical with Churchill's, and found himself more often than not in agreement with the leaders of the Labour Party, especially Attlee and Bevin. 'The Conservative Party was not his spiritual home,' Rhodes James writes, and Eden himself privately deplored 'the sordid medium of Tory party politics'. After the war, the continuity of British foreign policy became a matter of public comment. 'Hasn't Anthony Eden got fat,' was the Labour quip about Bevin. 'The Importance of Being Anthony' was the Tory taunt. Like Bevin, Eden did not foresee Britain's destiny as being in Europe: 'On the great issues of Western unity, strong defence and close links with the Americans, Bevin and Eden were in total agreement.'

There was, however, an important difference that is not brought out in this biography. For various reasons, including pragmatic ones, Bevin did not believe in intervention. Rhodes James does not directly discuss the political wisdom, or otherwise, of pursuing a policy of nonintervention, but it is central to the broader aspects of the Suez controversy. Restraint sometimes requires as much courage and determination as intervention.

When Eden returned as Foreign Sectary in 1952, one of the major issues he inherited was Musaddiq's nationalization of the Anglo-Iranian Oil Company. 'Certain clandestine steps', Rhodes James coyly writes, 'were taken to hasten Musaddiq's downfall.' This will not do. Was Eden directly involved in the planning that led to the MI6-CIA intervention in Iran in 1953? Was he a prime mover, or did he merely give the scheme his endorsement? 'It was . . . a superbly concealed operation', Rhodes James tells us, and adds, as if lamenting that the secret was not kept, it was 'to remain so for a long time.' He then remarks provocatively: 'This episode is perhaps not for the pure in heart and soul.' Certainly not. But he clearly believes that the toppling of the head of an independent state 'resolved' the problem of 'dictatorial and ruinous rule', without reflecting on the consequences of restoring the Shah or the long-term effect of intervention. In any case, the overthrow of Musaddiq was a precedent for the operation against Nasser. On the seamy side of Suez—the alleged assassination attempt on Nasser—Rhodes James also reveals nothing. We know that by 1956 Eden 'was now consumed with a real personal hatred of Nasser and all that he represented'. Was the passion so strong that it caused him to say that he actually wished to have Nasser 'murdered', as Anthony Nutting has recently stated? The reader will be none the wiser.

It would be unjust to pursue issues that lie beyond Rhodes James's purpose. The biography is rich in detail about Eden's uneasy and often tense relationship with 'a rapidly ageing and obstinate Prime Minster', the successful marriage to Churchill's niece Clarissa in 1952, and, in the following year, the disastrous operation in which his bile duct was accidentally cut. Here and elsewhere Rhodes James emphasizes that there was no abuse of alcohol, drugs, or hypnotics on Eden's part: 'It is absurd to portray Eden as being from this point a sick man, dependent on drugs and stimulants. He was not.' In 1954, Eden's greatest year of achievement, he helped prevent a war in Indo-China that might have involved atomic weapons, he contributed to the reorganization of the Iranian oil industry, and he concluded an agreement with the Egyptian government whereby British troops would be withdrawn from the Canal Zone. He secured disengagement from Egypt despite Churchill's sensitivity to the charge of 'scuttle' and 'appeasement' and despite the protest of the 'Suez group' within his own party. According to a contemporary account, 'seldom . . . [was] a man more nervous than Eden when he was sitting in the Commons corridor waiting to be invited into the room to meet his bitter critics—and bitter they were.' Yet Eden persevered. The agreement on Egypt in 1954 achieved the goal that he and Bevin before him had designed as the cornerstone of Britain's position in the Middle East. It marked the end of the period of British dominance and the beginning of a new era. Had Eden's career ended as Foreign Secretary in 1954, Rhodes James's assessment —'He brought honour and dignity, kindness and loyalty to the often grubby trade of politics'—which is the overall judgement of the book, would probably command hearty assent from all sides.

As it happened, Eden was responsible as Prime Minister (from April 1955) for one of the great catastrophes in Britain's Imperial history. Or was he? And was the Suez adventure such a bad idea after all? Rhodes James, for one, does not think that it was, but here he will probably not change many minds, either those for or against. On the former question, he will cause fair-minded readers to see the crisis of June to December 1956 in a new light, new not in the sense of discovery but in the sense of being sustained by evidence from the Eden Papers. The achievement of the book is to shift the responsibility for the failure of Suez from Eden, individually, to the Cabinet and military, collectively.

There are old scores to be settled. R. A. Butler (Lord Privy Seal and Leader of the House of Commons) is one of the few to emerge with credit, 'loyal, but doubtful and distant'. Mountbatten (First Sea Lord) 'did Eden the greatest disservice possible'—'virtually amounting to a dereliction of duty'—by not letting him know that he opposed the expedition and later by falsifying the historical record (for reasons that are not entirely clear; Eden later believed him to be 'a congenital liar'). Harold Macmillan (Chancellor of the Exchequer) from the out-set was 'the warlike fire-eater in the Cabinet', who saw 'the extreme military usefulness of working closely with the Israelis' and who 'whole-heartedly supported virtually any means of bringing Nasser down'. Later Macmillan became 'the key figure in the surrender'. Selwyn Lloyd (Foreign Secretary) is described as a 'competent lawyer' who 'disliked foreigners' and who was 'grossly over promoted and out of his sphere'. These assessments spill over marginally into the histori-ography of the subject. Rhodes James is at pains to correct Lloyd's account, *Suez 1956* (1979), and, especially (some will think unfairly), Anthony Nutting's *No End of a Lesson* (1967). These asides are rare. David Carlton's *Anthony Eden* (1981) is dismissed as unfriendly. Hugh Thomas's classic account, *The Suez Affair* (1967), is not mentioned. In-deed, it is difficult to judge from the skimpy notes and bibliography what Rhodes James has and has not read. For the most part the book stands on its own authority. But the disregard of conventional aca-demic trappings must not be allowed to detract from the insight into personalities. The judgement of character is consistent.

Nasser is portrayed as the villain. After 26 July 1956, the date of the nationalization of the Suez Canal Company, he was in 'a malignantly gloating mood'. In Eden's eyes, what Nasser had done 'was a callous betrayal of his solemn pledges and agreements, which was despicable in itself, and he was clearly a man without integrity or reason'. This view was not Eden's alone. Throughout the country there was outrage against Nasser, which Rhodes James places in Eden's perception:

> What he did believe, and on this there is no doubt whatever, is that he would have the strong support of a significant majority of the Brit-ish people, who cared little for niceties and wanted Nasser toppled and 'our' Canal returned to its rightful owners. His almost mystical love-affair with his countrymen was never so graphically demon-

strated. He believed that the British, like the French, were fed up
with humiliations from megalomaniac tinpot dictators. On this he
was also right, although the majority was not to be as large as he believe it would be.

From the minutes of the Cabinet, quoted extensively by Rhodes James,
it is also clear that Eden believed that he not merely represented but
also guided the collective sentiment of his colleagues, and bore the responsibility for implementing the decision, taken immediately after
Nasser's nationalization, 'to secure, by the use of force if necessary, the
reversal of the Egyptian Government's action'.

The Cabinet established a committee, according to the official record, 'as a kind of inner Cabinet . . . responsible for supervising the
military operations and plans'. The members of the 'Egypt Committee' were the Prime Minister, the Lord President (Lord Salisbury),
the Chancellor of the Exchequer (Macmillan), the Foreign Secretary
(Lloyd), the Commonwealth Secretary (the Earl of Home), and the
Minister of Defence (Sir Walter Monckton). Here Rhodes James presents vital new evidence. There was no pretence about using force as
'a last resort'. According to the minutes of 30 July: 'While our ultimate purpose was to place the Canal under international control, our
immediate [purpose] was to bring about the downfall of the present
Egyptian Government.' At a further meeting on 1 August, Macmillan
raised the question of involving Israel: 'It would be helpful if Egypt
were faced with the possibility of a war on two fronts.' At this stage
Eden was concerned that a military operation might be seen as 'anti-
Arab, or even worse, pro-Israel'. As the drama develops, he becomes
exasperated with the military planners, then in desperation grasps at
collusion with the French and Israelis, and finally meets his nemesis by
underestimating the response of Eisenhower and John Foster Dulles.
Throughout, Eden remains entirely consistent while becoming an increasingly isolated and tragic figure. In the end he stands heroically
alone, defeated, badly served by his advisers and colleagues, even his
friends.

Rhodes James is especially scathing about the military planners.
'We do not plan to become involved in the permanent occupation of
Egypt,' the Chiefs of Staff reported on 1 August. Nor did they wish to
take any unnecessary risks. A week and a half later they presented 'Plan
Musketeer', recommending a full-scale seaborne assault on Alexandria after the destruction of the Egyptian Air Force. The Egypt Committee approved the plan. On 7 September, however, the Chiefs of
Staff reversed themselves. In 'Musketeer Revise', they now urged an
attack on Port Said. Here is a mystery that Rhodes James has not been

able to solve. What was the reason for the volte-face that cost the British heavily in time and initiative? (Was it because of Lord Hailsham, at that time Lord of the Admiralty, or Selwyn Lloyd, both of whom wished to avoid civilian casualties at Alexandria?) 'This was to prove a decisive turning point,' Rhodes James writes. 'All Eden's military and political experience warned him against Musketeer Revise, and he argued against it with great vehemence, and, according to one of the chiefs, with considerable rudeness and anger.' Even Churchill during the war would not have overruled his military advisers on an issue of such magnitude. Eden angrily accepted the revised plan. In Rhodes James's judgement, the Chiefs of Staff 'let him down' because of the contradictory, cumbersome, and fatally slow military planning. One problem, as he points out, is that they knew of Israeli involvement only at a very late stage.

The political side of the operation was also marred, from Eden's own point of view, because of the formal agreement reached at Sèvres on 24 October between British, French, and Israeli representatives, coordinating military action against the Egyptians. Eden had wished nothing to be committed to paper. This incident is important, among other reasons, because it is damaging to Eden, and Rhodes James handles it judiciously. Eden was dismayed when he heard that Sir Patrick Dean of the Foreign Office had signed a document that became, in American parlance, the 'smoking gun'. When he learned of the written agreement, he sent another Foreign Office official, Donald Logan, to Paris to retrieve it. Logan failed in his mission, but the Israeli Prime Minister, David Ben Gurion, honoured Eden's wish for the secret accord not to be divulged. Eden thus partially succeeded in covering his tracks: he destroyed the British record. The general credibility of the biography is enhanced by the forthright discussion of this and comparable matters.

On the issue of collusion, Rhodes James quotes extensively from Cabinet minutes concerning Eden's explanation—or rationalization—of the secret agreement with the Israelis and French. On 25 October he revealed 'The Plan' to the full Cabinet:

> It now appears . . . that the Israelis were, after all, advancing their military preparation with a view to making an attack upon Egypt. They evidently felt that the ambitions of Colonel Nasser's Government threatened their continued existence as an independent State and that they could not afford to wait for others to curb his expansionist policies. The Cabinet must therefore consider the situation which was likely to arise if hostilities broke out between Israel and Egypt and must judge whether it would necessitate Anglo-French intervention in this area . . .

> We must face the risk that we should be accused of collusion with Is-
> rael. But this charge was liable to be brought against us in any event;
> for it could now be assumed that, if an Anglo-French operation were
> undertaken against Egypt, we should be unable to prevent the Israe-
> lis from launching a parallel attack themselves; and it was preferable
> that we should be seen to be holding the balance between Israel and
> Egypt rather than appear to be accepting Israeli co-operation in an
> attack on Egypt alone.

Perhaps there was an element of self-deception? In any case, Rhodes
James makes it clear that Eden was candid about the conspiracy and
that none of the members of the Cabinet had any reason to believe
that they had been misled. As for the conspiracy itself, Rhodes James
writes that Eden, in taking the plunge, had moved from 'an absolutely
legitimate position to what was perilously close to being an illegiti-
mate one'.

Perilously close? This is about as near as Rhodes James comes to an
unabashed stand on a matter that, as he says, divided families, broke
up friendships, and remains a dangerous topic for dinner conversation to the present day. What of another sensitive issue: Eden's lying
to the House of Commons, when he stated that there was 'no fore-
knowledge' of the Israeli attack on Egypt? Here the approach is persuasively sympathetic: 'There were those present who knew that it was
not true. Most seriously of all, Eden himself knew it was not true. He
was speaking under pressure, and he was ill; the mood of the House,
to which he was always acutely sensitive, was dismissive rather than
hostile.'

Rhodes James does not reveal anything about the post-Nasser or
collaborationist regime that would have been installed in Cairo, if indeed there were a plan for one. Could the Chiefs of Staff have avoided
their nightmare of another occupation? Did Eden and his advisers
have any firm ideas on the subject? Or were the long-range aims even
murkier than they appeared to be at the time? There is also little
new about the international or American dimension of the problem,
though it should be mentioned that in Rhodes James's demonology,
Dulles ranks close to Nasser. There are some parting shots at Macmillan, who, Eden believed, was 'excessively devoted to Anglo-American
unity at all costs'. The combined pressure from the Labour opposition
and the United States, as well as the run on the pound, paralyzed his
will to continue: 'Eden had been deserted by all his senior colleagues
except Lloyd, [Anthony] Head and [James] Stuart, and Macmillan's
defection had been crucial.' The underlying argument is not explicit,
but suggests that with greater loyalty and collective determination,
Suez need not have been a failure.

The theme of Sir Evelyn Shuckburgh's diaries, *Descent to Suez*, is that the drift towards Suez, or the collision course with the Arabs, was political folly of the highest order. This is not merely a retrospective judgement: it was a view he consistently held, day in and day out, though with increasing despair, during the time he served as Eden's Private Secretary and then as Under-Secretary dealing with Middle Eastern affairs in the Foreign Office.

Shuckburgh comes from an English family that has lived between Southam and Daventry since before the Norman Conquest. His father was Sir John Shuckburgh, the Colonial Office official responsible for Palestine in the inter-war years (and who at one stage had a breakdown because of it). He himself was educated at Winchester and King's College, Cambridge. One of his first posts was in Egypt in 1937; he retired as Ambassador to Italy in 1969. In insight and as an insider's record, his diaries are comparable in quality to those of Sir Alexander Cadogan, who in an earlier period dealt with many of the same problems. Like Cadogan's, the diaries served in part as a safety valve for the pressure of the job.

Had Shuckburgh known that he would become involved in the same 'insoluble problem' that had caused his father's breakdown, he reflected later, he probably would not have entered the public service. In an introductory note he quotes one of his own first reactions to the Palestine problem in a letter to his father-in-law, Lord Esher, in 1938: 'In Palestine we, with our own hands, are having to burn and explode villagers out of their village for the sake of what is, as usual a *theoretical* obligation [the Balfour Declaration], an interpreted, often misinterpreted, text of twenty years ago, of which no one knows the meaning. And why are we doing it considering that even the Cabinet know it is unjust and suicidal?' There is thus early on a strong commitment to the Arab cause, and if the view seems heady, it is no more so than many of the other comments in this book—for example, Churchill explaining to Eden how to handle the Egyptians: 'Rising from his chair, the old man advanced on Anthony with clenched fists, saying with the inimitable Churchill growl, "Tell them that if we have any more of their cheek we will set the Jews on them and drive them into the gutter, from which they should never have emerged".'

Some of the fascinating parts of the diary are about Churchill's deterioration and Eden's frustration as heir apparent, in which Shuckburgh saw the making of a tragedy. 'He starts confused and wrong on almost every issue', Shuckburgh wrote about 'the Old Man' in December 1953, 'hardly listens to argument and constantly reverts to wartime and post-war analogies.' Speaking to Eden about 'appeasement', Churchill said he never knew 'that Munich was situated on the Nile'.

Another refrain was 'we have thrown away our glorious Empire, our wonderful Indian Empire, we have cast it away'—the connecting idea being the futility of propping up the French in Indo-China (some of the absorbing sections of the diary deal with the Indo-China settlement of 1954). Eden at one time exploded: 'This simply cannot go on; he is gaga; he cannot finish his sentences.' Yet he did go on. Shuckburgh at times felt that Eden, whom he admired despite reservations about character and temperament, might never become Prime Minister. But finally the end came. 'The great thing is that he has gone from the active scene and can be a great man again without damage,' Shuckburgh wrote of Churchill's retirement. 'It was not a Greek tragedy after all.' At this stage Shuckburgh was optimistic about Eden's prospects: 'He is filling out with security and confidence.' One is reminded, however, of what Churchill said to Sir John Colville at about the same time, as related in Colville's *Fringes of Power* (1985): 'he [Churchill] stared at me and said with vehemence: "I don't believe Anthony can do it".'

Churchill believed, according to Shuckburgh, that the Foreign Office was 'riddled with Bevinism' on Middle East questions—in other words, 'anti-Jewish'. It is important to make Shuckburgh's own attitude clear. He was anti-Zionist (in the sense that he believed the creation of the State of Israel to have been a mistake) but not anti-Jewish. There are gloomy words about 'Israeli neurosis, their sense of isolation and frustration', but he was not anti-Israel. He believed that the Arabs no less than the Israelis would have to make substantial concessions to bring about a settlement acceptable to both sides. Shuckburgh devoted a critical part of his official life to the attempt to find, in his own view, a fair-minded solution. In 1955 he and Francis Russell of the State Department worked together on a highly secret project known as 'Alpha'. Shuckburgh described it as 'a full blueprint for a settlement, including territorial adjustments, compensations and resettlement of the refugees . . . and guarantees for both sides by the US and UK'. In March 1955 he recorded the Israeli response: 'no concessions of any sort . . . Keep off the grass.' Project Alpha eventually became one of the casualties of Suez. For his own effort, Shuckburgh recorded ruefully, 'I am regarded by the Jews and their friends as an evil counsellor to the Foreign Secretary.'

The diaries throw new light on the private thoughts of British officials on two of the landmarks on the road to Suez, the Czech arms deal of September 1955 and the sacking of General Sir John Glubb by King Hussein of Jordan in April of the next year. 'The folly and fragility of our Palestine policy is beginning to come home to roost at last,' Shuckburgh wrote about Nasser's purchase of weapons from

Czechoslovakia. 'As long as the Russians played no role in the ME we were able to run with the hares and hunt with the hounds. But now they are obviously beginning to make a bid for Arab support.' He relates a conversation between Macmillan (who served briefly as Foreign Secretary in the latter part of 1955) and Dulles in which outrage mounted against the Russians 'sitting on the airfields which we built', which was too much for Macmillan, and Nasser's duplicity, which was too much for Dulles: 'Dulles could not bear the Egyptian ingratitude for all the money US has spent on her.' Shuckburgh himself was by no means immune to the crescendo of the anti-Nasser mood. He now began to believe that he might have been mistaken in trying to reach an agreement with the Egyptians. The diaries end on a despondent note: 'Obviously my policy and efforts to save relations with Egypt have been all wrong.' At the time of the Czech arms deal, he had written, in words chosen deliberately to emphasize the importance of the event as a turning point: 'We must first try to frighten Nasser, then to bribe him, and if neither works, get rid of him.'

Glubb's dismissal as commander of the Arab Legion at the time seemed to be close to a national humiliation for the British because it was commonly assumed, erroneously, that Nasser was behind it. The diaries make it clear that Glubb himself was part of the problem. Shuckburgh regarded him as so anti-Israel that he had lost his balance. 'Alarmist', he had noted about Glubb's response to Israeli manoeuvres on the Jordanian border in 1954, and in April of the next year, 'Glubb is still wildly excited, and asking us to adopt a strictly anti-Israeli policy which we cannot do.' This is a repeated theme: 'Glubb seems to be near panic.' At the time of the actual dismissal, Shuckburgh wrote: 'I don't think it means Hussein is sold to the Egyptians or Saudis. For A. E. it is a serious blow, and he will be jeered at in the House of Commons.' This was another turning point. Shuckburgh recorded that Eden now became 'violently anti-Nasser'. For Shuckburgh himself this was also the last straw. He wrote on 8 March 1956: 'Today both we and the Americans really gave up hope of Nasser and began to look around for means of destroying him.'

Shuckburgh's diaries thus support one of Rhodes James's principal themes: responsibility for the anti-Nasser movement has to be shared with many others, including the mandarins of the Foreign Office. It is also clear that to the end Eden had the support of Sir Ivone Kirkpatrick, the Permanent Under-Secretary, who told Shuckburgh during the actual crisis:

> The PM was the only man in England who wanted the nation to survive; that all the rest of us have lost the will to live; that in two years'

time Nasser will have deprived us of our oil, the sterling area fallen apart, no European defence possible, unemployment and unrest in the UK and our standard of living reduced to that of the Yugoslavs or Egyptians.

Though Shuckburgh does not say so, Kirkpatrick was probably one of the central figures in the conspiracy with the Israelis. Here a clear distinction has to be drawn. The anti-Nasser campaign was one thing; collusion was another. The latter was fatal. It destroyed Britain's position in the Middle East and, even more importantly, jeopardized, in the eyes of the British themselves, the integrity of their own government. Only a handful knew of the conspiracy. Shuckburgh learned of it at the time from the Minister of State, Anthony Nutting: 'There was the fullest collusion with the Israelis. Selwyn Lloyd actually went to Paris incognito to meet Ben-Gurion with the French. It is true that he did not actually urge Ben-Gurion to make an attack, but he gave him to understand that we would not take a serious view. Later they even knew the date on which it was to take place. They deliberately deceived the Americans and everyone else.'

The portrait of Eden in Shuckburgh's contemporary account is quite different from Rhodes James's historical reconstruction. Shuckburgh wrote about Eden at the time of Glubb's dismissal: 'He seems to be completely disintegrated—petulant, irrelevant, provocative at the same time as being weak.' This was not a sudden development but one that Shuckburgh had observed since Eden became Prime Minister. And in perhaps the most poignant passage in the diaries, which stands as Shuckburgh's comment on the tragedy of it all: 'He has in my opinion greatly changed in the last two years. He is far away, thinking largely about the effect he is making, not in any way strengthened in character, as I hoped, by the attainment of his ambition.' One is led inescapably to the conclusion that the contemporary impression is closer to the mark than Rhodes James's romanticized version. As for Rhodes James's idea of collective responsibility and his vision of Eden as a tragic and isolated figure, here is how he appeared at the time through Shuckburgh's eyes: 'A. E. had broken down and gone off to Jamaica. This is the most extraordinary feature of the whole thing. Is he on his way out, has he had a nervous breakdown, is he mad? The captain leaves the sinking ship which he has steered personally on to the rocks.'

25

AN AMERICAN VOLCANO IN THE MIDDLE EAST: JOHN FOSTER DULLES AND THE SUEZ CRISIS

'We must never forget', Anthony Eden, the British Prime Minister, wrote in October 1956, 'that [John Foster] Dulles' purpose is different from ours.'[1] To Eden, the difference could be summed up in two words: 'Suez Canal', an artery of the British Empire that was critical to Britain's survival but 'in no sense vital to the United States'. Dulles's 'game', as it appeared to Eden, was 'to string us along' for reasons of American politics and not allow the Suez crisis to become an issue in the presidential election of 1956.[2] Thus there was a question of motive as well as the perception of national interest. Eden and other prominent British leaders believed that Dulles deliberately misled them. The phrases 'up the garden path', 'dishonest', and 'double cross' characterized British thought of the time, and the interpretation of Dulles as a devious politician has persisted. Dulles not only managed to poison Anglo-American relations but also, according to the extreme judgement of the time, bears responsibility for the catastrophe of Suez.[3]

Yet there was another British view, less dominant but equally significant, which held that he was an honourable man who differed from the British only in tactics. Sir Roger Makins, the British Ambassador in Washington, wrote during the early part of the Suez crisis: 'We agree about the substance of the policy, but differ on method and timing.'[4] This interpretation held that the 'special relationship' between the British and Americans had more than a symbolic meaning, and that Anglo-American friendship would ultimately survive the Suez crisis. These two views had one element in common: the issue of 'anticolonialism' exacerbated the situation. 'I have noticed before', Makins commented, 'this deep seated feeling about colonialism, which is common to so many Americans, occasionally welling up inside Foster [Dulles] like lava in a dormant volcano.'[5]

During the Suez crisis, the British were caught off guard by Dulles's volcanic sentiments about European colonialism, and Anthony Eden

---

[1] Eden to Selwyn Lloyd, Top Secret, 6 October 1956, PREM 11/1102.

[2] Ibid.

[3] 'Dulles has sometimes been saddled with the whole blame for Suez, and it is certainly hard to believe . . . that he was merely unconsciously rude' (Hugh Thomas, *The Suez Affair* [London, 1986 edn.], p. 174).

[4] 'We press for immediate action', Makins wrote, 'while the Americans are inclined to move with greater phlegm and deliberation. This is the opposite of what our natural temperaments are supposed to be' (Makins to Lloyd, Emergency Top Secret, 9 September 1956, FO 800/740).

[5] Makins to Eden, Secret and Personal, 4 October 1956, PREM 11/1174.

himself went so far as to describe his attitude as 'dishonest'.[6] Several questions arise from this harsh judgement. Did it only reflect the heat of the moment, a time when Eden's anger interfered with his discernment? For at least two years previously there had been friction between the two men. '[T]here is no doubt that Dulles and A.E. have got thoroughly on each other's nerves', wrote Sir Evelyn Shuckburgh (Eden's Private Secretary) during the Indo-China crisis of 1954, 'and are both behaving rather like prima donnas.'[7] Did their clash in temperament, and their difference in background and training, merely intensify the disagreement over issues of substance, or was there an unbridgeable gap in intent? How accurate was Eden's perception of the relationship between Dulles and Eisenhower? For that matter, how well did Dulles understand the British? Was there a misperception of motive or a conflict of purpose? What do recently released records reveal about one of Dulles's most acute dilemmas, in which he was caught between the expectations of the European allies and the nationalist aspirations of the non-European world? Perhaps most importantly of all, how should the historian assess Dulles as a statesman attempting to resolve these issues? The opening of the British archives at the Public Record Office in London affords the opportunity for a reconsideration of those questions.

This reinterpretation also derives from access to the Eisenhower Papers at the Presidential Library in Abilene, Kansas, and the Dulles Papers at the Seeley G. Mudd Manuscript Library at Princeton University.[8] These collections reveal an Eisenhower at variance with his public image in America, and even more with the predominant view of him in Britain, as a benign, slightly incoherent soldier-President somewhat out of his element. He cultivated that image. In fact he was highly intelligent, hard-working, and decisive. He had a keen sense of his own historical reputation, and he guarded it on all flanks. He had a genius for avoiding confrontation. His Secretary of State was his stalking horse. Dulles's dramatic language went down well with the right wing of the Republican Party. The American public could understand his Manichaean vision that identified the Soviet Union as an evil government of communist tyranny and the United States as the land of freedom and constructive capitalism. As a corrective to ideological interpretation, was there an underlying consistency of actual policy

[6] Eden's minute on Makins to Eden, 4 October 1956, PREM 11/1174.

[7] Evelyn Shuckburgh, *Descent to Suez: Diaries, 1951–1956* (London, 1986), p. 186.

[8] In an essay entitled 'Eisenhower, Dulles, and the Suez Crisis', Robert R. Bowie has examined these and other unpublished American sources (in *Suez 1956: The Crisis and Its Consequences*, ed. W. R. Louis and Roger Owen [New York, 1989]).

applied to specific events? If so, who controlled it—Eisenhower or Dulles?

In the case of Suez, the emphatic answer to the latter question is Eisenhower. It was Eisenhower who blocked the British and French and who, coincidentally, forced the Israelis to draw back, thus momentarily reversing the pro-Zionist thrust of American policy. Eisenhower was unalterably opposed to the invasion of Egypt. No doubt one of his motives was to keep the world's attention on the Soviet suppression of the Hungarian revolution. But above all he did not wish to antagonize nationalist sentiment in the Middle East, Asia, and Africa. He did not want to be associated in any way with the antiquated system of British and French 'colonialism' that the United States, in his view, had historic reason to oppose. He also believed that Britain and France no longer possessed the economic or military resources to dominate the Middle East. The United States would inevitably have to play an increasing part in Middle Eastern affairs, and Eisenhower was determined not be tarred by association with the British and French at Suez.

What then of Dulles? He agreed in principle and in detail with Eisenhower: their views were virtually identical. The two of them consulted closely on every issue, and there was indeed an underlying consistency of principle. But Dulles in every sense was the executor of the policy set by Eisenhower, even though he emerges from his secret letters and conversations as the more passionately anti-colonial of the two. This of course was the popular perception at the time, but one aspect was not apparent: it served Eisenhower's purpose to use Dulles as his lightning rod. Eisenhower wished to keep on good terms with the British government, though privately he was contemptuous of the British claim to be a 'world power'. He expected Dulles not only to oppose colonialism but also to support Britain and France as the oldest and most valued allies of the United States. Here was a challenge that tested even Dulles's intellectual agility and tore him emotionally.

We can now view the events of the 1950s from the perspective of three decades. Certain problems that faced Dulles are now much clearer than they were to contemporary observers. Two of these are the 'Palestine question', as it was called at the time, and the Baghdad Pact, which was conceived as an instrument of Western security in the Middle East. Dulles found himself mainly in agreement with the British over Palestine, but not in accord with them over the defence issue. It is useful briefly to study these two problems as part of the general background to the Suez crisis because they reveal Dulles's method and aims and because they establish his attitude towards the Arabs and the Israelis as well the British and the French. His pessimistic view of Rus-

sian intent was consistent, but his general outlook was nuanced and by
no means as unsubtle as some of his own rhetoric suggested.

Dulles was much less in sympathy with Zionist aims than he wished
to state in public. His attitude towards Israel probably explains part of
the reason for the vitriolic treatment in Herman Finer's indispensable
but unbalanced work, *Dulles over Suez*. Writing in 1964, and thus having
accumulated his evidence when emotions about the Suez crisis had by
no means subsided, Finer had read voluminously and had conducted
extensive interviews but had only scant access to secret records. He
believed that Dulles's 'Wilsonian missionary passion', together with a
characteristic determination to be even-handed, caused him to attach
too much significance to the Arab cause. Dulles's inflated assessment
of Arab nationalism led him to betray the Israelis and his European
allies, the British and the French. In turn, according to Finer, Dulles
jeopardized the Western position in the Middle East by giving the
advantage to the Soviet Union.[9] What Finer had no way of knowing
was that Dulles himself had played a leading part in the effort for a
comprehensive settlement between the Israelis and the Arabs. From
Dulles's point of view in 1956, the British had betrayed their own principles and the Israelis themselves had shattered the prospects of a lasting peace beyond repair. This explains in part what he meant when
he stated emphatically during the Suez crisis that 'what the British and
French had done was nothing but the straight old-fashioned variety of
colonialism of the most obvious sort.'[10] As will be seen, Dulles expected
as much from the French, but from the British this was a breach of
good faith.

The plan for a comprehensive settlement between the Israelis and
the Arabs was known as 'Project Alpha'. The full records of this venture are now accessible in London but not in Washington.[11] They reveal a determined effort by the State Department and Foreign Office
from late 1954 to solve the refugee problem by resettlement, mainly
in Arab countries. The United States would bear most of the cost of in-
demnity and repatriation. There would also be a territorial adjustment, which would include a revision of the frontiers to allow direct
land communication between Egypt and Jordan. The purpose was to

[9] Herman Finer, *Dulles over Suez: The Theory and Practice of His Diplomacy* (Chicago, 1964).

[10] Memorandum of National Security Council meeting, 1 November 1956, National Security
Council Series, Ann Whitman File, Eisenhower Papers.

[11] And in Jerusalem but not in Cairo. I have benefited from reading an essay that fully utilizes
Israeli as well as British sources: Shimon Shamir, 'The Collapse of Project Alpha and the End
of the Secret-Diplomacy Phase of the Search for an Egyptian Israeli Settlement', in Louis and
Owen, *Suez 1956*.

redress one of the principal Arab grievances of the 1948 war. The new boundaries would be guaranteed by both the United States and Britain. The Israelis would have to make concessions in the southern part of Israel, the Negev. In the view of the principal British architect of the scheme, Evelyn Shuckburgh, Israel's blocking of this solution led to the failure of the project. Egypt gave it one of the final blows in March 1956, but Israeli resistance to altering the frontiers was, in Shuckburgh's judgement, the fundamental reason why the scheme came to nothing.

During the latter stage of Eden's tenure as Foreign Secretary, Shuckburgh served as his Private Secretary. In late 1954, Shuckburgh took charge of Middle Eastern policy at the Foreign Office as Assistant Under-Secretary, a position of key responsibility. He never believed that the 'Alpha' plan had much chance of success, but his minutes reveal that whatever its hopes, they depended on Israeli willingness to arrive at a compromise between the boundaries proposed by the United Nations in 1947 and those established after the Israeli victories in the 1948–49 war. In retrospect, the assumption was extravagant. But Dulles himself at the time believed that some form of Israeli retreat from the 1949 armistice boundaries would be an essential ingredient of the settlement. On that point there was concurrence between the British and Americans: 'On the subject of Palestine', Shuckburgh summed up later, 'Eden and Dulles at this time saw eye to eye.'[12]

Shuckburgh has recently published his diaries, under the title *Descent to Suez*. They are an invaluable source for the study of Dulles in the mid-1950s, not merely because of the detail about British and American policies in the Middle East and other conflict-ridden regions, but also because of the fair-minded portrayal of Dulles. Here is an example of a British official upholding the view that Dulles did not, until Suez, view British and American policies as fundamentally incompatible. Misunderstanding and mutual irritation, much more than suspicion, characterized the relations between Dulles and Eden. Shuckburgh himself regarded Dulles as a methodical man of sound judgement. 'I had a sort of allegiance to Dulles', he wrote, 'and I had considerable respect for him. The trouble, so far as his [Dulles's] relations with Eden were concerned, was that the temper of his mind was entirely out of harmony with Eden's.'[13]

Shuckburgh and other British officials knew that on the Middle East, Dulles's views were virtually identical with Eisenhower's, above all

[12] Shuckburgh, *Descent to Suez*, p. 242.
[13] Ibid., p. 23.

on the Palestine question. Eisenhower once said privately at a Jewish
convention in 1954: 'I don't know what I would have done had I been
President when the question of Israel's independence came up . . .
but Israel is now a sovereign nation to which we have obligations. We
shall keep them.'[14] Like Eisenhower, Dulles did not dwell on historical controversies about the creation of the state of Israel, but rather
on the problems to be resolved between Israel and the Arab states.
Each nation would have to make sacrifices and commitments, including the United States. Dulles was willing for the American government
to guarantee Israel's security as part of the general settlement—but
after, and not before, agreement was reached with the Arab states as
well. He was explicit on this point: '[T]here should be no question of
giving the Israelis the guarantee . . . ahead of and apart from a general
settlement.'[15] In July 1955, Dulles explained to the British the reasons
why the plan should be publicly announced, the sooner the better. According to Shuckburgh's diary, which reveals relief about Dulles's determined attitude in the face of Jewish pressure in America:

> It is not, as I feared, that D. is weakening on the 'Alpha' demand for
> sacrifices from Israel, or is contemplating any abandonment of the
> position that Israel can only have a US guarantee after a settlement.

> His point is that only by getting the US Government publicly com-
> mitted to this policy now can he insure himself against being com-
> pelled later on, in the atmosphere of US elections, to make a much
> more pro-Israeli stand . . . There is a lot of force in this.[16]

Harold Macmillan, Eden's Foreign Secretary in 1955, wrote of Dulles's motives for wishing to make a public statement on the Palestine
problem:

> I am convinced that Dulles has impelling internal political reasons
> . . . The thing has risks, particularly from our point of view. But the
> situation in which we would find ourselves if, at a later date, the U.S.
> Administration were compelled by Jewish pressure and electoral con-
> siderations to move over towards a more obviously pro-Israeli policy,
> would be even more dangerous.[17]

[14] Quoted in Finer, *Dulles over Suez*, pp. 13–14.
[15] 'Record of Conversation . . . Alpha', 12 May 1955, FO 800/678.
[16] Shuckburgh, *Descent to Suez*, p. 266.
[17] Minute by Macmillan to Eden, 12 July 1955, FO 800/680.

The British thus understood Dulles's purpose. He was clearly a moving force behind the comprehensive settlement, despite the domestic opposition he was certain to encounter. If the plan succeeded, he would attempt to move the United States into the Baghdad Pact.[18]

Here then was Dulles's grand strategy: a settlement between Israel and the Arab states on the refugee question, and a territorial adjustment backed by the United States and Britain. The ground would thus be prepared for an effective alliance system in the Middle East in which the United States would adhere to a Baghdad Pact consisting of Britain, Iraq, Turkey, Iran, and Pakistan—and, it was hoped, eventually other Middle Eastern states if Project Alpha succeeded.

Dulles initially supported the plans for the Baghdad Pact as 'precisely [the] kind of basis from which full fledged regional defense organization could grow'.[19] But when it became clear that Project Alpha might fail, he became increasingly sceptical. Failing a settlement of the Palestine question, the Baghdad Pact, in his view, would divide the Arab states. The underlying political tensions had to be ameliorated before military security could become a reality. Otherwise, anti-Western Arab nationalists would denounce the military measures as designed to keep the Middle East under Western control. At the same time, the Soviet Union would become alarmed at a military alliance that paradoxically would not have the military unity or strength to serve its anti-Soviet purpose. '[B]etter to keep it a paper pact,' Dulles advised the British.[20]

This apparent vacillation exasperated Eden. 'I am sorry that Dulles is so hesitant', he wrote, 'I am afraid that we shall miss the tide once again.'[21] What seemed to Eden to be faintheartedness, and a wide gap between rhetoric and action, appeared to Dulles to be a matter of pragmatism and common sense. The Baghdad Pact was not developing into an effective military alliance. The divergence of views reflected different aims. Dulles wished to reconcile the nationalists' aspirations with the military requirements of the Western powers in the Middle East, thereby frustrating the expansionist ambitions of the Soviet Union. Eden of course was also wary of Russian aims, but he took a long-range historical view and believed American assessments to be

---

[18] 'Dulles has now assured me', Macmillan wrote, 'that he is willing to tell the Iraqis that if a Palestine settlement could be achieved the United States would be prepared to join the Pact' (minute by Macmillan to Eden, Top Secret, 16 July 1955, FO 800/687).

[19] Secretary of State to Embassy in Turkey, 31 December 1954, *Foreign Relations of the United States, 1952–1954*, IX, p. 2403.

[20] Shuckburgh, *Descent to Suez*, p. 299.

[21] Eden to Macmillan, Secret, 15 November 1955, FO 800/680.

overdrawn. Eden's priority was to preserve British power in the Middle
East and, in time, to secure a British line of defence along 'a frontier
stretching from the Mediterranean to the Himalayas'.[22]

'Distinctly disappointing' were the words used by Anthony Nutting
of the Foreign Office to sum up Dulles's attitude towards the Baghdad
Pact in March 1956.[23] Dulles now seemed to be interested in a UN solution; he appeared to be changing course. But the British were not
entirely certain; he spoke ambiguously. His rhetoric had a bearing on
substance, and here there were three British views. Perhaps American
legal training caused him to render his meaning opaquely. Perhaps he
made vague statements because of the danger of being misinterpreted
by Arab or Jew. Perhaps he merely preferred, like Eisenhower, to keep
options open. In any case, the British could not always be certain of
Dulles's intent. For example, what of the danger of Israeli aggression?
How would Dulles respond? Their reflections on a UN resolution
about the possibility of hostilities breaking out between Israel and the
Arab states presents an example of how the British attempted to de-
duce Dulles's purpose:

> His [Dulles's] unspoken thoughts may conceivably have been some-
> thing like this:—Israel is more likely to attack the Arab States than
> they are to attack her; it would be even more difficult for the United
> States to use force against Israel than against the Arab States; if this
> has to be done, there must be a clear finding on the part of the
> United Nations that Israel is responsible, and the United States must
> be able to vote for such a finding.[24]

That line of reasoning appealed to the Foreign Office. In March 1956,
Project Alpha and all hopes for a comprehensive settlement collapsed.
The immediate cause was Nasser's rejection of the basis for settlement,
which the Americans as well as the British interpreted as his smouldering ambitions against Israel. In Dulles's words, general agreement
'is impossible at the present time unless and until Arab hopes *vis-à-vis*
Israel are somewhat deflated'.[25] For preserving peace in the Middle
East, all that remained was the American, British, and French 'Tripartite Declaration' of May 1950, which was designed to regulate arms
shipments and prevent violations of the armistice frontiers of the previous year.

[22] Quoted in Robert Rhodes James, *Anthony Eden* (London, 1986), p. 398.
[23] Minute by Nutting, 6 March 1956, FO 800/734. Nutting was Minister of State.
[24] P. M. Crosthwaite to E. M. Rose, Secret, 11 February 1956, FO 371/121772.
[25] Dulles to Henry Cabot Lodge, 31 March 1956, Subject Series, 'Israeli Relations (3)', John
Foster Dulles Papers, Eisenhower Library.

To the British, the Tripartite Declaration had become a most unsatisfactory arrangement, and thus they responded positively to Dulles's
hint that the United Nations might play a greater part in keeping the
peace. A United Nations resolution, in other words, might supersede
the 1950 declaration. Shuckburgh now took into account the Czech
arms deal to supply Egypt with Soviet weapons, which the British and
Americans had learned about the previous autumn, as well as the 1950
tripartite pledge:

> We are left without a Middle East policy of any kind. The Tripartite
> Declaration is a mere stop-gap; its sole justification was that it held
> the ring while a settlement was sought. Now that no settlement is in
> sight, it operates only to sharpen the Israelis' dilemma. They now
> have no prospect of peace . . . they also have no prospect of arms,
> while their enemies grow strong.

The dilemma was acute for the Americans as well as for the British.
The Israelis might launch a pre-emptive attack. Then the three Western powers would be compelled, theoretically at least, to intervene
in order to fulfil the obligations of the 1950 declaration. Shuckburgh
continued, and as he wrote, his thoughts became more alarming:

> If the Jews attack, then perhaps we can find means of saving ourselves
> by falling upon them. But if they do not, the tension and despair of
> their position will grow rapidly and public opinion in the U.K. and
> U.S. will find it impossible not to support them and arm them, de-
> spite the appalling consequences of doing so. This will destroy the
> Baghdad Pact and put in jeopardy our oil supplies.

> It will lead us direct towards a conflict, with the West supporting Is-
> rael and Russia the Arabs. In fact, unless the Israelis commit an ag-
> gression, we are becoming daily more deeply committed to go to war
> against a Soviet-armed Arab world as soon as they feel strong enough
> or fanatical enough to attack Israel. Every time we refer to the Tri-
> partite Declaration as an 'obligation' to defend Israel, we get our-
> selves more deeply in this position.[26]

Shuckburgh therefore favoured an initiative through the United Nations, if only to circumvent the 'embarrassing' obligation of the Tripartite Declaration to uphold the 1949 frontiers.[27] The British records
reveal, however, that Anthony Eden did not see eye to eye with his For-

[26] Minute by Shuckburgh, Top Secret, 10 March 1956, FO 371/121235.
[27] Minute by Shuckburgh, Top Secret, 20 April 1956, FO 371/121738.

eign Office advisers on the virtue of the United Nations. Before, during, and after the Suez crisis, he despaired of effective UN action. He wrote in June 1956: 'The United Nations becomes an increasing source of trouble. I wish I could glimpse any good it does.'[28] On this point of transcendent importance there was a world of difference in the outlook of Eden and Dulles. In actual crises, for example in Guatemala in 1954, Dulles's tactics may have been manipulative and his attitude towards UN politics as cynical as Eden's.[29] Nevertheless, for Dulles the United Nations, despite its flaws, remained the cornerstone of the society of nations.

There was another fundamental difference. Eden believed much more than Dulles that the ruler of Egypt, Gamal Abdel Nasser, was at the heart of all Western troubles in the Middle East. In March 1956, King Hussein of Jordan kicked out Sir John Glubb, the Commander of the Arab Legion. Glubb represented the tradition of British Proconsuls in the Middle East; his dismissal was an affront; Eden held Nasser responsible. This was an error of judgement on Eden's part, for Hussein himself ousted Glubb, without Egyptian help, but to Eden it was an anti-British act of such calculated intent that it had to have been perpetrated by a villain comparable to Mussolini or Hitler—a comparison made frequently by Eden but rarely by Dulles.[30] Eden and many officials of the Foreign Office believed that the Americans had not learned the historical lesson of appeasement. 'It does not seem', wrote Anthony Nutting, 'that the Americans have yet hoisted in that appeasement of Nasser simply does not pay and that whatever "bargain" you make with him he will break.'[31]

A few weeks earlier, in January 1956, Eisenhower and Dulles had met with Eden and Selwyn Lloyd, the new Foreign Secretary. The President and Secretary of State mixed practical and, to the British, almost naive questions together with a sense of humour. Eisenhower asked, 'What kind of fellow is Nasser?' Lloyd answered, 'He is ambitious, dreams of an Arab empire from Atlantic to Persian Gulf under his leadership.'[32] Eisenhower expressed curiosity. Would other Arab leaders follow him? He suspected that the British view was alarmist,

[28] Minute by Eden, 6 June 1956, FO 800/737.

[29] Richard Immerman, *The CIA in Guatemala: The Foreign Policy of Intervention* (Austin, Tex., 1982), pp. 168–72.

[30] Dulles did refer to Nasser's 'Hitlerite personality' (Stephen E. Ambrose, *Eisenhower: The President* [New York, 1984], p. 334).

[31] Minute by Nutting, Secret, 6 March 1956, FO 800/734.

[32] This was one of Lloyd's insistent themes: Nasser 'aspired to have a pan-Arab union from the Atlantic to the Persian Gulf, dominated by Egypt and with all Western influences eliminated' (Lloyd to Jebb, Secret, 20 March 1956, FO 800/734).

but he saw a critical point: was Nasser falling irretrievably under Soviet influence? If so, the Americans would face the decision whether to support the British, French, Israelis, and anti-Nasser Arabs. Whatever might happen to Nasser, this course would further divide the Middle East. Lloyd replied by emphasizing an inflammatory anti-Western speech made by Nasser only the day before. Eisenhower appeared to be sceptical. This exchange was taking place two weeks after Dulles's celebrated statement about bringing the United States three times to the brink of war.[33] Eisenhower said that it was possible that Nasser 'doesn't have [a] good staff to go over his speeches'. There was a pause, then Dulles said, 'I wonder what you mean by that.'[34] The banter did not convince the British that Eisenhower and Dulles took Nasser seriously enough.

The Americans were in fact alarmed at Nasser, but they responded to some of the major issues differently. For example, the turning points in the background of the Suez crisis were the Czech arms deal and Glubb's dismissal. When Dulles learned of the arms deal in September 1955, his response was almost as indignant, and his sense of frustration was just as intense, as Eden's. Dulles remarked to Herbert Hoover, Jr., the Under Secretary of State:

> We have a lot of cards to play with Nasser—although they are mostly negative. The waters of the Upper Nile: we can strangle him if we want to. We can develop the Baghdad group and [we can] ruin the cotton market. We can switch this year's economic aid from Egypt to Iraq.[35]

Dulles nevertheless curbed his anger. He tried to woo Nasser away from the Russians by sending emissaries to Cairo and taking other measures, including coordinated efforts with the CIA. The British already doubted whether it was still possible to do business with Nasser, but the critical shift in their policy occurred in March 1956, when Glubb was cashiered. From that time onward, Eden became, in Shuckburgh's phrase, 'violently anti-Nasser'.[36] At one point Eden went so far as to exclaim that he wished to have Nasser 'murdered'.[37]

---

[33] James Shepley, 'How Dulles Averted War', *Life* (16 January 1956), p. 70 ff.

[34] Shuckburgh, *Descent to Suez*, p. 329. Shuckburgh continued in the vein of brinkmanship: 'The current joke about Dulles is—"three brinks and he's brunk"' (ibid.).

[35] Donald Neff, *Warriors at Suez* (New York, 1981), pp. 92–93.

[36] Shuckburgh, *Descent to Suez*, p. 341.

[37] Anthony Nutting's original version of this comment in his book *No End of a Lesson* (London, 1967) was that Eden wanted Nasser 'destroyed' (p. 34). In a recent interview for the Granada television series *End of Empire*, he stated that he had toned down Eden's comment and that the actual word was 'murdered' (Brian Lapping, *End of Empire* [London, 1985], p. 262).

Both Dulles and Eden agreed on the danger that Nasser represented, but they disagreed on the extent of the danger and the means to combat it. Eden regarded UN action as futile and resolved not to appease Nasser. His approach differed fundamentally from that of the more cautious Dulles, who made it clear throughout that he believed in the sanctity of the United Nations. He held that force should be employed only after all peaceful avenues had been explored and found to be dead ends. These were issues of profound substance, not style or timing, and they endured throughout the Suez crisis.

'Foster very gradually and very slowly came to realize what we were up against,' recalled George Humphrey, the Secretary of the Treasury in the Eisenhower administration. He was describing Dulles's reaction to the possibility that the Egyptians might turn to the Soviet Union for economic as well as military assistance. In the months following the Czech arms deal, the question of the High Dam at Aswan, a project that had been years in the planning, now acquired urgency—but to the British more than the Americans. Humphrey explained Dulles's reaction in October 1955:

> He [Dulles] had a cablegram from Eden which was . . . very sharp . . . demanding, practically—it was kind of half demand and half threat —that if we did not join them in building this Aswan Dam, that . . . the fat would be in the fire.[38]

So high were the stakes that Eden turned directly to Eisenhower. 'I hate to trouble you with this', Eden telegraphed to the President in November, 'but I am convinced that on our joint success in excluding the Russians from this [Aswan] contract may depend the future of Africa.'[39] Within a month, the American and British governments together with the International Bank for Reconstruction and Development offered a loan of $400 million towards the initial cost of the dam.

During the Aswan discussions, the question of colonialism emerged as an irritant in Anglo-American relations as well as in the negotiations with the Egyptians. Nasser inquired about the terms of the loan: would it be a means of regulating or interfering with the Egyptian economy? With the benefit of hindsight, it is clear that this was a real and not a fabricated concern, but at the time, officials within both the British and American governments believed that he was guilty not

---

[38] George Humphrey interview, John Foster Dulles Oral History Collection, Mudd Library, Princeton University.

[39] Quoted in Keith Kyle, 'Britain and the Crisis, 1955–1956', in Louis and Owen, *Suez 1956*.

merely of ingratitude but also of attempting to play the Western powers off against the Soviet Union. Dulles saw Nasser as an opportunist in the Cold War as well as an Egyptian nationalist rebelling against European dominance. The dilemma was acute. Sherman Adams, Eisenhower's principal assistant, summed it up after a visit by Eden to Washington in January 1956:

> Eden's visit to Washington did not resolve one serious difference between the American and British positions on the Middle East question; our firm opposition to colonialism made us sympathetic to the struggles which Egypt and the other Arab states were making to free themselves of the political and economic control that the British felt they had to maintain in the Middle East in their own self-interest.[40]

Eisenhower shared Dulles's aversion to British colonialism. On the other hand, members of the Eden government to a man believed that the Americans were misguided in this obsession. As Lord Blake has pointed out, it would be a mistake to lay too much emphasis on the conflict as a running battle between Dulles and Eden; the Suez crisis reflected differences of political judgement and national attitudes.[41]

Nevertheless the British, especially in retrospect, held Dulles responsible for the abrupt cancellation of the loan and for linking economic assistance with political alignment in the Cold War. It is true that he dealt the death blow to the loan in July 1956, but the British in the preceding months had been kept fully abreast of the reasons. From the Ambassador in Washington, Sir Roger Makins, the Foreign Office received accurate reports on the mounting domestic protests against the loan by the Israeli lobby, the cotton lobby, and the China lobby. In May, Nasser recognized Communist China, an action that antagonized both the Congress and the public. According to Makins, there was real doubt in Congress whether the Egyptian economy could bear the cost of the Czech arms deal together with a staggering new debt service that would be incurred by the Aswan project. To give but one example of the congressional pressure felt by Dulles, Otto Passman, a Democrat from Louisiana who chaired the foreign aid subcommittee in the House of Representatives, once said to a State Department official, 'Son, I don't smoke and I don't drink. My only pleasure in life is kicking the shit out of the foreign aid program of the United States of America.'[42] The dam in Egypt became a natural

[40] Sherman Adams, *Firsthand Report* (New York, 1961), p. 245.

[41] Lord Blake, *The Decline of Power, 1915–1964* (London, 1985), p. 349.

[42] Quoted in William J. Burns, *Economic Aid and American Policy toward Egypt, 1955–1981* (Albany, N.Y., 1985), p. 48.

target for such sentiment, especially since Nasser had aligned himself
with America's enemies in the Cold War. Dulles's cancellation of the
loan offer on 19 July 1956 came as no surprise to the British. They
were merely startled that he acted so quickly and decisively. According to William Clark, the Press Secretary who took the news to Eden:

> This came through, as messages tended to, on the Reuters tape be-
> fore it came through on the Foreign Office tape. I took it up, always
> glad to get credit for the press, to the Prime Minister in his bedroom.
> His comment was, 'Oh good, oh good for Foster. I didn't really think
> he had it in him.' Then there was a pause and, 'I wish he hadn't done
> it quite so abruptly.'[43]

The Foreign Office response indicates the alignment of the two countries at this stage: 'Mr. Dulles has taken the decision for us. We were
not absolutely in step at the last moment but the difference between
us was no more than a nuance.'[44]

Dulles was in Peru when he learned of Nasser's nationalization of
the Suez Canal Company on 26 July 1956. It is important to bear in
mind the word 'company' because Dulles correctly saw Nasser's action
as the takeover of a concession rather than, as in the widespread view
of the general public, an act of territorial aggression. On his return
to Washington a few days later, he quickly made his views known to
the British. 'Mr. Dulles sent for me this afternoon,' Sir Roger Makins
telegraphed to London on 30 July. The Secretary of State made clear
two points on which he remained consistent during the crisis:

> The United States Government thought it necessary to distinguish
> between the Suez Canal Convention of 1888, which was concluded
> in perpetuity, and the Canal Company concession, which had been
> granted for a fixed term. It was, therefore, *infractions* of the Conven-
> tion, *rather than the termination of the concession,* on which action could
> most appropriately be based.

> While he agreed that our attitude should be a firm one . . . his view
> was that so long as there was no interference with the navigation of
> the canal, and no threats to foreign nationals in Egypt, *there was no
> basis for military action.*[45]

---

[43] Lapping, *End of Empire,* p. 262. Eisenhower was also sceptical about Dulles's abrupt tactics.
See especially Townsend Hoopes, *The Devil and John Foster Dulles* (Boston, 1973), p. 343; and Ambrose, *Eisenhower,* p. 330.

[44] Minute by A. D. M. Ross (head of the Eastern Department of the Foreign Office), 20 July
1956, FO 371/119056.

[45] Makins to Lloyd, Top Secret, 30 July 1956, PREM 11/1098.

All of the underscoring was Eden's. 'Why?' he had written in the margin in response to Dulles's emphasis on the Suez Canal Convention of 1888, which secured the right of passage of vessels of the signatory states. Dulles was pointing out, implicitly at least, that each nation has the sovereign right to nationalize, which in his view could not be challenged effectively in international law unless questions arose about fair compensation or efficient management. Thus was there no basis for intervention, at least for the time being. On that point, at least, Eden was obviously clear about Dulles's meaning, even though it was open to the charge of hypocrisy in view of various acts of American intervention. Eden himself doubted that effective action could be taken on the basis of a nineteenth-century convention. 'Theft' was the straightforward word he used to describe Nasser's action.

The problem was that Dulles seemed to be speaking at two levels. One was the academic and legal, as if he were arguing his case before a court. The other was the popular and robust vernacular, which Eden and everyone else could easily comprehend. In meeting with Eden and others in London on 1 August, Dulles said: 'A way had to be found to make Nasser disgorge what he was attempting to swallow.' Here, as in the case of taking his country to the brink of war, Dulles's spontaneous remarks got him into trouble. Eden wrote in his memoirs about Dulles wishing to make Nasser disgorge: 'These were forthright words. They rang in my ears for months.' [46] Allowing for an element of exaggeration, what Eden wrote was no doubt true. Dulles gave the impression that he sympathized with the British and would support them, in the last resort with force, if they first pursued legal and peaceful methods to, in Eden's phrase, bring Nasser to his senses.

It will not be my purpose to discuss Dulles's tactics that led to the creation of the Suez Canal Users Association (SCUA), by which the waterway would be placed under international supervision.[47] I shall instead briefly examine the two incidents that revealed to the British what appeared to be his true sentiments. These episodes have had an adverse influence on Anglo-American relations to the present day. There is, however, a preliminary point that needs to be made about SCUA because it indicates Dulles's underlying purpose. It is one of the more important revelations from the opening of the British archives. Those officials in the British government who studied Dulles's methodical statements in writing and in committee, as well as his casual comments in conversation and his provocative remarks in press conferences, were certain of his intention. Adam Watson, the head of the

[46] *The Memoirs of Anthony Eden: Full Circle* (Boston, 1960), p. 487.
[47] For SCUA, see Robert R. Bowie, *Suez 1956* (New York, 1974), pp. 35–51.

African Department of the Foreign Office, wrote on the eve of the invasion by the expeditionary force in late October 1956: 'The fact is that he [Dulles] always really intended SCUA as a means for negotiating a settlement, not for pressure on Nasser.'[48]

Dulles and Eden both made basic miscalculations. Dulles believed that 'the danger of bellicose action would disappear if negotiations were prolonged.'[49] Eden assumed that if the British supported the proposal for a 'User's Club' (what became known as SCUA), then Dulles would back them in the application of economic sanctions and, if necessary, force. Eden said at one stage that SCUA was 'a cock-eyed idea, but if it brings the Americans in, I can go along'.[50] He wished to bring the crisis to a head as quickly as possible, thereby not losing momentum in protracted negotiations; Dulles, by contrast, hoped to gain time. But contrary to what might seem to be the natural course, he did not wish to turn to the UN, where the Soviet Union would be certain to block any chance of a peaceful resolution of the issue. According to a memorandum written by Dulles on 30 August 1956 after a conversation with Eisenhower, which summed up the basic points that they both endorsed:

> I [Dulles] said I had come to the conclusion that, regrettable as it might be to see Nasser's prestige enhanced even temporarily, I did not believe the situation was one which should be resolved by force.
>
> I could not see any end to the situation that might be created if the British and the French occupied the Canal and parts of Egypt. They would make bitter enemies of the entire population of the Middle East and much of Africa. Everywhere they would be compelled to maintain themselves by force and in the end their own economy would be weakened virtually beyond repair and the influence of the West in the Middle East and most of Africa lost for a generation, if not a century. The Soviet Union would reap the benefit of a greatly weakened Western Europe and would move into a position of predominant influence in the Middle East and Africa. No doubt it was for this reason that the Soviet were seeking to prevent a peaceful adjustment of the Suez problem.[51]

---

[48] Watson to G. E. Millard, Secret, 31 October 1956, PREM 11/1175.

[49] Robert Murphy, *Diplomat among Warriors* (London, 1964), p. 468.

[50] Thomas, *Suez Affair*, p. 83.

[51] Memorandum of conversation with the President, 30 August 1956, White House Memoranda Series, 'Meetings with the President, August–December 1956 (6)', John Foster Dulles Papers.

The Secretary of State noted for the record: 'The President said he entirely agreed with me in this basic analysis.'

Dulles's thoughts that he voiced intimately to Eisenhower were consistent with his public statement of 13 September 1956, affirming the premise of American policy. This extemporaneous comment was the first of the two incidents in which Dulles, in the British interpretation, revealed his true colours. It was the occasion of his famous remark that the United States would not force its way through the canal. In response to a question about the possibility of Egypt blocking passage of American ships sailing under the auspices of SCUA, Dulles had replied, in the phraseology of the headlines throughout the world, '*We do not intend to shoot our way through!*' [52] To Eden, the statement was an act of betrayal. He held to the end of his days that Dulles had misled him into believing that, if all else failed, the United States would support intervention.

The records recently released in London reveal that Sir Ivone Kirkpatrick, the Permanent Under-Secretary at the Foreign Office, was well aware of Dulles's attitude and was determined to take advantage of it. Eden trusted Kirkpatrick. He was one of the few officials within the Foreign Office who favoured intervention. He had written the week before Dulles's pronouncement against shooting one's way through the canal that the time had come to apply 'economic and psychological measures of pressure' against Nasser:

> We seem to me to be in a good position to do this because the Americans are so frightened that we may use force that we might bulldoze them into suitable economic and psychological measures simply by threatening that if they do not agree we shall have no alternative but to have recourse to force. [53]

Kirkpatrick thus gave careful thought to the ways in which the Americans might be manipulated. Though such evidence does not diminish Eden's genuine surprise at what he believed to be Dulles's treachery, it does indicate a deadly set of interlocking miscalculations. Kirkpatrick hoped that Dulles could be nudged from economic and psychological measures into political and military action, or at least into acquiescence in the British use of force. Kirkpatrick furthermore believed that the Americans would prefer not to know about the military plans against Nasser. According to another Foreign Office official,

[52] See Finer, *Dulles over Suez*, p. 229 (emphasis in original).
[53] Minute by Kirkpatrick, 4 September 1956, FO 371/119154.

'[N]othing had been said to the Americans because we assume that they did not wish to be told.'[54] In trying to understand Dulles and Eisenhower's reaction to the crisis, this was a fatal misjudgement.

The second occasion when Dulles revealed his true thoughts, in the British view, was at a press conference Dulles held on 2 October 1956. He elaborated on SCUA. If his previous public remarks had left any uncertainty, his comments now were explicit: SCUA would remain a voluntary association. Dulles's basic idea had always been that an international authority would schedule pilots to provide passage, collect tolls, and compensate the Egyptian government. The users of the canal would thus be in a position to bargain collectively with Egypt. But the international authority would have no power to enforce Nasser's compliance. 'There is talk', Dulles said, 'about teeth being pulled out of the plan, but I know of no teeth; there were no teeth in it.'[55] As if this further renunciation of the use of force were not enough, Dulles now connected the canal controversy with the volatile issue of colonialism. The United States, he stated, 'cannot be expected to identify itself 100 per cent either with the colonial Powers or the Powers uniquely concerned with the problem of getting independence as rapidly, and as fully, as possible'. All but suggesting that the British, together with the French, still possessed a nineteenth-century mentality, Dulles maintained that the colonial regimes should be dismantled. It should be the goal of the United States, in his view, to facilitate the shift from colonialism and 'to see that this process moves forward in a constructive, evolutionary way, and does not come to a halt or go forward through violent, revolutionary processes'.[56] Dulles was apprehensive about the instability that might be caused by decolonization, yet he also gave the impression that the European colonial powers were not moving fast enough towards a transfer of power.

Those comments caused great bitterness. To the British public, the Suez crisis did not represent a colonial issue but, in the words of *The Times* (London), 'one of elementary international law and order affecting a waterway which is many times as important for western Europe as the Panama Canal is for North America'. Beyond the merits of the canal dispute, Dulles had cast a slur on the British colonial record.

[54] Minute by Donald Logan (Private Secretary to the Foreign Secretary), 23 August 1956, FO 371/119123.

[55] *The Times*, 3 October 1956. According to Eden's recent biographer, Robert Rhodes James, 'In the unhappily long saga of Anglo-American duplicity, this ranks very high' (*Anthony Eden*, p. 515).

[56] *The Times*, 3 October 1956.

From the distance of some three decades it is difficult to recall the intensity of the debate about the end of the British Empire. The British, sometimes under American pressure and despite their better judgement, had quickened the pace of decolonization. For Dulles to call into question the British colonial record was entirely unjustified from both Tory and Labour points of view. His animosity now seemed almost to rival the ill will demonstrated by Nasser. *The Times* well expressed the sense of wounded pride and national indignation at Dulles's innuendo that Britain was not a progressive colonial power:

> Britain's record as a colonial Power stands in voluntarily bestowing independence on four great Asian countries after the war, in withdrawing from the Palestine mandate — at little benefit to peace in the Middle East — in 1947; in delaying settlement with Egypt because the latter refused to grant like independence to the Sudan, and in granting independence to Malaya and the Gold Coast next year at a time when even some nationalist politicians are forcibly expressing their doubts as to its immediate desirability.

> Britain has nothing to learn from anybody about the task of bringing progress, freedom, and self-government to the emergent peoples.[57]

With his remarks about colonialism, Dulles earned himself a permanent reputation as a hostile critic of Britain's Imperial mission. Eden was further exasperated, and he drew a practical lesson: 'We have been misled so often by Dulles' ideas that we cannot afford to risk another misunderstanding . . . Time is not on our side in this matter.'[58]

Eden received conflicting advice during the crisis. Sir Ivone Kirkpatrick represented one powerful view, cogently presented whenever the occasion arose, that whatever the Americans might do, the British would soon face a choice between 'the use of force or surrender to Nasser'.[59] On the other hand, Eden certainly did not lack counsel that intervention would be a mistake unless the Americans acquiesced. Certain officials knew the minds of Eisenhower and Dulles much better than others, and one of them stands vindicated in view of the events of late October through early November 1956. Sir Roger Makins wrote from Washington that he did not know the 'inner thoughts' of those in London making decisions about possible 'military action'

---

[57] Ibid.
[58] Eden to Selwyn Lloyd, Top Secret, 8 October 1956, FO 800/741.
[59] Kirkpatrick's draft telegram to Makins, 10 September 1956, FO 800/740.

—but 'to attempt it without full American moral and material support could easily lead to disaster'.[60]

Dulles's papers indicate that he had no knowledge of the British, French, and Israeli plans for the invasion. When he learned of the Israeli attack on 29 October, he explained his reaction to the British chargé d'affaires, John Coulson (Makins had completed his tour of duty, and his successor, Sir Harold Caccia, had not yet arrived). Dulles said he was appalled at not only the Israelis but also the French, whose brand of imperialism he warmly detested. According to Coulson, 'the French had in a sense involved us [the British] in their own Middle Eastern and African troubles and would try to use us further.' Both Eisenhower and Dulles, Coulson continued, harboured 'the profoundest suspicions' about the French.[61] At this initial stage of the invasion. Dulles still hoped that the Israelis and the French might be checked. He did not yet know the extent of British involvement. A record of a conversation among Eisenhower and others, shortly before Coulson's arrival, reveals what Dulles had in mind when he made his pointed remarks about the French: 'There has been a struggle between the French and ourselves to see who will have the British allied with them in the tense situations in the Middle East and North Africa . . . [T]here was still a bare chance to "unhook" the British from the French.'[62]

The British estimate of Dulles on the second day of the fighting reveals a man left with no doubt about the collusion. The British and French governments had issued an ultimatum for the Israelis and Egyptians each to withdraw from within ten miles of the canal, and to allow French and British troops to occupy the area of the canal itself. 'A pretty brutal affair,' Dulles said to Coulson. How could the Egyptians, who had been attacked, be expected to give up their own territory and submit again to occupation?[63] To Dulles, the veil of camouflaged intent had been lifted. He now had no doubt that the British were acting in concert with the French and the Israelis. Dulles's intuition and judgement were accurate on this point. He saw the true nature of the situation quicker than many of the British themselves. One can sympathize with Coulson, who in good faith believed that his government had issued the ultimatum in order to stop the fighting.

[60] Makins to Lloyd, Top Secret, 9 September 1956, FO 800/740.

[61] Coulson to Lloyd, Top Secret, 29 October 1956, FO 800/741.

[62] Memorandum of conference with the President, 29 October 1956, White House Memoranda Series, 'Meetings with the President, August–December 1956 (3)', John Foster Dulles Papers.

[63] Coulson to Lloyd, Top Secret, 30 October 1956, FO 800/741.

'Mr. Dulles was obviously profoundly disturbed and depressed,' Coulson reported on 31 October. Nothing could alter the view of Dulles or Eisenhower that they had been deceived. 'What rankles the most', Coulson concluded—and here he touched the heart of the matter— 'is what they believe to be deliberate concealment on our part, if not an actual plot with the French and Israelis.'[64] Some practitioners of international politics might have assumed that deception was part of the game, but Dulles and Eisenhower were genuinely offended.

On 1 November, Dulles explained to the members of the National Security Council the significance of the 'concerted moves' of the British, French, and Israelis. He again lashed out at the French, who had 'for some time been supplying the Israelis with far more military equipment than we knew anything about'. He then warmed to his subject. He spoke against the background of British bombers over Cairo and Molotov cocktails in Budapest. What the world had witnessed at Suez was a revival of European colonialism at a time when the Hungarians were in revolt against their own colonial masters. The United States now had to stand on its own historic principles. Summaries of NSC minutes do not ordinarily make for dramatic reading, but the following excerpt represents Dulles's creed as an American anti-imperialist. He spoke passionately—'with great warmth', in the euphemistic words of the minutes.

> For many years now the United States has been walking a tightrope between the effort to maintain our old and valued relations with our British and French allies on the one hand, and on the other trying to assure ourselves of the friendship and understanding of the newly independent countries who have escaped from colonialism . . . Unless we now assert and maintain this leadership, all of these newly independent countries will turn from us to the USSR. We will be looked upon as forever tied to British and French colonialist policies. In short, the United States would survive or go down on the basis of the fate of colonialism if the United States supports the French and the British on the colonial issue. Win or lose, we will share the fate of Britain and France . . .
>
> It is no less than tragic that at this very time, when we are on the point of winning an immense and long-hoped-for victory over Soviet colonialism in Eastern Europe, we should be forced to choose between following in the footsteps of Anglo-French colonialism in Asia and Africa, or splitting our course away from their course.[65]

[64] Coulson to Lloyd, Top Secret, 31 October 1956, FO 800/741.

[65] Memorandum of National Security Council meeting, 1 November 1956, National Security Council Series, Ann Whitman File, Eisenhower Papers.

Later the same day Dulles delivered a speech at the United Nations in which he reiterated, in a somewhat loftier tone, the same themes. It was one of the historic events of the Suez crisis. He later stated that he would stand by every word and indeed that he would choose the UN oration as his epitaph.[66] But for the vintage, unvarnished, anti-colonialist Dulles, his true epitaph was his comment earlier in the day to the National Security Council.

Within days after the UN speech Dulles fell ill and was taken to Walter Reed Hospital. The new British Ambassador, Sir Harold Caccia, reported later in November that though Herbert Hoover, Jr., the acting Secretary of State, wished to work back 'towards the old relationship', the State Department without Dulles seemed to be adrift: 'It does not look as if the Administration without Dulles has much idea of any coherent programme of action.'[67] What also seemed to emerge as an undeniable truth to the British was the control over the crisis exerted by Eisenhower himself. Eisenhower was a strong President served by a strong Secretary of State. According to a ranking British military officer who had served extended tours of duty in Washington, Air Chief Marshal Sir William Elliot: '[T]he President is the only man who matters, and there is no one near him, except Foster Dulles, who is the slightest good.'[68]

The impressions of Caccia and Elliott were not contradictory. In the British view, Dulles provided Eisenhower with the systematic policy that reinforced Eisenhower's own principles. In the emotionally charged debate about the Suez crisis in the NSC, the combination of Eisenhower and Dulles easily carried the anti-colonial sense of the meeting against those, notably Harold Stassen (the President's special assistant on disarmament), who wished to have a less condemnatory judgement on the British and French. So strongly did Eisenhower and Dulles feel about colonialism that they were prepared to nail the American colours to the mast, even though there might be adverse reactions during the election campaign. During the discussion on 29 October at the White House, the President had said (in the indirect words of the minutes of the meeting):

> [H]e does not care in the slightest whether he is re-elected or not. He feels we must make good on our word. He added that he did not

[66] Hoopes, *Devil and Dulles,* p. 379. For the speech, see especially Finer, *Dulles over Suez,* pp. 393–96. Finer attacks Dulles, here as elsewhere, for 'anger and excessive moralism', and lack of nerve and imagination: '[H]e was afraid of a world war, a figment of his own trepidation, and especially of the hostility of the Arab-Asian peoples' (p. 395).

[67] Caccia to Lloyd, Secret, 30 November 1956, FO 800/742.

[68] 'Record of Conversation', 18 November 1956, Top Secret and Guard [Guard = not for American eyes], PREM 11/1176.

really think the American people would throw him out in the midst of a situation like this, but if they did, so be it.[69]

Eisenhower may have been unduly modest about his political ambitions, but he was certainly right about the sentiment of the American public. Dulles interjected that one development would probably be 'a wave of anti-Semitism through the country'. Others at the meeting agreed. Eisenhower continued:

> The President next asked whether we should call Congress back into session, and specifically whether we could call them for the day following the election. He said that referral to the United Nations was not enough. We must take more definite action, since we are the only people the British and the French will listen to.[70]

So much for the view that Eisenhower and Dulles would hold back because of domestic political reasons. They were on solid political ground.

Even those who sympathized with the British purpose did little to end the rift. The Middle Eastern crisis had become a crisis in Anglo-American relations. Members of the Eisenhower administration believed that the Eden government had flouted the office of the U.S. Presidency by concealing the plans at Suez. According to Selwyn Lloyd, the traditional pro-British sentiment that usually characterized any administration in Washington had now been transformed:

> [T]he hard core of policy-makers, some of whom have been strongly pro-British in the past, are now against us . . . Their feeling is that we have to purge our contempt of the President in some way.

> [T]he Americans have no intention of lifting a finger to help to preserve us from financial disaster until they are certain that we are removing ourselves from Port Said quickly . . . Much of this American attitude is quite irrational and as they frankly admit contrary to their own long-term interests, but they . . . are temporarily beyond the bounds of reason and even threats to withdraw ourselves from the United Nations, N.A.T.O., etc. would not bring round those who have to make the decisions to a sense of reality.[71]

[69] Memorandum of conference with the President, 29 October 1956, White House Memoranda Series, 'Meetings with the President, August–December 1956 (3)', John Foster Dulles Papers.

[70] Ibid.

[71] Lloyd to R. A. Butler, Top Secret, 28 November 1956, FO 800/742.

In Washington, the new Ambassador agreed with that assessment. 'We have now passed the point where we are talking to friends,' Caccia reported. '[W]e are on a hard bargaining basis and we are dealing with an Administration of business executives who rightly or wrongly consider that they are animated by the highest principles.'[72] Those included, of course, Dulles. Once the British announced their plans to withdraw, he worked quickly and pragmatically to restore the alliance. In Caccia's judgement, Dulles's 'new found fervour for the Afro-Asians' would probably not interfere with a realistic approach to other problems, but Caccia was determined to review the relationship 'without mincing matters at any point'.[73]

On 16 November, Lloyd, together with Caccia, visited Dulles in the hospital. 'Dulles was up and looked remarkably well,' Lloyd wrote to Eden. What struck them on this occasion was Dulles's willingness to end the estrangement, repair the damage, and look towards the future. He emphasized that British and American policies differed not in aim but in method, not on the danger but on how to combat it. Here was the view that the British and Americans differed in timing and style, not the goal, which was, one way or another, to get rid of Nasser. There followed a startling remark. Dulles lamented that the British had not finished the job. This is a comment that has been discussed many times, but here is the excerpt from the original telegram:

> He [Dulles] agreed that there was no point in arguing about the past. The thing was to concentrate on the future. He said that he had no complaint about our objectives in our recent operations. In fact they were the same as those of the United States but he still did not think that our methods of achieving them were the right ones. Even so he deplored that we had not managed to bring down Nasser.[74]

What is one to make of the last sentence? Was Dulles merely saying, as did Churchill, that once begun the task should have been finished? Did he intend it as an interrogative comment, to discover why

---

[72] Caccia to Foreign Office, Top Secret, 28 November 1956, FO 800/742.

[73] Ibid.

[74] Lloyd to Eden, Secret, 18 November 1956, FO 371/118873. One of the more embroidered versions appears in Finer, *Dulles over Suez*, pp. 446–47: 'He [Dulles] said, *seriously*, "Well, once you started, why didn't you go through with it and get Nasser down?" Selwyn Lloyd answered, "Foster, why didn't you give us a wink?" Dulles answered, "Oh! I couldn't do anything like that!"' According to Lloyd's own posthumously published memoir in 1976, Dulles asked, 'Selwyn, why did you stop? Why didn't you go through with it and get Nasser down?' Lloyd replied, 'Well, Foster, if you had so much as winked at us we might have gone on' (Selwyn Lloyd, *Suez 1956: A Personal Account* [London, 1978], p. 219).

the British had pulled back? Did he mean to imply that the British had botched the operation, but said no more because of the obvious rejoinder that the Americans had caused them to do so? If he had been pressed by Caccia and Lloyd, how would he have reconciled the toppling of Nasser with the principle of anti-colonialism? Would he have replied that Nasser would have been best taken care of in the way that the CIA and MI6 had dislodged Musaddiq as the head of the Iranian government in 1953—in other words, by covert action? If so there was an echo of a previous conversation between Lloyd and Dulles: 'The Americans' main contention is that we can bring Nasser down by degrees rather on the Mossadeq lines.'[75] Unfortunately, Dulles did not elaborate, either earlier or later. But the British took his comment about the failure to bring down Nasser as further evidence of double-dealing.

There was no love lost between Caccia and Dulles. Caccia believed that the Suez expedition would have been a success had the United States not forced the British prematurely to withdraw. He held Dulles responsible. The root of the trouble, in Caccia's view, went back to Dulles's duplicity on SCUA. Early in 1957 he and Sir Antony Head, the Minister of Defence, decided to confront Dulles with the basic grievance:

> What we complained of most was the way in which we were misled by his scheme for a Users' Association. He had held this out to us as a method of bringing joint pressure to bear on Egypt: but, as soon as we accepted it, he had watered it down to nothing at all. I said that, frankly, we felt we had been 'led up the garden path' and that from that moment onwards the British Government had lost all confidence in the friendly intentions of the American Government.

Dulles seemed momentarily embarrassed by this.[76]

The occasion for the renewal of this acrimonious discussion was another of Dulles's spontaneous public comments. Appearing before the Senate Foreign Relations Committee in January 1957, he stated: '[I]f I were an American soldier who had to fight in the Middle East, I would rather not have a British and a French soldier, one on my right and one on my left.' To Caccia, this was an intolerable remark. He recalled Dulles's previous outburst on colonialism and other extemporaneous comments. He now reviewed the record: 'All [his words] have

[75] As alluded to in Eden to Macmillan, Top Secret, 23 September 1956, FO 800/740.
[76] Head to Macmillan, Secret, 28 January 1957, PREM 11/1178.

been said under pressure and the words have not been deliberately chosen. But after all allowances they do show a cast of thought which we should ignore at risk.'[77] Thus Dulles was a menace, and he had done harm—in Caccia's judgement, irreparable damage—to Anglo-American relations. That certainly was Eden's view as well.

Eden long outlived Dulles and continued to blame him for the fiasco at Suez. In his retirement he venomously referred to Dulles as 'tortuous as a wounded snake, with much less excuse'.[78] The language was poisonous, but it was consistent with the underlying attitude in his memoirs, which have had a lasting influence on historical interpretation. Dulles served as a convenient scapegoat. Eisenhower was still alive, and Eden had to be wary of him while writing *Full Circle*.[79] But Dulles could be painted, subtly but firmly, as the villain. This view persists. Whatever the more balanced judgement might be, one thing is certain. Dulles left an enduring impression on the public consciousness in Britain. The words of a contemporary critic sum it up: Dulles had a 'hypocritical obsession with the evils of British colonialism'.[80] He himself was responsible for this lasting reputation because of his extravagant rhetoric. But for those who studied Dulles's more careful language and consistent attitudes, they found a steadfast determination not to use force as well as views on colonialism shared widely by his countrymen. The Suez crisis caused his bedrock sentiments to erupt with the force of a volcano.

John Foster Dulles and the Diplomacy of the Cold War   1990

---

[77] Caccia to Lloyd, Secret, 26 January 1957, PREM 11/1178.
[78] Rhodes James, *Anthony Eden*, p. 617.
[79] See Blake, *Decline of Power*, p. 349. Blake assisted Eden in the writing of the memoirs.
[80] Quoted in Thomas, *Suez Affair*, p. 174.

26

THE UNITED NATIONS AND THE SUEZ CRISIS: BRITISH AMBIVALENCE TOWARDS THE POPE ON THE EAST RIVER

> There is only one motto worse than 'my country right or wrong' and that is 'the United Nations right or wrong'.
>
> Aneurin Bevan [1]

Aneurin Bevan's witty yet incisive comment cut to the heart of divided British sentiment at the height of the Suez crisis in November 1956. On the one side stood those who continued to believe in the supremacy of Britain's traditional national and Imperial mission. On the other were the champions of the United Nations, who held that the UN Charter had opened a new chapter in international law, indeed in human affairs, and that the United Nations therefore commanded the higher allegiance. In fact there was a great deal of ambivalence towards such passionate convictions, but feelings ran high— as high as on any other issue since the debate about appeasement in the late 1930s—and Bevan correctly detected the principal cleavage. At critical points in the Suez crisis, the debate centred as much on what was commonly assumed to be the new world order as on Gamal Abdel Nasser and the Suez Canal. To those who believed in the United Nations, the Suez confrontation represented a supreme test. Nasser's nationalization of the Suez Canal Company on 26 July 1956 not only created a crisis at the United Nations but also, it seemed to many at the time, represented a turning point in history, in which fidelity to international principle came irrevocably into conflict with the self-interest of the European colonial regimes.

In 1956 there was considerable wariness about approaching the United Nations to preserve the peace at Suez, not least because of the quite different motives of Britain and the United States. The Suez issue was not referred to the United Nations until 13 September, nearly two months into the crisis, and then on the initiative of Sir Anthony Eden, not John Foster Dulles or Gamal Abdel Nasser. This cautious approach to UN involvement was shared above all by the Secretary-General, Dag Hammarskjöld.[2] Though he later acquired the reputation as an activist Secretary-General, the qualities of circumspection

---

[1] Richard Crossman quoting Bevan in *Jewish Observer and Middle East Review*, 27 November 1964, cutting in FO 371/178598. Throughout this essay I rely heavily on the indispensable work on the subject, Keith Kyle, *Suez* (London, 1991).

[2] For Hammarskjöld, see Brian Urquhart, *Hammarskjold* (New York, 1972), a comprehensive and detailed biography based on the Hammarskjöld Papers and UN material.

and caution defined the early years of his tenure. The Suez crisis marked his emergence as a leader of broad vision and galvanizing, nervous energy. On the whole he managed to steer a steady and neutral course. His performance was all the more remarkable because of his critics' warnings, which would become ever more insistent later in his career, especially during the Congo crisis of 1960–61, that neither of the superpowers could rely on him to promote aims other than those of the United Nations. Neither Britain nor Egypt nor the United States could count on him to defend their interests. Hammarskjöld was his own man; the British referred to him sardonically as the Pope on the East River.[3]

Hammarskjöld had assumed office in 1953 at age forty-eight. He was a man of intellectual distinction, trained as an economist and in the law, and with refined interests in art and literature. He had chaired the Nobel Committee for Literature at the Swedish Academy. In a period when the United Nations had been weakened by the Korean War and the McCarthy anti-communist investigations, Hammarskjöld restored the morale of the UN Secretariat and transformed the chiefly administrative job of the Secretary-General into a position of political influence. The *Observer,* the foremost British newspaper championing the cause of the United Nations, wrote of him on 18 November 1956:

> He is an unemotional, minutely scrupulous and fastidious northern aristocrat. He does not possess any power of words—his speeches and his papers are said to be even more elliptical and obscure in Swedish than they are in English.

> He practises the sort of personal austerity that would be proper to a successful public priest. He avoids personal or emotional entanglements. He has a curious quality of solitariness at the centre of a vast and gregarious organisation.

Hammarskjöld to many was an enigmatic figure, but to those who knew him well there could be no doubt, in the words of the same 'Profile' in the *Observer,* that he was 'coldly devoted to his job without any of the romantic illusions about the brotherhood of man.'

Hammarskjöld in one sense took a minimalist attitude towards UN functions. In his view, if the United Nations were to survive, it had to be constantly on guard against taking on more than it could manage.

---

[3] For this theme, see Conor Cruise O'Brien, *The United Nations: Sacred Drama* (New York, 1968).

He strenuously resisted plans for converting the United Nations into a world police force or for adopting countries as permanent wards. Yet in a wider vision, Hammarskjöld also saw the potential of the United Nations as an independent institution that might achieve peaceful solutions to international problems in a way that would complement or surpass the efforts of individual states, large or small, which were each locked in narrow visions of self-interest. He worked relentlessly towards UN goals with creativity and resourcefulness. With careful calculation, the United Nations might play a critical part in solving not only the Suez crisis but even the more intractable problems of the Middle East. The Suez episode eventually represented a landmark in the history of the United Nations because it gave birth to the UN peace-keeping forces. To put it more negatively, as did Sir Pierson Dixon, the British Permanent Representative at the United Nations, Hammarskjöld sometimes gave the impression that he was 'fascinated by the idea of building up a U.N. police force under his command'.[4]

In all his UN affairs, Hammarskjöld believed that impartiality was essential, and he tried to embody that attribute. But he possessed a sceptical frame of mind, and to his critics he sometimes demonstrated a certain intellectual and ethical condescension that won him enemies, especially among those with equally strong personalities. Dixon was only one of several to collide with him over Egypt. Hammarskjöld, despite his attempt to remain unbiased towards all parties, eventually acquired among British officials a reputation for having, in Dixon's words, a 'notorious penchant for the Egyptians'.[5] At the beginning of the Suez crisis, however, the British regarded him on balance as anti-Nasser.

Hammarskjöld was sensitive to the United Nations being excluded from the debate about Suez, but he also recognized that the issues were so explosive that the organization itself might be wrecked if any of the protagonists succeeded in using it for their own purpose.[6] He had an unusually frank conversation with a member of the British delegation, Moore Crostwaite, in early August 1956. In Hammarskjöld's

[4] Diary entry for 5 November 1956, in Piers Dixon, *Double Diploma: The Life of Sir Pierson Dixon —Don and Diplomat* (London, 1968), p. 270. See also Edward Johnson, 'The Diplomats' Diplomat', *Contemporary British History*, 13, 2 (Summer 1999).

[5] Dixon to Lloyd, Top Secret, 19 June 1958, PREM 11/2387.

[6] The British Ambassador in Washington, Sir Roger Makins, recorded a conversation with John Foster Dulles that described Hammarskjöld's ambivalence: 'The Secretary-General was somewhat unhappy that the United Nations had been by-passed in the Suez affair' but did not want the administrative control over the canal 'to become too closely involved with the United Nations' (Makins to Lloyd, Secret, 11 August 1956, FO 371/119098).

subtle methods, candour was often an oblique rather than a conspicuous virtue, but in this exchange he made it clear that he had 'an unfavourable impression of Nasser'. Perhaps the crisis would end with
Nasser's enemies getting the upper hand, but not if the British and
French allowed it to become a confrontation between the colonial
powers and the rest of the world:

> He believed that there was a great deal of jealousy and distrust of Nas-
> ser among the other Arabs under the surface. He hoped that it would
> prove possible to exploit this. Making the issue one between the West
> and the East would solidify the Arabs behind Nasser, and indeed win
> him sympathy throughout Asia.

On this occasion Hammarskjöld was remarkably blunt: 'If the Suez
crisis led to the disappearance of Nasser, so much the better.'[7]

The initial British assessment of the prospect of turning to the
United Nations was negative. In the immediate aftermath of Nasser's
nationalization of the Suez Canal Company, Sir Harold Caccia had
summoned to his office, among others, the officials most concerned
with the United Nations, Sir Pierson Dixon and Sir Gerald Fitzmaurice.
Caccia was Deputy Under-Secretary and Ambassador-designate to the
United States. He would shortly depart, by sea, for Washington, where
he would arrive in November in the aftermath of the British and
French invasion of Egypt. Tough, aggressive, and competent, Caccia
was an Eden loyalist; he had been Eden's Private Secretary before the
Second World War.[8] Dixon was one of the ablest members of the diplomatic service of his generation.[9] He too had worked closely with
Eden, and continued to defend British policy at the United Nations,
even though personally he regarded it as misguided and, in the end,
disastrous. Fitzmaurice was the Legal Adviser at the Foreign Office,
with some twenty-five years experience in the legal department. Possessing a keen legal mind, he became the Prime Minister's most persistent and trenchant Foreign Office foe.[10]

This committee of Foreign Office worthies agreed unanimously that
it would be better to summon a conference of the maritime powers

---

[7] P. M. Crostwaite to A. D. M. Ross, Secret, 6 August 1956; Hammarskjöld to Selwyn Lloyd,
7 August 1956, FO 371/119114. Hammarskjöld stated in his letter to Lloyd that placing the issue
before the United Nations would be 'the only way to avoid making this a conflict between Europe
and Asia'.

[8] For Caccia in this context, see D. R. Thorpe, *Eden: The Life and Times of Anthony Eden* (London, 2003), esp. pp. 170–72.

[9] See Johnson, 'The Diplomat's Diplomat'.

[10] See Lewis Johnman, 'Playing the Role of a Cassandra: Sir Gerald Fitzmaurice, Senior Legal Advisor to the Foreign Office', *Contemporary British History*, 13, 2 (Summer 1999).

than to submit the matter to the United Nations. Though Dulles is usually given credit for convening the maritime conference, its origins can also be found in the Foreign Office. So too can the scepticism about the United Nations that characterized Anglo-American discussions at this stage. 'A special session of the General Assembly would be chancy,' according to Caccia and his colleagues, nor would the Security Council be satisfactory. In the Cold War atmosphere that prevailed at the United Nations, the Soviet Union would probably veto any proposal sponsored by the British. The Caccia committee also reached a negative conclusion on the possibility of confiding in the Secretary-General because whatever information they gave him 'would tend to reveal our intentions'. At this stage, the dominant British assumption, within the government at least, held that force might be necessary. The meeting ended on the further negative note that the Chinese President of the Security Council would probably vote with the Arabs. Clearly, not much could be expected from the United Nations.[11]

Nor did the Prime Minister think it expedient to turn to the United Nations. 'Please let us keep quiet about the UN,' he commented on 8 August.[12] In a manner entirely consistent with his earlier views about the League of Nations, Eden proclaimed himself to be an internationalist, but privately he had viewed both the League of Nations and especially the United Nations as organizations that might do more harm than good. In the 1930s he had regarded the League as an extension of the Foreign Office; the United Nations was much less malleable. Nevertheless, he needed to rely on the support of the United States and the Commonwealth, both of which would increasingly insist that Britain show good faith by referring the dispute to the United Nations. Eden did not want to appear as the aggressor in the judgement of world opinion. He therefore acquiesced in the idea of a maritime conference, and eventually agreed to submit the issue to the United Nations in order to prove that Britain had gone to every length to resolve the question by peaceful means. But ultimately there would be a fundamental and irrevocable difference between him and the United States, the Dominions, and not least the Labour Party. Many at

[11] Memorandum by J. D. Murray, 30 July 1956, FO 371/119118.
[12] Minute by Eden, 8 August 1956 on FO to Washington, 7 August 1956, PREM 11/1099. Eden's remark on keeping quiet about the United Nations arose because of the anxiety in the UN Department of the Foreign Office about the danger of Egypt taking the initiative in reporting to the Security Council the mobilization of massive British and French military forces in the Mediterranean. But Nasser feared that the United Nations would merely endorse the views of Britain and France and lead to an Egyptian defeat. Nasser also thought that the United States and the Soviet Union might try to settle the issue at the superpower level. At least in this respect he was partly right because, as will be seen, the unprecedented combination of the United States and the Soviet Union during the actual crisis helped determine its outcome.

the time assumed that the British government would abide by a UN solution to the problem. Yet Eden himself never wavered from the belief that the British must act in their own self-interest regardless of the United Nations.

Timing was one of Eden's principal preoccupations. By mid-September the weather in the eastern Mediterranean would begin to worsen, and, just as importantly, the passage of time would make it increasingly difficult to keep the troops mobilized and on alert. If Eden hoped to mount an attack on Egypt, with or without the blessing of the United Nations, then he would have to act sooner rather than later. Eden was as much aware as Dulles and Nasser that the momentum could not be sustained indefinitely. To keep things in play, he pursued two tactics that were difficult, probably impossible, to reconcile. One was to seek resolution of the conflict through peaceful means, which the Foreign Office now accepted as the overriding mission. Eden's other tactic was to plan for an invasion. The military objective was contingent upon a failure to secure a peaceful resolution of the problem. He would have to demonstrate that all reasonable means—including debate in the Security Council—had been exhausted before war could commence. To satisfy his own Cabinet as well as the House of Commons, the Labour Party, and the Commonwealth, Eden thus found it necessary to turn to the United Nations.

Within the Foreign Office, Harold Beeley, the Middle East expert, played a central part in shaping policy and expressed the pre-eminent goal: '[W]e must clearly aim at defeating Colonel Nasser without resort to force.'[13] At about the same time, Sir Gladwyn Jebb, the Ambassador in Paris, weighed in with the recommendation that Britain submit the issue to the United Nations. During the Second World War, Jebb had headed the Foreign Office's post-war planning department that helped create the United Nations.[14] After the war, he served as

---

[13] Minute by Beeley, 18 August 1956, FO 371/119128. In minutes on Beeley's analysis, Caccia and Sir Ivone Kirkpatrick (the Permanent Under-Secretary) reluctantly accepted this point, but the latter remained sceptical and asked for suggestions on how it might be achieved. The crisis now developed so rapidly that the British found themselves responding to events rather than guiding them. Beeley's plan rested on the assumption that Nasser might be provoked into action 'justifying military measures against him', by ships refusing to pay dues. Beeley noted in late August: 'We must work to a faster time-table' but had no further ideas (minute by Beeley, 31 August 1956, FO 371/119128).

[14] Brian Urquhart, who later became Under-Secretary at the United Nations, served under Jebb during the war and had a shrewd insight into his character:

He had a reputation for being supercilious and overbearing, but I soon discovered that his manner concealed an essentially kindly and humorous nature . . . He was both imaginative and realistic and knew better than most people that while a perfect inter-

Permanent Representative at the United Nations (1950–55). No one was more aware than he of the intricate politics of the Security Council and the General Assembly.[15] In addition to Beeley and Jebb, Sir Gerald Fitzmaurice persistently pointed out Britain's commitment to the UN Charter. Beeley, Jebb, and Fitzmaurice were all powerful figures in the Foreign Office. They believed that Britain must work in concert with the United Nations to resolve the issue. They and others, however, confronted a formidable personality, Sir Ivone Kirkpatrick, the Permanent Under-Secretary, who subtly, persistently, and firmly took the opposite view.

Kirkpatrick deftly parried suggestions about going to the United Nations so as to make them compatible with the plan for invasion. He stood second to none, not even Eden, in his belief that the United Nations must be kept subordinate to British aims. His tactic with Beeley and Fitzmaurice was to engage them in debate, often inconclusive, about the legal justification of force or the merits of proposals to keep Nasser in play. Sir Gladwyn Jebb is of particular interest in regard to this debate. Kirkpatrick—along with the Foreign Secretary and the Prime Minister—simply ignored him. At each stage Jebb was cut out of the discussions leading to major decisions. He naturally resented his status as a pariah, but Eden showed shrewd, instinctive judgement by ostracizing him. Jebb was one of the few people in the Foreign Office who, by sheer strength of personality, might have blocked, or at last made more difficult, the plans for the invasion. As it transpired, Kirkpatrick remained the dominant force within the Foreign Office. Eden trusted him and relied on him. Kirkpatrick regarded the United Nations with suspicion and even contempt, but was willing to exploit it to advantage.

Kirkpatrick believed that the time would come to apply 'economic and psychological measures of pressure' against Nasser that would command American assent:

---

national organization was impossible, an imperfect one was a great deal better than
nothing and might well be the indispensable factor in avoiding a nuclear world war.
Brian Urquhart, *A Life in Peace and War* (New York, 1987), pp. 91–92. See also Christopher Gold-smith, 'In the Know? Sir Gladwyn Jebb, Ambassador to France', *Contemporary British History*, 13, 2 (Summer 1999).

Jebb's sense of realism bore a similarity to Hammarskjöld's. Jebb wrote in 1951: 'One of the troubles about the United Nations . . . is that frustrated idealists tend to exaggerate wildly both its present powers and even its potential importance. In my own view it has, even now, a certain role to play . . . but it cannot, for a long time to come, expect to assume the powers and functions of a Super-State' (Jebb to Harold Nicolson, Strictly Personal, 6 November 1951, Gladwyn Jebb Papers, Churchill College, Cambridge, GLAD 1/1/1).

[15] See Jebb's memorandum 'Suez and the United Nations', 24 August 1956, FO 371/119177.

> We seem to be in a good position to do this because the Americans
> are so frightened that we may use force that we might bulldoze them
> into suitable economic and psychological measures simply by threat-
> ening that if they do not agree we shall have no alternative but to
> have recourse to force.[16]

Kirkpatrick thus gave careful thought to the ways in which the Americans might be manipulated. His ideas reveal a deadly set of interlocking miscalculations. He hoped that the United States could be
nudged from economic and psychological measures into political and
military action, or at least into acquiescence in the use of force. Kirkpatrick furthermore believed that Eisenhower and Dulles would prefer not to know about military plans against Nasser. According to another Foreign Office official, nothing had been said to the Americans
'because we assume that they did not wish to be told'.[17] This was a fatal misjudgement, which helps explain not only the reaction of Eisenhower and Dulles to the invasion, but also the British decision, taken
in some exasperation, to refer the Suez issue to the United Nations.

    During the crisis, Eden received conflicting advice. Kirkpatrick rep-
resented one powerful view, cogently presented whenever the occasion arose, that whatever the Americans might do, the British would
soon face a choice between 'the use of force or surrender to Nasser'.[18]
On the other hand, Eden certainly did not lack counsel that intervention would be a mistake unless the Americans acquiesced. Certain
British officials read the minds of Eisenhower and Dulles much better
than others, and one of them stands vindicated in view of the events
of late October through early November 1956. Sir Roger Makins wrote
from Washington that he did not know the 'inmost thoughts' of those
in London making decisions about possible 'military action'—but 'to
attempt it without full American moral and material support could
easily lead to disaster'.[19]

    By late August 1956, and even before, there were signs of internal
strain on the British side. Four out of five British voters believed that
the dispute should be submitted to the United Nations.[20] Most members of the Cabinet now thought that the issue should be submitted
to the United Nations before force could be used as an ultimate resort.
In explaining British wariness of the United Nations, Lord Home, the

[16] Minute by Kirkpatrick, 4 September 1956, FO 371/119154.

[17] Minute by Donald Logan (Private Secretary to the Foreign Secretary), 23 August 1956,
FO 371/119123.

[18] FO (Kirkpatrick) to Makins, Emergency Top Secret, 10 September 1956, FO 800/740.

[19] Makins to Lloyd, Emergency Top Secret, 9 September 1956, FO 800/740.

[20] Ralph Negrine, 'The Press and the Suez Crisis', *Historical Journal*, 25, 4 (1982), p. 978.

Secretary of State for Commonwealth Relations, succeeded more conspicuously with Australia and New Zealand than with Canada, Pakistan, and India.[21] Much would depend on the attitude of the United States. Within the Cabinet, Harold Macmillan, Chancellor of the Exchequer, held a position of particular significance not only because of his estimate of the crisis in relation to the British economy but also because of a visit he made to Washington in September and his assessment of Eisenhower and Dulles. If Eden misread the Americans, the error was all the more pronounced in Macmillan's celebrated misjudgement in September that Eisenhower was 'really determined, somehow or another, to bring Nasser down' and would not interfere with British plans.[22] Much more accurately, Macmillan wrote of Dulles's reaction in mid-September to Britain's submission of the Suez issue to the United Nations. The Secretary of State lost his temper: 'We should get nothing but trouble in New York; we were courting disaster.' As if to lend colour to the exchange, Macmillan added in his distinctive, racy style: 'From the way Dulles spoke you would have thought he was warning us against entering a bawdy-house.'[23] Nevertheless, Eden went ahead. The British decision on 13 September 1956 to refer the Suez issue to the United Nations marked a turning point in the crisis.[24]

Prelude to Crisis at the United Nations

In a visit to London in early August 1956, Dulles identified Lord Salisbury as one of the strongest personalities in the British Cabinet. The grandson of the great Victorian Prime Minister, Salisbury possessed aristocratic charm as well as a keen sense of principle. As much as anyone in the Eden government, he had an understanding of the way the colonial and Commonwealth system had evolved since the beginning of the Second World War. In 1942 he had served as Colonial Secretary, and in the last two years of the war as Dominions Secretary. As a British representative at the San Francisco conference, he helped create the trusteeship system of the United Nations.[25] He was thus one of the founders of the United Nations itself, but he was not uncritical of the

[21] See Peter Lyon, 'The Commonwealth and the Suez Crisis', in W. R. Louis and Roger Owen, eds., *Suez 1956* (Oxford, 1989).

[22] Macmillan to Eden, Top Secret, 26 September 1956, PREM 11/1102.

[23] Harold Macmillan, *Riding the Storm, 1956–1959* (New York, 1971), pp. 135–36.

[24] Eden stated in the House of Commons that if the Egyptians defaulted on international obligations, 'we should take them to the Security Council' (*Parliamentary Debates*, Commons, 13 September 1956, col. 305). Britain and France submitted letters to the United Nations on 23 September.

[25] See W. R. Louis, *Imperialism at Bay* (Oxford, 1977), chaps. 32–35.

organization. At San Francisco he had been on guard against establishing an international body that could interfere in the administration of the British colonies. Though an internationalist in the sense of wanting to learn from the mistakes of the League of Nations and establish an organization that would preserve peace by preventing aggression, he did not want the affairs of the British Empire discussed, in the phrase of the day, by 'a motley international assembly' or, in Salisbury's own words, by the 'rag tag and bobtail' Latin American countries and former colonies that increasingly made up the membership of the United Nations.[26] He wanted to avoid, in Churchill's phrase, Britain being put 'in the dock'. It is thus a matter of considerable irony that in November 1956, Britain was not only put in the dock but also widely condemned as a renegade that had rejected the UN code of international conduct. By bombing airfields and other military targets in and around Cairo while Soviet tanks were crushing Budapest, the British found themselves judged as possessing the same brutal and barbaric standards as the Russians.

Salisbury's support was critical to the Prime Minister. Not only was Salisbury one of Eden's few close friends, but he was also his trusted confidant and a central figure within the Cabinet. His concurrence or dissent could influence the Cabinet as a whole. On 27 August he had written to Eden that the UN Charter must prevail over all other considerations, at least before force could be brought to bear as a last resort:

> By my reading, the Charter says clearly—and again and again—that no member may embark on forceful action until he has referred his problem to the Security Council. I cannot feel that we can get out of that definite undertaking . . . I may be wrong. But, every time, I come up against that snag.[27]

Salisbury and most others in the Cabinet were willing ultimately to use force, but only if it were clear that a genuine effort had been made at the United Nations to resolve the issue peacefully. Another irony of the Suez crisis is that the Foreign Secretary, Selwyn Lloyd, nearly

---

[26] As Salisbury had put it to Eden in a letter of 6 November 1952, Salisbury Papers (Hatfield House). Salisbury elaborated on this theme in another letter written in 1953: 'The United Nations has become little more than a machine for enabling backward nations to press claims against the great powers to which they would normally not be entitled . . . As a result, I sadly fear that the strain that is put upon it may eventually kill the institution altogether, which would be a thousand pities' (Salisbury to Eden, Personal, 18 October 1953, Salisbury Papers).

[27] Salisbury to Eden, 27 August 1956, PREM 11/1100.

achieved the goal of a UN solution but abruptly became a key figure in the Franco-British-Israeli military alliance leading to war.

Selwyn Lloyd had become Foreign Secretary in late 1955 for the pre-eminent reason that Eden himself wanted to control foreign policy.[28] In Lloyd he found a compliant, competent, and loyal lieutenant. A lawyer by training, Lloyd had served as Minister of State in the Foreign Office (1951–54) during the Churchill government and had helped resolve the complex problems of Sudanese independence and British withdrawal from the Canal Zone. He thus had first-hand experience of Egypt, but he claimed no especial knowledge or expertise. He was modest in personality and reticent in conversation; his gruff banter concealed a natural shyness. He held no brief for the United Nations, but his inclination was to work towards a peaceful solution to the Suez crisis. Only because of his loyalty to Eden did he find himself pulled into the collusion with France and Israel.

In the earlier stages of the conflict, Lloyd had laboured tenaciously in the London maritime conference to discover principles acceptable to Egypt and the Soviet Union as well as the Western powers. At the United Nations, these points evolved into what became know as the six principles of 13 October 1956:

1. Free and open passage through the Canal;
2. Respect of Egypt's sovereignty;
3. Insulation of the operation of the Canal from the politics of any country;
4. Egypt and the users to agree on tolls and charges;
5. Allotment of a fair proportion of the dues to development of the Canal; and
6. Arbitration to settle affairs between Egypt and the old Canal Company.[29]

As in all comparable UN negotiations, the business of resolving the Suez crisis took place against the background of occasionally acrimonious debate, but at other times deliberately moderate discussion. In this case the debate was sometimes tempestuous because of the shrill voice of Krishna Menon of India, who championed the cause of Egypt but also stirred up general resentment, undermining India's influence.[30] The agreement on the six principles was essentially the work

[28] For Lloyd, see D. R. Thorpe, *Selwyn Lloyd* (London, 1989); and Lloyd's own substantial and valuable record, Selwyn Lloyd, *Suez 1956: A Personal Account* (London, 1978).

[29] These six principles are listed on pp. 167–68 of Urquhart, *Hammarskjold*, which contains the most detailed analysis of the evolution of the Suez crisis at the United Nations.

[30] The representative of the Commonwealth Relations Office in the British UN Delegation, Lord Lothian, commented on Menon in December 1956: 'One cannot help being impressed by the originality and liveliness of his mind, just as one is repelled by the authoritarianism and

of Lloyd, Hammarskjöld, and the Egyptian Foreign Minister, Mahmoud Fawzi.

Nasser was more willing to agree to a settlement than contemporary British and French participants in the crisis supposed at the time. The insistent Egyptian condition to any solution was sovereignty. The Egyptians would never agree to any international authority that would impinge on sovereign rights. Mahmoud Fawzi consistently and deftly upheld the Egyptian position and eventually suggested ways to reduce tensions within the Suez Canal Users Association: if the British and French would agree that the functions of SCUA would be limited to that of an international agency possessing no executive authority, Egyptian sovereignty would be maintained. But how could the canal be 'insulated' from Egypt without a derogation of sovereignty? This was the crucial point of conflict. While Britain and France insisted on measures of international control, Egypt guarded against encroachments on its sovereign rights.

Though Nasser made all major decisions, he relied on Fawzi both to maintain Egypt's prestige as a country in revolt against the colonial system and, if possible, to find a solution. Fawzi was recognized at the time as one of shrewdest and most experienced of the participants in the discussions at the United Nations in the autumn of 1956.[31] Hammarskjöld held him in esteem. Krishna Menon paid both of them an unintended compliment when he angrily commented that 'Hammarskjöld is just a Swedish edition of Fawzi, and Fawzi is just an Egyptian edition of Hammarskjöld.'[32] Menon thought them both second-rate, but this was entirely an erroneous judgement. Fawzi was a relic of King Farouk's regime, but he was also an Egyptian patriot as well as a master of international politics, and was thus keenly appreciated by Nasser. Fawzi became one of Hammarskjöld's few close friends at the United Nations.[33] It was the Hammarskjöld-Fawzi-Lloyd combination, despite the opposition of Krishna Menon and the French Foreign Minister, Christian Pineau, that brought the United Nations within a close distance of peacefully resolving the Suez conflict.

---

sanctimoniousness of his personality' (Lothian to Lord Home, Confidential and Personal, 17 December 1956, CO 936/320).

[31] According to Herman Finer, Fawzi was one of the subtlest of intelligences among all the foreign offices of the world, and one of the ablest debaters (*Dulles over Suez*, pp. 296–97).

[32] Muhammad Heikal, *Cutting the Lion's Tail: Suez through Egyptian Eyes* (London, 1986), p. 173.

[33] 'He saw that beneath Fawzi's urbanity and sophistication lay wisdom and goodness, and their friendship survived the disappointments of later years even the bitter experience of the Congo. Hammarskjold was privately criticized, especially in Great Britain for being too close to Fawzi and for being unduly influence by him, but . . . there seems little basis for these criticisms' (Urquhart, *Hammarskjold*, pp. 151–52).

The critical period for the shaping of the six principles was early to mid-October 1956; it was also the decisive phase in the strategic calculations. Military planners in Paris began making detailed arrangements for the secret alliance that began with France and Israel and then expanded to include Britain. At the same time, representatives sat around the horseshoe table at the Security Council to discuss a peaceful solution. Pineau knew of the military discussions in Paris and thus felt constrained to take a negative attitude in New York, though he would occasionally and unaccountably veer towards constructive comment. Lloyd did not at this stage know of the secret talks and thus genuinely worked towards accommodation with Fawzi. In the general debate in the Security Council, Cold War tactics were apparent when the Russian and Yugoslav representatives attacked the Anglo-French position and Krishna Menon attempted a compromise. Menon occupied a prominent place in the discussions because Egypt had refused to attend the London conference and India had stepped forward as Egypt's quasi-representative.[34] Menon at least demonstrated that there was a possible basis for understanding between Cairo and London, even if not Paris—for the French seemed as determined as ever to carry the Algerian war to Egypt.[35] Menon had Nehru's confidence, but virtually no one in New York trusted him because of his extravagant rhetoric and, in the common view, serpentine methods.[36]

The key to the actual compromise was Fawzi, whose conciliatory line probably reflected the pressures of India as well as the Arab oil-producing states. Perhaps the effect of the British and French freezing

[34] According to one of Krishna Menon's disciples, 'He argued for Egypt more powerfully than the Egyptian representative' (Kiran R. N. Kuttan Mahadevan, ed., *V. K. Krishna Menon: Man of the Century* [Delhi, 2000], p. 167).

[35] 'You have to be careful', Dulles warned Fawzi in October 1956: 'The French seem to be going towards waging the Algerian war in Egypt' (Mahmoud Fawzi, *Suez 1956: An Egyptian Perspective* [London, 1987], p. 108). Fawzi summed up the attitude of Pineau as 'very louche', mysterious as well as arrogant (Heikal, *Cutting the Lion's Tail*, p. 174).

[36] Fawzi held an equally balanced if jaded view of Nehru and Menon, on the one hand, and Dulles on the other: 'The moralizing of Nehru, which Menon shared, was as firm, as well-based, as articulately expressed, and as pontifical as Dulles's United States Christianity' (Fawzi, *Suez 1956: An Egyptian Perspective*, p. 116). For Nehru, Menon, and Suez, see especially Sarvepalli Gopal, 'India, the Crisis, and the Non-Aligned Nations', in Louis and Owen, *Suez 1956*. On Menon, most participants in the 1956 crisis would probably have agreed with the judgement of Judith Brown: 'He was psychologically unstable, very difficult to work with, incapable of delegating, self-willed and self-opinionated and thus liable to disastrous misjudgements' (Judith M. Brown, *Nehru: A Political Life* [New Haven, 2003], p. 248). On the other hand, Krishna Menon held a clear, intellectually vigorous, and consistent anti-colonial ideology that attracted a devoted band of followers. On his political thought, see Michael Brecher, *India and World Politics: Krishna Menon's View of the World* (London, 1968).

of Egyptian economic assets and the diminished revenue from the canal also played a part in tempering Egyptian aims. In any event, Hammarskjöld suggested that Fawzi, Lloyd, and Pineau meet privately. Hammarskjöld guaranteed to Fawzi that Lloyd honestly wished to have a settlement (after the British invasion of Egypt, Hammarskjöld felt that he had been double-crossed).[37] These were the dynamics behind the six principles, which were accepted by all sides until Britain and France added a clause to the effect that the Egyptian government must cooperate with the Users Association pending a settlement, thus again raising the issue of executive authority. Fawzi rejected the clause. Yugoslavia voted against it; the Soviet Union exercised its veto power. These skirmishes did not signify collapse, merely UN procedures. The door was left open: discussions would resume in Geneva in late October. By this time, however, British and French airplanes were preparing to bomb Egypt.

The acceptance of the six principles at the United Nations on 13 October 1956 occurred at a time when the Suez crisis reached a turning point. At a press conference, Eisenhower exclaimed that the work at the United Nations had saved the peace of the world: 'It looks as if a very great crisis is behind us.'[38] Dulles believed Eisenhower's comment to be too optimistic, as indeed it proved to be. No sooner did Lloyd arrive back in London than Eden commandeered him for a mission to Paris on 16 October. Thus began the fateful steps that led on to the secret military accord in a suburb of Paris, Sèvres, a week later.[39] Yet the odds on turning away from the United Nations in favour of military action would still have appeared to most contemporary observers as at least an equal bet. Military operations were by no means inevitable.

By September–October a declaration of war to reverse the nationalization of the Canal Company was no longer a matter of practical politics, though the directors of the company itself now took certain measures to force the issue. On 15 September the company withdrew

[37] Hammarskjöld's resentment surfaced in a savage letter written to Lloyd in 1958: 'The straight line often looks crooked to those who have departed from it' (Hammarskjöld to Lloyd, Secret, 10 July 1958, PREM 11/2387). The remark is reminiscent of Dean Acheson's comment, probably made in jest, about Lloyd as a 'crooked Welsh lawyer' (Evelyn Shuckburgh, *Descent to Suez: Diaries, 1951–1956* [London, 1986], p. 312). In any event, Acheson had a shrewd insight when he wrote of Lloyd's 'weakness' for 'abandoning the essence of one's own position and adopting the opposing one' (Dean Acheson, *Present at the Creation* [New York, 1969], p. 583). Acheson wrote of Lloyd in 1952, but it could just as well have been in October 1956.

[38] *The Times*, 13 October 1956.

[39] For this side of the story, see especially Avi Shlaim, 'The Protocol of Sèvres, 1956: Anatomy of a War Plot', *International Affairs*, 73, 3 (1997).

European pilots. Of a total of 205, there remained 26 Egyptian and 7 Greek pilots.[40] Contrary to many assumptions of what would happen, the Egyptians managed to operate the canal just as effectively as previously. They gave no ground for complaint. The pretext for declaring war on the issue of failing to run the canal now virtually disappeared.[41] The archival evidence is ambiguous, but there is good reason to believe that from mid-September Eden began to look for a way out. The country was divided and the House of Commons unmanageable. 'Difficult days in the House,' Eden wrote in his diary at one of his low points in the crisis.[42] Probably a majority in the House of Commons and the country at large would have been satisfied with Egyptian guarantees endorsed by the United Nations. When Eden decided, however reluctantly, that he must refer the issue to the Security Council on 13 September, he began to prepare the way for a peaceful solution that found expression in the six principles a month later.[43] But the military discussions came to a head at the same time. The French proposed an ingenious plan (so it seemed to Eden at the time) of intervention: encourage the Israelis to strike first, and thus provide the British and French with a pretext for advancing into Egypt to conduct a police operation. Eden, along with his loyal lieutenant, cast Britain's fate towards war rather than peace through the United Nations.

The British Ordeal in Late October and Early November

The climax at the United Nations in late October and early November took everyone by surprise, not least the British Ambassador, Sir Pierson Dixon. On 29 October, Israeli forces attacked the Egyptian army

[40] See D. A. Farnie, *East and West of Suez: The Suez Canal in History* (Oxford, 1969), pp. 726–27. See also especially Kennett Love, *Suez: The Twice-Fought War* (New York, 1969), pp. 421–24. Love gives slightly different figures but elaborates on the recruitment of German pilots from the Kiel Canal and Russian canal and river pilots who helped increase the traffic to 'the highest figure in the history of the canal'.

[41] The *New Statesman* summed up public sentiment on 15 September, the very day the European pilots left the canal: 'It is clear that most people now favour a negotiated settlement. The brief wave of chauvinism is over.'

[42] Eden MS Diary, 12 September 1956, Eden Papers AP 20/1/32.

[43] The diary entries by Harold Macmillan reveal Eden's uncertainty as well as his ambivalent attitude towards the United Nations. In Macmillan's impression, Eden uttered the phrase about taking the issue to the Security Council only after he became 'a little rattled'. A few days earlier Macmillan had written: 'To use force *without* going to the Security Council is really almost better than to use it *after* the Council has passed a resolution against it.' According to Macmillan's discerning interpretation of the British dilemma, Eden wavered indecisively and stumbled into the statement in the midst of conflicting pressures of the Parliamentary debate (Macmillan MS Diary entries, 10–13 September 1956).

in the Sinai. On the next day Britain and France issued an ultimatum
to Israel and Egypt to stop fighting within twelve hours and withdraw
ten miles from the canal. Israel would retreat from within enemy territory, but Egypt would withdraw from part of her own country under Egyptian sovereignty. British and French forces would occupy
strategic points at Port Said at the north end of the canal, Ismailia
towards the centre, and the port of Suez on the southern entrance. Israel accepted the ultimatum, but Egypt, not surprisingly, rejected it.
The subterfuge of Britain and France—conducting a police operation as peacemakers—deceived few people at the time. As one British
commentator put it later, 'If anybody in America believes the story of
mere "police action", let him stand up and be counted.'[44]

Dixon had no direct knowledge of the decisions to support the Israelis and then to invade; he was not in the inner circle (nor were the
British Ambassadors or representatives in Paris, Washington, Cairo, or
Tel Aviv). But he harboured no illusions about what was taking place.
According to Harold Macmillan, he possessed 'the most subtle mind
in Whitehall'.[45] Dixon was meticulous and cautious, outwardly unemotional, but temperamentally and intellectually highly sensitive.
Within the Foreign Office he had the reputation of having a quick
mind that reconciled divergent views and a personality that could
withstand difficult circumstances.[46] At the United Nations he was put
to the test. The normally gentle and congenial Dixon now had to use
the first veto ever exercised by the British. It sent a shock through the
British Isles, even among those usually indifferent to the United Nations. Britain, one of the founding members, now seemed to be undermining the purpose of the organization itself. Though he maintained
self-control and a dignified presence, Dixon occasionally revealed the
anguish of defending a position he believed to be false.

He learned of the Israeli attack in the late afternoon of 29 October. Hammarskjöld immediately engaged him in conversation along
with Henry Cabot Lodge, Jr. (the US Permanent Representative at the
United Nations), and Bernard Cornut-Gentille of France, who two
days later collapsed. Dixon and Cornut-Gentille were disconcerted at
the possibility of an emergency meeting of the Security Council—
understandably enough, since neither had instructions—and neither
welcomed the prospect of being put in the dock. That evening Lodge
and Dixon both attended the New York City Opera in formal dress.

---

[44] D. W. Brogan, in the *Spectator,* 30 November 1956.
[45] Macmillan MS Diary, 19 May 1962.
[46] See the perceptive entry by Evelyn Shuckburgh in the *Dictionary of National Biography,*
1961–70.

Lodge summoned Dixon out of a theatre stall to say that he now had instructions from Eisenhower himself to request an urgent meeting of the Security Council to demand Israeli withdrawal.[47] Dixon and Lodge had always regarded themselves as friendly colleagues, but Lodge remarked later the same night that the exchange with Dixon was 'one of the most disagreeable and unpleasant experiences' in his entire life:[48] 'Dixon until now had always been amiable but at this conference the mask fell off and he was virtually snarling.' Dixon said to Lodge: 'Don't be silly and moralistic. We have got to be practical.'[49] The remark is ironic because Dixon himself possessed a keen sense of ethical conduct. He had once written that Britain's place in the world depended largely on 'prestige', by which he meant 'what the rest of the world thinks of us'.[50] A veto would call universal attention to Britain's isolated moral position at the United Nations. Eisenhower himself commented to Eden that he was 'astonished' at Dixon's (and Cornut-Gentille's) 'completely unsympathetic' attitude.[51]

Dixon drafted a telegram to the Foreign Office on the back of the opera programme, a symbol of the way in which the crisis at the United Nations would become totally consuming. The next day the Security Council met morning, afternoon, and night. To Dixon's chagrin, he first learned of the British and French ultimatum from the Russian representative, who read an Associated Press report to the Security Council. Dixon could only extemporize that he expected to hear shortly from London about the statement the Prime Minister would make in the House of Commons. At the meeting in the afternoon, Dixon read verbatim from Eden's speech and tried as best he could to explain the

[47] For two slightly different but complementary accounts, see Henry Cabot Lodge, *The Storm Has Many Eyes* (New York, 1973), pp. 130–31, and Dixon, *Double Diploma*, pp. 263–64.

[48] But see Johnson, 'The Diplomats' Diplomat', p. 193, which is based on information from Douglas Hurd (at that time a member of the British delegation to the United Nations): 'Dixon did not like Lodge. Lodge was a politician and Dixon a diplomat and he found the American too forthright and to the point.' In any event, Dixon viewed Lodge as a representative American politician working within the constraints of the Eisenhower administration and reflecting a certain family tradition. Dixon wrote towards the end of the Suez crisis: 'The past weeks have shown that those directing United States policy are impervious to arguments and appeals to sentimental ties. Mr. Lodge, I suspect, has reverted to the isolationism of his grandfather and may have cast off for good the skin of liberal internationalism which he grew during his 4 years at the United Nations' (Dixon to FO, Top Secret and Guard [Guard = not for American eyes], 28 November 1956, FO 115/4550).

[49] *Foreign Relations of the United States, 1955–1957*, XVI, quoted in an editorial note on p. 841. Though he was no match for Dixon intellectually, Lodge was a New England gentleman. He wrote in his published account merely that Dixon's naturally ruddy face 'turned white' (*Storm Has Many Eyes*, p. 131).

[50] Minute by Dixon, 23 January 1952, FO 371/96920.

[51] Eisenhower to Eden, Top Secret, 30 October 1956, *Foreign Relations of the United States, 1955–1957*, XVI, p. 849.

rationale of the ultimatum. He was 'obviously shaken'.[52] Lodge then introduced a resolution demanding Israeli withdrawal. Dixon and Cornut-Gentille thereupon exercised the veto. 'We were opposed by the Americans on every point,' Dixon wrote in his diary.[53] In an extraordinary scene—unique in the annals of the Cold War—the Russian representative then embraced the American position by submitting virtually the same resolution, only to have it again vetoed by Britain and France. According to an American account, 'Both Dixon and Cornut-Gentille were white-faced and hostile to any conciliatory suggestions.'[54] In words that became famous in Foreign Office lore, Dixon wrote that casting the vetoes was the climax of 'a thoroughly unsatisfactory day's work'.[55] The world had witnessed the drama of Britain and France defying the United Nations. The *New Statesman* itself summed up at the time what many believed to be a shattering truth: 'The British government has broken the Charter of the U.N.' (3 November 1956).

On the next day, on the night of Wednesday, 31 October, Britain and France launched air attacks on Egypt. It is revealing to study Dixon's reaction to events at the United Nations because he as much as anyone else felt the tension between Britain's commitment to the UN Charter and the military operations in the Middle East. But it is also useful to keep in mind the more general background. From the time of the Anglo-French air bombardment to the ceasefire less than a week later, events in Egypt took place against the background of the Hungarian uprising and the entry into Budapest by Soviet forces. The British economy seemed to be spiralling towards collapse because of the drain on gold and dollar reserves. On 2 November, Israeli troops were on their way to completing the occupation of Gaza and the Sinai. On the same day, the General Assembly, where the veto does not apply, passed a US-sponsored resolution calling on Israel to withdraw and urging an immediate ceasefire. With 6 abstentions, the vote was 65 to 5. Only Australia and New Zealand voted with Britain and her two collusionist allies against the resolution. The resolution itself constituted one of the most emphatic censures ever voiced by the General Assembly. Eisenhower was re-elected President on 6 November, the same day that British and French seaborne troops landed at the northern

---

[52] The phrase is Brian Urquhart's in *Hammarskjold,* p. 173.

[53] Dixon, *Double Diploma,* p. 265.

[54] US Mission at the United Nations to State Department, Secret, 30 October 1956, *Foreign Relations of the United States, 1955–1957,* XVI, p. 859.

[55] Dixon to FO, 30 October 1956, FO 371/121746, quoted in Johnson, 'Diplomats' Diplomat', p. 182.

end of the canal. The Soviet Union now threatened rocket attacks on London and Paris. Less than twenty-four hours later, when the invasion forces had advanced only twenty-three miles down the canal, they received orders to cease fire.

Along with his British and French colleagues, Dixon found himself shunned as an outcast. Condemnation mingled with anger and sorrow in oblique glances. Scornful and embarrassed silence sometimes concealed genuine grief. Dixon recalled the emotionally tense general mood: 'Flanked by our faithful Australians and New Zealanders, we wandered about the U.N. halls like lost spirits. Our best friends averted their gaze or burst into tears as we passed.'[56] The British delegates were avoided as if they were lepers, but some proximity remained necessary. In the General Assembly the seating arrangement was alphabetical, the United Kingdom next to the United States. Dulles himself represented his country on 1 November. He entered while Dixon was attempting to persuade the General Assembly to allow British and French forces to fly the UN flag as peacemakers. Dixon paused on seeing him, perhaps in presentiment of impending danger: 'There was a strained moment as the two men eyed each other.'[57]

Dulles's speech to the General Assembly stands as one of the most eloquent statements made during the Suez crisis. He spoke urgently and simply but with deep reserves of sincerity and no ambiguity. He described the theme of his career as one of upholding international principles, at the Peace Conference in 1919 no less than the San Francisco Conference in 1945. He reaffirmed his commitment to the Charter of the United Nations. He expressed sorrow at the United States finding itself in disagreement with historic allies. He re-endorsed the purpose of the United Nations in such a way as to cause acute discomfort among the British, French, and Israelis:

> I doubt that any delegate ever spoke from this forum with as heavy a heart as I have brought here tonight. We speak on a matter of vital importance, where the United States finds itself unable to agree with three nations with whom it has ties, deep friendship, admiration, and respect, and two of whom constitute our oldest, most trusted and reliable allies . . .

[56] Dixon, diary entry for 7 January 1957, *Double Diploma*, p. 277.

[57] Leonard Mosley, *Dulles: A Biography of Eleanor, Allen, and John Foster Dulles and Their Family Network* (New York, 1978), p. 422. Mosley goes on, rather implausibly: 'Dixon was about to turn away abruptly when Foster held out his hand . . . He shook hands with Foster. But, as the photographers crowded in for a shot, a British aide shouted: "Don't smile, Sir!" and the expression went out of Dixon's good-humored face to become wooden as the cameras clicked.' In this case as in others, Mosley may have embellished his account, but it conveys psychological insight.

We thought when we wrote the charter in San Francisco in 1945 that we had seen perhaps the worst in war, that our task was to prevent a recurrence of what had been.[58]

He rejected the British solution of transferring authority from British and French forces to a UN peacekeeping operation. If the British proposal were accepted and the United Nations then failed to insist on a ceasefire and a renunciation of force, the General Assembly would have 'torn the Charter into shreds and the world would again be a world of anarchy.'[59] Dixon had forebodings that Britain would have to withdraw from the United Nations, perhaps even face expulsion.[60]

The UN problem was only one aspect of the extraordinarily complicated emergency that now faced the British Prime Minister. But resolving it was important for ending the crisis and salvaging his reputation as an international statesman. Eden made a television and radio broadcast on Saturday, 3 November, the day after the UN resolution condemning the British and their allies. With the Commonwealth torn asunder and the United States alienated, Eden also faced unprecedented public protest, a tempestuous House of Commons, and an economic crisis that threatened to destroy the sterling area as well as the British economy. Yet on television he appeared unruffled and decisive; some detected the spirit of Dunkirk. His calm and determined speech ranks along with Dulles's as one of the most memorable of the Suez crisis. He evoked memories of the 1930s and what appeared to him to be the ineluctable lessons of history. This passage became for ever famous:

> All my life I have been a man of peace, working for peace, striving for peace, negotiating for peace. I have been a League of Nations Man and a United Nations Man, and I am still the same man, with the same convictions, the same devotion to peace. I could not be other, even if I wished, but I am utterly convinced that the action we have taken is right.[61]

Eden left unspoken his premise that British self-interest must ultimately prevail, but he developed the theme that British and French

[58] Finer, *Dulles over Suez*, pp. 394–96.

[59] Joseph P. Lash, *Dag Hammarskjold: Custodian of the Brushfire Peace* (Garden City, N.Y., 1961), p. 83.

[60] Dixon's telegrams to the Foreign Office during these critical days are in FO 371/121746 and FO 371/121747. On the point of expulsion, see Bertjan Verbeek, *Decision-Making in Great Britain during the Suez Crisis* (Burlington, Vt., 2003), p. 122.

[61] Thorpe, *Eden*, p. 526. On Eden's television broadcast, see especially Tony Shaw, *Eden, Suez, and the Mass Media: Propaganda and Persuasion during the Suez Crisis* (London, 1996), p. 141.

action would prepare the way for a UN peacekeeping force. He said that the purpose of the military intervention was to put out the 'forest fire' in the Middle East. If the United Nations now wanted to take over from the British and French, 'we shall welcome it.'

The problem for the British was that there was no forest fire. The contrived rationale for the British and French presence no longer existed. The Israelis completed the conquest of Sinai and Gaza before the British and French invasion; accusations of collusion were already rampant.[62] The suggestion that the British and French forces might now form part of a UN peacekeeping operation had no appeal at all to most members of the United Nations. Lester Pearson, the Canadian Secretary of State for External Affairs, who played a leading part in creating the UN peacekeeping force, found that even the Canadians were regarded with suspicion.[63] The British, French, and Israelis were left with an unqualified ultimatum to evacuate.

The *Observer*, always the foremost advocate of the United Nations in Britain, wrote on Sunday, 4 November, the day after Eden's television broadcast, that the British government had 'flouted the United Nations' and 'dishonoured the name of Britain'. The most 'evil effect' of the crisis, according to the *Observer* (5 November 1956), could be seen in Hungary:

> The best chance that the Hungarians had of not suffering a return of the Red Army was Russia's obvious hesitation at playing the role of the oppressor before the eyes of the neutralist Asians. With the Anglo-French bombing of Egypt, that protection has been gravely weakened.[64]

Soviet archives have made it clear that the Suez crisis did not exert such a restraining influence as contemporaries had tended to be-

---

[62] For example, John Coulson of the British Embassy in Washington wrote:
It was naturally particularly galling to the Americans . . . that we should have chosen to cooperate with the French, a country for which they have the greatest contempt and whose policy they consider to be largely to blame for events in the Arab world. Our denials will never catch up with the belief that we and the French conspired with the Israelis to bring this incident about, and we are bound to suffer from the suspicion of deep, if not double, dealing.
J. E. Coulson to Harold Beeley, Confidential, 2 November 1956, FO 371/121794.

[63] For the Canadians and the creation of the UN peacekeeping force, see especially Michael G. Fry, 'Canada, the North Atlantic Triangle, and the United Nations', in Louis and Owen, *Suez 1956*. For the United Nations, chaps. 7 and 8 in Urquhart, *Hammarskjold*, are the best account.

[64] See Richard Cockett, *David Astor and 'The Observer'* (London, 1991), chap. 7.

lieve.[65] The Russians' threat of launching missiles against London and Paris or sending military forces to Egypt was put forward as bluff, but they certainly achieved their aim of heightening the tension.[66] At the United Nations, the British noted with alarm the comparisons being drawn between the Anglo-French bombing of Egypt and the Russian attack on Hungary. Dulles himself went so far as to say that he saw no difference between the British and French action in Egypt and the Russian move to crush Hungary.[67] Dixon felt the full brunt of such judgements. According to the *New Statesman* (10 November 1956), another champion of the UN cause in Britain: 'The pathetic figure of Sir Pierson Dixon, fighting back his tears . . . symbolised the dismay of all who had worked to weld the UN into an instrument of peace.'

The tension continued to mount. In the days following the Anglo-French paratroop drop on Monday, 5 November, and the landing of seaborne troops the following day, British and French aircraft continued to bomb military targets in and around Cairo. One bomb exploded near the central Cairo railway station. Krishna Menon seized the lead of the Afro-Asian group and gave voice to, as Dixon described it, the 'full cry for condemning us and the French for acts of war'.[68] Dixon himself now had a crisis of conscience. He came close to resigning.[69] In a series of urgent telegrams and telephone calls to London, he had already warned both the Foreign Secretary and Prime Minister that the bombing of non-military targets would create an atmosphere of moral revulsion against Britain at the United Nations.

[65] See Daniel F. Calhoun, *Hungary and Suez, 1956* (Lanham, Md., 1991).

[66] The young Tony Benn, for instance, wrote in his diary of the danger that even Communist China as well as the Soviet Union might intervene: 'Rumours of Russian troop and naval movements into the Mediterranean are very alarming. There are reports that a quarter of a million Chinese have volunteered to help Egypt. The whole thing has the nature of a nightmare and one wonders whether we are not within measurable sight of a racial war' (Ruth Winstone, ed., *Tony Benn, Years of Hope: Diaries, Letters, and Papers, 1940–1962* [London, 1994], p. 206).

[67] For example: On 30 October 1956 in a conversation with the French Ambassador, Hervé Alphand, Dulles stated 'that in his opinion there was no difference between Anglo-French intervention at Suez and the utilization of the Soviet army against the civilian population of Budapest.' In protest, Alphand thereupon got up to leave. Dulles then 'modified' the accusation to assuage him (*Foreign Relations of the United States, 1955–1957*, XVI, p. 868, note 3). On other hand, the Editor of the *Sunday Times*, H. V. Hodson, who was in the United States at the time, wrote in a balanced comment that would have applied to Dulles and Eisenhower as well as the American public: 'Americans are an emotional people and sentiment against Britain and France may flare; but it will take more than this to turn the people against the Anglo-American alliance' (*Sunday Times*, 5 November 1956).

[68] Dixon, diary entry, 5 November 1956, *Double Diploma*, p. 271.

[69] See *The Storm Has Many Eyes*, p. 131, which records that, as early as 30 October, during the air attack on Port Said, Dixon said to Cabot Lodge that if the bombing continued, 'he personally would resign'.

On 3 November he had emphasized that further air attacks 'would make a mockery of our repeated assertions that our intervention was an emergency police action confined to the occupation of a few key points along the Canal'.[70] On 4 November the Soviet army launched a major attack on Budapest. On 5 November, Dixon used the word 'butchery' to describe Russian behaviour. The same sort of language, to Dixon's distress, was now being used in the General Assembly to denounce the British. His moral turmoil spilled over into a telegram to the Foreign Office:

> Two days ago . . . I felt constrained to warn you that if there was any bombing of open cities with resulting loss of civilian life it would make our proposals seem completely cynical and entirely undermine our position here . . .

> We are inevitably being placed in the same low category as the Russians in their bombing of Budapest. I do not see how we can carry much conviction in our protests against the Russian bombing of Budapest, if we are ourselves bombing Cairo.[71]

Eden promised that the bombing would stop. On the next day, Tuesday, 6 November, he halted the advance of British troops down the canal. The Suez war abruptly ended. Dixon's warnings were hardly decisive in the decision to cease fire, but they certainly alerted the Cabinet to Britain's condemned position at the United Nations. Dixon himself later reflected in his diary that defending Britain's case before the General Assembly caused 'the severest moral and physical strain I have ever experienced'.[72]

Some of Dixon's most incisive comments during the Suez crisis focused on Hammarskjöld and the future of the United Nations. Though he reported under emotional stress and at a time of strained relations with Secretary-General, Dixon always wrote perceptively and realistically. He was relieved, for example, when he wrote on 5 November that Hammarskjöld seemed to be 'far more pre-occupied and incensed with the Israelis than with us'. It was at this time that Dixon observed, as has been mentioned earlier, that Hammarskjöld seemed fascinated by the emergence of a UN peacekeeping force—'a sort of peace brigade to put out world fires under the general direction of the head of the world organization'.[73] But the creation of the United

---

[70] Dixon to FO, Emergency Secret, 3 November 1956, FO 371/ 121747.

[71] Dixon to FO, Emergency Secret, 5 November 1956, FO 371/121748. Dixon's telegram is printed in full in Richard Lamb, *The Failure of the Eden Government* (London, 1987), pp. 265–66.

[72] *Double Diploma,* p. 278.

[73] Dixon to FO, Emergency Secret, 5 November 1956, FO 371/121748.

Nations Emergency Force proved to be a severe strain on both Hammarskjöld and the organization itself. One of the revealing features of Dixon's assessments is the extent to which Hammarskjöld came close to breakdown. Dixon wrote some weeks later that the Secretary-General told him that he did not possess 'the physical stamina or moral conviction' to continue:

> Hammarskjoeld, I think, is on the verge of collapse . . . Surprisingly enough this strange intellectual whom we have elevated into a superman is made of flesh and blood . . . He literally burst into tears this evening . . .[74]

> Allowance must, of course, be made for a very tired and nervous man but . . . he is a very obstinate creature with a unique gift for combining high moral principles with an obscurity of thought and expression which makes it almost impossible sometimes to understand what he is saying, let alone what he is driving at.[75]

But even Dixon recognized that Hammarskjöld had become a distinguished, creative, and indefatigable Secretary-General. Without him, the British position at the United Nations might have been much more hazardous: 'It may sound absurd but if this man collapses or turns against us our position will become immeasurably more complicated.'[76] In such faintly disguised praise, Hammarskjöld emerges, even in British assessments, as the key figure in the transformation of the United Nations of the mid-1950s. Though Hammarskjöld attempted to be even-handed, the members of the General Assembly and Hammarskjöld himself regarded 'Egypt as the victim'—with a resulting bias, especially in Dixon's view, against the Western colonial powers.[77] For at least the next decade, anti-colonialism—so marked a feature of the debates during the Suez crisis—became not only the dominant characteristic of the United Nations but one of the principles for ever associated with the organization.

Gurobaru Gabanansu no Rekishi-teki Henyo:
Kokuren to Kokusai-seiji-si   forthcoming

[74] Dixon to FO, Secret, 16 December 1956, FO 800/743.
[75] Dixon to Kirkpatrick, Secret, 22 December 1956, FO 371/119189.
[76] Dixon to FO, Secret, 16 December 1956, FO 800/743.
[77] Dixon to Kirkpatrick, Secret, 22 December 1956, FO 371/119189. Dixon's attempt to correct the perspective was as close as he came in reflecting on the causes of the Suez crisis. In this regard one of the more searching contemporary comments came from the pen of Sir William Strang (Kirkpatrick's predecessor as Permanent Under-Secretary): 'The Western world is now paying the price for the Balfour Declaration and all that flowed therefrom' (*Sunday Times*, 18 November 1956).

27

PUBLIC ENEMY NUMBER ONE:
BRITAIN AND THE UNITED NATIONS
IN THE AFTERMATH OF SUEZ

'I don't think they play at all fairly', Alice began, in rather a com-
plaining tone 'and they all quarrel so dreadfully one can't hear one-
self speak—and they don't seem to have any rules in particular; at
least, if there are, nobody attends to them.'[1]

Or, to use another literary allusion, as did Sir John Martin, the
Deputy Under-Secretary of State for the Colonies in 1964, 'No
man is an island.'[2] The Colonial Office drew up plans for territorial and economic configurations affecting millions throughout the
world; nationalist leaders in Asia, Africa, and the Caribbean made decisions attempting to set the pace for decolonization; and the United
States and the Soviet Union drew conclusions influencing the course
of the Cold War. In these interlocking circumstances, it is useful at the
international level to focus on the United Nations as a microcosm for
studying, in the British case, the relative weight of metropolitan infirmity, nationalist insurgency, and international interference.[3] The British public as well as successive governments, on the whole, endorsed
the idea of the United Nations as 'the finest conception that has yet
been born among mankind'.[4] But by 1960—and perhaps five years
before, when the membership had expanded from fifty-one to sixty-
seven—the United Nations was a quite different organization from
the one its founders had created in 1945. To add Mary Wollstone-
craft Shelley to Lewis Carroll and John Donne, the United Nations in
its colonial guise had become a Frankenstein's monster. In 1960 the

---

[1] Quoted in Report on the Proceedings in the Fourth (Trusteeship and Colonial) Committee at the 21st Session of the United Nations, enclosed in Lord Caradon (Ambassador to the
United Nations) to FCO, Confidential, 15 February 1967, FCO 58/87. John Sankey, 'Decolonisation: Cooperation and Confrontation at the United Nations', in Erik Jensen and Thomas Fisher,
eds., *The United Kingdom—The United Nations* (London, 1990), is a valuable work of reference.
Sankey for many years was the colonial adviser to the British delegation in New York and later
UK Permanent Representative to the United Nations in Geneva.

[2] Minute by Martin, 6 October 1964, CO 936/925.

[3] See W. R. Louis and R. E. Robinson, 'The Imperialism of Decolonization', *Journal of Imperial
and Commonwealth History*, 22, 3 (September 1994); John Darwin, 'Decolonization and the End
of Empire', in Robin W. Winks, ed., *Historiography* (vol. 5 in the *Oxford History of the British Empire*,
Oxford, 1999).

[4] Sir Alec Douglas Home in the House of Commons, 4 March 1965, *Parliamentary Debates*
(Commons), col. 1551, from which Christopher Eastwood in the Colonial Office drew the conclusion that 'there is no great division between the parties on this' (minute by Eastwood, 5 March
1965, CO 936/927).

General Assembly passed the notorious (at least to the British) Resolution 1514, calling for a speedy and unconditional end to colonialism.

In the United Nations no less than in Britain, the post-war history
of the British Empire divides into two phases, pre-Suez and post-Suez.
But the antecedents of the colonial problem at Turtle Bay (the loca-
tion of the United Nations on the East River in New York City) can be
traced to the founding of the organization itself. Sir Hilton Poynton,
the Permanent Under-Secretary at the Colonial Office (1959–66), had
attended the San Francisco conference that had created the United
Nations. He had wholeheartedly agreed with the Colonial Secretary of
the time, Oliver Stanley, that the United Nations must be kept out of
the affairs of the British Empire. 'A motley international assembly'—
Stanley's phrase—must not be allowed to put the Empire in the dock.[5]
No one was more consistent or adamant than Poynton in the view that
the United Nations must not be allowed to interfere in British colonial
administration. 'I have always been, and unashamedly remain, on the
extreme right wing over this,' he once wrote.[6] Even so, the commitment made by Britain to the United Nations was minimal. Under the
UN arrangements (Chapters XII and XIII of the Charter), the British
agreed to submit reports, hear petitions, and accept visiting missions
to the trust territories. Tanganyika was the only British trusteeship
dependency of any consequence, though British Togoland and British Cameroons had a certain relevance to the independence of the
Gold Coast and Nigeria. Despite the negligible significance of most
of the trusteeship territories, the debates were often acrimonious—
especially those regarding visiting missions. The Afro-Asian bloc, as
it became known, insisted that UN missions should be dispatched to
as many colonial dependencies as possible and not merely to the trust
territories. On this issue as on others, and above all on the invasion
of Egypt in 1956, the British inevitably found, in perhaps an understatement, that 'public debate at Turtle Bay exacerbates rather than
assuages'.[7]

In 1945 the British had also acquiesced in the Declaration regard-

---

[5] See W. R. Louis, *Imperialism at Bay* (Oxford, 1977), chaps. 33 and 34, especially p. 531, on
Poynton's dismay at the creation of the UN's Trusteeship Council, which was empowered to examine annual reports, receive petitions, and dispatch visiting missions. 'I am . . . disheartened
over the whole thing,' he wrote to Kenneth Robinson in the Colonial Office. 'I'm afraid we've
got ourselves into a ghastly jam. I expect you are all seething with rage in London.' On Poynton's
views, see also especially Sankey, 'Decolonisation', pp. 114–15.

[6] Quoted by Ronald Hyam in Ronald Hyam and W. R. Louis, eds., *British Documents on the End
of Empire: The Conservative Government and the End of Empire, 1957–1964* (2 vols., London, 2000),
I, p. lxxi (hereafter *BDEEP—Conservative Government*).

[7] Caradon to FCO, Confidential, 26 January 1965, FO 371/183521.

ing Non-Self-Governing Territories (Chapter XI of the Charter). They agreed to submit information on economic, social, and educational progress in British colonies; but as in the case of the trusteeship provisions, the Afro-Asian bloc insisted that the colonial powers also provide plans for independence. Here Poynton held a rigid view that 'independence' and 'self-determination'—phrases the British in 1945 had managed to keep to a subdued use in the UN Charter—should not be admitted into UN discourse. To Poynton's mind, emphasizing independence would encourage colonial subjects to break away from the Empire rather than to become self-governing within the Empire as a step towards Dominion Status within the Commonwealth. Recalling his early involvement, he stressed Britain's minimal obligation:

> I have a special personal interest in this in that I was myself representing the Colonial Office as an Adviser (Assistant Secretary) at the . . . San Francisco Conference and all the earlier meetings of the United Nations and the Trusteeship Council . . .

> The charter obliges us to transmit such information on social, economic and educational conditions, but not on political and constitutional progress . . . I confess I should be very sorry to see this point surrendered during my period as Permanent Secretary of the Colonial Office.[8]

On another occasion he remarked: 'I do not accept that the United Nations should have a right to meddle in our Colonial affairs.'[9] What Poynton feared most of all was that pressure by the United Nations would cause the British to grant independence before adequate political, economic, social, and educational preparation. His judgement on UN oratorical extravagance was unequivocal and emphatic: 'dangerous balderdash'.[10] But whatever the rhetoric, the UN Charter itself, even in its measured language, was, and is, a profoundly anticolonial document.

One of the ironies of the process of decolonization is that in 1945— as in 1919 at the time of the creation of the mandates system—the British had fiercely resisted the principle of self-determination, or, in the language of the UN Charter, 'the freely expressed wishes of the peoples concerned'.[11] Ultimately, however, the British came to rely on

[8] Minute by Poynton, 28 July 1961, CO 936/681.
[9] Minute by Poynton 9 May 1962, CO 936/727.
[10] Minute by Poynton, 2 November 1961, CO 936/683.
[11] The UN Charter does not refer explicitly to the principle of self-determination but rather to 'a full measure of self-government' (Chapter XI) and 'self-government or independence' (Chapter XII). Resolution 1541 of 1960 stated that non-self-governing territories could achieve

the formula of self-determination as an answer to their critics. In the rocks, shoals, and other remnants of Empire, what made more sense than to allow the inhabitants of Gibraltar or the Falklands to determine their own future? (Hong Kong was a unique exception.) In 1945, however, the wave of the future, to the British at least, seemed to lie in large economic and territorial units. Federations became the grand design of the two post-war decades. Whether in the West Indies, Nigeria, Central Africa, Aden, or Malaysia, the aim would be to make economic sense out of the arbitrary territorial boundaries by forging dependencies into viable nascent states. The British wanted to avoid the fragmentation that the United Nations seemed to be encouraging with its emphasis on individual sovereign states, whatever their size or capacity to stand on their own. Christopher Eastwood in the Colonial Office asked where would it all end? The logical progression, or absurdity, seemed to point to Pitcairn Island, a possibility he dismissed out of hand: 'Pitcairn Island, with 70 or 80 inhabitants, cannot really become independent.'[12] By the time of the decision to recall all British troops east of Suez in 1967, the United Nations had grown to 133 (as compared with 191 in 2004).[13] Clearly the future lay with the wave of independent states, but on the eve of the Suez crisis in 1956 the United Nations had not yet acquired its reputation as an aggressive anti-colonial champion of self-determination.

The public in Britain remained generally oblivious of the extent to which the United Nations in the mid-1950s was already being transformed into an organization whose purpose would be, in Conor Cruise O'Brien's classic formulation, multiracialism and decolonization as well as peace.[14] The moral authority of the United Nations

---

a full measure of self-government either by independence or by free association or integration with an independent state. See Sankey, 'Decolonisation', pp. 99–100.

[12] Minute by Eastwood, 20 October 1964, CO 936/925. Despite Eastwood's fears, Pitcairn Island, with a declining population—47 in 2003—has not yet become a member of the United Nations.

[13] To those within the British government watching the growth of the United Nations, there seemed to be a sort of Parkinson's law at work: the number of 'oppressed' would increase indefinitely in inverse proportion to the constant number of 'oppressors'. (See, for example, the minute by the young Philip Ziegler in the Foreign Office, 23 February 1962, FO 371/166850.)

[14] See Conor Cruise O'Brien, *The United Nations: Sacred Drama* (New York, 1968). On the decade of radical chic following the Suez crisis, O'Brien writes that 'these were the years when fair British royalty would be photographed dancing with jet-black African potentates' (p. 33, quoting the Brazilian journalist Hernane Tavares de Sá, who had Princess Margaret in mind). On the significance of O'Brien's book, see Adam Roberts and Benedict Kingsbury, *United Nations, Divided World* (Oxford, 1993), p. 21.

Here and in a few other passages I have drawn on a paper presented to a conference on the United Nations in Hokkaido, Japan, in December 2003. I have benefited from Asahiko Hanzawa,

endowed it with a charisma and a quasi-religious quality—with Dag Hammarskjöld as the secular Pope on the East River—that seemed, to those within the British government following its evolution closely, to be irrational yet compelling, and thus dangerous. This 'theological' quality was clearly detected in the Colonial Office.[15] In late 1954, Will Mathieson, who had previously served as the colonial adviser in the British delegation at the United Nations, commented that the UN membership would continue increasingly to reflect an anti-colonial and especially an anti-British bias. Mathieson later became head of the East African Department in the Colonial Office and still later served on the Executive Board of UNESCO. His minute of December 1954 reveals a certain intellectual acumen in dealing with the mythology of colonialism at the United Nations. Such was the power of UN emotional rhetoric that it could not 'be neutralised by rational argument'. There were five components:

> The myth that sovereign status is a sovereign remedy for all ills and that poverty and social injustices in dependent territories are attributable solely to their dependent status;

> The myth that expansion overseas is 'aggressive imperialism' whereas the assimilation of territory overland is the rightful and admirable prerogative of a vigorous state;

> The myth that 'colonialism', a term of abuse with historical origins in the relationship between metropolitan governments and peoples of the same stock in overseas settlements, still merits emotional application to the relationship between the remaining colonial powers and their wards of different race in their dependencies;

> The myth that professed altruism by Europeans towards coloured peoples must mask determined exploitation;

> And the myth that the major cause of war is the political subjection of one people by another of different pigmentation.[16]

'An Invisible Surrender: The United Nations and the End of the British Empire, 1956–1963' (D.Phil. thesis, Oxford University, 2002).

[15] 'Theological' was the word used by Christopher Eastwood in a letter to John Tahourdin of the Foreign Office, Confidential, 16 October 1959, FO 371/145269.

[16] Minute by Mathieson, 31 December 1954, CO 936/319. Mathieson's minute reflected many of the assumptions that had been developed by Poynton since late in the wartime period and that had become firmly established in departmental lore; see Louis, *Imperialism at Bay*, chap. 25.

Mathieson, a Scot, drew a dour conclusion. 'Perpetuating all these myths is the widely prevalent xenophobia or reverse colour prejudice of the non-European nations.' The 'motley crew' (the phrase had become standard usage in the Colonial Office) had become 'hag-ridden by prejudice' and 'willfully blind to fact and operating under a system which gives equal weight to the votes of all national units whatever the[ir] moral value.'[17] As Hilton Poynton later remarked when the anti-colonial movement reached its peak, there could be nothing but 'trouble ahead'.[18]

The immediate trouble came like a thunderclap with Gamal Abdel Nasser's nationalization of the Suez Canal Company on 26 July 1956.[19] But the eye of the storm did not move to Turtle Bay until several months later. Two of the principals, Anthony Eden and John Foster Dulles, were both wary of the United Nations, the latter because the United States could no longer control it, at least not always, and the former because he was planning military action against Egypt. But Eden needed to prove that he had exhausted all peaceful remedies before using force. In September he decided to refer the Suez issue to the United Nations. Such was the nature of the secret planning that virtually no one in the Colonial Office and few in the Foreign Office besides Sir Ivone Kirkpatrick, the Permanent Under-Secretary, along with a handful of others, were privy to Eden's plot to depose Nasser by force. When the news of referral reached the United Nations, Sir Pierson Dixon, the Ambassador, was uncertain whether to regard it as a genuine effort to resolve the issue or as a smokescreen.[20] Ironically, the British, French, and Egyptian delegates came close to finding a solution, but at the same time Eden plunged further into secret plans—collusion—with the French and Israelis for a coordinated invasion.[21] Those in the British delegation, which included Peter Ramsbotham (later Ambassador in Washington) and the young Douglas Hurd (later

[17] The motley crew moreover seemed to suffer from 'a colonial hangover'—another phrase used by Mathieson to sum up his conclusions. He went on: 'To put this in terms of Latin American oratory, in the lobbies of the United Nations the ring of the discarded fetter will always drown the cry of the starving child' (minute by Mathieson, 31 December 1954, CO 936/319).

[18] Minute by Poynton, 21 October 1964, CO 936/925.

[19] For the United Nations and the Suez crisis, see especially Michael G. Fry, 'Canada, the North Atlantic Triangle, and the United Nations', in W. R. Louis and Roger Owen, eds., *Suez 1956* (Oxford, 1989).

[20] See Piers Dixon, *Double Diploma: The Life of Sir Pierson Dixon—Don and Diplomat* (London, 1968); and Edward Johnson, 'The Diplomats' Diplomat', *Contemporary British History*, 13, 2 (Summer 1999).

[21] See especially Avi Shlaim, 'The Protocol of Sèvres, 1956: Anatomy of a War Plot', *International Affairs*, 73, 3 (1997); for the crisis itself, Keith Kyle, *Suez* (London, 1991) stands the test of time as the classic work.

Foreign Secretary), though they had their suspicions, knew nothing until the Israeli attack on Egypt on 29 October.[22] The next day Britain and France delivered an ultimatum to Israel and Egypt to withdraw from the Canal Zone. The Egyptians, if they complied, would be withdrawing from Egyptian sovereign territory. It was clear to most observers that the ultimatum was contrived and that it would be impossible for Egypt to accept it.

The world now witnessed the drama of Britain and France defying the United Nations by casting vetoes in the Security Council against an American resolution calling for the withdrawal of Israeli troops and —in an event unique in the annals of the Cold War—of the Soviet Union introducing virtually the same resolution, only to have it again vetoed by Britain and France. On 31 October, Britain and France launched air attacks on Egypt. Two days later the General Assembly (where the veto does not apply) voted 65 to 5 (with 6 abstentions) to call for an immediate ceasefire and the withdrawal of Israeli troops. Only Australia and New Zealand voted with Britain and her two collusionist allies against the resolution. The resolution itself constituted one of the most emphatic censures ever voiced by the General Assembly. Only a few days later, as the pound sterling deteriorated and the United States exerted heavy pressure, Eden halted the advance of British troops in the Canal Zone. The Suez war thus ended abruptly. The immediate crisis was over, but at an immense cost to Britain's reputation at the United Nations. The *New Statesman* perhaps best summed it up by stating a glaring truth: 'The British government has broken the Charter of the U.N.'[23]

The Suez crisis had two far-reaching consequences for the British Empire in the international community. One was short term, the other longer lasting. Both have to be understood in the temper of the time, when the United Nations still represented the hope of the world in an era under the enduring shadow of the Second World War. The first consequence was that the debate about the Suez Canal and the invasion of Egypt became transformed into a full-blown polemical yet searching discussion about colonialism. The British Empire was now not merely in the dock but reviled as a renegade. In a manner that previously would have been regarded as inconceivable to most people in Britain, at least in its intensity, the British Empire was now denounced as being just as immoral and vicious as the Soviet empire in Eastern Europe and Central Asia. The Suez crisis occurred at the same time that Russian tanks rolled through Budapest to crush the

[22] See Douglas Hurd, *Memoirs* (London, 2003).
[23] 3 November 1956.

Hungarian uprising. The British bombing of airfields in and around Cairo caused John Foster Dulles to remark that British and French methods were as brutal and barbaric as Russian tactics.[24] The moral turmoil of Sir Pierson Dixon spilled over into a telegram to the Foreign Office: 'We are inevitably being placed in the same low category as the Russians in their bombing of Budapest. I do not see how we can carry much conviction in our protests against the Russian bombing of Budapest, if we are ourselves bombing Cairo.'[25] Britain's ethical position at the United Nations had been shattered.

A few months later I. T. M. Pink of the Foreign Office assessed the damage. Pink had served in Tokyo and Berlin as well as Tehran, and thus had perspective on the historical evolution of the British Empire in world affairs. He reflected on the loss of Britain's good name:

> Our recent troubles over the Suez affair have seriously weakened our position in the United Nations, which was based not so much on our material power as on our reputation for wisdom, honesty, fair dealing and restraint. We may hope to regain the ground we have lost, but it will take time to re-establish our position.[26]

Ivor Pink was certainly right about the long-term implications. It was now clear, as if in a moment of revelation, that Britain could not act independently of the United States, nor did the British state possess the economic or military strength to be ranked as a great power. At the United Nations, the British Empire seemed to have revealed its true colours as a marauding, reactionary force. Here was the other consequence, which was entirely unexpected. For the next fifteen years or so, Britain became Public Enemy Number One at the United Nations.

Colonialism as a Menace to World Peace

International notoriety can be exhilarating, but in unpredictable ways. At the United Nations during the Suez crisis, the members of the British delegation were shunned. Scornful and embarrassed silence sometimes concealed genuine grief. Sir Pierson Dixon recalled the tense general mood: 'Flanked by our faithful Australians and New

[24] See *Foreign Relations of the United States, 1955–1957,* XVI, p. 868. Dulles made the remark to the French Ambassador in Washington, Hervé Alphand, who was so incensed that he stood up to leave the meeting. Dulles thereupon retracted, or, at least, according to the record, 'modified', his complaint.

[25] Dixon to FO, Emergency Secret, 5 November 1956, FO 371/121748. Dixon's telegram is printed in full in Richard Lamb, *The Failure of the Eden Government* (London, 1987), pp. 265–66.

[26] I. T. M. Pink, 'The United Nations: A Stocktaking', Confidential, 7 February 1957, CO 936/540.

Zealanders, we wandered about the U.N. halls like lost spirits. Our best friends averted their gaze or burst into tears as we passed.'[27] Britain, one of the principal founders of the United Nations, had undermined the purpose of the organization itself. The idea that the British had acted true to form by invading Egypt persisted through the next decade. During the Middle East war of 1967, Israeli forces defeated the armies of Egypt, Syria, and Jordan. The Arabs did not believe that the Israeli victory could have been possible without British (and American) assistance. This time, however, their suspicions were entirely unfounded. Their allegations were denounced by Britain and the United States as 'The Big Lie'. But Arab assumptions about British motives were easy to understand. British credibility had been destroyed in 1956. It was not until 1967, however, that the British paid the ultimate price for the Suez adventure. Apart from a few Commonwealth stalwarts, very few non-Western representatives at the United Nations were willing to give the British the benefit of the doubt when it came to motive. The Suez crisis thus provided the context for the anti-colonial movement as it gained momentum at the United Nations in the early 1960s.

The anti-colonial debate forced the British to centre stage. It compelled them to concentrate on large issues, such as the purpose of colonial rule and the fate of the non-Western world. The British, of course, were not alone, though the British Empire was still far and away the largest of the remaining Western maritime enterprises. The French were equally notorious, but with a difference. No one at the United Nations expected anything but colonialist behaviour from the French. By contrast, the British achievement, beginning with India in 1947, had demonstrated consecutive transfers of power conferring sovereign equality. 'Our colonial record tends to be forgotten,' lamented the British delegation at the United Nations.[28] As if in the worst of all possible worlds, the French continued to command the loyalty of their former colonies, whereas 'some of the Commonwealth countries are our most dangerous opponents in New York.'[29] Was this, asked John Beith in the Foreign Office, an example of 'French toughness and British flabbiness'?[30] The Foreign Office came to the conclusion that the French drew strength from their former colonies because of a greater willingness to continue a much higher degree of economic

[27] Dixon, diary entry for 7 January 1957, *Double Diploma*, p. 277.

[28] Sir Patrick Dean (Permanent Representative at the United Nations, 1960–64) to FO, Confidential, 25 January 1963, FO 371/172548.

[29] Minute by T. C. D. Jerrom, 19 September 1963, CO 936/921.

[30] Minute by Beith, 19 July 1962, FO 371/166803.

and military assistance than the British themselves were able or willing to provide. As the decade progressed, the British shared the colonial spotlight not only with the French but also with the South Africans and the Portuguese. In what was known as the 'Unholy Alliance', the British were suspected of indirectly supporting South African apartheid on the one hand and the antiquated Portuguese system on the other. According to the anti-colonialists, the British aimed to preserve the Central African Federation and along with it the profits of the mining industry as well as the supremacy of kith and kin in Southern Rhodesia.[31] Virtually no one would accept the explanation that the British hoped to achieve harmonious race relations based on equality and then to disengage. Being Public Enemy Number One was exhilarating but also exasperating.

The non-Western members of the United Nations appeared to have the long collective memories of the oppressed. They criticized British motives during and after the Suez crisis. They never allowed the British to minimize their buccaneering past or the exploitative nature of the British Empire. Nor did Britain's record of decolonization seem to hold up very well under the doctrine of 'neocolonialism', the theory that the metropolitan countries still held the colonies in thrall economically even after independence.[32] Much later, in the 1970s, Sir Colin Crowe reflected that the widespread obsession with colonialism could be traced to the decade before the First World War and the early years of British rule in Africa: 'At the turn of the century the British nanny was individually one of the most potent educative influences around the world, but what may be tolerable in the nursery causes resentment in international organisations and far too often we take on the role of universal governess.'[33]

[31] For the 'Unholy Alliance', see, for example, FO 371/172548, FO 371/172601, and FO 371/172606, especially the minutes produced by the powerful mind of C. W. Squire, who had served in the Nigerian Administrative Service as well as in the British delegation to the United Nations, and who later became Ambassador to Israel.

[32] See especially Brian Crozier, *Neo-Colonialism* (London, 1964), a book of interest because the Foreign Office commissioned it to disprove the theory of neocolonialism. (See Edward Youde to Sam Falle, Confidential, 27 May 1966, FO 371/189816.) Crozier, on the staff of *The Economist*, was a journalist of considerable repute, not least because of his highly acclaimed survey of the post-colonial world, *The Morning After* (London, 1963). *Neo-Colonialism* is an inferior work in comparison, but is nevertheless useful for its statistical comparisons of the former British and French colonies. For Foreign Office assessments of the theory, see for example FO 371/166835, FO 371/166842, and FO 371/172605. According to *The Times* on 23 August 1963: 'Neocolonialism is the prolongation of colonialism by other means, mainly but not wholly economic' (cutting in FO 371/172601).

[33] Sir Colin Crowe to FCO, Confidential, 23 May 1973, FCO 58/773. Crowe, a Supernumerary Fellow of St. Antony's College, Oxford, was Permanent Representative to the United Nations,

There certainly seemed to be a psychological dimension to the anti-colonial campaign of the 1960s. According to one of the most inter-esting explanations, the former colonial subjects still, on the whole, preferred the extended hand of the former nanny to the embrace of the Americans. Anti-colonialism, at least in Asia, was a cultural as well as political phenomenon:

> It is a frame of mind, resentment at patronage, resentment at fancied Western assumptions of superiority whether in social status or cul-ture, reaction to the Western impact on Asia in past centuries. This frame of mind, expressed in terms of opposition to western control or interference, explains the paradox of 'anti-colonialism' in coun-tries that have never been colonies, directed against countries that have never had them.

> Americans are sometimes baffled to find that Asian sentiment to-wards Britain, the greatest colonial power of all, is apt to be more cor-dial than towards the United States, despite their remarkable record of generosity and altruism in dealings with Asia.[34]

Looking suspiciously at Britain's place in the world as an Imperial power, the anti-colonialists not only condemned the British because of their colonial past but also despised them because of their post-Suez weakness and indecision. The enemies of imperialism would not let it be forgotten, as Sir Evelyn Shuckburgh summed it up, that the British had been 'great marauders in the past and are still a long way from having abandoned ill-gotten acquisitions'—while on the other hand, the lesson of Suez seemed to be that 'we are a poor, sad shadow of an influential past.'[35]

'It is important to us in all sorts of ways', wrote Sir John Martin, whose balanced judgement attracted respect throughout Whitehall, 'that the image of Britain should be that of a progressive modern State rather than of a feeble senescent power living in the past.'[36] What the British thought of themselves had a bearing on the Cold War and the Russian efforts to dismantle the British Empire, as well as on colonial

---

1970–73. He had begun his career in China before the Second World War and had post-1956 ex-perience in Egypt.

[34] Sir Robert Scott to Harold Macmillan, Secret, 13 November 1959, FO 371/143732. Scott was High Commissioner in South-East Asia, having served previously in China.

[35] Minute by Evelyn Shuckburgh, Confidential, 2 February 1962, FO 371/166819. Shuck-burgh was the Under-Secretary supervising Middle Eastern affairs until shortly before the Suez expedition, which he vehemently opposed. See Evelyn Shuckburgh, *Descent to Suez: Diaries, 1951–56* (London, 1986).

[36] Minute by Martin, 6 October 1964, CO 936/925.

nationalism and the attempts by nationalists, especially in Africa, to force the pace of decolonization. There were two widely held assumptions that are important for understanding why the British acted as they did in trying to regain the initiative at the United Nations and elsewhere after the Suez crisis. The first was the common belief that the British Empire would last a good deal longer than it in fact did. As late as 1959 the projected timetable for independence in East Africa was 1970 for Tanganyika, 1971 for Uganda, and 1975 for Kenya—as opposed to the actual dates of the early 1960s.[37]

The second assumption was that the international system at the United Nations was rigged against the British because of what was known as the 'double standard'. Representatives of the non-Western countries, above all India, held the Soviet Union to one standard, which was tolerant and forgiving, and Britain to another, which was harsh and exacting. Jawaharlal Nehru had been slow to criticize the Russians in Hungary but quick to condemn the British at Suez. At the United Nations, the anti-British and anti-American tone had been set by India's legendary representative in the 1950s, Krishna Menon, who spoke, according to a slightly jaded British description, as 'the mouthpiece of the world's conscience'. His unbridled and eloquent passion was usually directed, often to the relief of the British, against the United States.

> The long curved fingers, the curling lip, the limp and the stick, the sometimes almost incomprehensible but always earnest speech, seem to set him apart from other delegates. In some people . . . he inspires an instinctive dislike and mistrust. Almost all Americans regard him with intense suspicion . . . His anti-Americanism . . . sometimes verges on the hysterical.[38]

The first assumption regarding the longevity of the colonial system was shaken in 1960 by UN Resolution 1514, calling for immediate

[37] The United Nations had established the date of 1960 for the independence of the trust territory of Somalia, which in turn influenced the decision to grant independence to Tanganyika in 1961, with a knock-on effect of helping determine independence for Uganda in 1962 and Kenya in 1963. For the balance between political forces in East Africa and the causative effect of the trusteeship system, see W. R. Louis, 'The Dissolution of the British Empire', in Judith M. Brown and W. R. Louis, eds., *Oxford History of the British Empire: The Twentieth Century* (Oxford, 1999), pp. 351–52.

[38] These are the words of Sir Gladwyn Jebb, himself a grandiloquent and self-assured representative of Britain at the United Nations in the early 1950s (Jebb to FO, Confidential, 13 February 1954, CO 936/319). On the other hand, Krishna Menon held a clear, intellectually vigorous, and consistent anti-colonial ideology that attracted a devoted band of followers. On his political thought, see Michael Brecher, *India and World Politics: Krishna Menon's View of the World* (London, 1968).

liberation of all colonies. The second assumption continued to prove all too true. Resolution 1514 quickly gained a momentum in which the 'double standard' seemed conspicuous.

The year 1960 was the critical juncture between the Suez crisis and the end of the British colonial era. In May, riots broke out in South Africa in the town of Sharpeville, leaving 69 dead and 180 injured. The Sharpeville massacre marked the beginning of the thirty-year international campaign against apartheid. In June the Belgians left the Congo. The tempestuous events of 'Congo chaos' proved to Sir Hilton Poynton and others in the Colonial Office the perils of premature independence. The Congo became a cockpit of the Cold War. In September, Nikita Khrushchev visited Turtle Bay. He was followed by Harold Macmillan. In deciding to reiterate the message of the 'Wind of Change' blowing through Africa (the theme of his speech delivered earlier in the year in Cape Town), Macmillan deviated from usual UN procedure. Instead of reading a verbatim text, he deployed to memorable effect the House of Commons technique of directly addressing his audience and making references to previous speakers. He demonstrated a spontaneous and devastating wit, reaching one of the peaks of his occasional comic genius. It occurred when Khrushchev banged on a desk with his shoe. Macmillan paused. He said he had not quite understood—could he please have a translation?[39] The General Assembly erupted into hilarity. Public Enemy Number One could be entertaining as well as courteous and unflappable, though Macmillan's inner thoughts as recorded in the archival records reveal an anguished soul.

By the end of the year, the number of new African states in the United Nations increased by seventeen members.[40] The Colonial Office felt the time had come to warn Colonial Governors of adverse international circumstances and the unprecedented menace in the shape of the United Nations. 'Recent events in Africa and in the U.N.', Poynton wrote in September 1960, 'have been forcing us to think about the role which the United Nations is likely to play in future in relation to British territories.' He mentioned the Algerian revolution

---

[39] Harold Macmillan, *Pointing the Way: 1959–1961* (London, 1972), p. 279. According to the assessment at the time by the British delegation at the United Nations, Macmillan's speech represented far and away 'the most effective expression of a Western political philosophy', which was eye-opening, curiously enough, to 'Mr. Khrushchev himself'—though probably as much because of Macmillan's oratorical skills as because of the content (Sir Patrick Dean to FO, Confidential and Guard [Guard = not for American eyes], 14 January 1961, FO 371/160877).

[40] The new African members were Cameroon, the Central African Republic, Chad, the former Belgian Congo, the former French Congo, Dahomey, Gabon, the Ivory Coast, Madagascar, Senegal, Mali, Mauritania, Niger, Nigeria, Somalia, Togo, and Upper Volta. Cyprus also joined the United Nations in 1960.

as well as the Sharpeville massacre and the disaster in the Congo. He emphasized the changing 'international climate'. He believed the British themselves had consequently entered a period in which the United Nations would be 'a more decisive factor' in decolonization.[41] Poynton wrote only a few weeks before the passage of Resolution 1514, which echoed Khrushchev's demand for colonial liberation. The Russians helped sponsor the resolution, but the Africans themselves were now in full voice. According to another Colonial Office official: 'The Russians no longer need to push the band wagon, it rolls on without them.'[42]

Having resolved to end colonialism, the General Assembly in 1961 created what became known initially as the Committee of 17.[43] In the next year the Colonial Office, with considerable alarm, saw its membership increase to become the Committee of 24.[44] Though the British were represented, their frustration was palpable. The committee became famous in the history of the United Nations for its persistent, voluble, and impassioned attacks on the Western colonial powers, especially Britain. To the Colonial Office, it was, in Christopher's Eastwood's phrase, 'an infernal nuisance'.[45] It could become an outright danger by dispatching visiting missions that would whip up anti-British nationalism. Eastwood warned in January 1961 that 'colonialism' was now 'in the mainstream of United Nations affairs' and that colonies 'have become an international issue in a sense which they have not been hitherto'.[46] Later in the same year he wrote that there

[41] Poynton circular to Colonial Governors, 29 September 1960, *BDEEP—Conservative Government*, II, #405.

[42] Minute by D. J. Derx, 31 October 1963, CO 936/922. On the assumption that the members of the United Nations would sympathize with an animal that defended itself rather than submitting passively to slander, the British from time to time replied in kind to the Russians, pointing out the geographical and other circumstances of the Soviet empire. Much to their surprise, the British discovered that the Russians were taken aback: they were not used to being denounced as colonialists. 'The Russians have shown themselves to be pretty sensitive,' Patrick Dean wrote in December 1962 (Dean to FO, Confidential, 1 December 1962, FO 371/166842). On the other hand, the British did not carry the assault of 'pinpricks' too far, for reasons concerning China as well as the Soviet Union. According to the Governor of Hong Kong: 'If the Chinese are needled over Colonies, there is a possible danger of provoking them into some kind of action over Hong Kong' (Robin Black to J. D. Higham, Secret and Personal, 14 June 1963, CO 936/921).

[43] The seventeen original members of the Special Committee on Colonialism, created in November 1961, were Australia, Britain, Cambodia, India, Italy, Madagascar, Mali, Poland, the Soviet Union, Syria, Tanganyika, Tunisia, Syria, the United States, Uruguay, Venezuela, and Yugoslavia.

[44] The additional members were Bulgaria, Chile, Denmark, Iran, Iraq, the Ivory Coast, and Sierra Leone.

[45] Minute by Eastwood, 20 September 1963, CO 936/921.

[46] Eastwood to Sir Andrew Cohen, Confidential, 10 January 1961, FO 371/160902.

would be 'a harder and more sustained onslaught against the colonial powers' than ever before.[47]

It is useful to study briefly Eastwood's views on the Committee of 17 (or 24) because his association with the trusteeship issue went back to the early days of the Second World War.[48] In many ways he represented the best of the Colonial Office civil servants. He was respected for his intellect, his candour, and his willingness to take on difficult assignments.[49] By contrast with the rigid and uncompromising attitude of Poynton, Eastwood's temperament was accommodating and flexible. He held views in advance of his time; for example, as early as the wartime period he believed as a matter of principle that all 'races', or peoples, of the British Empire should be treated as equals. He tried to advance the cause of colonial subjects throughout the world. But his attitude towards the aim of the Committee of 24 to bring about immediate independence was unyielding: 'We must be the best judges of the pace of advance.'[50] Like many of his colleagues in the Colonial Office, Eastwood saw advantages to simply withdrawing from the Committee of 24 and leaving the discussion to evaporate in its own hot air at Turtle Bay; on the other hand, he respected the British commitment to world peace. As long as the United Nations remained one of Britain's principal obligations in international affairs, then the British delegation felt compelled to support all of its activities—even though the Colonial Office viewed the Committee of 24 as obnoxious. Loyalty to the higher purpose of the United Nations thus overrode the urge to walk out.

Only with great reluctance did Sir Hilton Poynton concede that the advantages of remaining in the Committee outweighed those of leaving it. Poynton's ideas, like Eastwood's, are of general interest, but for a different reason. Poynton perhaps more than anyone else embodied the official mind of the Colonial Office—in a specific sense. Passed on from one generation of officials to the next, the collective memory of the Colonial Office as an institution extended back to the eighteenth century. To Poynton, the consequences of the War of American Independence had led indirectly to the Committee of 24 because the

---

[47] Minute by Eastwood, 5 September 1961, CO 936/686.

[48] See Louis, *Imperialism at Bay,* especially chap. 6. Eastwood, among other things, was an acute observer of US aims in the colonial world. For example, he wrote in 1943: 'The Americans are quite ready to make their dependencies politically "independent" while economically bound hand and foot to them and see no inconsistency in this' (ibid., p. 247).

[49] The Eastwood Papers in Rhodes House, Oxford (MSS Brit. Empire. S. 509), contain records and diaries of his trips to various parts of the colonial empire together with a few reflective letters to Sir John Martin and others.

[50] Minute by Eastwood, 5 March 1965, CO 936/927.

Americans drew a false connection between their own anti-colonial heritage and the anti-colonial movement of the 1960s:

> The American War of Independence . . . was not a national up-rising of an indigenous population seeking independence from an alien occupying or protecting power. It was an up-rising of emigrants demanding independence from the Government of the Mother Country from which they had emigrated.

> Consequentially although Americans often invoke it in explanation of their traditional anti-colonial attitude it has no relevance whatsoever to the modern problem of building nations with indigenous populations.[51]

This curious historical lesson bore directly on the problem of American behaviour in the United Nations. Only the Americans had possessed sufficient influence to block the creation of the Committee of 24, and they were complicit in its birth, even if not in all its activities. If they could be made to see the error of the historical analogy, it might at least help instil some common sense into the Americans about the future task in Africa:

> The modern analogy would be an up-rising of Kenya or Rhodesian settlers to shake off control from London and I doubt whether the modern American would rally to this cause with the same enthusiasm as that with which his ancestors rallied to General Washington.[52]

From the vantage point of the British delegation in New York, the drift of such ideas had a certain absurdity. Sir Hugh Foot summed it up by writing of an anti-American, anti-United Nations bias at the Colonial Office: 'Poynton in particular seems entirely obsessed by the need to resist any attempt by people at the U.N. to interest themselves in British colonial affairs.'[53]

Sir Hugh Foot—elevated to the peerage in 1964 as Lord Caradon —was a former Colonial Governor who believed passionately and

---

[51] Minute by Poynton, 6 April 1962, CO 936/726.

[52] Ibid. Poynton was irrepressible. The lesson of the American Revolution, he believed, was that the Americans knew how to run their country: 'It is quite a different problem from trying to form a suitable government in a country like Uganda or Kenya. Thomas Jefferson is a rather different article from Thomas Mboya.'

[53] Foot to Dean, Confidential, 16 March 1962, FO 371/166822. The sentiment was mutual. 'With Sir Hugh Foot at the helm', Poynton once wrote, there would be all the more need for 'firmness' on the part of the Colonial Office (minute by Poynton, 7 February 1961, CO 936/679).

indefatigably in the cause of the United Nations. In the 1960s, the term 'Caradonian' came to signify total commitment to peace and decolonization. He came from a family of devout Christian outlook, tempered by philosophical radicalism. His brothers included the lawyer Dingle and the Labour politician Michael. He served in Palestine and Nigeria before becoming Governor of Jamaica (1951–57) and then Governor of Cyprus (1957–60).[54] In July 1961, after some thirty years in the colonial service, he succeeded Sir Andrew Cohen (another Colonial Governor) as British representative on the Trusteeship Council.[55] Foot was a man of good will and indestructible optimism. He would reply point by point to the allegations and denigrations of British motives by the Committee of 24, believing that every opportunity should be taken to establish the accuracy of the colonial record, of which the British had every right to be proud and not ashamed. In October 1962 he resigned over the Rhodesian issue, a decision that revealed his uncompromising commitment, in his own phrase, to African freedom. He stayed on at the United Nations to guide its development programme. In 1964 the Harold Wilson government appointed him Ambassador to the United Nations. He now rejoined the battle against the Committee of 24. He described his own determined tactic in Churchillian rhetoric: We shall fight on the resolutions. We shall fight in the corridors. We shall fight in the Committees. We shall never abstain.[56]

Sir Hugh Foot won the confidence of the US delegation and gained the respect of the Africans and other anti-colonialists by speaking to them without condescension. He also struck up a close friendship with

[54] See his autobiography, *A Start in Freedom* (London, 1964). The Foot (Caradon) Papers at Rhodes House, Oxford, contain documents relating only to Cyprus, but there are many examples of the principles that sustained him through his official career. For example, his friend (Sir) Eugene Melville in the Colonial Office wrote to him of the idealism of Milner: 'It helps to know that the cause is just and the motive unselfish and that, in the end, we shall come through all right' (Melville to Foot, Personal, 10 November 1958, Foot Papers, Box 8, MSS. Medit. S 25.)

[55] Cohen had been responsible for reshaping and modernizing British colonial policy in West Africa after the Second World War, and then became Governor of Uganda before his assignment to the United Nations (1957–60). The calibre of such men as Cohen and Foot is an indication of the importance the British government attached to the colonial problem in New York. On Cohen, see especially the entry by R. E. Robinson in the *Dictionary of National Biography, 1961–1970.*

[56] The Churchillian phrases are a paraphrase of Foot's 'tailpiece' summing up his outlook in his memorandum of 27 December 1961, *BDEEP— Conservative Government,* II, #409. According to Denis Greenhill (Permanent Under-Secretary at the Foreign and Commonwealth Office, 1969–73): 'He was a compelling speaker and was a major figure in the United Nations in New York to the benefit of the British reputation particularly in the Third World' (Greenhill, *More by Accident* [Bishop Wilton, UK, 1992], p. 112).

Ralph Bunche in the UN Secretariat.[57] But one of the problems of the United Nations after the death of Hammarskjöld in 1961 was the quality of leadership of the Secretary-General, U Thant, and of the US Ambassador, Adlai Stevenson.[58] And just as the UN Secretariat could do very little to curtail the extremism of the Committee of 24, so the American delegation seemed paralyzed because of what the British described as 'the revolt of the American negro'. Against the background and 'shocking impact' of 'dogs and fire hoses being turned on negro demonstrators', the members of the American delegation found it difficult to stand up to African nationalists. 'I regret', wrote Denis Greenhill of the British Embassy in Washington in 1963, 'that the present racial crisis has taken some of the stuffing out of the [US] Administration's will to resist African nationalist demands.'[59]

On the other hand, the British found active support in the middle ranks of the State Department and other parts of the bureaucracy in Washington. The inspiration of the British District Officer in Africa and elsewhere was apparent in the younger members of the Kennedy administration. The idealism and the 'same uncritical faith and hope' that had originally inspired the League of Nations spilled over into the Peace Corps of the 1960s. On issues affecting the British Empire, wrote the British Colonial Attaché in Washington, the Kennedy administration 'is shot through with a fundamental goodwill towards us'.[60] So it remained, more or less, in the LBJ era, but the American 'endemic naivety towards the Africans' began to wear off in the face of the onslaught of the Committee of 24, which from time to time could be as hostile to the United States as to Britain.[61] The Americans had helped the Africans along the path towards independence but now felt 'the

---

[57] For Bunche and Foot, see Brian Urquhart, *Ralph Bunche: An American Life* (New York, 1993), pp. 425 and 429. The FO Personalities Report noted that 'Dr. Bunche now wears a slightly melancholy air, and seems to lack some of the energy which he showed in earlier years' ('Leading Personalities in the United Nations', Confidential, 10 June 1959, FO 371/145243).

[58] The British delegation's assessment of U Thant was mixed: 'U Thant has not Mr. Hammarskjöld's intellect nor is he the dynamo that Mr. Hammarskjöld was. Unfortunately, he is not a very much better organizer. But he is a quiet, sensible, friendly man of great courage' (Dean to FO, Confidential, 25 January 1963, FO 371/172548). Sir Patrick Dean wrote of Stevenson: 'I acknowledge with respect his brilliance, his charm and his political experience and prestige, but even if he were ten years younger I doubt if he would be the right man to lead the United States delegation. As things are, he is not up to it; nor is he really interested. He gives the impression of disillusionment and lack of knowledge, and in negotiations he finds it impossible to get down to details or to stand firm' (Dean to FO, Confidential and Guard, 30 July 1963, FO 371/172634).

[59] Greenhill to FO, Confidential, 16 August 1963, FO 371/172634.

[60] J. D. Hennings to David Jerrom, Secret, 24 April 1962, CO 936/664.

[61] Dean to FO, Confidential and Guard, 30 July 1963, FO 371/172634.

sharp knife of ingratitude'.[62] Their patience, like that of the British, began to wear thin. As for Public Enemy Number One, enough was enough. It was time for a tougher line.

The British Revolt against the Committee of 24

'KEEP OFF THE GRASS', according to one observer of the Colonial Office attitude towards the United Nations, would be a good way to sum up the traditional outlook.[63] The Colonial Office had seen its position deteriorate, however, to the point of accepting visiting missions not merely to trust territories but also to other British dependencies, even though there was real enough risk of bloodshed. To some extent, the later stages of this development can be traced to Lord Caradon (Sir Hugh Foot). His energetic and persuasive tactics carried considerable weight within the British government. But the erosion of the Colonial Office position also reflected the dominance of the Foreign Office as well as the general consensus in official circles on the relationship between the United Nations and the British colonial empire. Caradon, for example, always held that Britain could not share or shift responsibility for the administration of colonial territories. But he nevertheless believed that the British should cooperate with the United Nations to the fullest extent possible, for reasons pragmatic and otherwise. Only by remaining on good terms with the United Nations in general could the British hope to minimize interference in the colonies, where tensions would continue to mount. He wrote in 1965: 'We are no doubt in for a very rough time in the United Nations this year since we shall not be able to move in the directions which the Afro-Asians wish on southern Africa, questions on which they feel intensely.'[64]

The anti-colonialists aimed increasingly at overthrowing the South African government, liquidating the Portuguese empire, and (after the declaration of unilateral independence by Southern Rhodesia in 1965) liberating Africans held in the grip of the Rhodesian white

[62] Benjamin Gerig, one of the central figures on the American side of the trusteeship issue, used this phrase several times in conversations with me in the early 1970s. For Gerig, see Louis, *Imperialism at Bay*, p. 91.

[63] Cecil King of the British delegation in New York to FO, Confidential, 26 September 1963, FO 371/72600. Ironically enough, the phrase 'keep off the grass' was the same one used by Lord Linlithgow, Viceroy of India, during the early part of the Second World War to warn the Americans not to interfere in India. See W. R. Louis, 'British Imperialism and the Partitions of India and Palestine', in Chris Wrigley, ed., *Warfare Diplomacy and Politics: Essays in Honour of A. J. P. Taylor* (London, 1986), p. 198.

[64] Caradon to Secretary of State for the Colonies, Confidential, 10 March 1965, CO 936/927.

settlers. A majority on the Committee of 24 embodied those ambitions. Caradon hoped to blunt the attack and to mediate. But the Committee would not be appeased. By early 1966 the Permanent Under-Secretary at the Foreign Office, Sir Paul Gore-Booth, believed the Committee to be so dishonest and dangerous that it was a disgrace for Britain to be associated with it any longer. He moved towards withdrawal, thus endorsing the position of the majority in the Colonial Office, but he thereby brought into play the larger issue of Britain's relations with the United Nations. The decision in 1966 was to soldier on with the Committee of 24, but in late 1967 Gore-Booth returned to the charge.

The problem was that the Committee of 24 was obsessed—in the British view, to a psychotic degree—with decolonization. As if reverting to an explanation that had endured since the late nineteenth century, the British believed that fundamental trouble in Asia and Africa could usually be traced to the French. At the centre of the ideological drive of the Committee of 24 stood the Tunisians. They viewed the worldwide quest for national liberation as a mirror reflection of the Tunisian and Algerian struggles against France. The Tunisians 'enjoy twisting our tail', according to Sir Herbert Marchant, the British Ambassador in Tunisia; but the fixation also revealed 'a national state of mind':

> For the last thirty years they have been engaged in an unhappy fight against the French. There have been some ugly incidents which have not reflected much glory on the colonialist power in question and they have had a ringside seat for the seven years' war in Algeria, where things have been even less savoury.

> Against this background British military bases, be they in Gibraltar, Malta, Cyprus, in the Middle East or in South East Asia, bear a strong resemblance in Tunisian eyes to French troops in Bizerta. They see in any country that has not yet got complete independence the image of themselves fighting their way to freedom—however dissimilar the cases may be. The whole emotional background makes this, I think, inevitable—and we are dealing with emotion rather than reason.[65]

---

[65] Marchant to Falle, Confidential, 10 February 1964, FO 371/178179. Marchant continued to explain the reasons for the Tunisian obsession with decolonization: 'This is a small country headed up by a number of physically small people—all of them full of bounce. Most have had a French education and on Arab and African standards are more than usually able. Perhaps it is because they are conscious of their superiority in their own continent that they are a little over anxious to cut a figure in the "big league" as well.' Marchant later became the British representative on the UN Committee for the Elimination of Racial Discrimination.

Within the committee, to give only a partial example, the Tunisians and Iraqis were cheered on by the Bulgarians and Poles while the Chileans and Venezuelans usually added their applause. The British could rely on firm support only from the Australians and the Danes, but, alas, the stalwart Danes eventually withdrew from the committee. Within a single year, 1963, the committee discussed Southern Rhodesia, Aden, Malta, Fiji, British Guiana, Kenya, Northern Rhodesia, Nyasaland, Zanzibar, Basutoland, Bechuanaland, Swaziland, Gibraltar, and the Gambia. One of their resolutions called for immediate independence for the Gambia.[66] On a much more serious note, they demanded visiting missions to, among other places, Aden, Fiji, and British Guiana, all of which had problems that could only be described, in the word of the Colonial Secretary, Reginald Maudling, as 'explosive'.[67]

'The wretched Committee of Twenty-Four', wrote David Jerrom, the head of the International Relations Department in the Colonial Office, had forced its way into a position of influence on all questions of decolonization. Here is a key passage from one of Jerrom's minutes on the extent to which international interference must be taken into account in the general process of decolonization:

> Many people still tend to look on the Committee as an anti-colonial pressure group divorced from the serious business of life. I think that this was a pretty sound view until the Committee took up Aden in 1963, since when *it has become a political factor of importance in all delicate colonial situations.*[68]

In Aden, British colonial officers could not but recall the visit, catastrophic in their view, by the United Nations Special Committee on Palestine in 1947. The Arabs had boycotted the mission, but the members of the Committee themselves prepared the way for a debate in the General Assembly and the end of the British mandate. In places such as Fiji or British Guiana, a visiting mission could easily upset, with violent results, the intricate ethnic balance between the indigenous inhabitants and immigrant populations. Visiting missions were thus, in Jerrom's phrase, the 'crux of the issue'.[69] What the Colonial Office

[66] See, for example, FO 371/178179 for very extensive documentation on the work of the committee.

[67] Minute by Maudling, 5 July 1962, FO 371/166829.

[68] Minute by Jerrom, 3 January 1964, CO 936/922 (emphasis added).

[69] Minute by Jerrom, 5 March 1965, CO 936/927. See also especially the minutes by A. N. Galsworthy, who emphasized not only 'a most unwelcome precedent for Rhodesia' but also '*the extreme danger*' of visiting missions in Basutoland and Mauritius as well as in Gibraltar, the Falklands, and British Honduras (minutes by Galsworthy, 29 and 30 June 1966, CO 936/960; emphasis

feared was that a visiting mission to Aden, for example, might set the precedent for another mission, this time to Southern Rhodesia.[70] Would the British thus not be shifting the very basis of colonial rule from one of accountability to Parliament to one of responsibility—in the Colonial Office phrase—to the motley international assembly? In such a way did the problem of visiting missions go to the heart of the British colonial system. It was an issue that had to be taken seriously in the Foreign Office, where the question of accountability ran in the direction of fulfilling the commitment to the United Nations.[71]

The counterpart of David Jerrom in the Foreign Office was Sam Falle, the head of the United Nations Department. Falle had extensive Middle East experience and was thus sensitive to the drift towards civil war in Aden. He had served in Iran, where he had formed close connections with MI6 and the CIA, and in Iraq, where he had been one of the few to predict the 1958 revolution. He viewed himself as a United Nations man, not quite a Caradonian, but one of Caradon's admirers.[72] Falle concurred in the Colonial Office's strongly held point that the Committee of 24 must not be allowed to dictate colonial policy. But he also agreed with Caradon on the enlightened nature of British colonial rule: '[I]f we have nothing in the colonies of which we are ashamed, we ought to welcome visits by United Nations bodies, to whom we could explain our problems.'[73] In the case of the Committee of 24, Falle proved to be far too optimistic, but it seemed to be a reasonable assumption that a UN visiting mission would be willing to listen and thus not take the extremist view echoed in the chambers of Turtle Bay. Falle also recognized that the Committee resembled, in the words of the British UN delegation, 'a whale stranded on a beach,

---

added). Galsworthy had a particular interest in the smaller territories of the colonial empire, and later (as High Commissioner to New Zealand) became Governor of Pitcairn.

[70] Aden and Rhodesia were the two principal preoccupations of the British delegation in New York: 'Aden, along with Southern Rhodesia, will be one of the main colonial crosses which we shall have to bear in the United Nations over the next few years' (Dean to FO, Confidential, 6 August 1963, FO 371/172591).

[71] This fundamental point was clearly expressed in a letter from Sir Leslie Monson (who had a long career in the Colonial Office and was High Commissioner in Zambia, 1964–66) to Percy Cradock, the head of the Planning Staff in the Foreign and Commonwealth Office (later Ambassador to China). Monson wrote: 'As an administrator I am conditioned to think primarily in terms of accountability to Parliament while you are more concerned naturally enough with accountability in the international sense under the UN Charter' (Monson to Craddock, 26 August 1971, FCO 49/322).

[72] See Sam Falle, *My Lucky Life in War, Revolution, Peace and Diplomacy* (Lewes, UK, 1996), p. 163: 'The idealistic Hugh Foot, Lord Caradon . . . really believed in what he was doing and some of his enthusiasm rubbed off.'

[73] Minute by Falle, 5 July 1963, FO 371/172591.

imposing in its bulk but helpless in action'.[74] In this view, it was better to let the Committee rot away or self-destruct rather than to declare war against a major body of the United Nations. This solution proved futile because of the Committee's own activist behaviour. Its members neither listened nor learned but took an increasingly theoretical or 'theological' view of British colonialism.

Sam Falle eventually became appalled at the violence of the rhetoric and the virulence of the personal insults, as did the Deputy Under-Secretary, Sir Martin Le Quesne. Falle prided himself on being thick-skinned, and his wartime service in the Royal Navy had made him about as tough as they came. But when he read of the experiences of Francis Brown, a member of the British UN delegation who had helped escort the Committee of 24 on its travels in Africa, he confessed to David Jerrom: 'Even after 3 1/2 years in this Department and the almost impenetrable hide I have grown during this time, this . . . brought tears to my eyes.'[75] In a similar vein, Le Quesne commented that the time had come to depart from the Committee of 24. Le Quesne, like Falle, had Middle East experience, but had also served as Ambassador to Mali and had become the Foreign Office's expert on radical African nationalism. He later served as Ambassador in Algeria. In retirement he achieved glory as Chairman of the Reform Club. At the time of the confrontation with the Committee of 24, he had definite ideas about gentlemanly behaviour and where to draw the line. He too commented on Francis Brown's experience with the Committee:

> The Committee's visit to Africa last year placed Mr. Brown in an intolerably difficult and embarrassing position, in which he conducted himself with superhuman patience and dignity. I do not believe, however, that, apart from such favourable impression as his display of British steadiness under fire may have created, he did us the slightest good so far as the question of securing understanding and sympathy for our problems and policies goes.[76]

Indignation began to mount from the middle ranks of the Foreign Office to the top. From early 1966 onwards the insults of the Committee

---

[74] Patrick Dean to FO, 6 August 1963, FO 371/172591. In another quirky judgement on the Committee, it was best to follow 'Confucius' advice to the girl about to be raped' (minute by C. W. Squire, 29 May 1963, FO 371/172591).

[75] Falle to Jerrom, Confidential, 8 June 1966, CO 936/959. For Brown's ordeal with the Committee, see also FO 371/189811. Brown had been educated at Wellington and at Trinity College, Cambridge, apparently good training against verbal assault and coarse behaviour.

[76] Minute by Le Quesne, 15 February 1966, FO 371/189811.

of the 24 began to catch the attention of the Permanent Under-Secretary, Sir Paul Gore-Booth.

Gore-Booth held strong convictions about the purpose of the United Nations. He had participated in its planning during the Second World War while at the British Embassy in Washington. He had attended the San Francisco conference in 1945. He viewed the Committee of 24 not only as a caricature of the United Nations but also as being at variance with his own sense of civilized international society. He had developed a set of ethics based on Christian Science, though with a detectible Eton and Balliol influence. His career had embraced long periods in Asia and other parts of the world. His early posts, before the Second World War, had included Japan, and he had learned Japanese. As Ambassador to Burma during the early 1950s, he (and his wife) had adopted the daughter of the assassinated nationalist leader Aung Sang (Suu Kyi Aung San, the Nobel Peace Prize winner and present-day Burmese prisoner of conscience). In India as High Commissioner a decade later, he had been treated with great respect by Nehru, in part because Nehru knew that he had opposed the Suez expedition. Gore-Booth became Permanent Under-Secretary in 1965, at about the time that Sam Falle began to write, by implication at least, of the moral obliquity of the Committee of 24. In February 1966, Falle recorded such acts as encouraging hostile petitioners, drumming up extremist groups, and calling for violence.[77] Gore-Booth at this stage noted that the British should either walk out of the Committee or themselves become more aggressive: 'The time for quiet reasonableness has passed.'[78]

Despite Gore-Booth's nudge towards withdrawal, the move to terminate Britain's connection with the Committee of 24 made no progress during the rest of the year. In a pattern that would recur, the combination of Lord Caradon and Eirene White, the Minister of State, prevailed over the United Nations Department and the Deputy Under-Secretary, Sir Denis Greenhill, as well as Gore-Booth. Sam Falle wrote in July 1966: 'As a determined U.N. man I am in favour of entering the ring on every possible occasion and defending our policy with vigour.' But Falle was also impressed with the 'violence of the debates' as well as the radical dissidence and 'inverse racism' affecting the United Nations itself. Falle therefore recommended withdrawal.[79]

[77] See, for example, minute by Falle, 14 February 1966, FO 371/189811.

[78] Minute by Gore-Booth, 15 February 1966, FO 371/189811. In Gore-Booth's autobiography, *With Great Truth and Respect* (London, 1974), he does not dwell especially on the United Nations, but see p. 160.

[79] Minute by Falle, 13 July 1966, FO 371/189814.

The advice did not commend itself to Lord Caradon, who held the rank of Minister of State as well as Ambassador to the United Nations. At the ministerial level of the Foreign Office, he effectively argued that withdrawal would be interpreted as a 'complete reversal' of British policy of cooperation with the United Nations on one of its most important missions—decolonization, the mission that affected the British most directly. This point had ramifications for Parliament as well as the British public. Here the influence of Eirene White, another Minister of State, was significant, since she too was passionately committed to the United Nations, though not so much as Caradon.[80] To her and Caradon, the act of withdrawal would stand symbolically as Britain reverting to true form—at least in the eyes of the enemies of British imperialism—to the Britain of Anthony Eden and the invasion of Egypt. So powerful was the memory of the recent past that no Labour Government could endorse a proposal that seemed to reverse course and re-establish Britain as a reactionary power. The British would take a tougher line with the Committee and 'soldier on', not withdraw.[81]

The Aden Mission and the Decision to Leave the Committee of 24

The debate on whether to abandon the Committee of 24 to its own fate took place against the background of a crisis within the United Nations and civil war in Aden. So severe was the UN budgetary shortfall in the mid-1960s that the organization itself was in peril. So desperate was the situation in Southern Arabia that the Foreign Office, and to some extent even the Colonial Office, began to think that the only way to provide any type of post-colonial stability would be through the United Nations. Here, then, were two further reasons not to leave the Committee of 24 to stew in its own juice. Desertion in a moment of financial crisis would further weaken the United Nations itself, and Britain could hardly strike with one hand while holding out the other for assistance.[82]

---

[80] Eirene White (later Baroness White) was the daughter of Thomas Jones, the aide to Lloyd George. She knew the history of the Committee of 24 because she had served as Parliamentary Secretary in the Colonial Office (1964–66) before becoming Minister of State at the Foreign Office (1966–67); but like Caradon, she consistently saw the problem of the Committee as subordinate to the larger issue of Britain's relations with the United Nations.

[81] The reasoning is laid out in Greenhill to Sir Roger Jackling, Confidential, 26 August 1966, CO 936/979.

[82] Eirene White had written while at the Colonial Office: 'The major troubles of the General Assembly cannot be cured by us, but the current danger of U.N. collapse makes it all the more necessary that, even in small ways, the United Kingdom should be seen to be supporting the ideals of international co-operation by deeds as well as words' (minute of 10 March 1965, CO 936/927).

The agony of the Foreign and Colonial Offices in making the decision to turn to Turtle Bay can be seen in these lines written by Sam Falle. Bringing in the United Nations would not only acknowledge British failure in Aden but would also remind the world of the disaster in Palestine two decades earlier:

> It might be argued that this is an ignominious scuttle, but since the alternative seems to be to maintain . . . a ramshackle, disunited and probably unviable South Arabian state, at great cost to the British taxpayer, there seems to be some advantage in swallowing our pride . . .
>
> This has, I admit, a nasty whiff of the Palestine scuttle about it . . . but it seems better to make an honest break now rather than to persist in setting up a Federation, which we know is going to fall to bits.[83]

The phrases 'ignominious scuttle' and 'United Nations involvement' evoked heart-wrenching emotions about where the British were in the world, where they did not want to be, and where they stood in the Middle East in relation to the United Nations. The intensity of these sentiments was captured in a few lines by one of the most experienced of the Middle East hands, Sir Roger Allen, who had served as Ambassador in Turkey, Greece, and Iraq. Allen wrote in despair:

> The United Nations has done nothing so far except make our task in Aden very much harder . . . Naturally, not all the members of the United Nations are hell-bent on this course, but I think that the majority would still be prepared to follow the lead of the extremists . . .
>
> If we were to bring in the United Nations . . . we should be likely to confirm the fears of our friends in the Middle East that we were simply scuttling out. I simply cannot believe that this would result in a change of heart by the United Nations, and a kind of idyllic period of peace and cooperation instead of vituperation and troublemaking.[84]

Sir Denis Greenhill, the Deputy Under-Secretary, intervened at this point to override Allen and others. Greenhill believed that a post-

---

On the fiscal woes of the United Nations, see especially the memorandum by Ralph Bunche for President Johnson, 2 February 1965, *Foreign Relations of the United States, 1964–1968*, XXXIII, pp. 724–29. LBJ recognized the seriousness of the crisis, commenting a few days later, 'I got a very distressing memo from Bunche.' He gave instructions to tell Bunche 'I'm as distressed as he is' (ibid., p. 733).

[83] Minute by Falle, 14 January 1966, FO 371/185180.

[84] Minute by Allen, 17 January 1966, FO 371/185180.

colonial state created by the British would be regarded by the rest of the world as a puppet.[85] The sooner the United Nations could be brought in to help give legitimacy to the successor state and stabilize it, the better. There would thus be a substantial UN civil and military presence during and after the British withdrawal.

In fact, the project of involving the United Nations in the post-colonial state came to nothing. But it was in this broader setting that the British agreed to a visiting mission by the Committee of 24. The call for a mission arose from a resolution of the Committee during a visit by some of its members to Cairo in June 1966.[86] In submitting to the request, the British were well aware that the significance of the problem extended beyond the United Nations and the Middle East. Egyptian subversion (or liberation, depending on one's point of view) in Aden now ranked in the same category as revolution in Vietnam, not only in the eyes of the Committee of 24, but also in the assessments of the US government. Earlier in the year, the Foreign Office had learned that Walt Rostow, the National Security Adviser in the Johnson administration, regarded the struggle in Aden as 'a national liberation war'. Though Aden could not be compared in size to Vietnam, it presented to the British 'the same kind of problem . . . as

[85] 'It would be open to the same sort of attacks, and with greater reason, as were directed against the Nuri régime in Iraq' (minute by Greenhill, 18 January 1966, FO 371/185178).

[86] It is useful to view the work of the Committee in relation to the agenda of the British delegation at the United Nations in order to keep the Aden mission in perspective and to bear in mind the changing nature of the United Nations itself towards ever-smaller states. Here is the calendar of some of the issues concerning colonial and post-colonial matters arising at the United Nations in the summer and autumn of 1966:

11–17 June	Committee of 24 sitting in Cairo calls for Visiting Mission to Aden.
17–22 June	Committee of 24 meets in Algiers.
18 July	International Court of Justice delivers judgement in the South-West Africa case.
1 August	Britain announces readiness to co-operate with a UN Mission to Aden.
4–16 August	Security Council meets on South Arabia.
20 September	Guyana (British Guiana) admitted to United Nations.
30 September	Security Council meets on Congo.
17 October	Botswana and Lesotho admitted to United Nations.
27 October	General Assembly adopts resolution on South-West Africa, terminating the mandate.
8–16 December	Security Council meets on question of Southern Rhodesia.
9 December	Barbados admitted to United Nations.
12 December	General Assembly requests Secretary-General to appoint immediately a special United Nations Mission to Aden.

These events follow the calendar in Caradon to FCO, Confidential, 6 January 1967, FCO 58/9.

Vietnam was for the United States Government'.[87] The British retorted that Aden was a colonial issue that would be resolved one way
or another, by independence or British withdrawal. But everyone
was aware that the mid-1960s was the era of Vietnam. Partly because
of the shadow of South-East Asia, but also because of the hostile, anti-
imperial spirit of the 1960s, the popularity of the British Empire
reached its nadir in Aden. As for the South-East Asian comparison,
the war in Southern Arabia turned out to be Nasser's Vietnam, not
Britain's.

To prepare the way for the visiting mission, Caradon wrote to the
High Commissioner in Aden, Sir Richard Turnbull. They were about
the same age (Caradon born 1907, Turnbull, 1909), and their careers
had marched in parallel, though with Turnbull tilling the soil of East
African self-government rather than emerging on the world stage. He
had worked his way up from District Officer in Kenya to Governor in
Tanganyika, 1959–61. His accelerated timetable for Tanganyikan independence and his good relations with Julius Nyerere provided for
one of the most successful transitions from colony to new African
state.[88] Turnbull was tough-minded, realistic, and willing to take risks;
but his virtues as an administrator in Africa did not necessarily translate into the skills required in the Middle East. He was cut from the authoritarian mould of Colonial Governor. Delegations from the United
Nations were not to his taste. But, he wrote to Caradon, he would do
his best:

> Everything now depends on the quality of the Mission. If it is co-
> operative and is genuinely seeking a solution all should go well. If it
> is cantankerous and difficult we shall still do our best; most of us here
> are old Colonial Civil Servants and have become accustomed to the
> current notion that nothing that the British do can conceivably be
> right.

> But if the Mission is so composed that it is likely to decide that it can
> have no truck with the 'unrepresentative Federal Government' it can
> cause nothing but the greatest damage.[89]

---

[87] C. H. D. Everett to FO, 9 April 1967, FO 961/30. 'It is typical of Rostow to take so wholehearted a view of a problem,' Everett commented. (FO 961 = records of the British delegation
at the United Nations. The Aden files are one of the few sets to have been preserved.)

[88] 'Turnbull in Tanganyika was widely recognised as a powerful and robust figure, performing for East African decolonisation a role comparable with that of Sir Charles Arden-Clarke ten
years earlier for West Africa' (Ronald Hyam in *BDEEP— Conservative Government,* I, p. xxi.

[89] Turnbull to Caradon, Confidential and Personal, 12 January 1967, FO 961/33.

Turnbull had placed his finger on the heart of the matter even before the arrival of the mission. As it transpired, the mission refused to deal with the British colonial state—known in Aden as the Federal government because of the unification of the port of Aden and the tribal hinterlands into a federation.

The short and unhappy history of the mission can be related briefly. Its chairman was Manuel Perez-Guerrero of Venezuela. Adbussattar Shalizi of Afghanistan and Moussa Leo Keita of Mali were the other two members. Perez-Guerrero was suspect in British eyes because he was on friendly terms with Nasser. Shalizi was the former Deputy Prime Minister of Afghanistan, whom Caradon had worked hard to get on the Committee as a moderate. Keita had the reputation of being a gentle and reserved man, but turned out to be an ideologue. The member of the British UN delegation who accompanied the mission was Peter Hope, whose background included Cambridge University, a distinguished war record, even service as Consul-General in Houston, Texas. He would later become Ambassador to Mexico.[90] All of his resources of tact and ingenuity were put to the test in Aden in 1967.

The mission arrived in Aden on 7 April but stayed only four days.[91] The beginning was not auspicious. Perez-Guerrero, Shalizi, and Keita were greeted by an unprecedented storm, which sent four feet of water pouring through the streets. All means of communications, including airstrips, became unusable. The fierce floodwaters burst open graves in the graveyards. Some 10,000 people were made homeless. The members of the mission then encountered a general strike, protesting their visit.[92] As if in a page of dark comedy—or in any event, in an egregious miscalculation—the two major contenders for power in Aden, the Front for the Liberation of Occupied South Yemen (FLOSY) and the National Liberation Front (NLF), regarded the UN trio as British stooges and refused to make contact. For their part, the members of the UN mission were committed to the ideological view of the Committee of 24 that the British or Federal jails were worse than Hitler's death camps. Therein lay the supreme irony: both the NLF and FLOSY regarded the UN visiting mission as a tool of British imperialism.

In its intensity, the anti-colonial sentiment of the Aden civil war

[90] Hope was knighted in 1972, the same year in which the Mexican government awarded him the Order of the Aztec Eagle, its highest recognition of a foreign citizen.

[91] See King-yuh Chang, 'The United Nations and Decolonization: The Case of Southern Yemen', *International Organization*, 26, 1 (Winter 1972); see also Sankey, 'Decolonisation at the UN', pp. 104-05.

[92] Memorandum by Peter Hope, 19 April 1967, FO 961/36.

resembled that of the Algerian revolution. In the spring of 1967 the
outcome was still uncertain, but it was clear that the British were fighting a rearguard action in a civil war that was acquiring a Cold War as
well as a regional dimension. The National Liberation Front, founded
in 1963, eventually acquired support from the Soviet Union. FLOSY,
created two years later, was sponsored by Egypt, and Nasser's rhetoric
soared to the level of his anti-British denunciations in 1956. In this
internecine struggle, the United Nations appeared to be irrelevant as
NLF and FLOSY gunmen battled for control of the streets in Aden
Town. The members of the UN mission, however, continued to regard
the Federal government as the source of all trouble. Faced on the one
hand with a boycott by the NLF and FLOSY, and on the other with
their own self-imposed embargo on the Federal government, they had
no one to talk to other than their ideological enemies, the British colonial officers.

Perez-Guerrero, Shalizi, and Keita found the security arrangements
oppressive. Their hotel, the Sea View, was surrounded by barbed wire
and machine-gun posts, reminiscent of the 'Bevingrads' in British Palestine. They left their hotel only twice. To the British colonial officers, they seemed to lack courage. In any event, they were not able to
make contact with terrorist suspects detained by the British or with
any of the FLOSY or NLF leaders. When they met with the High Commissioner, there was no meeting of the minds.[93] Turnbull had written
earlier that he hoped 'to woo them into a co-operative frame of mind
and get some realistic and practicable proposals out of them'.[94] He
was now flummoxed by their 'theoretical' and 'theological' responses.
Turnbull formed an exceedingly low opinion of the mission.[95] He
wrote afterwards in scathing self-mockery of his failure to talk sense to
the mission, describing his own written note of the encounter as 'a sad
record of ineffective flattery, futile sucking-up and quite unproductive
self-abasement.'[96]

[93] Perhaps the circumstances were not conducive to bonhomie, but the members of the mission were not invited, as far as I have been able to ascertain, to meet Turnbull's parrot, which
had been taught to swear before repeating the Lord's Prayer; see *BDEEP—Conservative Government*, I, p. xxi.

[94] Turnbull to Caradon, Confidential and Personal, 12 January 1967, FO 961/33.

[95] See his record of the meeting of 3 April 1967, written in formal and polite language but
seething with contempt for the mission members' ideological blinkers (FO 961/37).

[96] Turnbull to Donal McCarthy, Confidential, 11 April 1967, FO 961/37. Turnbull's infelici-
tous handling of the mission provoked Patrick Gordon-Walker (the Labour politician first appointed as Foreign Secretary in the Wilson government of 1964 and who then failed to win a seat
in the 1964 election and failed again to win two subsequent by-elections) to denounce Turnbull
for 'carrying out Tory policy of submerging the Aden people in the Federal proposals' and failing to demonstrate any originality in devising a solution: 'Perhaps it was too much to ask of him

The members of the mission thought they had been poorly treated by the British colonial administration and still worse by the Federal government. They took only one initiative, an abortive television broadcast, the purpose of which, according to Peter Hope, was 'to smoke out the leaders of the N.L.F. and FLOSY'. The Federal authorities, however, found the broadcast offensive and cancelled it, thus precipitating the end of the mission. Perez-Guerrero, Shalizi, and Keita departed, according to Hope, after an unceremonious encounter with British journalists, who used 'much heated and unparliamentary language'. Before leaving, a memorable exchange took place between Hope and Moussa Keita, who had established himself as the embodiment of the 'theological obsession' of the Committee of 24. Keita reproached Hope for, among other things, unsatisfactory transportation arrangements. Hope reminded him of the not inconsiderable difficulty of being caught in machine-gun fire between FLOSY and the NLF. Keita answered, in truly philosophical fashion, that since the British had invaded Aden in the first place, 'it was our fault that there was fighting'.[97]

After his return to New York, Peter Hope had a conversation with Ralph Bunche about 'the obvious failure of the mission'.[98] Bunche's mind raced back to the British withdrawal in Palestine and then forward to his premonitions that Aden might erupt into another Congo crisis.[99] He did not mince words about the cowardly behaviour of the mission, nor did he conceal depressing and anxious thoughts:

> Bunche commented that he thought the Mission had turned out to be craven (the word he used). They had either been craven physically or craven intellectually. They had shown no vigour. If Perez-Guerrero had been a rugged leader he would have gone at once to

---

after 32 years in East Africa and many years of dealing with Mau Mau.' In Gordon-Walker's judgement, Turnbull's bias and incompetence had contributed to the failure of the mission: 'Sir Richard carried his opposition to U.N. intervention into his dealings with the U.N.O. Mission when it actually went to Aden and showed himself incapable of taking effective action in admittedly difficult circumstances.' (See S. R. Ashton and W. R. Louis, eds., *BDEEP: East of Suez and the Commonwealth, 1964–1971* [3 vols., London, 2004], #64.) Turnbull was recalled a few weeks later.

[97] The fullest and certainly the most candid account of the mission is Hope's memorandum of 19 April 1967, FO 961/36. For a more benevolent view of the mission, see King-yuh Chang, 'The United Nations and Decolonization'.

[98] Minute by Hope, 26 April 1967, FO 961/36. It was Hope, rather than Caradon, who saw Bunche, because of Caradon's absence from New York. (Brian Urquhart of the UN Office of Special Political Affairs was also at the meeting.) Caradon always paid warm tribute to the efforts of his staff, and on this occasion wrote to Hope that he was aware of 'the strain and anxiety' caused by the mission. Hope replied that Caradon's note had given him 'much comfort' (minutes by Caradon and Hope, 24 and 25 April 1967, FO 961/36).

[99] Minute by Hope, 26 April 1967, FO 961/36.

the High Commissioner to argue all his problems out with him . . .
Bunche made no secret of his depression.

Bunche recalled our withdrawal from Palestine. He very much feared
that what would really happen would be an extension of the Yemen
civil war into South Arabia which could develop into another Congo
and be dropped in the U.N. lap.[100]

The UN mission to Aden damaged the public esteem of the United
Nations. Nor did it do any good for the reputation of the Committee
of 24. As for Public Enemy Number One, the end of the colonial era
drew closer. British troops gradually evacuated from the hinterland
into the great industrial port and military base at Aden Town. Their
departure under fire a few months later, in November 1967, marked
the liquidation of one of the few remaining major British colonial
commitments.

The civil war in Aden did not escalate into a crisis requiring UN
intervention, as had the emergency in the Congo, but the new state
—the People's Republic of South Yemen—relied heavily on military
and economic assistance from the Soviet bloc and China. The US
government, above all UN Ambassador Arthur Goldberg (Stevenson's
successor), held the Committee of 24 in part responsible for this adverse turn in the Cold War.[101] Goldberg told Caradon in December
1967 that 'the Committee was being used as an instrument to attack
the United States Government'. The time had come, Goldberg said,
for the British and Americans to withdraw from the Committee: 'It
had been largely captured by the radical elements amongst the Afro-
Asians and instead of being used for its proper purposes of encouraging and facilitating decolonisation it was being turned into a vehicle
for vituperous attacks, principally on Western powers.'[102]

Caradon, knowing that American withdrawal from the Committee
would provoke another round of debate in London, wrote, as always, in robust language in favour of the British remaining loyal to the

[100] Memorandum by Hope, 26 April 1967, FO 961/36.

[101] The British delegation had considerable respect for Goldberg and thought him a great
improvement over Stevenson; Goldberg was tragically portrayed by Sir Leslie Glass during a
debate about the 1967 war in the Middle East: 'One picture stands out—the stricken face of
Mr. Goldberg, profoundly vulnerable in this dispute, when taunted by the Syrian delegate as being the representative of Israel rather than of the United States' (Glass to FCO, Confidential,
9 August 1967, FCO 58/84; Glass was a former member of the Indian Civil Service, later High
Commissioner in Nigeria).

[102] Caradon to Goronwy Roberts, Confidential, 11 December 1967, FCO 58/100 (*BDEEP—
East of Suez*, #148). As events transpired, the United States decided to remain, temporarily at least,
on the Committee; see *Foreign Relations of the United States, 1964–1968*, XXXIII, #426.

principle of honestly defending the British colonial record, come thick or thin. 'I do not believe in walking out or running away,' he declared. 'We have stood our ground for many years and stated our case and answered back when attacks have been made. I should like to see this thing through.' The ill-informed and malicious attacks on the British Empire would continue, and if Britain left the Committee, the slander would remain unchallenged. So with considerable eloquence, Caradon argued in favour of staying the course and debating the issue of British colonialism 'even with the wildest men amongst the Afro-Asians'.[103]

The question of the Committee of 24 now moved into its most dramatic phase. Sir Paul Gore-Booth returned to the charge, once again bringing into play the larger stakes of Britain's support for the United Nations. Like others in the British government, Gore-Booth was appalled at the 'futile' mission to Aden and its attempt to cast a slur on the record of British rule. He believed that the time had come, once and forevermore, to put an end to Britain's participation in 'unfair, destructive nonsense'.[104] He found a powerful ally in presenting the case for withdrawal in George Thomson, later Lord Thomson, the head of the Commonwealth Office within the new Foreign and Commonwealth Office. Thomson also protested against the Committee's 'dogmatic anti-Colonialism'. Though some of the principal colonial difficulties had been resolved, there were still many British dependencies vulnerable to UN interference:

> We have now come practically to the end of our programme of decolonisation and we shall soon be left with territories too small and unviable to achieve independence and with a limited number of extremely difficult and delicate questions—the disputed territories of Gibraltar, Falklands, British Honduras, Fiji with its deep racial problem, Hong Kong and New Hebrides . . .
>
> Our continued presence in the Committee of 24 erodes our authority and confuses responsibilities.[105]

Sir Hilton Poynton could not have put the case better, but again it was a vain protest. The attempt to cut the connection with the Commit-

---

[103] Caradon to Goronwy Roberts, Confidential, 11 December 1967, FCO 58/100; *BDEEP—East of Suez*, #148.

[104] Minute by Gore-Booth, 27 December 1967, FCO 58/100; see also his minutes in FCO 58/101.

[105] George Thomson to George Brown, Confidential, 8 February 1968, FCO 58/101; *BDEEP—East of Suez*, #149.

tee of 24 failed, not least because of the tenacious, persuasive, and eloquent Lord Caradon.

In the final confrontation, Caradon found an ally in Goronwy Roberts, Minister of State in the Foreign and Commonwealth Office and one of the few who could consistently influence the erratic Foreign Secretary, George Brown. Caradon and Brown proved to be an unbreakable combination. Brown dealt with the issue only fleetingly, but his intellect penetrated to its heart. He grasped immediately, though 'reluctantly' and irritably, that Britain could not leave the Committee.[106] 'Our difference on these questions', he wrote, 'is not just with the Committee but with the majority at the United Nations.'[107] Brown's instinct was to remain loyal to the United Nations. The decisive words —indeed the rationale for the decision itself—were written by Goronwy Roberts: 'I do not wish you of all people to be the first Secretary of State to be associated with a retreat by Britain from full United Nations participation—for this is how it would look and how it would be regarded in this country and abroad.'[108] The Caradonian principle thus prevailed.

Gore-Booth did triumph on one point. He managed to persuade the Foreign Secretary to buck up Lord Caradon and to urge the delegation in New York to take a much more aggressive stance in the Committee—to 'play it tougher', in Gore-Booth's words.[109] But Gore-Booth did not think Caradon temperamentally capable of a sufficiently pugnacious attitude, even under direct order. This advice suited Brown's own belligerent disposition, drunk or sober.[110] They thus turned to Evan Luard (Parliamentary Under-Secretary at the Foreign and Commonwealth Office, MP for Oxford, and Supernumerary Fellow of St. Antony's College), who recently had been enlisted to help Caradon in the Committee of 24. Luard was a true believer in both the United Nations and the British Empire, though in a particular sense. He had been one of the few members of the Foreign Office to resign at the time of Suez in protest against Britain's flouting of the United Nations. He was second to none in defending Britain's colonial record, but he also upheld the principle of the orderly liquidation of the

[106] See his minute of *c*.24 January 1968 and other minutes in FCO 58/101.

[107] Brown to Thomson, 9 February 1968, FCO 58/102; *BDEEP—East of Suez,* #150.

[108] Roberts to Brown, Confidential, 1 February 1968, FCO 58/101.

[109] See Gore-Booth's minute of 2 February 1968, FCO 58/101: 'I do not think Lord Caradon would feel it easy to do this spontaneously unless there was some explicit expression from you . . . to take a really (and not nominally) tough line.'

[110] See Peter Paterson, *Tired and Emotional: The Life of Lord George-Brown* (London, 1993), especially p. 207, for his troubled relations with Gore-Booth.

Empire and its transformation into the Commonwealth. In fact, his attitude was identical with Caradon's, though he employed a more rough-and-tumble House of Commons debating technique and his comments had a confrontational edge. His earnest, plain speaking was much more to the taste of both Gore-Booth and Brown than Caradon's congenial rebuttals. Brown had written to Luard earlier: '[I]t was good to know that we had . . . someone who defended resolutely and counter-attacked boldly . . . It is certainly a tribute to you that, while giving no quarter, you were able to make and preserve many friendships among even our sharpest critics.'[111] With Luard speaking out at the United Nations, the Committee at least got some of the comeuppance that Gore-Booth thought it deserved.

The break with the Committee of 24 did finally occur, as Gore-Booth and others hoped it would, on 11 January 1971. The main reason was obvious to everyone at the time. Lord Caradon had retired after distinguished service as British Ambassador to the United Nations only a few months earlier, after the Conservative victory in the election of 1970. But there were other fundamental reasons as well. By the end of the 1960s, the anti-colonial movement had begun to run out of steam. Nasser's death in 1970 symbolized the end of the post-Suez era. By the beginning of the new decade, many of the problematical colonies, such as Fiji, had achieved independence or were on their way to it. There remained of course Hong Kong, Gibraltar, and the Falklands, as well as an array of island dependencies, such as St. Helena and Pitcairn, but even at the United Nations these were generally recognized as 'outposts without an empire'.[112] Britain remained 'shackled by the ball-and-chain of Rhodesia'.[113] But by the early 1970s the Committee of 24 itself had begun to suffer from a grave and deadly affliction: public boredom.

As if they were mates in a long-enduring but mismatched marriage, Britannia lost her reputation as an ongoing colonial predator and the Committee became 'pretty impotent'.[114] Not only was there a general view that the Committee of 24 had run its course, but in Britain there was an increasing disillusionment with the United Nations itself.[115] 'I am not at all a "Caradonian",' wrote F. A. Warner of the British dele-

---

[111] George Brown to D. E. T. Luard, 5 January 1968, FCO 58/87. This file is useful for letters to and from Luard on the subject of the Committee; see also FCO 58/310.

[112] Caradon to FCO, Confidential, 21 April 1970, FCO 58/587.

[113] Sir Colin Crowe to FCO, Confidential, 21 January 1971, FCO 58/642.

[114] Minute by J. H. Lambert (head of the United Nations Department), 27 July 1970, FCO 58/491.

[115] See, for example, Shirley Hazzard, *Defeat of an Ideal: A Study of the Self-Destruction of the United Nations* (Boston, 1973).

gation in New York in 1970, but it would be good, he argued, to keep things in perspective, neither overvaluing the United Nations nor writing it off as representing only 'a lot of hot air'.[116] The decision to leave the Committee reflected a balanced and hardheaded assessment that the British could now cautiously depart, safe in the knowledge—in the words of a much earlier Colonial Office judgement—that 'a rump committee composed of Communists, Afro-Asians and Latin Americans should not cause us much trouble.'[117] The British could thus listen with greater indifference to such accusations, in the mantra of the Committee of 24, as colonialism in any form is a crime against humanity. The British could now breathe easier, but without the exhilaration of being Public Enemy Number One.[118]

The British Empire in the 1950s: Retreat or Revival?   2006

---

[116] F. A. Warner to Sir Denis Greenhill, Personal and Confidential, 15 July 1970, FCO 58/586.

[117] Minute by D. J. Derx, 1 July 1964, CO 936/925. The US government had independently arrived at the same conclusion. The two delegations in New York now fixed their timing to leave on the same day, 11 January 1971. On the next day the *New York Times* carried a major story on the first page with these headlines: 'Britain and U. S. Pull Out of U.N. Colonialism Unit: Both Long Critical of Committee, Saying Resolutions Were Forced Through by the African-Asian and Red Blocs' (cutting in FCO 58/619, in which there is also a cutting from *The Times of Malta* with the headline 'End of an Era').

[118] For the last stage of the Committee and the decision of the 1974–79 Labour Government to resume cooperation with it but not to become a member, see Sankey, 'Decolonisation'.

THE MIDDLE EAST

28

MUSADDIQ, OIL, AND THE DILEMMAS
OF BRITISH IMPERIALISM

The overthrow of the Musaddiq government by the intelligence agencies of the United States and Britain in August 1953 is a subject that invites periodic reassessment.[1] The archive of the British Secret Intelligence Service (SIS) remains even more tightly sealed than that of the CIA, but the publication by the *New York Times* of a CIA historical study on the 1953 operation, written shortly after the event by Donald Wilber, an historian of Islamic architecture and art as well as an undercover agent, throws considerable new light on the British as well as the American side of the story.[2] In some ways the episode resembles a mosaic. The small pieces of evidence have long formed a general pattern, even though many of the British parts remain elusive and will probably remain so until sometime in the remote future, when the SIS disgorges its secrets of the 1950s. Nevertheless it is worth the effort, even on the basis of fragmented evidence, to reconsider the subject from a British vantage point. Significant parts of the mosaic have become more distinctly visible in the last decade.[3] The post–Cold War era, moreover, offers an opportunity to the historian to approach the subject from a different angle of vision. Greater distance in time and greater access to archival material encourage a more dis-

---

[1] My own analysis of the subject was made some twelve years ago: 'Musaddiq and the Dilemmas of British Imperialism', in James A. Bill and W. R. Louis, eds., *Musaddiq, Iranian Nationalism, and Oil* (London, 1988), pp. 228–60. For present purposes I have drawn from my earlier essay, but I have also reworked it extensively and have elaborated at length on the post–November 1952 part of the operation. For discussion and correspondence, I am indebted to four former British officials who were all involved in one way or another in the affairs of Iran in 1951–53: Sir Denis Wright, Lord Terrington (C. M. Woodhouse), Christopher Gandy, and Sir Sam Falle. They have enabled me to give the present essay a measure of detail and exactitude that would otherwise not have been possible. Woodhouse, alas, died February 13, 2001. There is a perceptive and useful obituary by Richard Clogg in the *Guardian*, 20 February 2001.

[2] *New York Times*, 16 April 2000. The title of the study is 'Overthrow of Premier Mossadeq of Iran: November 1952–August 1953'. According to a note at the beginning, the monograph was written in March 1954 by Donald N. Wilber, a Princeton University scholar and CIA consultant who participated in the operation. Only parts of the study were initially published by the *New York Times*. The full version eventually became electronically accessible but with certain names excised. The names have, on the whole, been restored, but there are problems in dealing with an electronic document that continues to evolve. For purposes of accuracy, this essay deals with my own copy, dated 18 August 2000. (There are several other CIA studies of the 1953 operation, but references to 'CIA History' in the text and footnotes are to Wilber's.) For Wilber's autobiographical account, see Donald N. Wilber, *Adventures in the Middle East: Excursions and Incursions* (Princeton, Darwin Press, 1986).

[3] This is true of the general subject as well, thanks mainly to the comprehensive work by Stephen Dorril, *MI6: Fifty Years of Special Operations* (London, 2000), especially part 6.

passionate view of a subject still riddled with ideological assumptions. Thus the purpose of this essay will be to reflect on the British involvement with Iran from the time of Mohammed Musaddiq's advent to power as Prime Minister in April 1951 to his overthrow in August 1953, and in a more general sense to restore British perspective to a story that has, on the Western side, been dominated by American comment.

One thing that intrigues the historian is how little is known of British intelligence activities conducted by the British Labour Government of 1945–51 and how little the underlying assumptions have been studied.[4] Did the Labour Government, when confronted with the issue of covert action, differ in principle from the successor Conservative Government? If so, then what led Herbert Morrison, who succeeded Ernest Bevin as Foreign Secretary in 1950, to endorse plans for subverting the Musaddiq government? Did the Prime Minister, C. R. Attlee, lose his grip, or had Attlee himself come round to the view that Musaddiq had to be removed from office? Who besides the Prime Minister and the Foreign Secretary made the decisions on covert operations during the time of the Labour Government? What of the influence of the local British experts in Iran? How did the chain of command differ from that of the Conservative Government under Sir Winston Churchill, who again became Prime Minister in late 1951? What comparisons can be made between MI6—the overseas arm of the British Secret Intelligence Service—and the CIA?

The key to British thought from the time of Musaddiq's ascendancy in April 1951 can be summed up in the description of him as a fanatically anti-British nationalist. But even the British granted that Musaddiq possessed certain qualities of leadership. First and foremost he was an Iranian patriot. When he became Prime Minister in 1951, he was seventy years old. His family belonged to the landed ruling class. He championed the Iranian constitutional movement and was a long-standing member of the Majlis, the Iranian Parliament. He was not corrupt. The British—and for that matter, the Americans—often misunderstood his principal motivation. The crucial set of events that determined his outlook was the virtual occupation of Iran by the British and the Russians twice in less than fifty years. Though often described in the West as a demagogue, and he did sometimes add drama to his oratory by pretending to faint, he consistently held that the Shah should reign and not rule and that the army and police should be subject to civil control. Musaddiq aimed to make the Majlis supreme.

---

[4] The best book generally on the Labour Government is Kenneth O. Morgan, *Labour in Power, 1945–1951* (Oxford, 1984); see also especially Alan Bullock, *Ernest Bevin: Foreign Secretary* (London, 1983). Neither mentions the Secret Intelligence Service.

He passionately opposed foreign intervention in Iran and above all wanted to end the domination of the Anglo-Iranian Oil Company. In this sense his goals were mainly negative. Though he worked for social, judicial, and economic reform, and he did possess gifts for constructive and creative work, he is remembered above all for his crusade against the British. In 1949 he became the architect of the plan to nationalize the oil industry and led a loose alliance known as the National Front, which in the Majlis consisted of representatives from most political parties in Iran, not least of whom was one of the most politically active clerics, the Ayatollah Abul Qasim Kashani. Musaddiq eventually broke with Kashani, but intermittently there existed an uneasy partnership. The British viewed both as irreconcilably anti-British. In fusing religion and politics, Kashani in a sense was a forerunner of the Ayatollah Khomeini. Musaddiq by contrast was a secular nationalist.

According to the British 'Oriental Counsellors'—the officials who spoke Persian and whose job it was to follow Iranian politics in the Embassy in Tehran—Musaddiq drew his strength from Iranians who shared not only his anti-British sentiment but also his vision of constitutional democracy.[5] As a populist leader, he had solid public support because of his stand on civil rights as well as his unswerving protest against foreign exploitation of Iranian oil. He fused the constitutional movement with that of anti-imperialism. The Shah found it difficult to oppose openly a populist Prime Minister who championed Iranian sovereign rights and freedom of the press. Musaddiq's dual stand on constitutional liberties and anti-imperialism appealed especially to the urban middle and working classes. His supporters also included some of the more important guilds and, in the business community or bazaar, owners of coffee houses and tea shops. Most important of all, not least for the British in their calculations of how to undermine, in their view, an anti-British fanatic, he controlled the police and had wide support in the army at all levels. He was, in short, a formidable political leader, one who presented the British and the Americans with a paradox. Why should Britain and the United States want to get rid of a statesman who stood for constitutional democracy and, according to Musaddiq himself, a fair-minded settlement of the oil issue?

Musaddiq was not a communist. There was no alliance between him and the Tudeh (the Iranian Communist Party) to achieve his goals. Nevertheless, Western contemporaries in Iran often portrayed him as sympathetic to communist aims. Such was his anti-British obsession, in

---

[5] The relevant series for studying the views of the Oriental Counsellors is FO 248 (Embassy Archives, Tehran).

the view that the Americans as well as the British came to espouse, that it blinded him to the dangers of communism through a takeover by the Tudeh, which the British estimated to have some 12,000 members and perhaps 50,000 sympathizers. To the British, the danger was that the communists would gain control over Musaddiq and then Iran. Musaddiq might thus wittingly or unwittingly enable the Soviet Union— in the words of C. M. Woodhouse, the head of MI6 in Iran in 1951– 52—'to take the country over as it [the Soviet Union] had just taken over Czechoslovakia.'[6] Some within the British government thought from the outset that it would be impossible to do business with the Musaddiq regime and that plans should be made as soon as possible for his removal from office. On the other hand, a few sympathized with his aspirations as an Iranian patriot and in any event believed it to be unethical to intervene in the affairs of other nations by covert means, at least in normal times. A good example is (Sir) Sam Falle, later High Commissioner in Singapore and then Nigeria. In 1949–52, Falle was a young Foreign Service officer in Iran: 'In the Foreign Service I was known as "Red Sam," because I believed in liberal causes, resurgent nationalism and the like . . . Thus Dr Musaddiq was initially a man after my own heart . . . So the fact that even I eventually became convinced that he had to go says something.'[7] It was the circumstances of the Cold War that brought even well-wishers such as Falle around to the view that Musaddiq must be toppled. By August 1953 there existed a virtual consensus within government circles that covert action was politically necessary and morally justified.

There is a vital chronological point within the 1951–53 period. In October 1952, Musaddiq expelled the British diplomatic mission from Iran on the grounds of interfering in domestic politics. Thereafter there existed no official British presence in the country. In October 1952, MI6 relinquished control of its intelligence network to the CIA. The British continued to monitor the situation in Iran from Cyprus as well as from London and Washington, but in the last part of the covert action, the British participated only indirectly. On the other hand, an equally emphatic point needs to be made about the origins of the operation. Before October 1952, the plan to destroy the Musaddiq government was British in inspiration, British in the covert financial assistance proffered to Musaddiq's enemies, and British in the actual attempts to replace him.

[6] C. M. Woodhouse, *Something Ventured* (London, 1982), p. 107.

[7] The CIA History, p. 1, mistakenly identifies him as an officer 'of the British Intelligence station in Tehran'. Falle had entered the Foreign Service in 1948, though it is true that he easily moved between the realms of the Foreign Office and MI6; for the quotation, see Sam Falle, *My Lucky Life in War, Revolution, Peace and Diplomacy* (Lewes, UK, 1996), pp. 84–85.

The historic British connection with Iran was based on India and on oil. The refinery of the Anglo-Iranian Oil Company at Abadan, an offshore island at the head of the Persian Gulf, was the largest installation of its kind in the world. It was Britain's single largest overseas asset. It was a source of national pride in the England of Attlee, Bevin, and Morrison. Even in the late 1940s and early 1950s some high British officials still believed that Persian oil was actually and rightly British oil because it had been discovered by the British, developed by British capital, and exploited through British skill and British ingenuity.[8] Hence the degree of outrage in 1951 at Musaddiq's nationalization of Anglo-Iranian.[9] His action had implications worldwide. If Musaddiq could get away with nationalizing the oil industry in Iran, might not Nasser be inspired to nationalize the Suez Canal Company? Musaddiq's challenge was basic in another sense. He held the foundation of Britain's position in Iran, the concession agreement of 1933, to be both illegal and immoral. Musaddiq stands as one of the forerunners of a later generation of Asian and African nationalists who believed that the Western powers had no right in the first place to impose conditions of economic exploitation.

In the political domain, the British Embassy in Tehran occupied fifteen acres in the heart of the city. The staff included political officers, consuls, economic and commercial officers, military attachés, and not least intelligence officers and cipher clerks. In short, the British compound was almost as much a world within itself as the cantonments of the Anglo-Iranian Oil Company. The British diplomatic enclave symbolized foreign dominance. Its members in 1952 could still joke that the Iranians believed its water supply contained miraculous life-invigorating qualities.[10] The power of the British Empire seemed to be

[8] This was especially true of Sir Donald Ferguson, Permanent Under-Secretary at the Ministry of Fuel and Power, who once wrote: 'It was British enterprise, skill and effort which discovered oil under the soil of Persia, which has got the oil out, which has built the refinery, which has developed markets for Persian oil in 30 or 40 countries, with wharves, storage tanks and pumps, road and rail tanks and other distribution facilities, and also an immense fleet of tankers. This was done at a time when there was no easy outlet for Persian oil in competition with the vastly greater American oil industry. None of these things would or could have been done by the Persian government or the Persian people'; quoted in W. R. Louis, *The British Empire in the Middle East* (Oxford, 1984), pp. 683–84.

[9] See J. H. Bamberg, *The History of the British Petroleum Company: The Anglo-Iranian Years, 1928–1954* (Cambridge, 1994), part 3; Mostafa Elm, *Oil, Power, and Principle: Iran's Oil Nationalization and Its Aftermath* (Syracuse, N.Y., 1992); and Mary Ann Heiss, *Empire and Nationhood: The United States, Great Britain, and Iranian Oil, 1950–1954* (New York, 1997).

[10] Denis Wright, who led the mission to restore relations with Iran in December 1953, commented that Iranian assumptions about the British had to be taken seriously: 'The situation is complicated by a continuing and widespread belief in our mystical and all-pervading powers' (Wright to Eden, Confidential, 13 February 1954, FO 248/1543).

all-pervasive, even though Iran was never a British colony. British influence in this sense was subtler but not less potent for being indirect.
There were good reasons why Iranians as well as the British themselves
regarded Iran as part of Britain's 'informal empire', in other words, as
being within the compass of the British Empire yet receiving none of
the benefits of direct British colonial administration that would have
been conferred by accountability to the British Parliament.

Musaddiq's own cosmology held British political hegemony and
economic exploitation to be a certainty. His belief in the British as a
source of *evil* helped explain his outlook and indeed his political philosophy. 'You do not know how crafty they are,' he once said in characteristic vein. 'You do not know how evil they are. You do not know
how they sully everything they touch.'[11] Melodramatic or not, Musaddiq thus expressed a deeply felt sentiment, though he meant it collectively and not individually. There could be no mistake that he was to
the core an anti-British nationalist. Though he opposed all foreign intervention, he believed specifically that the British had exploited Iran
through the Anglo-Iranian Oil Company and had exerted a political
control that had to be broken before Iran could be truly free and independent. There could be no compromise with the British. For the
most part, the Foreign Office in London as well as the Embassy in Tehran took Musaddiq's unremitting hostility as axiomatic. In the British
view, little or no reconciliation was possible. From 1951, plans to overthrow him were set in train.

The architects of the plan were no less than two distinguished British academics, Ann K. S. (Nancy) Lambton, author of the famous book
Landlord and Peasant in Persia (1953), and Robin Zaehner, who later
became Professor of Eastern Religions at All Souls College, Oxford.
Nancy Lambton believed that covert operations to overthrow Musaddiq would be the only way to achieve a stable and pro-Western government in Iran; she moved in high circles within the Foreign Office
and was a friend of Anthony Eden, who again became Foreign Secretary in late 1951. In the early 1950s she was Reader in Persian at the
School of Oriental and African Studies at the University of London.
She had served in an official capacity during the Second World War as
press attaché at the Embassy in Tehran. She was respected not only as
a scholar but also as an authority on contemporary Iranian affairs.[12]
In her view, the 'stupidity, greed and lack of judgement of the ruling
classes in Persia' caused the government to be corrupt and parasitic.[13]

[11] Quoted in Vernon A. Walters, *Silent Missions* (Garden City, New York, 1978), p. 247.

[12] For a slightly later example, see her article, 'The Impact of the West on Persia', *International Affairs*, 33, 1 (January 1957).

[13] *The Times*, 22 March 1951, in an anonymous article written by her.

The wealth of the country was entrenched in the hands of large-estate owners, who were linked by marriage or family with an elite of rich merchants and ranking military officers. Unless the social and economic system of the country could be reformed, Iran faced a revolutionary catastrophe.

Lambton believed that revolution might be averted because certain patriotic and intelligent Iranians held views that coincided with British concepts of national self-interest based on effective and responsible government, professional integrity, and respect for the rule of law. Yet they would be regarded as traitors if they publicly denounced Musaddiq. Hence the need for covert cooperation with those public-spirited Iranians, who would work towards reform in concert with the British. She thus expressed a fundamental aim of the Labour Government: to sustain Britain's own influence in Iran by economic and social reform. A harmony of interests could exist between the British and enlightened Iranians. Since the initiative had passed to Musaddiq, the collaboration had to be covert rather than open. Propaganda would play an important part. 'We discussed . . . with Nancy Lambton', wrote the head of the Eastern Department of the Foreign Office, Geoffrey Furlonge, 'effective lines of propaganda and . . . we decided that we should try to show that responsibility for failure to improve the lot of the ordinary Persian lies not with the AIOC nor with the British Government but with the successive Persian Governments, who, while professing to be interested in economic development, have done little or nothing to bring it about.'[14]

Robin Zaehner was the official in the British Embassy in Tehran appointed by Herbert Morrison in 1951 to plan and carry out the operation against Musaddiq. Zaehner was an improbable figure for such a job. He qualified for it because he had worked in covert operations in Tehran during the Second World War and thereafter with MI6 in Albania. He was fluent in Persian, indeed bilingual, and possessed an intimate knowledge of Iranian politics. According to a Foreign Office minute in 1951:

> Dr Zaehner was apparently extremely successful in covert propaganda in 1944 at the time that there was a serious threat that the Russians would take over Azerbaijan. He knows almost everyone who matters in Tehran and is a man of great subtlety. The line then was,

---

[14] Furlonge to Shepherd, Secret, 21 July 1951, FO 248/1528. Lambton herself, as if wary of future historians, rarely committed her thoughts on covert operations to writing. The quotations of her comments by various officials, however, are internally consistent and invariably reveal a hard-line attitude towards Musaddiq. I have the impression from the minutes that the officials quoting her sometimes wanted to invoke her authority to lend credibility to their own views.

of course, to mobilise public opinion from the bazaars upwards about the dangers of Russian penetration.[15]

Zaehner regarded Iranian politicians and political parties as part of a fascinating game, a constant jostling for supremacy in which the British, though in the background, played an almost natural part. As he saw it, the British and their allies in the internal political struggle could win out if they had the willpower and the skill to prevail in the perpetually shifting set of alliances and personalities. Like Lambton, Zaehner believed that he and his colleagues in the British Embassy had to align themselves decisively with influential and patriotic Iranians who perceived their own self-interest to be identical with that of the British. Zaehner possessed an extraordinary capacity to combine high thought with low living. He relished the lighter side of his duties. He held his own in gossip or discussion, whether about philosophy and religion or human foibles. He drank heavily.[16] To those who wished to learn about Iranian politics, he recommended Lewis Carroll's *Through the Looking-Glass*. He tended to tell his superiors what he believed they wanted to hear. His temperament did not draw him to the more sinister side of intelligence operations, nor did he have the discipline for rigorous secrecy. Zaehner was an Oxford bon vivant transmogrified into a quasi Secret Service agent.

The word 'quasi' is necessary to understand Zaehner's brief and the nature of his appointment. Though he had previously served in MI6, in 1951 he held a Foreign Office appointment as Acting Counsellor in Tehran.[17] In a strict sense the Foreign Office charged Zaehner to work for the overthrow of the Musaddiq government through legal and constitutional methods, but in fact a grey area existed in which Zaehner moved between intelligence and Foreign Office activities. Zaehner worked so closely with MI6 officers that he was often mistaken for

[15] Minute by Eric Berthoud (Assistant Under-Secretary supervising economic affairs), 15 June 1951, FO 371/91548.

[16] Rather in the tradition of Aldous Huxley, Zaehner also experimented with drugs to increase his sensory perception of eternal verities. Received into the Roman Catholic Church in 1946, he was profoundly religious. His last book, *Zen, Drugs, and Mysticism* (London, 1972; reprint by Vintage Books, 1974) is an attack on American drug cults. Zaehner believed that a mastery of the scriptures, not LSD, was a prerequisite to the quest for religious truth.

[17] One result of Zaehner's Foreign Office appointment (rather than a regular MI6 assignment) is that the records in the archives of the British Embassy in Tehran contain many of Zaehner's extant minutes and thus have left ajar a window that ordinarily, on the subject of covert activities, would have been closed. Zaehner wrote compulsively, and his minutes are omnipresent in the FO 248 series.

one of them. He made no secret of his assignment to have Musaddiq replaced by whatever means possible, short of force. Here is an important difference between the British Secret Intelligence Service and the CIA, for the lines between MI6 and the Foreign Office were more fluid than those between the CIA and other parts of the American government. The same might be said about the circumstances of his appointment, for it is difficult to imagine, for example, Dean Acheson (Secretary of State in the Truman administration) charging a member of the US Foreign Service with such an assignment. Zaehner's brief came directly from the Foreign Secretary, Herbert Morrison.

Morrison's advent as Foreign Secretary occurred at the same time as Musaddiq's rise to power, in the spring of 1951. The Persian oil crisis preoccupied Morrison during the eight months of his tenure. He experienced an unhappy time in his career. Famous for his leadership in the House of Commons, he failed to complement his mastery of domestic politics with a command of foreign affairs.[18] His interests did not extend much beyond British politics, though he did possess an aggressive attitude and a contempt for non-European peoples that put him at odds with some of his colleagues, not least Attlee. In 1943, while Home Secretary, Morrison had dismissed as 'nonsense' the possibility of granting independence to dependent territories under British sway: '[I]t would be like giving a child of ten a latch-key, a bank account, and a shot-gun.'[19] Morrison held the same paternalistic attitude towards Iran. After the nationalization of the Anglo-Iranian Oil Company on May 2, 1952, he took the lead in urging the British to launch an expeditionary force to seize the island of Abadan in retaliation. In an operation planned under the code name 'Buccaneer', the Royal Navy, the RAF, and the army assembled a virtual armada, ready for attack.[20] The plan reached an advanced stage when an MI6 officer, Norman Darbyshire (who, as will be seen, played an important part in the unfolding story of the 1953 operation), bribed the Iranian Commander-in-Chief to put up only token resistance.[21] Attlee himself now took charge, bringing the Cabinet to the conclusion that an invasion would not end the nationalization crisis but on the contrary would mobilize the Iranian nationalist movement against Britain. Attlee acted in part on a consistent non-interventionist principle of the

[18] See especially Bernard Donoughue and G. W. Jones, *Herbert Morrison: Portrait of a Politician* (London, 1973), chap. 36.

[19] Quoted in W. R. Louis, *Imperialism at Bay* (Oxford, 1977), p. 14.

[20] See James Cable, *Intervention at Abadan: Plan Buccaneer* (London, 1991).

[21] See Dorril, *MI6*, p. 561.

Labour Government, but in this case realpolitik assisted virtue because the US government opposed British military action. In effect,
Attlee vetoed the plans for an invasion. Morrison suffered a humiliating setback.[22]

   It is useful to place the decision in the broader setting of the Cold
War. To the British Chiefs of the Staff and those on the military committees who drew up the series of contingency plans culminating in
Buccaneer, there were grave issues of timing, manpower, and priorities. In this time of international crisis, as in others, intervention would
be most effective if it were done expeditiously. Apart from doubts
within the Cabinet about the legal basis for action, the Chiefs of Staff
lamented the lack of flexibility that had once allowed quick and decisive strokes by the Indian Army, a resource no longer at their disposal.
Political as well as military decisions proved to be protracted. The
Iranian crisis has to be seen against the background of the Korean
War: British troops there ranked numerically behind only those of the
United States and South Korea. What would be the extent of British
intervention in Iran? Could the British deploy troops there without
weakening their commitment in Korea? Would British forces occupy
the entire region of the oilfields, thereby requiring the call-up of reserves in Britain at a time of an economic crisis? Or if the aim were
limited to the seizure of Abadan, might not the British in any event be
drawn into a larger operation? Would the British occupation trigger a
Soviet invasion in the north?

   Musaddiq himself declared that British aggression would signal the
start of the Third World War, an eventuality that had a certain edge to
it in view of the open question whether American bombing in Korea
would extend to Manchuria. In the event, Buccaneer focused on the
capture of Abadan. Even this limited aim might have had the reverse
of the intended effect by unifying the Iranian people against British
imperialism. What would be the purpose of holding an enclave while
a hostile hinterland held the oil reserves? Those were the broad considerations that the Prime Minister had in mind when he explained to
the Cabinet that the US President had refused to endorse the use of
force. It was the American opposition to the British plan that proved
to be decisive in Attlee's own calculation of a complex problem. He
firmly led the Cabinet to this conclusion: 'We could not afford to break
with the United States on an issue of this kind.'[23] Dean Acheson, the
US Secretary of State, later remarked emphatically that it had been 'to
the great credit of the Labour Government' to stand 'against jingo

[22] See Louis, *British Empire in the Middle East*, pp. 686–89.
[23] Cabinet Minutes 60 (51), 27 September 1951, CAB 128/20.

pressures'.[24] He had in mind not only Churchill but specifically Herbert Morrison.

From Morrison's point of view, the entry of Robin Zaehner into the story represented a small but significant step. It is evidence of the seriousness with which the Foreign Secretary viewed the situation. The appointment passed virtually unnoticed because it involved only a relatively obscure assignment to the staff in the British Embassy in Tehran. Yet it eventually had ramifications that affected the British government as a whole as well as the Anglo-Iranian Oil Company and even the United States. Zaehner's name eventually came to symbolize subversive activity. It is important, however, to note some of the subtleties of distinction between covert and overt intervention and to establish the nature of the debate within the Labour Government in 1951. In the Cabinet, Attlee restrained the Foreign Secretary's impulse to punish Iran openly and forcibly and thereby to bring about a change in government. But Morrison by no means stood alone in believing that Musaddiq had to be toppled. The Minister for Defence, Emanuel Shinwell, spoke just as aggressively in favour of intervention. In slightly different circumstances, Morrison's line of 'sharp and forceful action' might have prevailed.[25] As events transpired, Morrison had to rely on covert means to achieve his goal. But even at the local level Zaehner's course of covert activity in attempting to unseat Musaddiq did not necessarily contradict Attlee's high policy. On the whole, by relying on influence or manipulation rather than force, Zaehner adroitly stayed within traditional Foreign Office boundaries.

There was tension within the Labour Government, as in the United States government, between those who favoured covert action as an extension of policy by other means and those who did not. In the Attlee era, the balance rested with those who did not, thereby making the Zaehner episode all the more significant by providing a small but vital element of continuity from Attlee to Churchill and from Morrison to Eden. In tracing the origins of the 1953 covert action against Musaddiq, however, we must consider the general context of the British and the politics of Iran; otherwise, our view of the intervention is likely to be distorted. It is also necessary to bear in mind that the Anglo-Iranian Oil Company played no part in either the origins of the intervention

---

[24] Dean Acheson, *Present at the Creation* (New York, 1969), p. 508. For the British decision in the context of plans to unseat Musaddiq, see Mark J. Gasiorowski, 'The 1953 Coup d'Etat in Iran', *International Journal of Middle East Studies*, 19 (1987), pp. 263–64. For a judgement on the decision in relation to the Suez crisis, see Cable, *Intervention at Abadan*, p. 118: 'If we think of the drastic pressure Eisenhower applied against Anglo-French intervention at Port Said in 1956 and the British débâcle that ensued, we must concede Attlee's prudence in 1951.'

[25] Herbert Morrison, *An Autobiography* (London, 1960), p. 281.

or its execution; otherwise, the covert action of the intelligence agencies is obscured by the persistent myth that the company participated in Musaddiq's overthrow.[26] In the British government, as in the American, covert action had its origin entirely within official circles.

The British and Iranian Politics

Almost from the beginning of the crisis in 1951 a strong current of thought in the Foreign Office held that Musaddiq's 'pathological' but shrewd anti-British attitude would make any discussion futile. In British eyes, Musaddiq himself was responsible for this deplorable state of affairs. Sir Francis Shepherd, who served as Ambassador in Iran from March 1950 through the crisis of 1951, regarded him as on the fringe of irrational or 'lunatic' behaviour.[27] Shepherd's view was representative. George Middleton, who acted as Chargé d'Affaires in 1952 and who was universally regarded as a man of balanced judgement, wrote that Musaddiq was 'no longer capable of rational thought'.[28] In London the Prime Minister himself referred to 'the emotional state of the Persian Prime Minister (who appeared to be on the lunatic fringe)'.[29] According to the *Observer*'s 'Profile': 'Moussadek is wholly impervious to common sense arguments of expediency . . . He is surrounded by crooks, adventurers and madmen. . . . He is truly a Frankenstein.'[30] Nor was this view restricted to British circles. The US Ambassador in Tehran, Loy Henderson, referred to Musaddiq as 'a madman'—and in a virtually identical vein, the Secretary of State, John Foster Dulles,

---

[26] There is no evidence of the Company's complicity. Bamberg, *British Petroleum Company*, pp. 588–89, note 115, independently confirms my own judgement that the company was not involved. It would be a mistake to assume, however, that there were no connections between individual members of the company and MI6. Two officials of the Company, Archibald Chisholm and Geoffrey Keating, had both served in Iran, and both were involved in the company's intelligence network, which was publicly known as the Central Information Bureau (CIB). The principal function of the CIB was propaganda, but it also included 'intelligence-gathering [and] bribing officials' (Dorril, *MI6*, p. 564). Both Chisholm and Keating moved in the same circles as MI6 officers. Chisholm had represented the company in Kuwait. A hint of Keating's influence can be found in a letter written by an official in the British Embassy in Washington to the Oriental Counsellor in Tehran: 'Geoffrey Keating is in our midst and being helpful' (N. W. H. Gaydon to Lance Pyman, Secret and Personal, 11 July 1951, FO 248/1528.)

[27] For example, Shepherd to Bowker, Confidential, 28 May 1951, FO 248/1514: 'The situation in Persia during the four weeks of Dr Musaddiq's premiership has been on the whole a good deal more lunatic than ever.'

[28] Middleton to Bowker, Personal and Secret, 1 September 1952, FO 371/98697.

[29] See minute by M. R. Starkey, 14 May 1951, FO 371/91534.

[30] 20 May 1951, news cutting in FO 248/1514.

exclaimed 'that madman Mossadegh!'[31] The growing consensus on Musaddiq's irrational behaviour is basic to understanding one of the reasons the British and American governments eventually decided to intervene.

In view of Sir Francis Shepherd's low opinion of 'Oriental character' and of Iran itself as a country of 'Oriental decadence', it is hardly surprising that he and Musaddiq found conversation difficult. One point that he did impress upon Musaddiq, and, it seems, on all other Iranians he met, was that Iran had not been allowed to develop 'at the hands of a virile and civilised nation'. The Iranians lacked the benefits of a nationalist movement that British imperialism might have inspired. There were at least two major underlying assumptions in Shepherd's quintessential British outlook: Iranian politics was irrational and the nationalist movement was not authentic but merely a 'preliminary flicker' of genuine nationalism.[32]

Both in Tehran and London the old Middle East hands of British officialdom developed more sophisticated interpretations of Musaddiq and Iranian nationalism. Shepherd's ideas 'may well have been sound at the time of Musaddiq's rise to power', wrote R. F. G. Sarell of the Eastern Department of the Foreign Office, but some nine months after Musaddiq's advent those assumptions no longer held true. Shepherd had believed that Iranian nationalism was a 'spurious' movement concocted by Musaddiq and a few other anti-British extremists to divert attention from the corruption of the ruling propertied classes. It had no roots and commanded no genuine popular support. Sarell took issue with that superficial analysis. Paraphrasing from an article by Nancy Lambton, he penned the most searching estimate of Iranian nationalism in the 'post-Shepherd' era (in fact, he wrote in the same month that Shepherd left Iran to become Ambassador to Poland, January 1952).[33] Sarell (closely following Lambton) argued that Shepherd was correct in holding that only a minority of the population supported the nationalist movement. But the explanation of Musaddiq's popular appeal lay in the genuine sentiment that existed against the Anglo-Iranian Oil Company. Musaddiq wished to expel the parasite of Western capitalism, and he exploited the 'xenophobia' and latent nationalism already present. He had been able to create a coherent

[31] James A. Bill, *The Eagle and the Lion: The Tragedy of American-Iranian Relations* (New Haven, 1988), pp. 88–89.

[32] See especially Shepherd to Furlonge, Confidential, 6 May 1951, FO 371/91459.

[33] I am grateful to Denis Wright for information about Sarell. For the article, see *The Times*, 22 March 1951.

national movement only because the religious leaders, especially the Ayatollah Kashani, had already expressed the sense of dissatisfaction in Iranian society. Musaddiq and Kashani roused nationalist sentiment and transformed the situation: '[B]y claiming to represent the real spirit of the nation against alleged foreign exploitation he [Musaddiq] and the other leaders of the movement, notably Kashani, were able to produce a state of emotional excitement in which criticism could be stifled'.[34]

By closely relying on Lambton's analysis, indeed on her very language, Sarell helped shape the collective estimate of the Eastern Department of the Foreign Office. The assessment included an historical analysis of the Iranian social forces that had produced both Musaddiq and the tensions between the 'classes' that might, or might not, sustain him:

> In the early period of the Nationalist movement as now many of its leaders in fact belonged to the religious classes. The other class from which the Nationalist leaders were drawn in the past was the middle-class bazaar merchants, to whom the exclusion of the West and restriction of competition offered the promise of financial gain; between this group and the religious classes there has been a traditional connection, and the support of leaders such as Kashani is still drawn largely from the bazaar.

Calculations about the response of the bazaar, as will be seen, played a critical part in British plans to topple Musaddiq. The Foreign Office (Lambton) assessment next discussed the 'classes' from which Musaddiq drew his support:

> The main support for the nationalist movement . . . comes from the military, professional, and bureaucratic classes, to whom nationalism opens the way to political power. In so far as nationalism is accepted by the masses it is probably because of their intuitive clinging to the Shia'. Nationalism appears to them as a reaction against the West, that is the non-Islamic world, but in so far as it penetrates to the masses it is transformed by their social traditions, and differs from the nationalism of the intellectuals . . . Any alliance between the intellectuals and the masses is likely to prove unstable, because the former

[34] R. F. G. Sarell, 'Nationalism in Persia', 13 February 1952, FO 371/98596. Sarell's estimate was a rejoinder to Shepherd's 'Comparison between Persian and Asian Nationalism in General', for which see Louis, *British Empire in the Middle East*, pp. 639–40. Shepherd had previously served in Indonesia (one of the bases of the 'comparison'), where the nationalist movement appeared to him to be much more fully developed.

are out of touch with the latter, and the intellectuals, failing to understand the masses, despise them.[35]

Such was the drift of British official thought as of January 1952.

Lambton's view of Musaddiq as a dangerously irrational anti-British nationalist also found expression in minutes written by Eric Berthoud, the Assistant Under-Secretary supervising economic affairs. Berthoud did not, however, usually address himself to day-to-day Iranian questions. Indeed, by a sort of gentleman's agreement he remained one step removed because he had been an employee of the Anglo-Iranian Oil Company early in his career. But whenever the occasion arose he freely ventured his opinion. It usually reinforced the judgement of Nancy Lambton, who characteristically urged the Foreign Office to boycott Musaddiq as far as possible and to deal with him only when necessary to preserve public order. This was an attitude she maintained consistently. 'Miss Lambton spent last weekend with us,' Berthoud wrote a year and a half after Musaddiq had been in office. She still held, as she had from the time of his ascendancy, that it was impossible to negotiate with him because his entire position was based on anti-British sentiment. If he began making concessions, he would destroy the foundation of his own power. Thus, in Lambton's judgement, 'It is still useless to accept any settlement with Dr Musaddiq', because he would immediately renege.[36]

Like Lambton, Zaehner believed that the British Embassy in Tehran had to align itself decisively with influential Iranians who perceived their own self-interest to be identical with that of the British. Zaehner's extensive minutes reveal that he regarded the wealthy Rashidian family—the brothers Seyfollah, Qodratollah, and Asadollah—as allies of that kind. They are well described by the leading historian of American-Iranian relations, James A. Bill: 'Seyfollah, the eldest and a musician and philosopher, was the brains of the triumvirate and a superb conversationalist and host. He was a student of political history and liked to quote verbatim from Machiavelli. Asadollah was the organizer, political activist, and confidante of the shah, while Qodratollah was the business man and entrepreneur.'[37] Asadollah became the key British contact—in the words of the CIA History, 'the principal SIS agent'.[38] The father of the three brothers had built a family fortune based on shipping, banking, real estate, and an array of business

[35] Sarell, 'Nationalism in Persia'.
[36] See minute by Berthoud, 13 October 1952, FO 371/98701.
[37] Bill, *The Eagle and the Lion*, p. 91.
[38] CIA History, p. 24.

ventures, including cinemas. During the Second World War, Zaehner had established contact with the Rashidian brothers while conducting covert anti-communist activities. By the early 1950s the Rashidians represented the operational arm of MI6 in Iran. From Zaehner they received a monthly sum of £10,000, which was used in part to influence attitudes in the bazaars but also in part for anti-Musaddiq articles and lampoons in the daily press.[39] The Rashidians were staunchly pro-British, quite apart from the money. They were also anti-American. One of the questions in the 1953 operation against Musaddiq was whether they would transfer their loyalty to the CIA. Until the British were evicted in November 1952 the Rashidians played the leading part in Zaehner's efforts to destabilize the Musaddiq government. The CIA History correctly notes that they had contacts 'in such fields as the armed forces, the Majlis (Iranian Parliament), religious leaders, the press, street gangs, politicians, and other influential figures'.[40] Their view of Musaddiq coincided with Zaehner's. Seyfollah Rashidian told Zaehner in January 1952 that 'even if Musaddiq were offered everything he wanted plus £100,000 he would still say "no".'[41]

As Zaehner saw it, much would depend on the Shah, whom the British at this time regarded as an unreliable ally, at once vacillating, indecisive, and opportunistic. It would be a mistake of the first magnitude to regard the authoritarian Shah of later decades as the same as the weak figure of 1951–53. The Shah, like Musaddiq and indeed like many other prominent Iranians, was suspicious of British influence. The CIA History refers not only to the Shah as 'a man of indecision' but also to his 'pathological fear of the "hidden hand" of the British'.[42] In any event the Shah did occupy a position at the centre of the Iranian political world. Any action on his part could help determine the course of events, but so also would any inaction. Thus the British attached importance to the Shah's twin sister, Princess Ashraf, who had a stronger personality than her brother and often influenced him.

The British, in particular Zaehner, were well informed of palace politics through the Shah's private secretary and *éminence grise*, Ernest Perron, a Swiss of long-standing influence with the royal family and 'probably the Shah's closest friend'.[43] Perron did not use his position

[39] The source for the figure of £10,000 is Woodhouse, *Something Ventured*, p. 118. This may seem in retrospect an extravagant amount, but the CIA's yearly budget for Iran was $1 million.

[40] CIA History, p. 7.

[41] Minute by Zaehner, 5 January 1952, FO 248/1531.

[42] CIA History, pp. vii and 22.

[43] Manucher Farmanfarmaian, *Blood and Oil* (New York, 1997), p. 226. This is a book with many shrewd insights into the British presence in Iran.

to acquire money, but he relished the glamour of the court and the social prestige, as well as the status of poet and philosopher conferred on him by the Shah. He was regarded by others in the Shah's circle as 'slippery as an eel'.[44] It was commonly known that he was a homosexual. He dressed 'like a musical comedy Bohemian'.[45] His lifestyle gave a certain racy reputation to the Shah's entourage. He cultivated the military officers and politicians close to the Shah as well as the prominent families who moved within the social circles of the court. On political issues, he calculated that the Shah's self-interest often coincided with that of the British, and he thus was an invaluable British source of delicate information. Like Zaehner, he loved to gossip. The two were compatible, though one can detect an element of wariness on both sides. 'Perron is admittedly not the ideal link' with the Shah, Zaehner noted in August 1951, 'but I can see no harm in keeping in close contact with him.'[46] Perron was the Shah's man, but he was also a vital British contact.[47]

There were two politicians whom the British regarded as possibilities to replace Musaddiq. They were Seyyid Zia and Qavam al-Saltana, both of whom had had long political careers and still commanded 'about an equal amount of support in the Majlis'.[48] Seyyid Zia was the British favourite. He had served briefly as Prime Minister as long ago as 1921 and had consistently aligned himself with the British in Iranian politics. One of Sir Francis Shepherd's predecessors, Sir John Le Rougetel, in 1949 had described Seyyid Zia as 'one of the few, in fact the only, outstanding personality in public life who is both competent, honest and sincere'.[49] 'The best man', commented the Oriental Counsellor.[50] In 1951, Seyyid Zia had emerged as one of Musaddiq's principal rivals, but he failed to receive the Shah's endorsement as Prime Minister. The British thus held the Shah partly responsible for Musaddiq's advent to power and saw the Shah's refusal to act as characteristically feckless. But the Shah had his reasons. Seyyid Zia's strength was also his weakness. He was so pro-British that the Iranian public would

---

[44] Dorril, *MI6*, p. 563.

[45] Daniela Meier, 'Between Court Jester and Spy: The Career of a Swiss Gardener at the Royal Court in Iran: A Footnote to Modern Iranian History', *Critique*, 16 (Spring 2000), p. 77.

[46] Minute by Zaehner, 27 August 1951, FO 248/1514.

[47] There was another long-standing British contact in the Palace, the head of the Royal household, Soleyman Behbudi. The evidence on this point is obscure, but apparently he came to the assistance of the Rashidians in the critical days of August 1953 by acting as intermediary between Princess Ashraf and the Shah; see CIA History, pp. 23–24.

[48] Minute by L. F. L. Pyman (Oriental Counsellor), 19 July 1951, FO 248/1515.

[49] Quoted in Fakhreddin Azimi, *Iran: The Crisis of Democracy* (New York, 1989), p. 212.

[50] Minute by Pyman, 22 September 1951, FO 248/1515.

have regarded him as no less than a traitor on the issue of oil. He did indeed offer assurances that he would attempt to reach a 'sensible' settlement. From about September 1951, however, the British learned that the US Embassy in Tehran increasingly had reservations about him for the same reasons that the Shah had opposed him. Seyyid Zia had so committed himself to the British that his ascendancy would be denounced as the high noon of US-British hegemony in Iran. Nevertheless he remained invaluable to Zaehner and others not only as a source of information and advice but also as an important pro-British yet independent figure in Iranian politics. Seyyid Zia could not be ordered about. He advised the British on how to conduct their affairs in Iran; he did not passively seek their advice. In different circumstances he might have been, from the British vantage point, an excellent replacement for Musaddiq.[51]

A tantalizing mention of a possible bribe to Seyyid Zia occurs in one of the British documents. It is in a telegram from the Ambassador to the Foreign Office in September 1951: Seyyid Zia expected 'to be helped with some fairly generous payment'.[52] In fact, no evidence exists that money changed hands, though Seyyid Zia may have expected, had he become Prime Minister, substantial but indirect financial gifts raked off from defence contracts. Nor is there any evidence of payments to the other two British candidates for high office in the 1951–54 period, Qavam al-Saltana and General Fazlollah Zahedi. There was no secret that all three, at different times, had had British sponsorship and that the British would have preferred any of them to Musaddiq. They were called the 'open opposition'. As public figures, they had their own reasons for being associated with the British, but to everyone concerned, the British as well as the Iranians, bribery at that level was dangerous, even in a culture that accommodated bribery as easily as Chicago politics of the same era.

There was an underlying principle in the British method.[53] With prominent politicians, the more the British could stay in the background, the better. Bribery, under whatever name, almost always took

---

[51] The British fascination with Seyyid Zia continued even after the overthrow of Musaddiq. Denis Wright, following an analysis by John Fearnley of the Embassy staff, wrote in 1955: 'Sayyed Zia has strength of character, experience, an imaginative understanding of his country and his fellow-countrymen, a plan of action, and loyal supporters in many different walks of life and in influential positions' (Wright to Macmillan, Secret, 3 August 1955, FO 371/114811).

[52] Shepherd to Strong, Confidential, 4 September 1951, FO 248/2529.

[53] I am grateful to Sir Sam Falle for clarification on this point and for much detailed information on the Rashidians. On matters where no written evidence exists, I have tried to verify factual detail with all four of the British officials mentioned in note 1: Falle, Wright, Gandy, and, before his death, Woodhouse.

place indirectly through the Rashidian brothers, but they in turn regarded Seyyid Zia, Qavam, and Zahedi as off-limits and left them to their political masters—at different times, Zaehner, Woodhouse, and Falle. The Rashidians, as has been mentioned, possessed a genius of sorts for securing political patronage. MI6 officers, particularly Norman Darbyshire, would occasionally make payments directly to deputies in the Majlis, but, to summarize, bribery was the domain of the Rashidians, who not only had a monthly retainer of £10,000 but could request more if necessary. So wealthy were the Rashidians, however, that they appeared to view the MI6 payments mainly as operational funds and did not hesitate to use their own bank accounts to promote operations against Musaddiq. At one time Musaddiq himself guessed that at least a third of the deputies in the Majlis were on the Rashidian payroll. The three brothers controlled, or at least manipulated, some twenty newspapers. They had contacts in the military and the police. Clerics as well as politicians and army officers were susceptible to their bribes. Asadollah Rashidian once spoke of his ability to promote a *coup d'état* against Musaddiq by enlisting 'the Army and the mullahs'.[54] The influence of the Rashidians was thus far-reaching. But it was by no means all-embracing, and the three brothers probably sometimes exaggerated their ability to influence events, as did, perhaps, the MI6 officers who worked with them. The CIA, for example, believed that MI6 overestimated the Rashidians' capabilities.[55] Nevertheless it is difficult to imagine how the 1953 operation against the Musaddiq government could have taken place without the Rashidian network.

Despairing of the prospect of replacing Musaddiq with Seyyid Zia, the British from the autumn of 1951 believed that the next suitable alternative was Qavam al-Saltana. In a famous chapter in his long political career, Qavam had been Premier at the time of the Azerbaijan crisis in 1946. He had managed to secure the withdrawal of Soviet troops by promising Stalin an oil concession in northern Iran. The Majlis later cancelled the concession. Whatever lessons the British might derive about Iran and the Soviet Union from that adept episode, which the Russians regarded as treacherous, it nevertheless seemed obvious that Qavam was far preferable to Musaddiq. Qavam, in the British view, was just as much a nationalist as Musaddiq, but more anti-Soviet and less anti-British. He had the positive advantage of not having a pro-British reputation. But the British approached him with a certain wariness.

[54] Minute by Falle, 28 July 1952, FO 248/1531. On this occasion Asadollah Rashidian had in mind Zahedi as a leader who could be put forward as a patriot with an appeal to diverse groups in Iranian society.

[55] CIA History, p. 7.

The overt campaign in favour of Seyyid Zia had proved to be coun-
terproductive. They now tried not to support Qavam too openly.
Qavam himself merely regarded the British as a means to gain power,
and was willing to do whatever necessary towards that end.

The following minute by Zaehner records a conversation with one
of Qavam's supporters, Abbas Iskandari, and gives a clear indication of
the mounting British intention, as of late 1951, to get rid of Musaddiq:

> After concluding our discussion on the ways and means of over-
> throwing Musaddiq, Iskandari went on to assure me (in Persian) that
> it was Qavam's desire to work in closely with the British and to pre-
> serve their legitimate interests in Persia without jeopardising Persia's
> political and economic independence.[56]

In the complex interplay of forces known as 'economic imperialism',
Qavam could be expected to follow the British lead despite the past
experience of the Anglo-Iranian Oil Company:

> I said that the independence of Persia had always been the corner-
> stone of our policy, but we were prepared to admit that economically
> Persia had been largely dependent on the A.I.O.C. just as we and Eu-
> rope in general were dependent on American aid. In the modern
> world no such thing as economic independence existed any more:
> and Persia must face this fact.

> Iskandari said that this was understood and that Qavam-us-Saltaneh
> greatly preferred that British influence should be exercised in Per-
> sia, rather than that of the Americans (who were foolish and without
> experience), or of the Russians who were Persia's enemies.

There was to be a firm, though implicit, alliance between Qavam and
the British. Qavam would have a free hand, and, with patience, the legitimate commercial interests of the British would be restored:

> If we were prepared to accept Qavam-us-Saltaneh's assurance that he
> would come to an agreement satisfactory to both sides [i.e. the Ira-
> nians and the British], we must give him a free hand in the use of
> methods. Public opinion had been worked up to such an intensity
> of anti-British feeling that it would need a month or two to change
> it. Qavam-us-Saltaneh did not wish to disclose in advance exactly
> what his methods would be, but we knew by experience that with him

[56] Minute by Zaehner, 10 November 1951, FO 248/1514.

everything came out right in the end, however curious the beginning might be.[57]

All of this, according to Zaehner, seemed to be 'very much on the cards'.

Here a general observation should be made about the British, Qavam, and Musaddiq. Zaehner was accurate in his estimate of Musaddiq. Economic dependence was precisely the point Musaddiq was not prepared to admit, at least to the British. In Qavam, the British hoped they had found a collaborator, perhaps a devious one, in the traditional mould.

In the circumstances of 1952, the youngest of the 'Oriental Counsellors', Sam Falle, consistently argued that the British would be acting in the best interests of the Iranians (as well as in their own legitimate self-interest) by promoting Qavam. Falle wrote in April: 'If Qavam comes to power he will try to act as a dictator—dissolve the Majlis and arrest dissident elements, among them probably Musaddiq and Kashani. On oil he is keen to reach an agreement with us.'[58] Through Falle's minutes may be traced the mounting excitement during the spring and summer of 1952, when it seemed to be a question of not *if* Musaddiq would fall but only a question of *when*. Having brought the country to the brink of economic ruin, Musaddiq, it now appeared, would be replaced by Qavam. The problem was the Shah's attitude. The Shah feared, rightly in the judgement of Zaehner and Falle, that he could not dominate Qavam. The British were indeed uncertain whether the Shah would support him. According to Falle:

> Even if Musaddiq falls the immediate future leaves plenty of room for anxiety. The Shah wants Musaddiq to go quietly without any fuss and seems to be determined that the new Prime Minister be a weak man . . . Such an appointment would in all probability be catastrophic and could not lead to the order and security which are vital if the country's problems are to be solved. Hence we come back to our problem which is that Qavam is the only man who can deal with the present situation, but that the Shah will not have him . . . The Shah's irresolution is extremely dangerous in these critical times.[59]

As the critical time of July 1952 approached, it looked as if Musaddiq might collapse mainly because of Qavam's own initiative. Falle

---

[57] Ibid.
[58] Minute by Falle, 28 April 1952, FO 248/1531.
[59] Minute by Falle, 30 June 1952, FO 248/1531.

748 The Middle East

judged that, whatever the Shah might do, the British should throw their weight behind Qavam; otherwise, 'there is a chance that the whole work of the country might be paralysed for a time and render an oil solution more difficult . . . My conclusion is that at the moment Qavam is the only man who can work effectively.'[60]

After much hesitation, the Shah decided to accept Qavam as Prime Minister after Musaddiq abruptly resigned in July, in what proved to be a skilful attempt to reconsolidate his authority. Here was the test of the Zaehnerian interlude in Iranian politics. Could British influence still be decisive? If so, it was an attempt to revert to the British doctrine of 'masterly inactivity', because they did very little. They remained aloof. As Zaehner himself explained the rationale: 'I think it would be a tactical mistake to do any overt campaign on behalf of Qavam; we did this with Sayyid Zia and this did him no good.'[61]

Qavam remained in power for less than a week. If the incident proved anything at all from the British side, it was that calculations could go radically wrong, not least Zaehner's. No one had championed Qavam as an anti-Soviet, anti-Musaddiq statesman more than Zaehner, but when Musaddiq triggered the crisis by his resignation, thus providing Qavam—and the British—with the opportunity to forge an anti-Musaddiq combination, the intelligence community and Zaehner himself were caught off guard. Woodhouse and Roger Goiran, the CIA Chief of Station, had left Tehran together on a trout-fishing holiday in the northern mountains. They returned to find that Musaddiq had been restored to power on a wave of popular support.[62] Woodhouse lamented in retrospect that the British had given Qavam virtually no assistance. Why had the British failed to rally to such a staunch anti-Musaddiqist? The Rashidians, for example, played no part at a critical juncture in which they could have made a difference, perhaps a decisive one.

The political crisis of July 1952 proved that British policy had been based on a drastic miscalculation. Zaehner and others had assumed that Qavam, as a national hero, would have far-reaching popular appeal. But the Qavam of 1952 was not the Qavam of 1946. He had neither the military nor the public support to sustain himself in office. He was ousted by pro-Musaddiq forces within a few days, on 21 July. Musaddiq himself returned to power buoyed up by mass demonstrations in which seventy-nine people were killed. In this test of strength, the remarkable outcome demonstrated the loyalty and perseverance of

---

[60] Minute by Falle, 2 July 1952, FO 248/1531.
[61] Quoted in Azimi, *Iran: The Crisis of Democracy,* p. 285.
[62] Woodhouse, *Something Ventured,* p. 115.

Musaddiq's followers as well as the skill of Musaddiq himself in consolidating his position against both the Shah and the British. After acquiring new plenary authority on an emergency basis, Musaddiq resolved to reform the political economy of Iran: not only by making the tax and land laws more equitable, but also by increasing the budgets for education and road construction, instituting rent control, nationalizing telephone companies, and creating a uniform bus service—matters of popular appeal. Musaddiq had greatly enhanced his popularity and authority while the Shah's had diminished. It is true that Musaddiq's euphoria was but brief. He soon began to quarrel with Kashani and other members of the National Front about his emergency powers and cabinet appointments. The morale of the army plummeted when Musaddiq purged officers sympathetic to Qavam. The Communists were now beyond Musaddiq's influence. The British were greatly discouraged at the time, above all because the Shah had proved to be an even more negligible force in Iranian politics than they had previously assumed.

George Middleton immediately described the events of 21 July as 'a turning point of Persian history'. Musaddiq had reconstituted his support by 'mob riots', which seemed to reveal a close coordination of forces within Iranian society that previously had regarded each other with hostility. Middleton wrote the day after:

> It seems clear to me that the bloody riot of the 21st July was a highly organized affair . . . The National Front demagogues, notably Kashani, gave an outward appearance of a spontaneous popular surge of feeling to these riots. But in fact I believe these were almost certainly organised by the Tudeh. Reports reaching me are that the demonstrations were as much anti-monarchical as anti-'imperialist' . . . Moreover there was a cold determination and ruthlessness behind the manifestations which is typically communist.

Mob rule, according to Middleton, now prevailed. The constitutional position of the Shah had been weakened. Middleton believed that the Shah himself bore large responsibility.

> The mob successfully defied the security forces and from now on the consent of the mob will be the decisive factor in judging the acceptability of any future government . . . In all this it seems to me that the influence and prestige of the Court has been fatally weakened. The Shah has I suppose been anxious to avoid bloodshed and to act in every respect as a constitutional sovereign who must bow to the majority of public opinion. In fact by his vacillations and weaknesses and in the absence of an informed and educated public he has

allowed the initiative to pass to the Tudeh and to the mob which the Tudeh controls.[63]

This was a black week, in Middleton's judgement, for the future of Western influence in Iran. The Shah and 'a small section of educated Persians' would probably continue to look to the United States and Britain for help, but, Middleton warned, 'I fear that their influence and consequently ours will be a declining one and that it may be beyond our power now to stop the drift towards communism.'[64]

Zaehner played a critical part in the Qavam episode, which in turn contributed to the expulsion of the British from Iran and the bringing together of MI6 and the CIA later in the year. The July crisis revealed not merely a lack of coordination but an uncertainty in estimating the extent of British power. In tracing the origins of British support for Qavam, it is clear that one of the motives was the search for a collaborator who would be able to conclude an agreement on oil satisfactory to Anglo-Iranian as well as to bring stability to the internal affairs of the country. This was a discussion that took place in London as well as in Tehran. One of Qavam's supporters had been Julian Amery, a Conservative Member of Parliament who had served in MI6 during the war.[65] He had longstanding contacts in the Middle East and elsewhere because of his father, Leopold Amery, who had served as Churchill's Secretary of State for India. Julian Amery is of interest not only because Qavam had made contact with him but also because of his perspective from the hard right of the Conservative Party. Amery believed that Britain still possessed the military and intelligence capacity to stand apart from the United States and exert an independent influence that would allow Qavam to dominate Iran. The trouble with this view was that it ascribed to the British in Iran much greater power than they possessed. It also assumed that the Shah would fall in with British plans. In the case of Qavam, he did not. In Zaehner's calculation, and especially Sam Falle's, it was the Shah's indecisiveness that undermined Qavam.[66] As has been mentioned, Qavam lasted only five days. The episode unnerved Zaehner, who decided shortly thereafter to return to academic life.

Since Robin Zaehner's name has acquired almost symbolic significance in the history of clandestine operations in Iran, it is worth briefly contemplating his achievements and his limitations. First and foremost he forged the Rashidian organization into a reliable and

---

[63] Minute by Middleton, 22 July 1952, FO 248/1531.
[64] Ibid.
[65] See Brian Lapping, *End of Empire* (London, 1985), p. 214.
[66] See Falle, *My Lucky Life*, p. 79.

effective British undercover network. He established an inside track to the palace through Perron. Not least, Zaehner developed firm friendships with younger members of the Embassy. He assisted the rise of Sam Falle, the junior Foreign Service officer who would play a critical part in the plans leading to Musaddiq's overthrow in 1953. Zaehner's legendary status as a hard-drinking opium-smoking *éminence grise* and bon vivant is entirely justified, but for those reasons Woodhouse, Falle, and others regarded him as an eccentric and ultimately unreliable academic who was unsuited for operational intelligence work.

Zaehner's lieutenant, Sam Falle, was fluent in Persian. Falle's specific assignment was to cultivate the younger anti-Musaddiqists. He sympathized with their nationalist aspirations. He had assisted Zaehner in sustaining contact with the Rashidians, and increasingly became the principal point of contact with them. Though he had no doubt that they represented the equivalent of the Mafia in their gang-like tactics and criminal activities, Falle liked them and regarded them as patriots. This may seem paradoxical. How could any Iranian recruited by the British Secret Intelligence be regarded as an Iranian patriot? In Falle's view no less than Zaehner and Lambton's, the Rashidians believed that Musaddiq's anti-British obsession would lead to a Communist takeover of Iran and with it the destruction of Iran itself. Iran's salvation as well as the Rashidians' fortune lay in cooperation with the British. In any event, Falle regarded them realistically as a means of getting rid of Musaddiq. It is not surprising that in late 1952 he was brought into the discussions with the CIA. Though only a junior officer, Falle's full-blooded and decisive views carried influence with his superiors, of whom the most significant was George Middleton, the Chargé d'Affaires from January 1952 until the rupture of relations between Iran and Britain in October.

Middleton had a broad outlook. By examining his assumptions, we can return to the larger themes of Iran's future in relation to the United States and the Soviet Union, and to the Anglo-Iranian Oil Company, as well as the conundrum of Musaddiq himself. While Middleton's colleagues often became caught up in Zaehnerian 'intrigue' (one of Zaehner's favourite words), usually with the anti-Musaddiqists, Middleton himself remained uncommitted to the view that Musaddiq was essentially irrational. Indeed, Middleton stood out conspicuously as recognizing in Musaddiq the qualities of a highly cultivated and intelligent human being. Among the British in Tehran, Middleton was almost alone in regarding Musaddiq as not merely an anti-British nationalist but also a nationalist figure attempting to bring about an Iranian renaissance. Musaddiq, in his view, had an almost mystical feeling towards nationalization. Both Musaddiq and Middleton had been educated in France, and they conversed easily in French. Middleton was then forty-two, Musaddiq seventy-one. The older man was cordial to the younger, even though they usually disagreed on almost everything. 'He was a highly civilised person,' Middleton recalled much later, in 1985.[67]

Musaddiq had such an inveterate mistrust of the British that no one who listened to his animated conversation could doubt that he actually believed the British to be somehow responsible for the poverty and general malaise of Iran.[68] Some remarks recorded in a confidential letter by Middleton in February 1952 well convey the flavour of Musaddiq's sentiments. As Musaddiq 'bounded up and down excitedly', he dwelt on the corruption of previous governments, the danger of Iran falling to the Communists, and the interference of the Anglo-Iranian Oil Company in the internal affairs of Iran. Corruption could be combated. Even the disaffected intellectuals, whom he denounced with contempt, could be prevented from turning Communist by providing them with a 'dole'. But the secret 'agents' exploiting the divisions of Iranian society seemed genuinely to worry Musaddiq. He held, according to Middleton, that Iranian society had certain distinct components:

> The Iranian people could be divided into three classes: communists, agents of the ex-Anglo-Iranian Oil Company and patriots. He would eliminate the first two and the nation would then be united and strong as never before. I remarked that the A.I.O.C. had already left.

[67] Transcript, 'End of Empire: Iran', Rhodes House, Oxford. This is a transcript of the interviews that Brian Lapping used in the television series and later the book, *End of Empire*.

[68] See for example Kingsley Martin (Editor of the *New Statesman*), 'Conversation with Dr. Mossadeq', *New Statesman,* 11 January 1952:

> Dr. Mossadeq received me in bed—a plain iron bed in which he bounced rather than lay . . . I saw no signs of the over-excitement or hysteria that some journalists have written about; he did not weep, though he laughed shrilly, stretching out his hand in a claw-like gesture that made him look at times like a benevolent pterodactyl. Here was a man of much force and capacity . . . He believed that it was not enough to get rid of a Company which had exploited his country, but that it was right to make sure that no other body or foreign Power would be in a position to exercise the influence in Iran that the Anglo-Iranian Company had possessed.

Martin was sympathetic. This was a view that hardly corresponded with *Through the Looking-Glass,* which had been recommended to him by Zaehner. Martin had been irritated by the suggestion. For another sympathetic British portrait of Musaddiq, see L. P. Elwell-Sutton, *Persian Oil: A Study in Power Politics* (London, 1955). In the 1975 edition Elwell-Sutton stated that he was content that the book 'should reappear in its original form as a record of the struggle of a small Asian country for independence and international recognition'.

Musaddiq replied that their agents were still everywhere and because they were all self-interested they were perhaps an even greater danger than the communists.[69]

Did Musaddiq actually believe his own conspiratorial rhetoric? If not, some sort of accommodation with the British might still be possible. Or was the anti-British obsession so integrated into his political personality (as Zaehner held) that Musaddiq could never come to terms with the British oil company? If so, then further discussion was virtually useless. Middleton, who probably knew him as well as any Englishman, had to admit that he saw no clear-cut answers. But he was willing to give Musaddiq the benefit of the doubt. The anti-British rhetoric was part of Musaddiq's political armour. The real question was whether Musaddiq intended to come to terms on the oil question.

To the British, Musaddiq may have been irrational about certain things, but at least he was consistent. He saw in the Anglo-Iranian Oil Company the personification of the evils of economic imperialism, and he never deviated from that view.[70] The British for their part were also consistent. From the outset of the crisis in 1951 they had been prepared to admit the principle of nationalization. With a Labour Government dedicated to nationalization, they could hardly do otherwise. But they insisted that the Anglo-Iranian Oil Company was entitled to fair compensation. Musaddiq himself agreed that the company should be compensated, but he flatly disagreed on the more fundamental point of the legality of the 1933 concession. By viewing the contractual arrangement as immoral as well as illegal, he challenged every aspect of the British commercial presence in Iran. It was difficult to see where there might be common ground. For the British, the Iranian oil dispute brought to a head the conflicting outlooks as represented by Musaddiq and the Anglo-Iranian Oil Company. The controversy brought home a basic point to the British, one they could not afford to concede: if Musaddiq's view prevailed, especially on the validity of the 1933 concession, then nationalists throughout the world could abrogate British concessions with impunity.

To George Middleton, the significance of the oil dispute was the sanctity of treaties. He was never in any doubt that the British had to hold firm on that point in all respects, legally, politically, and morally. But he did not think that the British could simply maintain a negative attitude, if only because the United States, while agreeing on the need

[69] Middleton to A. D. M. Ross, Confidential, 11 February 1952, FO 371/98618.

[70] For Musaddiq's economic views, see Homa Katouzian, *The Political Economy of Modern Iran* (New York, 1981), especially chap. 9.

to uphold the sanctity of treaties, would expect some kind of compromise. 'We cannot indefinitely maintain a basically negative attitude',
Middleton wrote in early 1952, 'nor do I suppose the Americans will
easily acquiesce in a policy of passive resistance to Musaddiq.' [71] As if
those things were not difficult enough, Middleton judged that there
was a further insidious, psychological stumbling block. The British recognized the principle of nationalization, but they continued to protest
the way it was carried out. They would accept nationalization as an
accomplished fact if the Iranians would agree to provide acceptable
compensation. But they also insisted that the oil industry be run 'efficiently'. Virtually no British expert believed that the Iranians could
manage a refinery as complex as the one at Abadan. Therein lay
Middleton's point about national psychology. The Iranians knew that
the British regarded them as inefficient, even incompetent—even,
perhaps, as inferior human beings. This was a psychological reality that
bore as much on the actual negotiations as did the abstract debate
about the validity of the 1933 agreement and the practical amount of
compensation to be paid to the company.

According to British calculations, the Iranian economy would take
a serious turn for the worse in the spring of 1952. Within a year after
Musaddiq's rise to power, British economic sanctions—the boycott
of Iranian oil and the successful denial of it to almost all foreign markets—would demonstrate the futility of the Musaddiq regime. Or so
it was hoped. According to Middleton's reports, the economy was sagging but not collapsing. If Musaddiq did not respond soon to economic pressure, there would be the danger that he might be replaced
by something worse, either a Communist regime or the fundamental-
ist religious faction led by Kashani, whom Middleton described as 'a
sly, corrupt and anti-Western demagogue'.[72] The spring and early summer of 1952 were also when the British awaited the result of Musaddiq's case against the Anglo-Iranian Oil Company before the International Court of Justice at The Hague.[73] When the court decided in July
1952 that the dispute lay beyond its jurisdiction, the ruling increased
rather than alleviated the tension. The international legal action coincided with rapidly developing events within Iran.

Middleton had always been sceptical of Musaddiq; scepticism now
hardened into disillusionment. 'His strength lies in his powers of

[71] Middleton to R. J. Bowker, Strictly Personal and Confidential, 4 January 1952, FO 371/98618.

[72] Middleton to Bowker, Secret and Personal, 28 July 1952, FO 371/98602. There is a persistent theme in British political reporting that Kashani was opportunistic and willing to be bribed.

[73] See Alan W. Ford, *The Anglo-Iranian Oil Dispute of 1951–1952* (Berkeley, 1954), part 2,
section 6.

demagogy', Middleton wrote in his report to the Foreign Office, 'and he has so flattered the mob as the source of his power that he has, I fear, made it impossible for a successor to oust him by normal consti-tutional methods.'[74] Middleton believed that the sense of power de-riving from the mob had gone to his head. Musaddiq thought he could control the Tudeh as well as Kashani. He was now more than ever incapable of 'reasonable' discourse:

> [H]e is surrounded by a gang as little amenable to reason as himself and there does not appear to be a single person in his entourage with whom one can discuss matters in a rational way . . . I think that his principal motivation just now is spite against the Americans and our-selves and he will stop at nothing to vent his dislike even though in effect it means alliance with the communists.[75]

Middleton wrote those lines during the July crisis in the immediate aftermath of Musaddiq's restoration. The chronology is significant be-cause it marks, in the testimony of the British official most willing to cooperate with him, Musaddiq's point of no return: 'Musaddiq ap-pears to be beyond reasonable thought and to be swayed entirely by emotion.' In other words, he had crossed the Rubicon into irrational-ity: '[H]is megalomania is now verging on mental instability'.[76]

Musaddiq had been well aware of the British attempt to dislodge him by aiding Qavam. Their days were now numbered. The oppor-tunity for expelling them came in September, when Britain and the United States presented a joint offer to settle the oil controversy. Musaddiq found the offer unacceptable. The British explanation was quite simple: whatever they held out, he demanded more. As the economy of the country deteriorated, he played on the emotions of the mob to retain power. The British in Tehran believed they were wit-nessing the virtual collapse of the Iranian state, a debacle that could be fatal because Musaddiq was playing the game of the Communists:

> Dr. Musaddiq by his own action has largely implemented the known programme of the communist Tudeh Party; the Shah has been re-duced to a cypher, the Army fatally weakened, the British 'imperial-ists' dispossessed, the central authority of the Government weakened and the economic and financial structure of the nation reduced al-most to chaos.

---

[74] Middleton to Eden, Confidential, 28 July 1952, FO 371/98602.
[75] Middleton to Bowker, Personal and Secret, 28 July 1952, FO 371/96802.
[76] Ibid.

Without having had to commit their forces in strength, the communists are in the fortunate position of seeing Persia reduced to the
point where the advent of a communist régime seems almost to be
part of the logic of history.[77]

Musaddiq now demanded £50 million in unpaid royalties from the
Anglo-Iranian Oil Company. He argued more dramatically than ever
that the concession of 1933 was invalid. 'The popular belief has been
carefully fostered', Middleton reported, 'that the A.I.O.C. is responsible for the existing ills of Persia and indeed for the miseries which
the country has suffered during the past 50 years.' Thus Britain owed
Iran reparations for past wrongs rather than Iran owing an indem-
nity for nationalizing a British company.[78] *Through the Looking-Glass*
now seemed to be an entirely accurate guide for viewing the situation
in Iran.

One year to the month after the eviction of the Anglo-Iranian Oil
Company, Musaddiq 'kicked out', in Middleton's explicit phrase, the
official British diplomatic mission in October 1952. Musaddiq had become the victim of 'his own brand of jingoistic nationalism'. Polite yet
melodramatic to the end, he explained to Middleton that 'he was a fa-
talist' and things would now have to take their own course. He had
'tears in his eyes' as he wished Middleton success in his future career.[79]
Middleton himself on the eve of his departure reflected that it might
have been a false assumption all along to believe that rationality could
prevail and that Musaddiq might come to terms. Lambton and Zaehner, it may be inferred, had been proved right. 'Perhaps it was a mistake', Middleton wrote, 'to fall in at all with the American view that
Musaddiq is "negotiable".'[80] Lambton expressed the point even more
emphatically: '[T]he United Kingdom policy of not making unjustifi-
able concessions to Dr. Musaddiq was right and would have been successful had it not been for American vacillations.'[81]

*The American Connection, the Anglo-Iranian Oil Company, and the
Dilemmas of the British Government*

Until the political crisis of July 1952 there had been a basic difference
in outlook between the British and American governments. From the

[77] Middleton to Eden, Confidential, 23 September 1952, FO 371/98604.
[78] Ibid.
[79] Middleton to Eden, 5 October 1952, FO 371/98700.
[80] Middleton to Ross, Personal and Confidential, 20 October 1952, FO 371/98605.
[81] See minute by Berthoud, 13 October 1952, FO 371/98701.

outset the Americans feared that the economic collapse of the Musaddiq regime might bring about the advent of Communist rule. Economic assistance was necessary to counter the Tudeh's exploitation of
chaos, poverty, and despair. The British were sceptical. They did not
minimize the danger of a Tudeh coup, but they did not believe that
Musaddiq could be appeased. Nor would economic assistance have any
tangible effect on the political situation. If anything, it would merely
delay the fall of Musaddiq. According to a Foreign Office assessment in
early 1952:

> The State Department's repeated reference to impending economic
> collapse in Persia seems to us to betray a misreading of the Persian
> situation and a diagnosis too much in terms of a Western industrial
> state. Their theories on this subject have no doubt been sedulously
> fed by Dr. Musaddiq's own propaganda . . . forecasting 'collapse in
> about 30 days'.

> It is our view that such terms are meaningless in Persia. A primitive
> agricultural community such as Persia, where some 80% of the pop-
> ulation are estimated to live off the land at bare subsistence level,
> does not 'collapse' economically. It sags, and no doubt more of the
> population will die of starvation than usual. We do not believe in the
> imminence of the catastrophic phenomenon forecast by the State
> Department.[82]

The crisis of July 1952 brought the British closer to the American assessment. To reiterate George Middleton's basic point, Musaddiq had
now 'worked himself up to a pitch of excitement' and was no longer
capable of 'rational thought'.[83] He might well play into the hands of
the Communists. The British thus now believed, again in Middleton's
words, that something was necessary 'to check Communist activity in
Persia'.

Nevertheless the British and the Americans remained poles apart
in their assessment of Musaddiq. The British continued to hold that
the end of the Musaddiq regime would not necessarily lead to communism, but the Americans believed that Musaddiq for all his faults
was the only person who might prevent a Communist revolution. In
the immediate aftermath of the July crisis, Bernard Burrows (a former
head of the Eastern Department of the Foreign Office, now serving
in Washington) reported a conversation with Charles Bohlen, a State

---

[82] Minute by Sarell, 22 January 1952, FO 371/98608.
[83] Middleton to Bowker, Personal and Secret, 1 September 1952, FO 371/98697.

Department official for whom the British had high respect. Bohlen had delivered an 'emotional tirade about Persia . . . his view seemed to be that Musaddiq and Co. were the only people left who could conceivably save Persia from Communism and we ought, therefore, to make up our minds that we must make a deal with them'.[84]

The British thought the Americans were responding excessively. Whatever might be happening in Iran could be explained more plausibly within the framework of Iranian politics than by the paramount American preoccupation at that time, the 'loss' of China. Nor did the British believe that the fate of Musaddiq would set off a chain reaction. Yet according to Bohlen, 'if Persia went Communist, Iraq and probably the rest of the Middle East would also, and our position would be lost anyway. We ought therefore to concentrate on saving Persia from Communism at all costs.'[85] This 'domino' theme also appeared in the American press, notably in articles written by Joseph and Stewart Alsop (a pair of reporters the British followed closely because their writing often revealed underlying assumptions of high American officials). The Alsops wrote after Musaddiq's return to power:

> [T]his country [the United States] may be faced with the choice of allowing Iran to go the way of China, or intervening forcefully to support any anti-Communist forces in Iran, however reactionary and blindly nationalist. It is believed in Washington that a Communist take-over in Iran must be averted at whatever cost, even the cost of a break with Britain on Middle East politics.[86]

The Americans seemed to believe that the British would rather see Iran go Communist than make an 'unsatisfactory' oil agreement with Musaddiq. This was the explicit challenge: 'whether we were now more interested in stopping Communism than in an oil settlement'.[87]

If there were to be an oil agreement, it would probably have to be based on the premise that the return of the Anglo-Iranian Oil Company was impossible. This was an American assumption as well as an Iranian one. But it was not necessarily a British assumption. As long as there seemed to be the prospect that Musaddiq might fall for reasons of his own making (because, for example, the Iranians themselves might see that he was leading the country to economic ruin), then there was hope that the Company might be reinstated under the

---

[84] Burrows to Bowker, Secret, 30 July 1952, FO 371/98603.

[85] Ibid.

[86] Article of 30 July 1952, enclosed in Burrows to Bowker, Secret, 30 July 1952, FO 371/98603.

[87] Burrows to Bowker, 30 July 1952.

façade of a new management company. In the first half of 1952 British policy pursued the hallowed course of 'masterly inactivity'—keeping the Americans in play (for example, through joint discussions with the World Bank as an intermediary with Musaddiq) and putting forward no constructive solution. There were good reasons for this negative approach. Any alternative to Anglo-Iranian would mean a breaking of the British monopoly. Thus the Americans were justified in their standard criticism that the British were merely 'standing pat'. Even before the July crisis, however, certain officials in the Foreign Office began to recognize that something had to be done, if only to counter the American suspicion that the British would allow Iran to drift into Communist revolution before giving up the concession. The driving force behind the effort to arrive at some solution, however unpalatable it might be to the company and the champions of privileged position, was the Deputy Under-Secretary at the Foreign Office, Sir Roger Makins (later Lord Sherfield). It came as a revelation to him that both the Treasury and the Ministry of Fuel and Power seemed to be just as hostile to compromise as the Company. 'We are indeed faced with a solid wall of Bourbonism and Micawberism in dealing with this question', Makins wrote in June 1952, 'of which the failure to deal with the reorganisation of the A.I.O.C. in the last six months is a symptom.'[88]

The actual architect of the reorganization of the Iranian oil industry, on the British side, was Peter Ramsbotham, then at the 'oil desk' of the Foreign Office. Through his minutes may be traced the steps that eventually led to the consortium agreement of 1954. Ramsbotham approached these problems with an eye towards a realistic settlement and with a sense of humour. 'A concession is probably neither definable in law nor as a term of art,' he once wrote.[89] Whatever a 'concession' might once have amounted to in Iran, it now had to be replaced. He had in mind a 'contractual arrangement' whereby a new company would negotiate a fifty-fifty principle of profit sharing with the Iranian government. The Anglo-Iranian Oil Company would receive compensation for losses (possibly through arbitration). Ramsbotham's language made explicit the nature of the proposed arrangement: the new managing company would be a 'façade' that would enable the Iranians to save face, and the new agreement would include a guarantee that would prevent them from interfering 'in the company's day to day operations'. He was well aware of the danger of attempting to make this fabrication a purely British façade: 'a reconstructed British com-

---

[88] Minute by Makins, 7 June 1952, FO 371/98690.
[89] Minute by Ramsbotham recording a FO meeting, 26 April 1952, FO 371/98689.

pany would not be able to operate as the sole company inside Persia as this would be a too transparent a restoration of British monopoly.'[90] Therefore American and perhaps other foreign oil companies would have to be allowed into the new arrangement. This proposal drew a protest from the Foreign Secretary himself. 'I do *not* like the idea of bringing American companies in,' Anthony Eden wrote in May 1952.[91]

Eden's past experiences help explain his attitude towards Iran in 1952. At Oxford he had studied Persian, which he continued to refer to as 'the Italian of the East'. He had served as Parliamentary Under-Secretary at the Foreign Office at the time of the Iranian oil crisis of 1933. He had been to Iran and had seen the oilfields. In 1951 he had denounced the Iranians for stealing British property. Upon becoming Foreign Secretary again after the fall of the Labour Government, one of his first major anxieties became 'Old Mossy'. Behind the caricature of Musaddiq as a buffoon in pyjamas negotiating from an iron bed-stead, Eden saw a shifty operator who was impervious to reason be-cause of his antipathy to the British. He occasionally referred to him as a megalomaniac (a word he usually reserved for Nasser). He cer-tainly regarded him as one of the shrewdest and most devious 'Orien-tals' he had ever encountered. Eden wrote in his memoirs: 'Interviews with Musaddiq, whether in bed or out of it, affable or corrosive, did not advance us one jot.'[92] The problem of Iran was of course only one of many that Eden faced, but in retrospect he regarded it as the most difficult to resolve. He wrote at the end of the critical year 1954, after the successful conclusion of negotiations on the Consortium:

> It is a strange thing about this year that though many people have written about the problems which we have, we hope, solved, Western European Union, Egypt, Indo-China, Iran, Arabia (Buraimi), very few have given much credit to Iran, which was, I believe, the tough-est of all.[93]

Eden's success in dealing with the Iranian crisis in fact derived in large part from delegating responsibility and listening to the advice of his permanent officials. In 1952 it was Sir Roger Makins, probably more than anyone else, who convinced him that he was wrong in his initial response to the question of the American oil companies. Makins held that the Americans would have to be allowed into the Iranian oil in-dustry or there would be no hope of a settlement.

---

[90] Minute by Ramsbotham, 26 April 1952, FO 371/98689.
[91] Minute by Eden, 4 May 1952, FO 371/98689.
[92] *The Memoirs of Anthony Eden: Full Circle* (Boston, 1960), p. 227.
[93] Ibid., p. 242.

The principal opponent to radical reorganization was Sir Donald Fergusson. From his position as Permanent Under-Secretary at the Ministry of Fuel and Power, he could effectively block any proposal the Foreign Office might put forward, or, conversely, he could be a key figure in shaping an outcome that would, in his view, correspond to the British national interest. Fergusson had been a member of the Stokes mission to Iran in 1951, when the British had made certain proposals to Musaddiq. The British would recognize the principle of nationalization and would relinquish the concession in favour of a contractual arrangement. In return for compensation, they would help establish a new management company that would efficiently run the Iranian oil industry on the basis of a fifty-fifty division of profits. This compromise represented the limit of Fergusson's generosity, which scarcely included the Americans. He was almost as distrustful of them as he was of the Iranians. After Makins wrote to him of the possibility of reopening discussion with both the Iranians and the Americans in the spring of 1952, Fergusson responded:

> I fear that we are in some danger of finding ourselves in a position where, having talked vaguely about resuming negotiations and making concessions, we shall be accused by the Americans of bad faith because we are unable to agree to specific concessions which their backroom boys will produce at short notice and in large quantities.
>
> The fact of the matter is that there is very little that we can do by way of making concessions.[94]

Only with extreme reluctance did Fergusson concur that somehow the Americans had to be accommodated, but not at the expense of the legitimate interests of the Anglo-Iranian Oil Company. He held that the British and American governments were not the appropriate parties to negotiate a settlement. Anglo-Iranian itself, in his view, was the only competent body to reach an agreement with the Iranians. Fergusson's attitude well represented what Makins referred to as 'Bourbonism'.

'I suppose one can never be certain of anything in Persia,' Makins wrote, but waiting like Mr. Micawber for something to turn up would surely not yield results favourable to the British. Both Makins and Fergusson could agree that there was no room for false optimism. Yet they were pulling in quite opposite directions—Makins towards collaborating with the Americans, Fergusson towards aligning the government's policy with the Company's, or at least remaining true to sound

---

[94] Fergusson to Makins, 27 May 1952, FO 371/98689.

British business principles. This was a first-class bureaucratic row. Makins eventually prevailed. He did so because of Eden's influence within the Cabinet and because of the transcendent importance of the political issue at stake. In Eden's own words, 'It is our national interest to obtain a settlement, not on account of the oil but because Persia's independence is very much our concern.' [95] Eden thus demonstrated the qualities of a statesman. And he exerted pressure on his colleagues. He spoke to the Chancellor of the Exchequer, R. A. Butler, and the Secretary of State for Co-ordination of Transport, Fuel, and Power, Lord Leathers. The latter, of course, was Fergusson's minister. Fergusson was a loyal, efficient, and extremely tenacious civil servant. From about mid-1952 onwards he began to redirect his energies towards bringing Anglo-Iranian into line with government policy, the Eden policy. He was exceedingly sceptical whether the Chairman of the company, Sir William Fraser, was capable of seeing beyond the strictly commercial limits of the problem. Fergusson minced words with no one. He told Fraser himself that he was 'a damn bad negotiator'.[96] After reading a report of one of Fergusson's conversations with Fraser, Eden made a memorable comment that will probably always be associated with the Iranian oil controversy: 'Fraser', noted the Foreign Secretary, 'is in cloud cuckoo land.' [97]

Sir William Fraser (Lord Strathalmond) holds a unique place in the history of British overseas expansion, not only because he dominated the Anglo-Iranian Oil Company, but also because of his autocratic personality. An exceptionally rugged Scottish individualist, he had been born and bred in the British oil industry. His father had been founder and managing director of the Pumpherston Oil Company, the leading Scottish shale-oil company. The younger Fraser personified the sense of adventure and enterprise that the British public associated with 'Anglo-Persian', as the company used to be called. He had been chairman since 1941. According to a notice in *The Times* after his death, he was 'a Scotsman to his fingertips . . . He had a razor-keen business brain combined with a Scottish sense of caution such that few, in an industry where tough bargaining is an accepted way of life, were likely to get the better of him.' [98] In business affairs, he was accustomed to having his way. It must therefore have been galling to confront Musaddiq's brand of Iranian nationalism, which aimed to repudiate everything Anglo-Iranian represented—even though Fraser maintained

[95] Quoted in a minute by Ramsbotham, 19 June 1952, FO 371/98690.
[96] As quoted in a minute by Bowker, 20 August 1952, FO 371/98694.
[97] Minute by Eden, 18[?] July 1952, FO 371/98690.
[98] Sir Eric Drake in *The Times*, 3 April 1970.

that nothing other than ingratitude should ever be expected from 'the Persians'. In fact, Musaddiq's estimation of him was probably not much different from Fergusson's: Fraser intended to exact as much as possible from Iran whatever the consequences. Fergusson believed that Fraser should be removed from the chairmanship of the company. So did most other officials, including the Governor of the Bank of England. Even the National Provincial Bank, the Company's bankers, believed that he had outserved his time.[99] Fraser, however, had great staying power. '[T]he retirement of Sir W. Fraser has been under consideration at various times in the past 2 years,' wrote Christopher Gandy of the Eastern Department in 1954: 'He is still there.'[100] He did not retire until 1956 and did not die until 1970, old enough for his friends to maintain that he had understood Iranian nationalism better than his critics and to claim credit for his reorganizing the Iranian oil industry in the form of the consortium arrangement of 1954.[101]

In fact, Fraser resisted from beginning to end. Part of the problem was his open contempt for civil servants. He was generally scornful of those who chose to earn their living by working for the state, and he was specifically disdainful of their knowledge of the oil industry. 'We had a pretty sticky meeting with Sir William Fraser last night,' Makins wrote on 19 July 1952.[102] The date is significant because this was the time of Qavam's brief advent to power. Fraser argued that Qavam would come to a reasonable agreement. The company did not wish to rush; indeed, as Fraser explained, there was no particular need for Anglo-Iranian to return to Iran. The losses at Abadan had already been more than recovered in the Kuwait fields. By the early 1950s, Kuwait reserves were estimated at 16 per cent of the world's total, compared with Saudi Arabia at about 10 per cent.[103] Thus the Foreign Office did not have a strong hand to play against the company. Fraser was not unresponsive to patriotism, but it was probable that his business instinct would prevail.[104] Nevertheless there was progress. By July 1952, Fraser

---

[99] George McGhee, *Envoy to the Middle World* (New York, 1983), p. 341.

[100] Minute by Gandy, 25 January 1954, FO 371/100078.

[101] Obituary in *The Times,* 2 April 1970: '[In] 1954 . . . a new international consortium was established in which the company held 40 per cent and was compensated for what it had relinquished. This scheme was devised by him and it was largely by his efforts that it was brought to a successful conclusion.'

[102] Minute by Makins, 19 July 1952, FO 371/98691.

[103] Benjamin Shwadran, *The Middle East, Oil and the Great Powers* (New York, 1959), p. 390.

[104] 'I have little doubt', wrote A. D. M. Ross of the Eastern Department, 'that both from motives of proper pride and from patriotism the Company would, in fact, bestir themselves to get into the Persian business again if they were asked to do so by Her Majesty's Government' (minute of 1 July 1953, FO 371/104616). Others were more sceptical.

had agreed in principle to a management company in which the major American oil companies might participate. The more he thought about it, the more Fraser thought it would be best for Anglo-Iranian to retain the initiative in this new arrangement. He himself would go to Iran to discuss the matter with Qavam. The following Foreign Office minute indicates Eden's response to Fraser's proposal: 'The Secretary of State had been horrified at the suggestion that Sir William Fraser should go out to Persia to conduct negotiations.' [105]

Speculation about Fraser bartering with the Iranians was short-lived. After Musaddiq's restoration in late July 1952, the calculations changed. As has been mentioned previously, this was the period when the American and British outlooks began to converge. The longer Musaddiq remained in power, the greater would be the danger of an eventual Communist takeover. There remained, however, serious differences between the American and British points of view. According to the British Ambassador in Washington, Sir Oliver Franks, the Americans distrusted the Anglo-Iranian Oil Company to the extent that they doubted whether any solution would be possible if Fraser remained a part of it. The Americans and the British also continued to disagree in assessing the stability of the Musaddiq regime. In the British view, economic assistance would sustain the Musaddiqists; in the American outlook, economic aid was necessary to prevent a Communist takeover. 'We must go on trying to restrain them,' Makins wrote of the Americans in August.[106] '[T]hey are agog for action,' reported Franks.[107] The result was the 'Truman-Churchill proposal' of September 1952, whereby the amount of compensation would be arbitrated; the Company would negotiate with the Iranian government for the resumption of oil production; and the United States would grant $10 million in budgetary aid. 'It is very important that we should not lose momentum', wrote R. J. Bowker, the Assistant Under-Secretary supervising the Eastern Department, for 'at any minute Musaddiq or the State Department may have another bright idea.' [108] The offer was presented. Musaddiq responded with a demand for £50 million as an advance against oil revenues.[109] This was another turning point: the Americans now moved still closer to the British assumption that it was impossible to do business with Dr. Musaddiq.

The autumn and winter of 1952 marked the critical period, when

[105] See minute of 23 July 1953, FO 371/98691.
[106] Minute by Makins, 9 August 1952, FO 371/98692.
[107] Franks to Eden, Secret, 24 August 1952, FO 371/98694.
[108] Minute by Bowker, 23 August 1952, FO 371/98694.
[109] See Heiss, *Empire and Nationhood,* pp. 141–50.

the British and Americans together began to plan covert operations against Musaddiq. Here a word must be said about the nature of the archival evidence. In late 1952 and early 1953 there occurs something like a sea change in the British documentation. It is not merely a coincidence that this was the beginning of the Eisenhower administration and the advent of Allen Dulles as head of the CIA. Until this time, British intelligence operations, if impinging on foreign policy, were discussed fully and candidly within the secret counsels of the Foreign Office. One can read minutes, for example, about the possibility of assassinating the Mufti of Jerusalem during the Second World War. For the Musaddiq period, the records have been suppressed. With the beginning of the Eisenhower presidency, Cold War secrecy was ratcheted up several notches. Even within the Foreign Office, officials stopped writing about matters they previously had debated in the ordinary course of minutes and private correspondence. The nature of historical analysis is thus affected. British policy remained constant, but it now had a deeper, subterranean dimension. Nevertheless, detailed points have emerged from accounts of the Cold War, not least from the CIA History.[110]

The British in 1953 detected a change in mood as well as a shift in policy in Washington. The Truman administration, in the British view, had been exceedingly cautious in dealing with Musaddiq. Indeed, Dean Acheson, the Secretary of State, and George McGhee, the Assistant Secretary who dealt with the Iranian question, seemed to the British to err in judgement by treating Musaddiq as a sort of charming oriental gentleman (rather than as a demented and extraordinarily devious and dangerous anti-British extremist). 'The difficulty with the previous administration', wrote Sir Pierson Dixon (the Deputy Under-Secretary who succeeded Makins when the latter became Ambassador to Washington in January 1953), 'was that we were continuously being pushed to make new concessions whenever Musaddiq shifted his ground. The new Administration, however, seem to realise that we have now reached the limit of concession.' This was a decided improvement over the 'vacillation' described by Lambton and Zaehner. 'Much more robust' were Dixon's words to sum up the change.[111]

It would suit one's taste for historical symmetry if a similar contrast could be made between the Tory government and its Labour predecessor. For better or worse, it was a Labour Foreign Secretary, Herbert Morrison, who had instructed Robin Zaehner to work for Musaddiq's overthrow by covert means, and it was Churchill himself, as will be

---

[110] For a general synthesis of the Cold War, see Dorril, *MI6*, passim, but especially chap. 28.
[111] Minute by Dixon, 19 February 1953, FO 371/104613.

seen, who sustained that course of action to its logical conclusion. On the other hand, Eden proved to be just as cautious and capable in his handling of the Iranian question, as distinct from the Egyptian, as any Labour Foreign Secretary might have been. There are no generalities that can be drawn other than that personalities and the quirks of fortune played a large part in the outcome of the Iranian question in 1953. So much has been made of the conspiracy to overthrow Musaddiq that it is well to bear in mind that things might have turned out quite differently with only a slight variation of circumstance. Indeed, as C. M. Woodhouse points out in his autobiography, *Something Ventured*, Musaddiq might well have fallen without any assistance from the British and Americans. Even so, Iran might have been doomed. Woodhouse's basic assumption was identical to that of the CIA History: 'Iran was in real danger of falling behind the Iron Curtain.'[112]

The British and the 1953 Covert Operation

From the vantage point of the CIA, 'Monty' Woodhouse was indispensable in planning the overthrow of the Musaddiq government because of his reputation, his competence, and his contacts, which extended to Churchill. Woodhouse was one of MI6's 'most highly esteemed officers', according to the CIA History.[113] He had fought with the Greek resistance during the Second World War. He was made colonel at the age of twenty-seven. He later became a Conservative Member of Parliament for Oxford, Chief Editor of Penguin Books, Director of Chatham House (the Royal Institute of International Affairs), and a distinguished historian of Greece. In 1951–52 he headed MI6 in Iran. He was trusted by the US Ambassador in Iran, Loy Henderson, and by certain key figures in the CIA, including Walter Bedell Smith (the Director of the CIA until 1953) and Allen Dulles (the Deputy Director who himself became Director in the Eisenhower years). Woodhouse got on well with Frank Wisner (the Director of Operations) and with Kermit Roosevelt (the head of CIA operations in the Middle East). In his general approach, Woodhouse took care to avoid the impression that the British merely aimed both to reverse Musaddiq's decision to nationalize the oil industry and to restore Anglo-Iranian. Since Woodhouse himself regarded the Company as 'stupid, boring, pigheaded and tiresome', this was not difficult.[114]

In Woodhouse's assessment, joint action by Britain and the United

---

[112] CIA History, p. iii.
[113] Ibid., p. 14.
[114] Dorril, *MI6*, p. 580.

States would be the only way to prevent the Soviet army from marching southwards and forging a satellite state in Iran on the model of Eastern Europe. Stalin might not actually have had that in mind, Woodhouse reflected later, but in the early 1950s it had certainly seemed possible. With the Shah and Kashani playing the parts of Hamlet and Thomas Becket respectively, Musaddiq appeared to Woodhouse as 'a wily theatrical, tragi-comic figure . . . [whose] abiding enemy . . . was Britain'.[115] The principal danger was not Musaddiq's crusade against the Anglo-Iranian Oil Company, which was serious enough from the British vantage point, but was not Woodhouse's main concern. From his background in the Greek civil war, the overarching menace was that of a Communist takeover: '[T]he longer he [Musaddiq] held office the more probable it became that Iran would pass under Soviet control.'[116] This, of course, was close to the American view, specifically the one held by Loy Henderson, who had long experience with the Russians and played a critical part in aligning the American and British positions: 'Loy Henderson changed the atmosphere in the US Embassy towards sympathy with the British case.'[117]

By late 1952, British and American views in Tehran closely approximated each other, but with a dissenting voice. The CIA Chief of Station in Tehran, Roger Goiran, believed that intervention would be a mistake. Goiran had carefully and skilfully built up an intelligence network in Iran, but its purpose, in his judgement, should remain anti-Soviet. He believed that intervention not only would be disastrous in the long run, but would also create the short-term impression that the United States supported 'Anglo-French colonialism'.[118] He was sensitive to that point because, among other reasons, he was a second-generation French American. He was also a man of principle and religious commitment. Woodhouse respected him, and the two of them worked in harmony despite a profound difference of outlook. He was an 'invaluable ally', Woodhouse commented in retrospect.[119]

Woodhouse had become head of MI6 in Tehran during the last months of the Labour Government in 1951. It is convenient at this point to review the relationship then existing between MI6 and the Foreign Office and to inquire into the ways in which the Conservative Government did or did not change things under the leadership of

---

[115] Woodhouse, *Something Ventured*, p. 106.

[116] Ibid., p. 114.

[117] Ibid., p. 110. For Henderson, see H. W. Brands, *Inside the Cold War: Loy Henderson and the Rise of the American Empire, 1918–1961* (New York, 1991), chaps. 15–17.

[118] Dorril, *MI6*, p. 584.

[119] Ibid., p. 577.

Churchill and Eden. Woodhouse owed his assignment to George Young, who had become head of MI6 operations in the Middle East earlier in the same year. Young has legendary status in MI6 lore as a man of unabashed contempt for Labour politicians, Arabs, and Iranians. 'A depressing experience,' he once commented on the Attlee government. He remarked about the 1951 election that 'the pall of negation' had lifted.[120] Those were revealing comments; Attlee and Bevin had held MI6 in check. There existed in any event a tension between MI6 and the Foreign Office, since officials of the latter were generally reluctant to endorse covert action. The Permanent Under-Secretary, Sir William Strang, had responsibility for coordinating intelligence operations with the head of MI6, 'C', Major-General Sir John 'Sinbad' Sinclair. Since Sinclair plays such a major part in the events of 1952–53, the following description of him is of interest: 'a tall, lean Scot with the angular, austere features of a Presbyterian minister, blue eyes behind horn-rimmed spectacles and a soft voice [that] gave him a kindly demeanour'.[121] Strang was the stronger of the two personalities. Sinclair often deferred to him on the Middle East, a region with which Strang had much greater familiarity. Strang submitted minutes to Bevin, who, in turn, characteristically and without fail, consulted Attlee on matters of importance. It is certain that Attlee directly concerned himself with intelligence operations during Morrison's tenure as Foreign Secretary (though Zaehner's appointment probably did not attract Attlee's attention). After the Conservative victory in 1951, the structure of decision making remained the same, but Eden acted with a much greater degree of independence than Morrison had been allowed. Indeed, Eden reasserted the prerogatives of covert action that he had held during 1941–45, his earlier term as Foreign Secretary. When he fell ill in 1953, the Prime Minister took charge. Churchill had an enthusiasm for clandestine operations that was entirely alien to Attlee. In such a way did the change of regime make a difference.

Within the Foreign Office, only a handful of officials knew of the plans to overthrow Musaddiq. These included the Deputy Under-Secretary, Sir Roger Makins, and his successor in early 1953, Sir Pierson Dixon, both of whom had strong reservations about the wisdom of covert action. Dixon objected not so much as a matter of principle, but because he doubted the efficacy of political intervention in Iran in both the short and the long term. As will be seen, he nearly throttled the Musaddiq project. Below Dixon in the chain of command was (Sir)

---

[120] George K. Young, *Masters of Indecision* (London, 1962), p. 15.
[121] Dorril, *MI6*, p. 494, quoting George Blake, the MI6 officer who provided the Soviet Union with vital intelligence secrets.

George Clutton, who acted as the Foreign Office liaison with MI6. Short-sighted and austere, Clutton had worked as an officer in the British Museum before the war. He was both efficient and humane, and his colleagues held him in esteem. Clutton controlled the circulation of intelligence papers, of which the further recipients included the Assistant Under-Secretary supervising the Middle East, Sir James Bowker; the head of the Eastern Department, Geoffrey Furlonge; and the officer in charge of the Iran desk, Christopher Gandy.

In Tehran, Woodhouse's predecessor, in practice and spirit, even if not in direct employment in MI6, was Colonel Geoffrey Wheeler, a former Indian Army officer whose intelligence career in Iran had begun during the Second World War.[122] Wheeler was a friend of Nancy Lambton. He had no more faith than she in the capacity of the Anglo-Iranian Oil Company to adjust to post-war circumstances, and he was in advance of most of his colleagues in recognizing the soundness of the fifty-fifty principle of profit sharing.[123] Not least, he was a source of inspiration to younger members in the British official community in Tehran. Woodhouse identified Wheeler as a man of kindred intellect and disposition and often conferred with him in London. At the beginning of his tenure in Tehran, Woodhouse found the British mission to be efficient and reliable, though he quickly developed doubts about both Zaehner and the Ambassador, Sir Francis Shepherd, who, he thought, perhaps unjustly, failed to rise to the challenge of the job.[124] Woodhouse got on well with Middleton and kept him fully apprised of MI6 activities.

When Woodhouse arrived in Iran there were standing plans to defend Iran from the threat of internal Communist subversion and from possible Soviet aggression in the event of another world war. Woodhouse himself was sceptical about the possibility of protecting the Western position in Iran during all-out war with the Soviet Union, but he saw it as one of his duties to carry forward such activities as surveillance on the Caspian Sea. In the Qavam crisis in July 1952, when the British feared the destabilization and possible collapse of the Iranian government, Woodhouse flew to Iraq to secure weapons for possible use by the tribes in northern Iran against a Soviet invasion.[125] There

---

[122] Like Zaehner, Wheeler held a Foreign Office appointment as Counsellor but had close links with MI6, if indeed he was not an MI6 officer. He is identified as such by Dorril, *MI6*, pp. 562 and 568.

[123] See Falle, *My Lucky Life,* p. 72.

[124] In his autobiography, Woodhouse referred to Shepherd as 'a dispirited bachelor dominated by his widowed sister' (*Something Ventured*, p. 109). For a much more favourable assessment of Shepherd, see Cable, *Intervention at Abadan*, e.g. pp. 17 and 81.

[125] Woodhouse, *Something Ventured*, pp. 115–16.

was also a tribal dimension to his work in the Abadan region of southern Iran, roughly in the oil-rich area controlled by the Bakhtiari. Derived from long, pre–Second World War antecedents, the plan involved the creation of an autonomous southern breakaway state under British overlordship. In the event of a collapse of the Iranian government, or the partition of Iran into informal spheres of Soviet and British influence, British control over the oilfields would remain intact. This plan carried over into the Woodhouse era. Though Woodhouse himself doubted its practicality, it remained part of his contingency planning in 1951–52.

Woodhouse devoted his principal attention to the danger of Communist, or Tudeh, subversion. He was assisted by Norman Darbyshire, the hard-drinking but able, Persian-speaking intelligence agent who had worked with Robin Zaehner during the war. Darbyshire's reputation later became clouded because of drunkenness, reckless behaviour, and abuse of his second wife, but at the time of his association with Woodhouse he was an energetic and exceedingly competent MI6 officer. The two of them divided their Iranian contacts roughly into those who spoke English and those who did not. While engaging the former, Woodhouse found members of the professional class who were willing not only to convey information but also to work actively against the Musaddiq regime.

As Nancy Lambton had anticipated, a significant number of lawyers, journalists, doctors, professors, bankers, and businessmen believed it to be in Iran's own interest to bring about the fall of Musaddiq. Many of them, it seemed to Woodhouse, were motivated above all by a sense of patriotism. This was certainly true of Woodhouse's three principal contacts. One, bearing the code name 'Omar', was the Director-General of a government department and eventually a member of Musaddiq's cabinet.[126] From 'Omar', Woodhouse learned some of the innermost secrets of the Musaddiq government. He had two other major contacts. One was Abbas Quli Neysari, Chairman of the Irano-British Bank.[127] The other was an ophthalmologist of international reputation, Hassan Alavi, who was also a deputy in the Majlis and never disguised his links with the British. Darbyshire helped in winning the support of other members of the Majlis, some with less

---

[126]See Woodhouse, *Something Ventured*, pp. 112–13. Omar's identity is still uncertain. He might have been Abdul Hussain Meftah, the Deputy Foreign Minister who attended Cabinet sessions in the absence of the Foreign Minister. I gained the impression from Woodhouse in the summer of 2001, however, that Omar might have been a composite figure constructed in recollection.

[127] George Young wrote in retrospect: '"Neys" did stand by us during the Mossadegh interlude' (Young to Denis Wright, 22 February 1981, Wright Papers, privately held).

than lofty motives, by distributing packages of biscuits, the centres of which had been removed and filled with banknotes.

When Woodhouse arrived in Tehran in August 1951, Robin Zaehner had already reestablished the alliance with the Rashidian brothers. Zaehner was now in the twilight of his Iranian career. Woodhouse recognized his skill in dealing with the Rashidians, but he regarded him as a dangerous amateur as far as serious undercover work was concerned. Zaehner did not possess the stamina or the ruthless determination to see his anti-Musaddiq plans through to completion. Nor did he prove to be especially adept at coordinating the activities of his branch of the Embassy with those of MI6. Before his departure, he turned over control of the Rashidian brothers to Woodhouse.[128] What Woodhouse would demonstrate was that the British, with careful planning, could still play a decisive part in Iran if they worked in concert with the Americans.

After Musaddiq evicted the British diplomatic mission in October 1952, Zaehner played his last hand, nearly upsetting Woodhouse's carefully laid plans. Having returned to London, Woodhouse made the mistake of inviting Zaehner to meet with him, Eden, and other high officials, including George Young, to discuss future operations. Zaehner gave a gloomy account. Plagued with self-doubt, he had been disillusioned with Qavam and now mistrusted the capacity of the Rashidians to dislodge Musaddiq. A late convert to the principle of non-intervention, Zaehner now emphatically believed that the British should let Iranian affairs take their own course. Woodhouse was appalled at Zaehner's defeatism. He responded to a casual remark made by Eden, who said that nothing could be done anyway without the help of the Americans. A less enterprising person than Woodhouse might have let things go at that. If Woodhouse himself had not seized the initiative at this point, there might never have been a coup against Musaddiq, at least one partly sponsored by the British.

Woodhouse interpreted Eden's comment to mean that he should explore possibilities with the Americans. He went to Washington in mid-November 1952. Before his departure, he conferred with Nancy Lambton, not Zaehner. Woodhouse was accompanied by Sam Falle, who had an intimate knowledge of Iranian politics and, since he had become the principal contact with the Rashidians, a familiarity with

---

[128] Another of Zaehner's contacts found useful by Woodhouse was (Sir) Shapoor Reporter, who later gained prominence in British-Iranian defence contracts. Reporter was a Zoroastrian (Parsee) whose family came from Bombay and who held dual British and Iranian citizenship. In 1953 he worked in the US Embassy in Tehran. It is possible that he helped provide the radio link with the MI6 Iranian station-in-exile in Cyprus.

the 'three larger-than-life brothers'.[129] In Washington, Woodhouse and Falle met with John Bruce-Lockhart, the MI6 station chief, who went with them to some of the meetings and cheerfully talked about the intricate relations between the State Department and the CIA but otherwise made no significant contribution to the discussions. Bedell Smith (Allen Dulles's predecessor) told Woodhouse, 'You may be able to throw out Musaddiq, but you will never get your own man to stick in his place.'[130] The question of Musaddiq's successor was by no means the only problem. The Rashidians were no less anti-American than previously. Woodhouse did not know how they would react until events actually unfolded. For their part, the Americans generally did not rule out the possibility of a combined move against Musaddiq, nor did they flinch at the price, which Woodhouse described as perhaps £500,000 plus the £10,000 a month already being paid to the Rashidians. Not all the American bureaucracy, however, fell in so wholeheartedly with these ideas. Woodhouse found the CIA officials ready to carry the discussions forward, even though they had been caught off guard by his raising the issue.[131] Those representing the State Department were hesitant to become involved. There was a lingering 'silliness' among some Americans, Woodhouse wrote later, who believed 'that Musaddiq could be retained and manipulated, and who dreaded the consequences of his downfall'.[132] This was at the end of 1952, a significant time because, among other reasons, the British had made contact with Kermit 'Kim' Roosevelt, who proved to be as enterprising on the American side as Woodhouse had been on the British.[133]

Woodhouse had made progress at the undercover level. Allen Dulles, though he could make no commitment in the transition between administrations, had seemed receptive to the idea of a combined operation against Musaddiq. And Woodhouse had found a powerful ally in Frank Wisner, a key figure in the CIA. At the other level, the one of high policy, the British were content to let things drift. 'We are in no hurry,' wrote Sir Pierson Dixon in December. 'Our Policy is to play the hand along until we can sound out the attitude of General Eisenhower's Administration to the Persian Oil problem.'[134]

In one of Eden's first conversations with Eisenhower in late 1952,

---

[129] Falle, *My Lucky Life*, p. 82.

[130] Woodhouse, *Something Ventured*, p. 118.

[131] See CIA History, p. 1.

[132] Woodhouse, *Something Ventured*, p. 121.

[133] See Kermit Roosevelt, *Countercoup: The Struggle for the Control of Iran* (New York, 1979), a book to be used with caution, but nevertheless a basic source.

[134] Minute by Dixon, 5 December 1952, FO 371/98703.

the President-Elect kept repeating, 'Then you don't think there is any-thing that can be done in the next sixty days?' Eden said he feared not, then and thereafter.[135] In his judgement the risks of interven-tion were too great. Yet the Americans insisted on some sort of action. 'The President kept repeating that we could not do nothing,' Eden reported to Churchill several months later, in March 1953. This was a ringing and persistent theme. 'The difficulty of this situation', Eden went on, 'remains that the Americans are perpetually eager to do something. The President repeated this several times.'[136] The British again acquiesced in another 'package deal' (as Eden described it to the Cabinet), whereby they once more adjusted their terms but main-tained their position that the company would have to receive 'fair compensation'.[137] The sticking point was now Musaddiq's reluctance to guarantee Anglo-Iranian compensation for future losses. Musad-diq himself seemed genuinely anxious to restore Iran's business repu-tation, and by all accounts, including his own, he desperately needed the money. But the Foreign Office believed that his anti-British an-tipathy would preclude his acceptance of any joint Anglo-American offer. This was probably an accurate judgement. As for Eisenhower, Eden concluded that he was 'obsessed' with the danger of a Commu-nist Iran, and far too solicitous of Musaddiq. When the final stalemate approached in the spring of 1953, Sir Pierson Dixon reflected: 'The plain fact is that we don't care how violent and unreasonable Musad-diq may be in announcing a breakdown. In fact the more unrestrained he is the more clearly our proposals will stand out as reasonable in the eyes of Persia & the world.'[138] On March 10, Musaddiq rejected the fi-nal offer. The 'high policy' of aligning American and British action in order to give Musaddiq a last chance had now come to an end, much to the relief of the British.

With such a concern for the reputation of Britain in 'the eyes of Persia' and the world at large, it is not surprising that Dixon and his Foreign Office colleagues were exceedingly wary of the other level of British policy, that of covert operations. In February 1953, Wood-house's plans were called to a halt. The principal influence in this de-cision was Dixon's. As Deputy Under-Secretary, he was proving himself to be just as 'robust' (one of his favourite words) as his predecessor, Makins, and just as influential with Eden. Dixon believed that if the

---

[135] See Eden to Sir C. Steel, Top Secret and Guard [Guard = not for American eyes], 4 De-cember 1952, FO 371/98703.

[136] As reported in Makins to FO, Top Secret, 7 March 1953, FO 371/104614.

[137] For this round of the abortive talks, see CAB 129/58 et seq.; and Eden, *Memoirs*, pp. 232–35.

[138] Minute by Dixon, 23 February 1953, FO 371/104613.

British and Americans sat tight, then the Musaddiq regime would fall of its own accord and they could then devise a solution to the oil problem with its successor. He was clear about priorities: '[T]he continuing tension in Persia', he wrote, 'is probably doing more harm in the M.E. than a "bad" settlement would cause.'[139] The Ministry of Fuel and Power and the Treasury did not agree. Here too Dixon saw a strong argument for biding one's time. The other departments would eventually concur in a settlement because the oil embargo could not be indefinitely sustained. He wanted to hold a steady course, 'always', in his own words, 'on the basic assumption that there must be a fair basis for compensation'.[140] He was a man of principle. He demanded respect for the British position. He wished above all to avoid compromising Britain's good name through underhanded actions of uncertain effectiveness and doubtful morality. Those were some of the reasons why, on 21 February, he curtailed the anti-Musaddiq conspiracy.[141] Yet his decision was shortly reversed. One cannot but pause to wonder how events would have transpired had Dixon not been overruled, or had Eden played a more aggressive part. Eden at the time was plagued with ill health and would be hospitalized in April for a gall bladder operation. He did not return to the Foreign Office until after Musaddiq's fall. What, then, was the reason for deciding not merely to resume covert operations but to pursue them with a vengeance? The answer can be summed up in one name: Churchill.

Churchill had been involved in the high politics of Persian oil since before the First World War. It was he who had championed the conversion of the Royal Navy from coal to oil and who had played a major part in the purchase by the British government of a majority of shares in the Anglo-Persian Oil Company. He had calculated at the time that the saving on the price paid for oil alone would amount to about £40 million. And he had stated:

> On this basis it may be that the aggregate profits, realised and potential, of this investment may be estimated at a sum not merely sufficient to pay all the programme of ships, great and small of that year and for the whole pre-war oil fuel installation, but are such that we may not unreasonably expect that one day we shall be entitled also to claim that the mighty fleets laid down in 1912, 1913, and 1914, the

[139] Minute by Dixon, 30 November 1952, FO 371/98703.
[140] Minute by Dixon, 19 March 1953, FO 371/104614.
[141] See Woodhouse, *Something Ventured*, p. 123, which does not, however, identify any of those involved in the decision except Eden.

greatest ever built by any power in an equal period, were added to the British Navy without costing a single penny to the taxpayer.[142]

Churchill therefore had every reason to take a renewed interest in the fate of Iranian oil in the early 1950s. After Eden became ill, Lord Salisbury assumed responsibility for foreign affairs, but in clandestine operations, he acted in effect as Churchill's lieutenant. As Woodhouse points out, it was Churchill who reversed the course: 'Churchill enjoyed dramatic operations and had no high regard for timid diplomatists. It was he who gave the authority for Operation Boot to proceed.'[143]

'Operation Boot' was the British term, 'Operation Ajax' the American, for the anti-Musaddiq plan.[144] It is certain that Eisenhower was fully aware of Operation Ajax and gave it his endorsement.[145] Like Churchill, Eisenhower worked from documents and mastered details. He knew his own mind and, contrary to the political mythology of the period, was by no means the captive of either Dulles brother, John Foster or Allen, though the latter certainly had his ear on this question. This is not the place for a discussion of the American side of the problem, but one point should be stressed. There was still an air of old-fashioned espionage about Operations Boot and Ajax. Musaddiq would be toppled. But neither Churchill nor Eisenhower was in the business of assassinating a fellow head of state. Specifically, there is no evidence that MI6 made plans to assassinate Musaddiq, as it did to kill Nasser three years later.[146]

Churchill merely endorsed plans that had developed since the meeting of Woodhouse and Falle with the officials of the CIA and State Department in November–December 1952. Despite Eden's ambivalent attitude, MI6 continued systematically to plan for Musaddiq's overthrow. Sir John Sinclair, 'C', in January 1953 lent his direct authority to Woodhouse, Darbyshire, and the Foreign Office liaison, George Clutton, to continue pursuing the possibility of a joint action with the CIA. Kermit Roosevelt attended some of their meetings in London. At almost the same time that Sir Pierson Dixon attempted to stop the operation, Sinclair and Clutton met in Washington with both CIA and

---

[142] Winston S. Churchill, *The World Crisis* (2 vols., New York, 1923), I, p. 140.

[143] Woodhouse, *Something Ventured*, p. 125.

[144] Technically, the American operation held the CIA classification of TPAJAX. The prefix TP designated the covert operation in Iran.

[145] See Stephen E. Ambrose, *Eisenhower: The President* (New York, 1984), p. 111.

[146] For a balanced discussion of the plots on Nasser's life, see Keith Kyle, *Suez* (London, 1991), pp. 149–51.

State Department officials on 18 February and proposed that Kermit Roosevelt be the 'Field Commander'.[147] A month later, on 18 March, MI6 received a message from Frank Wisner, Director of Plans, that the CIA would be prepared to discuss detailed tactics. The calendar now had a monthly ring to it. In mid-April, after a period of continued vacillation, the Foreign Office finally endorsed the project. In view of the combined pressure of the Prime Minister on the one hand, and of the CIA offering the equivalent of a full-blown Anglo-American alliance on the other, the Foreign Office now came aboard. George Clutton took the decisive step in giving the go-ahead to the Rashidian brothers. The coup was now underway.[148]

The candidate to replace Musaddiq was General Fazlollah Zahedi. In British and American discussions in Tehran after the collapse of the Qavam regime in July 1952, he had figured prominently as the only alternative to Musaddiq. During the Second World War, Zahedi had been seized by the British at gun point and interned for being pro-Nazi, which now turned out to be an advantage, since he was not tainted with a pro-British reputation.[149] Sam Falle had written about Zahedi:

In this country of weak men he is comparatively strong.

He is strongly anti-communist.

He was imprisoned by the British during the war and is not considered to be a British stooge.

He is on good terms with some members of the National Front—among these is Kashani . . .

He should be able to count on the support of a section of the Army.[150]

The British analysis as expressed by Falle coincided with the CIA assessment: 'Zahedi alone of potential candidates had the vigor and courage to make him worthy of support.'[151]

---

[147] These meetings are not mentioned in the CIA History, but see Dorril, *MI6,* pp. 580–83.

[148] It is at this point, April 1953, that the CIA History begins in substance (on p. 3).

[149] For the Second World War arrest of Zahedi, see Fitzroy Maclean, *Eastern Approaches* (London, 1949; 1964 edn.): 'He was . . . a really bad lot: a bitter enemy of the Allies, a man of unpleasant personal habits . . . he found himself looking down the barrel of my Colt automatic . . . Without further ado, I invited the General to put his hands up and informed him that I had instructions to arrest him and that, if he made any noise or attempt at resistance, he would be shot" (pp. 271–77).

[150] Minute by Falle, Confidential, 2 August 1952, FO 248/1531.

[151] CIA History, p. 8.

The British supported Zahedi in the same manner as they had Seyyid Zia and Qavam. Zahedi now represented the 'open opposition', in Falle's phrase, but too warm an embrace by the British would prove to be fatal: he would be regarded as a puppet. The British expulsion from Iran in October 1952 worked to Zahedi's advantage. In the preceding months the British had tried to keep their support for Zahedi as discreet as possible. Falle had made no secret that Zahedi was the British candidate, but there had been no direct bribes. Zahedi later received large amounts of money from the CIA—$1 million in cash after Musaddiq was ousted—but in the summer and autumn of 1952 the Rashidians had used bribes and other means of persuasion at a lower level. As with Seyyid Zia and Qavam, so with Zahedi: he was beyond the patronage of the three brothers. They had no contact with him up to the time of the British eviction.

One of Zahedi's principal virtues, in British eyes, was simply that he was willing to put himself forward. He was the only leading figure in public life bidding for the premiership. He attracted increasing support from disaffected members of the National Front, including clerics and merchants as well as the military. Nevertheless, the Shah distrusted him, and Zahedi himself seemed incapable of putting forward a plan of action (in the end, the CIA had to provide him with a military plan).[152] Musaddiq's coalition had become increasingly fragile, but he still commanded the general loyalty of the army and police. It was an open bet whether Musaddiq's enemies could combine to overpower him.

The Rashidians themselves were arrested and briefly imprisoned when Musaddiq cracked down on the pro-Zahedi movement shortly before the British expulsion: 'This in no way disconcerted the brothers, who continued to operate from jail, where they also obtained all the good food they desired.'[153] They were set free because of insufficient legal evidence to prosecute them, though as always in the case of the Rashidians, one suspects that a certain amount of bribery eased their release. To what extent did Musaddiq himself perceive the mounting danger? Musaddiq had always had a fatalistic streak in him, but in the autumn of 1952 fatalism seemed to merge with a certain complacency. When he finally acted to expel the British, his ruling coalition had already been fatally weakened by the rift between him and Kashani. In 1951 it had been the clerics who had helped Musaddiq to

[152] Falle, *My Lucky Life*, p. 82. In Falle's judgement, Zahedi was 'tough and clear headed'—an assessment more favourable than that of the local CIA officers, who found him 'lacking in drive, energy, and concrete plans' (CIA History, p. 27).

[153] Falle, *My Lucky Life*, p. 82.

power. They now played a vital part in his fall. In April 1953, Kashani helped Zahedi avoid arrest by providing him sanctuary in the Majlis. At an advanced stage of the planning for the coup, a joint MI6-CIA assessment concluded that 'nearly all the important religious leaders with large followings are firmly opposed to Mossadeq. Both the US field station and the British group have firm contacts with such leaders.'[154]

It is important to bear in mind that after October 1952 the British operated in Iran only indirectly. 'It's always unfortunate and makes things more difficult', Falle recalled with understatement in 1985, 'if you don't have diplomatic relations . . . [W]e couldn't negotiate on the spot, nor could we continue our contingency plan from an Iranian base.'[155] Anti-Musaddiq activities were now monitored from Cyprus, where Darbyshire kept in touch with the Rashidians by means of tri-weekly radio exchanges. The Rashidian organization swelled to full strength. It embraced not only deputies and senators of the Majlis but also ranking officers in the army and police, mullahs, merchants, newspapermen, and, not least, mob leaders. And as has been mentioned, there was another dimension to the British plan. In southern Iran the tribal leaders had maintained good relations with British consular officers. Both the urban and the rural components would be activated simultaneously to counter Tudeh support of Musaddiq. Here a major stroke of luck played to British advantage. The prelude to the Iranian crisis coincided with Stalin's death on 25 March. In the subsequent period of indecision, the Russians failed to succour the Communists in Iran. The Tudeh organization was cast adrift, leaving, among other things, a packing case of postage stamps overprinted with the words 'Republic of Iran'—a reminder of what might have happened had the Soviet Union intervened.

The key British figure to emerge on the operational side of the project was Norman Darbyshire, who after October 1952 became head of the MI6 Iran station-in-exile in Cyprus.[156] It fell to Darbyshire to make the initial contact with the CIA operatives in the field and to draw up the preliminary plan with his counterpart, Donald Wilber. It will be recalled that Wilber is the author of the CIA History. From the History there emerges a clear account of MI6 as a 'junior partner' entirely willing to follow the American lead.[157] There were good reasons

---

[154] CIA History, Appendix B, pp. 20–21.

[155] Transcript, 'End of Empire: Iran'.

[156] Darbyshire's second in command was (Sir) Dick Franks, who became head of the MI6 station in Tehran after relations were restored in December 1953. Franks rose to become Chief of the Service.

[157] 'Junior partner' is the phrase explicitly used in the CIA History, e.g. p. 87.

for this unaccustomed acquiescence. The CIA not only had the tactical advantage of a base in the US Embassy in Tehran but also possessed incomparably greater resources. Wilber describes his initial encounter with Darbyshire:

> Mr. Darbyshire held quite similar views of Iranian personalities and had made very similar estimates of the factors involved in the Iranian political scene. There was no friction or marked difference of opinion during the discussions. It also quickly became apparent that the SIS was perfectly content to follow whatever lead was taken by the Agency.

In letting the CIA take the initiative, Darbyshire and his colleagues betrayed hints of simultaneous satisfaction and jealousy:

> It seemed obvious to Wilber that the British were very pleased at having obtained the active cooperation of the Agency and were determined to do nothing which might jeopardize US participation.

> At the same time there was a faint note of envy expressed over the fact that the Agency was better equipped in the way of funds, personnel, and facilities than was SIS.[158]

The CIA History detects a pattern that recurred during the drafting of the two critical plans, the preliminary Cyprus plan prepared in Nicosia on June 1 and the major operational plan completed two weeks later on June 16 in London. On both occasions the British followed the American initiative.

In both meetings the British representatives carefully studied the language but merely endorsed the CIA version. Since the two views coincided, there was no need for elaborate exchanges, but American dominance was clear. At the meeting in mid-June in London, the CIA agents met with their counterparts at SIS headquarters at 54 Broadway, the inside of which was 'notable only for a large sign with the legend in red, "Curb Your Guests".' The CIA officials produced an expanded draft based on a conference in Beirut presided over by Kermit Roosevelt. Though Woodhouse was present, Darbyshire represented MI6 on the operational side.[159] The CIA History describes again the relatively passive part played by the British:

> From the moment the discussion began, it was clear that the SIS had no major comments of their own on the draft plan. Nor did they

---

[158] CIA History, p. 6.

[159] After the decision to launch the operation, Woodhouse withdrew into the background: 'I thought it best to absent myself from the scene, since the tactical control was in reliable hands and I did not want to be tempted to interfere with it' (Woodhouse, *Something Ventured*, p. 126).

have much to say on the Beirut version beyond a certain close attention to phraseology.

> As at Nicosia it was apparent that the Americans were to be placated and allowed to run things as they pleased.[160]

In the discussion of the 'assets' of the two organizations, it became clear that both MI6 and the CIA were rooted principally in the bazaar or business community, that the British had stronger contacts with the Shah, the military, and clergy, and that the Americans were effective in slightly different ways. The two networks now meshed.[161]

The approval of the operational plan took place on the British side on 1 July, when Churchill, Salisbury, and Sinclair gave formal endorsements. Eisenhower, John Foster Dulles, and Allen Dulles followed on 11 July, but not without extracting a further formal letter from the British Ambassador in Washington, stating that the British government would submit to international arbitration the issue of compensation for the nationalization of the Anglo-Iranian Oil Company. The Company had 'not been consulted', wrote the Ambassador, Sir Roger Makins, but he was convinced that 'a generous attitude' would be adopted.[162] This was a major statement because it meant that the British government would, if necessary, confront the Company and prepare the way for a settlement based in part on arbitration. According

---

[160] CIA History, p. 14.

[161] In the course of the discussions, the British revealed the details of the Rashidian network, but the Americans remained silent about their own undercover organization, which was also based on a pair of brothers, Ali Jalali and Farouk Keyvani, who had the code names Nerren and Cilley. 'To the best of our knowledge', concludes the CIA History on this point, the CIA agents in Iran 'were not uncovered by the Rashidian brothers or any other SIS agents during the course of this operation' (p. 8).

The names of Ali Jalali and Farouk Keyvani were not generally known until the late twentieth century, whereas the Rashidians, by contrast, were open about their connections with the British. Some further details clarify the contrast. Nerren and Cilley paid special attention to newspapers, though not necessarily the principal newspapers, and mob rousers. This concentrated effort to manipulate the press and control the street mirrored the CIA's aim in combating the Tudeh. The Rashidian network, by contrast, consisted largely of the elite and included members of the Majlis, government officials, clerics, and businessmen, though there was certainly a gangster and mob dimension as well. The British themselves were principally interested in influencing prominent Iranians; the Rashidian organization in turn reflected that aim. Nerren and Cilley had a network of at least 130 agents who, by Iranian standards, were effective. Their budget of $1 million was larger than that of the Rashidians, but Nerren and Cilley were not independently wealthy and probably did not invest any of their own resources. All in all, the strength of the two organizations was probably about equal. They overlapped but nevertheless complemented each other.

[162] CIA History, Appendix C, 23 July 1953.

to the CIA History, the purpose was to confirm that the British government would not rigidly follow the line of the Company but would be 'flexible' with Musaddiq's successor.[163] Lord Salisbury, who presided over the Foreign Office during Eden's illness, endorsed that principle and moreover stated to his colleagues in the Cabinet that it would be 'disastrous' to give the Americans the impression that 'we are only concerned with our oil.'[164] Arbitration seemed a small price to pay for American cooperation and, in the event, did not prove to be necessary.

When the plan for intervention became operational, no one knew how the Shah would react. This was the critical point. An earlier assessment of the part he might or might not play in the confrontation continued to hold true: 'The Shah still has some symbolic standing with the public throughout the country and the Army although the latter are angry with him because they think he has let them down. If he does not show some signs of decisiveness and manliness in the near future he will lose what little is left of his prestige.'[165] Whether the Shah would now steel himself for the showdown with Musaddiq, no one could predict. 'There still remained the problem of persuading the nervous Shah to play his role', Woodhouse wrote in getting to the heart of the matter, 'which would consist simply of signing two decrees (*firmans*), one dismissing Musaddiq and the other appointing Zahedi in his place.'[166] Much would depend on Kim Roosevelt, who in turn relied on the Rashidians as well as the CIA network. The Rashidians would be Roosevelt's means of access to the Shah and, from the British perspective, the key to his success.

Roosevelt secretly crossed the border into Iran on 19 July. It is at this stage worth reflecting on the balance of forces in Iran—the way they had shifted in the spring and summer of 1953—and the British and American calculation of the odds at the time. Part of the irony of the story is that the Musaddiq government was still popular, nationalist, and anti-communist. Musaddiq remained a figure who touched a basic chord of Iranian nationalism; according to one of the leading historians of Iran: 'Musaddiq's single-mindedness and intransigence were matched by his affectivity, compassion and sincerity, which made him the object of popular affection and esteem.'[167] He had powerful support from the population at large, in part because his social

---

[163] Ibid., p. 17.
[164] See Dorril, *MI6*, p. 587.
[165] Minute by Falle, Confidential, 2 August 1952, FO 248/1531.
[166] Woodhouse, *Something Ventured*, p. 126.
[167] Azimi, *Iran: The Crisis of Democracy*, p. 333.

reforms had now begun to take hold.[168] But some of the debate over social legislation increasingly antagonized the religious conservatives, not least the Ayatollah Kashani, with whom Musaddiq's relations by the spring of 1953 had deteriorated irretrievably. The National Front had cracked, and with it Musaddiq's precarious control over the Majlis. In April his chief of police, Muhammad Afshartus, had been assassinated. At least indirectly the Rashidians were involved in his murder, which contributed to the instability of the Musaddiq government.[169] Musaddiq nevertheless remained in control of the police and the army, though the latter included officers who might declare themselves loyal to the Shah if it came to a showdown.

The story of the actual intervention has been told many times, but two points of interest from the British vantage point emerge from the CIA History and other documentary evidence that has become accessible in the last decade. They concern Darbyshire and the Rashidians, who from beginning to end played a vital part in the unfolding events. Far from being reluctant to transfer their loyalties to the CIA, the Rashidians proved to be stalwart and indeed irrepressible in their anti-Musaddiq drive. When Sir Pierson Dixon managed to call a temporary halt to MI6 activities in February 1953, therewith curtailing the flow of money to the brothers, they carried on out of their own pocket. In the discussions with the CIA, Darbyshire gave assurances that the Rashidians would be willing 'to risk their possessions and their lives in an attempt against Mossadeq'.[170] The CIA History concludes: 'In the critical days of August 1953 the Rashidians did display such a willingness.'[171] Darbyshire himself was everywhere at once—in Nicosia,

---

[168] For Musaddiq's reforms, which included health and accident insurance as well as women's suffrage, see Homa Katouzian, *Musaddiq and the Struggle for Power in Iran* (London, 1990), chap. 10.

[169] There is no evidence of direct British involvement in the murder, but one of the motives of the Rashidians may have been that Afshartus had knowledge of their wide-ranging subversive activities—to a far greater extent than did Musaddiq. There are contradictory accounts of the murder itself, but the most interesting one on the British side is Darbyshire's. He was closer than any other MI6 officer to the internal developments in Iran at this time, and he could be relied on to relate the unvarnished truth as he saw it, though sometimes rather impulsively. According to Darbyshire, the Rashidians had helped certain Royalist army officers abduct Afshartus, but then things got out of hand: Afshartus 'was kidnapped and held in a cave. Feelings ran high and Afshartus was unwise enough to make derogatory remarks about the Shah. He was under guard by a young army officer and the young officer pulled out a gun and shot. That man was never part of the programme at all but that's how it happened' (Dorril, *MI6*, p. 585). Darbyshire's account glosses over the probability that the Rashidians may have had him murdered for their own reasons. Afshartus may have been about to move against them. By eliminating him, the Rashidians would have acted in self-interest while also attempting to destabilize the Musaddiq government.

[170] CIA History, p. 7.

[171] Ibid.

Baghdad, Geneva, and London. Yet when the crucial events began to unfold in mid-August and he requested authorization to return to Tehran, MI6 headquarters refused permission. If the operation failed, it would be just as well not to have direct MI6 involvement.

The basic weakness in the CIA-MI6 plan was the indecisiveness of the Shah. So feckless was he that MI6 and the CIA believed that the only way to goad him into signing the two decrees, the one dismissing Musaddiq, the other replacing him with Zahedi, would be for his twin sister, Princess Ashraf, to persuade him to take the plunge. The Princess had been forced into exile. She lived mainly in Switzerland, but she often went to the Riviera. Asadollah Rashidian now made contact with her, but left it to Darbyshire to provide a compelling lure.[172] When he presented her with a mink coat and a substantial though unspecified amount of cash, 'her eyes lit up'.[173] She returned to Tehran on 25 July and left again five days later for Europe. She was confident, according to Darbyshire, that she had persuaded her brother to take a decisive stand. But not quite. The Shah still insisted on guarantees from both the British and the Americans that they would come to his assistance. Darbyshire and Woodhouse helped arrange for the routine BBC Persian-language news broadcast to begin not with the usual 'It is now midnight in London' but with the phrase 'It is now exactly midnight'—a signal to the Shah that Britain would stand behind him.[174] He received similar assurance from Eisenhower himself. Everything then went off the track. After the Shah finally decided to issue the firmans, Musaddiq arrested the emissary handing him the decrees, thus preventing Zahedi from receiving the royal designation. The Shah fled the country. Zahedi went into hiding. The CIA-MI6 intervention seemed to have collapsed. Gloom and failure pervaded the two headquarters in Washington and London. Roosevelt was sent instructions to leave Iran, which he ignored. Churchill later referred to Nelson's blind eye.[175]

Again, the story has been related many times with different nuances and details emphasized, but Roosevelt managed to twist victory from

---

[172] The CIA was particularly interested in the way Asadollah Rashidian managed to obtain an exit visa and re-entry permit 'from no less a supporter of Mossadeq than Foreign Minister Hoseyn Fatemi'. It seemed to confirm that Fatemi had links with MI6. Fatemi in any event 'was certainly aware of Rashidian's agent status with the British' (CIA History, p. 10). It is, however, highly improbable that Fatemi had MI6 connections. He was one of the most radical of Musaddiq's ministers and the only one later to be executed.

[173] Dorril, *MI6*, p. 588.

[174] The CIA History attributes the BBC signal entirely to Darbyshire: 'In London the necessary arrangements had been made by Darbyshire to send the phrase over the BBC' (p. 24).

[175] CIA History, pp. 79–80.

defeat by rallying the anti-Musaddiq forces.[176] There is one passage that is frequently quoted because it vividly catches the bizarre mood as well as the technique used to rouse the mob to bring down the Musaddiq government on the morning of 19 August. It bears repeating here because it can now be placed in a British context:

> [W]ith the army standing close guard around the uneasy capital, a grotesque procession made its way along the street leading to the heart of Tehran. There were tumblers turning handsprings, weight-lifters twirling iron bars and wrestlers flexing their biceps. As specta-tors grew in number, the bizarre assortment of performers began shouting pro-Shah slogans in unison. The crowd took up the chant and there, after one precarious moment, the balance of public psy-chology swung against Musaddiq.[177]

Darbyshire's reaction to those events was immediate and joyous, and he knew the underlying reason for the success: it had been the Rashid-ians who had bribed and manipulated the mob, and it was they who had 'saved the day'.[178]

Over three hundred Iranians were killed in heavy street fighting. Musaddiq, true to style, carried on to the end by proclaiming that he

[176] The unpublished British documents unfortunately add little to well-known accounts. See, for example, the 'Tehran Situation Report Evening August 22 Secret' written by the official in charge of Iranian affairs, Christopher Gandy (FO 371/104570). Gandy knew of MI6 involve-ment, but he and his Foreign Office colleagues were careful to write all documents as if the change of government had been an entirely Iranian development. Thus, according to the ac-count prepared by the Eastern Department, 'Musaddiq rose to power on a platform of nation-alism and opposition to dictatorship. His collapse was due to his abandonment of the second of these principles and his increasingly dictatorial methods; and also to his failure as a nationalist, both by his inability to create a working oil industry of Persia's own and by his increasing reliance on a foreign-inspired organisation, the Tudeh (Communist) party' (memorandum of 24 Au-gust 1953, FO 371/104570). This became the standard line within the government as well as the interpretation given to the public. The British were much more discreet than the Americans. Until the publication of Woodhouse's book, hints of MI6 involvement came mainly from Amer-ican circles. In the first edition of *Countercoup*—the edition he was forced to withdraw—Roose-velt attempted to obscure the complicity of the British government by alleging, erroneously, that the conspiracy originated with the Anglo-Iranian Oil Company. See Thomas Powers, 'A Book Held Hostage', *Nation*, 12 April 1980.

[177] *Saturday Evening Post*, 6 November 1954, quoted in Woodhouse, *Something Ventured*, p. 129.

[178] Dorril, *MI6*, p. 592. This angle of vision on the events of August 1953 led later to a sim-plistic interpretation apparently endorsed by some MI6 officers: 'Roosevelt really did little more than show up in Iran with CIA funds to encourage agents the British had organized and then re-leased to American control' (Wilbur Crane Eveland, *Ropes of Sand: America's Failure in the Middle East* [New York, 1980], p. 109). See also Christopher Andrew, *Secret Service: The Making of the Brit-ish Intelligence Community* (London, 1985), p. 494.

would defend Iran against British and American tanks in the streets of Tehran, but acquiesced melodramatically in his arrest. At his trial he eloquently stated that he was being judged by the agents of foreigners for having struggled against the enemies of Iran. As the narrative of this essay has made clear, his accusation was not untrue, though British and American involvement in the coup was only one element and did not determine the subsequent set of events over the long run. Few at the time could have anticipated the Shah's later tyranny. Historians will long debate connections between the intervention of 1953 and the origins of the Iranian revolution.

In 1953, at least to MI6 and the CIA, the story appeared to have an entirely happy ending. Roosevelt arrived in London on 25 August. He was escorted immediately to Major-General Sir John Sinclair, the head of the Secret Intelligence Service, MI6. 'From the very beginning', according to the CIA History, 'it was made plain to him that SIS was grateful not only because of the success of the operation per se, but because of the effect its success had already had and would continue to have upon SIS's reputation and relations with its superiors.'[179] At the Foreign Office, Roosevelt received a frosty reception from the Assistant Under-Secretary supervising Middle Eastern affairs, Sir James Bowker, who probably represented traditional Foreign Office mistrust and disapproval of clandestine operations: 'It appeared that their [MI6] relationships, at least in this [Foreign Office] area, were neither close nor cordial at this level.'[180] On the other hand, the Permanent Under-Secretary, Sir William Strang, extended a warm greeting to Roosevelt and listened sympathetically as he explained why it had been necessary to take things into his own hands and, for four or five critical days, not to report to headquarters. This was a sensitive point. Had the intervention failed, Roosevelt would certainly have been held accountable not only for failing to communicate but also for not obeying orders to leave and thus risking capture. But in this case success justified local initiative and inspiration. The CIA History provides a fascinating account of the relationship between the Foreign Office and MI6 on that very point:

> He [Sinclair] explained that Strang was the source of his political guidance and such authorizations as were required from the Foreign Office . . . In the course of the conversation it became apparent that the portion of particular interest to Sinclair was the reason why

[179] CIA History, p. 78.
[180] Ibid., p. 80.

the station had not reported more fully from Tehran between 15 and 19 August.

> Sinclair is not a demonstrative person, but there was a definite glow emanating from him when Strang with apparent heartiness responded to the explanations, remarking that Roosevelt had done the only possible thing and that in matters of that sort decisions could only be made on the spot.[181]

Lord Salisbury, as Acting Secretary of State for Foreign Affairs, also greeted Roosevelt with a combination of courtesy and warmth of feeling that was memorable: 'As requested by Sinclair, Roosevelt gave Lord Salisbury the full treatment, and he appeared to be absolutely fascinated.'[182]

Salisbury, in fact, was one of the principal figures in a secret care-taker government, for Churchill along with Eden was incapacitated. Unknown to the CIA—and to the public—Churchill had suffered a stroke. But he rallied sufficiently to receive Roosevelt and to launch into a tirade against the Anglo-Iranian Oil Company, which, Churchill said, had 'fouled things up' and would no longer be allowed to do so. According to the CIA History, 'This was a most touching occasion.'

> The Prime Minister seemed to be in bad shape physically. He had great difficulty in hearing; occasional difficulty in articulating; and apparently difficulty in seeing to his left.

> In spite of this he could not have been more kind personally nor more enthusiastic about the operation. He was good enough to express envy of Roosevelt's role and a wish that he had been 'some years' younger and might have served under his command.[183]

Apart from Sir James Bowker, everyone seemed pleased, especially Churchill. From the vantage point of nearly half a century later, the CIA-MI6 operation appears basically misguided—indeed disastrous, since it strengthened the Shah and led to dictatorship and revolution. But that was not the contemporary judgement, which could be summed up in the contemporary view that the world had been spared

---

[181] CIA History, p. 83.
[182] Ibid., p. 80.
[183] Ibid., p. 81.

'a Communist Iran' and 'a second Korea'.[184] Churchill probably expressed the consensus as well as anyone when he said that it was 'the finest operation since the end of the war'.[185]

Mohammed Mosaddeq and the 1953 Coup in Iran   2004

---

[184] As, for example, in the CIA History, p. 34.
[185] Ibid., p. 81.

29

THE MIDDLE EAST CRISIS OF 1958

'**G**amal Abdel Nasser remains the hero of the Arab world,' observed the British Ambassador in Lebanon, Sir George Middleton, at the beginning of the Middle East crisis of 1958.[1] He wrote this in February, just a few days before the world's attention was galvanized by the joining of Egypt and Syria into the new state of the United Arab Republic. The significance of the merger, Middleton noted later, could be made clear by a glance at the map because it 'has brought Abdel-Nasser to within some fifty kilometres of Beirut'.[2] Neither Middleton nor virtually anyone else in British circles questioned the assumption that Nasser himself directed, indeed motivated, an expansionist pan-Arab movement or, later in the year, that he might be the hidden hand in the Iraqi revolution of 14 July.[3] For the British, the events in the spring and summer of 1958 posed dilemmas almost as severe as those during the Suez crisis, which Nasser had precipitated —two years previously to the month—by the nationalization of the Suez Canal Company in July 1956. He now appeared to be making a territorial bid for all the Middle East, not least the Persian Gulf. According to a Cabinet discussion in May 1958: 'If Lebanon was compelled to accede to the United Arab Republic, Iraq and Jordan might not be able to retain their independence.'[4] As the crisis reached its peak in July, the prospects seemed even more alarming: 'If we allowed the legitimate Government of the Lebanon to be overthrown and acquiesced in the armed insurrection in Iraq, disorder would rapidly develop in Jordan; Israel, Turkey and the Persian Gulf States would be

[1] Middleton to Lloyd, Confidential, 23 January 1958, FO 371/134116. For Nasser and the crisis of 1958, one of the most useful works remains Malcolm H. Kerr, *The Arab Cold War* (London, 1971 ed.). Another work that has stood the test of time is Patrick Seale, *The Struggle for Syria: A Study of Post-War Arab Politics* (Oxford, 1965). For recent scholarship, see especially Irene L. Gendzier, *Notes from the Minefield: United States Intervention in Lebanon and the Middle East, 1945–1958* (New York, 1997); Ulrich H. Brunnhuber, *Die Libanonkrise 1958: U.S. Intervention im Zeichen der Eisenhower Doktrin?* (Hamburg, 1997); Ritchie Ovendale, 'Great Britain and the Anglo-American Invasion of Jordan and Lebanon in 1958', *International History Review,* 16 (1994); Lawrence Tal, 'Britain and the Jordan Crisis of 1958', *Middle Eastern Studies,* 31 (January 1995); and Fawaz A. Gerges, *The Superpowers and the Middle East: Regional and International Politics, 1955–1967* (Boulder, Colo., 1994). See also especially J. C. Hurewitz, *Middle East Politics: The Military Dimension* (New York, 1969). For historiographical interpretation, see Douglas Little, 'Gideon's Band', *Diplomatic History,* 18, 4 (Fall 1994), pp. 513–40. I have benefited from Carolyn Attié, 'Lebanon in the 1950s: President Chamoun and Western Policy in Lebanon' (dissertation, University of Texas, 1996).

[2] Middleton to Lloyd, Confidential, 13 March 1958, FO 371/134116.

[3] For recent historical accounts, see Robert A. Fernea and W. R. Louis, *The Iraqi Revolution of 1958* (London, 1991).

[4] Cabinet Conclusions (58) 43, 15 May 1958, CAB 128/32, Part 1.

isolated'.[5] The question was whether Nasser could be stopped by force or whether intervention would merely repeat the disastrous Suez invasion of 1956, which stood in memory as an ignominious as well as frustrating defeat because of American insistence on the withdrawal of British and allied troops. Suez cast a shadow over all British thought and action.

In reflecting on the link between the events of 1956 and 1958, Middleton pondered the irony of the rise and decline of great powers, the winning of the Second World War, and the waning of British power. He was a man of incisive intellect and wide experience, which included tours of duty in Iran and India. His ideas represented a main current of thought. He believed that Western influence in the Middle East had gradually but ineluctably eroded. The power of the elites who had benefited from the British and French presence had diminished, thus leaving the British with only a remnant of their former power. 'The Suez intervention of 1956', he wrote, 'was the latest of the crises in this process of decline.'[6] He urged a realistic acknowledgement of Britain's limited capacity to influence the politics of the region. Sir Gladwyn Jebb, the Ambassador in Paris, agreed with him and held that 'the tough Suez type action' to prop up such states as Lebanon and Jordan simply would not work.[7] Those who had opposed Suez now not only questioned the effectiveness of another intervention but were uneasily aware of certain ethical issues. The lessons of Suez, for officials and ministers no less than for the public, were moral as well as political, at least in a minimal sense: everyone wished to avoid the 'moral obloquy' of Suez, in the phrase of Harold Macmillan, the Prime Minister.[8]

On the other hand, Sir William Hayter and others who shaped day-by-day as well as long-range Middle Eastern policy at the Foreign Office refused to accept 'defeatist assumptions'. Hayter was the Deputy Under-Secretary. 'We may flop', he wrote, 'but I hope we can avoid it, particularly as we now have the Americans on our side.'[9] This distinction between Suez in 1956 and the impending crisis of 1958 was vital. Had the Americans been on the side of the British in 1956, the outcome obviously would have been entirely different. In 1958 the

[5] Cabinet Conclusions (58), 55, 14 July 1958, CAB 128/32, Part 2.

[6] Middleton to Lloyd, Confidential, 11 June 1958, FO 371/134122.

[7] See Jebb to Hayter, Secret, 4 July 1958, FO 371/134130.

[8] Macmillan's comment in the Cabinet meeting of 16 July 1958, CC (58) 59, CAB 128/32, Part 2.

[9] Hayter to Jebb, Secret, 8 July 1958, FO 371/134130; W. R. Louis, 'Harold Macmillan and the Middle East Crisis of 1958', *Proceedings of the British Academy: 1996 Lectures and Memoirs*, 94 (London, 1996), pp. 207–28.

situation reversed itself. The Americans would now take the lead. Not without an element of sardonic humour mixed with anxiety, Macmillan noted that the Americans faced a crisis comparable to Britain's own encounter with Nasser. 'You are doing a Suez on me,' Macmillan remarked to Eisenhower in July 1958.[10]

After the British and French collapse in 1956, the United States emerged as the dominant Western power in the Middle East. Like those in London, officials in Washington recalled historical analogies of the 1930s and tended to see the Middle East through the prism of the Cold War. Arab politics, however, had a dynamic of their own, especially in relation to the Baghdad Pact of 1955 and the Eisenhower Doctrine of 1957. From Western perspectives, the Baghdad Pact would protect the Middle East against possible expansion by the Soviet Union as well as the danger of internal communist takeovers. The Pact included Iraq, Turkey, Iran, Pakistan, and Britain. The United States had acted as one of the sponsors but did not formally join the organization. John Foster Dulles, the Secretary of State, saw belatedly that Cold War alliances would divide rather than unite the Arab world and that the Baghdad Pact would have repercussions beyond the Middle East. Pakistan's adherence antagonized India and Afghanistan. Nasser regarded Iraq as a satellite of Britain. The Pact intensified Egypt's hostility to the West. In December 1955, Jordan had refused to join, thus dividing the Hashemite monarchies of Iraq and Jordan. Saudi Arabia allowed the United States access to an air base at Dhahran but opposed the Baghdad Pact, in part out of historic antagonism towards Iraq. After the events of Suez in late 1956, those rivalries took a different turn when Saudi Arabia shifted into the anti-Nasser camp. A loose royalist alliance of Iraq, Jordan, and Saudi Arabia now confronted the revolutionary force of Nasser's populist pan-Arab nationalism. Sir Charles Johnston, the Ambassador in Jordan, described the anti-Nasser coalition as a curious 'new "Arab caravan"' with which the British now travelled.[11] The metaphor of the caravan expressed a certain reality about Middle Eastern alliances, which shifted in and around the Baghdad Pact.

[10] According to Macmillan, Eisenhower laughed (Macmillan's Diary, 14 July 1958). But see Richard Lamb, *The Macmillan Years, 1957–1963* (London, 1995), p. 35; and Alistair Horne, *Macmillan, 1957–1986* (London, 1989), p. 93. I am grateful to Alistair Horne for allowing me to read typescript copies of the Macmillan Diaries, which have now been deposited in the Bodleian Library, Oxford. For recent assessments of Macmillan and issues of the Middle East, see Richard Aldous and Sabine Lee, *Harold Macmillan and Britain's World Role* (London, 1996); and Nigel John Ashton, *Eisenhower, Macmillan, and the Problem of Nasser* (London, 1997).

[11] Quoted in Elie Podeh, 'The Struggle over Arab Hegemony after the Suez Crisis', *Middle Eastern Studies*, 29, 1 (January 1993), pp. 91–110.

The survival of British influence as well as the very existence of some of the ruling elites in the Arab monarchies in the post-1956 period now depended on American support provided by the Eisenhower Doctrine. A makeshift proclamation in the wake of Suez in January 1957, it was originally a spontaneous utterance by Dulles, who had not conferred with regional experts at the State Department, the CIA, or the Pentagon. At one stroke he rekindled Arab suspicion of American motives and diminished the good will that the United States had built up by opposing the British, French, and Israelis during the Suez crisis.[12] The announcement of what became known as a 'Doctrine' progressed from a formal presidential address to a joint resolution by Congress. The resolution authorized the President to provide economic and military assistance to Middle Eastern countries that requested 'assistance against armed aggression from any country controlled by international communism'. The difficulty, which the British fully perceived, was that Nasser was not a communist, nor could it be proved that the Soviet Union 'controlled' Egypt. When Lebanon, Jordan, Saudi Arabia, and Iraq became open allies of the United States by adhering to the Eisenhower Doctrine, and thus qualifying for military and economic assistance, Nasser believed that a pro-Western alliance had encircled him. The polarization provided the regional background to the insurrection in Lebanon in May 1958 and to the military coup that liquidated the Iraqi monarchy in July.

From the British perspective there were three parts to the crisis of 1958. The first embraced the aftermath of the proclamation in Cairo on 1 February, merging Egypt and Syria into the United Arab Republic. Two weeks later, on 14 February, an Arab Federation between Iraq and Jordan was proclaimed in Amman. Less electrifying than the news of the Egyptian-Syrian merger, the Iraqi-Jordanian federation seemed to be a reflex reaction. The British doubted its effectiveness against Nasser. The second phase of the crisis began the week of 8 May with street riots in Lebanon protesting against the pro-Western policy of President Camille Chamoun and threatening civil war. The American and British governments made contingency plans; the Security Council of the United Nations on 11 June voted to send UN observers to Lebanon to guard against the illegal movement of troops or arms. The third phase began on 14 July with the outbreak of the Iraqi revolution. Lebanon and Jordan now appeared to be on the verge of dissolution

---

[12] In 1958, Middleton wrote that the Suez crisis remained 'a vivid memory', but that 'despite Lebanese adherence to the "Eisenhower Doctrine" and some increase in American aid to Lebanon, the United States signally failed to retain the popularity achieved at the time of the Suez crisis' (Middleton to Lloyd, Confidential, 3 March 1958, FO 371/134114).

because of pro-Nasser sentiment within the two countries and because of the revolutionary atmosphere spreading from Iraq. American marines from the Sixth Fleet landed near Beirut on 15 July, and British paratroops were dropped at the capital of Jordan, Amman, two days later. This last phase encompassed the return to stability in Lebanon, signified by the assumption of office by General Fuad Chehab as president on 23 September and the withdrawal of American and British troops by the end of October.

The underlying assumption common to both British and American officials held that Nasser, like Hitler, aimed at expansion and that he had to be confronted and made to desist, by force if necessary. Sir Harold Caccia, the Ambassador in Washington, reported that Dulles believed 'Nasser was following in Hitler's footsteps' and using similar methods to pursue a policy of expansion. Nasser 'could not afford to stop to consolidate the Syrian-Egyptian Union[,] because he was bound to encounter grave practical difficulties, and his only hope of maintaining his position and popularity was to gain external successes by further *coups* in the Middle East.'[13] The British generally agreed with that assessment. With various shades of sophistication, most British officials and statesmen, from lowly levels in Whitehall to the Prime Minister, shared the idea of Nasser as a latter-day dictator of 1930s vintage. Macmillan himself believed that Nasser was to some extent mentally unbalanced and thus, like Hitler, prone to unpredictable, irrational behaviour. Macmillan wrote in his diary in May 1958:

> [A] great crisis is blowing up in the Lebanon. Nasser is organising an internal campaign there against President Chamoun and his regime. This is partly Communist and partly Arab Nationalist.
>
> Russian arms are being introduced from Syria and the object is to force Lebanon to join the Egyptian-Syrian combination. In other words, after Austria—the Sudeten Germans. Poland (in this case Iraq) will be the next to go.

The Prime Minister added, 'Fortunately the Americans have learned a lot since Suez.'[14]

Another tenet in British thought, slightly at variance with the first, held that Nasser did not fully control his own destiny, because he had sold his political fortune, perhaps even his Arab soul, to the Soviet Union. Though not a predominant interpretation, it vied for ascen-

[13] As recounted in Caccia to Lloyd, Secret, 20 March 1958, FO 371/133789.
[14] Macmillan Diary, 13 May 1958.

dancy. Its high priest was Sir William Hayter, who had been Ambassador in Moscow in 1953–57. Hayter believed Nasser to be a dangerous dictator in his own right, one who had, by accepting Russian economic assistance and military advisers, forfeited some degree of political freedom and in any event had welcomed the Soviets into the Middle East as a means of undermining Britain and France. In early 1958, Hayter visited the Middle East and made a shrewd assessment of the interplay between Nasser and the Russians. In his reckoning, the Soviet Union figured as the enigma within the enigma of the Arab world. A week after the merger between Egypt and Syria, he reported from Baghdad that opinion throughout the region believed that neither Nasser nor the Russians had promoted the union and indeed did not want it to occur when it did. Nasser's hand had been forced by radical nationalists and military officers of the Arab Social Renaissance Party in Syria, the Baathists, who precipitated the merger. They argued that only Egypt and the pan-Arab movement could save Syria from anarchy and from the danger of a communist takeover. Hayter himself disparaged the idea that Nasser had merely responded to the crisis in Syria:

> My own opinion is that this is a superficial view; whether Nasser wanted it [union with Syria] or not, he is certainly now exploiting it to the full, while the Russians, through their control over Nasser, will no doubt be able to make much more of it than we ever could.

> Certainly the general view here [in Baghdad] is that it [the merger] represents a serious menace to our position in the Middle East and a still more immediate menace to the régimes in the Arab States favourable to the West.[15]

In this view, Nasser may have been reckless, and perhaps even irrational, but any assessment of him had to take into account a certain amount of Russian control over his actions, even though he had suppressed communism in Egypt and banned the Communist Party.

The last strain in British thought, exemplified perhaps by Harold Beeley, held that Nasser was not a Hitler or a stooge of the Russians but first and foremost an Arab nationalist who used the Soviet Union to achieve his own goals. Beeley later became Ambassador in Cairo. Throughout his career he was an astute observer of Nasser and the historical course of the Egyptian revolution. In the first part of 1958 he was Assistant Under-Secretary and, from June, Deputy Representative at the United Nations, where he exerted a moderating influence

---

[15] Hayter to Frederick Hoyer-Millar, Secret, 10 February 1958, FO 371/133806.

on the interpretation of Nasser and Egyptian aims. In Beeley's view, Nasser was essentially opportunistic and by no means in control of Arab nationalism, even though in the eyes of his followers he symbolized it. Beeley's Nasser was no demon, but neither was he benevolently disposed towards Britain. He had an inveterate suspicion of British motives and a remarkable capacity to read British conspiracies in each turn of events. He was inimical to British interests, especially those in oil. Nevertheless it might be possible to avoid confrontation.

The three interpretations were not necessarily contradictory, but it is useful to bear in mind that Beeley's was closest to the historical reality. The formative stage of Nasser's career had been before and during the Second World War, when he had graduated from the Egyptian Military Academy and had witnessed the humiliation of the Egyptians when the British forced them to create a pro-Allies government in 1942. Another motivating force in his personality was the lesson he learned from Egypt's humiliating defeat during the 1948 war against Israel, which he attributed to the corruption of the old regime and specifically to King Farouk. As one of the free officers in the revolution of 1952, Nasser had perfected the art of conspiracy. Those who met him were often struck by his transparent sincerity, but candour formed only one side of a complex personality. He was rational but also calculating and suspicious, especially of the British. His early experience as an anti-British nationalist continued to influence his judgement. He had great stamina, worked long hours, and was close to his family. Above all, he restored Egyptian pride and sense of dignity after decades of subjugation to the British. Contrary to the views of many critics, then and for ever after, he was not a megalomaniac, though he concentrated all power in his own hands. His ministers were often no more than glorified civil servants. He committed himself first and foremost to the social and economic development of Egypt, but even by 1958 the Egyptian debt had outstripped the capacity of the economy to service it. In foreign affairs he upheld the principle of non-alignment, but after 1955 he had become dependent on the Soviet Union for supplies for his armed forces and, later, for the construction of the high dam at Aswan. He aspired to be the leader of the Arab world. 'What he wants outside Egypt', Harold Beeley reflected some years later, 'is not provinces but Satellites.'[16] This may have pitched it a little high, but the interpretation was understandable enough.

[16] Beeley to Butler, Confidential, 19 August 1964, FO 371/178580. In a forecast of the 1958 crisis, Sir George Middleton in Beirut wrote in similar vein that the Lebanese Muslim leaders aimed at 'the "satellization" or "Nasserization" of Lebanon' (Middleton to Lloyd, Confidential, 11 June 1958, FO 371/134122).

Nasser was a charismatic orator whose rhetoric on Arab unity inspired his followers and caused Western observers to draw conclusions about his ambitions. His aims were not modest; neither were they especially coherent. As later reports were to make clear, he was as baffled and frustrated by the course of events in 1958 as the British and Americans.

The United Arab Republic and the Creation of the Arab Union

In a comment that perhaps reflected a consensus in British thought, Sir Michael Wright described what he believed to be Egyptian motives in creating the United Arab Republic (the British generally underestimated the Syrian initiative). It was a bid for regional economic hegemony: '[O]ne of Colonel Nasser's objectives was probably the control of the oil resources of the Mesopotamian plain and the Persian Gulf.' Wright was the Ambassador in Baghdad. He held views heavily influenced by Nuri Pasha es Said, the long-standing British ally, veteran premier of Iraq, and champion of plans for Arab unity in harmony with British interests. In British eyes, Nuri represented the counterweight to Nasser. Wright and his colleagues took a critical view of Nuri's weaknesses and limitations. Obsessed with political control, and perpetually on guard against conspiracies, Nuri paid only lip service to long-range social and economic development. He represented an older generation that at any time might have to yield to younger, anti-British nationalists. Yet Wright and others recognized in him attributes of political leadership that could not be found elsewhere in the Middle East except in his rival, Gamal Abdel Nasser. Nuri was not a puppet. He often created dilemmas for the British. In the estimate of the British Embassy in Baghdad, King Hussein of Jordan had taken the initiative in the creation of the Arab Union, but Nuri had become the driving force. If the new union were to collapse, 'the situation for Britain and America in the Middle East would be worse in the short term than it would have been if Iraq and Jordan had not come together.'[17] On the other hand there were grounds for optimism. The new union might succeed. General Sir Gerald Templer, the Chief of the Imperial General Staff, viewed the initiative as a stroke of luck that might help sustain British power: '[T]he Arab Union presented us with our very last chance to retain our position in the Middle East and to safeguard our oil.'[18]

From the Iraqi vantage point, the union of Egypt and Syria marked

[17] Wright to Lloyd, Confidential, 25 February 1958, FO 371/134025.
[18] Chiefs of Staff Meeting, Confidential Annex, 7 May 1958, DEFE 4/107.

an historic event. Wright placed the significance in the perspective of the evolution of power politics in the Middle East:

> In Iraqi eyes a new pattern has been taking shape since the begin-
> ning of the year and the map of the Middle East is being redrawn.
> Frontiers and groupings of population . . . decided by the West with-
> out full freedom of choice for those involved are now being called
> into question, and what may have been more or less sacrosanct since
> 1913, 1919 or the end of the second world war is no longer necessar-
> ily so. The map will be redrawn to their own liking by Nasser or the
> Communists or both, if they are not resisted jointly by those who wish
> to maintain their freedom.[19]

Nuri believed that the key to the struggle lay in the oil resources of Kuwait. Only by Kuwait's accession would the Iraqi-Jordanian combination be economically viable. Otherwise, Jordan would be a financial in-
cubus on Iraq. At the idea of Kuwait joining the union, 'Iraqi eyes tend
to light up'.[20] Unfortunately for Nuri and his colleagues, the Ruler of
Kuwait, Sheikh Sir Abdullah as-Salim as-Sabah, regarded himself as a
broker between Nasser and the West and seemed blind to the regional
danger of the new Egyptian-Syrian merger. By contrast, Nuri and Hussein saw themselves as upholding principles of Arab unity that ultimately offered the only alternative to Nasser. In this vision of the
Middle East, Iraq and Jordan formed a shield of resistance against
Egyptian encroachments in Yemen, in Lebanon, and possibly in Kuwait. According to Wright:

> In this situation the Iraqi and the Jordanian Governments and ré-
> gimes are fighting, not only for their own survival within the new
> Union based on friendly partnership, but also for the principles both
> of Arab unity on a basis of this kind and of the maintenance of active
> friendship with the West.

> If they fail, not only they themselves but Lebanon and Kuwait, are
> likely to go the way of Syria or at least of Yemen. Already Lebanon is
> in critical danger and Kuwait might be so at any moment. If they suc-
> ceed, Lebanon and Kuwait may be saved and Syria may be retrieved.[21]

The fate of the Middle East thus hung in the balance.

[19] Wright to Foreign Office, Secret, 8 June 1958, FO 371/132776.

[20] Sam Falle to R. M. Hadow, Confidential, 4 February 1958, FO 371/134387. On Kuwait and the crisis, see Mustafa M. Alani, *Operation Vantage: British Military Intervention in Kuwait, 1961* (Old Woking, UK, 1990), chap. 2.

[21] Wright to Foreign Office, Secret, 8 June 1958, FO 371/132776.

Shortly after the Iraqi-Jordanian union in mid-February 1958, Nuri was in London. Macmillan wrote in his diary:

> Nuri Pasha came to see me . . . He is full of plans—some of them rather dangerously vague—for detaching Syria from Egypt. He wants us to get the Ruler of Kuwait to join, in some form, the Irak-Jordan union.

> The problem we have is to head Nuri off impossible or dangerous schemes, which are bound to fail, without losing his confidence or injuring his will to resist Egypt and Russia.[22]

Nuri's plans bordered on the visionary. He hoped that the Iraqi-Jordanian union might lead to the incorporation of not merely Kuwait but also Saudi Arabia. The Arab Union eventually might succeed in wooing Syria away from Egypt. Nuri expected and demanded British support. But the British knew that to assist Nuri in furthering his extreme aims might lead to Soviet intervention on behalf of the Egyptian-Syrian union. According to Sir William Hayter: 'This would create a Spanish civil war situation, with dangerous consequences . . . for general peace in the Middle East.'[23]

One further comment on the Kuwaiti dimension of the regional problem helps establish the atmosphere of intellectual effervescence and commercial prosperity that characterized parts of the Middle East in the 1950s. The Ruler of Kuwait believed that 'the destiny of Kuwait is to become something like another Beirut'. Beirut was much more than a thriving centre of trade and commerce: intellectual debate and freedom of the press seemed to contribute to the ability of a small nation to prosper despite great-power rivalry and regional tension. The Ruler of Kuwait cared little for freedom of the press and still less for intellectuals, but the mystique of Lebanon exerted considerable influence on him. According to Bernard Burrows, the Resident at Bahrain, who was on close terms with the ruler of Kuwait, the Kuwaitis recognized 'that they cannot hope to rival the Lebanese climate but they think of Kuwait as a centre of communications and as a free market for finance and trade which with its much greater natural resources might fulfill some of the functions of Beirut in these matters.'[24] The idea of Kuwait as another Lebanon lasted at least until the troubles began in the spring of 1958. After the Iraqi revolution in July, the Ruler faced the prospect, which seemed real and by no means imagi-

---

[22] Macmillan Diary, 17 February 1958.

[23] Minute by Hayter, 29 May 1958, FO 371/134119.

[24] Burrows to Riches, Secret, 1 April 1958, FO 371/132775.

nary, that 'Kuwait might find itself entirely surrounded by a Nasser-controlled Iraq and a Nasser-controlled Saudi Arabia'.[25] Sir William Hayter had expressed that alarming thought as a worst-case scenario in May 1958. His words revealed the uncertainty of mood and the possibility of ominous events.

The British were willing to consider the membership of Kuwait in the Iraqi-Jordanian union, but the more they pondered the possible consequences, the less they were inclined to support Nuri's demands to exert pressure on the Ruler. Kuwait supplied the major part of Britain's oil, more than that of Iraq and Iran combined.[26] Nevertheless there were certain things to be said in favour of Kuwait's merger with Iraq and Jordan. It might not alter the oil relationship with Britain, and it might help the most impoverished of the three states, Jordan, through a sharing of the oil revenues. Kuwaiti accession, Hayter wrote, might give the Iraqi-Jordanian union more 'sex appeal' by helping correct the public impression that the merger had been brought about by the British in an attempt to preserve influence rather than by Iraq and Jordan in a genuine manifestation of Arab nationalism. According to Hayter, still on a positive note:

> The Iraqis, of course, see it [Kuwaiti accession] largely as a way of dealing with Jordan's chronic financial difficulties. For the Kuwaitis it would have at any rate the advantage that it might no doubt be possible as part of the bargain to extract from Iraq recognition of Kuwaiti sovereignty and frontiers.[27]

On the other hand, any assessment had to take into account the personality of the Ruler and the general anti-Iraq sentiment in Kuwait.

[25] Memorandum by Hayter, 14 March 1958, FO 371/132774. The assessment on Saudi Arabia pursued similar themes: 'If a pro-Egyptian Government' were installed in Saudi Arabia, it would probably join the United Arab Republic, 'and this would have the following effect:
  (i) The Hashemite Union would be outflanked, not to say more or less surrounded.
  (ii) The previous benevolent attitude of the Saudi Government towards the three shaikhdoms of Kuwait, Bahrain and Qatar would be replaced by pressure to join the United Arab Republic . . . The Ruling Families in Kuwait and Qatar would be ill-placed to resist such pressures given the state of public feeling. Bahrain would be a somewhat better case.
  (iii) The American tenure of Dhahran would become at the best insecure.'
Minute by D. M. H. Riches, 18 March 1958, FO 371/133154.
[26] The relative production of crude oil by the three states in 1957 in metric tons: Kuwait, 57 million; Iran, 35 million; and Iraq, 20 million. Value of total exports to Britain in 1957, including cotton, fruit, and grain as well as oil: Iran, £35 million; Iraq, £12 million; Kuwait, £134 million.
[27] Hayter to Hoyer-Millar, Secret, 10 February 1958, FO 371/133806.

The Ruler, in Hayter's view, held Nasser in esteem as a fellow Arab nationalist: 'He does not fear Nasser nor does he accept the thesis that his own fate is bound up with that of Iraq and the Union.'[28] On the contrary, the Ruler looked to Nasser for protection against the expansionist aims of Iraq:

> The Ruler does not see the need to stand with his fellow rulers of monarchical states in a common front against the threat of the United Arab Republic. He is suspicious of Iraqi policy in view of past history and sees no advantage in association with the Iraq-Jordan Union either politically or economically—rather the reverse.

> Popular feeling in Kuwait is strongly in favour of the [United Arab] Republic and indifferent or hostile to the Hashemite Union.[29]

Any British effort to persuade the Ruler to join Iraq and Jordan would jeopardize good relations between Britain and Kuwait. Better to have oil in hand than to risk the consequences of pushing Kuwait into an unpopular union. Ultimately, the calculation on oil determined the attitude. As will be seen, the British could even reconcile themselves to the loss of Iraqi oil if the oil of Kuwait remained secure.

It helps to see the Jordanian view of the possible membership of Kuwait in the Union, just as it is useful to focus briefly on Britain's specific relationship to Jordan as distinct from its connection to Iraq.[30] Jordan had become an independent kingdom in 1946 and had expanded its frontiers into former British Palestine by absorbing the West Bank during the war of 1948. Jordan then consisted of some 40,000 square miles (one-tenth of which were arable) with two million inhabitants, one-third of whom were refugees. The Palestinian issue dominated Jordanian politics. The radical pro-Nasser and anti-British atmosphere helps explain the mood at the time of the assassination of King Abdullah in 1951, the ruling Hashemite monarch since the creation of the state after the First World War. The element of radical nationalism weighed heavily in the calculations of his eventual successor, Abdullah's grandson, King Hussein, age eighteen at the time of his accession in 1953. In March 1956, Hussein dismissed General Sir John Glubb, the commander of Jordan's army, the Arab Legion, thereby sending a shock tremor throughout the Middle East. A Hashemite king had

[28] Minute by Hayter, 14 March 1958, FO 371/132774.

[29] FO memorandum, 3 March 1958, FO 371/132774.

[30] In general, see Uriel Dann, *King Hussein and the Challenge of Arab Radicalism: Jordan, 1955–1967* (New York, 1989); and more specifically, Tal, 'Britain and the Jordan Crisis of 1958'.

defied the British and disarmed critics who had denounced Jordan as a client state. In April 1957, Hussein ended the Anglo-Jordan treaty of 1946, and in the following month successfully suppressed a plot to depose him, led by the pro-Nasser nationalist Suleiman al-Nabulsi. Hussein thus proved himself to be a dexterous, an effective, and a ruthless force in Jordan's internal politics.

When Egypt and Syria merged into the United Arab Republic in January 1958, the external threat heightened. Damascus was little over an hour's drive from Amman. Hussein initiated the Arab Union as a means of countering Nasser. He appears to have placed less hope than Nuri in the prospect of Kuwait joining the Iraqi-Jordanian merger. As the ruler of one of the poorest states in the Middle East, he continued to look to the West for economic and military support. British influence, despite the ending of the formal treaty relationship a year earlier, remained significant, though Jordan relied increasingly on US economic assistance. According to the British Ambassador, Sir Charles Johnston, in 1957, Hussein 'seems to have perceived that his country could not survive economically on the basis of Arab aid only, and he therefore made no secret of his view that Jordan should at least consider the Eisenhower doctrine very carefully.'[31]

When Johnston commented on American assistance, he did not refer to a coherent policy of economic and military aid to pro-Western governments of the Middle East, but rather to a confused programme that nevertheless produced critical economic support. By the phrase 'Eisenhower Doctrine', he and others understood that the United States would come to the assistance of Middle Eastern states threatened by 'international communism', a phrase commonly assumed to have more meaning in American domestic politics than in the geopolitics of the Middle East. Nevertheless, the economic aid was vital. Looking back in December 1958, Johnston wrote: 'Jordan could never have survived without the financial and economic support of the United States.'[32]

Sir Charles Johnston himself is of interest because he consistently presented a closely reasoned case that the British must cooperate with the United States if Britain herself were to remain a regional power in the Middle East. The corollary was that Arab nationalism, especially in the case of Jordan, was not necessarily anti-Western or anti-British. Johnston, perhaps more than any of his contemporaries, saw that Hussein had to present himself as a full-blooded Arab nationalist and to

[31] Johnston to Lloyd, Confidential, 8 May 1957, FO 371/127880.
[32] Johnston to Lloyd, Secret, 4 December 1958, FO 371/134011.

some extent as an anti-British nationalist. But Johnston knew also that Hussein's own inclinations were moderate, that he was essentially conciliatory towards Israel as well as Britain, and that he still looked to the British for guidance and assistance, even though he might depend on the United States for economic aid. In this view, Jordan remained part of Britain's informal empire in the Middle East. The British had managed to free themselves from costly subsidies and military commitments, now assumed increasingly by the Americans. The significance of the crisis of 1958 for Jordan lay in part in the clear formation of power alignments in the Middle East involving Britain, the United States, and Israel. From the time of the Suez crisis through the period of the termination of the Anglo-Jordan treaty in April 1957, according to Johnston, 'we were neither liked here nor respected.' By the end of 1958, however, 'We were once more Jordan's greatest outside friend.'[33] Yet the British had always to bear in mind that 'the Jordanian Nasserites are more extreme than Nasser himself'.[34]

The issue of Palestine fuelled extremist sentiment in Jordan and elsewhere. In Jerusalem the British Consul, Charles Stewart, observed that the Arab inhabitants of the city displayed virtually no enthusiasm for the creation of the union of Jordan and Iraq: 'The Arabs are an emotional people who love celebration, yet the establishment of the Arab Federation aroused less spontaneous rejoicing than is normal during any of the Muslim holidays.' Stewart went on to explain that in time Jordan might benefit economically from the union, and thus might be in a stronger position against Israel. Palestinians generally would welcome the presence of Iraqi troops on Israel's borders. Yet there were underlying reasons why the Palestinians had reacted apathetically to the merger of the two Hashemite countries and why they continued to sympathize with Nasser:

> In the first place [Jordan's] union with the United Arab Republic would have been more logical from the point of view of geography (at least in so far as Syria is concerned).

> Secondly, the Palestinians have a greater cultural and racial affinity with the Syrians than with the Iraqis.

---

[33] Johnston to Lloyd, Secret, 4 December 1958, FO 371/134011.

[34] Johnston to Lloyd, Secret, 18 August 1858, PREM 11/2381. '[W]hatever Nasser's own private attitude may be, there is no doubt about the violent anti-Israeli fanaticism of his Jordanian supporters' (Johnston to Lloyd, Confidential and Guard [Guard = not for American eyes], 22 January 1959, FO 371/142100).

Thirdly, Egypt is regarded as the leader of Arab nationalism and the leading exponent of neutralism, both real forces here [in Jerusalem].

Fourthly, an united Arab Republic composed of Egypt, Jordan and Syria would encircle Israel, thus making more effective her containment and bringing nearer the day when the Arabs would be able to force the Jews to make the concessions or 'be swept into the sea'.[35]

Not all Arabs by any means held such extreme views on the destruction of Israel, but if given the option, Palestinian Arabs would choose the United Arab Republic over the Arab Union.

For all its intensity, the Palestine issue became relatively muted in the early months of 1958. 'The decision of Egypt and Syria to form a United Arab Republic', wrote Sir Michael Wright, in words that summed up everyone's preoccupation, 'changed the whole atmosphere.'[36] As the crisis deepened in Lebanon, the British asked not merely whether Jordan and Iraq could hold the line against Egyptian expansion but also whether the United States would recognize the gravity of the issues at stake. Sir William Hayter believed that behind Nasser lay the hand of the Soviet Union and that one could detect an historical pattern traceable to the inter-war years. In a sense, the Egyptian revolution could be seen as an extension of the Russian revolution, which as an ongoing world revolution continued to have an anti-British thrust to it. Hayter exaggerated the extent of Soviet control over Nasser, but his comment reveals a major element in British thought:

[A]ny extension of Nasser's influence means really an extension of Soviet influence. However much he and the Russians may distrust and dislike each other they seem bound to work together.

The Russians are using him as Stalin used Chiang Kai-shek in the twenties, as a Nationalist leader who can be relied upon to get rid of 'Western Imperialism influence' in what the Russians would regard as a semi-colonial area. They do not much mind if in so doing he is pretty rough with the local Communists too. But Nasser is much less capable than Chiang then was of turning against the Russians and standing on his own.[37]

[35] A. C. Stewart to E. M. Rose, Confidential, 19 February 1958, FO 371/134025.
[36] Wright to Lloyd, Confidential, 25 February 1958, FO 371/134025.
[37] Hayter to Sir Harold Caccia, Secret and Personal, 28 March 1958, FO 371/133799.

In view of such danger, why did the Americans, in Hayter's words, regard the situation with such 'torpor' and 'lethargy'? Did the Americans not sense the danger of revolution, held precariously at bay by Iraq and Jordan?[38] As the British approached the abyss in the spring of 1958, they regarded Jordan as more vulnerable than Iraq, certainly an ironic view in light of the revolution in July. One of the most remarkable comments on Britain's relationship with Jordan was made by David Ben Gurion, the Prime Minister of Israel, a few days after the outbreak of the revolution: 'The Lebanon was basically a democracy and would survive as such; Jordan was only the King and one bullet would finish him'—and the Jordanian state.[39]

Background to the Crisis in Lebanon

Lebanon was not merely a democracy but also, at least to the public at large in Britain and America in the 1950s, a sort of Christian Israel.[40] This was a misleading idea. But it formed part of the general view of Lebanon as a small but vital bulwark against communism in the Middle East. Here British and American views differed. Despite Sir William Hayter, whose ideas about the Middle East had crystallized during his time as Ambassador in Moscow, the British did not generally take the line that the Soviet Union used Nasser as a pawn. During the crisis in the spring and summer of 1958 there developed, in the words of a Foreign Office assessment, 'a basic but hitherto submerged difference between ourselves and the Americans'. It came into sharp focus during and after the Iraqi revolution, but had been implicit throughout:

> They [the Americans] have regarded Nasser as bad primarily because he seemed to be a tool of the Russians. We have regarded him as basically inimical to Western strategic, economic and political interests

[38] In fact the State Department at this time had concluded a balanced assessment of Middle Eastern dilemmas, concluding, among other things, 'The Arab Union has, undoubtedly, been handicapped by the bellicose and unrealistic policy which Nuri has pursued toward the United Arab Republic,' but nevertheless, 'The present regimes of Iraq and Jordan, while not popular, have created stability and appear to be the best able to bring about an alternative union to the United Arab Republic' (memorandum drafted by David Newsom, 26 March 1958, *Foreign Relations of the United States, 1958–1960*, XI, pp. 282–86).

[39] As related in Sir Francis Rundall to Foreign Office, 19 July 1958, FO 371/134284.

[40] For a useful essay that establishes the complexity of the situation in Lebanon in the present context, see Malcolm Kerr, 'The Lebanese Civil War', in Evan Luard, *The International Regulation of Civil Wars* (London 1972). See also especially J. C. Hurewitz, 'Lebanese Democracy in Its International Setting', *Middle East Journal*, 17, 5 (Autumn 1963), pp. 487–506, for an acute analysis of the confessional politics and system of government.

in the Middle East . . . particularly in the short run and especially in regard to oil.[41]

The crisis in Lebanon had many dimensions, oil among them. Tripoli was the terminal of the Iraq Petroleum Company's pipeline bringing crude oil from Iraq. Saida was the terminal of the Trans-Arabian Pipeline for oil from Saudi Arabia.

Despite the oil terminals, the British generally regarded Lebanon as a country not worth the bother that it caused in international affairs. Lebanon (3,400 square miles) was half the size of Israel (7,993 square miles) and by the same measure less than half the size of Wales. The country had a population of only 1.4 million, divided between Christians and Muslims, though these communities were by no means monolithic. The Lebanese exported citrus fruits, apples, olives, and tobacco, but the shipments to Britain in 1957 amounted only to £2 million, versus £11 million from Israel. The British Overseas Airways Corporation was Beirut's largest single customer. Nevertheless, even the most jaded British observer had to admit that Lebanon possessed an astonishing intellectual vitality as well as the commercial hustle and bustle of Beirut, which was already a principal financial centre of the Middle East. There were thirty-four daily newspapers, with a combined circulation of 100,000. Beirut was a thriving commercial port, the principal point of entry into Syria. As a strategically situated country that faced both sides in the Cold War, and as a Mediterranean as well as a Middle Eastern country, Lebanon attracted intelligence operatives. Beirut was thus a centre of the Arab Cold War as well as the larger Cold War between West and East.

Summing up Lebanon's years of independence since 1943, Sir George Middleton in 1958 observed that the country had 'achieved a quite remarkable level of material prosperity'. But affluence was a mixed blessing, the Christian half of the population benefiting more than the Muslim half. The economic disparity reflected and to some extent caused a basic tension: 'The Moslem element . . . resents the Western patronage and protection under which their Christian fellow-Lebanese have grown fat and seeks to redress the balance through a patron of its own (nowadays Nasser).'[42] Middleton's comment went to the heart of the matter. The 1950s were a period of economic growth and prosperity, but there nevertheless existed a grievance on the part of the less privileged, who now looked to Nasser. According to a later British comment: 'This Christian-dominated Lebanon rested

[41] Minute by R. M. Hadow, 18 December 1958, FO 371/133958.
[42] Middleton to Lloyd, Confidential, 11 June 1958, FO 371/134122.

on the assumption of Western support, the efficiency of which was generally taken for granted until the emergence in Egypt of Gamel Abdel-Nasser.'[43]

In the common Western stereotype, Lebanon represented an embattled Christian fortress in an Arab mass. But the Muslim population ranked substantially close numerically, and both Christians and Muslims regarded themselves as Arab. The official language of the country was Arabic. There were 792,000 Christians, 424,000 of whom were Maronites, the remainder Greek Orthodox, Armenians, and others, forming altogether some ten Christian communities. The Christians had been indigenous since the earliest time of Christianity. The Muslims numbered 536,000, of whom 286,000 were Sunnis and 250,000 Shias. The other principal community was that of the Druze, some 90,000. The country was divided along communal lines weighted since independence in favour of the Christians. By rigid convention, the President was always a Maronite Christian and the Prime Minister was always a Sunni Muslim. The Speaker of the Chamber of Deputies was always a Shia Muslim. In what Middleton described as a delicately balanced religious and political mosaic, 'the rise of Arab nationalism with its pan-Islamic overtones' now instilled fear in the Christian community.[44] But it was a basic mistake to regard Lebanese Christians as anything other than Arab. In a slightly paternalistic tone he commented on the better part of the population:

> The intelligent Christians do not want protection by the West from their Moslem Arab neighbours; they too are Arabs, resent colonialism (from which they have only recently emerged) and, for all their fears of Egypt, are mostly anti-Zionist and deeply shocked by attacks on other Arab peoples.

> The best elements in Lebanon are in sympathy with Western culture and philosophy, but Western policy sometimes appears to them as merely selfish and opportunistic and leading to the ruin of their small country as well as setting back the progress of the Arab world.[45]

The country's political system received a major shock after the merger of Egypt and Syria in early 1958, when Middleton reckoned that 85 per cent of the Lebanese Muslims 'must be counted as ardent supporters of the United Arab Republic.'[46]

[43] P. M. Crostwaite (Middleton's successor) to Lloyd, Confidential, 24 April 1959, FO 371/142208.

[44] Middleton to Lloyd, Confidential, 11 June 1958, FO 371/134122.

[45] Middleton to Lloyd, Confidential, 7 February 1957, FO 371/127996.

[46] Middleton to Lloyd, Confidential, 13 March 1958, FO 371/134116.

The key to Lebanon's intricate political system was the 'National Pact' of 1943, which essentially represented a compromise between the Maronite and Sunni communities on the issues of Lebanese independence.[47] It reflected a workable compromise within the context of internal Lebanese political rivalries and regional Arab politics. The National Pact eventually symbolized peaceful, democratic confessional coexistence as well as a reconciliation of the two faces of Lebanon, one side looking to the West, the other to Arab countries. In the first decade of independence, the National Pact held, though precariously, in part because of the system of checks and balances established in the constitution: a classic separation of powers between a President, a single Chamber of Deputies, and an independent judiciary. On the surface the system worked well, but it ossified the sectarian solution of 1943. Thereafter, the general Christian interpretation of the Pact remained unchanged, but regional developments greatly affected the Muslim view of it. Middleton made a perceptive comment in 1958 when he observed that the Lebanese political system probably needed to be basically revised: '[T]he Pact of 1943, which seemed the logical solution of sectarian differences when it was written, has with the passage of time had the unfortunate effect of freezing those divergencies and perpetuating the political fragmentation of Lebanon rather than resolving it.'[48] On another occasion he summed up what he believed to be the essence of the problem by stating that 'effective power remains in the hands of the Christians'.[49]

In 1952 the Chamber of Deputies elected Camille Chamoun for a six-year term. Chamoun regarded himself as a friend of Britain and the United States, but above all he viewed himself as an Arab nationalist and a Lebanese patriot. As the British saw it, his style of Arab nationalism, at its best, was a throwback to an earlier, more moderate type, one compatible with British interests and thus out of harmony with the radical nationalism of Nasser. Chamoun too had a problem of scarcely concealed ambition and an instinct for what the British described as Levantine intrigue. In the 1956–58 period he stood uncompromisingly for a pro-Western alignment, thus becoming the main target of those who sympathized with closer Arab unity. He was also, according to Middleton, 'a man of stubborn, sometimes obstinate, courage'. Unless he could find a successor who could be counted upon

[47] See Farid el-Khazen, 'The Communal Pact of National Identities: The Making and Politics of the 1943 National Pact' (Centre for Lebanese Studies, Papers on Lebanon, 12; Oxford, 1991); see also Albert Hourani, 'Lebanon: Development of a Political Society', in Albert Hourani, *The Emergence of the Modern Middle East* (Berkeley, 1981).

[48] Middleton to Lloyd, Confidential, 11 June 1958, FO 371/134122.

[49] Middleton to Lloyd, Confidential, 7 February 1957, FO 371/127996.

to follow his line of policy, he would succeed himself.[50] In the last phase of his career, Chamoun, in the British view, was almost in a class by himself in political ability and leadership. But by choosing to violate the conventional six-year term, he brought together Christians and Muslims, who increasingly held that 'whatever else may happen the present President should not be re-elected'.[51] The resolution of this issue by Chamoun's eventual, though hesitant, withdrawal from politics, and the restoration of the ever-more-fragile balance of the 1943 Pact, helps explain the success of the American intervention in the summer of 1958.

Until the time of Suez, the British had thought Chamoun a weak and indecisive personality. According to the collective wisdom of the confidential 'Personalities' report prepared each year by the Embassy in Beirut, 'he proved for a long time either too weak or too idle to pursue a persistent policy on the domestic front, and was a disappointment to the Opposition and the despair of the old political bosses whom he refused to consult, relying largely on his personal popularity and his talent for intrigue.'[52] In some circles Chamoun had the reputation of being a British tool. He disliked the French, having been arrested by them during the war. He had served as Minister in London during 1944–47, a critical period in the shaping of his general political outlook. But from the British point of view he was 'basically Lebanese and pro-Arab'. That was an essentially accurate judgement, though it hardly inspired confidence in the British, who, at least in the period up to 1956, had underestimated his strength. Chamoun's dominant sympathy, to the British, seemed to lie with Arab nationalism.[53] Perhaps because he was 'arabisant', the term of Middleton's predecessor, the British tended to underestimate the strength of his commitment to the Western powers. Middleton assessed Chamoun's strengths and weaknesses during the Suez crisis in August 1956, a little over two months before the invasion of Egypt:

> President Chamoun has done his best to exercise a moderating influence but he is basically a weak man and given to compromise and so far his voice has not been particularly effective. Indeed, if it should

[50] As Middleton reflected on one of the reasons for the May crisis in a dispatch of 11 June 1958, FO 371/134122.

[51] Middleton to Lloyd, Confidential, 3 March 1958, FO 371/134114.

[52] The 'Leading Personalities' reports are usually subjected to a fifty- rather than a thirty-year period of access denial, but one that eluded the censor's net is dated 18 July 1959 in FO 371/142209.

[53] See Chamoun's memoir, *Crise au Moyen-Orient* (Paris, 1963), in which pro-Arab sympathies are a prominent theme.

come to a show down in Egypt and we have to intervene with armed force, I am by no means sure that Chamoun will be strong enough to stand up to the outcry which is bound to follow and I should not be altogether surprised if he were to resign in such circumstances.[54]

Chamoun's resolute pro-British stand in November 1956 thus came as a welcome surprise. 'At this juncture', Middleton wrote, 'President Chamoun moved with gratifying courage and decision.' Despite earlier phases of indecision, he had proved himself a man of character and had transcended the limitations of what Middleton and others referred to as the Levantine personality: 'The President, frequently accused of weakness, vacillation and other Levantine failings, has shown himself able to take strong action when such action was needed.'[55]

It was the Suez crisis that gave Lebanese politics an international significance and shaped the background for the events of 1958. During the crisis itself, the development of conspicuous importance was, to British eyes, the sudden and ominous growth of Nasser's influence. Middleton reported in August 1956:

There is no doubt in my mind about the tremendous impetus which the Nasser bandwagon has now gained. All the latent anti-Western resentments, Arab xenophobia and 'anti-imperialist' hysteria is being given free rein . . . The Christian element especially feels that the very existence of Lebanon as an independent State is in danger.

Portraits of the Egyptian dictator are beginning to appear in all the shops and I should think that nearly half the taxis in Beirut also have his portrait displayed on the rear window.[56]

In November, after the British and French invasion of Egypt in concert with Israeli forces, the Lebanese Cabinet divided on the issue of whether or not to support Nasser. President Chamoun championed the Western powers, but the Prime Minister, Abdallah Yafi, and the Minister of the Interior, Saeb Salam, vehemently favoured Egypt. Chamoun rejected their recommendation to break relations with Britain and France, at which point they tendered their resignations. Middleton described this crucial development:

Yafi and his more powerful and sinister henchman, Saeb Salam, were strongly inclined towards a pro-Egyptian, pan-Arab and pan-Islamic policy. In Lebanon where communal affairs are so delicately bal-

[54] Middleton to Ross, Secret, 20 August 1956, FO 371/121607.
[55] Middleton to Lloyd, Confidential, 7 February 1957, FO 371/127996.
[56] Middleton to Ross, Secret, 20 August 1956, FO 371/121607.

anced, whose trade and prosperity depend upon free communications with the West and whose cultural and educational ties are largely European, this policy threatened to split the country into opposing camps . . .

At this juncture President Chamoun moved with gratifying courage and decision . . . The significance of the fall of the Yafi Cabinet lies in the fact that success for the pro-Egyptian section of the Moslem Arabs of Lebanon would have inevitably called into question the continuance of the Convention of 1943 under which effective power remains in the hands of the Christians. Once that position had been turned, it could probably never have been recovered.[57]

The Suez crisis thus touched the heart of Lebanese domestic politics while injecting a volatile element that would remain internationally significant.

There were two main aspects of Lebanese domestic politics, in Middleton's judgement, that had to be analysed against the changing international background. Chamoun had emerged from the Suez crisis as one of the few champions of the British in the Middle East. How did he stand, in consequence, in Lebanon itself? In answering that question, Middleton detected what he described as 'the underlying contradiction of the Lebanese political system'.[58] Chamoun's opponents had to be studied in this context. The second question was how the army might respond in a prolonged crisis. Here the answer turned on the Commander-in-Chief of the Armed Forces, General Fouad Chehab.

Chamoun's position as President had to be understood according to the Lebanese constitution of 1926. Modelled after the French constitution, it provided for a President and a Council of Ministers responsible to a Chamber of Deputies, but the President had inherited the executive authority of the High Commissioner in the mandate period, and was thus a more powerful figure than his French counterpart in the Third Republic. Though the system worked in favour of the Christians, they faced, in Middleton's slightly odd comment, a 'frustrating restriction' because they could never hope to have a Christian Prime Minister. From anyone's point of view, however, Chamoun was an active and aggressive President, and his rivals accused him of being 'un-neutral'. His opponents denounced him for violating the

---

[57] Middleton to Lloyd, Confidential, 7 February 1957, FO 371/127996. F. B. Richards, First Secretary in Bahrain but temporarily in the Foreign Office, commented: 'That our relations with Lebanon should now be as sound as they were a year ago is largely due to the efforts of President Chamoun' (minute by Richards, 14 February 1957, FO 371/127996).

[58] Middleton to Lloyd, Confidential, 5 June 1957, FO 371/127999.

consensus of the National Pact, which rested on the assumption that a Muslim Prime Minister would be able to represent the Sunni Muslims in the face of the extensive authority vested in a Christian President. Middleton dismissed the accusations against Chamoun as 'specious' because in the Lebanese political system, 'no President . . . can fail to play an active part in internal politics.' The question was whether Chamoun would overstep his authority to the point of destroying the consensus of the 1943 Pact. Middleton warned that there was serious 'confusion' between 'the chief executive and the chief legislative powers' and that this confusion of authority would be 'a source of weakness as regards future stability'.[59]

General Chehab had been brought into the government as Minister of Defence after the fall of the Yafi government in November 1956. According to Middleton, 'He commands respect among all communities, less because of his personal abilities than for his honesty and lack of ambition.' In 1952, Chehab had refused to allow the armed forces to become involved in politics, but by doing so had contributed to the collapse of the government. He had then served temporarily as Prime Minister. 'At that time', Middleton wrote, 'he loyally kept the ring and made no attempt to seize personal power or advantage.'[60] In general Middleton made measured assessments. Most of his colleagues in the Foreign Office would have agreed with him in 1956:

> The commonest estimate of General Chehab is that he is weak. He is certainly more given to reflection than to action but he has a strong streak of obstinacy and a well-known reluctance to commit himself hastily . . .

> In private conversation General Chehab is discursive, philosophic and, risking a pun, given to broad generalities. In all that does not immediately concern the Army he is by inclination cynical. But even as a military leader whose first concern is to maintain his beloved Army intact he allows himself no illusions and I was surprised when, at our first meeting . . . [in 1956] he quite cheerfully suggested that the Lebanese Army was capable, as a military force, of resisting the Syrians for one day and the Israelis for one hour . . .

> To sum up his character, General Chehab is too aristocratic to be ambitious, too lazy to descend to the common arena, too comfortable to seek martyrdom and too average to arouse jealousy.[61]

[59] Middleton to Lloyd, Confidential, 5 June 1957, FO 371/127999.
[60] Middleton to Lloyd, Confidential, 29 November 1956, FO 371/121607.
[61] Middleton to Lloyd, Confidential, 27 August 1956, FO 371/134133.

Chehab held as an axiom that any political intervention by the army
would cause its disintegration into Christian and Muslim factions and
might thereby destroy the Lebanese state itself. He resisted Chamoun's
political overtures and indeed, according to Middleton, held Chamoun in contempt as a politician who put ambition before country.
Middleton's judgement may have been generally too negative on Chehab himself, but on one point, at least, it was certainly accurate: 'The
General is a good Maronite Christian but I think he is also very conscious of his Arab heritage and of the need for Lebanon to be on good
terms with its neighbours.'[62]

Middleton respected Chehab as 'a sincere patriot', but he knew that
the mutual distrust of Chehab and Chamoun would lead to uneasy relations and perhaps trouble. What part might the army play in a time
of political turmoil? The British Chiefs of Staff held the Lebanese
armed forces in low esteem.[63] The army had only about 6,000 officers
and men and seemed to resemble a gendarmerie more than an effective military force. The army would, however, determine the balance
in any civil disturbance. Some months after Chehab had left the government in January 1957 and continued his duties as Commander-in-
Chief, Middleton commented on his leadership in relation to the lessons to be drawn elsewhere in the Middle East:

> General Chehab has been much praised publicly as the impartial
> guarantor of political freedom but the fact is that the Lebanese Army
> is a largely static body which can never expect to have a properly mil-
> itary function and whose duties are largely confined to the mainte-
> nance of internal order, in which promotion is almost non-existent
> and where dissatisfaction among the younger officers must exist.

> There have been the examples in neighbouring countries of the pre-
> ponderant part which the Army has been able to assume during time
> of political evolution, if not revolution. Hitherto the Lebanese army
> has fortunately remained largely divorced from day-to-day politics.
> But I seriously doubt whether this will remain the case in future and
> there is the real danger that . . . military cliques may be tempted to
> take over where politicians have failed.[64]

With the benefit of hindsight, it is clear that Middleton underestimated Chehab's political skill as well as his determination not to allow

---

[62] Middleton to Lloyd, Confidential, 27 August 1956, FO 371/134133.
[63] For the 'low opinion of the value of Lebanese forces held by the Chiefs of Staff', see COS
minutes and estimates in FO 371/110969.
[64] Middleton to Lloyd, Confidential, 5 June 1957, FO 371/127999.

the army to become a political instrument. Middleton's judgement, however, was representative. There was a general tendency among the British to underrate Chehab.[65]

To understand the crisis of 1958, it is necessary to study briefly the nature of post-Suez Lebanese politics. The prominent members of the November 1956 government, apart from Chamoun and Chehab, included Sami Solh (a Sunni Muslim) as Prime Minister, and Megid Arslan, a Druze leader who had previously been Minister of Defence but was now relegated to a minor post. Sami Solh had served before as Prime Minister, the first time as early as 1942. The son of an Ottoman official, he had been educated in Istanbul. The British regarded him as an aged and increasingly ineffectual politician with limited intellectual horizons. His loyalty to Chamoun made him vulnerable in his own Sunni Muslim community. He carried the portfolios of Interior, Justice, Information, and, after Chehab left the Cabinet in early 1957, Defence. To the British, Sami Solh appeared to be out of his depth, as did Megid Arslan, whom Middleton described as an affable nonentity. Arslan had been anti-German during the war and had resisted the Vichy regime. He had repeatedly represented the Druzes since 1943. According to the Personalities report, he was '[a] cheerful, uneducated and highly venal feudal chieftain with a boyish passion for dressing-up and firearms.'[66] In the British view, both Solh and Arslan were being used by Chamoun.

Part of the further political significance of Sami Solh and Megid Arslan lay in the way they had antagonized fellow politicians. By forcing the resignation of Abdallah Yafi and Saeb Salam, Chamoun had embittered two of the most prominent Muslim leaders, who now took an increasingly acerbic line towards both the British and himself. Yafi drifted more and more into the pro-Nasser camp. Saeb Salam, who was the far abler of the two, became one of stalwarts of the Muslim Opposition in 1958 and commanded the Basta quarter of Beirut, the Moslem district in the heart of the city. By including Megid Arslan in the Cabinet, Chamoun alienated Kemal Jumblatt, the highly intelligent and active Druze leader who stood in opposition to the Arslan clan. Jumblatt was the leader of the Socialist and Progressive Party and the foremost exponent of socialism in Lebanon. He urged radical reform

[65] A notable exception was Lord Mountbatten, from 1956 Admiral of the Fleet and from 1959 Chief of the Defence Staff. He stated to the Chiefs of Staff Committee in May 1958: 'General Chehab . . . in his view . . . was the only leader in the Lebanon whose patriotism and moral principles could be relied on. His army would be fully capable of maintaining internal security if the General wanted to do so' (Chiefs of Staff Committee, Confidential Annex, 13 May 1958, DEFE 4/107).

[66] FO 371/142209.

of what he viewed as a corrupt political system. It was difficult for the British to ascertain whether his influence derived more from his ideological views or from his position as a Druze chieftain, but in any event he was a dangerous opponent of Chamoun.

A special word needs to be said from the British perspective about Charles Malik, who became Foreign Minister in November 1956. He had been educated at the American University of Beirut and at Harvard University. A man of outstanding ability, Malik had returned from America to become Professor of Philosophy and Science at A.U.B. From 1945 to 1955 he had served as Ambassador in Washington and as Permanent Representative at the United Nations. He seemed, to the British at least, to fit awkwardly in the rough-and-tumble of Lebanese domestic politics. He had an unswerving commitment to what he called the values of Western society, and more particularly to those of the United States, which Middleton once described as 'the mecca of so many Lebanese'.[67] In a sense, Malik shared the passion of many of his countrymen for America, but he was in a class by himself. He had intellectual range and humane vision. Unfortunately for the British, he seemed temperamentally akin to the Americans, and intellectually he shared an outlook similar to that of John Foster Dulles. Middleton did not find him an easy colleague. Malik himself was politically vulnerable because of his long period as Ambassador in Washington. He had no substantial political base in Lebanon. Nor was his identification with the Americans a political asset, despite the number of Lebanese who had immigrated to the United States. In the aftermath of Suez, Anglo-Lebanese relations revived much more quickly than most contemporary observers would have believed possible. 'The United States', according to Middleton, 'signally failed to retain the popularity achieved at the time of the Suez crisis.'[68] Malik nevertheless supported wholeheartedly the Eisenhower Doctrine and the opportunity to associate Lebanon with the United States.

The post-Suez Lebanese political alignments seemed ominous because of the Lebanese elections to be held in June 1957. In view of the changed circumstances, the elections were bound to have international as well as local significance. Externally, the conflict reflected Chamoun's support of a pro-Western policy against the wishes of his opponents, who wanted to bring Lebanon into the orbit of Egypt and Syria. Internally, much revolved around Chamoun himself. His term of office was due to expire in October 1958, but Chamoun's predeces-

[67] Middleton to Lloyd, Confidential, 7 February 1957, FO 371/127996.
[68] Middleton to Lloyd, Confidential, 3 March 1958, FO 371/134144.

sor, Béchara el-Khoury, had set a precedent for re-election. Chamoun was anxious to consolidate support in the new Chamber of Deputies. Therein, in Middleton's view, lay one of the dangers. Chamoun had already acquired a reputation for manipulating people and rigging elections. He had an instinct for byzantine intrigue and a consuming suspicion of others—above all of General Chehab. Though Chamoun was a man of great charm, he also had a capacity that was astonishing, to Middleton at least, for stirring up political enemies in all communities. One was Hamid Frangié, a Maronite who had several times served as Minister for Foreign Affairs and who dissented from the pro-Western stance of the government. Another was the Maronite Patriarch, His Beatitude Boulos Meouschi, who was a relative of Béchara el-Khoury and who came into increasing conflict with Chamoun. If Chamoun too blatantly rigged the elections, Middleton commented, 'the Patriarch may feel impelled to side more and more openly with the political opponents of the President.'[69] Frangié and the Patriarch represented different strains of Lebanese political thought. But they held in common that Chamoun and Malik had tilted too far towards the West.

Middleton believed that the British should support Chamoun to the hilt: '[W]e must bring our weight to bear in support of the President and his followers and do what we can to frustrate the activities and influence of his opponents.' Opposition would not be confined to Lebanese factions: 'The Russians, the Egyptians and the Syrians are all making their preparations.'[70] Middleton attempted to rally the Americans to the cause. In May 1957 he reported that the American Ambassador now believed that 'full support' must be given to Chamoun. 'This is satisfactory', Middleton commented, 'as [the] American attitude towards the President has tended at times to be equivocal.' Middleton became increasingly alarmed at the extent of 'Egyptian, Syrian and possibly Russian interference, including bribery and distribution of arms'.[71] What kind of assistance did the British lend Chamoun? These matters are usually difficult to prove, and one of the ironies is that the British archives hold more evidence of the arrival of a consignment of arms at the Egyptian Embassy and of the half-million Syrian pounds distributed by the Egyptians than of the support contributed by the British themselves.[72] British assistance, however, must have been

---

[69] Middleton to Lloyd, Confidential, 27 February 1957, FO 371/127999.

[70] Ibid.

[71] Middleton to Lloyd, Confidential, 31 May 1957, FO 371/127999.

[72] For Middleton's discussion of the evidence of Egyptian bribery and arms shipments, see Middleton to Lloyd, Confidential, 5 June 1957, FO 371/127999.

substantial. Sir William Hayter noted afterwards: 'We were quite active in the recent elections.'[73]

The elections of June 1957 resulted in an overwhelming victory for Chamoun's supporters. The number of seats in the Chamber had been increased from forty-four to sixty-six. Fifty-three of them went to government-sponsored candidates. Among those returned were the Prime Minister, Sami Solh, and the Foreign Minister, Charles Malik, the latter despite his lack of domestic political experience or popular following. Yafi, Salam, Frangié, and Jumblatt were defeated. Chamoun's foremost political rivals had been driven into the political wilderness. They had not gone without protest. The elections had been marred by violence leading to thirty-one deaths. Middleton in fact described the violence as an attempted *coup d'état* because some of the leaders of the 'Opposition', including, he believed, Yafi and Salam, had brought in bands of supporters from southern Lebanon for demonstrations and had recruited Palestinian refugees to throw up barricades in the Muslim parts of Beirut. General Chehab had managed to restore order. The term 'Opposition' is significant. It included Muslims who refused to reconcile themselves to the events of Suez, but were nonetheless allied to Christians who wished to bring about a change of regime in Lebanon and to ensure that Chamoun would not be re-elected.

Middleton was dismayed by the results of the elections. He acknowledged that one of the problems in Lebanon was 'the subversive activities of outside Powers'.[74] But the real problem he believed to be internal. Chamoun had rigged the elections to an extent that had done irreparable damage to his own cause. His most vigorous opponents—including Yafi, Salam, Frangié, and Jumblatt—had been excluded from the Chamber of Deputies. 'I am afraid', Middleton wrote with considerable understatement about the fraud and corruption charges against Chamoun, 'that I have some doubt in my own mind as to whether some of these allegations may not have a basis of truth.'[75] Middleton was not naive. By Foreign Office standards, the Lebanese election had, on the whole, produced the desired results. What caused Middleton concern was the failure of Chamoun to see the wider issues at stake. Despite his electoral success, Chamoun faced a more determined opposition than previously. Political figures from all sects, Christian as well as Muslim, now gathered in loose alliance against Chamoun personally. Some, but not all, protested against the pro-

[73] Minute by Hayter, 20 December 1957, FO 371/128000.
[74] Middleton to Lloyd, Confidential, 31 May 1957, FO 371/127999.
[75] Middleton to Lloyd, Confidential, 12 June 1957, FO 371/127999.

Western orientation that he and Charles Malik represented. Others bore personal as well as electioneering resentments. In retrospect, Middleton viewed the elections of 1957 as the beginning of the troubles of 1958.

'The future looks black,' Middleton reported in January 1958. A wave of terrorism, which had begun the previous December, continued unabated with time bombs, dynamite detonations, and random murders. In themselves these incidents hardly constituted matters of international significance; but he believed them to be instigated by Syrian, Egyptian, and Russian agents who aimed 'to increase the public feeling of insecurity, disaffection and lack of confidence in the Chamoun régime'.[76] After the explosive news of the Egyptian-Syrian union in February, the public mood swung from jittery uncertainty to excitement.

> [T]here is no doubt that the announcement of this Union does much to satisfy a deeply-felt longing in the hearts of all Moslem Arabs. All Lebanese Moslems support it; and many of the Lebanese Christians who are dissatisfied, for a variety of reasons, with the way things are going in Lebanon or with President Chamoun personally are also prepared to support it.[77]

With the enemy within the gate, and with emotions now at a high pitch, how would Chamoun respond?

> [I]f Chamoun is goaded too far he will become more, rather than less, determined to stand for re-election. He has in his political make-up a courageous, almost reckless, streak and a readiness to take risk which is rare in his compatriots; and he is quite capable of allowing his irritation and amour-propre to affect his political judgement, and thus of overestimating his power to control 'the street'.[78]

The test came on 8 May with the assassination of an anti-government left-wing newspaper editor.

The Lebanese Troubles of May 1958

Strikes and violence immediately broke out in the cities of Sidon and Tripoli. The riots then spread to Beirut and other parts of Lebanon. Saboteurs cut the Iraq Petroleum Company's pipeline at Tripoli. The

[76] Middleton to Lloyd, Confidential, 23 January and 13 March 1958, FO 371/134116.
[77] Middleton to Lloyd, Confidential, 6 February 1958, FO 371/134387.
[78] Middleton to Lloyd, Confidential, 13 March 1958, FO 371/134116.

frontier with Syria closed. Opposition leaders demanded the resignation of Chamoun. From the British perspective the source of the agitation was obvious. According to a Foreign Office estimate:

> There is no doubt that these disorders are being fomented and sup-
> ported from the United Arab Republic. Arms have been smuggled in
> large quantities into the Lebanon, an Egyptian boat from Gaza has
> been caught landing arms and 500 armed men from Syria have at-
> tacked a Lebanese frontier post.[79]

Much of the situation now hinged on the President and on the
Commander-in-Chief of the Armed Forces. Chamoun and Chehab
not merely distrusted each other but were on exceedingly bad terms.
Unless the British, Americans, and perhaps the French took immediate action, according to Sir William Hayter, Chamoun would lose
power: 'Chehab might then hold the ring for a little but there will be
a slide towards Nasser.' The key would be with the Americans: 'American forces . . . will have to bear the burden.' In the wake of Suez,
the British could lend support but could not take the initiative. Hayter, who continued to supervise Middle Eastern affairs, believed that
the Americans should be urged to take action: 'Otherwise the Lebanon will drift into Nasser's camp and his forward march will become
unstoppable.'[80]

On the day of the riots, Chamoun informed Middleton that he
would seek re-election. The two issues of impending civil war and
Chamoun's ambition were thus joined. Both the British and American governments had been acutely aware of the buildup to the crisis.
'Mr. [John Foster] Dulles is worried about the situation in the Lebanon, which he thinks is critical,' the Foreign Office recorded in early
May.[81] Though the two governments had previously resisted Chamoun's demands for military assistance, they now prepared urgently
to deliver six fighter aircraft and eighteen tanks. Even before the outbreak of the crisis on 8 May, Lebanese affairs had acquired great significance. 'Chamoun has come to symbolize . . . the forces of resistance to Nasser,' Middleton reported.[82] In ringing words, the Secretary
of State himself, Selwyn Lloyd, had written earlier in the year that
'the continued independence of Lebanon is a pillar of British foreign
policy'.[83]

[79] Memorandum by the Levant Department, 13 May 1958, FO 371/134117.
[80] Minute by Hayter, 13 May 1958, FO 371/134116.
[81] Memorandum by the Levant Department, 1 May 1958, FO 371/134116.
[82] Middleton to FO, Secret, 5 May 1958, PREM 11/2386.
[83] Lloyd to Middleton, Secret, 8 February 1958, PREM/11/2386.

The Cabinet gave urgent attention to the Lebanese crisis on 13 May 1958. Macmillan's view coincided with Lloyd's. The Foreign Secretary took the lead in the discussion. The Commonwealth Secretary, Lord Home, and the Defence Minister, Duncan Sandys, contributed respectively to the wider discussion on international affairs and the mobilization of military forces. As during the Suez crisis, R. A. Butler, the Home Secretary, remained mostly passive but tacitly supported Macmillan and Lloyd. The latter stated that the situation continued to deteriorate. Syria and Egypt had 'deliberately fomented' strikes and disorders. Speaking to his brief, Lloyd described the political impasse created by Chamoun's insistence on seeking re-election and by Chehab's refusal to lend him political support. The Lebanese army still controlled the situation, but unless the British, American, and French governments responded to Chamoun's request for military assistance to preserve Lebanese independence, 'President Chamoun would probably be overthrown and the Lebanon would be compelled to accede to the United Arab Republic.'[84]

In the ensuing discussion, the lesson of Suez prevailed. Britain would act only in concert with the United States. Despite emphatic agreement on Nasser's responsibility for the crisis, and despite the premise of a free Lebanon as a 'pillar' of British foreign policy, the Cabinet would not intervene unilaterally. After the failure of the Suez expedition, Britain could no longer take the lead in major military operations in the Middle East. If the Americans were prepared to intervene, the British would offer their cooperation. This offer, however, contained a qualification. Western intervention would have to be acceptable to Britain's principal client, Nuri. The Cabinet warily cast an eye also towards the United Nations. It might be advisable for Chamoun to bring a case against Syrian aggression before the Security Council. But the British did not intend to get involved in 'procedural discussions' that would delay effective action. Nor were they convinced that France should be invited, as Chamoun suggested, to act along with the United States and Britain. The members of the Cabinet eventually concluded that the French should be dissuaded from taking part, 'since their participation would be liable to prejudice the attitude of the Arab States to the Western intervention.'[85]

Macmillan skilfully handled this phase of the crisis, but Lebanon by no means monopolized his attention. In mid-May 1958 an impending railway strike engaged much of his activity, and he nervously watched also the rise in the cost of potatoes and tomatoes as an index of polit-

---

[84] Cabinet Conclusions (58) 42, 13 May 1958, CAB 128/32, Part 1.
[85] Ibid.

ically unacceptable inflation. In Algeria, the French army had revolted against the Algerian policy of President Charles de Gaulle. In colonial affairs, Macmillan faced the problems of both Cyprus and Malta. Placing Lebanon in the context of his other overseas preoccupations, he wrote in his diary on 16 May:

> Lebanon still holds. Our forces are in readiness, in case the request for help comes. Malta is quieter—for the moment. Cyprus may boil over again at any moment. There have already been one or two murders. France is in a turmoil—no one knows whether it will lead to the collapse or the revival of the 4th Republic. The only solid thing we have to rely on is the Anglo-American co-operation, which is closer and more complete than ever before.[86]

It is a measure of Macmillan's success in restoring good will and trust between the British and American governments in the period after Suez, and an equal measure of Eisenhower's need for British collaboration, that the military experts almost immediately began planning joint operations. They anticipated having to deal with some 6,000 to 9,000 insurgents and some 1,000 armed 'volunteers' infiltrating from Syria. Estimates would vary, but the 'rebels' held one-half the country and all of the Basta quarter of Beirut. The US Sixth Fleet was in the Mediterranean. The British forces included an aircraft carrier and infantry as well as other troops in Cyprus.[87] There would be an American Commander-in-Chief, Admiral James L. Holloway. Some 2,000 British forces and 3,000 American troops would be deployed.[88]

The creation of an operational force, still in place at the time of the Iraqi revolution in July 1958, shaped perhaps more than anything else

---

[86] Macmillan Diary, 16 May 1958.

[87] The Defence Minister, Duncan Sandys, had sent the following message to the Prime Minister on 13 May 1958 (PREM 11/2386):

Prime Minister

1. You asked to be informed what forces could be sent rapidly to the Lebanon to support an American intervention . . .
    (a) Within 24 hours. 1 Marine Commando (600 men) and 2 Infantry battalions from Cyprus.
    (b) Within 2 days. 1 Parachute Brigade (3 battalions) from the United Kingdom.
    (c) Within 3 days. A small naval force including 1 aircraft carrier.
2. We are standing ready to alert these forces . . .

                                                                          D.S.

At the height of the interventions in July, the troop levels were 15,000 Americans in Lebanon and 3,000 British in Jordan.

[88] See *Foreign Relations of the United States, 1958–1960*, XI, p. 138, note 3.

the outcome of events. Selwyn Lloyd remarked at one stage that the British during the Suez crisis would have done better to respond immediately rather than to endure the buildup both of domestic and international protest. Failing to act immediately against Nasser, the British never again found the right moment to intervene. The pattern now seemed to be repeating itself. 'It is not clear that even our N.A.T.O. allies would support us,' Lloyd commented in June 1958. Yet if the crisis were resolved to Egypt's advantage, then the consequences would be as damaging as those at the time of Suez, as Lloyd well knew: 'If Nasser picks up the Lebanon like a ripe plum in three or four months' time, he will have won an even bigger victory than our evacuation from Port Said.'[89] British assumptions still rested on the premise that Nasser planned to annex Lebanon come what may, despite conflicting reports on his aims. The British assumed also that the experience at Suez offered enduring lessons. To the world at large, a genuine effort had to be made to present any intervention, in Middleton's words, as an action 'through the United Nations with Anglo-United States forces in the van'.[90] Only by keeping in step with the United Nations could the British hold together the Commonwealth and such 'difficult' members as Canada. 'We cannot be sure of Canadian support,' the Commonwealth Secretary, Lord Home, wrote in June. He described the Canadians as 'obsessed' with the United Nations.[91] Beyond the Commonwealth lay the even greater problem of Britain's allies. Any action with the French, not to mention the Israelis, would cause the Arab countries to rally to Nasser. In the context of the Middle East, France was now an unwelcome ally because of Arab protests against French colonial rule in Algeria and elsewhere. According to Selwyn Lloyd, French participation would be 'disastrous', since 'it would alienate all friendly Arabs'.[92]

The French knew, of course, about the concentration of military forces in the eastern Mediterranean. How could the British keep on good terms with President de Gaulle while discouraging any thought of the French joining in the intervention? Iraq played an important part in the equation. Sir Michael Wright reported from Baghdad that 'Nuri was staggered by the idea that Chamoun might invite or accept French participation,' and Nuri left no doubt 'that French participation would be ruinous'.[93] Chamoun in turn contributed to the

[89] Lloyd to Caccia, Secret, 23 June 1958, PREM 11/2387.
[90] Middleton to Lloyd, Top Secret, 29 May 1958, PREM 11/2386.
[91] Memorandum by Home, 26 June 1958, PREM 11/2387.
[92] Lloyd to Jebb, Top Secret, 24 June 1958, PREM 11/2387.
[93] Wright to Lloyd, Top Secret, 16 May 1958, PREM 11/2386.

complexity of the problem because he dealt with the French Ambassador in Lebanon the same as he did the British and American ambassadors. There was a certain logic in Chamoun's attitude: the Tripartite Declaration of 1950 by Britain, the United States, and France served to guarantee, at least in theory, the peace of the region. The French had every right to be consulted. Sir Gladwyn Jebb in Paris warned that if the 'Anglo-Saxon' powers landed troops in Lebanon, the French independently would send an expeditionary force. Jebb remarked that how the British had helped evict France from the Levant during the Second World War was still fresh in de Gaulle's memory: 'Syria is still written on his heart.' The only way, according to Jebb, to prevent de Gaulle from intervening was 'by threats or bribes, or both'.[94]

The Foreign Office ingeniously proposed to treat intervention as merely a hypothetical issue, but in the meantime to discuss fully with the French all issues concerning the local situation in Lebanon and political strategy at the United Nations. If it came to a showdown, then the British and Americans, presumably the latter more than the former, 'might frighten the French off'.[95] Macmillan and Lloyd in fact used the tactic of the 'hypothetical' in a conversation with de Gaulle in late June 1958. De Gaulle as usual confronted the issue directly. What did the British propose to do in 'the Orient'? Intervene? With considerable understatement, Macmillan answered that the situation had become 'difficult': 'At present our only possibility was to support any United Nations action.' Lloyd's response indicated how the ghost of Suez continued to hover over virtually all important discussions. He elaborated on the problem of the changing mood and the importance of finding the right moment to intervene:

> *The Secretary of State* said that operations of this kind were always easier if they were done at an early stage. If the Suez intervention had been carried out at the end of July, 1956, it would have been accepted by world opinion.

> But now the moment has passed in the Lebanon. The present Lebanese Government had shown themselves ineffective, Arab opinion had turned against us, and if we went in now we should find it very difficult to get out.[96]

As far as the poor timing of the intervention, the British in a sense were saved by the Iraqi revolution and by being able to act immediately. In the meantime de Gaulle's views coincided with those of the British,

[94] Jebb to Lloyd, Top Secret, 17 June 1958, PREM 11/2386.
[95] Lloyd to Jebb, Top Secret, 24 June 1958, PREM 11/2387.
[96] Record of conversation, 29 June 1958, PREM 11/2387.

at least on the future of Lebanon: 'Lebanon must not be allowed to disappear.' Macmillan agreed, adding that 'what must be avoided was control of the Lebanon by Nasser.'

In early June 1958 Nasser himself offered his services as peace-maker. He told the American Ambassador in Cairo, Raymond Hare, that Egypt had not stirred up the trouble in Lebanon, but that he would help end it. Chamoun would finish his term of office, Chehab would succeed him, and amnesty would be granted to the rebels.[97] These were reasonable terms. The British and Americans, however, greeted them with extreme suspicion. Macmillan happened to be in Washington on 11 June, when Dulles broke the news. What were Nasser's motives? If Nasser succeeded in bringing peace, Dulles asked, would it not bring him further prestige and discourage allies like Nuri? Macmillan suggested that the Russians might have told Nasser to call off the adventure lest it escalate into world war. Macmillan himself, always fond of historical analogy and always taking a hard line, at least tentatively, believed that American counsels divided between those who saw the need to stand up to the Egyptian dictator and those who wanted to appease him, such as William M. Rountree, the Assistant Secretary of State. Not only the ghost of Suez but the spectre of Munich appeared as Macmillan, Dulles, and Eisenhower debated Nasser's intent. Suspicion prevailed. The United States and Britain would not stand by while the United Arab Republic took over Lebanon as Germany had dismembered Czechoslovakia.

A more sophisticated, minority view also existed. Nasser's proposal that Chehab replace Chamoun represented the best solution that the Western powers could hope for. The problem of internal subversion would always be present, but failure to offer amnesty would further envenom Lebanese politics. Beyond the domestic Lebanese part of the problem, the British knew from various sources, including those at the United Nations, that Nasser might genuinely fear Anglo-American intervention. At Suez the British and Americans had been divided. Nineteen fifty-six had been Nasser's year for a miracle. In 1958 the combination of external forces did not augur a favourable outcome, nor could Nasser be certain that the Syrian initiative in Lebanon would work to his advantage. Selwyn Lloyd gained this perspective from Dag Hammarskjöld, the Secretary-General of the United Nations:

> [T]he Lebanese were geniuses at compromise and would find some way out which did not involve them in joining the United Arab

[97] See Macmillan to Lloyd, Top Secret and Guard, 11 June 1958, PREM 11/2386; Hare to Dulles, 7 June 1958, *Foreign Relations of the United States, 1958–1960*, XI, pp. 101–03.

Republic. In fact he [Hammarskjöld] thought the Syrians were much more in control of the operation than the Egyptians and might quite possibly even have the idea at the back of their minds of making things more difficult for Egypt.

Nasser was not happy about the situation.[98]

Despite this subtle, persuasive, and essentially accurate interpretation, the prevailing view simplified Nasser into a villain. Sir Harold Caccia, the Ambassador in Washington, summed up the dominant Western interpretation: the confrontation 'had become a personal contest between Chamoun, backed by the West, and Nasser by the Communists'.[99]

In the clash between the forces of darkness and light, Charles Malik played an important part. As Minister of Foreign Affairs, he projected into the international dimension of the struggle a vision as stark as that of John Foster Dulles. On 11 June the United Nations adopted a resolution calling for an observer team to be dispatched to Lebanon. By late that month it consisted of ninety-four military officers from eleven nations. Lebanon thus became, in Macmillan's phrase, a 'test case' for the United Nations. Malik, however, believed that the Secretary-General sympathized with Nasser, that the UN force represented subversion, and that 'a Munich was being prepared for his country'. He suspected Hammarskjöld of undermining Lebanon's alignment with the Western democracies:

> Hammarskjoeld evidently had exalted ideas about his role as a Scandinavian peace-maker in the Middle East, and Dr. Malik was sure he had been in continuous contact with Cairo. He feared that Hammarskjoeld might return from Beirut and Cairo with a scheme for a political settlement involving large concessions to Nasser.

> . . . Chamoun, like Benes [in Czechoslovakia], would have to submit, and Nasser would have scored another victory which would have serious consequences for the West and all its friends.[100]

In late June 1958, Malik visited Washington, where he met with Dulles. The two men were intellectually matched, and both had an interest in historical analogies, which ranged from Manchuria and Abyssinia to Munich and, more immediately, Beirut. Malik ably championed

---

[98] As related in Lloyd to Caccia, Top Secret, 19 June 1958, PREM 11/2387.

[99] Caccia to Lloyd, Top Secret, 19 June 1958, PREM 11/2387.

[100] As recounted in Sir Pierson Dixon (United Nations), Top Secret, 19 June 1958, PREM 11/2387.

Chamoun's position. But he went too far even for Dulles in attacking the United Nations. 'The activities of the UN and Hammarskjold', Dulles stated, 'have brought about a large cessation of infiltration.'[101] Nor did Malik convince either the Americans or the British when he spoke of 'something rotten in the Kingdom of Denmark', by which he meant the state of Lebanon and the hesitant part played by Lebanon's Hamlet, General Chehab.

By late June 1958 Chehab appeared to be the only person who could maintain Lebanese politics in its delicate balance, though the 'Chehab solution' had evolved gradually since the time of the outbreak of the insurrection in May. Against this background of a deteriorating political situation, Chamoun had only with extreme reluctance accepted that he could not stand for re-election. Chehab was the only figure in Lebanese public life who commanded unanimous respect; Middleton and others regarded him as the only possible candidate. Chamoun's impending withdrawal from politics and the election scheduled for 24 July 1958 prepared the way towards a national reconciliation, in Middleton's phrase, of 'all but the extremists'. Yet Chehab took no steps to consolidate his position or, in Western eyes, to exercise sufficient control over the armed forces. Middleton reported that the army as well as the Chamoun government was 'impotent'. Chamoun repeatedly contemplated sacking Chehab. Nevertheless, the only person who continued to command confidence was Chehab. But he appeared to suffer from several fatal defects. He was indecisive; he vacillated; he failed to come to grips with the situation. Furthermore his political ascendancy would mean a shift in the international alignment of Lebanon from a pro-Western state to one genuinely neutral, with a government composed of 'Lebanese of all colours and tendencies'.[102] Chehab, in other words, seemed to possess deficiencies of character that made the British and Americans themselves hesitant. But these were precisely the characteristics of moderation, caution, and fair-mindedness that made him the saviour of his nation. He believed that Lebanon should be genuinely neutral. Chehab's presence represented a return to the 1943 spirit of compromise. The British and Americans only slowly recognized his virtues.

The British and the United Nations

If the British got it wrong about Chehab, they got it even more disastrously wrong about Hammarskjöld. Little more than a decade old in

---

[101] Memorandum of conversation, 30 June 1958, *Foreign Relations of the United States, 1958–1960*, XI, p. 187.

[102] Middleton to Lloyd, Top Secret, 30 May 1958, PREM 11/2386.

1958, the United Nations commanded respect in part because of the prestige of the Secretary-General, who in one sense took a minimalist attitude towards UN functions. If the United Nations were to survive, it had constantly to be on guard against taking on more than it could manage. Hammarskjöld strenuously resisted plans for converting the United Nations into a world police force or for adopting countries as permanent wards. In another sense, Hammarskjöld saw the potential of the United Nations as an independent institution that might achieve peaceful solutions to international problems, complementing or surpassing the efforts of individual states, large or small, which were each locked in narrow visions of self-interest. Hammarskjöld worked towards UN goals relentlessly, creatively, and resourcefully. With careful calculation, the United Nations might play a critical part in solving not merely the problem of Lebanon, where it might establish a permanent observation team, but even the more intractable problems of the Middle East.

In all his affairs, Hammarskjöld held that absolute impartiality was essential. He embodied that attribute. But he combined with it a distrustful frame of mind and a certain intellectual and ethical condescension that won him enemies, especially among those with equally strong personalities. Sir Pierson Dixon, the British Ambassador at the United Nations, was only one of several to collide with him. In his attempt to remain unbiased towards all parties, Hammarskjöld acquired among British officials a reputation for having a 'notorious penchant for the Egyptians'.[103] In mid-June 1958 on his way to the Middle East, he paid a visit to Selwyn Lloyd. Both men had experienced the Suez crisis, the one as Secretary-General, upholding the ideals of the United Nations, the other as Foreign Secretary of one of the countries that had flouted them. Hammarskjöld and Lloyd regarded each other warily. But they seemed to see eye to eye on Lebanon. Hammarskjöld explained to Lloyd that the 'effective' members of the observation team would be from Europe and Canada and that, 'in view of Suez', he would not ask Australia and New Zealand to participate. Lloyd wrote afterwards:

> I wanted to assure him [Hammarskjöld] that there was no truth in any ideas current in some American quarters that we were longing to go into the Lebanon with the United States to prove how right we had been over Suez and how wrong the United States.[104]

[103] Dixon to Lloyd, Top Secret, 19 June 1958, PREM 11/2387.
[104] Lloyd to Dixon, Top Secret, 19 June 1958, PREM 11/2387.

Hammarskjöld then mentioned that he believed there would be revolutions in Iraq and Jordan. Lloyd disagreed, and the conversation moved on to the prospect of intervention in Lebanon. He attempted to make clear that intervention would be the last resort: 'Mr. Hammarskjoeld repeatedly said that everything I had said to him convinced him the more of the importance of making a success of the present United Nations operation. He saw our dilemma.'

If Hammarskjöld seemed to Lloyd to be favourably disposed towards the British predicament, evidence to the contrary soon reached the Foreign Office. From London, Hammarskjöld went on to the Middle East, where he stopped in Amman and visited the Jordanian Foreign Minister, Samir Rifai. In a report that the British acquired second-hand from the American Ambassador in Jordan, Hammarskjöld reportedly said 'that he was unalterably opposed to foreign intervention in Lebanon' and that he would attempt to persuade Nasser 'to take the heat off'. If Nasser refused, Hammarskjöld would consider economic sanctions by the United Nations.[105] He had thus contradicted the impression of sympathy for the British dilemma and seemed to imply that the British would force the Americans to act. Hammarskjöld had, Lloyd wrote, 'rather a devious mind'.[106] Lloyd wrote him the following letter:

> I have been told that you have said, after your arrival in the Middle East, that you were very depressed as a result of your conversation with me in London . . . I am told that you said you believed I was eager to involve America in an adventure in the Middle East to prove that I had been right about Suez and the United States wrong.[107]

Hammarskjöld took the letter as an insult. Responding with a spirited defence of the UN observation team, he commented that during the Suez crisis he had been accused of being 'fooled by, if not the stooge of, Nasser'. Hammarskjöld believed that the record clearly spoke for itself. He concluded with a stinging rebuke to Lloyd: 'The straight line often looks crooked to those who have departed from it.'[108] On the eve of the Iraqi revolution, Britain's relations with the United Nations, or at least with Hammarskjöld, were tense.

The question of Britain's ethics during the Suez crisis likewise clouded Lloyd's dealings with John Foster Dulles, who emerges with

[105] Mason to Lloyd, Top Secret, 23 June 1958, PREM 11/2387.
[106] Lloyd to Middleton, Secret, 24 June 1958, PREM 11/2387.
[107] Lloyd to Hammarskjöld, Secret, 24 June 1958, PREM 11/2387.
[108] Hammarskjöld to Lloyd, Secret, 10 July 1958, PREM 11/2387.

increased historical stature as one reads the records of the 1958 intervention. During the Suez crisis, Dulles had often contradicted himself and had certainly misled the British about his true intention of negotiating a solution with Nasser rather than forcing him, in Dulles's
inimitable phrase, to disgorge. In any event, Dulles warned the British
Ambassador at an early stage in the 1958 crisis that the public at large
suspected the British of pushing the United States into intervention
in revenge for Suez. Caccia responded indignantly, but the air was
cleared.[109] There evolved a harmony of British and American aims.
They would work together to sustain a Lebanon friendly to the West,
if possible, or failing that, a neutral Lebanon, but in any event a Lebanon free from domination by the United Arab Republic. The ultimate
step of military action would be taken only if all else failed. Dulles consistently followed that line, as if setting a precedent for defending all
small nations against insurrection caused by foreign powers, and as if
bearing in mind at all times the historical precedents of Manchuria,
Abyssinia, and Czechoslovakia. He weighed all sides of each issue, and
he moved ponderously, as was his nature, but he moved decisively. On
the whole his relations with the British in early July 1958 were satisfactory. If necessary, Britain and the United States were prepared to
intervene with a massive force that had been on standby for about two
months. In Dulles's mind, one thing was clear above all else, and the
British would have regarded it as ironic: if troops went in, 'it was important to avoid getting bogged down as the British had in Suez.'[110]

The British Response to the Iraqi Revolution

There is nothing like a revolution to concentrate the mind. After two
months of deliberating, the British and American governments now
acted immediately in response to the news on 14 July 1958 that about
five o'clock that morning a group of young army officers in Baghdad,
led by Brigadier Abdul Karim Qasim, had overthrown the monarchy
and the government of Nuri Pasha. Though at first the situation was
obscure, it soon became clear that the members of the royal family
had been executed and that Nuri had been killed while attempting
to escape. The British Embassy was set ablaze. The Royal Air Force ten-
uously held the base at Habbaniya, and King Hussein in Amman
spoke brave words to encourage Iraqi royalist forces, but the idea of
a counter-revolutionary force received only fleeting attention. What
the British at first called an 'insurrection' became at once a thorough-

---

[109] See Caccia to Lloyd, Top Secret, 23 May 1958, FO 371/134119.
[110] *Foreign Relations of the United States, 1958–1960,* XI, p. 252 note.

going social and political revolution that overturned the old order and broke the British connection of four decades. British policy now lay in ruins. The revolution threw the situation in Lebanon into an entirely new dimension. Chamoun immediately requested the landing of troops. But according to the Cabinet, the problem was now regional rather than restricted to Lebanon: 'A temporary Anglo-American intervention confined to the Lebanon alone would be to our disadvantage rather than to our benefit.'[111] The British urgently needed to defend their remaining clients in the Middle East, especially Jordan and above all Kuwait.

In Washington the reaction was the same as in London: if the Western powers failed to act, 'Nasser would take over the whole area.'[112] Dulles prepared for the worst. He had always believed, he remarked to Eisenhower, that the Arab world might be lost, but the United States had to consider the consequences for Turkey, Iran, and Pakistan[113] as well as for the rest of Asia: 'Our failure to respond would destroy the confidence in us of all the countries on the Soviet periphery throughout the Middle and Far East.'[114] The strategic aspect was also supremely important. The United States now held the edge militarily. As Dulles later explained in perhaps his clearest formulation of the problem, the Soviets 'had gambled on not developing many long-range bombers and had not yet adequate missiles in operation. We would probably not have another such chance.'[115] The balance might never again be so favourable. 'If we do not respond to the call from Chamoun', Dulles said on the critical day of 14 July, 'we will suffer the decline and indeed the elimination of our influence—from Indonesia to Morocco.' Eisenhower shared those cataclysmic thoughts: '[W]e must act, or get out of the Middle East entirely.' Vice President Richard Nixon warned of the danger of the United States now acquiring a 'Suez' reputation and urged that the President and Secretary of State meet with Congressional leaders. Dulles agreed, commenting that 'many will say we are simply doing what we stopped the British and the French from doing at the time of the Suez crisis'.[116] At the Congressional meeting, only Senator William J. Fulbright expressed scepticism about the extent of external aggression. Fulbright was a conspicuous exception. In Washington as in London, virtually everyone assumed,

[111] Cabinet Conclusions (58) 55, 14 July 1958, CAB 128/32, Part 2.

[112] Record of meeting of Dulles and others, 14 July 1958, *Foreign Relations of the United States, 1958–1960*, XI, p. 210.

[113] Dulles and Eisenhower telephone conversation, 14 July 1958, ibid., p. 209.

[114] Memorandum of conversation, 22 June 1958, ibid., p. 167.

[115] Ibid., p. 356, note 5.

[116] White House conference, 14 July 1958, ibid., pp. 211–15.

in the words of the British Cabinet discussion, 'that Lebanon was not primarily a civil war, but was a form of covert aggression promoted by the United Arab Republic.'[117]

Macmillan aimed to persuade Eisenhower that the Lebanon operation must now be expanded to include, if necessary, all of the Middle East. The showdown had come. In a telephone conversation with the President, Macmillan said: 'If this thing is done, which I think is very noble, dear friend, it will set off a lot of things throughout the whole area. I'm all for that as long as we regard it as an operation that has got to be carried through.' They would be driven into a much larger operation. Eisenhower would have none of that:

> Now just a minute so that there is no misunderstanding. Are you of the belief that unless we have made up our minds in advance to carry this thing on through to the Persian Gulf, that we had better not go in the first place? . . .

> If we are now planning the initiation of a big operation that could run all the way through Syria and Iraq, we are far beyond anything I have [the?] power to do constitutionally.

Macmillan reminded Eisenhower that crises could have unpredictable outcomes. 'I have seen these things go wrong,' Macmillan said.[118] 'I feel only this, my dear friend . . . it is likely that the trouble will destroy the oil fields and the pipelines and all the rest of it, and will blaze right through . . . [W]e are in it together.'[119] Eisenhower held firm. He could not commit the United States to more than the operation in Lebanon. But privately he told Dulles that he agreed with Macmillan: the crisis was a showdown between the West and Nasser. Though Eisenhower steeled himself to keep the conflict localized, he had to face the prospect of it widening and possibly engaging, at least indirectly, the Soviet Union.

Macmillan now knew that Eisenhower would attempt to limit the crisis to Lebanon and that he would proceed step-by-step in consultation with Congress and, as far as possible, in concert with the United Nations. Macmillan himself, as if consciously attempting to avoid Eden's mistakes during the Suez crisis, had kept all members of the Cabinet

[117] Cabinet Conclusions (58) 59, 14 July 1958, CAB 128/32, Part 2.
[118] Telephone conversation between Eisenhower and Macmillan, 14 July 1958, *Foreign Relations of the United States, 1958–1960*, XI, pp. 231–34.
[119] Record of conversation, Top Secret, 14 July 1958, PREM 11/2387.

as fully informed as possible and had tried to move in concert not merely with the United States but also with the United Nations, where British motives were generally suspect. But it was more than mere skullduggery in the General Assembly. Macmillan and Hammarskjöld operated on different assumptions. Contrary to the predominant view held in British and American circles—that Egypt or the United Arab Republic had inspired the insurrection in Lebanon—Hammarskjöld reckoned that Nasser had been wary of Lebanese politicians' using him to their own advantage, that he had been drawn in reluctantly, that he feared great-power involvement, and that he questioned whether the Syrian initiative would serve Egyptian purposes. Perhaps Hammarskjöld manipulated the intelligence reports, but the UN observation team found scant evidence of Syrian staff officers leading rebel troops armed with mortars and bazookas. On the other hand, the meagre reports perhaps reflected only the limited team the UN could field along the Syrian-Lebanese border. In any event, UN sources reported rival factions and fabricated estimates. Much of the trouble could be traced to the politicians ousted by Chamoun and to Chamoun himself, who exaggerated the strength of the opposition to secure external assistance. Hammarskjöld believed that if foreign influences were curtailed, and if the Lebanese were left more or less alone in their own goldfish bowl, they would devise their own solution.[120] That the exotic Lebanese goldfish bowl was being stirred by foreign hands, Hammarskjöld and Macmillan could both agree.

Where they disagreed, and where Eisenhower and Macmillan concurred, was on the extent of the external intervention. Even between Macmillan and Eisenhower there were differences, the latter regarding Nasser as a tool of the Soviets.[121] Macmillan acknowledged a degree of Soviet influence over Nasser, but, like the Foreign Office, he regarded Arab nationalism as the principal problem. As if all of this were not complicated enough—Macmillan, Hammarskjöld, Eisenhower, and others acting on different assumptions—there must be added the view that Chehab himself was a far subtler person than commonly supposed and that his motivations were to hold together the Lebanese army and beyond that the Lebanese nation. Towards that end he withheld intelligence reports from the United Nations. According to the American Deputy Under Secretary of State, Robert

[120] Many of these aspects of Hammarskjöld's thoughts are related in a conversation with Cabot Lodge, 26 June 1958, *Foreign Relations of the United States, 1958–1960,* XI, pp. 175–80.

[121] Eisenhower stated on 15 July that Nasser 'is so small a figure, and of so little power, that he is a puppet, even though he probably doesn't think so' (ibid., p. 245).

Murphy, who was sent to Lebanon at the height of the crisis, Chehab had telephone intercepts 'showing that Damascus is giving direct orders' to the rebel leaders in the Basta district of Beirut.[122]

Those conflicting interpretations were put to the test on 15 July 1958 when two battalions of US marines landed on the beaches of Beirut to the ringing of church bells. Hammarskjöld had a certain point when he commented on the extent to which the Lebanese problem above all else reflected domestic tensions. He believed that Lebanese of all political colours deliberately overestimated Nasser's influence. Middleton summed up Hammarskjöld's impression: '[T]he Lebanese were exaggerating the importance of the alleged infiltration from across the Syrian border in order to conceal their internal political disintegration.'[123]

The story of the landing of the US marines has been told many times from the American vantage point, but it gains fresh irony when related by Sir George Middleton. Middleton later recounted how 'the first wave of the American force, amounting to some 2,000 assault troops of the United States Marine Corps, land on Khaldé beach at about 2.30 p.m. on the 15th of July.' He went on:

> The ensuing scene which, but for the inherent gravity of the situation, must have come perilously near the ridiculous, was somehow symbolic of the whole crisis. The marines had been trained to land on enemy beaches in the face of stiff opposition; even those who had received some briefing expected to find some signs of civil war.
>
> They were totally unprepared for having to pick their way over recumbent sunbathers in their 'bikinis' or for grinning youths trying to help them drag their jeeps ashore. Still less were they prepared for the second shock wave of regiments of small boys jostling round to sell them chewing-gum while their older brothers followed with Coca-Cola.[124]

The American troops made their first contact with the Lebanese army at the airport, where Chehab negotiated a tense withdrawal of his forces. Middleton confirmed that Chamoun had not informed his Commander-in-Chief of the impending American invasion. Chehab had learned of the landing of troops from the American Ambassador, Robert L. McClintock, only two hours before. These were momentous transactions in Lebanese politics, beyond Western comprehension.

[122] Murphy to Dulles, 18 July 1958, ibid., p. 327.
[123] Middleton to Lloyd, Confidential and Guard, 30 July 1958, FO 371/134132.
[124] Ibid.

No less seriously, McClintock had to intervene with Chehab to prevent a coup by the army. Middleton and the British generally had regarded McClintock as an impulsive, though eloquent, American Ambassador, but on this occasion they had nothing but praise for the way in which he responded to the crisis. For the disciplined comportment of the American troops, Middleton wrote retrospectively in mild astonishment:

> In spite of their numbers I have nothing but praise for the Americans' behaviour. On the 9th of August they were given leave passes into the town; and for the first time in many months the enormous American taxis of Beirut came into their own with full cargoes of marines and sailors. Bars overflowed with white and grey-green uniforms, and everywhere one looked some grey-haired Turkish-trousered shoe-shine 'boy' was putting a final gloss on a pair of trans-Atlantic shoes.[125]

When British paratroopers were dropped in Amman on 17 June 1958, they faced difficulties of a different sort. In Macmillan's words, British forces had 'no port, no heavy arms, and no real mobility'.[126]

The same validity problem regarding intelligence sources arose in Jordan as it had in Lebanon. After a flicker of hope that all might not be lost in Iraq, British attention concentrated on Jordan and the Gulf. The British assumed, like the Americans, that 'the revolution in Iraq is clearly fostered and supported from Cairo.'[127] Nasser had good reason to throw his support behind those plotting to overthrow Hussein (as opposed to those causing trouble in Lebanon). The point of ambiguity, as Hammarskjöld had pointed out, was the extent of Nasser's involvement. Nasser himself was a conspirator as well as an opportunist, and he also calculated his self-interest against a possible British reoccupation of Jordan, as did Hussein. Nasser greatly increased his propaganda attacks against Jordan after the outbreak of the Iraqi revolution. For Jordan, the proof of the danger, though not of its ultimate source, lay in the Hussein's reckoning that he must obtain foreign assistance. But Hussein wanted the American as well as the British troops in order to guarantee a limited British presence. Dulles and Eisenhower were unwilling to expand the operation and thought that British intervention might have the opposite of the intended effect. The King might be overthrown rather than saved. The American Embassy in Amman had warned of a 'tidal wave' of Arab nationalism

---

[125] Middleton to Lloyd, Confidential, 26 August 1958, FO 371/134133.

[126] Macmillan to Eisenhower, 18 July 1958, *Foreign Relations of the United States, 1958–1960*, XI, p. 329.

[127] According to Macmillan in a message to Eisenhower, 14 July 1958, ibid., p. 301.

engulfing Jordan.[128] After the outbreak of the revolution in Baghdad, Hussein sent word requesting British and American military support if necessary. The next day, 15 July, British and American intelligence services learned 'that Nasser had instructed his agents in Jordan to assassinate Hussein and overthrow the Jordanian Government on July 16 or 17'.[129] Did these intercepts reflect Nasser's orders, or did they reveal the ambitions of anti-Hussein officers in the Jordanian army? In any event, the British Cabinet decided, after prolonged and agonized deliberations of over three hours, to send in troops.

The British force in Amman consisted of two battalions of paratroopers at the strength of 2,200 men and the support of a Guards Brigade, a potential 4,000 troops.[130] The object was to secure the airfield, the strategic bridgehead for all operations. Without the airfield, according to the British Cabinet minutes of 16 July, the British could not protect either the King or the government, and 'the opportunity for effective intervention would be lost'. Without intervention, 'Jordan would pass under the influence of the United Arab Republic.' Without Jordan, 'our position in the Gulf would at once be in jeopardy.' It was imperative to act immediately: 'Even a day's delay might rob us of the opportunity of seizing the airfield at Amman and establishing a bridgehead in Jordan.' But it was, in the Prime Minister's phrase, 'a difficult and dangerous operation'. If the Jordanian army attacked British troops, a counter-attack could come only from aircraft based on Cyprus.[131] Macmillan interrupted the Cabinet meeting to try to persuade the Americans to commit troops or at least aeroplanes to strengthen the tactical position at Amman and lend strategic support in the eastern Mediterranean. Dulles agreed only to 'moral support' and 'if needed, logistic support'.[132] At least the British were moving forward with American approval, but Macmillan nervously referred to it as 'a quixotic undertaking'. It was quixotic in the sense that British motives might be understood in the House of Commons, in the United Nations, and in America, but elsewhere it would be erroneously assumed that the British wished to reoccupy Jordan and launch a counter-revolutionary attack against Iraq. Macmillan was correct in assuming that these aims would be attributed to the British government.

As it later transpired, Macmillan and Dulles had entirely different conceptions about the purpose of interventions in Lebanon and in

---

[128] Embassy in Jordan to Department of State, 16 July 1958, *Foreign Relations of the United States, 1958–1960*, XI, p. 314.

[129] Ibid., p. 309, note 2.

[130] US forces assisted the British by airlifting oil and other logistical support.

[131] Cabinet Conclusions (58) 59, 16 July 1958, CAB 128/32, Part 2.

[132] *Foreign Relations of the United States, 1958–1960*, XI, p. 316.

Jordan. What would be the conditions of American and British withdrawal? Macmillan held that 'real United Nations safeguards' for both Lebanon and Jordan would have to be secured. Otherwise, 'if as soon as we withdrew, those countries fell into Nasser's lap our whole operation would have been a failure.' Dulles disagreed, in a statement that lucidly established the differences between British and American views on intervention:

> Nothing could cancel out the fact that we had achieved our main objectives which were, not so much to preserve Jordan and the Lebanon, as to show that our friends did not call on us for help in vain, to demonstrate to the Soviets that we could move quickly if we so wished and to show Nasser that he would not always assume that his plots could succeed without a reaction by us.[133]

Macmillan believed that the purpose of intervention went beyond the demands of the Cold War: the purpose was to save the two countries, especially Jordan, from Nasser. Dulles, by contrast, expressed ambivalence towards intervention, often recalling in 1958 the reasons he had opposed the British and French in 1956. Getting in was always easier than getting out, he said, and the presence of American troops in the Middle East would create 'strong anti-Western feeling and anti-Americanism'. No stable government there or elsewhere could last long if it were merely held in place by American or British bayonets. Dulles thus had two sharp reactions to a complex situation. The one pulled him in the direction of the British as part of a response to the Cold War, the other tugged him towards the position held by Henry Cabot Lodge, the US Ambassador at the United Nations, who believed as a matter of principle that intervention was fatal and that the United States should not be tainted by association with such powers as Britain and France. All in all, the British had good reason to be satisfied with the manifestation of what Selwyn Lloyd called the 'robust and realistic' side of Dulles's personality.[134]

In part to keep memories of Suez subdued, Britain now attempted to keep a distance from the two allies in 1956, France and Israel, even though the latter was directly concerned with the fate of Jordan. Dealing with the French proved easier than originally imagined because of the American insistence that the interventions in Lebanon and Jordan be kept separate. Sir Gladwyn Jebb had anticipated the failure of the operation if the French participated, or 'a blood row with de Gaulle'

---

[133] Record of a meeting between Macmillan, Dulles, and others, 27 July 1958, PREM 11/2388.
[134] Lloyd to Macmillan, Top Secret, 19 July 1958, PREM 11/2388.

if they did not.[135] After the American invasion of Lebanon, Jebb could say that the British would not participate but would reserve forces for action elsewhere, in other words, Jordan. Events then moved so fast that the British could but brace themselves for French protests against less than full consultation before the paratroop drop. 'It is impossible not to offend the French,' Jebb wrote on 18 July. Nevertheless, the separation of the two ventures helped considerably when the British came to argue that it had not been an allied operation under the terms of the Tripartite Declaration of 1950, but distinct manoeuvres. 'Given the General's determination to achieve tripartite consultation', Jebb reported, 'we must try to meet him somehow, or face the risk of his reverting to his 1940 methods.'[136] The answer was to involve the French as fully as possible in plans for the future of the Middle East. The British eventually took the same line with the Israelis, though with considerably more difficulty.

In the meeting on 16 July that decided in favour of the Jordan intervention, 'The Cabinet were informed that there was good reason to believe that in all the circumstances the Israel Government would find no difficulty in acquiescing in our over-flying their territory.'[137] The assumption proved too optimistic. Most of the British force arrived at the Amman airport at noon on 17 July, but Israeli fighters fired on the last of the transports and forced them back to Cyprus. The permission to fly over Israeli airspace still stood pending in Tel Aviv. The remainder of the brigade waited five hours in Cyprus until the United States government, responding to urgent British requests, secured permission from the Israelis for the over-flight into Jordan. The British quickly discovered that the problem went directly to the Prime Minister, David Ben Gurion, who found it 'humiliating' that 'we should ask to over-fly Israel at short notice'. Ben Gurion believed that the British reaped the advantage of an alliance without having concluded one. As during the Suez crisis, he placed great emphasis on being the 'moral equal' of Britain. He wanted a 'close working partnership' along the lines of the one between Israel and France.[138]

By acquiescing in the British over-flight, the Israelis had exposed themselves more than ever. They were aligned with the Western powers and more than ever opposed to Egypt and the Soviet Union. As Macmillan and Dulles both acknowledged, Ben Gurion's 'tacit agreement to the airlift was building up a backlog of Russian and Arab

---

[135] Jebb to Hoyer Millar, Top Secret, 19 June 1958, FO 371/134125.
[136] Jebb to Foreign Office, Secret, 18 June 1958, PREM 11/2388.
[137] Cabinet Conclusions (58) 59, 16 July 1958, CAB 128/32, Part 2.
[138] Sir Francis Rundall (Tel Aviv) to Foreign Office, Top Secret, 19 July 1958, FO 371/134284.

resentment . . . [W]hen American and British forces withdrew he would be left with no hard Western guarantee of Israel's position.' [139] Were Jordan to collapse, Israel would be drawn into the vortex of great-power confrontation. What did the British propose to do about it? Selwyn Lloyd attempted to answer that question in a surprisingly candid discussion with the Israeli Ambassador in London. Britain would consult closely with Israel on the question of the future of Jordan.[140] As to the 'partnership', the proposal produced some remarkable minutes in the Foreign Office. Sir Evelyn Shuckburgh, one of the key figures in British Middle Eastern policy in the earlier part of the decade, opposed closer association with Israel:

> [I]f we actually went on to create some sort of partnership on the lines proposed by the Israelis, it seems to me that we should simply be adding another heavy link to the chain hanging round our neck which started with the Balfour Declaration and has been steadily drowning us ever since.

> Whichever policy we adopt in the Middle East—whether to build up Iraq as a counter-weight to Egypt or to seek a *modus vivendi* with a more united Arab world under Egyptian leadership, association with Israel will be a fatal obstacle to its success.[141]

On the other hand, Sir William Hayter took a high moral line that coincided with British realpolitik.

> I confess I do not much like the idea of sucking up to the Israelis now when we need them and dropping them as soon as this need is over. It seems to me highly dishonest, and also liable to destroy any lingering trace of respect or confidence in us that the Israelis may retain . . .

> Our future relations with the Arabs will, or in my opinion at any rate should, be on the basis of hard-headed cooperation founded on mutual interests. They will need us, by which I mean the Americans and ourselves, as a counterpoise to Russian influence and as a market for their oil, and we shall need to buy their oil. We shall neither be able, nor be obliged to prop up unpopular regimes and to try to make them as little unpopular as possible by anti-Israeli gestures. It therefore

---

[139] Record of a meeting between Macmillan, Dulles, and others, 27 July 1958, FO 371/133823.
[140] Lloyd to Rundall, Secret, 23 July 1958, FO 371/134284.
[141] Minute by Shuckburgh, 28 July 1958, FO 371/134285. John Foster Dulles also described Israel as 'this millstone round our necks' (as reported in Hood to Hayter, Top Secret, 9 September 1958, FO 371/134279).

seems to be clear that we can even in the long term afford to be much less standoffish with the Israelis than we have been in the past.[142]

Britain emerged from the crisis of 1958 with a slightly more pro-Israeli, or, more accurately perhaps, a slightly less anti-Israeli policy than previously, in part for reasons concerning the Soviet Union.

Five days after the outbreak of the revolution in Iraq, Nikita Khrushchev wrote to Eisenhower, protesting the 'armed intervention' by the United States in Lebanon and by Britain in Jordan. To prevent a conflagration in the Middle East, he proposed a conference to be attended by the heads of government of the Soviet Union, the United States, Britain, France, and India. They would propose a solution to the Middle East crisis. Khrushchev suggested that Hammarskjöld participate. Sir William Hayter was extremely active in Washington, New York, and London, devising a reasoned course of action in response to what he believed to be Khrushchev's purpose. Assuming that Khrushchev would act rationally—as always, as with Nasser, a large assumption in the British view—the British did not think that the Soviet Union intended to go to war over Lebanon or Jordan, but that Khrushchev intended to make it clear that the Western powers must not embark on a counter-revolutionary invasion of Iraq. Hayter believed that there should be a United Nations solution.[143] This was the governing idea. He saw eye to eye with Hammarskjöld: Jordan, not Lebanon, was the heart of the problem. According to a record of a meeting between Hayter and other British officials with Hammarskjöld in New York, the Secretary-General 'viewed our presence in Jordan in a quite different light from the American presence in Lebanon'. The situation in Jordan was incomparably more serious.

> [Hammarskjöld] . . . sees that a collapse in Jordan, bringing it within Nasser's sphere of influence would at once create an acute problem for the Israeli Government and would probably lead them to occupy the West Bank, with incalculable consequences for the peace of the area.[144]

[142] Minute by Hayter, 29 July 1958, FO 371/134285.

[143] See e.g. memorandum of conversation at British Embassy, 19 July 1958, *Foreign Relations of the United States, 1958–1960*, XI, pp. 340–43.

[144] Dixon to Foreign Office, Secret, 21 July 1958, PREM 11/2388. In a conversation between Macmillan, Dulles, and others, Dulles commented: 'The disintegration of Jordan would lead probably to the Israelis seizing the West Bank and this in turn would mean an Arab/Israel war with a very dangerous chain reaction in the international field. It was possible that Khrushchev could be made aware of the dangers of such an upheaval and might agree to co-operate to prevent it. This, of course, was presupposing that Khrushchev was motivated by reason. But there were grave dangers that both Khrushchev and Nasser were inclined to act spontaneously without any rational approach' (record of meeting, 27 July 1958, PREM 11/2388).

The British discussed among themselves, and with others, various solutions, including Nasser's proposal to divide Lebanon along the lines of Vietnam or Korea and to divide Jordan as well, the Palestinian part to be absorbed into the United Arab Republic and the pre-1948 state of Transjordan to remain independent. The Levant Department of the Foreign Office, agreeing with Hammarskjöld, commented on the Jordan part of the proposal:

> Transjordan would be politically more viable, and economically no more unviable, than the present Jordan—and cheaper to maintain. But what on earth would the West Bank do—except fall into Israeli hands?[145]

The British discussed various other proposals in the wake of the Soviet demand for a conference. A neutralized Lebanon might become a ward of the United Nations, Jordan might be neutralized along the lines of Austria, and Kuwait might be guaranteed independence as a Switzerland in the Middle East. Whatever the solutions, they would be found through the United Nations. Thereby the British would have the support or at least the acquiescence of the international community, something they had so sorely lacked during the Suez crisis. As Macmillan described the plan to Dulles, the grand strategy bore a striking resemblance to Dulles's own manoeuvres in 1956, when he had attempted to let the crisis peter out through protracted negotiations. Macmillan wrote:

> If . . . the Russians accept a meeting of the Security Council, then I think it unlikely that desperate action will be taken by Nasser or the new Iraq Government to precipitate a crisis in the Middle East. We might look for a few weeks' pause before any further serious trouble develops—such as a coup in Jordan or a move against the Western interests in the Gulf.[146]

The immediate problem, however, was to be sure that Khrushchev did not misunderstand the intent of Britain and the United States. They would not intervene in Iraq. But they would defend at virtually any cost their access to the oil in the Gulf.

From beginning to end, the British aimed above all to preserve their position in the Gulf. They found to their great relief that the Americans agreed that this point had transcendent priority. After the outbreak of the revolution in Iraq, Selwyn Lloyd had flown to Washington. He reported jubilantly to Macmillan:

[145] Minute by Robert Tesh (Levant Department), 7 August 1958, FO 371/133826.
[146] Macmillan to Dulles 27 July 1958, *Foreign Relations of the United States, 1958–1960*, XI, p. 405.

One of the most reassuring features of my talks here has been the complete United States solidarity with us over the Gulf. They are assuming that we will take firm action to maintain our position in Kuwait. They themselves are disposed to act with similar resolution in relation to the Aramco oilfields in the area of Dhahran . . . They assume that we will also hold Bahrain and Qatar, come what may. They agree that at all costs these oilfields must be kept in Western hands.[147]

Eisenhower himself wrote to Macmillan that, beyond Lebanon and Jordan, 'we must also, and this seems to me even more important, see that the Persian Gulf area stays within the Western orbit. The Kuwait-Dhahran-Abadan areas become extremely important.'[148] Dulles entirely agreed: 'The thing we want to preserve is that Persian Gulf position.'[149] With the oil of the Gulf remaining in Western hands, the loss of Iraq could be taken more philosophically. Lloyd stated the problem at its most basic when he wrote of the agreement between him and Dulles: '[H]e was quite definite that the Gulf was the essential area, and that so long as we could hold it and its oil resources, the loss of Iraq was not intolerable.'[150]

In both Kuwait and Jordan the British had to face the prospect that the rulers might be swept away by waves of pro-Nasser Arab nationalism. 'If a *coup* could be carried out in Baghdad, as it had been', Lloyd remarked to Dulles, 'there was an equal danger of one in Kuwait.'[151] In that event, US marines based on Okinawa would secure Kuwait and, if the revolution reached Saudi Arabia, the oil installations at Dhahran. What would then happen? One course might be to rule Kuwait directly as a Crown Colony, though Lloyd pointed out the difficulties of occupying the country against the wishes of the ruling family:

> The labour force working in the oil area may strike. To produce tolerable conditions for a long-term operation, we should have to take control of the whole of Kuwait and run it as a Crown Colony. For a short-term operation we could hold the oil area alone, but that would no doubt mean a Nasserite régime in the rest of Kuwait with the inconveniences and pressures that happened when we held the Suez base but not the rest of Egypt.[152]

[147] Lloyd to Macmillan, Secret, 20 July 1958, FO 371/132776.
[148] Eisenhower to Macmillan, 18 July 1958, *Foreign Relations of the United States, 1958–1960*, XI, p. 330.
[149] Record of telephone conversation between Dulles and Eisenhower, 19 July 1958, ibid., p. 332.
[150] Lloyd to Foreign Office, Secret, 20 July 1958, PREM, 11/2388.
[151] Lloyd to Foreign Office, Top Secret, 18 July 1958, FO 371/133823.
[152] Lloyd to Macmillan, Secret, 20 July 1958, FO 371/132776.

Prudence prevailed.[153] British contingency planning proceeded on the assumption that Kuwait would become a sort of Switzerland. But the mere mention of the phrase 'Crown Colony' caused tremors in Washington, especially among those who viewed the new Anglo-American combination with distaste. The British were aware of a strong element of dissent from the general line taken by Dulles. It extended all the way from the upper echelons to low levels in the State Department, where one Edwin M. Kretzmann caused the British anguish. Kretzmann held strong opinions, especially about the Middle East. Recent commitments to the British, he said, by no means meant that the United States would maintain 'British political and military positions' in the Gulf.[154] What galled the British was not the existence of such views, but that they were so blatantly and publicly expressed. 'I find this disturbing evidence of the lack of discipline amongst State Department officials in dealing with policy issues on an off-the-record basis,' wrote P. H. G. Wright in the Foreign Office. 'There is nothing that we can do to alter what is in fact a fundamental American trait.' Suez, as usual, was part of the explanation for such robust views. Kretzmann merely vented openly what many other American officials expressed privately. To the British, a return to the subject of Suez was extremely unfortunate because it undermined the British position not merely in the Gulf but throughout the Middle East:

> One of the strongest propaganda cards which we can play at the present time in the Middle East is the fact that there is a joint Anglo-American policy, and that the Anglo-American difficulties of the Suez era are a thing of the past. But of course the value of this card is greatly weakened if the American part of this position is going to be undermined by an impression that the Americans themselves are not wholeheartedly behind their own policy.[155]

If Kuwait were to become the Switzerland of the Middle East, it would require strong backing of both the American and British governments. The trends in American policy by no means reassured the British.

The principal exponent of an alternative to Dulles's policy appeared to be William M. Rountree, the Assistant Secretary for Near

---

[153] The head of the Eastern Department, D. M. H. Riches, minuted: '[T]he political effects of running Kuwait as a colony are I think understated. I think that unless we can secure some kind of request for going into Kuwait we shall be in queer street not only with the Arab but also with the rest of the world' (22 July 1958, FO 371/133808).

[154] As quoted in Willie Morris to Riches, Secret and Guard, 6 August 1958, FO 371/132770.

[155] Minute by P. H. G. Wright, 12 September 1958, FO 371/132770.

Eastern and South Asian Affairs. Dulles himself liked and encouraged controversy. It provoked him to further thought, and in any event his own will always prevailed. But it disturbed the British to hear such a highly placed and influential adviser voice opinions at variance with Dulles's. Similar dissent was a vital part of the British tradition as well, but once policy had been decided, ministers and civil servants upheld it or resigned. To the British, Rountree represented an acute danger because he seemed to want to appease Nasser. In reality, Rountree's views were not far removed from Dulles's, but he did distrust the British and he did believe that eventually there had to be a reconciliation with Egypt. What drew British wrath regarding Jordan was Rountree's proposal that a referendum should be held to determine the country's future. The British Ambassador in Amman, Sir Charles Johnston, wrote with scarcely veiled contempt that Rountree knew nothing of the country or its traditions:

> Mr. Rountree perhaps imagines that the alternative to King Hussein could be a nice cosy pro-American and anti-British republic. If he does, he could not be more mistaken . . . If King Hussein went now there would be no halting the slide towards extremism . . . The result would be not only that Jordan would promptly join the U.A.R., but that its accession would give the whole U.A.R. a sharp twist to the left and indeed might replace Cairo's influence by Moscow's throughout Greater Syria. Mr. Rountree's advice would, in my view, lead straight to the establishment of Communist control over the Levant.[156]

The problem for the British in this case was one of mistaken identity. It was not merely Rountree but Dulles himself who wanted to examine the possibility of a referendum in Jordan. Dulles had become increasingly alarmed at the British position in Jordan. He now took that view that he had opposed the British intervention from the outset.[157] This was an exaggeration: he had been sceptical, and his scepticism had grown. He did not believe the British could now extricate themselves without pulling down the King and in consequence bringing about a Nasserite takeover. Dulles's doubts were fed by Macmillan and Lloyd, who also were extremely uneasy at the precarious British position in Jordan. Only Sir Charles Johnston took the robust stand that Hussein, and the British, could weather the storm.

Macmillan once said, agreeing with Dulles, that 'it is not really Jordan but Iraq which is the real problem'.[158] By the end of the year it was

---

[156] Johnston to Foreign Office, Secret, 18 August 1958, PREM 11/2381.

[157] Dulles stated on 23 July 1958 at a meeting with Eisenhower and others that 'we had not wanted the British to go in' (*Foreign Relations of the United States, 1958–1960,* XI, p. 377).

[158] Macmillan to Eisenhower, 18 July 1958, ibid., p. 329.

still not clear whether the revolutionary regime in Iraq would emerge as pro-Nasser or pro-Soviet. But there appeared to be the possibility, at least to the British, that Abdel Karim Qasim might be an Iraqi patriot first and thus an Arab nationalist with whom they could do business.[159] As it eventually transpired, they found him to be an erratic and oppressive tyrant, but certainly not the tool of either the Egyptians or the Soviets. Qasim apparently puzzled Nasser as well. As the British and Americans learned more of Nasser's reactions to the general crisis, the more they began to suspect that he had not been, after all, the mastermind behind the Iraqi revolution, or even in control of the anti-Hussein movement in Jordan, and still less directly involved in Lebanon. In a remarkable interview with Robert Murphy in August 1958, Nasser stated that 'frankly as a military man he just could not believe it earlier but was quite willing now to be convinced that US military intervention [was] limited to Lebanon.' He believed the Americans and certainly the British 'intended to attack Iraq'. Obviously, misperceptions were not limited to the West. On Jordan, Nasser stated that he simply did not know how to solve the problem, but that he failed to see how King Hussein could survive with 90 per cent of the population opposed to him. Nasser undoubtedly exaggerated the size of the opposition, but when he began talking about his own part in the plot against King Farouk in 1952, his words rang true. Nasser said that the overthrow of Farouk was in itself the best example of how wrong Hussein might be in his confidence in the fidelity of the Jordanian army.[160] Sir Charles Johnston would have disagreed. He believed that British intervention had not only strengthened Hussein's position but also consolidated the loyalty of the army.

The American and British interventions came to an end with the withdrawal of the last troops in late October–early November 1958. General Chehab's election as President on 31 July had begun a new era in Lebanese national history. In Jordan, King Hussein's regime did not collapse, contrary to fears in London and Washington. A UN 'presence' helped stabilize Jordan's relations with the neighbouring Arab states, and the United States agreed to economic assistance, thus providing the basis for Jordan's survival.

It is appropriate to end with the reflections on the significance of these events by the two British officials most closely concerned with

[159] Macmillan remarked that 'Iraq was a country of diverse elements, some of whom might be possible Kerenskys. We should not appear to drive them out, but rather see whether we could not gradually wean them away from Nasser' (record of a meeting between Macmillan, Dulles, and others, 27 July 1958, PREM 11/2400).

[160] Murphy's report of his interview, 8 August 1958, *Foreign Relations of the United States, 1958–1960*, XI, pp. 439–43.

Lebanon and Jordan, Sir George Middleton and Sir Charles Johnston. Both were extraordinarily able men, and their thoughts help provide perspective on the general crisis of 1958. Middleton was essentially a humane sceptic, both about Lebanon and about Britain's future in the Middle East. Johnston was robustly optimistic about Jordan. He was one of the last of a long line of British Proconsuls who believed that Britain's presence in the region could be compatible with Arab nationalism.

The end of the crisis coincided with the end of Middleton's tenure. In his valedictory dispatch he wrote of Lebanon with warm memories: 'It is impossible not to enjoy the splendid and dramatic scenery, the sparkling climate, the quick wit and innate courtesy of the country folk, the urbanity of the French-speaking upper class.' Nevertheless he wrote in despair. He believed that the national ordeal since May had been 'a moral crisis which had its origins in the independence of the Lebanon'. The internal crisis was basically a confessional issue: 'Christian and Moslem live in uneasy concord only so long as there is no obvious advantage to either side in seeking to change the balance or so long as one side has the clear mastery. So long as Islam and the West are not in conflict in the wider sphere of world politics, Lebanon manages to live quietly at home.'[161] He had written earlier of how the less privileged Shia had built up a standing grievance against the more affluent parts of the population, how the Suez crisis had injected an explosive element into Lebanese politics as many Muslims turned to Nasser as the leader of the Arab world, and how Chamoun had tilted the country too far to the West while driving his political opponents into armed opposition. Throughout the crisis, Middleton remained essentially favourably disposed to Chamoun and ambivalent, even hostile, to Chehab. He recognized in Chamoun, for all his faults, a patriot who had his country's interests at heart. He saw in Chehab a cynic who, though also a sincere patriot, could or would not rise to the occasion. This was a basic misjudgement. In fairness it must be said that Middleton acknowledged Chehab's potential greatness:

> General Chehab is descended from the emirs who once ruled much of south-central Lebanon and I think he is conscious of his inherited part in the history of this country. To his aristocracy of birth has been added the habit of command deriving from some twelve years as the senior officer in the Lebanese Army. Moreover he is conscious that by his aloofness from day-by-day affairs he has become something of

---

[161] Middleton to Lloyd, No. 129 Confidential, 27 August 1958, FO 371/134133.

a figurehead in Lebanese national life and widely regarded as a symbol of all that is most worthy in the Lebanese character . . .

History is his chosen reading and his family name is woven into the history of Lebanon in the same way as the name of Cecil is woven into that of England.[162]

With guarded words, Middleton summed up by stating that Chehab 'is by no means the ideal President but he is probably the best we can hope for in the circumstances'. This was a low assessment, for in Middleton's own words Chehab more than anyone else had worked 'to restore the national unity which had brought independence to the Lebanon in 1943, and which had inspired the National Pact'.[163] In their own way the Lebanese had again achieved a precarious balance of national unity with Chehab as their leader.

Though Middleton acknowledged the skill and the discipline of the American intervention, he believed it had only momentarily stabilized Lebanese politics and that the country might yet drift into Nasser's orbit. In their haste to patch together an accord, to outpace even the Lebanese in pursuit of a compromise that would allow for the withdrawal of the troops, the Americans had misjudged the tenacity of the pro-Nasser Muslims. Middleton remained pessimistic:

I do not see Lebanon settling down easily or quickly. I suspect that under American pressure the General [Chehab] may seek a drastic and pro-rebel solution to the present crisis rather than one of compromise which would be more natural to him. If he does, he may find himself faced with a new rebellious element on his hands and the temptation will then be to throw in his hand in disgust.

This will be exactly what the present Opposition have always wanted; first to get rid of Chamoun and then the General, so that the field is left open to the Moslem pro-Nasser nationalists.[164]

This again was too low an estimate of Chehab, but Middleton's comments reveal the suspicion prevalent in British circles that the Americans would eventually want to appease Nasser in order better to carry on the Cold War against the Soviet Union. The submerged differences between the British and American assessments of Nasser in relation to the Soviet Union had now come to the surface.

[162] Middleton to Lloyd, No. 128 Confidential, 27 August 1958, FO 371/134133.
[163] Middleton to Lloyd, Confidential, 26 August 1958, FO 371/134133.
[164] Middleton to Hayter, Confidential, 13 August 1958, FO 371/134133.

Those differences emerged sharply in the case of Jordan. British priorities there ranked much higher than in Lebanon, which Middleton referred to as a 'not very valuable' country.[165] Jordan lay in the strategic arc that extended through Iraq to Kuwait. After the revolution in Iraq, Sir Charles Johnston gave two reasons why Jordan continued to be important: '[I]f we did not hold on, first this whole area would go Nasserite, and secondly the remaining friends of Britain and America in the Arab World would regard us as useless and effete.'[166] Johnston believed that the Americans had been defeatist throughout the crisis. He complained especially about the US Chargé d'Affaires in Amman, Thomas K. Wright, whom Johnston regarded as 'the voice of doom'. Wright held that neither the United States nor the United Nations could continue to underwrite a bankrupt regime propped up by Bedouin bayonets. Wright happened to share that view, as did the Secretary of State himself. Dulles became increasingly nervous about the British position in Jordan. 'The British are getting into a dangerous situation in Jordan,' he commented a few days after the arrival of the British forces in Amman. 'They cannot leave without the situation collapsing.'[167] In London, Macmillan was jittery and Lloyd was pessimistic.[168] Despite those doubts and differences, the British and American combination held. Johnston drew a far-reaching conclusion: the intervention 'proved that Anglo-American cooperation in the Arab world is possible'.

Without the intervention, according to Johnston, 'Jordan would now be either Nasserite or Qassimite or a bit of both.' Again the conclusion was far-reaching:

> As it is, we have succeeded in preserving in the Arab world a régime which is both outspokenly pro-Western and at the same time acceptable in its country; at least it maintains normal stability by civilian methods and without the support of martial law, which is more than can be said for most other Middle East régimes. We have showed both types of Arab extremists [Nasserites and Qassimites] that we (the West in general and the British in particular) are people to be reckoned with.[169]

[165] Middleton to Lloyd, No. 129 Confidential, 27 August 1958, FO 371/134133.

[166] Johnston to Foreign Office, Secret, 12 August 1958, FO 371/134009.

[167] Record of a meeting at the White House, 20 July 1958, *Foreign Relations of the United States, 1958–1960*, XI, p. 348. Dulles said on another occasion to Eisenhower that 'We are hooked for 30–40 million a year to pay the budget deficit of Jordan' and that he would 'rather Nasser or the Soviets do that' (ibid., p. 332).

[168] On 23 July, Eisenhower remarked that Macmillan seemed to have 'lost his nerve'; and Lloyd at the end of September expressed the fear that 'Jordan would collapse shortly after the British withdrawal' (ibid., pp. 377 and 580).

[169] Johnston to Lloyd, Confidential and Guard, 22 January 1959, FO 371/142100.

Too much should not be made of Johnston's description of Jordan as a liberal regime, or for that matter of Jordan's independence. He recognized that Hussein presided over a police state and that 'to put it crudely, the Hashemite Kingdom is still a horse in the Western stable'.[170] Nevertheless, the instincts of King Hussein quite apart from Western influence were conciliatory, as if, Johnston wrote, he had inherited the realistic attitudes of his grandfather, King Abdullah, especially regarding Israel.

> [I]f King Hussein's régime collapsed, the Israelis would feel strongly tempted to seize some at least of the Jordanian territory on the West Bank, thereby at once transforming a Middle East dispute into a world crisis . . .

> To allow an Arab Government with such views [as Hussein's] . . . to be ousted by a gang of chauvinistic, irredentist demagogues like the Jordanian Nasserites . . . would be about the worst mistake that the West could commit.[171]

Johnston attributed the success in sustaining Hussein through the crisis in large part to Hussein himself, who possessed 'a certain doggedness which is rarely found in the Arab character'. Hussein, in Johnston's judgement, 'has now emerged as a leader of undoubted quality'. Such leaders might be rare in the Arab world, but they could be found. Johnston had written on numerous earlier occasions that it was defeatist to believe it impossible for Britain and the United States to reach an understanding with Arab nationalist leaders: 'The Arabs have more sense than their behaviour sometimes suggests. If properly handled by us, treated as equals, and helped where possible, but with tact and discretion, there is no reason why they should gravitate to eastward.'[172] Those ideas led to Johnston's ultimate conclusion, which helps explain the British view of the significance of the 1958 intervention: Arab nationalism was not necessarily anti-Western, and with the help of the United States, Britain could remain a great power in the Middle East.

A Revolutionary Year: The Middle East in 1958   2002

---

[170] Ibid.
[171] Johnston to Lloyd, Secret and Guard, 4 December 1958, FO 371/134011.
[172] Ibid.

30

THE ORIGINS OF THE IRAQI REVOLUTION

I n approaching the subject of British involvement in the origins of the Iraqi revolution of 1958, there are three useful points to bear in mind as well as a number of questions. The first point is that from the perspective of sheer self-interest, the British in Baghdad and in London were uneasily aware as early as the Second World War that too much depended on their principal collaborator, Nuri Pasha es Said. The long-range future, partly because of Nuri's dominant position in Iraqi politics—and no successor in sight—appeared to be unsatisfactory. Even two decades before 1958 there was an overarching question: could revolution be averted?

The second point is that the British in the post-1945 period miscalculated, as did Nuri, on the ways in which Iraq's resources should be developed and the revenues invested. The principal issue, to which the British gave sustained attention, was how to utilize the oil revenues to benefit the Iraqi population at large. The third point, certainly the most fundamental, is that the British had helped create the set of shifting alliances among the propertied classes, the sheikhs, and the political and military leaders of the country.[1] During the 1920s and 1930s and on into the post-war period, the British were part of the triangular basis of power in Iraq, and they rivalled the monarchy and the socially dominant landed classes. The institutional policies that they initiated continued to work in favour of the existing social order.

Until 1958, Britain remained the dominant foreign power in Iraq. Propping up the monarchy, stationing troops at air-force bases in Habbaniyah and Shaiba, and indirectly appointing officials to key posts in the Iraqi government, the British exerted informal control as well as influence. The Iraq Development Board was largely a British invention. The British position in Iraq was thus considerable, but it is important to distinguish between the institutional legacy of the earlier era, which continued to be significant, and the active part played in the 1950s by British soldiers and political advisers, who often asked whether British influence still counted. Could the British still intervene decisively, either directly or indirectly? Did the Iraqis still believe that they could? One is reminded of the feigned perplexity of Harold Beeley, who wrote as a member of the Foreign Office in 1951: 'I was often puzzled after my conversations in Iraq to know whether the

---

[1] Hanna Batatu, *The Old Social Classes and the Revolutionary Movements of Iraq* (Princeton, 1978), pp. 11–12.

complaint against us was that we interfered and ought not to interfere or that we ought to interfere and failed to do so.'[2]

What were the British assumptions, tacit as well as explicit, about Iraq? It is useful to begin with the thoughts of Sir John Troutbeck, the Ambassador in Baghdad in the period 1951–54. Troutbeck had a long record of service in the Middle East. From 1947 to 1950 he had been head of the Middle East Office in Cairo, where he had coordinated regional policy. He was thus familiar with general problems, such as the sort of Arab unity championed by the Arab League. He took it for granted that British influence in Iraq was beneficent, and indeed that the Iraqis owed their very independence to Britain. 'When all was said and done', he wrote in 1952, 'we had delivered Iraq from Turkish rule and given her her independence, provided a long succession of honest and able administrators for the country, built the railway system and handed it over practically free of charge, and created the oil industry upon which the financing of further development depended.'[3]

Though he may not have agreed with all of the implications, Troutbeck was expressing the rudiments of what has become known as the 'colonial state'.[4] During and after the First World War, Britain imposed a territorial unity on the three former Ottoman provinces of Basra, Baghdad, and Mosul; the boundaries of the new territory were policed by an army. Under the administration of the British, Iraq was a nascent modern state. It gradually possessed not only boundaries but also a system of administration and justice, a constitution, and a bicameral legislature. The British developed an infrastructure of roads, railways, and telegraph lines. They created a central bureaucracy with all of the trappings of Western government, including offices with files, typewriters, and telephones. The Iraqi Police Force, with its own Criminal Investigation Department, provided internal security. All of these measures in one way or another served British self-interest, yet British administrators could emphatically claim that they served the Iraqi government in the best tradition of the British civil service.

One function of the colonial state is to provide a basis of revenue, which the British did through the 1929 law dealing with the national tax system. It benefited their collaborators, the large landowners. Another function is to regulate land tenure, which the British did by

---

[2] Minute by Beeley, 30 March 1951, FO 624/199.

[3] Troutbeck to Eden, Confidential, 31 October 1952, FO 371/98747.

[4] For my own ideas on this useful concept in the African context, see Prosser Gifford and W. R. Louis, eds., *Decolonization and African Independence: The Transfers of Power, 1960–1980* (New Haven, 1988), introductory chap.

continuing to uphold the Ottoman land law of 1858 and overseeing the enactment of the land law of 1933.[5] Still another function of the colonial state is economic development. In 1925 a British, French, and American consortium called the Iraq Petroleum Company secured a concession over Iraqi oil. In 1950 the Iraq Development Board was created to invest a large part of the profits of the Iraqi government into such projects as irrigation and flood control, agricultural development, and land reclamation. Yet another fundamental function of the colonial state is to provide internal security. In 1941 the British responded to an uprising led by Rashid Ali by reoccupying the country and restoring the monarchy. Thus there was no doubt that Iraq was a puppet state.[6] Though the mandate had ended in 1932 and Iraq had become 'independent', it was clear that the Iraqi government was dependent on Britain. Troutbeck would have used a slightly different phrase—a 'friendly' rather than 'dependent' government, perhaps—but he would have recognized the functions of the Iraqi state as created or directed by the British. It would be unfair to Troutbeck, however, not to point out that he would probably have regarded the entire concept of the 'colonial state' as a convenient scapegoat for the Iraqis to use when blaming British imperialism for their own shortcomings.

Though Troutbeck was a man of equable temperament, it irritated him that Iraqis remained resentful and suspicious of the British presence. He was once provoked into reducing them to a racial stereotype:

> The Iraqi, it seems to me, or at any rate the townsman, will never forget a grievance. Being one of the laziest of mortals and having no family life, he will sit in his cafe for hours on end surrounded by his cronies, brooding over his grievances and talking interminable politics. By a mixture of tact and firmness one may keep him sane and good-humoured for a time, and a joke may turn his thoughts at a difficult moment. But there is a side to his nature which is embittered, frustrated and fanatical.

[5] The following works on land tenure in Iraq are particularly useful in understanding British assessments, which, in Troutbeck's case, invariably included the legacy of the Ottoman land law of 1858: T. Khalidi, ed., *Land Tenure and Social Transformation in the Middle East* (Beirut, 1984); Albertine Jwaideh, 'Midhat Pasha and the Land System of Lower Iraq', in Albert Hourani, ed., *St. Antony's Papers 16: Middle Eastern Affairs*, 3 (London, 1963); Doreen Warriner, *Land Reform and Development in the Middle East: A Study of Egypt, Syria, and Iraq* (London, 1957); and Joseph Sassoon, *Economic Policy in Iraq, 1932–1950* (London, 1987); see also especially Peter Sluglett, *Britain in Iraq, 1914–1932* (London, 1976), chap. 6.

[6] See Mohammad A. Tarbush, *The Role of the Military in Politics: A Case Study of Iraq to 1941* (London, 1982).

Seeing little but squalor and stagnation all round him, he will not admit even to himself the obvious answer, that he belongs to a peculiarly irresponsible and feckless race.[7]

The Iraqis did not seem capable, even in their own eyes, of keeping
pace with events in the Middle East. 'Bagdadi lawyers and coffee-
house politicians', Troutbeck observed after the Egyptian revolution
of 1952, 'seem to regard it as almost a matter of honour to have a
coup d'état. It has happened in Egypt and Syria, and even in the despised Lebanon. The Bagdadis are hanging their heads in shame; they
have not yet even murdered a Prime Minister.'[8]

Troutbeck was representative of his era. He held what Norman
Daniel has described as 'the theory of the two standards', by which the
British, so it was believed, had progressed to an advanced stage of civilization, whereas the Iraqis had developed only to an eighteenth-
century equivalent.[9] Troutbeck had no doubt whatever that the Iraqis
had been granted independence prematurely in 1932: 'There is not
the smallest doubt that Iraq achieved her independence too soon.'[10]
In holding that view, he was a quintessential British official. But he also
espoused more sophisticated and less paternalistic ideas that set him
apart from most of his contemporaries. Troutbeck believed that the
British should force the pace of reform and modernization in their
own self-interest as well as for the sake of Iraq. 'If nothing is done', he
wrote in April 1953,

> the position of the Royal House itself may be in danger. We are al-
> ways being accused here of interfering in Iraqi affairs in the wrong
> direction; I think that the moment has come when we must make a
> real effort to move things in the right direction both in our own in-
> terests and in those of Iraq.[11]

The issues that preoccupied him as he tried to exert a positive influence were the ethnic and religious composition of the Iraqi state, 'radical' nationalism as espoused by unemployed Iraqis with some degree
of education—the 'effendis'—and certain matters that needed to be
addressed urgently, such as tax reform.

Above all, Troutbeck was aware of what he called the 'artificiality' of

---

[7] Troutbeck to Eden, Confidential, 31 October 1952, FO 371/98747.

[8] Ibid.

[9] 'Caractacus' (Norman Daniel), *Revolution in Iraq* (London, 1959), p. 95.

[10] Troutbeck to Eden, Confidential and Guard [Guard = not for American eyes], 9 December 1954, FO 371/110991.

[11] Troutbeck to Sir James Bowker, Secret, 3 April 1953, FO 371/104678.

the Iraqi state. British rule had imposed a fragile unity over six and a half million diverse people who espoused disparate religious beliefs. Since agriculture provided the livelihood of the majority of the Iraqis, it was not surprising that Troutbeck called attention to the 'agrarian misery' of the rural areas. Traditionally, the British had upheld the authority of the tribal sheikhs, who were, in his phrase, 'horrified' at the idea of land reform. Quite another set of problems he identified with the Kurds of the northern part of the country; they formed about one-fifth the total population. 'In time of trouble', he observed, 'their loyalty could not be wholly guaranteed.'[12] The principal political element comprised the Sunni Arabs, who constituted only about one-quarter of the population but exercised a traditional dominance over the Shia Arabs, who formed about half the population. Troutbeck once gave a curious explanation of how British policy had enhanced Sunni supremacy: '[A] similar problem had arisen in the old days in India when the Hindus were much further advanced than the Muslims and were therefore being given all the appointments.'[13] Whenever he summarized the ethnic and religious reasons for unrest, Troutbeck recognized the part played by 'the politically conscious, truculent and unemployed effendi . . . [undermining] the stability of the country'.[14]

Troutbeck's interpretation was consistent and coherent. It may have been Anglocentric, and it may have used, for example, Indian analogies that today seem misguided, but it nevertheless made a persuasive point: Iraq was not a nationalistically cohesive state; the ideas of patriotism and nationalism were still weak.[15] Troutbeck believed that since 1932 the quality of administration in Iraq had steadily declined.

> So today we have a country with all the material means for progress at its disposal but with an administration so rotten and chaotic that it is more than doubtful whether it can take advantage of them . . . The British administration disappeared before new roots had time to establish themselves.[16]

In the face of administrative incompetence and corruption, how could fundamental problems be resolved? The question filled Troutbeck with despair as he reiterated in his own mind some of the larger issues: 'tax reform, the useful employment of the young effendis, the

[12] Troutbeck to Eden, Confidential, 9 December 1954, FO 371/110991.
[13] Troutbeck to Bowker, Confidential, 29 May 1953, FO 371/104678.
[14] Troutbeck to Bowker, Secret, 3 April 1953, FO 371/104678.
[15] See Batatu, *Old Social Classes*, p. 36.
[16] Troutbeck to Eden, Confidential, 9 December 1954, FO 371/110991.

low standard of efficiency and honesty in the administration and the moulding of the different races and religious sects into a united whole'. Troutbeck had begun his career in Turkey; he had witnessed the transformation of Turkish society under the leadership of Kemal Ataturk. In surveying the problems of Iraq, he reflected pessimistically that there was no leader of the same stature: 'No Ataturk has yet emerged in Iraq. Nuri Pasha, on the other hand, still has plenty of kick in him.'[17]

Part of the revolutionary indictment against Nuri was that he had irrevocably aligned himself with the forces of 'feudalism'. Troutbeck quite clearly regarded the issue of land as the basic problem of the country. Nuri supported the wealthy landowners and opposed agrarian reform that might have reduced the size of landholdings. Troutbeck estimated that the large 'landlords' held close to 70 per cent of the cultivable land, but small landholders or 'peasants' owned less than 15 per cent. The landowners were predominantly Sunni. The unequal relationship between Sunni and Shia Arabs pervaded all aspects of society and government. In Troutbeck's words, '[I]t is the Sunni minority that still holds most of the big jobs whether in Government, administration or army.'[18] This was his recurrent theme: '[T]he old guard of Sunnis . . . are neither greatly interested in internal reforms nor willing to share the sweets of office with the Shias.'[19] As if he were forecasting the eventual revolution, Troutbeck commented in 1953: 'The kind of things that were worrying me as likely in due course to lead to an explosive situation were the facts that the rich paid practically no taxes, that there were still innumerable peasants without land of their own, that the cost of living remained very high and that the split between the Sunnis and Shias seemed to be getting wider rather than otherwise.'[20]

Nuri dominated the shifting coalitions of the landed aristocracy and political or military leaders, many of whom, like Nuri himself, had served as young officers in the Ottoman Army.[21] The Iraqi elite in the professions, as well as in the civil service and the army, drew inspiration from an earlier age. Collectively, this miscellany of the 'old gang' —Troutbeck's phrase—exerted a fragile control over Iraqi society; but it was by no means comparable to the 'old guard' that existed, for

[17] Troutbeck to Eden, Confidential, 28 November 1952, FO 371/98736.
[18] Troutbeck to Eden, Confidential, 9 December 1954, FO 371/110991.
[19] Troutbeck to Bowker, Secret, 3 April 1953, FO 371/104678.
[20] Troutbeck to Bowker, Confidential, 29 May 1953, FO 371/104678.
[21] See David Pool, 'From Élite to Class: The Transformation of Iraqi Political Leadership', in A. Kelidar, ed., *The Integration of Modern Iraq* (London, 1978).

example, in Egypt.[22] The interlocking but variable Iraqi elites, in the British judgement, probably consisted of no more than four hundred men, of whom only about fifty were influential in national affairs. Again, they were mainly Sunnis. In 1953 almost all Iraqi army officers of Brigadier rank and above were Sunnis.[23] The problem for the British was that they themselves were so closely associated with Nuri and the monarchy that in turn they were inextricably linked with the coalition of interests that had grown up around the Hashemite regime. According to Troutbeck: '[O]ne of our major embarrassments here was that everyone tended to identify us with the elder statesmen.' In Troutbeck's view, Nuri himself frustrated all efforts to prove that the British were sincere in wishing for improvement in the standard of administration and the quality of life in Iraq:

> There is no sign that Nuri believes in reform. He believes rather in paternal government, the strong hand distributing gifts of welfare, which can be paid for not by taxing the rich but rather by extracting further revenues from the oil companies.[24]

Nuri believed that general prosperity and political stability would ensue from controlling and distributing the oil riches. Here Troutbeck was convinced that Nuri's attitude would be challenged by the younger generation of Iraqi nationalists. 'I find it hard to share his [Nuri's] confidence', Troutbeck concluded, 'that they [the Iraqis] will accept forever a position in which the wealthy landowners have so great privilege and so little burden of responsibility. It is certainly the view of the younger modern-educated Iraqi that this position cannot last.' [25]

Whatever the complexion of the actual government, Nuri and the 'old guard' continued to control the economy, the Parliament, and much of the political press. For example, from September 1953 to April 1954, Fadil Jamali presided over two governments as Prime Minister. The British followed the developments under his leadership with considerable interest because he represented a younger generation determined to introduce social and economic reform. Jamali was a Western-educated Shia; he held a Ph.D. from Columbia University; he did not have an anti-British reputation. Nevertheless, the British had ambivalent feelings about him, in part because of the nature of the Shia regime. Troutbeck commented:

[22] On the theme of the fragility of the Iraqi ruling group, see Elie Kedourie, 'The Kingdom of Iraq: A Retrospect', in his *The Chatham House Version* (London, 1970).

[23] Troutbeck to Bowker, Confidential, 29 May 1953, FO 371/104678.

[24] Troutbeck to Eden, Confidential, 9 December 1954, FO 371/110991.

[25] Troutbeck to Eden, Confidential, 6 October 1954, FO 371/110991.

> The old Ottoman-trained Iraqis were for the first time discarded and
> . . . Dr. Jamali's Government . . . marks something of an epoch in
> Iraq's history . . . The younger men are keener, work harder and . . .
> are less corrupt and more genuinely interested in reform than their
> seniors.

> On the other hand they are more parochial in outlook, more chau-
> vinistic and somehow smaller men. The Shias . . . bear all the marks
> of the underdog. The greater their power becomes, the more diffi-
> cult will Iraq be to deal with.[26]

Jamali, moreover, proved ineffective as a reformer because of the political basis of Nuri's strength. A Foreign Office minute summed up the
British perception of the static nature of the old social classes: 'Whatever the colour of the Prime Minister, Iraq is at present governed by
the old guard of landowners whose leader is Nuri Pasha es Said.'[27]
    Troutbeck's dispatches reveal that Jamali may have been an ineffec-
tive social reformer but that he was much more closely associated with
the origins of the Baghdad Pact than is commonly known. Troutbeck
wrote in December 1953 that Jamali was 'very anxious' to strengthen
Turco-Iraqi ties: 'Communism was a danger to them both and they
ought to combine to resist it.' Troutbeck was initially sceptical: 'Dr. Jamali is a man who scintillates brain-waves and this idea of his of wishing to strengthen Turco-Iraqi relations may prove nothing more than
a flash in the pan.'[28] The Foreign Office response, however, gives a
clue to more positive calculations, which were not only not ephemeral
but in fact led indeed to the creation of the Baghdad Pact:

> Iraq lies on the exposed south-eastern flank of N.A.T.O. and even
> out of the context of American plans to line up Turkey, Iraq, Persia
> and Pakistan, we should welcome any improvement in Turco-Iraqi
> relations . . .

> The Egyptians and the other members of the Arab League will be an-
> noyed but this should not worry us unduly: on the contrary it would
> be to our advantage to prevent the Iraqis from co-ordinating their
> policy on Middle East Defence with the Egyptians.[29]

Troutbeck had mixed sentiments about the wisdom of accentuating
differences in the Arab world over the issue of defence, but there was

[26] Troutbeck to Eden, Confidential, 11 January 1954, FO 371/110986.
[27] Minute by K. J. Simpson, 24 February 1954, FO 371/111007.
[28] Troutbeck to Roger Allen, Confidential, 23 December 1953, FO 371/110997.
[29] Minute by P. L. V. Mallet, 6 January 1954, FO 371/110997.

no doubt in his mind, or anybody else's, that Nuri was the driving force behind Iraq's eventual strategic alignment.

The main problem, as Troutbeck saw it at the end of his tour of duty as Ambassador in late 1954, was that Nuri could not endure as a permanent fixture. Though he regretted Nuri's reluctance to pursue social and economic reform, he believed that Iraq needed to be ruled by a strong hand and that Nuri, though no Ataturk, provided an indispensable stabilizing element. In one of his last dispatches Troutbeck discussed the issue of stability in relation to communism:

> Of course his [Nuri's] methods are not such as would appeal to nineteenth century liberals, and no doubt the cry will soon go up that Iraq has become a Fascist state. Nevertheless I am quite convinced that strong Government is essential in Iraq . . .

> The most alarming feature in Iraq today seems to me that stability still depends on one man—Nuri Said. He cannot last for ever, but no one of his calibre has appeared on the scene during my term of office and there seems no one else capable even of maintaining order. The Communists and their friends are quiet for the moment but, if Nuri were to disappear, there is no doubt that they would quickly raise their heads again.[30]

The communist movement in Iraq, in Troutbeck's judgement, might eventually bring about a revolution unless it could be effectively combated. Earlier in the year he had commented on the 'striking increase in left-wing and Communist sentiment'.[31]

Troutbeck devoted several passages to communism in Iraq in his swan song of 9 December 1954. He emphasized the spread of left-wing ideas not only among the urban population but also in religious circles and rural areas:

> It [Communism] is fed from many sources—the traditional resistance to Western imperialism, chronic indignation at the corruption and selfishness of the ruling classes, the hard living conditions of the poor, the lack of opportunity for the young men who pour out of the colleges year by year, and lastly the ideological gap left by the lessening influence of Islam.

> As a result, though there are few Communists in the strict sense of the word, the mass of the intelligentsia at least give a ready ear to Communist propaganda.

[30] Troutbeck to Eden, Confidential, 3 September 1954, FO 371/110991.
[31] Troutbeck to Eden, Confidential, 11 January 1954, FO 371/110986.

Nuri . . . believes that strong government is the answer. So it may be so long as the government remains strong. But when he is not Prime Minister, the government is weak. The most disturbing feature of my period of service here has been the steady growth of Communist sentiment from the time that Nuri relinquished the premiership in the summer of 1952 till he resumed power a couple of years later.[32]

In the eyes of the communists, and indeed for Iraqis generally, the British were identified indelibly with the Hashemite dynasty and Nuri.

Sir Michael Wright, like his predecessor, was a man of rigorous intellect. But Wright had less intellectual curiosity about Iraqi society. He was an 'old Middle East hand' by experience rather than by temperament. During the early part of the Second World War he had served in Cairo. Apparently the formality of the British Embassy under Lord Killearn left an inspirational mark on him. At least the way he ran the embassy in Baghdad bore a resemblance to Killearn's rigid style of pomp and Imperial circumstance. Wright himself was a man of courtly dignity. Even his wife referred to him as 'His Excellency', or less formally as 'H. E.' While Troutbeck was 'one of the best-loved members of the Diplomatic Service', Wright did not inspire personal warmth.[33]

Wright saw the affairs of Iraq in the context of the Cold War. He once described the Baghdad Pact as 'an agreement which committed Iraq to side with the Free World against possible Soviet aggression'.[34] No British official at the time would have taken exception to that obvious statement, but there was a world of difference in outlook between Wright and Troutbeck. The latter believed that the communist movement in Iraq and elsewhere in the Middle East was essentially nationalistic. Troutbeck once quoted from an Iraqi newspaper to sum up the Iraqi attitude towards the Cold War:

> The call of the West finds no echo in our hearts. We do not understand them because we do not feel ourselves to be part of the so-called 'free world' which they say they are defending. We are part of the oppressed world which is struggling against them to achieve its freedom and throw off their yoke.[35]

That attitude, Troutbeck continued, should not be confused with communism and did not imply identification with Moscow. The danger of

[32] Troutbeck to Eden, Confidential, 9 December 1954, FO 371/110991.

[33] The comment about Troutbeck was by Lord Hankey in *The Times*, 9 October 1971.

[34] Wright to Macmillan, Confidential, 17 May 1955, FO 371/115759.

[35] Quoted in W. R. Louis, *The British Empire in the Middle East, 1945–1951: Arab Nationalism, the United States, and Postwar Imperialism* (Oxford, 1984), p. 713.

a Soviet or communist takeover did not appear to most Iraqis to be an immediate threat. Wright, on the other hand, believed that most intelligent Iraqis recognized that 'Communism represented the greatest of the dangers to Iraq and to her development.' More specifically, he held that the events in Iran in 1953, when the Shah had been temporarily forced to flee the country, had awakened those in responsible positions in Iraq to the danger of 'a Communist or near-Communist Iran on her frontier'.[36]

Wright made certain assumptions about the nature of Iraqi society, and these influenced his views about other Arab countries and the Baghdad Pact. He believed that Iraq's 'natural orbit' caused the country to gravitate towards Iran and Turkey rather than towards the Middle East proper and 'the old and sterile policies of the Arab League'. If Iraq joined a new regional group that included Pakistan and Iran, then other countries, notably Egypt, might eventually see the light and be persuaded to throw in their lot on the 'right side'. Wright elaborated on the Shia-Sunni part of the equation:

> I do not feel so sure that the natural orbit of Iraq is purely an Arab one. I am becoming increasingly impressed by the degree to which Iraqi eyes are turned on Persia, to which the Shias look as the leading Shia power, and to some extent on Turkey, particularly in the case of the Sunnis.

> It was events in Persia which really awoke Iraq to the Communist danger . . . Turkish traditions are far from negligible; and links of sympathy with Britain are stronger than is often supposed. On these and other grounds . . . I question whether the Arab League, if that is more or less what we mean by the Arab fold, is, in fact, the right framework for Iraqi policy.[37]

That line of thought led Wright to the conclusion that it would be best to support Iraq as a pillar of the 'Free World', regardless of the reaction of the other Arab states. He was convinced of the emergency of the situation: 'Is it not better for us to have an Iraq prepared to take a staunch attitude, even if it is an independent one, on Communism and regional defence, rather than an Iraq more or less bound to accept policies of the Arab League . . . ?'[38]

Iraqis did not see their national destiny as coinciding with the fate of Iran and Turkey, and the Baghdad Pact itself isolated Iraq from the

[36] Wright to Lloyd, Confidential, 8 February 1957, FO 371/128038.
[37] Wright to Sir Evelyn Shuckburgh, Secret, 10 May 1955, FO 371/115511.
[38] Ibid.

most of the Arab world.[39] On the other hand, the Suez crisis of 1956 created a sense of regional sentiment against the Western invaders of Egypt. The impact of the Suez crisis of 1956 on Iraq requires a comment, not least because it caught the British in Baghdad by surprise and alarmed them.

'Disbelief and consternation' were the words Wright used to describe the Iraqi reaction to the invasion of Egypt by Britain, France, and Israel in November 1956. The problem was not that the British used force against Nasser, but that they consorted with France and Israel, 'the one regarded as the arch-colonizer and the other the arch-enemy of the Arabs'. As if expressing his own disapproval, Wright added: 'It was, as our friends said, un-British.' Part of the trouble, Wright explained, originated with the students, who had 'nothing to lose but their studies'.[40] In a much more serious vein, Wright described how the Suez invasion placed Nuri, the young King Faisal II, and the Crown Prince Abdulillah in mortal jeopardy:

> The action of Her Majesty's Government [at Suez], because it was linked with action by Israel, placed him [Nuri] personally, as well as the King and Crown Prince and all those in Iraq who had so actively pursued a policy of friendship with Her Majesty's Government, not only in the gravest political difficulty but in danger of their lives, and imperilled the continued existence of the régime and the monarchy.[41]

By all British accounts, Nuri took a stout-hearted attitude and precariously retrieved the situation. According to Wright: 'Nuri, growling like a wounded bear, took the line: "I will save the Iraqis from themselves and the British from themselves".' Wright specifically described how Nuri managed to hold the government and the monarchy intact:

> He put heart into his colleagues, into the Army, and into senior officials . . . He devoted his main attention to internal security and refused to yield an inch to demonstrations or criticism, the first time in the history of Iraq that a Prime Minister had maintained this attitude at a moment of critical tension.[42]

During this period of sustained crisis, Nuri held the position 'with a courage and a steadfastness beyond praise'. But it was a close call. Af-

---

[39] See Batatu, *Old Social Classes*, e.g. p. 766.

[40] Wright to Lloyd, Confidential, 7 December 1956, FO 371/121662.

[41] Wright to Lloyd, Confidential, 8 February 1957, FO 371/128038.

[42] Wright to Lloyd, Confidential and Guard, 11 July 1957, FO 371/128057.

ter the crisis had passed, Wright reported that Nuri was still in power, 'but with the ground heaving under his feet'.[43]

The following excerpts from the diaries and letters of Michael Ionides reveal the political consequences in Iraq of the Suez crisis, again from a British perspective but one that differed from Wright's. Ionides was the British member of the Iraq Development Board. He had been trained as an engineer and had Middle Eastern experience dating from the 1920s. He was sensitive to the criticism of younger Iraqis who felt aggrieved at Nuri's out-and-out support of the British. He wrote in December 1956:

> There are bitter complaints from the younger men, up to 30 or 40, that Nuri has never brought the next generation along, has kept everything to himself, never built up the structure of Government and Parliament, never even tried to make elections work as other emergent countries have done.

> He has given no outlet for discussion, they say, no means for the younger people to take any part, keeping them in suspense and in complete ignorance as to what is going on, laying Iraq open to charges of doing nothing for Egypt and everything for the British, charges they cannot find evidence to refute, however much they might wish to.

Commenting on the social structure of Iraq, Ionides continued: 'At the top of the pyramid there is the minority of diehard no-goods, fearing chiefly for their wealth and security, going with the wind as long as it is fair.' On another occasion he assessed Nuri's position after Suez:

> The gap between Nuri and the people of Iraq has been growing fast, and when he goes, it will not be just Nuri going out of power; it will be the end, or the near end of a phase when British influence, formerly dominant but steadily declining, clung on to the last solid pro-British rock, Nuri Pasha, while the tide of affairs went on, beyond his control and beyond British control.[44]

Ionides was thus an acute observer of Middle Eastern affairs. He emphasized the immediate political origins of the Iraqi revolution, though as an economic expert, he would have been the last to deny the underlying economic and social causes.

In reading contemporary evidence such as that of Wright and Ion-

---

[43] Wright to Lloyd, Confidential, 8 February 1957, FO 371/128038.
[44] Michael Ionides, *Divide and Lose: The Arab Revolt of 1955–1958* (London, 1960), pp. 188–89.

ides, one cannot but be struck by the deliberate political interpretation. This is more than a difference between officials or men of affairs, on the one hand, and a scholar on the other. This is a clash among those trying to understand the causes of revolution. Where does the balance lie between the immediate and the long-term, between the emphasis on certain individuals such as Nuri and the more impersonal economic and sociological forces? At one level there is no conflict. Contemporary British observers would certainly have identified the issue of the exploitation of oil wealth as playing a central part in the developing crisis. Wright wrote in the aftermath of Suez that Nuri had been lucky that 'the country was prosperous and that there was no economic discontent which others could exploit'.[45] Oil revenues had risen from £40.8 million in 1952 to £84.6 million in 1958.[46] Nuri's gamble was that this wealth would create prosperity and bring about a lasting political stability without unduly disturbing the basis of the land system. Through the eyes of British witnesses of the time, what in fact happened?

Most contemporary British observers of the 1956–58 period took it as an article of faith that a race was taking place between development and revolution. Wright wrote in 1957 about the progress in recent years:

> The benefits of the oil revenues were beginning to be felt in the lives of the ordinary people and whether in housing, education, health, flood control or irrigation, there was a sense of progress and expanding horizons, and of considerable pride in the manner in which the formidable tasks were being tackled.

At the same time, he was aware that the 'younger intellectuals', for example, 'considered that progress was too slow, and in particular that the somewhat feudal influence of the tribes, with their own law and their grip on land, must be made to give way more rapidly to more modern ideas'.[47] Nuri consistently gave the same answer to the charge that progress was too slow: Iraq needed a framework of 'internal stability' within which reforms could gradually be introduced. Wright summarized Nuri's outlook: 'to be over-hasty in undermining tribal structure and traditions before there was something adequate to put in their place would only lead to chaos'.[48] With the benefit of hindsight,

---

[45] Wright to Lloyd, Confidential, 11 July 1957, FO 371/128057.

[46] Edith and E. F. Penrose, *Iraq: International Relations and National Development* (London, 1978), p. 167.

[47] Wright to Lloyd, Confidential, 8 February 1957, FO 371/128038.

[48] Ibid.

one can state that Wright too easily acquiesced in Nuri's point of view. Thus he, and with him the British government, forfeited the opportunity to use what influence they still possessed to intervene, as Troutbeck would have put it, on the 'right side' of history.

Michael Ionides had insight into Nuri's temperament and limitations, especially in the area of economic development—its significance as well as the details:

> Despite his energy, he never found time enough to promote reforms which were getting more and more pressing. I do not mean only such things as land reform, springing from ideas of social advance, but also the kind of practical measures which were needed to bring all the new projects we [the Development Board] were building under efficient administrative control. I doubt if Nuri fully understood the need for these reforms.
>
> The complexity of affairs induced by this sudden economic expansion [in the 1950s] demanded a range of experience which he did not possess, and a concentration of thought and effort which he had no time to give.[49]

To do Nuri justice from a British point of view, Wright probably best summed it up when he wrote that 'he is a sincere patriot working according to his own lights for the betterment of all Iraqis.' He added that Nuri's plans definitely did not include 'the breaking up and sharing out' of the great landed estates.[50] Wright thus detected one of the underlying causes of the impending revolution. He was uneasily aware that the British, by continuing to align themselves with Nuri, had irrevocably identified themselves with 'the class and way of life which he represents'.[51]

Quite apart from the importance of certain individuals such as Nuri, what of the general spirit of the times? Can one understand the Iraqi revolution without taking fully into account the ideas about Arab nationalism that were prevalent in early 1958? On 14 February, King Faisal announced on radio and television the 'union' of Iraq and Jordan. The two 'sister countries', he proclaimed, thus offered proof that 'the Arab nation has awakened and is alert and determined to restore its glory'. The two branches of the Hashemite family would work together to provide common economic policies, customs laws,

[49] Ionides, *Divide and Lose*, p. 125.
[50] Wright to Lloyd, Confidential, 4 July 1957, FO 371/128041.
[51] Wright to Macmillan, Confidential, 17 May 1955, FO 371/115759.

educational curricula, perhaps even a unified military command. Sir Michael Wright summed up the essence of the scheme as 'a confederation plus economic and financial unification'.[52] 'The dream of Arab unity is as strong in Iraq as in the other Arab countries,' he reported, but on the other hand there could be little doubt that the Iraqi-Jordanian union was 'almost wholly' a response to the Egyptian and Syrian decision two weeks earlier to form the United Arab Republic.[53] People in Baghdad generally believed that the Iraqi-Jordanian union was 'imposed by the [two] Monarchies' or was 'Western inspired'. Nuri's ambition might be eventually to include Kuwait, Saudi Arabia, and other Arab countries in the union, but to the average Iraqi, the United Arab Republic represented the genuine path to Arab unity. According to Wright, '[T]here will be the problem of selling the confederation to the Iraqi man in the street, who is likely to be somewhat unimpressed by its advantages as compared with those of joining the United Arab Republic.'[54]

The creation of the Egyptian-Syrian union was a turning point in Middle Eastern affairs. Wright believed that it would influence the course of events in Iraq: 'The decision of Egypt and Syria to form a United Arab Republic changed the whole atmosphere.'[55] He had no doubt that Nasser was the catalyst of Arab nationalist thought, not merely on the question of unity but on such issues as Algeria. The years 1957–58 were of course critical ones in the Algerian revolution as well as in the impending Iraqi revolution. By all British accounts, the subject of Algeria was one of the principal topics of discussion among Iraqi intellectuals. Sam Falle, the Oriental Counsellor in the Baghdad Embassy, summed up the theme of conversation in the coffee houses of the city: 'The Baghdad Pact, Palestine and Algeria'.[56] In all those issues, the British detected the malevolent hand of Nasser. In Iraq there was no question of his immense popularity. 'Colonel Nasser is still the hero of the broad masses of the population,' Wright reported in February 1958.[57] Nasser appeared to be riding a wave of popular sentiment that would not be stopped by such artificial counter-currents as the Iraqi-Jordanian union. Wright related the

---

[52] Wright to Lloyd, Confidential, 14 February 1958, FO 371/134023. Wright and others believed that the proposal originated in Jordan: '[T]his Union resulted from an initiative of King Hussain' (Wright to Lloyd, Confidential, 25 February 1958, FO 371/134025).

[53] Wright to Lloyd, Confidential, 25 February 1958, FO 371/134025.

[54] Wright to Lloyd, Confidential, 14 February 1958, FO 371/134023.

[55] Wright to Lloyd, Confidential, 25 February 1958, FO 371/134025.

[56] Falle to R. H. Hadow, Confidential, 1 February 1958, FO 371/134197. R. H. Hadow in the Foreign Office noted that Falle had hit upon 'the kernel of the matter'.

[57] Wright to Lloyd, Confidential, 25 February 1958, FO 371/134025.

underlying sentiments of Iraqi politicians, businessmen, and tribal leaders as if there were almost an inevitability as well as a resolve behind Nasser's plans: '[T]he Egyptian revolution is not intended to be for domestic consumption only but to be followed by a similar form of revolution in Iraq, Jordan, Lebanon and ultimately Saudi Arabia.'[58] In any event, it appeared clear to the British in Baghdad that 'events outside Iraq' would play a large part in the domestic issues of the country.[59]

Wright attributed the creation of Nuri's last government in March 1958 to the external danger of Nasser and the United Arab Republic. 'The formation of this new Government [in Iraq] was a direct answer to President Nasser's challenge,' he wrote.[60] In comparison with previous regimes, Nuri's combination of ministers represented a strong alliance, which included politicians with progressive social and economic programmes. Two prominent figures were Fadil Jamali, the Foreign Minister, and Abdul Karim al-Uzri, the Minister of Finance. 'Dr. Jamali's words tend to be intemperate', Wright observed, but nevertheless Jamali was 'a firm believer in the dangers of Communist penetration in the area through Soviet co-operation with Nasser.' Wright regarded him as distinctly above the average cut of Iraqi politicians: '[H]e brings to the Government two most valuable qualities, courage in standing up for his convictions, however unpopular, a rare quality among Arab politicians, and a sincere belief in social reform.' Wright was beginning to attach increasing importance to the issue of economic inequity in Iraqi society. One of the reasons could be seen in Baghdad itself; 'ordinary people' migrating from the countryside were creating 'slums of mud huts' at a perturbing rate. Thus Wright welcomed the presence of the new Finance Minister as an indication that Nuri was at last beginning to take in earnest the question of social reform. Wright wrote of Abdul Karim al-Uzri:

> He is a somewhat doctrinaire economist and land owner with progressive views and many ideas . . . for carrying out social and economic reforms and for spreading the benefits of the oil revenues among all classes of the population.
>
> As Minister of Finance he is likely to press for reform of the tax structure and the introduction of land taxation, coupled with limitations on the size of estates, which will be popular with the ordinary people but may be strongly opposed by the tribal Shaikhs and large landed proprietors who will see their interests threatened.[61]

[58] Wright to Lloyd, Confidential, 28 December 1957, FO 371/134197.
[59] Wright to Lloyd, Confidential, 11 March 1958, FO 371/134198.
[60] Ibid.
[61] Ibid.

Wright therefore held out hope for social reform, but he did not want to be too optimistic: '[T]he Palace and Nuri will not wish to deliver too strong a frontal attack on one of the main groups to which the Government will look for support.' [62]

Wright's conscious effort to assess the influence of the United Arab Republic on Iraqi politics led him to a paradox. The British in their own self-interest did not wish to sharpen inter-Arab rivalries, despite the allegations of critics of British imperialism. Wright was fully aware of the charge that the British, by dividing the Arab world, sought to prolong the longevity of the British Empire. He regarded this hoary suspicion as nonsense. He thought that endemic tension was dangerous and might well jeopardize whatever influence the British still possessed. He believed Nasser to be a real danger to the British position in Iraq. Nasser's propaganda struck a sympathetic chord among the intellectuals, the younger generation of officials, and above all the poorer people, who believed that they were being excluded from the benefits of the oil wealth and the development projects. The paradox was that Nasser's challenge might at last galvanize Iraq's political elite into reforming the economy faster. Wright's expression of the 'paradox' is tortuous, but it repays study. It catches the delicate balance between the external and internal affairs of Iraq as perceived by the British in March 1958:

> We are confronted with the paradox that although we cannot wish for the continued sharpening of inter-Arab relations which President Nasser's present policy appears to involve, and although we may fear that in the long run the Iraqi régime will have the greatest difficulty in maintaining itself against the danger to it which President Nasser, working on a discontented population largely favourable to his aims, represents, yet by bringing together into one Government these disparate elements *he has perhaps produced the one combination which, given time, could carry through some of the internal reforms which are needed to give Iraq stability.* [63]

Again, Wright did not wish to be too optimistic. Nuri's past indifference to social reform hardly inspired confidence that there would be a dramatic change. But clearly the British believed that the game was still in play.

If Wright found it paradoxical that Iraq's salvation might come from the challenge of the United Arab Republic, he found it ironic,

[62] Wright to Lloyd, Confidential, 11 March 1958, FO 371/134198.
[63] Ibid.; emphasis added.

and depressing, that the regimes of Nuri and the Shah showed similarities. Both were authoritarian. The British might do their best to
press for reform in Iraq, but would they be any more successful than
they had been in pre-Musaddiq Iran? Perhaps it can be inferred from
Wright's sentiments that he would have agreed, at least in his moments of despondency, that the tensions in the structure of the post-
colonial state would determine the course of events more than the
policies or actions of the political elite. In any event, it gives one pause:
why did the Iraqi revolution take place in 1958 and the Iranian revolution some two decades later? According to Wright, the mounting
opposition in both countries had comparable middle-class strength.
Iraqis and Iranians alike held exaggerated notions about the extent of
British influence: 'There are striking similarities between the situation
in Iraq and Iran, such as the potentially explosive element of political frustration under an authoritarian régime, especially among the
growing middle class, as well as the belief in Britain's dominant and, to
some, sinister role.'[64]

Wright's reflections on the opposition to Nuri's regime led him to
conclude that Iraq was not in a revolutionary situation. He was confident in his assessment, both in reports to London and in conversation in Baghdad. It would not be fair to blame him for failing to
predict the revolution. Men of greater intellectual acumen did not
foresee the civil war in Lebanon or the revolution in Iran—or for that
matter, the American and French revolutions. Nevertheless, it is legitimate to inquire where Wright went astray in his judgement. Much of
his analysis on the eve of the revolution was shrewd, imaginative, and
balanced, but in retrospect it is clear that he erred on the problem of
the army and on the question of development.

Wright wrote his last full-blown report on the Iraqi political system
in April 1958; it reveals the strength and weakness of British political
analysis on the eve of the revolution. He believed that political power
resided in the 'Palace' (by which he meant Faisal II and Abdulillah).
The key to political balance lay in the skill with which the Palace
worked through the politicians, who were not organized in political
parties but rather revolved around a small political elite whose outstanding leader was Nuri. Wright compared Iraq with eighteenth-
century England:

> The King appoints and dismisses Prime Ministers and need not pay
> much attention to the two Houses of Parliament, for the Senators

[64] Wright to Lloyd, Confidential, 22 April 1958, FO 371/134198.

are appointed by him and the Deputies, although elected by a wider
suffrage than was the unreformed House of Commons in Britain, are
selected as candidates by a process in which the influence of the régime plays such a large part that in the countryside few elections are
contested and in the towns the opponents of the régime stand very
little chance of election.[65]

The only underlying principle from one regime to the next, Wright
thought, was probably 'the safety of the régime itself'.

In recent years a succession of governments had been drawn from
the professional politicians, 'who belong largely to the landed upper
class' but also included 'a certain number of self-made men', including Kurds. Whatever the change of government, all Iraqi politicians
embraced what Wright called 'a fundamental concept': only after
the successful exploitation of the oil wealth could a 'modern' political
structure replace the existing system. Here Wright offered a basic definition that may be taken as the sophisticated British view on the rudiments of Iraqi society in 1958: 'a feudal order based largely on the
tribes, the army and a strong monarchy'.[66] Wright thus explicitly identified the army as part of the triangular structure of power.

The analogy with the eighteenth century helped explain the rapid
turnover of Iraqi governments. Like Stewart Perowne, the Oriental
Counsellor in the British Embassy in Baghdad in 1947, Wright saw that
the Iraqi political groups did not represent political parties in the British sense but rather shifting alliances more like the Italian *combinazione*
(in Perowne's words, 'a transient association of a few interested individuals for a transient material end').[67] The Palace sought to preserve
its own influence, like George III, through prerogative and favour.
The principle at stake was nothing more and nothing less than self-
interest and survival:

> The Crown Prince has not believed in keeping any one man longer
> in office than a particular situation requires. The political objective
> of the Palace is in fact to preserve the position and influence of the
> Hashemite dynasty and to ensure that Governments depend on its
> favour rather than on parliament or on political parties; changes are
> therefore made with regularity so as to ensure that no group has a
> monopoly of power and can build up a position in which it can chal-
> lenge the prerogatives of the Palace itself.[68]

[65] Wright to Lloyd, Confidential, 22 April 1958, FO 371/134198.
[66] Ibid.
[67] Louis, *British Empire in the Middle East,* p. 320.
[68] Wright to Lloyd, Confidential, 22 April 1958, FO 371/134198.

The politicians who cooperated with the Palace shared political power from time to time; those who did not formed the opposition.

The principal flaw in Wright's judgement lay in his assessment of the forces opposing the regime. He characterized the 'Opposition' as consisting of a few prominent but ineffective public figures, including Mohammad Mahdi Kubba, the leader of the right-wing nationalist movement, and Kamil al-Chaderchi, a communist lawyer and journalist whom Nuri had jailed on the pretext of espousing anti-Suez sentiments.[69] For the most part, the politicians who protested against Nuri's regime belonged 'to the urban middle-class and are largely lawyers, businessmen, professors and teachers'. 'These men and their associates do not make up a "ragged band",' he wrote, 'for their material prosperity is marked.' Nor did he attach much importance to their political clichés regarding Arab nationalism; in his opinion, they were identical with the propaganda spread by Nasser's 'Radio Cairo'. He held, in short, that the 'Opposition' in Iraq merely effervesced the froth of Arab nationalism: 'passion for unity, strong opposition to Israel, revolutionary ardour against conservative régimes and xenophobia'. Nuri's opponents believed in liberalism and reform at home and neutralism abroad. Many of them thought that Iraq should have a British form of democracy. They did not necessarily oppose the monarchy. Most wished to introduce reform gradually. They all wanted a more equitable distribution of the oil profits, but so also did Nuri. With such critics, who needed a revolution? Only slightly did Wright veil his contempt for what he regarded as Nuri's main opponents. It is therefore not surprising that he came to an emphatic conclusion that revolution was improbable. His language is unequivocal: 'For it is quite certain that, today, a revolutionary situation does not exist.'[70]

Not everyone shared Wright's optimism. On the Foreign Office copy of his dispatch, one official, probably R. H. Hadow, inscribed next to Wright's non-revolutionary sentence a large exclamation mark—![71] Hadow was a member of the Levant Department. He held strong views on the need for internal reform. He was sceptical whether Wright had identified the true nature of Nuri's opposition. What of institutional loyalty? Here Wright made another comment that caused dissenting astonishment. He remarked that 'the Army, although it has in the past erupted into politics, is at present showing no signs of doing so . . . it is likely to go on supporting the régime.' Thereupon Hadow drew

[69] For Kubba and Chaderchi, see Batatu, *Old Social Classes*, especially pp. 300, 303, 306–07, 812–13.
[70] Wright to Lloyd, Confidential, 22 April 1958, FO 371/134198.
[71] Ibid.

another large exclamation mark—! What were Wright's reasons for arriving at conclusions that aroused such provocative comment in the Foreign Office? What led him to take such a favourable outlook on the army, which in turn coloured his assessment that Iraq was not in a revolutionary situation?

To some extent Wright relied on the judgement of his military attaché, Brigadier N. F. B. Shaw; he was not a man of outstanding ability. He competently managed the military side of his mission, but he was at sea in larger political issues, such as the loyalty of the officer corps.[72] His predecessor, Brigadier A. Boyce, had kept a sharp eye on possible subversive units or officers in the army.[73] By contrast, Shaw concentrated his attention on parades and ball bearings. It is an interesting question whether Wright, given better advice, might have modified the official assessment of the Embassy. It is true that on the subject of the army Wright had his own strong opinions, which in turn fortified his ideas about Nuri's successor. Taking a scornful view of the politicians, Wright saw the army as the possible salvation of Iraq. As for the collective military establishment, Wright wrote that both the army and air force 'have shown an example of loyalty and steadiness which has not been rivalled by the forces of any other Arab state'.[74]

No one could predict how long Nuri might last, but it was certain that it would be difficult to find a civilian counterpart. The problem with the army, Wright conceded, was that it might produce 'an Iraqi Nasser'. But a strong army leader might be the best that the British could anticipate. If, like Nuri, he remained loyal to the monarchy, the situation would not be unsatisfactory. Loyalty to the Hashemites was of course a large assumption, but Wright seems to have made it without too much mental agitation:

> When the time comes for Nuri to leave the political scene, there may be no alternative to a more authoritarian régime based on the Army with a soldier as the strong man behind a civilian figurehead. This is not an attractive prospect in view of the danger of instability through the emergence of an Iraqi Nasser or through competition among Army officers for power.

[72] Shaw wrote in a military assessment dated 26 February 1957: 'The British attack upon Egypt had a certain effect upon junior Army officers who were distressed at the British policy, but due to careful handling . . . there were no unpleasant incidents' (FO 371/128067).

[73] 'As far as the possibility of a *coup d'état* is concerned', Boyce wrote in 1954, 'I have still not noted any personality within the Army whose influence, bearing or actions lead me to believe that he might embark upon such an adventure' (Annual Report, Secret and Guard, 12 February 1954, FO 371/111023).

[74] Wright to Lloyd, Secret and Guard, 16 March 1957, FO 371/128067.

It would, of course, provide an easy target for the attacks of the Opposition and of Nasser, and it would be distasteful to those who remember the 1936–41 period which was dominated by the Army. But
it may be the best we can hope for. Provided it was based on the
Hashemite monarchy it would probably retain the Western connection and it might hold the fort for a time.[75]

Such was Wright's conclusion about the future of the army and Nuri's
successor. If it seems in retrospect too optimistic in its premise that the
army would remain loyal to the monarchy, it was no more so than
his other major conclusion about development. Wright appears to
have concurred entirely in Nuri's judgement that things would remain quiet in Iraq because of the benefits of development. Poverty itself would not be a cause of revolution. 'I do not believe', Wright concluded, 'that poverty or lack of economic opportunities by themselves
will, so long as the oil flows, produce an explosive situation.'[76]

It is easy to ridicule someone whose assessments proved to be wrong.
It is harder to recapture the spirit of the contemporary debate and to
bear in mind that it seemed plausible to uphold the points of view of
Wright and Nuri. Wright's outlook at the time commanded intellectual respect in part because of the conspicuous progress in building
textile factories, pumping stations, bridges, and river transport. Speaking to Wright's staff in March 1957, the Minister of Development took
pride in describing such projects as the new electricity powerhouse
in Baghdad. 'This is nothing', he said, 'wait till you see 1960.' Wright's
attitude was equally robust. 'The long-awaited results of planning and
spending are now becoming visible', he wrote, 'and Iraqis are taking
interest and pride in their country's development.'[77]

Unfortunately for Wright, the field reports by Sam Falle demonstrated that the evidence of material progress could be interpreted in
another way. Falle assessed the unevenness of development in different parts of the country and the ways that economic progress affected,
or did not affect, different parts of Iraqi society. His approach has
stood the test of time better than Wright's. Falle was one of the ablest
of the younger British officials. He was linguistically gifted, energetic,
and gregarious. He had an inquiring intellect. In late 1957 he had
reported on a trip he made by Land Rover to Kut and Amara, some
250 miles south of Baghdad. In the area around Kut he observed 'unemployment, widespread poverty and actual hunger'. There were no

[75] Wright to Lloyd, Confidential, 22 April 1958, FO 371/134198.
[76] Ibid.
[77] Wright to Lloyd, Confidential, 12 April 1957, FO 371/128061.

significant development projects under way, though test borings were being carried out for a new bridge. In Kut itself there were a few new buildings, including a school and a hospital. But he described the roads in the town as 'unspeakable'. In Amara about half the population of 54,000 lived in 'conditions of hideous squalor and poverty'. The only obvious development project was a new bridge. Falle took care not to present only one side of the picture. He spoke to some 'peasant smallholders' who were doing 'tolerably well'. But the general standard of living he could only describe as being 'shamefully low'.[78]

Wright would have been well advised to read Falle's report quite carefully. Instead he penned a perfunctory dispatch to the Foreign Office, commenting merely that he would do what he could to 'encourage' the Iraqi government to 'tackle' the issues raised by Falle.[79] These were problems, however, that the government in Baghdad usually found intractable. Falle raised questions that were basic to Iraqi society, not least the influence of the sheikhs and the issue of land tenure. Wright accepted Nuri's view that 'the tribal system', though not yet dead, was 'dying'.[80] The transition to the new social and economic order in Iraq would be facilitated by the reclamation of wastelands, which would open up opportunities for small landowners. Thus the old system of land tenure would be left to reform itself. 'New lands' became the shibboleth of the Nuri regime. They would be the supreme test of the development programme. In Amara, which was supposed to be the home of the pilot scheme, there were plans for draining and filling a large swamp, leaving land where 'the lower middle class' could build about 4,000 houses. Falle was exceedingly sceptical whether this plan was feasible: the local sheikh would have to provide free houses, which, according to Falle, he had no intention of doing.[81]

'The main cause of the trouble', Falle reported, 'is the large feudal landowners.' In the Amara scheme, the reclaimed land owned by the government would be distributed in equal measure to 'existing tribal leaders' and to 'fellaheen', or peasants.[82] The problem was that the local sheikhs received the better part of the 'new land', and their relatives most of the rest of it. Even among the three hundred 'peasant smallholders' to whom reclaimed land had been allocated, the sheikhs retained control over both the water pumps and the water itself. Falle

[78] 'Report on a Trip by Mr. S. Falle, Oriental Counsellor, to Kut and Amara, December 17–20, 1957', FO 371/134197.
[79] Wright to Lloyd, Confidential, 31 December 1958, FO 371/1134197.
[80] Wright to Lloyd, Confidential, 22 April 1958, FO 371/134198.
[81] Report by Falle, 17–20 December 1957, FO 371/134197.
[82] Ibid.

wrote: 'This system which puts the new smallholders at the mercy of the sheikhs, who have the pumping machinery, is clearly most unsatisfactory.' The conclusion he drew about the 'predatory landlords' carried him in the opposite direction from Wright's belief that Iraq was not in a revolutionary situation. 'The peasants are oppressed and hardly able to scrape a living,' he wrote. Falle's report dealt only with a district, but it is clear that he believed comparable conditions to exist throughout the country. These were circumstances that could well lead to 'Communism and anarchic nationalism', even revolution.[83] This was a clear warning; it was not heeded.

Straight to the end, Nuri and Wright were preoccupied with such external questions as whether Kuwait would join the Iraqi-Jordanian union, rather than with the more mundane issues of land distribution and water pumps. Nuri was in London two weeks before the July revolution. In conversation with Selwyn Lloyd, the Foreign Secretary, he ranged over topics such as the prospect of Lebanon joining the Iraqi-Jordanian union and the possibility of Iraqi intervention in Syria to break the link with Nasser.[84] For his part, Wright did not question fundamental assumptions. He continued to believe, like Nuri, in a firm, paternalistic internal policy as the best way to guide Iraq through a dangerous period. He thought that the union with Jordan fulfilled the Iraqi 'emotional demand for unity'.[85] He judged the monarchy to be 'the cementing factor' in Iraq's national life, failing to recognize how much the Iraqis themselves regarded it as an alien institution. The new union with Jordan fortified the old belief that behind the Hashemite dynasty stood the British. But Wright himself remained confident that Iraq was not in a revolutionary situation.

On 14 July 1958 at 7:10 A.M., Wright sent one of his last telegrams from the British Embassy in Baghdad. He stated simply that since 6:00 A.M. a revolutionary government had seized power. He reported fighting throughout the city. He did not know of the fate of the King, the Crown Prince, or Nuri.[86] The Station Commander at the Royal Air Force Base in Habbinayia, in a superb example of British understatement, reported later in the day that the situation was 'confused and interesting . . . we are minding our own business'.[87] The military

[83] Ibid.

[84] Lloyd to Wright, Secret, 4 July 1958, FO 371/134220.

[85] Wright to Lloyd, Confidential, 22 April 1958, FO 371/134198.

[86] Wright to Foreign Office, 14 July 1958, FO 371/134198.

[87] Political Office with Middle East Forces to Foreign Office, Emergency Top Secret, 14 July 1958, FO 371/134198.

community fared better than the British civilian population in Baghdad, though as revolutions go, it could have been worse. Only one member of Wright's staff of about twenty-four was killed—not deliberately, but by a stray bullet; the Embassy was looted and burned. Wright himself rose to the occasion. He acted honourably and courageously; by late afternoon he had evacuated his staff to the New Baghdad Hotel. The first news to reach London was through the American Ambassador in Baghdad, who reported that Sir Michael and Lady Wright were both 'remarkably calm and cheerful'.[88]

Two days later, having set up emergency headquarters in the New Baghdad Hotel, Wright reported that Nuri had been killed on the afternoon of 15 July: 'I understand he was discovered in woman's dress. He either shot himself or was killed by the mob.' It took a few more days to confirm the details, but on the 20th he telegraphed with certainty that the King and Crown Prince had been shot and that the 'bodies of Crown Prince and Nuri were dragged naked round the town'.[89] As if to confirm his own views on foreign influences on Iraqi politics, he noted that 'the town is full of photographs and emblems of Nasser especially on military vehicles.'[90] From Wright's point of view, it would have missed the spirit of the revolution not to associate it with Nasser and the sense of Arab nationalism with which Iraqis identified themselves.

Wright's initial assessments portrayed the events of 14 July as a *coup d'état* rather than a revolution. 'Certain Army Units', he reported, conducted the operation under the command of a 'very small' directorate or 'controlling group'.[91] It was clear from the outset that the leader was Brigadier Abdul Karim Qasim, who became the new Prime Minister. In an appreciation of the new leadership written a month after the takeover, Wright commented in balanced vein:

> The Prime Minister, Brigadier Abdul Karim Qassim, is soft-spoken and friendly to meet. He is said to be a devout Muslim and dedicated to the service of his country. He is unmarried and lives very simply. Apart from a few remarks in some of his speeches his conduct so far has been essentially moderate and restrained . . . He has a good reputation as a competent army officer and as far as it is possible to judge enjoys confidence in the army.[92]

[88] Viscount Hood to Foreign Office, Emergency Secret, 14 July 1958, FO 371/134198.
[89] Wright to Lloyd, Immediate Secret, 17 July 1958, FO 371/134199.
[90] Wright to Lloyd, Immediate Secret, 20 July 1958, FO 371/134200.
[91] Wright to Lloyd, Emergency Secret, 20 July 1958, FO 371/134200.
[92] Wright to Lloyd, Confidential, 19 August 1958, FO 371/134202.

Within a few weeks, Wright used the terms '*coup d'état*' and 'revolution' interchangeably. The analogy that sprang to his mind was with the Egyptian revolution of 1952. Qasim and his fellow officers, like the Free Officers rebelling against Farouk, were sincere, upright idealists who believed that they were acting in the best interests of their country. The new regime, Wright reported, 'is essentially an Administration of liberal reformers'.[93]

The Foreign Office came to a similar conclusion about the origins of the revolution and the aims of the Iraqi military officers:

> A revolutionary situation very similar to that existing in Egypt prior to the Neguib-Nasser *coup* of 1952 has been building up in Iraq for years. Wealth and power have remained concentrated in the hands of a few rich landowners and tribal sheikhs centred round the Court, while a growing middle class of politically conscious Arab 'intelligentsia', supporting the ideals of Arab Nationalism . . . have been denied an effective voice in the affairs of their country . . .

> As in Egypt, the *coup d'état* in Iraq seems to have been actually organised by a small number of army officers acting with great efficiency and secrecy.[94]

Revolutions in the Middle East often represent a shift of power from one generation to the next. In this sense, Wright actually anticipated the new order, though he did not foresee the revolutionary events. 'The group of politicians of the generation of Nuri with their roots in the 1920s', he had written in April 1958, were 'fading away'.[95]

Some of them, including Nuri, came to a much more brutal end than Wright or any of the other British observers of Iraq ever believed possible. One of the most striking descriptions of the revolution came from the pen of a British official in Jordan, C. H. Johnston. He related a detail about Nuri's death that conveyed the atmosphere of mob violence. After Nuri's body was dragged through the streets, 'a car was driven backwards and forwards over it until it was flattened into the ground'.[96] So ended Britain's principal collaborator in Iraq. 'I had the

---

[93] Wright to Lloyd, Immediate Secret, 23 July 1958, FO 371/134200.

[94] FO memorandum, 'The Immediate Outlook in Iraq', 24 July 1958, FO 371/123201.

[95] Wright to Lloyd, Confidential, 24 April 1958, FO 371/134195.

[96] C. H. Johnston to E. M. Rose, Secret, 28 July 1958, FO 371/134201. Batatu adds that the remains of Nuri's body were, 'after burial, disinterred by an angry crowd and, like that of the intensely hated crown prince, dragged through the streets, strung up, torn to pieces, and finally burnt' (*Old Social Classes*, p. 801).

impression', Johnston wrote, 'that if the Russian revolution had been put into execution by the Mau Mau the effect would not have been very much different.'[97]

The Iraqi Revolution of 1958 1991

[97] C. H. Johnston to E. M. Rose, Secret, 28 July 1958, FO 371/134201.

31

THE WITHDRAWAL FROM THE GULF

W hen the news broke on 16 January 1968 that Britain would withdraw all forces East of Suez by the end of 1971, the public responded with an awareness of the historic significance of the event. 'It is comparable in importance', according to the *New Statesman*, 'to Mr Attlee's granting of Indian independence and the Tory government's evacuation of British Africa.'[1] Critics quickly pointed out that the recall of troops from the Gulf seemed to be an afterthought to the closing down of the great base at Singapore, and that the cost of maintaining British forces in the Gulf, some £12 million yearly, was negligible compared to the immense revenues in oil: the Gulf States met nearly half of Britain's energy requirements. There was another vein of criticism, to some the most damning, which was expressed incisively by Iain Macleod, the former Colonial Secretary who had accelerated the pace of British decolonization in Africa. In the early 1960s, ironically enough, he had faced similar dilemmas regarding the promises given to the white settlers in Kenya and the Rhodesias; he had been accused of treachery. Macleod now declared that breaking pledges given to the Rulers in the Gulf would be 'shameful and criminal'.[2] Whatever the irony, Macleod expressed the ethical predicament involved in abandoning the Gulf. The dilemma seemed all the more acute because the Gulf represented, in the words of one of the Proconsuls, the 'last province of the Pax Britannica'.[3]

Economic stringency had forced the decision, but in another sense the retreat seemed to be yet another disastrous consequence of the events of the previous year. In the summer of 1967 the British had been accused, falsely, of assisting Israel in the Middle East war. In November of the same year, British troops were compelled to leave Aden. The issue of Aden became part of a larger debate on the withdrawal of British forces East of Suez and whether Britain could afford to remain

---

[1] *New Statesman*, 19 January 1968. For present purposes, the indispensable works on the Gulf are J. B. Kelly, *Arabia, the Gulf and the West* (New York, 1980); Glen Balfour-Paul, *The End of Empire in the Middle East: Britain's Relinquishment of Power in Her Last Three Arab Dependencies* (Cambridge, 1991); and Rosemarie Said Zahlan, *The Making of the Modern Gulf States: Kuwait, Bahrain, Qatar, the United Arab Emirates, and Oman* (Reading, UK, 1998 edn.). See also John Darwin, *Britain and Decolonisation* (London, 1988), chap. 7. Two contemporary articles by D. C. Watt remain invaluable both for analysis and for portraying the controversial nature of the debate in Britain at the time: 'The Decision to Withdraw from the Gulf', *Political Quarterly*, 39, 3 (July–September 1968); and, in the same journal, 'Britain and the Indian Ocean', 42, 3 (July–September 1971).

[2] *Parliamentary Debates* (Commons), 17 January 1968, col. 1819.

[3] Sir Geoffrey Arthur to Alec Douglas-Home, Confidential, 19 April 1971, FCO 8/1572. Arthur was the last Political Resident in the Gulf.

a world power. During the economic emergency in November 1967, the pound sterling was devalued from $2.80 to $2.40. The decision to end the British presence in the Gulf was directly due to the collapse in Aden and the simultaneous sterling crisis, yet there was also, more generally, a crisis of disillusionment with the British Empire. 'I am sure', wrote one British official in the Gulf, 'that most of our present difficulties stem from the appalling lack of confidence the Saudi Arabians and Gulf Arabs have in us, following devaluation and the decision to withdraw, not to mention the Aden *débacle*.'[4] The British did not plan to leave the Gulf because they wanted to, or for reasons concerning the Gulf itself; they left, in short, because of the decision of Harold Wilson's Labour Government to rescue the British economy by taking severe measures, including evacuating all troops from South-East Asia and the Gulf. Some of Wilson's colleagues in the Cabinet believed that the economic crisis compelled them to compromise their socialist principles by introducing charges for prescription medicine into the National Health Service; they in turn insisted on cutbacks in the defence budget. They preferred to preserve what they could of the welfare state rather than shore up the remaining parts of the British Empire. They were especially reluctant to agree to expenditures that would, in their view, continue to buoy up the 'oil-rich feudal sheikhs'.

In Britain, the public mood in 1967 reflected ambivalence about the end of the Empire and, later in the year, anxiety about devaluation. The High Commissioner in Aden referred to 'the tiresome air of guilt about our activities in Aden'.[5] The war in Aden, which concluded with the ignominy of evacuation, marked the nadir in the popularity of the British Empire, but it was by no means certain that the public or Parliament would tolerate the decision to leave the Gulf. From 1968 onwards, Conservative leaders, including the future Prime Minister, Edward Heath, and the former Prime Minister, Sir Alec Douglas-Home, threatened that the course might be reversed in the event of a Tory victory in the next election.

Besides taking into account the British and Middle Eastern dimensions of the problem, any analysis of the withdrawal from the Gulf would not be complete without touching on the United States and the Soviet Union. The year 1967 was a critical time in the escalation of the war in Vietnam. According to Michael Weir, the official at the Foreign

---

[4] R. H. M. Boyle to Political Resident, Confidential, 12 April 1968, FO 1016/860. The designation FO 1016 refers to the Gulf Residency archives.

[5] Sir Richard Turnbull at a meeting of the Chiefs of Staff Committee, 21 February 1967, FCO 8/183.

and Commonwealth Office who played a prominent part in the withdrawal from the Gulf: 'The U.S. Government continue to believe that the present British position in the Gulf is crucial to the stability of the area.'[6] When the British announced the decision to withdraw all forces East of Suez, the Americans regarded it as a betrayal. Again, an element of irony is present here as well, since earlier the Americans, as anti-colonialists, had urged the breakup of the European colonial empires. The Americans now fully appreciated the danger that the aftermath of British withdrawal from the Gulf could lead to instability, just as their similar pull-out had in South-East Asia. For the United States, British departure from the Gulf increased the danger of a Soviet takeover. The British themselves viewed the potential contest not only as a distinct episode in the Cold War but also as the last instalment in the Great Game in Asia, now being played out in the civil war in the Yemen. The late 1960s and early 1970s were revolutionary times: both the Soviet Union and Communist China supported the People's Democratic Republic of Yemen, as the new post-British Aden state was called. The revolution in Yemen might sweep through Arabia to the Gulf itself.

Julian Amery, a Member of Parliament who represented the imperialist wing of the Conservative Party, caught another part of the public mood by alluding to the Roman Empire: 'the Legions are under orders to return'.[7] He and many other critics believed the withdrawal to be a scuttle. In the confused circumstances, no one at the time could clearly answer the question, who would be the successor? The two major contenders were Iran and Saudi Arabia, now confronting each other, so it seemed to some observers, in a manner that portended a clash between Persian and Arab civilizations.[8] The traditional British aims had been to prevent the domination of either and to preserve the dynastic states of the Gulf by promoting some form of union, perhaps even a federation.

The British Protected States in the Gulf were remnants of the Brit-

---

[6] Memorandum by Michael Weir, Secret, 31 October 1967, FCO 8/78. The US Secretary of State, Dean Rusk, warned the British at one point: 'If there is any thought that we might be able to take on your commitments when you left, as we did in Greece, I must say at once that there is no sentiment in this country to take on additional commitments in any area' (memorandum by Rusk, Secret, 21 April 1967, *Foreign Relations of the United States, 1964–1968*, XII, pp. 565–66).

[7] Julian Amery, *Joseph Chamberlain and the Tariff Reform Campaign* (London, 1969), p. 1049.

[8] 'Differences between Arabs and Iranians are sharp. Two races, two civilizations, as well as political and commercial rivalries, are involved. Each looks across the inland sea which it regards as its own moat and mistrusts what the people on the other side are up to' (*The Times*, 17 August 1968).

ish Raj in India.[9] They enjoyed, according to some observers, the 'inflated status' of a bygone era.[10] The principalities in the Gulf, like others on the outer reaches of India, had been brought under British control during the nineteenth century (the exceptions were Kuwait and Qatar, which remained outside the British sphere until 1899 and 1916 respectively). The senior British official in the Gulf was the Political Resident in Bahrain, who supervised Political Agents in Bahrain itself, Kuwait, Qatar, the Trucial States (later the United Arab Emirates), and Oman, which in international law was an independent and sovereign state, but in effect a British Protected State. The Gulf system survived the Raj. At the time of Indian independence in 1947, protection of oil in the Gulf replaced the defence of India as a justification for the British presence. The Foreign Office took over the supervision of the Gulf territories from the India Office, though the Political Resident functioned more like a Colonial Governor. The British controlled defence and foreign affairs. Political Agents ruled some parts of the Gulf, such as the Trucial States, in the same way that District Officers administered other parts of the Empire; on the other hand, the degree of control in Qatar was minimal. British paramountcy was thus uneven, but throughout the Gulf the system of rule or control preserved the 'medieval' or 'fossilised' principalities, as they were commonly called, as well as the original pattern of local politics. Nevertheless there were significant changes: after 1947 the Foreign Office modernized the legal and social systems by revising the legal codes and abolishing slavery.[11]

The British military and naval presence was essentially regulatory:

[9] See Robert J. Blyth, 'Britain versus India in the Persian Gulf: The Struggle for Political Control, *c.*1928–48', *Journal of Imperial and Commonwealth History*, 28, 1 (January 2000), pp. 90–111.

[10] FCO circular despatch, Confidential, 15 December 1969, FO 1016/881.

[11] In a word, 'modernization' summed up the British aim, but a contradiction described in 1959 remained true a decade later:

> If we are to force the pace it will mean the appearance, if not the fact, of greater interference in internal affairs and the assumption of increased responsibility at a time when we are trying to build up the self-reliance of the Gulf States and actively encouraging rulers to widen the scope of their independence. There is, therefore, a certain basic contradiction which will tend to stultify any decisions of policy we may wish to make.

Sir George Middleton to Selwyn Lloyd, Confidential, 2 June 1959, DEFE 7/2200. For the issue of modernization in the post-1967 era, see especially Sir Stewart Crawford to FCO, 'The Modernisation of Her Majesty's Government's Relations with the Protected Gulf States', Confidential, 5 January 1968, FO 1016/885: 'I believe that our primary aim should be to improve the efficiency of the States' Administrations . . . Progress is still patchy.'

controlling or stabilizing the region, maintaining the peace, and keeping other powers out. The Gulf resembled a British lake. But only in 1949—a late development in Britain's Imperial history—did the term Protected States come into official usage. In Glen Balfour-Paul's words, it was a Foreign Office designation for an otherwise inexplicable status, describing a configuration of territories that were, even by Imperial Britain's standards, 'uniquely curious'.[12] The very titles 'Resident' and 'Political Agent' evoked the antiquated usage of the Government of India.

The public controversy over the withdrawal resounded with denunciations that the breach of faith with the Rulers of the Gulf States was a betrayal no less egregious than the abrogation of the treaties with the Indian Princes in 1947. As with the transfer of power in India in 1947, the setting of a deadline—the end of 1971—helped determine the outcome. Geoffrey Arthur, who served as the Under-Secretary supervising Middle Eastern affairs in the Foreign and Commonwealth Office and in 1970 became the last Political Resident, once commented that more progress was made in the two years after 1967 than the British had achieved 'in the twenty-two preceding years since World War Two'.[13]

What sort of progress did the British have in mind? Was it towards a federation, or some more modest type of unity? Federations were the grand design of the 1950s and 1960s, in the Caribbean and South-East Asia as well as in Africa and the Middle East. The breakup of the West Indies Federation in 1962 demonstrated that the trend probably would be towards fragmentation and the birth of tiny states, in the Commonwealth as well as the United Nations. Among the British Protected States of the Gulf, only Bahrain and perhaps Qatar held out much hope as viable units, and even they represented the type of 'micro-state', as the phenomenon later became known, that everyone wanted to avoid. There was little hope for effective unity, above all because the spectre of Aden hovered over the Gulf.[14] In view of the fate

---

[12] Balfour-Paul, *End of Empire in the Middle East*, pp. 101–02.

[13] Geoffrey Arthur to T. A. K. Elliot (Washington), Personal and Confidential, 19 June 1969, FCO 8/934.

[14] 'The fate of the West Indies Federation and the Federation in South Arabia was fresh in our minds' (Anthony Parsons, *They Say the Lion: Britain's Legacy to the Arabs: A Personal Memoir* [London, 1986], p. 121). Michael Weir commented: [C]learly there can be no question in the time we have left of trying . . . to promote another "Whitehall Federation" on the lines of South Arabia.' In searching for precedents for a political union that might or might not be the equivalent of federation, he turned over in his mind the possibility of 'a titular sovereign . . . on the Sudanese model' and 'a rotating Head of State on the Malaysian model' (Weir to Crawford, Confidential, 1 February 1968, FO 1016/855).

of Aden's federation, could one reasonably expect a similar scheme to succeed among the Protected States? Sir Kennedy Trevaskis, the former High Commissioner in Aden and mastermind of the plans for confederating the port of Aden with the sheikhdoms in the hinterland, visited the Gulf in 1968. According to Julian Bullard, the Political Agent in Dubai, Trevaskis drew a gloomy conclusion:

> Although the personalities [in the Gulf] were different, the problems were the same. The Southern Arabian Federation had failed, and if it had not been for pressure by the British Government it would never even have got off the ground. Trevaskis did not conceal his scepticism about the future.[15]

In Bahrain, Anthony Parsons, the Political Agent, reported that the Bahrainis regarded any type of unity among the sheikhdoms as 'a stock joke', though this generalization demanded a qualification. Among the younger generation in Bahrain, those below the age of thirty-five, there was 'a genuine emotional predilection for Arab unity in general and . . . for the unification of the Gulf States'.[16] The British were hardly optimistic, nor did they set their sights too high. If the exacting demands of a federation proved impossible, they would aim at the more amorphous goal of a lesser union, in part because it would be better than nothing: 'a union of some kind is better than complete chaos'.[17]

From 1967 onwards there were no illusions about the difficulty of unifying the nine or so rulers of the Gulf. In Qatar, the Political Agent compared the task ahead with the hero's quest in *Pilgrim's Progress:* '[T]he path to unanimity through the swamps, jungles and thickets of temptation, jealousy, and greed will make the Pilgrim's Progress look like a Sunday afternoon ramble of happiness and sunshine.'[18]

The announcement of abrupt departure seemed all the more jarring because only two months previously the British had given assurances that their presence would continue until political and security arrangements could be made for a post-British era. In November 1967, Goronwy Roberts, the Minister of State in the Foreign and Common-

---

[15] Julian Bullard to Michael Weir (Bahrain), Confidential, 26 November 1968, FCO 8/915. See also Parsons to Weir, Confidential, 3 December 1968, FO 1016/749, in which Parsons (Political Agent, Bahrain) related that, in a conversation with the Sheikh Isa of Bahrain, Trevaskis referred to Parsons himself as 'a slave of the Labour Party and cannot speak his own mind'.

[16] Parsons to Crawford, Confidential, 22 July 1968, FCO 8/16.

[17] Minute by Peter Hayman (Deputy Under-Secretary), 15 December 1969, FCO 8/925.

[18] R. H. M. Boyle (Qatar) to Sir Stewart Crawford (Bahrain), 12 May 1968, FCO 8/12.

wealth Office, had visited the Gulf. With unfailing canniness, Harold Wilson had shifted Roberts from the Welsh Office to the FCO because there were too many senior ministers from North Wales cluttering the Welsh Office. A kindly man, Roberts was out of his depth, but he was sent to the Middle East following a major discussion in Whitehall on the future of the British position in the Gulf. He reassured the Rulers —and the Shah of Iran—that rumours of an impending British departure were unfounded and that Britain would, in Roberts's words, remain in the Gulf 'so long as was necessary and desirable to ensure the peace and stability of the area'.[19] Roberts left no doubt at all: '[H]e was explicit that there was no thought of withdrawal in our minds.'[20]

The Rulers had been greatly relieved to learn that the British had no intention of leaving without making arrangements for their security. British forces would continue to provide the peaceful conditions necessary for economic development; the axe did not fall. But no sooner had the Rulers—and the Political Agents—taken in this good news than they learned that Roberts would again visit the region in January 1968, this time with the unhappy message that, mainly for financial reasons, the British military presence would end in 1971. Roberts insisted as a point of honour that he return to the Gulf to convey the bad news, though he himself did not seem to recognize the 'credibility gap' created in the minds of the Rulers by the reversal.[21] The date of the public announcement, 16 January 1968, lived then and for ever after in Gulf history in infamy. The Middle East hands at the Foreign and Commonwealth Office referred to the decision as the double-cross. Sir Stewart Crawford, the penultimate Political Resident in the Gulf (1966–70), reported that the Rulers felt betrayed.[22] So also did at least one of the Political Agents: Anthony Parsons in Bahrain wrote afterwards:

> The deed was done and that was that. But I was deeply troubled about my personal position and slept little that night . . . How could I now confront this volte-face and retain my own honour? I realized that, if

---

[19] According to the brief for Roberts: 'We have no plans for withdrawing, we have not set any time limit to our presence . . . It will probably not be in our interests to stay in the Gulf beyond the mid-1970s' (brief dated November 1967, FCO 8/142).

[20] Crawford to Paul Gore-Booth, Personal and Confidential, 3 February 1968, FO 1016/885. See also especially Crawford to FCO, Confidential, 27 January 1968, FCO 8/33.

[21] Crawford wrote that Roberts's previous reassurance 'only increased the magnitude of the reversal . . . It seems unfortunate that he is not aware of this himself' (Crawford to Paul Gore-Booth, Personal and Confidential, 3 February 1968, FO 1016/885).

[22] 'They are greatly perplexed about where to turn, and feel bitterly that we are letting them down' (Crawford to FCO, Confidential, 27 January 1968, FCO 8/33).

I were to resign, this act would change nothing and would not create
even a ripple on the surface of events. But these were not reasons for
failing to do the right thing.[23]

Parsons stayed on because the Ruler himself urged him not to quit.
But Parsons did so with strong feelings about the unethical behaviour
of the British government. Not only would Britain's military presence
be terminated but also the protective treaties.

The urgency of the situation led to comprehensive, intense discussions within the Foreign and Commonwealth Office about how best
to prepare for the British departure in view of the uncertainty of still
more defence cuts and the possibility that the British Army might be
drawn into a major operation in Northern Ireland.[24] In any event, the
withdrawal would be a complex process, varying from principality
to principality. The British had to deal immediately with the tense relations between Bahrain and Qatar, and the relations between those
two important sheikhdoms and what were then known as the Trucial
States (the word 'Trucial' derived from the treaty signed in 1854 by
the British and the ruling sheikhs, who agreed to a 'perpetual maritime truce'). The Trucial States—which became known as the United
Arab Emirates—were Abu Dhabi, Dubai, and the five northern or
small Trucial States of Ajman, Sharjah, Um al Qaiwain, Fujairah, and
Ras al Khaimah. Of these, the British were mostly concerned with Abu
Dhabi and Dubai, because of oil. The rest were impoverished, slight in
population and resources, but significant because they could cause
trouble by embracing radical Arab nationalism and perhaps block the
proposed union.

The British connection with Bahrain—and what was still called
the steel frame of British administration—was as sturdy as with any
other territory in the Middle East.[25] Bahrain was the seat of both the
Resident and the Political Agent; it was a miniature bastion for the
Royal Navy; the houses of British expatriates and service personnel
in Manamah, the capital, bore names such as 'Curzon, Piccadilly, and

[23] Parsons, *They Say the Lion*, p. 134.

[24] See especially Julian Bullard to Crawford, Confidential, 29 June 1970, FO 1016/757, for
reflection on some of the larger issues. For example, in view of their declining resources, should
the British 'merely stand back and watch, or try to take a hand in the knowledge that our intervention may in practice make things worse and not better?' Bullard identified one of the problems as the British rationalization that the plans for withdrawal had been undertaken in the interests of the Rulers themselves. But this line of argument 'carried little conviction' with the
Rulers, who saw clearly that the decision had been made purely for British reasons.

[25] See Bernard Burrows, *Footnotes in the Sand: The Gulf in Transition, 1953–1958* (Salisbury,
UK, 1990), chap. 4.

Britannia'.[26] British rule in Bahrain was more far-reaching than in any other Gulf state, in part because of the jurisdiction, inherited from the Raj, over the large foreign population of workers in the oilfields and in virtually all other sectors of the economy. Bahrain had developed as the first oil-producing state in the Gulf: oil began to flow in 1931, but the reserves proved to be minor compared to those in Kuwait and elsewhere. In the 1950s the ruling family, the Al Khalifah, had faced radical or militant demands for reform, but nationalist protest had, on the whole, been effectively dealt with, in the view of the British Resident, by 'first class British leadership'.[27] When Selwyn Lloyd, the Foreign Secretary in 1956, visited Bahrain shortly before the Suez crisis, he encountered violent denunciation, the event itself reflecting the turbulence in a society that included Iranians, Indians, Palestinians, and others who mainly worked in the oilfields. The currents of Arab nationalism ran deep, but so also did the undertow of cultural and religious affinity with Shia Iran. 'We employ a surprising number of Arabs who speak Arabic with a Persian accent', wrote the Resident in Bahrain, 'and read magazines from Tehran, not Cairo.'[28] But there could be no doubt about the Arab character of the population as a whole. According to Michael Weir, whose writings often reflected an awareness of problems in other parts of the British Empire: 'Bahrain is no Cyprus: it is demonstrably an Arab country.'[29]

The Resident judged that Bahrain was the most advanced of the Protected States but also the most complex. He drew a comparison with Qatar:

> By Gulf standards Bahrain is relatively sophisticated with a developed Government and educated population; on the other hand it is poor in oil resources . . .

> Qatar, far less sophisticated, only recently embarked on modern education, more dominated by its ruling family than is Bahrain, has nevertheless far greater oil resources and wealth and a clearer idea

---

[26] A. J. D. Stirling to Crawford, Confidential, 9 June 1969, FCO 8/1001.

[27] Crawford to FCO, Confidential, 12 June 1968, FCO 8/3.

[28] Arthur to FCO, Confidential, 19 April 1971, FCO 8/1572.

[29] Weir continued: 'In no sense, numerically or politically, does the Iranian community constitute a significant minority i.e. comparable to the Turkish Cypriots.' On another point of general interest, Weir commented on the Huwala, who had emigrated from southern Persia to Bahrain in the nineteenth and early twentieth centuries: 'They remind me in some ways of those Anglo-Irish families who . . . [have] the attitude of Protestant Anglo-Irish to the indigenous Catholics . . . The younger generation of Huwala . . . are generally speaking Arab nationalist and Nasserite' (Weir to Political Resident, Confidential, 17 June 1968, FO 1016/762).

of the policy to follow . . . The Al Khalifah of Bahrain and the Al Thani
of Qatar are . . . still, despite our efforts to bring them together, like
oil and water.[30]

The British accurately sensed that Bahrain marched out of step with
most of the other Protected States and would probably move towards
separate independence rather than inclusion in any possible union.
  In view of the danger of 'general upheaval' in Bahrain and of the
possibility of 'subversion' from Egypt and other radical Arab states, the
chances of inclusion in a union were problematical—above all because Iran claimed Bahrain as a lost province. Until Iran's territorial
claims to Bahrain and other minor islands could be resolved, the future of the unification plan would be in doubt.[31] Iran held an implicit
veto, or at least considerable influence, over the union because none
of the sheikhdoms could afford to be on bad terms with the major
power in the region. If the union were to come into being, it would
need, at a minimum, Iran's acquiescence.
  In contrast to Bahrain, Qatar represented one of the most minuscule portions of the British Empire. But the economic stakes were
large, as they were in Abu Dhabi and Dubai. By the 1960s, Qatar was
producing half the amount of oil of neighbouring Abu Dhabi, and
could rank as among the wealthiest states, per capita, in the world. Geoffrey Arthur once wrote of Qatar: 'It is the least attractive of the Gulf
States, its Rulers are the least pleasant and least responsive to British
pressures. They are also the most likely to last, for they are tough, pro-
lific, united, and above all capable of identifying, and ruthless in pursuing, their own interests.'[32]
  In wealth and prosperity, Abu Dhabi and Dubai, even in British
times, belonged to a class of their own. The discovery of oil in Abu
Dhabi in 1958 led to a growth rate in the 1960s four times that of Kuwait and to a position of unquestioned prominence in the region.
Dubai developed essentially as a city-state and eventually possessed
the largest dry dock in the world. It became one of the leading centres
of commerce in the Gulf, regarded by some contemporaries as having
the potential to become another Hong Kong. But Abu Dhabi and
Dubai had opposite political attractions within the larger Arab world.
Sheikh Rashid of Dubai thought that the natural ally of the Gulf States

[30] Crawford to Michael Stewart, Confidential, 9 July 1969, FCO 8/920.
[31] See Crawford to FCO, 'The Iranian Claim to Bahrain', Confidential, 25 June 1968,
FO 1016/865.
[32] Arthur to FCO, Confidential, 19 April 1971, FCO 8/1572.

was Saudi Arabia.[33] Sheikh Zaid of Abu Dhabi believed pragmatically that Gamal Abdel Nasser's Egypt not only should be recognized as the leader of revolutionary Arab nationalism, but also should be represented in the Gulf as part of the new, post-1968 order.[34] The idea of Egypt having a formal presence violated the basic British premise 'to keep Nasser out of the Gulf'.[35]

The fundamental or traditional British assumption about excluding Egypt needed to be reassessed. Should it not now be assumed that Britain's future in the larger reaches of the Middle East depended on better relations with Egypt? One Foreign Office official, D. J. Speares, wrote in July 1968: 'I am quite convinced that our over-all interests in the Middle East are likely to be furthered by . . . cultivating and maintaining good relations' with Egypt, 'rather than by the policies we followed in the past.'[36] What, then, to make of the overtures by some of the Gulf States to Egypt? The question placed those pondering the future of the Gulf in a quandary. Should the British 'allow our feckless clients to be seduced under our eyes'?[37] In any event, the Gulf states, in pursuing their local aims, formed quasi-alliances—or, to put it no higher, informal contacts—not only among themselves but with others beyond the Gulf as well: Qatar with Saudi Arabia, Dubai with Iran, Abu Dhabi and some of the lesser Sheikhdoms with Egypt and other Middle Eastern countries.[38] These were combinations or inclinations

---

[33] According to D. A. Roberts, Sheikh Rashid of Dubai:

> has personal links with Saudi Arabia, which he sees, rightly or wrongly, as the main guarantee of stability in the Arabian peninsula . . . He has also attributed to the Egyptians in general two motives; first, hatred of rulers and shaikhly regimes and, secondly, a longing somehow to get their hands on the wealth of Gulf states.

Roberts (Dubai) to British Residency Bahrain, Confidential, 27 May 1968, FO 1016/862.

[34] 'It looks as if Zaid is keeping his lines open in all directions' (Bullard to Weir, Confidential, 1 February 1970, FO 1016/739). On Sheikh Zaid and Egypt: 'He believes that he can handle any Egyptian mission that should arrive . . . We shall . . . remind him of the risks in supping with the devil' (Crawford memorandum of 1 June 1968, Confidential, FO 1016/862). 'Supping with the devil' was a recurrent theme, and not only in regard to Cairo. Michael Weir wrote in early 1971: 'At varying times most of the States which have felt threatened, Bahrain, Abu Dhabi and Ras al Khaimah, succumbed to the temptation to sup with the devil from Baghdad' (Weir to FCO, 1 January 1971, FCO 8/1570).

[35] For example, Crawford to Brenchley, Confidential, 11 April 1967, FCO 8/42.

[36] Minute by D. J. Speares, 2 July 1968, FCO 8/22.

[37] Minute by D. J. McCarthy, 5 July 1968, FCO 8/22.

[38] For example, from the vantage point of the Qataris: 'They see themselves as the main coordinator for co-operation with Saudi Arabia because of their traditional ties with that country. They also see themselves, with Dubai, as an ally of Iran' (Boyle to Political Resident, Confiden-

that shifted from issue to issue and sometimes from month to month, but throughout the Gulf itself the popular pro-Nasser or pan-Arab nationalist sentiment continued to trouble the British. It became clear only gradually that Nasser's eclipse created a more favourable climate for British withdrawal. According to a Foreign Office minute on the events of 1967: 'The June war was the turning point . . . we would never have had a chance of making an orderly withdrawal from the Gulf nor would the Sheikhs have had a chance of survival if the revolutionary Arabs had not been completely deflated by the results of the June war.'[39]

To the north, in the richest of the Gulf States, Kuwait faced ever-increasing pressures from the radical Arab world, above all from Nasser's Egypt, to invest its wealth in Middle East development rather than in London banks. Kuwait had become independent in 1961, but Iraq, which regarded Kuwait as an Iraqi province, immediately threatened to invade.[40] The British intervened to establish once and for all that Kuwait must be respected as a sovereign state, unconnected to Iraq, though, as will be seen, Iraqi ambitions again preoccupied the British before their departure from the Gulf—as did the possibility of revolution in Kuwait.[41]

The intervention in Kuwait in 1961 had left a lingering anti-British sentiment. Kuwait also had tense relations with its neighbours: its people saw themselves as being at the vortex of a troubled region. The British Ambassador, Sir Sam Falle, wrote in 1970, on the eve of withdrawal from the Gulf:

> Kuwait feels threatened in general terms by progressive Arab Social-
> ism and in specific terms by its manifestations in neighbouring States

---

tial, 12 April 1968, FO 1016/860). On the point about Egypt, again to use Qatar as an example: 'Qatar favoured Egypt in the past. This feeling is long since cold . . . The Qataris suspect most people's motives, but the Egyptians above all' (Boyle to British Residency Bahrain, Confidential, 1 June 1968, FO 1016/862). The Political Resident summed up the salient point: 'The truth is that everybody seems to suspect everybody else' (Crawford memorandum of 21 May 1968, Confidential, FO 1016/862).

[39] Fragment of a minute, May 1971, FCO 8/1311.

[40] See Simon C. Smith, *Kuwait, 1950–1965: Britain, the al-Sabah, and Oil* (Oxford, 1999).

[41] The Ambassador in Kuwait, Sir Sam Falle, believed Kuwait to be on the verge of revolution and thought in any event that the British should make contact with moderate 'evolutionaries' before they became revolutionaries. Falle had been in Baghdad in 1958 and had anticipated the Iraqi revolution. In the Gulf, however, his colleagues were mainly sceptical. 'Who are [the] moderate evolutionaries?' asked the Political Resident (Crawford to FCO, Confidential, 28 July 1970, FCO 8/1318). In London, the head of the Arabian Department, Antony Acland, held that prior connections with radicals would not 'deflect them . . . by having had contact with them before their advent to power' (Acland to Falle, Confidential, 2 July, 1970, FO 1016/757). On Falle, see his autobiography, *My Lucky Life in War, Revolution, Peace and Diplomacy* (Lewes, UK, 1996).

—Iraqi irredentism, pressure on the Sultan of Muscat inspired from Aden, discontent and subversion in Saudi Arabia and Bahrain . . . Again, there is fear of the Iranian empire and an arrogant Persian domination of the area. The insoluble and interminable Arab-Israel conflict continues to disturb even the placid waters of the Gulf . . . The rich Kuwaitis wonder what to do.[42]

The native Kuwaitis were outnumbered by the foreign population: Indians, Iranians, Palestinians, Iraqis, Syrians, Lebanese, Egyptians, and others from the lower Gulf—'Without them the State would collapse.'[43] Kuwait would probably not play a significant part in bringing about a union among the principalities in the lower Gulf, in part because of the historical evolution of the Gulf States: '[T]he Kuwaitis rightly or wrongly are disliked by the Rulers of the Southern States as arrogant and presumptuous upstarts'.[44]

To the far south, the Sultanate of Muscat and Oman was 'the odd state out', not merely because of its geographical position but because it would need 'about 600 years' to catch up with the other Gulf States.[45] Embroiled in civil war, and in any event self-absorbed, Oman played only a marginal part in the debate about the possible union. From 1965 the British had intervened decisively in the Dhofar rebellion; the Dhofar region was adjacent to the Aden Protectorate, as the territory was then known. By the mid-1960s the Yemeni civil war had engulfed Dhofar—described by the Resident in the Gulf as

the best guerilla country in the Middle East [where] . . . the Sultan's Armed Forces are fighting communist gangs supplied from Aden . . . [and who are] controlled by men dedicated to change of the most violent and radical kind, men who forbid prayer and whose reading, if they read at all, is not the Koran but the Thoughts of Chairman Mao.[46]

Part of the aim of the revolutionary movement was to destroy all of the dynastic states of the Gulf. The civil war had not yet worked its way to a conclusion by the time of the British withdrawal from the Gulf, but in 1970 the British had assisted in overthrowing Oman's ruler, Sultan bin Taimur—who, in the British view, was a dangerous anachronism—and in replacing him with his son, the present ruler of Oman,

[42] Sam Falle to FCO, Confidential, 1 January 1970, FCO 8/1387.

[43] Arthur to FCO, Confidential, 26 October 1968, FCO 8/1043.

[44] Crawford to FCO, Confidential, 13 May 1967, FCO 8/42.

[45] Crawford to FCO, Confidential, 14 January 1969, FCO 8/927; Anthony Parsons to A. J. D. Stirling, Confidential, 13 April 1968, FCO 8/11.

[46] Arthur to FCO, Confidential, 19 April 1971, FCO 8/1572.

Qaboos bin Said, who had been educated at Sandhurst and had served in the British Army. For our purposes, the significance of the Sultanate of Muscat and Oman is that it held the line against the Yemeni revolution during the period of British withdrawal from the Gulf.

Three regional powers claimed parts of the Gulf. Confronting Saudi Arabia, Iran, and Iraq, the British pursued a goal of triple containment, though this posture often seemed passive rather than active. They needed to keep Saudi Arabia reassured that their departure would not create a sort of Palestine in the Gulf. They hoped that Iran would not seize the disputed islands until after they had left. They viewed the possibility of Iraqi expansion as relatively dormant, but it nevertheless caused concern.

From the vantage point of Saudi Arabia, the decision to leave the Gulf reinforced impressions of the loss of British nerve in Aden. According to the British Ambassador, King Faisal of Saudi Arabia 'feels that by our actions in the Arabian Peninsula we have encouraged those who would endanger the security of his country and of its dynasty'.[47] Having watched the British leave Aden under humiliating circumstances and believing that their will to rule had cracked, King Faisal wondered whether the Gulf might now suffer the same fate. Might there be a domino effect from Aden to the Gulf, one principality toppling after the next? In responding to such questions, the Resident affirmed that the British position in the Gulf differed radically from the circumstances of British colonial rule in Aden. Sir Stewart Crawford, usually restrained and unemotional, had written with unusual passion during the actual withdrawal from Aden in late 1967:

> In the Gulf . . . we do not have, as we have had in Aden, to constitute a new government, the Rulers are all firmly in their saddles and can be counted on to show much more sense, guts and leadership than the Aden Amirs . . . Instead of a Yemen next door there is a reasonably solid and pretty inert Saudi Arabia.[48]

Such optimistic views, expressed without the insult about 'inertness', failed to make an impression on the Saudis. But the calculation that Saudi Arabia would remain 'inert' had a bearing on the outcome.

Saudi Arabia supported the effort to create a union, so the British believed, only because the sheikhdoms might otherwise fall prey to Iran. Indeed, the British sensed that if the union succeeded, the

---

[47] Morgan Man to FCO, Confidential, 20 February 1968, FCO 8/757.
[48] Crawford to Sir Richard Beaumont, Secret and Personal, 28 October 1967, FCO 8/41.

Saudis might be willing silently to forget but not forgive the long-
standing dispute over the Buraimi oasis, the point in the desert where
Oman, Saudi Arabia, and Abu Dhabi meet, and which reputedly sat
atop oil deposits. British departure might provide an 'escape hatch'
from the decades-old controversy, in which the three states were emotionally as well as strategically entangled. This estimate regarding Buraimi proved far too optimistic. The Saudis remained adamant on
their claims to the oasis, and they were also consistent in their outlook
on the Gulf. According to King Faisal, '[T]he Gulf sheikhdoms are
historically, geographically and politically Saudi Arabia's preserve and
no one else's.'[49] The British themselves were sceptical of these far-
reaching Saudi claims to the region: 'Saudi ignorance of the people
and territories on their borders and the inadequacies of their governmental machinery and personnel make it unlikely that they can quickly
assume any major role in the Gulf territories, and'—because of pan-
Arab nationalism—'perhaps risky for them to attempt it.'[50]

Revolutionary Arab nationalism posed a threat to the Shah of Iran
as well. In early 1967, Sir Denis Wright, the Ambassador in Tehran, had
remarked that the British were, 'in the Shah's eyes, still the only real
bulwark against Nasserite expansion'.[51] The decision to withdraw came
as a shock to the Shah no less than to King Faisal, though the British
had tried to prepare the way. Both the King and the Shah believed
the British to be acting not in their own best interest—indeed, irra-
tionally. Both regarded the Sheikhdoms in the Gulf as British puppets.
Each had suspicions of British motives, though the Saudi view of British abdication reflected a general Arab anxiety—that the British were
creating 'another Palestine' in the Gulf by supporting Iran's bid for
mastery of the region.

Just as the British denied giving aid and comfort to Israel, so they
also vigorously rejected charges of collaboration with Iran, especially
in the case of Bahrain. The British believed that the Shah had no actual ambition to take over Bahrain, but like any ancient claim, it could
not be easily repudiated: 'He does not wish to go down in history as
the man who lightly abandoned his country's "14th Province".'[52] But
he intended, in one way or another, to free himself, in his own words,

[49] Morgan Man to FCO, Confidential, 20 February 1968, FCO 8/757. This was a view reciprocated especially in Qatar: 'They see Saudi Arabia as Britain's natural inheritor in this area . . .
and their best defence against socialist and revolutionary subversion' (R. H. M. Boyle to Crawford, 12 April 1968, FCO 8/11).

[50] W. Morris to FCO, Confidential, 16 April 1969, FCO 8/1181.

[51] Sir Denis Wright to FCO, Confidential and Guard [Guard = not for American eyes],
10 February 1967, FCO 17/358.

[52] Wright to FCO, Confidential, 2 January 1969, FCO 17/849.

from the Bahrainian 'millstone'.[53] In contrast, there were other territorial claims that the Shah would relentlessly pursue. He aimed to annex the islands called the Tunbs in the narrow entrance to the Strait
of Hormuz, at the mouth of the Persian Gulf, and Abu Musa, an island
in the middle of the Gulf, slightly on the Arab side, that eventually became known as the farthest Iranian outpost in the Gulf. Sir Denis
Wright commented: 'I am quite certain that the Iranians will walk into
the Tunbs when we leave if no prior agreement has been reached, and
[I am] almost as certain that in those circumstances they would decide
they might as well go the whole hog and walk into Abu Musa as well.'[54]
Virtually all Iranian oil exports passed through the Strait, and it was
thus understandable that the Shah attached strategic significance to
the Greater and Lesser Tunbs.

In a larger sense, according to the British Embassy staff in Tehran,
'the Shah has never taken his eyes off Nasser'. Such was the Shah's
preoccupation with Nasser that it resembled a fixation:

> His obsessive hatred of Nasser . . . has grown steadily since the down-
> fall of the Nuri regime in Iraq in 1958. This the Shah transliterates
> into a major physical threat to Iran in the Persian Gulf.[55]

> Nasser . . . [is] enemy No. 1.[56]

The Shah carefully assessed each move made in response to Nasser,
and believed that the collapse in Aden was 'the beginning of the end'
for the British in the Gulf. The British were opting out; the Shah was
in the struggle to the end. The disputed islands were merely part of an
overall battlefield: 'What the Shah is really concerned with is who will
control the Gulf as a whole when we leave.'[57]

The other Middle Eastern state with a claim to the Gulf was Iraq.
Though the Iraqi dimension of the problem did not emerge until

---

[53] 'In private, the Shah regards Bahrain as a millstone round his neck and he has on the whole
in recent years tried to play the issue down . . . Come what may, it is most unlikely that the Shah
would attempt to seize Bahrain by force in any circumstances' (memorandum by C. D. Wiggin,
10 February 1967, FCO 17/358).

[54] Wright to A. R. Moore, Secret and Personal, 9 May 1968, FCO 8/28.

[55] Memorandum by C. D. Wiggin, 10 February 1967, FCO 17/358.

[56] Wright to FCO, Confidential, 11 January 1967, FCO 17/351.

[57] Memorandum by Wiggin, 18 February 1967, FCO 17/358. 'Our Middle East de Gaulle' was
the phrase Willie Morris (Ambassador in Saudi Arabia) used to sum up the Shah (Morris to FCO,
Confidential, 27 November 1968, FO 1016/870).

relatively late in the 1968–71 period, it was nevertheless significant because it represented the response of revolutionary Arab socialism — and with it, perhaps, the support of the Soviet Union. There was also a specific territorial claim: just as Iran regarded Bahrain as a lost province, so did Iraq view Kuwait as part of Iraq proper. Through intelligence sources, the British detected 'renewed Iraqi ambitions towards Kuwait'. And Iraqi influence extended far beyond the northern Gulf. Iraq also lent assistance to the rebels in the Dhofar province of Oman. The flashpoint in the Gulf itself might well be Bahrain: 'There is . . . a natural tendency for the Shi'a who form 50% of Bahrain's population to look towards Iraq.'[58] In sum, the Iraqis aspired to no less than 'a dominant position in the Arab Gulf' by promoting a revolution against the dynastic states. In so doing, they would not only advance the revolutionary socialist cause but also preserve the Gulf against Iranian invaders. According to the Ambassador in Baghdad, Glen Balfour-Paul, the problem had an obsessive quality to it:

> For the Iraqis, as for many other Arabs, safeguarding the Arabism of the Gulf means primarily the exclusion of Iranian influence from its western shores. But because of the rivalry, hostility and mistrust existing for other reasons between Iraq and Iran, the exclusion of Iranian influence takes on for the Iraqis a significance which it does not have for other interested Arab parties . . . For the Iraqis, who see an Iranian burglar under every bed, the Arabism of the Gulf States is . . . an obsession.

> To the pan-Arab revolutionaries of Iraq it is, like the struggle for Palestine, part and parcel of the single, all-embracing dogma of Arab revolution.[59]

Iraqi ambitions themselves might not have seemed so alarming had it not been for the context of the Cold War: 'There can scarcely be any

---

[58] Crawford to FCO, Secret, 22 July 1970, FCO 8/1309.

[59] Balfour-Paul to FCO, Confidential, 11 April 1970, FCO 8/1309. Balfour-Paul commented later on Iraqi ideology and the Gulf:

> A 'progressive' revolutionary Arab government has to have a forward policy somewhere. As I see it, therefore, the incentive to make a bid southwards must now be increasingly potent. Add to this their frantic resentment at Iranian ambitions in the Gulf and their ideological opposition to the shaikhly regimes ripe (as they believe) for subversion on the Arab side, and you have a pretty heady mixture.

Balfour Paul to FCO, Confidential, 21 November 1970, FCO 17/1539.

doubt that the Soviet Union would welcome the emergence of revolutionary regimes in the oil States of the Gulf'.[60]

In view of the obstacles to unifying the Gulf States, one is reminded of the reference to *Pilgrim's Progress*. Yet in the end the British left the Gulf with its political system of dynastic states intact and with the seven former Trucial States united in a federal structure known today as the United Arab Emirates. With the brief exception of the period of the Gulf War of 1991, when the state of Kuwait momentarily ceased to exist, the system has endured to the present. How, then, did the British manage to do it? What were the step-by-step measures taken from the time Britain announced her departure to the time the federal union of the Emirates was formed in late 1971? Until very late in the day it appeared that the Iranian claims to the disputed islands would prevent the emergence of a federation. Just as significant, the odds seemed to be overwhelmingly against the sheikhs themselves coming to an agreement on a federal constitution. On the British side, in January 1968 there was collective dismay at the Foreign and Commonwealth Office and among the Political Agents in the Gulf. But after British officials recovered from their initial consternation, they quickly and systematically, though not optimistically, began to work for a union of the sheikhdoms, including Bahrain and Qatar. Michael Weir wrote: 'We owe it to the Gulf States as well as ourselves to do the utmost in the time available.'[61]

After 16 January, the Rulers of the Gulf feared, not without reason, that the British would 'sell them down the river'. The Political Resident reported on the frantic exchanges between the Sheikhs about how best to defend themselves: 'All sorts of wild and impractical ideas are being ventilated.'[62] The first tangible step occurred in February 1968 when the Rulers of Abu Dhabi and Dubai abruptly agreed to unite and, without further consultation, invited the other rulers to join them. This move was 'greeted with fury by the ruler of Qatar'.[63] Seizing a short-lived initiative, the Ruler of Qatar secured the agreement of all nine Protected States to create, in principle, a union; this was known as the Dubai Agreement.[64] It marked a significant step towards unity, though there appeared to be no way of reconciling the

[60] Balfour-Paul to FCO, Confidential, 11 April 1970, FCO 8/1309.

[61] Weir to Crawford, 8 February 1968, FO 1016/754.

[62] Crawford to FCO, Confidential, 27 January 1968, FCO 8/33.

[63] Record of meetings, 25 and 26 March 1968, FCO 8/33.

[64] See Crawford to FCO, 'The Union of Arab Emirates', Confidential, 10 June 1968, FO 1016/865.

ancient animosities of Qatar and Bahrain. The British supported the idea of a 'loose confederation' that would include both Qatar and Bahrain plus the seven Trucial States.[65] The onus of failure would thus fall on the states refusing to join, or, conversely, the success would depend on those willing to combine, perhaps in a tighter union of Abu Dhabi, Dubai, and the five lesser, northern sheikhdoms. 'The Rulers of the five small and impecunious Northern Trucial States', the Political Resident reported, 'are in complete confusion and are looking in all directions to see where they can run for cover.'[66] The Ruler of Ras al Khaimah was especially vulnerable, since he exercised jurisdiction over the island of Abu Musa, one of the disputed islands claimed by Iran. Now that the British had declared their intention to leave the Gulf, when would Iran step in to occupy Abu Musa and the two Tunbs? If Iran seized the islands, the Shah—and the British—would be confronted with 'a united hostile [Arab] front'.[67] The move might precipitate a Saudi pre-emptive strike against Buraimi and thus upset the delicate territorial balance at the juncture of Abu Dhabi, Oman, and Saudi Arabia. The overall problem was proving to be as complicated and daunting as the British had anticipated.

Whatever the perils threatened by Iran or Saudi Arabia, or of the sheikhs failing to come to an agreement, there was also the hazard of the Conservative Party leaders attempting to reverse course and retain Britain's military presence in the Gulf beyond 1971—thus destroying the degree of unity that the Political Agents had been able to achieve against considerable odds. In 1968 the leader of the Conservative Party, Edward Heath, challenged the Labour Government's decision to withdraw all troops East of Suez. He continued his attack, with an increasing emphasis on the Gulf, to the time of the election in the summer of 1970. This created a problem for those now planning an orderly withdrawal. Whatever qualms one might have had personally—Anthony Parsons, for example, believing that the British government had betrayed its trust—a reversal might be even worse. Even if the British government decided to stay on, would the British now be welcomed by the Rulers of the Gulf? Parsons wrote about Bahrain in a comment that applied to other Gulf States as well: 'Virtually everyone . . . considered that the decision could not be reversed and that an attempt to do so might precipitate an Aden situation here.'[68]

No one of course could anticipate what a Conservative Govern-

[65] Memorandum by Goronwy Roberts, 28 March 1968, FCO 8/33.
[66] Crawford to FCO, Confidential, 27 January 1968, FCO 8/33.
[67] Record of meetings, 25 and 26 March 1968, FCO 8/33.
[68] Parsons to FCO, Confidential, 8 February 1969, FO 1016/755.

ment might actually do or what might take place in the meantime. The Middle East experts, however, were sceptical to a man that the *status quo ante* could be resumed. Though the Sheikhs under the initial shock had proclaimed themselves willing to do virtually anything to extend the British presence, including paying for the upkeep of British troops, the British detected a subtle change of attitude. Whatever the future might hold, things would never again be the same after 16 January. In one way or another, the Sheikhs would have to rely on their own devices. On the British side, the decision to withdraw had merely recognized, in Geoffrey Arthur's words, 'the writing on the wall'. The British system in the Gulf was already 'an anachronism'.[69] While still at the Foreign and Commonwealth Office, Arthur believed that neither Gulf nationalists nor the British public, on the whole, realistically would expect the British to stay on: 'Whereas surprisingly few elements in the Gulf, even among nationalists, welcomed our policy to withdraw, it is unlikely that any substantial body of opinion in the Gulf or around it would feel that the clock can now be turned back.'[70] Once made, a sweeping decision of that magnitude would be virtually impossible to reverse. And it was inevitable that dormant claims would be renewed, and that Iran, Iraq, Kuwait, and Saudi Arabia would all demand Britain's departure.

In the larger period of 1967–71 there were two turning points, both midway through the chronological sequence. One had to do with developments in the Gulf itself, the other with British politics. The first was the resolution in May 1970 of Iran's claim to Bahrain. Until this cloud over Bahrain's future could be dissipated, no substantial progress could be made: none of the Gulf States could afford to antagonize Iran. For Bahrain itself, there were internal ethnic and religious reasons why it was necessary to remain on as good terms as possible with Iran. From the beginning, soon after the announcement of the British departure, all nine Gulf States—the larger grouping including Bahrain and eventually even Qatar—had agreed to study the feasibility of a union. As has been mentioned, this was known as the Dubai Agreement, and it marked the beginning of detailed studies and talks on such matters as the pooling of sovereignty, representation and other

---

[69] Arthur to Elliot, Personal and Confidential, 19 June 1969, FCO 8/934. Though a certain sense of inevitability can be detected about the end of the British era, so also can the view that the aftermath would depend on the sheikhs themselves. If the possibility of a union of the nine (Bahrain and Qatar plus the Trucial States) proved impossible, would the remaining seven adopt, in Julian Bullard's words, 'a mood of hopeless dejection, or would a Dunkirk, we're-on-our-own-now spirit prevail?' (Bullard, 'The Future of the Trucial States', 8 July 1969, FO 1016/876).

[70] Arthur to Elliot, Personal and Confidential, 19 June 1969, FCO 8/934.

constitutional questions, defence, immigration, the choice of a capital, currency, and, not least, the question of a flag. These discussions paved the way for the eventual union. Julian Bullard commented on 'the confused and conspiratorial manner in which the talks have been conducted: mostly in whispers, on sofas, in odd corners . . . with messengers trotting from one little group to another'.[71] But until May 1970 it appeared that little progress was being made because the political issue of Bahrain remained unsettled and with it the nature and numbers of the union, indeed its very existence.

The British themselves appeared to be playing an essentially passive part; they, too, needed the good will of the Shah to make the union a success. They believed that the Shah would accept a face-saving device to resolve the issue of Bahrain (but would be unyielding on the other issue of the small islands). Yet no one could come up with a formula for Bahrain until the idea was put forward that the United Nations might come to the rescue. Sir Denis Wright in Iran played a crucial part in devising this formula by suggesting that the Iranians themselves might ask the United Nations to determine the actual sentiment of the Bahrainis. Wright relied on the principle that extraordinary things can be accomplished if someone else takes credit for them. This was an intricate task, but it worked. In late March 1970 a four-man UN mission under an Italian named Winspeare Guicciardi—who, by all accounts, did a brilliant job—established that virtually all Bahrainis were unanimous in wanting an independent Arab state.[72] On 9 May the Security Council unanimously endorsed the report and Iran formally abandoned its claim to Bahrain. Bahrain was now on its way to becoming a member of the United Nations. Qatar shortly afterwards declared its intention of becoming an independent state and applying for UN membership; with a population of 200,000, it met the minimum requirement. Thus the resolution of Bahraini sovereignty also broke the deadlock over Qatar and the Trucial States.

The other watershed occurred in British politics with the victory of the Conservative Party in the summer of 1970. The Prime Minister, Edward Heath, had been insistent that the Labour Government had broken pledges and abandoned its responsibilities.[73] He had himself visited the Gulf in 1969 and had repeatedly stated that the British must regain their nerve and restore Britain's good name. At one point he

[71] Bullard to Weir, Confidential, 29 April 1969, FO 1016/873.

[72] Visiting 'every corner of Bahrain' to ascertain public sentiment, Signor Winspeare Guicciardi 'conducted the operation impeccably' (Weir to FCO, Confidential, 31 December 1970, FCO 8/1638).

[73] On Heath and the possible reversal of British policy, see FCO 8/979.

said to Geoffrey Arthur: '[W]e're going to change policy and the F.O. should be working out how to do it.'[74] Heath's robust and consistent attitude, however, was not entirely shared by his colleagues. Sir Alec Douglas-Home, who had been the previous Tory Prime Minister, now returned to office as Foreign Secretary. Douglas-Home entirely sympathized with Heath's attitude, but he was also realistic. He took the view that he and his colleagues had inherited a situation not of their own making. He wanted neither to pursue Labour's aim, as he saw it, of cutting loose, nor to reverse course and become, in his own phrase, a permanent nanny. He aimed to impose as rigorous a control as possible over events in the Gulf, to move forward towards unifying the seven Trucial States without Bahrain and Qatar, and to retain rather than break the military and economic links. The British military presence would become less visible by the removal of land forces, but troops would still be available by sea and air. Douglas-Home also took a relatively open-minded view of the disputed islands in the Gulf. Shortly after assuming office, he and Denis Wright met with the Shah in Brussels; this was a crucial meeting. So adamant was the Shah, Home concluded, the British would simply have to hope that Iran would not seize the islands before the British departure.[75] Otherwise Britain would find itself at war with Iran because of the protective treaties. Home hoped to avoid a direct conflict by persuading the Iranians at least to wait until after the British departure before taking over the islands. He pitched his views on the Gulf in a way that would win the Prime Minister's acquiescence. But the main reason why the return of the Tories marked a watershed was because Home also persuaded Heath to summon Sir William Luce out of retirement to try to resolve the outstanding issues involving Iran and Saudi Arabia and to press forward towards union.

Luce was one of the last great Proconsuls.[76] He had a legendary reputation in the Sudan Political Service, where he began his career, and

---

[74] Quoted in McCarthy to Crawford, Confidential and Personal, 8 May 1969, FO 1016/756.

[75] Minute by Home, Confidential, 13 July 1970, PREM 15/538:

> For the Shah a satisfactory arrangement over the islands is the nub of his future relationship both with the Trucial States and with the Arabs as a whole . . . A satisfactory arrangement over the islands is, in the Shah's words, a *sine qua non* for the wholehearted Iranian support for a Union.

By repeating the word 'satisfactory' the Shah left no doubt that he meant annexation.

[76] For Luce, see especially Balfour-Paul, *End of Empire in the Middle East;* for the evolution of his views on the Gulf, see Kelly, *Arabia, the Gulf and the West,* pp. 80–82.

as Governor of Aden and later as Political Resident in the Gulf. In a sense, he is a controversial historical figure because in the 1960s he seemed to be a throwback to an earlier age. For example, those who knew him in the early 1960s, when the British had occupied Kuwait to prevent a takeover by Iraq, and who believed the British intervention to be a mistake, viewed him as a paternalistic Imperial personality whose time had past. These critics include (Sir) Marrack Goulding, who was in Kuwait at the time.[77] Others, such as Anthony Parsons, who were equally as anti-Empire, found him to be a forward-looking, pragmatic, and sympathetic personality. Parsons records in his memoirs how he was won over after initial scepticism and how Luce proved to be the saving grace in an exceedingly difficult and complicated situation.[78] There is evidence in the Gulf Residency archives that Luce's reappearance was welcomed among the Political Agents and that they themselves had pressed for his appointment. Parsons wrote in 1969 that he favoured 'enlisting the services of Bill Luce as a sort of father confessor and progress chaser'.[79] And there was another appointment of significance. Sir Geoffrey Arthur, who had served as Ambassador in Kuwait and then as Middle Eastern Under-Secretary at the Foreign and Commonwealth Office, now in the summer of 1970 became the last Political Resident in the Gulf. This was an exceptionally strong team.

Luce set out first and foremost to create a union of Bahrain, Qatar, and the seven Trucial States, even though Bahrain and Qatar would probably pursue separate paths to independence.[80] He knew that he could advise and cajole but had no authority to compel. But he used his powers of persuasion to the utmost. Luce could give the impression to Arabs and others, including the Americans, that he was taking them entirely into his confidence while giving away nothing. He indefatigably toured the Gulf, visiting all parties, and flew back and forth to London and to points as far away as Washington.[81] He was a figure

[77] Luce 'was not a man to whom the surrender of Empire came naturally' (Sir Marrack Goulding, 'Kuwait 1961', typescript, Middle East Centre, St. Antony's College, Oxford).

[78] Parsons, *They Say the Lion,* 107 ff.

[79] Parsons to Donal McCarthy, Confidential, 4 June 1969, FO 1016/756.

[80] For an important, detailed survey of this phase of the British disengagement (1969–71), see P. R. H. Wright to FCO, Confidential, 26 July 1971, FCO 8/1562.

[81] Luce visited Washington in January 1971. Guy Millard of the British Embassy wrote to him afterwards that the Americans were grateful for his providing 'a comprehensive picture' of the region because they

> realise that the Gulf will shortly change from a relative backwater in terms of U.S. political interests to a highly charged area of the world with all sorts of divisive problems
> . . . There is a widespread ignorance here about what goes on in that part of the world.

worthy of the description made earlier of the hero in *Pilgrim's Progress,* making his way through sloughs of jealousy and greed. The Political Agent who made that comment, Ranald Boyle, previously in the Sudan Political Service, wrote that 'the whole exercise seems to me . . . to be very "Arab". Everyone is trying to promote his own interest, and generating a tremendous amount of heat in the process.'[82] What Luce did was to reason patiently with each of the rulers, suggesting, in a way reminiscent of Benjamin Franklin during the American Revolution, that it was in their own interest to hang together because otherwise they would all hang separately. In the autumn and winter of 1970–71, the detailed discussions on constitutional and other matters among the rulers and the Political Agents began to pay off.

Luce was well placed with both the Shah, whose support he needed if there was going to be any form of union at all, and King Faisal, who was indispensable to the project, since both Bahrain and Qatar required Saudi backing to join the Arab League as well as the United Nations. Luce had ended his tenure as Political Resident before the collapse in Aden, and thus was not tarred with the brush, in Saudi eyes, of the Aden scuttle. To King Faisal, the paramount goal was to avoid another Aden, indeed another Palestine.[83] But though Luce was on good terms with both King Faisal and the Shah, there were certain

---

Even within the State Department, whose Arabists are very knowledgeable and experienced, there are few who know the Gulf.

Millard added that Joseph Sisco (the Assistant Secretary of State in charge of Middle Eastern affairs) 'showed a splendidly old-fashioned enthusiasm for British frigates and troops' (Millard to Luce, Confidential, 20 January 1971, FCO 8/1583).

Within the US government, the clearest response to the problem of British withdrawal came from Walt W. Rostow, the President's Special Assistant on National Security. 'We don't want to have to replace the British', he wrote in January 1968, 'and we don't want the Russians there.' The Americans would have to work with the Shah of Iran and with King Faisal of Saudi Arabia as well as the British to secure the continuing Western position in the Gulf: 'We must count on the Shah and Faisal.' As for the British, Rostow lamented the impending demise of the Pax Britannica, but it was not yet a spent force. The British would be in the Gulf for another three years. Before their departure in 1971, he hoped that they would get this message: '[D]on't rock the boat any more than you already have; help us buy time for the locals to work out their own arrangements for the future.' Rostow put forward two specific aims, using much the same language: 'First, we want the British to leave their treaties and political relationships intact to help calm local rulers' feelings of being deserted. Second . . . we think the best tack is for them to sit tight with their present relationships and let the locals come up with their own scheme for the future' (memoranda by Walt W. Rostow, Secret, 31 January and 6 February 1968, *Foreign Relations of the United States, 1964–1968,* XXI, pp. 268–69 and 278–79).

[82] Boyle to Balfour-Paul (Bahrain), Confidential, 28 March 1968, FO 1016/859.

[83] 'The two things about which the King felt strongly were Palestine and Aden. He kept on saying that a situation similar to that in Aden must be avoided in the Gulf' (minute by A. A. Acland, 13 May 1971, FCO 8/1558).

things that were intractable. These included the Saudi claim to the Buraimi oasis and Iran's claim to the disputed islands in the Gulf, which the British insisted belonged to the Rulers of Ras al Khaimah and Sharjah. Luce hoped that the Saudis would simply remain silent on the issue of the historic Buraimi dispute. At one point, far from staying passive, the Saudis actually increased their claims, but otherwise the British calculation that the Saudis would remain 'inert' proved accurate. The disputed islands were another matter. Luce wrote that the British had to avoid giving the Arabs the impression of a 'sell out' of the islands, 'or even one of the islands', to Iran because of the 'very serious effects indeed on our relations with the Arabs generally'.[84] The islands of Abu Musa and the Tunbs were regarded as Arab territory, especially by Iraq, but also by radical Arab states as far away as Libya. The takeover by Iran would be the surrender of Arab land.

Luce systematically studied the problem and submitted two complementary reports, which included best- and worst-case scenarios, but also stated clearly the British goal of maintaining access to Gulf oil.[85] The solution lay in the independence of Bahrain and Qatar and in the formation of a union of the seven Trucial States. The groundwork had been laid about a year before Luce's appointment, in a seminal study by Julian Bullard, the Political Agent in Dubai. Bullard held that a union of the seven Trucial States—without Qatar and Bahrain—would be a much more logical proposition.

> It is a much more modest objective, and in some ways a more plausible one. The Seven are geographically contiguous, and they already possess certain elements of a unitary structure . . . Movement of persons and goods from state to state is relatively free, and the only important gap in the main road system, between Abu Dhabi and Dubai, will soon be on the way to being closed.

> The seven states are at different stages of political development, perhaps; but their international status is the same. The history and tribal background are intermingled. All this is true of the Seven, but not the Eight or Nine.[86]

The defence force in the Trucial States, the Trucial Scouts, 1,700 men strong, would form the army of the new state. The British would withdraw military units but would enter into defence arrangements that

[84] Luce to Arthur, Secret and Personal, 17 December 1970, FO 1016/759.

[85] See 'Report on Consultations', Secret, 2 October 1970; and 'Policy in the Persian Gulf', Secret, 4 and 20 November 1970, PREM 15/538.

[86] J. L. Bullard, 'The Future of the Trucial States', Confidential, 8 July 1969, FO 1016/876.

would provide naval and air assistance, the training of new military and police units, and contract service by British military and police officers. The British presence would thus become less visible, but it would still be there.

On one point Luce came into conflict with the Prime Minister. Heath followed these matters with a far greater grasp of detail than had Harold Wilson, and Heath disagreed with Luce that all land forces should be withdrawn.[87] Heath believed, along with Julian Amery and others of the Imperialist wing of the Conservative Party, that Britain could continue to station battalions and hold enclaves regardless of world opinion. But in this respect Heath was like Churchill, and did not override his military and political advisers. The Cabinet decided that the withdrawal would take place by 1 December 1971. Heath defended the decision in the House of Commons in March.[88] The Luce plan of withdrawal survived intact, and the United Arab Emirates came into existence in December 1971 on target—with the exception of one of the northern sheikhdoms, Ras al Khaimah, which joined shortly afterwards the next year.

There was a dramatic prelude to independence. Sir Denis Wright had been consistently pessimistic about the disputed islands. He had reiterated that the Shah 'would go for the islands as soon as we left'.[89] Wright proved to be wrong in his prediction by one day. The British departed on schedule on 1 December. The day before, Iran had seized the disputed islands.[90] The Shah thus managed to deflect Arab anger towards the British on the last day of British sway. Iraq broke off relations with Britain, and Colonel Qaddafi appropriated the holdings of British Petroleum in Libya.[91] But the United Arab Emirates survived.

[87] See Heath's notation on Luce's memoranda of 4 November 1970, PREM 15/538.

[88] *Parliamentary Debates* (Commons), 2 March 1971, cols. 1423–24.

[89] FO meeting, 26 March 1968, FO 1016/955.

[90] Was there collusion between the British and the Shah that he would wait until the eve of British departure before taking over the Tunbs? All of the available evidence suggests the opposite. Luce explicitly stated in his communications to the Rulers as well as in his secret minutes within the FCO, both before and after the Iranian occupation, that there was no agreement. The situation probably appeared obvious that Iran had nothing to gain by going to war with Britain. By waiting until the day before the protective treaties expired, the Shah merely calculated that the British would still bear responsibility but could do nothing. Luce afterwards explained that 'HMG could not reasonably be expected to defend the Islands for one day, and then to withdraw' (record of meeting with representatives from Kuwait, Confidential, 3 December 1971, FCO 8/1777).

[91] It is useful to place the Libyan response in the context of the death of Nasser in 1970: 'Qadhafi . . . sees himself as Nasser's successor as leader of the Arab world' (minute by R. C. Hope-Jones, 19 April 1971, FCO 39/769). In Baghdad, the British Ambassador, Glen Balfour-Paul, shortly before he was expelled, summed up the mood in Iraq as well as the British dilemma:

It all turned out, as Sir Geoffrey Arthur commented, exactly as the British had hoped all along but could hardly dare to believe would happen: a new state on good terms with Britain, no sharp breaks or ruptures, and the new union still informally within the British Imperial system.[92]

Despite the genial courtesy, superficial or not, of that part of the populace . . . which has not yet been barbarised by misgovernment, and despite the cultivated charm of many of the better educated, the Iraqis do not laugh as readily as other Arab peoples I have lived with and there is always a detectable sense of suppressed rage or resentment in the Iraqi atmosphere . . . Almost by definition all Governments in Iraq are bad; and certainly by definition they govern by intimidation . . . The present Ba'athist model . . . is not, though nasty enough, as nasty as it is sometimes painted. And there is something to be said for keeping hold of it for fear of finding something worse.
Balfour-Paul to FCO, Confidential, 11 December 1971, FCO 17/1541.

[92] Arthur to FCO, 'The Independence of Bahrain', Confidential, 23 September 1971, FCO 8/1642.

HISTORIOGRAPHY

32

ROBINSON AND GALLAGHER
AND THEIR CRITICS

In 1953 John A. Gallagher and Ronald E. Robinson published their celebrated article 'The Imperialism of Free Trade', in which they argued that the nature of British imperialism in the nineteenth century remained constant. Seven years later appeared their magnum opus, *Africa and the Victorians*. The subtitle of the English edition, 'The Official Mind of Imperialism', reflects the content of the book. The subtitle of the American edition, 'The Climax of Imperialism in the Dark Continent', dramatizes the theme of continuity. In 1962 they sharply distilled their views on nineteenth-century expansion in a chapter in the *New Cambridge Modern History;* a decade later, Ronald Robinson advanced the argument into an 'excentric', or collaborative, theory of imperialism, which holds that imperialism in large part is the function of non-Western collaboration and resistance.[1] More than anything else, collaboration and resistance determine the incidence, the form, and the rise and fall of imperialism.

The accomplishment of Robinson and Gallagher has been hailed by Eric Stokes of Cambridge University as no less than a historiographical revolution, a new viewpoint in the history of the subject.[2] They themselves believe that they have achieved a unified theory of imperialism that is sustained in the case study of *Africa and the Victorians*. However one judges the work of Robinson, now the Beit Professor of the History of the British Commonwealth at Oxford University, and Gallagher, now Vere Harmsworth Professor of Imperial and Naval History at Cambridge University, there can be no question that their influence has been far-reaching.

In general, Robinson and Gallagher have attempted to replace

---

[1] John Gallagher and Ronald Robinson, 'The Imperialism of Free Trade', *Economic History Review,* 2nd series, 6, 1 (1953), pp. 1–15; Ronald Robinson and John Gallagher with Alice Denny [Mrs. Robinson], *Africa and the Victorians: The Official Mind of Imperialism* (London, 1961); for the transition between 'The Imperialism of Free Trade' and the book, see 'Imperial Problems in British Politics' by Ronald Robinson in *Cambridge History of the British Empire,* III, pp. 127–80; R. E. Robinson and J. Gallagher, 'The Partition of Africa', in *New Cambridge Modern History,* XI, chap. 22; Ronald Robinson, 'Non-European Foundations of European Imperialism: Sketch for a Theory of Collaboration', in E. R. J. Owen and R. B. Sutcliffe, eds., *Studies in the Theory of Imperialism* (London, 1972), chap. 5.

[2] Eric Stokes, 'Imperialism and the Scramble for Africa: The New View', a pamphlet published by the Historical Association of Rhodesia and Nyasaland (Local Series 10, 1963); see by the same author also especially 'Late Nineteenth-Century Colonial Expansion and the Attack on the Theory of Economic Imperialism: A Case of Mistaken Identity?' *Historical Journal,* 12, 2 (1969), pp. 285–301.

traditional interpretations of imperialism with a new set of hypotheses that, they believe, is nearer the facts. They have tried to bridge the gap between theory and the historical evidence. The bedrock idea that underlies all their later work is to be found in the 1953 article. It argues for the continuity of British expansion and policy, but it also suggests the discontinuity of imperialist activity and its form or mode of expansion, according to circumstances in countries beyond Europe. Increasingly in their later work they stress the trigger action of non-European resistance. Response and collaboration introduce a random element into the process of imperialism, which, before Robinson and Gallagher, had been regarded from a narrow, Eurocentric point of view. Some of their critics have charged that they have merely inverted the old chronology of mid-Victorian anti-imperialism and late-Victorian imperialism, paradoxically producing the 'Imperialism of Free Trade' and late-Victorian indifference to empire. What they have done, in fact, is something far more sophisticated and fundamental:

1. They have asserted that the urge to imperialism in Europe was merely one factor governing the timing and scope of imperialist activity abroad. Thereby they have challenged virtually all existing theories.
2. As they have developed their theories, they have argued that the process was governed as much as or more by non-European politics and economics than by European.
3. They have concluded that the phasing and changing forms of imperialism were unlikely to have conformed to chronological periods of opinion and policy in the expanding societies of Europe.

Africa and the Victorians was conceived as the acid test for this argumentation; it led them to unanticipated conclusions. In their investigation, they discovered that strategic considerations were the most common ones in the calculations of the men who carved up Africa. These strategic calculations were to an extent phantasmagorical, reflecting subjective interpretations of the history of European expansion. British statesmen in fact suffered from neuroses about holding what they had inherited. Misapprehension and blunders in dealing with non-European crises, without understanding them, often inadvertently turned decisions not to advance into advances; very often, high-flying strategic notions were covers for these blunders.

The result of *Africa and the Victorians* as a test case can be summed up in these propositions:

1. The greatest common factor in the partitioners' calculations was the search for strategic security in the world.

2. What compelled them to expand, however, were not these strategic interests as such, but crises in Egyptian and South African politics, which seemed to dictate that these interests must be secured by extension of territory.
3. The changes in Anglo-French relations and in the diplomacy within the European power balance stemming from the Egyptian crisis drove the partitioners in the same direction.
4. A distinction must be made between the 'motives' of the partitioners and the 'causes' of the African partition. The most compelling motives were strategic, although of course they did not exclude commercial interests or philanthropic interests in some regions. The causes of the partition of Africa, on the other hand, lie in the changes in Egyptian and South African domestic politics rather than in intensified expansion drives in Europe. These changes resulting from African crises in turn produced changes in the relations of Britain, France, and Germany.

The chapter in the *New Cambridge Modern History,* an elaboration of the book, attempts to generalize on these points from the British to the other European participants in the 'Scramble for Africa'. Robinson's 1972 essay develops the argument to its full implications, from acquiring empires to ruling and losing them.

More specifically, Robinson and Gallagher attack the traditional notion that 'imperialism' is the formal rule or control by one people or nation over others. In their view, historians have been mesmerized by formal empire and maps of the world with regions coloured red. The bulk of British emigration, trade, and capital went to areas outside the formal British Empire. A key to the thought of Robinson and Gallagher is the idea of empire 'informally if possible and formally if necessary'. In *Africa and the Victorians* they develop the argument of imperialism and sub-imperialisms—in other words, forces not fully amenable to metropolitan control, such as the foreign community and bondholders in Egypt, Cecil Rhodes in South Africa, and monopolistic commercial enterprises such as those of George Goldie on the Niger and King Leopold on the Congo. They argue that to understand late-nineteenth-century imperialism, it is important to grasp the significance of certain key events, such as the occupation of Egypt by the British in 1882. In this case in particular, British imperialism should be seen to some extent as a response to indigenous nationalism. The essay in the *New Cambridge Modern History* extends the argument of unanticipated local resistance, which drags in the metropolitan powers. What alters is not British policy but conditions abroad. Robinson and Gallagher do not deny that steadily mounting economic pressures led to a steady increase of colonies, but that the spectacle of the Scramble can be understood fully only by perceiving the difficulty of reining back sub-imperialisms and dealing with proto-nationalist movements. As the arguments develop and the emphasis shifts, it is useful to bear in mind that continuity is one of the dominant principles of 'the official mind'. Another is that of parsimony, or economy. British statesmen persistently exercised economy of effort and expense. The official mind itself can be described as the way in which the bureaucracy perceives its own history, the memory of past triumphs and past disasters. It possesses its own self-image and aspirations. It appraises present problems obliquely and subjectively. It is capable of translating economic interests into strategic concepts. It is a force in itself. It can be a cause of imperialism.

Theses of 'The Imperialism of Free Trade': Continuity and Regionalism

The point of overriding importance in 'The Imperialism of Free Trade' is the argument of continuity: 'a fundamental continuity in British expansion throughout the nineteenth century'. The character of this continuity or the nature of imperialism itself is determined by the changing circumstances at various times and in different regions—in their words, imperialism 'is largely decided by the various and changing relationships between the political and economic elements of expansion in any particular time and place'. The product of this interaction is imperialism, which remains constant. This interpretation constitutes a challenge to the basic idea of periodization in history and flies in the face of traditional views. Taking on at once the major analysts of the subject, Robinson and Gallagher attack the concept of the 'new imperialism' espoused by such diverse writers as John A. Hobson, V. I. Lenin, Leonard Woolf, Parker T. Moon, Robert L. Schuyler, and William L. Langer. Those students of imperialism, whatever their purpose in writing, all saw a fundamental difference between the imperialist impulses of the mid- and late-Victorian eras. Langer perhaps best summarized the importance of making the distinction of late-nineteenth-century imperialism when he wrote in 1935:

> Centuries hence, when interests in the details of European diplomacy in the pre-war period will have faded completely, this period will still stand out as the crucial epoch during which the nations of the western world extended their political, economic and cultural influence over Africa and over large parts of Asia . . . in the larger sense the story is more than the story of rivalry between European imperialisms; it is the story of European aggression and advance in the non-European parts of the world.[3]

[3] William L. Langer, *The Diplomacy of Imperialism* (New York, 1956 edn.), pp. 67 and 96.

In most important accounts, the partition of Africa in twenty years' time stands as the very symbol of new forces of imperialism and as a watershed in modern history.

With this watershed Robinson and Gallagher will have nothing to do. On the contrary, they demonstrate the disadvantages to the concept of the 'new imperialism'. Looking at maps in imperial colours in order to judge the nature of imperialism, they argue, is like gauging the size of icebergs only by the parts above the waterline. With this remarkable analogy, they are able immediately to expose the central error of earlier historians such as John R. Seeley and Hugh Edward Egerton and untold numbers of historians of the British Empire whose interpretations have been guided by constitutional and racial concepts—the same as those that originally inspired the imperial federation movement. The mid-Victorian empire was informal as well as formal, economic as much as it was political. Leaving aside for the moment the powerful argument of informal expansion and control, it is important to point out that Robinson and Gallagher rightly criticize many conventional historians who see the mid-Victorian empire almost exclusively as one of indifference towards colonial activity. Again, this time by use of an arresting series of facts, Robinson and Gallagher in a few sentences launch a frontal attack on the myth of the static nature of the mid-Victorian empire in even its formal and constitutional structure:

> Between 1841 and 1851 Great Britain occupied or annexed New Zealand, the Gold Coast, Labuan, Natal, the Punjab, Sind and Hong Kong. In the next twenty years British control was asserted over Berar, Oudh, Lower Burma and Kowloon, over Lagos and the neighbourhood of Sierra Leone, over Basutoland, Griqualand and the Transvaal; and new colonies were established in Queensland and British Columbia.[4]

[4] 'Imperialism of Free Trade', pp. 2–3. For an interesting review of the historiographical debate about the Free Trade era, see C. C. Eldridge, *England's Mission: The Imperial Idea in the Age of Gladstone and Disraeli, 1868–1880* (Chapel Hill, N.C., 1973). In general, Eldridge's book gives support to the Robinson and Gallagher thesis that events in the overseas world caused a defensive reaction and brought about a transformation of attitude towards empire. For another valuable recent survey, see B. A. Knox, 'Reconsidering Mid-Victorian Imperialism', *Journal of Imperial and Commonwealth History*, 1, 2 (January 1973). See also D. A. Low, *Lion Rampant* (London, 1973) and A. G. L. Shaw, ed., *Great Britain and the Colonies, 1815–1865* (London, 1970). One other recent publication also merits special comment in relation to Robinson and Gallagher's effort to reverse the traditional ethnocentric vision of the partition of Africa. G. N. Uzoigwe, in an account significant in his own view as the first attempt by an African to provide a comprehensive analysis of the Scramble, describes the approach of Robinson and Gallagher as only 'a more serious way of reasserting Seeley's thesis that Britain acquired its empire in a state of absentmindedness' (*Britain and the Conquest of Africa* [Ann Arbor, 1974], p. 24).

They thus provide a dazzling reminder that there should be nothing especially surprising about additional territorial acquisition during the last two or three decades of the century. The question is whether the case is strong enough to destroy the old concept of a 'new imperialism', or whether their theory of continuity can be applied—as later in the *New Cambridge Modern History* they emphatically imply it can— to the colonial experiences of other countries as well as to Great Britain. The force of the argument of 'The Imperialism of Free Trade' derives from the history of the British Empire. The test of its universality must lie in explaining not only the unique features of Great Britain as the greatest imperial power of the nineteenth century but also the imperialism of Europe and of the United States and Japan as well. The phenomenon of late-nineteenth-century imperialism was worldwide.

No one has more clearly expressed doubts about the universality of the Robinson and Gallagher concept than Professor Geoffrey Barraclough:

> The central fact about the 'new imperialism' is that it was a worldwide movement, in which all the industrialized nations, including the United States and Japan, were involved. If it is approached from the angle of Great Britain, as historians have largely been inclined to do, it is easy to underestimate its force and novelty; for the reactions of Britain, as the greatest existing imperial power, were primarily defensive, its statesmen were reluctant to acquire new territories, and when they did so their purpose was usually either to safe-guard existing possessions or to prevent the control of strategic routes passing into the hands of other powers. But this defensive, and in some ways negative, attitude is accounted for by the special circumstances of Great Britain, and was not typical. It was from other powers that the impetus behind the 'new imperialism' came—from powers that calculated that Britain's far-flung empire was the source of its might and that their own new-found industrial strength both entitled them to and necessitated their acquiring a 'place in the Sun'.[5]

As Barraclough points out, no one would deny the importance of the expansion of Europe's economy, technology, languages, and ideas throughout the world. The result probably constitutes the major revolution of our times. The legacies of European imperialism are undeniable. The question is whether there can be a single explanation and whether the theory of continuity has universal applicability. Put a different way, the question is whether late-nineteenth-century imperi-

[5] Geoffrey Barraclough, *An Introduction to Contemporary History* (Harmondsworth, 1967 edn.), pp. 56–67.

alism manifested an unprecedented urge to empire, or whether, for example, the partition of Africa merely represented the culmination of earlier expansionist tendencies. There lie some of the crucial areas of controversy raised by Robinson and Gallagher.

Imperial Security, Sub-Imperialisms, and Proto-Nationalisms

If the imperialism of the 1880s and 1890s represented no real break with previous patterns of expansion, what then were the immediate causes of the Scramble? The answer can be found in part in the term 'sub-imperialisms', or, in other words, the actions of the local agents of imperialism and their indigenous collaborators in such places as the frontiers of southern British Africa. 'Local crises' at the peripheries of the empire precipitate the intervention of the imperial power. Despite the importance of this theme, it is crucial to note that it is subordinate to the grand design of the book, which may be summed up as 'imperial security'. British statesmen acted on strategic calculations in a way quite differently from what they would have done had they based their decisions on economic advantages as such. Economic interests were involved but were not determinative. 'The official mind' translated economic calculations into strategic concepts drawn from long-rooted experience of the worldwide empire. Thus Robinson and Gallagher differ radically from those historians who emphasize designs for economic exploitation. Their view is also the reverse of those who hold that the calling of the 'white man's burden' played a central part in the European advance into the interior of Africa. Leaving aside for the moment their implicit attack on the theorists of economic imperialism, Robinson and Gallagher believe, as Sydney Kanya-Forstner has pointed out, that, far from espousing the 'civilizing mission', British statesmen saw that Africa could not be transformed in the British image. Lord Salisbury, like Lord Milner in the later era of the First World War, pessimistically adopted the policy of 'we hold what we have'. To protect the existing empire in the East, the British were driven into strategic annexations and spheres of influence that eventually extended British power and lines of communication through the 'Southern British World' from the Cape to Cairo to Singapore.

In 'The Partition of Africa', Robinson and Gallagher extend their arguments to apply to the European powers as well as the British, and they expand the dimension of their analysis to take account of the African (and Asian) side of the equation. The counter-theme of sub-imperialism is proto-nationalism. In the long run it develops into their ultimate argument that nationalism is a continuation of imperialism, which subsumes the argument of imperial security.

Robinson and Gallagher consistently held that the character of European imperialism fundamentally did not change but responded to non-European nationalist resistance of both neo-traditional and modern kinds. While taking into account rivalry with France and other powers in such areas as West Africa and the Congo, they contend that African resistance more than anything else brought about the transition from informal to formal empire and helped to trigger the Scramble.

> Imbroglios with Egyptian proto-nationalists and thence with Islamic revivals across the whole of the Sudan drew the powers into an expansion of their own in East and West Africa. Thousands of miles to the south, English efforts to compress Afrikaner nationalists into an obsolete imperial design set off a second sequence of expansion in southern Africa.[6]

As Eric Stokes has pointed out, this proposition reverses the Eurocentric interpretation of historians such as Moon, Langer, and A. J. P. Taylor, who hold that tensions within Europe generated the Scramble for colonies.[7] After the dramatic insight of *Africa and the Victorians* and 'The Partition of Africa', Africa can no longer be seen as a blank map on which Europeans freely wrote their will.[8] In overturning the traditional historiographical assumption that pressures within Europe produced European imperialism in Africa, Robinson and Gallagher attempt to prove that the idea of economic exploitation came after the event of political takeover, as if almost by afterthought.[9]

---

[6] 'The Partition of Africa', p. 594.

[7] For example, here is a classic statement of Europe's imperialism in Africa being no more than a 'safety valve' of Europe's energies and explosive troubles: 'All the Great Powers except Austria-Hungary found a safe channel for their exuberance outside Europe. They stumbled on this solution by chance, without foresight' (A. J. P. Taylor, *The Struggle for Mastery in Europe* [Oxford, 1954], p. 256). Taylor has remained singularly consistent in his argument that 'the age of imperialism' merely postponed the final struggle for mastery of Europe. See his comment below, 'The Meanings of Imperialism'.

[8] See Stokes, 'Late Nineteenth-Century Colonial Expansion', especially pp. 286–87, for the other principal assumptions that Stokes believes the authors have successfully challenged. Like Robinson and Gallagher's interpretation of Victorian statesmen, there may be a subjective element in what Stokes thinks they should have attacked.

[9] Ibid.: '[I]t was first and foremost a political phenomenon.' For clear objections to the political interpretation of Robinson and Gallagher in favour of one of economic factors being important but not determinative, see W. J. Mommsen, 'Nationale und ökonomische Faktoren im britischen Imperialismus vor 1914', *Historische Zeitschrift*, 206, 3 (1968). For another German commentary especially valuable for the perspective on continuity, see Karl Rohe, 'Ursachen und

This polemical argument against the theories of economic imperialism leads Robinson and Gallagher along with David Fieldhouse into a direct assault on Hobson, who viewed British expansion as synonymous with attempts at exploitation.[10] Here the point should be emphasized that Hobson's theory of imperialism differed from Lenin's. Lenin gave a subtler explanation. According to Eric Stokes:

> [I]t is too easily forgotten that the theory of economic or capitalist imperialism does not stand or fall on the authority of Hobson but of Lenin. A scrutiny of Lenin's principal writings reveals that no error could be more fundamental than to suppose that he was putting forward the same model of imperialism as Hobson. In the vital question of chronology Lenin made it plain that the era of monopoly finance capitalism did not coincide with the scramble for colonies between 1870 and 1900 but came after it.[11]

In this view, Robinson and Gallagher as well as Fieldhouse err in seeing 'the conflation of arguments of Hobson and Lenin . . . [as] a single model'. After reviewing Lenin's writings and concluding that he was less concerned with providing a theoretical analysis of the Scramble for colonies than in explaining the genesis of the First World War, Stokes goes on to isolate the economic argument of Robinson and Gallagher, thereby putting it into perspective:

> Robinson and Gallagher rightly pour scorn on the notion that economic interests were anything like powerful enough to bring about a historical phenomenon so remarkable as the scramble for Africa, but it is another thing to say they had no place at all, and *sub silentio* they admit their importance . . .
>
> Only in Egypt and East Africa were commercial interests clearly of subordinate importance. The 'official mind' may have placed considerations of strategy and security uppermost in its calculations of African policy, but it would be difficult to show that it acted very differently in that part of the world where Robinson and Gallagher regard the British economic stake as preponderant, and for whose

---

Bedingungen des modernen britischen Imperialismus vor 1914', in Wolfgang J. Mommsen, ed., *Der moderne Imperialismus* (Stuttgart, 1971).

[10] See D. K. Fieldhouse, '"Imperialism": An Historiographical Revision', *Economic History Review*, 2nd series, 14, 2 (1961); see also Harvey Mitchell, 'Hobson Revisited', *Journal of the History of Ideas*, 26, 3 (July–September 1965); Bernard Porter, *Critics of Empire: British Radical Attitudes to Colonialism in Africa, 1895–1914* (London, 1968); and Hugh Stretton, *The Political Sciences* (London, 1969), chap. 4.

[11] Stokes, 'Late Nineteenth-Century Colonial Expansion', p. 289.

strategic defence they argue Britain's African policy was shaped . . .
in Asia, as in Africa, the agencies of expansion were essentially economic and provoked the crises that drew the statesmen on to the
scene . . . when free of the elements of exaggeration Lenin's account
of the colonial scramble is not one of narrow economic determin-
ism, nor is Robinson's and Gallagher's one of simple non-economic
motivation.[12]

Reduced from complexity, the interpretations both of Lenin and of
Robinson and Gallagher have similarities. '[W]hen the arguments of
both Lenin and of Robinson and Gallagher have been freed from the
elements of caricature', Stokes concludes, 'their general analyses of
European colonialism between 1870 and 1914 exhibit a surprising degree of correspondence. Lenin, it would appear, was no Leninist; he
too stands the classical model of economic imperialism on its head.'[13]
If this interpretation is accurate, then Robinson and Gallagher might
be considered non-Leninist Leninists, and their contemptuous rejection of Marxist interpretation of imperialism deserves rescue from the
relegation of a single footnote in *Africa and the Victorians*.[14] It is a good
point about Lenin and a good joke on Robinson and Gallagher. They
are anything but Leninists.

With vivid recognition of the seriousness of the attack, V. G. Kiernan
in the *Socialist Register* commented on the way Robinson and Gallagher
have left Lenin's bones 'bleaching in the Sahara'.[15] Where else except
at the North and South poles could one find less evidence of capitalist
exploitation? According to this engaging and sardonic critique, Robinson and Gallagher have failed to meet Hobson and Lenin fairly on
their own ground. In a supremely sophisticated manner, the evidence
has been rigged. Robinson and Gallagher have based their interpretation on 'the official mind', which they erroneously assume is the

[12] Stokes, 'Late Nineteenth-Century Colonial Expansion', pp. 292–93.

[13] Ibid., p. 301.

[14] *Africa and the Victorians*, p. 15, note 1. For a Marxist critique of Robinson and Gallagher,
see Tom Kemp, *Theories of Imperialism* (London, 1967), p. 154. Since so many critics have commented on the theories of economic imperialism being compressed into a single note, perhaps
it is of interest to note that in the original manuscript the authors had devoted an entire chapter exposing what they believe to be the Eurocentric and false assumptions of existing theories
of imperialism. They argued that these theories are not based on empirical historical study but
are theories about European societies. The publishers, however, insisted on reducing the manuscript by one-third. The chapter was reduced to a note. Robinson and Gallagher did this on
grounds that it was more important to present the historical evidence than to debate, in their
view, already discredited theories. I am indebted to Professor Robinson for information on this
point.

[15] V. G. Kiernan, 'Farewells to Empire', *Socialist Register, 1964* (New York, 1964), pp. 259–79.

originator of policy: 'It is . . . a delusion of archive-searchers, who in-
hale a subtly intoxicating atmosphere and need its stimulus to keep
them going, to suppose that ministers and under-secretaries are careful to leave behind them all the documents required for a verdict on
their actions.'[16] Laying the ground rules that evidence must consist
mainly of the official records, Robinson and Gallagher next select the
part of the world where the capitalists could least expect to make a
profit. Kiernan thus blasts what he believes to be Robinson and Gallagher's specious reasoning.

> [O]ne acquittal leads easily to another. Capitalism did not really
> covet its neighbour's sand. Therefore capitalism cannot really have
> coveted its neighbour's oil, or his coal, or his rubber, or his ox, or
> his ass, or his manservant, or his maid-servant, or anything that was
> his. Henry VIII did not chop off the head of his last wife. Therefore
> Henry VIII cannot have chopped off the heads of any of his wives.
> Twice two is not five. Therefore twice three cannot be six.[17]

With logic of this sort, Robinson and Gallagher find that the defence
of India is the guiding thread through the diplomatic labyrinth. But
Kiernan believes it to be a subtly misleading explanation:

> What it overlooks is that the cry of 'India in danger' was a convenient
> one for financiers and concession-hunters, as well as historians; for
> anyone with an eye on Burmese timber, Yunnan railways, Malayan
> rubber, or Persian oil. It was a plausible excuse for all businessmen
> found in compromising situations, an unanswerable claim for offi-
> cial backing. If there had been space-travellers in those days India
> would have been a compulsory reason for Britain to take part in the
> race to the moon.[18]

Using official sources that echo the strategic defence of India, Robinson and Gallagher treat the policy makers as political computers
with no recognition of the immense influence of the financiers. Their
account of local crises thus, in Kiernan's judgement, totally misrepre-
sents the real forces at work:

> The assertion that the British Government did not desire to occupy
> Egypt only amounts to saying that it would have preferred to go on

[16] Ibid., p. 265. For similar comment, see Christopher Fyfe in *Irish Historical Studies,* 13 (March
1962), pp. 93–94. In Fyfe's view, *Africa and the Victorians* 'smells of the Public Record Office (a
nice but limited smell), not at all of Africa'.

[17] Kiernan, 'Farewells to Empire', p. 269.

[18] Ibid., p. 270.

with the cheaper and discreeter method of letting Egypt be exploited through a native puppet; just as U.S. marines are only sent into a banana-republic when the local dictator fails to deliver the bananas. Business interests wanting intervention could always provoke a situation, or help a situation to take shape, where ministers would have no choice about intervening, and could do so with a good or at least a brave conscience.[19]

For South Africa, Kiernan finds their explanation even more unsatisfactory than for Egypt. He makes his point in regard to Lord Salisbury, who at the end of his career wrote bitterly that Britain had to go to war 'for people whom we despise, and for territory which will bring no profit and no power to England'. Salisbury, in Kiernan's view, did not know why the Boer War was fought, and neither do Robinson and Gallagher, since they have been content 'to look through his spectacles'. Certainly they would not find the evidence in official documents, nor would their method lead them to it.

If Lenin deals out too summary a drumhead justice to capitalism, Robinson and Gallagher go to the opposite extreme. On their rules of evidence no conviction could ever be secured against any business lobby. Capitalism to be found guilty would have to be caught *in flagrante delicto* with a signed confession in its pocket properly witnessed by three ministers of the Crown.[20]

To Kiernan, Robinson and Gallagher give away their case when they acknowledge that British Africa was merely 'a gigantic footnote to the Indian Empire'. In India can be found the true and unabashed economic motives for empire, which Robinson and Gallagher have obscured by their analysis of strategy in Africa.[21] Kiernan thus emerges

---

[19] Kiernan, 'Farewells to Empire', p. 266.

[20] Ibid., pp. 267–68.

[21] Ibid., p. 270. In this regard, Tom Kemp comments:

However useful the new information available from such a work, no real analytical advance has been made, nor has the 'theory' of imperialism been refuted. In fact, as far as these authors are concerned, the question remains largely open because they do see African expansion as being a direct result of an already existing Imperialist interest in India. Clearly, any full analysis of British imperialism in this period would have to take into account India, what these authors have called the 'informal empire', as well as the newly-annexed territories which, if of little or no economic importance at the time, subsequently were economically appraised and became privileged markets and investment fields for British capitalism.

Kemp, *Theories of Imperialism*, p. 154. For Robinson and Gallagher's assessment of the importance of India, see *Africa and the Victorians*, pp. 10–13.

as the pre-eminent critic who charges that *Africa and the Victorians* is a whitewash of economic imperialism.

Writers who acknowledge the originality of Robinson and Gallagher's work, including Kiernan and Stokes, find themselves in at least implicit conflict with George Shepperson, co-author of *The Independent African*.[22] Just as Robinson and Gallagher emphasize the continuity of development of the British Empire, so Shepperson sees *Africa and the Victorians* as the logical and not especially earthshaking extension of ideas of previous writers. Writing in that elite journal of historical journals, *La Revue Belge de Philologie et d'Histoire*,[23] Shepperson points out that Robinson and Gallagher build the subtlety of their argument on works such as W. K. Hancock's *Wealth of Colonies*,[24] and he indicates that their inquiry overlaps with that of such writers as Hannah Arendt and Karl Deutsch, both of whom in different ways have made exceedingly important contributions to the subject of imperialism and nationalism.[25] It can be said that none of these writers was particularly concerned with non-European elements of imperialism, but it is true that their work finds little reflection in *Africa and the Victorians*. Above all, Shepperson judges Robinson and Gallagher weakest in that area in which they claim to have made a major contribution, the theory of imperialism. 'If, perhaps, there had been a preliminary review of the subject', writes Shepperson, who objects to economic theory being dismissed in a mere footnote, 'terms could have been defined at the start and subsequent theorization made easier.'[26] As it stands, *Africa and the Victorians* suffers from lack of analysis of economic motivation where it might have been most illuminating. For example, Robinson and Gallagher devote very little attention to the Berlin Congo Conference of 1884–85, the whole point of which was trade, and they neglect the role of King Leopold, whose founding of the Congo Free State at that time later made a mockery of the very phrase 'free trade'. If grand strategy more than hope of economic gain guided British statesmen, then '[i]t is strange . . . that there is no mention of Cecil Rhodes's attempts to secure Katanga, the overruling of which by the British government affords a striking demonstration of the authors' thesis.'[27] In

---

[22] George Shepperson and Thomas Price, *The Independent African* (Edinburgh, 1958).

[23] 'Africa, the Victorians and Imperialism', *Revue Belge de Philologie et d'Histoire*, 40, 4 (1962).

[24] Cambridge, 1950. For another major critical essay that also stresses the antecedents of Robinson and Gallagher's arguments, see A. P. Thornton, 'The Partition of Africa', in *For the File on Empire* (London, 1968). Thornton identifies the assumptions of Robinson and Gallagher with those of J. S. Keltie, *The Partition of Africa* (London, 1895).

[25] Hannah Arendt, *Origins of Totalitarianism* (London, 1958 edn.); Karl W. Deutsch, *Nationalism and Social Communication* (New York, 1953).

[26] *English Historical Review*, 78 (April 1963), pp. 345–47.

[27] Ibid.

cautious words, Shepperson accepts *Africa and the Victorians* as a contribution to the history of the expansion of Europe, and indeed to the history of Africa, but by no means as a revolutionary contribution. He sees the possibility of assimilating the arguments of Robinson and Gallagher with the ideas of such diverse writers as Schumpeter, Veblen, and Mannoni into a 'theory of imperialism and European partition of Africa'.[28]

No one recently has made more substantial contributions to the analysis of the theories of imperialism than David Fieldhouse, an historian who has devoted his career to the study of the economic factor in the expansion of Europe. He does not so much dissent from the views of Robinson and Gallagher as see their work essentially as an investigation into the political causes of the expansion of Europe. *Africa and the Victorians* confirms his own view that the partition of Africa occurred not only because of the dynamics of power politics and European diplomacy but also because of sub-imperialisms and crises in colonial areas. In 1962, Fieldhouse regarded *Africa and the Victorians* as 'perhaps the sanest and most convincing interpretation yet published of the real character of British imperialism in the late nineteenth century'.[29] More than any other commentator, he emphasized the Schumpeterian essence of the work—'the root of imperialist policies in this period was to be found in the special attitudes of the European aristocracy . . . the division of Africa showed how little British statesmen were interested in the acquisition of new colonies for purely economic reasons, which were always subordinated to strategic considerations.'[30] As for the contribution of Robinson and Gallagher to

---

[28] This is the title of a conference held at the Centre of African Studies, University of Edinburgh, November 1967, for the purpose, in Shepperson's words, to 'provide a group of recent case studies in certain aspects of the European partition of Africa, which may provide material for those historians and sociologists who believe theory to be possible'. The proceedings of the conference make fascinating reading on various aspects of imperialism, but the conference did not entirely succeed in moving towards a general theory. In Professor John Hargreaves's summing up: 'I fear some of our members may have been disappointed to find us apparently lost in the jungle of historical particulars' (*The Theory of Imperialism and the European Partition of Africa* [Edinburgh, 1967]). By contrast, Owen and Sutcliffe, *Studies in the Theory of Imperialism,* organizes the theme of discussion around Marxist interpretations of imperialism. It is a stimulating debate.

[29] See D. K. Fieldhouse, ed., *The Theory of Capitalist Imperialism* (London, 1967); *Economics and Empire* (Ithaca, N.Y., 1973).

[30] *Economic History Review,* 2nd series, 14, 3 (April 1962), pp. 574–76. In *Africa and the Victorians,* pp. 20–21, Robinson and Gallagher acknowledge Schumpeter's writings as brilliant. Following his analysis they write:

> The aristocrat by right, the official by *expertise,* both felt socially superior and functionally detached from those who pushed trade and built empires . . . England's rulers had inherited not only a world empire but the experience gained in bringing it to-

the theory of imperialism, Fieldhouse in *The Theory of Capitalist Impe-rialism* (1967) classified it as 'peripheral'—not in the sense of failing to get at the heart of the problem, but in the sense of explaining im-perialism by forces at the circumference of empires:[31] 'By no means all colonial acquisitions resulted from crises at the perimeter, and where the peripheral approach fails, the historian must turn back to Europe for his explanation.'[32] Since 1973, Fieldhouse has emerged as a pro-tagonist in the Robinson and Gallagher controversy by integrating the 'Eurocentric' and the peripheral theories. No other writer has given such powerful independent support to the general analysis of Robin-son and Gallagher, though he does not accept all of their arguments. It is important to note that in the historiography of the controversy, this is an original development and should be regarded as distinct from his interpretation in *The Theory of Capitalist Imperialism*. At the time, *The Theory* was significant, among other reasons, because it pro-voked Ronald Robinson into an elucidation of the Robinson and Gal-lagher position.

Ronald Robinson Clarifies the Argument

The idea of Robinson and Gallagher is precisely the opposite of Field-house's ultimate resort in *The Theory of Capitalist Imperialism* of finding the explanation of European imperialism within Europe. They aim to

---

gether, and the assumptions and prejudices accumulated from past successes and fail-ures inevitably influenced their behaviour in the partition.

For criticism of this interpretation, see especially Kiernan 'Farewells to Empire', p. 265:

A . . . fallacy is the treatment of the governing class as a separate caste of mandarins, aloof from the vulgar preoccupations of mere businessmen and absorbed in their 'high calling' . . . what the book fails to reckon with, just as it turns a blind eye to the transformation of capitalism in that epoch, was the development of a consolidated plutocracy in Britain and in Europe: a social stratum within which Scottish earls and Prussian junkers married Jewish heiresses, and politicians collected directorships in the City, and old-fashioned notions of gentility survived with less and less distinct meaning . . . Without reference to this process of fusion at the top of society, this mix-ing of the cream, the new imperialism cannot be comprehended.

For another observation on the influence of Schumpeter on Robinson and Gallagher, see George Lichtheim, *Imperialism* (New York 1971), p. 97, note 1, where he remarks that 'The Im-perialism of Free Trade' is 'an attempt to show that the partition of the globe among rival pow-ers after 1880 had no rational economic motivation'.

[31] In this connection, see also John S. Galbraith, 'The "Turbulent Frontier" as a Factor in British Expansion', *Comparative Studies in Society and History*, 2, 2 (January 1960); and W. David McIntyre, *The Imperial Frontier in the Tropics, 1865–75* (London, 1967).

[32] Fieldhouse, *Theory of Capitalist Imperialism*, p. 193.

replace the Eurocentric approach with a more satisfactory explanation of non-European elements of imperialism. Thus Fieldhouse's assessment as 'peripheral' (and perhaps the connotation) caused Ronald Robinson to elucidate the Robinson and Gallagher theory. Here is
the interpretation that may be taken as their most recent thoughts on
the subject:

> [I]t is what might be called an 'excentric' approach to European im-
> perialism. To borrow a figure from geometry, there was the Euro-
> centric circle of industrial strategy making varying intersections with
> circles centred in the implacable continuities of African and Asian
> history. Imperialism, especially in its time scale, was not precisely a
> true function of either circle. It was in many ways excentric to both.
> It should be emphasized that the Afro-Asian crises which evoked im-
> perialism were often not essentially the products of European forces
> but of autonomous changes in African and Asian domestic politics.
> Changing over to a mechanical analogy, imperialism was in another
> sense the 'centre of mass' or resultant of both circles. Hence the mo-
> tivation and modes of imperialism were functions of collaboration,
> non-collaboration, mediation and resistance of varying intersections
> of the two circles.[33]

Imperialism is thus in part a function of indigenous politics of the
non-European world. The argument is an expansion and reinforcement of the one first put forward in 'The Imperialism of Free Trade',
that imperialism is the political function of the process of integration
of various countries at various times into the world's economy. Their
position is thus consistent.

---

[33] Robinson, 'Non-European Foundations of European Imperialism', pp. 139–40. The circle
analogy is also used by John Fage in his essay in Prosser Gifford and W. R. Louis, eds., *Britain and
Germany in Africa: Imperial Rivalry and Colonial Rule* (New Haven, 1967). At the two Yale Conferences which produced this and the companion volume, *France and Britain in Africa: Imperial Rivalry and Colonial Rule* (New Haven, 1971), the ideas of Robinson and Gallagher were discussed
from time to time in regard both to imperial history and African history. Prosser Gifford draws
the conclusion:

> One important aspect of *Africa and the Victorians* is that the framework for imperial
> thought was established in the Cabinet and Parliament, often by reference to modes
> of thought developed in dealing with problems in Ireland or India that had little to
> do with Africa—or by reference to domestic political needs and alliances. This point
> is crucial because it explains why *British* interests shaped British imperialism. There
> were indeed national, rather than European, responses to imperial situations. To con-
> centrate upon African situations as Robinson and Gallagher do when they speak of
> collaboration is equally valid in explaining the final result, but the force of the origi-
> nal book is that it points to the origins of assumptions in the imperial mind.

D. C. M. Platt and the Attacks on 'The Imperialism of Free Trade'

Of the economic historians, D. C. M. Platt far and away remains the most persistent critic of Robinson and Gallagher. He is the author of the pioneering work *Finance, Trade, and Politics in British Foreign Policy, 1815–1914*.[34] Setting for himself the goal of estimating the extent to which commerce influenced foreign relations, Platt analyses the continuity of British foreign policy during the nineteenth century as an overriding concern for national security with a closely linked corollary of the creation and preservation of British trading opportunities. He thus finds himself more or less in agreement with the main theme of *Africa and the Victorians*. 'The official mind', bent on security of the routes to the east, gave way to other expansionist powers in the western part of the continent but nevertheless tried to safeguard trading interests there. But Platt questions whether Robinson and Gallagher have not distorted African problems at the expense of those of other regions. One of the merits of his detailed work is the examination of British policy throughout the world:

> There is . . . a danger that the new explanation of British official motives in Africa during the 'Age of Imperialism', while stressing, legitimately enough, such factors as the security of the routes to the East and of the Empire itself, will under-emphasize the part played in British policy by the need to protect the relative position of British trade in world markets. This need, which has already served as a constant, underlying theme in the description of British policy in Egypt, Turkey, and Persia, will be shown to have been of even greater importance in determining British policy in China and Latin America. Could it, then, have been so relatively unimportant in the Partition of Africa? . . .

> The point has been made by Robinson and Gallagher . . . that the minimal economic value of the new territories divided among the Powers during the Partition shows how slight a part economics must have played in determining international policy . . . The point is well taken, but it was the fear of being excluded from prospective as well as existing markets which prompted H.M. Government's policy in West and Central Africa, and nobody at the time could estimate precisely what these markets might be worth in future.[35]

[34] Oxford, 1968. For an analysis of the book in relation to the Robinson and Gallagher thesis, see Zara Steiner in the *Historical Journal*, 13, 3 (1970), pp. 542–52.

[35] Platt, *Finance, Trade, and Politics*, pp. 256–59.

On this well-taken point, Platt's criticism is identical with that of most prominent critics of Robinson and Gallagher. African dividends may eventually have been small, but this fact does not necessarily explain the motives for the partition; territories that remained largely unexplored during the Scramble might or might not eventually have paid large financial returns. On the whole, however, Platt's study of Africa (which is less extensive than that of other regions) confirms the resounding themes of *Africa and the Victorians:* 'The importance of British interests in India in the formulation of British policy in Uganda and the Upper Nile region is now undeniable.'[36]

Before turning to Platt's evaluation of 'The Imperialism of Free Trade', perhaps it would be well to restate the ideas of Robinson and Gallagher in relation to 'informal empire'.[37] According to them, 'the imperialism of free trade' covers one or more of the following links between an expanding and a receiving political economy:

1. The exertion of power or diplomacy to impose and sustain free trading conditions on another society against its will.
2. The exertion of capital or commercial attraction to bend economic organization and direction of growth in directions complementary to the needs and surpluses of the expanding economy.
3. The exertion of capital and commercial attraction directly upon foreign governments to influence them towards cooperation and alliance with the expanding country.
4. The direct intervention or influence of the export-import sector interests upon the politics of the receiving country in the direction of collaboration and political-economic alliance with the expanding power.
5. The taking over by European bankers and merchants of sectors of non-European domestic economies under cover of imposed free trade without accompaniment of large capital or export inputs from Europe, as in China.

If any one passage in 'The Imperialism of Free Trade' sums up their argument, perhaps it is this:

> British policy followed the principle of extending control informally if possible and formally if necessary. To label the one method 'anti-imperialist' and the other 'imperialist', is to ignore the fact that

[36] Platt, *Finance, Trade, and Politics*, p. 260.

[37] Robinson and Gallagher attribute the phrase 'informal empire' to C. R. Fay, but it is no exaggeration to say that it now has passed into the vocabulary of imperial history as a Robinsonian and Gallagherian concept. For discussion of early usage of the phrase, see Robin W. Winks, 'Toward a Theory on Decolonizing an Informal Empire', a paper presented at the meeting of the American Historical Association, December 1973.

whatever the method British interests were steadily safeguarded and extended. The usual summing up of the policy of the free trade empire as 'trade not rule' should read 'trade with informal control if possible; trade with rule when necessary'.[38]

It is remarkable, as Platt points out, that no historian took serious issue with that proposition during the 1950s, and even after the publication of *Africa and the Victorians,* few historians appeared to recognize that the theory of continuity and its corollary of informal empire had profound implications for the historiography of the era.

'[T]he point is that the character of this expansion *had* changed,' Platt exclaimed in April 1968 in *Past and Present,* as almost in a plea for sanity among fellow historians.

> The fashionable theory that British expansion was designed simply to maintain the security of the existing Empire against a new threat from the Continental Powers can explain a great deal . . . But the new threat which Britain faced in and after the 1880s was not confined to imperial frontiers and communications; it extended also to the security of British trade and finance . . . Before 1880 British statesmen had not been especially worried by foreign colonial expansion. Nor were they worried by expansion after that date provided that the markets remained open to British trade and investment and that no strategic interests were damaged.

So long as there were no restrictions on trade, the British Government tolerated foreign annexations.

> H.M. Government's part in the 'New Imperialism' might have been restricted entirely to areas of strategic interest if it had not been for

---

[38] 'Imperialism of Free Trade', p. 13. The argument continues that in Africa the imperialists scraped 'the bottom of the barrel'. On this point, David Landes has made an astute observation:
> While accepting this point about the persistence and indeed primacy of the economic pressures toward empire, especially informal empire, in nineteenth-century Britain, I would dissent from this interpretation on a ground . . . that it will account for only a part—an important but nevertheless insufficient part—of the facts. In particular, it will not account for a major historical phenomenon, the occupation of large areas of the world for noneconomic reasons. The correct observation that Africa was 'the bottom of the [imperialist] barrel', far from disposing of the significance of this occupation, only heightens it.

David S. Landes, 'Some Thoughts on the Nature of Economic Imperialism', *Journal of Economic History,* 21, 4 (1961). Landes's theory of imperialism perhaps can best conveyed by the phrase 'dynamic equilibrium model', by which he means that the expansion of empire, whether direct or indirect, formal or informal, into unprofitable as well as profitable areas, is inherent in the nature of imperialism as a response to disparity of power.

the revival of European Protectionism and the threat to the fair and equal treatment of British trade and finance ... Imperial expansion was only the most spectacular, and in Whitehall the least popular, of the remedies supplied. It was as simple as that.[39]

In same year, 1968, in the *Economic History Review,* Platt began to take on Robinson and Gallagher on grounds of his own expertise, Latin America. His criticism here is especially interesting because Latin America serves as one of the main props of their argument. It is simply not true, Platt argues, that mid-Victorian statesmen acted vigorously to open markets and to keep them open, in America, in China, or anywhere else. British policy in Latin America, for example, aimed at preserving neutrality, often in opposition to British financiers. After an abundance of examples from Latin America and China:

> Non-intervention and laissez-faire were the characteristic attitudes of mid-Victorian officialdom, and these attitudes were faithfully reflected overseas. It is *not* true, for example, that British government policy in Latin America was to obtain 'indirect political hegemony over the new regions for the purposes of trade', or to create 'a new and informal empire' in the interests of future British commercial expansion.[40]

In *Finance, Trade, and Politics:*

> It is not true, for example, that H.M. Government was prepared to exercise informal control in Latin America, whatever the provocation, and the examples quoted by Gallagher and Robinson go nowhere to prove their case.[41]

---

[39] D. C. M. Platt, 'British Policy during the "New Imperialism",' *Past and Present,* 39 (April 1968), pp. 134–38. The article is mainly an attack on Fieldhouse, who along with Robinson and Gallagher also stresses continuity rather than change; see Fieldhouse's 'Historiographical Revision'. For further support of the interpretation of continuity, see Bernard Semmel, *The Rise of Free Trade Imperialism* (Cambridge, 1970): 'From the standpoint of ideology ... from the perspective of theory and policy no less than from that of activities, it is possible to see continuity, rather than an interlude of anti-imperialism' (p. 4). Within the context of his earlier work, *Imperialism and Social Reform* (London, 1960), Semmel offered this criticism of 'The Imperialism of Free Trade': 'It tends too much to regard imperialism as all of one piece with the different imperialisms as responses to different conditions, one succeeding the other in almost mechanical fashion' (p. 133). Semmel's contribution to the debate about the imperialism of free trade has been summed up by D. R. Sardesai as providing 'a predominantly economic-oriented theoretical cushioning to the Robinson-Gallagher argument' (*American Historical Review,* 77, 2 [April 1972], p. 514).

[40] D. C. M. Platt, 'The Imperialism of Free Trade: Some Reservations', *Economic History Review,* 2nd series, 21, 2 (August 1968), p. 305.

[41] Platt, *Finance, Trade, and Politics,* p. 361.

And again in 'Further Objections', in the *Economic History Review,* in a full-blown reconsideration of the issue:

> The British government's role, in mid-Victorian England, was limited, and it was forced into an active promotional policy towards trade and investment overseas only under international pressure in the last decades of the century. Late-Victorian governments were *not* applying the same methods under new conditions, to achieve what remained the same goals. The whole concept of what was a 'legitimate' function for the Foreign Office and the Diplomatic Service had had to be altered and transformed under the competitive conditions and active foreign diplomacy of the 'eighties.[42]

According to Platt's view, the 'submerged part of the iceberg' of informal empire becomes less significant the more it is scrutinized and more and more the product of the fanciful imagination of Robinson and Gallagher. The 'informal empire' presumably existed above all in Latin America, the Levant, and China. Yet these are precisely the areas where, in the mid-nineteenth century, absence of returns checked expansion of trade. Arguing that 'the Imperialism of Free Trade' is an anachronism because it antedates by several decades the relative importance of the 'informal empire' as a place for investment and a source of raw materials and foodstuffs, Platt contends that the incentives for economic expansion simply did not exist. If 'The Imperialism of Free Trade' once served as a salutary corrective to the stereotyped conceptions of mid-Victorian empire, then Platt's articles are equally useful in keeping a balanced—and *relative*—view of mid-nineteenth-century imperialism.[43]

The first of the case studies testing the general ideas of Robinson

[42] D. C. M. Platt, 'Further Objections to an "Imperialism of Free Trade 1830–60",' *Economic History Review,* 2nd series, 26, 1 (February 1973), p. 87.

[43] One might argue that the difficulty is partly semantic, that Platt and Robinson and Gallagher are talking about two different things. To some extent, this is true. Platt seeks to explain the differences between mid- and late-Victorian expansion, while Robinson and Gallagher seek to explain the similarities of the two eras by the concept of imperialism as a function, but not a necessary function, of an expanding economy, and, as the concept is elaborated in the 'excentric theory', as the interaction between the expansive forces of the West and the collaborative elements of non-Western societies at no particular time. Platt is also clearly interested in establishing the purpose of British policy at given times, while Robinson and Gallagher are as much concerned with the reality of imperialism as they are with varying questions of motive. The ambiguity or ingenuity of the phrase 'imperialism of free trade' can be blamed for its share of semantic confusion. But the area of controversy is real enough. Platt emphasizes that the two eras distinctly differed; Robinson and Gallagher speak of the 'so called New Imperialism'. There are also true differences about the meaning of 'informal' that go beyond semantics. See Steiner's review article, *Historical Journal,* 13, 3, (1970), pp. 545–52.

and Gallagher is by Oliver MacDonagh, 'The Anti-Imperialism of Free Trade'.[44] It is about the ideas of Richard Cobden and the Manchester School in the years 1840–70. The general comments and conclusions are especially helpful in clearing up semantic and conceptual confusions that have run through the entire controversy. What, after all, do Robinson and Gallagher mean by 'informal empire'? To MacDonagh, it can be summed up by stating that both formal and informal empires are to some extent identical and interchangeable. The two kinds of empire express variable political functions of the extending patterns of overseas trade, investment migration, and culture (a seminal idea later reinforced in the 'excentric' theory). MacDonagh argues that this reasoning merely replaces old conceptual difficulties with new and unanticipated ones. Since the United States received much of British capital and emigrants during the nineteenth century, should the United States be included in the 'informal empire'? Even apart from the United States, a drastic recolouring of the imperial map might be required: 'We might find ourselves constrained to drain Canada of colour while the Balkans were being painted off-red.' And some cases defy categories. For example, was Ireland imperializing or being imperialized?

> Ireland was indeed the prime exporter of population from the United Kingdom; but she was also the major exporter of French Revolutionary ideology, Roman Catholic religion and anti-British sentiment. In fact, 'overseas trade, investment, migration and culture' were not four battalions in the same regiment: they did not even march in the same direction.[45]

Even apart from the difficult question of where to place and how to describe Ireland in any commentary on imperialism, is there perhaps a danger in not only the universality but also the depersonalization of the theory of Robinson and Gallagher? It did make a very real difference, as MacDonagh points out, that opportunity gave Disraeli and not Gladstone the chance to purchase the Suez canal shares in 1875. Gladstone probably would have refused, and the Egyptian crisis leading to the occupation in 1882 would have taken a substantially different form, whatever the role of the Egyptian nationalists. The idea of a constant and aggressive mid-Victorian imperialism has to be considered in relation to personalities and movements. Here MacDonagh

[44] Oliver MacDonagh, 'The Anti-Imperialism of Free Trade', *Economic History Review*, 2nd series, 14, 3 (April 1962), pp. 489–501.

[45] Ibid., p. 489, note 3.

develops his thesis: the free traders of the 1840–70 period clearly perceived the informal empire; but to imply that they promoted the growth of empire is basically to misread the history of the era.

> It is true that the pre-eminent free traders of the period 1840–70 were well aware of the development of 'informal empire', and discerned many of the features which Mr. Gallagher and Dr. Robinson have re-discovered. But they also pronounced them to be a sin against free trade, and opposed them with all the resources at their command.[46]

Free trade means, as MacDonagh clearly explains, the doctrine of specific associations and persons, of which the Manchester School and Richard Cobden in particular were at the centre. Cobden stood against all imperialism, formal and informal. The free-trade movement represented a force of Victorian society in perpetual conflict with the aristocracy and those principles associated with the aristocracy: unnecessary governmental expenditures, bellicosity, war as a solution to problems of colonial and international relations. The free-trade movement was more than a movement concerned with mere trade: it espoused moral principles and the idea of a society that would regulate itself if free from governmental interference. Not least it was a movement for peace, including support of international arbitration and disarmament. For Robinson and Gallagher to say that imperialism characterized the era of free trade—in other words, mid-Victorian England—is one thing, and to them goes the credit of destroying once and for all the myth of the mid-nineteenth century as anti-imperialist.[47] But for them to imply at least by ambiguity that the free-trade movement supported the forces of imperialism is misleading, even mischievous. The distinction is fundamental. In MacDonagh's judgement, the meaning conveyed by the phrase 'imperialism of free trade' is the opposite of the truth.[48]

[46] Ibid., p. 490.

[47] See, in this connection, John S. Galbraith, 'Myths of the "Little England" Era', *American Historical Review,* 67, 1 (October 1961).

[48] See, however, R. J. Moore, 'Imperialism and "Free Trade" Policy in India, 1853–4', *Economic History Review,* 2nd series, 17, 1 (August 1964), critical of MacDonagh. For the theory in regard to India, see also especially Peter Harnetty, *Imperialism and Free Trade: Lancashire and India in the Mid-Nineteenth Century* (Vancouver, 1972), which uses the idea as a 'conceptual tool'. The implicit rejoinder of Robinson and Gallagher to MacDonagh's line of argument can be found particularly in Robinson's expansion of the theory (in 'Non-European Foundations of European Imperialism'), that the mechanism of collaboration operates at various times in various regions, not necessarily in fixed historical eras or in regard to individuals. Even within the context of the 1953 essay it could be argued that MacDonagh has not taken all of the argument fully into

In 'The Imperialism of Free Trade—Peru, 1820–70', W. M. Mathew examines the viability of the thesis in a case study of an especially significant Latin American country.[49] Peru is a happy choice because one can evaluate the ideas of Robinson and Gallagher against a specific mid-Victorian problem in which the British Government remained aloof, and then proceed to the eve of the First World War, when Britain did intervene. Mathew asks whether the British Government employed economic and military measures in order to place Peru in a position of Imperial subordination, which is one way to test the straightforward idea of the imperialism of free trade (though not, perhaps, the 'excentric theory'). During the nineteenth century, Peru's guano trade with Britain reached sizable proportions. In the 1850s and 1860s the British imported more fertilizer from Peru than from any other Latin American country. And in the decade and a half of 1851–65, loans to Peru ranked greater than to any other Latin American country. But Peru behaved in a way that should have angered the free-trade imperialists of Robinson and Gallagher. The Peruvian Government demanded artificial prices for the guano and defaulted on obligations to British bondholders. How did the British respond?

> Farmers, agricultural commentators, and government alike in the early and mid-1850's all appear to have concurred that lower guano prices and more regular guano supplies would greatly assist the process of agricultural improvement in Britain—and to have accepted, too, that these could be secured through a degree of coercion which British governments, as it turned out, were simply not prepared to apply.[50]

About the defaults to the bondholders? 'In July 1857 Clarendon told a party of bondholders in London that "it would be inconsistent with the policy of the British government to enter into territorial guarantees with foreign governments."'[51] When the British Government did contemplate intervention, it appears to have been to redress breaches of international law, not to promote economic exploitation. Mathew

---

account. When he speaks of the inclusion of the United States in the informal empire as the *reductio ad absurdum* of their logic, it could be maintained that this is precisely what Robinson and Gallagher have in mind.

[49] W. M. Mathew, 'The Imperialism of Free Trade: Peru, 1820–70', *Economic History Review*, 2nd series, 21, 3 (December 1968).

[50] Ibid., p. 574.

[51] Ibid., p. 577.

concludes 'there is little in the historical record to justify viewing Peru as a victim of British imperialism, as part of Britain's "invisible empire of informal sway".' The history of mid-nineteenth-century Peru, in Mathew's view, does not sustain the themes of 'The Imperialism of Free Trade'.[52] Nor do any of the major themes of 'The Imperialism of Free Trade' or *Africa and the Victorians* help explain why Britain did intervene in Peru half a century later, in the era of the rubber atrocities. After the turn of the century the Peruvian Amazon Company, which was in fact a private British company, exploited the Indians of the Upper Amazon, in the Putumayo region, even more viciously than in the Congo. Rumours of atrocities appeared in the British press, and the Aborigines Protection Society pressed the Foreign Office for intervention. The Foreign Office felt sufficient humanitarian pressure to dispatch the British Consul in Brazil to investigate. The resulting report of 1912 constituted a damning indictment of the rubber regime of the Putumayo. Neither the Foreign Office nor the British public sympathized with rubber ruffians. Under parliamentary and public pressure, the company disbanded. There is no explanation of this episode other than humanitarian. This particular incident, of course, lies beyond the confines of their investigation, but it seems fair to say that the influence of the humanitarians and crusaders on 'the official mind' is a neglected dimension in the later works of Robinson and Gallagher.[53]

Historians of Latin America are deeply divided over the concept of 'imperialism of free trade'. Along with Platt and Mathew, H. S. Ferns in *Britain and Argentina in the Nineteenth Century* argues that the word 'imperialism' to be used in a meaningful sense must imply political subordination: 'If we accept the proposition that imperialism embraces the fact of control through the use of political power, then the

---

[52] Again, as in the case of the MacDonagh article, the implicit retort is that imperialism is not necessarily a function of economic expansion. See 'Imperialism of Free Trade', p. 6.

[53] This is not to deny the value of, for example, the chapter on 'Moral Suasion in Guinea and Zanzibar'. It is rather to say that in *Africa and the Victorians* Robinson and Gallagher are more interested in explaining why British statesmen intervened so infrequently instead of following the lead of the humanitarians: '[A]s the ambitious schemes of the humanitarians broke one by one against the facts of Africa, statesmen became more and more hard-headed. They saw clearly that no concrete national interest would be served by serious state intervention in tropical Africa' (p. 27). Compare with J. Gallagher, 'Fowell Buxton and the New African Policy, 1838–1842', *Cambridge Historical Journal*, 10 (1950), p. 58, where the emphasis is on 'the great political force which the humanitarians could employ'. The conclusion is of fundamental importance in understanding the sporadic influence of the humanitarians on governmental policy: 'Granted a weak Government and a stirring cause, they could for a time bend colonial policy away from its general pattern, and could force politicians who thought West Africa not worth the bones of one British Grenadier, to risk far more than that.'

verdict for Britain is unquestionably "Not Guilty".' [54] Ferns holds that the Argentine government always possessed sufficient strength to shape the course of British-Argentine relations and that economic facts of Argentina's financial power 'make nonsense of myths about British imperialism and Argentina as a semi-colony of a great and powerful state'.[55] In an article of lasting importance, 'Britain's Informal Empire in Argentina', written in the same year as Robinson and Gallagher's démarche in 1953, Ferns contended Britain's policy of political restraint had allowed Argentina to develop without the political friction that had characterized British relations with India, China, and Egypt. 'In a very real sense Argentina was the first community, substantially dependent economically on Great Britain, to achieve Dominion status.'[56] This positive interpretation would probably go beyond Platt's, but both are adamant that Britain pursued a policy of political neutrality.

By contrast, the writings of other Latin American historians, such as Peter Winn and Richard Graham, can be associated with Robinson and Gallagher. They stress 'informal empire' both as a British policy and a Latin American reality.[57] Along with Robinson and Gallagher, Graham emphasizes the importance of the role of the collaborator. Graham's interpretation in some ways is the opposite of Ferns's. Brazil may or may not have been on its way towards Dominion status, but in Graham's view there can be no doubt about the subordination of Brazil in the informal empire. It involved a transfer of values as well as economic exploitation.

> [T]he force of the imperial power is to be measured not only or even primarily by the overt acts of political control but by the degree to which the values, attitudes and institutions of the expansionist nation infiltrate and overcome those of the recipient one. In this process the native collaborator or sepoy is indispensable. It is when influential publicists and local politicians become convinced that the way of life of the imperial power is the best one imaginable that the strength of that nation is at its greatest, although the evidence may then be least noticeable. In nineteenth-century Brazil there were

---

[54] H. S. Ferns, *Britain and Argentina in the Nineteenth Century* (Oxford, 1960), p. 487. By the same author, *Argentina* (New York, 1969); and *The Argentine Republic* (New York, 1973).

[55] Ferns, *Britain and Argentina*, p. 489.

[56] H. S. Ferns, 'Britain's Informal Empire in Argentina, 1806–1914', *Past and Present*, 4 (November 1953), p. 63.

[57] Peter Winn, 'Uruguay and British Economic Expansion, 1880–1893' (Cambridge University Ph.D. thesis, 1972); Richard Graham, *Britain and the Onset of Modernization in Brazil, 1850–1914* (Cambridge, 1968).

both institutional and personal reflections of this mechanism of imperial control.[58]

Like Robinson and Gallagher, Graham sees the founts of British expansion as constant: 'The same forces that in the 1840's demanded the opening of Chinese ports had earlier taken a keen interest in breaking down the monopolies maintained by Spain and Portugal in the New World.'[59] Regardless of whether one endorses the interpretation of Ferns or Graham, it is important to keep the problem of the 'informal empire' in Latin America in worldwide perspective. Case studies may seem to prove Robinson and Gallagher both wrong and right, depending on other circumstances. To return to the case of Peru, for example, Clarendon made his statement of nonintervention in July 1857, when the British government faced the necessity of sending every available man to India to deal with the mutiny. It was a time immediately following the Persian expedition, the China war, and not long after the Crimean War. Intervention in South America had to be conceived of on a different order from that in Asia. In addition there was the possibility that intervention might interfere with relations with the United States. As in the case of Africa, British actions in Latin America have to be viewed as part of the problems facing British foreign policy and the British Empire as a whole.

In 'Economic Imperialism in West Africa: Lagos, 1880–92' by A. G. Hopkins, the interests of the economic historians and the African historians begin to mesh.[60] It is an illuminating article. The topic is specialized but the view is large. Hopkins argues that critics of the theory of economic imperialism, including Robinson and Gallagher, have been so eager to destroy conventional concepts that they fail to see the truly operative economic elements in the Scramble. This is especially true of West Africa, treatment of which most critics see as the weakest in *Africa and the Victorians*. Hopkins begins by asking the narrow and useful question: why did the Europeans partition not only Africa in general, but West Africa in particular? He is of course by no means the first to ask that question, but his line of reasoning is enlightening. The answer given by Robinson and Gallagher, he argues, has the advantages but also the disadvantages of seeing the connection between West Africa and other parts of the world; once they commit themselves

[58] Richard Graham, 'Sepoys and Imperialists: Techniques of British Power in Nineteenth-Century Brazil', *Inter-American Economic Affairs*, 23, 2 (Autumn 1969), pp. 23–37.

[59] Ibid., p. 24.

[60] A. G. Hopkins, 'Economic Imperialism in West Africa: Lagos, 1880–92', *Economic History Review*, 2nd series, 21, 3 (December 1968).

to explaining the partition of West Africa for reasons of grand strategy that have nothing to do with that particular area, then they do not permit themselves to see the full force of the economic reasons why the European powers partitioned West Africa. Another way of putting it is that Robinson and Gallagher help us understand why the British failed to paint all of West Africa red, but their explanation falls short of explaining how Britain managed to hold on to two of the richest areas, Nigeria and the Gold Coast. They underplay the significance of the economic depression of the 1880s because the very existence of a depression seems sufficient evidence to dispose of the aggressive economic imperialism of Hobson, for example, as a dynamic in the partition of West Africa. Robinson and Gallagher therefore search for and find non–West African explanations. On the other hand, if one starts with another set of suppositions:

> [S]uppose that the widespread depression in West African trade had a dynamic rather than a static effect on British and French interests; suppose that it upset the status quo, increased commercial rivalries, and led merchants and local officials to press for an alternative policy, a forward policy, in West Africa. There is a striking anticipation of this hypothesis in the history of Tudor England, for it was an economic crisis in the middle of the sixteenth century which encouraged English merchants to seek markets in new regions, including West Africa. If an economic crisis led the Elizabethans to the west coast, is it not possible that a similar motive encouraged the Victorians to move from the coast to the interior?[61]

The economic depression of the 1880s caused crises in commercial and manufacturing industries; British traders favoured partition as a means to prevent occupation by other powers. In sum, economic strategy played a major part in the Scramble for West Africa and cannot be cavalierly dismissed in the fashion of Robinson and Gallagher. In the course of his inquiry, Hopkins comes into collision with the views of Professor J. F. A. Ajayi of the University of Ibadan and with the Emin Pasha Professor of African History at the University of Chicago, Ralph Austen. They disagree with Hopkins about the internal history of the Yoruba states in the nineteenth century and the extent to which British intervention was caused by the West African merchants, whose influence Ajayi and Austen believe to be exaggerated.[62] But they do

---

[61] Hopkins, 'Economic Imperialism in West Africa', pp. 583–84.

[62] J. F. A. Ajayi and R. A. Austen, 'Hopkins on Economic Imperialism in West Africa', *Economic History Review*, 2nd series, 25, 2 (May 1972), pp. 303–06; and A. G. Hopkins, 'Economic Imperialism in West Africa: A Rejoinder', ibid., pp. 307–12. For Austen's views on Robinson and Gallagher within the context of African economic history, see Ralph A. Austen, 'Economic History', *African Studies Review*, 14, 3 (December 1971).

not dispute Hopkins's major conclusion, which in part takes exception to Ronald Robinson's description of 'the decrepit, mythological beast of economic imperialism'.[63] According to Hopkins:

> In the last analysis, the partition of West Africa may be thought of as a political act carried out to resolve the economic conflicts which had arisen as a result of the meeting of two disparate societies, one developing, the other underdeveloped. Seen in these terms, economic imperialism was not a mythical beast, a paper tiger, but a real, live creature after all.[64]

This is a rich investigation, important for changes in the economic structure of West Africa as well as for the ideas it generates about theories of economic imperialism and the value of the Robinson and Gallagher thesis.

The Arguments Recapitulated: Ronald Robinson Expands the Theory in 'Non-European Foundations'

Before this present discussion passes from aspects of the controversy that have preoccupied economic historians and goes on to points that have aroused the interest of historians of Africa as well as of European imperialism generally, perhaps it would be well to recapitulate the basic themes of the three works of 'The Imperialism of Free Trade', *Africa and the Victorians,* and the chapter in the *New Cambridge Modern History* in relation to one another. In the recapitulation can be seen the development of a basic idea undergoing considerable modification over a period of nine years. 'The Imperialism of Free Trade' essentially is an explanation of nineteenth-century British imperialism. Its basic theme is continuity. It makes no pretence of explaining the imperialisms of France or Germany, and it is entirely Anglocentric in outlook. It speaks of 'pseudonationalist' movements in Africa. Its ideas provide the framework of *Africa and the Victorians* as a case study. 'The Imperialism of Free Trade' becomes 'The Spirit of Victorian Expansion' as the authors restate their case 'more cautiously'.[65] With the premise of continuity we are given what the economic historians refer to as 'equilibrium analysis'. The European balance of power is disturbed and the result is the partition of Africa. The authors are not

[63] *Journal of African History,* 2 (1961), p. 158.

[64] Hopkins, 'Economic Imperialism in West Africa', p. 606; for Hopkins's enlarged analysis, see *An Economic History of West Africa* (New York, 1973). The interpretation in the book has much in common with Robinson's 'Non-European Foundations of European Imperialism'.

[65] W. L. Burn, *History,* 48, 163 (June 1963), p. 250.

inclined to accept the theory of economic imperialism as an explanation and do not emphasize increasing economic competition in western Africa as a major cause of the partition. In order to explain the upsetting of the equilibrium, they point to the Egyptian uprising, which
threatens Britain's short route to the East. Here we come to their main
thesis. The consequent British occupation of Egypt in 1882 directly
causes the Scramble for Africa. The wording of their argument is explicit: 'By altering the European balance, the occupation of Egypt inflated the importance of trivial disputes in tropical Africa and set off
a scramble.' The shattering of the Anglo-French Entente results in
French aggressive moves, especially in West Africa, in compensation. Bismarck, in his own phrase, using the 'Egyptian baton', joins
the Scramble, essentially for traditional diplomatic reasons. All of this,
they now argue, can be understood only by grasping the interaction
between European and African societies. In *Africa and the Victorians,* which appeared at a time when African history came of age as
a recognized academic discipline, the 'pseudonationalist' movements
of 'The Imperialism of Free Trade' become 'protonationalist' movements. The Egyptians in the north and the Boers in the south suck the
British into the extremities of the continent. The overriding purpose
of the British presence is the protection of their routes to the East, not
economic exploitation: 'They moved into Africa, not to build a new
African empire, but to protect the old empire in India . . . The decisive motive behind late-Victorian strategy in Africa was to protect the
all-important stakes in India and the East.'[66] In the article in the *New
Cambridge Modern History,* the argument appears in its most extreme
and aggressive form. The authors repeat the conclusion of 'The Imperialism of Free Trade', that the imperialists in Africa were scraping
the bottom of the barrel. The partition is described as a remarkable
freak. The imperialists, including Bismarck and Ferry, felt no new impulses to imperialize, the latter now being dragged into places such
as Tunisia by Muslim rebellion and the former still wielding the Egyptian baton.[67] This is history written with a vengeance. It is out for
the blood of the theorists of economic imperialism. As an alternative theory, it puts forth the signal hypothesis of European imperialism as a reflex to proto-nationalist movements not only in northern
and southern Africa, but now also in such places as the western Sudan
and Ethiopia.[68] They see the interaction of Western imperialism and

---

[66] *Africa and the Victorians*, p. 464.

[67] 'The Partition of Africa', pp. 595 and 604.

[68] Ibid., pp. 609–10 and 626. For an important critical assessment of the theory in regard to
the western Sudan, see A. S. Kanya-Forstner. *The Conquest of the Western Sudan: A Study in French
Military Imperialism* (Cambridge, 1969), especially pp. 268–69.

indigenous polities in places such as China and India. Here is the bid of Robinson and Gallagher for an explanation of imperialism as a worldwide phenomenon.

> The defter nationalisms of Egypt and the Levant, the 'Scholars of New Learning' in Kuang-Hsü China, the sections which merged into the continental coalition of the Indian Congress, the separatist churches of Africa—in their different ways, they all planned to reform their personalities and regain their powers by operating in the idiom of the westerners.[69]

In sum, imperialism becomes a powerful engine of social change. Nationalism becomes a continuation of imperialism.[70]

The argument is clarified, developed, and modified in Robinson's 'Non-European Foundations'. Here is the clarification:

> Any new theory must recognise that imperialism was as much a function of its victims' collaboration or non-collaboration—of their indigenous politics, as it was of European expansion. The expansive forces generated in industrial Europe had to combine with elements within the agrarian societies of the outer world to make empire at all practicable.[71]

Imperialism occurs when the expansive forces of the West interact with indigenous polities. There are three parts to the formula: European strategy and economics make two components, indigenous collaboration or resistance the third. Here Robinson more explicitly develops the idea of collaboration:

> Without the voluntary or enforced cooperation of their governing elites, economic resources could not be transferred, strategic interests protected or xenophobic reaction and traditional resistance to change contained. Nor without indigenous collaboration, when the time came for it, could Europeans have conquered and ruled their non-European empires. From the outset that rule was continuously resisted; just as continuously native mediation was needed to avert resistance or hold it down.[72]

[69] 'The Partition of Africa', p. 640.

[70] On the imperialism-nationalism theme, see especially Anil Seal, *The Emergence of Indian Nationalism* (Cambridge, 1968), chap. 8.

[71] 'Non-European Foundations of European Imperialism', p. 118.

[72] Ibid., p. 120. The word 'collaboration' is not, of course, used in a pejorative sense: 'It is as false to interpret the "collaborating class" as a dependent compradore "quisling" element as it is to suppose . . . that it hoisted itself into the saddle and rode the blinkered imperial war horse as it chose' (Eric Stokes, 'Traditional Resistance Movements and Afro-Asian Nationalism: The Context of the 1857 Mutiny Rebellion in India', *Past and Present*, 48 (August 1970), p. 102. For an example of work done in the field of nationalism, see T. O. Ranger, 'African Reactions to the Im-

Thus the central mechanism of imperialism is collaboration. The collaborative elements in non-Western societies succeed or fail in integrating Western and non-Western economies. Their success leads eventually to conversion against alien rule and the ousting of the Europeans. Here the theory is modified, in that it becomes more distinctly ahistorical. Imperialism is best understood by use of geometrical or mechanical analogies that can be applied regardless of time or place. The element of collaboration makes the mechanism work. Imperialism is thus a formula or a static concept. As a conceptual tool, it can be used to comprehend the European takeover, the period of colonial rule, decolonization, and even 'neocolonialism'. Robinson's concept is free from the shackles of historical causality that make *Africa and the Victorians* such an intensely fascinating work. The 'excentric' theory has the advantages of the insight of social science but the disadvantage of attempting to deal with such colourful personalities as Rosebery or Goldie with a formula. In *Africa and the Victorians* the artistic brilliance of the pen portraits unique to the Victorian age is at war with the proclivity to search for an underlying principle or determining chain of events.

The Onslaught against 'Africa and the Victorians'

The breadth and sweep of *Africa and the Victorians* in all its originality and complexity can best be examined by reviewing specific attacks. If critics of the book are agreed upon anyone point, it is that Robinson and Gallagher overargue their case in regard to Egypt. They attempt to establish a direct, causal relationship between the British occupation in 1882 and the subsequent partition of the continent. In the vanguard against this interpretation, Jean Stengers pointed out in one of the first major commentaries on the book that commercial and political rivalry in the basin of the Congo existed independently from the Egyptian question.[73] Merely to give a precis of his essay is to present an entirely different idea of how the history of the Scramble might be written. It restores vitality to the notion of the 'new imperialism' so warmly scorned by Robinson and Gallagher. Are we to believe, Stengers asks, that the Scramble was merely a myth, that circum-

---

position of Colonial Rule in East and Central Africa', in L. H. Gann and Peter Duignan, eds., *Colonialism in Africa,* I (Cambridge, 1969). In 'Traditional Resistance Movements and Afro-Asian Nationalism', Stokes discusses the 'populist' conception of Ranger in contrast to the 'elitist' conception of Robinson and Gallagher. For a list of relevant articles, see the notes in Robinson, 'Non-European Foundations of European Imperialism'.

[73] Jean Stengers, 'L'Impérialisme Colonial de la Fin du XIXe Siècle', *Journal of African History,* 3, 3 (1962).

stances change but not the spirit of the times? Did imperialists casu-ally partition Africa merely because of a chain of circumstances be-ginning in Egypt? Not in the least. First of all the European powers scrambled not only for Africa but also for the Pacific, which geo-graphically strains the credibility of the Egyptian argument. Further-more, the atmosphere of international relations concerning Africa had changed in a short period of time, as Stengers illustrates in a com-ment of Lord Salisbury: 'When I left the Foreign Office in 1880, no-body thought about Africa. When I returned to it in 1885, the nations in Europe were almost quarrelling with each other as to the various portions of Africa which could obtain.'[74] Who took initiative and where? One might well suspect King Leopold in the Congo, but his earlier schemes aimed at commercial exploitation, not political sov-ereignty. We must look to France for the explanation, and two epi-sodes are instructive. In 1882, Brazza unfurled the French flag on the Congo, and in 1883 France embarked on a protectorate policy on the western coast. Brazza had concluded a treaty with an African chief at Stanley Pool, an area of strategic and commercial importance because it commands the head of the navigable Congo. The French Parliament approved this treaty in the autumn of 1882, and this act began the po-litical appropriation of central Africa. What moved the French Parlia-ment? In a phrase, 'public opinion'—a theme that runs profoundly contrary to the interpretation of Robinson and Gallagher. The Egyp-tian issue raised its head south of the Equator in a way not perceived in *Africa and the Victorians*. The occupation of Egypt wounded French national pride. With a sense of humiliation in Egypt, the press clam-oured for success in the Congo. Journalists proclaimed Brazza a na-tional hero, defending French commerce and civilization; 'National pride, national amour-propre, and chauvinism, all poured into colo-nial affairs with unprecedented force.' In the autumn of 1882 the flames of colonial enthusiasm waxed intense for the first time in mod-ern history. The sparks soon ignited public opinion in other countries. Even Bismarck eventually felt the heat of the public's passion for col-onies. Did England remain isolated from the colonial 'fire', 'fever', 'mania', or whatever term one might use to describe the phenome-non that swept Europe during the 1880s? According to Stengers, defi-nitely not. There may have been a lag in the force with which colonial enthusiasm hit England, and British statesmen such as Salisbury may have acted primarily for defensive reasons of strategy. But the appro-priation of the non-Western world fascinated even Salisbury, whose political study of African cartography fired such participants as Harry

[74] Ibid., p. 471.

Johnston. In other words, there was an emotional dimension of the Scramble, not least to the builders of the British Empire in Africa. In Stengers's view, *Africa and the Victorians* emphasizes the slowness, the deliberation, and the indifference of British statesmen at the expense of the sense of mission or 'sacred fire' motivating such men as Cecil Rhodes. The charge is fundamental. Robinson and Gallagher have failed to convey that intangible but all-important element in history, the spirit of the times.

According to historians of West Africa, the general thesis of imperialism as a political phenomenon and the specific argument of Egypt setting off the Scramble founders on the complexities of economic history.[75] No one has written with greater authority on trade and commerce in West Africa than Colin Newbury.[76] 'If it is true', he wrote in the *Journal of African History,* quoting the resounding conclusion of Robinson and Gallagher,

> that 'the theory of economic imperialism puts the trade before the flag, the capital before the conquest, the cart before the horse', then the theory requires modification and a reappraisal of its terms, at least in the West African context. But neither was any 'horse' goaded into the interior by a *bâton égyptien.* And until a history of West African trade and commerce has been written the question of motive at any point in the expansion of Europe in that area, is still open.[77]

[75] See, for example, John E. Flint, 'Nigeria: The Colonial Experience', in Gann and Duignan, *Colonialism in Africa,* I, pp. 224–25, note 1: The view of 'territorial partition of Africa as a "repercussion" of the British occupation of Egypt in 1882 . . . would not be acceptable to most scholars who have worked in the West African documents in detail; they would regard it as an oversimplification.' Flint has developed this line of criticism into a major attack in the Festschrift for Gerald Graham, where he attempts

> to show that an almost exactly opposite thesis can provide a more acceptable explanation for Britain's West African role in the partition; that the British occupation of Egypt in 1882 was not a basic consideration of British strategy in West Africa during partition; that far from neglecting her role in West Africa, or conceding claims there in return for Nile security, British decisions in West Africa were based solidly on considerations of commercial advantage; and that the territorial expansion of Britain in West Africa may be regarded as a classic case study of commercial imperialism.

John E. Flint, 'Britain and the Partition of West Africa', in John E. Flint and Glyndwr Williams, eds., *Perspectives of Empire* (London, 1973).
[76] See, for example, Colin W. Newbury, 'Trade and Authority in West Africa from 1850 to 1880', in Gann and Duignan, *Colonialism in Africa,* I.
[77] Colin W. Newbury, 'Victorians, Republicans, and the Partition of West Africa', *Journal of African History,* 3, 3 (1962), p. 501.

There was no direct connection between the Egyptian issue and the partition, as he indicates by an extensive examination of both French and British documents. Robinson and Gallagher may be right in saying the trade followed the flag—with this important qualification: 'But not quite all trade or all capital.' And not necessarily the national flag.[78] Contradictions abound, whether in the theories of economic imperialism or of Robinson and Gallagher. The fundamental argument put forward by Newbury is that the Scramble for West Africa did not originate merely in political or military calculations by the strategy makers in London or Paris. Fear of rising tariff barriers played an important part.

Anglo-French trade rivalry in West Africa forms one of the main themes of John D. Hargreaves's *Prelude to the Partition of West Africa,*[79] which appeared shortly after *Africa and the Victorians.* As Ronald Hyam has pointed out in a major critical essay, the two works complement each other.[80] In a straightforward and noncontroversial vein, Hargreaves traces the commercial negotiations that shaped the colonial boundaries after 1885. Though he does not explicitly enter the lists with Robinson and Gallagher, he has noted the exaggeration of the Egyptian thesis and their 'very British view'. In his review of *Africa and the Victorians,* he made the superb observation that the detailed research at the Public Record Office produces an effect 'as if *Ulysses* had been compiled from the records of the Dublin police force'.[81] Hargreaves's own work, in contrast to Robinson and Gallagher's, manifests a diligent effort fully to take account of the French as well as the British side and to evaluate without preconceptions the objectives and methods of African rulers during the partition. Henri Brunschwig, who reviewed the *Prelude* in the *Journal of African History,* commented that if one took together the works of Hargreaves, Stengers, and Newbury, the consensus does not favour Robinson and Gallagher: whatever the emphasis, France, not Britain, set in motion the partition of the continent.[82] Essentially in agreement with Stengers, Brunschwig argues in his own work that deals with the subject, *L'Avènement de*

---

[78] Colin W. Newbury, 'The Tariff Factor in Anglo-French West African Partition', in Gifford and Louis, *France and Britain in Africa,* p. 221.

[79] London, 1963.

[80] Ronald Hyam, 'The Partition of Africa', *Historical Journal,* 7, 1 (1964).

[81] John D. Hargreaves, 'British and French Imperialism in West Africa, 1885–1898', in Gifford and Louis, *France and Britain in Africa,* p. 276, note 42; his review of *Africa and the Victorians* is 'Victorians in Africa', *Victorian Studies,* 6 (1962/63), pp. 75–80.

[82] Henri Brunschwig, 'Les Origines du Partage de l'Afrique Occidentale', *Journal of African History,* 5, 1 (1964), pp. 121–25.

l'Afrique Noire,[83] that Brazza on the Congo with his treaty of 1882, not the British with the occupation of Egypt, sparked the chain of events of the political partition. 'So much for Robinson and Gallagher!' exclaimed Roland Oliver in the *Journal of African History.*[84]

Hence a controversy within a controversy. Though emphasizing the British invasion of Egypt as the direct cause of the partition of West Africa, Robinson and Gallagher find themselves in agreement with Stengers and Brunschwig that French naval and consular initiatives in the Gulf of Guinea in the winter of 1882–83 stimulated the immediate Scramble in that region.[85] Colin Newbury and A. S. Kanya-Forstner, however, have reviewed the entire question on the basis of extensive research in French archives and have challenged this view. Their article in the *Journal of African History* is remarkable for its comprehensive grasp of the basic issues of French expansion.[86] The crucial change in French policy, they argue, did not occur in 1882 but in 1879–80. At this time Charles de Freycinet (Minister of Public Works and later Prime Minister) and Admiral Jean Jauréguiberry (Minister of Marine and Colonies) inaugurated the era of French imperialism in West Africa by making specific decisions to establish French political as well as economic claims to territory and to assume military burdens of responsibility. The result of this investigation leads the authors to adjust the themes of Robinson and Gallagher to the counterpoint of French imperialism:

> The policies of Freycinet and Jauréguiberry contained the very essence of late-nineteenth-century imperialism; they were the Gallic 'doctrine of tropical African estates' enunciated fifteen years before Chamberlain came to office. And this difference in timing was vital. By 1895 the scramble for West Africa was virtually over; in 1880 it had yet to begin. Chamberlain's doctrine may have 'inspired the beginning of . . . modern administration' in Britain's African territories; its French counter-part inspired the actual process of expansion. The beginnings of British imperialism in West Africa may have been a

[83] Paris, 1963.

[84] *Journal of African History*, 5, 1 (1964), p. 134. Oliver's review of *Africa and the Victorians* is in the *Observer* of 27 August 1961. Here he makes the point, among others, that Robinson and Gallagher's preoccupation with strategy has led them to misinterpret the Scramble in East Africa: 'The strategic importance of Kenya and Uganda was a secondary discovery, made when it was known that the chartered company was failing. It was an excuse to hold on rather than an incentive to go in.'

[85] *Africa and the Victorians*, p. 166.

[86] C. W. Newbury and A. S. Kanya-Forstner, 'French Policy and the Origins of the Scramble for West Africa', *Journal of African History*, 10, 2 (1969), pp. 253–76.

consequence of the partition; the beginnings of French imperialism were its cause.[87]

Though it alters crucial causes and dates, this interpretation supports the thesis of continuity of Robinson and Gallagher: 'the initiatives of 1882–3 were a less radical departure from previous policies than has hitherto been assumed.' With a French twist it also expands the dimension of the argument. It is an ingenious analysis of 'the official mind' of French imperialism. It helps immensely in clarifying the chronology of the partition. Henri Brunschwig, again acting as moderator, suggests that at least everyone can agree that responsibility for the Scramble rests with France. He draws the distinction between the terms 'Scramble' and 'Course au Clocher' (steeplechase), the latter phrase appearing in the vocabulary of politics later than the former. For the decisive dates in the *dual* Anglo-French rivalry and the French initiative, Newbury and Kanya-Forstner correctly point to the years 1879–80. In 1882 the Scramble became truly *multinational,* a steeplechase whose competitors included King Leopold and eventually Bismarck.[88]

The years 1879–82 also represent the shattering of the *dual* Anglo-French control in Egypt and the beginning of the subsequent *multinational* competition in tropical Africa. Robinson and Gallagher are undoubtedly correct in emphasizing the way in which the emergency of the Egyptian crisis loomed over the minor issues of the partition. The question is whether they correctly establish a causal relationship between the Egyptian invasion and the partition and whether they are right in their interpretation of Egyptian nationalism or 'proto-nationalism'. On the latter point, the student of this controversy might do well to remember the balanced interpretation of Langer:

> It would be erroneous . . . to regard the troubles which arose in Egypt in 1881 and 1882 purely as a mutinous movement of discontented officers . . . A native press sprang up, and before long something resembling a national, constitutional party appeared on the scene. Of course, one must not look for absolute unity of purpose or for consistency in a rudimentary movement of this sort. Religious, political, and social factors were all intertwined in it, and within the group itself there were ill-concealed contradictions and antagonisms. The ecstatic partisanship of European Arabophils, like Wilfrid Scawen

---

[87] Ibid., p. 275.

[88] Henri Brunschwig, '"Scramble" et "Course au Clocher",' *Journal of African History,* 12, 1 (1971), pp. 139–41; *Le Partage de l'Afrique Noire* (Paris, 1971), pp. 153–56.

Blunt, harmed the movement perhaps more than it helped it, for by idealizing it these men made it rather ridiculous in the disillusioned eyes of the Westerner . . . The movement was, in fact, directed primarily against the domination of the country by foreign interests.[89]

The interpretation of Robinson and Gallagher does not contradict Langer's, but it is much more insistent. The emphasis is different: 'A recognisably modern nationalist revolution was sweeping the Nile Delta by 1882.'[90] Where lies the correct balance? In Langer's view that *if one event more than another* gave impetus to British imperialism in the late nineteenth century it was the *British* occupation of Egypt? Or in the thesis of Robinson and Gallagher, that the occupation was the *decisive event* caused by *Egyptian nationalism?* Agatha Ramm, as an authority probably more familiar with Gladstone's foreign policy than anyone else, and with no particular axe to grind in this controversy, has given her judgement in regard to those questions. In a full review of the collapse of the Anglo-French condominium, she examines British policy in the context of the distinct traditions of Palmerston and Gladstone and the varying French responses. Noting that in the *New Cambridge Modern History* Robinson and Gallagher call attention to national and Muslim revolt against alien and Christian rule in Tunisia[91] as well as Egypt, Ramm points out that Frenchmen saw this revolt more clearly than the British, who remained more sceptical. In the historiography of the subject, Robinson and Gallagher have performed a valuable service in giving greater dimension to the indigenous North African part of the problem. But essentially her own interpretation comes closer to Langer's: 'The ultimate causes of the establishment and of the end of the Dual Control in Egypt lay in the foreign policies of the Great Powers. The immediate causes lay in Egypt

---

[89] William L. Langer, *European Alliances and Alignments* (New York, 1956 edn.), pp. 262–64. It should be noted that Langer himself found the arguments of *Africa and the Victorians* persuasive. He wrote in 1962:

> A new analysis of the partition of Africa contends convincingly that Britain, concerned by the disturbance of the European balance of power by the German victories of 1870–1871, was driven primarily by concern for its communications with India to assume control of Egypt, and that this move in turn had such repercussions on international relations as to precipitate the 'Scramble for Africa'.

William L. Langer, 'Farewell to Empire', *Foreign Affairs*, 41, 1 (October 1962).

[90] 'The Partition of Africa', p. 597.

[91] For the Tunisian question in relation to the Egyptian, see Jean Ganiage, 'France, England, and the Tunisian Affair', in Gifford and Louis, *France and Britain in Africa,* and *Les origines du protectorat français en Tunisie, 1861–1881* (Paris, 1959).

itself.'[92] In regard to the connection between the occupation of Egypt and the Scramble for Africa, Ramm endorses the explanation of Robinson and Gallagher without accepting their premise of a causal relationship: 'The partition of Africa took place in the context of Anglo-French ill feeling. Bismarck was able to embark upon a colonial policy with a much greater degree of freedom than he would have enjoyed had the Anglo-French entente and the Anglo-French condominium in Egypt continued to exist.'[93]

European Imperialisms and African Nationalisms

Historians probably have spilled more ink over Bismarck's colonial policy than any other episode of the Scramble. Perhaps because of this extensive treatment, Robinson and Gallagher treat it in the same manner as the theories of economic imperialism and give it short shrift in two pages.[94] They merely accept the conclusions of the works of diplomatic historians, including A. J. P. Taylor's *Germany's First Bid for Colonies,* which is the epitome of the diplomatic approach.[95] In 1967 Henry A. Turner delivered a scathing attack on Taylor, and since Robinson and Gallagher accept his interpretation, on them as well.[96] Turner denounces the Taylor and Robinson-Gallagher position as an acceptance of the *Primat der Aussenpolitik,* or in other words, the idea that foreign affairs governed Bismarck's actions. The Taylor and Robinson-Gallagher thesis explains within the framework of international diplomacy Bismarck's sudden conversion from a staunch opponent of colonial expansion to the founder of Germany's overseas empire. At a time when Bismarck pursued reconciliation with France, he quarrelled with Britain over colonial issues such as South-West Africa, in which he had no real interest. France and Germany would unite together against the imperialism of Great Britain. This explanation takes account to some extent of Bismarck's exploitation of a popular issue

---

[92] Agatha Ramm, 'Great Britain and France in Egypt, 1876–1882', in Gifford and Louis, *France and Britain in Africa,* p. 77. For the Egyptian argument in relation to Egyptian and African history, see especially Roger Owen, 'Egypt and Europe: From French Expedition to British Occupation', in *Studies in the Theory of Imperialism.* As an expert on the Middle East, Owen believes that the Arabi movement, far from being indigenous, was in fact the result of a long period of interaction between Europe and Egypt. Therefore Robinson and Gallagher must be wrong in their argument that Africa's history is autonomous.

[93] Ramm, 'Great Britain and France in Egypt', p. 119.

[94] *Africa and the Victorians,* pp. 173–174.

[95] London, 1938.

[96] Henry Ashby Turner, Jr., 'Bismarck's Imperialist Venture: Anti-British in Origin?' in Gifford and Louis, *Britain and Germany in Africa,* chap. 2.

for electioneering purposes, and his personal pique at Gladstone and Lord Granville, the Foreign Secretary.[97] But it fails to encompass the powerful economic reasons for Bismarck's abrupt change of course. Though he remained sceptical, who was to say that the colonial enthusiasts in Germany might not be right in maintaining that colonies would eventually prove to be valuable? According to Turner, 'Bismarck was also not immune to the *Torschlusspanik* that was to play such an important role in the partition of the non-European world—the fear that the gate was rapidly closing and that the last chance was at hand.'[98] Bismarck aimed to protect German merchants, who faced rising protective tariffs abroad, and he sought to secure economic opportunities overseas at a time when the other Western nations were appropriating the rest of the non-Western world. Hans-Ulrich Wehler gives massive support to this interpretation in *Bismarck und der Imperialismus,* a landmark in the economic history of modern Europe as well as a conclusive examination of the socio-economic and political ingredients of Bismarck's imperialism.[99] He also specifically attacks the explanation of Robinson and Gallagher. German imperialism can be seen in no other way than as the result of socio-economic forces within Europe and by no means as a response to indigenous nationalist movements abroad. Robinson and Gallagher, Wehler argues, uncritically take over the 'simplistic theory' of Taylor because it suits their purpose.[100] Bismarck aimed to support Germany's foreign trade in pragmatic style; he tried to unite the German people by picking up the

[97] 'I now incline to believe that the principal explanation lay in Bismarck's bad temper, when the British government failed to do what he wanted. This explanation sounds trivial, but there is more evidence for it than for any other' (A. J. P. Taylor in response to Turner's attack, *English Historical Review,* 84 [October 1969], p. 816).

[98] Turner, 'Bismarck's Imperialist Venture', p. 51.

[99] Hans-Ulrich Wehler, *Bismarck und der Imperialismus* (Cologne, 1969).

[100] According to Wehler, even apart from the uncritical and entirely unsatisfactory account of German imperialism:

> Their model cannot successfully be defended either theoretically or empirically; even British imperialism during those years poses numerous questions which are excluded by their model. Apart from the fact that the description of policy in South Africa undercuts the authors' theories, their theories take no account of the many domestic and foreign interests which everywhere are the basis of certain stereotypes of political language and which condition the political horizon of ruling élites—the self-evident economic importance of India, for instance. In many respects their book is an exercise in belated historicism, with subtle apologetics.

Hans-Ulrich Wehler, 'Bismarck's Imperialism, 1862–1890', *Past and Present,* 48 (August 1970), pp. 125–26, note 11; the article is a synopsis of the main interpretations of *Bismarck und der Imperialismus.*

theme of colonial enthusiasm and Anglophobism; and he attempted to defend the traditional social structures of the Prussian state by diverting abroad the forces of social imperialism. All of this complex explanation of Bismarck's imperialism must be seen within the context of European history. So far as Bismarck is concerned, African nationalism as a causal factor in European imperialism did not exist.

In the view of Jean Stengers, African nationalism played no part in the imperialism of King Leopold and the creation of the Congo Free State. Probably the Congo State more than any other example can be put forward as a case in which the imperialists partitioned Africa in total disregard of the wishes or influences of the indigenous inhabitants.

> The Congo is the archetype of a political entity brought into being on African soil completely by the will of a European. One would seek in vain for any African substructure, any autochthonous base for this state as it appeared toward the end of the nineteenth century. It had nothing in common—save the name—with the Congo of former times, the Congo that had two or three centuries earlier been an important African kingdom. Its origins are to be found entirely in the will of one man—Leopold II of Belgium.
>
> In 1884–5 Leopold traced its boundaries firmly on the map of Africa. These extended to the very heart of the Black Continent and included regions largely unexplored up to that time. These borders were recognized by the powers and thus the Congo was born.[101]

King Leopold was motivated by greed, economic and territorial. He dreamed of an empire on the Nile as well as on the Congo. His imagination knew no bounds. He combined the idealism of a Rhodes with the business acumen of a Rockefeller. He was a patriotic imperialist, his purpose the exploitation of the Congo for the embellishment and glory of Belgium. So idiosyncratic and indeed unique was King Leopold's blend of imperialism that it defies classification by theory.[102] Nor can King Leopold's imperialism in any way be regarded as a response to local conditions in Africa, proto-nationalistic or other: 'All the features peculiar to the Free State . . . derived their origin from the person of its sovereign. The influence of the African environment was negligible, that of the metropolitan milieu scarcely less so.'[103]

[101] Jean Stengers, 'The Congo Free State and the Belgian Congo before 1914', in Gann and Duignan, *Colonialism in Africa*, I, p. 261.

[102] See Jean Stengers, 'King Leopold's Imperialism', in Owen and Sutcliffe, *Studies in the Theory of Imperialism,* chap. 11.

[103] Stengers, 'Congo Free State and Belgian Congo', p. 287.

Henri Brunschwig makes the same point of the imperialists' disregard of African conditions by beginning *Le Partage d'Afrique Noire* with reference to the disposal of Poland, Finland, and the Baltic states by Hitler and Stalin in 1939.[104] Blatant violation of Europe's own political and national boundaries puts into perspective the lack of scruple in drawing boundaries in black Africa. It is no doubt true that Africans influenced the course of the partition more than has been commonly recognized.[105] But most critics would argue that to shift the emphasis and impetus of nationalism from Europe to Africa is to produce a distortion of history. It is to caricature a fundamental truth of the modern expansion of Europe. European imperialism originated in Europe. No one is more insistent about the ultimate causes of French nationalism and imperialism than is Brunschwig. Galvanized by the defeat of 1871, 'the French people as a whole were not interested in colonization for its own sake but only in relation to everyone's major preoccupation—the German menace.'[106]

While the historians of European imperialism have criticized Robinson and Gallagher for distorting the non-European dimension of the nationalist theme, the Africanists have attacked them for basically misinterpreting early nationalist or resistance movements. T. O. Ranger has analysed the subject in an essay which Robinson and Gallagher themselves regard as among the most stimulating of the commentaries by their critics.[107] Ranger recapitulates the argument as it is especially developed in 'The Partition of Africa'. Nationalism is a continuation of imperialism; but primary resistance movements were essentially backward-looking and traditional. Recalcitrance represented the reactionary element of tribal life. In Robinson and Gallagher's own words, resistance movements were 'romantic reactionary struggles against the facts, the passionate protest of societies which were shocked by a new age of change and would not be comforted.' In his full-scale critique of this view, Ranger first points out that recent studies by

---

[104] *Le Partage d'Afrique Noire,* p. 21. The observation holds true for Africa as well. The imperialists still envisaged a repartition as late as the 1930s. See Klaus Hildebrand, *Vom Reich zum Weltreich* (Munich, 1969); for the British side, see W. R. Louis, 'Colonial Appeasement, 1936–1938', *Revue Belge de Philologie et d'Histoire,* 49, 4 (1971).

[105] See, for example, John D. Hargreaves, 'West African States and the European Conquest', in Gann and Duignan, *Colonialism in Africa,* I, chap. 6.

[106] Henri Brunschwig, 'French Exploration and Conquest in Tropical Africa from 1865 to 1898', in Gann and Duignan, *Colonialism in Africa,* I, p. 141; on the general theme, see Henri Brunschwig, *French Colonialism, 1871–1914* (London, 1966), with an introduction by Ronald Robinson. Cf. Raoul Girardet, *L'Idée coloniale en France,* (Paris, 1972).

[107] T. O. Ranger, 'Connexions between "Primary Resistance" Movements and Modern Mass Nationalism in East and Central Africa', *Journal of African History,* 9, 3 (1968).

other scholars, including Thomas Hodgkin, would greatly qualify this interpretation in West Africa. There was an immediate significance of the resistance for later nationalist movements by, for example, not only the memory of the earlier struggles but also the surviving structure of the anti-European movements. Ranger goes on to indicate at length the ways in which Robinson and Gallagher should be challenged in central and eastern Africa:

> [H]aving made this point of the continuing significance of memories of defeat, it is at once necessary to go on to say that not all resistances were doomed to total failure and crushing suppression. Some of them preserved liberties, wrung concessions or preserved pride. In so doing they made their own very important contributions to the creation of the environment in which later politics developed.[108]

The Hehe in German East Africa, for example, did not twist the colonial situation particularly to their advantage, but they certainly maintained their pride. Resistance movements contributed to the environment of later, modern nationalist politics. Thus Robinson and Gallagher's contrast between the backward-looking resistance movements and forward-looking 'defter nationalisms' is overdrawn. Nevertheless, Ranger has obviously found the concept extraordinarily useful in formulating his own basic ideas on the subject, even though he arrives at almost the opposite conclusion: resistance movements, even in the form of witchcraft, were 'often revolutionary in method and in purpose and sought to transcend tribal limitations'.[109]

One could argue that the theme of nationalism also goes askew in relation to the major 'proto-nationalist' movements of *Africa and the Victorians*. Even if one grants the attractiveness of the argument of Egyptian provocation in the north, Afrikaner nationalism as the catalyst of British imperialism is open to doubt. According to Leonard Thompson, Afrikaner national consciousness did not exist before the 1870s. British intervention created the combination of nationalistic fear and pride—not vice versa.[110] This view is upheld by one of the leading Afrikaner historians of the subject, F. A. van Jaarsveld. British imperialism stimulated Afrikaner nationalism.[111] In the judgement of

---

[108] Ibid., p. 441.

[109] Ibid., p. 452.

[110] Leonard Thompson, in Monica Wilson and Leonard Thompson, eds., *Oxford History of South Africa* (Oxford, 1971), II, p. 301.

[111] F. A. Van Jaarsveld, *The Awakening of Afrikaner Nationalism, 1868–1881* (Cape Town, 1961).

C. F. Goodfellow, whose book is an extensive study of South Africa in the 1870s, British policy 'arose from no unforeseen incident, and was in reaction against no nationalist challenge'. Again, the reverse of the thesis of Robinson and Gallagher is true: 'So far as the inter-relationship between British imperialism and Afrikaner nationalism is concerned, it seems much more plausible to say that the nationalism of the 1880s and later was in reaction against the impact of British imperialism during the 1870s.' [112] The same conclusion is reached by D. M. Schreuder, whose *Gladstone and Kruger* aims in part at testing the idea of Afrikaner nationalism as a stimulus of British imperialism. He concludes that Afrikaner unity was no more than a mirage: 'What Professor Gallagher and Dr. Robinson have taken as a major theme of their *Africa and the Victorians* . . . was no more than a momentary aberration in Afrikaner behaviour in the nineteenth century.' [113] In fact one can conclude in regard to nationalism, in Schreuder's words—he writes about Victorians and Afrikaners, but the same might be said of Robinson and Gallagher—'The historian is left with a supreme irony.' Upon careful examination, the general themes of *Africa and the Victorians* still flash brilliantly, but the more the specific cases are studied, the more luminous appear the older and more traditional accounts of the expansion of Europe.

[112] Clement Francis Goodfellow, *Great Britain and South African Confederation, 1870–1881* (Oxford, 1966), p. 218.

[113] D. M. Schreuder, *Gladstone and Kruger: Liberal Government and Colonial 'Home Rule', 1880–85* (London, 1969), p. 475, note 2. For a commentary on the validity of the argument in regard to the Western Sudan, see Kanya-Forstner, *Conquest of the Western Sudan*, p. 269.

In fairness to Robinson and Gallagher, it should be added that the complexities of South African history as illuminated by such historians as Goodfellow and Schreuder also can be interpreted to give support to other interpretations of *Africa and the Victorians*. For example, Goodfellow clearly establishes that British policy in the 1870s was essentially imperialist in the sense of pursuing a federal goal, and he thus indicates a continuity in imperial policy that links earlier imperialists such as Carnarvon and Frere to the imperialists of the 1890s such as Chamberlain and Milner. On Schreuder's argument that Afrikaner nationalism was a 'mirage', Afrikaner republicanism and the will for its defence did exist during the war of 1880–81. If Afrikaner nationalism seemed to be a mirage in the 1880s, it was in part because of the Liberal policy of conciliating the Afrikaners by restoring their independence. After the Jameson Raid, when Afrikaner nationalism definitely ceased to be a mirage, the general themes of both Schreuder and Robinson and Gallagher hold true: Britain as a world power in relative decline had to respond not only to the imperialism of her European rivals but also to crises of local nationalisms throughout the Empire. I am indebted to Professor Noel Garson for his comments on these points. For his contribution to the Robinson and Gallagher debate, see his essay, 'British Imperialism and the Coming of the Anglo-Boer War', *South African Journal of Economics*, 30, 2 (June 1962).

The Achievement of Robinson and Gallagher

Let it be said at once and finally that whatever reservations one might have about the themes of *Africa and the Victorians,* they do not detract from the accomplishment of Robinson and Gallagher. Anyone who writes about imperialism must take account of their work. *Africa and the Victorians* is a classic. Like most masterpieces, it bears the stamp of the age in which it was written. No one would want to exaggerate the extent to which historians are prisoners of their eras, but perhaps it is helpful in explaining the more exuberant inspirations of Robinson and Gallagher to remember that 'The Imperialism of Free Trade' was written during the time of Marshall aid and that the chapter on the British occupation of Egypt was drafted during Nasser's nationalization of the canal and the Suez crisis of 1956.[114] Ronald Robinson's more sober reassessment of the occupation and its consequences is a modification but by no means a repudiation: the breakdown of collaborative indirect rule was the 'imperative' for the British invasion 'and incidentally for much of the subsequent rivalry impelling the partition of Africa'.[115] The element of collaboration is the vital key.[116] The work of Robinson and Gallagher has made it clear—above all—that indigenous collaboration and recalcitrance helped shape European penetration into some non-Western societies, that collaboration guided the direction and form of colonial control, and, by extension, that the inversion of collaboration into non-cooperation determined in large part the process of decolonization. Their insights can be applied to various regions and different eras.[117] Whatever the merit of the critics' objections, Robinson and Gallagher have provided an intellectual framework in which an array of difficult problems can

---

[114] I am grateful to Professor Gallagher for discussion of these points.

[115] Robinson, 'Non-European Foundations of European Imperialism', p.130.

[116] Collaboration is the vital key to Robinson and Gallagher, but not to historians such as T. O. Ranger, who hold that *resisters* rather than collaborators are more significant in the colonial situation. For comment on Robinson and Gallagher perhaps inadvertently opening the floodgates of ideological history in this regard, see Donald Denoon and Adam Kuper, 'The "New Historiography" in Dar Es Salaam', *African Affairs,* 69, 277 (October 1970).

[117] For example, Keith Sinclair, 'Hobson and Lenin in Johore: Colonial Office policy towards British Concessionaires and Investors, 1878–1907', *Modern Asian Studies,* 1,4 (October 1967), p. 352: 'One need merely mention the route to the East and the tendency of established colonies to expand their borders to see that Robinson and Gallagher are more at home in Johore than Hobson and Lenin.' W. R. Louis, *Great Britain and Germany's Lost Colonies, 1914–1919* (Oxford, 1967), p. 159: 'The powerful theme of *Africa and the Victorians* is even more true of British statesmen of the First World War period than for those of the partition era: "Over and over again, they show an obsession with security, a fixation on safeguarding the routes to the East".'

fruitfully be discussed. Their work carries the study of 'imperialism' a long way forward.

Unresolved Problems: Imperialism in War and in Worldwide Perspective; the Work of Robinson and Gallagher as Social Science, or History as Art?

The unresolved problems can be defined by comment on Robinson and Gallagher's method. If there is paradox in such central concepts as 'the imperialism of free trade', considerable sophistication also characterizes their handling of the general themes of economic motives during the Scramble and imperialism as a cause of war. Though *Africa and the Victorians* can be read as a polemic against the theorists of economic imperialism, nowhere do Robinson and Gallagher deny the economic essence of empire. In the accounts of the Fashoda crisis,[118] and the origins of the Boer War,[119] the reader can rightly draw the general conclusion that the Continental powers subordinated their colonial activity to European concerns. Colonial expansion was

[118] The key work to be compared with Robinson and Gallagher is G. N. Sanderson, *England, Europe and the Upper Nile, 1882–1899* (Edinburgh, 1965). Sydney Kanya-Forstner has written:
> Throughout his treatment of British policy, Professor Sanderson's implicit intention has been at least in part to challenge the whole interpretation of *Africa and the Victorians:* that British policy on the Upper Nile was from beginning to end determined by the need to protect the security of Egypt and was formulated by an élite largely immune from outside influences. This is why he stresses the influence of private interest and public opinion.

Historical Journal, 9, 2 (1966), pp. 251–54. See Jean Stengers, 'Aux Origines de Fachoda; L'Expedition Monteil', *Revue Belge de Philologie et d'Histoire,* 36 (1958), pp. 436–50; 38 (1960), pp. 366–404 and 1040–65; R. G. Brown, *Fashoda Reconsidered* (London, 1970); and Marc Michel, *La Mission Marchand, 1895–1899* (Paris, 1972). For an important review article, see J. Stengers, 'Une Facette de la Question du Haut-Nil: Le Mirage Soudanais', *Journal of African History,* 10, 4 (1969), which has references useful for the Robinson-Gallagher controversy.

[119] See J. S. Marais, *The Fall of Kruger's Republic* (Oxford, 1961), which is compared with Robinson and Gallagher by N. G. Garson in 'British Imperialism and the Anglo-Boer War'; see also L. M. Thompson, *The Unification of South Africa, 1902–1910* (Oxford, 1960); G. H. L. LeMay, *British Supremacy in South Africa, 1899–1907* (Oxford, 1965); and G. Blainey, 'Lost Causes of the Jameson Raid', *Economic History Review,* 2nd series, 18, 1 (August 1965), which by contrast to Robinson and Gallagher argues that Rhodes risked political power in order to preserve economic power. Other important recent articles are J. S. Galbraith, 'The British South Africa Company and the Jameson Raid', *Journal of British Studies,* 10, 1 (1970); Robert V. Kubicek, 'The Randlords in 1895: A Reassessment', *Journal of British Studies,* 11, 2 (1972); Andrew Porter, 'Lord Salisbury, Mr. Chamberlain, and South Africa, 1895–9', *Journal of Imperial and Commonwealth History,* 1, 1 (1972); and 'Sir Alfred Milner and the Press, 1897–1899', *Historical Journal,* 16, 2 (1973).

no more than a marginal activity for France and Germany and never of any substantial economic importance. This holds true as well for the British, for whom imperialism in Africa was clearly more than a fringe activity yet always subordinate to Britain's non-colonial role, Robinson and Gallagher do not emphasize the poisoning of international relations by internecine rivalry in Africa, and it is beyond their scope to examine the extent to which the emotions generated by the Boer War contributed to the atmosphere of the decade before the war. We will not know the answers to such problems until thorough studies are made of the changing climate of opinion. To what extent did contemporaries alter their views about the problems and consequences of colonial expansion as a result of the Boer War? Robinson and Gallagher probably would minimize the significance of such an investigation, just as Jean Stengers would affirm its fundamental importance. The split is between those who wish to stress the continuity of historical experience and those who emphasize the changing perceptions of fundamental historical problems. There can be no ultimate resolution of the issue of continuity—one of the major differences, in other words, between Robinson and Gallagher and some of their critics—because it hinges on approach and temperament as well as the answers sought.

The Robinson and Gallagher controversy provides insight into the universality of the problems of imperialism even in such areas as Japanese expansion in the Far East,[120] while it also indicates that the debate about continuity is by no means restricted to British imperialism. The controversy about American expansion has similarities. William Appleman Williams, Walter LaFeber, and Thomas McCormick emphasize the conscious pursuit of informal empire as a constant theme in American history,[121] while Ernest May espouses an analogous interpretation to Stengers's explanation of imperialism as a phenomenon most usefully associated with a particular era.[122] On the one hand, imperialism can be seen as an ever-present, all-pervasive, and perhaps even unconscious urge for empire. Perhaps a universal formula or satisfactory theory of imperialism may never be found, but the search is worthwhile. On the other hand, some historians are as much

---

[120] The book to be read in this regard to the Robinson and Gallagher controversy is Akira Iriye, *Pacific Estrangement: Japanese and American Expansion, 1897–1911* (Cambridge, Mass., 1972).

[121] William Appleman Williams, *The Tragedy of American Diplomacy* (New York, 1962 edn.); Walter LaFeber, *The New Empire: An Interpretation of American Expansion, 1860–1898* (Ithaca, N.Y., 1963); and Thomas J. McCormick, *China Market: America's Quest for Informal Empire, 1893–1901* (Chicago, 1967).

[122] Ernest R. May, *American Imperialism: A Speculative Essay* (New York, 1968).

interested in the differences as the similarities of historical eras and are more concerned to paint the last two decades of the nineteenth century as possessing unique characteristics of an age which will be remembered for its exuberant enthusiasm for colonies, the racial arrogance of the Europeans, and the belief that Europeans were somehow divinely destined to rule the world. The controversy is at least in part a collision between those with the approach and temperaments of social scientists who believe in the search for universal explanations or theory and historians who believe that history is best considered an art and not a science. In the works of Robinson and Gallagher there are elements of both.

The Robinson and Gallagher Controversy 1976

33

THE HISTORIOGRAPHY
OF THE BRITISH EMPIRE

I n this essay the word 'historiography' is used in the sense of the evolving or changing interpretations of the history of the British Empire. The term thus means the history of the British Empire's history. It represents the effort to portray the Zeitgeist, or the spirit of the time, in which historians wrote and the influences on them. In another sense, it deals with the art of writing Imperial history and the development or professionalization of the discipline. The essay is therefore concerned with the ways historians have responded to the problems of the British Empire. How did historians of the Empire go about their tasks and what were their assumptions? How were their accounts influenced by the political and cultural climate of their times? Above all, which of the historians of the Empire had the strength of intellect and personality to write works that have endured? This essay addresses itself to those questions up through the period of the historiographical revolution of the early 1960s.

In tracing the antecedents of British Imperial history, the era of the Enlightenment is critical. Historians since Herodotus had grappled with the problem of how to write history, but modern historiography had its birth in the Enlightenment's axiom that historical truth could be ascertained through the exercise of reason and, for Edward Gibbon, by fidelity to written evidence. Reaching its zenith of optimism in the nineteenth century, the idea developed that history might be perfected as a science, whereby events would be recorded not only as they actually happened but in a true and universal account. Yet history also continued to be used for political purposes. Though few historians of quality have betrayed themselves as propagandists, many have been caught up, consciously or unconsciously, in the ideological struggles of their times. Most historians today probably recognize that there is an element of subjectivity in virtually all historical accounts. Those who have the good fortune of being able to pursue their calling according to their own lights face the same perplexities as the nineteenth-century academic historians who created the modern profession. From then onwards the aim of professional historians has been to interpret events and analyse institutions and traditions as accurately and as free from overt bias as possible. This essay reveals the dilemmas of historians who have attempted to explain 'imperialism', sometimes at the risk of public condemnation. It conveys not only the dominant intellectual passions as they carried over from one generation to the next, but also the way in which preoccupation with national and world affairs influenced historical writing on the British Empire.

Leopold von Ranke was the father of the modern historical profession, British as well as German. By founding one of the first scholarly seminars in the mid-nineteenth century in Berlin, he played a major part in the historical revolution that trained students to examine documents systematically and to write history in a spirit of detachment and precision. The great English historians during most of the nineteenth century, like many historians of the British Empire to the present, were fairly oblivious of German historical scholarship. But by the last two decades of the century, British historians had taken steps towards creating the discipline as it is known today. The year 1886, when the *English Historical Review* was founded at the initiative of James Bryce, may be taken as a symbolic date.[1] 'The object of history', proclaimed the anonymous preface, penned by Bryce, in the first issue, 'is to discover and set forth facts.' After noting that English historical scholarship was 'as thorough in quality as that even of the Germans', he stated the aim of the new journal in a way that bears remarkable similarity to that of the *Oxford History of the British Empire:* the *EHR* would be devoted 'to the person called the "general reader"', as well as scholars, and would present historical essays 'which an educated man, not specially conversant with history, may read with pleasure and profit'.[2] The hope met with disappointment. The *EHR* failed to arouse the interest of the general public, but it did mark the arrival of the academic or professional historian in Britain, and it set the standard of excellence in the field.[3]

[1] The *Historische Zeitschrift* had been founded in 1859; the *Revue Historique* in 1876; and the *Rivista storica italiana* in 1884. The first issue of the *American Historical Review* appeared in 1895. (Lord) Bryce had a long-standing interest in America, later publishing *The American Commonwealth* (1888) and serving as Ambassador in Washington (1907–13). He hoped that the *EHR* would provide a common forum for American as well as British historians and would be a historical journal for 'the whole race'.

[2] 'Prefatory Note', *EHR*, 1 (January 1886), pp. 1–6.

[3] See Philippa Levine, *The Amateur and the Professional: Antiquarians, Historians and Archaeologists in Victorian England, 1838–1886* (Cambridge, 1986), chap. 7. See also especially Rosemary Jann, 'From Amateur to Professional: The Case of the Oxbridge Historians', *Journal of British Studies*, 22, 2 (Spring 1983), pp. 122–47; and Doris S. Goldstein, 'The Origins and Early Years of the English Historical Review', *EHR*, 101, 398, (January 1986), pp. 6–19. Llewellyn Woodward makes the essential point that in the latter part of the nineteenth century, college tutors rather than professors in Oxford and Cambridge controlled the curriculum, which was designed more to prepare students for competitive examinations for entry into the Home and Indian Civil Service than to advance knowledge. In 1895, Oxford established a research degree of B.Litt., requiring a thesis, but not the more advanced degree of Doctor of Philosophy until 1917 (Llewellyn Woodward, 'The Rise of the Professional Historian in England', in K. Bourne and D. C. Watt, eds., *Studies in International History* [London, 1967], pp. 16–34).

Among the greatest works by past masters in British history—Lord Clarendon, David Hume, Edward Gibbon, Thomas Carlyle, Thomas Babington Macaulay, and J. R. Seeley—there are three that are especially significant for the historical background. They are Gibbon's *Decline and Fall of the Roman Empire* (1776–88), Macaulay's *History of England* (1849–55), and Seeley's *Expansion of England* (1883). The three works have a central bearing on the interpretation of the Empire's end, its purpose as well as its beginning, and they all continue to inspire debate.

Gibbon set a high standard of accuracy, he had a perspective that extended over centuries, and he possessed an incomparable literary style. His *Decline and Fall* casts a long shadow that falls even on the *Oxford History of the British Empire*. Readers expect to know whether Gibbon helps them understand not only the end but also the course of the British Empire. He wrote in the era of the American Revolution, but he was austere in not projecting the lessons of the past into the present: he did not necessarily think that the loss of the American colonies was the beginning of the end, in the Roman sense, for the British Empire.[4] Nevertheless there is a key question that has captivated the historian's imagination: was there an undeviating line of decline that characterized the British Empire? The question is significant because it has haunted generations. Was there in the British Empire a period of tolerant and benevolent rule comparable to Gibbon's golden age in Antonine Rome? Did Britain—the first industrialized nation, possessor of the greatest navy and a worldwide empire—decline because of moral weakness at the centre and a failure of the will to resist the onslaught at the periphery? Gibbon might or might not have agreed with the trajectory of descent as portrayed by Correlli Barnett and other recent historians who believe that, with greater determination, British statecraft after 1945 might have modernized Britain's industry and reversed the process of economic decline.[5] On the question of the Empire's collapse—of determining whether there was infirmity of will in the metropole as well as insurgency in the provinces—Gibbon continues to provoke thought.

The issue of economic decline has been the specific Gibbonian theme applied to the history of the Empire. On this point, Adam Smith provides a clue to the complexity of the problem: he held that the loss

---

[4] See J. G. A. Pocock, 'Between Machiavelli and Hume: Gibbon as Civic Humanist and Philosophical Historian', in G. W. Bowersock, John Clive, and Stephen R. Graubard, eds., *Edward Gibbon and the Decline and Fall of the Roman Empire* (Cambridge, Mass., 1977), pp. 103–19.

[5] See especially Correlli Barnett, *The Lost Victory: British Dreams, British Realities, 1945–1950* (London, 1995).

of the colonies would not endanger Britain's long-term economic prospects.[6] Smith was probably more accurate than Gibbon, since empires revive as well as fall and Britain's long-term economic prosperity was not necessarily dependent on her colonies. In view of the natural resources, population, and geographical extent of the British Isles, what seems surprising in retrospect is that the British maintained the Empire as long as they did. One significant point in assessing Gibbon is that his contemporaries did not believe that the Empire, and Britain's place in the world, were doomed to inevitable decline. Gibbon's interpretation would have left the British people with little choice other than defeatism; it would have denied them any significant voice in their own fate. The emotional and creative energy of the post–Second World War period can be explained only by the determination to halt the decline and collapse of the economy and to prevent Britain from sinking into the status of 'a second-class European power'. Contrary to Gibbon, decline is a relative concept. Barry Supple, one of the foremost authorities on British economic performance, points out that national decline and degradation, if it can be so described, was replaced with something else. He quotes a concluding passage in A. J. P. Taylor's *English History*:

> [In the Second World War] the British people came of age . . . Imperial greatness was on the way out; the welfare state was on the way in. The British empire declined; the condition of the people improved. Few now sang 'Land of Hope and Glory'. Few even sang 'England Arise'. England had risen all the same.[7]

What would Gibbon have made of that? He had a habit of ignoring criticism, but he might have been jolted by John Gallagher's argument in the Ford Lectures in Oxford in 1974 that in history, at least in the history of the British Empire, there is no 'unbroken movement' in the same direction:

> Edward Gibbon said of the Roman empire that 'the causes of destruction multiplied with the extent of conquest; and, as soon as time and accident had removed the artificial supports, the stupendous

---

[6] Max Beloff discusses Gibbon and Smith in relation to the *OHBE* in 'Empire Reconsidered', *History Today*, 46, 2 (February 1996), pp. 13–20. For Smith in the context of the British Empire, see especially Donald Winch, *Classical Political Economy and Colonies* (London, 1965), chap. 2.

[7] Supple quoting Taylor in Peter Clarke and Clive Trebilcock, eds., *Understanding Decline: Perceptions and Realities of British Economic Performance* (Cambridge, 1997), p. 16. On the theme of economic decline, this is the key work that connects with the history of the Empire.

fabric yielded to the pressure of its own weight.' 'Time and accident'. We might look at the fall of the British empire in a briskly function-alist way, and conclude that it was simply the damage of the Second World War which brought the British empire down. But . . . a result of the Second World War was (temporarily) to reintegrate the system, reversing the trend and turning it back from influence towards em-pire before the downfall.[8]

Empires can revive as well as die, and the British Empire attempted to resurrect itself in the form of the Commonwealth. The themes of de-cline and fall, revival and collapse, and the nature of the post-colonial era recur in the historiography of the subject. Paul Kennedy's *Rise and Fall of the Great Powers: Economic Change and Military Conflict from 1500 to 2000,* a major work of synthesis, is a case in point. The inspiration, however, derives explicitly from Ranke's empirical treatment of the rise and decline of nations and implicitly rejects Gibbon's unwavering line of descent.[9]

Thomas Macaulay holds a place of unique importance in the his-tory of the British Empire, not least because of the way he linked the Empire's purpose with that of progress. Macaulay was the pre-eminent historian in nineteenth-century England. His name is indelibly asso-ciated with the Whig interpretation of history, and as a civil servant in India, he devised the Indian penal code and penned the famous Min-ute on Education. Seminal ideas—for example 'informal empire'—can be traced to his work. Macaulay held arrogant but representative views on England's cultural ascendancy in the world and on what he believed to be the benevolent impact of British rule in India and else-where. The controversial Minute on Education, written in India in 1835, managed to reconcile British realpolitik and idealism in a way that left a lasting mark on subsequent interpretations of British rule:

> It is impossible for us, with our limited means, to attempt to educate the body of the people. We must at present do our best to form a class who may be interpreters between us and the millions whom we gov-ern; a class of persons, Indian in blood and colour, but English in taste, in opinions, in morals, and in intellect.[10]

[8] John Gallagher, *The Decline, Revival and Fall of the British Empire,* Anil Seal, ed. (Cambridge, 1982), p. 73. R. G. Collingwood makes the same point in assessing the work of Arnold Toynbee: 'There are no mere phenomena of decay: every decline is also a rise' (R. G. Collingwood, *The Idea of History* [Oxford, 1946], p. 164). Collingwood was a philosopher as well as historian, and his book remains the indispensable general work on historiography.

[9] Paul Kennedy, *The Rise and Fall of the Great Powers: Economic Change and Military Conflict from 1500 to 2000* (New York, 1987), p. xxiv.

[10] See John Clive, *Macaulay: The Shaping of the Historian* (New York, 1973), chap. 12.

On another occasion Macaulay proclaimed the progress of India towards order and rationality, and said of the Indian desire for British institutions:

> [N]ever will I attempt to avert or to retard it. Whenever it comes, it will be the proudest day in English history. To have found a great people sunk in the lowest depths of slavery and superstition, to have so ruled them as to have made them desirous and capable of all the privileges of citizens, would indeed be a title to glory all our own.[11]

In advance of most others of his time, but with his characteristic streak of arrogance, Macaulay anticipated eventual Indian independence, believing that it would come as a result of beneficent collaboration and, specifically, of the use of English education to transform Indian society.[12] Eric Stokes, Smuts Professor of the History of the British Commonwealth at Cambridge (1970–81), once wrote that Macaulay's writing 'with its shrewd blend of altruism and self-interest . . . represented the permanent political instinct of British colonial policy.'[13]

Macaulay was an unabashed supporter of the Whig cause, holding throughout his life that the party of reform had saved England from revolution and that the Whigs championed principles of English liberty, toleration, and improvement. In short, he believed in progress. A distinction must be made, however, between Macaulay as a Whig historian and the Whig school of history. Whig history is history reflecting the anxieties and preoccupations of the present and emphasizing the evolution of certain principles—as if, for example, English history should be read as the unfolding triumph of liberty.[14] Macaulay's writings embodied all of those things, and he certainly would have defended the celebration of liberty, but he cannot be held responsible

[11] Quoted in Ronald Hyam, *Britain's Imperial Century, 1815–1914: A Study of Empire and Expansion* (London, 1976), p. 220; see also especially Thomas R. Metcalf, *Ideologies of the Raj* (Cambridge, 1994), pp. 39–40.

[12] Though he was in advance of his time, he was not alone. James Mill also anticipated that Indians might eventually achieve self-government, but on the basis of good government, just law, and 'scientific' taxation. For Macaulay in relation to James Mill and John Stuart Mill, see Hyam, *Britain's Imperial Century,* e.g. p. 55.

[13] Eric Stokes, 'Macaulay: The Indian Years, 1834–38', *A Review of English Literature,* 1, 4 (October 1960), pp. 41–50; Stokes, *The English Utilitarians and India* (Oxford, 1959), pp. 46–47.

[14] See Herbert Butterfield, *The Whig Interpretation of History* (London, 1931); his much more substantial work is *Man on His Past: The Study of the History of Historical Scholarship* (Cambridge, 1955). For a fair assessment that has implications for Imperial history, see G. R. Elton, 'Herbert Butterfield and the Study of History', *Historical Journal,* 27, 3 (1984), pp. 729–43. In the 1960s, Elton generally opposed the expansion of the Cambridge curriculum into 'Third World' studies, or, as he put it, 'bits of history' from 'Mexico to Malawi'.

for the reductionist interpretations perpetuated by subsequent historians.[15] Macaulay remains in a class by himself.[16]

The Whig interpretation of history has a direct bearing on Imperial history, in which it forms a respected tradition. Even in the time of Adam Smith and the era of the American Revolution, historical works reflected the belief of progress in the Empire. Historians in the nineteenth century generally held that British rule brought to indigenous peoples the benefits of civilization. British colonies would advance towards self-governing status or what was later called Dominionhood. In the early twentieth century the same idea was applied to India. Ramsay MacDonald of the Independent Labour Party, among others, advocated Dominion Status for India before the First World War. The cause was later championed by historians, above all by Lionel Curtis, Reginald Coupland, and W. K. Hancock. The Empire would justify itself by its result: equal nations, freely associating in the British Commonwealth. The tradition reached its apogee after the Second World

[15] For example Robert Mackenzie, *The Nineteenth Century* (London, 1880), caricatured as a work

> depicting that century as a time of progress from a state of barbarism, ignorance and bestiality which can hardly be exaggerated to a reign of science, enlightenment, and democracy . . . everybody was rapidly getting happier and happier until a culmination of joy was reached in the dazzling victories of the Crimea. But the victories of peace were no less dazzling; they include the splendours of the cotton trade, the magnificent conception of steam locomotion, which awakened the dormant love of travel and taught people in distant parts of the earth to love one another instead of hating one another as before.

Collingwood, *Idea of History*, p. 145.

[16] As may be gathered from Lord Acton, the Regius Professor of Modern History at Cambridge, 1895–1902, recounting conversations with William Stubbs, the foremost English historian of his time, and Mandell Creighton, the first Editor of the *EHR;* and later with two equally distinguished German historians:

> I was once with two eminent men, the late bishop of Oxford [William Stubbs] and the present Bishop of London [Mandell Creighton]. On another occasion I was with two far more eminent men, the two most learned men in the world. I need hardly tell you their names—they were [Theodore] Mommsen and [Adolf von] Harnack. On each occasion the question arose: who was the greatest historian the world had ever produced. On each occasion the name first mentioned, and on each occasion the name finally agreed upon, was that of Macaulay.

James Westfall Thompson, *A History of Historical Writing* (2 vols., New York, 1942), II, p. 300.

Who among the historians of the British Empire would hold the comparable place of honour? There is obviously an element of subjectivity in any such judgement, but on the basis of the formal and informal discussions among historians of the *OHBE,* it is Sir Keith Hancock.

War in the works of Nicholas Mansergh, who accepted the progress of the Commonwealth as an article of faith and achieved the highest level of scholarly accuracy and balanced treatment.[17] The idealism of Mansergh and others is far removed from the crude Whig interpretations of the nineteenth century.[18] But there is a teleology in much of the historical writing on the Empire, whether Whig or, eventually, Marxist.[19]

The founders of the *English Historical Review* objected to Macaulay not because he was a Whig historian, but because he championed the cause of the Whig party in his history. They criticized Gibbon not because he had portrayed Rome as falling before the forces of barbarism and religion, but because of his bias in favour of pagan Rome.[20] This era saw the rise of the academic historians, of William Stubbs and Frederic Maitland, Lord Acton and Seeley. Seeley, especially severe, referred to Macaulay as a 'charlatan'; he warmly and pointedly despised Macaulay's romanticism. Of the historians associated with the creation of the *EHR,* all of whom were more or less in open rebellion against Macaulay, Seeley is of particular interest because he has a fair claim to be regarded as the founder of the field of Imperial history, though he would not have described himself as having such a purpose.[21] His *Expansion of England* (1883) provided inspiration for men of affairs as well as for historians. He spoke for his generation when he stated that lessons or morals could be drawn from the study of history to instruct politicians and statesmen, not least servants of the Empire.

Seeley was not an historian of the same rank as Gibbon or Macaulay, but his work had a comparable intellectual rigour, and *Expansion of*

---

[17] See especially Nicholas Mansergh, *The Commonwealth Experience* (London, 1969). Constitutional progress to Mansergh was a cardinal principle, but he saw a tension between empire and liberty. For him, the Colonial Empire did not inevitably give way to Commonwealth: liberty and equality had to be fought for and won. The Commonwealth, in Mansergh's view, should be regarded as the achievement of anti-imperial nationalists such as Smuts of South Africa, Mackenzie King of Canada, de Valera of Ireland, and Nehru of India.

[18] See also the works by D. A. Low, especially *Eclipse of Empire* (London, 1991), for 'the profound sense of positive achievement' and 'positive sense of direction [that] lasted right through to the end of empire and beyond' (p. xiii). 'The last of the great Whig historians!' according to Sarvepalli Gopal, the historian of British rule in India, only half in jest describing Low (*OHBE* Archives).

[19] For an important reassessment of the idea of progress in a Marxist context, see Barrington Moore, Jr., 'On the Notion of Progress, Revolution, and Freedom', *Ethics*, 72, 2 (January 1962), pp. 106–19. For general Marxist interpretation of the Empire, see especially V. G. Kiernan, *Marxism and Imperialism* (London, 1974).

[20] See Collingwood, *Idea of History*, pp. 146–47.

[21] See Peter Burroughs, 'John Robert Seeley and British Imperial History', *Journal of Imperial and Commonwealth History*, 1, 2 (January 1973), pp. 191–211. On Seeley's life and career, see Deborah Wormell, *Sir John Seeley and the Uses of History* (Cambridge, 1980).

England remained in print until 1956, the year of the Suez crisis.[22] It was the first systematic account of the eighteenth-century Empire. Seeley was Regius Professor of Modern History at Cambridge from 1869 until his death at sixty-one in 1895. He passionately believed in empirical method, reasoned argument, and impartiality. In the spirit of the new scholarship, he conducted research at the Public Record Office. He was an admirer of Ranke's accuracy and rigorous use of evidence. A student of German as well as British history, he also had a general grasp of European history since antiquity as well as an impressive command of the history of the European colonial empires. He disliked the phrase 'British Empire', preferring instead 'Greater Britain' to convey the idea that the colonies of white settlement were an extension of England overseas. In that sense he believed the British Empire to be organic: whether in Britain or abroad, everyone 'British' belonged to a single Imperial nation. The British Empire was thus an empire of kith and kin, in which India formed a perplexing and alien part. Like other writers since the 1860s, including Charles Dilke and J. A. Froude, Seeley held that Imperial federation might be England's destiny, depending in part on whether the British were prepared to see themselves as a world power rather than merely as part of Europe:

> If the United States and Russia hold together for another half century, they will at the end of that time completely dwarf such old European States as France and Germany and depress them into a second class. They will do the same to England, if at the end of that time England still thinks of herself as simply a European State.[23]

He did not commit himself to federation. He merely debated it vigorously, just as he inquired into whether India might be too large a defence commitment for the British government. What if a Russian invasion of India were to spark another mutiny? One of the reasons for the continued success of his book was his ability to ask provocative questions and to appeal for imaginative answers. Seeley was a publicist. He believed that the British government had a responsibility to answer difficult questions honestly and to acknowledge that the state itself had ethical responsibilities. Seeley's work thus had a moral as well as a

---

[22] It was republished in 1971 by the University of Chicago Press with a useful introduction by John Gross.

[23] *Expansion of England* (Chicago edn.), p. 62. For Dilke, see *Greater Britain* (London, 1868); for Froude, *Oceana* (London, 1885). For Dilke, Froude, and other nineteenth-century writers who provided the antecedents of such concepts as the 'special relationship' with the United States and the 'informal empire' of British influence beyond the Empire, see Hyam, *Britain's Imperial Century*.

clear intellectual thrust, which appealed to Cecil Rhodes and others committed to British expansion.

There were many ways in which Seeley's work had a lasting historiographical influence. One is quite simple. His famous phrase that the British seemed 'to have conquered and peopled half the world in a fit of absence of mind' caused historians as well as the general public to reflect on the origins of the Empire. Perhaps no other single phrase in the Empire's history is so famous or has had such a stimulating effect in the classroom. As is clear from his general style, Seeley intended it as a provocative remark on the dynamics of British expansion. He was drawing attention to the unconscious acceptance by the English public of the burdens of Empire, particularly in India. Economic history was not Seeley's strength, but he clearly grasped the commercial principles of 'the old colonial system', and by using that phrase he lent his academic authority to a lasting and useful concept.[24] Although he lamented the American Revolution, he took heart that the United States had inherited 'the language and traditions of England' and that the British had learned the lesson not to regard colonies as mere estates 'out of which the mother-country is to make a pecuniary profit'. There had gradually developed, he believed, 'a better system', whereby colonies could over time achieve 'emancipation'. Despite his repudiation of Macaulay, Seeley was still enough of a Whig historian to see progress over the course of the nineteenth century. But he did not believe that human progress was inevitable; it required statesmanship and determination. Thus, again, there was the moral ring to his work, especially in the passages in *Expansion of England* concerning liberty.

The concept of liberty is another reason why Seeley's work has a permanent historiographical significance. He drew inspiration from John Stuart Mill's idea that democracy and despotism are incompatible. Seeley faced squarely the central contradiction of the British Empire: how could the British reconcile the despotism of the Indian Empire with the democracy enjoyed by the colonies of white settlers? The famous passage reads:

> How can the same nation pursue two lines of policy so radically different without bewilderment, be despotic in Asia and democratic in Australia, be in the East at once the greatest Musulman Power in the world . . . and at the same time in the West be the foremost champion of free thought and spiritual religions, stand out as a great mil-

[24] See John S. Galbraith, 'The Empire since 1783', in Robin W. Winks, ed., *The Historiography of the British Empire–Commonwealth: Trends, Interpretations, and Resources* (Durham, N.C., 1966), pp. 46–68.

itary Imperialism to resist the march of Russia in Central Asia at the same time that it fills Queensland and Manitoba with free settlers?[25]

By posing so clearly the conjunction of liberty and despotism, Seeley's work continued to engage subsequent generations of readers.

Seeley's successor in Cambridge was Lord Acton, whose achievement at the beginning of the twentieth century, the *Cambridge Modern History*, was a culmination of nineteenth-century historical thought. In time, it inspired other Cambridge series, including the *Cambridge History of the British Empire*. Acton himself was a dignified man possessed of vast erudition and an epigrammatic style. With the rigour of a German background and training tempered by his association with the *English Historical Review*, he seemed to be the best possible editor for a series that would set the standard for the next century. He believed, or at least hoped, that the *CMH* would be definitive. He took as a premise that the opening of the archives in the nineteenth century made possible the revelation of historical truth—in the words of the preface to the first volume, composed by his successors but with him in mind: 'the long conspiracy against the revelation of truth has gradually given way.'[26] It seemed obvious to Acton and his colleagues that it lay beyond the grasp of any single individual to write the history of the modern world.[27] He recruited 160 authors, mainly British, but also prominent European and American historians, including Woodrow Wilson, then President of Princeton University. Acton found the planning of the series and the preliminary editing a heavy responsibility. He died in 1902, two years before the publication of the first installment. The *CMH* appeared in thirteen volumes from 1904 to 1912. E. A. Benians, one of the assistant editors and eventually Master of St. John's College and Vice-Chancellor of Cambridge University, became one of the three editors of the *Cambridge History of the British Empire*.

The first volume of the *Cambridge History of the British Empire* (1929) opened by quoting Macaulay on the greatness of England and commenting on the forty-five years that had elapsed since Seeley's *Expansion of England*.[28] Benians and his two fellow editors, J. Holland

---

[25] *Expansion of England* (Chicago edn.), p. 141.

[26] For the beginning of the project, see especially G. N. Clark, 'The Origins of the Cambridge Modern History', *Cambridge Historical Journal*, 8, 2 (1945), pp. 57–64.

[27] The assumption did not command universal agreement, either at the time or later. In 1949, Max Beloff commented that the planning and execution of the *Cambridge Modern History* marked the beginning of 'the decadence of English historical writing' (quoted in Gertrude Himmelfarb, *Lord Acton: A Study in Conscience and Politics* [Chicago, 1952], p. 228).

[28] The *CHBE* followed chronologically from the *Cambridge History of India* (6 vols., Cambridge, 1922–32); two of the *CHI* volumes (V: *British India, 1497–1858,* and VI: *The Indian*

Rose (Vere Harmsworth Professor of Imperial and Naval History at Cambridge) and A. P. Newton (Rhodes Professor of Imperial History in London), planned the series on Acton's model.[29] Appearing in nine volumes, the last installment of the *CHBE* was not published until 1959.[30] None of the original editors lived to see its completion. Though some of the chapters by younger scholars in volume III, on the Empire–Commonwealth, reflected the changing mood after 1945, the *CHBE* in its entirety was essentially a work of the inter-war years. Its planning and ideas reflected the era of the aftermath of the First World War, the international depression, and the drift towards war in the 1930s. Though not quite so confident in tone as that of the generation of Acton, it does have a ring of certainty, especially on the nature of the British Empire–Commonwealth as a benevolent and progressive force in human history. Perhaps the ethos of the *CHBE* as a collective work tended to muffle dissent and to encourage consensus on what was believed to be the underlying, essentially noble, purpose of the Empire. The general commitment of the historians who contributed to the *CHBE* in the inter-war years is well brought out in a comment by Benians on Holland Rose, who seemed to epitomize the generation of *CHBE* historians: he was 'intensely loyal to the British Empire, and [had] . . . a strong faith in its historical and future significance to mankind.'[31]

In assessing the historiography up to 1914, it is useful to note significant works that capture the spirit of the times as well as the issues of substance, including, for example, the problem of imperialism as a cause of war. The ideological battle lines regarding the Empire had

---

Empire, 1858–1918) served as the two Indian volumes in the *CHBE*. For the landmarks in Indian historiography, see Vincent A. Smith, *The Oxford History of India: From the Earliest Times to the End of 1911* (Oxford, 1919) and H. Dodwell, *A Sketch of the History of India from 1858 to 1919* (London, 1925).

[29] Much of the detailed planning was done by Newton, who had begun his career as a physicist and whose 'scientific method' is reflected in the project. In the inter-war period, Newton also took the lead in the supervision of research students.

[30] The eight volumes of the *CHBE* were published in nine books, volume VII appearing in two parts: *Australia* and *New Zealand*.

[31] E. A. Benians in the *Dictionary of National Biography, 1941–1950*. R. E. Robinson—Beit Professor of Commonwealth History at Oxford (1971–87) and himself a contributor to the *CHBE*—has written: 'These tomes stand as the classic historiographical monument to the Seeleyan unity of organic empire . . . Their standpoint was anglocentric and their values Anglo-Saxon, although there was much of value in their pioneer narrative' (Ronald Robinson, 'Oxford in Imperial Historiography', in Frederick Madden and D. K. Fieldhouse, eds., *Oxford and the Idea of Commonwealth: Essays Presented to Sir Edgar Williams* [London, 1982], p. 33).

long been drawn between those upholding the idealism of the Empire and those who attacked the system of European imperialism. How did the academic historians of the late nineteenth century respond to shifting public moods as they studied earlier periods in the Empire's history? How did they begin to re-evaluate 'the old colonial system' up to the American Revolution and the 'second British Empire' in the century thereafter, 1783–1870?

Hugh Egerton was the pioneer in the field after Seeley, publishing *A Short History of British Colonial Policy* in 1897 and becoming the first Beit Professor of Colonial History in Oxford in 1905. His book reached a twelfth edition in 1950. His clear and systematic narrative dealt with such major issues as the commercial system of the first British Empire, the rise of British power in India, the abolition of slavery, the influence of Gibbon Wakefield's colonization schemes in New Zealand, the beginnings of constitutional government in Australia, and the attainment of Canadian self-government.[32] Egerton's history reflected the preoccupations of the time. He was a cautious federationist. His ideas in many ways were an extension of Seeley's. According to *The Times*: 'The publication of Seeley's "Expansion of England" in 1883 had made a deep impression on public opinion in this country: and Egerton was one of those who accepted Seeley's dictum that the maintenance of the unity of the British Empire was the great question of the age.'[33] But there was already a shift in the background. While Seeley had emphasized Britain's historic antagonism towards Russia and France, Egerton wrote in the era of naval rivalry with Germany and the extension of colonial control into Africa.

During Egerton's career as an historian, powerful books by politicians called for unity of the Empire and the fulfilment of Britain's Imperial destiny. They included Alfred Milner's *England in Egypt* (1893), George N. Curzon's *Problems of the Far East* (1894), and, in the next decade, the Earl of Cromer's *Modern Egypt* (2 vols., 1908). For the evolving historiography, Milner is the critical figure. Many held him responsible for the war in South Africa at the turn of the century, a conflict that split British society. Egerton wrote of Milner in the 1907 edition of *British Colonial Policy*:

> The time has not yet come to form the final judgment on the great
> Governor, who, after eight years of arduous labour retired in 1905

[32] Egerton wrote also with a certain historiographical purpose: for example, in commenting on Thomas Carlyle, Egerton believed his interest in the Empire to have been more negligible than commonly assumed, and his comment on certain personalities 'most unfair' (*British Colonial Policy*, p. 307, note 3).

[33] *The Times* obituary of Egerton, 23 May 1927.

from South Africa. His doings are still involved in the smoke of controversy. But if, in the fullness of time British South Africa works out
its own salvation, and Dutch racial patriotism takes a more sentimental form, compatible with political patriotism to a common Empire,
it will largely be due to the determination and courage, which shirked
no difficulty, and looked squarely in the face even the horrors of war,
rather than that South Africa should remain an exception to the
general history of British development, along the lines of progress
and freedom.[34]

In 1905 Milner had served as one of Egerton's electors to the Beit Professorship, but without enthusiasm. Milner was exceedingly sceptical
whether academic historians could rise to the occasion and produce
history worthy of the Empire—in other words, history of high quality
with a political purpose. He did not doubt Egerton's enthusiasm, only
the quality of his intellect.[35]

With a vision combining 'race patriotism' and Empire idealism, Milner inspired a younger generation of British Imperialists who became
known in the aftermath of the South African war, or Boer War, as the
Kindergarten.[36] In 1909 they created the Round Table movement, and
published a quarterly of the same name, dedicated to the strengthening and eventual unification of the Empire. Among the ablest of Milner's disciples, and the most dynamic in the new movement, was Lionel Curtis, who held the Beit Lectureship in Oxford from 1912, and
from 1921 a Fellowship at All Souls College. Curtis stands in the historiography as the central figure who believed—to his ever-lasting
credit—that India and other dependencies should eventually achieve
the same status of equality as the old Dominions. In that sense, he
clearly envisaged the British Commonwealth of Nations.[37] From Curtis's arrival in Oxford can also be dated the birth of Imperial history as
it is known today, with the seminar, the visitors, and the camaraderie.
Curtis had a vigorous intellect and a compelling force of personality.
Egerton complained that Curtis made him feel 'like a country rec-
tor with the Prophet Isaiah as his curate'.[38] Among Curtis's recruits

[34] Egerton, *British Colonial Policy*, p. 501; quotation from 1908 edn.

[35] See Colin Newbury, 'Cecil Rhodes and the South African Connection: "A Great Imperial
University"?' and Madden, 'The Commonwealth', in *Oxford and the Idea of Commonwealth*.

[36] Milner used the words 'Imperialist' and 'Imperialism' in a positive sense. See, for example,
his speech 'The Imperialist Creed', in Lord Milner, *The Nation and the Empire* (London, 1913).
For the negative as well as the positive use of the words, and for an important historiographical
investigation, see Richard Koebner and Helmut Dan Schmidt, *Imperialism: The Story and Significance of a Political Word, 1840–1960* (Cambridge, 1964).

[37] See especially *The Commonwealth of Nations* (London, 1916) and *Dyarchy* (London, 1920).

[38] Deborah Lavin, *From Empire to International Commonwealth: A Biography of Lionel Curtis* (Oxford, 1995), p. 119. On the debate among historians on the Round Table movement, see espe-

were historians of such diverse backgrounds and personalities as Lewis Namier, whose research was sponsored by the Round Table and the Rhodes Trust;[39] Frank Underhill, who became one of the leading Canadian historians;[40] and George Louis Beer, one of the outstanding American historians of the British colonial system before the American Revolution.[41] The historiographical influence of Curtis, the Round Table, and Oxford was considerable. But the response to Curtis's political commitment was ambiguous. Curtis—far more than Milner—held that the Empire must unite or disintegrate. This view had implications for historical studies, both for historians in Britain and for those in the Dominions. C. P. Lucas, one of the Round Table stalwarts and a Colonial Office official as well as the editor of a three-volume edition of Lord Durham's Report on Canada, resented, for example, Canadian historians who described 'the development of Canada from a dependency to a nation as something which was wrung by clear-sighted, freedom-loving Canadians from purblind politicians in a repressive Mother Country'.[42]

Curtis's dogmatism on the need to 'unite or bust' divided the members of the Round Table, some of whom, notably Leopold Amery, believed the development of Dominion nationalism to be compatible with Empire nationalism. 'Britannic' nationalism would emerge as a common bond if the British encouraged the leaders of Canada, Australia, New Zealand, and South Africa—and eventually India—to develop their own sense of identity and allowed them to retain control over tariffs, defence, and external affairs. Amery formed his ideas over the course of a long career: he began as a correspondent for *The Times*

---

cially John E. Kendle, *The Round Table Movement and Imperial Union* (Toronto, 1975); Leonie Foster, *High Hopes: The Men and Motives of the Australian Round Table* (Melbourne, 1986); and Alexander C. May, 'The Round Table, 1910-66' (unpublished D.Phil. thesis, Oxford 1995).

[39] Namier won a Beit Prize in 1913 and received further assistance from the Rhodes Trust, which enabled him eventually to publish *The Structure of Politics at the Accession of George III* (2 vols., London, 1929) and *England in the Age of the American Revolution* (London, 1930), the two works that placed him in the front rank of British historians. Vehemently anti-ideological, unlike many other historians of his era, Namier demonstrated no commitment to the sense of progress in the British Empire, and he later opposed, like Geoffrey Elton, the development of the fields of Asian and African history. He gave the general impression, according to his obituary in *The Times* (22 August 1960), 'of combining his Jewish character with a sturdy British Imperialism'.

[40] Underhill's aim, like that of others of his generation, was not 'the breaking of the tie with Great Britain but the changing of its nature to that of a free association of equals'; see Frank H. Underhill, *The British Commonwealth: An Experiment in Co-Operation among Nations* (Durham, N.C., 1956).

[41] Beer's books include *The Origins of the British Colonial System, 1578–1660* (New York, 1908).

[42] Quoted in Carl Berger, *The Writing of Canadian History: Aspects of English-Canadian Historical Writing, 1900–1970* (Toronto, 1976), p. 45. C. P. Lucas, ed., *Lord Durham's Report on the Affairs of British North America* (3 vols., Oxford, 1912).

during the Boer War and peaked as Churchill's Secretary of State for India, 1940–45. While Secretary of State for the Colonies, 1924–1929, he championed the protectionist principles expressed by Joseph Chamberlain. Above all, Amery saw himself as carrying forward the work of Lord Milner.[43] Amery rendered 'signal service to the cause of sovereign equality and national freedom in the Dominions and India'.[44] He thus holds a particular place in the historiography; and his own view on accounts of the Empire before 1914 is acute. Amery acknowledged inspiration from the work of Richard Jebb, the author of *Studies in Colonial Nationalism* (1905).[45] Jebb had originally popularized the idea of Britannic nationalism. Travelling in Australia, New Zealand, Canada, and later South Africa, he recognized earlier than most that the 'White Dominions' would develop their own sense of identity and would expect to retain control over internal affairs and defence, not relinquish them, as parts of a federation such as proposed by Curtis. Jebb did not believe that the self-governing colonies wished to break with Britain, but that they would if confronted with the stark choice between federation or separatism. Jebb advocated a partnership or alliance between Britain and the Dominions. He believed, for example, that the separate Dominion navies would willingly cooperate with the Royal Navy. Like Amery, he stood for tariff reform as a means of unity. In measuring Jebb's historiographical influence, it is useful to bear in mind that the developments after 1914 took place along the lines he had anticipated a decade earlier. The vision of Jebb and Amery, not Curtis, proved to be closer to the reality of the emerging Commonwealth.

In the turbulent years before the First World War, British radicals began to attack the system of European imperialism and to offer theories that have had an influence on historical interpretation to the present day. Drawing inspiration from William Cobbett, John Bright, and Richard Cobden—names 'redolent of our English past'[46]—the economist J. A. Hobson wrote *Imperialism: A Study* (1902), a book that overshadows in popular influence all other works on the British

[43] See W. R. Louis, *In the Name of God, Go! Leo Amery and the British Empire in the Age of Churchill* (New York, 1992). For Amery's own thought, see especially L. S. Amery, *The Forward View* (London, 1935).

[44] W. K. Hancock, *Smuts: The Sanguine Years, 1870–1919* (Cambridge, 1962); *Smuts: The Fields of Force, 1919–1950* (Cambridge, 1968); quotation from *Sanguine Years*, p. 459.

[45] For Jebb, see J. D. B. Miller, *Richard Jebb and the Problem of Empire* (London, 1956), and especially John Eddy and Deryck Schreuder, eds., *The Rise of Colonial Nationalism: Australia, New Zealand, Canada, and South Africa First Assert Their Nationalities, 1880–1914* (Sydney, 1988).

[46] A. J. P. Taylor, *The Trouble Makers: Dissent over Foreign Policy, 1792–1939* (London, 1957), p. 14.

Empire in the twentieth century. In 1935, William L. Langer of Harvard wrote: 'Hobson was the ablest critical writer on the subject in his time, and his *Imperialism* is perhaps the best book yet written on the subject. The most divergent theories can be traced back to his writings.' [47] Hobson's shadow fell on Lenin as well on the economist Joseph Schumpeter, whose sociological interpretation offers the principal alternative to Marxist theory.[48] In his attack on imperialism, Hobson unwittingly laid the eventual ideological basis for Soviet foreign policy. Above all, he popularized the idea that the causes of war—of the Boer War in particular—originated in a conspiracy of financiers who profited from investments and the arms industry.

Ironically, Hobson has been a somewhat discredited figure in the historiography of the Empire, at least until recently, because of D. K. Fieldhouse's disproving of his theory when applied in southern and tropical Africa.[49] Many assumed that if Hobson stood convicted as wrong on investment in tropical Africa and as misleading on the flow of capital to Latin America and the Dominions, then not only Hobson's authority but all economic explanations had been undermined. Hobson's theory on the Boer War, however, must be seen against a half-century of writing that proliferated until his death in 1940. Hobson refined his views, continued to challenge orthodox economic thought, and acquired the reputation of a saint of rationalism. *Imperialism* remains his most important work. It reads as well at the end of the century as it did at the beginning, if regarded not as social science theory but as an ethical and intellectual inquiry into the nature, in his famous phrase, of 'The Economic Taproot of Imperialism'. One of the virtues of P. J. Cain and A. G. Hopkins's recent *British Imperialism* is that they demonstrate the continuing vitality of Hobson's ideas. Along with resuscitating him, they have produced an assessment of the British Empire on the eve of the First World War with which Hobson would have agreed: '[D]espite her many problems, Britain was still formidably strong when war broke out.' [50]

[47] William L. Langer, *The Diplomacy of Imperialism* (2 vols., New York, 1935; 2nd edn., with supplementary bibliographies, 1950); quotation from 2nd edn., p. 97.

[48] Joseph Schumpeter, 'Zur Soziologie der Imperialismen', *Archiv für Sozialwissenschaft und Sozialpolitik*, 47 (1918–19), pp. 1–39, 275–310; translated as *Imperialism and Social Classes* (Cambridge, Mass., 1951).

[49] D. K. Fieldhouse, '"Imperialism": An Historiographical Revision', *Economic History Review*, 2nd series., 14 (December 1961), pp. 187–209; see also D. K. Fieldhouse, ed., *The Theory of Capitalist Imperialism* (London, 1967).

[50] P. J. Cain and A. G. Hopkins, *British Imperialism: Innovation and Expansion, 1688–1914;* and *British Imperialism: Crisis and Deconstruction, 1914–1990* (London, 1993); quotation from *Innovation and Expansion*, p. 464.

In catching the spirit of the frenzied nationalism before 1914, the radical British writers on imperialism rather than the historians of the Empire provided the historiographical landmarks.[51] Norman Angell in *The Great Illusion* (1910) and H. N. Brailsford in *The War of Steel and Gold* (1914) both agreed with Hobson's arguments that wars were essentially irrational and were exploited by those profiting from munitions and armaments. It was an illusion to believe that wars for overseas empire would benefit the aggressor. In an era when the German navy and German colonial ambitions seemed to threaten the British Empire, the arguments of Hobson, Angell, and Brailsford were unpopular and misunderstood. They were not pacifists, nor did they want to liquidate the Empire; they were courageous writers who wished to reform the Empire and make it humane. They believed that rational men could arrive at rational solutions, even for Ireland. In the Home Rule crisis in the two years before 1914, there were still grounds for optimism on Ireland, though it was left to a later writer, George Dangerfield (in *The Strange Death of Liberal England* [1935]) to pose the unanswerable question: would Britain have plunged into civil war over Ireland had it not been for the outbreak of the First World War?[52]

The outbreak of the First World War marked the beginning of a new phase in the historiography, in part because historians began to undermine the popular view that British rule had entered a golden age. Historians and other writers dissented from the myth of the Pax Britannica establishing peace and harmony in India and Africa, though their work did not find full expression until the inter-war period. As in the preceding section, it is necessary to bear in mind not only historians but also writers such as Lytton Strachey and T. E. Lawrence,[53]

[51] See Bernard Porter, *Critics of Empire: British Radical Attitudes to Colonialism in Africa, 1895–1914* (London, 1968); and Norman Etherington, *Theories of Imperialism: War, Conquest and Capital* (London, 1984).

[52] Two of the key works on Ireland in this period are by Erskine Childers, powerfully putting forward the Irish case in *The Framework of Home Rule* (London, 1911), and F. S. Oliver, a respected and influential member the Round Table, in *The Alternatives to Civil War* (London, 1913).

[53] Strachey's *Eminent Victorians* (London, 1918) placed him in the forefront of the reaction against the Victorian age and the debunking of such heroes as General Charles Gordon. His book was an anti-imperialist as well as anti-Victorian work, but it was also written with such quirkiness, occasional stylistic brilliance, and irony that it was read with interest by Lord Curzon and others of the Lloyd George government.

Apart from aspiring to write literary masterpieces, Lawrence's aim in *Revolt in the Desert* (London, 1926) and *Seven Pillars of Wisdom: A Triumph* (London, 1935) was to establish his place in history as the leader of the Arab uprising against the Turks and also to lament the lost opportunity of securing a place in the Empire or Commonwealth for 'our brown [Arab] brothers'. For a critical view, see especially Albert Hourani, 'The Myth of T. E. Lawrence', in W. R. Louis, ed., *Adventures with Britannia* (London, 1995), pp. 9–24. The best general study is John E. Mack, *A*

who influenced historical interpretation. It is useful also to note the two novels that most contributed to the anti-Empire spirit of the times: *A Passage to India* by E. M. Forster (1924) and *Burmese Days* by George Orwell (1935). Scholarly interest in the inter-war years ranged over the chronological and geographical extent of the Empire, though in the public debate on 'imperialism'—the word now commonly used by radicals but not yet accepted by most British historians—there were certain preoccupations. In the 1920s, Africa emerged in the public eye as a problem almost of the same magnitude as India. In the realm of international affairs, historians used previously inaccessible documents to begin studying economic imperialism as a cause of war.[54] In the 1930s, the Great Depression generated debate on the possibility of shoring up the Empire by devising measures of economic protection that eventually became known as the Ottawa system. Throughout the entire period, the problem of the constitutional future of the Empire stirred the historical imagination.

Most historians during the First World War found the wartime experience too overwhelming and too distracting to allow them to get on with their own work, still less to assess long-term significance.[55] During the war itself, patriotism prevailed over reason, though Hobson, Brailsford, Angell, and other radicals held their own against such champions of the British colonial mission as Sir Harry Johnston.[56] To most British writers, Germany virtually overnight had become a barbaric power, forfeiting the right to rule over indigenous peoples in Africa and the Pacific.[57] Public revulsion against the Turks, though

---

Prince of Our Disorder: The Life of T. E. Lawrence (London, 1976), a work that probably comes as close as any other to applying successfully the methods of clinical psychiatry to history.

[54] Responding to Allied propaganda that Germany had caused the First World War, the German government in 1922 began publishing documents from the German archives: Johannes Lepsius, Albrecht Mendelssohn-Bartholdy, and Friedrich Thimme, eds., *Die Große Politik der Europäischen Kabinette, 1871–1914* (40 vols., Berlin, 1922–27). The German series marked a revolution in access to recent documentary evidence. The British began a comparable series in 1927: G. P. Gooch and Harold Temperley, eds. *British Documents on the Origins of the War, 1898–1914* (11 vols., London, 1927–38). For other series, see the bibliography in A. J. P. Taylor, *The Struggle for Mastery in Europe, 1848–1918* (Oxford, 1954).

[55] C. P. Lucas is an exception, a transitional figure from the pre-war period. During the war he wrote *The Beginnings of English Overseas Enterprise* (London, 1917), and afterwards *The Partition and the Colonization of Africa* (Oxford, 1922). He also edited with great and subtle skill the major work begun during the war *The Empire at War* (5 vols., London, 1921–26).

[56] A Proconsul during the Scramble for Africa, Johnston wrote a knowledgeable, encyclopedic, and lucid but entirely Eurocentric book ('superior races' is a representative phrase) that survived into the post-Second World War era in Nigerian schools: Sir Harry H. Johnston, *A History of the Colonization of Africa by Alien Races* (Cambridge, 1899). On Johnston as polymath as well as Proconsul, see Roland Oliver, *Sir Harry Johnston and the Scramble for Africa* (London, 1957).

[57] See W. R. Louis, *Great Britain and Germany's Lost Colonies, 1914–1919* (Oxford, 1967).

slower to crystallize, led irrevocably to the same conclusion: the former Ottoman territories could not be returned. Here was an opportunity not merely to secure lines of British communication but to create a national home in Palestine for the Jewish people.[58] The war was being fought for a purpose, the Imperial aims of which were complex. At one level the purpose could be summed up in the phrase 'security of the Empire'; at another level it found expression in the insistence by the Dominions on equal status, a demand that eventually culminated in the Statute of Westminster of 1931.

Above all, the wartime debate on colonial issues centred on the question of accountability. Should the conquered territories be placed under the supervision of an international body to be known as the League of Nations? Or should national trusteeship prevail? On the whole, the consensus in Britain held British rule to be superior to that of others, and Parliament to be the highest authority. At least obliquely, much of the historiography of the inter-war years reflects such concerns. Accountable only to themselves, the British faced little significant nationalist dissent except in India and Egypt, and had little to fear from international interference by either the League of Nations or rival powers, at least until the challenges by Japan, Italy, and Germany in the 1930s. After 1929, economic turbulence shook assumptions about the Empire's commercial viability; defence commitments placed the armed forces as well as the economy under further strain, especially after the British began seriously to plan for a possible war in the Eastern as well as in the Western Hemisphere; and the potential of major unrest in India preoccupied British officials throughout the entire period. Nevertheless, the British Empire in 1939 remained intact. It appeared to many as a permanent institution in British public life. Churchill, in a famous speech rallying morale against a possible German invasion in 1940, expressed the hope that the Empire would last for a thousand years. Subsequent historical interpretation had to take into account the buoyancy of hope for the Empire's future as well as the deep strain of pessimism regarding the possibility of resolving the economic and military predicaments of the Imperial system.

Leonard Woolf's *Empire & Commerce in Africa* (1920) sustained the radical argument that the League of Nations should supervise colonial administration. His book is significant because of the rigour of the analysis as well as the thesis that international supervision would assist in reforming the colonial system and perhaps help root out economic

---

[58] See especially John Darwin, *Britain, Egypt, and the Middle East: Imperial Policy in the Aftermath of War, 1918–1922* (London, 1981). More generally, the key work in the historiography is Elizabeth Monroe, *Britain's Moment in the Middle East, 1914–1956* (London, 1963; 2nd. edn. 1981, with a comment on the consequences of Suez crisis of 1956).

imperialism as a cause of war.[59] Woolf had a powerful intellect informed by his service, in John Flint's phrase, as 'a renegade former colonial official' in Ceylon. But his major historiographical significance is that he founded, along with his wife, Virginia, the Hogarth Press. The books and pamphlets on colonial issues published by the Press included three books by Norman Leys, attacking the colonial administration in Kenya;[60] four books by Sydney Olivier, including *Anatomy of African Misery* (1927);[61] Leonard Barnes's *New Boer War* (1932); C. R. Buxton's *Race Problem in Africa* (1931); Horace Samuel's pro-Zionist indictment of the British administration in Palestine;[62] and three books critical of British rule in India.[63] At the Hogarth Press, Woolf published his own *Imperialism and Civilization* (1928) and *The League and Abyssinia* (1936). Many other works could be listed.[64] The anti-imperialist outlook of the Hogarth Press and the group of Bloomsbury writers associated with Leonard and Virginia Woolf represented a major dimension of British intellectual and literary life in the inter-war period.

The First World War, like the Second, witnessed a revival of the

[59] Historians in America picked up on the same themes. Parker Thomas Moon's *Imperialism in World Politics* (New York, 1926) is an outstanding example, serving as a standard college text and running to its 20th edition in 1964. Other significant American books pursing the economic theme include Leland Hamilton Jenks, *The Migration of British Capital to 1875* (New York, 1927), and Herbert Feis, *Europe the World's Banker, 1870–1914: An Account of European Foreign Investment and the Connection of World Finance with Diplomacy before the War* (New Haven, 1930); J. Fred Rippy, who began his career in the inter-war years, eventually published *British Investment in Latin America, 1822–1949: A Case Study in the Operations of Private Enterprise in Retarded Regions* (Minneapolis, 1959).

One American historian in the 1930s set the standard for detachment as well as comprehensive analysis and stands in a class by himself in the attempt to take account of economic developments, military calculations, national sentiment, and individual leadership: William L. Langer, especially his *The Diplomacy of Imperialism*. Chapter 3, 'The Triumph of Imperialism', is perhaps the single most brilliant essay on the subject.

[60] Norman Leys, *Kenya* (London, 1924), *A Last Chance in Kenya* (London, 1931), and *The Colour Bar in Africa* (London, 1941). On Leys, see John W. Cell, *By Kenya Possessed: The Correspondence of Norman Leys and J. H. Oldham, 1918–1926* (Chicago, 1976).

[61] The others were *The Empire Builder* (London, 1927); *White Capital and Coloured Labour* (London, 1929, a revision of an earlier work published in 1906); and *The Myth of Governor Eyre* (London, 1933), an account of Eyre's suppression of the 1865 rebellion in Jamaica. Olivier had served in the Colonial Office and as Governor of Jamaica, but was an outspoken critic on economic and racial issues. See Francis Lee, *Fabianism and Colonialism: The Life and Political Thought of Lord Sydney Olivier* (London, 1988).

[62] Horace Barnett Samuel, *Beneath the Whitewash: A Critical Analysis of the Report of the Commission on the Palestine Disturbances of August, 1929* (London, 1930).

[63] Edward Thompson, *Other Side of the Medal* (London, 1925); Graham Pole, *India in Transition* (London, 1932); and K. M. Panikhar, *Caste and Democracy* (London, 1933).

[64] See J. H. Willis, Jr., *Leonard and Virginia Woolf as Publishers: The Hogarth Press, 1917–41* (Charlottesville, Va., 1992), especially chap. 6.

British colonial mission. The affirmation of moral purpose found full expression in the writings of Sir Frederick (Lord) Lugard (1858–1945) and his disciple (Dame) Margery Perham (1895–1982). Lugard was the Proconsul whose name is indelibly associated with the creation of British Nigeria and the system of colonial administration known as Indirect Rule. Margery Perham was an Oxford don and eventually the first woman Fellow of Nuffield College.[65] Regarded in Oxford and indeed throughout the world as a formidable intellect, she had close connections with British colonial officials throughout the Empire. Working together and individually in the 1930s, Lugard and Perham emphasized the duties and responsibilities of colonial administration. The earlier publication of Lugard's *Dual Mandate in Tropical Africa* (1922) can be taken as a critical point in the development of the cult of the British District Officer, who was idealized as being almost single-handedly able to preside with fairness and justice over vast regions in the tropics. The District Officer, like the British nation, had a dual duty to protect indigenous subjects and to promote economic development for the benefit of the world at large.[66]

Then as now the doctrine of the Dual Mandate had fierce critics.[67] But it also had wide acceptance, in part because of its ethical appeal to the British to act as wards for less fortunate peoples. According to Lugard, Africans would be ruled best through their own institutions, thus

[65] On her place in the historiography, see Anthony Kirk-Greene, 'Margery Perham and Colonial Administration: A Direct Influence on Indirect Rule', in Madden and Fieldhouse, *Oxford and the Idea of Commonwealth*. See also especially Alison Smith and Mary Bull, eds., *Margery Perham and Colonial Rule in Africa* (London, 1991).

[66] Lugard wrote *The Dual Mandate* to serve as, among other things, a handbook for District Officers. It can thus be read as a systematic attempt to place problems of local administration within the context of the worldwide British Imperial system. In that sense, it bears contrast with the work of the American political scientist Raymond Leslie Buell, *The Native Problem in Africa* (2 vols., New York, 1928), a remarkable pioneering survey that remains indispensable to the present day.

[67] The contemporary criticism by Leonard Barnes (like Leonard Woolf, a former colonial official) is representative:

> To rob and exploit the 'lesser breeds' too weak for self-defence against machine guns and high explosives, to disintegrate their distinctive cultures, to pull down their traditional livelihoods, to conscript them as protesting and bewildered auxiliaries of industrialism—all this was seen not as a chaotic fury of looting (which is what it in fact was), but as a beneficent process of tidying up a disorderly world, of spreading the salt of civilization more easily over the earth and of sweeping the scum of barbarism away from inconspicuous corners.

Leonard Barnes, *The Duty of Empire* (London, 1935), p. 87. See also the same author's *Soviet Light on the Colonies* (London, 1944), which expressed admiration for the achievement of Soviet rule in the former Tsarist empire. For the scholarly deconstruction of Indirect Rule, see I. F. Nicolson, *The Administration of Nigeria, 1900–1960: Men, Methods, and Myths* (Oxford, 1969).

preserving traditions and drawing on the African genius for adaptation. The high tide of Indirect Rule may be marked by the publication of Perham's *Native Administration in Nigeria* (1937), which, among other things, reveals the collaborative basis of British rule. In their own time both Lugard and Perham were immensely influential figures, suspicious of rapid change yet champions of gradual reform. Part of their aim was to forestall the advent of 'hot-headed' Indian-type nationalism in Africa. To a later age, they seemed to be no less than agents of British imperialism, striving to perpetuate the Empire indefinitely by propping up traditional rulers and frustrating African nationalists; but to many contemporaries they were colonial reformers locked in combat with the Colonial Office.[68] There is a certain irony in Lugard, the champion of national trusteeship yet endlessly at odds with the Colonial Office, having served from 1922 to 1936 as the British representative on the Mandates Commission of the League of Nations.[69] Margery Perham became the foremost authority on Africa of her generation. She explicated the theory of Indirect Rule, and she wrote a two-volume biography of Lugard; but her most effective writing found expression in letters to *The Times*.[70] In the aftermath of the fall of Singapore in 1942, Perham called for a renewal of Britain's Imperial mission. As a preliminary step, she urged the abolition of the 'Colour Bar', a phrase officially denied but which expressed a reality in the British colonial world.[71] In late life she demonstrated great courage by travelling

[68] Though both were closely associated with the Colonial Office, there was no love lost for the bureaucracy. *The Dual Mandate* can be read in a sense as an extended complaint by Lugard on the trammelling of local administration by an ignorant and arbitrary Colonial Office. Perham believed that the government in London (especially the Foreign Office in relation to the Sudan) sacrificed Imperial obligations to larger issues of foreign policy. Her scepticism of Colonial Office motives perhaps reached a culmination when, after examining the evidence in R. E. Robinson's unpublished Ph.D. thesis ('The Trust in British Central African Policy, 1889–1939', Cambridge, 1951), she commented: 'I'll never again trust the Colonial Office' (information from R. E. Robinson).

[69] In fact Lugard and Perham as colonial reformers had much in common with the British radicals. They all thought that uncontrolled capitalist enterprise would damage the political economy of indigenous societies. But Hobson held that exploitation was the aim of Empire, whereas Lugard believed that the Empire needed to protect Africans and others from capitalist exploitation. Norman Etherington has written: '[T]he difference between Hobson and Lugard is in fact no more than a sheet of paper' (Etherington, *Theories of Imperialism*, p. 75). This is a shrewd insight; but it was a pretty thick piece of paper.

[70] For Perham on Indirect Rule, see especially her introduction to the 1965 edn. of *The Dual Mandate*. The Lugard biography was published as *Lugard: The Years of Adventure, 1858–1898* (London, 1956) and *Lugard: The Years of Authority, 1898–1945* (London, 1960). For the letters, see Margery Perham, *Colonial Sequence, 1930 to 1949: A Chronological Commentary upon British Colonial Policy, Especially in Africa* (London, 1967).

[71] See W. R. Louis, *Imperialism at Bay, 1941–1945: The United States and the Decolonization of the British Empire* (Oxford, 1977), pp. 135–38.

to Nigeria in 1968 in an attempt to end the Nigerian civil war. She was in many respects the embodiment of the British colonial conscience.

The inter-war years can be described not merely as the age of Lugard and Perham but also as the Coupland era in Imperial history. (Sir) Reginald Coupland succeeded Egerton in 1920 as Beit Professor in Oxford. Coupland's electors deliberately chose 'a first-class mind' to raise the level of scholarship above that of Egerton, whom they regarded as too much of a specialist. Coupland had a distinguished career. But in the end it was clouded by the attack on him by Eric Williams, who in 1938 became the first student from the West Indies to receive an Oxford D.Phil. and who later became Prime Minister of Trinidad and Tobago. No one could have worked harder than Coupland to bring 'colonial history' up to the standard of Stubbs, Maitland, and the others who had founded the *English Historical Review*.[72] A Fellow of All Souls, Coupland contributed to the College's reputation as a place where important decisions were made on the Empire as well as on national and world affairs; and by sponsoring the Ralegh Club (an undergraduate society that debated colonial issues on Sunday evenings at Rhodes House), he attempted to recruit outstanding Oxford students into Imperial service. He was, however, a Proconsul *manqué*. He did his best work in a semi-official capacity as a member of the Peel Commission on Palestine, drafting its report with such historical sweep and exactitude of detail that it stands as one of the great state papers in modern times. He conducted research at the Public Record Office, and his two major works on East Africa stand as solid, though unimaginative, accounts based on archival records and private papers.[73] One of Coupland's lasting contributions to historical scholarship was his study of the interaction between the British and the Arab empire extending from Oman to Zanzibar and the East African coast. In his last book, *Welsh and Scottish Nationalism: A Study* (1954, posthumous), his exploration of tensions within British society reflected his knowledge of multinational identities in Palestine, India, South Africa, and Canada.

Coupland was an idealist. He believed in the moral capacity of the British Empire to shape a better world and help dependent peoples

---

[72] 'Under Coupland, colonial history came of age and took its place beside the older historical studies' (*The Times*, 7 November 1952, Coupland's obituary).

[73] *East Africa and Its Invaders: From the Earliest Times to the Death of Seyyid Said in 1856* (Oxford, 1938); *The Exploitation of East Africa, 1856–1890: The Slave Trade and the Scramble* (London, 1939). Coupland's accounts of missionary activity left subsequent historians in his debt. See especially Roland Oliver, *The Missionary Factor in East Africa* (London, 1952). Oliver can be seen as working in the tradition of Coupland, but, in A. D. Roberts's phrase, as a Coupland 'leavened by irony'.

advance towards self-government. He was almost, but not quite, as un-abashed as Macaulay in believing in the history of the Empire as the story of unfolding liberty. In his work on India, he was the first writer to make clear to the general public the significance of the Pakistan movement.[74] He also wrote more generally on humanitarian issues, such as Wilberforce and the abolition of the slave trade. It was his latter-day championing of the British humanitarian mission that brought him into collision with Eric Williams. In 1944, Williams published *Capitalism and Slavery,* a revised version of his D.Phil. thesis, challenging the primacy of the humanitarian motive by arguing that the end of the slave trade came about essentially for economic reasons: sugar was no longer profitable. In mounting the attack against Coupland, Williams charged him with indulging in 'poetic sentimentality', deliberately presenting 'a distorted view of the abolitionist movement', and suffering from a 'deplorable tendency' to confuse supposed humanitarian aims with veiled economic motives.[75] The problem, however, was not the attack but that Williams had much the better part of the argument, or so it appeared to many at the time.[76] The confrontation was not entirely personal. It represented a clash between generations as well as between Oxford Imperial history and the beginning of what became known as area studies.[77]

The development of area studies in relation to Imperial history can be traced to the 1930s. Parts of the *Cambridge History of the British Empire* anticipated later regional specialization—for example, the work by Cornelius de Kiewiet.[78] Above all, the books by W. M. Macmillan are

[74] See his *The Indian Problem: Report on the Constitutional Problem in India* (3 vols., Oxford, 1942–43), and *India: A Re-Statement* (London, 1945).

[75] Eric Williams, *Capitalism and Slavery* (Chapel Hill, N.C., 1944), pp. 45, 178, 211. Coupland's Oxford colleagues thought the comments to be entirely unjustified and indeed scandalous. According to Frederick Madden, Coupland's relations with 'Rhodes Scholars, Indians, and the few Africans around were easy and friendly: the more bitterly did he feel Eric William's personal attack on him' (Madden, 'The Commonwealth, Commonwealth History, and Oxford', p. 13).

[76] Williams's economic argument in turn received substantial criticism. In the context of the Empire, see especially Roger Anstey, *The Atlantic Slave Trade and British Abolition, 1760–1810* (Cambridge, 1975).

[77] Williams defined his own purpose as a contribution to 'West Indian and Negro history' as well as economic history. It is significant that he dedicated his book to Lowell Joseph Ragatz, the author of *The Fall of the Planter Class in the British Caribbean, 1763–1833: A Study in Social and Economic History* (New York, 1928), which was a pioneering work in the field.

[78] See his chapters in *CHBE,* VIII, especially chapter 30, 'Social and Economic Developments in Native Tribal Life': 'The significance of the nineteenth century in native history is that it produced a black proletariat' (p. 828). See also especially C. W. de Kiewiet, *A History of South Africa: Social and Economic* (Oxford, 1941).

Though the South African volume in the *CHBE* did foreshadow later regional research, it

significant for his coherent general interpretation and specifically because of his radical line of class analysis on such issues as the 'industrial colour bar'. His work inspired a later generation of historians of southern Africa.[79] In *The Cape Colour Question: A Historical Survey* (1927) and *Bantu, Boer, and Britain: The Making of the South African Native Problem* (1929), Macmillan tenaciously pursued social and economic research—with Marxist overtones, or at least with a line of analysis not incompatible with Marxism, a stance that made him unwelcome in many British academic circles as well as in South Africa. In *Warning from the West Indies: A Tract for Africa and the Empire* (1936), he challenged Lugard's idea of static trusteeship and minimal colonial government, demanding that the Colonial Office accept responsibility for educational as well as economic and social development. Macmillan's work, like A. P. Newton's before him, represents a historiographical connection between Africa and the West Indies.[80]

In other regions, historians in the 1930s began to deal with non-European nationalism in a manner that marked the beginning of a new era. George Antonius's *Arab Awakening: The Story of the Arab National Movement* (1938) provided the first sympathetic account in English of the development of Arab nationalism, challenging the optimistic assumption of the Balfour Declaration and thus the basis of British rule in Palestine: '[T]he logic of facts is inexorable. It shows that no room can be made in Palestine for a second nation except by dislodging or exterminating the nation in possession.'[81] On India, Edward Thompson and G. T. Garratt's *Rise and Fulfillment of British Rule in India* (1934) was the first major British attempt to understand the Indian nationalist movement on its own terms. The authors also occasionally drew historical parallels: in the early twentieth century, 'most Englishmen began to understand that there was an Indian "problem", just as there was an Irish "problem", and that, as in the case of Ireland,

---

should also be said that this was an exception in the series. With the further exception of some of the younger authors in volume III, notably Frederick Madden, most of the contributors to the *CHBE* had little to say about such areas as Africa or the Pacific. What did emerge from the *CHBE* in relation to other scholarship on the Empire in the 1930s was the outstanding regional work on Canada, Australia, New Zealand, and South Africa.

[79] See Hugh Macmillan and Shula Marks, eds., *Africa and Empire: W. M. Macmillan, Historian and Social Critic* (London, 1989).

[80] Newton's books included *The European Nations in the West Indies, 1493–1688* (London, 1933).

[81] George Antonius, *The Arab Awakening: The Story of the Arab National Movement* (London, 1938), p. 412. For an historiographical assessment of Antonius, see especially Albert Hourani, 'The Arab Awakening Forty Years After', in Albert Hourani, *The Emergence of the Modern Middle East* (London, 1981).

it was based on a national movement.'[82] On South-East Asia, from a radically different perspective, Rupert Emerson of Harvard wrote *Malaysia: A Study in Direct and Indirect Rule* (1937), the scope of which included the Netherlands East Indies as well as British Malaya. Emerson, like W. M. Macmillan, later inspired a new generation of scholars to pursue questions of nationalism and independence.[83] In dealing with the political economy of South-East Asia, Emerson rigorously challenged the assumptions of the colonial administration in Malaya on such issues as monopolies in tin mining and rubber production as well as favouritism shown to 'European and Chinese land seekers'.[84] The 1930s also witnessed the publication of some the most original work of J. S. Furnivall, an administrator-scholar in Burma: for example, *An Introduction to the Political Economy of Burma* (1931). His later book, *Colonial Policy and Practice: A Comparative Study of Burma and Netherlands India* (1948), lent academic credibility to the voguish but exceedingly

[82] Edward Thompson and G. T. Garratt, *Rise and Fulfillment of British Rule in India* (London, 1934), p. 550. On the 'problem' of Indian and Irish nationalism, Nicholas Mansergh later became the acknowledged authority. In 1967 he became Editor-in-Chief of *Constitutional Relations between Britain and India: The Transfer of Power, 1942–7* (12 vols., London, 1970–83). Though he is remembered above all for the transfer-of-power series and his work on the Commonwealth, from the 1930s he had written on Ireland and he stands as 'one of the finest historians of Ireland' (David Harkness, 'Philip Nicholas Seton Mansergh 1910–1991', *Proceedings of the British Academy,* 82 [London, 1993]). See especially Nicholas Mansergh, *The Unresolved Question: The Anglo-Irish Settlement and Its Undoing, 1912–72* (New Haven, 1991). See also *Nationalism and Independence: Selected Irish Papers by Nicholas Mansergh,* Diana Mansergh, ed. (Cork, 1997).

[83] See, for example, Crawford Young, *The African Colonial State in Comparative Perspective* (New Haven, 1994), which is the key work on the idea of the colonial state. For example, on Lugard and the assumptions of European colonial administration (p. 165):

> As a Platonic guardian class, colonial officialdom represented itself as the disinterested servant of the subject population, basking as philosopher-king in the full sunlight of wisdom, ruling firmly but justly over those still enclosed in the cave of ignorance, who could see only distorted shadows of their true interests flickering on the darkened walls.

[84] Emerson used deft quotations to let British administrators speak for themselves, sometimes with unwitting irony. For example on the appointment of Malays to the Malayan Civil Service:

> [T]he new High Commissioner, Sir Shenton Thomas, replied [in 1936] in language worthy of precise analysis: 'This is the sixth country in which I have served, and I do not know of any country in which what I may call a foreigner—that is to say, a person not a native of the country or an Englishman—has ever been appointed to an administrative post.'

Malaysia, p. 515.

useful phrase 'plural society', which conveyed the meaning of separate peoples with different purposes that were determined in large part by the economic functions of the colonial state.[85] Many other authors might be mentioned. The decade of the 1930s, in short, was a seminal period for comparative studies and for works more favourably disposed to emergent nationalism.

The new trends in the historiography of the 1930s by no means represented the inter-war period as a whole. If one single vein of interpretation predominated, it was the constitutional. In this field there looms in the historiography a giant whose erudition matches that of any other: the Sanskrit scholar and constitutional lawyer (Sir) Arthur Berriedale Keith. The historian with whom he should be compared is (Sir) Kenneth Wheare, whose books on the constitutional history of the Empire will probably continue to be read more widely than Keith's. The third scholar to bear in mind is Frederick Madden, whose work continues to the present. In this specialized and now neglected field, it is useful to ask: why did constitutional history figure so largely in the history of the Empire in the inter-war years? The short answer is that constitutional history was the dominant mode of study in British schools and universities, but beyond that people generally believed that constitutional solutions could be found to problems of such magnitude as Ireland, India, and Palestine. Like their Victorian predecessors—above all Stubbs and Maitland—historians such as Curtis, Coupland, and Perham, along with Keith, continued to view Imperial history from the perspective of British constitutions and administration. They generally 'read back into the imperial past the gradual but inevitable triumph of Commonwealth institutions and ethics.'[86] It might require time, perhaps even centuries, but even the African dependencies could be launched on the course of self-government and eventual democracy. Disillusionment with the ideals of the Empire and Commonwealth—or at least with common British ethical and constitutional assumptions about the colonies—is essentially a post-Imperial phenomenon. Historians of the inter-war years, with varying degrees of scepticism, continued to affirm the Whig idea of progress. It would do them an injustice to be measured against the Zeitgeist of a later age.

In 1914, Keith was appointed Regius Professor of Sanskrit and Comparative Philology at the University of Edinburgh. His recondite

---

[85] Furnivall anticipated the idea of the colonial state by using the concept of the 'Leviathan'; see J. S. Furnivall, *The Fashioning of Leviathan: The Beginnings of British Rule in Burma* (Canberra, 1991), reprinted from the *Journal of Burma Research Society,* 24 (1939), pp. 3–137.

[86] Ronald Robinson, 'Oxford in Imperial Historiography', p. 37.

knowledge and his scholarly works on Sanskrit were already legendary, but in the previous decade he had also worked as a civil servant in the Dominions Department at the Colonial Office, where he began systematically to study the constitutional law of the Empire. His greatest work in this field was his first: *Responsible Government in the Dominions* (1909), which he expanded in subsequent editions until its final two-volume version appeared in 1928. Like Antonio Vivaldi, Keith continued to reshape the same themes in many different works. Among his outstanding publications are a constitutional history of the Empire from the beginning to the time of the loss of the American colonies, *Constitutional History of the First British Empire* (1930), and *A Constitutional History of India, 1600–1935* (1936). Yielding to no other perspective, he wrote with a legal insistence that sometimes approached belligerence, and with such density of style and crabbed exposition of obscure evidence that his work was read mainly by other learned scholars. Like Margery Perham, some of his most effective writing for a general audience found expression in letters to *The Times,* to which, in Keith's case, should be added *The Scotsman.*[87] He had no rival to the time of his death in 1942, though Wheare's first book, *The Statute of Westminster, 1931* appeared in 1933 and his second, *The Statute of Westminster and Dominion Status,* in 1938. Wheare was the Gladstone Professor of Government and Public Administration at Oxford (1944–57) and a Fellow of All Souls. He placed the subject of the British constitution in a much broader perspective than Keith by studying political as well as constitutional traditions. By taking into account the world of politics and administration, he raised the field of the constitutional history of the Empire 'to it highest intellectual level'.[88] He was a stylist who wrote concisely and elegantly.[89] His most stimulating work was *Government by Committee: An Essay on the British Constitution* (1955), which remains mandatory reading. As a genre, the constitutional history of the Empire has perhaps quietly reached its apex in the ongoing series by Frederick Madden, assisted by D. K. Fieldhouse and John Darwin, *Select Documents on the Constitutional History of the British Empire and Commonwealth.*[90] In scholarly detail and insight, the series sustains in every sense the tradition of Keith and Wheare.

[87] See for example Arthur Berriedale Keith, *Letters on Imperial Relations, Indian Reform, Constitutional and International Law, 1916–1935* (Oxford, 1935).

[88] David Fieldhouse, in *Oxford and the Idea of Commonwealth,* p. 159.

[89] He was also, in Max Beloff's words, 'the model of a true Oxford don' (*Dictionary of National Biography, 1971–1980*).

[90] Seven volumes to date, Greenwood Press, Westport, Conn., 1985–94. This is a labour of love, representing Madden's decades of dedication to the subject. The last volume in the series will deal with the final stage of decolonization from 1948.

In the late 1930s, the work of W. K. (Sir Keith) Hancock transformed the subject of Imperial history by integrating its component parts—especially the constitutional, economic, demographic, and religious—into a single, coherent, and comprehensive interpretation. More than that of any other historian of the British Empire, his historiographical influence bridged the period of the 1930s to the 1950s and beyond. Hancock arrived in Oxford at Balliol as a Rhodes Scholar, and in 1924 became the first Australian to be elected a Fellow of All Souls. There Lionel Curtis influenced him but failed to convert him to the belief that the Empire must federate or disintegrate. Hancock from early on developed the view that Dominion nationalism must be respected as much as Imperial patriotism. In *Australia* (1930) he attempted to reconcile *imperium et libertas* by writing that 'it is not impossible for Australians . . . to be in love with two soils'; he also developed the three resounding themes of mastering a continent, framing a polity, and forging an identity. These grand ideas reflected his wide reading in American as well as European, specifically Italian, history.[91] After holding the post of Professor of Modern History in Adelaide, he accepted a chair in Birmingham in 1934, explicitly to come to grips with the economic history of the Empire. This was his most creative period. At the invitation of Arnold Toynbee, he wrote the *Survey of British Commonwealth Affairs*.[92] In the Second World War, Hancock undertook the editing of the civil series in the official war histories, which were eventually published in twenty-eight volumes.[93] He returned to Oxford as Chichele Professor of Economic History at All Souls (1944–49), then became the first Director of the Institute of Commonwealth Studies at the University of London (1949–56), and finally returned to Australia to be the Director of the Research School of Social Sciences

[91] His first book was *Ricasoli and the Risorgimento in Tuscany* (London, 1926).

[92] Published by the Oxford University Press for the Royal Institute of International Affairs (Chatham House) in two volumes, 1937–42. The first volume (1937) carries the subtitle *Problems of Nationality, 1918–1936;* the second was published in two parts (1940–42), both subtitled *Problems of Economic Policy, 1918–1939.* Hancock viewed publication by the RIIA as an opportunity to influence policy not only in Britain but also in the Dominions, an ambition that distinguished him from virtually all other historians then and later. The connection with Toynbee is significant. Hugh Trevor-Roper's attack on Toynbee in the 1950s has obscured the esteem and gratitude felt by those, such as Albert Hourani and Hancock, who worked with Toynbee at Chatham House in the 1930s. See the biography by William H. McNeill, *Arnold J. Toynbee: A Life* (New York, 1989), especially p. 239 for the attack by Trevor-Roper (later Lord Dacre).

[93] The full title of the series is *History of the Second World War: United Kingdom Civil Series;* with M. M. Gowing, Hancock wrote *British War Economy* (London, 1949). The standards of the series were exceptionally high. Unlike Acton and the Editors of the *Cambridge History of the British Empire,* Hancock did not die before his editorial duties were completed, but his experience appears to have resembled that of the *OHBE* Editors, emerging with 'white hair and . . . exhaustion' (K. S. Inglis, quoting Margaret Gowing in the *Dictionary of National Biography, 1986–1990*).

at the Australian National University (1957–61). In the latter part of his career, he published a two-volume biography of J. C. Smuts, ultimately a flawed work because it stops short of exploring the African dimension of the subject, but nevertheless one of the great biographies of the twentieth century.

Unlike most of his predecessors, Hancock mastered the art of the case study. Following Acton's maxim that one should study problems, not subjects, in the *Survey* Hancock began immediately with Ireland and progressed to Palestine. In his analysis of the settler colonies of Kenya and Rhodesia, he brought into sharp focus the part played by missionaries and (in the case of Kenya) the immigrant community of Indians as well as the land policies of the colonial governments. With a capacious knowledge of the breadth and scope of the Empire's history, he used case studies to draw conclusions on universal issues, including those of the world economy. Partly on the basis of his own understanding of the Australian economy, but largely because of the power of his intellect, he was able brilliantly to assess the protectionist policies of the 1930s.[94] In short, he established the interaction of what are now called the centre and the periphery, reminding the reader constantly of the historian's virtues of attachment (empathy with the subject), justice, and span.[95] Yet for all his reach, there are two aspects of his work that are unsatisfactory. Despite his efforts to see the Empire as a worldwide system, the Indian dimension of his work is curiously limited. He never assimilated India into his general analysis in the same way that he did Palestine or West Africa.[96] And though his West African case study is a tour de force, it is flawed by the same blind spot that mars his masterpiece on Smuts. Hancock never quite got the African side of the problem into focus or saw the full force of the Africans' initiative in shaping their own history. In the biography, Africans are conspicuous by their absence.[97] Yet despite those shortcomings

---

[94] Hancock's treatment of the Ottawa system remained for decades the most incisive analysis and still must be read, along with Ian M. Drummond's *Imperial Economic Policy, 1917–1939: Studies in Expansion and Protection* (London, 1974). The single best comment on Hancock as an economic historian is David Fieldhouse, 'Keith Hancock and Imperial Economic History', in *Oxford and the Idea of Commonwealth.*

[95] 'Attachment, justice, and span' were the words Hancock used to describe the work of Mary Kingsley, but they could well be used to characterize his own work. Mary H. Kingsley was the author of *Travels in West Africa: Congo Français, Corisco and Cameroons* (London, 1897), and to her he attributed part of his intellectual heritage; see *Problems of Economic Policy*, part 2, appendix A. Kingsley was a pioneer in the field of anthropology, and she advanced scientific knowledge in such areas as disease, diet, and malnutrition.

[96] In part, perhaps, because he intended to move on to India as one of his future case studies.

[97] See the review by Roland Oliver: 'Blinkered Genius', *Journal of African History*, 9, 3 (1968), pp. 491–94.

Hancock remains, like Macaulay, in a class by himself. As has already been mentioned, there would probably be a consensus among the historians involved in the *Oxford History of the British Empire* that he was far and away the greatest historian of the Empire and Commonwealth.

On the eve of the Second World War, Lord Hailey's *African Survey* was published.[98] This massive account, written in effect by a team of experts, immediately became a classic. It provided a full discussion of the colonial policies of France, Belgium, and Portugal as well as Britain, and it covered such topics as law and education as well as such technical subjects as soil erosion, crops, and mining. It helped define what later became known as the field of African studies. Above all, it had a historiographical significance. In the words of Hailey's biographer: 'It was a pivotal work, looking both ways.' Looking forward, it argued for 'constructive' trusteeship rather than the static system of minimal government and non-intervention. It anticipated the colonial reforms of the wartime era and even 'the postwar transfer of power'. Looking backward, it distilled the inter-war generation's discussion of such African problems as 'race, culture, primitiveness, and what would later be called colonial dependency'.[99] Hailey believed it inevitable that Africans at some distant point would master their own destinies. He regarded Indirect Rule as a temporary stage in the process of political evolution; it had already, in his view, become an anachronism except as a form of local government.[100] He came to these conclusions after dispassionate deliberation. During a distinguished career in the Indian Civil Service, Hailey rose to the rank of Governor of the Punjab and subsequently of the United Provinces. In retirement he became Lugard's successor as British representative on the Permanent Mandates Commission, 1936–39.

Hailey possessed a rare ability to synthesize great amounts of material and, like Margery Perham, a capacity to present general views on

---

[98] With the subtitle *A Study of Problems Arising in Africa South of the Sahara* (London, 1938). Hailey made extensive changes for the revised edition published in 1957, when he was eighty-six years old. In this edition he referred to emergent African nationalism as 'Africanism', to suggest that it was a 'racial' idea rather than one reflecting the concept of the nation-state. The revised edition of the *Survey* appeared in the year after the historiographical landmark, Thomas Hodgkin, *Nationalism in Colonial Africa* (London, 1956), which argued persuasively that African nationalism possessed the same 'universal' attributes of nationalism elsewhere.

[99] John W. Cell, *Hailey: A Study in British Imperialism, 1872–1969* (Cambridge, 1992), p. 217.

[100] According to John Flint, 'an elaboration of indirect rule institutions could, at most, have led to "self-administration" of small units . . . The concept had a good deal in common with that of the "Bantustans" in South Africa today' (John Flint, 'Planned Decolonization and Its Failure in British Africa', *African Affairs*, 82, 328 [1983], pp. 389–411).

controversial subjects in a persuasive manner. Hailey proved especially effective with American audiences. He emerged during the war,
along with Perham, as one of the most influential speakers on the
future of the British Empire. In late 1942 a Colonial Office report expressed well the consensus on Hailey's public stature and caught the
mood of British sensitivity to American criticism of the Empire. The
report dealt with a conference convened in Canada to debate 'the
colonial issue', a phrase summing up a major point of wartime tension
between the British and the Americans, as reflected in much of the
historiography.

> Hailey throughout was truly superb . . . [and] without a trace of
> condescension. I was lost in admiration at the whole ten-day per-
> formance and many times as I watched him cross swords with the
> American 'Professors' and gracefully prick one balloon after another,
> I thought what a stupid tragedy it would be to take the manage-
> ment of great affairs from men like Hailey and give them over to
> the [American] boys with thick-lensed glasses, long hair and longer
> words nasally intoned.[101]

Margery Perham and others identified Hailey as the moving spirit behind the colonial reforms in progress during the war despite, in the
contemporary view, intolerable official delay and incompetence. Hailey, however, moved at a stately pace. He had little personal warmth,
and though he spoke cogently and convincingly, he did not convey the
sincerity of Perham's dedication to the cause. If any single person can
be said to represent the revival of Britain's colonial mission during the
war, it would be Margery Perham. But the two of them in the public
eye rather stood out as superintendents of the British Empire.

The Second World War distracted historians from their research
and writing, but more works of substance appeared than during the
First World War.[102] It is illuminating to note briefly the wartime experiences of a few historians and future historians of the British Empire. For some, the war was merely an impediment to scholarly work;
for others, a formative experience. A few, such as J. C. Beaglehole in

---

[101] Report by D. M. MacDougall (Colonial Office), 22 December 1942, quoted in Louis, *Imperialism at Bay*, p. 13.

[102] In addition to books already mentioned by C. W. de Kiewiet and Eric Williams, these
works included Arthur J. Marder, *The Anatomy of British Sea Power: A History of British Naval Policy
in the Pre-Dreadnought Era, 1880–1905* (New York, 1940); S. E. Crowe, *The Berlin West African Conference, 1884–1885* (London, 1942); John Bartlet Brebner, *North Atlantic Triangle: The Interplay
of Canada, the United States and Great Britain* (New York, 1945); and Robert Livingston Schuyler,
The Fall of the Old Colonial System: A Study in British Free Trade, 1770–1870 (New York, 1945).

New Zealand, managed to persevere. Beaglehole, a 'casually dressed scholar, somewhat resembling E. M. Forster',[103] continued to work on the editions of the *Journals of Captain James Cook* later published by the Hakluyt Society. Many prominent historians were drawn by the war into the vortex of the bureaucracy in London. Vincent Harlow worked during the war years in the Ministry of Information. Richard Pares, who had produced *War and Trade in the West Indies* (1936), spent the war at the Board of Trade, as did Lucy Sutherland, who was already acknowledged as an authority on the East India Company. The young Jack Gallagher served in the Royal Tank Regiment in North Africa. Rather like a latter-day T. E. Lawrence (choosing in the 1920s to enlist in the ranks in the RAF), Gallagher refused to be commissioned as an officer. He later said that he wanted his epitaph to read simply 'Tank Soldier and Historian'. The young Ronald Robinson served in the Royal Air Force and won the Distinguished Flying Cross. At war's end, Robinson was inspired—to his later embarrassment—by a book by Eric A. Walker, *The British Empire: Its Structure and Spirit*. Walker's book seemed to imply that God had stood on the side of the Empire during the war.[104]

Keith Hancock took enough time off from his job supervising the beginning of the civil histories to write *Argument of Empire* (published in 1943 as a 'Penguin Special'), a didactic book of some interest because of its teleology, because of its distillation of some of the more controversial elements in the *Survey of British Commonwealth Affairs*, and also because of its clarity on the regeneration of Britain's colonial purpose. Hancock wanted Americans to reflect on the ideals of the British Empire and Commonwealth. In powerful words, he defined the purpose of the Empire as being to guard liberty: 'Freedom is something which unites men. In our own history it has united English and Scots and Welsh, French-Canadians and British-Canadians, Dutch-South-Africans and British-South-Africans, white New Zealanders and Maoris.'[105] To Americans, it might appear that the British were fighting to preserve the Empire, perhaps even to add to it, but the reality,

---

[103] E. H. McCormick in the *Dictionary of National Biography, 1971–1980*.

[104] The Empire's 'Faith, hope and charity were justified in the long run' (p. 236, 1947 edn.). The book was first published in 1943, went through its 4th impression in 1947, and was republished in extended form in 1953. It was perhaps the best text on the Empire of its time. Walker was the Vere Harmsworth Professor of Naval and Imperial History at Cambridge. He was a major contributor to the volume on South Africa in the *CHBE* (VIII, Cambridge, 1936).

[105] *Argument of Empire*, p. 137. The key to Hancock's argument on India was that Canada, Australia, New Zealand, and South Africa had all achieved national unity. In India there was still no national consensus: 'The future of India rests upon Indian decision' (p. 38). This was a representative British view during the wartime period.

according to Hancock, was that the Empire represented the most extensive system of freedom that had ever existed in human history: 'Monarchy grows into democracy, empire grows into commonwealth, the tradition of a splendid past is carried forward into an adventurous future.'[106] The Empire's history as the unfolding story of liberty continued to be the dominant mode of interpretation by Imperial historians. The major shift in the teleology did not occur until ten years later, emblazoned in the historiography by the publication of Gallagher and Robinson's article 'The Imperialism of Free Trade' in 1953.[107]

At the end of the Second World War there was a resurgence of interest in the Pacific as well as Africa. In the historiography of the Pacific, the name of J. C. Beaglehole is writ large, but it is useful to consider briefly the works of J. W. Davidson as well. In 1942 Davidson had completed his Cambridge Ph.D. thesis, 'The European Penetration of the South Pacific, 1779–1842'. About a decade earlier, Beaglehole had decided to write a biography of Captain James Cook, including a full account of Cook's voyages and exploration of the Pacific. As a prelude, in a task that would take well over a quarter of a century, Beaglehole began editing Cook's *Journals,* the first of which was published in 1955 and the last in 1967. Beaglehole's editing was a model of scholarly exactitude. The biography appeared posthumously in 1974.[108] Beaglehole wrote with a style that sometimes had a poetic ring to it, and, in his own words describing the early explorers, with 'a passion to see and to report truly'.[109] Devoted to the history of exploration in the Pacific, he stands as one of the principal historians of the eighteenth century. In a sense, J. W. Davidson's work reflected the intellectual interests of the next generation. Davidson attempted to shift the focus from the Europeans to the islanders and, rather like Hancock, used the method of the case study to achieve his aims. Western Samoa became the microcosm. Davidson argued that Samoan resentment of European intrusion had existed from early on and that the presence of missionaries, traders, and colonial administrators galvanized and shaped the Samoan national movement. Davidson has a fair claim to be described as the founder of Pacific Studies, which

[106] Hancock's thought already bore a remarkable similarity to that of J. C. Smuts, who, in a famous interview with *Life* magazine in December 1942, had spoken along those lines; for the quotation, see *Argument of Empire*, p. 12.

[107] *Economic History Review*, 2nd series, 6, 1 (1953), pp. 1–15.

[108] J. C. Beaglehole, *The Life of Captain James Cook* (London, 1974). The book appeared as volume 4 in *The Journals of Captain James Cook on His Voyages of Discovery*, Hakluyt Society Extra Series, no. 37.

[109] J. C. Beaglehole, *The Exploration of the Pacific* (London, 1934), p. 3. His other books include *The Discovery of New Zealand* (Wellington, 1939).

emerged the 1960s along with African Studies. In 1949 he was appointed Professor of Pacific History at the Australian National University, and in 1967 he published *Samoa mo Samoa,* the pioneer work on nationalism in the Pacific.[110]

Of the historians of the 1950s, Richard Pares and Lucy Sutherland are exceptional because of the quality of their work. Both were concerned with the major issues of the Empire in the eighteenth century, and each in different ways wove the politics of the era into the fabric of economy and society in a manner that few historians have achieved before or since. But they were slightly removed from the mainstream of Imperial history. Both were what might be called *EHR* historians, from whom a line could be drawn back to Bryce, Stubbs, and others who created the journal. The point is significant because until the 1960s—before the proliferation of area journals—historians of the Empire continued to measure their own work against the standard set by the *EHR.* Pares was in fact Editor of the *EHR* from 1939 to the time of his death in 1958. He had begun his career as an historian while a Fellow of All Souls, 1928–45. Thereafter he was Professor of History at the University of Edinburgh until 1954, when he returned to All Souls because of ill health. He was progressively crippled by paralysis. His 1936 book, *War and Trade in the West Indies, 1739–1763,* pursued thematic issues of finance and trade based on private business papers as well as official archives. His work had both a Caribbean and a European focus, but he made no attempt at a conventional synthesis of the subject. 'It is much to be regretted', complained A. P. Newton, that Pares 'flinched' from the historian's duty to provide a general history.[111] Pares's method indeed pointed to the economic and social history of future decades.[112] Sutherland's approach to history had a complementary but quite different thrust. Born in Australia but raised in South Africa, she had studied under W. M. Macmillan. At Oxford

[110] J. W. Davidson, *Samoa mo Samoa: The Emergence of the Independent State of Western Samoa* (Melbourne, 1967). Davidson's work generally built on the accounts of earlier historians, such as Ralph S. Kuykendall, *The Hawaiian Kingdom, 1778–1854: Foundation and Transformation* (Honolulu, 1938); and Harold Whitman Bradley, *The American Frontier in Hawaii: The Pioneers, 1789–1843* (New York, 1942). For a more strictly British context, see W. P. Morrell, *Britain in the Pacific Islands* (Oxford, 1960).

[111] *English Historical Review,* 53 (January 1938), p. 143. Pares's other books included *A West-India Fortune* (London, 1950); *Yankees and Creoles: The Trade between North America and the West Indies before the American Revolution* (London, 1956); and *Merchants and Planters* (Cambridge, 1960). See also especially 'The Economic Factors in the History of the Empire', *Economic History Review,* 7 (1937), pp. 119–44.

[112] In intellectual rigour he stood unsurpassed and was an inspiration to his fellow historians. 'He was the best and most admirable man I have ever known' (Isaiah Berlin, *Personal Impressions* [London, 1949]; quotation from 1981 New York edn., p. 95).

she was a Fellow of Somerville, 1928–45, and then Principal of Lady Margaret Hall, 1945–1971. Macmillan's influence can be traced in her work, but it was to Namier that she owed her inspiration. Her significance for Imperial history is that she used Namier's conceptual framework to analyse the finances and politics of the East India Company.[113] At once an economic, a social, and an administrative history, *The East India Company in Eighteenth-Century Politics* (1952) established the relationships of pressure groups both in Parliament and in the Company from London to Calcutta. Her work, like that of Pares, had an uncompromising academic integrity.

The leading Imperial historian of the 1950s was Vincent Harlow, and it was Pares who provided the most searching critique of his work. Harlow was pre-eminently a Public Record Office historian. No one of his era better mastered the records of the various departments, including the Board of Trade and the Admiralty and above all the Colonial Office, but his reliance on official records was at once his weakness as well as his strength. One does not gain from *The Founding of the Second British Empire*, as one does from Hancock's work, a sense of demography and emigration or of religion and the work of missionaries. One does find a keen mastery of the official documents and a grasp of the full geographical scope of the Empire. Harlow was among the first to study the element of continuity in the minds of the policy makers and to define the nature of the Empire at specific times. He followed the thinking of British statesmen through the linked crises of imperialism and nationalism in Ireland, North America, and India, thus dealing with the interconnected emergencies in the Empire as a whole. His scholarly and original interpretation set the debate for subsequent historians.[114]

There are two general problems in Harlow's historical interpretation, one of which was clearly identified by Pares. Harlow powerfully argued that a transition was already in progress, even before the American Revolution, from colonization to trade—a transition summed up in the phrase 'We prefer trade to dominion'. In short, the thesis holds that the British renounced formal control in favour of trade, bases, and influence—informal rather than formal Empire—with an emphasis on the East rather than the West. The argument rested on the assumption of Britain's industrial supremacy and her competitive

---

[113] Like Pares, Sutherland was a disciple of Namier, though she far more consciously than Pares followed Namier's method. She was not, however, uncritical. See Lucy S. Sutherland, 'Sir Lewis Namier, 1888–1960', *Proceedings of the British Academy, 1962* (London, 1963), pp. 371–85.

[114] See especially the comprehensive assessment of Harlow's work by Ronald Hyam, 'British Imperial Expansion in the Late Eighteenth Century', *Historical Journal*, 10, 1 (1967), pp. 113–31.

power. With a certainty of touch confirmed by later historians, Pares challenged Harlow's thesis by questioning the extent of Britain's lead in the industrial revolution and the confidence of British businessmen and traders. The second problem is that Harlow was seduced by the power of his own argument on the dynamism of the shift to the East, with trade replacing dominion. The old Empire resting on conquest and subjugation seemed to be giving way to a more enlightened yet 'authoritative' rule.[115] His work does not satisfactorily take into account the plantation economies in the Caribbean based on slavery, still less the slave trade itself. The West Indies and the slave trade do not fit easily into his general scheme, but force continued to play an important part in sustaining the Empire. But let there be no doubt that *The Founding of the Second British Empire* is one of the great works in the literature. Pares described the first volume as 'not only a *magnum opus* but also, in certain respects, a masterpiece'.[116]

The 1950s give the impression of being a claustrophobic decade paradoxically bursting with new ideas. Its confined dimension is well represented by Harlow. Harlow presided over the Imperial history seminar in Oxford with an almost 'suffocating' sense of moral purpose.[117] He was a learned scholar and a master in his field, but he was also a martinet who wanted his followers to march in the traditional and, ultimately, narrow lines of the subject, which would be shaped by a study of documents and would still be, essentially, Anglocentric.[118] Anthony Low, for example, studied under Harlow in the 1950s for his D.Phil. thesis, 'The British in Uganda, 1862–1900' (1957). Low wanted to place his Imperial subject in the context of African history. Harlow

[115] For Harlow's use of this term, see C. A. Bayly, *Imperial Meridian: The British Empire and the World, 1780–1830* (London, 1989), which comments (p. 8) on the 'curious paradox' of Harlow drawing a conclusion at variance with the evidence presented. Harlow concludes that there was a steady growth of order and justice within the colonial system under a structure of 'authoritative' rule. But Bayly argues that 'Harlow could not bring himself to say "authoritarian"' for what was really a systematic attempt to centralize power. In my own view, Harlow may have used the word 'authoritative' to mean 'legitimate', in the sense of the rule of law prevailing over authoritarian force, but refrained from saying so explicitly. The idea that Imperial rule could be 'legitimate' was already unpopular by the 1950s.

[116] Pares in *English Historical Review*, 68, 267 [April 1953], pp. 282–85. I am much indebted to P. J. Marshall for an exchange of views on Harlow.

[117] According to Frederick Madden, Harlow's seminars were 'more than a little serious and morally earnest . . . week after week it could be school-masterly and suffocating' ('The Commonwealth, Commonwealth History, and Oxford', pp. 19–20).

[118] Pares picked up on this point. Like C. P. Lucas before him, Harlow resisted the initiatives taken on what is now called the periphery. According to Pares, Harlow demonstrated 'a courage . . . unusual among imperial historians. Many of them write as if there were no such place as the mother-country' (*English Historical Review*, 68, 267 [April 1953], p. 283).

resisted the new trends; he deplored the development of area studies. Low went on to bridge the fields of African and Indian history, to become Hancock's spiritual successor in Canberra, and later, as Smuts Professor in Cambridge (1983–87), to hold the balance between Imperial history and area studies.[119]

In the decade of the 1950s dozens of historians were pushing the subject of Imperial history beyond its traditional boundaries. A good example can be found in the work of Gerald Graham and the historians in the Imperial History Seminar in the Institute of Historical Research at London University.[120] Graham was a Canadian who combined the history of the Empire with that of sea power.[121] He took a prominent part in the new direction of research in the 1950s, including the supervision of Africans working towards the Ph.D. The London historians included John Flint, Glyndwr Williams, and, later, P. J. Marshall.[122] Merely to list some of the work coming to completion in the late 1950s and early 1960s gives an indication of the continuing vitality in the field. In Cambridge, Gallagher and Robinson stimulated new research in area studies as well as Imperial history, and Anil Seal later wrote his creative and influential work on Indian nationalism.[123] In Oxford, David Fieldhouse had already become famous as the economic historian of the Empire, and Colin Newbury had conducted extensive research on comparative studies in emigration, land, and labour in French as well as British archives.[124] In Canada, A. P. Thornton

---

[119] See especially D. A. Low, *Lion Rampant: Essays in the Study of British Imperialism* (London, 1973); *Congress and the Raj: Facets of the Indian Struggle, 1917–45* (London, 1977); *Britain and Indian Nationalism: The Imprint of Ambiguity, 1929–1942* (Cambridge, 1997); and *Eclipse of Empire* (London, 1991). Low played a critical part in the launching of the *British Documents on the End of Empire*, which began publication in 1992.

[120] Another equally good example would be the seminar at the Institute for Commonwealth Studies, London, where Kenneth Robinson succeeded Hancock as Director (1957–65). Robinson wrote one of the most useful and concise analytical works on the Empire: *The Dilemmas of Trusteeship: Aspects of British Colonial Policy between the Wars* (London, 1965).

[121] See especially Gerald S. Graham, *Empire of the North Atlantic: The Maritime Struggle for North America* (Toronto, 1950); and *Great Britain in the Indian Ocean: A Study of Maritime Enterprise, 1810–1850* (Oxford, 1967). See also especially *The China Station: War and Diplomacy, 1830–1860* (Oxford, 1978).

[122] The Africans included J. F. A. Ajayi, who later published *Christian Missions in Nigeria, 1841–1891: The Making of a New Elite* (London, 1965). For the works of the London historians, see John E. Flint, *Sir George Goldie and the Making of Nigeria* (London, 1960); Glyndwr Williams, *The British Search for the Northwest Passage in the Eighteenth Century* (London, 1962); P. J. Marshall, *The Impeachment of Warren Hastings* (Oxford, 1965).

[123] For example, see Thomas R. Metcalf, *The Aftermath of Revolt: India, 1857–1870* (Princeton, 1964); Anil Seal, *The Emergence of Indian Nationalism* (Cambridge, 1968).

[124] See especially Fieldhouse's later work, *Economics and Empire, 1830–1914* (Ithaca, N.Y., 1973). For Newbury, see *The Western Slave Coast and Its Rulers: European Trade and Administration*

completed his inquiry into the reasons for the decline of British power.[125] In New Zealand, Keith Sinclair wrote on the Maori wars; in Australia, J. D. B. Miller pursued the international politics of the Commonwealth.[126] In South Africa, Leonard Thompson studied the consequences of the Boer War; in Southern Rhodesia, Eric Stokes brought to conclusion his book on the Utilitarians and India.[127] In South-East Asia, Cyril Parkinson traced the absorption of the Malay States into the Empire.[128] John Hargreaves had begun the research in Africa, France, and Britain that would make him one of the principal historians of the partition of Africa.[129] Not least, in the 1950s John Fage and Roland Oliver prepared the field of African history and successfully countered the attacks by the Regius Professor of History at Oxford, Hugh Trevor-Roper, who declared with a Gibbonian ring that Africa had no history other than that of the unrewarding gyrations of barbarous tribes. The launching of the *Journal of African History* by Oliver and Fage in 1960 symbolically marked the coming of age of area studies. But above all the 1950s will be remembered in Imperial history because of the revolution in the historiography brought about by Robinson and Gallagher.

There were two parts to the revolution: one was the article published in 1953, 'The Imperialism of Free Trade'; the other, their book *Africa and the Victorians* (1961).[130] 'The Imperialism of Free Trade' is far and away the most frequently cited article in the historiography. It is a model of its kind in stating a clear yet complex and sophisticated thesis. First is the argument of 'informal empire',[131] and second is that

---

among the Yoruba and Adja-Speaking Peoples of South-Western Nigeria, Southern Dahomey, and Togo (Oxford, 1961).

[125] A. P. Thornton, *The Imperial Idea and Its Enemies: A Study of British Power* (London, 1959).

[126] Keith Sinclair, *The Origins of the Maori Wars* (Wellington, 1957); J. D. B. Miller, *The Commonwealth in the World* (London, 1958). Miller had actually completed this book at the University of Leicester before returning to Australia to become Professor of International Relations at the Australian National University.

[127] L. M. Thompson, *The Unification of South Africa, 1902–1910* (Oxford, 1960); Stokes, *The English Utilitarians and India* (Oxford, 1959).

[128] C. Northcote Parkinson, *British Intervention in Malaya, 1867–1877* (Singapore, 1960); see also especially C. D. Cowan, *Nineteenth-Century Malaya: The Origins of British Political Control* (London, 1961).

[129] John D. Hargreaves, *Prelude to the Partition of West Africa* (London, 1963).

[130] 'Imperialism of Free Trade', *Economic History Review*, 2nd series, 6, 1 (1953), pp. 1–15. Ronald Robinson and John Gallagher with Alice Denny, *Africa and the Victorians: The Official Mind of Imperialism* (London, 1961). The American edition had a more dramatic but less revealing subtitle: *The Climax of Imperialism in the Dark Continent*.

[131] Robinson and Gallagher's most persistent critic was the economic historian D. C. M. Platt. See 'The Imperialism of Free Trade: Some Reservations', *Economic History Review*, 2nd series, 21,

of continuity. Both these ideas had already been expressed by Harlow, to whom, among others, Robinson and Gallagher acknowledged their debt; but no previous author had written so sharply or so lucidly—or with such unforgettable metaphors, such as that of the Empire as an 'iceberg'. The iceberg represented, below the waterline, the empire of informal trade and influence; above the waterline was the formal Empire, obvious to everyone because it was painted red on the map. Robinson and Gallagher denied the conventional, sharply chronological divisions of mid- and late-Victorian imperialism, thereby affirming the continuity of the forces of imperialism throughout the century and indeed to the present. The theory thus helps one understand the era of decolonization as well as the nineteenth century, and, perhaps, American as well as British imperialism. All of this was a lasting and controversial achievement.

The circumstances around the creation of both the article and the book help explain the thrust of their thought as well as the ongoing controversy. The essay was very much the product of its time. The two young authors were committed British socialists, wary of both the red sickle and hammer of Soviet communism and the red claw of American capitalism. They wrote at a time when both feared the consequences of American economic assistance to Europe—the Marshall Plan—and the attempt, in their view, by the United States to reduce Britain to an economic satellite. A similar anxiety can be detected in their masterpiece, *Africa and the Victorians,* which was written mainly in the aftermath of the Suez crisis of 1956. Arabi Pasha became the forerunner of Gamal Abdel Nasser, and proto-nationalism in Egypt anticipated the full-blown Egyptian nationalism of the 1950s. Was it anachronistic to relate the problems of the 1950s to those of the 1880s so emphatically, though implicitly? The arguments and themes remain as provocative today as when conceived. The historiographical significance of both the article and the book lies in the brilliance of the writing as well as the boldness of the ideas. What *Africa and the Victorians* accomplished once and for ever more was to destroy the European notion of causation—that the springs of British action, for example, lay in Britain alone. Africa and the world at large can no longer be seen as a blank map on which Europeans freely wrote their will. Robinson and Gallagher overturned the traditional historiographical assumption that European expansion originated wholly within Europe; from the time of their work onwards, the history of British imperialism

---

2 (August 1968); and 'Further Objections to an "Imperialism of Free Trade", 1830–60', *Economic History Review,* 2nd series, 26, 1 (February 1973).

would be the history of the interaction between the British and indigenous peoples.[132]

In 1948 Robinson had married Alice Denny, an American with a radical determination to uphold civic virtues and an unwavering faith in the constitutional principles of the US government. Without her persistence and accuracy—and typing skills—*Africa and the Victorians* might never have seen the light of day. Both authors were responsible in equal measure for the shaping of the book, though in Robinson's methodical reasoning can be found the connecting links in the argument that the response by British imperialism to the two crises in Egypt and in Southern Africa set off a tertiary crisis in tropical Africa. From Gallagher came the wit of Jonathan Swift and the deft pen portraits of Salisbury, Chamberlain, Rhodes, and other 'fabulous artificers' who galvanized the African continent in the same tradition of their predecessors in America, Australia, and Asia.[133]

In 1963 Gallagher became Harlow's successor as the Beit Professor in Oxford. Gallagher was a beloved figure. One of his former students provided a Falstaffian dedication to 'sweet Jack, kind Jack, true Jack, valiant Jack'.[134] Gallagher returned to Cambridge in 1971 to hold the Vere Harmsworth Chair until his death in 1980. Robinson succeeded him in Oxford as Beit Professor, 1971–87. Robinson's colleagues and former students throughout the world attested to his uncompromising intellectual standards and diligence as a supervisor.[135] Each continued to exert immense influence, Gallagher concentrating especially on the study of the history of Indian nationalism, Robinson making a seminal contribution on collaboration as the basis of British rule.[136] Both of course are famous in their own right, but in the historiography

---

[132] For a full discussion, see W. R. Louis, ed., *Imperialism: The Robinson and Gallagher Controversy* (New York, 1976).

[133] *Africa and the Victorians*, p. 472.

[134] D. M. Schreuder, *Gladstone and Kruger: Liberal Government and Colonial 'Home Rule', 1880–85* (London, 1969), p. xvi.

[135] See the Festschrift in the *Journal of Imperial and Commonwealth History*, 16, 3 (May 1988): 'Theory and Practice in the History of European Expansion Overseas: Essays in Honour of Ronald Robinson'.

[136] See Gallagher, *The Decline, Revival and Fall of the British Empire*. Ronald Robinson, 'Non-European Foundations of European Imperialism: Sketch for a Theory of Collaboration', in Roger Owen and Bob Sutcliffe, eds., *Studies in the Theory of Imperialism* (London, 1972). For Robinson's more recent work, see especially 'The Conference in Berlin and the Future of Africa, 1884–1885', in Stig Förster, Wolfgang J. Mommsen, and Ronald Robinson, eds., *Bismarck, Europe and Africa: The Berlin Africa Conference, 1884–1885, and the Onset of Partition* (Oxford, 1988); and 'Railways and Informal Empire', in Clarence B. Davis and Kenneth E. Wilburn, Jr., with Ronald E. Robinson, eds. *Railway Imperialism* (Westport, Conn., 1991).

they are, in Frederick Madden's phrase, as inseparable as the panto-mime horse.

We live today in the shadow of the reshaping of Imperial history by Robinson and Gallagher and others in the 1950s and 1960s. Despite this creative effort, there was great foreboding that with the end of the Empire the history of British imperialism might become a dead subject. Beyond that anxiety, and much more significantly, Imperial history appeared to be cracking up because of the emergence of area studies in India, Africa, and elsewhere. Looking at the subject over the long haul, however, it is clear that there was no crisis in the historiography. Area studies naturally developed when the consequences as well as the causes of Empire began to be studied systematically. What has seemed to be the supremacy of area studies in recent decades can now be viewed as part of a much longer history of scholarship on the British and other European empires as well as the emergence of fields of concentration in their own right. Imperial history can only benefit from the wider perspectives offered by area studies, literary criticism, and cultural studies. Whichever direction academic fashions may turn, there will always be an interest in the history of the British Empire: human curiosity about the domination of one people or nation over others, and about the interaction of peoples and cultures, is unquenchable. The historiography of the Empire as it enters a new century is as rich and diverse as ever before.

Oxford History of the British Empire   1999

34

THE PAX AMERICANA:
SIR KEITH HANCOCK, THE BRITISH EMPIRE,
AND AMERICAN EXPANSION

I n his lifetime, Sir Keith Hancock was—and perhaps in reputation
still is—the greatest historian of the British Empire and Commonwealth.[1] He had a long life (1898–1988), and in his last two
decades he reflected on themes in world history, such as the Pax Britannica, that had preoccupied him much earlier in his career. There
is a remarkable consistency to Hancock's thought, and from about the
1970s onwards, other historians, drawing on recently released archival
material, produced works that not only tended to confirm what he
had written earlier but also revealed more clearly the nature of American economic and military aims. He could now judge the old Pax Britannica in relation to the new Pax Americana, which he saw in the
context of the dissolution of the British Empire, the ambiguous fate of
the Commonwealth, and the nuclear stalemate between the United
States and the Soviet Union. In the 1970s he asked the question: what
would succeed the British Empire? Even if one assumed that it might
be the global reach of the United States, the answer was complicated:
the Pax Americana seemed mainly to be a protective shield against the
Soviet Union and, at the same time, a danger to countries such as Australia. Hancock wrote late in life: 'I see my country as a Subject Ally of
the United States of America.'[2]

Hancock's first attempt to clarify the concept of the Pax Britannica
in relation to the United States came in a short book written during

This article has its origins in a Chichele Lecture at All Souls College, Oxford, in May 2003
and, in a slightly different form, in the keynote address to the conference of the Australasian
Modern British Historians Association in Canberra the following July. I wish to thank the ar-
chivists and holders of copyright who have assisted me, as well as several friends and fellow historians for their suggestions.

[1] W. R. Louis in *Oxford History of the British Empire*, vol. 5: *Historiography*, ed. Robin Winks (Oxford, 1998–99), p. 30: '[T]here would probably be a consensus among the [some 125] historians
involved in the *Oxford History of the British Empire* that he was far and away the greatest historian
of the Empire and Commonwealth.' This claim needs a slight qualification: the post-publication
OHBE consensus proved to be a little more muted.

[2] W. K. Hancock, *Testimony* (Canberra, 1985), p. 101. The single most revealing source on
Hancock's life and writing is D. A. Low, ed., *Keith Hancock: The Legacies of an Historian* (Melbourne,
2001), hereafter *Legacies*. The best assessment of him in his own field as an economic historian
is by David Fieldhouse, 'Keith Hancock and Imperial Economic History', in Frederick Madden
and D. K. Fieldhouse, eds., *Oxford and the Idea of Commonwealth* (London, 1982). There is a full-
scale biography underway by J. H. Davidson.

the Second World War, *Argument of Empire.*[3] He later refined his ideas, but he uniformly used the phrase Pax Britannica to convey the conditions of relative peace and stability throughout large parts of the world under British sway, an orderliness that allowed the indigenous inhabitants to learn to rule themselves in modern circumstances. Individual states under British tutelage might take many decades to achieve the economic development necessary for viability. Hancock never doubted that self-government was the goal, but he did not view the Empire as having a predestined course. The Empire would not necessarily transform itself into a Commonwealth. He did not believe that straightforward progress towards independence was inevitable. But he thought it could be made to happen.

In getting a bearing on Hancock's politics as well as his personality —'puckishly cheerful' is the single phrase that perhaps best describes him—and status as an historian, it is useful to bear in mind that in the 1920s he wrote his first book on Tuscany and the emergence of the unified Italian state in the mid-nineteenth century.[4] He believed, as he later summed it up, that 'the Risorgimento constitutes one of the noblest chapters in the history of modern Europe.'[5] He held throughout his life that nations represent the intrinsic qualities of their people and that national sovereign equality creates the bedrock of international politics. He thought that federations or superstates would diminish the qualities of hard-won national freedom and independence. He was thus, late in life, as suspicious of the prospect of a federated Europe as he was, in his early career, of attempts to forge a unified British Empire.

In the history of the British Empire, or for that matter of modern Britain, Hancock stands in the forefront of the historiographical revolution of the 1940s and 1950s. He helped lay the foundation for later work by John Gallagher and Ronald Robinson, for example, by shaping clear analytical concepts of Britain's imperial economy and by demonstrating the cultural links among English-speaking peoples that

---

[3] W. K. Hancock, *Argument of Empire*, published in 1943 as a 'Penguin Special'. The title of the American edition is *Empire in a Changing World*, published in New York in the same year. Hancock wrote to a friend in September 1943: '75,000 copies of the first printing have been disposed of' (Hancock to Colin Badger [a former pupil in Adelaide with whom Hancock corresponded without inhibition from the mid-1920s onwards], 5 September 1943, Australian National University Archives at the Noel Butlin Archives Centre [Canberra], P96/23 [hereafter Hancock Papers ANU]). There is another set of Hancock Papers at the National Library of Australia, Deposit MS 2886 (hereafter Hancock Papers NLA).

[4] W. K. Hancock, *Ricasoli and the Risorgimento in Tuscany* (London, 1926). 'Puckishly cheerful' and 'pugnaciously cheerful' were phrases used to describe Hancock during the Second World War. See Ann Oakley, *Man and Wife: Richard and Kay Titmuss* (London, 1996), pp. 230, 234.

[5] W. K. Hancock, *Perspective in History* (Canberra, 1982), p. 136.

continue to be reflected in studies on the British diaspora.[6] In the words of a recent writer taking measure of Hancock's enduring influence: 'His comments are as pertinent today in their discussion of the scope, objects and methodology of historical writing, as when they were written during the Second World War—and indicate the continuing relevance of rigorous historical scholarship in difficult times.'[7] Hancock was also a public figure, confident in his own judgement and determined to influence in his own way the emergence of new states in Africa, as for example in his leadership of an official mission to Uganda in 1954. In this as in all other cases Hancock's thought and action revealed, in his own words, 'my very British preoccupation with right conduct'.[8] He believed that the British Empire was, or should be, a force for good in world affairs and in the administration of the colonies. His code of conduct is of historical interest because it stood for moral responsibility and vigilance against abuses in the colonial era from the 1920s to the 1960s. If one thing is more certain than any other from a survey of his life in the context of the British Empire, it is that he would have been deeply disturbed by the recent books by David Anderson and Caroline Elkins, which present evidence of systematic brutality by the colonial government in Kenya in the 1950s.[9]

Hancock's ideas about the Empire and Commonwealth can of course be traced to his early life and writing, above all to his time as a Fellow of All Souls College, Oxford, 1924–1930—the decisive phase in his development as an historian—and to his period of greatest creativity in the 1930s and early 1940s, when he taught in Adelaide and then in Birmingham. At All Souls he became acquainted with two College luminaries whose thought on Imperial issues pulled in entirely different directions. One was L. S. Amery, the Colonial and Dominions Secretary of the 1920s; the other was Lionel Curtis, the dynamo behind the movement to federate the Empire and Commonwealth.[10] Both Amery and Curtis aimed to strengthen the British Imperial sys-

---

[6] For a recent reassessment of the work of Gallagher and Robinson, see John Darwin, 'Gallagher's Empire', in W. R. Louis, ed., *Yet More Adventures with Britannia* (London, 2005). For the British diaspora, see Carl Bridge and Kent Fedorowich, eds., *The British World: Diaspora, Culture and Identity* (London, 2003).

[7] A. D. Harvey, 'Historians in The National Archives', *Oxford Magazine* (Hilary Term, 2005), p. 12.

[8] W. K. Hancock, *Politics in Pitcairn* (London, 1947), p. v.

[9] David Anderson, *Histories of the Hanged: Britain's Dirty War in Kenya and the End of the Empire* (London, 2005); Caroline Elkins, *Britain's Gulag: The Brutal End of Empire in Kenya* (New York, 2005).

[10] For Hancock and Curtis, see Deborah Lavin, *From Empire to International Commonwealth: A Biography of Lionel Curtis* (Oxford, 1995); for the relationship with Amery, see W. R. Louis, *In the Name of God, Go! Leo Amery and the British Empire in the Age of Churchill* (New York, 1992).

tem. Amery, however, believed that the achievement of sovereign equality (a key phrase in Hancock's vocabulary) could be harmonious with the growth of a 'British' Imperial consciousness. An Australian patriot and British nationalist in equal measure, Hancock held ideas compatible with Amery's.[11] Curtis, on the other hand, thought that the British Empire and Commonwealth would evolve towards a federation in which there would be, in the very nature of federalism, a central authority, but in this case an authority that would bring not only order but spiritual fulfilment as well. Hancock never became a convert to the cause of Imperial federation. He regarded the Commonwealth as something quite different: 'a cooperative confederacy', a phrase he used as early as 1930.[12] Nevertheless, Curtis's vision of the Commonwealth, apart from the organizing principle of federation, had an inspirational appeal to Hancock. And it was Curtis who had an incomparable impact on Hancock's career: he persuaded Arnold Toynbee to recruit Hancock to write the two-part *Survey of Commonwealth Affairs*, which was eventually published in 1937–42.[13]

Toynbee, too, played an important part in Hancock's early life as an historian. As Director of Studies at the Royal Institute of International Affairs, Toynbee had to decide on Hancock's appointment. He resisted the view that Hancock was 'temperamentally not suited' for the project.[14] As Toynbee wrote later, he took the gamble that 'Australian irreverence' combined with a reach of knowledge would produce 'a

[11] In his biography of J. S. Smuts, Hancock paid tribute to Amery by recognizing the 'signal service' he rendered 'to the cause of sovereign equality and national freedom in the Dominions and India' (W. K. Hancock, *Smuts,* 2 vols., London, 1962 and 1968, I, p. 459) On another occasion, Hancock described Amery as 'that serene realist' (W. K. Hancock, *Four Studies of War and Peace in this Century* [Cambridge, 1961], p. 47).

[12] W. K. Hancock, *Australia* (London, 1930), p. 148.

[13] The correspondence between Hancock and Curtis on this point is in the Curtis Papers, Box 10, Bodleian Library, Oxford. For Hancock's insistence that the work be more than a book of reference and have 'a point of view', see Hancock to Curtis, 6 February 1934. At an earlier stage in Hancock's life, Curtis had exerted another kind of decisive influence. According to Hancock's later recollection of the 1920s: 'Curtis . . . said to me one day, as we sat together on a garden bench outside the Common Room: "Research! I want all you young men to do research! No matter what conclusions you come to." From that day on I followed my own path of research' (W. K. Hancock, *All Souls, 1923–1982: Recollections and Reflections* [1982], privately published with very limited circulation, p. 11; copies may be found in the Codrington Library, All Souls, and in the Hancock Papers ANU, P96/22).

[14] The negative voices included those of Professor Charles Webster of the London School of Economics and Professor (Sir) Reginald Coupland, Hancock's fellow historian at All Souls ('Survey of British Commonwealth Affairs', publications committee meeting, 13 February 1934, Royal Institute of International Affairs Archives, hereafter RIIA, 14/1). 'He has a strongly individualist personality and viewpoint,' Coupland wrote in moderately negative vein (Coupland to Toynbee, 2 February 1934, RIIA 14/4).

book which had a real historical colour and perspective'.[15] Both Toynbee and Curtis are today rather neglected figures, but to historians of their generation they were immensely influential. Toynbee encouraged Hancock to pursue his idiosyncratic and iconoclastic style. 'I think I understand your general method of work,' Toynbee wrote. 'As I see it, you are telling a story, and throwing in your information, in an illustrative way, in order to spin the thread.'[16]

As for Curtis, though Hancock disagreed with him on the issue of federation, on the more basic point of 'ordinary, vulgar Imperial patriotism'—as Hancock expressed it in order to get to the heart of his complex feelings—he found Curtis's vision uplifting. Hancock was usually reticent on such matters, but he divulged this very private view in the mid-1920s, when he had returned to Australia to teach in Adelaide. Frustrated by living in a place where he found life difficult and conversation limited, he poured out his innermost thoughts to a friend at All Souls, the historian A. L. Rowse. The letter, almost a political credo, is of interest because, among other reasons, it gives Hancock's views on the rise of the Pax Americana—'Yank-land'—and the problem of Japan. Above all, it expresses his love for Australia:

> I love the mountains and forests and even some of the plains of this country just for themselves and am keen on this community for what it may become. Joined with this is my devotion to England. If I want to do something, someday, to help interpret Australia to the outside world, I can do a little, every day, to help interpret England to Australia—by teaching history . . .
>
> I don't want Australia to drift vaguely round in the south Pacific, falling under the shadow of the Yank-land, or getting blown up by yellow men, or going on her own isolated narrow self-assertive way. I want her to become more and more an effective part of the British community; give her contribution to that, and through that to Christendom—yes, I admit that I am a very thorough 'British Commonwealth' person—an imperialist of the Lionel Curtis type.[17]

It was one of the most revealing passages Hancock ever wrote.[18]

---

[15] Toynbee to Hancock, 5 December 1935, RIIA 14/4. Toynbee also remarked that Hancock could 'bait the New Zealanders' in a manner unthinkable for an English writer.

[16] Toynbee to Hancock, 20 June 1935, RIIA 14/4.

[17] Hancock to A. L. Rowse, 20 November 1926, Rowse Papers, MS 113/3/1/H, University of Exeter.

[18] It also helps explain other references in Hancock's letters that refer to Curtis virtually as a father figure. Hancock wrote to Curtis after the publication of the first part of the *Survey* in 1935:

Of course, sons develop characteristics and attitudes distinct from those of their parents, but the real relationship is not shaken off. I wonder if you see this relationship

Hancock was very much a man of the 1920s, and some of his life-long characteristics were shaped at All Souls, specifically the puckish or flippant Common Room banter that characterized his conversation. Though he mellowed over time, there was always an identifiable tone, at once confident and didactic yet nonchalant and usually aggressively light-hearted.[19] These characteristics perhaps disguised a natural shyness, and he struck many of his contemporaries as a man of almost impenetrable reserve.[20] He once wrote that he preferred scenes to people.[21] A. L. Rowse, one year his junior at All Souls, wrote, slightly unfairly, that Hancock's autobiography, *Country and Calling* (1954) was 'too self-conscious, defensive, pussy-footing'.[22] Certainly the autobiography is less than candid, but like R. G. Collingwood's *Idea of History,* it usefully reflects on the historian's craft.[23]

---

of me to you in my volume. It is there. Your thought is throughout the centre of reference, even when the reference is critical.
Hancock to Curtis, 23 September 1937, Box 11; quoted in Deborah Lavin, 'Lionel Curtis and the Idea of Commonwealth', in Madden and Fieldhouse, *Oxford and the Idea of Commonwealth,* p. 117, and in Leonie Foster, *High Hopes: The Men and Motives of the Australian Round Table* (Melbourne, 1986), p. 159. *High Hopes* is an invaluable guide to an unfashionable topic.

[19] Or, to put it more positively, in Margaret Gowing's words: 'He was . . . equable, courteous, yet very tough . . . His personality, including his enquiring smile and his calm, beautifully modulated voice, quite apart from his deeply probing mind and common sense, made him welcome everywhere' ('The Civil Histories of the Second World War', p. 16, unpublished seminar paper, Hancock Papers ANU, P96/22). Margaret Gowing, later Professor of the History of Science at Oxford, worked with Hancock in the Historical Section of the Cabinet Office during the war and became a lifelong friend. Her papers are deposited at the Museum of the History of Science, Oxford, and contain a valuable, indeed unique, set of letters from Hancock from the wartime years to the time of his death (hereafter Gowing Papers).

[20] Hancock's 'cold blue eyes never gave much away' (Gerald Walsh, 'Recording "The Australian Experience": Hancock and the *Australian Dictionary of Biography*', in Low, *Legacies,* p. 264).

[21] Doug Munro perceptively comments that Smuts's 'profound love of the landscape' helped create a common bond between biographer and subject (*Journal of Imperial and Commonwealth History,* 31, 1 [January 2003], p. 150).

[22] A. L. Rowse, *All Souls in My Time* (London, 1993), p. 139. One dominant concern of the autobiography is Hancock's own moral code of conduct, a theme that can be traced in many of his other writings. On Rowse, Hancock disliked his *All Souls and Appeasement* (London, 1961): 'I am well aware that the choices between right and wrong policies were not so clearcut as Rowse believed them to be' (Hancock, *All Souls, 1923–1982,* p. 14) The two had long fallen out because Hancock voted for a rival candidate for the Chichele Professorship of Modern History in 1950. Rowse consequently regarded Hancock as a traitor and thereafter 'turned the cold shoulder to him' (Rowse's notation on diary entry of 14 February 1950, Rowse Papers, MS 113/2/2/1).

[23] 'Like R. G. Collingwood, I ask myself the question *what is history for?* and I answer that question as he did, *history is for human self-knowledge*' (W. K. Hancock, *Professing History* [Sidney, 1976], p. 170; Hancock's italics). *Professing History* is the sequel to *Country and Calling.*

Hancock was a complicated and driven man. In my own view—I knew him from the mid-1960s onwards—there were two Hancocks. One was the intimidating public personage of strong opinions, pompous formality, and impeccable courtesy. 'Professor Sir Keith Hancock', as he would introduce himself, insisted on wearing academic gowns at formal dinners at University House in Canberra.[24] The other side of his personality was the private Hancock: candid, open-minded, and friendly, though intellectually exacting. A pussy-footer he certainly was not. To those admitted to his circle of friendship, he was affectionate, steady, and loyal. The Governor of Uganda, Sir Andrew Cohen, described him as 'an acute observer'.[25] He had a habit of presenting his ideas under a cloak of self-deprecation, though in fact he was remarkably self-centred, or at least had a keen sense of his own importance. He was amusing and incisive yet hard to pin down. His research and writing sometimes had an obsessive quality to it. Occasionally there was a ruthless side to his character.[26] But despite his complex nature, he came across on the whole as remarkably straightforward. Again to use A. L. Rowse's words, 'Happily there was none of the boring headache about being colonial.'[27]

Yet it is Hancock's Australian background that is critical for understanding his work as well as his personality. He was the son of an Australian rural pastor, later Archdeacon of Melbourne. Throughout his work on the Empire and Commonwealth there is an insistent emphasis on the importance of religion and especially of missionar-

[24] The recent but already classic account of the history of the Australian National University has a revealing passage on Hancock's influence with students and as well as fellow historians: 'In relations with students, whether in his own department or others, Hancock was a great encourager, always stimulating, always concerned. His comments in seminars were searching, demanding, constructive. He drove himself, and others followed his example' (S. G. Foster and Margaret M. Varghese, *The Making of the Australian National University* [St. Leonards, Australia, 1996], p. 130).

[25] Cohen to Secretary of State, Top Secret and Personal, 18 September 1954, CO 822/751.

[26] 'Hancock . . . could be ruthless when he wanted to be' (Foster and Varghese, *Making of the Australian National University*, p. 134).

[27] A. L. Rowse, *Historians I Have Known* (London, 1995), p. 179. Hancock did once refer to 'the inequality-complex' of Australia, Canada, and other countries that felt 'a thwarted passion for equality'. But this was one of his rare lapses into what he called fashionable jargon (W. K. Hancock, *Survey of British Commonwealth Affairs* [2 vols., Oxford, 1937–42], I, p. 263). On Bloomsbury and the literary fashions of the era, Hancock had a low opinion of 'the pseudo-biographical performances of Lytton Strachey' (*Professing History*, p. 54). Indeed, he appears to have had something of a fixation on Strachey. He once wrote: 'I'm not a Lytton Strachey type; his portrait of Florence Nightingale . . . is in my view an outrage. Sober and significant truth is what I am after' (Hancock to Lady Daphne Moore, 4 March 1963, Hancock Papers NLA, Series 1B).

ies.[28] In 1923, while still a Rhodes Scholar at Balliol, he met Curtis and thus became aware of the quasi-religious or mystical vision of the Commonwealth. At All Souls, Hancock became a member of the Round Table, the group of scholars, government officials, and writers who met regularly to discuss the problems of the Empire and who published articles in the journal of the same name. In a more general sense he was thus part of the 'Milner Group' or the 'Empire Builders' (the sardonic phrase used by Hancock and others of his generation). These are epithets that must be used with caution. Among his college friends and acquaintances were not only Amery and Curtis but also Geoffrey Dawson (editor of *The Times*), (Sir) Dougal Malcolm (one of the stalwarts of the Round Table), and (Lord) Robert Brand (the banker), as well as his own contemporaries (Sir) Penderel Moon (later of the Indian Civil Service) and Harry Hodson (later editor of the *Sunday Times*). But this was by no means a unified group. Indeed Hancock grew ever more hostile to some of the underlying ideas of expansion, consolidation, and appeasement.[29] Over the years, he increasingly held Milner to be responsible for the Boer War.[30]

It would be a mistake to regard All Souls as a sort of inner sanctum where self-selected elites made decisions on the Empire. The College provided the opportunity for camaraderie and the exchange of information and ideas, no more, no less. The cohesiveness of the Round

[28] 'Few economic historians today would preface an inquiry into "men, money and markets" with the question "What had Christian evangelism to do with economic policy?"' (Ronald Robinson, 'Oxford in Imperial Historiography', in Madden and Fieldhouse, *Oxford and the Idea of Commonwealth*, p. 41).

[29] Hancock states in his autobiography that he withdrew from the Round Table group in 1936 in protest against the prevailing sentiment in favour of appeasement (*Country and Calling*, p. 181). But his memory played him false on this point. He later put it right in *All Souls, 1923–1982*. He resigned in 1935 in the wake of the Abyssinian crisis after Lord Lothian (Philip Kerr, who had been active in the Round Table from the outset and shortly would become Ambassador in Washington) declared at a meeting: 'We must get Hitler onto the Brenner Pass to keep Mussolini in order.' Giving point to a general attitude, this singular remark was the cause of Hancock's withdrawal: 'Next morning I posted to the Secretary of the Round Table my letter of resignation' (p. 14). On another occasion, he reflected, correctly, that his reaction to the appeasement of Germany had been the same as radical critics of Hitler, ranging from Aneurin Bevan to Churchill (Hancock to Curtis, 14 September 1949, Curtis Papers, Box 31).

[30] For example: 'Milner wanted the Transvaal just as much as Hitler wanted Austria, Czechoslovakia and Poland. In anticipation of Hitler, Milner planned a war of brutal aggression' (Hancock, *Perspective in History*, p. 164). This radical vein in Hancock's personality, sometimes submerged but always present, bore a certain similarity to A. J. P. Taylor's, though the two otherwise disagreed on many things. Hancock wrote privately after the publication of Taylor's *Troublemakers* (London, 1958): 'Taylor uses the term quite affectionately, and believes, as I do, that the people whom the Foreign Office called "trouble makers" are very often the salt of the earth' (Hancock to Mrs. M. C. Gillett, 2 May 1958, Hancock Papers NLA, Series 1B).

Table group was limited because Curtis dominated it by sheer force of personality; it thus had a definite strength but also a narrow appeal. Hancock was a welcome interlocutor not only because of his sceptical, inquiring intellect but precisely because he came from Australia. He brought to bear an Australian perspective. On the other hand, his academic work focused on Italian history, and only by chance did he shift towards the study of Australia and, later, the Empire. He wrote his classic book *Australia* because he taught in Adelaide in the late 1920s. His seminal work on the Commonwealth, which culminated in the *Survey of Commonwealth Affairs,* originated in an invitation, not his own initiative. Hancock once said that he could not resist walking through open doors. After he had conducted his investigation on a particular topic, he tended to lose interest, though on some points of principle he remained ever vigilant. He demonstrated constant hostility, for example, to the idea of the Empire and Commonwealth as a single sovereign state.

It is worth pursuing briefly Hancock's intellectual inheritance or assumptions as he went through the two separate but adjacent doors of Australian and Commonwealth history. *Australia,* published in 1930, is in a popular sense his best work, a wonderful book, sparkling with brilliant details that support effervescent, still-famous themes: mastering a continent, framing a polity, and forging an identity.[31] It has often been assumed that Hancock must have been influenced by Frederick Jackson Turner's work on the American frontier, since *Australia* embraces a similar interpretation of the 'moving frontier'. It is a measure of Hancock's originality that he had not read Turner, yet almost intuitively employed similar concepts.[32] Hancock was a man of his time and a writer abreast of most of the ideas of his era. He had certain limitations that, to the present-day reader, are most apparent in the lack

[31] One of the virtues of *Australia* is its vivid and colloquial language. Throughout his writings Hancock was a careful, sometimes whimsical, wordsmith. In the case of *Australia,* he asked his loyal friend Badger to write to him about contemporary slang. See Badger's 'A Tribute from a Grateful Pupil' (no date, but probably 1989, Hancock Papers ANU, P96/22/6). For assessments of *Australia,* see Stuart Macintyre, '"Full of Hits and Misses": A Reappraisal of Hancock's *Australia*', in Low, *Legacies;* and Tim Rowse, *Australian Liberalism and National Character* (Malmsbury, Australia, 1978), in part a hostile critique of Hancock's economic interpretation, but also containing certain insights into his personality, including 'an apparently engaging talent for buffoonery' (p. 90).

[32] See *Survey of British Commonwealth Affairs,* II, pt. 1, p. 4, note 2: 'I used the idea of the moving frontier in . . . *Australia* . . . without any conscious borrowing from American historians, with whose work I was not then familiar.' See also his essay 'The Moving Metropolis', in A. R. Lewis and T. F. McGann, eds., *The New World Looks at its History* (Austin, Tex., 1963), in which Hancock discusses 'the splendour, span, audacity' of Walter Prescott Webb's *Great Frontier* (Boston, 1951).

of any sustained attention given to the Aborigines. Yet he did state quite clearly that the Australian continent had been invaded, implying that the Aborigines had been dispossessed. The young Hancock is remarkable also because of his unease about the 'vulgar' phase of Australian expansion in the late nineteenth century (similar to the spirit of British jingo expansion in southern Africa, which he also deplored). He scorned the type of Australian nationalism that upheld 'White Australia' as preferable to 'nigger-infested England'.[33] But he uncritically accepted the White Australia policy of restricting immigration for 'economic and racial necessity'.[34] In this regard he was indeed very much a man of his time. Still, in other ways he stands above, or at least apart from, most other historians then and later by believing that Australia could become a 'radical democracy' yet remain loyal to Britain. In his own well-known words, 'it is not impossible for Australians . . . to be in love with two soils.'[35]

The *Survey* is Hancock's greatest work.[36] No one before him had given the subject such imaginative, systematic, and exacting treatment. He was one of the first major historians of his time to use case studies to illuminate a larger universe. Ireland thus becomes a microcosm of the British Empire. ('Microcosmic' was one of Hancock's favourite words.) There is, however, a weakness as well as a strength to this approach. The case studies stand somewhat apart from the general chapters and sometimes, as in the Whiggish treatment of Malta, do not seem sufficiently integrated into the sustained theme of how the Commonwealth developed over time.[37] The microcosmic approach affords

[33] *Australia,* p. 66.

[34] He later reflected on the rationale: 'Racial impartiality at that time [early in the twentieth century] would have spelt "white capital and coloured labour"—an inhuman combination that has created a heap of trouble' (W. K. Hancock, *Today, Yesterday, and Tomorrow: The 1973 Boyer Lectures* [Sydney, 1973], p. 57).

[35] *Australia,* p. 68. Some of his colleagues in Australia, at least later, found Hancock's emotional tone a little excessive. The geographer J. M. Powell notes his 'patriotic puffing' (Low, *Legacies,* p. 214). Hancock was steadfast. He wrote towards the end of his life: 'I remained and shall remain until I die in love with two soils' (*All Souls, 1923–1982,* p. 18).

[36] For the historiographical context of the *Survey,* see W. David McIntyre, 'The Commonwealth', in *OHBE,* V. See also Mary Beth Norton, ed., *The American Historical Association's Guide to Historical Literature* (2 vols., New York, 1995, 3rd edn.), I, p. 813: 'Often called the best book ever written in [the] British imperial field.' Hancock himself at the time of its completion (at least the first part of it) seems to have felt that he was on the cusp of an inspired, original work. 'I think the thing is about 800% better than "Australia": indeed it is in a different class' (Hancock to Badger, 23 September [1936], Hancock Papers ANU, P96/23).

[37] See Dennis Austin, 'Malta and the Maltese', unpublished seminar paper, Hancock Memorial Seminar, 8–9 December 1988, Institute of Commonwealth Studies, London (hereafter ICS Seminar Papers 1988), which dismisses Hancock's assumptions as historical Whiggery. Austin argues that self-interest, not progress within the Commonwealth, explains Maltese motivation, and

acute insight, but it takes stamina to get through the case studies. Part of the problem lies in Hancock's magisterial style. Reading his work today is like returning to an earlier age, when an author could proceed at a leisurely pace, examine evidence in exhaustive detail, and go off on tangents and discursive comment without having to worry, it seems, about editorial sanctions on length. If the chapter happens to coincide with the reader's subject of immediate interest, then Hancock's detailed analysis is incisive and rewarding. For example, on Palestine, on which he had strong feelings, one can detect the tension he described in his private correspondence:

> I sympathise with both Jews & Arabs: but what is the use of that? One has to decide what is best on the merits of the case. I decide violently for the Arabs. I do not think we are bound to make them a minority by the methods of frightfulness.[38]

But in general the marathon treatment makes it difficult to read from cover to cover. Hancock is probably an historian more talked about than comprehensively read.

By virtue of the breadth of his reading, the scope of his interests, and the rigour of his analysis, Hancock stands in a class of his own. The *Survey* represents a watershed in the history of the subject, as does the work of Ronald Robinson and Jack Gallagher two decades or so later. Robinson and Gallagher helped bring about the revolution in historical writing in the 1950s and 1960s. They argued that the 'informal empire' of trade, commerce, and indirect control was just as important to the British Imperial system as the territories under formal British jurisdiction. But all the elements of the informal Empire are present in Hancock. Robinson and Gallagher, or at least Robinson, acknowledged Hancock's influence.[39] Hancock wrote of the 'invisible empire' of trade and commerce as well as the formal Empire of

---

that the Maltese, determined to twist the relationship to their advantage, responded to the British as they had to previous conquerors.

[38] Hancock to Badger, 23 September [1936], Hancock Papers ANU.

[39] The other direct influences were those of Vincent T. Harlow, *The Founding of the Second British Empire* (2 vols., Oxford, 1952 and 1964), and, more specifically on collaboration, Margery Perham, *Native Administration in Nigeria* (London, 1937). Hancock wrote to Margery Perham while preparing the *Survey:*

> We must be temperamentally akin as well as allies in our present work, for it's a habit of mine to cheer as lustily as you do when I come on work that in [historical] matters or method hits home . . . A dangerous trait, enthusiasm, but I would not be without it.

Hancock to Perham, 7 December 1939, Perham Papers, Box 27, Rhodes House, Oxford.

protectorates and Crown Colonies. As he put it in 1950, 'economic and political dependence are matters of degree'.[40] He insisted on the significance of cooperative arrangements, or what Robinson and Gallagher called 'collaboration'.[41] This is the recognizable domain of 'The Imperialism of Free Trade', but Hancock stopped short of integrating his thoughts into the concept of a worldwide British Imperial system, perhaps for a particular reason. He concluded that the non-territorial Empire of indirect influence did *not* reveal political or indirect control.[42] But indirect control eventually proved to be the essence of Robinson and Gallagher's argument. Hancock thus did not provide much of a model for Robinson and Gallagher's paradigm, even though he certainly emphasized the extent of the non-territorial empire. He simply did not pursue this line of inquiry. Indeed, his purpose differed fundamentally. He wanted to justify the Empire and to improve it; he was committed to the cause of self-government and, in the phrase he used repeatedly, sovereign equality. Hancock's moral and didactic purpose is a far cry from Robinson and Gallagher's standpoint of ironic detachment.[43]

Taking Hancock's measure on Imperial themes can perhaps best be done by direct comparison with that of other 1930s historians of the Empire, two of whom happened to be at All Souls. These were (Sir) Reginald Coupland and Richard Pares. This contrast proves useful because Hancock, apart from his concentration on the Dominions, focused mainly on Africa and the Mediterranean. One significant gap belies the breadth of his knowledge. He never mastered India as a field of study.[44] By contrast, Coupland devoted much of his attention to the Empire at large, and to India and East Africa as well as Palestine.

---

[40] W. K. Hancock, *Wealth of Colonies* (Cambridge, 1950), preface.

[41] On the theme of collaboration, see the recent work by Colin Newbury, *Patrons, Clients, and Empire: Chieftaincy and Over-Rule in Asia, Africa, and the Pacific* (Oxford, 2003), a book of great originality and historiographical significance, dedicated to Robinson and Gallagher.

[42] *Survey*, II, pt. I, p. 27.

[43] But it is not far removed from Nicholas Mansergh's sense of commitment to the ideals of the Commonwealth in, for example, *The Commonwealth Experience* (London, 1969). To Mansergh as to Hancock, the Empire did not willingly concede independence, which had to be firmly claimed and jealously guarded. On Mansergh himself, Hancock wrote that he was 'a man of one hundred per cent. reliability', presumably as both a scholar and a colleague (Hancock to Lord Bruce, 11 May 1961, Hancock Papers NLA, Series VII) Among his fellow historians, Hancock also had an especially high regard for Henry Pelling: '[H]e is a humane influence' (Hancock to Barry Smith, 4 June 1971, Hancock Papers ANU, P96/26).

[44] While discussing the progress of the *Survey* with Arnold Toynbee, Hancock wrote: 'India terrifies me. I have done no work on it and I dare not plunge into the manifold problems of that vast country' (Hancock to Toynbee, 12 May 1938, quoted in Peter Lyon, 'Hancock's Survey of British Commonwealth Affairs', ICS Seminar Papers 1988). On Hancock and India, see D. A. Low, '*Imperium et Libertas* and Hancock's *Problems of Nationality*', in Low, *Legacies*, pp. 70–78.

Pares, the historian of the West Indies, had, in Hancock's judgement, an 'unrivalled knowledge of the patterns of trade within and beyond the West Indies'.[45] Among the three of them, they covered most of the world. Coupland brought the subject of the Empire's history up to the academic standards of comparable fields in modern history at Oxford.[46] He and Hancock shared the same assumptions, but no one who reads their books can be left with any doubt that Hancock possessed the sharper mind. Here the real comparison is with Richard Pares, whose analytical ability matched Hancock's.[47] Pares, however, usually refused to be drawn into generalizations beyond his own field.[48] No one was more highly respected, in part because he was an editor of the *English Historical Review*, 1939–58.[49] But neither Pares nor Coupland could match Hancock's chronological scope, breadth of vision, or mastery of historical literature. Hancock's *Survey* achieves universality because he always presses his arguments beyond their immediate context, as when he uses a case study of the anthropologist Mary Kingsley to demonstrate the historian's three virtues of attachment, justice, and span.[50] Present-day historians use the work he did in the 1930s more often than that of most of his contemporaries.

Leaving aside for the moment his short wartime book *Argument of Empire,* Hancock's principal achievement of the 1940s was the editing of the *Civil Histories* in the official history of the Second World War.[51]

[45] Hancock, *Professing History,* p. 140. Pares, almost as if anticipating a future trend among historians, had, according to A. L. Rowse, 'an inhibition about dynamic characters in history' and maintained 'that they in fact do nothing very much' (Richard Ollard, ed., *The Diaries of A. L. Rowse* [London, 2003], p. 220).

[46] See W. R. Louis, 'Introduction', in *OHBE,* V, pp. 23–24; Coupland's books include *The Exploitation of East Africa, 1856–1890* (London, 1939); and *The Indian Problem: Report on the Constitutional Problem in India* (3 vols., Oxford, 1942–43).

[47] See especially Richard Pares, *War and Trade in the West Indies, 1739–1763* (Oxford, 1936).

[48] But see his article 'The Economic Factors in the History of the Empire', *Economic History Review,* 7 (1937), which is an exceptional essay that helped lay the foundation for Robinson and Gallagher's work.

[49] Pares died in 1958. In his last years he was almost entirely paralyzed below the neck, though his mind remained as alert as ever. Hancock remembered seeing him, shortly before his death, with a pole strapped to his head in a manner that brought to mind a unicorn. By moving his head, Pares manipulated the unicorn's horn to turn the pages of Toynbee (*All Souls, 1923–1982,* p. 7). I have heard a similar account, but of Pares with great dedication turning the pages of *EHR* proof.

[50] Hancock developed his idea of the three virtues in a rare diary (he seldom kept diaries) during a trip to West Africa in 1940. Of particular interest is the way he kept reformulating the concept of 'attachment', which he eventually took to mean the way in which an historian lives 'inside' the thoughts and problems of his subject (1940 Diary, Hancock Papers ANU, P96/14).

[51] See José Harris, 'Thucydides amongst the Mandarins: Hancock and the World War II Civil Histories', in Low, *Legacies.* This is a seminal essay. See also especially Gowing, 'The Civil Histories of the Second World War'.

He owed the appointment to Sir Edward (Lord) Bridges, Secretary to the War Cabinet and one of the most powerful figures in the civil service.[52] Bridges had been a Fellow of All Souls in the 1920s. His sponsorship (and protection) of Hancock during the war exemplifies the effectiveness of All Souls connections. He defended Hancock's project against the bureaucrats who wanted to eviscerate the histories or block their publication. When published, the series consisted of twenty-eight volumes and included as authors such talented historians as Michael (Munia) Postan on war production, Richard Titmuss on social policy, Betty Behrens on shipping, and Margaret Gowing, who came to Hancock's rescue by helping complete his own volume on the wartime economy. Hancock made false starts on *British War Economy* (published with Gowing as a joint author in 1949) because he attempted to apply the same discursive methods he had used in the *Survey*. Why should a study of wartime economy, asked Sir Norman Brook of the War Cabinet Secretariat, be 'interlarded' with 'digressions on strategy and institutions'? Brook urged Hancock to tell a more 'straightforward story'.[53] As José Harris has pointed out, Hancock was then intellectually adrift and close to exhaustion.[54] In any event he received

---

[52] Hancock later wrote of Bridges: 'To me he was the embodiment of all the virtues of the British civil service at their highest' (*Country and Calling*, p. 196). Hancock's gratitude to Bridges is also a theme in his private correspondence—for example: 'Bridges . . . in times of trial was always vigilant' (Hancock to Margaret Gowing, 14 November 1986, Gowing Papers).

[53] Brook to Sir Gilbert Laithwaite, Confidential, 23 June 1945, CAB 103/122. Brook (who succeeded Bridges as Secretary to the War Cabinet) was far more formal and distant than Bridges. The relations between Brook and Hancock were sometimes tempestuous, but eventually they worked together effectively.

[54] See Harris, 'Thucydides amongst the Mandarins', pp. 129–30. Hancock was also affected, then and subsequently, by the illness of his wife, Theaden, who often hovered near collapse because of nervous anxiety and depression. Anthony Low has written perceptively: 'She was a remarkable woman; at least as intelligent as he was; a much better judge of people; tall, handsome, invariably well groomed . . . But with him she was impatient, irascible, jealous' (Anthony Low, 'Country and Calling Cohere', ICS Seminar Papers 1988). Part of Hancock's own stress, at least according to his own account, was caused simply by wartime conditions of bad beds and broken chairs. In 1944 he wrote a revealing letter about the difficulties of writing history in London and Oxford:

> I never seem to find a bed that isn't sagging or [hasn't] broken springs: this is a menace, because I can't sleep properly on a sagging bed . . . Take All Souls. Despite the monastic austerity of its bedrooms, it used to have a certain magnificence, or at least elegance in Hall and Common Room . . . But now alas . . . leaky rusting cisterns and the broken chairs, the frowsty Common Room and the shivering corridors where a few old Fellows and two old servants scuffle around: and the Domestic Bursar (Grant Robertson) eyes me coldly when I appear and says: Have you brought your margarine?

Hancock to Badger, 17 September 1944, Hancock Papers ANU, P96/23.

detailed, exacting criticism from both Brook and Bridges. They helped temper Hancock's style and give the loose writing more focus, though they did not press him too far.[55] But it was Margaret Gowing who saved the day, drafting chapters on clear and relevant economic themes. 'It would have been quite impossible', Hancock wrote, 'to have finished the job without the succour of M.G.'[56]

In a certain sense Hancock was always a loner, working alone and striking out in an individual way. He once commented: 'It remains my practice as an historian to hew my own wood and draw my own water.'[57] But beyond his own work, he organized research projects and stimulated other scholars with indefatigable energy and purpose. As D. A. Low has written, he gathered about him 'clusterings of people of ability and of widely different backgrounds'.[58] Twice in his life he found himself fully immersed in major projects of historical collaboration.[59] During the war, and much later in the project on the *Australian Dictionary of Biography*, he proved to be an effective editor,

[55] Hancock found an ally in Sir Gilbert Laithwaite, a consummate bureaucrat who later became Permanent Under-Secretary at the Commonwealth Relations Office. 'We must not tie him up too closely,' Laithwaite wrote (minute by Laithwaite, 11 August 1944, CAB 103/122). One of the criticisms of the final draft was that Hancock conveyed the impression of 'muddle, improvisation and fortuitous decisions' and a picture of 'internecine warfare between Departments' (note by Sir Donald Vandepeer, Ministry of Agriculture and Fisheries, 26 July 1948, CAB 102/86). Though Hancock met specific points, the volume in its published form still leaves the reader in no doubt that the impression of historical accident and makeshift planning usually conformed to reality.

[56] Hancock to Betty Behrens, 6 August 1947, Behrens Papers, Churchill College, Cambridge, BEHR/ADD/17. Hancock wrote to Gowing herself to thank her for 'doing all the work, all the research and thought and construction of the second half of the book' (Hancock to Gowing, 14 May 1948, Gowing Papers).

[57] *Smuts*, II, p. xiii. Hancock made this declaration of scholarly independence specifically in regard to the help he received with the biography of Smuts; but he might have emphasized his dependence on others even further if he had reviewed the files on the *Survey* in the RIIA Archive, which contain evidence of massive research assistance. Still, Hancock was surely right when he wrote: '[A]lthough a biographer may here and there devolve a limited and particular job on somebody else, basically, he has to do his own work' (Hancock to Lord Bruce, 11 May 1961, Hancock Papers NLA, Series VII).

[58] Low, *Legacies*, p. 7.

[59] To put it in broader context:

> Hancock's story . . . [is] a tale of the mass accumulation of historical information, the production of extensive series of books of reference and analysis, the management of institutions devoted to research and postgraduate training, the administrative direction and intellectual leadership of teams of researchers, and the writing of influential syntheses, an exhaustive biography and a pioneering regional history.

Julian Thomas, 'Keith Hancock: Professing the Profession', in Stuart Macintyre and Julian Thomas, eds., *The Discovery of Australian History, 1890–1939* (Melbourne, 1995), p. 152.

lining up his authors, giving them guidance, and encouraging mutual criticism.[60] With his fellow authors he could be affectionate as well as encouraging.[61]

In the case of the *Civil Histories* as well as with the *Australian Dictionary of Biography,* he came to grief in dealing with certain individuals.[62] But during the saga of the *Civil Histories* he proved himself an adept infighter in Whitehall against entrenched civil servants, even though the series was ultimately less candid and forthright than he had intended. One crisis occurred because of the Air Ministry's determination to block, on grounds of national security, the publication of Munia Postan's book on air production. Had the obstruction been successful, according to Margaret Gowing, Hancock 'would, I am sure, have resigned'.[63] As a result of the harrowing editorial experience perhaps as much as from the stress of the war itself, Hancock's distinctive shock of hair turned white.

On the whole, the *Civil Histories* constitute a remarkable historical

---

[60] In one notable case in the wartime series, Betty Behrens of Cambridge wrote a detailed critique of Hancock's own draft, summing up her criticism by remarking that it struck her as 'paste & scissors history'. Hancock dismissed much of what she wrote as 'poppycock', but it was a telling comment that the broad-gauged and rambling narrative of the *Survey* would not work in a study of wartime economic policy; see Behrens to Hancock, 16 and 20 August 1947, CAB 102/86, and Hancock to Behrens, n.d. but August 1947, Behrens Papers, BEHR/ADD/17. His exchange with Behrens reveals certain anxieties. Hancock feared that mutual criticism might be damaging to the project if it went beyond the authors themselves:

> I don't mind you telling me that my draft up to date is muck—that partly is what you are for—but I must warn you not to tell Cambridge that you think it is muck. That would be a breach of friendship and a damaging disloyalty to the Historical Section.

The friendship survived the exchange about muck. Hancock later wrote: 'Her book *Merchant Shipping and the Demands of War* [1955] .... is a masterpiece of the historian's craft' (Hancock to Edward Miller, 21 July 1983, Hancock Papers ANU, P96/31).

[61] See, for example, Ann Moyal, *Breakfast with Beaverbrook: Memoirs of an Independent Woman* (Sydney, 1995), p. 148.

[62] On the wartime series, see Harris, 'Thucydides amongst the Mandarins' in Low, *Legacies;* on the *Australian Dictionary of Biography,* see Moyal, *Breakfast with Beaverbrook.* On the other hand, Hancock possessed a remarkable ability to get on with difficult or temperamental colleagues. In Canberra, he appears to have had a relationship of mutual respect with the radical historian Manning Clark, just as he previously had with A. J. P. Taylor in Oxford: 'Manning Clark . . . never took kindly to rivals; but so long as Hancock was in charge of History . . . his resentments were largely suppressed' (Foster and Varghese, *Making of the Australian National University,* p. 178). Though Hancock disagreed with Clark on politics (as he certainly did with Taylor), they were kindred spirits. The radical streak in Hancock's own personality remained with him through his life. For his part, Clark described Hancock as a 'kind man, a warm-hearted man' (C. M. H. Clark, *A History of Australia,* vol. 6: *'The Old Dead Tree and the Young Tree Green'* [Melbourne, 1987], p. 301).

[63] 'The Civil Histories of the Second World War', p. 17.

venture. Most of the volumes have an interdepartmental theme, and each has its own individual focus and methodological coherence.[64] Part of the success of the series in relating a rounded account of the war effort can be attributed to Hancock's determination to have books on *subjects* (such as war production) rather than government departments. The overarching themes have a ring similar to *Australia*'s, but he now recast the formula to fit British wartime circumstances: national unity, state intervention, centralization, and reconstruction. The *Civil Histories* became indispensable sources for such historians as A. J. P. Taylor, Alan Bullock, and Henry Pelling.

Apart from his later excursions into environmental history, Hancock's last major work was the biography of Smuts that appeared in two volumes in 1962 and 1968. This is perhaps one of the distinguished biographies of the twentieth century, though ultimately it is a flawed work. Reread today, it perhaps reminds one of Ralf Dahrendorf's history of the London School of Economics.[65] Both Hancock and Dahrendorf deal with their subjects in such a way as to write universal history. Hancock's biography can be read as a history of the late nineteenth and early twentieth centuries as seen through the eyes of Smuts —with Hancock providing the focus. It also gives the impression, as more than one critic has suggested, of one great man writing about another great man. Smuts was an Afrikaner patriot but also an international statesman; Hancock, an Australian patriot and citizen of the Commonwealth. Hancock was now at the height of his powers, having left Oxford as the Chichele Professor of Economic History (1944– 49) to become the founding Director of the Institute of Commonwealth Studies at the University of London in 1949.[66] By the time he

[64] Harris, 'Thucydides amongst the Mandarins', in Low, *Legacies*, p. 131. Munia Postan, for example, knew that his method 'would have to combine the technique of an historian with that of an anthropologist, and should have to supplement documentary source with direct field work among the savage tribes I was investigating' (Postan to W. S. Farren, Secret, 23 October 1945, CAB 102/43). Of all his fellow historians working on the wartime project, Hancock held Postan in highest esteem: 'His decision that he would best serve his country in Hitler's war by practicing his own craft was for me an uncovenanted mercy' (Hancock to Edward Miller, 21 July 1983, Hancock Papers ANU, P96/31).

[65] Ralf Dahrendorf, *A History of the London School of Economics and Political Science, 1885–1995* (Oxford, 1995).

[66] In one of the seismic shifts in his career, when he moved to Oxford in 1944, Hancock felt 'compelled to read in three months 300 books on the Industrial Revolution' in order to lecture on 'this uninviting theme' (note by Hancock, 23 June 1944, CAB 102/86). On another occasion Hancock wrote that the Oxford appointment would protect him from the historian's great enemy, sloth: 'It means also that I shall have to spend some years learning my subject as I teach it, and that is excellent at my time of life, when I could too easily become lazy' (Hancock to Badger, 25 March 1944, Hancock Papers ANU, P96/23).

completed the biography, he had long since returned to Australia to become, in 1957, Director of the School of Social Sciences at the Australian National University.[67] He wrote the biography of Smuts over a fifteen-year period, from the early 1950s to the late 1960s.[68]

Hancock's reputation as a biographer probably remains secure, despite changing intellectual traditions. He still wrote in the historical vein of those who believed that knowledge based on wide reading—from the Bible to Shakespeare, from Aristotle to Machiavelli—could and should be assimilated into the work at hand. The biography of Smuts no less then the *Survey* is filled with literary allusions that now strike the reader as mannered, though certainly learned. Hancock moreover believed that writing about a historical personage who also happened to be a hero of the Commonwealth would command public attention and would, he hoped, further the cause of the Commonwealth itself. He threw himself into the task with characteristic commitment and thoroughness. Measured by Hancock's own criteria of attachment, justice, and span, the biography succeeds: it is a critical as well as sympathetic treatment of Smuts, who then as later was regarded by his enemies as 'slim' (the Afrikaner word for devious or unprincipled).[69] Commanding a knowledge of international as well as British and South African affairs in the first half of the twentieth century, Hancock attempted to be scrupulously fair to such figures as Gandhi as well as Smuts.

'Blinkered Genius', a review written by Roland Oliver, sharply assesses of one of the biography's deficiencies. Oliver develops the theme that Smuts from early in his life not only regarded the black African inhabitants of South Africa as barbarians but that he never altered his view.[70] He was 'blinkered' in the sense of never being able to

[67] For Hancock and the ANU, Foster and Varghese, *Making of the Australian National University*, is indispensable.

[68] Hancock reflected late in life that the biography had been 'hard labour indeed—but without it, life would have been empty' (Hancock to Margaret Gowing, 14 November 1986, Gowing Papers).

[69] Hancock nevertheless failed to discover persuasive evidence of devious or unethical behaviour. He wrote to the historian Leonard Thompson: 'My trouble with "slimness" . . . [is] on the whole, I do not find them [the accusations] convincing, except in the sense that Smuts wanted power and fought for it by methods which are the ordinary stuff of politics' (Hancock to Thompson, 17 February 1960, Hancock Papers NLA, Series 1B).

[70] Roland Oliver, 'Blinkered Genius', *Journal of African History*, 9, 3 (1968), pp. 491–94. See also the extraordinary review by Eric A. Walker in the *Historical Journal*, 9 (1968), pp. 565–81. On another critical point—Hancock's treatment of Smuts and the aftermath of the Boer War—see Ronald Hyam and Peter Henshaw, *The Lion and the Springbok: Britain and South Africa since the Boer War* (Cambridge, 2003), pp. 60–75: 'Smuts . . . certainly exaggerated the extent of his influence in claiming for the remainder of his life that he had persuaded Campbell-Bannerman to grant immediate responsible government.' Hancock in turn 'most unfortunately' en-

see the black African side of the problem, other than from an Afrikaner point of view. Hancock had a similar blind spot. He did not endorse Smuts's racist attitudes, but neither did he explicitly challenge
them.[71] It was not that Hancock was unaware of the way in which
the whites dealt with the black Africans. As long ago as the *Survey,* he
had trenchantly analysed the impact of the capitalist system 'in sweeping Bantu away from their lands to live in compounds and work in
mines'.[72] In the post-war era, Hancock treated black Africans as equals
and championed their cause.

Yet in the Smuts biography he does not deal fully with the black
African dimension of the problem, nor does he appear to have comprehended it. The extent of the gap between his work and the developing scholarship of the 1950s and 1960s is puzzling, but it can be understood at least in part by examining some of Hancock's own implicit
preconceptions.[73] He brought to South Africa the same assumptions
that he held about Australia. In the *Survey,* for example, there is a striking contrast between the lack of empathy ('attachment', in Hancock's
phrase) with the South African blacks working in the mines, and the
sympathetic treatment of black African commodity producers in West
Africa. The duality in Hancock's approach reflects the two sides of
his personality. His reaction to the black Africans of South Africa reflected the conventional Australian attitude towards 'blackfellows' in
Australia, whereas his response to the Africans of Nigeria and the Gold
Coast revealed the progressive ideas of London in the 1930s.

As Shula Marks has written, '"[W]hiteness" in Australia or Britain
was not the same as whiteness in South Africa.'[74] One difference was

---

dorsed Smuts's own interpretation of the 'myth of magnanimity'. *The Lion and the Springbok* is a
work of fundamental importance, not least for its careful tracing of historiographical issues.

[71] On this point, Hancock had a crisis of historical conscience. Many observers of Smuts, including Smuts's own son, told Hancock that Smuts ultimately had to be counted as a white su-
premacist. But Hancock could find no evidence that satisfied him on this point, and indeed he
believed that Smuts grew or progressed in race relations just as he had in other fields. Hancock wrote in the early 1960s: 'It is very important for me to get the public record straight. It is
extraordinary how little J. C. S. gives away in his private letters. I just don't know yet whether or
not he believed in white supremacy' (Hancock's note to Joan Bradley, research assistant, n.d.,
but probably 1963, Hancock Papers NLA, Box 4). On another occasion he wrote: 'My feeling
is that he held to no principle at all on this issue but followed short term expediency' (Hancock
to Lady Daphne Moore, 11 March 1963, Hancock Papers NLA, Series 1B).

[72] *Survey*, I, p. 178.

[73] Hancock's lack of awareness of developing trends in African history can also be explained
by his obsessive attention to Smuts. He wrote to Leonard Thompson: 'I am out of touch with historians of West Africa'—a comment that would have been true for all other parts of Africa except
South Africa (Hancock to Thompson, 16 October 1962, Hancock Papers NLA, Series 1B).

[74] Shula Marks, 'Jan Smuts, Race, and the South African War', in W. R. Louis, ed., *Still More
Adventures with Britannia* (Austin, Tex., 2003), p. 76. See also Shula Marks and Saul Dubow, 'Patriotism of Place and Race: Hancock on South Africa', in Low, *Legacies.*

that in South Africa there were, from Smuts's perspective, '100,000,000 [*sic*] barbarians' and only half a million whites. In his book on Australia in 1930, Hancock regarded the diminishing number of Aborigines as so insignificant that he did not bother to discuss the demography.[75] Just as in the 1930s, when he had remained more or less oblivious of the question of the Aborigines, so in the 1950s he was left relatively untouched by the intellectual and academic currents that led, in the 1960s, to the creation of African history as a new field.[76] It is interesting to reflect on how Hancock might have responded later to further stimulus about black Africans, as he did with the Aborigines when in the 1970s he pressed forward his work in environmental history in Australia.[77]

Hancock completed the biography at a time when the international campaign against apartheid was beginning to take off. He could perhaps not have chosen a worse moment to publish a major biography about a man whose reputation already seemed tarnished simply because he was a South African. But Hancock did not think it the historian's job to condemn apartheid; his aim was to explain it. His own views about the futility—indeed the absurdity—of the Afrikaner system of racial separation are manifest in his carefully reasoned lecture, based on legal precedent and economic analysis, delivered in Cape Town in 1966.[78] Especially in the lecture and rather more implicitly in the biography, Hancock took his stand on legal and demographic evidence while attempting to be evenhanded in his treatment of Smuts. He did not have the benefit of a post-apartheid vantage point, which would have made clear the far more precarious situation in South Africa. He held out hope, as would have Smuts himself, that the Afrikaner regime could reform itself. This is now an exploded view,

[75] But he wrote in 1943: 'We in Australia did not even have Red Indians to reckon with: the scanty population of stone-age aborigines—alas, its helplessness and decline lie heavy upon our conscience—was quite unable to oppose the stockmen who drove their flocks over the old hunting grounds. Civilised opponents we had none' (*Argument of Empire*, p. 67).

[76] His aloofness from the new field of African history is all the more remarkable because he had helped sponsor seminars in African history and had a high regard for Roland Oliver, who became the first Professor of African History at the University of London. Hancock once wrote to Margery Perham: 'I have . . . an immense respect for his learning and character' (Hancock to Perham, Personal, 13 December 1956, Perham Papers, Box 266).

[77] See W. K. Hancock, *Discovering Monaro: A Study of Man's Impact on Environment* (Cambridge, 1972); and *The Battle of Black Mountain: An Episode of Canberra's Environmental History* (Canberra, 1974). For a critique of Hancock's work on the environment, see J. M. Powell, '"Signposts to Tracks?" Hancock and Environmental History', in Low, *Legacies*. See also the comment by Tom Griffiths in the same volume that in the 1970s Hancock awoke 'to the ancient Aboriginal presence and influence' (p. 243).

[78] The Hoernlé Lecture: 'Are There South Africans?' (Cape Town, 1966).

but it matters not for the integrity of Hancock's scholarship. The biography is a powerfully argued and coherent work, but a book of its time. He did not pretend to look into the future, nor should he have. Historians could no more foresee the collapse of the Afrikaner regime than they could the disintegration of the Soviet Union.[79]

Argument of Empire, written in 1943 after the war turned in favour of the Allies, reveals Hancock's ideas about a Pax Britannica.[80] It also contains a streak of anti-Americanism; indeed, it is a full-scale attack on American anti-colonialism. Almost from the time of the American entry into the war, the debate on war aims included the future of the European colonies. One thing was certain from the American vantage point: the United States did not wage war for the purpose of preserving the British Empire. To many Americans, British imperialism seemed to be an eighteenth-century anachronism as well as an instrument of oppression and exploitation. Hancock believed that the Americans were dead wrong. He aimed to straighten them out. He reminded them that George III was dead and that Dominion Status conferred sovereignty. 'My own country, Australia, is every bit as independent and free as the United States.'[81] Though the British Empire like all institutions needed to be improved, he believed that it was a progressive force in world affairs.

By the phrase 'Pax Britannica', Hancock meant the conditions of peace in the colonies that permitted economic development and allowed the inhabitants to be trained in the art of self-government; these propositions he put forward in a somewhat hectoring tone.[82] Here

[79] For example, in a useful book written in the early 1980s Dan O'Meara states: 'Despite claims that "apartheid as you know it is dying", [apartheid] . . . remains unshaken' (Dan O'Meara, *Volkskapitalisme: Class, Capital, and Ideology in the Development of Afrikaner Nationalism, 1934–1948* [Cambridge, 1983], p. 257).

[80] See R. F. Holland, 'Keith Hancock and the Argument for Empire', ICS Seminar Papers 1988. The book had its origins in a series of broadcasts, which perhaps explains its conversational tone and loose structure. This was one of Hancock's most ill-considered ventures, written under great pressure during the air bombardment of London. Usually Hancock demonstrates scepticism towards the Whiggish view of Empire, but in this work his belief in the Empire and Commonwealth as a force for progress in world affairs achieves unabashed expression: 'Monarchy grows into democracy, empire grows into commonwealth, the tradition of a splendid past is carried forward into an adventurous future.' He adds, as if slightly embarrassed, 'Well, that is how I see it' (*Argument of Empire,* p. 12). The social historian Richard Titmuss once commented that a little of Hancock's 'uplift' went a long way (Titmuss to Behrens, 26 August 1947, BEHR/ADD/17). On Titmuss and Hancock, see Margaret Gowing, 'Richard Morris Titmuss', *Proceedings of the British Academy,* 61 (1975), pp. 401–28. See also Ann Oakley, *Man and Wife: Richard and Kay Titmuss* (London, 1996), which provides rare glimpses into Hancock's private life during the war.

[81] *Argument of Empire,* p. 12.

[82] For example: 'I am an Australian. I think my country no less democratic than the United States—and quite a lot more socialistic. In Australia, our governments and parliaments and

as elsewhere the anti-American thrust to Hancock's thought is usually veiled but always detectable. In *Argument of Empire* this is apparent in the title of his first chapter: 'The Americans Cut In'. Though he argued that American intervention in the debate on the future of colonies would be salutary, in fact he merely stated in polite language what the Viceroy of India, Lord Linlithgow, wrote in more forthright words —that the Americans should 'keep off the grass'.[83] That made up one part of Hancock's message. The other was that the Americans and British had to find a way to cooperate in the development of the colonial world. Two sides of Hancock's personality struggled for ascendancy: the one conciliatory, the other combative and certainly resistant to interference in the affairs of the Empire.

Before the war, Hancock shared with many of his colleagues at Oxford and Cambridge a genteel anti-Americanism. It was common, then as now, to think of Americans as unsophisticated, loud, and crude.[84] During the war, this condescension or snobbery sometimes took the form of resentment. Hancock's own anti-Americanism was muted: he accepted individual Americans as friends and academic colleagues, but he shared with many others in Britain an uneasy reaction to the American insistence that the Empire must be liquidated.[85] He deplored the advice that a timetable like that used for the Philippines should be set for the independence of the British colonies. Hancock, and probably most of his British compatriots, believed not only that it would take many decades before the African dependencies could stand on their own, but also that colonial rule was a necessary institution at this time in world history. To set the record straight, he

---

courts, state and federal, do their business in the King's name. That suits us well enough. We intend to keep on that way' (ibid., p. 12).

[83] Cited in W. R. Louis, 'British Imperialism and the Partitions of India and Palestine', in Chris Wrigley, ed., *Warfare, Diplomacy, and Politics: Essays in Honour of A. J. P. Taylor* (London, 1986), p. 198. One incident concerning Linlithgow early in the war made an indelible impression on Hancock. In 1941, Gandhi admitted that he had never read the India Act of 1935. He now 'discovered to his surprise that it gave to a united India all the essentials of self-government.' Had he studied it earlier, according to Linlithgow, much of the conflict with the British might never have arisen. The Viceroy believed that Gandhi's statement was 'the saddest thing he had ever heard' since arriving in India. Hancock repeated this episode several times. See, for example, Hancock to Amery, 20 May 1953, Hancock Papers NLA, Box 4. Cf. *Smuts,* II, p. 454.

[84] For example, see Ronald A. Knox, *Let Dons Delight: Being Variations on a Theme in an Oxford Common-Room* (London, 1939) on 'Colonials' and 'Rhodes scholars': 'I wonder who did the talking at societies before the Rhodes bequest?' (p. 238).

[85] In his private correspondence, at least to his friend Badger, Hancock was less restrained. He wrote in March 1943: 'There are of course some features of American life which are in my view a menace. There is crudity in American big business as well as in some of the methods of American thought and discussion. In this crudity there are elements of brutality, vulgarity and naivete' (Hancock to Badger, 9 March 1943, Hancock Papers ANU, P96/23).

emphasized British achievements in agriculture, animal health, forestry, and mining as well as medicine and education.[86] But he did not stop at correcting American misperceptions: he wanted to persuade the Americans to play a part in the development of the African continent. The modernization of Africa and Asia was a project that lay beyond Britain's capacity. Hancock may have felt ambivalent about American power, but he knew for certain that only the resources of the United States could produce the investment necessary to achieve full-scale economic development in the colonial world.[87]

Hancock sometimes used 'Pax Britannica' as a shorthand expression to convey Britain's place in the world. In the nineteenth century, the sheet anchor was the Royal Navy, which along with the Army and later the Royal Air Force secured relatively stable and peaceful conditions, sometimes in regions far beyond formal British jurisdiction.[88] Besides suppressing piracy and providing stability, the aim was to keep hostile powers out of areas such as the Persian Gulf. The remarkable thing about Hancock's thought in this regard is the way in which he adopted a Victorian view of the world, in which a harmony of interests might prevail. In the *Survey* he referred several times to a famous statement by Sir Eyre Crowe of the Foreign Office before the First World War.[89] The gist of Crowe's argument was a harmony of interests. Britain could remain paramount in different parts of the world only by harmonizing commercial and other activities with those of other nations.[90] As Hancock brought his ideas to bear on contemporary circumstances, his political philosophy became identical with that of the Attlee government (1945–51).[91] In the 1940s he argued that Britain's Imperial aims must be made compatible with the aspirations of colonial nationalists—whether in Asia, Africa, or the Caribbean—by

[86] *Argument of Empire*, p. 118.

[87] 'Great Britain does not possess the resources to finance . . . all her African Empire, let alone the West Indies and other places as well.' Hancock's views brought him into collision with the economic expert in the Colonial Office, Sir Gerald Clauson, who commented that Hancock proposed 'great nonsense'. American investment would bring with it interference in British management of development. See W. R. Louis, *Imperialism at Bay* (Oxford, 1977), pp. 104–05.

[88] 'The fact that we [Australians] grew up in the shelter of the *Pax Britannica* is the best reason we have for calling Australia "the lucky country"' (Hancock, *Professing History*, p. 160).

[89] For Crowe, see Zara S. Steiner, *The Foreign Office and Foreign Policy, 1898–1914* (Cambridge, 1969).

[90] *Survey*, I, p. viii.

[91] In Hancock's view, 'the best peace-time government which had served the nation since the time of Sir Henry Campbell-Bannerman' (*Perspective in History*, p. 170). Hancock's unpublished notes include a description of Attlee as 'not v. interested in econ. matters. Much more interested in political things like India . . . v. high character' (Hancock, note on 'Personalities', n.d., but at the end of file following 1948 documents, CAB 102/86).

promising them eventual self-government and independence. The British had to demonstrate that colonial rule brought tangible advantages of not only economic development and political rights, but also, in a word, welfare. No less that Attlee, Bevin, and Cripps, Hancock believed in the welfare state, and, as far as Hancock was concerned, not only for Britain but for the colonies. To bring the welfare state to Asia and Africa, the British would have to hitch their wagon to the rising star of American economic expansion, try to provide a direction to fit their own purposes, and demonstrate to the Americans that the 'harmonization' of British and American goals would satisfy mutual self-interest.

During the 1950s and 1960s, while working on the biography of Smuts, Hancock seldom commented on the dissolution of the Empire and what he came to view as the transition from the Pax Britannica to the Pax Americana. One of the rare exceptions came on the eve of the Suez crisis. In February 1956 he delivered the Cust Lecture at the University of Nottingham.[92] The title of the lecture was 'Colonial Self-Government'. He reaffirmed his belief that the most urgent and rewarding task of the British Empire was to prepare its inhabitants for self-government. He possessed, of course, a paternalistic attitude, as did most others of his era; Hancock, however, was more explicit than most about Britain's paternalistic duty. In recent years he has been out of fashion precisely because he argued for the ethical justification of the Empire. In the Cust Lecture he raised questions that must surely arise today as historians begin to assess the controversial issue of the Empire's moral worth. What of the colonial structures that by keeping a measure of social and political order, allowed for social mobility, outside contacts, open markets, and a reasonably free press? In 1956, Britain still had self-imposed responsibilities in such places as the Gold Coast and Malaya: 'Their frontiers may be artificial in origin; but they contain the framework of emergent states—orderly administrations, coherent systems of transport and marketing, a field of tolerable security for the attraction of capital and skill—all the things that belong to economic viability which is . . . a condition of political independence.'[93]

He made certain assumptions about dependencies such as Uganda. Hancock had led a mission to Uganda in 1954 to deal with the explosive issue of Buganda and its possible secession from the Uganda Protectorate. He always hoped that his writings would influence policy; in a most unusual assignment for an historian, he not only went to

---

[92] The lecture is republished with Hancock's 1981 notes in *Perspective in History*.
[93] Ibid., p. 63.

Uganda but assisted in shaping the future of the state, at least in the short term.[94] He contributed significantly to the stability of the country, thereby helping set it on the road towards a unified, independent state.[95] He upheld the principle, as did Sir Andrew Cohen, that old attitudes must change and that the British must regard Africans as equals.[96] He assumed that the British would continue to preside over an orderly process of decolonization and could assist Uganda and other new states in the post-colonial period.

Hancock commented a quarter of a century later that he had been far too sanguine, though he remained at heart an optimist.[97] The outcome of the Suez crisis had proved that Imperial power had diminished so much that the British could no longer control orderly decolonization, certainly not according to their own timetable. He also took note of Idi Amin's regime in Uganda. He offered the two examples of Suez and Uganda as 'cautionary tales' against excessive optimism.[98] Perhaps he judged his own writing a little too soon after events that seemed to prove him wrong. From today's vantage point, the waning of the Pax Britannica does not appear so cataclysmic as it seemed in the immediate aftermath of the British collapse at Suez and the

[94] Hancock wrote to Lionel Curtis later in the year that he hoped he had helped 'to lay the foundation' for a self-governing African state, 'but the building [of it] is bound to be slow' (Hancock to Curtis, 9 December 1954, Curtis Papers, Box 95).

[95] See Hancock, *Professing History,* chap. 5; D. A. Low, '*Imperium et Libertas*', in Low, *Legacies,* pp. 78–80; and, by the same author, *Buganda in Modern History* (London, 1971), chap. 4. Colonial Office officials regarded Hancock at first with some reserve and believed that he was politically naive; the Governor of Uganda, Sir Andrew Cohen, commented at one point that Hancock had a 'sentimental' view of Africans. But in the end Cohen professed admiration for his 'modest' personality as well as the objective and analytical way in which he led the Africans into agreement: 'He has done a magnificent job for us' (Cohen to Secretary of State, Top Secret and Personal, 18 September 1954, CO 822/751). The files on Uganda in the Hancock Papers at the ANU are an invaluable supplement to the official papers. Among other things, there is a correspondence between Roland Oliver and Hancock on 'what went wrong' with the 1954 settlement, as well as Hancock's assessment that the Colonial Secretary, Alan Lennox-Boyd, did not move with the times. See, for example, Oliver to Hancock, 25 May 1958, and Hancock to Oliver, 18 June 1958, Hancock Papers ANU, P96/28. For published documentary background, see David Goldsworthy, ed., *British Documents on the End of Empire: The Conservative Government and the End of Empire, 1951–1957* (3 vols., London, 1994), II, documents 293–95.

[96] See note of conversation with Anthony Low, Confidential, 24 February 1955, CO 822/897. The young Anthony Low at that time was a correspondent of *The Times*. Roland Oliver, for one, believed that British attitudes had changed not at all. While visiting Uganda in 1958, he wrote to Hancock that British officials still referred to 'the Niggers' (Oliver to Hancock, 3 April 1958, Hancock Papers ANU, P96/28).

[97] 'He struck me . . . as an historical optimist': this is the judgement of the veteran journalist Michael Davie, who had a long conversation with Hancock in 1978 (Michael Davie, *Anglo-Australian Attitudes* [London, 2000], p. 219).

[98] *Perspective in History,* p. 64.

breakdown of civil society in Uganda—nor does his disillusionment seem quite so justified.[99] In one of his last comments on the Commonwealth, he remarked that at least it represented more than the smile on the face of the Cheshire Cat.[100] But perspectives on the Commonwealth change from decade to decade. It would now appear that one of his earlier assessments came closer to the mark: in 1960 he wrote that the Commonwealth was 'an interesting segment of international society, not a bloc, but a group of sovereign nations whose members have developed to an unusual degree the habit of mutual consultation.'[101]

Hancock wrote of the Pax Americana in a specific way.[102] He thought of it as a shield against the expansion of the Soviet Union and Communist China, specifically against the use of nuclear weapons. He did not believe either the Pax Britannica or the Pax Americana to be the equivalent of a Leviathan or an all-powerful state. Indeed he embraced a minimalist interpretation of empire. He once wrote on the uneven nature of the British Empire by describing it as 'an untidy patchwork of naval bases, coaling-stations, trading companies, Protectorates, Crown colonies and self-governing Dominions rapidly advancing to equality with Great Britain both in law and in fact.'[103] He apparently never used the phrase 'American Empire', but if he had, he would have restricted its meaning, in accordance with his exact usage of definitions, to the American dependencies of the Philippines and in the Caribbean. An empire rules and can enforce decisions. He

[99] Hancock was able to write in 1979 in the aftermath of Idi Amin: 'Today is a great day for me. Lule, the new President of Uganda, is an intimate friend . . . a man of remarkable integrity' (Hancock to Margaret Gowing, 23 April 1979, Gowing Papers). Yusufu Lule, the former Vice-Chancellor of Makerere University, had helped Hancock achieve the political settlement in 1954.

[100] *Perspective in History*, p. 178.

[101] Hancock, *Four Studies of War in This Century*, p. 113.

[102] He did so, on the whole, with an independence of mind unencumbered by much knowledge of the American scholarship on the subject. He appears to have been unaware of Ronald Steele's *Pax Americana* (New York, 1967), an ironically titled book that was immensely influential at the time. Nor does he seem to have read the imaginative and stimulating work by Robert W. Tucker and Robert E. Osgood; see their *Force, Order, and Justice* (Baltimore, 1967), and especially Tucker's *Nation or Empire? The Debate over American Foreign Policy* (Baltimore, 1968). Hancock was similarly silent on the remarkable, original work by radical American historians—for example, Walter LaFeber, *The New Empire: An Interpretation of American Expansion, 1860–1898* (Ithaca, N.Y., 1963). Nor did he read Ernest R. May's searching essay, *American Imperialism* (New York, 1968). The list could be expanded at length. As in the case of the 'moving frontier' (when he had shaped his views without having read Frederick Jackson Turner), Hancock formed his ideas while taking little account of American authors. But on the Pax Americana, he did not, as previously, obsessively assimilate new information. His views are of considerable interest simply because of his insight into the British side of the question.

[103] *Perspective in History*, p. 164.

would not have meant 'empire' to apply generally to American military and economic power, but instead would, as he did in the case of the British, distinguish between informal and formal empire. What the United States appears to be doing today in the Middle East is remarkably similar to the British attempt after the First World War to create an informal Empire in the region. But if commenting today, Hancock would not rate the chances of success very high, if only because, in the post-war decades, he failed to detect any coherence within the American government. He saw instead a set of conflicting bureaucracies operating without any overall, guiding principle or purpose. He once compared the United States to the elephant in a West African parable:

> A kind-hearted she-elephant, who, while walking out one day, inadvertently trod upon a partridge and killed it, and observing near at hand the bird's nest full of callow fledglings, dropped a tear, and saying 'I have the heart of a mother myself', sat down upon the brood.[104]

This was not an unfair comment and, for Hancock, it was a charitable one.[105]

In the 1970s, Hancock was much preoccupied with the question of 'unjust war', a category in which he now placed the Vietnam conflict as well as the Boer War. He examined international problems in the light of historical scholarship on an earlier era. During the decade when Britain withdrew all troops East of Suez and the United States faced disaster in Vietnam, there occurred a revolution in the historiography of the Second World War, brought about by the release of British documents of the wartime period. Hancock began to assess the crises of the 1970s in Asia and the Pacific in view of historical scholarship on the 1940s. The dismantling of British bases East of Suez and the American evacuation of Vietnam had grave implications for Australia's own defence. With a view towards the more distant past, Hancock had no doubt that the Australian government had made the right decision to turn to the United States after the fall of Singapore in 1942. He believed unequivocally in the justice of the American cause in both the Second World War and the Cold War. Despite his condemnation of the war in Vietnam, he knew that the United States and Australia were allies in the struggle against the Soviet Union and Communist China.

[104] Ibid., p. 171.
[105] 'There are quite a lot of *good* Americans', he wrote later. 'But they cut little ice in the Pentagon, or the Department of State, or the White House' (Hancock to Margaret Gowing, 23 January 1985, Gowing Papers).

Nevertheless Hancock's anti-Americanism and suspicion of the United States resurfaced in the 1970s. My own work played a part in his new view of the United States because he carefully read *Imperialism at Bay,* a study of the colonial question during the Second World War. It deals with, among other things, the economic and military expansion of the United States in such areas as the south-west Pacific. It presents evidence that the US Navy aimed to annex or control islands in the vicinity of Australia. Hancock wrote a two-part review of the book for the *Canberra Times;* he repeated the main points at least three times in later essays.[106] According to his last book, *Testimony* (1983): 'Roger Louis . . . tells a story which I still find astonishing.'[107] During the war, the strategic outposts of the United States moved closer and closer to Australia. Since the 1960s, the Australian government had permitted the United States to establish scientific and intelligence installations on Australian soil: Hancock believed not only that they made Australia a possible target in a nuclear war but that they encroached on Australian sovereignty.[108]

Hancock had a complicated personality, and his approach to history reflected a complex and powerful intellect. He was a driven man— though, as he might have retorted, 'to be a trifle crazy can be quite profitable'.[109] He was a moralist but also a realist. If there is one concern more than any other that emerges from his writing, it is the preoccupation with economic and military power as the central themes in modern history.[110] His later works focus more specifically on the dilemmas arising from the contraction of British power.[111] He saw clearly the significance of Indian independence in 1947 for Britain's military position: 'She no longer has Indian divisions at her disposal to send to South East Asia or the Aden Protectorate or East Africa or the fringes

---

[106] *Canberra Times,* 10 July, 7–8 September 1980. He reworked the review article and republished it in *Perspective in History,* pp. 163–79; he then compressed it as 'Our Interests and Obligations', in Robert O'Neill and D. M. Horner, eds., *Australian Defence Policy for the 1980s* (Brisbane, 1982), pp. 114–23. The last version is in *Testimony,* pp. 73 ff.

[107] *Testimony,* p. 73.

[108] This is a continuous theme in Hancock's thought, but for the more general Australian intellectual climate at the time, see Coral Bell, ed., *Agenda for the Eighties: Contexts of Australian Choices in Foreign and Defence Policy* (Canberra, 1980).

[109] *Country and Calling,* p. 233.

[110] In a sense, A. P. Thorton's *Imperial Idea and Its Enemies* (London, 1959) can thus be regarded as a parallel work on one of Hancock's main themes; see especially pp. xiii–iv.

[111] On this theme, see D. A. Low, 'The Contraction of England' (Inaugural Lecture, Cambridge, 1984), in which there is a reference to Hancock, four years before his death, as 'still the doyen of our limb of the profession' (p. 1).

of the Mediterranean.'[112] He recognized that recurring sterling crises would undermine plans for economic development in the colonies as well as the foundation of colonial rule itself. Military and economic weakness demonstrated to him the limited scope of the colonial state, as it is now called, rather than the unbridled power of a Leviathan. British paramountcy in the past had rested on the cooperative arrangements that he called harmonization, and he believed that American hegemony would also be limited by the necessity to reach accommodation with individual states throughout the world. Even a superpower cannot be all-powerful. But to Hancock, the power of the United States was alarming enough, especially if it threatened to impinge on Australian sovereignty.

During the last decade of his life he continued to be as zealously concerned with Australia's sovereign equality as when he began his career as an historian at All Souls. He remained intellectually engaged with friends and colleagues, but sometimes he gave the impression of a man not entirely happy, as if the world had passed him by. One critic has recently written that he fell into obscurity even before his death because of 'an outdated mindset' that was out of tune with 'the cutting edge of fashionability'.[113] It could well be that his magisterial style seemed a throwback to an earlier age, but he nevertheless continued to work at the forefront of historical research by turning to environmental history, and he certainly remained at the centre of historical controversy in Australia in the era of the Cold War. He did not relish Australia's position as an outpost of the Pax Americana. The Americans could not be trusted, he believed, to come to Australia's defence. The Australians would have to rely on themselves and to be on guard against any danger to their national sovereignty. Australian security might depend on the Pax Americana, he concluded, but the Australians would do well 'to trust God and to keep our powder dry'.[114] From beginning to end, from All Souls to the Australian National University, Hancock was an Australian and a British patriot, ever vigilant of Australian sovereign independence but at the same time a champion of the British Empire and Commonwealth.

---

[112] *Perspective in History*, p. 55.
[113] Doug Munro, *Journal of Imperial and Commonwealth History*, 31, 1 (January 2003), 150.
[114] *Perspective in History*, 187.

INDEX

Index

Casement, (Sir) Roger (*cont.*):
outset of his trip into the interior, 132; reasons for emotional change of attitude during his trip, 135; and the question of evidence for the lopped-off hand, 135, 143–44; submits report, 137–39; feels betrayed by the Foreign Office, 140; protests the edited version of his report as 'cooked and garbled', 142; contemplates resigning, 142; described A. J. Balfour as a 'cur . . . incapable of any honest or straightforward act of human sympathy', 142; critical of Sir Constantine Phipps, 142–43; writes a check for £100 to help create the Congo Reform Association, 145; 'sleeping partner' in the Association, 148; defended by the Foreign Office, 150; and the end of the Congo Reform Association, 151; his formula: 'Leopold = Hades = Hell', 152; Manichaean vision of evil in the Congo, 152; his report unites British public, 155; describes Sir Alfred Jones as a 'bold and original liar', 158; reaction to Commission of Inquiry report, 162; and the post-Leopoldian Congo, 180; believes E. D. Morel has defeated 'the Principalities of Powers of Darkness', 181

Cecil, Lord Robert, on the German colonies in 1917, 196, 202; on the French and Italians as imperialists, 205; on the irony of the colonial settlement in 1919, 224; on the symbolism of a 'trustee flag', 253; does not believe League can intervene in mandated territories but can serve to call public's attention to abuses, 274

Central African Federation, economic significance in the Cold War, 463; problem of white settlers, 494

Central Intelligence Agency, and Eisenhower, 607; believes MI6 exaggerates the influence of the Rashidians, 745; intricate relations with the State Department, 772; and support of General Zahedi, 777; assets combine with MI6's, 780; acknowledgement that the Rashidians were willing to risk their lives, 782

Ceylon, and Indian membership in the Commonwealth, 418

Chamberlain, Neville, hopes to revive Anglo-Japanese friendship, 294; believes that a renewed alliance with Japan might save Britain and the British Empire, 305; thinks a hostile Japan will destroy the British Empire in Asia, 306; and the explanation of why appeasement failed in the Far East, 313; believes candid discussion of dilemmas of defence will split the Common-

wealth, 319, 328; mistrust of U.S., 319; and Roosevelt's quarantine speech, 321; and the ghost of the Manchurian crisis, 321; 'We are a very rich and a very vulnerable Empire', 323; and Roosevelt in 1938, 323; values Craigie's reports as a corrective to the anti-Japan bias of the Foreign Office, 330; relieved at Churchill's attitude towards Japan in 1940, 335

Chamoun, Camille, pro-Western, 792; regards himself as Arab nationalist and Lebanese patriot, 807; British assessment of in 1958, 808; and the Suez crisis, 808–09; on bad terms with Chehab, 818; symbolizes the forces of resistance against Nasser, 818

Chehab, General Fouad, his background and personality, 811–12, underrated by British, 813; on bad terms with Chamoun, 818; his stature in Lebanese public life and the return to the 1943 spirit of compromise, 825; his election as President begins a new era in Lebanese history, 843; his family compared by George Middleton with the Cecils of England, 844–45

Chiang Kai-shek, and Hong Kong, 342–43, 345, 350, 351; his effectiveness and influence exaggerated by the British, 356–57

Chiefs of Staff (British), assessment of strategic position in the Far East in 1937, 318; decision to defend Hong Kong in the event of Japanese attack, 318; and the balance between the Foreign Office and the Colonial Office on Palestine, 423; on the need to preserve Arab good will, 432–33; hope to preserve strategic rights in Palestine, 433; believe that the British can impose a solution by force on one part of the community in Palestine but not both, 435–36; on Palestine as 'a screen for the defence of Egypt', 435; on the emergence of Libya as an independent state, 515; on 9,500 troops in the Canal Zone and 11,000 in Cyrenaica in 1949, 516; assess Suez base, 622; during Suez crisis, 632–33

China, and British treaty rights, 294, British hold out hope for unity and prosperity with, 298; problem of 'violent' resentment in the event of reviving the Anglo-Japanese alliance, 309; currency crisis and the problem of possible British recognition of Manchukuo, 312; passive, elastic resistance, 325; memories of the Chinese 'are almost as long as Irish', 342; civil war and Hong Kong, 352; and the question of Singapore, 567

Churchill, Winston, on the U.S. as a naval power, 209; on Mesopotamia and Pales-

Index

Peretti, de, 'You will see what these mandates will develop into in ten years', 235

Perham, Margery, courageous stand on equalitarian principle after the fall of Singapore, 2 n. 4, 977; described by Leo Amery as 'a clever and rather good-looking girl', 385; has an inquiring mind with a sense of the absurd, 529; admiration for Sir Douglas Newbold, 532–34; publishes *Government of Ethiopia* in 1948, 532; on the Sudan as a microcosm of the British Empire, 532; and the southern policy in the Sudan, 533; and the connection between the fall of Singapore in 1942 and the future of the Sudan as a crisis in the British colonial conscience, 535; fears the Foreign Office might sell the Sudan to promote agreement with Egypt, 536; points of tension with Sir James Robertson, 537; reduced almost to tears by the 'utter unreasonableness of young coloured nationalism', 538; and Mekki Abbas, 538–40; and 'premature' Sudanese independence, 541; on General Neguib, 544; compares the transfers of power in India and the Sudan, 545–46; hopes Creech Jones might 'do a Mountbatten' in the Sudan, 546; on Nkrumah and the lessons to be drawn from Ghanaian independence, 547; believes the Foreign Office to be responsible for scuttle in the Sudan, 548; *Native Administration in Nigeria*, 977; 'I'll never again trust the Colonial Office', 977 n. 68; embodiment of the British colonial conscience, 978; temperamentally akin to Hancock, 1009 n. 39

Perowne, Stewart, useful description of shifting alliances in Iraq, 868

Perron, Ernest, 'slippery as an eel' but important contact with the Shah, 742–43

Phillips, William, believes Linlithgow to be a descendant of George III, 401

Phipps, Sir Constantine, describes Casement's dispatches as 'febrile, almost hysterical', 134; doubts that Belgians are guilty of systematic cruelty, 143; denounced by Casement as a 'complacent mouthpiece' of King Leopold, 143; Casement's description as a 'cur', 144; acknowledges Casement's ability, 149; believes in cooperation with the Congo government, 159

Pineau, Christian, and the Suez crisis, 676–78, 'very louche', 677 n. 35

Pink, I. T. M., on the loss of Britain's good name, 696

Platt, D. C. M., attacks 'Imperialism of Free Trade', 923–27

Portugal, colonies viewed by Sir Edward Grey as 'sinks of iniquity', 35; scope and nature of colonial rule, 47–48; claims to the Congo, 52–55; public regards colonial concessions as tantamount to treason, 54; 'frantic' at the suggestion of international supervision in the Congo, 55; placed as a scarecrow on the mouth of the Congo to keep away France, 59; denounced as a cat's paw of Britain, 96; and boundaries of the Congo Free State, 109, 111; and the colonial settlement of 1919, 221–22, 242–44

Postan, Munia, an 'uncovenanted mercy' that he stuck to history during the Second World War, 1015 n. 64

Poynton, (Sir) Hilton, on the need for US economic assistance, 456; dislikes international interference in British colonies, 690; fears premature independence, 691; on the changing 'international climate' of opinion on colonies, 701–02; embodies the official mind of the Colonial Office, 703; on the lessons of the American Revolution, 703–04

Pratt, Sir John, on Britain's position in China vis-à-vis Japan, 312; believes Hong Kong should be relinquished to China, and British trade and commerce protected by treaty, 350

'prestige', defined by Sir John Brennan as 'respect inspired by military strength', 337; defined by Sir Pierson Dixon as 'what the rest of the world thinks of us', 598

Prince of Wales, loss symbolizes collapse of British power in Far East, 337

Princes (Indian), detect British willingness to sacrifice them, 394; and the India Act of 1935, 396

protectorates, discussed by Sir Travers Twiss, 114; useful definition by the Earl of Selborne, 115; untrammelled by administrative and judicial responsibilities, 119

'public opinion', definition as news and opinion 'published in the principal newspapers', 75 n. 1; 'Stands England where she did?', a theme in the mid-1880s, 78; a favorite motto: 'a fair field and no favour', 85; 'VICTORY ON THE NIGER', 101; united in 1904 in favor of reform in the Congo, 155; Congo crusade the last chapter in the history of the anti-slavery movement, 182; and the mandates system, 274 n. 72; and the 'full glare of the noonday sun', 276; and *Africa and the Victorians*, 940